McGRAW-HILL
CONCISE
ENCYCLOPEDIA OF
BIOSCIENCE

McGRAW-HILL

CONCISE
ENCYCLOPEDIA OF
BIOSCIENCE

McGraw-Hill

New York   Chicago   San Francisco   Lisbon   London   Madrid   Mexico City
Milan   New Delhi   San Juan   Seoul   Singapore   Sydney   Toronto

Library of Congress Cataloging in Publication Data

McGraw-Hill concise encyclopedia of bioscience.
    p.   cm.
  Includes bibliographical references and index.
  ISBN 0-07-143956-0
    1. Biology—Encyclopedias.

QH302.5.M378   2004
570′.3—dc22   2004049947

This material was extracted from the *McGraw-Hill Encyclopedia of Science & Technology*, Ninth Edition, © 2002 by The McGraw-Hill Companies, Inc. All rights reserved.

5

:hBooks, Fairfax, Virginia.

The book was printed and bound by RR Donnelley, The Lakeside Press.

CONTENTS

EDITORIAL STAFF

EDITING, DESIGN, AND PRODUCTION STAFF

CONSULTING EDITORS

Dr. Milton B. Adesnik. *Department of Cell Biology, New York University School of Medicine, New York.* CELL BIOLOGY.

Prof. William P. Banks. *Chairman, Department of Psychology, Pomona College, Claremont, California.* PHYSIOLOGICAL AND EXPERIMENTAL PSYCHOLOGY.

Dr. Paul Barrett. *Department of Palaeontology, The Natural History Museum, London.* VERTEBRATE PALEONTOLOGY.

Dr. Mark Chase. *Molecular Systematics Section, Jodrell Laboratory, Royal Botanic Gardens, Kew, Richmond, Surrey, United Kingdom.* PLANT TAXONOMY.

Dr. J. John Cohen. *Department of Immunology, University of Colorado School of Medicine, Denver.* IMMUNOLOGY.

Dr. Peter J. Davies. *Professor, Department of Plant Biology, Cornell University, Ithaca, New York.* PLANT PHYSIOLOGY.

Dr. John P. Harley. *Department of Biological Sciences, Eastern Kentucky University, Richmond.* MICROBIOLOGY.

Prof. Terry Harrison. *Department of Anthropology, Paleoanthropology Laboratory, New York University, New York.* ANTHROPOLOGY AND ARCHEOLOGY.

Dr. Ralph E. Hoffman. *Associate Professor, Yale Psychiatric Institute, Yale University School of Medicine, New Haven, Connecticut.* PSYCHIATRY.

Dr. S. C. Jong. *Senior Staff Scientist and Program Director, Mycology and Protistology Program, American Type Culture Collection, Manassas, Virginia.* MYCOLOGY.

Dr. Peter M. Kareiva. *Director of Conservation and Policy Projects, Environmental Studies Institute, Santa Clara University, Santa Clara, California.* ECOLOGY AND CONSERVATION.

Dr. Arnold G. Kluge. *Division of Reptiles and Amphibians, Museum of Zoology, Ann Arbor, Michigan.* SYSTEMATICS.

Prof. Robert E. Knowlton. *Department of Biological Sciences, George Washington University, Washington, DC.* INVERTEBRATE ZOOLOGY.

Dr. Donald W. Linzey. *Wytheville Community College, Wytheville, Virginia.* VERTEBRATE ZOOLOGY.

Dr. Orlando J. Miller. *Professor Emeritus, Center for Molecular Medicine and Genetics, Wayne State University School of Medicine, Detroit, Michigan.* GENETICS AND EVOLUTION.

Prof. Arthur N. Popper. *Department of Biology, University of Maryland, College Park.* NEUROSCIENCE.

Dr. Kenneth P. H. Pritzker. *Pathologist-in-Chief and Director, Head, Connective Tissue Research Group, and Professor, Laboratory Medicine and Pathobiology, University of Toronto, Mount Sinai Hospital, Toronto, Ontario, Canada.* MEDICINE AND PATHOLOGY.

Dr. Roger M. Rowell. *USDA-Forest Service, Forest Products Laboratory, Madison, Wisconsin.* FORESTRY.

Dr. Steven A. Slack. *Associate Vice President for Agricultural Administration, Director, Ohio Agricultural Research and Development Center, and Associate Dean for Research, College of Food, Agricultural, and Environmental Sciences, Ohio State University, Wooster.* PLANT PATHOLOGY.

Prof. Arthur A. Spector. *Department of Biochemistry, University of Iowa, Iowa City.* BIOCHEMISTRY.

Dr. Bruce A. Stanley. *Director, Scientific Programs, Section of Technology Development and Research Resources,*

Penn State College of Medicine, Hershey, Pennsylvania. PHYSIOLOGY.

Dr. Trent Stephens. *Department of Biological Sciences, Idaho State University, Pocatello.* DEVELOPMENTAL BIOLOGY.

Prof. John F. Timoney. *Department of Veterinary Science, University of Kentucky, Lexington.* VETERINARY MEDICINE.

Dr. Bruce A. Voyles. *Professor, Department of Biological Chemistry, Grinnell College, Iowa.* VIROLOGY.

Dr. Sally E. Walker. *Associate Professor of Geology and Marine Science, University of Georgia, Athens.* INVERTEBRATE PALEONTOLOGY.

Dr. Nicole Y. Weekes. *Pomona College, Claremont, California.* NEUROPSYCHOLOGY.

PREFACE

For more than four decades, the *McGraw-Hill Encyclopedia of Science & Technology* has been an indispensable scientific reference work for a broad range of readers, from students to professionals and interested general readers. Found in many thousands of libraries around the world, its 20 volumes authoritatively cover every major field of science. However, the needs of many readers will also be served by a concise work covering a specific scientific or technical discipline in a handy, portable format. For this reason, the editors of the *Encyclopedia* have produced this series of paperback editions, each devoted to a major field of science or engineering.

The articles in the *McGraw-Hill Concise Encyclopedia of Bioscience* cover all the principal topics of this field. Each one is a condensed version of the parent article that retains its authoritativeness and clarity of presentation, providing the reader with essential knowledge in the biological sciences without extensive detail. The authors are international experts, including Nobel Prize winners. The initials of the authors are at the end of the articles; their full names and affiliations are listed in the back of the book.

The reader will find over 900 alphabetically arranged entries, many illustrated with images or diagrams. Most include cross references to other articles for background reading or further study. Dual measurement units (U.S. Customary and International System) are used throughout. The Appendix includes useful information complementing the articles. Finally, the Index provides quick access to specific information in the articles.

This concise reference will fill the need for accurate, current scientific and technical information in a convenient, economical format. It can serve as the starting point for research by anyone seriously interested in science, even professionals seeking information outside their own specialty. It should prove to be a much used and much trusted addition to the reader's bookshelf.

MARK D. LICKER
Publisher

ORGANIZATION OF THE ENCYCLOPEDIA

Alphabetization. The more than 900 article titles are sequenced on a word-by-word basis, not letter by letter. Hyphenated words are treated as separate words. In occasional inverted article titles, the comma provides a full stop. The index is alphabetized on the same principles. Readers can turn directly to the pages for much of their research. Examples of sequencing are:

Biological specificity	**Plant-animal interactions**
Biologicals	**Plant cell**
Cell (biology)	**Plant viruses and viroids**
Cell biology	**Plants, life form of**

Cross references. Virtually every article has cross references set in CAPITALS AND SMALL CAPITALS. These references offer the user the option of turning to other articles in the volume for related information.

Measurement units. Since some readers prefer the U.S. Customary System while others require the International System of Units (SI), measurements in the Encyclopedia are given in dual units.

Contributors. The authorship of each article is specified at its conclusion, in the form of the contributor's initials for brevity. The contributor's full name and affiliation may be found in the "Contributors" section at the back of the volume.

Appendix. Every user should explore the variety of succinct information supplied by the Appendix, which includes conversion factors, measurement tables, fundamental constants, and a biographical listing of scientists. Users wishing to go beyond the scope of this Encyclopedia will find recommended books and journals listed in the "Bibliographies" section; the titles are grouped by subject area.

Index. The 6200-entry index offers the reader the time-saving convenience of being able to quickly locate specific information in the text, rather than approaching the Encyclopedia via article titles only. This elaborate breakdown of the volume's contents assures both the general reader and the professional of efficient use of the *McGraw-Hill Concise Encyclopedia of Bioscience*.

Abscission The process whereby a plant sheds one of its parts. Leaves, flowers, seeds, and fruits are parts commonly abscised. Almost any plant part, from very small buds and bracts to branches several inches in diameter, may be abscised by some species. However, other species, including many annual plants, may show little abscission, especially of leaves.

Abscission may be of value to the plant in several ways. It can be a process of self-pruning, removing injured, diseased, or senescent parts. It permits the dispersal of seeds and other reproductive structures. It facilitates the recycling of mineral nutrients to the soil. It functions to maintain homeostasis in the plant, keeping in balance leaves and roots, and vegetative and reproductive parts.

In most plants the process of abscission is restricted to an abscission zone at the base of an organ (see illustration); here separation is brought about by the disintegration of the walls of a special layer of cells, the separation layer. The portion of the abscission zone which remains on the plant commonly develops into a corky protective layer that becomes continuous with the cork of the stem.

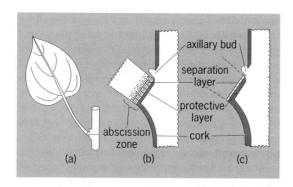

Diagrams of the abscission zone of a leaf. (*a*) A leaf with the abscission zone indicated at the base of the petiole. (*b*) The abscission zone layers shortly before abscission and (*c*) the layers after abscission.

Auxin applied experimentally to the distal (organ) side of an abscission zone retards abscission, while auxin applied to the proximal (stem) side accelerates abscission. The gibberellins are growth hormones which influence abscission. When applied to young fruits or to leaves, they tend to promote growth, delay maturation, and thereby indirectly prevent or delay abscission. Abscisic acid has the ability to promote abscission and senescence and to retard growth. Small amounts of ethylene have profound effects on the growth of plants and can distort and reduce growth and promote senescence and abscission.   [F.T.A.]

Absorption (biology)   The net movement (transport) of water and solutes from outside an organism to its interior. The unidirectional flow of materials into an animal from the environment generally takes place across the alimentary tract, the lungs, or the skin, and in each location a specific cell layer called an epithelium regulates the passage of materials.

Absorption across epithelia may occur by several different passive and active processes. Simple diffusion is the net movement of molecules from the apical to basolateral surfaces of an epithelium down chemical and electrical gradients without the requirement of cellular energy sources. Facilitated diffusion across the epithelium is similar to simple diffusion in that energy is not required, but in this process, molecular interaction with protein binding sites (carriers) in one or both membranes must occur to facilitate the transfer. Active molecular transport involves the use of membrane protein carriers as well as cellular energy supplies to move a transported molecule up an electrochemical gradient across the epithelium. Endocytosis and phagocytosis are also examples of active transport because metabolic energy is required, but in these processes whole regions of the cell membrane are used to engulf fluid or particles, rather than to bring about molecular transfer using single-membrane proteins. See CELL MEMBRANES; ENDOCYTOSIS; OSMOREGULATORY MECHANISMS; PHAGOCYTOSIS.

Although a wide variety of ions are absorbed by different types of epithelial cells, the mechanisms of Na^+ and Cl^- transport in mammalian small intestine are perhaps best known in detail. Transepithelial transport of these two ions occurs in this tissue by three independent processes: active Na^+ absorption, not coupled directly to the flow of other solutes but accompanied indirectly by the diffusional absorption of Cl^-; coupled NaCl absorption; and cotransport of Na^+ with a wide variety of nutrient molecules. See ION TRANSPORT.

Net water transport across the epithelium is coupled to net ion transport in the same direction. Pump sites for Na^+ are believed to be located along the lateral borders of epithelial cells. Energy-dependent Na^+ efflux from the cells to the intercellular spaces creates a local increase in osmotic pressure within these small compartments. An osmotic pressure gradient becomes established here, with greatest solute concentrations located nearest the tight junctions. Water flows into the cell across the brush border membrane and out the lateral membranes in response to the increased osmotic pressure in the paracellular spaces. Once water is in the intercellular compartment, a buildup of hydrostatic pressure forces the transported fluid to the capillary network.   [G.A.A.]

Acanthocephala   A distinct phylum of helminths, the adults of which are parasitic in the alimentary canal of vertebrates. They are commonly known as the spiny-headed worms. The phylum comprises the orders Archiacanthocephala, Palaeacanthocephala, and Eocanthocephala. Over 500 species have been described from all classes of vertebrates, although more species occur in fish than in birds and mammals and only a relatively few species are found in amphibians and reptiles. The geographical distribution of acanthocephalans is worldwide, but genera and species do not have a uniform distribution because some species are confined to limited geographic areas. Host specificity is well established in some species, whereas others exhibit a wide range of host tolerance. The same species never occurs normally, as an adult, in coldblooded and warm-blooded definitive hosts. More species occur in fish than any other vertebrate; however, Acanthocephala have not been reported from elasmobranch fish. The fact that larval development occurs in arthropods gives support to the postulation that the ancestors of Acanthocephala were parasites of primitive arthropods during or before the Cambrian Period and became parasites of vertebrates as this group arose and utilized arthropods for food.

Adults of various species show great diversity in size, ranging in length from 0.04 in. (1 mm) in some species found in fish to over 16 in. (400 mm) in some mammalian species.

The body of both males and females has three subdivisions: the proboscis armed with hooks, spines, or both; an unspined neck; and the posterior trunk. The proboscis is the primary organ for attachment to the intestinal wall of the host. In most species the proboscis is capable of introversion into a saclike structure, the proboscis receptacle. The proboscis receptacle and neck can be retracted into the body cavity but without inversion. The body cavity, or pseudocode, contains all the internal organs, the most conspicuous of which are the reproductive organs. There is no vestige of a digestive system in any stage of the life cycle. The reproductive organs of the male consist of a pair of testes and specialized cells, the cement glands. The products of the testes and cement glands are discharged through a penis. Female Acanthocephala are unique in that the ovary exists as a distinct organ only in the very early stages of development and later breaks up to form free-floating egg balls. The eggs are fertilized as they are released from the egg balls and are retained within the ligament sacs until embry-onation is complete. The nervous system is composed of a chief ganglion or brain located within the proboscis receptacle. Two nerve trunks pass through the wall of the proboscis receptacle to innervate the trunk wall. Modified protonephridial organs are found closely adherent to the reproductive system, but in most species specialized excretory organs are completely lacking.   [D.V.Mo.]

Acetylcholine   A naturally occurring quaternary ammonium cation ester, with the formula $CH_3(O)COC_2H_4N(CH)_3^+$, that plays a prominent role in nervous system function. The great importance of acetylcholine derives from its role as a neurotransmitter for cholinergic neurons, which innervate many tissues, including smooth muscle and skeletal muscle, the heart, ganglia, and glands. The effect of stimulating a cholinergic nerve, for example, the contraction of skeletal muscle or the slowing of the heartbeat, results from the release of acetylcholine from the nerve endings.

Acetylcholine is synthesized at axon endings from acetyl coenzyme A and choline by the enzyme choline acetyltransferase, and is stored at each ending in hundreds of thousands of membrane-enclosed synaptic vesicles. When a nerve impulse reaches an axon ending, voltage-gated calcium channels in the axonal membrane open and calcium, which is extremely low inside the cell, enters the nerve ending. The increase in calcium-ion concentration causes hundreds of synaptic vesicles to fuse with the cell membrane and expel acetylcholine into the synaptic cleft (exocytosis). The acetylcholine released at a neuromuscular junction binds reversibly to acetylcholine receptors in the muscle end-plate membrane, a postsynaptic membrane that is separated from the nerve ending by a very short distance. The receptor is a cation channel which opens when two acetylcholine molecules are bound, allowing a sodium current to enter the muscle cell and depolarize the membrane. The resulting impulse indirectly causes the muscle to contract.

Acetylcholine must be rapidly removed from a synapse in order to restore it to its resting state. This is accomplished in part by diffusion but mainly by the enzyme acetylcholinesterase, which hydrolyzes acetylcholine.

Acetylcholinesterase is a very fast enzyme: one enzyme molecule can hydrolyze 10,000 molecules of acetylcholine in 1 s. Any substance that efficiently inhibits acetylcholinesterase will be extremely toxic.   [I.B.W.]

Acquired immune deficiency syndrome (AIDS)   A viral disease of humans caused by the human immunodeficiency virus (HIV), which attacks and compromises the body's immune system. Individuals infected with HIV proceed through a spectrum of stages that ultimately lead to the critical end point, acquired immune deficiency syndrome. The disease is characterized by a profound progressive irreversible depletion of T-helper-inducer lymphocytes (CD4+ lymphocytes), which leads to the onset of multiple and recurrent opportunistic infections by other viruses, fungi, bacteria, and protozoa, as well as various tumors (Kaposi's sarcoma, lymphomas). HIV infection is transmitted by sexual intercourse (heterosexual and homosexual), by blood and blood products, and perinatally from infected mother to child (prepartum, intrapartum, and postpartum via breast milk).

Since retroviruses such as HIV-1 integrate their genetic material into that of the host cell, infection is generally lifelong and cannot be eliminated easily. Therefore, medical efforts have been directed toward preventing the spread of virus from infected individuals. *See* RETROVIRUS.

Approximately 50–70% of individuals with HIV infection experience an acute mononucleosis-like syndrome approximately 3–6 weeks following primary infection. In the acute HIV syndrome, symptoms include fever, pharyngitis, lymphadenopathy, headache, arthralgias, myalgias, lethargy, anorexia, nausea, and erythematous maculopapular rash. These symptoms usually persist for 1–2 weeks and gradually subside as an immune response to HIV is generated.

Although the length of time from initial infection to development of the clinical disease varies greatly from individual to individual, a median time of approximately 10 years has been documented for homosexual or bisexual men, depending somewhat on the mode of infection. Intravenous drug users experience a more aggressive course than homosexual men and hemophiliacs because their immune systems have already been compromised.

As HIV replication continues, the immunologic function of the HIV-infected individual declines throughout the period of clinical latency. At some point during that decline (usually after the CD4+ lymphocyte count has fallen below 500 cells per microliter), the individual begins to develop signs and symptoms of clinical illness, and sometimes may demonstrate generalized symptoms of lymphadenopathy, oral lesions, herpes zoster, and thrombocytopenia.

Secondary opportunistic infections are a late complication of HIV infection, usually occurring in individuals with less than 200 CD4+ lymphocytes per microliter. They are characteristically caused by opportunistic organisms such as *Pneumocystis carinii* and cytomegalovirus that do not ordinarily cause disease in individuals with a normally functioning immune system. However, the spectrum of serious secondary infections that may be associated with HIV infection also includes common bacterial pathogens, such as *Streptococcus pneumoniae*. Secondary opportunistic infections are the leading cause of morbidity and mortality in persons with HIV infection. Tuberculosis has also become a major problem for HIV-infected individuals. Therefore, HIV-infected individuals are administered protective vaccines (pneumococcal) as well as prophylactic regimens for the prevention of infections with *P. carinii, Mycobacterium tuberculosis*, and *M. avium* complex. *See* OPPORTUNISTIC INFECTIONS; PNEUMOCOCCUS; STREPTOCOCCUS; TUBERCULOSIS.

Antiretroviral treatment with deoxyribonucleic acid (DNA) precursor analogs—for example, azidothymidine (AZT), dideoxyinosine (ddI), and dideoxycytidine (ddC)—has been shown to inhibit HIV infection by misincorporating the DNA precursor analogs into viral DNA by the viral DNA polymerase. Nevertheless, these agents are not curative and do not completely eradicate the HIV infection.   [A.M.Ma.; E.P.Go.]

Acquired immunological tolerance An induced state in which antigens originally regarded as foreign become regarded as self by the immune system. Tolerance can be induced (tolerization) in all of the cells of the immune system, including T cells (also known as T lymphocytes), the antibody-forming B cells (also known as B lymphocytes), and natural killer cells. Artificially induced immunological tolerance can be helpful in a number of clinical settings. Inducing self-tolerance in the immune system could be an approach to curing autoimmune diseases.

Tolerization can also be used to facilate organ transplantation. Despite improvements in immunosuppressive drug therapy, teaching the immune system to regard a set of foreign antigens presented by the organ graft as self (that is, tolerance induction) has become an important goal for several reasons: (1) It would eliminate the need for chronic immunosuppressive therapy, which is associated with lifelong increased risks of infection and malignancy, and other side effects. (2) It would prevent chronic rejection (a major problem even with immunosuppressive therapy), which often leads to late graft loss. (3) It presents a less toxic alternative to the unacceptably high levels of nonspecific immunosuppressive therapy that would likely be required to prevent rejection of xenografts (grafts from a donor of another species). See TRANSPLANTATION BIOLOGY.

Many strategies for inducing immunological tolerance involve reproducing the mechanisms involved in natural central tolerance—the phenomenon by which self-tolerance is maintained among immature lymphocytes developing in the central lymphoid organs. For developing T cells, tolerance occurs in the thymus, the central organ for T cell development. For B cells, development occurs in the bone marrow, and an encounter with self antigens can induce tolerance there among the immature cells.

The transplantation of bone marrow or other sources of hematopoietic (blood cell-producing) stem cells provides a very powerful means of inducing T cell central tolerance. The clinical potential of bone marrow or other types of hematopoietic cell transplantation for the induction of transplantation tolerance in humans has not yet been realized.

Peripheral tolerance comprises mechanisms to prevent immune responses among mature lymphocytes in the peripheral tissues. One major mechanism of T cell and B cell peripheral tolerance is anergy, in which the cells cannot be fully activated by encounter with the antigens that their receptors recognize. Numerous methods of inducing T and B cell anergy have been described.

Another major mechanism of peripheral tolerance is suppression, in which both B cells and T cells may be rendered tolerant of a specific antigen through the activity of substances or cells that actively suppress the lymphocyte's function. Numerous means of inducing B cell and T cell suppression have been described, and convincing evidence implicates cells with the ability to suppress T cell alloresponses (immune responses to alloantigens) in transplantation models. See IMMUNOSUPPRESSION. [M.Sy.]

Actinobacillus A genus of gram-negative, immotile and nonspore-forming, oval to rod-shaped, often pleomorphic bacteria which occur as parasites or pathogens in mammals (including humans), birds, and reptiles. They are facultatively aerobic, capable of fermenting carbohydrates (without production of gas) and of reducing nitrates. The genomic DNA contains between 40 and 47 mol % guanine plus cytosine. The actinobacillus group shares many biological properties with the genus *Pasteurella*. See PASTEURELLA.

Actinobacillus (Pasteurella) ureae and *A. hominis* occur in the respiratory tract of healthy humans and may be involved in the pathogenesis of sinusitis, bronchopneumonia, pleural empyema, and meningitis. *Actinobacillus actinomycetemcomitans* occurs in the human oral microflora, and together with anaerobic or capnophilic organisms may cause endocarditis and suppurative lesions in the upper alimentary tract. Actinobacilli are susceptible to most antibiotics of the β-lactam family, aminoglycosides, tetracyclines, chloramphenicol, and many other antibacterial chemotherapeutics. *See* ANTIBIOTIC; MEDICAL BACTERIOLOGY.   [W.Ma.]

Actinomycetes   A heterogeneous collection of bacteria that form branching filaments. The actinomycetes encompass two different groups of filamentous bacteria: the actinomycetes per se and the nocardia/streptomycete complex. Historically, the actinomycetes were called the ray fungi and were thought to be related to the true fungi, such as bread molds, because they formed mats (mycelia) of branching filaments (hyphae). However, unlike the true fungi, the actinomycetes have thin hyphae (0.5– 1.5 micrometers in diameter) with genetic material coiled inside as free DNA. The cell wall of the hyphae is made up of a cross-linked polymer containing short chains of amino acids and long chains of amino sugars. In general, actinomycetes do not have membrane-bound cell organelles. Actinomycetes are susceptible to a wide range of antibiotics that are used to treat bacterial diseases, such as penicillin and tetracycline. *See* AMINO SUGAR; ANTIBIOTIC.

Members of the genus *Actinomyces* are most often found in the mouth and gastrointestinal tract of humans and other animals. *Actinomyces* do not require oxygen for growth and are sometimes referred to as anaerobic bacteria. It is actually the requirement for elevated levels of carbon dioxide rather than the negative effect of oxygen that characterizes *Actinomyces*. When displaced from their normal sites within the mouth or gastrointestinal tract, *Actinomyces* may cause diseases in humans, such as lung abscesses, appendicitis, and lumpy jaw, which is also seen in cattle. Serious ulcers of the cornea of the eye have been caused by contact lens contaminated with saliva containing *Actinomyces*.

The nocardia/streptomycete complex constitutes a continuous spectrum of organisms from those most like true bacteria to those that are superficially most like fungi. The nocardiae represent the transition, having members that resemble the bacteria that cause diphtheria (*Corynebacterium*) and tuberculosis (*Mycobacterium*). Members of the genus *Nocardia* require oxygen for growth, are found in soil and water, and have the ability to use a wide range of organic material as a source of energy. A few species of *Nocardia* cause disease in humans. Nocardiae inhaled from the soil may cause a disease of the lungs similar to tuberculosis. A few species produce clinically useful antibiotics. The streptomycetes have long branching filaments and two types of mycelia. The cell walls are typical bacterial cell walls and do not contain the fatty acids found in nocardiae and mycobacteria. Streptomycetes require oxygen for growth, are found in soil and water, and have the ability to utilize a wide range of organic materials as nutrients. The streptomycetes are particularly important in degradation of dead plant materials in soil; the aroma of fresh soil and newly dug potatoes is actually due to streptomycetes. Streptomycetes do not produce disease in humans or animals and are best known for producing many clinically useful antibiotics, including streptomycin, tetracycline, and cephalosporin. There are many other genera of actinomycetes, defined on the bases of morphology, chemical composition of cell walls, or unique roles in nature. *See* BACTERIA; DIPHTHERIA; MEDICAL BACTERIOLOGY; TUBERCULOSIS.   [S.G.B.]

Actinopterygii   A group of bony fishes, also known as actinops or ray-finned fishes, containing about half of all vertebrate species and about 96% of all living "fishes" (a nonmonophyletic group derived from more than one lineage when tetrapods are excluded). Living Actinopterygii comprise Polypteriformes (bichirs and reedfish),

Acipenseriformes (sturgeons and paddlefishes), Lepisosteiformes (gars), Amiiformes (bowfins), and Teleostei (teleosts). Actinops are characterized by the presence of a single dorsal fin, an enclosed sensory canal in the dentary bone, a specialized tissue called ganoin, and several other anatomical characters. About 40% of living actinopterygian species live exclusively or almost exclusively in fresh water. The rest inhabit mostly marine, brackish, or combination environments.

The fossil record indicates that actinopterygians are at least as old as the Late Silurian (about 420 million years before present). Fossil actinopterygians are speciose and extremely abundant, making up the majority of vertebrate fossils that are known by complete skeletons. Many major radiations of early actinopterygians, such as pycnodonts, semionotiforms, and palaeonisciforms, have been extinct for tens of millions of years. Other early actinopterygian groups, such as the Cheirolepiformes, have been extinct for hundreds of millions of years. Based on the fossil record, the most major differentiation of the group began in the late Mesozoic.   [L.G.]

Adaptation (biology)   A characteristic of an organism that makes it fit for its environment or for its particular way of life. For example, the Arctic fox (*Alopex lagopus*) is well adapted for living in a very cold climate. Appropriately, it has much thicker fur than similar-sized mammals from warmer places; measurement of heat flow through fur samples demonstrates that the Arctic fox and other arctic mammals have much better heat insulation than tropical species. Consequently, Arctic foxes do not have to raise their metabolic rates as much as tropical mammals do at low temperatures. The insulation is so effective that Arctic foxes can maintain their normal deep body temperatures of 100°F (38°C) even when the temperature of the environment falls to −112°F (−80°C). Thus, thick fur is obviously an adaptation to life in a cold environment. See THERMOREGULATION.

In contrast to that clear example, it is often hard to be sure of the effectiveness of what seems to be an adaptation. For example, the scombrid fishes (tunnies and mackerel) seem to be adapted to fast, economical swimming. The body has an almost ideal streamlined shape. However, some other less streamlined-looking fishes are equally fast for their sizes. There are no measurements of the energy cost of scombrid swimming, but measurements on other species show no clear relationship between energy cost and streamlining.

Evolution by natural selection tends to increase fitness, making organisms better adapted to their environment and way of life. It might be inferred that this would ultimately lead to perfect adaptation, but this is not so. It must be remembered that evolution proceeds by small steps. For example, squids do not swim as well as fish. The squid would be better adapted for swimming if it evolved a fishlike tail instead of its jet propulsion mechanism, but evolution cannot make that change because it would involve moving down from the lesser adaptive summit before climbing the higher one.   [R.M.Al.]

Adaptive management   An approach to management of natural resources that emphasizes how little is known about the dynamics of ecosystems and that as more is learned management will evolve and improve. Natural systems are very complex and dynamic, and human observations about natural processes are fragmentary and inaccurate. As a result, the best way to use the available resources in a sustainable manner remains to be determined. Furthermore, much of the variability that affects natural populations is unpredictable and beyond human control. This combination of ignorance and unpredictability means that the ways in which ecosystems respond to human interventions are unknown and can be described only in probabilistic terms. Nonetheless, management decisions need to be made. Adaptive management proceeds despite this uncertainty by treating human interventions in natural systems as large-scale experiments from which more may be learned, leading to improved management in the future.

A key first step in the development of an adaptive management program is the assessment of the problem. During this stage, existing knowledge and interdisciplinary experience is synthesized and formally integrated by developing a dynamic model of the system. This modeling exercise helps to identify key information gaps and to postulate hypotheses about possible system responses to human intervention consistent with available information. Different management policies have to be screened in order to narrow down the alternatives to a few plausible candidates.

The second stage involves the formal design of a management and monitoring program. To the extent that new information can result in improved future management, adaptive management programs may include large-scale experiments deliberately designed to accelerate learning. Some management actions may be more effective than others at filling the relevant information gaps. In cases where spatial replication is possible (such as small lakes, patches of forest, and reefs), policies that provide contrasts between different management units will be much more informative about the system dynamics than those that apply the same rule everywhere. There are other barriers to the implementation of large-scale management experiments. Experiments usually have associated costs; thus, in order to be worthwhile, benefits derived from learning must overcompensate short-term sacrifices. Choices may be also restricted by social concerns or biological constraints, or they may have unacceptably high associated risks.

Once a plan for action has been chosen, the next stage is to implement the program in the field. This is one of the most difficult steps, because it involves a concerted and sustained effort from all sectors involved in the use, assessment, and management of the natural resources. Beyond the implementation of specific initial actions, putting in place an adaptive management program involves a long-term commitment to monitoring the compliance of the plan, evaluating the effects of management interventions, and adjusting management accordingly.

No matter how thorough and complete the initial assessment and design may have been, systems may always respond in manners that could not be foreseen at the planning stage. Ecosystems exhibit long-term, persistent changes at the scale of decades and centuries; thus, recent experience is not necessarily a good basis for predicting future behavior. The effects of global climatic change on the dynamics of ecosystems, which are to a large extent unpredictable, will pose many such management challenges. Adaptive management programs have to include a stage of evaluation and adjustment. Outcomes of past management decisions must be compared with initial forecasts, models have to be refined to reflect new understanding, and management programs have to be revised accordingly. New information may suggest new uncertainties and innovative management approaches, leading to another cycle of assessment, design, implementation, and evaluation.   [A.M.Pa.]

Addictive disorders   Addictive disease disorders are characterized by the chronic use of a drug (such as heroin, cocaine, or amphetamines), alcohol, or similar substances. These disorders usually result in (1) the development of tolerance for the substance, with the need for increasing amounts to achieve the desired effect; (2) physical dependence, characterized by a sequence of well-defined signs and physiological symptoms, such as the withdrawal or abstinence syndrome on cessation of use of the substance; and (3) compulsive drug-seeking behavior, with chronic, regular, or intermittent use, despite possible harm to self or others. Since the early 1960s, research has been increasing in the biology of addictive diseases, and emphasis has shifted from only psychological, sociological, and epidemiological studies to investigations of the metabolic, neurobiological, and molecular bases of addiction.

The four major addictive diseases are alcoholism, narcotic (or opiate) addiction, cocaine and other stimulant addiction, and nicotine addiction. Drug addiction may also occur after chronic use of other types of agents such as barbiturates, benzodiazepines, and marijuana.

Opiate receptors (cell structures that function as an intermediary between the opioid and the physiological response) were conclusively identified in mammals (including humans) in 1973. Since then, it has been determined that there are at least three different types of opioid receptors—mu receptors, delta receptors, and kappa receptors. The genes encoding each of these were cloned for the first time in 1992, beginning with the delta opioid receptor. Subsequent to the discovery of specific opioid receptors, endogenous ligands which bind to these receptors, the so-called endogenous opioids, were discovered. Opioids include substances that are produced endogenously (such as the enkephalins, endorphins, and dynorphins) and may be produced synthetically. Exogenous synthetic opioids are used extensively in the treatment of pain. See ENDORPHINS.

It is not known to what extent the endogenous opioids play a role in addictive diseases. It has been suggested that narcotic addiction may be a disorder characterized by (1) a relative or absolute deficiency of endogenous opioids; (2) an end organ or receptor failure to respond to normal or possibly increased levels of endogenous opioids; (3) genetic or acquired (for example, short-acting opiate or stimulant drug–induced) abnormalities in the feedback control of the synthesis, release, and processing, or degradation of one or more types of the endogenous opioids; or (4) genetic variations in the opioid receptors.

The possible role of endogenous opioids in alcoholism is also not clear. It has been shown that a specific opioid antagonist, naloxone, may reverse or ameliorate some of the signs and symptoms and physical abnormalities of the acute alcohol intoxication syndrome. However, this apparent beneficial effect of an opioid antagonist may not be related to the addictive disease per se, but may be due to the counteracting of the possible acute release of large amounts of endogenous opioids in response to excessive acute alcohol ingestion. Whether there are some common mechanisms with a genetic, metabolic, or purely behavioral basis underlying these two addictive diseases has not yet been defined.

There are three approaches to the management of opiate (primarily heroin) addiction: pharmacological treatment, drug-free treatment following detoxification, and incarceration. Statistical data over the last century reveal that after release from prison, completion of drug-free treatment, or discontinuation of chronic pharmacological treatment with methadone or other mu agonists, partial agonists, or antagonists, fewer than 30% of former long-term heroin addicts are able to stay drug-free. (Long-term addiction is defined as more than 1 year of daily use of several doses of heroin, with tolerance, physical dependence, and drug-seeking behavior.)

Since the 1960s, methadone maintenance treatment has been documented to be medically safe and the most effective available treatment for heroin addiction. Unlike heroin, which has a 3-min half-life in humans, and its major metabolite, morphine, which has a half-life of 4–6 h, methadone has a 24-h half-life. Therefore, when given orally daily, methadone prevents the signs and symptoms of narcotic abstinence and also prevents drug hunger, without causing any narcotic-induced euphoria during the 24 h between doses. Steady moderate to high doses of methadone can be used in the treatment of addiction over long periods of time without tolerance developing to these desired effects. Because of the high degree of cross-tolerance developed for other narcotics, a patient receiving methadone maintenance treatment does not experience any narcotic high or other effects after self-administration of a dose of short-acting narcotic such as heroin. Through this cross-tolerance mechanism, methadone blocks any illicit narcotic effect. 60–90% of heroin addicts who have entered into methadone maintenance treatment will stay in treatment voluntarily for 1 year or more. Illicit opiate abuse drops to less than 15% during such treatment when adequate doses of methadone (usually 60–150 mg per day) are administered. Cocaine or polydrug abuse or alcohol abuse may persist in 20–30% of patients even in excellent methadone programs, since methadone maintenance is specific for treatment of narcotic dependency. Chronic methadone treatment also brings about the normalization of the multiple physiological alterations caused by chronic heroin abuse. Methadone-maintained patients, who are not chronic abusers of other drugs or alcohol, are able to work, to attend school, and to take part in normal socialization, including restoration of family life. However, when maintenance treatment is discontinued, over 70% of all patients will return to opiate abuse within 2 years.

A second type of pharmacological treatment of narcotic addiction is chronic treatment with a specific narcotic antagonist, naltrexone. This drug also prevents any narcotic effect from illicitly administered heroin, but does so by way of direct opioid receptor blocking, with displacement of endogenous or exogenous opioids from receptor binding. Naltrexone treatment has limited acceptance by unselected opiate addicts; only 15–30% of former narcotic addicts entering treatment with this agent remain in treatment for 6 months or more. Therefore, although it may be a worthwhile treatment for some small defined special populations, it does not seem to be an effective treatment for the majority of unselected long-term heroin addicts.

Drug-free treatment involving either long-term institutionalization in a drug-free residence or, less frequently, attendance at an outpatient resource, has resulted in long-term success in approximately 10–30% of all unselected heroin addicts who enter treatment.

Alcoholism has been difficult to treat over a long-term period. There is no specific pharmacological replacement treatment for alcoholism. Disulfiram (Antabuse) is an agent which blocks the metabolism of acetaldehyde, the major metabolite of ethanol. When a person treated with Antabuse drinks alcohol, there is a rapid buildup of acetaldehyde and a severe physiological syndrome ensues, which frequently prevents or modifies further immediate drinking behavior.

The most widely used treatment of alcoholism is self-help groups, such as Alcoholics Anonymous (AA), where mutual support is available on a 24-h basis, along with group recognition of chronic problems with alcohol. However, only around 20–40% of severe chronic alcoholics are able to stay alcohol-free for more than 2 years even under such management. Early studies of the use of an opioid antagonist naltrexone or nalmefene for the treatment of chronic alcoholism have shown that about 50% of the subjects had reduced numbers and magnitudes of relapse events. Ethanol, unlike heroin and other narcotics, has many well-defined severes, specific toxic effects on several organs, including the liver, brain, and reproductive system, so even relatively short drug-free intervals will decrease exposure to this toxin. Therefore, it has been suggested that success in treatment of alcoholism be measured in part by increasing lengths of alcohol-free intervals, and not just by permanent restoration of the alcohol-free state.

Cocaine addiction may also involve disruption of the endogenous opioid system in addition to the well-known primary effect of cocaine in blocking reuptake of dopamine by the synaptic dopamine transporter protein. This effect results in the accumulation of dopamine in the synapse and similar actions at the serotonin and norepinephrine reuptake transporter. Demonstrated changes in the mu and kappa endogenous opioid system increase the complexity of the effect of cocaine and may contribute to its resultant reinforcing properties leading to addiction, as well as to the drug craving and relapse. This may explain in part the resultant difficulties in developing a pharmacotherapeutic approach for the treatment of cocaine addiction.   [M.J.Kr.]

Adenohypophysis hormone   Of the endocrine glands, the anterior pituitary, or adenohypophysis, occupies the prime place because, through the secretion of various hormones, it controls the functioning of certain other endocrine glands, namely, the adrenal cortex, the thyroid, and the gonads. In addition, hormones from the anterior pituitary influence the growth and metabolism of the organism through direct action on skeletal, muscular, and other tissues. The pituitary maintains control over the various target organs by a feedback mechanism which is sensitive to circulating levels of hormones from the target organs. Pituitary hormones are also released in response to metabolic conditions which they help to control. One factor influencing the secretion of growth hormone, for example, is the level of blood glucose.

There are eight anterior pituitary hormones whose existence has been firmly established for some time. They include the two gonadotropic hormones, interstitial-cell stimulating hormone (ICSH, or luteinizing hormone, LH) and follicle-stimulating hormone (FSH); thyrotropic hormone (thyroid-stimulating hormone, TSH); lactogenic hormone (prolactin); growth hormone (GH, or somatotropin, STH); adrenocorticotropic hormone (ACTH, or adrenocorticotropin, or corticotropin); and the two melanocyte-stimulating hormones (α-MSH and β-MSH). In addition, two peptides have been isolated which are structurally related to ACTH and the MSHs. These peptides have been designated β-lipotropic hormone (β-LPH) and γ-lipotropic hormone (γ-LPH). The hormones of the adenohypophysis are composed of amino acids in peptide linkage and are therefore classed as either polypeptides or proteins, depending on their size. In addition, three of the hormones, TSH, ICSH, and FSH, contain carbohydrate and are therefore categorized as glycoproteins. *See* AMINO ACIDS; HORMONE; PROTEIN.

In the female, FSH initiates the development of ovarian follicles. ICSH, acting synergistically with FSH, is necessary for the final stages of follicular maturation and the production of estrogen. ICSH also stimulates the development of the corpus luteum. In the male, FSH stimulates spermatogenesis through its action on the germinal epithelium of the testis, and ICSH primarily activates the Leydig cells which produce androgen.

TSH stimulates the growth of the thyroid gland and the secretion of thyroid hormones.

Through a process which requires other hormones as well, lactogenic hormone stimulates the mammary gland to secrete milk. There is evidence that in some species of mammals lactogenic hormone also plays a role in maintaining the corpus luteum in the ovary. In contrast to all nonprimate species investigated, a distinct lactogenic hormone has never been isolated from the pituitaries of the monkey or the human. In these two species a hormone containing lactogenic activity can indeed be isolated from the pituitary, but it also has growth-promoting activity and in major respects corresponds to growth hormones isolated from nonprimate species. Thus, in nonprimates, a distinct growth hormone, having no lactogenic activity, can be isolated from the pituitary gland. In the primates, however, growth-promoting and lactogenic activities are present in the same molecule. In spite of its dual activities, the primate hormone is usually referred to simply as growth hormone, which promotes an increase in body size. It stimulates the growth of bones, muscles, and other tissues and enhances the effects of other pituitary hormones on their target organs. Although certain cellular effects of growth hormone are known, such as increasing incorporation of amino acids into muscle protein, the biochemical mechanisms whereby this hormone exerts its effects at the cellular level remain a mystery.

The hormone ACTH stimulates the growth of the adrenal cortex and the secretion of cortisol and other cortical hormones. An interesting aspect of the ACTH molecule is that it contains in part a sequence found in the melanocyte-stimulating hormones and lipotropic hormones (see below). In accordance with their chemical similarities, it is not surprising that all of these hormones exhibit both melanocyte-stimulating and lipolytic activities.

The melanocyte-stimulating hormones are also called intermedins, since they can be isolated from the intermediate lobe of the pituitary in those animals which have a distinct intermediate lobe. Melanocyte-stimulating activity refers to the ability of these hormones to cause dispersion of pigment granules in melanocytes, producing a darkening of the skin. Two types of MSHs have been isolated. α-MSH is the most potent melanocyte-stimulating hormone; β-MSH has about 50% of the activity of α-MSH, while ACTH and the LPHs have about 1%.

In 1965–1966, β-lipotropic hormone and γ-lipotropic hormone, were isolated from the pituitaries of sheep and chemically characterized. The term lipotropic refers to the lipolytic activity of these substances on adipose tissue. Subsequently, it was learned that they also possessed melanocyte-stimulating activity. Lipolytic activity refers to the ability of certain hormones to stimulate the breakdown of lipid in adipose tissue to free fatty acids and glycerol. As has been mentioned, ACTH and the MSHs are also lipolytic hormones, and are, in fact, of greater potency in this regard than the LPHs. *See* LACTATION; PITUITARY GLAND; THYROID GLAND.   [C.H.L.]

Adenosine diphosphate (ADP)

Adenosine diphosphate (ADP)   A coenzyme and an important intermediate in cellular metabolism as the partially dephosphorylated form of adenosine triphosphate. The compound is 5′-adenylic acid with an additional phosphate group attached through a pyrophosphate bond. ADP is produced from adenosine triphosphate and reconverted to this compound in coupled reactions concerned with the energy metabolism of living systems. ADP is also produced from 5′-adenylic acid by the transfer of a phosphate group from adenosine triphosphate in a reaction that is catalyzed by an enzyme, myokinase. *See* METABOLISM.   [M.D.]

Adenosine triphosphate (ATP)

Adenosine triphosphate (ATP)   A coenzyme and one of the most important compounds in the metabolism of all organisms, since it serves as a coupling agent between different enzymatic reactions. Adenosine triphosphate is adenosine diphosphate (ADP) with an additional phosphate group attached through a pyrophosphate linkage to the terminal phosphate group (see illustration). ATP is a powerful donor of phosphate groups to suitable acceptors because of the pyrophosphate nature of the bonds between its three phosphate radicals. For instance, in the phosphorylation of glucose, which is an essential reaction in carbohydrate metabolism, the enzyme hexokinase catalyzes the transfer of the terminal phosphate group.

ATP serves as the immediate source of energy for the mechanical work performed by muscle. In its presence, the muscle protein actomyosin contracts with the formation of adenosine diphosphate and inorganic phosphate. ATP is also involved in the activation of amino acids, a necessary step in the synthesis of protein. *See* MUSCLE.

In metabolism, ATP is generated from adenosine diphosphate and inorganic phosphate mainly as a consequence of energy-yielding oxidation-reduction reactions. In respiration, ATP is generated during the transport of electrons from the substrate to

Structure of adenylic acid and phosphate derivatives ADP and ATP.

oxygen via the cytochrome system. In photosynthetic organisms, ATP is generated as a result of photochemical reactions. *See* CARBOHYDRATE METABOLISM; CYTOCHROME.

By virtue of its energy-rich pyrophosphate bonds, ATP serves as a link between sources of energy available to a living system and the chemical and mechanical work which is associated with growth, reproduction, and maintenance of living substance. For this reason, it has been referred to as the storehouse of energy of living systems. Because ATP, ADP, and adenylic acid are constantly interconverted through participation in various metabolic processes, they act as coenzymes for the coupled reactions in which they function. *See* BIOCHEMISTRY; COENZYME; METABOLISM.   [M.D.]

Adenoviridae   A family of viral agents associated with pharyngoconjunctival fever, acute respiratory disease, epidemic keratoconjunctivitis, and febrile pharyngitis in children. A number of types have been isolated from tonsils and adenoids removed from surgical patients. Although most of the illnesses caused by adenoviruses are respiratory, adenoviruses are frequently excreted in stools, and certain adenoviruses have been isolated from sewage. Distinct serotypes of mammalian and avian species are known. These genera contain 87 and 14 species, respectively. *See* ANIMAL VIRUS.

Infective virus particles, 70 nanometers in diameter, are icosahedrons with shells (capsids) composed of 252 subunits (capsomeres). No outer envelope is known. The genome is double-stranded deoxyribonucleic acid (DNA), with a molecular weight of $20–25 \times 10^6$. Three major soluble antigens are separable from the infectious particle by differential centrifugation. These antigens—a group-specifc antigen common to all adenovirus types, a type-specific antigen unique for each type, and a toxinlike material which also possesses group specificity—represent virus structural protein subunits that are produced in large excess of the amount utilized for synthesis of infectious virus.

The known types of adenoviruses of humans total at least 33, and previously unrecognized types continue to be isolated. The serotypes are antigenically distinct in neutralization tests, but they share a complement-fixing antigen, which is probably a smaller soluble portion of the virus.

The virus does not commonly produce acute disease in laboratory animals but is cytopathogenic, that is, destroys cells, in cultures of human tissue. Certain human adenovirus serotypes produce cancer when injected into newborn hamsters.

Base ratio determinations have revealed three distinct groups of adenoviruses: those with a low guanine plus cytosine (G + C) content (48–49%); those with an intermediate

G + C content (50–53%); and those with a high G + C content (56–60%). The strongly oncogenic adenovirus types 12, 18, and 31 are the only members of the group with low G + C, and certain adenoviruses in the intermediate group (types 3, 7, 14, 16, and 21) are mildly oncogenic. The adenovirus mRNA observed in transformed and tumor cells has a G + C content of 50–52% in the DNA. This suggests that viral DNA regions containing 47–48% G + C are integrated into the tumor cells or that such regions are preferentially transcribed. However, the mRNA from tumor cells induced by one subgroup such as the highly oncogenic adenoviruses (types 12 and 18) do not hybridize with DNA from the other two subgroups. Apparently, different viralcoded information is involved in carcinogenesis by the three different groups of adenoviruses.

With simian adenovirus 7 (SA7), the intact genome, as well as the heavy and light halves of the viral DNA, is capable of inducing tumors when injected into newborn hamsters. Extensive studies have failed to demonstrate adenovirus DNA or viral-specific mRNA in human tumors.

Live virus vaccines against type 4 and type 7 have been developed and used extensively in military populations. When both are administered simultaneously, vaccine recipients respond with neutralizing antibodies against both virus types. *See* ANTIGEN; COMPLEMENT-FIXATION TEST; NEUTRALIZATION REACTION (IMMUNOLOGY); VIRUS CLASSIFICATION. [J.L.Me.; M.E.Re.]

Adrenal gland   A complex endocrine organ in proximity to the kidney. Adrenal gland tissue is present in all vertebrates. The adrenal consists of two functionally distinct tissues: steroidogenic cells and catecholamine-secreting cells. While "adrenal" refers to the gland's proximity to the kidney, significant variation exists among vertebrates in its anatomic location as well as the relationship of the two endocrine tissues which make up the gland. In mammals, steroidogenic cells are separated into distinct zones that together form a cortex. This cortical tissue surrounds the catecholamine-secreting cells, constituting the medulla. In most other vertebrates, this unique anatomic cortical-medullary relationship is not present. In species of amphibians and fish, adrenal cells are found intermingling with kidney tissue, and the steroidogenic cells are often termed interrenal tissue.

Development. The adrenal gland forms from two primordia: cells of mesodermal origin which give rise to the steroid-secreting cells, and neural cells of ectodermal origin which develop into the catecholamine-secreting tissue (also known as chromaffin tissue). In higher vertebrates, mesenchymal cells originating from the coelomic cavity near the genital ridge proliferate to form a cluster of cells destined to be the adrenal cortex. During the second month of human development, cells of the neural crest migrate to the region of the developing adrenal and begin to proliferate on its surface. The expanding cortical tissue encapsulates the neural cells forming the cortex and medulla. In mammals, three distinct zones form within the cortex: the outermost zona glomerulosa, the middle zona fasiculata, and the inner zona reticularis. The glomerulosa cells contain an enzyme, aldosterone synthase, which converts corticosterone to aldosterone, the principal steroid (mineralocorticoid) secreted from this zone. The inner zones (fasiculata and reticularis) primarily secrete glucocorticoids and large amounts of sex steroid precursors. In many lower vertebrates, the two tissues form from similar primordia but migrate and associate in different ways to the extent that in some cases the two tissues develop in isolation from each other.

Comparative anatomy. While the paired adrenals in mammals have a characteristic cortical-medullary arrangement with distinct zonation present in the cortex, such distinctions are lacking in nonmammalian species. In more primitive fishes, chromaffin cells form in isolation from steroidogenic tissue. A general trend is present, however, throughout vertebrates for a closer association of chromaffin and steroidogenic tissues. Zonation in steroidogenic tissue is largely confined to mammals, although suggestions of separate cell types have been postulated in birds and in some other species.

Comparative endocrinology. Hormones are secreted from the cells of both the medulla and the cortex.

Chromaffin cells. In all vertebrates, chromaffin cells secrete catecholamines into circulation. In most species, the major catecholamine secreted is epinephrine, although significant amounts of norepinephrine are released by many animals. Some dopamine is also secreted. No phylogenetic trend is obvious to explain or predict the ratio of epinephrine to norepinephrine secreted in a given species. A given species may release the two catecholamines in different ratios, depending on the nature of the stimulus. The great majority of the norepinephrine in circulation actually originates from that which is released from non-adrenal sympathetic nerve endings and leaks into the bloodstream. In addition to catecholamines, chromaffin cells secrete an array of other substances, including proteins such as chromogranin A and opioid peptides. *See* EPINEPHRINE.

Biologic effects of catecholamines are mediated through their binding to two receptor classes, α- and β-adrenergic receptors. Further examination of these receptors has revealed that subclasses of each type exist and likely account for the responses on different target tissues. In general, biologic responses to catecholamines include mobilization of glucose from liver and muscle, increased alertness, increased heart rate, and stimulation of metabolic rate.

Steroid hormones. In broad terms, most steroids secreted by adrenal steroidogenic cells are glucocorticoids, mineralocorticoids, or sex hormone precursors. However, these classes have been established largely on the basis of differential actions in mammals. The principal glucocorticoids are cortisol and corticosterone, while the main mineralocorticoid is aldosterone. This division of action holds for mammalian species and likely for reptiles and birds. In other vertebrates, such as fish and amphibians, steroids from the interrenal tissue do not show such specialized actions; instead, most show activities of both glucocorticoid and mineralocorticoid type. Mammals, birds, reptiles, and amphibians secrete cortisol, corticosterone, and aldosterone. The ratios of the two glucocorticoids vary across species; in general, corticosterone is the more important product in nonmammalian species. Even within mammals, a large variation exists across species, due to the relative ratio of cortisol to corticosterone from the adrenal cortex.

Effects of adrenal-derived steroids in lower vertebrates involve a diverse array of actions, including control of distribution and availability of metabolic fuels such as glucose, and regulation of sodium and extracellular fluid volume. In nonmammalian vertebrates, corticosterone, cortisol, and aldosterone possess mineralocorticoid effects. Other areas where adrenal steroids likely contribute to biologic processes include control of protein, fat, and carbohydrate balance; reproduction; and growth and development. *See* STEROID.

[R.J.K.]

Aeromonas   A bacterial genus in the family Vibrionaceae comprising oxidase-positive, facultatively anaerobic, monotrichously flagellated gram-negative rods. The mesophilic species are *A. hydrophila*, *A. caviae*, and *A. sobria*; the psychrophilic one is *A. salmonicida*. Aeromonads are of aquatic origin and are found in surface and waste water but not in seawater. They infect chiefly cold-blooded animals such as fishes, reptiles, and amphibians and only occasionally warm-blooded animals and humans. Human wound infections may occur following contact with contaminated water. Septicemia has been observed mostly in patients with abnormally low white blood counts or liver disease. There is evidence of intestinal carriers. The three mesophilic species are also associated with diarrheal disease (enteritis and colitis) worldwide. *See* DIARRHEA.

A related lophotrichous genus, *Plesiomonas* (single species, *P. shigelloides*), is also known as an aquatic bacterium and is associated with diarrhea chiefly in subtropical and tropical areas. It is also found in many warm-blooded animals. Systemic disease in humans is rare. *See* MEDICAL BACTERIOLOGY.   [A.W.C.V.G.]

Affective disorders   A group of psychiatric conditions, also known as mood disorders, characterized by disturbances of affect, emotion, thinking, and behavior. Depression is the most common of these disorders, and about 10–20% of those affected also experience manic episodes. The affective disorders are not distinct diseases but are psychiatric syndromes that likely have multiple or complex etiologies.

Clinical syndromes. The most common form of affective disorder is a major depressive episode. The episode is defined by a pervasively depressed or low mood (which is experienced most of the day over a period of 2 weeks or longer) and at least four associated symptoms affecting sleep, appetite, hedonic capacity, interest, and behavior.

Major depressive episodes have several clinical forms. Melancholia is a severe episode characterized by anhedonia, marked anorexia with weight loss, early morning awakening, observable motor disturbances (extreme slowing, or retardation, or pacing and stereotypic agitated behaviors), and diurnal mood variation (mood is worse in the morning). *See* ANOREXIA NERVOSA.

Common among young patients, especially women, is a milder syndrome historically referred to as atypical depression. Atypical depression is characterized by intact mood reactivity (one's spirits can go up or down in response to day-to-day events) and reverse symptoms: oversleeping, overeating, or gaining weight. Significant anxiety symptoms, including phobias and panic attacks, also are common in atypical depression.

A more chronic, insidious form of depression known as dysthymia "smolders" at a subsyndromal level (that is, there are three or four daily symptoms) for at least 2 years. Dysthymia often begins early in life and, historically, has been intertwined with atypical and neurotic characteristics.

A manic episode is heralded by euphoric or irritable mood and at least four of the following: increased energy, activity, self-esteem, or speed of thought; decreased sleep; poor judgment; and risk-taking. About one-half of manic episodes are psychotic. The delusions of mania typically reflect grandiose or paranoid themes. Most people who have manic episodes also experience recurrent depressive episodes.

The term bipolar affective disorder has largely replaced the old term manic-depression, although both names convey the cyclical nature of this illness. The classical presentation (which includes full-blown manic episodes) is known as type 1 disorder. The diagnosis of bipolar type 2 disorder is used when there are recurrent depressive episodes and at least one hypomania. The diagnosis of cyclothymia is used when neither hypomanias nor depressions have reached syndromal levels.

Two variations of bipolar episodes are increasingly recognized. A mixed episode is diagnosed when the symptoms of mania and depression coexist. The term rapid cycling is used when there have been four or more episodes within a time frame of 1 year.

A number of affective disorders follow a seasonal pattern. A pattern of recurrent fall/winter depressions (also known as seasonal affective disorder) has generated considerable interest because it may be treated with bright white light, which artificially lengthens the photoperiod.

Literally all forms of affective disorder can be caused by general medical illnesses and medications that affect brain function (such as antihypertensives, hormonal therapies, steroids, and stimulant drugs). The diagnosis "mood disorder associated with a general medical condition" is applied to these conditions.

Pathophysiology. The affective disorders have diverse biopsychosocial underpinnings that result, at least in part, in extreme or distorted responses of several neurobehavioral systems. The neurobehavioral systems of greatest relevance regulate a person's drives and pursuits, responses to acute stress, and capacity to dampen or quiet pain or distress.

Although there is considerable evidence that affective disorders are heritable, vulnerability is unlikely to be caused by a single gene. It is likely that some combination of genes conveys greater risk and, like an amplifier, distorts the neural signals evoked by stress and distress. See BEHAVIOR GENETICS; HUMAN GENETICS.

Research permits several firm conclusions about brain neurochemistry in stress and depression. Acute stress mobilizes the release of three vital brain monoamines—serotonin, norepinephrine, and dopamine—as well as glucocorticoids such as cortisol. Sustained and unresolvable stress eventually depletes the neurotransmitters (cortisol levels remain high), inducing a behavioral state of learned helplessness. Severe depression, especially recurrent episodes of melancholia, affects the brain similarly.

Psychosocial and neurobiologic vulnerabilities, no doubt, intersect. For example, harsh early maltreatment, neglect, or other abuses can have lasting effects on both self-concept and brain responses to stress.

Epidemiology. The lifetime rates of affective disorders are increasing, with an earlier age of onset. The onset of major depression most often occurs in the late 20s to mid-30s; dysthymia and bipolar disorder typically begin about a decade earlier. However, no age group is immune to an affective disorder. Vulnerability is not related to social class or race, although the affluent are more likely to receive treatment.

Treatment. Most episodes of dysthymia and major depressive disorder respond to treatment with either psychotherapy or antidepressant medication, either singly or in combination. Many experts now recommend the newer forms of psychotherapy, including cognitive behavior therapy and interpersonal therapy, because they have been better studied than more traditional psychoanalytic therapies and because they have been found to be as effective as medications.

Nearly 30 antidepressant medications are available worldwide, with most falling into three classes: tricyclic antidepressants (TCAs), selective serotonin reuptake inhibitors (SSRIs), and monoamine oxidase reuptake inhibitors (MAOIs). Most classes of antidepressants enhance the efficiency of serotonin or norepinephrine neurotransmission. Antidepressants are not habit-forming and have no mood-elevating effects for nondepressed people. See PSYCHOPHARMACOLOGY; PSYCHOTHERAPY.

Acute manic episodes are usually treated with either lithium salts or divalproex sodium. Psychotic symptoms and severe agitation sometimes warrant the acute use of antipsychotic drugs. Although psychotherapy does not have a major role in the acute treatment of mania, it may help people come to terms with their illness, cope more effectively with stress, or curb minor depressive episodes.

When pharmacotherapies are not effective, the oldest proven treatment of the affective disorders, electroconvulsive therapy (ECT), still provides a powerful alternative. Today, ECT is a highly modified and carefully monitored treatment that has little in common with its depictions in the movies. Nevertheless, confusion and transient amnesia are still problems.

[M.E.T.]

Aflatoxin   Any of a group of secondary metabolites produced by the common molds *Aspergillus flavus* and *A. parasiticus* that cause a toxic response in vertebrates when introduced in low concentration by a natural route. The group constitutes a type of

(a)

(b)

(c)

(d)

Structures of major naturally occurring aflatoxins. (*a*) B_1. (*b*) B_2. (*c*) G_1. (*d*) G_2.

mycotoxin. The naturally occurring aflatoxins are identified in physicochemical assays as intensely blue (aflatoxins B_1 and B_2) or blue-green (aflatoxins G_1 and G_2) fluorescent compounds under long-wave ultraviolet light. The common structural feature of the four major aflatoxins is a dihydrodifurano or tetrahydrodifurano group fused to a substituted coumarin group (see illustration). The relative proportions of the four major aflatoxins synthesized by *Aspergillus* reflect the genetic constitution of the producing strain and the parameters associated with fungal growth. In addition, derivative aflatoxins are produced as metabolic or environmental products. *See* TOXIN.

Aflatoxins are formed through a polyketide pathway involving a series of enzymatically catalyzed reactions. In laboratory cultures, aflatoxins are biosynthesized after active growth has ceased, as is typical for secondary metabolites. By using blocked mutants and metabolic inhibitors, many of the intermediates have been identified as brightly colored anthraquinones.

Aflatoxins are potent molecules with many biological effects. They are toxigenic, carcinogenic, mutagenic, and teratogenic in various animal species. Aflatoxin B_1 is usually the most abundant naturally occurring member of the family, and most studies on the pharmacological activity of aflatoxin have been conducted with this congener. Aflatoxin B_1 is the most potent hepatocarcinogenic agent known, although the liver by no means is the only organ susceptible to aflatoxin carcinogenesis. Aflatoxin is listed as a probable human carcinogen by the International Agency for Research on Cancer. *See* PLANT PATHOLOGY.

Aflatoxins are a major agricultural problem. Contamination can occur in the field, during harvest, or in storage and processing. Corn, rice, cottonseed, and peanuts are the major crops regularly displaying high levels of aflatoxin contamination. Since *A. flavus* and *A. parasiticus* are nearly ubiquitous in the natural environment, numerous other grain, legume, nut, and spice crops, as well as coffee and cocoa, have been reported to contain aflatoxins. Given the potential of aflatoxins as human carcinogens and their known activity as toxins in animal feeds, many international regulatory agencies monitor aflatoxin levels in susceptible crops. Prevention is the main line of defense against aflatoxins entering the food chain. Moisture, temperature, and composition of the substrate are the chief factors affecting fungal growth and toxin production. In the field, insect damage is often involved. Detoxification is a last line of defense. Several commercially feasible methods of ammoniation have been developed for reducing levels of aflatoxin contamination in animal feeds. *See* AGRONOMY; MYCOTOXIN.   [J.W.Be.]

Agar   A major constituent of the cell walls of certain red algae, especially members of the families Gelidiaceae and Gracilariaceae. Extracted for its gelling properties, it is one of three algal polysaccharides of major economic importance, the others being alginate and carrageenan. Agar is composed of two similar fractions, agarose and agaropectin, in which the basic unit is galactose, linked alternately α-1,3-(D-galactose) and β-1,4-(α-L-galactose).

Agar is prepared by boiling the algae in water, after which the filtered solution is cooled, purified, and dried. It is an amorphous, translucent material that is packaged in granules, flakes, bricks, or sheets. One of its chief uses is as a gelling agent in media for culturing microorganisms. It is also used in making confections, as an emulsifier in cosmetics and food products, as a sizing agent, as an inert carrier of drugs in medicine, and as a laxative. *See* CULTURE.   [P.C.Si; R.L.Moe.]

Agglutination reaction   A reaction in which suspended particles are aggregated or clumped. It occurs upon the admixture of another type of particle, a change in the composition of the suspending fluid, or the addition of a soluble agent that acts as a bridge between two or more particles. The reaction is a secondary one in that the process resulting in agglutination occurs after the primary antigen-antibody linkage has taken place.

The particles undergoing agglutination may be either unicellular or microscopic multicellular organisms (such as bacteria and parasites), individual cells of multicellular organisms (such as erythrocytes and lymphocytes), or artificial particles (such as beads of plastic, glass, or polysaccharide). The immunological specificity of agglutination depends upon the uniqueness of the reaction between a marker substance on one type of particle and a receptor on either another type of particle or a specific antibody in solution. The marker can be a usual biological component of the surface of the particle or blood group substance on red cells. It can be an enzymatically or a chemically modified chemical group on the surface of biological particles. It can also be an adsorbed or a chemically attached substance. The attachment can be to biological particles or artificial ones. The receptor can be a biological component of the particle, an attached antibody, or antibody in solution. A reverse reaction is one in which the antibody is attached to a particle and the addition of the antigen causes the mixture to clump. Inhibition of agglutination can also be used to test for antigens, especially of low molecular weight, in a manner similar to that for agglutination itself. *See* ANTIGEN-ANTIBODY REACTION; IMMUNOASSAY.   [A.B.]

Agglutinin   A substance that will cause a clumping of particles such as bacteria or erythrocytes. Of major importance are the specific or immune agglutinins, which are antibodies that will agglutinate bacteria containing the corresponding antigens on their surfaces. Agglutinins are readily determined, and their presence is of diagnostic value to indicate present or past host contact with the microbial agent sufficient to result in antibody formation. *See* AGGLUTINATION REACTION; ANTIBODY.

Analogous reactions involve erythrocytes and their corresponding antibodies, the hemagglutinins. Hemagglutinins to a variety of erthyrocytes occur in many normal sera, and their amounts may be increased by immunization. The blood group isoagglutinins of humans and animals are important special cases which must be considered in all proposed blood transfusions lest transfusion reactions result. *See* BLOOD GROUPS.
                                                                    [H.P.T.]

Aggression   Behavior that is intended to threaten or inflict physical injury on another person or organism; a broader definition may include such categories as verbal attack, discriminatory behavior, and economic exploitation. The inclusion of intention in defining aggression makes it difficult to apply the term unequivocally to animals in which there is no clear means of determining the presence or absence of intention. As a result, animal violence is usually equated with aggression. There are four main approaches to understanding the causes or origins of human aggression. First, the basis may be differences among people, due either to physiological difference or to early childhood experiences. Second, there are sociological approaches which seek the causes of aggression in social factors such as economic deprivation and social (including family) conflicts. Third, causes may be found in the power relations of society as whole, where aggression arises as a function of control of one group by another. Fourth, aggression may be viewed as an inevitable (genetic) part of human nature; this approach has a long history and has produced extensive arguments. Given the wide variation in aggressive behavior in different societies and the occasional absence of such behavior in some groups and some individuals, a general human genetic factor is unlikely. However, some genetic disposition to react with force when an individual is blocked from reaching a goal may provide an evolutionary basis for the widespread occurrence of violence and aggression. The existence of different kinds of aggression suggests that different evolutionary scenarios need to be invoked and that aggression is not due to a single evolutionary event; it is likely that aggression is multidetermined and rarely, if ever, due to a single factor. *See* BEHAVIOR GENETICS.

Aggression in humans ranges through fear-induced aggression, parental disciplinary aggression, maternal aggression, and sexual aggression. One clearly biologically adaptive type, defensive aggression, occurs when fight responses are mobilized in defense of an organism's vital interests, such as obtaining food or the protection of its young. The aim of defensive aggression is not destruction but the preservation of life. Thus, aggression can serve both destructive and constructive purposes. Among animals, the varieties of aggression include most of the human types as well as predatory aggression, territorial defense, and sexually related aggression in competition for a mate.   [G.M.]

Agnosia   An impairment in the recognition of stimuli in a particular sensory modality. True agnosias are associative defects, where the perceived stimulus fails to arouse a meaningful state. An unequivocal diagnosis of agnosia requires that the recognition failure not be due to sensory-perceptual deficits, to generalized intellectual impairment, or to impaired naming (as in aphasia). Because one or more of these conditions frequently occur with agnosia, some clinical scientists have questioned whether pure recognition disturbances genuinely exist; but careful investigation of appropriate cases has affirmed agnosia as an independent entity which may occur in the visual, auditory, or somesthetic modalities. *See* APHASIA.

The patient with visual object agnosia, though quite able to identify objects presented auditorily or tactually, cannot name or give other evidence of recognizing visually presented objects. Because visual object agnosia is a rather rare disorder, knowledge of its underlying neuropathology is incomplete. Most reported cases have shown bilateral occipital lobe lesions, with the lesion extending deep into the white matter and often involving the corpus callosum. Prosopagnosia is the inability to recognize familiar faces. Persons well known to the individual before onset of the condition, including members of the immediate family, are not recognized. In many instances, individuals fail to recognize picture or mirror images of themselves. Isolated impairment of reading is frequently considered to be an exotic form of aphasia. Logically, however, it may be considered as a visual-verbal agnosia (also referred to as pure word blindness or alexia without agraphia). Individuals with this disorder show a marked reduction in their ability to read the printed word, though their writing and other language modalities remain essentially intact.

The term auditory agnosia is most often used to indicate failure to recognize non-verbal acoustic stimuli despite adequate hearing sensitivity and discrimination. In most well-documented cases of agnosia for sounds, the subjects have had bilateral temporal lobe lesions. Auditory-verbal agnosia (or pure word deafness) is a disturbance in comprehension of spoken language, in the presence of otherwise intact auditory functioning and essentially normal performance in other language modalities. The person's speech expression is remarkably intact in comparison with the gross impairment in understanding speech. Like its visual analog, visual-verbal agnosia, this is a disconnection syndrome. It is produced by damage to the left primary auditory cortex (or the tracts leading to it) coupled with a lesion to the corpus callosum. Phonagnosia is a disturbance in the recognition of familiar voices. The person has good comprehension of what is spoken, but the speaker cannot be identified. *See* BRAIN; HEARING (HUMAN); HEMISPHERIC LATERALITY; PSYCHOACOUSTICS; VISION.   [G.J.C.]

Agonomycetes   Mitosporic or anamorphic (asexual or imperfect) fungi (Deuteromycotina) that not only lack fruit bodies but also fail to produce conidia, the thallus consisting of septate hyphae. Somatic structures of propagation or survival, termed propagules, are varied and include chlamydospores and bulbils. Hyphae are modified to form sclerotia, pseudosclerotia, rhizomorphs, strands, and cords. About 40 genera (with +30 synonyms) containing 220 species are recognized. The Agonomycetes constitute an artificial group that does not consist of closely related genera and is recognized for its practicality rather than homogeneous taxonomic composition. They are circumscribed not only by what they lack, such as conidia, asci and ascospores, basidia and basidiospores, and zygospores, but also by the apparent superficial similarity between some of the members in, for example, hyphal, chlamydospore, and sclerotial form.

Agonomycetes are generally considered to be combative species which are persistent and long-lived, largely because of the resistant nature of their vegetative structures and their slow and intermittent reproduction or complete absence of reproduction. Whether they are capable of defending captive resources and have good enzymatic competence, which are other features of combative species, is largely unknown. However, they occupy diverse ecological niches, including aquatic habitats, soil, wood in various stages of decay, other decaying plant material, and dung. They also function as root and foliar pathogens, and many cause serious diseases in terms of host damage and economic loss, especially of roots, corms, and bulbs. Agonomycetes sometimes cause damage in commercial mushroom-growing environments, and *Papulaspora byssina* in particular is associated with the brown plaster mold problem in mushroom beds. *Armillaria*, a basidiomycete with a *Rhizomorpha* agonomycete state, is a severe parasite of a wide range of woody and herbaceous plants. *See* DEUTEROMYCOTINA; PLANT PATHOLOGY.

[B.C.S.]

Agriculture   The art and science of crop and livestock production. In its broadest sense, agriculture comprises the entire range of technologies associated with the production of useful products from plants and animals, including soil cultivation, crop and livestock management, and the activities of processing and marketing. The term agribusiness has been coined to include all the technologies that mesh in the total inputs and outputs of the farming sector. In this light, agriculture encompasses the whole range of economic activities involved in manufacturing and distributing the industrial inputs used in farming; the farm production of crops, animals, and animal products; the processing of these materials into finished products; and the provision of products at a time and place demanded by consumers.

Many different factors influence the kind of agriculture practiced in a particular area. Among these are climate, soil, water availability, topography, nearness to markets, transportation facilities, land costs, and general economic level. Climate, soil, water availability, and topography vary widely throughout the world. This variation brings about a wide range in agricultural production enterprises. Certain areas tend toward a specialized agriculture, whereas other areas engage in a more diversified agriculture. As new technology is introduced and adopted, environmental factors are less important in influencing agricultural production patterns. Continued growth in the world's population makes critical the continuing ability of agriculture to provide needed food and fiber.

The primary agricultural products consist of crop plants for human food and animal feed and livestock products. The crop plants can be divided into 10 categories: grain crops (wheat, for flour to make bread, many bakery products, and breakfast cereals; rice, for food; maize, for livestock feed, syrup, meal, and oil; sorghum grain, for livestock feed; and oats, barley, and rye, for food and livestock feed); food grain legumes (beans, peas, lima beans, and cowpeas, for food; and peanuts, for food and oil); oil seed crops (soybeans, for oil and high-protein meal; and linseed, for oil and high-protein meal); root and tuber crops (principally potatoes and sweet potatoes); sugar crops (sugarbeets and sugarcane); fiber crops (principally cotton, for fiber to make textiles and for seed to produce oil and high-protein meal); tree and small fruits; nut crops; vegetables; and forages (for support of livestock pastures and range grazing lands and for hay and silage crops). The forages are dominated by a wide range of grasses and legumes, suited to different conditions of soil and climate.

Livestock products include cattle, for beef, tallow, and hides; dairy cattle, for milk, butter, cheese, ice cream, and other products; sheep, for mutton (lamb) and wool; pigs, for pork and lard; poultry (chiefly chickens but also turkeys and ducks) for meat and eggs; and horses, primarily for recreation.   [J.J.]

Agroecosystem   A model for the functionings of an agricultural system, with all inputs and outputs. An ecosystem may be as small as a set of microbial interactions that take place on the surface of roots, or as large as the globe. An agroecosystem may be at the level of the individual plant-soil-microorganism system, at the level of crops or herds of domesticated animals, at the level of farms or agricultural landscapes, or at the level of entire agricultural economies.

Characteristics. Agroecosystems differ from natural ecosystems in several fundamental ways. First, the energy that drives all autotrophic ecosystems, including agroecosystems, is either directly or indirectly derived from solar energy. However, the energy input to agroecosystems includes not only natural energy (sunlight) but also processed energy (fossil fuels) as well as human and animal labor. Second, biodiversity in agroecosystems is generally reduced by human management in order to channel as much energy and nutrient flow as possible into a few domesticated species. Finally, evolution is largely, but not entirely, through artificial selection where commercially desirable phenotypic traits are increased through breeding programs and genetic engineering. Agroecosystems are usually examined from a range of perspectives including energy flux, exchange of materials, nutrient budgets, and population and community dynamics.

Solar energy influences agroecosystem productivity directly by providing the energy for photosynthesis and indirectly through heat energy that influences respiration, rates of water loss, and the heat balance of plants and animals. See BIOLOGICAL PRODUCTIVITY; ECOLOGICAL ENERGETICS; PHOTOSYNTHESIS.

Nutrient uptake from soil by crop plants or weeds is primarily mediated by microbial processes. Some soil bacteria fix atmospheric nitrogen into forms that plants can assimilate. Other organisms influence soil structure and the exchange of nutrients, and still other microorganisms may excrete ammonia and other metabolic by-products that are useful plant nutrients. There are many complex ways that microorganisms influence nutrient cycling and uptake by plants. Some microorganisms are plant pathogens that reduce nutrient uptake in diseased plants. Larger organisms may influence nutrient uptake indirectly by modifying soil structure or directly by damaging plants. See SOIL MICROBIOLOGY.

Although agroecosystems may be greatly simplified compared to natural ecosystems, they can still foster a rich array of population and community processes such as herbivory, predation, parasitization, competition, and mutualism. Crop plants may compete among themselves or with weeds for sunlight, soil nutrients, or water. Cattle overstocked in a pasture may compete for forage and thereby change competitive interactions among pasture plants, resulting in selection for unpalatable or even toxic plants. Indeed, one important goal of farming is to find the optimal densities for crops and livestock. See HERBIVORY; POPULATION ECOLOGY.

Widespread use of synthetic chemical pesticides has bolstered farm production worldwide, primarily by reducing or eliminating herbivorous insect pests. Traditional broad-spectrum pesticides such as DDT, however, can have far-ranging impacts on agroecosystems. For instance, secondary pest outbreaks associated with the use of many traditional pesticides are not uncommon due to the elimination of natural enemies or resistance of pests to chemical control. Growers and pesticide developers in temperate regions have begun to focus on alternative means of control. Pesticide developers have begun producing selective pesticides, which are designed to target only pest species and to spare natural enemies, leaving the rest of the agroecosystem community intact. Many growers are now implementing integrated pest management programs that incorporate the new breed of biorational chemicals with cultural and other types of controls.

Genetic engineering. The last few decades have seen tremendous advances in molecular approaches to engineering desirable phenotypic traits in crop plants. Although artificially modifying crop plants is nothing new, the techniques used in genetic engineering allow developers to generate new varieties an order-of-magnitude faster than traditional plant breeding. In addition, genetic engineering differs from traditional breeding in that the transfer of traits is no longer limited to same-species organisms. Scientists are still assessing the effects that the widespread deployment of these traits may have on agroecosystems and natural ecosystems. There is some concern, for instance, that engineered traits may escape, via genes in pollen transferred by pollinators, and become established in weedy populations of plants in natural ecosystems, in some cases creating conservation management problems and new breeds of superweeds. As with pesticides, there is evidence that insects are already becoming resistant to some more widespread traits used in transgenic plants, such as the anti-herbivore toxin produced by the bacterium *Bacillus thuringiensis*. *See* BIOTECHNOLOGY; GENETIC ENGINEERING.   [C.R.Ca.; C.A.H.; J.E.Ba.]

Agronomy   The science and study of crops and soils. Agronomy is the umbrella term for a number of technical research and teaching activities: crop physiology and management, soil science, plant breeding, and weed management frequently are included in agronomy; soil science may be treated separately; and vegetable and fruit crops generally are not included. Thus, agronomy refers to extensive field cultivation of plant species for human food, livestock and poultry feed, fibers, oils, and certain industrial products. *See* AGRICULTURE.

Agronomic studies include some basic research, but the specialists in this field concentrate on applying information from the more basic disciplines, among them botany, chemistry, genetics, mathematics, microbiology, and physiology. Agronomists also interact closely with specialists in other applied areas such as ecology, entomology, plant pathology, and weed science. The findings of these collaborative efforts are tested and recommended to farmers through agricultural extension agents or commercial channels to bring this knowledge into practice. This critical area is now focused on the efficiency of resource use, profitability of management practices, and minimization of the impact of farming on the immediate and the off-farm environment. *See* AGROECOSYSTEM.
                    [C.A.F.]

Albumin   A type of globular protein that is characterized by its solubility in water and in 50% saturated aqueous ammonium sulfate. Albumins are present in mammalian tissues, bacteria, molds, and plants, and in some foods. Serum albumin, which contains 584 amino acid residues, is the most abundant protein in human serum, and it performs two very important physiological functions. It is responsible for about 80% of the total osmotic regulation in blood, and it transports fatty acids from adipose tissue to muscle. When excessive amounts of albumin are found in the urine upon clinical examination, some form of kidney disease is usually indicated. Another important albumin, ovalbumin, is found in egg white. This protein is about two-thirds the size of serum albumin, and it contains sugar residues in addition to amino acid residues (that is, it is a glycoprotein). *See* PROTEIN.   [J.M.M.]

Aldosterone   The steroid hormone found in the biologically active amorphous fraction that remains after separation of the various crystalline steroid substances, such as cortisol and corticosterone, from adrenal extracts. In solution, aldosterone exists as an equilibrium mixture of aldo and lactol forms (see illustration).

Structures for two forms of aldosterone in an equilibrium mixture, (*a*) aldo and (*b*) lactol.

The chief function of aldosterone is the regulation of electrolyte metabolism, that is, promotion of sodium retention and enhancement of potassium excretion. Aldosterone is the most potent of the hormones which are concerned in this type of metabolism. *See* ADRENAL GLAND; HORMONE; STEROID.

[C.H.L.]

Algae   An informal assemblage of predominantly aquatic organisms that carry out oxygen-evolving photosynthesis but lack specialized water-conducting and food-conducting tissues. They may be either prokaryotic (lacking an organized nucleus) and therefore members of the kingdom Monera, or eukaryotic (with an organized nucleus) and therefore members of the kingdom Plantae, constituting with fungi the subkingdom Thallobionta. They differ from the next most advanced group of plants, Bryophyta, by their lack of multicellular sex organs sheathed with sterile cells and by their failure to re-tain an embryo within the female organ. Many colorless organisms are referable to the algae on the basis of their similarity to photosynthetic forms with respect to structure, life history, cell wall composition, and storage products. The study of algae is called al-gology (from the Latin *alga*, meaning sea wrack) or phycology (from the Greek *phykos*, seaweed). *See* BRYOPHYTA; PLANT KINGDOM; THALLOBIONTA.

General form and structure.   Algae range from unicells 1–2 micrometers in diam-eter to huge thalli [for example, kelps often 100 ft (30 m) long] with functionally and structurally distinctive tissues and organs. Unicells may be solitary or colonial, attached or free-living, with or without a protective cover, and motile or nonmotile. Colonies may be irregular or with a distinctive pattern, the latter type being flagellate or nonmotile. Multicellular algae form packets, branched or unbranched filaments, sheets one or two cells thick, or complex thalli, some with organs resembling roots, stems, and leaves (as in the brown algal orders Fucales and Laminariales). Coenocytic algae, in which the protoplast is not divided into cells, range from microscopic spheres to thalli 33 ft (10 m) long with a complex structure of intertwined siphons (as in the green algal order Bryopsidales).

Classification.   Sixteen major phyletic lines (classes) are distinguished on the basis of differences in pigmentation, storage products, cell wall composition, flagellation of motile cells, and structure of such organelles as the nucleus, chloroplast, pyrenoid, and eyespot. These classes are interrelated to varying degrees, the interrelationships being expressed by the arrangement of classes into divisions (the next-higher category). Among phycologists there is far greater agreement on the number of major phyletic lines than on their arrangement into divisions.

Superkingdom Prokaryotae
   Kingdom Monera
      Division Cyanophycota (= Cyanophyta, Cyanochloronta)
         Class Cyanophyceae, blue-green algae
      Division Prochlorophycota (= Prochlorophyta)
         Class Prochlorophyceae
Superkingdom Eukaryotae
   Kingdom Plantae
      Subkingdom Thallobionta
         Division Rhodophycota (= Rhodophyta, Rhodophycophyta)
            Class Rhodophyceae, red algae
         Division Chromophycota (= Chromophyta)
            Class: Chrysophyceae, golden or golden-brown algae
                  Prymnesiophyceae (= Haptophyceae)
                  Xanthophyceae (= Tribophyceae), yellow-green algae
                  Eustigmatophyceae
                  Bacillariophyceae, diatoms
                  Dinophyceae, dinoflagellates
                  Phaeophyceae, brown algae
                  Raphidophyceae, chloromonads
               Cryptophyceae, cryptomonads
         Division Euglenophycota (= Euglenophyta, Euglenophycophyta)
            Class Euglenophyceae
         Division Chlorophycota (= Chlorophyta, Chlorophycophyta)
            Class: Chlorophyceae, green algae
                 Charophyceae, charophytes
                 Prasinophyceae

    Placing more taxonomic importance on motility than on photosynthesis, zoologists traditionally have considered flagellate unicellular and colonial algae as protozoa, assigning each phyletic line the rank of order. *See* PROTOZOA.

    Although some unicellular algae are naked or sheathed by mucilage or scales, most are invested with a covering (wall, pellicle, or lorica) of diverse composition and construction. These coverings consist of at least one layer of polysaccharide (cellulose, alginate, agar, carrageenan, mannan, or xylan), protein, or peptidoglycan that may be impregnated or encrusted with calcium carbonate, iron, manganese, or silica. They are often perforated and externally ornamented. Diatoms have a complex wall composed almost entirely of silica. In multicellular and coenocytic algae, most reproductive cells are naked, but vegetative cells have walls whose composition varies from class to class. *See* CELL WALLS (PLANT).

Characteristics. Prokaryotic algae lack membrane-bounded organelles. Eukaryotic algae have an intracellular architecture comparable to that of higher plants but more varied. Among cell structures unique to algae are contractile vacuoles in some freshwater unicells, gas vacuoles in some planktonic blue-green algae, ejectile organelles in dinoflagellates and cryptophytes, and eyespots in motile unicells and reproductive cells of many classes. Chromosome numbers vary from $n = 2$ in some red and green algae to $n \geq 300$ in some dinoflagellates. The dinoflagellate nucleus is in some respects intermediate between the chromatin region of prokaryotes and the nucleus of eukaryotes and is termed mesokaryotic. Some algal cells characteristically are multinucleate, while others are uninucleate. Chloroplasts, which always originate by division of pre-existing chloroplasts, have the form of plates, ribbons, disks, networks, spirals, or stars and may be positioned centrally or along the cell wall. Photosynthetic membranes (thylakoids) are arranged in distinctive patterns and contain pigments diagnostic of individual classes. *See* CELL (BIOLOGY); CELL PLASTIDS; CHROMOSOME; PHOTOSYNTHESIS; PLANT CELL.

In all classes of algae except Prochlorophyceae, there are cells that are capable of movement. The slow, gliding movement of certain blue-green algae, diatoms, and reproductive cells of red algae presumably results from extracellular secretion of mucilage. Ameboid movement, involving pseudopodia, is found in certain Chrysophyceae and Xanthophyceae. An undulatory or peristaltic movement occurs in some Euglenophyceae. The fastest movement is produced by flagella, which are borne by unicellular algae and reproductive cells of multicellular algae representing all classes except Cyanophyceae, Prochlorophyceae, and Rhodophyceae.

Internal movement also occurs in algae in the form of cytoplasmic streaming and light-induced orientation of chloroplasts. *See* CELL MOTILITY; CILIA AND FLAGELLA.

Sexual reproduction is unknown in prokaryotic algae and in three classes of eukaryotic unicells (Eustigmatophyceae, Cryptophyceae, and Euglenophyceae), in which the production of new individuals is by binary fission. In sexual reproduction, which is found in all remaining classes, the members of a copulating pair of gametes may be morphologically indistinguishable (isogamous), morphologically distinguishable but with both gametes motile (anisogamous), or differentiated into a motile sperm and a relatively large nonmotile egg (oogamous). Gametes may be formed in undifferentiated cells or in special organs (gametangia), male (antheridia) and female (oogonia). Sexual reproduction may be replaced or supplemented by asexual reproduction, in which special cells (spores) capable of developing directly into a new alga are formed in undifferentiated cells or in distinctive organs (sporangia). *See* REPRODUCTION (PLANT).

Most algae are autotrophic, obtaining energy and carbon through photosynthesis. All photosynthetic algae liberate oxygen and use chlorophyll *a* as the primary photosynthetic pigment. Secondary (accessory) photosynthetic pigments, which capture light energy and transfer it to chlorophyll *a*, include chlorophyll *b* (Prochlorophyceae, Euglenophyceae, Chlorophycota), chlorophyll *c* (Chromophycota), fucoxanthin among other xanthophylls (Chromophycota), and phycobiliproteins (Cyanophyceae, Rhodophyceae, Cryptophyceae). Other carotenoids, especially β-carotene, protect the photosynthetic pigments from oxidative bleaching. Except for different complements of accessory pigments (resulting in different action spectra), photosynthesis in algae is identical to that in higher plants. Carbon is predominantly fixed through the C_3 pathway. *See* CAROTENOID; CHLOROPHYLL.

The source of carbon for most photosynthetic algae is carbon dioxide (CO_2), but some can use bicarbonate. Many photosynthetic algae are also able to use organic substances (such as hexose sugars and fatty acids) and thus can grow in the dark or in the absence of CO_2. Colorless algae obtain both energy and carbon from a wide variety of organic compounds in a process called oxidative assimilation.

Numerous substances are liberated into water by living algae, often with marked ecological effects. These extracellular products include simple sugars and sugar alcohols, wall polysaccharides, glycolic acid, phenolic substances, and aromatic compounds. Some secreted substances inhibit the growth of other algae and even that of the secreting alga. Some are toxic to fishes and terrestrial animals that drink the water.

Occurrence. Algae are predominantly aquatic, inhabiting fresh, brackish, and marine waters without respect to size or degree of permanence of the habitat. They may be planktonic (free-floating or motile) or benthic (attached). Benthic marine algae are commonly called seaweeds. Substrates include rocks (outcrops, boulders, cobbles, pebbles), plants (including other algae), animals, boat bottoms, piers, debris, and less frequently sand and mud. Some species occur on a wide variety of living organisms, suggesting that the hosts are providing only space. Many species, however, have a restricted range of hosts and have been shown to be (or are suspected of being) at least partially parasitic. All reef-building corals contain dinoflagellates, without which their calcification ability is greatly reduced. Different phases in a life history may have different substrate preferences. Many fresh-water algae have become adapted to a nonaquatic habitat, living on moist soil, masonry and wooden structures, and trees. A few parasitize higher plants (expecially in the tropics), producing diseases in such crops as tea, coffee, and citrus. Thermophilic algae (again, chiefly blue-greens) live in hot springs at temperatures up to 163°F (73°C), forming a calcareous deposit known as tufa. One of the most remarkable adaptations of certain algae (blue-greens and greens) is their coevolution with fungi to form a compound organism, the lichen. See LICHENS; PHYTOPLANKTON.

Geographic distribution. Fresh-water algae, which are distributed by spores or fragments borne by the wind or by birds, tend to be widespread if not cosmopolitan, their distribution being limited by the availability of suitable habitats. Certain species, however, are characteristic of one or another general climatic zone, such as cold-temperate regions or the tropics. Marine algae, which are spread chiefly by water-borne propagules or reproductive cells, often have distinctive geographic patterns. Many taxonomic groups are widely distributed, but others are characteristic of particular climatic zones or geographic areas. See PLANT GEOGRAPHY.

Economic importance. Numerous red, brown, and green seaweeds as well as a few species of fresh-water algae are consumed by the peoples of eastern Asia, Indonesia, Polynesia, and the North Atlantic. Large brown seaweeds may be chopped and added to poultry and livestock feed or applied whole as fertilizer for crop plants. The purified cell-wall polysaccharides of brown and red algae (alginate, agar, carrageenan) are used as gelling, suspending, and emulsifying agents in numerous industries. Some seaweeds have specific medicinal properties, such as effectiveness against worms. Petroleum is generally believed to result from bacterial degradation of organic matter derived primarily from planktonic algae.

Planktonic algae, as the primary producers in oceans and lakes, support the entire aquatic trophic pyramid and thus are the basis of the fisheries industry. Concomitantly, their production of oxygen counteracts its uptake in animal respiration. The ability of certain planktonic algae to assimilate organic nutrients makes them important in the treatment of sewage. See FOOD WEB.

On the negative side, algae can be a nuisance by imparting tastes and odors to drinking water, clogging filters, and making swimming pools, lakes, and beaches unattractive. Sudden growths (blooms) of planktonic algae can produce toxins of varying potency. In small bodies of fresh water, the toxin (usually from blue-green algae) can kill fishes and livestock that drink the water. In the ocean, toxins produced by dinoflagellate blooms (red tides) can kill fishes and render shellfish poisonous to humans.

Fossil algae. At least half of the classes of algae are represented in the fossil record, usually abundantly, in the form of siliceous, calcareous, or organic remains, impressions, or indications. Blue-green algae were among the first inhabitants of the Earth, appearing in rocks at least as old as 2.3 billion years. Their predominance in shallow Precambrian seas is indicated by the extensive development of stromatolites.

All three classes of seaweeds (reds, browns, and greens) were well established by the close of the Precambrian, 600 million years ago (mya). By far the greatest number of fossil taxa belong to classes whose members are wholly or in large part planktonic. Siliceous frustules of diatoms and endoskeletons of silicoflagellates, calcareous scales of coccolithophorids, and highly resistant organic cysts of dinoflagellates contribute slowly but steadily to sediments blanketing ocean floors, as they have for tens of millions of years. Cores obtained in the Deep Sea Drilling Project have revealed an astounding chronology of the appearance, rise, decline, and extinction of a succession of species and genera. From this chronology, much can be deduced about the climate, hydrography, and ecology of particular geological periods. [P.C.Si.; R.L.Moe.]

Alkaloid   A cyclic organic compound that contains nitrogen in a negative oxidation state and is of limited distribution among living organisms. Over 10,000 alkaloids of many different structural types are known; and no other class of natural products possesses such an enormous variety of structures. Therefore, alkaloids are difficult to differentiate from other types of organic nitrogen-containing compounds.

Simple low-molecular-weight derivatives of ammonia, as well as polyamines and acyclic amides, are not considered alkaloids because they lack a cyclic structure in some part of the molecule. Amines, amine oxides, amides, and quaternary ammonium salts are included in the alkaloid group because their nitrogen is in a negative oxidation state (the oxidation state designates the positive or negative character of atoms in a molecule). Nitro and nitroso compounds are excluded as alkaloids. The almost-ubiquitous nitrogenous compounds, such as amino acids, amino sugars, peptides, proteins, nucleic acids, nucleotides, prophyrins, and vitamins, are not alkaloids. However, compounds that are exceptions to the classical-type definition (that is, a compound containing nitrogen, usually a cyclic amine, and occurring as a secondary metabolite), such as neutral alkaloids (colchicine, piperine), the β-phenylethylanines, and the purine bases (caffeine, theophylline, theobromine), are accepted as alkaloids.

Alkaloids often occur as salts of plant acids such as malic, meconic, and quinic acids. Some plant alkaloids are combined with sugars, for example, solanine in potato (*Solanum tuberosum*) and tomatine in tomato (*Lycopersicum esculentum*). Others occur as amides, for example, piperine from black pepper (*Piper nigrum*), or as esters, for example, cocaine from coca leaves (*Erythroxylum coca*). Still other alkaloids occur as quaternary salts or tertiary amine oxides.

While most alkaloids have been isolated from plants, a large number have been isolated from animal sources. They occur in mammals, anurans (frogs, toads), salamanders, arthropods (ants, millipedes, ladybugs, beetles, butterflies), marine organisms, mosses, fungi, and certain bacteria.

Many alkaloids exhibit marked pharmacological activity, and some find important uses in medicine. Atropine, the optically inactive form of hyoscyamine, is used widely in medicine as an antidote to cholinesterase inhibitors such as physostigmine and insecticides of the organophosphate type; it is also used in drying cough secretions. Morphine and codeine are narcotic analgesics, and codeine is also an antitussive agent, less toxic and less habit-forming than morphine. Colchicine, from the corms and seeds of the autumn crocus, is used as a gout suppressant. Caffeine, which occurs in coffee, tea, cocoa, and cola, is a central nervous system stimulant; it is used as a cardiac and respiratory stimulant and as an antidote to barbiturate and morphine poisoning. Emetine, the key alkaloid of ipecac root (*Cephaelis ipecacuanha*), is used in the treatment of amebic dysentery and other protozoal infections. Epinephrine or adrenaline (see structure),

produced in most animal species by the adrenal medulla, is used as a bronchodilator and cardiac stimulant and to counter allergic reactions, anesthesia, and cardiac arrest. *See* EPINEPHRINE.   [S.W.Pe.]

Allantois   A fluid-filled sac- or sausagelike, extraembryonic membrane lying between the outer chorion and the inner amnion and yolk sac of the embryos of reptiles, birds, and mammals. It is composed of an inner layer of endoderm cells, continuous with the endoderm of the embryonic gut, or digestive tract, and an outer layer of mesoderm, continuous with the splanchnic mesoderm of the embryo. It arises as an outpouching of the ventral floor of the hindgut and dilates into a large allantoic sac which spreads throughout the extraembryonic coelom. The allantois remains connected to the hindgut by a narrower allantoic stalk which runs through the umbilical cord. *See* AMNION; CHORION; GERM LAYERS.

The allantois eventually fuses with the overlying chorion to form the compound chorioallantois, which lies just below the shell membranes in reptiles and birds. The chorioallantois is supplied with an extensive network of blood vessels and serves as an important respiratory and excretory organ for gaseous interchange. The allantoic cavity also serves as a reservoir for kidney wastes in some mammals, in reptiles, and in birds. In the latter two groups the allantois assists in the absorption of albumin. In some mammals, including humans, the allantois is vestigial and may regress, yet the homologous blood vessels persist as the important umbilical arteries and veins connecting the embryo with the placenta. *See* FETAL MEMBRANE; PLACENTATION.   [N.T.S.]

Allele   Any of a number of alternative forms of a gene. Allele is a contraction of allelomorph, a term used to designate one of the alternative forms of a unit showing mendelian segregation. New alleles arise from existing ones by mutation. The diversity of alleles produced in this way is the basis for hereditary variation and evolution. The different alleles of a given gene determine the degree to which the specific hereditary characteristic controlled by that gene is manifested. The particular allele which causes that characteristic to be expressed in a normal fashion is often referred to as the wild-type allele. Mutations of the wild-type allele result in mutant alleles, whose functioning in the development of the organism is generally impaired relative to that of the wild-type allele. *See* DEOXYRIBONUCLEIC ACID (DNA); GENE; GENE ACTION; GENETIC CODE; MENDELISM; MUTATION.

An allele occupies a fixed position or locus in the chromosome. In the body cells of most higher organisms, including humans, there are two chromosomes of each kind and hence two alleles of each kind of gene, except for the sex chromosomes. Such organisms and their somatic cells are said to carry a diploid complement of alleles. A diploid individual is homozygous if the same allele is present twice, or heterozygous if two different alleles are present. Let *A* and *a* represent a pair of alleles of a given gene; then *A/A* and *a/a* are the genetic constitutions or genotypes of the two possible homozygotes, while *A/a* is the genotype of the heterozygote. Usually the appearance or phenotype of the *A/a* individuals resembles that of the *A/A* type; *A* is then said to be the dominant allele and *a* the recessive allele. In the case of the sex chromosomes, one sex (usually the male in most higher animals, with the exception of birds) has only one X chromosome, and the Y lacks almost all of the genes in X. The male thus carries only one dose of X-linked genes and is said to be hemizygous for alleles carried on his X chromosome. As a result, if a male inherits a recessive mutant allele such as color blindness on his X chromosome, he expresses color blindness because he lacks the wild-type allele on his Y chromosome. *See* CHROMOSOME; SEX-LINKED INHERITANCE.

In a population of diploid individuals, it is possible to have more than two alleles of a given gene. The aggregate of such alleles is called a multiple allelic series. Since genes are linear sequences of hundreds or even thousands of nucleotide base pairs, the potential number of alleles of a given gene which can arise by base substitution alone is enormous. [E.B.L.]

Allelopathy   The biochemical interactions among all types of plants, including microorganisms. The term is usually interpreted as the detrimental influence of one plant upon another but is used more and more, as intended originally, to encompass both detrimental and beneficial interactions. At least two forms of allelopathy are distinguished: (1) the production and release of an allelochemical by one species inhibiting the growth of only other adjacent species, which may confer competitive advantage for the allelopathic species; and (2) autoallelopathy, in which both the species producing the allelochemical and unrelated species are indiscriminately affected. The term allelopathy, frequently restricted to interactions among higher plants, is now applied to interactions among plants from all divisions, including algae. Even interactions between plants and herbivorous insects or nematodes in which plant substances attract, repel, deter, or retard the growth of attacking insects or nematodes are considered to be allelopathic. Interactions between soil microorganisms and plants are important in allelopathy. Fungi and bacteria may produce and release inhibitors or promoters. Some bacteria enhance plant growth through fixing nitrogen, others through providing phosphorus. The activity of nitrogen-fixing bacteria may be affected by allelochemicals, and this effect in turn may influence ecological patterns. The rhizosphere must be considered the main site for allelopathic interactions.

Allelopathy is clearly distinguished from competition: In allelopathy a chemical is introduced by the plant into the environment, whereas in competition the plant removes or reduces such environmental components as minerals, water, space, gas exchange, and light. In the field, both allelopathy and competition usually act simultaneously. [M.Ru.]

Allergy   Altered reactivity in humans and animals to allergens (substances foreign to the body that cause allergy) induced by exposure through injection, inhalation, ingestion, or skin contact. The most common clinical manifestations of allergy are hay fever, asthma, hives, atopic (endogenous) eczema, and eczematous skin lesions caused by direct contact with allergens such as poison ivy or certain chemicals.

A large variety of substances may cause allergies: pollens, animal proteins, molds, foods, insect venoms, foreign serum proteins, industrial chemicals, and drugs. Most natural allergens are proteins or polysaccharides of moderate molecular size (molecular weights of 10,000 to 200,000). Chemicals or drugs of lower molecular weight (haptens) have first to bind to the body's own proteins (carriers) in order to become fully effective allergens.

For the development of the hypersensitivity state underlying clinical allergies, repeated contact with the allergen is required. Duration of the sensitization period is usually dependent upon the sensitizing strength of the allergen and the intensity of exposure. Some allergens (for example, saliva, urine, and hair proteins of domestic animals) are more sensitizing than others. In most instances, repeated contact with minute amounts of allergen is required; several annual seasonal exposures to grass pollens or ragweed pollen usually occur before an overt manifestation of hay fever. On the other hand, allergy to cow milk proteins in infants can develop within a few weeks. When previous contacts with allergens have not been apparent (for example, antibiotics in food), an allergy may become clinically manifest even upon the first conscious encounter with the offending substance.

Besides the intrinsic sensitizing properties of allergens, individual predisposition of the allergic person to become sensitized also plays an important role. Clinical manifestations, such as hay fever, allergic asthma, and atopic (endogenous) dermatitis, occur more frequently in some families. In other clinical forms of allergy, genetic predisposition, though possibly present as well, is not as evident.

Exposure to sensitizing allergens may induce several types of immune response, and the diversity of immunological mechanisms involved is responsible for the various clinical forms of allergic reactions which are encountered in practice. Three principal types of immune responses are encountered: the production of IgE antibodies, IgG or IgM antibodies, and sensitized lymphocytes. See ANTIBODY; IMMUNOGLOBULIN.

Diagnosis of allergic diseases encompasses several facets. Since many clinical manifestations of allergy are mimicked by nonallergic mechanisms, it is usually necessary to use additional diagnostic procedures to ascertain whether the person has developed an immune response toward the incriminated allergen. Such procedures primarily consist of skin tests, in which a small amount of allergen is applied on or injected into the skin. If the individual is sensitized, a local immediate reaction ensues, taking the form of a wheal (for IgE-mediated reactions), or swelling and redness occurs after several hours (for delayed hypersensitivity reactions). The blood may also be analyzed for IgE and IgG antibodies by serological assays, and sensitized lymphocytes are investigated by culturing them with the allergen.

Since the discovery of the responsible allergens markedly influences therapy and facilitates prediction of the allergy's outcome, it is important to achieve as precise a diagnosis as possible. Most tests indicate whether the individual is sensitized to a given allergen, but not whether the allergen is in fact still causing the disease. Since in most cases the hypersensitive state persists for many years, it may well happen that sensitization is detected for an allergen to which the individual is no longer exposed and which therefore no longer causes symptoms. In such cases, exposition tests, consisting of close observation of the individual after deliberate exposure to the putative allergen, may yield useful information.

The most efficient treatment, following identification of the offending allergen, remains elimination of allergen from the person's environment and avoidance of further exposure. This form of treatment is essential for allergies caused by most household and workplace allergens. *See* ANTIGEN; HYPERSENSITIVITY.   [A.L.deW.]

Allosteric enzyme   Any one of the special bacterial enzymes involved in regulatory functions. End-product inhibition is a bacterial control mechanism whereby the end product of a biosynthetic pathway can react with the first enzyme of the pathway and prevent its activity. This end-product inhibition is a device through which a cell conserves its economy by shutting off the synthesis of building blocks when too many are present.

A model to explain the action of allosteric enzymes suggests that the enzyme molecule is a complex consisting of identical subunits, each of which has a site for binding the substrate and another for binding the regulatory substance. These subunits interact in such a way that two conformational forms may develop. One form is in a relaxed condition (R state) and has affinity for the substrate and activator; the other form is in a constrained or taut condition (T state) and has affinity for the inhibitor. The forms exist in a state of equilibrium, but this balance can be readily tipped by binding one of the reactants. The substrate and activator are bound by the relaxed form; when this happens, the balance is tipped in favor of that state. Conversely, the inhibitor will throw the balance toward the constrained state. The balance is thus tipped one way or the other, depending on the relative concentrations of substrate and inhibitor. Since the two states require subunit interaction for their maintenance, it can be seen why dissociation of the subunits leads to a simple monomeric enzyme which no longer exhibits allosteric effects. The model also shows how the binding sites may interact in either a cooperative or antagonistic manner. *See* ENZYME.   [J.S.G.]

Alzheimer's disease   A disease of the nervous system characterized by a progressive dementia that leads to profound impairment in cognition and behavior. Dementia occurs in a number of brain diseases where the impairment in cognitive abilities represents a decline from prior levels of function and interferes with the ability to perform routine daily activities (for example, balancing a checkbook or remembering appointments). Alzheimer's disease is the most common form of dementia, affecting 5% of individuals over age 65. The onset of the dementia typically occurs in middle to late life, and the prevalence of the illness increases with advancing age to include 25–35% of individuals over age 85.

Memory loss, including difficulty in remembering recent events and learning new information, is typically the earliest clinical feature of Alzheimer's disease. As the illness progresses, memory of remote events and overlearned information (for example, date and place of birth) declines together with other cognitive abilities. In the later stages of Alzheimer's disease, there is increasing loss of cognitive function to the point where the individual is bedridden and requires full-time assistance with basic living skills (for example, eating and bathing). Behavioral disturbances that can accompany Alzheimer's disease include agitation, aggression, depressive mood, sleep disorder, and anxiety. *See* MEMORY.

The major neuropathological features of Alzheimer's disease include the presence of senile plaques, neurofibrillary tangles, and neuronal cell loss. Although the regional distribution of brain pathology varies among individuals, the areas commonly affected include the association cortical and limbic regions.

Deficits in cholinergic, serotonergic, noradrenergic, and peptidergic (for example, somatostatin) neurotransmitters have been demonstrated. Dysfunction of the cholinergic neurotransmitter system has been specifically implicated in the early occurrence of memory impairment in Alzheimer's disease, and it has been a target in the development of potential therapeutic agents. *See* ACETYLCHOLINE; NEUROBIOLOGY; NORADRENERGIC SYSTEM.

A definite diagnosis of Alzheimer's disease is made only by direct examination of brain tissue obtained at autopsy or by biopsy to determine the presence of senile plaques and neurofibrillary tangles. A clinical evaluation, however, can provide a correct diagnosis in more than 80% of cases. The clinical diagnosis of Alzheimer's disease requires a thorough evaluation to exclude all other medical, neurological, and psychiatric causes of the observed decline in memory and other cognitive abilities.

Although the cause of Alzheimer's disease is unknown, a number of factors that increase the risk of developing this form of dementia have been identified. Age is the most prominent risk factor, with the prevalence of the illness increasing twofold for each decade of life after age 60. Research in molecular genetics has shown that Alzheimer's disease is etiologically heterogeneous. Gene mutations on several different chromosomes are associated with familial inherited forms of Alzheimer's disease.

A major strategy for the treatment of Alzheimer's disease has focused on the relation between memory impairment and dysfunction of the acetylcholine neurotransmitter system. Other treatment strategies to delay or diminish the progression of Alzheimer's disease are being explored. Behavioral and pharmacological interventions are also available to treat the specific behavioral disturbances that can occur in Alzheimer's disease.   [G.Al.]

Ameba   Any protozoon moving by means of protoplasmic flow. In their entirety, the ameboid protozoa include naked amebas, those enclosed within a shell or test, as well as more highly developed representatives such as the heliozoians, radiolarians, and foraminiferans. Ameboid movement is accomplished by pseudopods—cellular extensions which channel the flow of protoplasm. Pseudopods take varied forms and help distinguish among the different groups. A lobe-shaped extension or lobopod is perhaps the simplest type of pseudopod. The shapelessness and plasticity of these locomotory organelles impart an asymmetric, continually changing aspect to the organism. Other, more developed, representatives have pseudopodial extensions containing fibrous supporting elements (axopods) or forming an extensive network of anastomosing channels (reticulopods). Though involved in locomotion, these organelles are also functional in phagocytosis—the trapping and ingesting of food organisms (usually bacteria, algae, or other protozoa) or detritus. *See* FORAMINIFERIDA; PHAGOCYTOSIS; RADIOLARIA.

Amebas range from small soil organisms, such as *Acanthamoeba* (20 micrometers), to the large fresh-water forms *Amoeba proteus* (600 μm; see illustration) and *Pelomyxa* (1 mm, or more). Some types, such as *Amoeba*, are uninucleate; others are multinucleate. Reproduction is by mitosis with nuclear division preceding cytoplasmic division to produce two daughters. Multinucleate forms have more unusual patterns of division, since nuclear division is not immediately or necessarily followed by cytoplasmic division. Transformation of the actively feeding ameba into a dormant cyst occurs in many species, particularly those found in soil or as symbionts. The resting stages allow survival over periods of desiccation, food scarcity, or transmission between hosts. *See* REPRODUCTION (ANIMAL).

Amebas are found in a variety of habitats, including fresh-water and marine environments, soil, and as symbionts and parasites in body cavities and tissues of vertebrates and invertebrates. Because of their manner of locomotion, amebas typically occur on surfaces, such as the bottom of a pond, on submerged vegetation, or floating debris. In soil, they are a significant component of the microfauna, feeding extensively on bacteria and small fungi. Amebas in marine habitats may be found as planktonic forms adapted for floating at the surface (having oil droplets to increase bouyancy and projections to

Phase-contrast photomicrograph of *Amoeba proteus*, a large fresh-water ameba. The organism is seen moving by means of a single lobose pseudopod.

increase surface area), where they feed upon bacteria, algae, and other protozoa. Several species of amebas may be found in the human intestinal tract as harmless commensals (for example, *Entamoeba coli*) or as important parasites responsible for amebic dysentery (*E. histolytica*).   [F.L.Sc.]

Amino acids   Organic compounds possessing one or more basic amino groups and one or more acidic carboxyl groups. Of the more than 80 amino acids which have been found in living organisms, about 20 serve as the building blocks for the proteins.

All the amino acids of proteins, and most of the others which occur naturally, are α-amino acids, meaning that an amino group ($-NH_2$) and a carboxyl group ($-COOH$) are attached to the same carbon atom. This carbon (the α carbon, being adjacent to the carboxyl group) also carries a hydrogen atom; its fourth valence is satisfied by any of a wide variety of substitutent groups, represented by the letter R in the structural formula below.

$$\begin{array}{c} R \\ | \\ CH \\ \diagup \quad \diagdown \\ H_2N \quad\quad COOH \end{array}$$

In the simplest amino acid, glycine, R is a hydrogen atom. In all other amino acids, R is an organic radical; for example, in alanine it is a methyl group ($-CH_3$), while in glutamic acid it is an aliphatic chain terminating in a second carboxyl group ($-CH_2-CH-COOH$). Chemically, the amino acids can be considered as falling roughly into nine categories based on the nature of R (see table).

Occurrence. Amino acids occur in living tissues principally in the conjugated form. Most conjugated amino acids are peptides, in which the amino group of one amino acid is linked to the carboxyl group of another. Amino acids are capable of linking together to form chains of various lengths, called polypeptides. Proteins are polypeptides

Amino acids of proteins, grouped according to the nature of R	
Amino acids	R
Glycine	Hydrogen
Alanine, valine, leucine, isoleucine	Unsubstituted aliphatic chain
Serine, threonine	Aliphatic chain bearing a hydroxyl group
Aspartic acid, glutamic acid	Aliphatic chain terminating in an acidic carboxyl group
Asparagine, glutamine	Aliphatic chain terminating in an amide group
Arginine, lysine	Aliphatic chain terminating in a basic amino group
Cysteine, cystine, methionine	Sulfur-containing aliphatic chain
Phenylalanine, tyrosine	Terminates in an aromatic ring
Tryptophan, proline, histidine	Terminates in a heterocyclic ring

*See articles on the individual amino acids listed in the table.

ranging in size from about 50 to many thousand amino acid residues. Although most of the conjugated amino acids in nature are proteins, numerous smaller conjugates occur naturally, many with important biological activity. The line between large peptides and small proteins is difficult to draw, with insulin (molecular weight = 7000; 50 amino acids) usually being considered a small protein and adrenocorticotropic hormone (molecular weight = 5000; 39 amino acids) being considered a large peptide.

Free amino acids are found in living cells, as well as the body fluids of higher animals, in amounts which vary according to the tissue and to the amino acid. The amino acids which play key roles in the incorporation and transfer of ammonia, such as glutamic acid, aspartic acid, and their amides, are often present in relatively high amounts, but the concentrations of the other amino acids of proteins are extremely low, ranging from a fraction of a milligram to several milligrams per 100 g wet weight of tissue. The presence of free amino acids in only trace amounts points to the existence of extraordinarily efficient regulation mechanisms. Each amino acid is ordinarily synthesized at precisely the rate needed for protein synthesis.

General properties. The amino acids are characterized physically by the following: (1) the pK_1, or the dissociation constant of the various titratable groups; (2) the isoelectric point, or pH at which a dipolar ion does not migrate in an electric field; (3) the optical rotation, or the rotation imparted to a beam of plane-polarized light (frequently the D line of the sodium spectrum) passing through 1 decimeter of a solution of 100 grams in 100 milliliters; and (4) solubility.

Since all of the amino acids except glycine possess a center of asymmetry at the α carbon atom, they can exist in either of two optically active, mirror-image forms, or enantiomorphs. All of the common amino acids of proteins appear to have the same configuration about the α carbon; this configuration is symbolized by the prefix L-. The opposite, generally unnatural, form is given the prefix D-. Some amino acids, such as isoleucine, threonine, and hydroxyproline, have a second center of asymmetry and can exist in four stereoisomeric forms.

At ordinary temperatures, the amino acids are white crystalline solids; when heated to high temperatures, they decompose rather than melt. They are stable in aqueous solution, and with few exceptions can be heated as high as 120°C (248°F) for short periods without decomposition, even in acid or alkaline solution. Thus, the hydrolysis of proteins can be carried out under such conditions with the complete recovery of most of the constituent free amino acids.

Biosynthesis. Since amino acids, as precursors of proteins, are essential to all organisms, all cells must be able to synthesize those they cannot obtain from their environment. The selective advantage of being able rapidly to shift from endogenous to exogenous sources of these compounds has led to the evolution of very complex and precise methods of adjusting the rate of synthesis to the available level of the compound. An immediately effective control is that of feedback inhibition. The biosynthesis of amino acids usually requires at least three enzymatic steps. In most cases so far examined, the amino acid end product of the biosynthetic pathway inhibits the first enzyme to catalyze a reaction specific to the biosynthesis of that amino acid. This inhibition is extremely specific; the enzymes involved have special sites for binding the inhibitor. This inhibition functions to shut off the pathway in the presence of transient high levels of the product, thus saving both carbon and energy for other biosynthetic reactions. When the level of the product decreases, the pathway begins to function once more.

The metabolic pathways by which amino acids are synthesized generally are found to be the same in all living cells investigated, whether microbial or animal. Biosynthetic mechanisms thus appear to have developed soon after the origin of life and to have remained unchanged through the divergent evolution of modern organisms.

Biosynthetic pathway diagrams reveal only one quantitatively important reaction by which organic nitrogen enters the amino groups of amino acids: the reductive amination of α-ketoglutaric acid to glutamic acid by the enzyme glutamic acid dehydrogenase. All other amino acids are formed either by transamination (transfer of an amino group, ultimately from glutamic acid) or by a modification of an existing amino acid. An example of the former is the formation of valine by transfer of the amino group from glutamic acid to α-ketoisovaleric acid; an example of the latter is the reduction and cyclization of glutamic acid to form proline.

Importance in nutrition. The nutritional requirement for the amino acids of protein can vary from zero, in the case of an organism which synthesizes them all, to the complete list, in the case of an organism in which all the biosynthetic pathways are blocked. There are 8 or 10 amino acids required by certain mammals; most plants synthesize all of their amino acids, while microorganisms vary from types which synthesize all, to others (such as certain lactic acid bacteria) which require as many as 18 different amino acids. *See* PROTEIN METABOLISM.   [E.A.Ad.; P.T.M.; R.G.M.]

Amino sugar   A sugar in which one or more nonglycosidic hydroxyl groups is replaced by an amino or substituted amino group. The most abundant example is D-glucosamine (2-amino-2-deoxy-D-glucose) [see illustration].

Structural formula of D-glucosamine (α-pyranose ring form).

A linear polymer of N-acetyl-D-glucosamine is widely distributed as chitin, the exoskeletal material of arthropods. The glycoproteins of higher animals, which are components of the proteoglycans of cartilage and skin, consist of polysaccharides that are generally sulfated and have *N*-acetylated glucosamine or galactosamine alternating with a uronic acid.

Amino sugars are important constituents of glycoproteins and oligosaccharides involved in biological recognition. Amino sugars of the greatest structural diversity are found in microorganisms as constituents of cell walls, in antigenic carbohydrates produced at the cell surface, and as antibiotic substances secreted from the cell. Streptomycin is the first demonstrated example of numerous amino-sugar-containing antibiotics produced notably by Actinomycetes (bacteria). *See* CHITIN; GLYCOPROTEIN; OLIGOSACCHARIDE; POLYSACCHARIDE.   [D.Ho.]

Amnesia   A significant but relatively selective inability to remember. Amnesia can be characterized along two dimensions with respect to its onset: an inability to remember events that occurred after the onset of amnesia is referred to as anterograde amnesia, and a deficit in remembering events that occurred prior to the onset of amnesia is referred to as retrograde amnesia. Amnesia can be due to a variety of causes and can be classified according to whether the cause is primarily neurological or psychological in origin. Neurological amnesias are the result of brain dysfunction and can be transient or permanent. They are usually characterized by a severe anterograde amnesia and a relatively less severe retrograde amnesia. Transient amnesias are temporary memory disturbances and can range in duration from hours to months, depending on the cause and severity. They can be caused by epilepsy, head injury, and electroconvulsive therapy (most frequently used for the treatment of depression). In cases of transient global amnesia, an extensive amnesia that is usually sudden in onset and resolves within a day, the cause is still not known, although many believe that it is vascular in origin.

Permanent amnesia usually occurs following brain damage to either the diencephalons or the medial temporal lobe. Amnesia resulting from impairment to the medial temporal lobe can occur following anoxia, cerebrovascular accidents, head injury, and viral infections to the brain. The primary structures involved in the processing of memory within the medial temporal lobe are the hippocampus and the amygdala. One of the most common causes of diencephalic amnesia is Wernicke-Korsakoff syndrome, a disorder caused by a thiamine deficiency, usually related to chronic alcoholism.

Memory impairment that is not associated with brain damage is referred to as functional amnesia. Functional amnesia can be classified according to whether the amnesia is nonpathological or pathological. Nonpathological functional amnesia is a normal memory loss for events occurring during infancy and early childhood, sleep, hypnosis, and anesthesia. Pathological functional amnesia is an abnormal memory loss found in cases of functional retrograde amnesia and multiple personality. In contrast to neurological amnesia, pathological functional amnesia is usually associated with more severe retrograde than anterograde amnesia. *See* BRAIN; MEMORY.   [R.S.Le.]

Amnion   A thin, cellular, extraembryonic membrane forming a closed sac surrounding the embryo in all reptiles, birds, and mammals. It is present only in these forms; the collective term amniotes is applied to these animals. The amnion contains a serous fluid in which the embryo is immersed. *See* AMNIOTA.

Typically, the amnion wall is a tough, transparent, nerve-free, and nonvascular membrane consisting of two layers of cells: an inner, single-cell-thick layer of ectodermal epithelium and an outer covering of mesodermal, connective, and specialized smooth muscular tissue. Early after the formation of the amnion, waves of contraction of the muscles pass over the amniotic sac and produce a characteristic rocking of the embryo. *See* GERM LAYERS.

The major function of the amnion and its fluid is to protect the delicate embryo. Thus, developmental stages of terrestrial animals are provided with the same type of cushioning against mechanical shock as is provided by the water environment of aquatic forms. *See* FETAL MEMBRANE.   [N.T.S.]

Amniota   A collective term for the classes Reptilia (reptiles), Aves (birds), and Mammalia (mammals) of the subphylum Vertebrata. The remaining vertebrates, including the several classes of fishes and the amphibians, are grouped together as the Anamnia. Members of the Amniota are characterized by having a series of specialized protective extraembryonic membranes during development. Three of the membranes—amnion, chorion or serosa, and allantois—occur only in this group, but a fourth, the yolk sac, is sometimes present and is found in many anamniotes. The presence of the extraembryonic membranes makes it possible for the embryonic development of the amniotes to take place out of the water. In the most primitive forms the early stages of development take place inside a shell-covered egg that is deposited on land. This pattern is typical of most reptiles, all birds, and some mammals. In these animals the amnion and chorion form fluid-filled sacs which protect the embryo from desiccation and shock. The allantois usually acts as a storage place for digestive and nitrogenous wastes and, in conjunction with the chorion, as a respiratory structure. In viviparous reptiles and mammals the chorion and allantois generally fuse and become more or less intimately associated with the uterine lining of the mother. Nutritive, excretory and respiratory exchanges take place across the chorioallantoic membrane between the allantoic circulation of the embryo and the uterine circulatory vessels of the mother. *See* ALLANTOIS; AMNION; ANAMNIA; CHORION; VERTEBRATA; YOLK SAC.   [J.M.S.]

Amphibia   One of the four classes composing the superclass Tetrapoda of the subphylum Vertebrata, the other classes being Reptilia, Aves, and Mammalia. The living amphibians number approximately 2460 species, and are classified in three orders: the Anura or Salientia (frogs and toads, slightly less than 2000 species); Urodela or Caudata (salamanders, 300 species); and Apoda or Gymnophiona (caecilians, about 160 species). The orders in the subclasses Labyrinthodontia and Lepospondyli existed in the geologic past and are now extinct. A classification scheme for the Amphibia follows:

Class Amphibia
  Subclass Labyrinthodontia
    Order: Ichthyostegalia
         Temnospondyli
         Anthracosauria
  Subclass Lepospondyli
    Order: Nectridea
         Aistopoda
         Microsauria
         Lysorophia
  Subclass Lissamphibia
    Order: Anura
         Urodela
         Apoda

A typical amphibian is characterized by a moist, glandular skin, the possession of gills at some point in its life history, four limbs, and an egg lacking the embryonic membrane called the amnion. *See* AMNION; ANAMNIA.

The closest relatives of the amphibians are the fishes, from which they evolved, and the reptiles, to which they gave rise. Present-day amphibians, however, are highly specialized animals, rather different from the primitive forms that probably first arose from crossopterygian fishes and far removed from those that gave rise to the earliest reptiles.

In general, modern amphibians as adults differ from fishes in lacking scales, breathing by means of the skin and lungs instead of gills, and having limbs in place of fins. There are many exceptions to these generalizations, however. Reptiles usually have a dry, scaly skin that is relatively impervious to water loss and very different from the amphibians with their moist skin that permits much evaporation. Young (larval) amphibians have gills, but there is no comparable gill-breathing, larval stage in the life history of a reptile. A most important difference between the two groups is the absence of the amnion in the Amphibia, and its presence in the Reptilia. Lacking this membrane, amphibian eggs must be laid in water or in very moist places. The amnion of the reptile egg makes it more able to resist desiccation, and the eggs can be laid in relatively dry places. The ability to resist water loss through the skin and the development of a land egg are perhaps the differences between reptiles and amphibians that are of the greatest evolutionary significance. See REPTILIA.

The all-important factor in amphibian life is water. Most species must return to the water to breed, and all must have access to water (even if only in the form of rain or dew) or die of dehydration in a short time. An important consequence of this basic fact of physiology is that vast arid and semiarid areas of the Earth are inhabited by a relatively few specialized amphibians. The majority of amphibian species are found in moist, tropical regions.

Amphibians are among the so-called cold-blooded animals; that is, the temperature of the body of an amphibian is not regulated internally to a high level as is that of mammals and birds, but fluctuates with that of the environment. An animal such as an amphibian that burns none of its food energy in keeping warm is able to get along on much less food than a bird or mammal of similar size. This advantage is offset by the inability of amphibians to be active under cold conditions that do not inhibit a warm-blooded animal. Thus the far northern and southern parts of the world which support large populations of birds and mammals are almost devoid of amphibian life. The amphibians mark a significant point in the evolution of the vertebrates, the transition from aquatic to terrestrial life. As animals neither divorced from the water nor fully at home on land, they suffer from their intermediate mode of life. Reptiles, and later mammals, came to dominate the land, and fishes the waters, leaving the amphibians of today as a relatively unimportant but nevertheless highly interesting group of vertebrates. See THERMOREGULATION.   [R.G.Z.]

The fossil record of the three groups of living amphibians is extensive, and the earliest member of each has been found in Mesozoic rocks. However, no intermediary forms linking the three groups together have been found in the Mesozoic, and it is necessary to look in the Paleozoic, some 100 million years earlier, for the common ancestor of modern amphibians, with the earliest known amphibians having been found in the Upper Devonian rocks of Greenland.

It is clear that modern amphibians have a very long history extending back almost to the time of the origin and radiation of land vertebrates 340 million years ago. Their unique sensory biology and specialized glands must have evolved at that time and remained unchanged to the present day.   [T.R.Sm.]

Amylase   An enzyme which breaks down (hydrolyzes) starch, the reserve carbohydrate in plants, and glycogen, the reserve carbohydrate in animals, into reducing fermentable sugars, mainly maltose, and reducing nonfermentable or slowly fermentable dextrins. Amylases are classified as saccharifying (β-amylase) and as dextrinizing (α-amylases). The α- and β-amylases are specific for the α- and β-glucosidic bonds which connect the monosaccharide units into large aggregates, the polysaccharides. The α-amylases are found in all types of organs and tissues, whereas β-amylase is found almost exclusively in higher plants. *See* CARBOHYDRATE; ENZYME; GLYCOGEN; MALTOSE.

In animals the highest concentrations of amylase are found in the saliva and in the pancreas. Salivary amylase is also known as ptyalin and is found in humans, the ape, pig, guinea pig, squirrel, mouse, and rat.

In plants, starch is broken down during the germination of seeds (rich in starch) by associated plant enzymes into sugars. These constitute the chief energy source in the early development of the plant. β-Amylase occurs abundantly in seeds and cereals such as malt. It also is found in yeasts, molds, and bacteria.   [D.N.La.]

Anaerobic infection   An infection caused by anaerobic bacteria (organisms that are intolerant of oxygen). Most such infections are mixed, involving more than one anaerobe and often aerobic or facultative bacteria as well. Anaerobes are prevalent throughout the body as indigenous flora, and virtually all anaerobic infections arise endogenously, the principal exception being *Clostridium difficile* colitis. Factors predisposing to anaerobic infection include those disrupting mucosal or other surfaces (trauma, surgery, and malignancy or other disease), those lowering redox potential (impaired blood supply, tissue necrosis, and growth of nonanaerobic bacteria), drugs inactive against anaerobes (such as aminoglycosides), and virulence factors produced by the anaerobes (toxins, capsules, and collagenase, hyaluronidase, and other enzymes). Anaerobic gram-negative bacilli (*Bacteroides, Prevotella, Porphyromonas, Fusobacterium*) and anaerobic gram-positive cocci (*Peptostreptococcus*) are the most common anaerobic pathogens. *Clostridium* (spore formers) may cause serious infection. The prime pathogen among gram-positive nonsporulating anaerobic bacilli is *Actinomyces*. Of the infections commonly involving anaerobes, the oral and dental pleuropulmonary, intraabdominal, obstetric-gynecologic, and skin and soft tissue infections are most important in terms of frequency of occurrence. To document anaerobic infection properly, specimens for culture must be obtained so as to exclude normal flora and must be transported under anaerobic conditions. Therapy includes surgery and antimicrobial agents. *See* ANTIBIOTIC; INFECTION.   [S.M.F.]

Anamnia   Those vertebrate animals, sometimes called Anamniota, which lack an amnion in development. The amnion is a protective embryonic envelope that encloses the embryo and its surrounding liquid, the amniotic fluid, during fetal life. An amnion is present in mammals, birds, and reptiles (collectively called the Amniota), but is absent in fishes and amphibians. *See* AMNION; AMNIOTA; AMPHIBIA; PISCES (ZOOLOGY).   [R.M.B.]

Anaphylaxis   A generalized or localized tissue reaction occurring within minutes of an antigen-antibody reaction. Similar reactions elicited by nonimmunologic mechanisms are termed anaphylactoid reactions. In humans, the clinical manifestations of anaphylaxis include reactions of the skin with itching, erythema, and urticaria; the upper respiratory tract with edema of the larynx; the lower respiratory tract with dyspnea, wheezing, and cough; the gastrointestinal tract with abdominal cramps, nausea, vomiting, and diarrhea; and the cardiovascular system with hypotension and shock. Individuals undergoing anaphylactic reactions may develop any one, a combination, or all of the signs and symptoms. Anaphylaxis may be fatal within minutes, or may occur days or weeks after the reaction, if the organs sustained considerable damage during the hypotensive phase.

Anaphylaxis in humans is most often the result of the interaction of specific IgE antibody fixed to mast cells and antigen. Two molecules of IgE are bridged by the antigen, which may be a complex protein or chemical (hapten) bound to protein. The antigen-antibody interaction leads to increased cell-membrane permeability, with influx of calcium and release of either preformed or newly formed pharmacologic mediators from the granules. Preformed mediators include histamine and eosinophilic or neutrophilic chemotactic factors. Newly formed molecules include leukotrienes or slow-reacting substance of anaphylaxis and prostaglandins. The mediator action induces bronchoconstriction, vasodilation, cellular infiltration, and increased mucus production.

Another mechanism for induction of anaphylaxis in humans occurs when antigen binds to preformed IgG antibody and complement components interact with the antigen-antibody complex. The early components of the complement system bind to the antibody molecule, leading to activation of other complement components. During the activation, components known as anaphylatoxins (C3a and C5a) are released which may directly cause bronchoconstriction with respiratory impairment, and vasodilation with hypotension or shock. *See* COMPLEMENT; EICOSANOIDS.

Anaphylaxis due to IgE mechanisms has been associated with foreign proteins such as horse antitoxins, insulin, adrenocorticotropic hormone (ACTH), protamine, and chymopapain injected into herniated discs; drugs such as penicillin and its derivatives; foods such as shellfish, nuts, and eggs; and venom of stinging insects. Anaphylaxis mediated by IgG is seen in blood-transfusion reactions and following the use of cryoprecipitate, plasma, or immunoglobulin therapy.

After the identification of the inciting agent for the anaphylactic reaction, prevention is the best mode of therapy. Immunotherapy with insect venom and desensitization with certain drugs are effective prophylactic measures. Individuals with recurrent episodes of anaphylaxis, when the etiological cause is unknown and preventive measures are impractical, should be provided with epinephrine in a form that can be self-administered whenever symptoms occur. *See* EPINEPHRINE.

The treatment of anaphylaxis is aimed at reducing the effect of the chemical mediators on the end organs and preventing further mediator release. The drug of choice for this is epinephrine given subcutaneously in repeated doses. Additionally, a clear airway and appropriate oxygenation must be maintained; hypotension should be treated, as should any cardiac arrhythmia. *See* ANTIGEN-ANTIBODY REACTION; HYPERSENSITIVITY.

[S.B.Se.; J.N.F.]

Androgen   One of a class of steroid hormones. Androgens play a major role in the development and maintenance of masculine secondary sexual characters, for example, the seminal vesicle and prostate gland of the male mammal, and the comb, wattles, and spur of the male fowl. They also influence certain other secondary sexual characters, such as hair growth pattern and voice quality in humans. In the fowl, they affect the pattern and seasonal coloration of its feathers, as well as crowing. In addition, androgens affect nitrogen metabolism (anabolic). Androgens are produced in the testis, ovary, adrenal, and most likely, in the placenta. A small portion of the androgen is from corticoids, or adrenal cortex steroids, and from other C_{21} steroids, such as progesterone. *See* HORMONE; OVARY; PROGESTERONE; STEROID; TESTIS.   [R.I.D.]

Animal   Any living organism which possesses certain characteristics that distinguish it from plants. There is no single criterion that can be used to distinguish all animals from all plants. Animals usually lack chlorophyll and the ability to manufacture foods from raw materials available in the soil, water, and atmosphere. Animal cells are usually delimited by a flexible plasma or cell membrane rather than a cell wall. Animals generally are limited in their growth and most have the ability to move in their environment at some stage in their life history, whereas plants are usually not restricted in their growth and the majority are stationary.

The presence or lack of chlorophyll in an organism does not determine its affinity to the plant or animal kingdom. Among the protozoa, the class Phytamastigophora includes animals, such as the euglenids, which have chromatophores containing chlorophyll. These organisms are considered to be animals by zoologists and plants by phycologists. Higher parasitic plants and the large plant group Fungi also lack chlorophyll. Another borderline group is the slime molds: the Mycetozoa of zoologists and the Myxomycophyta of the botanists; these organisms exhibit both plant and animal characteristics during their life history. Movement is not a characteristic restricted to the animal kingdom; many of the thallophytes such as *Oscillatoria*, numerous bacteria, and colonial chlorophytes are motile.

Classifying organisms as plants or animals is difficult. Today biologists recognize up to five kingdoms. Most place the one-celled animals and plants, sometimes along with algae and certain other groups, into the Protista. Other kingdoms are the Monera for the bacteria and blue-green algae, and the Fungi for the slime molds and true fungi. These schemes for recognizing additional kingdoms have the practical advantage of eliminating the difficulties of delimiting and describing the kingdoms of multicellular animals and plants. *See* ANIMAL KINGDOM; PLANT; PLANT KINGDOM.   [W.J.B.]

Animal communication   A discipline within the field of animal behavior that focuses upon the reception and use of signals. Animal communication could well include all of animal behavior, since a liberal definition of the term signal could include all stimuli perceived by an animal. However, most research in animal communication deals only with those cases in which a signal, defined as a structured stimulus generated by one member of a species, is subsequently used by and influences the behavior of another member of the same species in a predictable way (intraspecific communication). In this context, communication occurs in virtually all animal species.

The field of animal communication includes an analysis of the physical characteristics of those signals believed to be responsible in any given case of information transfer. A large part of this interest is due to technological improvements in signal detection, coupled with analysis of the signals obtained with such devices.

Information transmission between two individuals can pass in four channels: acoustic, visual, chemical, and electrical. An individual animal may require information from two or more channels simultaneously before responding appropriately to reception of a signal. Furthermore, a stimulus may evoke a response under one circumstance but be ignored in a different context.

Acoustic signals have characteristics that make them particularly suitable for communication, and virtually all animal groups have some forms which communicate by means of sound. Sound can travel relatively long distances in air or water, and obstacles between the source and the recipient interfere little with an animal's ability to locate the source. Sounds are essentially instantaneous and can be altered in important ways. Both amplitude and frequency modulation can be found in sounds emitted by animals; in some species sound signals have discrete patterns due to frequency and timing of utterances. Since a wide variety of sound signals are possible, each species can have a unique set of signals in its repertoire. *See* PHONORECEPTION.

Sound signals are produced and received primarily during sexual attraction, including mating and competition. They may also be important in adult–young interactions, in the coordination of movements of a group, in alarm and distress calls, and in intraspecific signaling during foraging behavior. *See* REPRODUCTIVE BEHAVIOR.

Visual signaling between animals can be an obvious component of communication. Besides the normal range of human vision (visible light), visual signals include additional frequencies in the infrared and ultraviolet ranges. The quality of light that is often considered is color, but other characteristics are important in visual communication. Alterations of brightness, pattern, and timing also provide versatility in signal composition. The visual channel suffers from the important limitation that all visual signals must be line of sight. Information transfer is therefore largely restricted to the daytime (except for animals such as fireflies) and to rather close-range situations.

Intraspecific visual signaling appears to occur primarily during mate attraction. The color dimorphism of birds, the patterns of butterfly wings, the posturing of some fish, and firefly flashing are examples. Some parent–young interactions involve visual signaling. A young bird in the nest may open its mouth when it sees the underside of its parent's beak. Other examples are the synchronized behavior observed in schooling fish and flocking birds.

Chemical signals, like visual and sound signals, can travel long distances, but with an important distinction. Distant transmission of chemical signals requires a movement of air or water. Therefore, an animal cannot perceive an odor from a distance; it can only perceive molecules brought to it by a current of air or water. Animals do not hunt for an odor source by moving other than upwind or upcurrent in water because chemical signals do not travel in still air or water since diffusion is far too slow.

The fact that chemical signals comprise molecules means that, unlike acoustical or visual signals, chemical signals have a time lag. Chemical signals have to be of an appropriate concentration if they are to be effective. A chemical normally considered to be an attractant can serve as a repellent if it is too strong. Chemical signals may persist for a while, and time must pass before the concentration drops below the threshold level for reception by a searching animal. Since molecules of different sizes and shapes have varying degrees of persistence in the environment, the chemical channel is often involved in territorial marking, odor trail formation, and mate attraction. This channel is particularly suitable where acoustical or visual signals might betray the location of a signaler to a potential predator.

The array of molecular structure is essentially limitless, permitting a species-specific nature for chemical signals. Unfortunately, that specificity can make interception and analysis of chemical signals a difficult matter for research.

Pheromones are chemical signals that are produced by an animal and are exuded to influence the behavior of other members of the same species. If pheromones are incorporated into a recipient's body (by ingestion or absorption), they may chemically alter the behavior of such an individual for a considerable period of time. *See* CHEMICAL ECOLOGY; CHEMORECEPTION; PHEROMONE.

Some electric fish and electric eels live in murky water and have electric generating organs that are really modified muscle bundles. Communication by electric signaling is rapid; signals can travel throughout the medium (even murky water), and rather complex signals can be generated, permitting species-specific communication during sexual attraction. However, the electrical mode is apparently restricted to those species that have electric generating organs.

Animal communication is one of the most difficult areas of study in science for several reasons. First, experiments must be designed and executed in such a manner that extraneous cues (artifacts) are eliminated as potential causes of the observed results. Second, once supportive evidence has been obtained, each hypothesis must be tested. In animal communication studies, adequate tests often rely upon direct evidence—that is, evidence obtained by artificially generating the signal presumed responsible for a given behavioral act, providing that signal to a receptive animal, and actually evoking a specific behavioral act in a predictable manner. *See* ETHOLOGY; PSYCHOLINGUISTICS.

[A.M.We.]

Animal evolution   The theory that modern animals are the modified descendants of animals that formerly existed and that these earlier forms descended from still earlier and different organisms.

Animals are multicellular organisms that feed by ingestion of other organisms or their products, being unable to derive energy through photosynthesis or chemosynthesis. Animals are currently classed into about 30 to 35 phyla, each of which has evolved a distinctive body plan or architecture.

All phyla began as invertebrates, but lineages of the phylum Chordata developed the internal skeletal armature, with spinal column, which was exploited in numerous fish groups and which eventually gave rise to terrestrial vertebrates. The number of phyla is uncertain partly because most of the branching patterns and the ancestral body plans from which putative phyla have arisen are not yet known. For example, arthropods (including crustaceans and insects) may have all diversified from a common ancestor that was a primitive arthropod, in which case they may be grouped into a single phylum; or several arthropod groups may have evolved independently from nonarthropod ancestors, in which case each such group must be considered a separate phylum. So far as known, all animal phyla began in the sea. *See* ANIMAL; ANIMAL KINGDOM.

Some features of the cells of primitive animals resemble those of the single-celled Protozoa, especially the flagellates, which have long been believed to be animal ancestors. Molecular phylogenies have supported this idea and also suggest that the phylum Coelenterata arose separately from all other phyla that have been studied by this technique. Thus animals may have evolved at least twice from organisms that are not themselves animals, and represent a grade of evolution and not a single branch (clade) of the tree of life. Sponges have also been suspected of an independent origin, and it is possible that some of the extinct fossil phyla arose independently or branched from sponges or cnidarians. *See* COELENTERATA; PORIFERA; PROTOZOA.

The earliest undoubted animal fossils (the Ediacaran fauna) are soft-bodied, and first appear in marine sediments nearly 650 million years (m.y.) old. This fauna lasted about 50 m.y. and consisted chiefly of cnidarians or cnidarian-grade forms, though it contains a few enigmatic fossils that may represent groups that gave rise to more advanced phyla. Then, nearly 570 m.y. ago, just before and during earliest Cambrian time, a diversification of body architecture began that produced most of the living phyla as well as many extinct groups. The body plans of some of these groups involved mineralized skeletons which, as these are more easily preserved than soft tissues, created for the first time an extensive fossil record. The soft-bodied groups were markedly diversified, though their record is so spotty that their history cannot be traced in detail. A single, exceptionally preserved soft-bodied fauna from the Burgess Shale of British Columbia that is about 530 m.y. old contains not only living soft-bodied worm phyla, but extinct groups that cannot be placed in living phyla and do not seem to be ancestral to them.

Following the early phase of rampant diversification and of some concurrent extinction of phyla and their major branches, the subsequent history of the durably skeletonized groups can be followed in a general way in the marine fossil record. The composition of the fauna changed continually, but three major associations can be seen: one dominated by the arthropodlike trilobites during the early Paleozoic, one dominated by articulate brachiopods and crinoids (Echinodermata) in the remaining Paleozoic, and one dominated by gastropod (snail) and bivalve (clam) mollusks during the Mesozoic and Cenozoic. The mass extinction at the close of the Paleozoic that caused the contractions in so many groups may have extirpated over 90% of marine species and led to a reorganization of marine community structure and composition into a modern mode. Resistance to this and other extinctions seems to have been a major factor in the rise of successive groups to dominance. Annelids, arthropods, and mollusks are the more important invertebrate groups that made the transition to land. The outstanding feature of terrestrial fauna is the importance of the insects, which appeared in the late Paleozoic and later radiated to produce the several million living species, surpassing all other life forms combined in this respect. *See* ANNELIDA; ARTHROPODA; INSECTA; MOLLUSCA.   [J.W.V.]

The phylum Chordata consists largely of animals with a backbone, the Vertebrata, including humans. The group, however, includes some primitive nonvertebrates, the protochordates: lancelets, tunicates, acorn worms, pterobranchs, and possibly the extinct graptolites and conodonts. The interrelationships of these forms are not well understood. With the exception of the colonial graptolites, they are soft-bodied and have only a very limited fossil record. They suggest possible links to the Echinodermata in developmental, biochemical, and morphological features. In addition, some early Paleozoic fossils, the carpoids, have been classified alternatively as chordates and as echinoderms, again suggesting a link. In spite of these various leads, the origin of the chordates remains basically unclear. *See* VERTEBRATA.

Chordates are characterized by a hollow, dorsal, axial nerve chord, a ventral heart, a system of slits in the larynx that serves variously the functions of feeding and respiration, a postanal swimming tail, and a notochord that is an elongate supporting structure lying immediately below the nerve chord. The protochordates were segmented, although sessile forms such as the tunicates show this only in the swimming, larval phase.

The first vertebrates were fishlike animals in which the pharyngeal slits formed a series of pouches that functioned as respiratory gills. An anterior specialized mouth permitted ingestion of food items large in comparison with those of the filter-feeding protochordates. Vertebrates are first known from bone fragments found in rocks of Cambrian age, but more complete remains have come from the Middle Ordovician. Innovations, related to greater musculoskeletal activity, included the origin of a supporting skeleton of cartilage and bone, a larger brain, and three pairs of cranial sense organs (nose, eyes, and ears). At first the osseous skeleton served as protective scales in the skin, as a supplement to the notochord, and as a casing around the brain. In later vertebrates the adult notochord is largely or wholly replaced by bone, which encloses the nerve chord to form a true backbone. All vertebrates have a heart which pumps blood through capillaries, where exchanges of gases with the external media take place. The blood contains hemoglobin in special cells which carry oxygen and carbon dioxide. In most fishes the blood passes from the heart to the gills and thence to the brain and other parts of the body. In most tetrapods, and in some fishes, blood passes to the lungs, is returned to the heart after oxygenation, and is then pumped to the various parts of the body.

The jawless fish, known as Agnatha, had a sucking-rasping mouth apparatus rather than true jaws. They enjoyed great success from the Late Cambrian until the end of the Devonian. Most were heavily armored, although a few naked forms are known. They were weak swimmers and lived mostly on the bottom. The modern parasitic lampreys and deep-sea scavenging hagfish are the only surviving descendants of these early fish radiations. *See* DEVONIAN.

In the Middle to Late Silurian arose a new type of vertebrate, the Gnathostomata, characterized by true jaws and teeth. They constitute the great majority of fishes and all tetrapod vertebrates. The jaws are modified elements of the front parts of the gill apparatus, and the teeth are modified bony scales from the skin of the mouth. With the development of jaws, a whole new set of ecological opportunities was open to the vertebrates. Along with this, new swimming patterns appeared, made possible by the origin of paired fins, forerunners of which occur in some agnathans.

Four groups of fishes quickly diversified. Of these, the Placodermi and Acanthodii are extinct. The Placodermi were heavily armored fishes, the dominant marine carnivores of the Silurian and Devonian. The Acanthodii were filter-feeders mostly of small size. They are possibly related to the dominant groups of modern fishes, the largely cartilaginous Chondrichthyes (including sharks, rays, and chimaeras) and the Osteichthyes (the higher bony fishes). These also arose in the Late Silurian but diversified later. *See* ACANTHODII; CHONDRICHTHYES.

The first land vertebrates, the Amphibia, appeared in the Late Devonian and were derived from an early group of osteichthyans called lobe-finned fishes, of which two kinds survive today, the Dipnoi or lungfishes, and the crossopterygian coelacanth *Latimeria*. They were lung-breathing fishes that lived in shallow marine waters and in swamps and marshes. The first amphibians fed and reproduced in or near the water. True land vertebrates, Reptilia, with a modified (amniote) egg that could survive on land, probably arose in the Mississippian. *See* AMNIOTA; AMPHIBIA; CROSSOPTERYGII; DIPNOI.

By the Middle Pennsylvanian a massive radiation of reptiles was in process. The most prominent reptiles belong in the Diapsida: dinosaurs, lizards and snakes, and pterosaurs (flying reptiles). The birds, Aves, which diverged from the dinosaur radiation in the Late Triassic or Early Jurassic, are considered to be feathered dinosaurs, and thus members of the Diapsida, whereas older authorities prefer to treat them as a separate case. In addition, there were several Mesozoic radiations of marine reptiles such as ichthyosaurs and plesiosaurs. Turtles (Chelonia) first appeared in the Triassic and have been highly successful ever since. *See* AVES; REPTILIA.

The line leading to mammals can be traced to primitive Pennsylvanian reptiles, Synapsida, which diversified and spread worldwide during the Permian and Triassic. The first true mammals, based on characteristics of jaw, tooth, and ear structure, arose in the Late Triassic. Derived mammals, marsupials (Metatheria) and placentals (Eutheria), are known from the Late Cretaceous, but mammalian radiations began only in the early Cenozoic. By the end of the Eocene, all the major lines of modern mammals had become established. Molecular analyses (blood proteins, deoxyribonucleic acid, ribonucleic acid) of living mammals show that the most primitive group of placentals is the edentates (sloths, armadillos, and anteaters). An early large radiation included the rodents, primates (including monkeys, apes, and humans), and bats, possibly all closely related to the insectivores and carnivores. The newest radiations of mammals are of elephants and sea cows, while the whales are related to the artiodactyls (cattle, camels). *See* MAMMALIA. [K.S.Th.]

Animal kingdom   One of five kingdoms of organisms: Animalia, Plantae, Fungi, Protista, and Monera. Animals are eukaryotic multicellular organisms that take food into their bodies and that develop from blastula embryos. Animal species are organized into phyla that are defined according to comparative patterns of development, body structures, behavior, biochemical pathways, modes of nutrition, and ancestry. *See* AN-IMAL SYSTEMATICS.

Traditionally, animals have been grouped into invertebrates (without backbones) and vertebrates (with backbones). Vertebrates include mammals, amphibians, reptiles, birds, and fish. Members of all other animal phyla, more than 98% of all animal species, are invertebrates. Although invertebrates lack backbones, they achieve physical support by structures ranging from delicate glass spicules, to tough rings and rods, to hydrostatic pressure. The phylum Arthropoda alone comprises more than 1 million known species. If tropical species were better described, the arthropods might include as many as 10 million living species. *See* AMPHIBIA; AVES; CHONDRICHTHYES; CHORDATA; MAMMALIA; OSTEICHTHYES; REPTILIA.   [K.V.S.]

Animal morphogenesis   The development of form and pattern in animals. Animals have complex shapes and structural patterns which are faithfully reproduced during the embryonic development of each generation. Morphogenesis takes place by the generation of progressively more complex structures from a single cell: the fertilized egg, or zygote. The zygote divides repeatedly to form a multicellular embryo, within which groups of cells undergo structural and functional specialization (differentiation) in the precise spatial patterns that are recognized as tissues and organs.

Cell differentiation involves the differential expression of genes in the nuclear deoxyribonucleic acid (DNA) which code for the production of proteins specifying the structure and function of each cell type. During cleavage, nuclei divide equivalently so that all cells of the embryo receive the total complement of genes contained in the DNA of the zygote nucleus. However, cells in different regions of the embryo contain cytoplasm which differs in composition. The cytoplasmic composition of a cell controls which genes will be expressed in each region of the embryo, resulting in a patterned differentiation. Initially, different cell types arise because cells come to occupy unique positions; some cells are on the inside and others on the outside of the group of cells produced by the early divisions of the zygote. Interactions between subpopulations of cell types thus produced further alter regional cytoplasmic compositions, resulting in new patterns of gene expression. By means of many such interactions, all of the 200 or so different cell types of an animal body gradually emerge in the proper spatial patterns. *See* CELL DIFFERENTIATION; DEOXYRIBONUCLEIC ACID (DNA); GENE ACTION.

The structural patterns of animals and their parts exhibit polarity; that is, they display structural differences along one or more axes. In many animals, the overall polarities of the embryo are established during oogenesis and the period between fertilization and the first cleavage. For example, as the amphibian egg grows in the ovary, its posterior half becomes laden with yolk, and a dark pigment is deposited in the cortical cytoplasm of its anterior half. The line between the poles of these two halves defines the anterior-posterior axis of the future embryo. *See* FERTILIZATION; OOGENESIS; OVUM.

The dorsal-ventral axis develops perpendicular to the anterior-posterior axis, and is established by a reorganization of the zygote cytoplasm initiated by the events of fertilization. This axis can form in any of the planes which contain the anterior-posterior axis. The plane in which it actually forms is determined by the meridian at which the sperm enters the egg. Cytoplasmic reorganization occurs after fertilization. A tongue of yolky cytoplasm is formed on the elevated side as the heavy yolk flows down under the influence of gravity, and a new gray crescent appears on this side, its dorsal midline coinciding with the plane in which the anterior-posterior axis was tilted. The dorsal-ventral axis established by sperm entry becomes determined shortly before the first cleavage.

Two major cell types are formed during cleavage of the amphibian egg: large, yolky endoderm cells, and smaller, pigmented ectoderm cells, including the cells formed from the gray crescent region.

At the mid-blastula state, when the embryo consists of several thousand cells, an inductive interaction takes place between the endoderm cells and the gray crescent cells, causing the latter to become mesoderm cells. During gastrulation, these three cell types are rearranged to form three concentric layers, with ectoderm on the outside, endoderm on the inside, and mesoderm in between. The ectoderm develops into the skin epidermis and nervous system, endoderm into the organs of the alimentary tract, and mesoderm into muscles, skeleton, heart, kidneys, and connective tissue. *See* BLASTULATION; GASTRULATION; GERM LAYERS.

Prior to gastrulation, the prospective organ regions of the ectoderm and endoderm are not yet determined. Mesodermal organ regions, however, are highly self-organizing under these conditions. Ectodermal and endodermal organ regions become determined during and after gastrulation by the inductive action of the mesoderm. For example, dorsal mesoderm normally invaginates and stretches out along the dorsal midline where it differentiates as notochord and trunk muscles. The ectoderm overlying the dorsal mesoderm differentiates as the central nervous system. *See* FATE MAPS (EMBRYOLOGY).

Once induced, organ regions can themselves induce additional organs from undetermined tissue. For example, the retina and iris of the eye develop from a vesicle growing out of the forebrain. This vesicle induces a lens from the overlying head ectoderm, and the lens then induces the cornea from head ectoderm to complete the eye. By means of such cascades of inductive interactions, all the organs of the body are blocked out. *See* EMBRYONIC INDUCTION.

Once determined, an organ region constitutes a developmental system, called a morphogenetic field, which specifies the detailed pattern of cell differentiation within the organ. Cells differentiate in patterns dictated by their relative positions within the field. It is generally accepted that graded molecular signals, or cues, are the basis of this positional information. It is proposed that the source of the signals is a set of boundary cells which define the limits of the field. All the cells of a field thus derive their positional information from a common set of boundary cells.

Most fields become inactive after the pattern they specify begins to differentiate; the ability to form normal organs after removal or interchange of cells is then lost. However, in some animals, the fields of certain organs can be reactivated by loss of a part, even in the adult. The missing part is then redeveloped in a process called regeneration. *See* REGENERATION (BIOLOGY).

Different kinds of cells secrete molecules of protein and protein complexed with carbohydrate which constitute specific types and patterns of extracellular matrix. The matrix stabilizes tissue and organ structure, guides migrating cells to their proper locations, and is a medium through which cell interactions take place. Cell interactions take place at cell surfaces, the molecular composition of which is distinct from one cell type to another, allowing them to recognize one another. These differences are reflected in varying degrees of adhesivity between different kinds of cells, and between cells and different kinds of extracellular matrix. Differential adhesivity is the property upon which cell migration, clustering, and rearrangement is based, and is thus important in creating the conditions for cell-cell and cell-matrix interactions. *See* CELLULAR ADHESION.

Another important mechanism for the development of complex patterns and shapes is the differential growth of organs and their parts. Differential growth is evident as soon as embryonic organ regions begin to develop. During the early part of their development, the growth rates of organs are controlled by intrinsic factors. At later stages of development, including postnatal life, organ growth is largely under the control of hormones secreted by cells of the endocrine glands.

Programmed cell death (apoptosis) is an important feature in the shaping of such structures as the head, limbs, hands, and feet of some animals. A striking example is foot development in ducks and chickens. Ducks have webbed toes while chickens do not. This difference results because as the chicken leg bud grows and forms the toes, the cells between the developing digits die. Various grafting and culturing experiments have indicated that it is a cell's relative position in the limb bud which establishes its fate to die at some later time in development. *See* DEVELOPMENTAL BIOLOGY; MOLECULAR BIOLOGY.   [D.L.S.]

Animal systematics   The comparative analysis of living and fossil species, including their discovery, description, evolutionary relationships to other species, and patterns of geographic distribution.

Systematics can be divided into four major fields. Taxonomy, often equated with systematics, is the discipline concerned with the discovery, description, and classification of organism groups, termed taxa (singular, taxon). Classification is the clustering of species into a hierarchical arrangement according to some criterion, usually an understanding of their relationships to other species. Phylogenetic analysis, an increasingly important aspect of systematics, is the discovery of the historical, evolutionary relationships among species; this pattern of relationships is termed a phylogeny. The fourth component of systematics is biogeography, the study of species' geographic distributions. Historical biogeography examines how species' distributions have changed over time in relationship to the history of landforms, ocean basins, and climate, as well as how those changes have contributed to the evolution of biotas (groups of species living together in communities and ecosystems).

Systematic data and interpretations underlie progress in all of biology. An understanding of relationships, in particular, is fundamental for interpreting comparative data across different kinds of organisms, whether those data be morphological, physiological, or biochemical.   [J.Cr.]

Animal virus   A small infectious agent that is unable to replicate outside a living animal cell. Unlike other intracellular obligatory parasites (for example, chlamydiae and rickettsiae), they contain only one kind of nucleic acid, either deoxyribonucleic acid (DNA) or ribonucleic acid (RNA). They do not replicate by binary fission. Instead, they divert the host cell's metabolism into synthesizing viral building blocks, which then self-assemble into new virus particles that are released into the environment. During the process of this synthesis, viruses utilize cellular metabolic energy, many cellular enzymes, and organelles which they themselves are unable to produce. Animal viruses are not susceptible to the action of antibiotics. The extracellular virus particle is called a virion, while the name virus is reserved for various phases of the intracellular development. *See* RIBONUCLEIC ACID (RNA).

Morphology. Virions are small, 20–300 nanometers in diameter, and pass through filters which retain most bacteria. However, large virions (for example, vaccinia, which is 300 nm in diameter) exceed in size some of the smaller bacteria. The major structural components of the virion are proteins and nucleic acid, but some virions also possess a lipid-containing membranous envelope. The protein molecules are arranged in a symmetrical shell, the capsid, around the DNA or RNA. The shell and the nucleic acid constitute the nucleocapsid.

In electron micrographs of low resolution, virions appear to possess two basic shapes: spherical and cylindrical. High-resolution electron microscopy and x-ray diffraction studies of crystallized virions reveal that the "spherical" viruses are in fact polyhedral in their morphology, while the "cylindrical" virions display helical symmetry. The polyhedron most commonly encountered in virion structures is the icosahedron, in which the protein molecules are arranged on the surface of 20 equilateral triangles. Based on these morphological features, viruses are classified as helical or icosahedral. Certain groups of viruses do not exhibit any discernible features of symmetry and are classified as complex virions. Further distinction is made between virions containing RNA or DNA as their genomes and between those with naked or enveloped nucleocapsids.

Viral nucleic acid. The outer protein shell of the virion furnishes protection to the most important component, the viral genome, shielding it from destructive enzymes (ribonucleases or deoxyribonucleases). The viral genome carries information which specifies all viral structural and functional components required for the initiation and establishment of the infectious cycle and for the generation of new virions. This information may be contained in a double-stranded or single-stranded (parvoviruses) DNA, or double-stranded (reoviruses) or single-stranded RNA. The viral DNA may be linear or circular, and the viral RNA may be a single long chain or a number of shorter chains (fragmented genomes), each of which contains different genetic information. Furthermore, some RNA viruses have the genetic information expressed as a complementary nucleotide sequence. These are classified as negative-strand RNA viruses. Finally, the RNA tumor viruses have an intracellular DNA phase, during which the genetic information contained in the virion RNA is transcribed into a DNA and integrated into the host cell's genome. The discovery of this process came as a surprise, since it was believed that the flow of genetic information was unidirectional from DNA to RNA to protein and could not take place in the opposite direction. The transcription of RNA to DNA was termed reverse transcription, and the RNA tumor viruses are sometimes referred to as retroviruses. See GENETIC CODE.

When introduced into a susceptible cell by either chemical or mechanical means, the naked viral nucleic acid is in most cases itself infectious. Two exceptions are the negative-strand RNA viruses and the RNA tumor viruses. In these cases the RNA has to be first transcribed and reverse-transcribed, respectively, into the proper form of genetic information before the infectious process can take place. This task is carried out by means of an enzyme which is contained in the protein shell of the virion nucleocapsid. The whole nucleocapsid is therefore required for infectivity.

Viral infection is composed of several steps: adsorption, penetration, uncoating and eclipse, and maturation and release. Adsorption takes place on specific receptors in the membrane of an animal cell. The presence or absence of these receptors determines the tissue or species susceptibility to infection by a virus. Enveloped viruses exhibit surface spikes which are involved in adsorption; however, most animal viruses do not possess obvious attachment structures. Penetration takes place through invagination and ingestion of the virion by the cell membrane (phagocytosis or viropexis). Penetration is followed by uncoating of the nucleic acid, or in some cases by uncoating of the nucleocapsid. At this stage, the identity of the virion has disappeared, and viral infectivity cannot be recovered from disrupted cells. See PHAGOCYTOSIS.

The absence of infectious particles in cell extracts is characteristic of the eclipse period. During the eclipse the biochemical processes of the cell are manipulated to synthesize viral proteins and nucleic acids. The eclipse period in infections with DNA viruses starts with the transcription of the genetic information in the nucleus of the cell (except poxviruses), processing into mRNAs, and their translation into proteins (in the cytoplasm). This process is divided into early and late transcription. The early proteins are virus-encoded functional proteins which will participate in the synthesis of viral DNA and of intermediate and late viral proteins, as well as in the shutoff of various cellular functions which might be detrimental to viral synthesis. The major late products are the structural proteins of the nucleocapsid. Almost as soon as these proteins are synthesized, they assemble with newly synthesized DNA molecules into virion nucleocapsids.

The events of the eclipse period in infections with RNA viruses are similar, except that they take place in the cytoplasm (influenza virus excepted), and a division into early and late transcription cannot be made. In the case of positive-strand RNA viruses, the viral RNA is itself the mRNA. In infections with negative-strand RNA viruses, the virion RNA in the nucleocapsid is first transcribed into positive mRNAs. Intracellular nucleocapsids are present throughout the entire infectious cycle, and the eclipse period cannot be defined in the classical sense. RNA tumor viruses reverse-transcribe their RNA into DNA, which enters the cell nucleus and becomes integrated into the cellular DNA. All viral mRNAs and genomic RNAs are generated by transcription of the integrated DNA.

The event characteristic of the maturation step is virion assembly and release. In many cases the protein shell is assembled first (procapsid) and the nucleic acid is inserted into it. During this insertion, processing of some shell proteins by cleavage takes place and is accompanied by a modification of the structure to accommodate the nucleic acid. Unenveloped viruses which mature in the cytoplasm (for example, poliovirus) often exit the cell rapidly by a reverse-phagocytosis process, even before the breakdown of the cell. In some cases, however, a large number of virus particles may accumulate inside the cell in crystalline arrays called inclusion bodies. Viruses that mature in the nucleus are usually released slowly, and the damage to the cell is extensive. Enveloped viruses exit the cell by a process of budding. Viral envelope proteins (glycoproteins) become inserted at various sites into the cell membrane, where they also interact with matrix proteins and with nucleocapsids. The cellular membrane then curves around the complex and forms a bud which detaches from the rest of the cell (see illustration).

Effect of viral infections. Two extreme types of effects are identified with viral infections: lytic infections, which cause cell death by a variety of mechanisms with cell lysis as the most common outcome, and persistent infections, accompanied either by no apparent change in the host cell or by some interference with normal growth control, as in transformation of normal to cancer cells. In animals, extensive destruction of tissue may accompany an infection by a lytic virus. *See* LYTIC INFECTION.

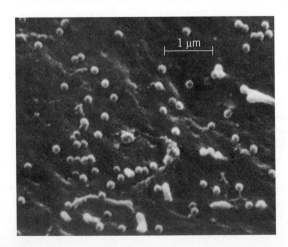

1 μm

Scanning electron micrograph of the surface of a mouse cell infected with murine leukemia virus. A large number of virus particles are shown in the process of budding. (*Courtesy of R. MacLeod*)

As a defense to certain conditions of infection, animal cells generate a group of substances called interferons which, by a complex mechanism, inhibit replication of viruses. They are specific to the cell species from which they were derived but not to the virus which elicited their generation. (Mouse interferon will protect mouse but not human cells from any viral infection.)

Pathology. Virus infections spread in several ways: through aerosols and dust, by direct contact with carriers or their excretions, and by bites or stings of animal and insect vectors. At the point of entry, infected cells undergo viremia. From there, the virus becomes disseminated by secretions. It is carried through the lymphatic system and bloodstream to other target organs, where secondary viremias occur (except in localized infections like warts). In most cases viral infections are of short duration and great severity. However, persistent infections are not uncommon (herpes, adeno, various paramyxoviruses like measles).

The afflicted organism mounts a variety of defenses, the most important of which is the immune response. Circulating antibodies against viral proteins are generated. Those interacting with virion surface proteins neutralize the infectious potential of the virus. Although the antibodies are specific against the virus which has elicited them, they will cross-react with closely related virus strains. The specificity of neutralizing antibodies obtained from experimentally injected animals is utilized for diagnostic purposes or in quantitative assays. In addition to the circulating antibodies, cell-mediated immune responses also take place. The most important of these is the production of cytotoxic thymus-derived lymphocytes, found in the lymph nodes, spleen, and blood. They destroy all cells which harbor in their membrane viral glycoproteins. The cell-mediated immunity has been demonstrated to be more important to the process of recovery than circulating antibodies. In spite of their beneficial role, immune responses often seriously contribute to the pathology of the disease. Circulating antigen-antibody complexes can lodge in organs and cause inflammation; cell-mediated responses have been known to produce severe shock syndromes in patients with a history of previous exposures to the virus. *See* ANTIBODY; AUTOIMMUNITY; IMMUNITY.

Control. Viruses are resistant to the antibiotics commonly used against bacterial infections. The use of chemotherapeutic agents with antiviral activity is plagued by their toxicity to the animal host. However, the application of vaccines has been successful in the control of several viruses. The vaccines elicit immune responses and provide sometimes life-long protection. Two types of vaccines have been applied: inactivated virus and live attentuated virus. Various inactivation procedures are available. An attentuated laboratory strain of smallpox has been applied so successfully that the disease is considered to be eradicated. A small probability of back mutations of the attenuated virus to a virulent strain makes applications of live vaccines somewhat riskier. On the other hand, protection is longer-lasting and, by virtue of spread to nonvaccinated individuals, more beneficial to the population group (herd effect). *See* POLIOMYELITIS; VACCINATION.

In order to achieve full protection, it is important that the vaccine contain all the distinct antigenic types of the virus. Development of monoclonal antibodies led to a better characterization of these types in naturally occurring viruses. This information will undoubtedly lead to better vaccines. Moreover, monoclonal antibodies have aided investigations into the molecular structure of viral antigenic groups and brightened future prospects for synthetic vaccines. *See* MONOCLONAL ANTIBODIES; VIRUS; VIRUS CLASSIFICATION.   [M.E.Re.]

Annelida   The phylum comprising the multisegmented, invertebrate wormlike animals, of which the most numerous are the marine bristle worms and the most familiar the terrestrial earthworms. The Annelida (meaning little annuli or rings) include the Polychaeta (meaning many setae); the earthworms and fresh-water worms, or Oligochaeta (meaning few setae); the marine and fresh-water leeches or Hirudinea; and two other marine classes having affinities with the Polychaeta: the Archiannelida (meaning primitive annelids), small heteromorphic marine worms, and the Myzostomaria (meaning sucker mouths), parasites of crinoid echinoderms. These five groups share few common characters and little resemblance except that most have a wormlike body. Typically they are bilaterally symmetrical, lack a skeleton, and have a short to long linear body divided into rings or segments, which are separated from one another by transverse walls or septa. The mouth is an anteroventral or anterior vent at the forward end of the alimentary tract, and the anus posterodorsal or posterior at the hind end of the gut. *See* HIRUDINEA; OLIGOCHAETA; POLYCHAETA.

The linear series of segments, or metameres, from anterior to posterior ends constitute the annelid body. These segments may be similar throughout, resulting in an annulated cylinder, as in earthworms and *Lumbrineris*. More frequently the successive segments are dissimilar, resulting in regions modified for particular functions. Each segment may be simple (uniannular) corresponding to a metamere, or it may be divided (multiannulate). The total number of segments varies from five to several hundred. Segments may have lateral fleshy outgrowths called parapodia (meaning side feet), armed with special secreted bristles or rods, called setae and acicula; they provide protection and aid in locomotion. Setae are lacking in Hirudinea and some polychaetes. The body is covered by a thin to thick epithelium which is never shed.

The ability to replace lost parts is highly developed in annelids. Most frequent is the replacement of tail, parapodia, and setae. The anterior end may be replaced provided the break is postpharyngeal. The torn end is first covered over with scar tissue, then differentiated into epithelial cells and all other tissues characteristic of the whole animal.

Depending on the species, reproduction may be sexual, asexual, or both. Sexual reproduction may be dioecious, in which male and female are similar, rarely dissimilar. Individuals may be hermaphroditic, both male and female, but with cross fertilization. Some annelids are protandric hermaphrodites, in which the sexual stages alternate.

[O.H.]

Anthozoa   A class of the phylum Coelenterata. These organisms are marine, solitary or colonial, and exclusively polypoid coelenterates with no traces of a medusoid stage. Most anthozoans live attached to some firm object of the shore or on the sea bottom; some embed in the soft sediment. Anthozoans have a cylindrical body with an oral disk, mouth, stomodeum, hollow tentacles, endodermal gonad, and cellular mesoglea. The gastrovascular cavity is partitioned longitudinally into radial compartments by endodermal mesenteries or septa whose free edges, particularly, thicken and differentiate into mesenteric or septal filaments. The nervous system is a diffuse network of scattered nerve cells over the ectoderm and the endoderm. No localized sense organs are present.

Both sexual and asexual reproduction occurs. The germ cells are derived from the endoderm, and fertilization occurs either in the female gastrovascular cavity or in the sea. The zygote develops into either a ciliated swimming larva, the planula, or a young polyp.

The class Anthozoa includes the soft, horny, stony, and black corals, the sea pens, and sea anemones. The horny corals include the sea fans, sea whips, and sea feathers. The Anthozoa may be classified as listed here.

Class Anthozoa
　　Subclass Alcyonaria (Octocorallia)
　　　　Order: Stolonifera
　　　　　　Telestacea
　　　　　　Coenothecalia
　　　　　　Alcyonacea
　　　　　　Gorgonacea
　　　　　　Pennatulacea
　　Subclass Zoantharia (Hexacorallia)
　　　　Order: Actiniaria
　　　　　　Scleractinia (Madreporaria)
　　　　　　Zoanthidea
　　　　　　Antipatharia
　　　　　　Ceriantharia
　　　　　　Rugosa
　　　　　　Tabulata

All anthozoans are marine and most are sedentary, except the free-swimming larval stages, while actinians, cerianthids, and pennatulans are somewhat movable. They are widely distributed over the world, extending from the Arctic to the Antarctic; however, they predominate in the tropic and subtropic areas of the Indo-Pacific Ocean. Actinians also inhabit colder water areas from which deep-sea species of gorgonians, pennatulans, and scleractinians have been collected.

Anthozoans seldom tolerate desiccation or heavy sedimentation. They are so sensitive to reduced salinity that they usually do not live near coastal areas where there is river drainage. Tropical corals are able to endure high temperatures and are adversely affected by low temperatures. Therefore, coral reefs are commonly located in tropic and subtropic regions. *See* COELENTERATA; HYDROZOA.　　　　　　　　　　　　　　　[K.At.]

Anthrax　　An acute infectious zoonotic disease caused by the bacterium *Bacillus anthracis* and primarily associated with herbivorous mammals. Carnivorous mammals, birds, reptiles, amphibians, fish, and insects are generally resistant to anthrax infection. However, carnivorous and omnivorous mammals often succumb after ingestion of infected meat containing the anthrax toxins, which can cause swelling in the throat and suffocation. Humans primarily present with cutaneous lesions, appearing as black scabs or eschars, after contact with infected animals, carcasses, or animal products. *See* ZOONOSES.

Anthrax is responsible for the deaths of thousands of domesticated and wild herbivorous animals annually. Parts of Africa, Asia, southern Europe, and North and South America are subject to repeated outbreaks. In the Western Hemisphere, anthrax is well controlled in livestock.

Bacillus anthracis is a gram-positive, rod-shaped, endospore-forming bacterium, approximately 1.0–1.2 micrometers in diameter and 3–8 μm long. The spores resist drying, cold, heat, and disinfectants, and can remain viable for many years in soil, water, and animal hides and products. *Bacillus anthracis* possesses three virulence factors: lethal toxin, edema toxin, and a poly-D-glutamic acid capsule. Lethal toxin is composed of two proteins, lethal factor and protective antigen. The protective antigen is produced by the anthrax bacillus at a molecular weight of 83 kDa, but must be cleaved by either serum or target cell surface proteases to 63 kDa before it complexes with lethal factor to form lethal toxin. The edema toxin is composed of edema factor and protective antigen, and it is believed to complex in a manner similar to that seen for lethal toxin. Protective antigen plays a central role in that it is required for transport of lethal factor and edema factor into host target cells. The macrophage appears to be the primary host target cell for lethal toxin, whereas the neutrophil appears to be the target cell for edema toxin in addition to other cells involved in edema formation. The third virulence factor is the capsule, which inhibits phagocytosis through its negatively charged poly-D-glutamic acid composition. All three toxin components are encoded by a plasmid, pXO1, whereas the enzymes required for capsule synthesis are encoded for by the pXO2 plasmid. Strains lacking either or both plasmids are avirulent, such as the veterinary vaccine Sterne strain, which lacks the pXO2 plasmid.

Anthrax consists of two clinical forms, cutaneous and septicemic. The cutaneous form begins as a blisterlike lesion that eventually becomes an intensely dark, relatively painless, edematous lesion forming a black eschar. The lesions rapidly become sterile after antibiotic therapy and take several weeks to resolve, even with treatment. The cutaneous form is reported only in humans, rabbits, swine, and horses.

The septicemic form arises from various initial sites of infection, including cutaneous, oropharyngeal, gastrointestinal, or inhalational exposures. The course of septicemic disease depends on the exposure route and the susceptibility of the animal host. The vast majority of systemic anthrax cases in herbivorus animals occur from trauma to mucosal linings of the mouth and upper alimentary canal caused by ingested fibrous foods. Inhalation anthrax is believed to be initiated by phagocytosis of spores within the lungs by alveolar macrophages. Spore-laden macrophages pass through lymphatic channels to the sinuses of regional lymph nodes or migrate to the spleen, where the spores germinate within the macrophages, multiply, and overwhelm and escape the macrophages to invade the efferent lymphatics. For other portals of entry, mesenteric lymph nodes become involved. The bacilli move to the spleen, where they induce pronounced splenomegaly (enlargement of the spleen), and finally enter the bloodstream, where they induce secondary sites of infection, massive bacillemia, toxemia, and sudden death. Failure of the blood to clot, hemorrhages of skin, hemorrhagic meningitis, and reduced rigor mortis are frequently found in anthrax-infected carcasses. Exposure of contaminated body fluids to the lower atmospheric levels of carbon dioxide results in sporulation of the bacilli. Therefore, opening of infected carcasses should be avoided.

Besides its central role for binding the lethal and edema toxins to target cells, protective antigen plays an important role in the host's protective immune response against anthrax, hence the term protective antigen. Vaccines lacking protective antigen are not protective. For United States and United Kingdom human anthrax vaccines, protective antigen bound to aluminum salts is the principal immunogen. However, veterinary vaccines are composed of viable spores of B. anthracis Sterne strain, a nonencapsulated toxigenic variant. Full protection against anthrax with the veterinary vaccine is afforded by primary and annual booster vaccinations. See INFECTIOUS DISEASE.   [J.W.Ez.]

Antibiotic   The original definition of an antibiotic was a chemical substance that is produced by a microorganism and, in dilute solutions, can inhibit the growth of, and even destroy, other microorganisms. This definition has been expanded to include similar inhibitory substances that are produced by plants, marine organisms, and total- or semisynthetic procedures. Since the discovery of penicillin by A. Fleming in 1928, thousands of antibiotics have been isolated and identified; some have been found to be of value in the treatment of infectious disease. They differ markedly in physicochemical and pharmacological properties, antimicrobial spectra, and mechanisms of action.

Production. Penicillin is produced by strains of the fungus *Penicillium notatum* and *P. chrysogenum*. Most of the other antibiotics in clinical use are produced by actinomycetes, particularly streptomycetes (natural antibiotics). Other antibiotics are produced by chemical synthesis (synthetic antibiotics). Based on structure, the major antibiotic classes are the β-lactams (penicillins and cephalosporins), aminoglycosides, macrolides, tetracyclines, quinolones, rifamycins, polyenes, azoles, glycopeptides, and polypeptides.

The key step in the production of natural antibiotics is a fermentation process. Strains of microorganisms, selected by elaborate screening procedures from randomly isolated pure cultures, are inoculated into sterile nutrient medium in large vats and incubated for varying periods of time. Different strains of a single microbial species may differ greatly in the amounts of antibiotics they produce. Strain selection is thus the most powerful tool in effecting major improvements in antibiotic yield. In addition, variations in culturing conditions often markedly affect the amount of antibiotic that is produced by a given strain. Chemical modifications of antibiotics produced by fermentation processes have led to semisynthetic ones with improved antimicrobial activity or pharmacological properties. *See* BACTERIAL PHYSIOLOGY AND METABOLISM; FERMENTATION.

Antimicrobial activity. All microorganisms can cause infectious diseases in animals and humans, though the majority of infections are caused by bacteria. Most antibiotics are active against bacteria. Although for the proper treatment of serious infections cultures and antibiotic sensitivities are required, antibiotic therapy is often empiric, with etiology being inferred from the clinical features of a disease.

Bacteria are divided into the gram positive and the gram negative; each group comprises a wide variety of different species. Staphylococci, pneumococci, and streptococci are the more common gram-positive organisms, while enterobacteria, *Pseudomonas*, and *Hemophilus* are the most common gram negative. Certain antibiotics are effective only against gram-positive bacteria. Others are effective against both gram-positive and gram-negative bacteria and are referred to as broad-spectrum antibiotics. *See* BACTERIA; MEDICAL BACTERIOLOGY.

Pathogenic fungi may be divided on the basis of their pathogenicity into true pathogens and opportunistic pathogens. The opportunistic occur mainly in debilitated and immunocompromised patients. Clinically useful antibiotics include amphotericin B, nystatin, griseofulvin and the azole antifungals. *See* FUNGI; MEDICAL MYCOLOGY; OPPORTUNISTIC INFECTIONS.

With some viruses that cause mild infections, such as the common-cold viruses (rhinoviruses), treatment is symptomatic. With others, such as the polio, smallpox (now eradicated), and hepatitis B viruses, the only way to prevent disease is by vaccination. With still other viruses, antibiotics, mostly synthetic, are the appropriate treatment. Clinically useful antibiotics are ribavirin, acyclovir, and zidovudine, which are active against, respectively, respiratory, herpes, and human immunodeficiency viruses. *See* ANIMAL VIRUS; VACCINATION.

Protozoa may be divided, on the basis of the site of infection, into intestinal, urogenital, blood, and tissue. Protozoan diseases such as malaria, trypanosomiasis, and amebiasis are particularly common in the tropics, in populations living under poor housing and sanitary conditions. In the developed countries, *P. carinii* is the most important opportunistic pathogen, being associated almost exclusively with acquired immune deficiency syndrome (AIDS). Antibiotics active against protozoa include metronidazole, trimethoprim-sulfamethoxazole, and quinine. *See* ACQUIRED IMMUNE DEFICIENCY SYNDROME (AIDS); MEDICAL PARASITOLOGY; PROTOZOA.

Antitumor activity. The observation of the antitumor activity of actinomycin sparked an intensive search for antitumor antibiotics in plants and microorganisms.

Among the antibiotics used clinically against certain forms of cancer are daunorubicin, doxorubicin, mitomycin C, and bleomycin.

Mechanism of action. Antibiotics active against bacteria are bacteriostatic or bacteriocidal; that is, they either inhibit growth of susceptible organisms or destroy them. On the basis of their mechanism of action, antibiotics are classified as (1) those that affect bacterial cell-wall biosynthesis, causing loss of viability and often cell lysis (penicillins and cephalosporins, bacitracin, cycloserine, vancomycin); (2) those that act directly on the cell membrane, affecting its barrier function and leading to leakage of intracellular components (polymyxin); (3) those that interfere with protein biosynthesis (chloramphenicol, tetracyclines, erythromycin, spectinomycin, streptomycin, gentamycin); (4) those that affect nucleic acid biosynthesis (rifampicin, novobiocin, quinolones); and (5) those that block specific steps in intermediary metabolism (sulfonamides, trimethoprim). *See* ENZYME; SULFONAMIDE.

Antibiotics active against fungi are fungistatic or fungicidal. Their mechanisms of action include (1) interaction with the cell membrane, leading to leakage of cytoplasmic components (amphotericin, nystatin); (2) interference with the synthesis of membrane components (ketoconazole, fluconazole); (3) interference with nucleic acid synthesis (5-fluorocytosine); and (4) interference with microtubule assembly (griseofulvin). *See* FUNGISTAT AND FUNGICIDE.

For an antibiotic to be effective, it must first reach the target site of action on or in the microbial cell. It must also reach the body site at which the infective microorganism resides in sufficient concentration, and remain there long enough to exert its effect. The concentration in the body must remain below that which is toxic to the human cells. The effectiveness of an antibiotic also depends on the severity of the infection and the immune system of the body, being significantly reduced when the immune system is impaired. Complete killing or lysis of the microorganism may be required to achieve a successful outcome. *See* IMMUNITY.

Antibiotics may be given by injection, orally, or topically. When given orally, they must be absorbed into the body and transported by the blood and extracellular fluids to the site of the infecting organisms. When they are administered topically, such absorption is rarely possible, and the antibiotics then exert their effect only against those organisms present at the site of application.

Microbial resistance. The therapeutic value of every antibiotic class is gradually eroded by the microbial resistance that invariably follows broad clinical use.

Some bacteria are naturally resistant to certain antibiotics (inherent resistance). Clinical resistance is commonly due to the emergence of resistant organisms following antibiotic treatment (acquired resistance). This emergence, in turn, is due to selection of resistant mutants of the infective species (endogenous resistance) or, usually, to transfer of resistance genes from other, naturally resistant species (exogenous resistance). A major challenge in antimicrobial chemotherapy is the horizontal spread of resistance genes and resistant strains, mostly in the hospital but also in the community. The consequences are increased patient morbidity and mortality, reduced drug options, and more expensive and toxic antibiotics.

Rapid detection of resistance and pathogen identification are critical for the rational use of antibiotics and implementation of infection control measures. In the absence of such information, treament is empiric, usually involving broad-spectrum agents, which exacerbates resistance development. Inadequate infection control measures encourage dissemination of resistant strains.

Importance. It is estimated that the average duration of many infectious diseases and the severity of certain others have decreased significantly since the introduction of antibiotic therapy. The dramatic drop in mortality rates for such dreaded diseases as meningitis, tuberculosis, and septicemia offers striking evidence of the effectiveness of these agents. Bacterial pneumonia, bacterial endocarditis, typhoid fever, and certain sexually transmitted diseases are also amenable to treatment with antibiotics. So are infections that often follow viral or neoplastic diseases, even though the original illness may not respond to antibiotic therapy. *See* EPIDEMIOLOGY.

Antibiotics in small amounts are widely used as feed supplements to stimulate growth of livestock and poultry. They probably act by inhibiting organisms responsible for low-grade infections and by reducing intestinal epithelial inflammation. Many experts believe that this use of antibiotics contributes to the emergence of antibiotic-resistant bacteria that could eventually pose a public health problem.

In cattle, sheep, and swine, antibiotics are effective against economically important diseases. The use of antibiotics in dogs and cats closely resembles their use in human medical practice. In fish farms, antibiotics are usually added to the food or applied to the fish by bathing. The incidence of infections in fish, and animals in general, may be reduced by the use of disease-resistant stock, better hygiene, and better diet.

Although effective against many microorganisms causing disease in plants, antibiotics are not widely used to control crop and plant diseases. Some of the limiting factors are instability of the antibiotic under field conditions, the possibility of harmful residues, and expense. Nevertheless, antibiotic control of some crop pathogens is being practiced, as is true of the rice blast in Japan, for example. *See* PLANT PATHOLOGY.

[N.H.G.]

Antibody   A protein found principally in blood serum and characterized by a specific reactivity with the corresponding antigen. Antibodies are important in resistance against disease, in allergy, and in blood transfusions, and can be utilized in laboratory tests for the detection of antigens or the estimation of immune status.

Antibodies are normally absent at birth unless derived passively from the mother through the placenta or colostrum. In time, certain antibodies appear in response to environmental antigens. Antibodies are also induced by artificial immunization with vaccines or following natural infections. The resulting antibody level declines over a period of months, but rapidly increases following renewed contact with specific antigen, even after a lapse of years. This is known as an anamnestic or booster response. *See* ALLERGY; BLOOD GROUPS; HYPERSENSITIVITY; ISOANTIGEN; VACCINATION.

Antibody reactivity results in precipitation of soluble antigens, agglutination of particulate antigens, increased phagocytosis of bacteria, neutralization of toxins, and dissolution of bacterial or other cells specifically sensitive to their action; the antibodies so revealed are termed precipitins, agglutinins, opsonins, antitoxins, and lysins. One antibody may give many such reactions, depending on conditions, so these classifications are not unique or exclusive.

Three principal groups (IgG, IgM, IgA) and two minor groups (IgD, IgE) of antibodies are recognized. These all form part of the wider classification of immunoglobulins. Antibody diversity is generated by amino acid substitutions that result in unique antigen-binding structures. *See* CELLULAR IMMUNOLOGY; IMMUNOGLOBULIN.

The development of the technology for producing monoclonal antibodies, which can bind to specific sites on target antigens, revolutionized the uses of antibodies in biology and medicine. Unfortunately, almost all monoclonal antibodies originate in mice, and the murine immunoglobulin serves as an antigen, frequently acting immunogenic in human recipients. *See* ANTIGEN; MONOCLONAL ANTIBODIES.

[M.J.Po.]

Antigen A substance that initiates and mediates the formation of the corresponding immune body, termed antibody. Antigens can also react with formed antibodies. Antigen-antibody reactions serve as host defenses against microorganisms and other foreign bodies, or are used in laboratory tests for detecting the presence of either antigen or antibody. *See* ANTIBODY; ANTIGEN-ANTIBODY REACTION.

A protein immunogen (any substance capable of inducing an immune response) is usually composed of a large number of antigenic determinants. Thus, immunizing an animal with a protein results in the formation of a number of antibody molecules with different specificities. The antigenicity of a protein is determined by its sequence of amino acids as well as by its conformation. Antigens may be introduced into an animal by ingestion, inhalation, sometimes by contact with skin, or more regularly by injection into the bloodstream, skin, peritoneum, or other body part.

With a few exceptions, such as the autoantigens and the isoantigens of the blood groups, antigens produce antibody only in species other than the ones from which they are derived. All complete proteins are antigenic, as are many bacterial and other polysaccharides, some nucleic acids, and some lipids. Antigenicity may be modified or abolished by chemical treatments, including degradation or enzymatic digestion; it may be notably increased by the incorporation of antigen into oils or other adjuvants. *See* ISOANTIGEN.

Bacteria, viruses, protozoans, and other microorganisms are important sources of antigens. These may be proteins or polysaccharides derived from the outer surfaces of the cell (capsular antigens), from the cell interior (the somatic or O antigens), or from the flagella (the flagellar or H antigens). Other antigens either are excreted by the cell or are released into the medium during cell death and disruption; these include many enzymes and toxins, of which diphtheria, tetanus, and botulinus toxins are important examples. The presence of antibody to one of these constituent antigens in human or animal sera is presumptive evidence of past or present contact with specific microorganisms, and this finds application in clinical diagnosis and epidemiological surveys. *See* BOTULISM; DIPHTHERIA; TOXIN.

Microbial antigens prepared to induce protective antibodies are termed vaccines. They may consist of either attenuated living or killed whole cells, or extracts of these. Since whole microorganisms are complex structures, vaccines may contain 10 or more distinct antigens, of which generally not more than one or two engender a protective antibody. Examples of these are smallpox vaccine, a living attenuated virus; typhoid vaccine, killed bacterial cells; and diphtheria toxoid, detoxified culture fluid. Several independent vaccines may be mixed to give a combined vaccine, and thus reduce the number of injections necessary for immunization, but such mixing can result in a lesser response to each component of the mixture. *See* VACCINATION.

Allergens are antigens that induce allergic states in humans or animals. Examples are preparations from poison ivy, cottonseed, or horse dander, or simple chemicals such as formaldehyde or picryl chloride. *See* HYPERSENSITIVITY; IMMUNOLOGY.   [M.J.Po.]

Antigen-antibody reaction A reaction that occurs when an antigen combines with a corresponding antibody to produce an immune complex. A substance that induces the immune system to form a corresponding antibody is called an immunogen. All immunogens are also antigens because they react with corresponding antibodies; however, an antigen may not be able to induce the formation of an antibody and therefore may not be an immunogen. For instance, lipids and all low-molecular-weight substances are not immunogenic. However, many such substances, termed haptens, can be attached to immunogens, called carriers, and the complex then acts as a new immunogen. *See* ANTIBODY; ANTIGEN.

A molecule of antibody has two identical binding sites for one antigen or more, depending on its class. Each site is quite small and can bind only a comparably small portion of the surface of the antigen, which is termed an epitope. The specificity of an antibody for an antigen depends entirely upon the possession of the appropriate epitope by an antigen. The binding site on the antibody and the epitope on the antigen are complementary regions on the surface of the respective molecules which interlock in the antigen-antibody reaction. The intensity with which an antibody binds to the antigen depends on the exactitude of the fit between the respective binding site and epitope, as well as some inherent characteristics of the reacting molecules and factors in the environment. The epitope must be continuous spatially, but not structurally: in other words, if the molecule of the antigen consists of several chains, then an epitope may be formed by adjacent regions on two different chains, as well as by adjacent regions on the same chain. If the epitope is now modified either chemically (for example, by altering the hapten) or physically (for example, by causing the chains to separate), then its fit in the binding site will be altered or abolished, and the antigen will react with the antibody either less strongly or not at all.

The immune complex formed in the reaction consists of closely apposed, but still discrete, molecules of antigen and antibody. Therefore, the immune complex can dissociate into the original molecules. The proportion of the dissociated, individual molecules of antigen and antibody to those of the immune complex clearly depends on the intensity of the binding. These proportions can be measured in a standardized procedure, so that the concentration of antigen [Ag], antibody [Ab], and the immune complex [AgAb] becomes known. A fraction is then calculated and called either the dissociation constant or the association constant. The magnitude of either of these constants can be used subsequently to assess the intensity of the antigen-antibody reaction. *See* IMMUNOASSAY.

Only one epitope of its kind generally occurs on each molecule of antigen, other than that which consists of multiple, identical units, though many epitopes of different configuration are possible. Particles, however, either natural ones such as cells or suitably treated artificial ones made of, for example, latex or glass, typically carry multiple identical epitopes, as well as nonidentical ones, because their surfaces contain many molecules of the same antigen. Immune complexes comprising many molecules eventually reach sufficient size to scatter light, at which point they can be detected by nephelometry or turbidimetry; if their growth continues, they become visible as precipitates, which can also be assayed by such methods as immunodiffusion. Since particles typically carry many molecules of antigen, they can be, in principle, aggregated and the reaction can be detected by inspection. Antigen-antibody reactions can also be detected at very low concentration of reactants through special techniques such as immunofluorescence and radioimmunoassay. *See* IMMUNOASSAY; RADIO-IMMUNOASSAY.

The reaction between antigen and antibody is followed by a structural change in the remainder of the antibody molecule. The change results in the appearance of previously hidden regions of the molecule. Some of these hidden regions have specific functions, such as binding complement. Fixation of complement by immune complexes has been used to detect and measure antigen-antibody reactions. *See* COMPLEMENT.

The chief use of antigen-antibody reactions has been in the determination of blood groups for transfusion, serological ascertainment of exposure to infectious agents, and development of immunoassays for the quantification of various substances. *See* BLOOD GROUPS; IMMUNOLOGY; SEROLOGY.   [A.B.]

Antihistamine   A type of drug that inhibits the combination of histamine with histamine receptors. These drugs are termed either H-1 or H-2 receptor antagonists depending on which type of histamine receptor is involved. H-1 receptor antagonists are used largely for treating allergies, and H-2 receptor antagonists are used to treat peptic ulcer disease and related conditions. *See* HISTAMINE.

The primary therapeutic use of H-1 receptor antagonists is to antagonize the effects of histamine released from cells by antigen-antibody reactions; they can thus inhibit histamine-induced effects, such as bronchoconstriction, skin reactions, for example, wheals and itching, and nasal inflammation. These drugs, therefore, are quite effective in reducing allergy signs and symptoms, especially if they are administered before contact with the relevant antigen; however they are not effective in treating asthma. Their effects vary widely, both among the drugs and from individual to individual; in young children excitement may be seen. Another common set of effects caused by many of these drugs, including dry mouth, blurred vision, and urinary retention, can be ascribed to their anticholinergic actions. H-1 receptor antagonists have low toxicity. The chief adverse effect is sedation. Overdoses of H-1 receptor antagonists may be associated with excitement or depression, and although there is no pharmacologic antidote for these drugs, good supportive care should be adequate in managing cases of poisoning. *See* ALLERGY; ANTIGEN-ANTIBODY REACTION.

H-2 receptor antagonists are much newer. Histamine stimulates gastric acid secretion by combining with H-2 receptors. By preventing this combination, H-2 antagonists can reduce acid secretion in the stomach, an effect that makes these drugs useful in managing various conditions, such as peptic ulcer disease.

Other conditions in which H-2 antagonists are used to lower gastric acidity include reflux esophagitis, stress ulcers, and hypersecretory states such as the Zollinger-Ellison syndrome, in which tumor cells secrete large amounts of the hormone gastrin, which stimulates gastric acid secretion. In these conditions, administration of H-2 antagonists reduces symptoms and promotes healing.

The toxicity of H-2 antagonists is quite low, and adverse effects are reported by only 1-2% of patients. The most common side effects are gastrointestinal upsets, including nausea, vomiting, and diarrhea.   [A.Bur.]

Antimicrobial agents   Chemical compounds biosynthetically or synthetically produced which either destroy or usefully suppress the growth or metabolism of a variety of microscopic or submicroscopic forms of life. On the basis of their primary activity, they are more specifically called antibacterial, antifungal, antiprotozoal, antiparasitic, or antiviral agents. Antibacterials which destroy are bactericides or germicides; those which merely suppress growth are bacteriostatic agents. *See* ANTIBIOTIC.

Of the thousands of antimicrobial agents, only a small number are safe chemotherapeutic agents, effective in controlling infectious diseases in plants, animals, and humans. A much larger number are used in almost every phase of human activity: in agriculture, food preservation, and water, skin, and air disinfection. A compilation of some common uses for antimicrobials is shown in the table.

The most important antimicrobial discovery of all time, that of the chemotherapeutic value of penicillin, was made in 1938. In the next 20 years, more than a score of new and useful microbially produced antimicrobials entered into daily use. New synthetic antimicrobials are found today by synthesis of a wide variety of compounds, followed by broad screening against many microorganisms. Biosynthetic antimicrobials, although first found in bacteria, fungi, and plants, are now being discovered primarily in actinomycetes.

Common antimicrobial agents and their uses

Use	Agents
Chemotherapeutics (animals and humans)	
Antibacterials	Sulfonamides, isoniazid, p-aminosalicylic acid, penicillin, streptomycin, tetracyclines, chloramphenicol, erythromycin, novobiocin, neomycin, bacitracin, polymyxin
Antiparasitics (humans)	Emetine, quinine
Antiparasitics (animal)	Hygromycin, phenothiazine, piperazine
Antifungals	Griseofulvin, nystatin
Chemotherapeutics (plants)	Captan (N-trichlorothio-tetrahydrophthalimide), maneb (manganese ethylene bisdithiocarbamate), thiram (tetramethylthiuram disulfide)
Skin disinfectants	Alcohols, iodine, mercurials, silver compounds, quaternary ammonium compounds, neomycin
Water disinfectants	Chlorine, sodium hypochlorite
Air disinfectants	Propylene glycol, lactic acid, glycolic acid, levulinic acid
Gaseous disinfectants	Ethylene oxide, β-propiolactone, formaldehyde
Clothing disinfectants	Neomycin
Animal-growth stimulants	Penicillin, streptomycin, bacitracin, tetracyclines, hygromycin
Food preservatives	Sodium benzoate, tetracycline

Antimicrobial agents contain various functional groups. No particular structural type seems to favor antimicrobial activity. The search for correlation of structure with biological activity goes on, but no rules have yet appeared with which to forecast activity from contemplated structural changes. On the contrary, minor modifications may lead to unexpected loss of activity. [G.M.S.]

Antioxidant A substance that, when present at a lower concentration than that of the oxidizable substrate, significantly inhibits or delays oxidative processes, while being itself oxidized. In primary antioxidants, such as polyphenols, this antioxidative activity is implemented by the donation of an electron or hydrogen atom to a radical derivative, and in secondary antioxidants by the removal of an oxidative catalyst and the consequent prevention of the initiation of oxidation.

Antioxidants have diverse applications. They are used to prevent degradation in polymers, weakening in rubber and plastics, autoxidation and gum formation in gasoline, and discoloration of synthetic and natural pigments. They are used in foods, beverages, and cosmetic products to inhibit deterioration and spoilage. Interest is increasing in the application of antioxidants to medicine relating to human diseases attributed to oxidative stress.

The autoxidation process is shown in reactions (1), (2), and (3). Lipids, mainly

$$RH + \text{initiator (L)} \rightarrow R\cdot + LH \tag{1}$$

$$R\cdot + O_2 \rightarrow ROO\cdot \tag{2}$$

$$ROO\cdot + RH \rightarrow ROOH + R\cdot \tag{3}$$

those containing unsaturated fatty acids, such as linoleic acid [RH in reaction (1)], can undergo autoxidation via a free-radical chain reaction, which is unlikely to take place with atmospheric oxygen (ground state) alone. A catalyst (L) is required, such as light, heat, heavy-metal ions (copper or iron), or specific enzymes present in the biological system [reaction (1)]. The catalyst allows a lipid radical to be formed (alkyl radical R·) on a carbon atom next to the double bond of the unsaturated fatty acid. This radical is very unstable and reacts with oxygen [reaction (2)] to form a peroxyl radical (ROO·), which in turn can react with an additional lipid molecule to form a hydroperoxide [ROOH in reaction (3)] plus a new alkyl radical, and hence to start a chain reaction. Reactions (2) and (3), the propagation steps, continue unless a decay reaction takes place (a termination step), which involves the combination of two radicals to form stable products.

When lipid autoxidation occurs in food, it can cause deterioration, rancidity, bad odor, spoilage, reduction in nutritional value, and possibly the formation of toxic by-products. Oxidation stress in a lipid membrane in a biological system can alter its structure, affect its fluidity, and change its function, causing disease.

An antioxidant can eliminate potential initiators of oxidation and thus prevent reaction (1). It can also stop the process by donating an electron and reducing one of the radicals in reaction (2) or (3), thus halting the propagation steps. A primary antioxidant can be effective if it is able to donate an electron (or hydrogen atom) rapidly to a lipid radical and itself become more stable then the original radical. The ease of electron donation depends on the molecular structure of the antioxidant, which dictates the stability of the new radical. Many naturally occurring polyphenols, such as flavonoids, anthocyanins, and saponins, which can be found in wine, fruit, grain, vegetables, and almost all herbs and spices, are effective antioxidants that operate by this mechanism.

A secondary antioxidant can prevent reaction (1) from taking place by absorbing ultraviolet light, scavenging oxygen, chelating transition metals, or inhibiting enzymes involved in the formation of reactive oxygen species, for example, NADPH oxidase and xanthine oxidase (reducing molecular oxygen to superoxide and hydrogen peroxide), dopamine-β-hydroxylase, and lipoxygenases. The common principle of action in the above examples is the removal of the component acting as the catalyst that initiates and stimulates the free-radical chain reaction. *See* ENZYME.

Among antioxidants, the synthetic compounds butylated hydroxyanisole (BHA), propyl gallate, ethoxyquin, and diphenylamine are commonly used as food additives. Quercetin belongs to a large natural group of antioxidants, the flavonoid family, with more than 6000 known members, many acting through both mechanisms described above. Ascorbic acid is an important water-soluble plasma antioxidant; it and the tocopherols, the main lipid soluble antioxidants, represent the antioxidants in biological systems. β-Carotene belongs to the carotenoid family, which includes lycopene, the red pigment in tomatoes; the family is known to be very effective in reacting with singlet oxygen ($^1O_2$), a highly energetic species of molecular oxygen. *See* ASCORBIC ACID; CAROTENOID; FLAVONOID.   [J.Va.; L.P.]

Antitoxin   An antibody that will combine with and generally neutralize a particular toxin. When the manifestations of a disease are caused primarily by a microbial toxin, the corresponding antitoxin, if available in time, may have a pronounced prophylactic or curative effect. Apart from this, the other properties of an antitoxin are those of the antibody family (IgG, IgA, IgM) to which it belongs. *See* ANTIBODY; BIOLOGICALS; IMMUNOGLOBULIN.

Antitoxins have been developed for nearly all microbial toxins. Diphtheria, tetanus, botulinus, gas gangrene, and scarlatinal toxins are important examples. Antitoxins may be formed in humans as a result of the disease or the carrier state, or following vaccination with toxoids, and these may confer active immunity. The status of this can be evaluated through skin tests, or by titration of the serum antitoxin level. *See* BOTULISM; DIPHTHERIA; IMMUNITY; TOXIN-ANTITOXIN REACTION. [H.P.T.]

Anura   One of the three living orders (sometimes called Salientia) of the class Amphibia, which includes the frogs and toads. About 2400 species of frogs are known. Only the frozen polar regions and remote oceanic islands are without native frogs, and 80% of the species live in the tropics.

Frogs are short-bodied animals with a large mouth and protruding eyes. The externally visible part of the ear, absent in some forms, is the round, smooth tympanum situated on the side of the head behind the eye. There are five digits on the hindfeet and four on the front. Teeth may be present on the upper jaw and the vomerine bones of the roof of the mouth, but are found on the lower jaw of only one species. Often teeth are totally lacking, as in toads of the genera *Bufo* and *Rhinophrynus*. The short vertebral column consists of from 6 to 10 vertebrae, usually 9, and the elongate coccyx. The sacral vertebra precedes the coccyx and bears more or less enlarged lateral processes with which the pelvic girdle articulates. A characteristic feature of frogs is the fusion of the bones in the lower arm and lower leg, so that a single bone, the radioulna in the arm and the tibiofibula in the leg, occupies the position of two in most other tetrapods.

The one character of frogs that comes to the attention of most persons, including many who may never see a frog, is the voice. Most frogs have voices and use them in a variety of ways. In the breeding season great numbers of male frogs may congregate in favorable sites and call, each species giving its own characteristic vocalization. Because no two species breeding at the same time and place have identical calls, it is assumed that the call is important in aiding individuals to find the proper mate. In some species it appears that the female is active in selecting the mate and may be responding to the mating call, but the call may not act in exactly the same way in other species. The mating call is given with the mouth closed. Air is shunted back and forth between the lungs and the mouth, so frogs can call even though submerged. Many species possess one or two vocal sacs, which are expansible pockets of skin beneath the chin or behind the jaws. The sacs (Fig. 1), which may be inflated to a volume as great as that of the frog itself, serve as resonators.

Other noises made by frogs include the so-called fright scream given with the mouth open, and the warning chirp, which evidently serve as a sex recognition signal when one male contacts another. Some calls evidently serve as territorial signals.

Breeding and development typically take place in the following manner. The male grasps the female about the body with the forelegs, a procedure called amplexus, and fertilizes the eggs externally as they are extruded. The number of eggs may be quite large (up to 20,000 in the bullfrog or 25,000 in a common toad) or may be as few as one in a frog of the West Indies. The larva, called a tadpole, is at first limbless and has external gills and a muscular tail with dorsal and ventral fins (Fig. 2). At hatching there is no mouth opening present, but one soon forms that develops a horny beak and several rows of labial teeth not at all like the true teeth of the adult frog. Shortly after the tadpole hatches, the gills become enclosed within chambers and are no longer visible externally. Except for the gradual development of the hindlimbs, no additional external changes take place as the tadpole grows until the time for metamorphosis. The anterior limbs, which have been forming hidden in the gill chambers, break through the covering skin as metamorphosis begins. The tail dwindles in size as it is absorbed, while the mouth assumes the shape of that of the adult frog. Many other changes are taking

Fig. 1. Toad of the genus *Bufo* giving mating call with vocal sac expanded. (*American Museum of Natural History*)

place internally, including shortening of the intestine and adapting it to the carnivorous diet of the adult frog.

All frogs are carnivorous. The kind of food seems to depend largely upon the size of the frog, whose capacious mouth permits somewhat astonishing feats of swallowing. A large bullfrog, for example, may snap up low-flying bats, ducklings, snakes, and turtles. Insects and other invertebrates form the bulk of the diet of most frogs. The tongue, moistened by a sticky secretion from the intermaxillary gland in the roof of the mouth, is used to catch smaller prey, while larger items of food may bring the front limbs into play. When swallowing, a frog will usually depress the eyeballs into the head to aid in forcing the food down the pharynx. In contrast to transformed frogs, most tadpoles are vegetarian and feed on algae. A few are largely carnivorous or sometimes cannibalistic, and even vegetarian species will scavenge for dead animal matter.

The habitats of frogs are as various as the places where fresh water accumulates. Lakes and streams are tenanted year-round by many species, and others migrate to these places in the breeding season. Any permanent source of water in the desert is likely to support a population of one or more species, and when rainstorms occur, the air around a temporary pool may be filled with mating calls for a few nights, while the frogs take advantage of the water for breeding. As often as not, the pool goes dry before the tadpoles metamorphose, and the adult frogs retreat underground to await another rain. Moist tropical regions provide an abundance of habitats little known to temperate regions, such as the air plants (bromeliads) that hold water and so provide a moist home and breeding site for frogs that may never leave the trees.

Fig. 2. The tadpole, or larval, stage of the frog *Rana pipiens*. (*After W. F. Blair et al., Vertebrates of the United States, 2d ed., McGraw-Hill, 1968*)

Although the majority of frogs fall into fairly well-defined familial categories, the arrangement of the families into subordinal groups by different authorities is not consistent, and there is controversy about the relationships of some smaller groups.   [R.G.Z.]

Anxiety disorders   A group of distinct psychiatric disorders characterized by marked emotional distress and social impairment, including generalized anxiety disorder, panic disorder, obsessive-compulsive disorder, and posttraumatic stress disorder.

Generalized anxiety disorder (GAD) is characterized by excessive worry, tension, and anxiety. Accompanying physical symptoms include muscle tension, restlessness, fatigability, and sleep disturbances. GAD occurs in around 4–6% of the population and is the most frequently encountered anxiety disorder in primary care, where sufferers may seek help for the physical symptoms of the disorder. Studies of fear in animals and clinical studies of people with GAD suggest that similar brain circuits are involved in both cases. For example, numerous complex connections to other brain areas allows the amygdala to coordinate cognitive, emotional, and physiological responses to fear and anxiety. Thus in the "fight or flight" response, the organism makes cognitive-affective decisions about how to respond to the perceived danger and has a range of somatic (increased heart and respiration rate) and endocrine (release of stress hormones) responses that act together to increase the likelihood of avoiding the danger. Various neurotransmitter systems are responsible for mediating the communication between the functionally connected regions. Medications acting on these systems are thus effective in treating GAD. Although benzodiazepines have often been used, selective serotonin reuptake inhibitors (SSRIs) and noradrenergic/serotonergic reuptake inhibitors (NSRIs) are currently viewed as first-line options because of their favorable safety profile. Psychotherapy has also proven effective in the treatment of GAD. Cognitive-behavioral psychotherapy focuses on using behavioral techniques and changing underlying thought patterns.

Panic disorder (PD) is characterized by repeated, sudden, and unexpected panic attacks. Panic attacks are accompanied by a range of physical symptoms, including respiratory (shortness of breath), cardiovascular (fast heart rate), gastrointestinal (nausea), and occulovestibular (dizziness) symptoms. The prevalence of PD is approximately 2% in the general population, is more common in women, and is often complicated by depression. The same brain circuits and neurotransmitters implicated in fear and GAD are also likely to play a role in PD. For treatment the first-line choice of medication should be an SSRI or NSRI. Benzodiazepines are effective alone or in combination with SSRIs, but their use as the only medication is generally avoided due to the potential for dependence and withdrawal. Cognitive-behavioral principles that address avoidance behavior and irrational dysfunctional beliefs are also effective.

Obsessive-compulsive disorder (OCD) is characterized by obsessions (unwanted, persistent, distressing thoughts) and compulsions (repetitive acts to relieve anxiety caused by obsessions). The disorder occurs in 2–3% of the population and often begins in childhood or adolescence. OCD is also seen in the context of certain infections, brain injury, and pregnancy. A range of evidence now implicates a brain circuit between the frontal cortex, basal ganglia, and thalamus in mediating OCD. Key neurotransmitters in this circuit include the dopamine and serotonin neurotransmitter system. SSRIs are current first-line treatments for OCD, with dopamine blockers added in those who do not respond to these agents. Behavioral therapy focuses on exposure and response prevention, while cognitive strategies address the distortions in beliefs that underlie the perpetuation of symptoms.

Social anxiety disorder (SAD) is characterized by persistent fears of embarrassment, scrutiny, or humiliation. People with SAD may avoid social situations and performance situations, resulting in marked disability. For some, symptoms are confined to one or more performance situations, while others may be generalized to include most social and performance situations. Generalized SAD is usually more severe and sufferers are more likely to have a family history of SAD. SAD is particularly common, with prevalence figures in some studies upwards of 10%. SAD is often complicated by depression, and people with SAD may self-medicate their symptoms with alcohol, leading to alcohol dependence. Brain-imaging studies have found that effective treatment with medication and psychotherapy normalizes activity in the amygdala and the closely related hippocampal region in SAD. SSRIs, NSRIs, and cognitive-behavioral therapy are all effective in the treatment of SAD. Monoamine oxidase inhibitors (MAOIs) and benzodiazepines are also known to be effective treatments, but have a number of disadvantages.

Posttraumatic stress disorder (PTSD) is an abnormal response to severe trauma. PTSD is characterized by distinct clusters of symptoms: reexperiencing of the event (for example, in flashbacks or dreams), avoidance (of reminders of the trauma), numbing of responsiveness to the environment, and increased arousal (for example, insomnia, irritability, and being easily startled). Although exposure to severe trauma occurs in more than 70% of the population, PTSD has a lifetime prevalence of 7–9% in the general population. Risk factors for developing PTSD following exposure to severe trauma include female gender, previous psychiatric history, trauma severity, and absence of social support after the trauma. Brain-imaging studies have suggested that in PTSD frontal areas of the brain may fail to effectively dampen the "danger alarm" of the amygdala. Whereas stress responses ordinarily recover after exposure to trauma, in PTSD they persist. There is growing evidence that functioning of the hypothalamic-pituitary-adrenal hormonal axis is disrupted in PTSD. However, other systems, such as serotonin and noradrenaline, may also be involved. Both SSRIs and cognitive-behavioral therapy are effective in decreasing PTSD symptoms. Behavioral techniques (using different forms of exposure in the safety of the consultation room) or cognitive retraining (addressing irrational thoughts on the trauma and its consequences) can both be helpful.   [P.D.C.; D.J.St.]

Aphasia   Impairment in the use of spoken or written language caused by injury to the brain which cannot be accounted for by paralysis or incoordination of the articulatory organs, impairment of hearing or vision, impaired level of consciousness, or impaired motivation to communicate. The language zone in the brain includes the portion of the frontal, temporal, and parietal lobes surrounding the sylvian fissure and structures deep to these areas. In right-handed persons, with few exceptions, only injury in the left cerebral hemisphere produces aphasia. Lateralization of language function is variable in left-handers, and they are at greater risk for becoming aphasic from a lesion in either hemisphere. *See* HEMISPHERIC LATERALITY.

Distinctive recurring patterns of deficit are associated with particular lesion sites within the language zone. These patterns may entail selective impairment of articulation, ability to retrieve concept names, or syntactic organization. Other dissociations affect principally the auditory comprehension of speech, the repetition of speech, or the recognition of written words. The erroneous production of unintended words in speech (paraphasia), oral reading (paralexia), or writing (paragraphia) is a feature of some forms of aphasia.

Mixed forms of aphasia, caused by multiple lesions or lesions spanning anterior and posterior portions of the speech zone, are quite common, and massive destruction of the entire language area results in a global aphasia. Further, individual variations in behavioral manifestations of similar lesions have set limits on the strict assignment of function to structures within the language area.

Preadolescent children suffering aphasia after unilateral injury usually recover rapidly, presumably by virtue of the capacity of the right cerebral hemisphere early in life to acquire the language functions originally mediated by the left hemisphere. Capacity for recovery of function decreases during later adolescence and young adulthood.

Complete recovery in adults after a severe injury is much less common, and severe aphasia may persist unchanged for the duration of the person's life. Many patients are aided by remedial language training, while others continue severely impaired. *See* MEMORY.

[H.G.]

Apical meristem Permanently embryonic tissue involved in cell division at the apices of plant roots and stems, and forming dynamic regions of growth. These apical meristems, usually consisting of small, densely cytoplasmic cells, become established during embryo development. Thereafter they divide, producing the primary plant body of root and shoot. Below the apical meristems, tissue differentiation begins: the protoderm gives rise to the epidermal system, the procambium to the primary vascular system, and the ground meristem to the pith and cortex (see illustration). Plant apical meristems have been the object of experiments on development similar to those carried out on animal embryos.

Root apical meristem is covered by a root cap, a region of parenchymatous, cells which has a protective function and is responsible for perceiving gravitational changes. Root tips have been shown to possess a central region, usually hemispherical, which consists of cells which rarely divide or synthesize deoxyribonucleic acid (DNA), and have less ribonucleic acid (RNA) and protein than adjacent cells; this region is known as the quiescent center. The cells which divide and give rise to root tissues lie around the periphery of this region. Cells in the quiescent center are regarded as cells that are mitotically young and genetically sound; they can renew the initial cells from time to time.

Shoot apices vary greatly in size and shape. The diameter can vary from about 50 micrometers to 0.14 in. (3.5 mm); the shape may be elongated and conical, dome-shaped, flat, or even slightly concave. The distance from the center of the apex to

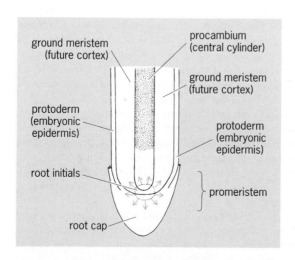

Diagram of a root apical meristem. Cortex and central cylinder have separate initials; epidermis and root cap have a common origin.

the youngest leaf primordium also varies considerably. Apices increase in size during the development of a single plant; for example, the apical meristem of flax *(Linum usitatissimum)* increases in area 20-fold from the seedling up to the time of flowering. Apices may also change in size during the time between the formation of one leaf primordium and the next. A single apical cell is present in shoot apices of bryophytes and vascular cryptogams; however, surrounding cells are also mitotically active, and these plants have multicellular apical meristems. In flowering plants, the outer layer or layers of cells (tunica) may divide predominantly by walls at right angles to the surface; the inner tissue (corpus), in less regular planes. Regions of the apical meristem may react differently to certain stains, reflecting so-called cytohistological zonation.

Cells in the central terminal region of the vegetative shoot apex divide less actively than those on the flanks or at the periphery, where leaf and bud primordia are formed. Various surgical experiments, involving incision of the apical meristem, have shown that new apices can be regenerated from portions of the flank. Excised apical meristems, devoid of leaf primordia, can be successfully grown on agar nutrient medium, in the presence of auxin, and will eventually yield new plants. *See* BUD; LEAF.   [E.G.C.]

Apoda   The smallest order (sometimes called Gymnophiona) of the class Amphibia, known as the caecilians. These are wormlike, legless animals with indistinct or even hidden eyes. A series of annular grooves is usually present along the length of the body, heightening the resemblance to an earthworm. Most caecilians lead a burrowing existence, though members of one genus, *Typhlonectes*, are aquatic. Some species have the eyes hidden beneath the bones of the skull and probably are blind, but others at least are able to distinguish movement. A unique feature of the caecilians among modern Amphibia is the presence of scales buried in the skin of some species. There are more than 160 species of caecilians confined to tropical regions of both Eastern and Western hemispheres. Many species are less than 1 ft (0.3 m) in length, but three species of the genus *Caecilia* grow to over 3 ft (0.9 m). Some species lay eggs, while others bring forth their young alive. The embryos of the species that bear living young are nourished in the later part of their embryonic development by "uterine milk," which is secreted by the mother. In some of the species that lay eggs there is an aquatic larval stage. Caecilians are carnivorous, but little is known of their food habits. Captive specimens have fed on earthworms, and in the natural state caecilians have eaten lizards. *See* AMPHIBIA; ANURA; URODELA.   [R.G.Z.]

Apraxia   An impairment in the performance of voluntary actions despite intact motor power and coordination, sensation and perception, and comprehension. The apraxic person knows the act to be carried out, and has the requisite sensory-motor capacities, yet performance is defective. The abnormality is highlighted when the act must be performed on demand and out of context. Defects in performance vary from total inability to initiate the action, to incorrect serial ordering of elements, to partial approximations. A common apraxic behavior is the use of a body part as an object. Pantomiming the act of brushing the teeth, for example, a person may run the index finger across the teeth as though it were a toothbrush, while in normal performance, the hand assumes the posture of holding and moving the brush.

Apraxia is usually observed in both upper extremities. When it occurs unilaterally, it is usually the left arm and hand that are affected. This has been explained by assuming that the left cerebral hemisphere is specialized in the organization of voluntary movements, just as it is in language. The left hand is under the immediate control of the right hemisphere, but for skilled voluntary actions, the right hemisphere is dependent on information transmitted from the dominant left hemisphere over the corpus callosum. Callosal lesions produce apraxia of the left hand, because the right hemisphere is incapable of organizing the plan of movement independently. With an appropriately placed left-hemisphere lesion, a bilateral apraxia will result. When the left-hemisphere lesion also destroys the primary motor zone, the right arm is paralyzed and the apraxia is masked. The observable apraxia on the left side is referred to as sympathetic apraxia. This is seen in many individuals with right hemiplegia (unilateral paralysis of the body) and Broca's aphasia. Another apraxia often coupled with Broca's aphasia is nonspeech oral apraxia (or buccofacial apraxia). Individuals with this disorder can be observed to struggle to perform such simple acts as protruding the tongue or licking the lips on command or imitation, even though these movements are executed easily as part of the act of eating. *See* APHASIA; HEMISPHERIC LATERALITY.

There are several disorders that are controversial with regard to their interpretation as forms of apraxia. The nonfluent speech pattern of Broca's aphasia, often riddled with speech-sound errors, is considered as apraxia of speech by some authorities, while others view it as an integral part of the linguistic deficit of the aphasia. In dressing apraxia and in some types of constructional apraxia, the defect appears to be perceptually based. Limb-kinetic apraxia is widely interpreted today as a mild spastic paresis, while ideational apraxia, commonly associated with dementia, is likely due to conceptual confusion rather than to a disturbance of motor organization. *See* AGNOSIA.   [G.J.C.]

Arboviral encephalitides   A number of diseases, such as St. Louis, Japanese B, and equine encephalitis, which are caused by arthropod-borne viruses (abbreviated "arboviruses"). In their most severe human forms, the diseases invade the central nervous system and produce brain damage, with mental confusion, convulsions, and coma; death or serious aftereffects are frequent in severe cases. Inapparent infections are common.

The arbovirus "group" comprises more than 250 different viruses, many of them differing fundamentally from each other except in their ecological property of being transmitted through the bite of an arthropod. A large number of arboviruses of antigenic groups A and B are placed in the family Togaviridae, in two genera, alphavirus (serological group A) and flavivirus (serological group B). Still other arboviruses, related structurally and antigenically to one another but unrelated to Togaviridae, are included in the family Bunyaviridae, consisting chiefly of the numerous members of the Bunyamwera supergroup—a large assemblage of arboviruses in several antigenic groups which are cross-linked by subtle interrelationships between individual members. The nucleic acid genomes of all arboviruses studied thus far have been found to be RNA.

Members of serological group A include western equine encephalitis, eastern equine encephalitis, and Venezuelan equine encephalitis viruses; and Mayaro, Semliki Forest, Chikungunya, and Sindbis viruses, which have nonencephalitic syndromes. Group A viruses are chiefly mosquito-borne. Serological group B viruses include Japanese B, St. Louis, and Murray Valley encephalitis viruses (mosquito-borne), and the viruses of the Russian tick-borne complex, some of which produce encephalitis (Russian spring-summer), whereas others cause hemorrhagic fevers (Omsk, Kyasanur Forest) or other syndromes, such as louping ill. Also in group B are the nonneurotropic viruses of West Nile fever, yellow fever, dengue, and other diseases. *See* YELLOW FEVER.

There is no proved specific treatment. In animals, hyperimmune serum given early may prevent death. Killed virus vaccines have been used in animals and in persons occupationally subjected to high risk. A live, attenuated vaccine against Japanese B encephalitis virus, developed in Japan, has been used experimentally with some success, not only in pigs to reduce amplification of the virus in this important vertebrate reservoir but also in limited trials in humans. In general, however, control of these diseases continues to be chiefly dependent upon elimination of the arthropod vector. *See* VIRUS.   [J.L.Me.]

Archaebacteria   A group of prokaryotic organisms that are more closely related to eukaryotes than bacteria. Based on comparative analyses of small subunit ribosomal ribonucleic acid (rRNA) sequences and selected protein sequences, the three primary lines of descent from the common ancestor are the Archaea (archaebacteria), the Bacteria, and the Eucarya (eukaryotes). Although the Archaea look like Bacteria cytologically (they are both prokaryotes), they are not closely related to them.

The Archaea can be divided into two evolutionary lineages on the basis of rRNA sequence comparisons, the Crenarchaeotae and the Euryarchaeotae. The crenarchaeotes are organisms that grow at high temperatures (thermophiles) and metabolize elemental sulfur. Most are strict anaerobes that reduce sulfur to hydrogen sulfide (sulfidogens), but a few can grow aerobically and oxidize sulfur to sulfuric acid. The euryarchaeotes have a number of different phenotypes. *Thermococcus* and *Pyrococcus* are sulfidogens like many crenarchaeotes. *Archaeoglobus* reduces sulfate to sulfide. *Thermoplasma* grows under acidic conditions aerobically or anaerobically (as a sulfidogen). Many euryarchaeotes are methane-producing anaerobes (methanogens) and some grow aerobically in the presence of very high concentrations of salt (halophiles). *See* METHANOGENESIS (BACTERIA).

The thermophilic archaea are found in high-temperature environments around the world. They have been isolated from soils and shallow marine sediments heated by nearby volcanoes and from deep-sea hydrothermal vents. Some are used as a source for heat-stable enzymes useful for industrial applications. The methanogenic archaea inhabit the digestive tracts of animals (especially ruminants like cows), sewage sludge digesters, swamps (where they produce marsh gas), and sediments of marine and fresh-water environments. They are of interest commercially because of their ability to produce methane from municipal garbage and some industrial wastes. Halophilic archaea live in the Great Salt Lake, the Dead Sea, alkaline salt lakes of Africa, and salt-preserved fish and animal hides. They are also commonly found in pools used to evaporate seawater to obtain salt.

The discovery of the Archaea caused a major revision in the understanding of evolutionary history. It had previously been thought that all prokaryotes belonged to one evolutionary lineage. Since their cellular organization is simpler, prokaryotes were assumed to be ancestors of eukaryotes. The discovery of the relationship of the Archaea to the Eucarya revealed that prokaryotes do not comprise a monophyletic group since they can be divided into two distinct lineages. Although the three descended from a common ancestor, modern eukaryotes may have arisen from fusions of bacterial and archaeal endosymbionts with ancestral eukaryotes. Chloroplasts and mitochondria arose from free-living bacteria which became endosymbionts. The discovery of the Archaea has also given microbiologists a better picture of the common ancestor. The deepest-branching eukaryotes (like *Giardia*) are strict anaerobes that lack mitochondria, and they diverged much later than the deepest-branching bacteria and archaea. The earliest archaea and bacteria (*Thermotoga* and *Aquifex*) are also anaerobes and are also extreme thermophiles. Therefore the common ancestor of these groups was probably also an extremely thermophilic anaerobe. Therefore, it is possible that life may have arisen in a relatively hot environment, perhaps like that found in deep-sea hydrothermal vents. *See* BACTERIA; EUKARYOTAE; PROKARYOTAE.

                                                                                              [K.M.N.]

Arthropoda A phylum that includes the well-known insects, spiders, ticks, and crustaceans, as well as many smaller groups, some of which are known only as fossils. Arthropodous animals make up about 75% of all animals that have been described. The estimated number of known species exceeds 780,000. Of this number the class Insecta alone contains about 700,000 described species. Arthropods vary in size from the microscopic mites to the giant decapod crustaceans, such as the Japanese crab with an appendage span of 5 ft (1.5 m) or more.

The adult arthropod typically has a body composed of a series of ringlike segments, muscularly movable on each other. The integument is sclerotized by the formation of hardening substances in the cuticle, and the segmental limbs are many-jointed. These characteristics, taken together, distinguish the arthropods from all other animals. Young stages may be quite different from the adults, and some parasitic species differ very radically from their relatives.

Arthropod evolution is no longer the clear-cut subdivision of a single phylum, Arthropoda, into three structurally divergent subphyla. Advances in functional morphology, comparative embryology, spermatology, serology, and paleontology have brought an array of new hypotheses about relationships of arthropodous animals. At the center of debate is the question of monophyly versus polyphyly: Did all arthropodous animals evolve from a common ancestor or did several distinct lineages evolve along similar pathways? Two opposing classification schemes are presented; numerous variations on these schemes can be found in the literature. The first pair of classifications is as follows:

> Phylum Uniramia
>   Subphylum: Onychophora
>   Myriapoda
>   Hexapoda (Insecta)
> Phylum Trilobita (Trilobitomorpha)
> Phylum Crustacea
> Phylum Chelicerata

Versus

> Phylum Arthropoda
>   Subphylum Arachnata
>   Superclass: Trilobita
>   Chelicerata
>   Subphylum Mandibulata
>   Superclass: Crustacea
>   Myriapoda
>   Insecta
> Phylum Onychophora

Alternatively, a slightly different and expanded pair of classifications is as follows:

> Phylum Uniramia
>   Subphylum Onychophora
>   Subphylum Myriapoda
>   Class: Chilopoda
>   Diplopoda
>   Symphyla
>   Pauropoda

Superclass: Arthropleurida
Subphylum Hexapoda
Class: Protura
Collembola
Diplura
Thysanura
Pterygota (Insecta)
Phylum Crustacea
Class: Cephalocarida
Remipedia
Branchiopoda
Ostracoda
Tantulocarida
Maxillopoda
Malacostraca
Phylum Cheliceriformes
Subphylum Pycnogonida
Subphylum Chelicerata
Class: Merostomata
Arachnida
Phylum Trilobitomorpha
Class: Trilobitoidea
Trilobita

Versus

Phylum Onychophora
Phylum Arthropoda
Subphylum Cheliceromorpha
Infraphylum: Pycnogonida
Chelicerata
Superclass: Xiphosurida
Cryptopneustida
Class: Eurypterida
Archnida
Subphylum Ganthomorpha
Infraphylym: Trilobitomorpha
Class: Trilobita
Trilobitodea
Infraphylum: Mandibulata
Class: Cheloniellida
Crustacea
Myriapoda
Insecta

Body segmentation, or metamerism, is the most fundamental character of the arthropods, but it is shared by the annelid worms, so there can be little doubt that these two groups of animals are related. The limbs of all modern arthropods develop in the embryo from small lateroventral outgrowths of the body segments that lengthen and become jointed. Hence it may be inferred that the arthropods originated from some segmented worm that acquired similar lobelike limb rudiments and thus, as a crawling or walking animal, became distinguished from its swimming relatives. Then, with sclerotization of the integument, the limbs could lengthen and finally become jointed, providing greater locomotor efficiency. In their later evolution, some of these limbs became modified for many other purposes, such as feeding, grasping, swimming, respiration, silk spinning, egg laying, and sperm transfer. The body segments, corresponding to specialized sets of appendages, tend to become consolidated or united in groups, or tagmata, forming differentiated body regions, such as head, thorax, and abdomen. Annelida; Metameres.

Sclerotization of the cuticle may be continuous around the segments. More usually, it forms discrete segmental plates, or sclerites. A back plate of a segment is a tergum, or notum; a ventral plate is a sternum; and lateral plates are pleura. The consecutive tergal and sternal plates, unless secondarily united, are connected by infolded membranes, and are thus movable on each other by longitudinal muscles attached on anterior marginal ridges of the plates. Since nearly all the body and limb muscles are attached on integumental sclerites, there is little limit to the development of skeletomuscular mechanisms.

All arthropods have all the internal organs essential to any complex animal. An alimentary canal extends either straight or coiled from the subapical ventral mouth to the terminal anus. Its primary part is the endodermal stomach, or mesenteron, but there are added ectodermal ingrowths that form a stomodeum anteriorly and a proctodeum posteriorly. The nervous system includes a brain and a subesophageal ganglion in the head, united by connectives around the stomodeum, and a ventral nerve cord of interconnected ganglia. Some of the successive ganglia, however, may be condensed into composite ganglionic masses. Nerves proceed from the ganglia. Internal proprioceptors and surface sense organs of numerous kinds are present, chiefly tactile, olfactory, and optic. A usually tubular pulsatory heart lies along the dorsal side of the body and keeps the blood in circulation. In some arthropods arteries distribute the blood from the heart; in others it is discharged from the anterior end of the tube directly into the body cavity. The blood reenters the heart through openings along its sides.

Aquatic arthropods breathe by means of gills. Most terrestrial species have either flat air pouches or tubular tracheae opening from the outside surface; some have both. A few small, soft-bodied forms respire through the skin. Excretory organs open either at the bases of some of the appendages or into the alimentary canal. Most arthropods have separate sexes, but some are hermaphroditic, and parthenogenesis is of common occurrence. The genital openings differ in position in different groups and are not always on the same body segment in the two sexes. See CHELICERATA; CRUSTACEA; INSECTA; ONYCHOPHORA. [J.C.Ro.]

Ascomycota   A phylum in the kingdom Fungi, representing the largest of the major groups of fungi, and distinguished by the presence of the ascus, a specialized saclike cell in which fusion of nuclei and reduction division occur and the resulting nuclei form ascospores. In most ascomycetes, each ascus contains eight ascospores, but the number may vary from one to several hundred. In the simplest ascomycetes (yeasts), the vegetative body (thallus) is unicellular; however, in the majority of ascomycetes, the thallus is more complex and consists of a tubular, threadlike hypha with cross walls which grows in or on the substrate. These hyphae eventually form structures called ascomata (ascocarps), on or in which the asci are formed. In addition to their sexual reproduction, most ascomycetes reproduce asexually by means of conidia.

Traditionally, the structure of the ascoma and ascus has served as the basis for subdividing the Ascomycota into five classes: Hemiascomycetes, Plectomycetes, Pyrenomycetes, Discomycetes, Loculoascomycetes. The introduction of molecular data, however, is changing concepts of the relationships of different groups of ascomycetes and will eventually lead to a much-revised classification scheme.

The ascomycetes occur throughout the world in all types of habitats and on both living and dead substrates. An estimated 33,000 species are arranged in about 3300 genera, with new species being described regularly. Ecologically ascomycetes function as primary decomposers of plant materials, but they also are important as plant and human pathogens; in baking, brewing, and winemaking; in enzyme and acid production; and as sources of antibiotics and other drugs. *See* EUMYCOTA; FUNGI; PLANT PATHOLOGY; YEAST.   [R.T.Ha.]

Ascorbic acid   A white, crystalline compound, also known as vitamin C. It is highly soluble in water, which is a stronger reducing agent than the hexose sugars, which it resembles chemically. Vitamin C deficiency in humans has been known for centuries as scurvy. The compound has the structural formula shown below.

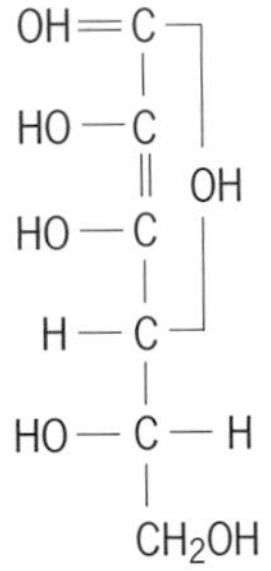

$$
\begin{array}{l}
OH = C \\
\ \ \ \ \ \ \ | \\
HO - C \\
\ \ \ \ \ \ \ \| \ \ OH \\
HO - C \\
\ \ \ \ \ \ \ | \\
H - C \\
\ \ \ \ \ \ \ | \\
HO - C - H \\
\ \ \ \ \ \ \ | \\
\ \ \ \ \ CH_2OH
\end{array}
$$

The stability of ascorbic acid decreases with increases in temperature and pH. This destruction by oxidation is a serious problem in that a considerable quantity of the vitamin C content of foods is lost during processing, storage, and preparation.

While vitamin C is widespread in plant materials, it is found sparingly in animal tissues. Of all the animals studied, only a few, including humans, require a dietary source of vitamin C. The other species are capable of synthesizing the vitamin in such tissues as liver and kidneys. Some drugs, particularly the terpene-like cyclic ketones, stimulate the production of ascorbic acid by rat tissues.

Vitamin C–deficient animals suffer from defects in their mesenchymal tissues. Their ability to manufacture collagen, dentine, and osteoid, the intercellular cement substances, is impaired. This may be related to a role of ascorbic acid in the forma- tion of hydroxy-proline, an amino acid found in structural proteins, particularly collagen. People with scurvy lose weight and are easily fatigued. Their bones are fragile, and their joints sore and swollen. Their gums are swollen and bloody, and in advanced stages their teeth fall out. They also develop internal and subcutaneous hemorrhages.

There is evidence that vitamin C may play roles in stress reactions, in infectious disease, or in wound healing. Therefore, many nutritionists believe that the human intake of ascorbic acid should be many times more than that intake level which produces deficiency symptoms. The recommended dietary allowances of the Food and Nutrition Board of the National Research Council are 30 mg per day for 1- to 3-month infants, 80 mg per day for growing boys and girls, and 100 mg per day for pregnant and lactating women. These values represent an intake which tends to maintain tissue and plasma concentrations in a range similar to that of other well-nourished species of animals. *See* VITAMIN.   [S.N.G.; W.A.Li.]

Attention deficit hyperactivity disorder A common psychiatric disorder of childhood characterized by attentional difficulties, impulsivity, and hyperactivity; known earlier as attention deficit disorder. Other older names for this disorder include minimal brain dysfunction, minimal brain damage, hyperactivity, hyperkinesis, and hyperactive child syndrome. Over time, these names were modified due to their implications about etiology and core symptoms: minimal brain dysfunction seemed to imply that children with this disorder were brain-damaged, while hyperactivity and its synonyms named a feature seen in many but not all of these children.

The three defining symptoms of attention deficit disorder are as follows:

(1) *Attentional deficits.* The child is described as having a short attention span. The child often fails to finish things he or she starts, does not seem to listen, and is easily distracted or disorganized. In more severe instances the child is unable to focus attention on anything, while in less severe cases attention can be focused on things of interest to the child.

(2) *Impulsivity.* The child is often described as acting before thinking, shifting excessively and rapidly from one activity to another, or having difficulty waiting for a turn in games or group activities.

(3) *Hyperactivity.* Many children with this disorder are hyperactive—and indeed, may have been noted to be so prior to birth. They may fidget, wiggle, move excessively, and have difficulty keeping still. This excessive activity is not noticeable when the children are playing; however, in the classroom or other quiet settings, the child cannot decrease his or her activity appropriately. Some affected children are active at a normal level or even sluggish. On the basis of the predominating symptoms, children with attention deficit hyperactivity disorder are subcategorized as having hyperactive symptoms (hyperactive type), lacking hyperactivity (inattentive type), and having both inattention and hyperactivity or impulsivity (combined type).

Many children with attention deficit hyperactivity disorder frequently show an altered response to socialization. They are often described by their parents as obstinate, impervious, stubborn, or negativistic. With peers, many affected children are domineering or bullying, and thus may prefer to play with younger children. Another characteristic often seen in children with the disorder is emotional lability. Their moods change frequently and easily, sometimes spontaneously, and sometimes reactively. Because of their behavioral difficulties, children with the disorder often have conflicts with parents, teachers, and peers. Commonly, difficulties in discipline and inadequacies in school-work lead to reproof and criticism. As a consequence, children with the disorder usually also have low self-esteem. Attention deficit hyperactivity disorder is frequently associated with other disorders, including disruptive behavior disorders, internalizing (mood and anxiety) disorders, and developmental disorders. *See* Affective disorders.

Formerly believed to be largely caused by brain damage, and more recently believed by some to be caused by food allergy, attention deficit hyperactivity disorder is now considered to be mainly hereditary. It is estimated that 3–10% of children of elementary school age (roughly 6–19 years) manifest significant symptoms of attention deficit hyperactivity disorder. About twice as many boys as girls are affected with the disorder. The girls are much less likely than the boys to be aggressive and have serious behavioral difficulties, making the girls vulnerable to underidentification and undertreatment. It was formerly believed that attention deficit hyperactivity disorder was out-grown during adolescence. Although some signs of the disorder such as excessive activity may diminish or disappear in some affected children, other signs such as attentional difficulties, impulsivity, and interpersonal problems may persist. Despite the fact that this disorder is not uncommon in adults, the lower rates of hyperactivity in adults may result in the condition being frequently overlooked.

The treatment of the child or adult with this disorder involves three steps: evaluation, explanation of the problem to parents and child, and therapeutic intervention. Evaluation requires a detailed history of the child's psychological development and current functioning. Next, because the disorder is frequently associated with learning problems in school, it is desirable to obtain an individual intelligence test as well as a test of academic achievement. Since attention deficit hyperactivity disorder is often associated with other psychiatric disorders, it is important to carefully evaluate the presence of these other conditions. If a diagnosis of attention deficit hyperactivity disorder is confirmed, the parents or family should be educated regarding the nature of the condition and other associated conditions. Medication and guidance are the mainstays of the treatment. Approximately 70–80% of the children manifest a therapeutic response to one of the major stimulant drugs, such as amphetamines and methylphenidate. When effective, these medications increase attention, decrease impulsivity, and usually make the child more receptive to parental and educational requests and demands. Hyperactivity, when present, is usually diminished as well. Although usually less effective, other medications can be helpful to individuals who cannot tolerate or do not respond to stimulants. The common mechanism of action for such medications is their impact upon the neurotransmitters dopamine and norepinephrine.   [J.Bi.]

Audiometry   The quantitative assessment of individual hearing, either normal or defective. Three types of audiometric tests are used: pure tone, speech, and bone conduction tests. Such tests may serve various purposes, such as investigation of auditory fatigue under noise conditions, human engineering study of hearing aids and communication devices, screening of individuals with defective hearing, and diagnosis and treatment of defective hearing. In all of these situations, individual hearing is measured relative to defined standards of normal hearing.

The pure-tone audiometer is the instrument used most widely in individual hearing measurement. It is composed of an oscillator, an amplifier, and an attenuator to control sound intensity. For speech tests of hearing, word lists called articulation tests are reproduced on records or tape recorders. Measurements of detectability or intelligibility can be made by adjusting the intensity of the test words. To make bone conduction tests, sound vibrations from the audiometer activate a vibrator located on the forehead or mastoid bone.

Scientific advance in audiometry demands careful control of all environmental sound. Two types of rooms especially constructed for research and measurement of hearing are the random diffusion, or reverberation, chamber and the anechoic room. In the reverberation chamber, sounds are randomly reflected from heavy nonparallel walls, floor, and ceiling surfaces. In the anechoic room, the fiber glass wedges absorb all but a small percent of the sound.

The measurement of hearing loss for pure tones in defective hearing is represented by the audiogram (see illustration). Sounds of different frequencies are presented separately to each ear of the individual, and the intensity levels of the absolute thresholds for each frequency are determined. The absolute threshold is the lowest intensity which can be detected by the individual who is being tested.

In clinical audiometry the status of hearing is expressed in terms of hearing loss at each of the different frequency levels. In the audiogram the normal audibility curve, representing absolute thresholds at all frequencies for the normal ear, is represented as a straight line of zero decibels. Amount of hearing loss is then designated as a decibel value below normal audibility. The audiogram in the illustration reveals a hearing loss for tones above 500 Hz. Automatic audiometers are now in use which enable individuals to plot an audiogram for themselves.

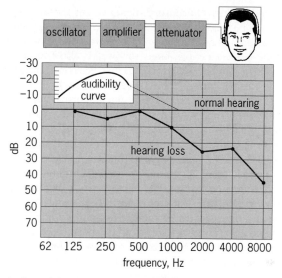

Audiogram for determining the audibility curve for pure-tone hearing loss at various frequency levels.

Articulation tests are speech perception or speech hearing tests used to assess hearing and loss of hearing for speech. The threshold of intelligibility for speech is defined as the intensity level at which 50% of the words, nonsense syllables, or sentences used in the articulation test are correctly identified. The hearing loss for speech is determined by computing the difference in decibels between the individual intelligibility threshold and the normal threshold for that particular speech test. Discrimination loss for speech represents the difference between the maximum articulation score at a high intensity level (100 dB), expressed in percent of units identified, and a score of 100%. The measure of discrimination loss is important in distinguishing between conduction loss and nerve deafness.

Bone conduction audiograms are compared with air conduction audiograms in order to analyze the nature of deafness. Losses in bone conduction hearing generally give evidence of nerve deafness, as contrasted to middle-ear or conduction deafness. *See* EAR (VERTEBRATE); HEARING IMPAIRMENT.   [K.U.S.]

Autistic disorder   A severe neuropsychiatric disorder of early childhood onset, historically regarded as a psychosis of childhood but now classified as a pervasive developmental disorder. While autism has been the most intensively studied pervasive developmental disorder, other conditions are now included in this class of conditions: Asperger's syndrome (sometimes referred to as autistic psychopathy), Rett's syndrome, and childhood disintegrative disorder (Heller's syndrome).

Symptoms of autism generally are apparent within the first 2 years of life and may occasionally be noted from the time of birth. Characteristic disturbances include disruption of social, cognitive, linguistic, motor, and perceptual development. Affected individuals fail to develop appropriate interpersonal relationships. In about half of the cases, language fails to develop; when it does develop, it is characterized by pronoun confusion (for example, the use of "you" for "I"), abnormal speech tone or rhythm, and an impaired ability to use abstract terms or communicate symbolic information. Unusual responses to the environment are common and may include resistance to change, exaggerated reactions to sensory stimuli or changes in the environment, ritualistic behavior, and peculiar attachments to inanimate objects. Motor abnormalities include unusual posturing and stereotyped (purposeless and repetitive) movements; self-injurious behavior (for example, head banging) is also common. Although some islets of unusual ability (in memory, drawing, or calculation) may be present, about 80% of individuals score in the mentally retarded range on tests of intelligence. Autistic individuals do not experience delusions and hallucinations; however, the metaphorical and bizarre language of verbal individuals may mistakenly suggest the kind of thought disturbance that is found in schizophrenia. See SCHIZOPHRENIA.

In Rett's syndrome, a short period of normal development is followed by loss of developmental skills and marked psychomotor retardation. A brief autisticlike phase may be observed during the preschool period, but the subsequent course and clinical features are markedly different from those of autism. Rett's syndrome has been observed only in females. The validity of Asperger's syndrome apart from autism has been more controversial. Individuals with Asperger's syndrome appear to have relatively much more preserved verbal and cognitive skills. Unusual circumscribed interests are common (for example, in maps, the weather, or train or bus schedules). In childhood disintegrative disorder, development in the first several years of life is unequivocally normal and is followed by a marked developmental regression (a child who previously had been speaking in sentences becomes totally mute), and various autistic features develop.

Autism is chronic and incapacitating. Only one autistic individual in six is able to make a good adjustment in adulthood and engage in regular, gainful employment. Approximately two-thirds of children remain severely handicapped as adults and need constant supervision and support. Even for those autistic individuals who make the best adjustment as adults, residual deficits in social, affective, and cognitive development remain. Factors related to better prognosis include the development of communication skills by age 5 and intellectual achievement. In Asperger's syndrome, the prognosis is apparently better than in autism, probably reflecting, in some part, the preservation of cognitive abilities in this condition. In Rett's syndrome and childhood disintegrative disorder, the prognosis is worse than in autism.

The "purest" form of autism, where the child has higher IQ, some islets of normal or near-normal behavior, and profound social detachment, affects only 1 child in 2000; however, the broader spectrum of communication and developmental disorders associated with autism and requiring similar care may affect 1 in every 750 children. Although males outnumber females (by four or five times), females with autism tend to be more severely affected. Predisposing factors include congenital infections (for example, maternal rubella) and metabolic and genetic illnesses (for example, phenylketonuria). A history of prenatal or perinatal complication is not uncommon, but in many cases no specific predisposing factor or associated mental condition is found. See RUBELLA.

For the majority of cases of autism, the cause remains unknown. Theoretical explanations have emphasized either a primary psychological or biological vulnerability in the child, the role of environmental factors, and an interaction between an inborn vulnerability and the child's environment. The high incidence of neurological signs, electroencephalographic abnormalities, and the fact that seizures develop in 25% of children during adolescence (especially in lower-IQ children) tend to support the role of a biological vulnerability. The final behavioral expression of the syndrome may be a function of multiple factors. Individuals with Rett's syndrome and childhood disintegrative disorder also are at increased risk for developing seizures, and exhibit other signs of central nervous system dysfunction. The history of a prolonged period of normal development in childhood disintegrative disorder often prompts extensive medical investigation, which usually does not reveal a specific medical condition that might account for the deterioration.

Treatment modalities that have been used in the management of individuals with autism and related conditions include psychotherapy, pharmacotherapy, behavior therapy, various somatic treatments, and educational interventions. Certain drugs may be effective in controlling certain maladaptive behavioral features, such as hyperactivity, aggression, and stereotyped behaviors. Behavior modification procedures may be quite useful. Educational interventions with highly structured, intensive remediation are of greatest overall benefit. However, even with the best of interventions there are no cures and most autistic individuals remain severely impaired. *See* PSYCHOTHERAPY.   [D.J.C.; F.R.Vo.]

Autoimmunity   The occurrence in an organism of an immune response to one of its own tissues, that is, a response to a self constituent. Efficient discrimination between self and nonself, the basis of normal immune function, depends upon a function known as immune tolerance (inertness to substances that could be capable of provoking an immune response). Failure of immune tolerance to self constituents results in an autoimmune response which is often, although not invariably, associated with autoimmune disease. Autoimmune disease occurs when the autoimmune response to self constituents has damaging effects of a structural or functional character.

Lymphocytes that participate in immune responses belong to two major groups. One group, which matures in the thymus gland, comprises thymic or T lymphocytes, of which there are several subsets. These subsets have different functions and carry unique surface molecules: (1) helper T lymphocytes, marked by the CD4 molecule, respond to antigens by releasing stimulatory cytokines (intercellular hormones) that can amplify the number and activity of lymphocytes participating in the immune response; (2) cytolytic T lymphocytes, marked by the CD8 molecule, can directly recognize and kill cellular targets, usually virus-infected cells; and (3) suppressor T lymphocytes, which also carry the CD8 molecule, release molecules that reduce the intensity of immune responses, or switch these off altogether. The other major group of lymphocytes, which mature in the bone marrow, are B lymphocytes. After stimulation with antigen molecules, and under the influence of factors released by helper T cells, B lymphocytes proliferate and later secrete the antibody molecules which, when circulating in the blood, provide for humoral immune responses. The normal immune system remains in a state of balance conditioned by positive signals and negative signals. Positive signals are provided by antigen in low dose and the amplifying factors released by activated helper T lymphocytes, while negative signals are provided by antigen present in excess, which causes an overload paralysis, and by suppressor T lymphocytes which are generated preferentially when self antigens are presented. There is still a lack of full understanding of the mechanism by which immune responses to self antigens are suppressed so as to provide for natural tolerance to self. The major processes are (1) permanent deletion, or functional inactivation in early life, of cells capable of responding to self antigens; and (2) regulatory controls, which inhibit the activity of self-reactive lymphocytes that escape the deletion process. The relative contribution of these two mechanisms for specific self antigens appears to differ, and both probably operate to control autoimmunity. There are low background levels of immunologic reactivity to many self antigens in healthy subjects, indicating that suppressor activity over immune responses to autoantigens must be continuously operative. *See* IMMUNITY.

Failure of immune regulation is responsible for autoimmune disease. Inheritance may account for 25–50% of the risk for autoimmune diseases. It is known that autoimmune disease, or at least the tendency to produce autoantibodies, runs in families. There are many genetic determinants, and they are poorly understood. One set is in some way associated with major histocompatibility complex (MHC; called HLA in humans), a gene complex that codes for cell-surface molecules which confer biological uniqueness on cells of an individual. Since products of HLA genes normally function to direct T lymphocytes to cells with which they should interact, it is not surprising that autoimmune diseases are associated with the presence of particular HLA types; examples include B8 (thyrotoxicosis), DR4 (rheumatoid arthritis, type 1 diabetes mellitus), and DR2 (multiple sclerosis). The reason may be that the autoantigen readily associates with the MHC (HLA) molecule on cells which present antigen to helper T lymphocytes. The MHC influences the occurrence of autoimmunity in other ways. Release of cytokines by T lymphocytes may induce aberrant expression of molecules on tissue cells which then can present their own antigens, and these become inducers of an autoimmune response. In addition to the MHC, there are other inherited determinants of autoimmunity, including genes specifying immunoglobulin structure and genes specifying weakness in the down-regulation of immune reactions. There may also be somatic genetic causes of autoimmunity (random mutations in later life) among genes that code for immunoglobulins that function as recognition structures on the surface of B lymphocytes; such a mutation may generate a cell with a receptor structure with exquisite specificity for a self antigen which is resistant to regulation. Environmental causes could include infection with microorganisms that carry antigenic structures closely resembling those of self; these could provoke an uncontrolled response to the related self structures of the body. See IMMUNOGENETICS.

Any autoimmune response must become self-sustaining, which implies coexisting failure of normal regulatory processes, either by reason of genetic predisposition or by an acquired disruption of immune function. Once self-sustaining, the autoimmune reaction can cause damage or dysfunction in one of several ways. First, autoantibody molecules circulate in the blood and, by attaching to self antigens on cell surfaces, either damage cells or interfere with important cell-surface receptor molecules. Second, antibodies can unite with their autoantigen, which results in the binding of a serum factor, complement, to form immune complexes that are capable of provoking inflammatory responses. Third, there may be generated T lymphocytes with the capacity for cellular destruction, and these may cause the progressive inflammatory damage that characterizes autoimmune reactions in solid organs. Many human diseases can be attributed to autoimmune reactions. Circulating autoantibodies are responsible for diseases in which there is intravascular destruction of elements of the blood, for example, the red blood cells in hemolytic anemia. T lymphocytes may be responsible for some types of thyroid goiter, such as Hashimoto's disease; a stomach mucosal degeneration that results in nonabsorption of vitamin B_{12} and thus the blood disease pernicious anemia; the insulin-dependent or juvenile type of diabetes mellitus; and one type of chronic hepatitis. Immune complexes cause glomerulonephritis and most of the features of systemic lupus erythematosus, in which autoantibodies are formed to various constituents of cell nuclei. In Sjogren's disease, in which salivary and lacrimal glands are destroyed, damage by T lymphocytes within the glands may be accompanied by damage by immune complexes throughout the body. Some autoimmune diseases are caused by antibodies to cell receptors, which either block neuromuscular transmission, as in myasthenia gravis, or stimulate thyroid cells to overactivity, as in Graves' disease. Some important human diseases may be autoimmune disorders, although demonstration of an autoimmune basis is not yet adequate: these include rheumatoid arthritis, multiple sclerosis, and ulcerative colitis. See HEPATITIS.

Autoimmune diseases are alleviated by treatment, though these diseases are seldom curable. At the simplest level, replacement of the specific secretions of tissues or organs damaged by autoimmune reactions may help. For multisystem autoimmune disease, such as lupus, there are drugs, particularly cortisone derivatives, that modify the harmful effects of humoral or cellular autoimmune attack on tissues and so allow the body to reestablish immunologic homeostasis. Also used are cytotoxic immunosuppressive drugs, which are given specifically to inhibit the activity of immunologically active cells responsible for autoantibody formation or for cytolytic damage to tissues. *See* IMMUNOLOGY.

[I.R.M.]

Autonomic nervous system   The part of the nervous system that innervates smooth and cardiac muscle and the glands, and regulates visceral processes including those associated with cardiovascular activity, digestion, metabolism, and thermoregulation. The autonomic nervous system functions primarily at a subconscious level. It is traditionally partitioned into the sympathetic system and the parasympathetic system, based on the region of the brain or spinal cord in which the autonomic nerves have their origin. The sympathetic system is defined by the autonomic fibers that exit thoracic and lumbar segments of the spinal cord. The parasympathetic system is defined by the autonomic fibers that either exit the brainstem via the cranial nerves or exit the sacral segments of the spinal cord. *See* PARASYMPATHETIC NERVOUS SYSTEM; SYMPATHETIC NERVOUS SYSTEM.

The defining features of the autonomic nervous system were initially limited to motor fibers innervating glands and smooth and cardiac muscle. This definition limited the autonomic nervous system to visceral efferent fibers and excluded the sensory fibers that accompany most visceral motor fibers. Although the definition is often expanded to include both peripheral and central structures (such as the hypothalamus), contemporary literature continues to define the autonomic nervous system solely as a motor system. However, from a functional perspective, the autonomic nervous system includes afferent pathways conveying information regarding the visceral organs and the brain areas (such as the medulla and the hypothalamus) that interpret the afferent feedback and exert control over the motor output back to the visceral organs. *See* HOMEOSTASIS.

[S.W.P.]

Autoradiography   A photographic technique used to localize a radioactive substance within a solid specimen; also known as radioautography.

A photographic emulsion is placed in contact with the object to be tested and is left for several hours, days, or weeks, depending on the suspected concentration of the radioactive material to be measured. The emulsion, which is a gel containing silver halide, is then developed, fixed, and washed as in the usual photographic process. At sites where the emulsion was close enough to the radioactive substance, it appears dark because of the presence of silver grains. When the number of grains is insufficient to darken the film to the unaided eye, the film may be examined with the aid of a microscope. The individual silver grains may then be seen. The pattern formed by the grains depends on the type of radiation and the nature of the photographic emulsion. Alpha particles produce short, straight rows or tracks of grains. Beta particles as well as x-rays and gamma rays, which affect film by producing beta particles, produce tortuous tracks whose lengths and grain densities depend on the energy of the beta particles. Low-energy particles produce shorter tracks with higher grain densities. Very low energy particles like those from tritium (3-hydrogen) may produce only a single grain very close to the site of decay.

Autoradiography can be used to detect, and measure semiquantitatively, the radioactive materials in almost any object that can be placed in contact with film or photographic emulsion in some form. However, in biological research the object may be (1) a whole plant or animal that can be flattened against a film; (2) the cut surface of a plant or animal, or one of its organs; (3) thin sections of tissues or cells; (4) squashed or otherwise flattened cells; (5) surface films produced by spreading on water the protein monolayers containing DNA or ribonucleic acid (RNA) that are picked up on grids for electron microscopy; (6) sheets of paper or other materials on which radioactive substances have been separated by chromatography or electrophoresis; or (7) acrylamide gels in which DNA, RNA, or proteins have been separated by electrophoresis.

[J.H.T.]

Aves Modern birds are a class of vertebrates characterized by being feathered, warm-blooded (endothermic), and bipedal (two-legged); and by having very high metabolic rates and a forelimb modified into a wing which, together with a long tail, forms part of a flight mechanism. Such a definition, however, as with any group of vertebrates, characterizes the living forms and is blurred by the fossil record, which contains species with characteristics close to those of the reptilian ancestors of birds. The feathers of birds are filamentous, lightweight modifications of the outer skin that have remarkable aerodynamic qualities. They serve not only as flight structures by generating lift and thrust but also as insulation to maintain high body temperatures. In addition, birds have lightweight hollow bones, a well-developed air-sac system and flow-through lungs, a wishbone or furcula (fused clavicles), and a hand reduced to three digits (comparable to digits 2, 3, and 4 of the human hand). Birds are known to have evolved from some group of reptiles within the larger group of ancient diapsid reptiles known as archosaurs. However, debate still centers on whether they are derived from a common ancestor with the theropod (meat-eating) dinosaurs (a group known as basal archosaurs), or later in time directly from theropod dinosaurs.

Feathers are unique to birds. These lightweight structures made of keratin are the most complex appendages produced by the skin of any vertebrate. The bird wing comprises two sets of flight feathers, the outer primary feathers which are attached to the hand, and the inner secondary feathers which are attached to the ulna. The vanes of the wing feathers are asymmetric with a smaller outer vane and larger inner vane, producing lift in flight. The body feathers provide small aerodynamic contours which result in laminar airflow in flight. Most of the vane is stiff and tightly bound, like flight feathers. However, the basal portion can by fluffed up to trap body heat next to the skin. In warm conditions the body feathers can be flattened to allow heat to escape. Thus, feathers form an insulatory pelt to cover the surface of the avian body. The tail feathers resemble the flight feathers of the wing and provide lift in flight. The tail feathers of modern birds are attached to a specialized bone known as the pygostyle, which is formed by a number of fused tail vertebrae. The pygostyle (sometimes called the plowshare bone) also accommodates the uropygial gland, or oil gland, an essential part of the anatomy of birds that provides a rich waterproofing oil for preening the feathers. In addition to their primary functions of flight and insulation, feathers can serve other functions, ranging from the production of color patterns and structural forms that allow for species recognition and courtship displays, to color patterns that serve a cryptic purpose for protection. *See* FEATHER.

The once-toothed jaws of birds have evolved into the lighter beak in which the upper and lower jaws are covered by a horny rhamphotheca, which may vary in texture from the rock-solid beaks of predatory raptors to relatively soft beaks of shorebirds and ducks. Beaks have a great variety of adaptive forms, including the flesh-tearing hooked beaks of hawks and eagles, the filter-feeding straining beaks of flamingos and ducks, the fish-trapping beaks of pelicans, the climbing and nut-cracking beaks of parrots, the hammering beaks of woodpeckers, and the seed-eating beaks of finches. Birds have developed a muscular gizzard (also found in their relatives, crocodiles and dinosaurs) for grinding and processing food into small pieces. The grinding is often assisted by the addition of gizzard stones, which are ingested.

Birds have varied feet. The most primitive avian foot, found in the earliest known bird, *Archaeopteryx*, is the perching foot also found in most modern tree-dwelling birds. Three toes point forward, and a reversed first toe, or hallux, opposes them in perching on a branch. This type of foot is called anisodactyl. Other modifications include the zygodactyl feet of woodpeckers with two forward and two rearward pointing toes, and the webbed feet of ducks with the three forward pointing toes united by a web that serves as a paddle. The varied birds in the order Pelecaniformes have a foot in which all four toes are united by webbing, a totipalmate foot. Ostriches are unique in the bird world in having a foot with only two toes. The ankle and foot bones are fused and elongated in birds, so that the avian leg consists of a femur, tibiotarsus, and fibula, then a fusion of three bones into a tarsometatarsus, and finally the toes. Thus, birds walk on their toes, and the equivalent to the human foot is a long bone, the tarsometatarsus, which is off the ground.

Birds have keen senses of vision and hearing. The sense of smell (olfaction) is not particularly well developed, although in some birds there is a good sense of smell. Birds have developed a flow-through lung and an extensive air-sac system. Modern flying birds have a well-developed sternum with a keel, or carina, for the attachment of the large flight musculature.

Birds are found over the entire Earth. One of the most intriguing aspects of bird biology is the ability to migrate exceptional distances. Birds possess highly specialized directional senses for orientation, navigation, homing, and migration, including the ability to detect the Earth's magnetic field. These uncanny abilities permit birds to occupy distinctive wintering and nesting grounds, thus expanding their usable habitats. Some migrations, such as that of the Arctic tern, involve a circumatlantic migration from Alaska to the South Pole. *See* FLIGHT.

There are some 9700 species of birds living today, and most species are particularly well known. However, the relationships of the higher categories of birds are still debated. Of the 9700 species, some 5000 species belong to the order Passeriformes, the perching birds or songbirds. The number of avian orders is still controversial, and texts show different arrangements. Because the situation is in flux, a fairly conservative system is used below (fossil groups are designated by a dagger).

> Class Aves
>   Subclass Sauriurae
>   Infraclass Archaeopterygiformes[†]
>   Order Archaeopterygiformes (late Jurassic reptile-birds)[†]
>   Order Confuciusornithiformes (lower Cretaceous,
>   beaked reptile-birds)[†]
>   Infraclass Enantiornithes (archaic Mesozoic land birds)
>   Subclass Ornithurae
>   Infraclass Odontornithes (or Odontoholcae)[†]
>   Order Hesperornithiformes (Cretaceous toothed divers)[†]
>   Infraclass Neornithes (or Carinata)
>   Superorder Ambiortimorphae (gull-like, Mesozoic toothed
>   birds)[†]

Incertae sedis (*Gansus, Chaoyangia*, etc., archaic modern-
  type birds)[†]
Palaeognathae (ostrich and allies)
Neognathae (modern birds)
   Order: Sphenisciformes (penguins, 17 species)
        Procellariiformes (tube-nose seabirds, 114)
        Pelecaniformes (pelicans and allies, 66)
        Ciconiiformes (storks and allies, 86)
        Falconiformes (hawks, eagles, and vultures, 309)
        Galliformes (chickens and allies, 282)
        Gruiformes (rails, cranes and allies, 214)
        Podicipediformes (grebes, 22)
        Charadriiformes (shorebirds, gulls and allies, 349)
        Pteroclidiformes (sand grouse, 16)
        Threskiornithiformes (ibis, spoonbills, 33)
        Anseriformes (waterfowl, 161)
        Phoenicopteriformes (flamingos, 5 or 6)
        Gaviiformes (loons, 5)
        Columbiformes (pigeons and doves, 316)
        Psittaciformes (parrots, 360)
        Coliiformes (mousebirds, 6)
        Musophagiformes (turacos, or plaintain-eaters, 23)
        Cuculiformes (cuckoos, 142)
        Opisthocomiformes (hoatzin, 1)
        Strigiformes (owls, barn owls, 173)
        Caprimulgiformes (nightjars and allies, 116)
        Apodiformes (hummingbirds and swifts, 425)
        Trogoniformes (trogons, quetzals, 39)
        Coraciiformes (kingfishers, bee-eaters and allies,
          219)
        Piciformes (woodpeckers and allies, 407)
        Passeriformes (perching birds, songbirds, passerines,
          5739)

The classification system presented above coordinates with most major treatises on birds. The subclass Sauriurae contains the archaic birds of the Mesozoic Era, the Age of Reptiles, which includes the toothed fossil *Archaeopteryx*, or *Urvogel*, the oldest known bird (150 million years ago). Other Mesozoic birds included the ancient or- nithurine birds more closely allied with the modern radiation of birds, among them such forms as the hesperornithiforms, the Cretaceous toothed divers, which superfi- cially resembled loons. They became extinct at the end of the Cretaceous along with their gull-like contemporaries, the Ambiortimorphae. Also included in this group is the Lower Cretaceous *Ambiortus* from Mongolia, which was a fully volant ornithurine bird about the size of a pigeon. It possessed a well-developed sternal keel and other features of the pectoral region typical of modern birds, indicating that true flying birds existed some 12 million years after the appearance of *Archaeopteryx*.

The extinction of the dinosaurs 65 million years ago is now believed to have been due to the collision of a large extraterrestrial body, a meteor or some other object, with Earth, causing catastrophic effects, including the extinction of numerous bird species. It is likely that the very few types that survived, possibly related to shorebirds, were the wellspring of the modern evolution of birds; and modern birds, like their mammalian counterparts, probably evolved explosively during the early part of the Tertiary Period, perhaps over a period of some 5–10 million years. Among the first birds to appear were the strange *Diatrymas*, large, predatory, flightless birds that had a head the size of that of a horse. They are thought to have taken over the niche left vacant by predatory dinosaurs, and they fed on the small archaic mammals of the Paleocene and Eocene.

By the Eocene, approximately 50 million years ago, all the major orders of modern birds were present. By the Oligocene, most of the families were present, and by the Miocene, the genera of modern birds were well established.   [A.Fe.]

B

Bacillary dysentery A highly contagious intestinal disease caused by rod-shaped bacteria of the genus *Shigella*. Bacillary dysentery is a significant infection of children in the developing world, where it is transmitted by the fecal-oral route. The global disease burden is estimated as 165 million episodes and 1.3 million deaths annually. Common-source outbreaks occasionally occur in developed countries, usually as a result of contaminated food. The most common species isolated in developed countries is *S. sonnei*, while *S. flexneri* serotypes predominate in endemic areas. Epidemics of *S. dysenteriae* 1 occur in equatorial regions, and these outbreaks can involve adults as well as children.

When ingested even in very small numbers, shigellae multiply in the intestine and invade the epithelial lining of the colon. Infection of this tissue elicits an acute inflammatory response (colitis) that is manifested as diarrhea or bloody, mucoid stools (dysentery). The virulence of all *Shigella* species, and *Shigella*-like enteroinvasive *Escherichia coli*, depends on an extrachromosomal genetic element (virulence plasmid) that encodes four invasion plasmid antigen (Ipa) proteins and a secretory system (Type III) for these proteins. Secreted Ipa proteins help shigellae to initiate colonic invasion through specialized endocytic intestinal cells (M cells). After shigellae pass through these M cells, they are phagocytized by tissue macrophages in the underlying lymphoid tissue. Ipa proteins then induce apoptosis (programmed cell death) in infected macrophages, releasing cytokines (primarily IL-1) that initiate an acute, localized inflammatory infiltrate. This infiltrate of polymorphonuclear leukocytes destabilizes tight junctions between absorptive epithelial cells (enterocytes), making the tissue more susceptible to additional *Shigella* invasion. Secreted Ipa proteins induce uptake of shigellae by the colonic enterocytes. The virulence plasmid also encodes an intercellular spread protein (IcsA) that recruits mammalian cytoskeletal elements (primarily actin) to the bacterial surface. This actin is organized into a cytoplasmic motor that facilitates spread of shigellae to adjacent enterocytes. *See* ESCHERICHIA.

In otherwise healthy individuals, bacillary dysentery is typically a short-term disease lasting less than a week. The symptoms can be truncated by appropriate antibiotic therapy (such as oral ampicillin or cyprofloxacin) that rapidly eliminates shigellae from the intestinal lumen and tissues. When *S. dysenteriae* 1 is the etiologic agent, however, hemolytic uremic syndrome can be manifested as a serious consequence of disease. This species produces a cytotoxin (Shiga toxin or Stx) that is functionally identical to the toxin of enterohemorrhagic *E. coli* (for example, O157:H7). Stx inhibits protein synthesis, damaging endothelial cells of the intestinal capillary bed; the toxin may also damage renal tubules, causing acute renal failure with chronic sequela in up to one-third of hemolytic uremic syndrome patients. *See* MEDICAL BACTERIOLOGY.

[T.L.Ha.]

Bacteria   Extremely small—usually 0.3 to 2.0 micrometers in diameter—and relatively simple microorganisms possessing the prokaryotic type of cell construction. Although traditionally classified within the fungi as Schizomycetes, they show no phylogenetic affinities with the fungi, which are eukaryotic organisms. The only group that is clearly related to the bacteria are the blue-green algae. Bacteria are found almost everywhere, being abundant, for example, in soil, water, and the alimentary tracts of animals. Each kind of bacterium is fitted physiologically to survive in one of the innumerable habitats created by various combinations of space, food, moisture, light, air, temperature, inhibitory substances, and accompanying organisms. Dried but often still living bacteria can be carried into the air. Bacteria have a practical significance for humans. Some cause disease in humans and domestic animals, thereby affecting health and the economy. Some bacteria are useful in industry, while others, particularly in the food, petroleum, and textile industries, are harmful. Some bacteria improve soil fertility. As in higher forms of life, each bacterial cell arises either by division of a preexisting cell with similar characteristics or through a combination of elements from two such cells in a sexual process. *See* INDUSTRIAL MICROBIOLOGY.

Descriptions of bacteria are preferably based on the studies of pure cultures, since in mixed cultures it is uncertain which bacterium is responsible for observed effects. Pure cultures are sometimes called axenic, a term denoting that all cells had a common origin in being descendants of the same cell, without implying exact similarity in all characteristics. Pure cultures can be obtained by selecting single cells, but indirect methods achieving the same result are more common.

If conditions are suitable, each bacterium grows and divides, using food diffused through the gel, and produces a mass of cells called a colony. Colonies always develop until visible to the naked eye unless toxic products or deficient nutrients limit them to microscopic dimensions. *See* CULTURE.

The morphology, that is, the shape, size, arrangement, and internal structures, of bacteria can be distinguished microscopically and provides the basis for classifying the bacteria into major groups. Three principal shapes of bacteria exist, spherical (coccus), rod (bacillus), and twisted rod (spirillum). The coccus may be arranged in chains of cocci as in *Streptococcus*, or in tetrads of cocci as in *Sarcina*. The rods may be single or in filaments. Stains are used to visualize bacterial structures otherwise not seen, and the stain reaction with Gram's stain provides a characteristic used in classifying bacteria.

Many bacteria are not motile. Of the motile bacteria, however, some move by means of tiny whirling hairlike flagella extending from within the cell. Others are motile without flagella and have a creeping or gliding motion. Many bacteria are enveloped in a capsule, a transparent gelatinous or mucoid layer outside the cell wall. Some form within the cell a heat- and drought-resistant spore, called an endospore. Cytoplasmic structures such as reserve fat, protein, and volutin are occasionally visible within the bacterial cell.

The nucleus of bacteria is prokaryotic, that is, not separated from the rest of the cell by a membrane. It contains the pattern material for forming new cells. This material, deoxyribonucleic acid (DNA), carrying the information for synthesis of cell parts, composes a filament with the ends joined to form a circle. The filament consists of two DNA strands joined throughout their length. The joining imparts a helical form to the double strand. The double-stranded DNA consists of linearly arranged hereditary units, analogous and probably homologous with the "genes" of higher forms of life. During cell division and sexual reproduction, these units are duplicated and a complete set is distributed to each new cell by an orderly mechanism.

The submicroscopic differences that distinguish many bacterial genera and species are due to structures such as enzymes and genes that cannot be seen. The nature of these structures is determined by studying the metabolic activities of the bacteria. Data are accumulated on the temperatures and oxygen conditions under which the bacteria grow, their response in fermentation tests, their pathogenicity, and their serological reactions. There are also modern methods for determining directly the similarity in deoxyribonucleic acids between different bacteria. *See* FERMENTATION; PATHOGEN; SEROLOGY.

Bacteria are said to be aerobic if they require oxygen and grow best at a high oxygen tension, usually 20% or more. Microaerophilic bacteria need oxygen, but grow best at, or may even require, reduced oxygen tensions, that is, less than 10%. Anaerobic bacteria do not require oxygen for growth. Obligatorily anaerobic bacteria can grow only in the complete absence of oxygen. Some bacteria obtain energy from the oxidation of reduced substances with compounds other than oxygen (O_2). The sulfate reducers use sulfate, the denitrifiers nitrate or nitrite, and the methanogenic bacteria carbon dioxide as the oxidizing agents, producing H_2S, nitrogen (N_2), and methane (CH_4), respectively, as reduction products.

Interrelationships may be close and may involve particular species. Examples are the parasitic association of many bacteria with plant and animal hosts, and the mutualistic association of nitrogen-fixing bacteria with leguminous plants, of cellulolytic bacteria with grazing animals, and of luminous bacteria with certain deep-sea fishes. *See* POPULATION ECOLOGY.   [R.E.H.]

Endospores are resistant and metabolically dormant bodies produced by the gram-positive rods of *Bacillus* (aerobic or facultatively aerobic), *Clostridia* (strictly anaerobic), by the coccus *Sporosarcina*, and by certain other bacteria. Sporeforming bacteria are found mainly in the soil and water and also in the intestines of humans and animals. Some sporeformers are found as pathogens in insects; others are pathogenic to animals and humans. Endospores seem to be able to survive indefinitely. Spores kept for more than 50 years have shown little loss of their capacity to germinate and propagate by cell division. The mature spore has a complex structure which contains a number of layers. The unique properties of bacterial spores are their extreme resistance to heat, radiation from ultraviolet light and x-rays, organic solvents, chemicals, and desiccation. The capacity of a bacterial cell to form a spore is under genetic control, although the total number of genes specific for sporulation is not known. The actual phenotypic expression of the spore genome depends upon a number of external factors. For each species of sporeforming bacteria, there exist optimum conditions for sporogenesis which differ from the optimal conditions for vegetative growth. These conditions include pH, degree of aeration, temperature, metals, and nutrients. The three processes involved in the conversion of the spore into a vegetative cell are (1) activation (usually by heat or aging), which conditions the spore to germinate in a suitable environment; (2) germination, an irreversible process which results in the loss of the typical characteristics of a dormant spore; and (3) outgrowth, in which new classes of proteins and structures are synthesized so that the spore is converted into a new vegetative cell.   [H.O.H.; K.Hu.; C.O.]

Bacterial genetics   The study of gene structure and function in bacteria. Genetics itself is concerned with determining the number, location, and character of the genes of an organism. The classical way to investigate genes is to mate two organisms with different genotypes and compare the observable properties (phenotypes) of the parents with those of the progeny. Bacteria do not mate (in the usual way), so there is no way of getting all the chromosomes of two different bacteria into the same cell. However, there are a number of ways in which a part of the chromosome or genome from one bacterium can be inserted into another bacterium so that the outcome can be studied. *See* GENETICS.

All organisms have diverged from a common ancestral prokaryote whose precise location in the evolutionary tree is unclear. This has resulted in three primary kingdoms, the Archaebacteria, the Eubacteria, and the Eukaryotae. All bacteria are prokaryotes, that is, the "nucleus" or nucleoid is a single circular chromosome, without a nuclear membrane. Bacteria also lack other membrane-bounded organelles such as mitochondria or chloroplasts, but they all possess a cytoplasmic membrane. Most bacteria have a cell wall that surrounds the cytoplasmic membrane, and some bacteria also contain an outer membrane which encompasses the cell wall. Duplication occurs by a process of binary fission, in which two identical daughter cells arise from a single parent cell. Every cell in a homogeneous population of bacterial cells retains the potential for duplication. Bacteria do not possess the potential for differentiation (other than spore formation) or for forming multicellular organisms. *See* ARCHAEBACTERIA; BACTERIA; RIBONUCLEIC ACID (RNA).

One of the most frequently used organisms in the study of bacterial genetics is the rod-shaped bacillus *Escherichia coli*, whose normal habitat is the colon. Conditions have been found for growing *E. coli* in the laboratory, and it is by far the best understood of all microorganisms. The single circular chromosome of *E. coli* contains about 4.5×10^6 base pairs, which is enough to make about 4500 average-size genes (1000 base pairs each). In regions where mapping studies are reasonably complete, the impression is obtained of an efficiently organized genome. Protein coding regions are located adjacent to regulatory regions. There is no evidence for significant stretches of nonfunctional deoxyribonucleic acid (DNA), and there is no evidence for introns [regions that are removed by splicing the messenger RNA (mRNA) before it is translated into protein] in the coding regions. Very little repetitive DNA exists in the *E. coli* chromosome other than the seven sequence-related rRNA genes that are dispersed at different locations on the chromosome. *See* CHROMOSOME; DEOXYRIBONUCLEIC ACID (DNA); GENETIC CODE.

The first step in performing genetic research on bacteria is to select mutants that differ from wild-type cells in one or more genes. Then crosses are made between mutants and wild types, or between two different mutants, to determine dominance-recessive relationships, chromosomal location, and other properties. Various genetic methods are used to select bacterial mutants, antibiotic-resistant cells, cells with specific growth requirements, and so on.

Certain genes that have the function of modulating the expression of other genes are known as regulatory genes. Mutations that affect the action of regulatory proteins are of two types: those that occur in the genes that encode the regulatory proteins, and those that affect the genetic loci where the regulatory protein interacts to modulate the level of gene expression. Some regulatory gene mutations cause overproduction and some cause underproduction of gene products. This is the hallmark of a mutation that influences the functioning of a regulatory protein or regulatory factor-binding site; it affects the quantity but not the quality of other gene products. Furthermore, regulatory gene mutations are frequently pleiotropic, that is, they influence the rate of synthesis of several gene products simultaneously. *See* GENE ACTION; PROTEIN.

Frequently, geneticists want to increase the number or types of mutants that can be obtained as a result of spontaneous mutagenesis. In such instances, they treat a bacterial population with a mutagenic agent to increase the mutation frequency. This is called induced mutagenesis. The simplest techniques of induced mutagenesis involve measured exposure of the bacteria to a mutagenic agent, such as x-rays or chemical mutagenic agents. Such procedures have a general effect on the increase in the mutation rate. More sophisticated procedures involve isolating the gene of interest and making a change in the desired location. This is called site-directed mutagenesis. The goal is usually to determine the effects of a change at a specific gene locus. The gene in question is isolated, modified, and reinserted into the organism. Discrete alterations can be made in a variety of ways on any DNA in cell-free culture, and the effect of such alterations can be subsequently tested in the organism. *See* GENETIC ENGINEERING; MUTAGENS AND CARCINOGENS.

Bacteria do not mate to form true zygotes, but they are able to exchange genetic information by a variety of processes in which partial zygotes (merozygotes) are formed. The first type of genetic exchange between bacteria to be observed was transformation. Naturally occurring transformation involves the uptake of DNA. This phenomenon is observed only for a limited number of bacterial species and is a relatively difficult technique to use for gene manipulation. In 1946 direct chromosomal exchange by conjugation between *E. coli* cells was discovered by J. Lederberg and E. Tatum, and in 1951 transduction, the virus-mediated transfer of bacterial genes, was discovered. Both conjugation and transduction provide facile, generally applicable methods for moving part of the bacterial chromosome from one cell to another. The discovery of bacterial transposons (a class of mobile genetic elements commonly found in bacterial populations) in the 1970s has been useful in marking and mobilizing genes of interest. The purely genetic approaches to mapping have been supplemented by the biochemical approaches of hybrid plasmid construction and DNA sequence analysis. *See* TRANSFORMATION (BACTERIA); TRANSPOSONS.

At any given time, only a small percentage of the *E. coli* genome is being actively transcribed. The remainder of the genome is either silent or being transcribed at a very low rate. When growth conditions change, some active genes are turned off and other, inactive genes are turned on. The cell always retains its totipotency, so that within a short time (seconds to minutes), and given appropriate circumstances, any gene can be fully turned on. The maximal activity for transcription varies from gene to gene. For example, a β-galactosidase gene makes about one copy per minute, and a fully turned-on biotin synthase gene makes about one copy per 10 min. In the maximally repressed state, both of these genes express less than one transcript per 10 min. The level of transcription for any particular gene usually results from a complex series of control elements organized into a hierarchy that coordinates all the metabolic activities of the cell. For example, when the rRNA genes are highly active, so are the genes for ribosomal proteins, and the latter are regulated in such a way that stoichiometric amounts of most of the ribosomal proteins are produced. When glucose is abundant, most genes involved in processing more complex carbon sources are turned off in a process called catabolite repression. If the glucose supply is depleted and lactose is present, the genes involved in lactose breakdown (catabolism) are expressed. In *E. coli* the production of most RNAs and proteins is regulated exclusively at the transcriptional level, although there are notable exceptions. [G.Z.]

Bacterial growth The processes of both the increase in number and the increase in mass of bacteria. Growth has three distinct aspects: biomass production, cell production, and cell survival. Biomass production depends on the physical aspects of the environment (water content, pH, temperature), the availability of resources (carbon and energy, nitrogen, sulfur, phosphorus, minor elements), and the enzymatic machinery for catabolism (energy trapping), anabolism (biosynthesis of amino acid, purines, pyrimidines, and so forth), and macromolecular synthesis [proteins, ribonucleic acid (RNA), and deoxyribonucleic acid (DNA)]. Cell production is contingent on biomass production and involves, in addition, the triggering of chromosome replication and subsequent cell division. The cells may or may not separate from each other, and the division may partition the cell evenly or unevenly. Alternatively, growth may occur by budding (unequal division). Most cells so produced are themselves capable of growing and dividing; consequently, viability is usually very high when growth conditions are favorable. Moreover, in many cases the incidence of death is surprisingly low in the absence of needed nutrients. Many bacteria differentiate into resistant resting forms (such as spores); others may simply reduce their rate of metabolism and persist in the vegetative state for long times.   [A.L.Ko.]

Bacterial physiology and metabolism   The biochemical reactions that together enable bacteria to live, grow, and reproduce. Strictly speaking, metabolism describes the total chemical reactions that take place in a cell, while physiology describes the role of metabolic reactions in the life processes of a bacterium. The study of bacteria has significance beyond the understanding of bacteria themselves. Since bacteria are abundant, easily grown, and relatively simple in cellular organization, they have been used extensively in biological research. Functional analyses of bacterial systems have provided a foundation for much of the current detailed knowledge about molecular biology and genetics. Bacteria are prokaryotes, lacking the complicated cellular organization found in higher organisms; they have no nuclear envelope and no specialized organelles. Yet they engage in all the basic life processes—transport of materials into and out of the cell, catabolism and anabolism of complex organic molecules, and the maintenance of structural integrity. To accomplish this, bacteria must obtain nutrients and convert them into a form of energy that is useful to the cell.   [M.R.J.S.]

Enzymes. A list of bacterial enzymes (organic catalysts) includes many of the enzymes found in mammalian tissues, as well as many enzymes not found in higher forms of life. By combining with such enzymes, many antibiotics are able to exert a selective killing or inhibition of bacterial growth without causing toxic reactions in the mammalian host. The great capability of the bacterial cell to metabolize a wide variety of substances, as well as to control to some extent the environment in which the cell lives, is reflected in its ability to form inducible enzymes. The majority of bacterial enzymes require cofactors for activity. These cofactors may be inorganic cations of organic molecules called coenzymes. See COENZYME; ENZYME.

Bacterial enzymes may be classified in numerous ways, for example, on the basis of (1) whether they are inducible or constitutive (constitutive enzymes are defined as those enzymes formed by the bacterial cell under any or all conditions of growth, whereas inducible enzymes are formed by the bacterial cell only in response to an inducer); (2) whether they are degradative (catabolic; resulting in the release of energy) or synthetic (anabolic; using energy to catalyze the formation of macromolecules); or (3) whether they are exoenzymes (enzymes secreted from the cell to hydrolyze insoluble polymers— wood, starch, protein, and so on—into smaller, soluble compounds which can be taken into the cytoplasm of the bacterium).

In addition, bacterial enzymes are involved in the transport of substrates across the cell wall, in the oxidation of inorganic molecules to provide energy for the cell, and in the destruction of a large number of antibiotics.

Many pathogenic microorganisms excrete enzymes which may play an important role in pathogenesis in some cases (see table). The α-toxin (lecithinase) of *Clostridium perfringens* illustrates a highly active enzyme which is responsible for the necrotizing action associated with gas gangrene infections due to this microorganism. *Streptococcus pyogenes* excretes hyaluronidase which degrades ground substance (polymer of hyaluronic acid), and streptokinase, which activates plasmin resulting in a system that lyses fibrin. Other examples include coagulase of the *Staphylococcus*, which activates

Enzymes excreted by microorganisms of medical importance

Organism	Enzyme	Substrate	End products
Clostridium	Lecithinase	Lecithin	Diglyceride, phosphoryl choline
	Collagenase	Collagen	?
Streptococcus	Hyaluronidase	Hyaluronic acid polymer	Hyaluronic acid
	Streptodornase	Deoxyribonucleic acid	Nucleotides
	Streptokinase	Activates plasminogen to plasmin	Results in lysis of fibrin clots
Staphylococcus	Coagulase	Coagulase reacting factor	Results in coagulation of plasma
Proteus	Urease	Urea	Ammonia and carbon dioxide
Corynebacterium diphtheriae	Diphtheria toxin	Nicotinamide dinucleotide (NAD)	Splits NAD and adds ADP-ribose to elongation factor 2 to prevent protein synthesis by freezing ribosome movement

clotting of plasma, urease of *Proteus vulgaris*, which splits urea to ammonia and carbon dioxide, and collagenase of *Clostridium*, which hydrolyzes collagen. *See* DIPHTHERIA; STAPHYLOCOCCUS.

Many bacteria are able to synthesize enzymes which will hydrolyze or modify an antibiotic so that it is no longer effective. Essentially all of these enzymes are coded by DNA that exists in bacterial plasmids. As a result, the ability to produce enzymes which destroy antibiotics can be rapidly passed from one organism to another either by conjugation in gram-negative organisms or by transduction in both gram-negative and gram-positive bacteria. [W.A.V.]

Bacterial catabolism. Bacterial catabolism comprises the biochemical activities concerned with the net breakdown of complex substances to simpler substances by living cells. Substances with a high energy level are converted to substances of low energy content, and the organism utilizes a portion of the released energy for cellular processes. Endogenous catabolism relates to the slow breakdown of nonvital intracellular constituents to secure energy and replacement building blocks for the maintenance of the structural and functional integrity of the cell. This ordinarily occurs in the absence of an external supply of food. Exogenous catabolism refers to the degradation of externally available food. The principal reactions employed are dehydrogenation or oxygenation (either represents biological oxidation), hydrolysis, hydration, decarboxylation, and intermolecular transfer and substitution. The complete catabolism of organic substances results in the formation of carbon dioxide, water, and other inorganic compounds and is known as mineralization. Catabolic processes may degrade a substance only part way. The resulting intermediate compounds may be reutilized in biosynthetic processes, or they may accumulate intra- or extracellularly. Catabolism also implies a conversion of the chemical energy into a relatively few energy-rich compounds or "bonds," in which form it is biologically useful; also, part of the chemical energy is lost as heat.

Bacterial intermediary metabolism relates to the chemical steps involved in metabolism between the starting substrates and the final product. Normally these intermediates, or precursors of subsequent products, do not accumulate inside or outside the bacterial cell in significant amounts, being transformed serially as rapidly as they are formed. The identification of such compounds, the establishment of the coenzymes and enzymes catalyzing the individual reaction steps, the identity of active forms of the intermediates, and other details of the reaction mechanisms are the objectives of a study of bacterial intermediary metabolism. [J.W.Fo./R.E.K.]

Many bacteria are able to decompose organic compounds and to grow in the absence of oxygen gas. Such anaerobic bacteria obtain energy and certain organic compounds needed for growth by a process of fermentation. This consists of an oxidation of a suitable organic compound, using another organic compound as an oxidizing agent in place of molecular oxygen. In most fermentations both the compounds oxidized and the compounds reduced (used as an oxidizing agent) are derived from a single fermentable substrate. In other fermentations, one substrate is oxidized and another is reduced. Different bacteria ferment different substrates. Many bacteria are able to ferment carbohydrates such as glucose and sucrose, polyalchohols such as mannitol, and salts of organic acids such as pyruvate and lactate. Other compounds, such as cellulose, amino acids, and purines, are fermented by some bacteria.   [H.A.B.]

Bacterial anabolism. Bacterial anabolism comprises the physiological and biochemical activities concerned with the acquisition, synthesis, and organization of the numerous and varied chemical constituents of a bacterial cell. Clearly, when a cell grows and divides to form two cells, there exists twice the amount of cellular components that existed previously. These components are drawn, directly or indirectly, from the environment around the cell, and (usually) modified extensively in the growth processes when new cell material is formed (biosynthesis). This build-up, or synthesis, begins with a relatively small number of low-molecular-weight building blocks which are either assimilated directly from the environment or produced by catabolism. By sequential and interrelated reactions, they are fashioned into different molecules (mostly of high molecular weight, and hence called macromolecules), for example, lipids, polysaccharides, proteins, and nucleic acids, and many of these molecules are in turn arranged into more complex arrays such as ribosomes, membranes, cell walls, and flagella. Other typical anabolic products, of lower molecular weight, include pigments, vitamins, antibiotics, and coenzymes. The enzymes responsible for the sequential reactions in any one biosynthetic pathway or assembly sequence are often located on or in cellular structures and thus in physical proximity to the preceding and succeeding enzymes, and their products, and to the site(s) where cellular structures are to be formed. Anabolism also includes the transport of molecules into cells, of building blocks to reaction sites, energetic activations, and the transfer and incorporation of the finished products to their ultimate sites in or outside the cell.   [E.R.L.]

Bacterial taxonomy   The classification, nomenclature, and identification of bacteria; sometimes used as a term to indicate the theory of classification. The bacteria are members of the kingdom Prokaryotae, which is defined in terms of the unique structural and biochemical properties of their cells; more specifically, the organization of the deoxyribonucleic acid (DNA) in the nucleus, the lack of a nuclear membrane, the lack of independent membrane-bounded cytoplasmic organelles, the lack of endocytosis and exocytosis, and the chemical nature of some components of plasma membrane and cell walls.

Classification involves the recognition of similarities and relationships as a basis for the arrangement of the bacteria into taxonomic groups or taxa. The basic taxon is the species. Identification involves the recognition of a bacterium as a member of one of the established taxa, appropriately named, by the comparison of a number of characters with those in the description. *See* BACTERIA; TAXONOMIC CATEGORIES.

A bacterial species is a conceptual entity that is hard to define, despite its role as the basic taxonomic grouping. Bacteriologists accept the imprecision and recognize that a species represents a cluster of clones exhibiting some variations in minor properties. They have developed a formal approach to the description of the taxon while trying to solve the problems encountered in the process of recognizing and naming species. The description is an assembly of such structural, chemical, physiologic, genetic, and ecologic characteristics as can be determined for the available strains that closely resemble each other. A strain is any pure culture of an organism isolated from nature, and the collected strains may then be conserved as cultures in the laboratory for study and comparison. In addition to the description, one strain must be designated by the author and preserved in a culture collection as a type strain, or permanent example, of the species and available to all who study bacteria. If that type strain is lost or succumbs, a formal proposal of a substitute strain (neotype) must be published. In general, bacterial taxonomy is built around the living type specimen: a species consists of the type strain and, whenever available, all other strains sufficiently similar to the type strain to be considered as included in the species. There is a provision for the description and naming of a distinctive species that is not yet cultivable, with the requirement for a suitably preserved type specimen.

A new species, validly described, must be assigned to a genus in order to accord with the binomial system of nomenclature initiated by C. Linnaeus. Thus, a species assigned to the genus *Bacillus* would be referred to as, for example, *Bacillus subtilis*. Such formal names of taxa are italicized to indicate that they are considered to accord with the formal description. If there is no appropriate genus available, a new genus must be named in accord with the *International Code of Nomenclature of Bacteria* and provided with a description that circumscribes the included species, and a type species must be designated as the exemplary representative of the genus.

The lowest nomenclatural rank that is recognized by the *Code* is subspecies, which is a subdivision of the species recognizing consistent variations in otherwise stable characters in the species description, for example, *Bacillus cereus* ssp. *mycoides*. There are times, however, when even finer but unofficial subdivisions of the species are useful and contribute to science, for example, for the epidemiology of pathogenic species. Then, groups of strains may be recognized by some special character as a variety of the species. These may be based on a biological property (biovar), antigenic variation (serovar), pathogenicity (pathovar), or susceptibility to particular bacterial viruses (phagovar). These characters have no formal standing in nomenclature.

Several new techniques are presently used in modern approaches to taxonomy. Numerical taxonomy (taxometrics) is a first approach for the analysis of phenotype. It implies the existence of programs for computer-assisted identification, either as recognizable phenons or by relation into a computer-stored classification and key program. Either of these methods has found considerable application in dealing with masses of isolates (for example, in studies of pollution or of sediments), or in dealing with results of automated systems for identification of pathogens in clinical bacteriology. *See* NUMERICAL TAXONOMY.

Chemotaxonomy applies systematic data on the molecular architecture of components of the bacterial cell to the solution of taxonomic problems. This has been a powerful tool since the 1950s, and a number of chemotaxonomic markers have been identified, ranging from molecules unique to the Prokaryotae or specific groups of bacteria to mechanisms or products of metabolism that characterize genera or species. The availability, and relative simplicity of techniques for amino acid analysis, for sequential analysis of polymers, for gas and thin-layer chromatography, for fermentation products and lipids, and so on, have made the systematic studies possible. These have led to a more effective definition of taxonomic groups based on biochemical assessment of cell wall composition, lipid composition of membranes, the types of isoprenoid quinones, the amino acid sequences of select proteins, and the characterization of proteins, such as the cytochromes and many other macromolecules. *See* CHEMOTAXONOMY.

Nucleic acid studies have been by far the most potent generators and arbiters of data on relatedness, with distinct capability for applications to the phylogenetic assessment of taxonomic arrangements. *See* DEOXYRIBONUCLEIC ACID (DNA); RIBONUCLEIC ACID (RNA).

[R.G.E.M.]

Bacteriology   The science and study of bacteria, and hence a specialized branch of microbiology. It deals with the nature and properties of the bacteria as living entities, their morphology and developmental history, ecology, physiology and biochemistry, genetics, and classification.

The major subjects that have consecutively occupied the forefront of bacteriological research have been the origin of bacteria, the constancy or variability of their properties, their role as causative agents of disease and of spoilage of foods, their significance in the cycle of matter, their classification, and their physiological, biochemical, and genetic features. *See* BACTERIA; MICROBIOLOGY.   [C.B.V.N.]

Bacteriophage   Any of the viruses that infect bacterial cells. They are discrete particles with dimensions from about 20 to about 200 nanometers. A given bacterial virus can infect only one or a few related species of bacteria; these constitute its host range. Bacteriophages consist of two essential components: nucleic acid, in which genetic information is encoded (this may be either ribonucleic acid or deoxyribonucleic acid), and a protein coat (capsid), which serves as a protective shell containing the nucleic acid and is involved in the efficiency of infection and the host range of the virus.

The description of a bacterial virus involves a study of its shape and dimensions by electron microscopy (see illustration), its host range, the serological properties of its capsid, the kind of nucleic acid it contains, and the characters of the plaques it forms on a given host. Both the nucleic acid and the capsid proteins are specific to the individual virus; in the case of the capsid proteins this specificity is the basis for serological identification of the virus.

The most striking form of phage infection is that in which all of the infected bacteria are destroyed in the process of the formation of new phage particles. This results in the clearing of a turbid liquid culture as the infected cells lyse. When lysis occurs in cells fixed as a lawn of bacteria growing on a solid medium, it produces holes, or areas of clearing, called plaques. These represent colonies of bacteriophage. The size and other

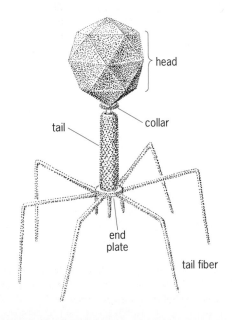

Diagram of a T4 bacteriophage.

properties of the plaque vary with individual viruses and host cells. *See* LYSOGENY; LYTIC INFECTION; VIRUS.   [L.B.]

Basidiomycota   A phylum in the kingdom fungi; commonly known as basidiomycetes. Basidiomycetes traditionally included four artificial classes: Hymenomycetes, Gasteromycetes, Urediniomycetes, and Ustilaginomycetes. They are mostly filamentous fungi characterized by the production of basidia. These are microscopic, often club-shaped end cells in which nuclear fusion and meiosis usually take place prior to the maturation of external, typically haploid basidiospores, which are then disseminated. Common basidiomycetes are the rusts and smuts, which cause severe plant diseases, mushrooms (edible and poisonous), boletes, puffballs, stinkhorns, chanterelles, false truffles, jelly fungi, bird's-nest fungi, and conk or bracket fungi. Basidiomycetes are the most important decayers of wood, living or dead, in forests or buildings, causing either brown rot (for example, dry rot) or white rot. Many, especially mushrooms and boletes, are the primary fungal partners in symbiotic ectomycorrhizal associations with tree roots. Plant litter and soil are other major habitats. A few basidiomycetes are cultivated for food. Some are luminescent, hallucinogenic, lichenized, nematophagous, or aquatic. Some are cultivated by ants or termites, or are symbiotic with captured scale insects. Some can convert to a yeast (or single-cell) phase, one of which causes cryptococcosis in humans and animals. *See* MUSHROOM; MYCORRHIZAE; RUST (MICROBIOLOGY).

[S.A.R.]

Bean   Any of several leguminous plants, or their seeds, long utilized as food by humans or livestock. Some 14 genera of the legume family contain species producing seeds termed "beans" which are useful to humans. Twenty-eight species in 7 genera produce beans of commercial importance, which implies that the bean can be found in trade at the village level or up to and including transoceanic commerce.

The principal Asiatic beans include the edible soybeans, *Glycine* sp., and several species of the genus *Vigna*, such as the cowpea and mung, grams, rice, and adzuki beans. The broad bean (*Vicia faba*) is found in Europe, the Middle East, and Mediterranean region, including the North African fringe. Farther south in Africa occur *Phaseolus* beans, of the *vulgaris* (common bean) and *coccineus* (scarlet runner) species. Some *Phaseolus* beans occur in Europe also. The cowpea, used as a dry bean, is also found abundantly in Nigeria.

In the Americas, the *Phaseolus* beans, *P. vulgaris* and *P. lunatus* (lima bean), are the principal edible beans, although the blackeye cowpea, mung bean, and chick pea or garbanzo (*Cicer arietinum*) are grown to some extent. *Phaseolus coccineus* is often grown in higher elevations in Central and South America, as is *Vicia faba*. The tepary bean (*P. acutifolius*) is found in the drier southwestern United States and northern Mexico.

Bean plants may be either bush or vining types, with white, yellow, red, or purple flowers. The seed itself is the most differentiating characteristic of bean plants. It may be white, yellow, black, red, tan, cream-colored, or mottled, and range in weight from 0.0044 to over 0.025 oz (125 to over 700 mg) per seed. Seeds are grown in straight or curved pods (fruit), with 2–3 seeds per pod in *Glycine* to 18–20 in some *Vigna*.

Beans are consumed as food in several forms. Lima beans and snap beans are used as fresh vegetables, or they may be processed by canning or freezing. Limas are also used as a dry bean. Mung beans are utilized as sprouts. Usage of dry beans (*P. vulgaris*) for food is highly dependent upon seed size, shape, color, and flavor characteristics, and is often associated with particular social or ethnic groups.   [M.W.A.]

Behavior genetics   The study of the hereditary factors of behavior. Charles Darwin, who originated the theory that natural selection is the basis of biological evolution, was persuaded by Francis Galton that the principles of natural selection applied to behavior as well as physical characteristics. Members of a species vary in the expression of certain behaviors because of variations in their genes, and these behaviors have survival value in some environments. One example of such a behavior is curiosity—some organisms are more curious than others, and in some settings curiosity is advantageous for survival. The science of behavior genetics is an extension of these ideas and seeks (1) to determine to what extent the variation of a trait in a population (the extent of individual differences) is due to genetic processes, to what extent it is due to environmental variation, and to what extent it is due to joint functions of these factors (heredity-environment interactions and correlations); and (2) to identify the genetic architecture (genotypes) that underlies behavior.

Traditionally, some of the clearest and most indisputable evidence for a hereditary influence on behavior comes from selective-breeding experiments with animals. Behavior genetic research has utilized bacteria, paramecia, nematodes, fruit flies, moths, houseflies, mosquitoes, wasps, bees, crickets, fishes, geese, cows, dogs, and numerous other organisms. Breeding of these organisms allows genetically useful types of relationships, such as half-sibs, to be produced easily. Artificial selection (selective breeding) can be used to obtain a population that scores high or low on specific traits. Inbred strains of many animals, particularly rodents, are readily available, and the study of various types of crosses among them can provide a wealth of information. An experimental design using the recombinant inbred-strain method shows great promise for isolating single-gene effects. This procedure derives several inbred strains from the F_2 generation (grandchildren) produced by a cross between two initial inbred strains. Since it is possible to exert a great deal of control over the rearing environments, the experimenter can manipulate both heredity and environment.

Other work has focused on the effects of the environment and genotype-environment interactions. For example, experiments with mice have shown that, with respect to several learning tasks, early environmental-enrichment effects and maternal effects were quite small, relative to the amount of normal genetic variation found in the strains of mice tested. Only a few genotype-environment interactions were found. Still other work has shown that early experiences affect later behavior patterns for some strains but not others (a genotype-environment interaction).

An increasing role for animals in genetic research is to provide models of human genetic diseases, many of which have behavioral features. Such animal models may occur naturally or may be engineered in the laboratory. Animal models are available for many neurobehavioral disorders, including narcolepsy, various epilepsies, and alcoholism. The availability of animal models allows researchers to obtain information about the development of genetic disorders and the effects of different environments on this development, as well as to explore treatment options. While it is not always prudent or desirable to generalize from animal results to humans, it is assumed that basic genetic systems work in similar ways across organisms, and it is likely that these types of animal studies will play a key role in elucidating the ways in which environment influences phenotypic variation. With advances in genetic technology, it is possible to observe genetic variation more directly by locating, identifying, and characterizing genes themselves.

The effects of a single gene on behavior have been most extensively studied in the domain of mental retardation. Research has shown that there are a large number of metabolic pathways which have defects due to a single gene. Over 100 of these defects influence mental ability. One such single-gene defect is classic phenylketonuria (PKU), an autosomal recessive disorder, which also illustrates the role that environment can play in the expression of a trait. Individuals who are homozygous (having two copies of the PKU allele) are unable to make the enzyme phenylalanine hydroxylase, which converts the essential amino acid phenylalanine to tyrosine, a nonessential amino acid. Instead, the excess phenylalanine builds up in the blood and is converted into phenylpyruvic acid, which is toxic to the developing nervous system in large amounts. The main effect of untreated PKU is severe mental retardation, along with a distinctive odor, light pigmentation, unusual gait and posture, and seizures. Many untreated individuals with PKU show fearfulness, irritability, and violent outbursts of temper. *See* MENTAL RETARDATION.

Every organism develops in a particular environment, and both genes and environment control development. It is, therefore, not possible to state that a particular behavioral trait is either genetic or environmental in origin. It is possible, however, to investigate the relative contributions of heredity and environment to the variation among individuals in a population. With humans, it is possible to obtain approximate results by measuring the similarity among relatives on the trait of interest. Twins are often used in such studies. One method compares the similarity within pairs of both identical twins and fraternal twins reared together. Identical twins have all their genes in common by descent, since they arise from a single fertilized egg. Fraternal twins arise from two fertilized eggs and so share on average one-half of their genes. If it is assumed that the effects of the shared environments of the two types of twins are equal (a testable assumption), greater resemblance between identical twins than fraternal twins should reflect the proportion of genes they share, and the difference between the correlations of the two twin types should represent about one-half the genetic effect.

A second type of twin study compares not only twins reared together but twins who have been reared apart. The degree of similarity between identical twins reared in the same home would reflect the fact that all their genes are identical and that they share a common family environment. On the other hand, if identical twins can be located who had been adopted by different families chosen at random (an unlikely event, since adopted children tend to be selectively placed), a measure of their degree of similarity would reflect only the effect of their common genes. If it were true that an individual's level on a measure (for example, extroversion) is determined in large part by the characteristics of his or her family and the opportunities that the family makes available to him or her, reared-apart identical twins should be no more alike than pairs of individuals chosen at random. If they do exhibit some degree of similarity, it would reflect genetic effects alone. The existence of even very large genetic effects, however, would in no way imply that the environment was unimportant in the development of the trait; it would simply imply that environment was less important than genes in determining the variation among individuals on the trait in question at the time of measurement. That is, the individuals would differ more because of the genes they carry than because of the particular environments to which they were exposed. In another range of environments, the results might be different. *See* TWINS (HUMAN).

Developmental psychologists are finding that differences in children's behavioral phenotypes are due more to their different genotypes than to their different rearing environments, as long as those environments are within a normal range of experiences. Identifying environmental variables from this normal range that have an important effect on the behavioral phenotype may be even more difficult than identifying contributing genes. Advances in theory and new technologies, combined with information from more traditional methodologies, will continue to provide insight into the contributions of genes and environment to behavior. [K.J.W.; T.J.B.]

Behavioral ecology   The branch of ecology that focuses on the evolutionary causes of variation in behavior among populations and species. Thus it is concerned with the adaptiveness of behavior, the ultimate questions of why animals behave as they do, rather than the proximate questions of how they behave. The principles of natural selection are applied to behavior with the underlying assumption that, within the constraints of their evolutionary histories, animals behave optimally by maximizing their genetic contribution to future generations. For example, animals must maintain their internal physiological conditions within certain limits in order to function properly, and often they do this by behavior. Small organisms may avoid desiccation by living under logs or by burrowing. Many insects must raise body temperatures to 86–95°F (30–35°C) for effective flight, and achieve this by muscular activity such as the shivering of butterflies in the early morning or by orienting to the Sun. Other adaptive behaviors that are studied may fall in the categories of habitat selection, foraging, territoriality, and reproduction. *See* BEHAVIOR GENETICS; ETHOLOGY; MIGRATORY BEHAVIOR; REPRODUCTIVE BEHAVIOR. [H.Di.; P.Fr.]

Behavioral psychophysics   The use of behavioral methods to measure the sensory capacities of animals and nonverbal humans such as infants. The observations are analogous to those obtained from adult human subjects who are asked to observe appropriate stimuli and report what they see. The behavioral methods differ primarily in that stimulus-response associations are established by means other than verbal instructions, either as unlearned reflexes or through conditioning. Any sense or species may be studied, but most work has been done on the vision and hearing of primates, cats, pigeons, and rats. Typical investigations determine (1) the absolute threshold (the minimum intensity needed to elicit a standard response); (2) the difference threshold (the minimum change in a stimulus needed to elicit a standard response); and (3) points of apparent equality (values of stimuli that elicit no response because a change in one aspect compensates for a change in another). A few investigations have determined stimulus scales that express quantitative relations between the physical stimulus and the perceptual effect over a range of stimulus values. These various measures provide a picture of the sensory function, such as visual acuity, color sensitivity, loudness or pitch perception, and odor discrimination. Efficiency and sensitivity to the sensory function of interest are the major factors that govern the choice of method in behavioral psychophysics.

Reflex methods are the most convenient since no training is required. An example is the preferential looking response in infants. Without training, infants spend more time looking at patterned stimuli than at blank fields. Two stimulus fields are placed before the infant, and the relative time spent looking at each is determined. A preference for one pattern according to this measure indicates that the infant can detect a difference between the two.

Unconditioned reflex methods are limited to sensory functions for which appropriate reflexes may be found; also, they usually impose severe limits on the specific stimulus conditions that may be used. Conditioning methods add considerable flexibility. In Pavlovian conditioning, the stimulus of interest becomes the conditioned stimulus through its association with a stimulus that elicits a clear-cut reflexive response (the unconditioned stimulus).

Operant conditioning offers still more flexibility. Typically the subject is rewarded for making an indicator response in the presence of one stimulus value; reward is withheld (or another response rewarded) in the presence of other stimulus values. The responses are selected to suit the species and the stimulus under study.

Interest in the development of sensory function has spurred the use of behavioral methods in infants and young children, while the effects of controlled sensory input during development have been extensively monitored in nonhuman subjects. Applications to the prevention and control of sensory disorders also are increasing. For example, a number of toxicants, drugs, and environmental stressors have been related to sensory disorders; the methods of behavioral psychophysics are used to follow the development of these disorders under controlled conditions, and to uncover potential preventive and therapeutic measures. See PSYCHOLOGY; SENSATION. [D.Bl.]

Bilirubin The predominant orange pigment of bile. It is the major metabolic breakdown product of heme, the prosthetic group of hemoglobin in red blood cells, and other chromoproteins such as myoglobin, cytochrome, and catalase. The breakdown of hemoglobin from the old red cells takes place at a rapid rate in the reticuloendothelial cells of the liver, spleen, and bone marrow. The steps in this breakdown process include denaturation and removal of the protein globin, oxidation and opening of the tetrapyrrole ring, and the removal of iron to form the green pigment biliverdin, which is then reduced to bilirubin by the addition of hydrogen. The formed bilirubin is transported to the liver, probably bound to albumin, where it is conjugated into water-soluble mono- and diglucuronides and to a lesser extent with sulfate. See LIVER.

In mammalian bile essentially all of the bilirubin is present as a glucuronide conjugate. Bilirubin glucuronide is passed through the liver cells into the bile caniculi and then into the intestine. The bacterial flora further reduces the bilirubin to colorless urobilinogen. Most of the urobilinogen is either reduced to stercobilinogen or oxidized to urobilin. These two compounds are then converted to stercobilin, which is excreted in the feces and gives the stool its brown color. See HEMOGLOBIN. [M.K.S.]

Bioassay A method for the quantitation of the effects on a biological system by its exposure to a substance, as well as the quantitation of the concentration of a substance by some observable effect on a biological system. The biological material in which the effect is measured can range from subcellular components and microorganisms to groups of animals. The substance can be stimulatory, such as an ion increasing taxis behavior in certain protozoans, or inhibitory, such as an antibiotic for bacterial growth. Bioassays are most frequently used when there is a number of steps, usually poorly understood, between the substance and the behavior observed, or when the substance is a complex mixture of materials and it is not clear what the active components are. Bioassays can be replaced, in time, by either a more direct measure of concentration of the active principle, such as an analytical method (for example, mass spectrometry, high-pressure liquid chromatography, radioimmunoassay), or a more direct measurement of the effect, such as binding to a surface receptor in the case of many drugs, as the substance or its mechanism of action is better characterized.

Assays to quantitate the effects of an exposure model the effect of a substance in the real world. Complex biological responses can be estimated by laboratory culture tests, which use, for example, bacteria or cells cultured in a petri dish (usually to model an effect either on the organism of interest, such as bacteria, or on some basic cellular function); by tissue or organ culture, which isolates pieces of tissue or whole organs in a petri dish (usually to model organ function); or in whole animals (usually to model complex organismic relationships). [R.W.Har.; A.Tu.]

Biocalorimetry   The measurement of the energetics of biological processes such as biochemical reactions, association of ligands to biological macromolecules, folding of proteins into their native conformations, phase transitions in biomembranes, and enzymatic reactions, among others. Two types of instruments have been developed to study these processes: differential scanning calorimeters and isothermal titration calorimeters. Differential scanning calorimeters measure the heat capacity at constant pressure of a sample as a continuous function of temperature. Isothermal titration calorimeters measure directly the energetics (through heat effects) associated with biochemical reactions or processes occurring at constant temperatures. In all cases, the uniqueness of calorimetry resides in its capability to measure directly and in a model-independent fashion the heat energy associated with a process.   [E.Fr.]

Biochemistry   The study of the substances and chemical processes which occur in living organisms. It includes the identification and quantitative determination of the substances, studies of their structure, determining how they are synthesized and degraded in organisms, and elucidating their role in the operation of the organism.

Substances studied in biochemistry include carbohydrates (including simple sugars and large polysaccharides), proteins (such as enzymes), ribonucleic acid (RNA) and deoxyribonucleic acid (DNA), lipids, minerals, vitamins, and hormones. *See* CARBOHYDRATE; DEOXYRIBONUCLEIC ACID (DNA); ENZYME; HORMONE; LIPID; PROTEIN; RIBONUCLEIC ACID (RNA); VITAMIN.

Metabolism and energy production. Many of the chemical steps involved in the biological breakdown of sugars, lipids (fats), and amino acids are known. It is well established that living organisms capture the energy liberated from these reactions by forming a high-energy compound, adenosine triphosphate (ATP). In the absence of oxygen, some organisms and tissues derive ATP from an incomplete breakdown of glucose, degrading the sugar to an alcohol or an acid in the process. In the presence of oxygen, many organisms degrade glucose and other foodstuff to carbon dioxide and water, producing ATP in a process known as oxidative phosphorylation. *See* CARBOHYDRATE METABOLISM; LIPID METABOLISM.

Structure and function studies. The relationship of the structure of enzymes to their catalytic activity is becoming increasingly clear. It is now possible to visualize atoms and groups of atoms in some enzymes by x-ray crystallography. Some enzyme-catalyzed processes can now be described in terms of the spatial arrangement of the groups on the enzyme surface and how these groups influence the reacting molecules to promote the reaction. It is also possible to explain how the catalytic activity of an enzyme may be increased or decreased by changes in the shape of the enzyme molecule. An important advance has been the development of an automated procedure for joining amino acids together into a predetermined sequence. This technology will permit the synthesis of slightly altered enzymes and will improve the understanding of the relationship between the structure and the function of enzymes. In addition, this procedure permits the synthesis of medically important polypeptides (short chains of amino acids) such as some hormones and antibiotics.

Molecular genetics. A subject of intensive investigation has been the explanation of genetics in molecular terms. It is now well established that genetic information is encoded in the sequence of nucleotides of DNA and that, with the exception of some viruses which utilize RNA, DNA is the ultimate repository of genetic information. The sequence of amino acids in a protein is programmed in DNA; this information is first transferred by copying the nucleotide sequence of DNA into that of messenger RNA, from which this sequence is translated into the specific sequence of amino acids of the protein. See GENETIC CODE; MOLECULAR BIOLOGY.

The biochemical basis for a number of genetically inherited diseases, in which the cause has been traced to the production of a defective protein, has been determined. Sickle cell anemia is a striking example; it is well established that the change of a single amino acid in hemoglobin has resulted in a serious abnormality in the properties of the hemoglobin molecule. See DISEASE.

Regulation. Increased understanding of the chemical events in biological processes has permitted the investigation of the regulation of these proceses. An important concept is the chemical feedback circuit: the product of a series of reactions can itself influence the rates of the reactions. For example, the reactions which lead to the production of ATP proceed vigorously when the supply of ATP within the cell is low, but they slow down markedly when ATP is plentiful. These observations can be explained, in part, by the fact that ATP molecules bind to some of the enzymes involved, changing the surface features of the enzymes sufficiently to decrease their effectiveness as catalysts. It is also possible to regulate these reactions by changing the amounts of the enzymes; the amount of an enzyme can be controlled by modulating the synthesis of its specific messenger RNA or by modulating the translation of the information of the RNA molecule into the enzyme molecule. Another level of regulation involves the interaction of cells and tissues in multicellular organisms. For instance, endocrine glands can sense certain tissue activities and appropriately secrete hormones which control these activities. The chemical events and substances involved in cellular and tissue "communication" have become subjects of much investigation.

Photosynthesis and nitrogen fixation. Two subjects of substantial interest are the processes of photosynthesis and nitrogen fixation. In photosynthesis, the chemical reactions whereby the gas carbon dioxide is converted into carbohydrate are understood, but the reactions whereby light energy is trapped and converted into the chemical energy necessary for the synthesis of carbohydrate are unclear. The process of nitrogen fixation involves the conversion of nitrogen gas into a chemical form which can be utilized for the synthesis of numerous biologically important substances; the chemical events of this process are not fully understood. See NITROGEN CYCLE; PHOTOSYNTHESIS.

[A.S.L.H.]

Biodegradation   The destruction of organic compounds by microorganisms. Microorganisms, particularly bacteria, are responsible for the decomposition of both natural and synthetic organic compounds in nature. Mineralization results in complete conversion of a compound to its inorganic mineral constituents (for example, carbon dioxide from carbon, sulfate or sulfide from organic sulfur, nitrate or ammonium from organic nitrogen, phosphate from organophosphates, or chloride from organochlorine). Since carbon comprises the greatest mass of organic compounds, mineralization can be considered in terms of CO_2 evolution. Radioactive carbon-14 (^{14}C) isotopes enable scientists to distinguish between mineralization arising from contaminants and soil organic matter. However, mineralization of any compound is never 100% because some of it (10–40% of the total amount degraded) is incorporated into the cell mass or products that become part of the amorphous soil organic matter, commonly referred to as humus. Thus, biodegradation comprises mineralization and conversion to innocuous products, namely biomass and humus. Primary biodegradation is more limited in scope and refers to the disappearance of the compound as a result of its biotransformation to another product.

Compounds that are readily biodegradable are generally utilized as growth substrates by single microorganisms. Many of the components of petroleum products (and frequent ground-water contaminants), such as benzene, toluene, ethylbenzene, and xylene, are utilized by many genera of bacteria as sole carbon sources for growth and energy.

The process whereby compounds not utilized for growth or energy are nevertheless transformed to other products by microorganisms is referred to as cometabolism. Chlorinated aromatic hydrocarbons, such as diphenyldichloroethane (DDT) and polychlorinated biphenyls (PCBs), are among the most persistent environmental contaminants; yet they are cometabolized by several genera of bacteria, notably *Pseudomonas*, *Alcaligenes*, *Rhodococcus*, *Acinetobacter*, *Arthrobacter*, and *Corynebacterium*. Cometabolism is caused by enzymes that have very broad substrate specificity. See BACTERIAL GROWTH.

The use of microorganisms to remediate the environment of contaminants is referred to as bioremediation. This process is most successful in contained systems such as surface soil or ground water where nutrients, mainly inorganic nitrogen and phosphorus, are added to enhance growth of microorganisms and thereby increase the rate of biodegradation. The process has little, if any, applicability to a large open system such as a bay or lake because the nutrient level (that is, the microbial density) is too low to effect substantive biodegradation and the system's size and distribution preclude addition of nutrients.

Remediation of petroleum products from ground waters is harder to achieve than surface soil because of the greater difficulty in distributing the nutrients throughout the zone of contamination, and because of oxygen (O_2) limitations.   [D.D.Fo.]

Biodiversity   The variety of all living things; a contraction of biological diversity. Biodiversity can be measured on many biological levels ranging from genetic diversity within a species to the variety of ecosystems on Earth, but the term most commonly refers to the number of different species in a defined area.

Numbers of extant species for selected taxonomic groups				
Kingdom	Phylum	Number of species described	Estimated number of species	Percent described
Protista		100,000	250,000	40.0
Fungi	Eumycota	80,000	1,500,000	5.3
Plantae	Bryophyta	14,000	30,000	46.7
	Tracheophyta	250,000	500,000	50.0
Animalia	Nematoda	20,000	1,000,000	2.0
	Arthropoda	1,250,000	20,000,000	5.0
	Mollusca	100,000	200,000	50.0
	Chordata	40,000	50,000	80.0

*With permission, modified from G. K. Meffe and C. R. Carroll, *Principles of Conservation Biology*, 1997.

Recent estimates of the total number of species range from 7 to 20 million, of which only about 1.75 million species have been scientifically described. The best-studied groups include plants and vertebrates (phylum Chordata), whereas poorly described groups include fungi, nematodes, and arthropods (see table). Species that live in the ocean and in soils remain poorly known. For most groups of species, there is a gradient of increasing diversity from the Poles to the Equator, and the vast majority of species are concentrated in the tropical and subtropical regions.

Human activities, such as direct harvesting of species, introduction of alien species, habitat destruction, and various forms of habitat degradation (including environmental pollution), have caused dramatic losses of biodiversity; current extinction rates are estimated to be 100–1000 times higher than prehuman extinction rates.

Some measure of biodiversity is responsible for providing essential functions and services that directly improve human life. For example, many medicines, clothing fibers, and industrial products and the vast majority of foods are derived from naturally occurring species. In addition, species are the key working parts of natural ecosystems. They are responsible for maintenance of the gaseous composition of the atmosphere, regulation of the global climate, generation and maintenance of soils, recycling of nutrients and waste products, and biological control of pest species. Ecosystems surely would not function if all species were lost, although it is unclear just how many species are necessary for an ecosystem to function properly. [M.A.Ma.]

Biofilm An adhesive substance, the glycocalyx, and the bacterial community which it envelops at the interface of a liquid and a surface. When a liquid is in contact with an inert surface, any bacteria within the liquid are attracted to the surface and adhere to it. In this process the bacteria produce the glycocalyx. The bacterial inhabitants within this microenvironment benefit as the biofilm concentrates nutrients from the liquid phase. However, these activities may damage the surface, impair its efficiency, or develop within the biofilm a pathogenic community that may damage the associated environment. Microbial fouling or biofouling are the terms applied to these actual or potentially undesirable consequences.

Microbial fouling affects a large variety of surfaces under various conditions. Microbial biofilms may form wherever bacteria can survive; familiar examples are dental plaque and tooth decay. Dental plaque is an accumulation of bacteria, mainly streptococci, from saliva. The process of tooth decay begins with the bacteria colonizing fissures in and contact points between the teeth. Dietary sucrose is utilized by the bacteria to form extracellular glucans that make up the glycocalyx and assist adhesion to the tooth. Within this microbial biofilm or plaque the metabolic by-products of the bacterial inhabitants are trapped; these include acids that destroy the tooth enamel, dentin, or cementum. [H.L.Sc.; J.W.C.]

Biogeography A synthetic discipline that describes the distributions of living and fossil species of plants and animals across the Earth's surface as consequences of ecological and evolutionary processes. Biogeography overlaps and complements many biological disciplines, especially community ecology, systematics, paleontology, and evolutionary biology.

Based on relatively complete compilations of species within well-studied groups, such as birds and mammals, biogeographers identified six different realms within which species tend to be closely related and between which turnovers in major groups of species are observed (see table). The boundaries between biogeographic realms are less distinct than was initially thought, and the distribution of distinctive groups such as parrots, marsupials, and southern beeches (*Nothofagus* spp.) implies that modern-day biogeographic realms have been considerably mixed in the past. *See* ANIMAL EVOLUTION; PLANT EVOLUTION; SPECIATION.

Two patterns of species diversity have stimulated a great deal of progress in developing ecological explanations for geographic patterns of species richness. The first is that the number of species increases in a regular fashion with the size of the geographic area being considered. The second is the nearly universal observation that there are more species of plants and animals in tropical regions than in temperate and polar regions.

In order to answer questions about why there are a certain number of species in a particular geographic region, biogeography has incorporated many insights from

Biogeographic realms		
Realm	Continental areas included	Examples of distinctive or endemic taxa
Palearctic	Temperate Eurasia and northern Africa	Hynobiid salamanders
Oriental	Tropical Asia	Lower apes
Ethiopian	Sub-Saharan Africa	Great apes
Australian	Australia, New Guinea, and New Zealand	Marsupials
Nearctic	Temperate North America	Pronghorn antelope, ambystomatid salamanders
Neotropic	Subtropical Central America and South America	Hummingbirds, antbirds, marmosets

community ecology. Species number at any particular place depends on the amount of resources available there (ultimately derived from the amount of primary productivity), the number of ways those resources can be apportioned among species, and the different kinds of ecological requirements of the species that can colonize the region. The equilibrium theory of island biogeography arose as an application of these insights to the distribution of species within a specified taxon across an island archipelago. This theory generated specific predictions about the relationships among island size and distance from a colonization source with the number and rate of turnover of species. Large islands are predicted to have higher equilibrium numbers of species than smaller islands; hence, the species area relationship can be predicted in principle from the ecological attributes of species. Experimental and observational studies have confirmed many predictions made by this theory. *See* ECOLOGICAL COMMUNITIES; ISLAND BIOGEOGRAPHY.

The latitudinal gradient in species richness has generated a number of explanations, none of which has been totally satisfactory. One explanation is based on the observation that species with more temperate and polar distributions tend to have larger geographic ranges than species from tropical regions. It is thought that since species with large geographic ranges tend to withstand a wider range of physical and biotic conditions, this allows them to penetrate farther into regions with more variable climates at higher latitudes. If this were true, then species with smaller geographic ranges would tend to concentrate in tropical regions where conditions are less variable. While this might be generally true, there are many examples of species living in high-latitude regions that have small geographic regions.

Biogeography is entering a phase where data on the spatial patterns of abundance and distribution of species of plants and animals are being analyzed with sophisticated mathematical and technological tools. Geographic information systems and remote sensing technology have provided a way to catalog and map spatial variation in biological processes with a striking degree of detail and accuracy. These newer technologies have stimulated research on appropriate methods for modeling and analyzing biogeographic patterns. Modern techniques of spatial modeling are being applied to geographic information systems data to test mechanistic explanations for biogeographic patterns that could not have been attempted without the advent of the appropriate technology.   [B.A.M.]

Biological clocks   Self-sustained circadian (approximately 24-hour) rhythms regulating daily activities such as sleep and wakefulness were described as early as 1729. By the midtwentieth century it had become clear that the period of self-sustained (free-running) oscillations usually does not match that of the Earth's rotation (environmental cycle), therefore the expression "approximately 24 hours." Moreover, the free-running period varies among species and also somewhat from one individual to another. Circadian rhythmicity is often referred to as the biological clock. *See* PHOTOPERIODISM.

Almost all organisms display circadian rhythms, indicating an evolutionary benefit, most likely facilitating adaptation to the cyclic nature of the environment. Physiological processes that occur with a circadian rhythm range from conidiation (spore production) in the bread mold, *Neurospora crassa*, and leaf movements in plants to rest-activity behavior in animals. Despite the diversity of these phenomena, the basic properties of the rhythms are the same—they synchronize to environmental cues, predominantly light, but are maintained in the absence of such cues, and they display a constant periodicity over a wide temperature range.

In humans, circadian rhythmicity is manifested in the form of sleep-wake cycles, and control of body temperature, blood pressure, heart rate, and release of many endocrine hormones. It is increasingly apparent that temporal ordering is a fundamental aspect of physiological processes. In fact, several disorders such as asthma, stroke, and myocardial infarction also tend to occur more frequently at certain times of the day. Awareness of circadian control has led to the concept of chronotherapeutics, which advocates drug delivery timed to the host's circadian rhythms.

In mammals the "master clock" controlling circadian rhythms is located in the hypothalamus, within a small group of neurons called the suprachiasmatic nucleus. Available data suggest that the suprachiasmatic nucleus transmits signals in the form of humoral factors as well as neural connections. For many years the suprachiasmatic nucleus was thought to be the only site of a clock in mammals. This was in contrast to several other vertebrates where clocks were known to be present in the pineal gland and the eye as well. However, it is now clear that the mammalian eye also contains an oscillator (something that generates an approximately 24-h cycle) whose activity can be assayed by measuring melatonin release in isolated retinas. *See* NERVOUS SYSTEM (INVERTEBRATE); NERVOUS SYSTEM (VERTEBRATE).

The genetic basis of circadian rhythms was established through the identification of altered circadian patterns that were inherited. Such mutants were found first in *Drosophila* and then in *Neurospora* in the early 1970s. In addition, there is now an impetus to identify circadian abnormalities or naturally occurring variations in human populations. For instance, the difference between people that wake up and function most effectively in the early morning hours as opposed to those who prefer to sleep late into the morning may well lie in polymorphisms within clock genes.

It is now known that a feedback loop composed of cycling gene products that influence their own synthesis underlies overt rhythms in at least three organisms (*Drosophila*, *Neurospora*, and cyanobacteria) and most likely in a fourth (mammals). Similar feedback loops have also been found in plants, although it is not clear that they are part of the clock.

[A.Se.]

Biological productivity   The amount and rate of production which occur in a given ecosystem over a given time period. It may apply to a single organism, a population, or entire communities and ecosystems. Productivity can be expressed in terms of dry matter produced per area per time (net production), or in terms of energy produced per area per time (gross production = respiration + heat losses + net production). In aquatic systems, productivity is often measured in volume instead of area. *See* BIOMASS.

Ecologists distinguish between primary productivity (by autotrophs) and secondary productivity (by heterotrophs). Plants have the ability to use the energy from sunlight to convert carbon dioxide and water into glucose and oxygen, producing biomass through photosynthesis. Primary productivity of a community is the rate at which biomass is produced per unit area by plants, expressed in either units of energy [joules/$(m^2)(day)$] or dry organic matter [kg/$(m^2)(year)$]. The following definitions are useful in calculating production: Gross primary production (GPP) is the total energy fixed by photosynthesis per unit time. Net primary production (NPP) is the gross production minus losses due to plant respiration per unit time, and it represents the actual new biomass that is available for consumption by heterotrophic organisms. Secondary production is the rate of production of biomass by heterotrophs (animals, microorganisms), which feed on plant products or other heterotrophs. *See* PHOTOSYNTHESIS.

Productivity is not spread evenly across the planet. For instance, although oceans cover two-thirds of Earth's surface, they account for only one-third of the Earth's productivity. Furthermore, the factors that limit productivity in the ocean differ from those limiting productivity on land, producing differences in geographic patterns of productivity in the two systems. In terrestrial ecosystems, productivity shows a latitudinal trend, with highest productivity in the tropics and decreasing progressively toward the Poles; but in the ocean there is no latitudinal trend, and the highest values of net primary production are found along coastal regions.   [D.C.C.; E.Gry.]

Biological specificity   The orderly patterns of metabolic and developmental reactions giving rise to the unique characteristics of the individual and of its species. Biological specificity is most pronounced and best understood at the cellular and molecular levels of organization, where the shapes of individual molecules allow them to selectively recognize and bind to one another. The main principle which guides this recognition is termed complementarity. Just as a hand fits perfectly into a glove, molecules which are complementary have mirror-image shapes that allow them to selectively bind to each other.

This ability of complementary molecules to specifically bind to one another plays many essential roles in living systems. For example, the transmission of specific hereditary traits from parent to offspring depends upon the ability of the individual strands of a deoxyribonucleic acid (DNA) molecule to specifically generate two new strands with complementary sequences. Similarly, metabolism, which provides organisms with both the energy and chemical building blocks needed for survival, is made possible by the ability of enzymes to specifically bind to the substrates whose interconversions they catalyze. During embryonic development, individual cells associate with each other in precise patterns to form tissues, organs, and organ systems. These ordered interactions are ultimately dependent upon the ability of individual cells to recognize and specifically bind to other cells of a similar type. *See* DEOXYRIBONUCLEIC ACID (DNA); ENZYME; METABOLISM.

In addition to binding to one another, cells can interact by releasing hormones into the bloodstream. Though all of an organism's cells are exposed to hormones circulating in the bloodstream, only a small number of target cells respond to any particular hormone. This selectivity occurs because the specific receptor molecules to which hormones bind are restricted to certain cell types. Thus each hormone exerts its effects on a few selected cell types because only those cells contain the proper receptor. Specific receptors are also involved in interactions between neurotransmitters and the cells they stimulate or inhibit, between certain types of drugs and the cells they affect, and between viruses and the cells they infect. This last phenomenon has an important influence on the susceptibility of individuals to virally transmitted diseases. *See* ENDOCRINE MECHANISMS; HORMONE.

Although most examples of biological specificity are based upon interactions occurring at the molecular level, such phenomena affect many properties manifested at the level of the whole organism. The ability of individuals to defend against infectious diseases, for example, requires the production of antibody molecules which specifically bind to bacteria and viruses. The fertilization of an egg by a sperm is facilitated by specific recognition between molecules present on the surfaces of the sperm and egg cells. Even communication between organisms can be mediated by specific chemical signals, called pheromones. Such chemical signals are utilized in trail marking by ants and bees, in territory marking by certain mammals, and as sexual attractants. Specific molecular interactions thus exert influences ranging from the replication of genes to the behavior of organisms. *See* IMMUNOLOGY; MOLECULAR BIOLOGY; PHEROMONE.   [L.J.Kl.]

Biologicals   Biological products used to induce immunity to various infectious diseases or noxious substances of biological origin. The term is usually limited to immune serums, antitoxins, vaccines, and toxoids that have the effect of providing protective substances of the same general nature that a person develops naturally from having survived an infectious disease or having experienced repeated contact with a biological poison. As a matter of governmental regulatory convenience, certain therapeutic substances which have little to do with conferring immunity have been classified as biological products primarily because they are derived from human or animal sources and are tested for safety by methods similar to those used for many biological products. *See* IMMUNITY.

One major class of biologicals includes the animal and human immune serums. All animals, including humans, develop protective substances in their blood plasma during recovery from many (but not all) infectious diseases or following the injection of toxins or killed bacteria and viruses. These protective substances, called antibodies, usually are found in the immunoglobulin fraction of the plasma and are specific since they react with and neutralize only substances identical or closely similar to those that caused them to be formed. *See* ANTIBODY; IMMUNOGLOBULIN; SERUM.

Antibody-containing serum from another animal is useful in the treatment, modification, or prevention of certain diseases of humans when it is given by intramuscular or intravenous injection. The use of these preformed "borrowed" antibodies is called passive immunization, to distinguish it from active immunization, in which each person develops his or her own antibodies. Passive immunization has the advantage of providing immediate protection, but it is temporary because serum proteins from other animals and even from other humans are rapidly destroyed in the recipient.

Serums which contain antibodies active chiefly in destroying the infecting virus or bacterium are usually called antiserums or immune serums; those containing antibodies capable of neutralizing the secreted toxins of bacteria are called antitoxins. Immune serums have been prepared to neutralize the venoms of certain poisonous snakes and black widow spiders; they are called antivenins.

Because all products used for passive immunization are immune serums, or globulin fractions from such serums, they are named to indicate the diseases that they treat or prevent, the substances that they inhibit or neutralize, the animal from which they came, and whether they are whole serums or the globulin fractions thereof. Thus there is, for example, antipertussis immune rabbit serum, measles immune globulin (human), diphtheria antitoxic globulin (horse), tetanus immune globulin (human), and anti-Rh$_0$ (D) gamma globulin (human).

The use of animal immune serums for prevention of therapy in humans has certain disadvantages. The serum proteins themselves may cause the production of specific antibodies in the recipient of the immune serum, and thus the person may become allergically sensitized to the serum protein of this animal species. *See* ANAPHYLAXIS; HYPERSENSITIVITY.

Products used to produce active immunity constitute the other large class of biological products. They contain the actual toxins, viruses, or bacteria that cause disease, but they are modified in a manner to make them safe to administer. Because the body does not distinguish between the natural toxin or infectious agent and the same material when properly modified, immunity is produced in response to injections of these materials in a manner very similar to that which occurs during the natural disease. Vaccines are suspensions of the killed or attenuated (weakened) bacteria or viruses or fractions thereof. Toxoids are solutions of the chemically altered specific bacterial toxins which cause the major damage produced by bacterial infections. Biological products producing active immunity are usually named to indicate the disease they immunize against and the kind of substance they contain: thus typhoid vaccine, diphtheria toxoid, tetanus toxoid, measles vaccine, mumps vaccine, and poliomyelitis vaccine. *See* VACCINATION.

Another group of biological products consists of reagents used in the diagnosis of infectious diseases. These include immune serums for the serological typing and identification of pathogenic bacteria and viruses, and various antigens for the detection of antibodies in patients' serums as a means of assisting in diagnosis.   [L.F.S.]

Biology   A natural science concerned with the study of all living organisms. Although living organisms share some unifying themes, such as their origin from the same basic cellular structure and their molecular basis of inheritance, they are diverse in many other aspects. The diversity of life leads to many divisions in biological science involved with studying all aspects of living organisms. The primary divisions of study in biology consist of zoology (animals), botany (plants), and protistology (one-celled organisms), and are aimed at examining such topics as origins, structure, function, reproduction, growth and development, behavior, and evolution of the different organisms. In addition, biologists consider how living organisms interact with each other and the environment on an individual as well as group basis. Therefore, within these divisions are many subdivisions such as molecular and cellular biology, microbiology (the study of microbes such as bacteria and viruses), taxonomy (the classification of organisms into special groups), physiology (the study of function of the organism at any level), immunology (the investigation of the immune system), genetics (the study of inheritance), and ecology and evolution (the study of the interaction of an organism with its environment and how that interaction changes over time).

The study of living organisms is an ongoing process that allows observation of the natural world and the acquisition of new knowledge. Biologists accomplish their studies through a process of inquiry known as the scientific method, which approaches a problem or question in a well-defined orderly sequence of steps so as to reach conclusions. The first step involves making systematic observations, either directly through the sense of sight, smell, taste, sound, or touch, or indirectly through the use of special equipment such as the microscope. Next, questions are asked regarding the observations. Then a hypothesis—a tentative explanation or educated guess—is formulated, and predictions about what will occur are made. At the core of any scientific study is testing of the hypothesis. Tests or experiments are designed so as to help substantiate or refute the basic assumptions set forth in the hypothesis. Therefore, experiments are repeated many times. Once they have been completed, data are collected and organized in the form of graphs or tables and the results are analyzed. Also, statistical tests may be performed to help determine whether the data are significant enough to support or disprove the hypothesis. Finally, conclusions are drawn that provide explanations or insights about the original problem. By employing the scientific method, biologists aim to be objective rather than subjective when interpreting the results of their experiments. Biology is not absolute: it is a science that deals with theories or relative truths. Thus, biological conclusions are always subject to change when new evidence is presented. As living organisms continue to evolve and change, the science of biology also will evolve. *See* ANIMAL; BOTANY; CELL BIOLOGY; ECOLOGY; GENETICS; IMMUNOLOGY; MICROBIOLOGY; PLANT; TAXONOMY; ZOOLOGY.   [L.Co.]

Bioluminescence   The emission of light by living organisms that is visible to other organisms. The enzymes and other proteins associated with bioluminescence have been developed and exploited as markers or reporters of other biochemical processes in biomedical research. Bioluminescence provides a unique tool for investigating and understanding numerous basic physiological processes, both cellular and organismic.

Although rare in terms of the total number of luminous species, bioluminescence is phylogenetically diverse, occurring in many different groups (see table). Luminescence

Major groups having luminous species	
Group	Features of luminous displays
Bacteria	Organisms glow constantly; system is autoinduced
Fungi	Mushrooms and mycelia produce constant dim glow
Dinoflagellates	Flagellated algae flash when disturbed
Coelenterates	Jellyfish, sea pansies, and comb jellies emit flashes
Annelids	Marine worms and earthworms exude luminescence
Mollusks	Squid and clams exude luminous clouds; also have photophores
Crustacea	Shrimp, copepods, ostracodes; exude luminescence; also have photophores
Insects	Fireflies (beetles) emit flashes; flies (Diptera) glow
Echinoderms	Brittle stars emit trains of rapid flashes
Fish	Many bony and cartilaginous fish are luminous; some use symbiotic bacteria; others are self-luminous; some have photophores

is unknown in higher plants and in vertebrates above the fishes, and is also absent in several invertebrate phyla. In some phyla or taxa, a substantial proportion of the genera are luminous (for example, ctenophores, about 50%; cephalopods, greater than 50%). Commonly, all members of a luminous genus emit light, but in some cases there are both luminous and nonluminous species.

Bioluminescence is most prevalent in the marine environment; it is greatest at midocean depths, where some daytime illumination penetrates. In these locations, bioluminescence may occur in over 95% of the individuals. Where high densities of luminous organisms occur, their emissions can exert a significant influence on the communities and may represent an important component in the ecology, behavior, and physiology of the latter. Above and below midocean depths, luminescence decreases to less than 10% of all individuals and species; among coastal species, less than 2% are bioluminescent. Firefly displays of bioluminescence are among the most spectacular, but bioluminescence is rare in the terrestrial environment. Other terrestrial luminous forms include millipedes, centipedes, earthworms, and snails, but the display in these is not very bright.

While not metabolically essential, light emission can confer an advantage on the organism. The light can be used in diverse ways. Most of the perceived functions of bioluminescence fall into four categories: defense, offense, communication, and dispersal to enhance propagation.

Bioluminescence does not come from or depend on light absorbed by the organism. It derives from an enzymatically catalyzed chemiluminescence, a reaction in which the energy released is transformed into light energy. One of the reaction intermediates or products is formed in an electronically excited state, which then emits a photon.

Bioluminescence originated and evolved independently many times, and is thus not an evolutionarily conserved function. It has been estimated that present-day luminous organisms come from as many as 30 different evolutionarily distinct origins. In the different groups of organisms, the genes and proteins involved are unrelated, and it may be confusing that the substrates and enzymes, though chemically different, are all referred to as luciferin and luciferase, respectively. To be correct and specific, each should be identified with the organism.

Luminous bacteria typically emit a continuous light, usually blue-green. When strongly expressed, a single bacterium may emit 10^4 or 10^5 photons per second. A primary habitat where most species abound is in association with another (higher) organism, dead or alive, where growth and propagation occur. Luminous bacteria are ubiquitous in the oceans and can be isolated from most seawater samples. The most exotic specific associations involve specialized light organs (for example, in fish and squid) in which a pure dense culture of luminous bacteria is maintained. In teleost fishes, 11 different groups carrying such bacteria are known, an exotic example being the flashlight fish.

Of the approximately 70,000 insect genera, only about 100 are classed as luminous. But their luminescence is impressive, especially in the fireflies and their relatives. Fireflies possess ventral light organs on posterior segments; the South American railroad worm, *Phrixothrix*, has paired green lights on the abdominal segments and red head lights; while the click and fire beetles, Pyrophorini, have both running lights (dorsal) and landing lights (ventral). The dipteran cave glow worm, in a different group and probably different biochemically, exudes beaded strings of slime from its ceiling perch, serving to entrap minute flying prey, which are attracted by the light emitted by the animal. The major function of light emission in fireflies is for communication during courtship, typically involving the emission of a flash by one sex as a signal, to which the other sex responds, usually in a species-specific pattern. The time delay between the two may be a signaling feature; for example, it is precisely 2 s in some North America species. But the flashing pattern is also important in some cases, as is the kinetic character of the individual flash (duration; onset and decay kinetics).

The firefly system was the first in which the biochemistry was characterized. In 1947 it was discovered that adenosine triphosphate (ATP) functions to form a luciferyl adenylate intermediate from firefly luciferin. This then reacts with oxygen to form a cyclic luciferyl peroxy species, which breaks down to yield CO_2 and an excited state of the carbonyl product (thus emitting a photon). Luciferase catalyzes both the reaction of luciferin with ATP and the subsequent steps leading to the excited product.

Bioluminescence and chemiluminescence have come into widespread use for quantitative determinations of specific substances in biology and medicine. Luminescent tags have been developed that are as sensitive as radioactivity, and now replace radioactivity in many assays. The biochemistry of different luciferase systems is different, so many different substances can be detected. One of the first, and still widely used, assays involves the use of firefly luciferase for the detection of ATP. The amount of oxygen required for bioluminescence in luminescent bacteria is small, and therefore the reaction readily occurs. Luminous bacteria can be used as a very sensitive test for oxygen, sometimes in situations where no other method is applicable. An oxygen electrode incorporating luminous bacteria has been developed.

Luciferases have also been exploited as reporter genes for many different purposes. Analytically, such systems are virtually unique in that they are noninvasive and nondestructive: the relevant activity can be measured as light emission in the intact cell and in the same cell over the course of time. Examples of the use of luciferase genes are the expression of firefly and bacterial luciferases under the control of circadian promoters; and the use of coelenterate luciferase expressed transgenically (in other organisms) to monitor calcium changes in living cells over time. Green fluorescent protein is widely used as a reporter gene for monitoring the expression of some other gene under study, and for how the expression may differ, for example at different stages of development or as the consequence of some experimental procedure. [J.W.H.]

Biomagnetism   The production of a magnetic field by a living object. The living object presently most studied is the human body, for two purposes: to find new techniques for medical diagnosis, and to gain information about normal physiology. Smaller organisms studied include birds, fishes, and objects as small as bacteria; many scientists believe that biomagnetics is involved in the ability of these creatures to navigate. The body produces magnetic fields in two main ways: by electric currents and by ferromagnetic particles. The electric currents are the ion currents generated by the muscles, nerves, and other organs. For example, the same ion current generated by heart muscle, which provides the basis for the electrocardiogram, also produces a magnetic field over the chest; and the same ion current generated by the brain, which provides the basis for the electroencephalogram, also produces a magnetic field over the head. Ferromagnetic particles are insoluble contaminants of the body; the most important of these are the ferromagnetic dust particles in the lungs, which are primarily Fe_3O_4 (magnetite). Magnetic fields can give information about the internal organs not otherwise available.

These magnetic fields are very weak, usually in the range of 10^{-14} to 10^{-9} tesla; for comparison, the Earth's field is about 10^{-4} T (1 T $= 10^4$ gauss, the older unit of field). The fields at the upper end of this range, say stronger than 10^{-4} T, can be measured with a simple but sensitive magnetometer called the fluxgate; the weaker fields are measured with the extremely sensitive cryogenic magnetometer called the SQUID (superconducting quantum interference device). The levels of the body's fields, whether they are fluctuating or steady, are orders of magnitude weaker than the fluctuating or steady background fields. They can, however, be measured by using either a magnetically shielded room or two detectors connected in opposition so that much of the background is canceled, or a combination of both methods. The organs producing magnetic fields which are of most interest are the brain, the lungs, and the liver. *See* ELECTROENCEPHALOGRAPHY; MIGRATORY BEHAVIOR. [D.C.]

Biomass   The organic materials produced by plants, such as leaves, roots, seeds, and stalks. In some cases, microbial and animal metabolic wastes are also considered biomass. The term "biomass" is intended to refer to materials that do not directly go into foods or consumer products but may have alternative industrial uses. Common sources of biomass are (1) agricultural wastes, such as corn stalks, straw, seed hulls, sugarcane leavings, bagasse, nutshells, and manure from cattle, poultry, and hogs;

(2) wood materials, such as wood or bark, sawdust, timber slash, and mill scrap; (3) municipal waste, such as waste paper and yard clippings; and (4) energy crops, such as poplars, willows, switchgrass, alfalfa, prairie bluestem, corn (starch), and soybean (oil). *See* BIOLOGICAL PRODUCTIVITY.

Biomass is a complex mixture of organic materials, such as carbohydrates, fats, and proteins, along with small amounts of minerals, such as sodium, phosphorus, calcium, and iron. The main components of plant biomass are carbohydrates (approximately 75%, dry weight) and lignin (approximately 25%), which can vary with plant type. The carbohydrates are mainly cellulose or hemicellulose fibers, which impart strength to the plant structure, and lignin, which holds the fibers together. Some plants also store starch (another carbohydrate polymer) and fats as sources of energy, mainly in seeds and roots (such as corn, soybeans, and potatoes).

A major advantage of using biomass as a source of fuels or chemicals is its renewability. Utilizing sunlight energy in photosynthesis, plants metabolize atmospheric carbon dioxide to synthesize biomass. An estimated 140 billion metric tons of biomass are produced annually.

Major limitations of solid biomass fuels are difficulty of handling and lack of portability for mobile engines. To address these issues, research is being conducted to convert solid biomass into liquid and gaseous fuels. Both biological means (fermentation) and chemical means (pyrolysis, gasification) can be used to produce fluid biomass fuels. For example, methane gas is produced in China for local energy needs by anaerobic microbial digestion of human and animal wastes. Ethanol for automotive fuels is currently produced from starch biomass in a two-step process: starch is enzymatically hydrolyzed into glucose; then yeast is used to convert the glucose into ethanol. About 1.5 billion gallons of ethanol are produced from starch each year in the United States.   [B.Y.Ta.]

Biome   A major community of plants and animals having similar life forms or morphological features and existing under similar environmental conditions. The biome, which may be used at the scale of entire continents, is the largest useful biological community unit. In Europe the equivalent term for biome is major life zone, and throughout the world, if only plants are considered, the term used is formation. *See* ECOLOGICAL COMMUNITIES.

Each biome may contain several different types of ecosystems. For example, the grassland biome may contain the dense tallgrass prairie with deep, rich soil, while the desert grassland has a sparse plant canopy and a thin soil. However, both ecosystems have grasses as the predominant plant life form, grazers as the principal animals, and a climate with at least one dry season. Additionally, each biome may contain several successional stages. A forest successional sequence may include grass dominants at an early stage, but some forest animals may require the grass stage for their habitat, and all successional stages constitute the climax forest biome. *See* DESERT; ECOLOGICAL SUCCESSION; ECOSYSTEM; GRASSLAND ECOSYSTEM.

Distributions of animals are more difficult to map than those of plants. The life form of vegetation reflects major features of the climate and determines the structural nature of habitats for animals. Therefore, the life form of vegetation provides a sound basis for ecologically classifying biological communities. Terrestrial biomes are usually identified by the dominant plant component, such as the temperate deciduous forest. Marine biomes are mostly named for physical features, for example, for marine upwelling, and for relative locations, such as littoral. Many biome classifications have been proposed, but a typical one might include several terrestrial biomes such as desert, tundra, grassland, savanna, coniferous forest, deciduous forest, and tropical forest. Aquatic biome examples are fresh-water lotic (streams and rivers), fresh-water lentic (lakes and ponds), and marine littoral, neritic, upwelling, coral reef, and pelagic. *See* FRESH-WATER ECOSYSTEM; MARINE ECOLOGY; PLANTS, LIFE FORMS OF. [P.Ri.]

Biomechanics   A field that combines the disciplines of biology and engineering mechanics and utilizes the tools of physics, mathematics, and engineering to quantitatively describe the properties of biological materials. One of its basic properties is embodied in so-called constitutive laws, which fundamentally describe the properties of constituents, independent of size or geometry, and specifically how a material deforms in response to applied forces. For most inert materials, measurement of the forces and deformations is straightforward by means of commercially available devices or sensors that can be attached to a test specimen. Many materials, ranging from steel to rubber, have linear constitutive laws, with the proportionality constant (elastic modulus) between the deformation and applied forces providing a simple index to distinguish the soft rubber from the stiff steel. While the same basic principles apply to living tissues, the complex composition of tissues makes obtaining constitutive laws difficult.

Most tissues are too soft for the available sensors, so direct attachment not only will distort what is being measured but also will damage the tissue. Devices are needed that use optical, Doppler ultrasound, electromagnetic, and electrostatic principles to measure deformations and forces without having to touch the tissue.

All living tissues have numerous constituents, each of which may have distinctive mechanical properties. For example, elastin fibers give some tissues (such as blood vessel walls) their spring-like quality at lower loads; inextensible collagen fibers that are initially wavy and unable to bear much load become straightened to bear almost all of the higher loads; and muscle fibers contract and relax to dramatically change their properties from moment to moment. Interconnecting all these fibers are fluids, proteins, and other materials that contribute mechanical properties to the tissue.

The mechanical property of the tissue depends not only upon the inherent properties of its constituents but also upon how the constituents are arranged relative to each other. Thus, different mechanical properties occur in living tissues than in inert materials. For most living tissues, there is a nonlinear relationship between the deformations and the applied forces, obviating a simple index like the elastic modulus to describe the material. In addition, the complex arrangement of the constituents leads to material properties that possess directionality; that is, unlike most inert materials that have the same properties regardless of which direction is examined, living tissues have distinct properties dependent upon the direction examined. Finally, while most inert materials undergo small (a few percent) deformations, many living tissues and cells can deform by several hundred percent. Thus, the mathematics necessary to describe the deformations is much more complicated than with small deformations. [F.C.P.Y.]

The biomechanical properties and behaviors of organs and organ systems stem from the ensemble characteristics of their component cells and extracellular materials, which vary widely in structure and composition and hence in biomechanical properties. An example of this complexity is provided by the cardiovascular system, which is composed of the heart, blood vessels, and blood. *See* CARDIOVASCULAR SYSTEM.

Blood is a suspension of blood cells in plasma. The mammalian red blood cell consists of a membrane enveloping a homogeneous cytoplasm rich in hemoglobin, but it has no nucleus or organelles. While the plasma and the cytoplasm behave as fluids, the red blood cell membrane has viscoelastic properties; its elastic modulus in uniaxial deformation at a constant area is four orders of magnitude lower than that for areal deformation. This type of biomechanical property, which is unusual in nonbiological materials, is attributable to the molecular structure of the membrane:

the lipid membrane has spanning proteins that are linked to the underlying spectrin network. The other blood cells (leukocytes and platelets) and the endothelial cells lining the vessel wall are more complex in composition and biomechanics; they have nuclei, organelles, and a cytoskeletal network of proteins. Furthermore, they have some capacity for active motility. *See* BLOOD; CYTOSKELETON.

Cardiac muscle and vascular smooth muscle cells have organized contractile proteins that can generate active tension in addition to passive elasticity. Muscle cells, like other cells, are surrounded by extracellular matrix, and cell-matrix interaction plays an important role in governing the biomechanical properties and functions of cardiovascular tissues and organs. The study of the overall performance of the cardiovascular system involves measurements of pressure and flow. The pressure-flow relationship results from the interaction of the biomechanical functions of the heart, blood, and vasculature. To analyze the biomechanical behavior of cells, tissues, organs, and systems, a combination of experimental measurements and theoretical modeling is necessary. *See* MUSCLE.

Other organ systems present many quantitative and qualitative differences in biomechanical properties. For example, because the cardiovascular system is composed of soft tissues whereas bone is a hard tissue, the viscoelastic coefficients and mechanical behaviors are quite different. Cartilage is intermediate in stiffness and requires a poroelastic theory to explain its behavior in lubrication of joints. In general, living systems differ from most physical systems in their nonhomogeneity, nonlinear behavior, capacity to generate active tension and motion, and ability to undergo adaptive changes and to effect repair. The biomechanical properties of the living systems are closely coupled with biochemical and metabolic activities, and they are controlled and regulated by neural and humoral mechanisms to optimize performance. While the biomechanical behaviors of cells, tissues, and organs are determined by their biochemical and molecular composition, mechanical forces can, in turn, modulate the gene expression and biochemical composition of the living system at the molecular level. Thus, a close coupling exists between biomechanics and biochemistry, and the understanding of biomechanics requires an interdisciplinary approach involving biology, medicine, and engineering.   [S.Chi.; R.Sk.]

Biophysics   A hybrid science involving the overlap of physics, chemistry, and biology. A dominant aspect is the use of the ideas and methods of physics and chemistry to study and explain the structures of living organisms and the mechanisms of life processes. The recognition of biophysics as a separate field is relatively recent, having been brought about, in part, by the invention of physical tools such as the electron microscope, the ultracentrifuge, and the electronic amplifier, which greatly facilitate biophysical research. These tools are peculiarly adapted to the study of problems of great current importance to medicine, problems related to virus diseases, cancer, heart disease, and the like.

The major areas of biophysics are the following:

Molecular biophysics has to do with the study of large molecules and particles of comparable size which play important roles in biology. The most important physical tools for such research are the electron microscope, the ultracentrifuge, and the x-ray diffraction camera. *See* MOLECULAR BIOLOGY.

Radiation biophysics consists of the study of the response of organisms to ionizing radiations, such as alpha, beta, gamma, and x-rays, and to ultraviolet light. The biological responses are death of cells and tissues, if not of whole organisms, and mutation, either somatic or genetic.

Physiological biophysics, called by some classical biophysics, is concerned with the use of physical mechanisms to explain the behavior and the functioning of living organisms or parts of living organisms and with the response of living organisms to physical forces.

Mathematical and theoretical biophysics deals primarily with the attempt to explain the behavior of living organisms on the basis of mathematics and physical theory. Biological processes are being examined in terms of thermodynamics, hydrodynamics, and statistical mechanics. Mathematical models are being investigated to see how closely they simulate biological processes. See BIOMECHANICS; BIOPOTENTIALS AND IONIC CURRENTS; MATHEMATICAL BIOLOGY; MUSCLE PROTEINS; MUSCULAR SYSTEM; THERMOREGU-LATION.
[M.A.L.]

Biopotentials and ionic currents   The voltage differences which exist between separated points in living cells, tissues, organelles, and organisms are called biopotentials. Related to these biopotentials are ionic charge transfers, or currents, that give rise to much of the electrical changes occurring in nerve, muscle, and other electrically active cells. Electrophysiology is the science concerned with uncovering the structures and functions of bioelectrical systems, including the entities directly related to biological potentials and currents. According to their function, these structures are given descriptive names such as channels, carriers, ionophores, gates, and pumps.

The potential difference measured with electrodes between the interior cytoplasm and the exterior aqueous medium of the living cell is generally called the membrane potential or resting potential (E_{RP}). This potential is usually in the order of several tens of millivolts and is relatively constant or steady. The range of E_{RP} values in various striated muscle cells of animals from insects through amphibia to mammals is about -50 to -100 mV (the voltage is negative inside with respect to outside). Nerve cells show a similar range in such diverse species as squid, cuttlefish, crabs, lobsters, frogs, cats, and humans. Similar potentials have been recorded in single tissue culture cells.

Biopotentials arise from the electrochemical gradients established across cell membranes. In most animal cells, potassium ions are in greater concentration internally than externally, and sodium ions are in less concentration internally than externally. Generally, chloride ions are in less concentration inside cells than outside cells, even though there are abundant intracellular fixed negative charges. While calcium ion concentration is relatively low in body fluids external to cells, the concentration of ionized calcium internally is much lower (in the nanomolar range) than that found external to the cells.

Sodium pump. Measurements of ionic movements through cell membranes of muscle fibers by H. B. Steinbach and by L. A. Heppel in the late 1930s and early 1940s found that radioisotopically labeled sodium ion movement through the cell membrane from inside to outside seemed to depend upon the metabolism of the cell. I. M. Glynn showed that the sodium efflux from red cells depended on the ambient glucose concentration, and A. L. Hodgkin and R. D. Keynes demonstrated in squid and *Sepia* giant axons that the sodium efflux could be blocked by a variety of metabolic inhibitors (cyanide, 2,4-dinitrophenol, and azide). It was proposed that a metabolic process (sodium pump) located in the cell membrane extruded sodium from the cell interior against an electrochemical gradient. P. C. Caldwell's experiments on the squid's giant axon in the late 1950s indicated that there was a close relation between the activity of the sodium pump and the intracellular presence of high-energy compounds, such as adenosine triphosphate (ATP) and arginine phosphate. Caldwell suggested that these compounds might be directly involved in the active transport mechanism. Evidence by R. L. Post for red cells and by Caldwell for the giant axon also suggested that there was a coupling between sodium extrusion and potassium uptake. Convincing evidence has been presented that ATP breakdown to adenosine diphosphate and phosphorus (ADP + P) provides the immediate energy for sodium pumping in the squid giant axon. It seems that the sodium pump is a sufficient explanation to account for the high internal potassium and the low internal sodium concentrations in nerve, muscle, and red blood cells. *See* ABSORPTION (BIOLOGY); CELL PERMEABILITY.

Channels. In living cells there are two general types of ion transport processes. In the first, the transported ionic species flows down the gradient of its own electrochemical potential. In the second, there is a requirement for immediate metabolic energy. This first category of bioelectrical events is associated with a class of molecules called channels, embedded in living cell membranes. It is now known that cell membranes contain many types of transmembrane channels. Channels are protein structures that span the lipid bilayers forming the backbones of cell membranes. The cell membranes of nerve, muscle, and other tissues contain ionic channels. These ionic channels have selectivity filters in their lumens such that in the open state only certain elementary ion species are admitted to passage, with the exclusion of other ion species. *See* CELL MEMBRANES.

There are two general types of channels, and these are classified according to the way in which they respond to stimuli. Electrically excitable channels have opening and closing rates that are dependent on the transmembrane electric field. Chemically excitable channels (usually found in synaptic membranes) are controlled by the specific binding of certain activating molecules (agonists) to receptor sites associated with the channel molecule.

Calcium channels are involved in synaptic transmission. When a nerve impulse arrives at the end of a nerve fiber, calcium channels open in response to the change in membrane potential. These channels admit calcium ions, which act on synaptic vesicles, facilitating their fusion with the presynaptic membrane. Upon exocytosis, these vesicles release transmitter molecules, which diffuse across the synaptic cleft to depolarize the postsynaptic membrane by opening ionic channels. Transmitter activity ceases from the action of specific transmitter esterases or by reabsorption of transmitter back into vesicles in the presynaptic neuron. Calcium channels inactivate and close until another nerve impulse arrives at the presynaptic terminal. Thus biopotentials play an important role in both the regulation and the genesis of synaptic transmission at the membrane channel level.

Ionic currents flow through open channels. The ion impermeable membrane lipid bilayer acts as a dielectric separating two highly conductive salt solutions. Ionic channels have the electrical property of a conductance between these solutions. The membrane conductance at any moment depends on the total number of channels, the type of channels, the fraction of channels found in the open state, and the unit conductances of these open channels. The most common channels directly giving rise to biopotentials are those admitting mainly sodium ions, potassium ions, chloride ions, or calcium ions. These channels are named after the predominant charge carrier admitted in the open state, such as potassium channels. It is now known that there are charged amino acid groups lining the channel lumen that determine the specificity of the channel for particular ions. These selectivity filters admit only ions of the opposite charge.

Hodgkin and A. F. Huxley proposed in 1952 that there were charged molecular entities responsible for the opening and closing of the ionic conductance pathways. These structures had to be charged to be able to move in response to changing electrical forces when the membrane voltage changed. Any movement of the gating structures would require a movement of charge and hence should have a detectable component of current flow across the membrane. It was not until 1973 that the existence of a gating current in squid axon sodium channels was demonstrated, and gating currents and their significance became a lively endeavor in membrane biophysics. *See* BIOPHYSICS.

[W.J.A.]

Biorheology   The study of the flow and deformation of biological materials. The behavior and fitness of living organisms depend partly on the mechanical properties of their structural materials. Thus, biologists are interested in biorheology from the point of view of evolution and adaptation to the environment. Physicians are interested in it in order to understand health and disease. Bioengineers devise methods to measure or to change the rheological properties of biological materials, develop mathematical descriptions of biorheology, and create new practical applications for biorheology in agriculture, industry, and medicine.

The rheological behavior of most biological materials is more complex than that of air, water, and most structural materials used in engineering. Air and water are viscous fluids; all fluids whose viscosity is similar to that of air and water are called newtonian fluids. Biological fluids such as protoplasm, blood, and synovial fluid behave differently, however, and they are called non-newtonian fluids. For example, blood behaves like a fluid when it flows, but when it stops flowing it behaves like a solid with a small but finite yield stress.

Most materials used in engineering construction, such as steel, aluminum, or rock, obey Hooke's law, according to which stresses are linearly proportional to strains. These materials deviate from Hooke's law only when approaching failure. A structure made of Hookean materials behaves linearly: load and deflection a relinearly proportional to each other in such a structure. Some biological materials, such as bone and wood, also obey Hooke's law in their normal state of function, but many others, such as skin, tendon, muscle, blood vessels, lung, and liver, do not. These materials, referred to as non-Hookean, become stiffer as stress increases. *See* BONE.

In biorheology, so-called constitutive equations are used to describe the complex mechanical behavior of materials in terms of mathematics. At least three kinds of constitutive equations are needed: those describing stress-strain relationships of material in the normal state of life; those describing the transport of matter, such as water, gas, and other substances, in tissues; and those describing growth or resorption of tissues in response to long-term changes in the state of stress and strain. The third type is the most fascinating, but there is very little quantitative information available about it except for bone. The second type is very complex because living tissues are nonhomogeneous, and since mass transport in tissues is a molecular phenomenon, it is accentuated by nonhomogeneity at the cellular level. The best-known constitutive equations are therefore of the first kind. *See* BIOMECHANICS.

[Y.C.F.]

Biosensor   An integrated device consisting of a biological recognition element and a transducer capable of detecting the biological reaction and converting it into a signal which can be processed. Ideally, the sensor should be self-contained, so that it is not necessary to add reagents to the sample matrix to obtain the desired response. There are a number of analytes (the target substances to be detected) which are measured in biological media: pH, partial pressure of carbon dioxide (pCO_2), partial pressure of oxygen (pO_2), and the ionic concentrations of sodium, potassium, calcium, and chloride. However, these sensors do not use biological recognition elements, and are considered chemical sensors. Normally, the biological recognition element is a protein or protein complex which is able to recognize a particular analyte in the presence of many other components in a complex biological matrix. This definition has since been expanded to include oligonucleotides. The recognition process involves a chemical or biological reaction, and the transducer must be capable of detecting not only the reaction but also its extent. An ideal sensor should yield a selective, rapid, and reliable response to the analyte, and the signal generated by the sensor should be proportional to the analyte concentration.

Biosensors are typically classified by the type of recognition element or transduction element employed. A sensor might be described as a catalytic biosensor if its recognition element comprised an enzyme or series of enzymes, a living tissue slice (vegetal or animal), or whole cells derived from microorganisms such as bacteria, fungi, or yeast. The sensor might be described as a bioaffinity sensor if the basis of its operation were a biospecific complex formation. Accordingly, the reaction of an antibody with an antigen or hapten, or the reaction of an agonist or antagonist with a receptor, could be employed. In the former case, the sensor might be called an immunosensor.

Since enzyme-based sensors measure the rate of the enzyme-catalyzed reaction as the basis for their response, any physical measurement which yields a quantity related to this rate can be used for detection. The enzyme may be immobilized on the end of an optical fiber, and the spectroscopic properties (absorbance, fluorescence, chemiluminescence) related to the disappearance of the reactants or appearance of products of the reaction can be measured. Since biochemical reactions can be either endothermic (absorbing heat) or exothermic (giving off heat), the rate of the reaction can be measured by microcalorimetry. Miniaturized thermistor-based calorimeters, called enzyme thermistors, have been developed and widely applied, especially for bioprocess monitoring.

In the case of affinity biosensors, as is true of catalytic biosensors, many physical techniques can be used to detect affinity binding: microcalorimetry (thermometric enzyme-linked immunosorbent assay, or TELISA), fluorescence energy transfer, fluorescence polarization, or bioluminescence.

The quality of the results obtained from sensors based on biological recognition elements depends most heavily on their ability to react rapidly, selectively, and with high affinity. Antibodies and receptors frequently react with such high affinity that the analyte does not easily become unbound. To reuse the sensor requires a time-consuming regeneration step. Nonetheless, if this step can be automated, semicontinuous monitoring may be possible.   [G.S.W.]

Biosynthesis   The synthesis of more complex molecules from simpler ones in cells by a series of reactions mediated by enzymes. The overall economy and survival of the cell is governed by the interplay between the energy gained from the breakdown of compounds and that supplied to biosynthetic reaction pathways for the synthesis of compounds having a functional role, such as deoxyribonucleic acid (DNA), ribonucleic acid (RNA), and enzymes. Biosynthetic pathways give rise to two distinct classes of metabolite, primary and secondary. Primary metabolites (DNA, RNA, fatty acids, α-amino acids, chlorophyll in green plants, and so forth) are essential to the metabolic functioning of the cells. Secondary metabolites (antibiotics, alkaloids, pheromones, and so forth) aid the functioning and survival of the whole organism more generally. Unlike primary metabolites, secondary metabolites are often unique to individual organisms or classes of organisms. *See* ENZYME; METABOLISM.

The selective pressures that drive evolution have ensured a diverse array of secondary metabolite structures. Secondary metabolites can be grouped to some extent by virtue of their origin from key biosynthetic pathways. It is often in the latter stages of these pathways that the structural diversity is introduced. All terpenes, for example, originate from the C_5 (five-carbon) intermediate isopentenyl pyrophosphate via mevalonic acid. The mammalian steroids, such as cholesterol, derive from the C_{30} steroid lanosterol, which is constructed from six C_5 units. Alternatively, C_{10} terpenes (for example, menthol from peppermint leaves) and C_{15} terpenes (for example, juvenile hormone III from the silk worm) are derived after the condensation of two and three C_5 units, respectively, and then with further enzymatic customization in each case. *See* CHOLESTEROL; ORGANIC EVOLUTION; STEROID.

[D.O'H.]

Biotechnology   Generally, any technique that is used to make or modify the products of living organisms in order to improve plants or animals, or to develop useful microorganisms. In modern terms, biotechnology has come to mean the use of cell and tissue culture, cell fusion, molecular biology, and in particular, recombinant deoxyribonucleic acid (DNA) technology to generate unique organisms with new traits or organisms that have the potential to produce specific products. Some examples of products in a number of important disciplines are described below.

Recombinant DNA technology has opened new horizons in the study of gene function and the regulation of gene action. In particular, the ability to insert genes and their controlling nucleic acid sequences into new recipient organisms allows for the manipulation of these genes in order to examine their activity in unique environments, away from the constraints posed in their normal host. Genetic transformation normally is achieved easily with microorganisms; new genetic material may be inserted into them, either into their chromosomes or into extrachromosomal elements, the plasmids. Thus, bacteria and yeast can be created to metabolize specific products or to produce new products. *See* GENE; GENE ACTION; PLASMID.

Genetic engineering has allowed for significant advances in the understanding of the structure and mode of action of antibody molecules. Practical use of immunological techniques is pervasive in biotechnology. *See* ANTIBODY.

Few commercial products have been marketed for use in plant agriculture, but many have been tested. Interest has centered on producing plants that are resistant to specific herbicides. This resistance would allow crops to be sprayed with the particular herbicide, and only the weeds would be killed, not the genetically engineered crop species. Resistances to plant virus diseases have been induced in a number of crop species by transforming plants with portions of the viral genome, in particular the virus's coat protein.

Biotechnology also holds great promise in the production of vaccines for use in maintaining the health of animals. Interferons are also being tested for their use in the management of specific diseases.

Animals may be transformed to carry genes from other species including humans and are being used to produce valuable drugs. For example, goats are being used to produce tissue plasminogen activator, which has been effective in dissolving blood clots.

Plant scientists have been amazed at the ease with which plants can be transformed to enable them to express foreign genes. This field has developed very rapidly since the first transformation of a plant was reported in 1982, and a number of transformation procedures are available.

Genetic engineering has enabled the large-scale production of proteins which have great potential for treatment of heart attacks. Many human gene products, produced with genetic engineering technology, are being investigated for their potential use as commercial drugs. Recombinant technology has been employed to produce vaccines from subunits of viruses, so that the use of either live or inactivated viruses as immunizing agents is avoided. Cloned genes and specific, defined nucleic acid sequences can be used as a means of diagnosing infectious diseases or in identifying individuals with the potential for genetic disease. The specific nucleic acids used as probes are normally tagged with radioisotopes, and the DNAs of candidate individuals are tested by hybridization to the labeled probe. The technique has been used to detect latent viruses such as herpes, bacteria, mycoplasmas, and plasmodia, and to identify Huntington's disease, cystic fibrosis, and Duchenne muscular dystrophy. It is now also possible to put foreign genes into cells and to target them to specific regions of the recipient genome. This presents the possibility of developing specific therapies for hereditary diseases, exemplified by sickle-cell anemia.

Modified microorganisms are being developed with abilities to degrade hazardous wastes. Genes have been identified that are involved in the pathway known to degrade polychlorinated biphenyls, and some have been cloned and inserted into selected bacteria to degrade this compound in contaminated soil and water. Other organisms are being sought to degrade phenols, petroleum products, and other chlorinated compounds. *See* GENETIC ENGINEERING; MOLECULAR BIOLOGY.   [M.Z.]

Biotin   A vitamin, widespread in nature. It is only sparingly soluble in water; it is stable in boiling water solutions, but can be destroyed by oxidizing agents, acids, and alkalies. Under some conditions, it can be destroyed by oxidation in the presence of rancid fats. Biotin's occurrence in nature is so widespread that it is difficult to prepare a natural deficient diet. Biotin deficiency in animals is associated with dermatitis, loss of hair, muscle incoordination and paralysis, and reproductive disturbances. Biotin deficiency produced in humans by feeding large amounts of egg white resulted in dermatitis, nausea, depression, muscle pains, anemia, and a large increase in serum cholesterol. *See* COENZYME.   [S.N.G.]

Bivalvia   One of the five classes in the phylum Mollusca, sometimes known as Pelecypoda. All bivalves are aquatic, living at all depths of the sea and in brackish and fresh waters. With about 25,000 living species, Bivalvia is second to class Gastropoda (over 74,000) in molluscan species diversity. However, the total biomass of bivalves is much greater, and certain bivalve species are numerically dominant in many benthic ecosystems. The most primitive bivalves are infaunal, burrowing into soft sediments, but many families are epifaunal, attached to rocks or shells or residing on the sediment surface. Bivalves are well represented in the fossil record from the early Paleozoic because of their calcareous shells.

In general, bivalves are bilaterally symmetrical and laterally compressed. They have a fleshy mantle that secretes the shell enclosing the body (see illustration). The mouth is located anteriorly in bivalves; and in the Lamellibranchiata, the largest subclass, the mouth is flanked by paired labial palps that act to sort food prior to ingestion. Sensory organs are located on the outer mantle margin that has the closest contact with the environment. Frequently these sensory organs are borne on tentacles, and they are sensitive to tactile and chemical stimuli. Certain species of scallops have highly developed light-sensing organs or "eyes" on their mantle tentacles.

The shell consists of two valves with a noncalcified connecting ligament holding the valves together at a hinge plate. The shell layers consist of an outer horny periostracum (protective layer) that can be either absent or eroded in some species, a middle prismatic layer consisting of crystalline calcium carbonate, and an inner lamellar or nacreous layer. In some families such as the Mytilidae (mussels) or the Pteriidae (winged or pearl oysters), the nacreous layer can exhibit a beautiful iridescent sheen, whereas in most bivalves the inner layer is smooth but with a chalky appearance. Hinge ligament tension holds the valves in a gaping position, with valve closure effected by adductor muscles.

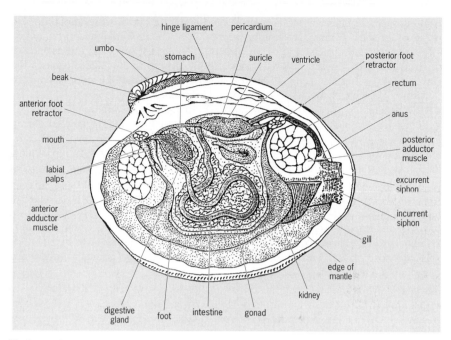

Bivalve anatomy.

   The ciliated molluscan gills, properly called ctenidia, are enlarged in the subclass Lamellibranchiata and occupy a substantial portion of the mantle cavity. The ctenidia consist of layered filaments which function primarily to pump water into the mantle cavity and to filter particulate food from the incurrent water stream. The ctenidia of bivalves of the subclass Protobranchia also serve to pump water, but they are smaller and less developed than in the lamellibranchs and do not serve to filter food particles. Protobranch bivalves are deposit feeders that gather food by extending thin muscular palp proboscides to probe soft sediments and entrap organic detrital particles. Bivalves of the subclass Septibranchia (sometimes called Anomalodesmata) have highly modified ctenidia that lack filaments. A septum divides the mantle cavity into dorsal and ventral chambers, and water is pumped by muscular contraction of the septum wall.

   Some bivalves have a foot for locomotion. If present, the foot can be extended from the shell by blood pressure and dilated to act as an external anchor while movement is effected by contraction of retractor muscles. Some bivalves of the family Pectinidae (scallops) lack a foot but are highly active swimmers through clapping their valves and jetting water through orifices (openings) near the hinge. Some bivalves, such as oysters and giant clams, are sedentary and lack a foot as adults.

   Bivalves exhibit a wide range of reproductive strategies. Most bivalves are dioecious or have separate sexes, while others exhibit various forms of hermaphrodism. For example, as mature adults, scallops carry both eggs and sperm, while oysters exhibit protandric hermaphrodism in which the oysters first develop as males and in subsequent years change sex to develop ovaries. Most species of bivalves shed eggs and sperm directly into the water, where fertilization occurs; in others, eggs may be held in a brood chamber, where they are fertilized by sperm in incurrent water, and released as well-developed larvae into the water. Most bivalves go through several planktonic stages prior to settlement and metamorphosis to their benthic form.

Many species of bivalves are actively farmed either for human consumption of the meats or for shell products. Most of the gem-quality pearls sold in the world originate from farmed pearl oysters of the genus *Pinctada* in Japan, Australia, and islands of the tropical Pacific. Fresh-water pearls are produced from fresh-water mussels in the United States, China, and Japan. Other species of bivalves are of economic concern by virtue of being pest organisms or biological invaders.

The fossil record of the Bivalvia can be traced to the Lower Cambrian *Fordilla*. The Ordovician was a major period of bivalve speciation, but throughout the Paleozoic the Bivalvia remained second to bivalves of the phylum Brachiopoda in species diversity and abundance. During the Mesozoic Era, the brachiopods declined in importance. It is probable that diverse adaptations of the Bivalvia to avoid predatory gastropods, arthropods, and fish evolving during the Mesozoic were a major factor in the replacement of the more exposed brachiopods as the dominant bivalves. The evolutionary radiation occurring during the Mesozoic includes the emergence of many species of bivalves that bore into rocks, hard corals, and wood. The Mesozoic emergent family Ostreidae, which includes oysters, remains to the present. The transition from the Mesozoic to Cenozoic began with the extinction of many ancient families and the emergence of several modern families. *See* MOLLUSCA.   [M.A.Ric.]

Blastomycetes   A class of the subdivision Deuteromycotina comprising anamorphic (asexual or imperfect) yeast fungi that lack fruit bodies (conidiomata), have no dikaryophase, and are usually unicellular rather than filamentous. The thallus consists of individual cells. Approximately 80 genera comprising about 600 species are recognized.

The Blastomycetes, like other groups of deuteromycetes, are artificial, composed entirely of anamorphic fungi of ascomycete or basidiomycete affinity. Taxa are referred to as form genera and form species because the absence of sexual, perfect, or meiotic states forces classification and identification by artificial rather than phylogenetic means. Black yeasts are distinguished from anamorphic yeasts by the presence of melanin in the cell walls, abundant production of septate mycelium (filamentous), and aerial dispersal of conidia. Unlike other deuteromycetes, the number of morphological and developmental features for classification of Blastomycetes, although useful, is limited. The emphasis in yeast systematics has therefore been on physiological and biochemical tests, supplemented extensively by serological, electrophoretic, and molecular techniques.

Anamorphic yeasts can be recovered from most ecological niches—animals, plants and their surfaces, fresh and marine water, soils, and environments such as manufacturing plants, tanning fluids, and mineral oils. Blastomycetes are of great economic importance in two respects: the production of products and the spoilage of raw materials and products. Selected strains of *Saccharomyces cerevisiae* are used in the baking, brewing, distilling, and wine industries.

Blastomycetes are also recognized pathogens in medicine. Both *Candida*, causing candidiasis or candidosis, and *Cryptococcus*, causing cryptococcosis, are opportunistic pathogens that cause systemic infections only in individuals with lowered resistance. Esophageal candidiasis and cryptococcosis of the central nervous system are both regarded as being particularly strong indicators of AIDS. *See* DEUTEROMYCOTINA; EUMYCOTA; FUNGI; YEAST.   [B.C.S.]

Blastulation   The formation of a segmentation cavity or blastocoele within a mass of cleaving blastomeres and rearrangement of blastomeres around this cavity in such a way as to form the type of definitive blastula characteristic of each species.

The blastocoele originates as an intercellular space which sometimes arises as early as the four- or eight-cell stage. Thus blastulation is initiated during early cleavage stages, and formation of the definitive blastula is thought to terminate cleavage and to initiate gastrulation. Initially the diameter of the blastula is no greater than that of the activated egg; subsequently it increases. See GASTRULATION.

The blastula is usually a hollow sphere. Its wall may vary from one to several cells in thickness. In eggs which contain considerable amounts of yolk the blastocoele may be eccentric in position, that is, shifted toward the animal pole. The animal portion of its wall is always completely divided into relatively small cells, whereas the vegetative portion tends to be composed of relatively large cells and may be incompletely cellulated in certain species. The blastocoele contains a gelatinous or jellylike fluid, which originates in part as a secretion by the blastomeres and in part by passage of water through the blastomeres or intercellular material, or both, into the blastocoele.

The wall of the blastula is a mosaic of cellular areas, each of which will normally produce a certain structure during subsequent development. In other words, each area of cells in the wall of the blastula has a certain prospective fate which will be realized in normal development.   [R.L.W.]

Blood   The fluid that circulates in the blood vessels of the body. Blood consists of plasma and cells floating within it. The cells are derived from extravascular sites and then enter the circulatory system. They frequently leave the blood vessels to enter the extravascular spaces, where some of them may be transformed into connective tissue cells. The fluid part of the blood is in equilibrium with the tissue fluids of the body. The circulating blood carries nutrients and oxygen to the body cells, and is thus an important means of maintaining the homeostasis of the body. It carries hormones from their sites of origin throughout the body, and is thus the transmitter of the chemical integrators of the body. Blood plasma also circulates immune bodies and contains several of the components essential for the formation of blood clots. Finally, blood transports waste products to excretory organs for elimination from the body. Because of its basic composition (cells surrounded by a matrix), development, and ability to modify into other forms of connective tissues, blood can be regarded as a special form of connective tissue. See CONNECTIVE TISSUE.

Formed elements. The cells of the blood include the red blood cells and the white blood cells. In all vertebrates, except nearly all mammals, the red blood cells or corpuscles contain a nucleus and cytoplasm rich in hemoglobin. In nearly all mammals the nucleus has been extruded during the developmental stages.

In normal adult men the blood contains about 5,000,000 red blood corpuscles or erythrocytes per cubic millimeter; in normal adult women, about 4,500,000. Human erythrocytes are about 8 micrometers in diameter and about 2 μm at their thickest and have a biconcave shape. They contain hemoglobin, which imparts to them their color, and possess an envelope. When circulating in the blood vessels, the red blood cells are not evenly dispersed. In the capillaries the erythrocytes are often distorted. In certain conditions they may be densely aggregated. This is known as a sludge. The erythrocytes respond to changes in osmotic pressure of the surrounding fluid by swelling in hypotonic fluids and by shrinking irregularly in hypertonic fluids. Shrunken red blood cells are referred to as crenated cells. The average life of the mature red blood cells is surprisingly long, having a span of about 120 days. See HEMOGLOBIN.

In humans the white blood cells in the blood are fewer in number. There are about 5000–9000/mm^3. In general, there are two varieties, agranular and granular. The agranular cells include the small, medium, and large lymphocytes and the monocytes

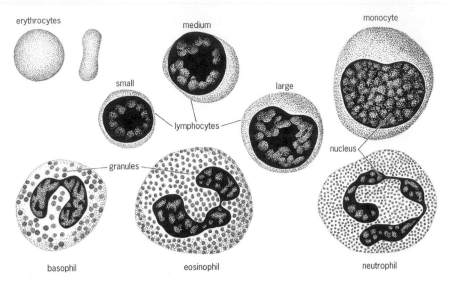

erythrocytes

medium

monocyte

small

large

lymphocytes

nucleus

granules

basophil

eosinophil

neutrophil

Diagrammatic representation of human blood cells.

(see illustration). The small lymphocytes are spherical, about the diameter of erythrocytes or a little larger, and constitute about 20–25% of the white blood cells. The medium and large lymphocytes are relatively scarce. In all lymphocytes the nucleus occupies nearly the whole volume of the cell, and the cytoplasm which surrounds it forms a thin shell. The typical monocyte is commonly as large as a large lymphocyte (12 μm), and constitutes 3–8% of the white blood cells. The nucleus is relatively small, eccentric, and oval or kidney-shaped. The cytoplasm is relatively larger in volume than that in lymphocytes.

The granular leukocytes are of three varieties: neutrophil, eosinophil, and basophil. Their structure varies somewhat in different species, and the following applies to those of humans. The neutrophils make up 65–75% of the leukocytes. They are about as large as monocytes with a highly variable nucleus, consisting of three to five lobes joined together by threads of chromatin. The cytoplasm contains numerous minute granules which stain with neutral dyes and eosin. The eosinophils (also called acidophils) are about the same size as the neutrophils but are less numerous, constituting about 1% of the leukocytes. The nucleus commonly contains but two lobes joined by a thin thread of chromatin. The granules which fill the cytoplasm are larger than those of the neutrophils and stain with acid dyes. The basophils are about the same size as the other granular leukocytes. The nucleus may appear elongated or with one or more constrictions. The granules are moderately large, stain with basic dyes, and are water-soluble.

The functions of the leukocytes while they are circulating in the blood are not known. However, when they leave the blood vessels and enter the connective tissue, they constitute an important part of the defense mechanism and of the repair mechanism. Many of the cells are actively phagocytic and engulf debris and bacteria. Lymphocytes are of two major kinds, T cells and B cells. They are involved in the formation of antibodies and in cellular immunity.

The blood platelets are small spindle-shaped or rodlike bodies about 3 μm long and occur in large numbers in circulating blood. In suitably stained specimens they consist of a granular central portion (chromomere) embedded in a homogeneous matrix (hyalomere). They change their shape rapidly on contact with injured vessels or foreign surfaces and take part in clot formation. The platelets are not to be regarded as cells and are thought to be cytoplasmic bits broken off from their cells of origin in bone marrow, the megakaryocytes.   [I.G.]

Plasma. Plasma is the residual fluid of blood left after removal of the cellular elements. Serum is the fluid which is obtained after blood has been allowed to clot and the clot has been removed. Serum and plasma differ only in their content of fibrinogen and several minor components which are in large part removed in the clotting process. *See* SERUM.

The major constituents of plasma and serum are proteins. The total protein concentration of human serum is approximately 7 g/ml, and most other mammals show similar levels. By various methods it can be demonstrated that serum protein is a heterogeneous mixture of a large number of constituents. Only a few are present in higher concentrations, the majority being present in trace amounts. More than 60 protein components have been identified and characterized. Albumin makes up more than one-half of the total plasma proteins and has a molecular weight of 69,000. Because of its relatively small molecular size and its high concentration, albumin contributes to 75–80% of the colloid osmotic pressure of plasma. The immunoglobulins, which represent approximately one-sixth of the total protein, largely constitute the γ-globulin fraction. The immunoglobulins are antibodies circulating in the blood, and therefore are also called humoral antibodies. They are of great importance in the organism's defense against infectious agents, as well as other foreign substances. *See* IMMUNOGLOBULIN.

In addition to the proteins, many other important classes of compounds circulate in the blood plasma. Most of these are smaller molecules which diffuse freely through cell membranes and are, therefore, more similarly distributed throughout all the fluids of the body and not as characteristic for plasma or serum as the proteins. In terms of their concentration and their function, the electrolytes are most important. They are the primary factors in the regulation of the osmotic pressure of plasma, and contribute also to the control of the pH. The chief cations are sodium, potassium, calcium, and magnesium. The chief anions are chloride, bicarbonate, phosphate, sulfate, and organic acids. The circulating blood also contains the many small compounds which are transported to the sites of synthesis of larger molecules in which they are incorporated, or which are shifted as products of metabolic breakdown to the sites of their excretion from the body.   [H.Cl.]

Coagulation. When mammalian blood is shed, it congeals rapidly into a gelatinous clot of enmeshed fibrin threads which trap blood cells and serum. Modern theories envision a succession of reactions leading to the formation of insoluble fibrin from a soluble precursor, fibrinogen (factor I). Blood also clots when it touches glass or other negatively charged surfaces, through reactions described as the intrinsic pathway. Several of the steps in this process are dependent upon the presence in blood of calcium ions and of phospholipids, the latter derived principally from blood platelets. The coagulation of blood can also be induced by certain snake venoms which either promote the formation of thrombin or clot fibrinogen directly, accounting in part for their toxicity.

Platelets, besides furnishing phospholipids for the clotting process, help to stanch the flow of blood from injured blood vessels by accumulating at the point of injury, forming a plug. Platelets participate in the phenomenon of clot retraction, in which the blood clot shrinks, expelling liquid serum. Although the function of retraction is unknown, individuals in whom this process is impaired have a bleeding tendency.

Hereditary deficiencies of the function of each of the protein-clotting factors have been described, notably classic hemophilia and Christmas disease, which are disorders of males and clinically indistinguishable. The various hereditary functional deficiencies are associated with a bleeding tendency with one inexplicable exception. Acquired deficiencies of clotting factors, sometimes of great complexity, are also recognized. Therapy for bleeding due to deficiencies of clotting factors often includes the transfusion of blood plasma or fractions of plasma rich in particular substances the patient may lack. *See* HUMAN GENETICS.

Clinical tests of the coagulability of the blood include (1) determination of the clotting time, that is, the time elapsing until shed blood clots; (2) the prothrombin time, the time elapsing until plasma clots in the presence of tissue thromboplastin (and therefore a measure of the extrinsic pathway of clotting); (3) the partial thromboplastin time, the time elapsing until plasma clots in the presence of crude phospholipid (and therefore a measure of the intrinsic pathway of clotting); (4) the enumeration of platelets; and (5) crude quantification of clot retraction and of the various plasma protein-clotting factors.

Heparin, a polysaccharide–sulfuric acid complex found particularly in the liver and lungs, impairs coagulation; its presence in normal blood is disputed. Both coumarin and heparin are used clinically to impede coagulation in thrombotic states, including thrombophlebitis and coronary heart disease. *See* FIBRINOGEN.   [O.D.R.]

Blood groups   Genetically determined markers on the surface of cellular blood elements (red and white blood cells, platelets). In medicine, the matching of ABO and Rh groups of recipients and donors before blood transfusion is of paramount importance; other blood groups also can be implicated in incompatibility. Markers on white cells (histocompatibility antigens) are shared by a number of body tissue cells; these markers are important to the survival of transplanted organs and bone marrow. In law, the recognition of identity between bloodstains found at the scene of a crime and those on clothing of a suspect has resulted in many convictions, and blood typing has served to resolve paternity disputes. From an anthropologic standpoint, some blood groups are unique to specific populations and can be a reflection of tribal origin or migration patterns. Blood groups are also valuable markers in gene linkage analysis, and their study has contributed enormously to the mapping of the human genome.

Table 1. ABO blood group system

Blood group	RBC antigens	Possible genotypes	Plasma antibody
A	A	A/A or A/O	anti-B
B	B	B/B or B/O	anti-A
O	—	O/O	Anti-A and anti-B
AB	A and B	A/B	—

Antibodies. Human blood can be classified into different groups based on the reactions of red blood cells with blood group antibodies (Table 1). Naturally acquired antibodies, such as anti-A and anti-B antibodies, are normally found in serum from persons whose red blood cells lack the corresponding antigen. It is thought that they are stimulated by antigens present in the environment, and are acquired by infants within months of birth. Because anti-A and anti-B antibodies can cause rapid, life-threatening destruction of incompatible red blood cells, blood for transfusion is always selected to be compatible with the plasma of the recipient. *See* ANTIBODY; ANTIGEN.

Most blood group antibodies, including Rh antibodies, are immune in origin and do not appear in serum or plasma unless the host is exposed directly to foreign red

Table 2. Human blood group systems

System name	ISBT* symbol	System number	Antigens in system	Chromosome location[†]	Gene products
ABO	ABO	001	4	9q34.1-q34.2	$A = \alpha$-N-acetylgalactosaminyl transferase $B = \alpha$-galactosyl transferase
MNS	MNS	002	43	4q28-q31	GYPA = glycophorin A; 43-kDa single-pass glycoprotein GYPB = glycophorin B; 25-kDa single-pass glycoprotein
Rh	RH	004	45	1p36.13-p34	RHD and RHCE, 30–32-kDa multipass polypeptides
Lutheran	LU	005	18	19q13.2	78- and 85-kDa single-pass glycoproteins
Kell	KEL	006	23	7q33	93-KDa single-pass glycoprotein
Duffy	FY	008	6	1q22-q23	38.5-kDa multipass glycoprotein
Diego	DI	010	18	17q12-q21	95–105-kDa multipass glycoprotein
Xg	XG	012	1	Xp22.32	22–29-kDa single-pass glycoprotein

*International Society of Blood Transfusion.
[†]Chromosome locations of genes/loci are identified by the arm (p = short; q = long), followed by the region, then by the band within the region, in both cases numbered from the centromere; ter = end.

blood cell antigens. The most common stimulating event is blood transfusion or pregnancy. Because of the large number of different blood group antigens, it is impossible, when selecting blood for transfusion, to avoid transfusing antigens that the recipient lacks. However, these foreign antigens may or may not be immunogenic. A single-unit transfusion of Rh D-positive to an Rh D-negative recipient causes production of anti-D in about 85% of cases. Consequently, in addition to matching for ABO types, Rh D-negative blood is almost always given to Rh D-negative recipients. In pregnancy, fetal red blood cells cross the placenta and enter the maternal circulation, particularly at delivery. The fetal red blood cells may carry paternally derived antigens that are foreign to the mother and stimulate antibody production. These antibodies may affect subsequent pregnancies by destroying the fetal red blood cells and causing a disease known as erythroblastosis fetalis.

Antigens, genes, and blood group systems. Approximately 700 distinct blood group antigens have been identified on human red blood cells. Biochemical analysis has revealed that most antigen structures are either protein or lipid in nature; in some instances, blood group specificity is determined by the presence of attached carbohydrate moieties. The human A and B antigens, for example, can be either glycoprotein or glycolipid, with the same attached carbohydrate structure. With few exceptions, blood group antigens are an integral part of the cell membrane.

A number of different concepts have been put forth to explain the genetics of the human blood groups. The presence of a gene in the host is normally reflected by the presence of the corresponding antigen on the red blood cells. Usually, a single locus determines antigen expression, and there are two or more forms of a gene or alleles (for example, a and b) that can occupy a locus. Each individual inherits one allele from each parent. For a given blood group, when the same allele (for example, allele a) is inherited from both parents, the offspring is homozygous for a and only the antigen structure defined by a will be present on the red blood cells. When different alleles are inherited (that is, a and b), the individual is heterozygous for a (and b), and both a and b antigens will be found on the red blood cells. In some blood group systems, several loci govern the expression of multiple blood group antigens within that system. These loci are usually closely linked, located adjacent to each other on the chromosome. Such complex loci may contain multiple alleles and are referred to as haplotypes.

Some 200 antigens have been assigned to 25 different blood group systems. Eight such systems are shown in the Table 2. For a system to be established, the genes involved must be distinct from other blood group system genes, and either they must be polymorphic (that is, two or more alleles, each with an appreciable frequency in a population) or the chromosome location must be known. Antigens that do not meet the criteria for assignment to a specific blood group system have been placed into collections, based primarily on biochemical data or phenotypic association, or into a series of either high- or low-frequency antigens.

ABO was the first human blood group system to be described. Three major alleles at the *ABO* locus on chromosome 9 govern the expression of A and B antigens. Gene *A* encodes for a protein (α-*N*-acetylgalactosaminyl transferase) that attaches a blood group–specific carbohydrate (α-*N*-acetyl-D-galactosamine) and confers blood group A activity to a preformed carbohydrate structure called H antigen. Gene *B* encodes for an α-galactosyl transferase that attaches α-D-galactose and confers blood group B activity to H antigen. In both instances, some H remains unchanged. The *O* gene has no detectable product; H antigen remains unchanged and is strongly expressed on red blood cells. These three genes account for the inheritance of four common phenotypes: A, B, AB, and O. A and O blood types are the most common, and AB the least common. The *A* and *B* genes are codominant; that is, when the gene is present the antigen can be detected. The *O* gene is considered an amorph since its product cannot be detected. When either A or B antigens are present on red blood cells, the corresponding antibody or antibodies should not be present in the serum or plasma. In adults, when A or B or both are absent from the red blood cells, the corresponding naturally acquired antibody is present in the serum. This reciprocal relationship between antigens on the red blood cells and antibodies in the serum is known as Landsteiner's law. Other ABO phenotypes do exist, but these are quite rare. Further, the A blood type can be subdivided, based on strength of antigen expression, with A_1 red blood cells having the most A antigen.

Currently 45 antigens are assigned to the Rh blood group system, although D is the most important. Red blood cells that carry D are called Rh-positive; red blood cells lacking D are called Rh-negative. Other important Rh antigens are C, c, E, and e. Rh antigen expression is controlled by two adjacent homologous structural genes on chromosome 1 that are inherited as a pair or haplotype. The *RhD* gene encodes D antigen and is absent on both chromosomes of most Rh-negative subjects. The *RhCE* gene encodes CE protein. Nucleotide substitutions account for amino acid differences at two positions on the CE protein, and result in the Cc and Ee polymorphisms.

Biological role. The function of blood group antigens has been increasingly apparent. Single-pass proteins such as the LU and XG proteins are thought to serve as adhesion molecules that interact with integrins on the surface of white blood cells. Multipass proteins such as band 3, which carries the DI system antigens, are involved in the transportation of ions through the red blood cell membrane bilipid layer. Some blood group antigens are essential to the integrity of the red blood cell membrane, for their absence results in abnormal surface shape; for example, absence of KEL protein leads to the formation of acanthocytes, and absence of RH protein results in stomatocytosis and hemolytic anemia. Many membrane structures serve as receptors for bacteria and other microorganisms. For example, the FY or Duffy protein is the receptor on red blood cells for invasion by *Plasmodium vivax*, the cause of benign tertian malaria. Particularly significant is the fact that Fy(a-b-) phenotype is virtually nonexistent among Caucasians but has an incidence of around 70% among African-Americans.

Presumably, the Fy(a-b-) phenotype evolved as a selective advantage in areas where *P. vivax* is endemic. Similarly, the S-s-U-red blood cell phenotype in the MNS blood group system affords protection against *P. falciparum*, or malignant tertian malaria. Yet other blood group antigens can be altered in disease states; A, B, and H antigens are sometimes weakened in leukemia or may be modified by bacterial enzymes in patients with septicemia. *See* BLOOD; IMMUNOLOGY.   [W.J.J.]

Blood vessels   Tubular channels for blood transport, of which there are three principal types: arteries, capillaries, and veins. Only the larger arteries and veins in the body bear distinct names. Arteries carry blood away from the heart through a system of successively smaller vessels. Capillaries are the smallest but most extensive blood vessels, forming a network everywhere in the body tissues. Veins carry blood from the capillary beds back to the heart through increasingly larger vessels. In certain locations blood vessels are modified for particular functions, as the sinusoids of the liver and the spleen and the choroid plexuses of the brain ventricles. *See* LYMPHATIC SYSTEM.   [W.J.B.]

Bone   The hard connective tissue that, together with cartilage, forms the skeleton of humans and other vertebrates. It is made of calcium phosphate crystals arranged on a protein scaffold. Bone performs a variety of functions: it has a structural and mechanical role; it protects vital organs; it provides a site for the production of blood cells; it serves as a reserve of calcium. *See* CONNECTIVE TISSUE.

There are two types of bone in the skeleton: the flat bones (for example, the bones of the skull and ribs) and the long bones (for example, the femur and the bones of the hand and feet). Both types are characterized by an outer layer of dense, compact bone, known as cortical bone, and an inner spongy bone material made up of thin trabeculae, known as cancellous bone. Cortical bone consists of layers of bone (lamellae) in an orderly concentric cylindrical arrangement around tiny Haversian canals. These interconnecting canals carry the blood vessels, lymph vessels, and nerves through the bone and communicate with the periosteum and the marrow cavity. The periosteum is a thin membrane covering the outer surface of bone and consisting of layers of cells that participate in the remodeling and repair of bone. The cancellous bone is in contact with the bone marrow, in which much of the production of blood cells takes place. The interface between the cancellous bone and the marrow is called the endosteum, and it is largely at this site that bone is removed in response to a need for increased calcium elsewhere in the body.

Bone is formed by the laying down of an osteoid matrix by osteoblasts, the bone-forming cells, and the mineralization of the osteoid by the development and deposition of crystals of calcium phosphate (in the form of hydroxyapatite) within it. It is the mineral, organized in a regular pattern on a collagen scaffold, that gives bone its stiffness. Osteoid contains largely fibers of type I collagen and lesser amounts of numerous noncollagenous proteins. Although the role of these proteins in bone is not well understood, it is thought that their particular combination in bone gives this tissue the unique ability to mineralize. It is clear that these proteins interact with each other and that collagen and several of the noncollagenous proteins can bind to specialized receptors on the surface of bone cells. This binding is important for the adhesion of the cells to the bone matrix, and also delivers behavioral signals to the cells. *See* COLLAGEN.

The primary cell types in bone are those that result in its formation and maintenance (osteoblasts and osteocytes) and those that are responsible for its removal (osteoclasts). Osteoblasts form from the differentiation of multipotential stromal cells that reside in the periosteum and the bone marrow. Under the appropriate stimuli, these primitive stromal cells mature to bone-forming cells at targeted sites in the skeleton. Under different stimuli, they are also capable of developing into adipocytes (fat cells), muscle cells, and chondrocytes (cartilage cells). Osteocytes, which are osteoblasts that become incorporated within the bone tissue itself, are the most numerous cell type in bone. They reside in spaces (lacunae) within the mineralized bone, forming numerous extensions through tiny channels (cannaliculi) in the bone that connect with other osteocytes and with the cells on the endosteal surface. Osteocytes are therefore ideally placed to sense stresses and loads placed on the bone and to convey this information to the osteoblasts on the bone surface, thus enabling bone to adapt to altered mechanical loading by the formation of new bone. Osteocytes are also thought to be the cells that detect and direct the repair of microscopic damage that frequently occurs in the bone matrix due to wear and tear. Failure to repair the cracks and microfractures that occur in bone, or when this microdamage accumulates at a rate exceeding its repair, can cause the structural failure of the bone, such as in stress fractures. A large number of molecules that regulate the formation and function of osteoblastic cells have been identified. Circulating hormones, such as insulin, growth hormone, and insulinlike growth factors, combine with growth factors within the bone itself, such as transforming growth factor beta (TGFβ) and bone morphogenetic proteins (BMPs), to influence the differentiation of osteoblasts.

Osteoclasts are typically large, multinucleated cells, rich in the intracellular machinery required for bone resorption. This is accomplished when the cells form a tight sealing zone by attachment of the cell membrane against the bone matrix, creating a bone-resorbing compartment. Into this space, the cell secretes acid to dissolve the bone mineral, and enzymes to digest the collagen and other proteins in the bone matrix. The removal of bone by osteoclasts is necessary to enable the repair of microscopic damage and changes in bone shape during growth and tooth eruption. Osteoclast-mediated bone resorption is also the mechanism for releasing calcium stored in bone for the maintenance of calcium levels in the blood. Most agents that promote bone resorption act on osteoblastic cells, which in turn convey signals to osteoclast precursors to differentiate into mature osteoclasts. These agents include the active form of vitamin D, parathyroid hormone, interleukin-1, interleukin-6, and interleukin-11, and prostaglandins such as prostaglandin E_2. Differentiation to fully functional osteoclasts also requires close contact between osteoclast precursors and osteoblastic cells. This is due to a molecule called osteoclast differentiation factor (ODF) which is located on the surface of osteoblasts, binds to receptors on the surface of osteoclast precursor cells, and induces their progression to osteoclasts.

Flat bones and long bones are formed by different embryological means. Formation of flat bones occurs by intramembranous ossification, in which primitive mesenchymal cells differentiate directly into osteoblasts and produce bony trabeculae within a periosteal membrane. The initial nature of this bone is relatively disorganized and is termed woven bone. Later, this woven bone is remodeled and replaced by the much stronger mature lamella bone, consisting of layers of calcified matrix arranged in orderly fashion. Long bones are formed by intracartilaginous development in which the future bone begins as cartilage. The cartilage template is gradually replaced by bone in an orderly sequence of events starting at the center of the growing bone. Cartilage remains at the ends of long bones during growth, forming a structure at each end termed the growth plate. Cartilage cells (chondrocytes) that arise in the growth plates proliferate and add to the length of the bone. This occurs during a complex series of events, with expansion both away from and toward the center of the bone. When the bone achieves its final length in maturity, expansion from the growth plate ceases. Cartilage persists at the ends of the long bones in a specific form called articular cartilage, which provides the smooth bearing surfaces for the joints.

Bone is a dynamic tissue and is constantly being remodeled by the actions of osteoclasts and osteoblasts. After bone removal, the osteoclasts either move on to new resorption sites or die; this is followed by a reversal phase where osteoblasts are attracted to the resorption site. It is thought that growth factors that are sequestered in an inactive form in the bone matrix are released and activated by the osteoclast activity and that these in turn promote fresh osteoid production by the recruited osteoblasts. The new osteoid eventually calcifies, and in this way the bone is formed and replaced in layers (lamellae), which are the result of these repeated cycles. In growing bone, the activities of bone cells is skewed toward a net increase in bone. However, in healthy mature bone there is an equilibrium between bone resorption and bone formation. When the equilibrium between these two cell types breaks down, skeletal pathology results.

The most common bone disease is osteoporosis, in which there is a net loss of bone due to osteoclastic bone resorption that is not completely matched by new bone formation. The best-understood cause of osteoporosis is that which occurs in women due to the loss of circulating estrogen after menopause. Another cause of osteoporotic bone loss is seen in disuse osteoporosis. Just as bone can respond to increased loading with the production of additional bone, bone is also dependent on regular loading for its maintenance. Significant bone loss can occur during prolonged bed rest or, for example, in paraplegia and quadriplegia. Likewise, an unloading of the skeleton (due to a lack of gravitational pull) in space flight results in severe bone loss in astronauts unless the effects of gravity are simulated by special exercises and devices. *See* Osteoporosis.

Many metabolic and genetic diseases can affect the amount and quality of bone. Metabolic diseases such as diabetes, kidney disease, oversecretion of parathyroid hormone by the parathyroid glands, anorexia nervosa, and vitamin D-dependent rickets may cause osteopenias (the reduction in bone volume and bone structural quality). Immunosuppressive therapy in organ transplant patients can lead to reduced bone mass, as can tumors of bone and other sites. Tumors can produce substances that cause the activation of osteoclastic bone resorption. In the genetically based disease osteogenesis imperfecta, mutations in the gene for type I collagen result in the production of reduced amounts of collagen or altered collagen molecules by osteoblasts. Other common diseases of the skeleton are diseases of the joints, such as rheumatoid arthritis and osteoarthritis. *See* Thyroid gland.   [D.M.Fi.]

Bordetella   A genus of gram-negative bacteria which are coccobacilli and obligate aerobes, and fail to ferment carbohydrates. These bacteria are respiratory pathogens. *Bordetella pertussis*, *B. parapertussis*, and *B. bronchiseptica* share greater than 90% of their deoxyribonucleic acid (DNA) sequences and would not warrant separate species designations except that the distinctions are useful for clinical purposes. *Bordetella pertussis* is an obligate human pathogen and is the causative agent of whooping cough (pertussis). *Bordetella parapertussis* causes a milder form of disease in humans and also causes respiratory infections in sheep. *Bordetella bronchiseptica* has the broadest host range, causing disease in many mammalian species, but kennel cough in dogs and atrophic rhinitis, in which infected piglets develop deformed nasal passages, have the biggest economic impact. *Bordetella avium* is more distantly related to the other species. A pathogen of birds, it is of major economic importance to the poultry industry.

Infection by all four species is characterized by bacterial adherence to the ciliated cells that line the windpipe (trachea), *B. pertussis* releases massive amounts of peptidoglycan, causing an exaggerated immune response that is ultimately deleterious, resulting in self-induced death of the ciliated cells. *Bordetella* also produces protein toxins. The best-characterized is pertussis toxin, made only by *B. pertussis*. This toxin interferes with the mechanisms used by host cells to communicate with one another.

Bordetella pertussis is spread by coughing and has no environmental reservoir other than infected humans. Culturing the organism is difficult. Erythromycin is the antibiotic used most frequently to treat whooping cough. Unfortunately, antibiotic treatment improves the patient's condition only if given early, when the disease is most difficult to diagnose, and does not help after whooping has begun. This is consistent with the concept that the early symptoms of the disease result from bacterial damage to the respiratory tract and the later symptoms are due to toxins released by the bacteria. Antibiotics can eradicate the microorganisms but cannot reverse the effects of toxins, which can cause damage far from the site of bacterial growth.

Vaccines have been developed for whooping cough and kennel cough. Multicomponent pertussis vaccines consisting of inactivated pertussis toxin and various combinations of filamentous hemagglutinin, pertactin, and fimbriae are now replacing the older whole-cell vaccines consisting of killed bacteria, which were suspected but not proven to cause rare but serious side effects. Vaccination programs have greatly reduced the incidence of whooping cough in affluent nations, but worldwide nearly half a million deaths occur each year, most of which are vaccine-preventable. *See* ANTIBIOTIC; MEDICAL BACTERIOLOGY. [A.We.]

Borrelia   A genus of spirochetes that have a unique genome composed of a linear chromosome and numerous linear and circular plasmids. Borreliae are motile, helical organisms with 4–30 uneven, irregular coils, and are 5–25 micrometers long and 0.2–0.5 μm wide. All borreliae are arthropod-borne. Of the 24 recognized species, 21 cause relapsing fever and similar diseases in human and rodent hosts; two are responsible for infections in ruminants and horses; and the remaining one, for borreliosis in birds. *See* BACTERIA.

The borreliae of human relapsing fevers are transmitted by the body louse or by a large variety of soft-shelled ticks of the genus *Ornithodoros*. The species *B. burgdorferi*, the etiologic agent of Lyme disease and related disorders, is transmitted by ticks of the genus *Ixodes. Borrelia anserina*, which causes spirochetosis in chickens and other birds, is propagated by ticks of the genus *Argas*. Various species of ixodid ticks are responsible for transmitting *B. theileri* among cattle, horses, and sheep. *Borrelia coriaceae*, isolated from *O. coriaceus*, is the putative cause of epizootic bovine abortion in the western United States.

Polyacrylamide gel electrophoresis of spirochetes has shown that the outer surface of the microorganisms contains numerous variable lipoproteins of which at least two are abundant. The antigenic variability is well known for the relapsing fever borreliae. A switch in the major outer-surface proteins leads to recurrent spirochetemias. Tetracyclines, penicillins, and doxycycline are the most effective antibiotics for treatment of spirochetes. Two vaccines consisting of recombinant *B. burgdorferi* have been evaluated in subjects of risk for Lyme disease. Both proved safe and effective in the prevention of this disease. *See* ANTIBIOTIC; MEDICAL BACTERIOLOGY. [W.Bu.; P.Ro.]

Botany   That branch of biological science which embraces the study of plants and plant life. Botanical studies may range from microscopic observations of the smallest and obscurest plants to the study of the trees of the forest. One botanist may be interested mainly in the relationships among plants and in their geographic distribution, whereas another may be primarily concerned with structure or with the study of the life processes taking place in plants.

Botany may be divided by subject matter into several specialties, such as plant anatomy, plant chemistry, plant cytology, plant ecology (including autecology and synecology), plant embryology, plant genetics, plant morphology, plant physiology, plant taxonomy, ethnobotany, and paleobotany. It may also be divided according to the group of plants being studied; for example, agostology, the study of grasses; algology (phycology), the study of algae; bryology, the study of mosses; mycology, the study of fungi; and pteridology, the study of ferns. Bacteriology and virology are also parts of botany in a broad sense. Furthermore, a number of agricultural subjects have botany as their foundation. Among these are agronomy, floriculture, forestry, horticulture, landscape architecture, and plant breeding. See Agriculture; Agronomy; Bacteriology; Cell biology; Ecology; Genetics; Plant anatomy; Plant growth; Plant morphogenesis; Plant pathology; Plant physiology; Plant taxonomy.   [A.Cr.]

Botulism   An illness produced by the exotoxin of *Clostridium botulinum* and occasionally other clostridia, and characterized by paralysis and other neurological abnormalities. There are seven principal toxin types involved (A–G); only types A, B, E, and F have been implicated in human disease. Types C and D produce illness in birds and mammals. Strains of *C. barati* and *C. butyricum* have been found to produce toxins E and F and have been implicated in infant botulism. See Virulence.

The three clinical forms of botulism are classic botulism, infant botulism, and wound botulism. Classic botulism is typically due to ingestion of preformed toxin, infant botulism involves ingestion of *C. botulinum* spores with subsequent germination and toxin production in the gastrointestinal tract, and wound botulism involves production of toxin by the organism's infecting or colonizing a wound. The incubation period is from a few hours to more than a week (but usually 1–2 days), depending primarily on the amount of toxin ingested or absorbed.

There is classically acute onset of bilateral cranial nerve impairment and subsequent symmetrical descending paralysis or weakness. Commonly noted are dysphagia (difficulty in swallowing), dry mouth, diplopia (double vision), dysarthria (a neuromuscular disorder affecting speech), and blurred vision. Nausea, vomiting, and fatigue are common as well. Ileus (impaired intestinal motility) and constipation are much more typical than diarrhea; there may also be urinary retention and dry mucous membranes. Central nervous system function and sensation remain intact, and fever does not occur in the absence of complications. Fever may even be absent in wound botulism. See Toxin.

In food-borne botulism, home-canned or home-processed foods (particularly vegetables) are commonly implicated, with commercially canned foods involved infrequently. Outbreaks usually involve only one or two people, but may affect dozens. In infant botulism, honey and corn syrup have been implicated as vehicles. Therapy involves measures to rid the body of unabsorbed toxin, neutralization of unfixed toxin by antitoxin, and adequate intensive care support. See Food poisoning.   [S.M.F.]

Brachiopoda   A phylum of solitary, exclusively marine, coelomate, bivalved animals, with both valves symmetrical about a median longitudinal plane. They are typically attached to the substrate by a posteriorly located fleshy stalk or pedicle. Anteriorly, a relatively large mantle cavity is always developed between the valves, and the filamentous feeding organ, or lophophore, is suspended in it, projecting forward from the anterior body wall (see illustration).

There are two clearly defined groups within the phylum, a division that is particularly marked if only Recent animals are considered. These two groups are regarded as classes; several names have been given to them, but Inarticulata and Articulata are

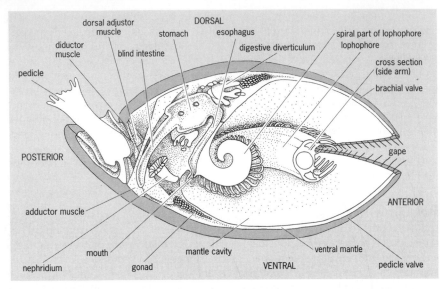

The principal organs of a brachiopod as typified by *Terebratulina.* **(***After R. C. Moore, ed., Treatise on Invertebrate Paleontology, pt. H, Geological Society of America, Inc., and University of Kansas Press, 1965***)**

the most widely used and are based on one of the most readily observed differences between them, the presence or absence of articulation between the two valves of the shell. Among the Articulata the valves are typically hinged together by a pair of teeth with complementary sockets in the opposing valve; these hinge teeth are lacking in the Inarticulata, whose valves are held together only by the soft tissue of the living animal. The phylum is currently classified into the following groups:

Class Inarticulata   Class Articulata
Order: Lingulida   Order: Orthida
Acrotretida   Strophomenida
Obolellida   Pentamerida
Paterinida   Rhynchonellida
Class Incertae Sedis   Spiriferida
Order Kutorginida   Terebratulida

The pedicle is the only organ protruding outside the valves, while the remainder of the animal is enclosed in the space between them. This space is divided into two unequal parts, a smaller posteriorly located body cavity and an anterior mantle cavity. The two mantles approach each other and ultimately fuse along the posterior margin of articulate brachiopods; in contrast, the mantles are invariably discrete in the inarticulates and are separated by a strip of body wall.

The body cavity contains the musculature; the alimentary canal; the nephridia, which are paired excretory organs also functioning as gonoducts; the reproductive organs; and primitive circulatory and nervous systems. Except for the openings through the nephridia, the body cavity is enclosed, but the mantle cavity communicates freely with the sea when the valves are opened. The lophophore is suspended from the anterior body wall within the mantle cavity and is always symmetrically disposed about the median plane. The lophophore consists of a variably disposed, ciliated, filament-bearing tube, with the ciliary beat producing an ordered flow of water within the cavity, flowing across the filaments. The latter trap food particles which are carried along a groove in the lophophore to the medially situated mouth.

All modern brachiopods are marine, and there is little doubt from the fossil record that brachiopods have always been confined to the sea. Recent brachiopods occur most commonly beneath the relatively shallow waters of the continental shelves, which seems to have been the most favored environment, but the bathymetric range of the phylum is large. A few modern species live intertidally and, at the other extreme, a limited number have been dredged from depths of over 16,000 ft (5000 m).

The majority of brachiopods form part of the sessile benthos and are attached by their pedicle during postlarval life. *Glottidia* and *Lingula* are exceptional in being infaunal and making burrows. A commoner modification involves loss of the pedicle, either complete suppression or atrophy early in the life history of the individual. Such forms either lie free on the sea floor, are attached by cementation of part or all of the pedicle valve, or are anchored by spines. The geographic distribution and geological setting of some fossil species suggest that they may have been epiplanktonic, attached to floating weed, but such a mode of life is unknown in modern faunas.   [A.J.R.]

Brain   A collection of specialized cells (neurons) in the head that regulates behavior as well as sensory and motor functions. The three main parts of the brain in vertebrates are the cerebrum, the cerebellum, and the brainstem that connects them with each other and with the spinal cord (see illustration). The two cerebral hemispheres are separated by a midline fissure that is bridged by a massive bundle of axons running in both

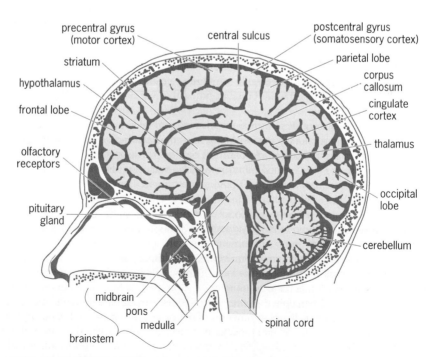

Midsagittal (midline, medial) section through the human brain. (*After C. R. Noback, The Human Nervous System, 4th ed., McGraw-Hill, 1991***)**

directions, the corpus callosum. Each hemisphere has a core of groups of neurons (the basal ganglia); an outer shell of neurons in layers (the cerebral cortex); and massive bundles of axons for communication within the cerebrum and with the rest of the brain. These bundles are called white matter because of the waxy myelin sheaths surrounding the axons.

The basal ganglia comprises three main groups. (1) The thalamus receives axons from all sensory systems and transmits information to the cortex. It also receives feedback from cortical neurons during sensory processing. (2) The striatum, comprising bundles of axons cutting through the groups of neurons, also has two-way communication with the cortex and assists in the organization of body movement. (3) The hypothalamus receives orders from the cortex and organizes the chemical systems that support body movement. One output channel is hormonal, and controls the pituitary gland (hypophysis) which in turn controls the endocrine system. The other channel is neural, comprising axons coursing through the brainstem and spinal cord to the motor neurons of the autonomic nervous system, which regulates the heart, blood vessels, lungs, gastrointestinal tract, sex organs, and skin. The autonomic and endocrine systems are largely self regulating, but they are subject to control by the cortex through the hypothalamus. *See* AUTONOMIC NERVOUS SYSTEM; ENDOCRINE SYSTEM (VERTEBRATE); NEUROBIOLOGY.

The cortex is also called gray matter because it contains the axons, cell bodies, and dendrites of neurons but there is very little myelin. An index of the capacity of a brain is cortical surface area. In higher mammals, the cortical surface increases more rapidly than the volume during fetal development; as a result the surface folds, taking the form of convexities (gyri) and fissures (sulci) that vary in their details from one brain to another. However, they are sufficiently reliable to serve as landmarks on the cerebral hemisphere that it can be subdivided into lobes. Four lobes make up the shell of each hemisphere, namely the frontal, parietal, temporal, and occipital lobes. Each lobe contains a motor or sensory map (an orderly arrangement of cortical neurons associated with muscles and sensory receptors on the body surface). The central sulcus delimits the frontal and parietal lobes. The precentral gyrus contains the motor cortex whose neurons transmit signals to motor neurons in the brainstem and spinal cord which control the muscles in the feet, legs, trunk, arms, face, and tongue of the opposite side of the body. The number of neurons for each section is determined by the fineness of control, not the size of the muscle; for example, the lips and tongue have larger areas than the trunk. Within the postcentral gyrus is the primary somatosensory cortex. Sensory receptors in the skin, muscles, and joints send messages to the somatosensory cortical cells through relays in the spinal cord and the thalamus to a map of the opposite side of the body in parallel to the map in the motor cortex. The lateral fissure separates the temporal lobe from the parietal and frontal lobes. The cortex on the inferior border of the fissure receives input relayed through the thalamus from the ears to the primary auditory cortex. The occipital lobe receives thalamic input from the eyes and functions as the primary visual cortex.

In humans, the association cortex surrounds the primary sensory and motor areas that make up a small fraction of each lobe. The occipital lobe has many specialized areas for recognizing visual patterns of color, motion, and texture. The parietal cortex has areas that support perception of the body and its surrounding personal space. Its operation is manifested by the phenomenon of phantom limb, in which the perception of a missing limb persists for an amputee. Conversely, individuals with damage to these areas suffer from sensory neglect. The temporal cortex contains areas that provide recognition of faces and of rhythmic patterns, including those of speech, dance, and music. The frontal cortex provides the neural capabilities for constructing patterns of motor behavior and social behavior. It was the rapid enlargement of the frontal and temporal lobes in human evolution over the past half million years that supported the transcendence of humans over other species. This is where the capacity to create works of art, and also to anticipate pain and death, is located. Insight and foresight are both lost with bilateral frontal lobe damage, leading to reduced experience of anxiety, asocial behavior, and a disregard of consequences of actions.

A small part of frontal lobe output goes directly to motor neurons in the brainstem and spinal cord for fine control of motor activities, such as search movements by the eyes, head, and fingers, but most goes either to the striatum from which it is relayed to the thalamus and then back to the cortex, or to the brainstem from which it is sent to the cerebellum and then through the thalamus back to the cortex. In the cerebellum, the cortical messages are integrated with sensory input predominantly from the muscles, tendons, and joints, but also from the eyes and inner ears (for balance) to provide split-second timing for rapid and complex movements. The cerebellum also has a cortex and a core of nuclei to relay input and output. Their connections, along with those in the cerebral cortex, are subject to modification with learning in the formation of a working memory (the basis for learned skills). See MEMORY; MOTOR SYSTEMS.

The cerebellum and striatum do not set goals, initiate movements, store temporal sequences of sensory input, or provide orientation to the spatial environment. These functions are performed by parts of the cortex and striatum deep in the brain that constitute another loop, the limbic system. Its main site of entry is the entorhinal cortex, which receives input from all of the sensory cortices, including the olfactory system. The input from all the sensory cortices is combined and sent to the hippocampus, where it is integrated over time. Hippocampal output returns to the entorhinal cortex, which distributes the integrated sensory information to all of the sensory cortices, updates them, and prepares them to receive new sensory input. This new information also reaches the hypothalamus and part of the striatum (the amygdaloid nucleus) for regulating emotional behavior. Bilateral damage to the temporal lobe including the hippocampus results in loss of short-term memory. Damage to the amygdaloid nucleus can cause serious emotional impairment. The Papez circuit is formed by transmission from the hippocampus to the hypothalamus by the fornix, then to the thalamus, parietal lobe, and entorhinal cortex. The limbic system generates and issues goal-directed motor commands, with corollary discharge to the sensory systems that prepares them for the changes in sensory input caused by motor activity (for example, when one speaks and hears oneself, as distinct from another).

Each hemisphere has its own limbic, Papez, cortico-thalamic, cortico-striatal, and cortico-cerebellar loops, together with sensory and motor connections. When isolated by surgically severing the callosum, each hemisphere functions independently, as though two conscious persons occupied the same skull, but with differing levels of skills in abstract reasoning and language. The right brain (spatial)-left brain (linguistic) cognitive differences are largely due to preeminent development of the speech areas in the left hemisphere in most right- and left-handed persons. Injury to Broca's area (located in the frontal lobe) and Wernicke's area (located in the temporal lobe) leads to loss of the ability, respectively, to speak (motor aphasia) or to understand speech (sensory aphasia). Studies of blood flow show that brain activity during intellectual pursuits is scattered broadly over the four lobes in both hemispheres. See APHASIA; CENTRAL NERVOUS SYSTEM; HEMISPHERIC LATERALITY.   [W.J.F.]

Breast   The human mammary gland, usually well developed in the adult female but rudimentary in the male. Each adult female breast contains 15–20 separate, branching glands that radiate from the nipple. During lactation their secretions are discharged through separate openings at the base of the nipple.

In the female, hormonal changes in adolescence cause enlargement of breast tissue, but much of this is connective tissue although some glandular buds form. With the advent of full menstruation ovarian estrogenic hormones influence breast development. If pregnancy ensues, the glandular tissue reaches full development and full lactation begins shortly after birth. After cessation of lactation the breasts regress considerably and once again reflect cyclic regulation. See LACTATION.　　　　　　　　[W.J.B.]

Breast disorders may result from congenital or developmental abnormalities, inflammations, hormonal imbalances, and, most important, from tumor formation.

Congenital defects are usually unimportant except for their psychic or cosmetic implications. Supernumerary nipples and breasts or accessory breast tissue are common examples.

Inflammations are not encountered frequently and usually result from a staphylococcal or streptococcal invasion incurred during lactation. A special form of inflammation may result from fat necrosis. Although any age is susceptible, older women show a slightly higher incidence of fat necrosis, the commonest cause of which is injury from trauma. See STAPHYLOCOCCUS; STREPTOCOCCUS; SYPHILIS; TUBERCULOSIS.

Hormonal imbalances are believed to be responsible for the variants of the commonest nontumorous breast disorder of women, cystic hyperplasia. The changes are thought to result from exaggeration or distortion of the normal cyclic alterations induced during the menstrual interval. Although a wide range of clinical and pathologic variation is commonplace, three major types or tendencies prevail. The first, called fibrosis or mastodynia, is marked by an increase of connective tissue in the breast, without a proportionate increase in glandular epithelium. The second, cystic disease, is characterized by an increase in the glandular and connective tissues in local areas, with a tendency toward formation of cysts varying in size. The third major type is adenosis, in which glandular hyperplasia is predominant. Each major form of cystic hyperplasia has its own clinical characteristics, ages of highest incidence, and distribution. Each is important because the breast masses which occur require differentiation from benign and malignant tumors. These lesions also have been found to predispose to the subsequent development of carcinoma.

Breast cancer is the most significant lesion of the female breast, accounting for 25,000–30,000 deaths in the United States each year. It rarely occurs before the age of 25, but its incidence increases each year thereafter, with a sharper climb noted about the time of menopause. Early breast cancer may appear as a small, firm mass which is nontender and freely movable. Diagnosis at this time carries a more favorable prognosis than later, when immobility, nipple retraction, lymph node involvement, and other signs of extension or spread are noted. Paget's disease of the nipple is a special form of breast cancer, in which there are early skin changes about the nipple. See HORMONE.
　　　　　　　　[E.G.St./N.K.M.]

Breeding (animal)　The application of genetic principles to improving heredity for economically important traits in domestic animals. Examples are improvement of milk production in dairy cattle, meatiness in pigs, feed requirements or growth rate in beef cattle, and egg production in chickens. Selection permits the best parents to leave more offspring in the next generation than do poor parents.

Selection is the primary tool for generating directed genetic changes in animals. It may be concentrated on one characteristic, may be directed independently on several traits, or may be conducted on an index or total score which includes information on several traits. In general, the third method is preferable when several important heritable traits need attention. In practice, selection is likely to be a mixture of the second and third methods.

Heritability, the fraction of the total variation in a trait that is due to additive genetic differences, is a key parameter in making decisions in selection. Most traits are strongly to moderately influenced by environmental or managemental differences. Therefore, managing animals to equalize environmental influences on them, or statistically adjusting for environmental differences among animals, is necessary to accurately choose those with the best inheritance for various traits.

The improvement achieved by selection is directly related to the accuracy with which the breeding values of the subjects can be recognized. Accuracy, in turn, depends upon the heritabilities of the traits and upon whether they can be measured directly upon the subjects for selection (mass selection), upon their parents (pedigree selection), upon their brothers and sisters (family selection), or upon their progeny (progeny testing). For traits of medium heritability, the following sources of information are about equally accurate for predicting breeding values of subjects: (1) one record measured on the subject; (2) one record on each ancestor for three previous generations; (3) one record each on five brothers or sisters where there is no environmental correlation between family members; and (4) one record each on five progeny having no environmental correlations, each from a different mate.

Propagation of improved animal stocks is achieved primarily with purebred strains descended from imported or locally developed groups or breeds of animals which have been selected and interbred for a long enough period to be reasonably uniform for certain trademark characteristics, such as coat color. Because the number of breeding animals is finite and because breeders tend to prefer certain bloodlines and sires, some inbreeding occurs within the pure breeds, but this has not limited productivity in most of these breeds. Crossbreeding makes use of the genetic phenomenon of heterosis. Heterosis is improved performance of crossbred progeny, exceeding that of the average performance of their parents. Most commercial pigs, sheep, and beef cattle are produced by crossbreeding. *See* GENETICS.

Advances in a variety of technologies have application for improvement of domestic animals, including quantitative genetics, reproductive physiology, and molecular genetics. Quantitative geneticists use statistical and genetic information to improve domestic animals. Typically a statistical procedure is used to rank animals based on their estimated breeding values for traits of economic importance. The statistical procedures used allow ranking animals across herds or flocks, provided the animals in different herds or flocks have relatives in common. The primary contribution of reproductive physiology to genetic improvement is to reduce the generation interval. If genetic improvement is increasing at the same rate per generation, more generations can be produced for a fixed time, and thus more gain per unit of time. The most important development was artificial insemination, which allows extensive use of superior males. Another development was embryo transplantation, which allows more extensive use of females. Cloning is a relatively new technique, by which whole and healthy animals have been produced that have the same DNA as the animal from which the cells were taken.

Due to advances in molecular genetics, knowledge is increasing regarding the location of genes on chromosomes and the distance between the genes. In domestic animals, polymorphisms (changes in the order of the four bases) that are discovered in the DNA may be associated with economic traits. When the polymorphisms are associated with or code for economic traits, they are called quantitative trait loci (QTL). When a few or several quantitative trait loci are known that control a portion of the variability in a trait, increasing the frequencies of favorable alleles can enhance the accuracy of selection and augment production. Another use of molecular genetics is to detect the genes that code for genetically predetermined diseases. An example is the bovine leukocyte deficiency gene, which does not allow white blood cells to migrate out of the blood supply into the tissues to fight infection. The calves perish at a young age. Screening all sires that enter artificial breeding organizations and not using sires that transmit the defect has effectively controlled this condition.   [A.E.Fr.]

Breeding (plant)   The application of genetic principles to improve cultivated plants. New varieties of cultivated plants can result only from genetic reorganization that gives rise to improvements over the existing varieties in particular characteristics or in combinations of characteristics. Thus, plant breeding can be regarded as a branch of applied genetics, but it also makes use of the knowledge and techniques of many aspects of plant science, especially physiology and pathology. Related disciplines, like biochemistry and entomology, are also important, and the application of mathematical statistics in the design and analysis of experiments is essential. *See* GENETICS.

The cornerstone of all plant breeding is selection, or the picking out of plants with the best combinations of agricultural and quality characteristics from populations of plants with a variety of genetic constitutions. Seeds from the selected plants are used to produce the next generation, from which a further cycle of selection may be carried out if there are still differences. Conventional breeding is divided into three categories on the basis of ways in which the species are propagated. First come the species that set seeds by self-pollination; that is, fertilization usually follows the germination of pollen on the stigmas of the same plant on which it was produced. The second category of species sets seeds by cross-pollination; that is, fertilization usually follows the germination of pollen on the stigmas of different plants from those on which it was produced. The third category comprises the species that are asexually propagated; that is, the commercial crop results from planting vegetative parts or by grafting. The procedures used in breeding differ according to the pattern of propagation of the species. Several innovative techniques have been explored to enhance the scope, speed, and efficiency of producing new, superior cultivars. Advances have been made in extending conventional sexual crossing procedures by laboratory culture of plant organs and tissues and by somatic hybridization through protoplast fusion.

The essential attribute of self-pollinating crop species, such as wheat, barley, oats, and many edible legumes, is that, once they are genetically pure, varieties can be maintained without change for many generations. When improvement of an existing variety is desired, it is necessary to produce genetic variation among which selection can be practiced. This is achieved by artificially hybridizing between parental varieties that may contrast with each other in possessing different desirable attributes. This system is known as pedigree breeding, and it is the method most commonly employed, and can be varied in several ways.

Another form of breeding often employed with self-pollinating species involves backcrossing. This is used when an existing variety is broadly satisfactory but lacks one useful and simply inherited trait that is to be found in some other variety. Hybrids are made between the two varieties, and the first hybrid generation is crossed, or backcrossed, with the broadly satisfactory variety which is known as the recurrent parent. Backcrossing has been exceedingly useful in practice and has been extensively employed in adding resistance to diseases, such as rust, smut, or mildew, to established and acceptable varieties of oats, wheat, and barley.

Natural populations of cross-pollinating species are characterized by extreme genetic diversity. No seed parent is true-breeding, first because it was itself derived from a fertilization in which genetically different parents participated, and second because of the genetic diversity of the pollen it will have received. In dealing with cultivated plants with this breeding structure, the essential concern in seed production is to employ systems in which hybrid vigor is exploited, the range of variation in the crop is diminished, and only parents likely to give rise to superior offspring are retained.

Plant breeders have made use either of inbreeding followed by hybridization or of some form of recurrent selection. During inbreeding programs normally cross-pollinated species, such as corn, are compelled to self-pollinate by artificial means. Inbreeding is continued for a number of generations until genetically pure, true-breeding, and uniform inbred lines are produced. During the production of the inbred lines, rigorous selection is practiced for general vigor and yield and disease resistance, as well as for other important characteristics. To estimate the value of inbred lines as the parents of hybrids, it is necessary to make tests of their combining ability. The test that is used depends upon the crop and on the ease with which controlled cross-pollination can be effected.

Breeding procedures designated as recurrent selection are coming into limited use with open-pollinated species. In theory, this method visualizes a controlled approach to homozygosity, with selection and evaluation in each cycle to permit the desired stepwise changes in gene frequency. Experimental evaluation of the procedure indicates that it has real possibilities. Four types of recurrent selection have been suggested: on the basis of phenotype, for general combining ability, for specific combining ability, and reciprocal selection. The methods are similar in the procedures involved, but vary in the type of tester parent chosen, and therefore in the efficiency with which different types of gene action (additive and nonadditive) are measured.

Varieties of asexually propagated crops consist of large assemblages of genetically identical plants, and there are only two ways of introducing new and improved varieties: by sexual reproduction and by the isolation of somatic mutations. (A very few asexually propagated crop species are sexually sterile, like the banana, but the majority have some sexual fertility.) The latter method has often been used successfully with decorative plants, such as chrysanthemum, and new forms of potato have occasionally arisen in this way. When sexual reproduction is used, hybrids are produced on a large scale between existing varieties; the small number that have useful arrays of characters are propagated vegetatively until sufficient numbers can be planted to allow agronomic evaluation.   [R.Ri.]

Cell technologies have been used to extend the range and efficiency of asexual plant propagation. For example, plant cell culture involves the regeneration of entire mature plants from single cells or tissues excised from a source plant and cultured in a nutrient medium. In micropropagation and cloning, tissues are excised from root, stem, petiole, or seedling and induced to regenerate plantlets. All regenerants from tissues of one source plant constitute a clone. Microspore or anther culture is the generation of plants from individual cells with but one set of chromosomes, haploid cells, as occurs in the development of pollen. Microspores are isolated from anthers and cultured on nutrient media, or entire anthers are cultured in this manner. Doubling of chromosomes that may occur spontaneously or can be induced by treatment with colchicine leads to the formation of homozygous dihaploid plants. *See* PLANT PROPAGATION; POLLEN.

Breeding for new, improved varieties of crop plants is most often based on cross-pollination and hybrid production. Such breeding is limited to compatible plants, and compatibility lessens with increasing distance in the relationship between plants. Breeding would benefit from access to traits inherent in sexually noncompatible plants. Biotechnological techniques such as in vitro fertilization and embryo rescue (the excision and culture of embryos on nutrient media) have been employed to overcome incompatibility barriers, as have somatic hybridization and DNA technologies. Somatic hybridization involves enzymatic removal of walls from cells of leaves and seedlings to furnish individual naked cells, that is, protoplasts, which can then be fused to produce hybrids. Similarity of membrane structure throughout the plant kingdom permits the fusion of distantly related protoplasts. Cell fusion may lead to nuclear fusion, resulting in amphi-diploid somatic hybrid cells. Fusion products of closely related yet sexually incompatible plants have been grown to flowering plants; the most famous example is the potato + tomato hybrid = pomato (*Solanum tuberosum* + *Lycopersicon esculentum*). DNA technologies enable the isolation of desirable genes from bacteria, plants, and animals (genes that confer herbicide resistance or tolerance to environmental stress, or encode enzymes and proteins of value to the processing industry) and the insertion of such genes into cells and tissues of target plants by direct or indirect uptake has led to the genetic transformation of plant cells. The regeneration of transformed plant cells and tissues results in new and novel genotypes (transgenic plants). Contrary to hybrids obtained by cross-pollination, such plants are different from their parent by only one or two single, defined traits.   [F.Co.]

Brucellosis   An infectious, zoonotic disease of various animals and humans caused by *Brucella* species. Each species tends to preferentially infect a particular animal, but several types can infect humans. *Brucella melitensis* (preferentially infects goats and sheep), *B. suis* (infects pigs), and *B. abortus* (infects cattle) are the most common causes of human brucellosis. *Brucella melitensis* is the most virulent for humans, followed by *B. suis* and *B. abortus*. *Brucella canis* and *B. ovis*, which infect dogs and sheep respectively, rarely infect humans. Although brucellosis is found all over the world, in many countries the disease has been eradicated. The brucellae are small, gram-negative coccobacilli which are defined as facultative intracellular parasites since they are able to replicate within specialized cells of the host.

In animals the brucellae often localize in the reproductive tract, mammary gland, and lymph node. They have a particular affinity for the pregnant uterus, leading to abortion and reduced milk production with resultant economic loss to the farmer. Wildlife, including elk, feral pigs, bison, and reindeer, can become infected and can spread the disease to domestic livestock.

Brucellosis in humans is characterized by undulant fever, cold sweats, chills, muscular pain, and severe weakness. Some individuals may have recurrent bouts of the disease in which a variety of organs may be affected, sometimes resulting in death. The disease can be contracted by consuming unpasteurized milk or cheese, or via the introduction of organisms through small skin lesions or as an aerosol through the conjunctiva and the respiratory system. Treatment with tetracycline and other antibiotics is most successful if started early after symptoms occur. Development of the disease can be prevented if treatment is initiated immediately after contact with potentially infected material.

At present there are no effective vaccines for humans. The disease can be eliminated only by eradicating it in animals. A major source of brucellosis in humans is the consumption of *B. melitensis*–infected milk and cheese from goats. Incidence can be reduced by pasteurizing milk. Animals can be vaccinated to increase their immunity against brucellosis and therefore reduce abortions and disease transmission. *See* EPIDEMIOLOGY; MEDICAL BACTERIOLOGY.   [W.W.Sp.]

Bryophyta   A division that consists of some 23,000 species of small and relatively simple plants commonly known as mosses, granite mosses, peat mosses, liverworts, and hornworts (see illustration). The bryophytes display a distinct alternation of sexual and asexual generations; the sexual gametophyte, with a haploid chromosome number,

Moss plant, *Polytrichum juniperinum*. (*General Biological Supply House*)

is the more diversified. The sporebearing, diploid sporophyte is reduced in size and structure, attached to the gametophyte, and partially or almost completely dependent on it.

The gametophytes may consist of leafy stems or flat thalli. They have no roots but are anchored to the substrate by hairlike rhizoids. Vascular tissue is at best poorly differentiated, with no lignification of cells. Growth results from the divisions of single cells (rather than meristematic tissues) located at stem tips or in notches at the margins of thalli. The sex organs are multicellular and have a jacket of sterile cells surrounding either the single egg produced in flask-shaped archegonia or the vast number of sperms produced in globose to cylindric, stalked antheridia. The sperms swim by means of two flagella. The sporophyte commonly consists of a capsule that produces a large number of spores, a stalklike seta, and a swollen foot anchored in the gametophyte. The spores, nearly always single-celled, are dispersed in the air, except in the case of a small number of aquatics. They germinate directly or produce a juvenile stage called a protonema. *See* REPRODUCTION (PLANT).

The division can be divided into five classes: Sphagnopsida (peat mosses), Andreaeopsida (granite mosses), Bryopsida (true mosses), Hepaticopsida (liverworts), and Anthocerotopsida (hornworts). The mosses have radially organized leafy gametophytes that develop from a protonema and have multicellular rhizoids with slanted crosswalls. The liverworts and hornworts are mostly flat and dorsiventrally organized and have no protonematal stage; the rhizoids are unicellular. Though obviously related, as evidenced by similar sex organs and attachment of a simplified sporophyte to a more complex and independent gametophyte, the classes differ greatly in structural detail. *See* PLANT KINGDOM.   [H.Cr.]

Bryozoa   A phylum of sessile aquatic invertebrates (also called Polyzoa) which form colonies of zooids. Each zooid, in its basic form, has a lophophore of ciliated tentacles situated distally on an introvert, a looped gut with the mouth inside the lophophore and the anus outside, a coelomic body cavity, and (commonly) a protective exoskeleton. The colonies are variable in size and habit. Some are known as lace corals and others as sea mats, but the only general name is bryozoans (sea mosses).

The colony may be minute, of not more than a single feeding zooid and its immediate buds, or substantial, forming masses 3 ft (1 m) in circumference, festoons 1.6 ft (0.5 m) in length, or patches 2.7 ft^2 (0.25 m^2) in area. Commonly the colonies form incrustations not more than a few square centimeters in area, small twiggy bushes up to about 1.2 in. (3 cm) in height, or soft masses up to about 0.3 ft (0.1 m) in the largest dimension. In many colonies much of the bulk consists of the zooid exoskeletons which may persist long after the death of the organism and account for the abundance of fossilized bryozoan remains.

Many bryozoans display polymorphism, having certain zooids adapted in particular ways to perform specialized functions, such as protection, cleaning the surface, anchoring the colony, or sheltering the embryo. The evolution of nonfeeding polymorphs is dependent upon some form of intercommunication between zooids.

Bryozoa is the name of a phylum for which Ectoprocta is generally regarded as a synonym, these names being used by zoologists according to personal preference. Entoprocta (synonym Callyssozoa) is likewise regarded as an independent phylum. A minority regard Ectoprocta and Entoprocta as subphyla within the Bryozoa, while others maintain Ectoprocta and Entoprocta as phyla but link them under Bryozoa as a name of convenience.

The phylum contains some 20,000 described species, one-fifth of them living. These are distributed among three classes and a somewhat variable number of orders:

> Phylum Bryozoa
>   Class Phylactolaemata
>   Order Plumatellida
>   Class Gymnolaemata
>   Order Ctenostomata
>   Suborder Cheilostomata
>   Class Stenolaemata
>   Order Cyclostomata
>   Suborder Cystoporata (extinct)
>   Suborder Trepostomata
>   Suborder Cryptostomata
>   Suborder Hederellida

Fresh-water bryozoans are present on submerged tree roots and aquatic plants in most lakes, ponds, and rivers, especially in clear water of alkaline pH. Most other bryozoans are marine, although some gymnolaemates inhabit brackish water. They are common in the sea, ranging from the middle shore to a depth of over 26,000 ft (8000 m), and are maximally abundant in waters of the continental shelf. Most attach to firm substrata, so that their distribution is primarily determined by the availability of support. Mud is unfavorable and so is sand unless well provided with stone, dead shells, hydroids, or large foraminiferans.

Colony form in bryozoans is to some extent related to habitat. Encrusting and bushy flexible species are adapted to wave exposure; brittle twiglike and foliaceous species are found deeper; some erect branching species tolerate sediment deposition. One group of tiny discoid species lives on sand in warm seas, and in one genus the colonies are so small that they live actually among the sand grains; a few species live anchored in mud. A number of stolonate ctenostomes bore into the substance of mollusk shells; other species are associated only with hermit crabs, and a few are commensal with shrimps or polychaete worms.

Bryozoans have few serious predators. Nudibranch mollusks and pycnogonids (sea spiders) specialize in feeding on zooids but are rarely destructive of entire colonies. Loxosomatids (Entoprocta) and a hydroid (*Zanclea*) are common commensals.

Life spans vary. Small algal dwellers complete their life cycle in a few months. Many species survive a year but have two overlapping generations; others are perennial, with one known to survive for 12 years.

Bryozoans may be a nuisance in colonizing ship hulls and the insides of water pipes, and one species has caused severe dermatitis in fishers. Recently some delicate kinds have been used in costume jewelry, and green-dyed clumps of dried *Bugula* are often sold as "everlasting plants." [J.S.R.]

Fossil Bryozoa have a long geological history, from early in the Ordovician Period [500 million years ago (Ma)] to the Recent. Individual fossils range in size from a few millimeters to several meters in maximum dimension. Various encrusting or erect growth forms are common, though some were free-living. Representatives of the marine orders that secreted calcareous skeletons (Cryptostomata, Cyclostomata, Cystoporata, Trepostomata, and Cheilostomata) commonly are abundant in sedimentary rocks formed where benthic organisms flourished. Skeletons generally are calcite, though some are aragonite or mixed calcite and aragonite. Ctenostomata have nonmineralized skeletons, so they have been preserved only as excavations or borings in marine shells or on the undersides of other organisms that overgrew them. The fresh-water Phylactolaemata have gelatinous skeletons, but their tough statoblasts (dormant reproductive bodies) have been reported from sediments as old as the Jurassic (at least 150 Ma). During the Ordovician, Carboniferous, and Permian periods, bryozoans were important parts of many fossil reefs, reef flanks, and other carbonate buildups in shallow (less than 100 m depth) tropical waters. Bryozoans commonly dominate and may reach very high diversities in post-Paleozoic cool-temperate carbonate deposits, indicating a shift in primary environment after the Paleozoic.

Although colonies of many bryozoan species are large, the individual skeletons of each zooid (unit of the colony) range from less than 0.1 to about 1 mm in diameter. The smaller diameters are typical for cross sections of elongate tubes that characterize zooids in stenolaemate bryozoans, and the larger diameters are typical for the more equidimensional zooids of cheilostomes. Identification is based on numerous external and, for most stenolaemates, internal features that require study with a microscope. Features of the colonial skeletons (zoaria) as well as the morphology of the individual zooidal skeletons (zooecia) are used to classify bryozoans. Many fossil bryozoans had only one type of zooid (autozooids), which apparently could feed and carry out all other necessary biological functions of the colony. Others were polymorphic, with various types of specialized zooids supplementing the autozooids. Number, types, and morphology of polymorphs is important in classification. Other characters important in classification of fossil bryozoans are wall structure, reproductive chambers, general growth habit or specific shape of colonies, and for some, surface topography of the colony. [F.K.McK.]

Bud An embryonic shoot containing the growing stem tip surrounded by young leaves or flowers or both, and the whole frequently enclosed by special protective leaves, the bud scales.

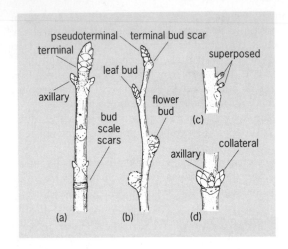

Bud positions. (*a*) Terminal and axillary (buckeye). (*b*) Pseudoterminal (elm). (*c*) Superposed (butternut). (*d*) Collateral (red maple).

The bud at the apex of the stem is called a terminal bud (illus. *a*). Any bud that develops on the side of a stem is a lateral bud. The lateral bud borne in the axil (angle between base of leaf and stem) of a leaf is the axillary bud (illus. *a* and *d*). It develops concurrently with the leaf which subtends it, but usually such buds do not unfold and grow rapidly until the next season. Because of the inhibitory influence of the apical or other buds, many axillary buds never develop actively or may not do so for many years. These are known as latent or dormant buds. Above or beside the axillary buds, some plants regularly produce additional buds called accessory, or supernumerary, buds. Accessory buds which occur above the axillary bud are called superposed buds (illus. *c*), and those beside it collateral buds (illus. *d*). Under certain conditions, such as removal of terminal and axillary buds, other buds may arise at almost any point on the stem, or even on roots or leaves. Such buds are known as adventitious buds. *See* PLANT GROWTH.

Buds that give rise to flowers only are termed flower buds, or in some cases, fruit buds. If a bud grows into a leafy shoot, it is called a leaf bud, or more accurately, a branch bud. A bud which contains both young leaves and flowers is called a mixed bud.

Buds of herbaceous plants and of some woody plants are covered by rudimentary foliage leaves only. Such buds are called naked buds. In most woody plants, however, the buds are covered with modified protective leaves in the form of scales. These buds are called scaly buds or winter buds. In the different species of plants, the bud scales differ markedly. They may be covered with hairs or with water-repellent secretions of resin, gum, or wax. Ordinarily when a bud opens, the scales fall off, leaving characteristic markings on the stem (bud scale scars). *See* LEAF.   [N.A.]

C

Carbohydrate   A term applied to a group of substances which include the sugars, starches, and cellulose, along with many other related substances. This group of compounds plays a vitally important part in the lives of plants and animals, both as structural elements and in the maintenance of functional activity. Plants are unique in that they alone in nature have the power to synthesize carbohydrates from carbon dioxide and water in the presence of the green plant chlorophyll through the energy derived from sunlight, by the process of photosynthesis. This process is responsible not only for the existence of plants but for the maintenance of animal life as well, since animals obtain their entire food supply directly or indirectly from the carbohydrates of plants. *See* CARBOHYDRATE METABOLISM; PHOTOSYNTHESIS.

The term carbohydrate originated in the belief that naturally occurring compounds of this class, for example, D-glucose ($C_6H_{12}O_6$), sucrose ($C_{12}H_{22}O_{11}$), and cellulose ($C_6H_{10}O_5)_n$, could be represented formally as hydrates of carbon, that is, $C_x(H_2O)_y$. Later it became evident that this definition for carbohydrates was not a satisfactory one. New substances were discovered whose properties clearly indicated that they had the characteristics of sugars and belonged in the carbohydrate class, but which nevertheless showed a deviation from the required hydrogen-to-oxygen ratio. Examples of these are the important deoxy sugars, D-deoxyribose, L-fucose, and L-rhamnose, the uronic acids, and such compounds as ascorbic acid (vitamin C). The retention of the term carbohydrate is therefore a matter of convenience rather than of exact definition. A carbohydrate is usually defined as either a polyhydroxy aldehyde (aldose) or ketone (ketose), or as a substance which yields one of these compounds on hydrolysis. However, included within this class of compounds are substances also containing nitrogen and sulfur. *See* DEOXYRIBOSE; FRUCTOSE.

The properties of many carbohydrates differ enormously from one substance to another. The sugars, such as D-glucose or sucrose, are easily soluble, sweet-tasting, and crystalline; the starches are colloidal and paste-forming; and cellulose is completely insoluble. Yet chemical analysis shows that they have a common basis; the starches and cellulose may be degraded by different methods to the same crystalline sugar, D-glucose.

The carbohydrates usually are classified into three main groups according to complexity: monosaccharides, oligosaccharides, and polysaccharides. Monosaccharides are simple sugars that consist of a single carbohydrate unit which cannot be hydrolyzed into simpler substances. These are characterized, according to their length of carbon chain, as trioses ($C_3H_6O_3$), tetroses ($C_4H_8O_4$), pentoses ($C_5H_{10}O_5$), hexoses ($C_6H_{12}O_6$), heptoses ($C_7H_{14}O_7$), and so on. Oligosaccharides are compound sugars that are condensation products of two to five molecules of simple sugars and are subclassified into disaccharides, trisaccharides, tetrasaccharides, and pentasaccharides, according to the number of monosaccharide molecules yielded upon hydrolysis. Polysaccharides comprise a heterogeneous group of compounds which represent large aggregates of monosaccharide units, joined through glycosidic bonds. They are tasteless, nonreducing, amorphous substances that yield a large and indefinite number of monosaccharide units on hydrolysis. Their molecular weight is usually very high, and many of them, like starch or glycogen, have molecular weights of several million. They form colloidal solutions, but some polysaccharides, of which cellulose is an example, are completely insoluble in water. On account of their heterogeneity they are difficult to classify. *See* MONOSACCHARIDE; OLIGOSACCHARIDE; POLYSACCHARIDE.

The sugars are also classified into two general groups, the reducing and nonreducing. The reducing sugars are distinguished by the fact that because of their free, or potentially free, aldehyde or ketone groups they possess the property of readily reducing alkaline solutions of many metallic salts, such as those of copper, silver, bismuth, mercury, and iron. The most widely used reagent for this purpose is Fehling's solution. The reducing sugars constitute by far the larger group. The monosaccharides and many of their derivatives reduce Fehling's solution. Most of the disaccharides, including maltose, lactose, and the rarer sugars cellobiose, gentiobiose, melibiose, and turanose, are also reducing sugars. The best-known nonreducing sugar is the disaccharide sucrose. Among other nonreducing sugars are the disaccharide trehalose, the trisaccharides raffinose and melezitose, the tetrasaccharide stachyose, and the pentasaccharide verbascose.

The sugars consist of chains of carbon atoms which are united to one another at a tetrahedral angle of $109°28'$. A carbon atom to which are attached four different groups is called asymmetric. A sugar, or any other compound containing one or more asymmetric carbon atoms, possesses optical activity; that is, it rotates the plane of polarized light to the right or left.   [W.Z.H.]

Carbohydrate metabolism   Many aspects of biochemistry and physiology have to do with the breakdown and synthesis of simple sugars, oligosaccharides, and polysaccharides, and with the transport of sugars across cell membranes and tissues. The breakdown or dissimilation of simple sugars, particularly glucose, is one of the principal sources of energy for living organisms. The dissimilation may be anaerobic, as in fermentations, or aerobic, that is, respiratory. In both types of metabolism, the breakdown is accompanied by the formation of energy-rich bonds, chiefly the pyrophosphate bond of the coenzyme adenosine triphosphate (ATP), which serves as a coupling agent between different metabolic processes. In higher animals, glucose is the carbohydrate constituent of blood, which carries it to the tissues of the body. In higher plants, the disaccharide sucrose is often stored and transported by the tissues. Certain polysaccharides, especially starch and glycogen, are stored as endogenous food reserves in the cells of plants, animals, and microorganisms. Others, such as cellulose, chitin, and bacterial polysaccharides, serve as structural components of cell walls. As constituents of plant and animal tissues, various carbohydrates become available to those organisms which depend on other living or dead organisms for their source of nutrients. Hence, all naturally occurring carbohydrates can be dissimilated by some animals or microorganisms. *See* ADENOSINE TRIPHOSPHATE (ATP); CARBOHYDRATE; CHITIN; GLYCOGEN.

Certain carbohydrates cannot be used as nutrients by humans. For example, cellulose cannot be digested by humans or other mammals and is a useful food only for those, such as the ruminants, that harbor cellulose-decomposing microorganisms in their digestive tracts. The principal dietary carbohydrates available to humans are the simple sugars glucose and fructose, the disaccharides sucrose and lactose, and the polysaccharides glycogen and starch. Lactose is the carbohydrate constituent of milk and hence one of the main sources of food during infancy. The disaccharides and polysaccharides that cannot be absorbed directly from the intestine are first digested and hydrolyzed by enzymes, glycosidases, secreted into the alimentary canal. *See* FRUCTOSE; LACTOSE.

The simple sugars reach the intestine or are produced there through the digestion of oligosaccharides. They are absorbed by the intestinal mucosa and transported across the tissue into the bloodstream. This process involves the accumulation of sugar against a concentration gradient and requires active metabolism of the mucosal tissue as a source of energy. The sugars are absorbed from the blood by the liver and are stored there as glycogen. The liver glycogen serves as a constant source of glucose in the bloodstream. The mechanisms of transport of sugars across cell membranes and tissues are not yet understood, but they appear to be highly specific for different sugars and to depend on enzymelike components of the cells.

The degradation of monosaccharides may follow one of several types of metabolic pathways. In the phosphorylative pathways, the sugar is first converted to a phosphate ester (phosphorylated) in a reaction with ATP. The phosphorylated sugar is then split into smaller units, either before or after oxidation. In the nonphosphorylative pathways, the sugar is usually oxidized to the corresponding aldonic acid. This may subsequently be broken down either with or without phosphorylation of the intermediate products. Among the principal intermediates in carbohydrate metabolism are glyceraldehyde-3-phosphate and pyruvic acid. The end products of metabolism depend on the organism and, to some extent, on the environmental conditions. Besides cell material the products may include carbon dioxide (CO_2), alcohols, organic acids, and hydrogen gas. In the so-called complete oxidations, CO_2 is the only excreted end product. In incomplete oxidations, characteristic of the vinegar bacteria and of certain fungi, oxidized end products such as gluconic, ketogluconic, citric, or fumaric acids may accumulate. Organic end products are invariably found in fermentations. The amount of biosynthesis and mechanical work that an organism can do at the expense of a given amount of sugar is many times greater in respiration than in fermentation. *See* FERMENTATION; RESPIRATION.

The principal phosphorylative pathway involved in fermentations is known as the glycolytic, hexose diphosphate, or Embden-Meyerhof pathway (see illustration). This sequence of reactions is the basis of the lactic acid fermentation of mammalian muscle and of the alcoholic fermentation of yeast. For every molecule of glucose fermented through the glycolytic sequence, two molecules of ATP are used for phosphorylation, while four are produced. Thus, fermentation results in the net gain of two energy-rich phosphate bonds as ATP at the expense of inorganic phosphate esterified. The excess ATP is converted back to ADP and inorganic phosphate through coupled reactions useful to the organism, such as the mechanical work done by the contraction of muscle or biosynthetic reactions associated with growth. *See* ADENOSINE DIPHOSPHATE (ADP); NICOTINAMIDE ADENINE DINUCLEOTIDE (NAD).

The oxidative or respiratory metabolism of sugars differs in several respects from fermentative dissimilation. First, the oxidative steps, that is, the reoxidation of NADH, are linked to the reduction of molecular oxygen. Second, the pyruvic acid produced through glycolytic or other mechanisms is further oxidized, usually to CO_2 and H_2O. Third, in most aerobic organisms, alternative pathways either supplement or completely replace the glycolytic sequence of reactions for the oxidation of sugars. Where pyruvic acid appears as a metabolic intermediate, it is generally oxidatively decarboxylated to yield CO_2 and the two-carbon acetyl fragment which combines with coenzyme A. The acetyl group is then further oxidized via the Krebs cycle. The principal alternative pathways by which sugars are dissimilated involve the oxidation of glucose-6-phosphate to

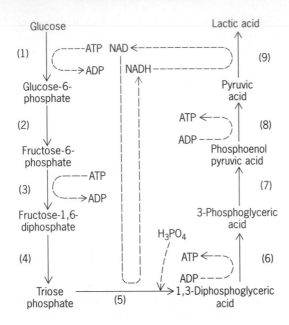

Glucose

Lactic acid

(1)

ATP NAD
ADP NADH

(9)

Glucose-6-
phosphate

Pyruvic
acid

(2)

ATP
ADP

(8)

Fructose-6-
phosphate

Phosphoenol
pyruvic acid

(3)

ATP
ADP

(7)

Fructose-1,6-
diphosphate

3-Phosphoglyceric
acid

H_3PO_4

(4)

ATP
ADP

(6)

Triose
phosphate

(5)

1,3-Diphosphoglyceric
acid

**Glycolysis in lactic acid
fermentation.**

the lactone of 6-phosphogluconic acid and are known as the hexose monophosphate pathways. *See* CITRIC ACID CYCLE.

The metabolism of simple sugars other than glucose usually involves the conversion of the sugar to one of the intermediates of the phosphorylative pathways described for glucose metabolism. For example, fructose may be phosphorylated to fructose-6-phosphate, which can then be degraded via the glycolytic pathway or converted to glucose-6-phosphate and oxidized through the hexose monophosphate pathway.

The dissimilation and biosynthesis of the oligosaccharides are effected through the enzymatic cleavage or formation of glycosidic bonds between simple monosaccharide constituents of the complex carbohydrates. The principal types of enzyme which split or synthesize glycosidic bonds are the hydrolases or glycosidases, phosphorylases, and transglycosylases. The enzymes are generally highly specific with respect to the glycosidic portion, or moiety, and the type of linkage of the substrates which they attack. The essential function of all three types of enzymes is the transfer of the glycosyl moiety of the substrate to an appropriate glycosyl acceptor. The phosphorylases catalyze the reversible phosphorolysis of certain disaccharides, polysaccharides, and nucleosides by transferring the glycosyl moieties to inorganic phosphate. The breakdown of glycogen and starch by the enzymes known as amylophophorylases is an example of biologically important phosphorolytic reactions.   [M.D.]

Cardiovascular system   Those structures, such as the heart, or pumping mechanism, and the arteries, veins, and capillaries, which provide channels for the flow of blood. The cardiovascular system is sometimes called the blood-vascular system. The circulatory system includes both the cardiovascular and lymphatic systems; the latter consists of lymph channels (lymphatics), nodes, and fluid lymph which finally empties into the bloodstream. *See* BLOOD; HEART (VERTEBRATE); HEMATOPOIESIS; LYMPHATIC SYSTEM.   [C.K.W.]

Circulatory physiology describes the structure and operation of the circulation in living animals, and enquires as to how or why the circulatory system may have evolved.

The circulatory system in all vertebrates has multiple functions, but all functions are involved in regulating the internal environment of the animal (promoting homeostasis). In all vertebrates the circulatory system consists of a central pump, the heart, which drives a liquid transport medium, the blood, continuously around a closed system of tubes, the vascular system. The arterial portion of this system is divided into larger elastic and smaller resistance vessels (arterioles) which distribute blood to specialized regions or organs where transfer of nutrients, oxygen, or waste products takes place across the walls of a fine network of microscopic capillaries. Blood from the capillaries passes through the venules (small venous vessels) into the main vein and returns to the heart. The arterioles, venules, and capillaries make up the microcirculation, which is arguably the most important functional role of the vertebrate circulatory system from a functional point of view.

Cardiovascular system disorders are those disorders which involve the arteries, veins, and lymphatics.

[D.R.J.]

Carnivora   One of the larger orders of placental mammals, including fossil and living dogs, raccoons, pandas, bears, weasels, skunks, badgers, otters, mongooses, civets, cats, hyenas, seals, walruses, and many extinct groups organized into 12 families, with about 112 living genera and more than twice as many extinct genera. The subdivision of the order into three superfamilies has long been practiced and the following groups seem appropriate: Miacoidea, Canoidea, and Feloidea. The primary adaptation in this order was for predation on other vertebrates and invertebrates. A few carnivorans (for example, bear and panda) have secondarily become largely or entirely herbivorous, but even then the ancestral adaptations for predation are still clearly evident in the structure of the teeth and jaws. The Carnivora have been highly successful animals since their first appearance in the early Paleocene.

Structural adaptations involve the teeth and jaws. The dentition is sharply divided into three functional units. The incisors act as a tool for nipping and delicate prehension, and the large, interlocking upper and lower canines for heavy piercing and tearing during the killing of prey. The cheek teeth are divided into premolars (for heavy prehension) and molars (for slicing and grinding), which may be variously modified depending on the specific adaptation, but there is a constant tendency for the last (fourth) upper premolar and the first lower molar to enlarge and form longtitudinal opposed shearing blades (the carnassials). In all carnivorans the jaw articulation is arranged in such a manner that movement is limited to vertical hinge motions and transverse sliding. The temporal muscle dominates the jaw musculature, forming at least one-half of the total mass of the jaw muscles.

The earliest fossil records are early Paleocene, but the earliest well-represented material comes from the middle Paleocene of North America. During the Paleocene and Eocene the stem-carnivorans or miacoids underwent considerable diversification in both the Old and New World. At the end of Eocene and beginning of Oligocene time throughout the Northern Hemisphere, a dramatic change took place within the Carnivora; this was the appearance of primitive representatives of modern carnivoran families. *See* MAMMALIA; PINNIPEDS.

[R.H.T.]

Carotenoid   Any of a class of yellow, orange, red, and purple pigments that are widely distributed in nature. Carotenoids are generally fat-soluble unless they are complexed with proteins. In plants, carotenoids are usually located in quantity in the grana of chloroplasts in the form of carotenoprotein complexes. Carotenoprotein complexes give blue, green, purple, red, or other colors to crustaceans, echinoderms, nudibranch mollusks, and other invertebrate animals. Some coral coelenterates exhibit purple, pink, orange, or other colors due to carotenoids in the calcareous skeletal material. Cooked or denatured lobster, crab, and shrimp show the modified colors of their carotenoproteins.

The general structure of carotenoids is that of aliphatic and aliphatic-alicyclic polyenes, with a few aromatic-type polyenes. Most carotenoid pigments are tetraterpenes with a 40-carbon (C_{40}) skeleton. More than 300 carotenoids of known structure are recognized, and the number is still on the rise.

There are several biochemical functions in which the role of carotenoids is well understood. These include carotenoids in the photosynthetic apparatus of green plants, algae, and photosynthetic bacteria, where carotenoids function as a blue light-harvesting pigment (antenna or accessory pigment) for photosynthesis. Thus carotenoids make it possible for photosynthetic organisms more fully to utilize the solar energy in the visible spectral region. *See* CHLOROPHYLL; PHOTOSYNTHESIS.

Another function of carotenoids is to protect biological systems such as the photosynthetic apparatus from photodynamic damage. This is done by quenching the powerful photodynamic oxidizing agent, singlet oxygen, produced as an undesirable by-product of the exposure of pigmented organisms to light.

Perhaps the most important industrial application of carotenoids is in safe coloration of foods, as exemplified in the coloring and fortification of margarine and poultry feedstuff.   [P.-S.S.; T.Y.L.]

Cartilage   A firm, resilient connective tissue of vertebrates and some invertebrates. Isolated pieces act to provide support and anchor muscles, or with bone to contribute its resilience and interstitial growth to skeletal functions. Cartilage comprises a firm extracellular matrix synthesized by large, ovoid cells (chondrocytes) located in holes called lacunae. The matrix elements are water bound by the high negative charge of extended proteoglycan (protein-polysaccharide) molecules, and a network of fine collagen fibrils. The elements furnish mechanical stability, give, and tensile strength, but allow the diffusion of nutrients and waste to keep the cells alive. *See* BONE; COLLAGEN.

Cartilage is modified in several ways. In elastic cartilage, elastic fibers in the matrix increase resilience, as in cartilages supporting the Eustachian tube, mammalian external ear, and parts of the larynx. Where cartilage joins bones tightly at certain joints with limited mobility, for example, at the pubic symphysis and between vertebrae, the matrix of fibrocartilage contains prominent collagen fibers and has less proteoglycan than the typical hyaline variety. Hyaline cartilage, named for its glassy translucence, is the major support in the airway; and throughout the embryo, pieces of it develop as a precursor to the bony skeleton, except in the face and upper skull. *See* EAR (VERTEBRATE); LARYNX.

The primitive cartilaginous skeleton undergoes another modification, by locally calcifying its matrix. At sites of calcification, invading cells destroy the cartilage and mostly replace it by bone, leaving permanent hyaline cartilage only at the joint or articular surfaces, in some ribs, and, until maturity, at growth plates set back from the joints and perpendicular to the long axis of limb bones. The precarious physiological balance between chondrocytes and matrix materials in the heavily loaded articular cartilage breaks down in old age or in inflamed joints. *See* CONNECTIVE TISSUE; JOINT (ANATOMY).   [W.A.Be.]

Catalytic antibody   An antibody that can cause useful chemical reactions. Catalytic antibodies are produced through immunization with a hapten molecule that is usually designed to resemble the transition state or intermediate of a desired reaction.

Antibodies are the recognition arm of the immune system. They are elicited, for example, when an animal is infected with a bacterium or virus. The animal produces antibodies with binding sites that are exactly complementary to some molecular feature of the invader. The antibodies can thus recognize and bind only to the invader, identifying it as foreign and leading to its destruction by the rest of the immune system. Antibodies are also elicited in large quantity when an animal is injected with molecules, a process known as immunization. A small molecule used for immunization is called a hapten. Ordinarily, only large molecules effectively elicit antibodies via immunization, so small-molecule haptens must be attached to a large protein molecule, called a carrier protein, prior to the actual immunization. Antibodies that are produced after immunization with the hapten-carrier protein conjugate are complementary to, and thus specifically bind, the hapten. *See* ANTIBODY; ANTIGEN-ANTIBODY REACTION; IMMUNITY.

Ordinarily, antibody molecules simply bind; they do not catalyze reactions. However, catalytic antibodies are produced when animals are immunized with hapten molecules that are specially designed to elicit antibodies that have binding pockets capable of catalyzing chemical reactions. For example, in the simplest cases, binding forces within the antibody binding pocket are enlisted to stabilize transition states and intermediates, thereby lowering a reaction's energy barrier and increasing its rate. This can occur when the antibodies have a binding site that is complementary to a transition state or intermediate structure in terms of both three-dimensional geometry and charge distribution. This complementarity leads to catalysis by encouraging the substrate to adopt a transition-state-like geometry and charge distribution. Not only is the energy barrier lowered for the desired reaction, but other geometries and charge distributions that would lead to unwanted products can be prevented, increasing reaction selectivity.

Making antibodies with binding pockets complementary to transition states is complicated by the fact that true transition states and most reaction intermediates are unstable. Thus, true transition states or intermediates cannot be isolated or used as haptens for immunization. Instead, so-called transition-state analog molecules are used. Transition-state analog molecules are stable molecules that simply resemble a transition state (or intermediate) for a reaction of interest in terms of geometry and charge distribution. To the extent that the transition-state analog molecule resembles a true reaction transition state or intermediate, the elicited antibodies will also be complementary to that transition state or intermediate and thus lead to the catalytic acceleration of that reaction.

Catalytic antibodies bind very tightly to the transition-state analog haptens that were used to produce them during the immunization process. The transition-state analog haptens only bind and do not react with catalytic antibodies. It is the substrates, for example, the analogous ester molecules, that react. For this reason, transition-state analog haptens can interfere with the catalytic reaction by binding in the antibody binding pocket, thereby preventing any substrate molecules from binding and reacting. This inhibition by the transition-state analog hapten is always observed with catalytic antibodies, and is used as a first level of proof that catalytic antibodies are responsible for any observed catalytic reaction.

The important feature of catalysis by antibodies is that, unlike enzymes, a desired reaction selectivity can be programmed into the antibody by using an appropriately designed hapten. Catalytic antibodies almost always demonstrate a high degree of substrate selectivity. In addition, catalytic antibodies have been produced that have regioselectivity sufficient to produce a single product for a reaction in which other products are normally observed in the absence of the antibody. Finally, catalytic antibodies have been produced by immunization with a single-handed version (only left- or only right-handed) of a hapten, and only substrates with the same handedness can act as substrates for the resulting catalytic antibodies. The net result is that a high degree of stereoselectivity is observed in the antibody-catalyzed reaction.   [B.I.]

Cell (biology)   Cells can be separated into prokaryotic and eukaryotic categories. Eukaryotic cells contain a nucleus. They comprise protists (single-celled organisms), fungi, plants, and animals, and are generally 5–100 micrometers in linear dimension. Prokaryotic cells contain no nucleus, are relatively small (1–10 μm in diameter), and have a simple internal structure. They include two classes of bacteria: eubacteria (including photosynthetic organisms, or cyanobacteria), which are common bacteria inhabiting soil, water, and larger organisms; and archaebacteria, which grow under unusual conditions. *See* EUKARYOTAE; PROKARYOTAE.

    Prokaryotic (bacterial) cells. All eubacteria have an inner (plasma) membrane which serves as a semipermeable barrier allowing small nonpolar and polar molecules such as oxygen, carbon dioxide, and glycerol to diffuse across (down their concentration gradients), but does not allow the diffusion of larger polar molecules (sugars, amino acids, and so on) or inorganic ions such as Na^+, K^+, Cl^-, Ca^{2+} (sodium, potassium, chlorine, calcium). The plasma membrane, which is a lipid bilayer, utilizes transmembrane transporter and channel proteins to facilitate the movement of these molecules. Eubacteria can be further separated into two classes based on their ability to retain the dye crystal violet. Gram-positive cells retain the dye; their cell surface includes the inner plasma membrane and a cell wall composed of multiple layers of peptidoglycan. Gram-negative bacteria are surrounded by two membranes: the inner (plasma) membrane and an outer membrane that allows the passage of molecules of less than 1000 molecular weight through porin protein channels. Between the inner and outer membranes is the peptidoglycan-rich cell wall and the periplasmic space. *See* CELL PERMEABILITY.

    Eubacteria contain a single circular double-stranded molecule of deoxyribonucleic acid (DNA), or a single chromosome. As prokaryotic cells lack a nucleus, this genomic DNA resides in a central region of the cell called the nucleoid. The bacterial genome contains all the necessary information to maintain the structure and function of the cell.

    Many bacteria are able to move from place to place, or are motile. Their motility is based on a helical flagellum composed of interwoven protein called flagellin. The flagellum is attached to the cell surface through a basal body, and propels the bacteria through an aqueous environment by rotating like the propeller on a motor boat. The motor is reversible, allowing the bacteria to move toward chemoattractants and away from chemorepellants.

    Eukaryotic cells. In a light microscopic view of a eukaryotic cell, a plasma membrane can be seen which defines the outer boundaries of the cell, surrounding the cell's protoplasm or contents. The protoplasm includes the nucleus, where the cell's DNA is compartmentalized, and the remaining contents of the cell (the cytoplasm). The eukaryotic cell's organelles include the nucleus, mitochondria, endoplasmic reticulum, Golgi apparatus, lysosomes, peroxisomes, cytoskeleton, and plasma membrane (Fig. 1). The organelles occupy approximately half the total volume of the cytoplasm. The remaining compartment of cytoplasm (minus organelles) is referred to as the cytosol or cytoplasmic ground substance. Eukaryotic cells also differ from prokaryotic cells in having a cytoskeleton that gives the cell its shape, its capacity to move, and its ability to transport organelles and vesicles from one part of the cell cytoplasm to another. Eukaryotic cells are generally larger than prokaryotic cells and therefore require a cytoskeleton and membrane skeleton to maintain their shape, which is related to their functions.

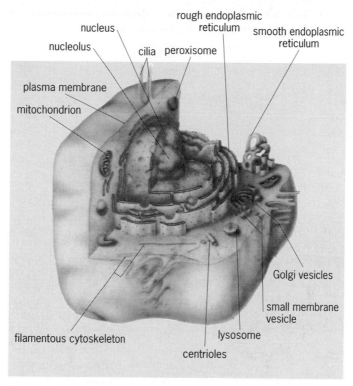

Fig. 1. Artist's rendition of a eukaryotic animal cell. (*Modified from H. Lodish et al., Molecular Cell Biology, 3d ed., Scientific American, New York, 1995*)

Eukaryotic cells contain a large amount of DNA (about a thousandfold more than bacterial cells), only approximately 1% of which encodes protein. The remaining DNA is structural (involved in DNA packaging) or regulatory (helping to switch on and off genes).

Plasma membrane. The plasma membrane serves as a selective permeability barrier between a cell's environment and cytoplasm. The fundamental structure of plasma membranes (as well as organelle membranes) is the lipid bilayer, formed due to the tendency of amphipathic phospholipids to bury their hydrophobic fatty acid tails away from water. Human and animal cell plasma membranes contain a varied composition of phospholipids, cholesterol, and glycolipids. *See* CELL MEMBRANES.

Cytoskeleton. The cytoskeleton is involved in establishing cell shape, polarity, and motility, and in directing the movement of organelles within the cell. The cytoskeleton includes microfilaments, microtubules, intermediate filaments, and the two-dimensional membrane skeleton that lines the cytoplasmic surface of cell membranes. *See* CYTOSKELETON.

Nucleus. One of the most prominent organelles within a eukaryotic cell is the nucleus. The nuclear compartment is separated from the rest of the cell by a specialized membrane complex built from two distinct lipid bilayers, referred to as the nuclear envelope. However, the interior of the nucleus maintains contact with the cell's cytoplasm via nuclear pores. The primary function of the nucleus is to house the genetic apparatus of the cell; this genetic machinery is composed of DNA (arranged in linear units called chromosomes), RNA, and proteins. Nuclear proteins aid in the performance of nuclear functions and include polypeptides that have a direct role in the regulation of gene function and those that give structure to the genetic material. *See* CELL NUCLEUS.

Endoplasmic reticulum. The endoplasmic reticulum is composed of membrane-enclosed flattened sacs or cisternae. The enclosed compartment is called the lumen. The endoplasmic reticulum is morphologically separated into rough (RER) and smooth (SER). PER is studded with ribosomes and SER is not. RER is the site of protein synthesis, while lipids are synthesized in both RER and SER. *See* ENDOPLASMIC RETICULUM.

Golgi apparatus. The final posttranslational modifications of proteins and glycolipids occur within a series of flattened membranous sacs called the Golgi apparatus. Vesicles which bud from the endoplasmic reticulum fuse with a specialized region of the cis Golgi compartment called the cis Golgi network. In the trans Golgi network, proteins and lipids are sorted into transport vesicles destined for lysosomes, the plasma membrane, or secretion. *See* GOLGI APPARATUS.

Lysosomes. Lysosomes are membrane-bound organelles with a luminal pH of 5.0, filled with acid hydrolyses. Lysosomes are responsible for degrading materials brought into the cell by endocytosis or phagocytosis, or autophagocytosis of spent cellular material. *See* ENDOCYTOSIS; LYSOSOME.

Mitochondria. The mitochondrion contains a double membrane: the outer membrane, which contains a channel-forming protein named porin, and an inner membrane, which contains multiple infolds called cristae. The inner membrane, which contains the protein complexes responsible for electron transport and oxidative phosphorylation, is folded into numerous cristae that increase the surface area per volume of this membrane. The transfer of electrons from nicotinamide adenine dinucleotide (NADH) or flavin adenine dinucleotide ($FADH_2$) down the electron transfer chain to oxygen causes protons to be pumped out of the mitochondrial matrix into the intermembrane space. The resulting proton motive force drives the conversion of ADP plus inorganic orthophosphate (P_i) to ATP by the enzyme ATP synthetase. *See* MITOCHONDRIA.

Peroxisomes. Within the peroxisome, hydrogen atoms are removed from organic substrates and hydrogen peroxide is formed. The enzyme catalase can then utilize the hydrogen peroxide to oxidize substrates such as alcohols, formaldehydes, and formic acid in detoxifying reactions. *See* PEROXISOME.

Plant cells. Plant cells are distinguished from other eukaryotic cells by various features. Outside their plasma membrane, plant cells have an extremely rigid cell wall. This cell wall is composed of cellulose and other polymers and is distinct in composition from the cell walls found in fungi or bacterial cells. The plant cell wall expands during cell growth, and a new cell wall partition is created between the two daughter cells during cell division. Similar cell walls are not observed in animal cells (Fig. 2).

Most plant cells contain membrane-encapsulated vacuoles as major components of their cytoplasm. These vacuoles contain water, sucrose, ions, nitrogen-containing compounds formed by nitrogen fixation, and waste products.

Chloroplasts are the other major organelle in plant cells that is not found in other eukaryotic cells. Like mitochondria, they are constantly in motion within the cytoplasm. One of the pigments found in chloroplasts is chlorophyll, which is the molecule that absorbs light and gives the green coloration to the chloroplast. Chloroplasts, like mitochondria, have an outer and inner membrane. Within the matrix of the chloroplast there is an intricate internal membrane system. The internal membranes are made up of flattened interconnected vesicles that take on a disc-like structure (thylakoid vesicles). The thylakoid vesicles are stacked to form structures called grana, which are separated by a space called the stroma. Within the stroma, carbon dioxide (CO_2) fixation occurs, in which carbon dioxide is converted to various intermediates during the production of

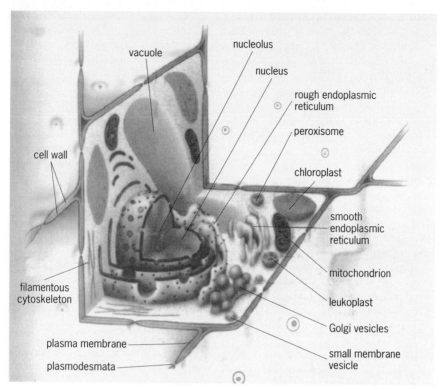

Fig. 2. Artist's rendition of a typical plant cell. (*Modified from H. Lodish et al., Molecular Cell Biology, 3d ed., Scientific American, New York, 1999***)**

sugars. Chlorophyll is found within the thylakoid vesicles; it absorbs light and, with the involvement of other pigments and enzymes, generates ATP during photosynthesis. *See* PLANT CELL.

[S.R.G.]

Cell biology   The study of the activities, functions, properties, and structures of cells. Cells were discovered in the middle of the seventeenth century after the microscope was invented. In the following two centuries, with steadily improved microscopes, cells were studied in a wide variety of plants, animals, and microorganisms, leading to the discovery of the cell nucleus and several other major cell parts. By the 1830s biologists recognized that all organisms are composed of cells, a realization that is now known as the Cell Doctrine. The Cell Doctrine constitutes the first major tenet upon which the contemporary science of cell biology is founded. By the late 1800s biologists had established that cells do not arise de novo, but come only by cell division, that is, division of a preexisting cell into two daughter cells. This is the second major tenet upon which the modern study of cells is based.

By the end of the nineteenth century chromosomes had been discovered, and biologists had described mitosis—the distribution at cell division of chromosomes to daughter cells. Subsequent studies showed that the chromosomes contain genes and that mitosis distributes a copy of every chromosome and hence every gene to each daughter cell during cell division. This established the basis of cell heredity and ultimately the basis of heredity in multicellular organisms. *See* CHROMOSOME; MITOSIS.

Microscope studies established that some kinds of organisms are composed of a single cell and some, such as plants and animals, are made up of many cells—usually many billions. Unicellular organisms are the bacteria, protozoa, some fungi, and some algae. All other organisms are multicellular. An adult human, for example, consists of about 200 cell types that collectively amount to more than 10^{14} cells.

All modern research recognizes that in both unicellular and multicellular organisms the cell is the fundamental unit, housing the genetic material and the biochemical organization that account for the existence of life. Many millions of different species of cells exist on Earth. Cells as different as a bacterium, an ameba, a plant leaf cell, and a human liver cell appear to be so unrelated in structure and life-style that they might seem to have little in common; however, the study of cells has shown that the similarities among these diverse cell types are more profound than the differences. These studies have established a modern set of tenets that bring unity to the study of many diverse cell types. These tenets are: (1) All cells store information in genes made of deoxyribonucleic acid (DNA). (2) The genetic code used in the genes is the same in all species of cells. (3) All cells decode the genes in their DNA by a ribonucleic acid (RNA) system that translates genetic information into proteins. (4) All cells synthesize proteins by using a structure called the ribosome. (5) Proteins govern the activities, functions, and structures in all cells. (6) All cells need energy to operate; all use the molecule adenosine triphosphate (ATP) as the currency for transfer of energy from energy sources to energy needs. (7) All cells are enclosed by a plasma membrane composed of lipid and protein molecules. See CELL MEMBRANES; GENETICS; RIBOSOMES.

In the twentieth century the study of cells, which had been dominated for more than 200 years by microscopy, has been enormously expanded with many other experimental methods. The breaking open of a large mass of cells and the separation of released cell parts into pure fractions led to the discovery of functions contributed by different structures and organelles.

Contemporary research in cell biology is concerned with many problems of cell operation and behavior. Cell reproduction is of special concern because it is essential for the survival of all unicellular and multicellular forms of life. Cell reproduction is the means by which a single cell, the fertilized egg, can give rise to the trillions of cells in an adult multicellular organism. Disrupted control of cell reproduction, resulting in accumulation of disorganized masses of functionally useless cells, is the essence of cancer. Indeed, all diseases ultimately result from the death or misfunctioning of one or another group of cells in a plant or animal. The study of cells pervades all areas of medical research and medical treatment. Great advances have been made in learning how cells of the immune system combat infection, and the nature of their failure to resist the acquired immune deficiency syndrome (AIDS) virus. See ACQUIRED IMMUNE DEFICIENCY SYNDROME (AIDS); CELL SENESCENCE AND DEATH.

The development of methods to grow plant and animal cells in culture has provided new ways to study cells free of the experimental complications encountered with intact plants and animals. Cell culture has greatly facilitated analysis of abnormal cells, including transformation of normal cells into cancer cells. Cultured cells are also used extensively to study cell differentiation, cell aging, cell movement, and many other cell functions.   [D.M.Pr.]

Cell constancy   The condition in which the entire body of an adult animal or plant consists of a fixed number of cells that is the same in all members of the species. This phenomenon is also called eutely. The largest group of animals exhibiting eutely are the nematode worms, one of the largest of all animal phyla, and of great medical and agricultural importance as parasites of plants, animals, and humans. A plant that exhibits eutely is usually called a coenobium. Many species of semimicroscopic aquatic green algae exist as coenobia, such as the common *Volvox* and *Pandorina*.

Numerical limitation occurs in certain organs and organ systems, notably the brain and muscles of annelid worms, mollusks, and vertebrates. A related but different phenomenon, observed for many animal cells when cultured, is that normal cells divide some specific number of times and then stop dividing. Thus the life-span, as measured by number of cell cycles, is limited; for many human cell types this is about 50 cell generations.

In annelids and vertebrates, cell proliferation is more or less continuous throughout life only in those tissues that are subject to wear. Thus, in adults, cell division may be found in the germinative zones of the skin, hair, finger and toe nails, the lining of the alimentary canal, and especially in the blood cell-forming tissues. The muscles and nervous system, however, appear to undergo no cell division after early embryonic or fetal stages. In both earthworms and mammals, including humans, it has been demonstrated that the number of muscle nuclei and muscle fibers, but not fibrils, is fixed early and does not increase with subsequent growth. An earthworm hatches from its egg cocoon with the adult number of muscle fibers and nuclei. A human fetus, about 5 in. (13 cm) from crown to rump, has as many muscle fibers and nuclei as an adult. It has been shown that the number of glomeruli in each kidney of a rat or human, and therefore presumably of any mammal, is fixed before birth, and that the subsequent growth of the glomeruli, either normally or resulting from compensatory hypertrophy after unilateral nephrectomy, is due entirely to the enlargement of cells already present. The same holds true for the cells of the ciliated nephrostomes of earthworms.   [G.B.M.]

Cell cycle   The succession of events that culminates in the asexual reproduction of a cell; also known as cell division cycle. In a typical cell cycle, the parent cell doubles its volume, mass, and complement of chromosomes, then sorts its doubled contents to opposite sides of the cell, and finally divides in half to yield two genetically identical offspring. Implicit in the term "cycle" is the idea that division brings the double-sized parent cell back to its original size and chromosome number, and ready to begin another cell cycle. This idea fits well with the behavior of many unicellular organisms, but for multicellular organisms the daughter cells may differ from their parent cell and from each other in terms of size, shape, and differentiation state.

The time required for completion of a eukaryotic cell cycle varies enormously from cell to cell. Embryonic cells that do not need to grow between divisions can complete a cell cycle in as little as 8 min, whereas cycling times of 10–24 h are typical of the most rapidly dividing somatic cells. Many somatic cells divide much less frequently; liver cells divide about once a year, and mature neurons never divide. Such cells may be thought of as temporarily or permanently withdrawing from the cell cycle.

Eukaryotic phases. The cell cycle is divided into two main parts: interphase and mitosis (see illustration). During interphase, the cell grows and replicates its chromosomes. Interphase accounts for all but an hour or two of a 24-h cell cycle, and is subdivided into three phases: gap phase 1 (G1), synthesis (S), and gap phase 2 (G2). Interphase is followed by mitosis (nuclear division) and cytokinesis (cell division). This relatively brief part of the cell cycle includes some of the most dramatic events in cell biology.

G1 phase. Gap phase 1 begins at the completion of mitosis and cytokinesis and lasts until the beginning of S phase. This phase is generally the longest of the four cell cycle phases and is quite variable in length. During this phase, the cell chooses either to replicate its deoxyribonucleic acid (DNA) or to exit the cell cycle and enter a quiescent state (the G0 phase).

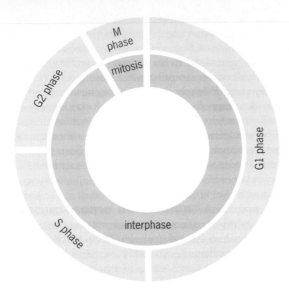

Phases of the eukaryotic cell cycle.

S phase. Replication of the chromosomes is restricted to one specific portion of interphase, called S phase (DNA synthesis phase), which typically lasts about 6 h. In mammalian cells, the start of S phase—the actual initiation of DNA synthesis—takes place several hours after the cell has committed to carrying out DNA synthesis. During S phase, each chromosome replicates exactly once to form a pair of physically linked sister chromatids. In animal cells, a pair of centrioles is also duplicated during S phase. *See* CHROMOSOME; GENETICS.

G2 phase. The portion of interphase that follows S phase is called gap phase 2. Some cells can exit the cell cycle from G2 phase, just as they can from G1 phase.

M phase. M phase includes the overlapping processes of mitosis and cytokinesis. Mitosis is divided into five stages: prophase, prometaphase, metaphase, anaphase, and telophase. Cytokinesis usually begins during anaphase and ends at a point after the completion of mitosis. At the end of cytokinesis, the parent cell has formed its two G1 phase progeny and the cell is ready to repeat the cycle. *See* CYTOKINESIS; MITOSIS.

Control of cell cycle. The network of proteins that regulate DNA synthesis (G1/S), mitotic entry (G1/M), and mitotic exit (the transition from mitotic metaphase to anaphase and then out of mitosis) appears to be well conserved throughout eukaryotic evolution. At the heart of these cell cycle transitions is the periodic activation and inactivation of cyclin-dependent protein kinases. In addition, in multicellular eukaryotes, pathways regulating entry into and exit from the cell cycle entrain these central cyclin-dependent kinases to extrinsic signals.   [J.E.F.]

Cell differentiation   The mechanism by which cells in a multicellular organism become specialized to perform specific functions in a variety of tissues and organs. Specialized cells are the product of differentiation. The process can be understood only from a historical perspective, and the best place to start is the fertilized egg. Different kinds of cell behavior can be observed during embryogenesis: cells double, change in shape, and attach at and migrate to various sites within the embryo without any obvious signs of differentiation. Cleavage is a rapid series of cell cycles during which the large egg cell is divided into a ball of small cells that line the primitive body cavity as a single layer of embryonic cells. This blastula stage is followed by gastrulation, a complex coordinated cellular migration which not only shapes the embryo but segregates the single-cell layer of the blastula into the three germ layers: endoderm, mesoderm, ectoderm. They give rise to specific cell types; for example, skin and nerves from the ectoderm, the digestive tract from the endoderm, and muscle and connective tissue from the mesoderm. *See* BLASTULATION; CELL CYCLE; CLEAVAGE (EMBRYOLOGY); EMBRYOGENESIS; GASTRULATION.

The stable differentiated state is a consequence of multicellularity. A complex organism maintains its characteristic form and identity because populations of specialized cell types remain assembled in a certain pattern. Thus several kinds of cells make up a tissue, and different tissues build organs. The variable assortment of about 200 cell types allows for an almost infinite variety of distinct organisms.

Epithelia, sheets of cells of specific structure and function, cover the outer surface of the vertebrate body and line the lungs, gut, and vascular system. The stable form of a vertebrate is due to its rigid skeleton built from bone and cartilage, forming cells to which the skeletal muscles adhere. All other organs, such as liver and pancreas, are embedded in connective tissue that is derived from fibroblast cells which secrete large amounts of soft matrix material.

Some cells, like nerve cells, are so specialized that they need divide no longer in order to maintain a complex network. Their finite number decreases even during embryonic development. Other cell types are constantly worn out and must be replaced; for example, fibroblasts and pancreas cells simply divide as needed, proving that the differentiated state of cells is heritable, as the daughter cells remember and carry out the same special functions. The renewal of terminally differentiated cells that are unable to divide anymore, such as skin and blood cells, is carried out by stem cells. They are immortal and choose, as they double, whether to remain a stem cell or to embark on a path of terminal differentiation. Most stem cells are unipotent because they give rise to a single differentiated cell type. However, all cell types of the blood are derived from a single blood-forming stem cell, a pluripotent stem cell. A fertilized egg is a totipotent stem cell giving rise to all other cell types that make up an individual organism. *See* EMBRYONIC DIFFERENTIATION; EMBRYONIC INDUCTION; OOGENESIS.   [H.Sa.]

Cell lineage   A type of embryological study in which the history of individual blastomeres (cells formed during division of the zygote) or meristem cells is traced to their ultimate differentiation into tissues and organs.

The question of how the animal genome can be regulated to produce the various cell types found in the larval and adult organism is a central concern in developmental biology. A possible approach to this problem would involve tracing the structural fates of the descendants of each of a population of progenitor cells, and then trying to determine which gene products are required for particular steps in the process of cell differentiation.

Some of the most promising cell lineage studies are conducted on a nematode worm, *Caenorhabditis elegans*, which is a small (1 mm or 0.04 in. in length), nearly transparent worm that lives in soil. Adults are either males or hermaphrodites; the hermaphrodites contain 959 somatic nuclei. The origin of each somatic cell can be traced back to a single blastomere, and the clonal history of each cell has been determined. A detailed genetic map for the 80,000-kilobase genome has been worked out. *See* CLEAVAGE (EMBRYOLOGY); FATE MAPS (EMBRYOLOGY).   [S.J.B.]

Cell lineage analysis in plants, as in animals, involves tracing the origin of particular cells in the adult body back to their progenitor cells. The adult body of a typical plant consists primarily of leaves, stems, and roots. Cells arise continuously during plant life from specialized dividing cell populations called meristems. A shoot apical meristem produces the leaves and stem, and a root apical meristem produces root tissue. The shoot apical meristem will also produce specialized structures, such as cones, flowers, and thorns. Because plant cells do not move during development, and in many cases the plane of cell division is constant, lines of cells, called cell files, all derive from a single meristem cell at the base of the file. [V.W.]

Cell membrane The membrane that surrounds the cytoplasm of a cell; it is also called the plasma membrane or, in a more general sense, a unit membrane. This is a very thin, semifluid, sheetlike structure made of four continuous monolayers of molecules. The plasma membrane and the membranes making up all the intracellular membranous organelles display a common molecular architectural pattern of organization, the unit membrane pattern, even though the particular molecular species making up the membranes differ considerably. All unit membranes consist of a bilayer of lipid molecules, the polar surfaces of which are directed outward and covered by at least one monolayer of nonlipid molecules on each side, most of which are protein, packed on the lipid bilayer surfaces and held there by various intermolecular forces. Some of these proteins, called intrinsic proteins, traverse the bilayer and are represented on both sides. The segments of the polypeptide chains of these transverse proteins within the core of the lipid bilayer may form channels that provide low-resistance pathways for ions and small molecules to get across the membrane in a controlled fashion. Sugar moieties are found in both the proteins and lipids of the outer half of the unit membrane, but not on the inside next to the cytoplasm. The molecular composition of each lipid monolayer making up the lipid bilayer is different. The unit membrane is thus chemically asymmetric. *See* CELL ORGANIZATION.

Unit membrane. The unit membrane of a cell is a continuous structure having one surface bordered by cytoplasm and the other by the outside world. It appears in thin sections with the electron microscope as a triple-layered structure about 7.5–10 nanometers thick consisting of two parallel dense strata each about 2.5 nm thick separated by a light interzone of about the same thickness. The plasma membrane may become tucked into the cytoplasm and pinch off to make an isolated vesicle containing extracellular material by a process called endocytosis. During endocytosis the membrane maintains its orientation, with its cytoplasmic surface remaining next to cytoplasm. In this sense the contents of intracellular organelles, such as the endoplasmic reticulum, Golgi apparatus sacs, nuclear membrane, lysosomes, peroxisomes, and secretion granules, are material of the outside world, since at some time the space occupied by this material may become continuous directly or indirectly with the outside world. Hence the surface of the membrane bordering such material and lying between it and cytoplasm is topographically an external membrane surface even though it may be contained completely within the cell. *See* ENDOCYTOSIS.

Eukaryotic cells are characterized by the triple-layered nature of the unit membrane. The genetic material is segregated into a central region bounded by the nuclear membrane that is penetrated by many pores containing special proteins. Bacteria (prokaryotes) do not contain such elaborate systems of internal membranes, but some have an external unit membrane separated from the plasma membrane by a special material called periplasm. The membrane does not normally flip over, so that the surface that borders the outside world, either at the cell surface or inside the cell, comes to border cytoplasm. This principle is maintained in all membranous organelles.

Mitochondria are a special case because the inner mitochondrial membrane is believed to be the membrane of a primitive one-celled organism that is symbiotically related to the cell and lies inside a cavity containing material of the outside world as defined above. The outer mitochondrial membrane is in this sense a membrane of the cell analogous to a smooth endoplasmic reticulum membrane, and the inner membrane of the mitochondrion is the plasma membrane of the included organism, which normally does not become continuous with the membrane of the cell. Thus it has its own unit membrane, and again the orientation of this unit membrane is always maintained, with one side directed toward the cytoplasm, in this case the cytoplasm of the mitochondrion. *See* MITOCHONDRIA.

Function. The cell membrane functions as a barrier that makes it possible for the cytoplasm to maintain a different composition from the material surrounding the cell. The unit membrane is freely permeable to water molecules but very impermeable to ions and charged molecules. It is permeable to small molecules in inverse proportion to their size but in direct proportion to their lipid solubility. It contains various pumps and channels made of specific transverse membrane proteins that allow concentration gradients to be maintained between the inside and outside of the cell. For example, there is a cation pump that actively extrudes sodium ions (Na^+) from the cytoplasm and builds up a concentration of potassium ions (K^+) within it. The major anions inside the cell are chlorine ions (Cl^-) and negatively charged protein molecules, the latter of which cannot penetrate the membrane. The presence of the charged protein molecules leads to a buildup of electroosmotic potential across the membrane. Action potentials result from the transient opening of Na^+ or calcium ion (Ca^{2+}) channels depolarizing the membrane, followed by an opening of K^+ channels leading to repolarization. This is one of the most important functions of membranes, since it makes it possible for the brain to work by sending or receiving signals sent over nerve fibers for great distances, as well as many other things. *See* BIOPOTENTIALS AND IONIC CURRENTS.

The plasma membrane contains numerous receptor molecules that are involved in communication with other cells and the outside world in general. These respond to antigens, hormones, and neurotransmitters in various ways. For example, thymus lymphocytes (T cells) are activated by attachment of antigens to specific proteins in the external surfaces of the T cells, an important part of the immune responses of an organism. Hormones such as epinephrine and glucagon attach to a receptor protein in the surfaces of cells and cause the activation of adenylate cyclase, which in turn causes the formation of cyclic adenosine monophosphate. Neurotransmitters attach to the postsynaptic membrane in synapses and mediate the transfer of information between neurons. There is a class of membrane proteins called cell adhesion molecules, components of the outer surfaces of cell membranes in the developing nervous system, that is thought to be involved in guiding embryonic development.

Membrane lipids. The major lipids of membranes are phospholipids with a glycerol backbone including phosphophatidyl ethanolamine, phosphatidyl choline, phosphatidyl serine, phosphatidyl inositol, and cardiolipin. Cardiolipin is more complex because it contains two glycerols and four fatty acids. It is important in bacterial membranes and is also found in the mitochondrial inner membrane.

The sphingolipids are another class of membrane lipids having the compound sphingosine as their backbone structure instead of glycerol. Ceramide is a fatty acid derivative of sphingosine that is the parent substance of many important membrane lipids. Sphingomyelin is ceramide with phosphatidyl choline added. This molecule, like phosphatidyl choline and phosphatidyl ethanolamine, is a zwitterion at pH 7; that is, it is uncharged. Phosphatidyl serine is negatively charged.

The glycolipids are an important class of lipid not containing phosphorus and based on ceramide. These include the uncharged cerebrosides that have only one sugar group, either glucose or galactose, and the gangliosides that may contain branched chains of as many as seven sugar residues including sialic acid, which is charged.

Cholesterol is a very important membrane lipid. It is present only in eukaryotes and is a prominent constituent of red blood cells, liver cells, and nerve myelin. *See* CHOLESTEROL.

The different lipid molecules are not equally distributed on both sides of the bilayer. The amino lipids, glycolipids, and cholesterol are located primarily in the outer mono-layer, and the choline and sphingolipids are located mainly in the internal monolayer. The fatty acids of the outer half of the bilayer tend to have longer, more saturated carbon chains than those of the inner half.

The lipid bilayer has a considerable degree of fluidity, with the lipid molecules tend-ing to rotate and translate easily, but they do not ordinarily flipflop from one side of the bilayer to the other. Furthermore, some lipids are firmly attached to mem-brane proteins and translate laterally only as the proteins do so. Some membrane proteins form extended two-dimensional crystals, and their lateral movement is thus restricted. Nevertheless, there is a considerable degree of fluidity in membranes overall. *See* LIPID.

Membrane proteins. The ratio of protein to lipids in membranes is often about 1:1, but in some cases, such as nerve myelin, there is only about 20% protein. Usually polypeptide chains are folded into a globular structure with hydrophilic amino acid side chains to the outside and hydrophobic ones tucked inside. For this reason the common globular protein is hydrophilic. Sometimes stretches of hydrophobic amino acids occur in the chain and may divide it into two hydrophilic domains. If there is a stretch of hydrophobic amino acids long enough (about 20) to stretch across the hydrophobic interior of a membrane bilayer, the extrusion of the protein across the bilayer during protein synthesis may stop, leaving a hydrophilic part of the protein on the cytoplasmic side and another hydrophilic part on the outside. This protein then becomes an intrinsic amphiphilic transmembrane protein. Such proteins can be removed only with chaotropic agents that destroy the bilayer.

The classification of membrane proteins as intrinsic and extrinsic is not always easy. Some proteins clearly become attached to either the inside or outside of the bilayer by more specific interactions with the polar heads of the lipid molecules, and sometimes it is not clear whether such proteins should be called extrinsic or intrinsic. They are extrinsic in that they can be removed without using detergents to disrupt the lipid bilayer completely, but they are intrinsic in that they are permanent parts of the membrane and retain some tightly bound lipids when removed. Spectrin and anchorin in the erythrocyte membrane are firmly bound to the cytoplasmic surfaces presumably by polar head group interactions and can thus be regarded as intrinsic. *See* CELL (BIOLOGY); PLANT CELL; PROTEIN. [J.D.Ro.]

Cell metabolism The sum of chemical reactions which transpire within cells. The cell performs chemical, osmotic, mechanical, and electrical work, for which it needs energy. Plant cells obtain energy from sunlight; using light energy, they convert simple compounds such as carbon dioxide and various nitrogen, phosphate, and sul-fur compounds into more complex materials. The energy in light is thus "stored" as chemical substances, mostly carbohydrates, within plant cells. Animal cells cannot use sunlight directly, and they obtain their energy by breaking down the stored chemical compounds of plant cells. Bacterial cells obtain their energy in various ways, but again mostly by the degradation of some of the simple compounds in their environment. *See* BACTERIAL PHYSIOLOGY AND METABOLISM; PHOTOSYNTHESIS; PLANT METABOLISM.

Cells have definite structures, and even the chemical constituents of these struc-tures are being constantly renewed. This continuing turnover has been called the dynamic state of cellular constituents. For example, an animal cell takes in carbohydrate molecules, breaks down some of them to obtain the energy which is necessary to replace the chemical molecules that are being turned over, while another fraction of these molecules is integrated into the substance of the cell or its extracellular coverings. The cell is constantly striving to maintain an organized structure in the face of an environment which is continuously striving to degrade that structure into a random mixture of chemical molecules.

All the large molecules of the cell have specific functions: Carbohydrates, fats, and proteins constitute the structures of the cells; these, particularly the former two, are also used for food, or energy, depots; the nucleic acids are the structures involved in the continuity of cell types from generation to generation. All these large molecules are really variegated polymers of smaller molecules. These smaller molecules interact with one another in chemical reactions which are catalyzed at cellular temperature by enzymes. All these reactions are very specific each enzyme only reacting with its own specified substrate or substrates. At present, about a thousand chemical reactions are known which occur within cells; thus, about a thousand specific enzymes are known. By studying how enzymes operate and what substrates they attack, the biochemist has learned in general, and in many cases in specific, how fats, carbohydrates, proteins, and nucleic acids are synthesized and degraded in cells. Mainly through the use of radioactive tracer atoms, the pathways of many chemical compounds within the cell have been realized. For example, it is known what part of the carbohydrate molecule is used for energy production, what part is used in fat storage, and what parts end up in proteins and nucleic acids. See CARBOHYDRATE METABOLISM; ENZYME; LIPID METABOLISM; NUCLEIC ACID; PROTEIN METABOLISM.

Via the vast array of enzymatic reactions which go on inside cells, the substances which a cell brings in are completely changed, becoming transformed into cell substance. This changeover needs energy for accomplishment. This energy comes from a chemical compound called adenosine triphosphate (ATP); it is synthesized enzymatically by the cell in a number of reactions in which various compounds coming from foodstuffs are oxidized, and the energy gained as a result is stored in ATP. Subsequently, all cellular reactions which require synthesis of cell-specific substances use this ATP as a source of energy. See ADENOSINE TRIPHOSPHATE (ATP).

Remarkably, even with these constant replacements going on, the cell never loses its own distinctive structure and function. The reason is that the ordering of the cell resides in a code of nucleic acids, which directs the syntheses of specific enzymes designed to do specific tasks; when these enzymes are degraded and have to be resynthesized, they are made again in exactly the same way as before. In this way continuity is ensured. See DEOXYRIBONUCLEIC ACID (DNA); GENETICS; RIBONUCLEIC ACID (RNA).

Although a great deal is known of the metabolism of a large variety of compounds (their degradation, syntheses, and interactions), little is known of how these multitudinous reactions are regulated within the cell to effect growth, particular size, and division into daughter cells having the same structure and functioning characteristics as those of the parent cells. It is known that enzymatic reaction activities within cells are strictly governed so that in quite a few cases knowledge has been gained of how a cell shuts off the synthesis of a compound of which it has enough, or speeds up the syntheses of those in short supply. This is done by an enzyme so constructed that the compound which it synthesizes, say, can interact with the enzyme to inhibit its further activity.

Almost the sole justification for cell metabolism is the functioning of a vehicle whose major task is to reproduce as precise a replica of itself as possible. The efficiency of this metabolism has been maximized with this goal in view. See CELL (BIOLOGY).   [P.Si.]

Cell motility   The movement of cells, changes in cell shape including cell division, and the movement of materials within cells. Many free-living protozoa are capable of movement, as are sperm and ameboid cells of higher organisms. Coordinated movement of cells occurs during embryogenesis, wound healing, and muscle contraction in higher organisms. Cell division is observed in all organisms and is a requirement for reproduction, growth, and development. Many cells also undergo structural changes as they differentiate, such as the outgrowth of axonal and dendritic processes during nerve cell differentiation. A more subtle form of cell motility involves the active transport of membranous organelles within the cytoplasm. This form of movement is required for proper organization of the cytoplasmic contents, and the redistribution of metabolites, hormones, and other materials within the cell.

There are two basic molecular systems responsible for producing a variety of forms of movement in a wide range of cell types: one system involves filamentous polymers of the globular protein actin; the other involves hollow, tube-shaped polymers of the globular protein tubulin, known as microtubules. Associated with both actin filaments and microtubules are accessory enzymes that convert the chemical energy stored in adenosine triphosphate (ATP) into mechanical energy. Other proteins are responsible for regulating the arrangement, assembly, and organization of actin filaments and microtubules within the cell.

Actin and myosin. Muscle contraction represents one of the most extensively studied forms of cell movement, and it is from muscle that much basic knowledge of actin-based movement has been derived. Striated muscle cells found in skeletal muscle and heart muscle contain highly organized arrays of actin filaments interdigitating with filaments of the protein myosin. Myosin has an enzymatic activity that catalyzes the breakdown of ATP to adenosine diphosphate (ADP) and phosphate. The released energy is used to produce force against the actin filaments, which results in sliding between the actin and myosin filaments. *See* MUSCLE PROTEINS.

These proteins have by now been found in virtually all cell types. Actin is involved in a wide variety of movements in many cell types, such as ameboid movement, lamellipodial extension, cytoplasmic streaming, and cytokinesis. *See* CYTOKINESIS.

Microtubules, dynein, and kinesin. Like actin filaments, microtubules have by now been found within the cytoplasm of almost all eukaryotic cells. They are involved in a variety of forms of movement, including ciliary and flagellar movement in eukaryotes, organelle movement in cytoplasm, and chromosome movement during mitosis. *See* CILIA AND FLAGELLA; MITOSIS.

Two different molecules, dynein and kinesin, have been identified as enzymes that break down ATP to ADP and phosphate to produce force along microtubules. Dynein is a large enzyme complex that was initially identified in cilia and flagella. It has also been found associated with cytoplasmic microtubules. Kinesin is a force-producing enzyme that was initially found in microtubules prepared from neuronal cells. It is now also known to be widespread.

Despite the basic similarity in how the three force-producing enzymes (myosin, dynein, and kinesin) work, they differ from each other in structure and enzymatic properties and there is no evidence that they are evolutionarily related. Kinesin and dynein differ from each other in another important way: they produce force in opposite directions along microtubules. This suggests that they play complementary roles in the cell. As yet, no enzyme has been identified that produces force along actin filaments in the direction opposite to myosin.

Other motile proteins. Other motile mechanisms certainly exist. For example, bacterial flagella are very fine helical hairs, unlike the more substantial flagella and cilia of eukaryotic cells. Bacterial flagella rotate about their axis and propel the bacterium by a corkscrewlike mechanism, unlike the bending and whiplashing movements of eukaryotic cilia and flagella. Bacterial flagella are hollow filamentous polymers, like microtubules, but are composed of the protein flagellin, which has no apparent relationship to tubulin. *See* BACTERIA.

Other forms of bacteria glide over solid substrata by using an excreted slime for propulsion; the mechanism of gliding is not understood. Gliding motility is also seen in a number of algae and blue-green algae.

The sperm cells of roundworms differ from other types of sperm cells in that they lack flagella and exhibit a form of ameboid movement. These cells, however, contain neither actin, which is involved in ameboid movement in other ameboid cells, nor tubulin. Movement may be produced by insertion of lipid in the forward region of the plasma membrane and rearward flow of the membrane.

A contractile protein, spasmin, has been identified in *Vorticella* and related ciliated protozoa. Spasmin is organized into a long, thick fiber within the stalk portion of the organism. In response to calcium, the fiber undergoes a rapid, drastic contraction. It is not known whether spasmin exists in other organisms. *See* CELL (BIOLOGY).

Disease. Understanding how cells move increases the ability to control abnormal cell behavior, such as the increased level of cell division responsible for cancer and the migration of cancer cells from their site of origin in the body. Errors in chromosome segregation are also known to be responsible for Down syndrome, and are prevalent during the progression of neoplastic tumors.

Because the normal functioning of cells is so dependent on proteins that compose and regulate microtubules and actin filaments, defects in these proteins are expected to have severe effects on cell viability. An example of a microtubule defect has been identified in Alzheimer's disease: a microtubule-associated protein (termed tau) is found to be a prominent component of abnormal neurofibrillary tangles seen in affected nerve cells. However, it remains unknown whether the defect involving tau is part of the cause of the disease or represents one of its effects. *See* ALZHEIMER'S DISEASE; DOWN SYNDROME.

[R.V.]

Cell nucleus   The largest of the membrane-bounded organelles which characterize eukaryotic cells; it is thought of as the control center since it contains the bulk of the cell's genetic information in the form of deoxyribonucleic acid (DNA). The nucleus has two major functions: (1) It is the site of synthesis of ribonucleic acid (RNA), which in turn directs the formation of the protein molecules on which all life depends; and (2) in any cell preparing for division, the nucleus precisely duplicates its DNA for later distribution to cell progeny. *See* DEOXYRIBONUCLEIC ACID (DNA); EUKARYOTAE; RIBONUCLEIC ACID (RNA).

The diameter of nuclei ranges from 1 micrometer in intracellular parasites and yeast cells to several millimeters in some insect sperm. Spherical or ellipsoidal nuclei are found in most cell types, although occasionally spindle-shaped, lobulated, disc-shaped, or cup-shaped nuclei may be observed. Although nuclear size and shape are somewhat consistent features of a particular cell type, these features are more variable in cancer cells. In addition, tumor cell nuclei are characterized by indentation, furrowing, elongation, and budding.

The nucleus is bounded by a double membrane (the nuclear envelope) and contains several major components: chromatin, which is composed of DNA and chromosomal proteins; the nucleolus, which is the site of ribosomal RNA (rRNA) synthesis; and nucleoplasmic fibrils and granules, some of which are involved in the processing and

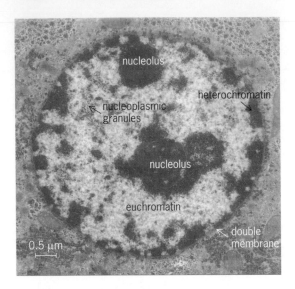

Transmission electron micrograph of a thin section of a rat liver cell nucleus.

transport of messenger RNA out of the nucleus (see illustration). The constituents of the nucleus are contained within a framework referred to as the nuclear matrix. [D.L.S]

Cell organization   Cells are divided into several compartments, each with a characteristic structure, biochemical composition, and function (see illustration). These compartments are called organelles. They are delimited by membranes composed of phospholipid bilayers and a number of proteins specialized for each type of organelle. All eukaryotic cells have a nucleus surrounded by a nuclear envelope, and a plasma membrane that borders the whole cell. Most eukaryotic cells also have endoplasmic reticulum, a Golgi apparatus, lysosomes, mitochondria, and peroxisomes. Plant cells have chloroplasts for photosynthesis in addition to the organelles that both they and animal cells possess. These organelles are suspended in a gellike cytoplasmic matrix composed of three types of protein polymers called actin filaments, microtubules, and intermediate filaments. In addition to holding the cell together, the actin filaments and microtubules act as tracks for several different types of motor proteins that are responsible for cell motility and organelle movements within the cytoplasm.

A major challenge in the field of cell biology is to learn how each organelle and the cytoplasmic matrix are assembled and distributed in the cytoplasm. This is a very complex process since cells consist of more than 2000 different protein molecules together with a large number of lipids, polysaccharides, and nucleic acids, including both deoxyribonucleic acid (DNA) and many different types of ribonucleic acid (RNA). *See* NUCLEIC ACID.

The cell must possess enough information to specify which molecules are to be associated in a specific compartment, to route the appropriate groups of molecules to their compartments, and then to position each type of component appropriately in the cell. As a result of intense research on each of these topics, a number of specific chemical reactions that contribute to organizing cells are now recognized, but even more important, a small number of general principles that explain these complex processes of life can be appreciated.

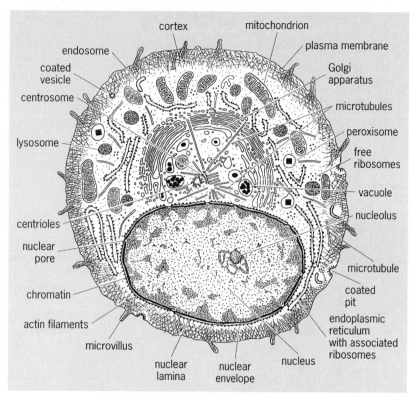

endosome
cortex
mitochondrion
plasma membrane
coated vesicle
Golgi apparatus
centrosome
microtubules
lysosome
peroxisome
free ribosomes
vacuole
nucleolus
centrioles
nuclear pore
microtubule
chromatin
coated pit
actin filaments
endoplasmic reticulum with associated ribosomes
microvillus
nuclear lamina
nuclear envelope
nucleus

Section through an animal cell showing the major components visible by electron microscopy. To simplify, a few important components, including intermediate filaments, have been omitted.

Normal cells regulate the production and degradation of all of their constituent molecules so that the right balance of molecules is present at any given time. The genes stored in nuclear DNA are duplicated precisely once per cell cycle. The supply of each of thousands of proteins is usually regulated at the level of the genes at the time of biosynthesis and by the rate of degradation. These proteins serve as enzymes that determine the rate of synthesis of themselves as well as of other cellular components such as nucleic acids, carbohydrates, and lipids. Each of these processes is regulated by molecular feedback loops to assure the proper levels of each cellular constituent. *See* CELL CYCLE; CELL METABOLISM.

A large majority of cellular components are generated by the self-assembly of their constituent molecules. Self-assembly means that the information required for molecules to bind together in the proper orientation is contained in the molecules themselves. Some examples include the binding of histones to DNA, the formation of bilayers from phospholipids, and the polymerization of actin molecules into filaments. The molecules are usually brought together by diffusion. The energy required to hold them together derives from the exclusion of water from their complementary surfaces as well as from the formation of ionic bonds and hydrogen bonds. The variety of molecular structures found in proteins allows each type to self-assemble specifically, only with their correct partner molecules.

After biosynthesis, proteins and nucleic acids are routed to their proper cellular compartment by specific recognition signals consisting of parts of the molecule or, in the case of some proteins, by sugar side chains. These signals are recognized by compartment-specific receptors that guide the molecules to the correct compartment. For example, proteins destined for lysosomes have a specific sugar side chain added in the Golgi apparatus that guides them to lysosomes. Similarly, proteins destined for the nucleus all contain short sequences of amino acids that target the proteins for uptake by the nucleus. These so-called nuclear recognition sequences most likely bind to specific receptors associated with the nuclear pores, the channels through the nuclear envelope that connect the nucleus with the cytoplasm.

Most molecules move to their correct compartment by the process of diffusion down concentration gradients, but organelles generally require transport systems composed of microtubules or actin filaments together with specific motor proteins to position them correctly in the cytoplasm. For example, a protein molecule destined to be part of a mitochondrion will diffuse from the site of biosynthesis through the cytoplasm to a mitochondrion, where it will bind to a receptor that guides its incorporation into the mitochondrion. On the other hand, the mitochondrion itself is too large to diffuse through the network of protein fibers in the cytoplasmic matrix, and so it must be pulled through the matrix by a motor protein that moves along microtubules to the correct place in the cell.

Some cellular components, such as ribosomes and the filaments in the cytoplasmic matrix, assemble afresh from their constituent molecules, but all organelles composed of membranes form only by the growth and division of preexisting organelles. The reason that these organelles require precursors is that biological membranes composed of phospholipids can grow only by expansion of preexisting bilayers. As a consequence, organelles such as mitochondria and the endoplasmic reticulum are inherited maternally starting from the egg and expanding into every cell in the body by continued growth and partition into both daughter cells at every cell division. Other membrane-bound organelles, such as lysosomes, form by budding off the Golgi apparatus.

Many of the individual self-assembly reactions required for normal cell growth can be reproduced in the test tube, but the cell is the only place known where the entire range of reactions, including biosynthesis, targeting, and assembly, can go to completion. Thus, cells are such a special environment that the chain of life has required an unbroken lineage of cells stretching from all living cells back through their ancestors to the earliest forms of life. This requirement for cellular continuity explains why extinction is an irreversible process.   [T.Po.]

Cell permeability   The permitting or activating of the passage of substances into, out of, or through cells, or from one cell to another. These materials traverse either the cell surface that demarcates the living cytoplasm from the extracellular space or the boundaries between adjacent cells. In many cases the materials also traverse the cell wall. See CELL WALLS (PLANT).

The cell can control many properties of its membranes, including those related to permeability. Control can be exerted in the following ways: (1) by varying the number and variety of membranes; (2) by varying the specific nature of the lipid components in the membrane; (3) by varying the glycocalyx proteins or lipid-associated sugar molecules on the outside of the cell, or the membrane-associated proteins on the inside; (4) by causing large areas of membrane to flow from one place to another, or to fold, indent, evert, or pinch off, carrying with these movements substances bound to one or the other surface of the membrane, or embedded in it; (5) by selectively moving integral membrane proteins in the plane of the membrane, allowing these proteins to carry with them substances, particles, molecules, or other materials bound to them; (6) by varying the properties of a single integral membrane protein or of a closely associated group of them so as to allow or prevent the passage across the membrane of substances such as ions or proteins of a specific character. *See* CELL MEMBRANES.   [H.S.Be.]

Cell plastids   Specialized structures found in the cytoplasm of plant cells, diverse in distribution, size, shape, composition, structure, function, and mode of development. A number of different types are recognized. Chloroplasts occur in the green parts of plants and are responsible for the green coloration, for they contain the chlorophyll pigments. These pigments, along with certain others, absorb the light energy that drives the processes of photosynthesis, by which sugars, starch, and other organic materials are synthesized. Amyloplasts, nearly or entirely colorless, are packed with starch grains and occur in cells of storage tissue. Proteoplasts are less common and contain crystalline, fibrillar, or amorphous masses of protein, sometimes along with starch grains. In chromoplasts the green pigment is masked or replaced by others, notably carotenoids, as in the cells of carrot roots and many flowers and fruits. *See* CAROTENOID; CHLOROPHYLL.

All types of plastids have one structural feature in common, a double envelope consisting of two concentric sheets of membrane. The outer of these is in contact with the cytoplasmic ground substance; the inner with the plastid matrix, or stroma. They are separated by a narrow space of about 10 nanometers.

Another system of membranes generally occupies the main body of the plastid. This internal membrane system is especially well developed in chloroplasts, where the unit of construction is known as a thylakoid. In its simplest form this is a sac such as would be obtained if a balloon-shaped, membrane-limited sphere were to be flattened until the internal space was not much thicker than the membrane itself. It is usual, however, for thylakoids to be lobed, branched, or fenestrated.

The surface area of thylakoids is very large in relation to the volume of the chloroplast. This is functionally significant, for chlorophyll molecules and other components of the light-reaction systems of photosynthesis are associated with these membranes. A chloroplast, however, is much more than a device for carrying out photosynthesis. It can use light energy for uptake and exchange of ions and to drive conformational changes. The stroma contains the elements of a protein-synthesizing system—as much deoxyribonucleic acid (DNA) as a small bacterium, various types of ribonucleic acid (RNA), distinctive ribosomes, and polyribosomes. There is evidence to indicate that much of the protein synthesis of a leaf takes place within the chloroplasts. *See* PHOTOSYNTHESIS; PROTEIN; RIBOSOMES.

One of the most challenging problems in cell biology concerns the autonomy of organelles, such as the plastids. Chloroplasts, for instance, have their own DNA, DNA-polymerase, and RNA-polymerase; can make proteins; and, significantly, can mutate. All this suggests a measure of independence. It is known, however, that some nuclear genes can influence the production of molecules that are normally found only in chloroplasts, so their autonomy cannot be complete. It remains to be seen whether they control and regulate their own morphogenetic processes.   [B.E.S.G.]

Cell senescence and death   The limited capacity of all normal human and other animal cells to reproduce and function. The gradual decline in normal physiological function of the cells is referred to as aging or senescence. The aging process ends with the death of individual cells and then, generally, the whole animal. Aging occurs in all animals, except those that do not reach a fixed body size such as some tortoises and sharks, sturgeon, and several other kinds of fishes. These animals die as the result of accidents or disease, but losses in normal physiological function do not seem to occur. Examples of cells that do not age are those composing the germ plasm (sex cells) and many kinds of cancer cells. These cells are presumed to be immortal.

Although cultured normal human and other animal cells are mortal, they can be converted to a state of immortality. The conversion can be produced in human cells by the SV40 virus and in other animal cells by other viruses, chemicals, and irradiation. This conversion from mortality to immortality is called transformation, and is characterized by the acquisition of many profoundly abnormal cell properties, including changes in chromosome number and form, and the ability of the cells to grow unattached to a solid surface. These changes, and many more, are characteristic of most cancer cells. *See* TUMOR VIRUSES.   [L.H.]

Cell walls (plant)   The cell wall is the layer of material secreted by the plant cell outside its plasma membrane. All plants have cell walls that are generally very similar in chemical composition, organization, and development. The walls of the Chlorophyta (green algae) show characteristics virtually identical to those of flowering plants, an indication that flowering plants are derived evolutionarily from this division of algae. The wall serves as the first point of entry of materials into cells, functions in the movement of water throughout the plant, and is one of the major mechanical strengthening factors. In addition, the wall must be sufficiently flexible and plastic to withstand mechanical stresses while still permitting the growth of the cell. *See* CELL MEMBRANES.

The plant primary wall is initiated during the process of cell division. After chromosomes line up along the metaphase plate and begin to be pulled apart toward the poles of the cells by the spindle fibers (the anaphase portion of mitosis), a cell plate or phragmoplast can be observed at the equator of the dividing cell. Vesicles line up on both sides of the equator to form the proteinaceous cell plate. Elements of the endoplasmic reticulum fuse with the cell plate, marking the location of plasmodesmatal pores and pits which will eventually provide the intercellular connections between adjacent cells. The cell plate forms the matrix within which the middle lamella and primary walls are formed. The middle lamella is composed of pectic substances which are polymers of pectins plus smaller amounts of other sugars. The middle lamella provides some of the observed plasticity and extensibility of cell walls during cell growth, and it has also been suggested that pectins are capable of hydrogen-bonding to the cellulose that forms the plant cell primary wall. During the early stages in cell wall formation, the cellulose wall is isotropic without any ordered orientation, but as cell walls continue to develop in area and in thickness and the cell grows to mature size, the walls become anisotropic, or highly ordered. *See* CYTOKINESIS.

Cellulose, like starch, is basically a polymer of glucose, a six-carbon monosaccharide. Each chain of cellulose may be as long as 8000 to 12,000 glucose monomers, or up to 4 micrometers long. These are arranged linearly, with no side branching. Cellulose chains are aggregated into bundles of approximately 40 chains each, the cellulose micelles, which are held together by hydrogen bonds. The micelle is a very regular, quasicrystalline structure.

The micelles are embedded in a matrix of other polysaccharides, the hemicelluloses. Hemicellulose serves to bind the micelle into a fairly rigid unit which retains a good deal of flexibility. Micelles, in bundles of variable number, are bound together into the cellulose microfibril, a unit sufficiently large to be seen under the electron microscope; these, in turn, are bound together into macrofibrils which are observable under the light microscope.

During the formation of the primary wall, at locations predetermined by attachments of endoplasmic reticulum to the middle lamella, cellulose microfibrillar deposition is minimal, leaving a thin place in the primary wall which forms the plasmodesmatal connections. Running through these pores are fine strands of protoplasm, the plasmodesmata proper, which contain a tube of endoplasmic reticulum–like material. The plasmodesmata provide a cytoplasmic connection between adjacent cells. Such connections are found among all the living cells of a plant, a fact which has led to the concept that all plant cells are so interconnected that the entire plant is a cytosymplast or single unit.

Although there are differences in nomenclature and terminology, secondary walls of plant cells are defined as those laid down after the primary wall has stopped increasing in surface area, essentially at that time when the plant cell has reached mature size. This is particularly true of those cells that, at maturity, have irreversibly differentiated into specialized cells, some of which are destined to lose their cytoplasm and become functional only as dead cells, including xylem vessels and tracheids, and sclereids. The secondary wall of most plants seems to have the same chemical structure and physical orientation of fibrils and hemicelluloses as do primary walls. While there may be little orientation of fibrils in young primary walls, the secondary walls are composed of fibrils that are highly ordered. In most secondary walls, and particularly those of the xylem, the fibrillar structure of the primary as well as the secondary walls may become impregnated with more substances, the most prominent of these being lignin. The chemical nature and biological role of lignin is of considerable interest because of the use of wood in the lumber and pulpwood-paper industries. The primary roles of the lignins include their ability to render walls mechanically strong, rigid, and—at least to some extent—water-impermeable. It has been suggested that lignins may also serve to make wood less subject to microbially caused decay. *See* PLANT CELL; PLANT GROWTH; WOOD ANATOMY.
[R.M.K.]

Cellular adhesion   The process whereby cells interact and attach to other cells or to inanimate surfaces, mediated by interactions between the molecules on the surface of the cell. This process has been studied extensively in embryonic cells of higher organisms, where species and tissue specificity of adhesion has been shown. However, adhesion is a common feature in the life of most organisms.

Prokaryotic microorganisms do not frequently exhibit cell-to-cell interactions, but adhere to surfaces forming biofilms. In these interactions with a surface, some microorganisms cause corrosion of metal by adhering and producing corrosive acid by-products as a result of their metabolism. Adhesion of microorganisms to the cells of higher plants and animals is often a prerequisite for causing disease. Eukaryotic microorganisms often exhibit specific cell-to-cell interactions, allowing complex colonial forms and multicellular organisms to be constructed from individual or free-living cells. Adhesion between different plant cells is apparent in several cases, as in the interaction between a pollen grain and the stigma during fertilization.

Interactions between two cell surfaces may be quite specific, involving certain types of cell-surface protein molecules, or general, involving production of a sticky extracellular matrix that surrounds the cell, as frequently occurs in bacterial adhesion. Cellular adhesion is important in cellular recognition, in the generation of form or pattern, and possibly in regulation of cellular differentiation. *See* CELL (BIOLOGY); CELL DIFFERENTIATION.

All adhesion is mediated by the cell surface, either directly involving integral components of the plasma membrane, or indirectly through material excreted and deposited on the outside of the cell. Most theories of cellular adhesion suggest that cell-surface glycoproteins serve as ligands involved in attaching cell surfaces together. When a specific cell interacts with an identical cell, the attachment is said to be homotypic. Heterotypic adhesion involves interactions between different cell types. If the ligand-specific attachment involves interaction between identical cell-surface ligands, it is homophilic, and between two different ligands, heterophilic. The interaction between a pollen grain and the stigma cells described previously is an example of a heterotypic, heterophilic interaction.

Many studies of species and tissue specificity have been done with embryonic chick and mouse systems. In general, it would seem that homotypic adhesion is stronger that heterotypic adhesion. Also, tissue and species specific adhesion can be shown, but tissue specificity seems to be more frequent. For example, when dissociated embryonic neural retina of mouse and chick are mixed and allowed to aggregate, there is very little sorting, and mosaic tissue is formed. This is not true in all tissues, as heart and liver tissue show much greater species specificity than neural retina.

Throughout development, it is necessary for specific adhesion among cells to establish and maintain form. It is also important during development that cells change position, as occurs during gastrulation, or migrate, as with neural crest cells that move from the neural tube to various positions, forming ganglia. In these cases, it would seem to be necessary for certain cells to dissociate or alter their adhesive properties in response to the proper developmental cues. Throughout development, there are a series of primary and secondary inductions that affect cellular differentiation and pattern formation. These inductions depend on interactions between cell types having different histories, either due to being in different embryonic layers or due to interaction between cells derived from the same layer but previously differentiated. These changes in form are related to specific changes in cell-adhesion molecules.   [M.Ha.]

Cellular immunology   The field concerning the interactions among cells and molecules of the immune system, and how such interactions contribute to the recognition and elimination of pathogens. Humans (and vertebrates in general) possess a range of nonspecific mechanical and biochemical defenses against routinely encountered bacteria, parasites, viruses, and fungi. The skin, for example, is an effective physical barrier to infection. Basic chemical defenses are also present in blood, saliva, and tears, and on mucous membranes. True protection stems from the host's ability to mount responses targeted to specific organisms, and to retain a form of "memory" that results in a rapid, efficient response to a given organism upon a repeat encounter. This more formal sense of immunity, termed adaptive immunity, depends upon the coordinated activities of cells and molecules of the immune system.

Cells involved. Several types of cells play a role in protecting the body from infection, and they are found primarily in the blood and lymph. Specific immune responses mainly involve the activities of T-lymphocytes and B-lymphocytes, two types of white blood cells. A response is initiated when a pathogen triggers the activity of one or both of the two major types of T-cells: CD4+ cells, also known as helper T-cells (T_H); and CD8+ cells, also known as cytotoxic T-lymphocytes (CTL) [see illustration].

When CD4+ T-cells are triggered, they release factors called cytokines, which in turn stimulate B-lymphocytes to make and secrete antibodies. See ANTIBODY; CYTOKINE.

When CD8+ T-cells are triggered, they release factors that kill a cell harboring an infectious agent, and they also release cytokines. Virus-infected cells commonly are the targets of cytotoxic T-lymphocytes, since viruses need to get inside a cell in order to reproduce.

Antigen recognition. The immune system must detect a pathogen before a response can be made. This phase of the response is shown in the interaction between a T-cell and an antigen-presenting cell (APC) [see illustration]. An antigen is a molecule, or portion of a molecule, that is recognized by a T-cell receptor (TCR) or antibody molecule. The cell surface molecules involved in antigen recognition by T-cells are the T-cell receptor and class I or class II molecules of the major histocompatibility complex (MHC). Each T-cell expresses a unique T-cell receptor that will interact specifically with

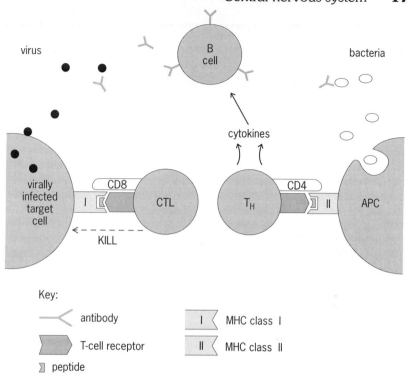

Key:

antibody

T-cell receptor

peptide

I ⟨ MHC class I

II ⟨ MHC class II

Key processes in a specific immune response.

a limited set of antigens. The antigens recognized by T-cell receptors are short peptides bound to MHC molecules. *See* Histocompatibility.

Co-stimulation. Antigen recognition, as mediated by the T-cell receptor–MHC–peptide interaction, is necessary, but generally it is not sufficient for the initiation of an immune response. Several other molecular interactions occur between molecules on the T-cell surface and those on the antigen-presenting cells. The co-stimulation provided by these additional interactions drives the production of cytokines by T-cells and induces their proliferation.

Memory. Once an immune response has been initiated, T-cells and B-cells proliferate and become mature responder cells. These cells do not have the same requirement for co-stimulation once a response is under way. As pathogen elimination nears completion, many of the T- and B-cells involved in the response die. However, a subset of cells remain as memory cells, which can be quickly called into action if the same pathogen is encountered on a future occasion. *See* Acquired immunological tolerance; Cellular immunology; Immunity; Immunology. [D.J.L.]

Central nervous system   That portion of the nervous system composed of the brain and spinal cord. The brain is enclosed in the skull, and the spinal cord within the spinal canal of the vertebral column. The brain and spinal cord are intimately covered by membranes called meninges and bathed in an extracellular fluid called cerebrospinal fluid. Approximately 90% of the cells of the central nervous system are glial cells which support, both physically and metabolically, the other cells, which are the nerve cells or neurons.

Functionally similar groups of neurons are clustered together in so-called nuclei of the central nervous system. When groups of neurons are organized in layers (called laminae) on the outer surface of the brain, the group is called a cortex, such as the cerebral cortex and cerebellar cortex. The long processes (axons) of neurons course in the central nervous system in functional groups called tracts. Since many of the axons have a layer of shiny fat (myelin) surrounding them, they appear white and are called the white matter of the central nervous system. The nuclei and cortex of the central nervous system have little myelin in them, appear gray, and are called the gray matter of the central nervous system. *See* BRAIN; NERVOUS SYSTEM (VERTEBRATE).   [D.B.W.]

Centriole   A morphologically complex cellular organelle at the focus of centrosomes in animal cells and some lower plant cells. Prokaryotes, some lower animal cells, higher plant cells, and a few exceptional higher animal cells do not have centrioles in their centrosomes. Centrioles typically are not found singly; the centrosome of higher animal cells contains a pair of centrioles (together called the diplosome), arranged at right angles to each other and separated by a distance ranging from 250 nanometers to several micrometers. *See* CENTROSOME.

Centrioles are typically 300–700 nm in length and 250 nm in diameter. Although they can be detected by the light microscope, an electron microscope is required to resolve their substructure. At the electron microscopic level, a centriole consists of a hollow cylinder of nine triplet microtubules in a pinwheel arrangement (see illustration). Within each triplet, one microtubule (the A tubule) is a complete microtubule, while the others (the B and C tubules) share a portion of their wall with the adjacent tubule. In some cells these nine triplet microtubules are embedded in a densely staining cylindrical matrix that is spatially distinct from the pericentriolar material of the centrosome. Structures found in the lumen or core of the centriole include linkers between the triplets, granules, fibers, a cartwheel structure at one end of the centriole, and sometimes a small vesicle.

Centrioles have a close structural similarity to basal bodies, which organize the axoneme of cilia and flagella. In many types of mammalian somatic cells, the older of the two centrioles in the centrosome can act as a basal body during the interphase portion of the cell cycle. In such cases, tapered projections, called basal feet, are often observed on the external surface of the centriole that is acting as the basal body. Microtubules are attached to the globular tips of the basal feet and may serve to anchor this centriole in the cell.

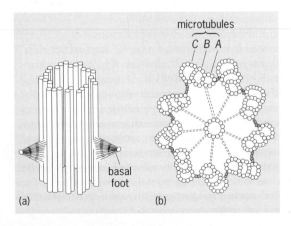

Diagrams of centriole showing (a) arrangement of microtubules and (b) cross section of proximal end, with nine triplet microtubules (A, B, and C) and central cartwheel structure.

During interphase the centrosome nucleates the array of cytoplasmic microtubules; later in the cell cycle the centrosome duplicates, and the daughter centrosomes form the poles of the mitotic (or meiotic) spindle. The terms "centriole" and "centrosome" are sometimes erroneously used interchangeably; centrioles are not the centrosome itself, but a part of it. The centrosome of higher animal cells has at its center a pair of centrioles, arranged at right angles to each other and separated by 250 nm or less.

The only clearly demonstrated role for the centriole is to organize the axoneme (central microtubular complex) of the primary cilium in cells having this structure, and the flagellar axoneme in sperm cells. Other possible functions for centrioles are a matter of debate. Some authorities assert that when present in the centrosome, centrioles contain activities that serve to organize the centrosome, determine the number of centrosomes in a cell, and control the doubling of the centrosome as a whole before mitosis. Others believe that centrioles have no role in the formation and doubling of the centrosomes but are associated with the centrosomes only to ensure the equal distribution of basal bodies during cell division. *See* CELL (BIOLOGY).   [G.Slu.]

Centrosome   An organelle located in the cytoplasm of all animal cells and many plants, fungi, and protozoa that controls the polymerization, position, and polar orientation of many of the cell's microtubules throughout the cell cycle. There is usually one centrosome per cell, located near the cell's center; it doubles during interphase, so there are two when the cell divides. At the onset of mitosis, each centrosome increases the number of microtubules it initiates. These mitotic microtubules are more labile and generally shorter than their interphase counterparts, and as they rapidly grow and shrink they probe the space around the centrosome that initiated them. When the nuclear envelope disperses, the microtubules extend from the centrosome into the former nucleoplasm where the chromosomes have already condensed. Some of these microtubules attach to the chromosomes, while others interact with microtubules produced by the sister centrosome, forming a mitotic spindle that organizes and segregates the chromosomes. During anaphase, sister centrosomes are forced apart as the spindle

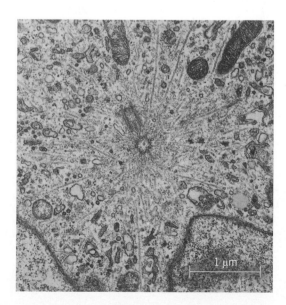

Centrosome of a mammalian cell. Many microtubules radiate from the cloud of pericentriolar material which surrounds one of the two centrioles. (*Courtesy of Kent McDonald*)

elongates, allowing each daughter cell to receive one centrosome to organize its microtubules in the next cell generation. *See* CELL CYCLE; CELL MOTILITY.

The shapes of centrosomes differ widely between organisms. The centrosomes of animal cells (see illustration) usually contain a pair of perpendicular centrioles including a parent centriole formed in an earlier cell generation and a daughter centriole formed during the most recent interphase. Centrioles can serve as basal bodies for the initiation of a cilium or flagellum in the cells that make them. They appear to be essential for the formation of these motile appendages, so centriole inheritance by both daughters at cell division is analogous to the transmission of a gene. *See* CENTRIOLE; CILIA AND FLAGELLA; CYTOSKELETON.

Centrosome action is regulated as a function of time in the cell cycle. The increase in microtubule number that occurs prior to mitosis is correlated with a significant increase in the extent of phosphorylation of several centrosomal proteins. The protein kinase p34^{cdc2}, which helps to regulate the cell cycle, is concentrated at the centrosome, together with cyclin-B, a positive regulator of this kinase. *See* MITOSIS.   [J.R.Mc.]

Cephalopoda   The most highly evolved class of the phylum Mollusca. It consists of squids, cuttlefishes, octopuses, and the chambered nautiluses. The earliest known cephalopods are small, shelled fossils from the Upper Cambrian rocks of northeast China that are 500 million years old. Cephalopods always have been marine, never fresh-water or land, animals. Most fossil cephalopods, among them the subclasses Nautiloidea and Ammonoidea, had external shells and generally were shallow-living, slow-moving animals. Of the thousands of species of such shelled cephalopods that evolved, all are extinct except for four species of the only surviving genus, *Nautilus*. All other recent cephalopods belong to four orders of the subclass Coleoidea, which also contains five extinct orders.

Living cephalopods are bilaterally symmetrical mollusks with a conspicuously developed head that has a crown of 8–10 appendages (8 arms and 2 tentacles) around the mouth. These appendages are lined with one to several rows of suckers or hooks. *Nautilus* is exceptional in having many simple arms. The mouth contains a pair of hard chitinous jaws that resemble a parrot's beak and a tonguelike, toothed radula (a uniquely molluscan organ). Eyes are lateral on the head; they are large and well developed. The "cranium" contains the highly developed brain, the center of the extensive, proliferated nervous system. The shell of ancestral cephalopods has become, in living forms, internal, highly modified, reduced, or absent; and is contained in the sac- or tubelike, soft muscular body, the mantle. A pair of fins may occur on the mantle as an aid to locomotion, but primary movement is achieved through jet propulsion in which water is drawn into the mantle cavity and then forcibly expelled through the nozzlelike funnel. Fewer than 1000 species of living cephalopods inhabit all oceans and seas.

The classification given here concentrates on the living groups and lists only the major fossil groups.

> Class Cephalopoda
>> Subclass Nautiloidea
>> Subclass Ammonoidea
>> Subclass Coleoidea
>>> Order Belemnoidea
>>> Order Sepioidea
>>> Order Teuthoidea
>>>> Suborder Myopsida

Suborder Oegopsida
Order Vampyromorpha
Order Octopoda
Suborder Cirrata
Suborder Incirrata

Species of cephalopods inhabit most marine habitats. Cephalopods inhabit tide pools, rocky patches, sandy bottoms, coral reefs, grass beds, mangrove swamps, coastal waters, and the open ocean from the surface through the water column to depths on the abyssal bottom at over 16, 000 ft (5000 m). *See* NERVOUS SYSTEM (INVERTEBRATE).

Cephalopods are high-level, active predators that feed on a variety of invertebrates, fishes, and even other cephalopods. The relatively sluggish nautiluses feed primarily on slow-moving prey such as reed shrimps, and even are scavengers of the cast-off shells of molted spiny lobsters. Cuttlefishes prey on shrimps, crabs, and small fishes, while squids eat fishes, pelagic crustaceans, and other cephalopods. Benthic octopuses prey mostly on clams, snails, and crabs. Salivary glands secrete toxins that subdue the prey and, in octopuses, begin digestion.

To protect themselves from predators cephalopods would rather hide than fight. To this end they have become masters of camouflage and escape. Benthic forms especially (for example, *Sepia* and *Octopus*) have evolved an intricate, complex system of rapid changes in color and patterns via thousands of individually innervated chromatophores (pigment cells) that allow precise matching to the color and pattern of the background. In addition, they regulate the texture of their skins by erecting papillae, flaps, and knobs that simulate the texture of the background. Many midwater oceanic squids camouflage against predation from below by turning on photophores (light organs) that match the light intensity from the surface and eliminate their silhouettes. *See* CHROMATOPHORE; PROTECTIVE COLORATION.

Cephalopods have perfected jet propulsion for many modes of locomotion, from hovering motionless, to normal cruising, to extremely rapid escape swimming. Water enters the mantle cavity through an opening around the neck when the muscular mantle (body) expands. The mantle opening seals shut as the mantle contracts and jets the water out through the hoselike funnel, driving the cephalopod tail-first through the water.

The sexes are separate in cephalopods, and many species display complex courtship, mating, spawning, and parental care behavior. At mating, the male of most species transfers the spermatophores to the female with a specially modified arm, the hectocotylus. The spermatophores are implanted into the female's mantle cavity, around the neck, under the eyes, or around the mouth, depending on the species. Incubation takes a few weeks to a few months depending on the species.

Cephalopods are extremely important in the diets of toothed whales (sperm whales, dolphins), pinnipeds (seals, sea lions), pelagic birds (petrels, albatrosses), and predatory fishes (tunas, billfishes, groupers). For example, pilot whales in the North Atlantic feed almost exclusively on one species of squid, *Illex illecebrosus*, that aggregates for spawning in the summer. *See* MOLLUSCA. [C.F.E.R.]

Cetacea A mammalian order comprising approximately 90 living species of whales, dolphins, and porpoises and their fossil relatives. Like all other mammals but unlike all fish, cetaceans nurse their young with milk produced by the mother, are endothermic (warm-blooded), breathe air, have a lower jaw that consists of a single bony element (the dentary), and have three small bones (hammer, anvil, and stirrup) subserving sound transmission within the ear.

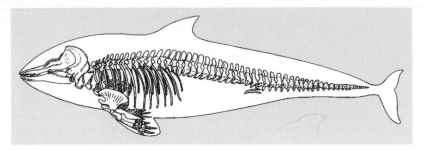

Skeleton of a porpoise, highly specialized for an aquatic life. (*After Guide to the Hall of Biology of Mammals, Amer. Mus. Nat. Hist. Guide Leafl. Ser. 76, 1933*)

Living cetaceans are aquatic animals that cannot live on land. They have streamlined bodies, with the nasal opening (blowhole) on top of the head (see illustration). Their forelimbs are modified into flippers, they lack external hindlimbs, and their tail forms a flat horizontal fluke. Modern cetaceans lack hair except for whiskers in the young of some species. Many of these features are common in aquatic vertebrates, and they have evolved convergently as adaptations for life in water.

The brain of cetaceans is large and highly developed, and they are thought to be very intelligent. The cetacean sense of smell is nearly or totally absent. In most species the nerve that carries olfactory information to the brain is absent, which is very unusual among mammals. The eyes of most species are well developed. The ear is the most important sense organ. Toothed whales (Odontoceti) echolocate, emitting high-frequency sounds and using the echoes to determine shapes and distances in their surroundings. Odontocetes do not emit sounds with their voice box (larynx) like other mammals, but have modified nasal passages through which bursts of air are forced. Mysticetes (baleen whales) do not echolocate; rather, they produce low-frequency sounds with their larynx. These sounds can travel through the ocean for hundreds of miles and are used for communication.

The two extant suborders of cetaceans, odontocetes and mysticetes, have different dietary specializations. Most odontocetes have simple, pronglike teeth which are used to grab and hold, but not chew, large prey items. Prey includes a variety of fish of all sizes, crustaceans, and squid and other mollusks. Some of the larger odontocetes, such as the killer whale (*Orcinus orca*), eat large prey, including sea lions and dolphins. A pod of killer whales will also hunt together, attacking much larger prey such as gray whales. Modern mysticetes do not have teeth and are filter feeders, straining water filled with clouds of marine organisms (krill) through a network of baleen. Baleen is a keratinlike substance that hangs down in plates from the upper jaws of the whale.

All modern cetaceans swim by swinging their horizontal tail fluke through the water, while their forelimbs are used for steering and navigating. The flippers of modern cetaceans resemble flat oars, although the bones for five fingers are present internally. The dorsal fin stabilizes the body during swimming. Under the skin of cetaceans is a layer of blubber, a fatty tissue that serves to insulate the animal and affects its buoyancy and streamlining. Some species are capable of diving to great depths [commonly more than 5000 ft (1500 m) in the sperm whale], yet all cetaceans must come to the surface to breathe. Whales have a number of adaptations for diving and staying underwater for long periods of time. They exhale before they dive, allowing them to submerge faster. They store oxygen in the muscle (myoglobin) and not in the lungs or blood (hemoglobin) and change circulation patterns of blood to save oxygen. Their chests can easily collapse under increasing pressure (with depth) without causing permanent damage. *See* HEMOGLOBIN.

A variety of social structures are found among cetaceans. Two examples are marine dolphins and sperm whales. Most marine dolphins live in schools that may contain dozens of animals, sometimes composed of multiple species. Herds of sperm whales consist of related females and juveniles. Clusters of young males form bachelor groups, and adult males, much larger than the females, are solitary.

Cetaceans are found in all oceans and seas. Some species are restricted to coastal environments (such as bottlenosed dolphins), whereas others live only in the open sea (such as sperm whales). Some species live in all seas and oceans of the world (such as killer whales). Many mysticetes and sperm whales are migratory. A number of dolphin species have left the sea and live permanently in rivers.

Cetaceans originated from a four-footed terrestrial ancestor. This predecessor, a mesonychian, may have resembled a wolf or a hyena and lived approximately 55 million years ago. Modern odontocetes are diverse, ranging from the enormous sperm whales [up to 20 m (66 ft) long and 52,000 kg (114,500 lb)] to the tiny porpoises [Phocaenidae, smallest around 9 kg (20 lb), length 1.5 m (5 ft)]. Dolphins (Delphinidae, which includes the killer whale), porpoises (Phocaenidae), and fresh-water dolphins (Iniidae, Pontoporidae, Platanistidae) are the smallest odontocetes. The largest animal ever to live on Earth is the blue whale (*Balaenoptera musculus*), a baleen whale that is 25 m (82 ft) long and weighs 130,000 kg (286,340 lb). Other examples of mysticetes are humpback whales, right whales, gray whales, and minke whales. *See* MAMMALIA.

[J.G.M.B.]

Chaetognatha A phylum of abundant planktonic arrow-worms. Their bodies are tubular and transparent, and divided into three portions: head, trunk, and tail. The head possesses one or two rows of minute teeth anterior to the mouth and usually 7–10 larger chaetae, or seizing jaws, on each side of the head. One or two pairs of lateral fins and a caudal fin are present.

Nine genera and about 42 species are recognized by some specialists. Most species belong to the genus *Sagitta*, which can be recognized by the presence of two pairs of teeth and two pairs of lateral fins.

Chaetognaths are cosmopolitan forms which live not only at the surface but also at great depths; however, no one species is found in all latitudes and at all depths. One of the Arctic species, *Eukrohnia hamata*, may extend to the Antarctic by way of deep water across the tropics. A few species are neritic and are not found normally beyond the continental shelf. Their food consists principally of copepods and other small planktonic crustaceans; however, they are very predacious and will even eat small fish larvae and other chaetognaths on rare occasions.

Studies have shown them to be useful as indicator organisms. Certain species appear to be associated with characteristic types or masses of water, and when this water is displaced into an adjacent water mass, the chaetognaths may be used as temporary evidence for such displacement.

[E.L.P.]

Chelicerata A subphylum of the phylum Arthropoda. The Chelicerata can be defined as those arthropods with the anteriormost appendages as a pair of small pincers (chelicerae) followed usually by pedipalps and four pairs of walking legs, and with the body divided into two parts: the prosoma (corresponding approximately to the cephalothorax of many crustaceans) and the opisthosoma (or abdomen). There are never antennae or mandibles (lateral jaws). The Chelicerata comprise three classes:

the enormous group Arachnida (spiders, ticks, mites, scorpions, and related forms); the Pycnogonida (sea spiders or nobody-crabs); and the Merostomata (including the Xiphosurida or horseshoe crabs).

Both Merostomata and Pycnogonida are marine, but the enormous numbers and varied forms of the Arachnida are almost entirely terrestrial. The respiratory structures of chelicerates include gills, book-lungs, and tracheae. Sexes are normally separate, with genital openings at the anterior end of the opisthosoma. Some mites and other small chelicerates are omnivorous scavengers, but the majority of species of larger chelicerates are predaceous carnivores at relatively high trophic levels in their particular ecotopes. *See* ARTHROPODA.   [W.D.R.H.]

Chelonia   An order of the Reptilia, subclass Anapsida, including the turtles, terrapins, and tortoises. This order is also known as the Testudines. The group first appeared in the Triassic, and its representatives are among the commonest fossils from that time on. Members of the order are most frequently found in fresh-water streams, lakes, and ponds or in marshy areas. However, a number of strictly terrestrial species are known, and several are marine. Turtles occur on all the major continents and continental islands in tropic and temperature regions. The marine forms are basically tropical in distribution, but some individuals stray into temperate waters.

The living turtles are usually divided into two major groups, the suborders Pleurodira and Cryptodira, based upon the structures of the head and neck. The pleurodires have spines on the most posterior cervicals (neck vertebrae) and the head is retractile laterally. In the cryptodires the cervical spines are uniformly reduced and the head is folded directly back to within the shell. In several cryptodires, notably in the marine turtles, the neck is secondarily nonretractible because of a reduction in the shell.

The Chelonia differ from most other vertebrates in possessing a hard bony shell which encompasses and protects the body. The shell is made up of a dorsal portion, the carapace, and a ventral segment, the plastron, connected by soft ligamentous tissue or a bony bridge. The carapace is composed of the greatly expanded ribs and dorsal vertebrae overlain by a series of enlarged dermal ossifications and an outer covering of tough skin or horny scales. The plastron is similarly arranged with remnants of the interclavicle, clavicles, and gastralia fused with dermal ossifications and covered by skin or scales. Other peculiarities associated with the shell include the fusion of the ribs to the vertebrae and the reduction of trunk muscles, the presence of the pectoral girdle completely inside the ribs (found in no other animal), the highly modified short, thick humerus and femur, and the lungs attached dorsally to the shell. In addition, living turtles differ from the tuatara, snakes, lizards, and crocodilians in having an anapsid skull, no true teeth but horny beaks on the jaws, an immovable quadrate, and a single median penis in males.

The rigid bony shell of turtles imposes a basic body plan subject to relatively little variation. The principal obvious differences between them are in the shell shape, limbs, head, and neck. The general outline of the shell is variable, but in most forms the shell is moderately high-arched and covered with epidermal scales. The majority of turtles have limbs more or less adapted to aquatic or semiaquatic life with moderate to well-developed palmate webbed feet. However, in strictly terrestrial forms such as the tortoises, the limbs are elephantine with the weight of the body being borne on the flattened sole of the feet.

Associated with the tendency of most turtles toward a life in or near water is the auditory apparatus. Even though an eardrum is present, hearing is adapted to picking up sounds transmitted through the water or substratum. However, there is evidence that airborne sound can be heard. Vision is also important, and turtles have color vision. Most of the species are gregarious and diurnal, and territoriality is unknown in the order.

The courtship patterns of various turtles are distinctive. In general, aquatic forms mate in the water, but tortoises breed on land. The male mounts the female from above, and fertilization is internal. Sperm may be stored in the cloacal region of the female for extended periods before fertilization. Because of the presence of the large median penis in males, the sexes of many species can be distinguished by the longer and broader tail of the male. All turtles lay shelled eggs which are buried in sand or soil in areas where females congregate. The shell is calcareous in most forms, but the marine turtles have leathery shells. Eggs are rather numerous, as many as 200 being laid by a single individual in some species, and are highly valued as human food. Incubation takes 60–90 days, and the little turtle cuts its way out of the shell with a small horny egg caruncle at the end of the snout.

Turtles feed on all types of organisms. Aquatic species may eat algae, higher plants, mollusks, crustaceans, insects, or fishes; terrestrial forms are similarly catholic in tastes. Most species are omnivores, but some have very specialized diets. The edges and internal surfaces of the horny beaks of these reptiles are frequently denticulate and modified to form specialized mechanisms adapted to handle particular food items. [J.M.S.]

Chemical ecology The study of ecological interactions mediated by the chemicals that organisms produce. These substances, known as allelochemicals, serve a variety of functions. They influence or regulate interspecific and intraspecific interactions of microorganisms, plants, and animals, and operate within and between all trophic levels—producers, consumers, and decomposers—and in terrestrial, fresh-water, and marine ecosystems.

Function is an important criterion for the classification of allelochemicals. Allelochemicals beneficial to the emitter are called allomones; those beneficial to the recipient are called kairomones. An allomone to one organism can be a kairomone to another. For example, floral scents benefit the plant (allomones) by encouraging pollinators, but also benefit the insect (kairomones) by providing a cue for the location of nectar.

The chemicals involved are diverse in structure and are often of low molecular weight ($<10,000$). They may be volatile or nonvolatile; water-soluble or fat-soluble. Proteins, polypeptides, and amino acids are also found to play an important role.

Plant allelochemicals are often called secondary compounds or metabolites to distinguish them from those chemicals involved in primary metabolism, although this distinction is not always clear.

Chemical defense in plants. Perhaps to compensate for their immobility, plants have made wide use of chemicals for protection against competitors, pathogens, herbivores, and abiotic stresses. A chemically mediated competitive interaction between higher plants is referred to as allelopathy. Allelopathy appears to occur in many plants, may involve phenolics or terpenoids that are modified in the soil by microorganisms, and is at least partly responsible for the organization of some plant communities. *See* ALLELOPATHY.

Chemicals that are mobilized in response to stress or attack are referred to as active or inducible chemicals, while those that are always present in the plant are referred to as passive or constitutive. In many plants, fungus attack induces the production of defensive compounds called phytoalexins, a diverse chemical group that includes isoflavonoids, terpenoids, polyacetylenes, and furanocoumarins. *See* PHYTOALEXINS.

Defensive chemicals can be induced by herbivore attack. There has been increasing evidence that inducible defenses, such as phenolics, are important in plant-insect interactions.

Constitutive defenses include the chemical hydrogen cyanide. Trefoil, clover, and ferns have been found to exist in two genetically different forms, one containing cyanide (cyanogenic) and one lacking it (acyanogenic); acyanogenic forms are often preferred by several herbivores. *See* ALKALOID; FLAVONOID.

Chemical defenses frequently occur together with certain structures which act as physical defenses, such as spines and hairs. While many chemicals protect plants by deterring herbivore feeding or by direct toxic effects, other defenses may act more indirectly. Chemicals that mimic juvenile hormones, the antijuvenile hormone substances found in some plants, either arrest development or cause premature development in certain susceptible insect species.

Plant chemicals potentially affect not only the herbivores that feed directly on the plant, but also the microorganisms, predators, or parasites of the herbivore. For example, the tomato plant contains an alkaloid, tomatine, that is effective against certain insect herbivores. The tomato hornworm, however, is capable of detoxifying this alkaloid and can thus use the plant successfully—but a wasp parasite of the hornworm cannot detoxify tomatine, and its effectiveness in parasitizing the hornworm is reduced. Therefore, one indirect effect of the chemical in the plant may be to reduce the effectiveness of natural enemies of the plant pest, thereby actually working to the disadvantage of the plant.

Most plant chemicals can affect a wide variety of herbivores and microorganisms, because the modes of action of the chemicals they manufacture are based on a similarity of biochemical reaction in most target organisms (for example, cyanide is toxic to most organisms). In addition, many plant chemicals may serve multiple roles: resins in the creosote bush serve to defend against herbivores and pathogens, conserve water, and protect against ultraviolet radiation.

It is argued that there are two different types of defensive chemicals in plants. The first type occurs in relatively small amounts, is often toxic in small doses, and poisons the herbivore. These compounds may also change in concentration in response to plant damage; that is, they are inducible. These kinds of qualitative defensive compounds are the most common in short-lived or weedy species that are often referred to as unapparent. They are also characteristic of fast-growing species with short-lived leaves. In contrast, the second type of defensive chemicals often occurs in high concentrations, is not very toxic, but may inhibit digestion by herbivores and is not very inducible. These quantitative defenses are most common in long-lived, so-called apparent plants such as trees that have slow growth rates and long-lived leaves. Some plants may use both types of defenses.

There is accumulating evidence that marine plants may be protected against grazing by similar classes of chemicals to those found in terrestrial plants. One interesting difference in the marine environment is the large number of halogenated organic compounds that are rare in terrestrial and fresh-water systems.

Through evolution, as plants accumulate defenses, herbivores that are able to bypass the defense in some way are selected for and leave more offspring than others. This in turn selects for new defenses on the part of the plant in a continuing process called coevolution.

Animals that can exploit many plant taxa are called generalists, while those that are restricted to one or a few taxa are called specialists. Specialists often have particular detoxification mechanisms to deal with specific defenses. Some generalists possess powerful, inducible detoxification enzymes, while others exhibit morphological adaptations of the gut which prevent absorption of compounds such as tannins, or provide reservoirs for microorganisms that accomplish the detoxification. Animals may avoid eating plants, or parts of plants, with toxins.

Some herbivores that have completely surmounted the plant toxin barrier use the toxin itself as a cue to aid in locating plants. The common white butterfly, *Pieris rapae*, for example, uses mustard oil glycosides, which are a deterrent and toxic to many organisms, to find its mustard family hosts.

Chemical defense in animals. Many animals make their own defensive chemicals—such as all of the venoms produced by social insects (bees, wasps, ants), as well as snakes and mites. These venoms are usually proteins, acids or bases, alkaloids, or combinations of chemicals. They are generally injected by biting or stinging, while other defenses are produced as sprays, froths, or droplets from glands.

Animals frequently make the same types of toxins as plants, presumably because their function as protective agents is similar. Other organisms, particularly insects, use plant chemicals to defend themselves. Sequestration may be a low-cost defense mechanism and probably arises when insects specialize on particular plants.

Microbial defenses. Competitive microbial interactions are regulated by many chemical exchanges involving toxins. They include compounds such as aflatoxin, botulinus toxin, odors of rotting food, hallucinogens, and a variety of antibiotics. *See* ANTIBIOTIC; TOXIN.

Microorganisms also play a role in chemical interaction with plants and animals that range from the production of toxins that kill insects, such as those produced by the common biological pest control agent *Bacillus thuringiensis*, to cooperative biochemical detoxification of plant toxins by animal symbionts.

Information exchange. A large area of chemical ecology concerns the isolation and identification of chemicals used for communication. Pheromones, substances produced by an organism that induce a behavioral or physiological response in an individual of the same species, have been studied particularly well in insects. These signals are compounds that are mutually beneficial to the emitter and sender, such as sex attractants, trail markers, and alarm and aggregation signals. Sex pheromones are volatile substances, usually produced by the female to attract males. Each species has a characteristic compound that may differ from that of other species by as little as a few atoms.

Pheromones are typically synthesized directly by the animal and are usually derived from fatty acids. In a few cases the pheromone or its immediate precursors may be derived from plants, as in danaid butterflies.

Very little work has been done in identifying specific pheromones in vertebrates, particularly mammals. It is known, however, that they are important in marking territory, in individual recognition, and in mating and warning signals. Chemical communication may also occur among plants and microorganisms, although it is rarer and less obvious than in animals. *See* REPRODUCTIVE BEHAVIOR; TERRITORIALITY.   [C.G.J.; A.C.L.]

Chemical senses   In vertebrates, the senses of smell (olfaction) and taste (gustation) plus the so-called common chemical sense constitute the external chemical senses (as contrasted with internal chemoreceptors). The olfactory cells of vertebrates, usually located in the olfactory mucosa of the upper nasal passages, are specialized neural elements that are responsive to chemicals in the vapor phase. Taste buds of the oral cavity, especially the tongue, are composed of modified epithelial cells responsive to chemicals in solution. The common chemical senses are composed of free nerve endings in the mucous membrane of the eye, nose, mouth, and digestive tract and are responsive to irritants or other chemicals in either the vapor or liquid phase. *See* CHEMORECEPTION.

Among invertebrates, sense organs occur as specialized hairs and sensilla, or minute cones supplied with sensory nerves and nerve cells. Characteristic of male moths, for example, are their distinctive bushy antennae, by which they detect and locate females by sex pheromones. Rodents, ungulates, carnivores, and other mammals also show sexual attraction to female odors produced by specialized glands. Whether humans in general are susceptible to pheromonal influences from other humans is debatable. *See* PHEROMONE.

Taste plays an important role in selection and acceptance of food. Besides the protective, inborn aversion to bitter (many poisons, but not all, are bitter), a single experience with the particular taste of a toxic substance which caused illness may establish a strong and persistent learned taste aversion. By contrast, a compensatory salt hunger may occur in persons or animals suffering salt deficiency.

The limbic system of the brain, which modulates appetitive and emotional behavior and hedonic (pleasant vs. unpleasant) experiences, has both taste and olfactory neural pathways to it, providing the neural substrate for the pleasure or displeasure of sensations. *See* NEUROBIOLOGY; OLFACTION; SENSATION; TASTE.   [C.P.]

Chemiosmosis   The coupling of metabolic and light energy to the performance of transmembrane work through the intermediary of electroosmotic gradients. Processes include synthesis of adenosine triphosphate (ATP) by oxidative phosphorylation or by photosynthesis, production of heat, accumulation of small molecules by active transport, movement of bacterial flagella, uptake of deoxyribonucleic acid (DNA) during bacterial conjugation, genetic transformation and bacteriophage infection, and insertion or secretion of proteins into or through membranes.

Mitochondria are the powerhouses of the eukaryotic cell and the site of synthesis of ATP by oxidative phosphorylation. In the oxidation portion of ATP synthesis, reductants, such as reduced nicotinamide adenine dinucleotide (NADH) and succinate, are generated during metabolism of carbohydrates, lipids, and protein. These compounds are oxidized through the series of redox reactions performed by membrane-bound complexes, called electron transport or respiratory chains. *See* ADENOSINE TRIPHOSPHATE (ATP); MITOCHONDRIA.

Bacteria do not contain mitochondria, but many of the functions of the mitochondrial membrane are carried out by the bacterial cytoplasmic membrane. Many bacteria also use respiratory chains. This resemblance to mitochondria is more than chance. The evidence, although mostly circumstantial, suggests that mitochondria, chloroplasts, and perhaps other eukaryotic organelles were originally free-living bacteria. These bacteria and larger proto-eukaryotic cells became mutually symbiotic, so that neither was complete or viable without the other. The animal and plant kingdoms arose from these endosymbiotic events.

Photosynthesis is the conversion of light energy into chemical energy. Overall photosynthetic bacteria and the chloroplasts of eukaryotic plants capture sunlight or other light and use that energy to generate both ATP and a reductant for use in biosynthesis. The mechanism of photophosphorylation, that is, the use of light energy to drive the phosphorylation of adenosine diphosphate (ADP) to ATP, resembles that of oxidative phosphorylation. *See* PHOTOSYNTHESIS.

Oxidative phosphorylation and photophosphorylation are but specialized examples of chemiosmotic energy coupling. Among the forms of useful energy are chemical energy, such as that derived from fossil fuels, and light energy in the case of solar cells. Electricity is transmitted to motors, which couple electrical energy to the performance of work. Bacterial cells, mitochondria, and chloroplasts have protonic generators and protonic motors. Respiratory and photosynthetic electron transport chains are generators of proton currents' proton motive forces, which then drive the various motors of the cell or organelle. When the H^+-translocating ATPase is "plugged in," the proton current drives phosphorylation. There are other motors present in the cell. Most membranes contain specific transport systems for small molecules, such as ions, sugars, and amino acids. Many of these transport systems are protonic; that is, they use the energy of the proton motive force to drive the accumulation or extrusion of their substrate.   [B.Ro.]

Chemoreception   The ability of organisms to detect changes in the chemical composition of their exterior or interior environment. It is a characteristic of every living cell, from the single-celled bacteria and protozoa to the most complex multicellular organisms. Chemoreception allows organisms to maintain homeostasis, react to stimuli, and communicate with one another. See HOMEOSTASIS.

At the single-cell level, bacteria orient toward or avoid certain chemical stimuli (chemotaxis); algal gametes release attractants which allow sperm to find oocytes in a dilute aqueous environment; and unicellular slime molds are drawn together to form colonial fruiting bodies by use of aggregation pheromones. See CELLULAR ADHESION; TAXIS.

In multicellular organisms, both single cells and complex multicellular sense organs are used to homeostatically maintain body fluids (interoreceptors) as well as to monitor the external environment (exteroreceptors). The best-studied interoreceptors are perhaps the carotid body chemoreceptors of higher vertebrates, which monitor the levels of oxygen, carbon dioxide, and hydrogen ions in arterial blood. The best-studied exteroreceptors are those associated with taste (gustation) and smell (olfaction). Internal communication is also effected by chemical means in multicellular organisms. Thus both hormonal and neural control involve the perception, by cells, of control chemicals (hormones and neurotransmitters, respectively). See CHEMICAL SENSES; OLFACTION; SENSE ORGAN; TASTE.

The basic mechanism underlying chemoreception is the interaction of a chemical stimulus with receptor molecules in the outer membrane of a cell. These molecules are believed to be proteins which, because of their three-dimensional shapes and chemical properties, will have the right spatial and binding "fit" for interaction with only a select group of chemicals (the same basic mechanism by which enzymes are specific for various substrates). The interaction between a chemical stimulus and a receptor molecule ultimately leads to structural changes in membrane channels. The net result is usually a change in membrane conductance (permeability) to specific ions which changes both the internal chemical composition of the cell and the charge distribution across the cell membrane. In single-celled organisms, this may be sufficient to establish a membrane current which may elicit responses such as an increase or decrease in ciliary movement. In multicellular organisms, it usually results in changes in the rate of release of hormones or the stimulation of neurons. See CELL MEMBRANES.

The basic characteristics of all chemoreceptors are specificity (the chemicals that they will respond to); sensitivity (the magnitude of the response for a given chemical stimulus); and range of perception (the smallest or largest level of stimulus that the receptor can discriminate). Specificity is a consequence of the types of proteins found in the membrane of a receptor cell. Each cell will have a mosaic of different receptor molecules, and each receptor molecule will show different combinations of excitatory or inhibitory responses to different molecules. In an excitatory response, there is a net flux of positive ions into the cell (depolarization); for an inhibitory response, there is a net flux of negative ions into the cell (hyperpolarization). The stronger the stimulus—that is, the more of the chemical present—the more receptors affected, the greater the change in conductance, and the larger the membrane current. In animals with nervous systems, these changes in conductance of primary sensory cells can lead to one of two events. In some receptors, if the current is excitatory and sufficient in magnitude (threshold), an action potential will be generated at a spike-initiating zone on the neuron. Other receptors respond by releasing a neurotransmitter that acts on a second-order neuron which is excitable and therefore can generate action potentials. *See* BIOPOTENTIALS AND IONIC CURRENTS.

The sensitivity of a chemoreceptor reflects both the amount of chemical substance required to initiate a change in membrane potential or discharge of the receptor cell, and the change in potential or discharge for any given change in the level of the chemical stimulus. There are real limits as to the extent of change in membrane conductance or firing frequency. Thus, for more sensitive cells, there is a smaller range over which they can provide information about the change in concentration of any given chemical before it has reached its maximum conductance or discharge rate and has saturated.

In animals, the responsiveness of some chemoreceptors can be either enhanced or attenuated by other neural input. These influences come in the form of efferent inputs from the central nervous system, from neighboring receptors, or even from recurrent branches of the chemoreceptor's own sensory axons. The net effect is either (1) to increase the acuity of the receptors (excitatory input brings the membrane potential of the receptor cell closer to threshold, requiring less chemical stimulus to elicit a response); or (2) to extend the range of responsiveness of the receptors (inhibitory input lowers the membrane potential of the receptor cell, requiring more chemical stimulus to bring the cell to threshold). For example, chemical sensitivity is greatly heightened in most animals when they are hungry.

Any given chemoreceptor cell can have any combination of receptor proteins, each of which may respond to different chemical molecules. Thus, chemoreceptor cells do not exhibit a unitary specificity to a single chemical substance, but rather an action spectrum to various groups of chemicals. The ability of animals to distinguish such a large number of different, complex, natural chemical stimuli resides in the ability of higher centers in the nervous system to "recognize" the pattern of discharge of large groups of cells. Sensory quality does not depend on the activation of a particular cell or group of cells but on the interaction of cells with overlapping response spectra.

Despite the common, basic mechanism underlying chemoreception in all organisms, there is a great diversity in the design of multicellular chemoreceptive organs, particularly in animals. The complex structures of most of these organs reflect adaptations that serve to filter and amplify chemical signals. Thus, the antennae in many insects, and the irrigated protective chambers, such as the olfactory bulb of fishes and nasal passages of mammals, increase the exposure of chemoreceptor cells to the environment. At the same time, they allow the diffusion distances between chemoreceptive cells and the environment to be reduced, thereby increasing acuity. In terms of filtering, they may serve to convert turbulent or dispersed stimuli into temporal patterns that can be more easily interpreted. The extent to which such structural adaptations are seen in various organisms tends to reflect the relative importance of chemoreception to the organism, which, to a large extend, reflects the habitat in which the organism lives. *See* CHEMICAL ECOLOGY.   [W.Mil.]

Chemostat   An apparatus (see illustration) for the continuous cultivation of microorganisms or plant cells. The nutrients required for cell growth are supplied continuously to the culture vessel by a pump connected to a medium reservoir. The cells in the vessel grow continuously on these nutrients. Residual nutrients and cells are

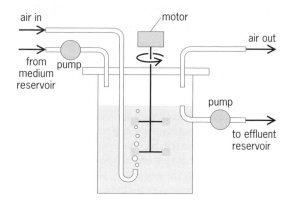

air in

motor

air out

from
medium
reservoir

pump

pump

to effluent
reservoir

**Schematic representation of
chemostat apparatus.**

removed from the vessel (fermenter) at the same rate by an overflow, thus maintaining the culture in the fermenter at a constant volume.

An important feature of chemostat cultivation is the dilution rate, defined as the volume of nutrient medium supplied per hour divided by the volume of the culture. During chemostat cultivation, an equilibrium is established (steady state) at which the growth rate of the cells equals the dilution rate. The higher the dilution rate, the faster the organisms are allowed to grow. Above a given dilution rate the cells will not be able to grow any faster, and the culture will be washed out of the fermenter. The chemostat thus offers the opportunity to study the properties of organisms at selected growth rates. *See* FERMENTATION.

The nutrient medium which is fed to the fermenter contains an excess of all growth factors except one, the growth-limiting nutrient. The concentration of the cells (biomass) in the fermenter is dependent on the concentration of the growth-limiting nutrient in the medium feed. Upon entering the fermenter, the growth-limiting nutrient is consumed almost to completion, and only minute amounts of it may be found in the culture and the effluent. Initially, when few cells have been inoculated in the growth vessel, even the growth-limiting nutrient is in excess. Therefore, the microorganisms can grow at a rate exceeding their rate of removal. This growth of cells causes a fall in the level of the growth-limiting nutrient, gradually leading to a lower specific growth rate of the microorganisms. Once the specific rate of growth balances the removal of cells by dilution, a steady state is established in which both the cell density and the concentration of the growth-limiting nutrient remain constant. Thus the chemostat is a tool for the cultivation of microorganisms almost indefinitely in a constant physiological state.

To achieve a steady state, parameters other than the dilution rate and culture volume must be kept constant (for example, temperature and pH). The fermenter is stirred to provide a homogeneous suspension in which all individual cells in the culture come into contact with the growth-limiting nutrient immediately, and to achieve optimal distribution of air (oxygen) in the fermenter when aerobic cultures are in use.

Laboratory chemostats usually contain 0.5 to 10.5 quarts (0.5 to 10 liters) of culture, but industrial chemostat cultivation can involve volumes up to 343,000 gal (1300 m^3) for the continuous production of microbial biomass.

The chemostat can be used to grow microorganisms on very toxic nutrients since, when kept growth-limiting, the nutrient concentration in the culture is very low. The chemostat can be used to select mutants with a higher affinity to the growth-limiting nutrient or, in the case of a mixed population, to select the species that are optimally adapted to the growth limitation and culture conditions. The chemostat is of great use in such fields as physiology, ecology, and genetics of microorganisms. *See* BACTERIAL GENETICS; BACTERIAL PHYSIOLOGY AND METABOLISM; MICROBIOLOGY. [J.Gi.]

Chemotaxonomy The use of biochemistry in taxonomic studies. Living organisms produce many types of natural products in varying amounts, and quite often the biosynthetic pathways responsible for these compounds also differ from one taxonomic group to another. The distribution of these compounds and their biosynthetic pathways correspond well with existing taxonomic arrangements based on more traditional criteria such as morphology. In some cases, chemical data have contradicted existing hypotheses, which necessitates a reexamination of the problem or, more positively, chemical data have provided decisive information in situations where other forms of data are insufficiently discriminatory. *See* ANIMAL SYSTEMATICS.

Modern chemotaxonomists often divide natural products into two major classes: (1) micromolecules, that is, those compounds with a molecular weight of 1000 or less, such as alkaloids, terpenoids, amino acids, fatty acids, flavonoid pigments and other phenolic compounds, mustard oils, and simple carbohydrates; and (2) macromolecules, that is, those compounds (often polymers) with a molecular weight over 1000, including complex polysaccharides, proteins, and the basis of life itself, deoxyribonucleic acid (DNA).

A crude extract of a plant can be separated into its individual components, especially in the case of micromolecules, by using one or more techniques of chromatography, including paper, thin-layer, gas, or high-pressure liquid chromatography. The resulting chromatogram provides a visual display or "fingerprint" characteristic of a plant species for the particular class of compounds under study.

The individual, separated spots can be further purified and then subjected to one or more types of spectroscopy, such as ultraviolet, infrared, or nuclear magnetic resonance or mass spectroscopy (or both), which may provide information about the structure of the compound. Thus, for taxonomic purposes, both visual patterns and structural knowledge of the compounds can be compared from species to species. *See* SPECTROSCOPY.

Because of their large, polymeric, and often crystalline nature, macromolecules (for example, proteins, carbohydrates, DNA) can be subjected to x-ray crystallography, which gives some idea of their three-dimensional structure. These large molecules can then be broken down into smaller individual components and analyzed by using techniques employed for micromolecules. In fact, the specific amino acid sequence of portions or all of a cellular respiratory enzyme, cytochrome *c*, has been elucidated and used successfully for chemotaxonomic comparisons in plants and especially animals.

Cyctochrome *c* is a small protein or polypeptide chain consisting of approximately 103–112 amino acids, depending on the animal or plant under study. About 35 of the amino acids do not vary in type or position within the chain, and are probably necessary to maintain the structure and function of the enzyme. Several other amino acid positions vary occasionally, and always with the same amino acid substitution at a particular position. Among the remaining 50 positions scattered throughout the chain, considerable substitution occurs, the number of such differences between organisms indicating how closely they are related to one another. When such substitutional patterns were subjected to computer analysis, an evolutionary tree was obtained showing the degree of relatedness among the 36 plants and animals examined. This evolutionary tree is remarkably similar to evolutionary trees or phylogenies constructed on the basis of the actual fossil record for these organisms. Thus, the internal biochemistry of living organisms reflects a measure of the evolutionary changes which have occurred over time in these plants and animals. Since each amino acid in a protein is the ultimate product of a specific portion of the DNA code, the substitutional differences in this and other proteins in various organisms also reflect a change in the nucleotide sequences of DNA itself. *See* GENETIC CODE; PHYLOGENY.

In the case of proteins, it is often not necessary to know the specific amino acid sequence of a protein, but, rather, to observe how many different proteins, or forms of a single protein, are present in different plant or animal species. The technique of electrophoresis is used to obtain a pattern of protein bands of spots much like the chemical fingerprint of micromolecules. Because each amino acid in a protein carries a positive, negative, or neutral ionic charge, the total sum of charges of the amino acids constituting the protein will give the whole protein a net positive, negative, or neutral charge.

By using other techniques of molecular biology, such as DNA hybridization and genetic cloning, the specific gene function of individual fragments may be identified. Their nucleotide sequences can be determined and then compared for different taxa. Such data may prove useful at several different taxonomic levels. *See* GENETIC ENGINEERING.

While the organellar DNA does not contain the number of genetic messages of the organism that nuclear DNA does, and its transmission from parent to offspring may vary somewhat depending on the organism, the convenient size of organellar DNA and its potential for direct examination of the genetic code suggest that it is a potent macromolecular approach to chemosystematics. *See* GENETIC CODE.   [D.E.G.]

Chickenpox and shingles   Chickenpox (varicella) and shingles (herpes zoster) are two different forms of disease caused by the varicella-zoster virus, which is a deoxyribonucleic acid (DNA) virus closely related to herpes simplex and *Epstein-Barr viruses*. Initial infection causes varicella, a common childhood infection characterized by fever, malaise, and a rash consisting of dozens to hundreds of small fluid-filled lesions (vesicles) that are individually surrounded by reddened skin. Successive crops of lesions appear that eventually ulcerate and crust over during the two-week course of the disease. The virus is spread from person to person by the highly infectious respiratory secretions and lesion drainage. Varicella is rarely a serious disease in normal children but can be severe in immunocompromised individuals or in the rare adult who escaped childhood infection. Primary infection results in immunity to a new varicella-zoster virus, but the original virus lies dormant in nerve ganglia cells. *See* EPSTEIN-BARR VIRUS; HERPES.

At some time in their life, approximately 10% of the population suffers subsequent reactivation of latent virus, which spreads to the skin overlying the affected nerve and causes a localized eruption of vesicles called herpes zoster. The vesicles are similar in appearance and in infectiousness to varicella lesions. This syndrome is usually well tolerated, although elderly persons may develop chronic pain at the site of reactivation. Herpes zoster in immunocompromised individuals may be prolonged or may disseminate to vital organs.

Varicella or herpes zoster in a normal host is self-limited and does not typically require antiviral therapy. In individuals with underlying immune disorders, treatment with the antiviral drug acyclovir decreases the duration and severity of disease. *See* ANIMAL VIRUS.   [F.P.H.]

Chimera   An individual animal or plant made up of cells derived from more than one zygote or otherwise genetically distinct.

Animals. Although some chimeras do arise naturally, most are produced experimentally, either by mixing cells of very early embryos or by tissue grafting in late embryos or adults. Experimental chimeras have been used to study a number of biological questions, including the origin and fate of cell lineages during embryonic development, immunological self-tolerance, tumor susceptibility, and the nature of malignancy.

Two techniques used to form chimeras by mixing embryo cells are aggregation and injection.

Aggregation chimeras are produced by a technique that involves removing the zonae pellucidae from around 8–16 cell embryos of different strains of mice and pushing the morulae together so that the cells can aggregate. After a short period of laboratory culture, during which the aggregate develops into a single large blastocyst, the embryo is returned to a hormone-primed foster mother. Chimeric offspring are recognized in several ways. If derived from embryos of pigmented and albino strains, they may have stripes of pigmented skin and patches of pigment in the eye. Internal chimerism can be detected by use of chromosomal markers or genetically determined enzyme variants. Chimeras accept skin grafts from the two component strains, but reject grafts from third-party strains.

Injection chimeras are produced by a technique in which a blastocyst of the host mouse strain of mouse embryos is removed from its zona pellucida and held on a suction pipette. Cells of the donor strain are injected through a fine glass needle, either into the blastocoele cavity or into the center of the inner cell mass (the group of cells from which the fetus is derived). After a short period of culture, the blastocyst is returned to a foster mother.

Another kind of cell—the pluripotent stem cell of mouse teratocarcinomas—was found to give rise to normal tissues in adult chimeras after injection into the mouse blastocyst. Teratocarcinomas are tumors consisting of a disorganized mixture of adult and embryonic tissues. They develop spontaneously from germ cells in the gonads of certain mouse strains, or from cells in early embryos transplanted to ectopic sites. All the differentiated tissues in the tumor arise from pluripotent stem cells known as embryonal carcinoma (EC) cells. When embryonal carcinoma cells are injected into a genetically marked host blastocyst, they continue to divide and participate in normal development, and give rise to fully differentiated cells in all tissues of the adult, including skin, muscle, nerve, kidney, and blood. Embryonal carcinoma cells from several sources, including spontaneous and embryo-derived tumors and cultured lines selected to carry specific mutations or even human chromosomes, have contributed to normal chimeras. However, embryonal carcinoma cells from some other sources fail to integrate, but produce teratocarcinomas in the newborn animal or adult. The fact that certain embryonal carcinoma cells give rise to tumors when injected under the skin or into the body cavity, but behave normally in the blastocyst, has been used to support the idea that cancers can develop not only as a result of gene mutations but also as a result of disturbances in environmental factors controlling normal cell differentiation (epigenetic theory of cancer).

Animals that have accepted skin or organ grafts are technically chimeras. Radiation chimeras are produced when an animal is exposed to x-rays, so that blood-forming stem cells in the bone marrow are killed and then replaced by a bone marrow transplant from a genetically different animal. Lymphoid cells in the process of differentiating from stem cells in the donor marrow recognize the recipient as "self" and do not initiate an immune response against the host cells. *See* TRANSPLANTATION BIOLOGY.

Naturally occurring chimeras in humans are not rare and are most easily recognized when some cells are XX and others XY. Such individuals are usually hermaphrodite and probably result from fertilization of the egg by one sperm and the second polar body by another, with both diploid cells then contributing to the embryo (the small polar bodies normally degenerate). Blood chimeras are somewhat more common in animals such as cattle where the blood vessels in placentas of twins fuse, so that blood cells can pass from one developing fetus to the other.   [B.Hog.]

Plants. In modern botanical usage a chimera is a plant consisting of two or more genetically distinct kinds of cells. Chimeras can arise either by a mutation in a cell in some part of the plant where cells divide or by bringing together two different plants so that their cells multiply side by side to produce a single individual. They are studied not only because they are interesting freaks or ornamental, but also because they help in the understanding of many of the developmental features of plants that would otherwise be difficult to investigate.

The first type of chimera to be used in this way resulted from grafting. Occasionally a bud forms at the junction of the scion and stock incorporating cells from both, and it sometimes happens that the cells arrange themselves so that shoots derived from the bud will contain cells from both plants forever.

Flowering plants have growing points (apical meristems) where the outer cells are arranged in layers parallel to the surface. This periclinal layering is due to the fact that the outer cells divide only anticlinally, that is, by walls perpendicular to the surface of the growing point. In many plants there are two such tunica layers and, because cell divisions are confined to the anticlinal planes, each layer remains discrete from the other and from the underlying nonlayered tissue called the corpus. The epidermis of leaves, stems, and petals is derived from the outer layer of the growing point. *See* APICAL MERISTEM.

With a periclinal chimera it is possible to trace into stems, leaves, and flowers which tissues are derived from each layer in the growing point. For leaves, this can also be done with variegated chimeras where the genetic difference between the cells rests in the plastids resulting from mutation whose effect is to prevent the synthesis of chlorophyll. Tracts of cells whose plastids lack this pigment appear white or yellow. A common form of variegated chimera has leaves with white margins and a green center (see illustration). The white margin is derived from the second layer of the tunica, and the green center is derived from inner cells of the growing point. The white leaf tissue overlies the green in the center of the leaf, but does not mask the green color. Chimeras with green leaf margins and white centers are usually due to a genetically green tunica proliferating abnormally at the leaf margin in an otherwise white leaf.

Since the somatic mutation that initiates chimeras would normally occur in a single cell of a growing point or embryo, it often happens that it is propagated into a tract of mutant cells to form a sector of the plant. If the mutation resulted in a failure to form green pigment, the tract would be seen as a white stripe. Such chimeras are called sectorial, but they are normally unstable because there is no mechanism to isolate the mutant sector and, in the flux that occurs in a meristem of growing and dividing cells, one or other of the two sorts of cells takes over its self-perpetuating layer in the growing point. The sectorial chimera therefore becomes nonchimerical or else a periclinal chimera.

However, in one class of chimera an isolating mechanism can stabilize the sectorial arrangement. This propagates stripes of mutant tissue into the shoot, but because the tunica and corpus are discrete from each other, the plant is not fully sectored and is called a mericlinal chimera. Many chimeras of this type have a single tunica layer; those with green and white stripes in the leaves have the mutant cells in sectors of the corpus. They are always plants with leaves in two ranks, and consequently the lateral growth of the growing point occurs by cell expansion only in the plane connecting alternate leaves. This results in the longitudinal divisions of the corpus cells being confined to

Variegated *Pelargonium*, a periclinal chimera whose second tunica layer is genetically white and whose corpus is genetically green.

planes at right angles to the plane containing the leaves. A mutation in one cell therefore can result in a vertical sheet of mutant cells which, in the case of plastid defect, manifests itself as a white stripe in every future leaf.

The growing points of roots may also become chimerical, but in roots there is no mechanism to isolate genetically different tissues as there is in shoots, and so chimeras are unstable.

Since the general acceptance of the existence of organisms with genetically diverse cells, many cultivated plants have been found to be chimeras. Flecks of color often indicate the chimerical nature of such plants. Color changes in potato tubers occur similarly because the plants are periclinal chimeras. *See* SOMATIC CELL GENETICS.   [F.A.L.C.]

Chiroptera   An order of mammals (bats) in which the front limbs are modified as wings, thus making the chiropterans the only truly flying mammals. Bats form the second largest order of living mammals (16 families, 171 genera, some 840 species). They range from the limit of trees in the Northern Hemisphere to the southern tips of Africa, New Zealand, and South America, but most species are confined to the tropics. On many oceanic islands they are the only native land mammals.

The wing is formed by webs of skin running from the neck to the wrist (propagatium, or antebrachial membrane), between the greatly elongated second, third, fourth,

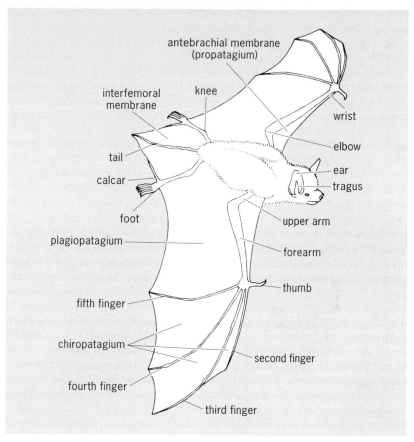

Features of the bat. (*From R. Peterson, Silently by Night, McGraw-Hill, 1964*)

and fifth fingers (chiropatagium), and from the arm and hand to the body (usually the side) and hindlegs (plagiopatagium). There is also usually a web between the hindlegs (uropatagium, or interfemoral membrane) in which the tail, if present, is usually embedded for at least part of its length (see illustration).

Bats have a poor fossil record, but have been distinct at least since the Eocene, some 50,000,000 years ago. *See* MAMMALIA.   [K.F.K.]

Chitin A polysaccharide found abundantly in nature. Chitin forms the basis of the hard shells of crustaceans, such as the crab, lobster, and shrimp. The exoskeleton of insects is also chitinous, and the cell walls of certain fungi contain this substance.

Chitin is a long, unbranched molecule consisting entirely of N-acetyl-D-glucosamine units linked by β-1,4 bonds (see illustration). It may be thought of as cellulose in which the hydroxyl groups on the second carbon are replaced with $NHCOCH_3$ groups. Chitin is considered to be synthesized in nature by an enzyme which is capable of effecting a glycosyl transfer of the N-acetyl-D-glucosamine from β-*N*-acetyl-D-glucosamine unit of chitin.

uridinediphosphate-*N*-acetyl-D-glucosamine to a preformed chitodextrin acceptor, forming the polysaccharide. This stepwise enzymic transfer results in the production of the long chain of β-*N*-acetyl-D-glucosamine units, which is insoluble chitin. *See* POLYSACCHARIDE.   [W.Z.H.]

Chlamydia   A genus of bacteria with a growth cycle differing from that of all other microorganisms. Chlamydiae grow only in living cells and cannot be cultured on artificial media. Although capable of synthesizing macromolecules, they have no system for generating energy; the host cell's energy system fuels the chlamydial metabolic processes. The genome is relatively small; the genomes of *C. pneumoniae* and *C. trachomatis* have been completely sequenced.

The chlamydial infectious particle, called the elementary body, is round and about 350–450 nanometers in diameter. It enters a susceptible host cell and changes to a metabolically active and larger (approximately 800–1000 nm in diameter) reticulate body that divides by binary fission. The entire growth cycle occurs within a vacuole that segregates the chlamydia from the cytoplasm of the host cell. The reticulate bodies change back to elementary bodies, and then the cell lyses and the infectious particles are released. The growth cycle takes about 48 h.

Human diseases are caused by three species of *Chlamydia*. *Chlamydia trachomatis* is almost exclusively a human pathogen, and one of the most common. Infections occur in two distinct epidemiologic patterns. In many developing countries, *C. trachomatis* causes trachoma, a chronic follicular keratoconjunctivitis. It is the world's leading cause of preventable blindness, affecting approximately 500 million people. In areas where this condition is highly endemic, virtually the entire population is infected within the first few years of life. Most active infections are found in childhood. By age 60, more than 20% of a population can be blinded as a result of trachoma. *See* EYE DISORDERS.

Chlamydia trachomatis is the most common sexually transmitted bacterial pathogen; an estimated 3–4 million cases occur each year in the United States, and there are close to 90 million worldwide. The most common manifestation is nongonococcal urethritis in males. The cervix is the most commonly infected site in women. Ascending infections can occur in either sex, resulting in epididymitis in males or endometritis and salpingitis in females. Chlamydial infection of the fallopian tube can cause late consequences such as infertility and ectopic pregnancy, even though the earlier infection is asymptomatic. The infant passing through the infected birth canal can acquire the infection and may develop either conjunctivitis or pneumonia. A more invasive form of *C. trachomatis* causes a systemic sexually transmitted disease called lymphogranuloma venereum. *See* SEXUALLY TRANSMITTED DISEASES.

Chlamydia psittaci is virtually ubiquitous among avian species and is a common pathogen among lower mammals. It is economically important in many countries as a cause of abortion in sheep, cattle, and goats. It causes considerable morbidity and mortality in poultry. *Chlamydia psittaci* can infect humans, causing the disease psittacosis. Psittacosis can occur as pneumonia or a febrile toxic disease without respiratory symptoms.

Chlamydia pneumoniae appears to be a human pathogen with no animal reservoir. It is of worldwide distribution and may be the most common human chlamydial infection. It appears to be an important cause of respiratory disease.

Azithromycin is the drug of choice for uncomplicated chlamydial infection of the genital tract. Two therapeutic agents require longer treatment regimens: doxycycline, a tetracycline antibiotic, is the first alternate treatment; erythromycin may be used for those who are tetracycline-intolerant, as well as for pregnant women or young children. *See* MEDICAL BACTERIOLOGY.   [J.S.]

Chlorophyll   The generic name for the intensely colored green pigments which are the photoreceptors of light energy in photosynthesis. These pigments belong to the tetrapyrrole family of organic compounds.

Five closely related chlorophylls, designated *a* through *e*, occur in higher plants and algae. The principal chlorophyll (Chl) is Chl *a*, found in all oxygen-evolving organisms; photosynthetic bacteria, which do not evolve O_2, contain instead bacteriochlorophyll (Bchl). Higher plants and green algae contain Chl *b*, the ratio of Chl *b* to Chl *a* being 1:3. Chlorophyll *c* (of two or more types) is present in diatoms and brown algae. Chlorophyll *d*, isolated from marine red algae, has not been shown to be present in the living cell in large enough quantities to be observed in the absorption spectrum of these algae. Chlorophyll *e* has been isolated from cultures of two algae, *Tribonema bombycinum* and *Vaucheria hamata*. In higher plants the chlorophylls and the above-mentioned pigments are contained in lipoprotein bodies, the plastids. *See* CAROTENOID; CELL PLASTIDS; PHOTOSYNTHESIS.

Chlorophyll molecules have three functions: They serve as antennae to absorb light quanta; they transmit this energy from one chlorophyll to another by a process of "resonance transfer;" and finally, this chlorophyll molecule, in close association with enzymes, undergoes a chemical oxidation (that is, an electron of high potential is ejected from the molecule and can then be used to reduce another compound). In this way the energy of light quanta is converted into chemical energy.

The chlorophylls are cyclic tetrapyrroles in which four 5-membered pyrrole rings join to form a giant macrocycle. Chlorophylls are members of the porphyrin family, which plays important roles in respiratory pigments, electron transport carriers, and oxidative enzymes. *See* PORPHYRIN.

It now appears that the chlorophyll *a* group may be made up of several chemically distinct Chl *a* species. The structure of monovinyl cholorophyll *a*, the most abundant of the Chl *a* species, is shown in the illustration.

The two major pigments of protoplasm, green chlorophyll and red heme, are synthesized from ALA (δ-aminolevulinic acid) along the same biosynthetic pathway to protoporphyrin. ALA is converted in a series of enzymic steps, identical in plants and animals, to protoporphyrin. Here the pathway branches to form (1) a series of porphyrins chelated with iron, as heme and related cytochrome pigments; and (2) a series of porphyrins chelated with magnesium which are precursors of chlorophyll. *See* HEMOGLOBIN.

Chlorophylls reemit a fraction of the light energy they absorb as fluorescence. Irrespective of the wavelength of the absorbed light, the emitted fluorescence is always on the long-wavelength side of the lowest energy absorption band, in the red or infrared region of the spectrum.

The fluorescent properties of a particular chlorophyll are functions of the structure of the molecule and its immediate environment. Thus, the fluorescence spectrum of

**Structure of chlorophyll *a*
($C_{55}H_{72}O_5N_4Mg$).**

chlorophyll in the living plant is always shifted to longer wavelengths relative to the fluorescence spectrum of a solution of the same pigment. This red shift is characteristic of aggregated chlorophyll.   [G.; S.Gr.; G.P.]

Cholera   A severe diarrheal disease caused by infection of the small bowel of humans with *Vibrio cholerae*, a facultatively anaerobic, gram-negative, rod-shaped bacterium. Cholera is transmitted by the fecal-oral route. Cholera has swept the world in seven pandemic waves. These involved the Western Hemisphere several times in the 1800s, and again in Peru in 1991. Whereas previous cholera outbreaks were associated with high mortality rates, through understanding of its pathophysiology it can now be said that no one should die of cholera who receives appropriate treatment soon enough.

Cholera produces a secretory diarrhea caused by the protein cholera enterotoxin (CTX). The toxin causes hypersecretion of chloride and bicarbonate and inhibition of sodium absorption in host membranes leading to the secretion of the large volumes of isotonic fluid which constitute the diarrhea of severe cholera. Treatment consists of replacing the fluids and electrolytes lost in the voluminous cholera stool. This can be done intravenously or orally. Appropriate antibiotics can also be used. The incubation period may be less than one day or up to several days; properly treated, the patient should recover in 4 or 5 days. The disease produces immunization, and convalescents rarely get cholera again.

Despite the fact that the cholera bacteria were first discovered by Robert Koch in 1883 and a cholera vaccine was introduced 3 years later, there is still no effective, economical, and nonreactogenic vaccine. Use of a killed whole-cell vaccine administered parenterally (via injection) was eliminated because of expense, reactogenicity, and lack of efficacy. Experimental vaccines currently being evaluated include genetically engineered living attenuated preparations administered orally (or intranasally), killed whole-cell vaccines administered orally, and conjugated vaccines (polysaccharide and toxin antigens) administered parenterally. Efforts are also being made to include cholera antigens transgenically in edible plants.

A complicating feature is the fact that of approximately 150 recognized serogroups of *V. cholerae*, until 1992 only two, classical (first described by Koch) and El Tor (recognized later), of serogroup O1 have been responsible for all epidemic cholera. In 1992 a recently recognized serogroup, O139, caused epidemic cholera in India and Bangladesh and, for a time, replaced the resident El Tor vibrios. O139 and El Tor are antigenically distinct, so a new vaccine will be required for O139. The emergence of O139 raises the specter that other serogroups of *V. cholerae* may acquire virulence and epidemicity.

The best ways to avoid cholera are by chlorination of water, sanitary disposal of sewage, and avoidance of raw or improperly cooked seafood, which may have become infected by ingesting infected plankton in epidemic areas.   [R.A.Fin.]

Cholesterol   A cyclic hydrocarbon alcohol commonly classified as a lipid because it is insoluble in water but soluble in a number of organic solvents. It is the major sterol in all vertebrate cells and the most common sterol of eukaryotes. In vertebrates, the highest concentration of cholesterol is in the myelin sheath that surrounds nerves and in the plasma membrane that surrounds all cells. *See* LIPID.

Cholesterol can exist either in the free (unesterified) form (see structure below) or in

the esterified form, in which a fatty acid is bound to the hydroxyl group of cholesterol by an ester bond. The free form is found in membranes. Cholesteryl esters are normally found in lipid droplets either within the cells of steroidogenic tissues, where it can be converted to free cholesterol and then to steroid hormones, or in the middle of spherical lipid-protein complexes, called lipoproteins, that are found in blood. *See* CELL MEMBRANES.

Cholesterol, together with phospholipids and proteins, is important in the maintenance of normal cellular membrane fluidity. At physiological temperatures, the cholesterol molecule interacts with the fatty acids of the membrane phospholipids and causes increased packing of the lipid molecules and hence a reduction of membrane fluidity. Thus, all vertebrate cells require cholesterol in their membranes in order for the cell to function normally. Cholesterol is also important as a precursor for a number of other essential compounds, including steroid hormones, bile acids, and vitamin D. *See* LIPID METABOLISM; STEROID.

Cellular cholesterol is obtained both from the diet, following its absorption in the intestine, and from synthesis within all cells of the body. Foods that are particularly high in cholesterol include eggs, red meat, and organs such as liver and brain. About 40–50% of the dietary cholesterol is absorbed from the intestine per day. In contrast, plant sterols are very poorly absorbed. Cholesterol synthesis occurs in all vertebrate cells but is highest in the liver, intestine, and skin, and in the brain at the time of myelination.

Cholesterol and cholesteryl esters are essentially insoluble in water. In order to transport these compounds around the body in the blood, the liver and intestine produce various lipid-protein complexes, called lipoproteins, which serve to solubilize them. Lipoproteins are large, complex mixtures of cholesterol, cholesteryl esters, phospholipids, triglycerides (fats), and various proteins. The major lipoproteins include chylomicrons, very low density lipoprotein (VLDL), low-density lipoprotein, and high-density lipoprotein (HDL).

Total plasma cholesterol levels of less than 200 mg/100 ml are considered desirable. Values of 200–239 or greater than 239 mg per 100 ml are considered, respectively, borderline high or high risk values, indicating the potential for a heart attack. High levels of low-density lipoprotein in the plasma are associated with increased risk of atherosclerosis, ("hardening of the arteries"), which involves deposition of cholesterol and other lipids in the artery wall. Diets low in cholesterol and saturated fats often result in a reduction in total plasma and LDL cholesterol levels. Such changes in blood cholesterol levels are thought to be beneficial and to reduce the incidence of heart attacks.

[P.A.E.]

Choline   A compound, trimethyl-β-hydroxyethylammonium hydroxide, used by the animal organism as a precursor of acetylcholine and as a source of methyl groups. It is a strongly basic hygroscopic substance with the formula

$$(CH_3)_3 \equiv \overset{+}{N} - CH_2 - CH_2OH$$

Choline deficiency in animals is associated with fatty livers, poor growth, and renal lesions. It is a lipotropic agent. There is no direct evidence of disease in humans due to choline deficiency, although there have been suggestions that some of the liver, kidney, or pancreas pathology seen in various nutritional deficiency states may be related to choline insufficiency. Choline is found in acetylcholine, which is necessary for nerve impulse propagation, and in phospholipids.

Humans eat 50–600 mg of choline per day, but only excrete 2–4 mg. Thus, conventional tests are of no value in studying choline requirements, and no knowledge of human choline requirements exists. See Acetylcholine.

[S.N.G.]

Chondrichthyes   A class of vertebrates comprising the cartilaginous, jawed fishes. The Chondrichthyes have traditionally included the subclasses Elasmobranchii (sharks, skates, and rays) and Holocephali (ratfishes). A classification scheme for the Chondrichthyes follows.

Class Chondrichthyes
Subclass Elasmobranchii
Order: Cladoselachii
Pleurocanthodii
Selachii
Batoidea
Subclass Holocephali
Order Chimaeriformes

A group of Devonian armored fishes, the Placodermi, has usually been regarded as ancestral to the Chondrichthyes, but this derivation is not certain. Another group of primitive jawed fishes called acanthodians, which are considered by many as ancestral to the higher bony fishes, exhibit certain primitive elasmobranch-like features. In any case it is probable that the elasmobranchs and ratfishes arose independently of each other sometime during the Silurian or Early Devonian. *See* ACANTHODII; PLACODERMI.

The most distinctive feature shared by the elasmobranchs and ratfishes is the absence of true bone. In both groups the endoskeleton is cartilaginous; in some cases it may be extensively calcified. Because even calcified cartilage is rarely preserved, the fossil record of the Chondrichthyes is represented mainly by teeth and spines, with only occasional associated skeletons.

Other characteristics of the Chondrichthyes include placoid scales, clasper organs on the pelvic fins of males for internal fertilization, a urea-retention mechanism, and the absence of an air (swim) bladder. Both groups have primarily always been marine predators, although they have repeatedly invaded fresh water throughout their long history. The elasmobranchs have probably always fed as they do today, on other fishes as well as on soft and hard-bodied invertebrates. The ratfishes have most likely concentrated on invertebrates, although modern forms occasionally also feed on smaller fishes. *See* RAY; SWIM BLADDER.   [B.S.]

Chordata   The highest phylum in the animal kingdom, which includes the lancelets or amphioxi (Cephalochordata), the tunicates (Urochordata), the acorn worms and pterobranchs (Hemichordata), and the vertebrates (Craniata) comprising the lampreys, sharks and rays, bony fish, amphibians, reptiles, birds, and mammals. Members of the first three groups, the lower chordates, are small and strictly marine. The vertebrates are free-living; the aquatic ones are primitively fresh-water types with marine groups being advanced; and the members include animals of small and medium size, as well as the largest of all animals. *See* VERTEBRATA.

The typical chordate characteristics are the notochord, the dorsal hollow nerve cord, the pharyngeal slits, and a postanal tail. The notochord appears in the embryo as a slender, flexible rod filled with gelatinous cells and surrounded by a tough fibrous sheath, and contains, at least in some forms, transverse striated muscle fibers; it lies above the primitive gut. In lower chordates and the early groups of vertebrates, the notochord persists as the axial support for the body throughout life, but it is surrounded and gradually replaced by segmental vertebrae in the higher fish.

The dorsal hollow nerve cord grows from a specialized band of ectoderm along the middorsal surface of the embryo by a folding together of two parallel ridges. The anterior end enlarges slightly in larval tunicates and somewhat more in lancelets, but enlarges greatly in the vertebrates to form the brain. Vertebral evolution is characterized by continual enlargement of the brain. *See* NERVOUS SYSTEM (VERTEBRATE).

Paired slits develop as outpocketings of the posterior end of the mouth on the sides of the embryonic pharynx, a part of the digestive system, and are retained in all aquatic chordates. Pharyngeal slits originated as adaptations for filter feeding but soon became the primary respiratory organ, as blood vessels line the fine filaments on the margins of each slit. Water passing over the gills serves for gas exchange in addition to the original filter-feeding function, which was soon lost in the vertebrates. Internal gills were lost with the origin of tetrapods; larval and some adult amphibians possess external gills which are different structures. The pharyngeal slits in embryonic tetrapods close early in life, with the pharyngeal pouches becoming the site for development of glands, for example, the thyroid and the tonsils. *See* RESPIRATORY SYSTEM.

The chordate tail is part of the skeletal support, muscles, and nervous system which continues posteriad to the anus or posterior opening of the digestive system. It is a feature not found in any other animal group and serves to increase the force available to the animal for locomotion.

Much controversy still exists about the limits, origin, and affinities of the chordates. For example, opinions differ considerably as to whether the Hemichordata and the Pogonophora are related to the Chordata, although there is no question that the Hemichordata are closely related and part of the pharyngeal-slit filter-feeding radiation; the Hemichordata are here considered as members of the phylum Chordata, not as a separate phylum. Almost all workers agree that the Echinodermata are the closest relatives of the Chordata because of evidence ranging from embryonic development to biochemical resemblances, but there is dispute over which group is the more primitive. *See* ECHINODERMATA; POGONOPHORA.

The Chordata apparently arose from a group of elongated, segmented worms with three sets of body musculature (longitudinal, circular, and transverse) and transverse septa. The first change was the evolution of a segmented coelom, associated with improved locomotion; these animals possessed a hydrostatic skeleton and moved with a sinusoidal or peristaltic locomotion. The first chordate feature to appear was the notochord, which provided a stronger skeleton and permitted the reduction of the transverse and circular muscles. A notochord resulted in a fixed body length and the loss of peristaltic locomotion. The dorsal longitudinal muscles enlarged, and with this modification came the evolution of the dorsal hollow nerve cord. Having a notochord for support rather than a hydrostatic skeleton permitted the appearance of pharyngeal slits through the lateral walls of the anterior parts of the body, which served for increased filter feeding and subsequently for respiration. The presence of the notochord also permitted the appearance of a postanal tail and increased force for locomotion.

The earliest chordate with all of the typical features of the phylum probably looked much like the present-day lancelet or amphioxus (Cephalochordata), which burrows in shifting sands and needs considerable force to move through the heavy sand. Presumably all other chordates developed from this ancestral type, with their differing characteristics evolving because of conditions of their differing habitats.   [W.J.B.]

Chorion   The outermost of the several extraembryonic membranes in amniotes (reptiles, birds, and mammals) enclosing the embryo and all of its other membranes. The chorion, or serosa, is composed of an outer layer of ectodermal cells and an inner layer of mesodermal cells, collectively the somatopleure. Both layers are continuous with the corresponding tissue of the embryo. The chorion arises in conjunction with the amnion, another membrane that forms the outer limb of the somatopleure which folds up over the embryo in reptiles, birds, and some mammals. The chorion is separated from the amnion and yolk sac by a fluid-filled space, the extraembryonic coelom, or body cavity. In those mammals in which the amnion forms by a process of cavitation in a mass of cells, instead of by folding, the chorion forms directly from the trophoblastic capsule, the extraembryonic ectoderm, which becomes gradually underlain by extraembryonic mesoderm.

In reptiles and birds the chorion fuses with another extraembryonic membrane, the allantois, to form the chorioallantois, which lies directly below the shell membranes. An extensive system of blood vessels develops in the mesoderm of this compound membrane which serves as the primary respiratory and excretory organ for gaseous interchanges. In all mammals above the marsupials, the chorion develops special fingerlike processes (chorionic villi) extending outward from its surface. To a varying degree in different species of mammals, the villous regions of the chorion come into more or less intimate contact with the uterine mucosa, or uterine lining, of the mother, thereby forming the various placental types. *See* ALLANTOIS; AMNIOTA; FETAL MEMBRANE; GERM LAYERS.   [N.T.S.]

Chromatophore   A pigmented structure found in many animals, generally in the integument. The term is usually restricted to those structures that bring about changes in color or brightness. A majority of chromatophores are single cells that are highly branched and contain pigment granules that can disperse or aggregate within the cell. However, in coleoid cephalopod mollusks (all mollusks except *Nautilus*), the chromatophores function as miniature organs, and changes in the dispersion of pigment are brought about by muscles. Although the mode of action of the two types of chromatophore is completely different, the effect is the same: pigment either is spread out over a large area of the body or is retracted into a small area.

The movement of pigment takes place in many chromatophores simultaneously, so that the effect is a change in the quality of light reflected from the surface of the animal. The color change functions as a camouflage from predator or prey, but it may also serve for regulating temperature, protecting against harmful radiation, and in signaling. Light stimulates the responses of chromatophores, generally indirectly via the eyes and central nervous system.

Single-cell chromatophores are found in some annelids, insects, and echinoderms. They are much more conspicuous in crustaceans (shrimps and prawns), in fishes (especially in bony fish and teleosts), in anuran amphibians (frogs and toads), and in a few reptiles. The chromatophores may be uniformly distributed in the skin (chameleons), or they may occur in patches (flounders) or lines (around the abdomen in shrimps). Chromatophores of various colors may be distributed unevenly across the body, and occur at different depths in the skin.

Chromatophores produce their colors by reflection after absorption of light. Generally, the light comes from above, but it may come from below after reflection from an underlying structure. The most common type of chromatophore contains melanin (and is, therefore, often called a melanophore), which absorbs all wavelengths so that the chromatophore appears black; other types have red (erythrophores) or yellow (xanthophores) pigments. These pigments generally derive from carotenoids in vertebrates.

Chromatophores contain pigment granules that move within them, giving them an appearance that ranges from spotted to fibrous on the five-stage scale that is widely used to measure the degree of chromatophore expansion. If the pigment within the particular cell is black or brown, the integument takes on a dark appearance when most of the chromatophores are in the last stage of dispersion (stage 5). If the pigment color is yellow or cream, the animal tends to look paler if all the chromatophores are at that stage.

In crustaceans, elasmobranch fishes, anurans, and lizards, control of the chromatophores is thought to be exclusively hormonal. Such hormonal control is true also of some teleosts; in others the control is part hormonal and part neural; while in still others control is purely neural, as in the chameleon. Where nerves are involved, the speed of the response is faster, the chromatophores responding in minutes rather than hours. *See* NEUROSECRETION.

Each cephalopod chromatophore organ comprises an elastic sac containing pigment granules. Attached to the sac is a set of 15–25 radial muscles that are striated and contract rapidly. Associated with the radial muscles are axons from nerve cell bodies that lie within the brain. Active nerve cells cause the radial muscles to contract and the chromatophore sac expands; when the nerves are inactive, energy stored in the elastic sac causes the chromatophore to retract as the muscles relax. The chromatophores receive only nerve impulses, and there is no evidence that they are influenced by hormones. The chromatophores are ultimately controlled by the optic lobe of the brain under the influence of the eyes.

Two consequences follow from the fact that cephalopod chromatophores are under the direct control of the brain. First, color change is instantaneous. Second, patterns can be generated in the skin in a way impossible in other animals. Thus, cephalopods can use the chromatophores not just to match the background in general color but to break up the body visually (disruptive coloration) so that a predator does not see the whole animal. Because the chromatophores are neurally controlled and patterns can be produced in the skin, they can also be used for signaling. *See* PIGMENTATION; PROTECTIVE COLORATION. [J.B.M.]

Chromosome Any of the organized components of each cell which carry the individual's hereditary material, deoxyribonucleic acid (DNA). Chromosomes are found in all organisms with a cell nucleus (eukaryotes) and are located within the nucleus. Each chromosome contains a single extremely long DNA molecule that is packaged by various proteins into a compact domain. A full set, or complement, of chromosomes is carried by each sperm or ovum in animals and each pollen grain or ovule in plants. This constitutes the haploid (*n*) genome of that organism and contains a complete set of the genes characteristic of that organism. Sexually reproducing organisms in both the plant and animal kingdoms begin their development by the fusion of two haploid germ cells and are thus diploid (2*n*), with two sets of chromosomes in each body cell. These two sets of chromosomes carry virtually all the thousands of genes of each cell, with the exception of the tiny number in the mitochrondria (in animal), and a few plant chloroplasts. *See* DEOXYRIBONUCLEIC ACID (DNA); GENE.

Chromosomes can change their conformation and degree of compaction throughout the cell cycle. During interphase, the major portion of the cycle, chromosomes are not visible under the light microscope because, although they are very long, they are extremely thin. However, during cell division (mitosis or meiosis), the chromosomes become compacted into shorter and thicker structures that can be seen under the microscope. At this time they appear as paired rods with defined ends, called telomeres, and they remain joined at a constricted region, the centromere, until the beginning of anaphase of cell division. *See* CELL CYCLE; MEIOSIS; MITOSIS.

Chromosomes are distinguished from one another by length and position of the centromere. They are metacentric (centromere in the middle of the chromosome), acrocentric (centromere close to one end), or telocentric (centromere at the end, or telomere). The centromere thus usually lies between two chromosome arms, which contain the genes and their regulatory regions, as well as other DNA sequences that have no known function. In many species, regional differences in base composition and in the time at which the DNA is replicated serve as the basis for special staining techniques that make visible a series of distinctive bands on each arm, and these can be used to identify the chromosome.

Compaction. Each nucleus in the cell of a human or other mammal contains some 6 billion base pairs of DNA which, if stretched out, would form a very thin thread about 6 ft (2 m) long. This DNA has to be packaged into the chromosome within a nucleus that is much smaller than a printed dot (Fig. 1). Each chromosome contains a single length of DNA comprising a specific portion of the genetic material of the organism. Tiny stretches of DNA, about 140 base pairs long and containing acidic phosphate groups, are individually wrapped around an octamer consisting of two molecules of each of the four basic histone proteins H2a, H2b, H3, and H4. This arrangement produces small structures called nucleosomes and results in a sevenfold compaction of the DNA strand. Further compaction is achieved by binding the histone protein H1 and several nonhistone proteins, resulting in a supercoiled structure in which the chromosome is shortened by about 1600-fold in the interphase nucleus and by about 8000-fold

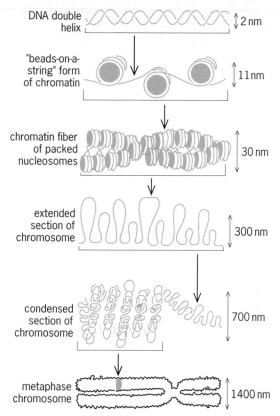

DNA double helix — 2 nm

"beads-on-a-string" form of chromatin — 11 nm

chromatin fiber of packed nucleosomes — 30 nm

extended section of chromosome — 300 nm

condensed section of chromosome — 700 nm

metaphase chromosome — 1400 nm

Fig. 1. Organization of DNA into chromosomes. (*From B. Alberts et al., Molecular Biology of the Cell, 2d ed., Garland Publishing, 1989*)

during metaphase and anaphase, where the genetic material must be fully compacted for transport to the two daughter cells. At the point of maximum compaction, human chromosomes range in size from about 2 to 10 micrometers in length, that is, less than 0.0004 in. *See* NUCLEOSOME.

Number and size. Each diploid ($2n$) organism has a characteristic number of chromosomes in each body (somatic) cell, which can vary from two in a nematode worm and one species of ant, to hundreds in some butterflies, crustaceans, and plants. The diploid number of chromosomes includes a haploid (n) set from each parent. Many one-celled organisms are haploid throughout most of their life cycle. The human diploid number is 46.

There is some relationship between the number of chromosomes and their size. Some of the chromosomes in certain classes of organisms with large numbers of chromosomes are very tiny, and have been called microchromosomes. In birds and some reptiles, there are about 30–40 pairs of microchromosomes in addition to 5–7 or so pairs of regular-sized macrochromosomes. The number of microchromosomes is constant in any species carrying them, and only their size distinguishes them from the widespread macrochromosomes. At least seven microchromosomes in birds have been shown to contain genes, and all are thought to.

In some species of insects, plants, flatworms, snails, and rarely vertebrates (such as the fox), the number of chromosomes can vary because of the presence of a variable number of accessory chromosomes, called B chromosomes. It is not clear what role, if any, B chromosomes play, but they appear to be made primarily of DNA that neither contains functional genes nor has much effect on the animal or plant even when present in multiple copies.

Structure. A telomere caps each end of every chromosome and binds specific proteins that protect it from being digested by enzymes (exonucleases) present in the same cell. Most important, the telomere permits DNA replication to continue to the very end of the chromosome, thus assuring its stability. The telomere is also involved in attachment of the chromosome ends to the nuclear membrane and in pairing of homologous chromosomes during meiosis. The structure of telomeric DNA is very similar in virtually all eukaryotic organisms except the fruit fly (*Drosophila*). One strand of the DNA is rich in guanine and is oriented toward the end of the chromosome, and the other strand is rich in cytosine and is oriented toward the centromere. In most organisms, the telomere consists of multiple copies of a very short DNA repeat.

The centromere is responsible for proper segregation of each chromosome pair during cell division. The chromatids in mitosis and each pair of homologous chromosomes in meiosis are held together at the centromere until anaphase, when they separate and move to the spindle poles, thus being distributed to the two daughter cells. The kinetochore, which is the attachment site for the microtubules that guide the movement of the chromosomes to the poles, is organized around the centromere. The molecular structures of centromeres in most species are still unclear. The repetitive DNA making up and surrounding the centromere is called heterochromatin because it remains condensed throughout the cell cycle and hence stains intensely.

One or more pairs of chromosomes in each species have a region called a secondary constriction which does not stain well. This region contains multiple copies of the genes that transcribe, within the nucleolus, the ribosomal RNA (rRNA). The number of active rRNA genes may be regulated, and an organism that has too few copies of the rRNA genes may develop abnormally or not survive. *See* RIBOSOMES.

Staining. Staining with quinacrine mustard produces consistent, bright and less bright fluorescence bands (Q bands) along the chromosome arms because of differences in the relative amounts of CG (cytosine-guanine) or AT (adenine-thymine) base pairs. The distinctive Q-band pattern of each chromosome makes it possible to identify every chromosome in the human genome. Quinacrine fluorescence can also reveal a difference in the amount or type of heterochromatin on the two members of a homologous pair of chromosomes, called heteromorphism or polymorphism. Such differences can be used to identify the parental origin of a specific chromosome, such as the extra chromosome in individuals who have trisomy 21. Two other methods involve treating chromosomes in various ways before staining with Giemsa. Giemsa or G-band patterns are essentially identical to Q-band patterns; reverse Giemsa or R-band patterns are the reverse, or reciprocal, of those seen with Q or G banding. In humans, most other mammals, and birds (macrochromosomes only), the Q-, G-, and R-banding patterns are so distinctive that each chromosome pair can be individually identified, making it possible to construct a karyotype, or organized array of the chromosome pairs from a single cell (Fig. 2). The chromosomes are identified on the basis of the banding patterns, and the pairs are arranged and numbered in some order, often based on length. In the human karyotype, the autosomes are numbered 1 through 22, and the sex chromosomes are called X and Y. The short arm of a chromosome is called the p arm, and the long arm is called the q arm; a number is assigned to each band on the arm. Thus, band 1q23 refers to band 23 on the long arm of human chromosome 1.

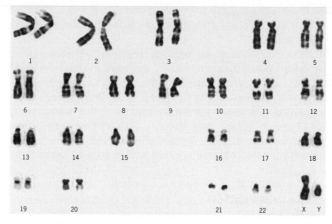

Fig. 2. G-banded metaphase karyotype of a human male cell. Every chromosome pair can be identified by its banding pattern. Chromosome 1 is about 12 μm long.

Imprinting. A chromosome carries the same complement of genes whether it is transmitted from the father or the mother, and most of these genes appear to be functionally the same. However, a small number of mammalian genes are functionally different depending on whether they were transmitted by the egg or by the sperm. This phenomenon is known as imprinting. It appears to be caused by the inactivation of certain genes in sperm or ova, probably by methylation of cytosine residues within the regulatory (promotor) region of the imprinted gene. As a result of imprinting, normal development of the mammalian embryo requires the presence of both a maternal and a paternal set of chromosomes. Parthenogenesis, the formation of a normal individual from two sets of maternal chromosomes, is therefore not possible in mammals.

Sex chromosomes. In most mammals, the sex of an individual is determined by whether or not a Y chromosome is present because the Y chromosome carries the male-determining *SRY* gene. Thus XX and the rare XO individuals are female, while XY and the uncommon XXY individuals are male. In contrast, sex in the fruit fly depends on the balance of autosomes (non-sex chromosomes) and X chromosomes. Thus, in diploids, XX and the rare XXY flies are female, while XY and the rare XO flies are male. In both mammals and fruit flies, males are the heterogametic sex, producing gametes that contain either an X or a Y chromosome; and females are the homogametic sex, producing only gametes containing an X. In birds and butterflies, however, females are the heterogametic sex and males the homogametic sex. Other sex-determining systems are used by some classes of organisms, while sex in some species is determined by a single gene or even by environmental factors such as temperature (some turtles and alligators) or the presence of a nearby female (*Bonellia*, a marine worm) rather than by a chromosome-mediated mechanism.

More than 900 gene loci have been mapped to the human X chromosome. If the genes on both X chromosomes were fully expressed in female mammalian cells, then male cells, which have only one X, would exhibit only half as much gene product as female cells. However, dosage compensation is achieved, because genes on only one X chromosome are expressed, and genes on any additional X chromosomes are inactivated. This X inactivation randomly occurs during an early stage in embryonic development, and is transmitted unchanged to each of the daughter cells. Mammalian females are therefore mosaics of two types of cells, those with an active maternally derived X and those with an active paternally derived X. Species other than mammals do not show this type of dosage compensation mechanism for sex-linked genes, and some show none at all.

The Y chromosome is one of the smallest chromosomes in the genome in most mammalian species. Usually the mammalian Y chromosome has a very high proportion of heterochromatin, as does the large Y chromosome in *Drosophila*. Very few genes are located on the Y chromosome in mammals or in *Drosophila*, and most of these genes are concerned with either sex determination or the production of sperm. In some species of insects and other invertebrates, no Y chromosome is present, and sex in these species is determined by the X:autosome balance (XX female, XO male). *See* CELL NUCLEUS; GENETICS; HUMAN GENETICS; SEX DETERMINATION; SEX-LINKED INHERITANCE.

[O.J.M.; D.A.Mi.]

Chromosome aberration   Any numerical or structural change in the usual chromosome complement of a cell or organism.

Heteroploidy. Numerical changes (heteroploidy) are of two types, polyploidy and aneuploidy. Polyploidy is a change in the number of chromosome sets. Triploidy ($3n$), for example, occurs in about 1% of human pregnancies, but it is almost always an embryonic lethal condition. *See* MEIOSIS; MITOSIS; POLYPLOIDY.

Aneuploidy is a change in the number of chromosomes from the diploid ($2n$) number (usually found in the somatic cells of sexually reproducing organisms) or the haploid (n) number (usually found in germ cells and the haplophase of some unicellular organisms.) It usually involves a single chromosome, and any chromosome in the complement can be involved. Aneuploidy is the result of aberrant segregation of one or more chromosomes during meiosis or mitosis. If malsegregation or nondisjunction occurs during meiosis, one daughter cell receives two copies of the chromosome and the other daughter cell receives none. Fertilization of such an aneuploid germ cell by a euploid gamete will produce a zygote that has either three copies (trisomy) or one copy (monosomy) of the chromosome. Malsegregation of a chromosome can also take place during a mitotic division in a somatic cell, producing trisomic or monosomic cells in an otherwise euploid individual. This outcome is important primarily in the origin and progression of some forms of cancer.

The most common trisomy of autosomes (non-sex chromosomes) in human liveborns is trisomy 21, or Down syndrome, which is a major cause of mental retardation and congenital heart disease. Individuals with trisomy 18 and trisomy 13 also occur but are much less common. Most autosomal trisomies are lethal to embryos, leading to spontaneous abortion. The incidence of trisomy for any autosome increases exponentially with maternal age. *See* CHROMOSOME; DOWN SYNDROME.

In humans, there are more types of aneuploidy involving the sex chromosomes than the autosomes. The most common is XO, occurring in about 1% of pregnancies. Although 99% of XO fetuses die early in pregnancy, the other 1% (about 1 in 10,000 liveborn females) survive. Adults who are XO tend to be short, with some webbing of the neck. They rarely develop secondary sexual characteristics or have children because the germ cells essential for ovarian development are usually absent. These features are characteristic of Turner syndrome. Trisomy for the human X chromosome, commonly called XXX, is not associated with embryonic death or congenital malformations. The reason is that in all mammals only a single X chromosome is active in each somatic cell. *See* HUMAN GENETICS.

In contrast to autosomal trisomy, sex chromosome aneuploidy increases only slightly with maternal age, and the extra X chromosome comes from the mother in only about 60% of the cases. An additional X chromosome can be present in either egg or sperm;

additional Y chromosomes can be present only in sperm. The XXX and XXY individuals display minimal phenotypic manifestations of their increased number of chromosomes. Individuals who are XYY generally are indistinguishable from XY individuals. The presence of a Y chromosome leads to male sex differentiation no matter how many X chromosomes are present, because of the presence of a single, critical gene, called *SRY*, on the Y chromosome. A mutation of this gene has been found in some XY individuals who developed as females.

Structural abnormalities. Structural abnormalities (chromosome mutations) involve the gain, loss, or rearrangement of chromosome segments after the continuity of the deoxyribonucleic acid (DNA) strand in one or more chromosomes is disrupted. A deletion involves the loss of a chromosome segment and the genes it carries. A terminal deletion involves the loss of a segment extending from the point of disruption (breakpoint) to the end of the same arm of a chromosome, and it is relatively uncommon. An interstitial deletion involves the loss of the segment between two breakpoints in one arm of a chromosome. The effect of such a loss depends on the genes that are included in the missing segment.

When one break occurs in each arm of a chromosome, the broken ends of the internal centromeric fragment may join, resulting in the formation of a stable ring chromosome. Each of the two end segments lacks a centromere, and such acentric fragments are lost during cell division. Ring chromosomes are subject to reduction in size, as well as doubling. An individual who has a ring chromosome may thus show phenotypic effects not only of deletion but of duplication of part of the chromosome. A duplication more commonly occurs in other ways. For example, a chromosome segment can undergo tandem or inverted duplication at the usual chromosome site, or the second copy of the segment may be carried on another chromosome.

An inversion is generated by disrupting the DNA strand in a chromosome at two breakpoints and rejoining the broken ends with the interstitial segment in the opposite orientation. This process will invert the order of the genes on the segment.

A translocation involves the interchange of one or more chromosome segments between two or more chromosomes. If a translocation breakpoint disrupts a gene, the gene's function will be blocked or abnormal, and such can have deleterious effects on development or function. Sometimes a normally silent gene is activated by a chromosome rearrangement that places it next to a strong promoter of gene expression, and this change is important as a cause of cancer. If a translocation does not block the function of an essential gene or activate a normally silent gene, the individual carrying the rearrangement will be normal.

Structural aberrations can occur spontaneously or be induced by agents that break chromosomes, such as x-rays, radioactive substances, ultraviolet rays, and certain chemicals. The most frequent cause may be the presence of enormous numbers of a few types of short interspersed elements (SINES), that is, DNA sequences that occur once every few thousand base pairs throughout the genome of most metazoans, including humans. These elements predispose to the occurrence of errors during DNA replication or genetic recombination at meiosis that can lead to the deletion or duplication of the region between two nearby interspersed repeats on one chromosome. They may also play a role in the formation of inversions and, possibly, translocations. *See* GENE AMPLIFICATION; MUTAGENS AND CARCINOGENS; MUTATION.

Another cause of structural aberrations is also inherent in the genome: the great abundance of short repeats of a 2-, 3-, or 4-base-pair unit. Some trinucleotide repeats, such as $(CGG)_n$ or $(CAG)_n$, can undergo expansion during meiotic and mitotic cell divisions. This expansion sometimes affects gene function and leads to disease. The most common type of X-linked mental retardation in humans is the result of heritable expansions, in the *FMR-1* gene, of a specific trinucleotide repeat, $(CGG)_n$, where the number of expansions (n) is increased from the normal 8–20 or so to 50–200 or more. For unknown reasons, this expanded region tends to undergo breakage under some conditions, and this particular form of mental retardation is called the fragile X syndrome. There are dozens, if not hundreds, of similar fragile sites in the human and other genomes.   [O.J.M.; D.A.Mi.]

Cilia and flagella   Centriole-based, motile cell extensions. These organelles are usually indistinguishable in fine structure as seen with the electron microscope, but quantitatively there are many (several hundred) cilia, and few or fewer (usually one or two) flagella, on one cell. Bacterial or prokaryotic flagella are entirely different organelles that are not considered in this article, which concerns only eukaryotic flagella.

Flagella move with undulatory motion in which successive bending waves progress along the length of the organelle, whereas cilia move with flexural motion consisting of a planar effective stroke, with the organelle extended perpendicular to the cell body, followed by a nonplanar curving recovery stroke, with the organelle pulled parallel to the cell body. Both organelles function to move water past the cell. Their action may bring food and oxygen into an animal, or it may propel the cell to a new environment.

The words cilium (eyelash) and flagellum (whip) are accurate descriptions of the appearance of these cell organelles when they are seen under the light microscope. Cilia are present on protozoa, such as *Paramecium*, and on metazoan cells of many different tissue types. A flagellum is present on human sperm; in fact, the sperm of most animals possess a flagellum, and, correspondingly, male gametes of many lower plants are flagellated. In addition, many ordinary types of cells of vertebrates, for example, from the thyroid, the kidney, or the pituitary gland, possess modified nonmotile derivatives that resemble cilia. *See* CILIOPHORA; EPITHELIUM; SPERM CELL.

Relative to cell size, both cilia and flagella are very long organelles. Flagella may be over 50 micrometers long. Certain compound cilia, such as the comb plates of ctenophores, are macroscopic structures, visible to the naked eye. Usually, however, cilia range from 10 to 15 μm in length.

The electron microscope reveals that the cilium or flagellum is really an internal organelle since it is bounded by the cell membrane and enclosed at the tip. The main internal structure of the cilium is the axoneme. Under the electron microscope, a single

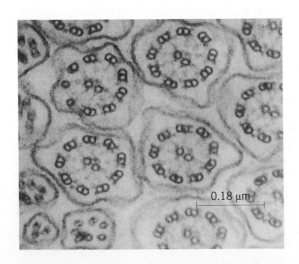

0.18 μm

Electron micrograph of cilia showing 9 + 2 pattern of axoneme. (*From P. Satir, Studies on Cilia, II: Examination of the distal region of the ciliary shaft and the role of the filaments in motility, J. Cell Biol., 26:805–834, 1965*)

axoneme appears to contain a fixed pattern of microtubules. The microtubules are not simple single units; rather, nine doublet microtubules are found on the periphery of the axoneme surrounding two central elements. This is the so-called 9 + 2 pattern (see illustration). Each peripheral doublet is composed of one complete and one partial microtubule. The microtubules are themselves composed of subunits arranged into microfibers or protofilaments.

At the base of the cilium or flagellum there is a basal body, or kinetosome, that is similar to, and sometimes derived from, a centriole. The basal body may have extensions of various sorts attached to it, notably a basal foot that indicates effective stroke direction and prominent striated rootlet fibers in many cilia. Ordinarily, the ciliary axoneme originates and grows in a membrane protrusion which forms just above the basal body, either at the cell surface or deeper inside the cytoplasm. The basal body remains attached to the cell membrane throughout morphogenesis by a structure that extends from the microtubules to the membrane, where it is seen as a ciliary necklace. *See* CENTRIOLE.

[P.S.; I.Gi.]

Ciliophora   A subphylum of the Protozoa. The ciliates are a fairly homogeneous group of highly differentiated, unicellular organisms. Over 5000 species have been described, and many more surely exist but remain to be discovered. Typically, ciliates are larger than most other protozoans, ranging from 10 to 3000 micrometers (about 1/2500 to 1/8 in.). Some larger species are easily visible to the naked eye. The majority of them are free-living forms, found abundantly in a variety of fresh- and salt-water habitats, although a few entire groups live in association with other organisms, generally as harmless ecto- or endocommensals. Their principal value to humans is as experimental animals in a host of biological investigations.

The usual ciliate life cycle is fairly simple. An individual feeds and undergoes binary fission, and the resulting filial products repeat the process. Some commensal or parasitic forms have a more complicated life history. Some ciliates, including free-living species, have a cystic stage in their cycle. As in other kinds of Protozoa this stage often serves as a protective phase during adverse environmental conditions, such as desiccation or lack of food. It also may be important in distribution, and thus possibly in preservation, of the species.

Six major characteristics aid in distinguishing the Ciliophora from other protozoan groups. Not all of these are entirely unique, but when taken together they are definitely distinctive of ciliates: mouth, ciliation, infraciliature, nuclear apparatus, fission, and reproduction.

Most Ciliophora possess a true mouth or cytostome often associated with a buccal cavity containing compound ciliary organelles. However, some ciliates are completely astomatous, that is, mouthless. Nutrition is heterotrophic in ciliates.

The Ciliophora possess simple cilia or compound ciliary organelles, often in abundance, in at least one stage of their life cycle. Morphologically, cilia are relatively short and slender hairlike structures, whose ultrastructure is known, from electron microscope studies, to be composed of nine peripheral and two central fibrils. Membranes and membranelles are characteristically associated with the mouth or buccal areas and serve to bring food into the oral opening, although they sometimes aid in locomotion as well. *See* CILIA AND FLAGELLA.

Infraciliature is present, without exception, at a subpellicular level in the cortex. The infraciliature consists essentially of basal bodies, or kinetosomes, associated with cilia and ciliary organelles at their bases, plus certain more or less interconnecting fibrils.

Ciliophora possess two kinds of nuclei, and at least one of each is usually present. The smaller, or micronucleus, contains recognizable chromosomes and behaves much as the single nucleus in cells of metazoan organisms. The larger, or macronucleus, is considered indispensable in controlling metabolic functions, and is recognized as having genic control over all phenotypic characteristics of ciliates.

Ciliophora exhibit a type of binary fission commonly known as transverse division. In ciliates the splitting results in two filial organisms, the anterior or proter and the posterior or opisthe which, geometrically speaking, show homothety with respect to identical structures possessed by each. Thus, homothetogenic is both a broader and most exact descriptive term.

Ciliophora lack true sexual reproduction. Ciliates do not show syngamy, with fusion of free gametes. Processes such as conjugation are considered to be sexual phenomena, since meiosis and chromosome recombination are involved, but not sexual reproduction. In addition to conjugation, certain ciliates exhibit forms of sexual phenomena known as autogamy and cytogamy. See PROTOZOA; REPRODUCTION (ANIMAL).   [J.O.C.]

Circulation   Those processes by which metabolic materials are transported from one region of an organism to another. Ultimately, the essential gases, nutrients, and waste products of metabolism are exchanged across cell membranes by diffusion. Diffusion is the movement of material, by random motion of molecules, from a region of high concentration to one of low concentration. The amount of material moved from one place to another depends on the difference in concentrations and on the distance between the two points. The greater the distance, the less movement of material per unit time for a given difference in concentration. Consequently, in all but the smallest animals, convection (or bulk circulation) of materials to the cell must be employed to supplement diffusion.

Protoplasmic movement aids diffusion at the intracellular level. In multicellular animals, however, either the external medium or extracellular body fluids, or both, are circulated. In sponges and coelenterates, water is pumped through definite body channels by muscular activity or, more often, by cilia or flagella on the cells lining the channels.

Coelenterates have a body wall derived from two cell layers; an outer ectoderm is separated from an inner endoderm by a noncellular gelatinous material (mesoglea). All higher animals have bodies consisting of three cell layers, with the ectoderm being separated from the endoderm by a cellular layer of mesoderm. The mesoderm proliferates and separates to develop a fluid-filled body cavity or coelom. The coelom separates the ectoderm (together with an outer layer of mesoderm) from the endoderm (which has an inner layer of mesoderm). Coelomic fluid is moved around by body movements or ciliary activity, but in larger animals this movement is usually inadequate to supply the metabolic requirements of the organs contained within the coelom. These needs are provided for by pumping a fluid, blood, to them through vessels, the blood vascular system. See BLOOD.

When the blood is in a separate compartment from the rest of the extracellular fluid, the vascular system is described as closed. The two principal components of such systems are hearts and blood vessels. In such a system, the blood is circulated by a pump, the heart, through special channels, blood vessels; it comes into close association with the tissues only in the capillaries, fine vessels with walls only one cell thick. In some tissues or regions, larger blood spaces may exist, called sinuses. A closed vascular system is found in most annelids (segmented worms and leeches), cephalopod mollusks (squids and octopods), holothurian echinoderms (sea cucumbers), and vertebrates. See BLOOD VESSELS; HEART (VERTEBRATE).

In vertebrates, a functional but anatomically closed connection exists between the extracellular spaces (between the cells) and the blood vascular system in the form of lymph channels. Lymph is derived from the noncellular component of blood (plasma), modified in its passage through the tissues, and is conducted to the veins by blind-ending lymphatic vessels, which are separate from blood vessels and coelomic space. *See* LYMPHATIC SYSTEM.

In most arthropods (crustaceans, insects), most mollusks (shellfish), and many ascidians (sea squirts), the extracellular spaces are confluent with the blood system. In these animals, blood is pumped through a limited network of vessels into a body cavity called a hemocoel. After bathing the tissues, blood (called hemolymph in these organisms) collects in sinuses and returns to the heart. This is the open vascular system. In animals with open circulatory systems, the coelom is much reduced.   [D.R.J.]

Citric acid cycle   In aerobic cells of animals and certain other species, the major pathway for the complete oxidation of acetyl coenzyme A (the thioester of acetic acid with coenzyme A); also known as the Krebs cycle or tricarboxylic acid cycle. Reduced electron carriers generated in the cycle are reoxidized by oxygen via the electron transport system; water is formed, and the energy liberated is conserved by the phosphorylation of adenosine diphosphate (ADP) to adenosine triphosphate (ATP). Reactions of the cycle also function in metabolic processes other than energy generation. The role of the cycle in mammalian tissues will be emphasized in this article. *See* ADENOSINE DIPHOSPHATE (ADP); COENZYME; ENZYME.

The first step in the cycle involves the condensation of the acetyl portion of acetyl coenzyme A (CoA) with the four-carbon compound oxaloacetate to form citrate, a tricarboxylate containing six carbons (see illustration). A shift of the hydroxyl group of citrate to an adjacent carbon results in the formation of D-threo-isocitrate, which in turn is oxidized to the five-carbon compound α-ketoglutarate and carbon dioxide (CO_2). In a second oxidative decarboxylation reaction, α-ketoglutarate, in the presence of CoA, is converted to succinyl CoA and another molecule of CO_2. In the subsequent formation of the four-carbon compound succinate and CoA, the energy in the thioester bond of succinyl CoA is conserved by the formation of guanosine triphosphate (GTP) from guanosine diphosphate (GDP) and inorganic phosphate. Fumarate is formed from succinate by the removal of two atoms of hydrogen, and the unsaturated compound is then hydrated to L-malate. The dehydrogenation of malate forms oxaloacetate, the starting four-carbon compound of the metabolic cycle. Thus, beginning with the two-carbon acetyl group, one completion of the cycle results in the formation of two molecules of carbon dioxide.

The oxidation of acetyl CoA to CO_2 in the cycle occurs without direct reaction with molecular oxygen. The oxidations occur at dehydrogenation reactions in which hydrogen atoms and electrons are transferred from intermediates of the cycle to the electron carriers nicotinamide adenine dinucleotide (NAD^+) and flavin adenine dinucleotide (FAD). The electrons from NADH and $FADH_2$ are transferred to molecular oxygen via a series of electron transport carriers, with regeneration of NAD^+ and FAD. The energy liberated in the electron transport chain is partially conserved by the formation of ATP from ADP and inorganic phosphate, by a process called oxidative phosphorylation. The energy generated as oxygen accepts electrons from the reduced coenzymes generated in one turn of the cycle results in the maximal formation of 11 molecules of ATP. Because GTP obtained by phosphorylation of GDP at the succinyl CoA to succinate step of the cycle is readily converted to ATP by nucleotide diphosphokinase, the yield is 12 molecules of ATP per molecule of acetyl CoA metabolized. *See* NICOTINAMIDE ADENINE DINUCLEOTIDE (NAD).

The electron transport and oxidative phosphorylation systems and the enzymes required for the citric acid cycle are located in the mitochondria of cells, which are the major source of ATP for energy-consuming reactions in most tissues. The citric acid cycle does not occur in all cells. For example, mature human red blood cells do not contain mitochondria and the cycle is absent. In these cells, ATP is formed by the anaerobic conversion of glucose to lactate (anaerobic glycolysis). *See* MITO-CHONDRIA.

Acetyl CoA is formed from carbohydrates, fats, and the carbon skeleton of amino acids. The origin of a precursor and the extent of its utilization depend on the metabolic capability of a specific tissue and on the physiological state of the organism. For example, most mammalian tissues have the capacity to convert glucose to pyruvate in a reaction called glycolysis. Pyruvate is then taken up from cellular cytosol by mitochondria and oxidatively decarboxylated to acetyl CoA and carbon dioxide by pyruvate dehydrogenase. Acetyl CoA is also the end product of fatty acid oxidation in mitochondria. However, the fatty acid oxidation pathway occurs in fewer tissues than does glycolysis or the citric acid cycle. The amino acids follow varied pathways for forming compounds that can enter the citric acid cycle. *See* AMINO ACIDS.

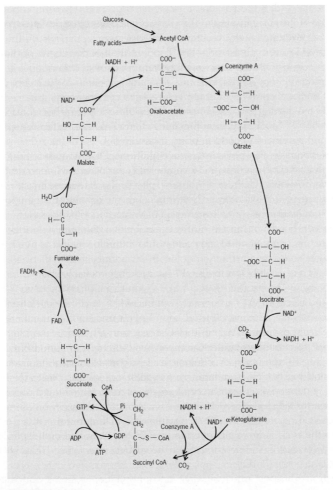

Citric acid cycle.

In addition to the cycle's role in yielding catabolic energy, portions of it can supply intermediates for synthetic processes, such as the synthesis of the fatty acid moiety of triglycerides from glucose (lipogenesis), and formation of glucose from the carbon skeletons of certain amino acids, lactate, or glycerol (gluconeogenesis). *See* CARBOHYDRATE METABOLISM; CELL (BIOLOGY); GLUCOSE; GLYCOGEN; LIPID METABOLISM; METABOLISM.

[G.E.W.P.]

Classification, biological

Classification, biological   A human construct for grouping organisms into hierarchical categories. The most inclusive categories of any classification scheme are called kingdoms, which are delimited so that organisms within a single kingdom are more related to each other than to organisms grouped in the other kingdoms. Classification (grouping) is a part of biological systematics or taxonomy, science that involves naming and sorting organisms into groups.

Historically, organisms have been arranged into kingdoms based on practical characteristics, such as motility, medicinal properties, and economic value for food or fiber. In the nineteenth and twentieth centuries, advances such as electron and light microscopy, biochemistry, genetics, ethology, and greater knowledge of the fossil record provided new evidence upon which to construct more sophisticated classification schemes. Proposals were made to assign organisms into four, five, and even thirteen kingdoms. Earlier two-kingdom and three-kingdom systems were devised without awareness of the profound distinction between prokaryotes and eukaryotes, which Edouard Chatton (1937) recognized as a fundamental evolutionary discontinuity. Prokaryotic cells do not have either a nucleus or any other internal membrane-bounded structures, the so-called organelles. By contrast, eukaryotic cells have both a nucleus and organelles. The deoxyribonucleic acid (DNA) of eukaryotes is combined with protein to form chromosomes. All bacteria are prokaryotes. Plants, fungi, animals, and protoctists are eukaryotes. *See* EUKARYOTAE; PROKARYOTAE.

By the late 1990s, biologists widely accepted a system that classifies all organisms into five kingdoms based on key characteristics of function and structure. These are Superkingdom Prokarya [Kingdom Bacteria (Monera) with two subkingdoms, Archaea and Eubacteria] and Superkingdom Eukarya with four kingdoms, Protoctista (or Protozoa in some classification schemes), Fungi, Animalia, and Plantae. Key charactistics used to classify organisms into these categories include the mode by which the organism obtains its nutrients; presence or absence of an embryo; and whether and how the organism achieves motility.

Cladistics may be defined as an approach to grouping organisms that classifies them according to the time at which branch points occur along a phylogenetic tree. Such a phylogenetic tree is represented by a diagram called a cladogram. In this approach, classification is based on a sequence of phylogenetic branching. In a cladogram, the phylogenetic tree branches dichotomously and repeatedly, reflecting cladogenesis (production of biological diversity by evolution of new species from parental species).

Modern classification is based on evidence derived from developmental pattern, biochemistry, molecular biology, genetics, and detailed morphology of extant organisms and their fossils. Because information is drawn from such diverse sources, and because 10–30 million (possibly 100 million) species are probably alive today, informed judgments must be made to integrate the information into classification hierarchies. Only about 1.7 million species have been formally classified in the taxonomic literature of biology to date. Thus, as new evidence about the evolutionary relationships of organisms is weighed, it must be anticipated that biological classification schemes will continue to be revised. *See* ANIMAL SYSTEMATICS; BACTERIAL TAXONOMY; PLANT TAXONOMY; VIRUS CLASSIFICATION.

[K.V.S.]

Cleavage (embryology)   The subdivision of eggs into cells called blastomeres. It occurs in eggs activated by fertilization or parthenogenetic agents. Cleavages follow one another so rapidly that there is little opportunity for daughter cells to grow before they divide again. Consequently the size of blastomeres diminishes progressively, although many times unequally, during cleavage. By contrast, the nucleus of each daughter cell enlarges following each cleavage with the result that the ratio of the volume of the nucleus to the volume of cytoplasm (the nucleoplasmic ratio) progressively increases. The cleavage period is said by some authorities to terminate when the nucleoplasmic ratios of various blastomeres attain values characteristic of adult tissues. Cells continue to divide thereafter, but each daughter cell then undergoes a period of growth prior to its division with the result that the nucleoplasmic ratio tends to remain approximately constant for each cell type following termination of cleavage. According to others, cleavage terminates with formation of the definitive blastula. Cleavage appears to be an essential step in development. Although some differentiation occurs in eggs of certain animals when cleavage is blocked experimentally, it is limited and infrequent. See BLASTULATION.

Cleavage does more than merely subdivide the substance of the egg quantitatively into smaller units, the blastomeres, which are then of such a size that they can readily undergo the subsequent events of blastulation, gastrulation, and interaction that are involved in formation of tissues and organs. Sooner or later, cleavage segregates different cytoplasmic areas into different blastomeres, thus subdividing the substance of the egg qualitatively. These qualitative cytoplasmic differences among blastomeres are then sufficient to account for the initial establishment of different lines of differentiation in the progeny of different blastomeres, even though the genetic content of all blastomeres is identical. See CELL LINEAGE.   [R.L.W.]

Clinical immunology   A branch of clinical pathology concerned with the role of the immune defense system in disease. The subject encompasses diseases where a malfunction of the immune system itself is the basic cause, together with diseases where some external agent is the initiating factor but an excessive response by the immune system produces the actual tissue damage. It also extends to the monitoring of the normal immune response in infectious diseases and to the use of immunological techniques in disease diagnosis. See ALLERGY; AUTOIMMUNITY; HYPERSENSITIVITY; IMMUNOLOGICAL DEFICIENCY.

Many features of the immune system make it prone to shift from protecting the body to damaging it. This complex system not only must distinguish between the body's own cells and a foreign invader but must also recognize and eliminate the body's own cells if they are damaged or infected with a virus. The recognition receptors used to make this fine distinction between "self" and "not self" are not encoded in the genes. Rather, they are assembled following random rearrangement of information carried in small gene segments. During their development, immune system cells are subjected to a selective process, those bearing potentially useful receptors being preserved while those bearing dangerous, self-reactive receptors are eliminated. This process is closely balanced, and some potentially self-reactive cells often persist. See CELLULAR IMMUNOLOGY.

There are several approaches to suppressing excessive immune reactivity. Desensitization, or modifying the nature of the response by injecting small amounts of the foreign antigen, is sometimes used to treat allergic states. In contrast, there are few therapies for enhancing immune responses. Bone marrow transplantation is used to restore the immune system in some immunodeficiency diseases. Passive transfer of preformed antibody protects against some infections, and transfusion of immunoglobulin is used to treat immunoglobulin deficiencies. However, vaccination or immunization is one of the most effective of all medical procedures. See IMMUNOSUPPRESSION.   [K.Sh.]

Clinical microbiology   The adaptation of microbiological techniques to the study of the etiological agents of infectious disease. Clinical microbiologists determine the nature of infectious disease and test the ability of various antibiotics to inhibit or kill the isolated microorganisms. In addition to bacteriology, a contemporary clinical microbiologist is responsible for a wide range of microscopic and cultural studies in mycology, parasitology, and virology. The clinical microbiologist is often the most competent person available to determine the nature and extent of hospital-acquired infections, as well as public-health problems that affect both the hospital and the community. See ANIMAL VIRUS; MEDICAL BACTERIOLOGY; MEDICAL MYCOLOGY; MEDICAL PARASITOLOGY; VIRUS.

Bacteriology. Historically, the diagnosis of bacterial disease has been the primary job of clinical microbiology laboratories. Many of the common ailments of humans are bacterial in nature, such as streptococcal sore throat, diphtheria, and pneumococcal pneumonia. The bacteriology laboratory accepts specimens of body fluids, such as sputum, urine, blood, and respiratory or genital secretions, and inoculates the specimens onto various solid and liquid growth media. Following incubation at body temperature, the microbiologist examines these agar plates and tubes and makes a determination as to the relative numbers of organisms growing from the specimen and their importance in the disease process. The microbiologist then identifies these alleged causes of disease and determines their pattern of antibiotic susceptibility to a few chosen agents.

Clinical microbiologists also microscopically examine these body fluids. They report on the presence of bacteria in body fluids and the cellular response to infection, such as the numbers or types of white blood cells observed in the specimen.   [R.C.T.]

Nonculture methods. While direct microscopy and culture continue to be methodological mainstays in diagnostic microbiology laboratories, nonculture methods are growing in the variety of applications and the sophistication of the technology. For example, polyclonal antibodies raised in animals such as mice, sheep, goats, and rabbits, and monoclonal antibodies produced by hybridization technology are used to detect bacteria, fungi, parasites, or virus-infected cells by using direct or indirect fluorescent techniques. Additional methods include latex agglutination tests to detect particulate antigens and enzyme immunoassays to detect soluble antigens. See IMMUNOASSAY; MONOCLONAL ANTIBODIES.

Probes for deoxyribonucleic acid (DNA) or messenger ribonucleic acid (mRNA) are available for various applications. Probes are used for direct detection of organisms in clinical material and for culture confirmation.

Further increases in analytical sensitivity have been achieved by nucleic acid amplification techniques. In polymerase chain reaction (PCR), double-stranded DNA is denatured; oligonucleotide probes bind to homologous strands of single-stranded DNA, and the enzyme polymerase extends the probes using deoxyribonucleotides in the milieu. In ligase chain reaction (LCR), the enzyme ligase fills the 3-nucleotide gap between two probes that attach to homologous, target, single-stranded DNA. In nucleic acid sequence–based amplification (NASBA), reverse transcriptase is used to make double-stranded complementary DNA (cDNA) and the target RNA is digested by ribonuclease H.

Analysis of lipopolysaccharides and proteins by sodium dodecyl sulfate–polyacrylamide gel electrophoresis (SDS-PAGE) and cellular fatty acid analysis by gas-liquid chromatography have given way to nucleic acid–based methods. Restriction enzymes, which cut DNA at a constant position within a specific recognition site usually composed of four to six base pairs, are used to cut chromosomal DNA; the resulting fragments are compared by pulse field gel electrophoresis (PFGE) or ribotyping. Electrophoresis of isolated plasmid DNA is another method for comparing organisms. DNA sequencing can also compare segments of the DNA of organisms from the same genus and species.

DNA chip or microarray technology is expected to have a greater effect on medicine than either DNA sequencing or PCR. Over 30,000 small cDNA clones of expressed fragments of individual genes are spotted onto a thumbnail-sized glass chip. Fluorescein-labeled genomic or cDNA from the sample being evaluated is passed over the chip to allow hybridization. A laser measures the fluorescent emissions and a computer analyzes the data.   [C.A.Sp.]

Clostridium   A genus of bacteria comprising large anaerobic spore-forming rods that usually stain gram-positive. Most species are anaerobes, but a few will grow minimally in air at atmospheric pressure.

The clostridia are widely distributed in nature, and are present in the soil and in the intestinal tracts of humans and animals. They usually live a saprophytic existence, and play a major role in the degradation of organic material in the soil and other nature environments. A number of clostridia release potent exotoxins and are pathogenic for humans and animals. Among the human pathogens are the causative agents of botulism (*Clostridium botulinum*), tetanus (*C. tetani*), gas gangrene (*C. perfringens*), and an antibiotic-associated enterocolitis (*C. difficile*). *See* ANAEROBIC INFECTION; BOTULISM; TOXIN.

Clostridial cells are straight or slightly curved rods, 0.3–1.6 micrometers wide and 1–14 μm long. They may occur singly, in pairs, in short or long chains, or in helical coils. The length of the cells of the individual species varies according to the stage of growth and growth conditions. Most clostridia are motile with a uniform arrangement of flagella. *See* CILIA AND FLAGELLA.

The endospores produced by clostridia are dormant structures capable of surviving for prolonged periods of time, and have the ability to reestablish vegetative growth when appropriate environmental conditions are provided. The spores of clostridia are oval or spherical and are wider than the vegetative bacterial cell. Among the distinctive forms are spindle-shaped organisms, club-shaped forms, and tennis racket-shaped structures:

Clostridia are obligate anaerobes: they are unable to use molecular oxygen as a final electron acceptor and generate their energy solely by fermentation. Clostridia exhibit varying degrees of intolerance of oxygen. Some species are sensitive to oxygen concentrations as low as 0.5%, but most species can tolerate concentrations of 3–5%. The sensitivity of clostridia to oxygen restricts their habitat to anaerobic environments; habitats that contain large amounts of organic matter provide optimal conditions for their growth and survival.

A primary property of all species of *Clostridium* is their inability to carry out a dissimilatory reduction of sulfate. Most species are chemoorganotrophic. The substrate spectrum for the genus as a whole is very broad and includes a wide range of naturally occurring compounds. Extracellular enzymes are secreted by many species, enabling the organism to utilize a wide variety of complex natural substrates in the environment.
                                                                    [H.P.W.]

Coelenterata   That group of the Radiata whose members typically bear tentacles and possess intrinsic nematocysts. The name Cnidaria is also used for this phylum and is preferred by some because the name Coelenterata, as first used, included the sponges

(Porifera) and the comb jellies (Ctenophora), as well as the animals called coelenterates. *See* CTENOPHORA; PORIFERA.

The coelenterates are mainly marine organisms and are best known as jellyfish or medusae, sea anemones, corals, the Portuguese man-of-war, small polypoid forms called hydroids, and the fresh-water hydras. Taken together, the phylum is divisible into three classes as follows: (1) Hydrozoa, the hydroids, hydras, and hydrozoan or craspedote jellyfish (hydromedusae); (2) Scyphozoa, the acraspedote jellyfish; and (3) Anthozoa, the sea anemones, corals, sea fans, sea pens, and sea pansies. *See* ANTHOZOA; HYDROZOA.

It is convenient to recognize two basic body forms in this phylum, the polyp and the medusa, into which all coelenterates can be classified. The polyp and the medusa, however, have many features in common (see illustration).

The polyp is a radially, biradially, or radiobilaterally symmetrical individual having a longitudinal oral-aboral axis and is usually sessile. The mouth is at the free end and is surrounded by one to many whorls or sets of tentacles which may be hollow or solid. The aboral end is commonly developed as an adhesive device for attachment and is conveniently referred to as a base. The central body cavity is the gastrovascular cavity, also called the enteron or coelenteron.

The medusa is a tetramerously or polymerously radial individual and is free-swimming. The body is usually bell- or bowl-shaped with the mouth suspended in the center of the underside of the bell on a stalk. Instead of directly surrounding the mouth as in the polyp, the tentacles are located at the margin of the bell. The outer or aboral part of the bell is recognized as the exumbrella and the under or oral part as the subumbrella. The mouth leads to the central stomach which in turn gives rise to four or more radial canals. These radial canals run through the umbrella, on the subumbrellar side, and commonly lead to a ring canal at the margin which is continuous around the margin.

The unique and most distinctive feature of coelenterates is the possession of intracellular, independent effector organelles called nematocysts, but also known as stinging cells or nettle cells. A coiled thread tube in each cell may be rapidly everted under proper stimulation and used for food gathering and for defense against predators, intruders, or enemies. Nematocysts are produced within cells called cnidoblasts. The morphologically simplest coelenterates, the Hydrozoa, have nematocysts limited to their outer epidermis whereas the more complex Scyphozoa and Anthozoa bear nematocysts in both the outer epidermis and inner gastrodermis.

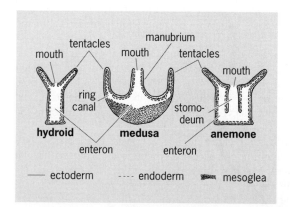

Comparison of hydroid polyp, medusa (inverted), and anthozoan polyp. (*After T. I. Storer and R. L. Usinger, General Zoology, 3d ed., McGraw-Hill, 1957*)

The phylum is characterized by its carnivorous diet, made possible first by the possession of nematocysts which make the predaceous habit successful. After food has been trapped, movements of the tentacles carry it to the mouth, where with the help of ciliary and muscular devices the food is moved to the coelenteron. Here extracellular proteases prepare the way for final intracellular digestion. No herbivorous coelenterates are known.

The reproductive system of coelenterates consists of specialized areas of epithelia, the gonads, which periodically appear and produce gametes. There are no ducts for the sex products or any accessory sexual structures. Fertilization usually occurs in the water surrounding the animal, although a few coelenterates have their eggs fertilized in place and may then brood their young.

The ability to regenerate lost parts is characteristic of coelenterates. Pieces cut from almost any part of polyps will in time grow into new polyps. The regenerative powers of medusae are much less well developed, and not only will the excised piece not develop but it may not even be replaced by the medusa. Gradients of regenerative ability in polyps exist with the ability for a piece to reconstitute a new whole organism decreasing from the mouth to the base. *See* REGENERATION (BIOLOGY).   [C.H.]

Coelom   The mesodermally lined body cavity of most animals above the flatworms and nonsegmented roundworms. Its manner of origin provides one basis for classifying the major higher groups.

Annelids, arthropods, and mollusks have a coelom which develops from solid mesodermal bands. Within the trochophore larva of annelids, a single pole cell proliferates two strips of mesoblast lying on either side of the ventral midline. These bands subdivide transversely into bilateral solid blocks, the somites. Each somite then splits internally to form a hollow vesicle, the cavity of which is the coelom. The mollusks also form bands of mesoderm from a single pole cell, but these bands do not segment. They split internally to form single right and left coelomic sacs, but the cavities are soon reduced and the surrounding mesoblast disperses as separate cells, many of which become muscle. The only remnants of the coelom in the adult are the pericardial cavity and the cavities of the gonads and their ducts. In arthropods paired bands of mesoblast may proliferate from a posterior growth center or may separate inward from a blastoderm, a superficial layer of cells, on the ventral surface of the egg. These bands divide into linear series of somites which then hollow out. Their cavities represent the coelom.

Echinoderms and chordates constitute a second major group, characterized by the origin of the coelom from outpocketings of the primitive gut wall. In echinoderms one pair of bilateral pouches evaginates and separates from the archenteron or primitive digestive cavity. Each pouch constricts into three portions, not homologous to the metameres of other animals.

The protochordates of the groups Hemichordata and Cephalochordata have three coelomic pouches formed by separate evaginations of the archenteral roof. In hemichordates the head cavity remains single as the cavity of the proboscis and has a pore to the exterior on each side. The second pouches form cavities within the collar and also acquire external pores. The third pair is contained within the trunk and forms the major perivisceral cavity.

In cephalochordates the head cavity divides into lateral halves. The left side communicates, by a pore, to an ectodermal pit called the wheel organ. The second pair of pouches forms the pair of mesoblastic somites, and the third pouches subdivide transversely to give rise to the remainder of the linear series of somites. The upper or myotomic portion of each somite remains metameric and forms the segmental muscles.

As it enlarges, the coelomic space is displaced ventrally and expands above and below the gut to form the perivisceral cavities and mesenteries, as described for annelids.

In vertebrates the mesoderm arises as a solid sheet from surface cells that have been involuted through the blastopore. Lateral to the notochord, beginning at about the level of the ear, the mesoderm subdivides into three parts: (1) the somites; (2) the nephrotomic cord, temporarily segmented in lower vertebrates, which will form excretory organs and ducts; and (3) the unsegmented lateral plate. The coelom arises as a split within the lateral plate. *See* ANIMAL KINGDOM; GASTRULATION.   [H.L.H.]

Coelomycetes   Mitosporic or anamorphic (asexual or imperfect) fungi (Deuteromycotina) with sporulation occurring inside fruit bodies (conidiomata) that arise from a thallus consisting of septate hyphae. About 1075 genera containing more than 10000 species are recognized.

The Coelomycetes, like other groups of deuteromycetes, is artificial, comprising almost entirely anamorphic fungi of ascomycete affinity. Some are known anamorphs of Ascomycotina, although there are a few (*Fibulocoela, Cenangiomyces*) with Basidiomycotina affinities because they have clamp connections or dolipore septa. Taxa are referred to as form genera and form species because the absence of a teleomorph (sexual or perfect) state means that they are classified and identified by artificial rather than phylogenetic means. The unifying feature of the group is the production of conidia inside cavities lined by fungal tissue, or by a combination of fungal and host tissue which constitutes the conidioma. *See* ASCOMYCOTA.

Differences in conidiomatal structure traditionally have been used to separate three orders: the Melanconiales, the Sphaeropsidales, and the Pycnothyriales. However, differences in the ways that conidia are produced are now used in classification and identification.

Coelomycetes are known mainly from temperate and tropical regions. They grow, reproduce, and survive in a wide range of ecological situations and can be categorized as either stress-tolerant or combative species. They are commonly found in and recovered from soils, leaf litter and other organic debris from both natural and manufactured sources (as biodeteriogens and biodegradative organisms), and saline and fresh water; and on other fungi and lichens. Several are of medical importance, associated with acute conditions in humans and animals, often as opportunistic organisms causing infection in immunocompromised patients. Coelomycetes are consistently isolated from or associated with disease conditions in all types of vascular plants, often in association with other organisms. *See* PLANT PATHOLOGY.   [B.C.S.]

Coenzyme   An organic cofactor or prosthetic group (nonprotein portion of the enzyme) whose presence is required for the activity of many enzymes. The prosthetic groups attached to the protein of the enzyme (the apoenzyme) may be regarded as dissociable portions of conjugated proteins. Neither the apoenzyme nor the coenzyme moieties can function singly. In general, the coenzymes function as acceptors of electrons or functional groupings, such as the carboxyl groups in α-keto acids, which are removed from the substrate. *See* PROTEIN.

Well-known coenzymes include the pyridine nucleotides, nicotinamide adenine dinucleotide (NAD) and nicotinamide adenine dinucleotide phosphate (NADP); thiamine pyrophosphate (TPP); flavin mononucleotide (FMN) and flavinadenine dinucleotide (FAD); iron protoporphyrin (hemin); uridine diphosphate (UDP) and UDP-glucose; and adenosine triphosphate (ATP), adenosine diphosphate (ADP), and adenosine monophosphate (AMP). Coenzyme A (CoA), a coenzyme in certain condensing enzymes, acts in acetyl or other acyl group transfer and in fatty acid synthesis and oxidation. Folic acid coenzymes are involved in the metabolism of one carbon unit. Biotin is the coenzyme in a number of carboxylation reactions, where it functions as the actual carrier of carbon dioxide. *See* ADENOSINE DIPHOSPHATE (ADP); ADENOSINE TRIPHOSPHATE (ATP); BIOTIN; ENZYME; HEMOGLOBIN; NICOTINAMIDE ADENINE DINUCLEOTIDE (NAD); NICOTINAMIDE ADENINE DINUCLEOTIDE PHOSPHATE (NADP).   [M.B.McC.]

Cognition   The internal structures and processes that are involved in the acquisition and use of knowledge, including sensation, perception, attention, learning, memory, language, thinking, and reasoning. Cognitive scientists propose and test theories about the functional components of cognition based on observations of an organism's external behavior in specific situations.

Cognition throughout life can be broadly described as an interaction between knowledge-driven processes and sensory processes; and between controlled processes and automatic processes. Over time, there is a trade-off between the amount of surface information that is retained in the internal representation of objects or events (bottom-up processing) and the amount of meaning that is incorporated (top-down processing). Following exposure to a stimulus, a sensory representation (sometimes called an image, icon, or echo) is constructed that encodes nearly all the surface characteristics of the stimulus (for example, color, shape, location, pitch, and loudness). The information is short lived, lasting less than a second. Much evidence suggests that extraction of information from this representation takes place in two stages, a feature analysis stage and an object recognition stage. It is during the latter stage that attention (controlled processing) and previous knowledge come into play. *See* MEMORY; PERCEPTION.

Conceptual knowledge is needed to classify objects and events in the world. Some aspects of conceptual knowledge are innate or emerge very early in development, while others are acquired through learning and inference.

A primary cognitive function of all social species is communication, which can be accomplished by a combination of vocal, gestural, and even hormonal signals. Of all species on Earth, only humans have developed a communication system based on abstract signs. This evolutionary development is closely tied to the greater reasoning capacity of humans as well. All reasoning can be broadly described as pattern recognition and search. Conceptual knowledge base are searched for relevant information in order to draw a conclusion, solve a problem, or guide behavior. Thinking often takes the form of a chain of associations among concepts in long-term memory, with one thought retrieving others to which it is related. The most common reasoning strategies include direct retrieval, imaging, means-ends analysis, analogy, classification, deduction, and formal procedures.

Reasoning by direct retrieval involves retrieving a known fact from memory to solve a problem. Reasoning imagistically involves constructing or retrieving images from conceptual memory and examining or manipulating them to solve a problem. For example, individuals reason imagistically when they determine how many windows there are in their living rooms by retrieving an image of the room and counting the windows in the image.

Means-ends analysis is typically employed when solving problems in unfamiliar domains. When a solution is not immediately apparent, reasoners typically compare the goal to the current situation and select means with which to reduce the differences between the two situations.

The restructuring of a problem representation that allows an available means to be used in a novel way or a seemingly unrelated bit of knowledge to be accessed to solve the probem is called insight.

Reasoning by analogy is used when a current situation allows an individual to recall another, similar situation that has a known solution or other information relevant to the task at hand. It is a technique that is powerful but error prone.

Reasoning by classification involves making inferences about an object or event based on its category membership.

Deductive reasoning involves drawing a conclusion based on its logical relation to one or more premises. A second common use for deduction is testing hypotheses.

Formal procedures for reasoning and for solving problems include logic, mathematics, probability theory and statistics, and scientific investigation. Understanding of the behavior and properties of physical, biological, and cognitive systems has been greatly enhanced through the use of these techniques. See PSYCHOLINGUISTICS.

By using noninvasive techniques such as positron emission tomography (PET scan), magnetic resonance imaging, electrical skin conductance, invasive surgical and chemical investigations of animal brains, and data from clinically observed syndromes associated with brain injury, cognitive neuroscientists have pieced together information concerning the role that specific brain regions play in the processing of emotional and cognitive events. High-level visual processing, such as object recognition, takes place in the occipital lobes of the cortex, although recognition of certain highly complex visual stimuli, such as faces, is handled by the right cerebral hemisphere. Auditory stimuli in general are processed by the temporal lobes of the cortex, and written and spoken word recognition and syntactical components of language processing are handled by certain regions of the left hemisphere of the cerebral cortex, notably Broca's and Wernicke's areas; while emotional, idiomatic, and prosodic aspects of language are handled by corresponding regions in the right hemisphere. Higher cognition, such as reasoning and problem solving, involves the frontal lobes of the cortex. Memory and the processing of emotional stimuli are handled by the combined effort of the cortex (notably the anterior and frontal regions) and subcortical structures (notably the limbic system).

One particular subcortical structure—the hippocampus—plays a major role in the formation of new explicit memories. It is believed that an intact hippocampus is needed to temporarily bind together distributed sites of activation in the cortex that together make up a whole, explicit memory for an event. See BRAIN.

Theories of cognition are often tested by building computer models that embody the theories and then comparing the model's performance with human performance on selected tasks. These models tend to be of two types. Rule-based models consist of a long-term memory containing rules which specify actions to take in the presence of particular input patterns, a short-term memory that encodes input patterns and temporarily stores data structures constructed by the rules, and a control structure that guides the process and resolves conflicts when more than one rule applies to the current input. Neural network models simulate cognition as a strengthening and weakening of associations among cognitive events. They consist of a network of interconnected nodes, a mathematical formula for modifying the connections, and a mathematical formula for propagating activation through the network. See INTELLIGENCE.   [D.D.C.]

Collagen   The major fibrous protein in animals, present in all types of multicellular animals and probably the most abundant animal protein in nature. It is estimated that collagen accounts for about 30% of the total human body protein. Collagen is located in the extracellular matrix of connective tissues. It is part of the interacting network of proteoglycans and proteins that provides a structural framework for both soft and calcified connective tissues. By self-associating into fibrils and by binding to proteoglycans and other matrix components, collagen contributes to tissue integrity and mechanical properties. Collagen interacts with cells through the integrin cell receptors and mediates cellular adhesion and migration. Important roles for collagen have been identified in development, wound healing, platelet aggregation, and aging. Its commercial importance in leather and the production of gelatin and glue have long been recognized. More recently, it is being used as a basis for biomaterials. Examples of its biomedical applications include injectable collagen to lessen facial wrinkles and defects; surgical collagen sponges to increase blood clotting; and artificial skin for the treatment of burns.

The classification of an extracellular matrix protein as a collagen is based on the presence of a domain with a distinctive triple-helical conformation. The collagen triple helix consists of three polypeptide chains supercoiled about a common axis and linked by hydrogen bonds. At least 19 distinct molecules have been classified as collagens, and specific types are associated with particular tissues. The most prevalent and well-studied collagens belong to the fibril-forming or interstitial collagen family. The molecules in a fibril are covalently cross-linked by an enzymatic mechanism to strengthen and stabilize them. Inhibition of the enzyme involved in cross-linking results in a dramatic decrease in the tensile strength of tissues, a condition known as lathyrism.

Type I is the most common fibril-forming collagen. Its fibrils make up the mineralized matrix in bone, the strong parallel bundles of fibers in tendon, and the plywoodlike alternating layers in the transparent cornea. Type II is the major fibril-forming collagen in cartilage, while type III is found in blood vessels and skin, together with type I. Basement membranes, which serve to separate cell layers and act as filtration barriers, contain a distinctive group of collagens, denoted as type IV collagens, which are organized into a network or meshlike sheet structure. In the kidney glomerulus, the network based on type IV collagen acts as a filter to determine which molecules will pass from the blood into the urine. *See* BONE; CONNECTIVE TISSUE.

An orderly breakdown of collagen is necessary during development and tissue remodeling. For instance, following childbirth, the uterus reduces in size, which involves a massive degradation of collagen. An abnormal increase in the degradation of cartilage collagen is seen in osteoarthritis. Collagen breakdown also appears to be essential for tumor metastases. A number of hereditary diseases have been shown to be due to mutations in specific collagen genes. Osteogenesis imperfecta (brittle bone) disease is characterized by fragile bones and is due to mutations in type I collagen. Some cartilage disorders are caused by mutations in type II collagen. Ruptured arteries are found in Ehlers-Danlos syndrome type IV, which arises from mutations in type III collagen. [B.Bro.]

Collenchyma   A primary, or early differentiated, supporting tissue of young shoot parts appearing while these parts are still elongating. It is located near the surface, usually just under the epidermis. When observed in transverse sections, it is characterized structurally by cell walls that are intermittently thickened, generally in the corners or places of juncture of three or more cells. Collenchyma is typically formed in the petioles and vein ribs of leaves, the elongating zone of young stems, and the pedicels of flowers. *See* CELL WALLS (PLANT).

As in parenchyma, the cells in collenchyma are living and may contain chloroplasts and starch grains. The cell wall of a collenchyma cell is its most striking feature structurally and functionally. It is composed of cellulose and pectic compounds plus a very high proportion of water. The cytoplasm is very rich in ribosomes and ribonucleic acids in the early stages of development. Another striking feature of collenchyma cell walls is their plasticity. They are capable of great elongation during the period of growth in length of the plant. The plasticity of collenchyma is associated with a tensile strength comparable to that shown by fibers of sclerenchyma. The combination of strength and plasticity makes the collenchyma effective as a strengthening tissue in developing stems and leaves having no other supporting tissue at that time. *See* EPIDERMIS (PLANT); PARENCHYMA.   [R.L.Hu.]

Colon   The portion of the intestine that runs from the cecum to the rectum; in some mammals, it may be separated from the small intestine by an ileocecal valve. It is also known as the large intestine. The colon is usually divided into ascending, transverse, and descending portions. In the human a fourth section, the sigmoid, is found. The colon is longer in herbivores and shorter in carnivores, and is about 4 to 6 ft (1.2 to 1.8 m) long in humans. No digestive enzymes are secreted in the colon. Much digestion (for example, all breakdown of cellulose) occurs by bacteria, of which *Escherichia coli* is the most common. Most of the fluid added to the food during digestion is reabsorbed into the body in the colon. All digestive action, water absorption, and so on, is completed before the food materials pass out of the colon into the rectum. *See* DIGESTIVE SYSTEM.   [W.J.B.]

Color vision   The ability to discriminate light on the basis of wavelength composition. It is found in humans, in other primates, and in certain species of birds, fishes, reptiles, and insects. These animals have visual receptors that respond differentially to the various wavelengths of visible light. Each type of receptor is especially sensitive to light of a particular wavelength composition. Evidence indicates that primates, including humans, possess three types of cone receptor, and that the cones of each type possess a pigment that selectively absorbs light from a particular region of the visible spectrum. The trichromatic system of colorimetry, using only three primary colors, is based on the concept of cone receptors with sensitivities having their peaks, respectively, in the long, middle, and short wavelengths of the spectrum.

Color is usually presented to the individual by the surfaces of objects on which a more or less white light is falling. A red surface, for example, is one that absorbs most of the short-wave light and reflects the long-wave light to the eye. A set of primary colors can be chosen so that any other color can be produced from additive mixtures of the primaries in the proper proportions. Thus, red, green, and blue lights can be added together in various proportions to produce white, purple, yellow, or any of the various intermediate colors. Three-color printing, color photography, and color television are examples of the use of primaries to produce plausible imitations of colors of the original objects.

Colors lying along a continuum from white to black are known as the gray, or achromatic, colors. They have no particular hue. Whiteness is a relative term; white paper, paint, and snow reflect some 80% or more of the light of all visible wavelengths, while black surfaces typically reflect less than 10% of the light. The term white is also applied to a luminous object, such as a gas or solid, at a temperature high enough to emit fairly uniformly light of all visible wavelengths.

Color blindness is a condition of faulty color vision. It appears to be the normal state of animals that are active only at night. It is also characteristic of human vision when the level of illumination is quite low or when objects are seen only at the periphery of the retina. Under these conditions, vision is mediated not by cone receptors but by rods, which respond to low intensities of light. In rare individuals, known as monochromats, there is total color blindness even at high light levels. Such persons are typically deficient or lacking in cone receptors, so that their form vision is also poor.

Dichromats are partially color-blind individuals whose vision appears to be based on two primaries rather than the normal three. Dichromatism occurs more often in men than in women because it is a sex-linked, recessive hereditary condition. One form of dichromatism is protanopia, in which there appears to be a lack of normal red-sensitive receptors. Red lights appear dim to protanopes and cannot be distinguished from dim yellow or green lights. A second form is deuteranopia, in which there is no marked reduction in the brightness of any color, but again there is a confusion of the colors normally described as red, yellow, and green. A third and much rarer form is tritanopia, which involves a confusion among the greens and blues. *See* HUMAN GENETICS.

Many so-called color-blind individuals might better be called color-weak. They are classified as anomalous trichromats because they have trichromatic vision of a sort, but fail to agree with normal subjects with respect to color matching or discrimination tests. Protanomaly is a case of this type, in which there is subnormal discrimination of red from green, with some darkening of the red end of the spectrum. Deuteranomaly is a mild form of red-green confusion with no marked brightness loss. Nearly 8% of human males have some degree of either anomalous trichromatism or dichromatism as a result of hereditary factors; less than 1% of females are color-defective.

Color blindness is most commonly tested by the use of color plates in which various dots of color define a figure against a background of other dots. The normal eye readily distinguishes the figure, but the colors are so chosen that even the milder forms of color anomaly cause the figure to be indistinguishable from its background.

Techniques of microspectrophotometry have been used to measure the absorption of light by single cone receptors from the eyes of primates, including humans. The results confirm that three types of cone receptors are specialized to absorb light over characteristic ranges of wavelength, with maximum absorption at about 420, 530, and 560 nanometers. In addition there are rod receptors sensitive to low intensities of light over a broad range of wavelengths peaking at about 500 nm. In each of the four types of receptor there is a photosensitive pigment that is distinguished by a particular protein molecule. This determines the range and spectral location of the light which it absorbs.

Central nervous system factors are also evident. Color vision, like other forms of perception, is highly dependent on the experience of the observer and on the context in which the object is perceived. *See* EYE (INVERTEBRATE); EYE (VERTEBRATE); NERVOUS SYSTEM (VERTEBRATE); PERCEPTION; PHOTORECEPTION; VISION.   [L.A.R.]

Common cold   An acute infectious disorder characterized by nasal obstruction and discharge that may be accompanied by sneezing, sore throat, headache, malaise, cough, and fever. The disorder involves all human populations, age groups, and geographic regions; it is more common in winter than in summer in temperate climates. Most people in the United States experience at least one disabling cold (causing loss of time from work or school or a physician visit) per year. Frequencies are highest in children and are reduced with increasing age.

Most, or possibly all, infectious colds are caused by viruses. More than 200 different viruses can induce the illness, but rhinoviruses, in the picornavirus family, are predominant. Rhinoviruses are small ribonucleic acid-containing viruses with properties similar to polioviruses. Other viruses commonly causing colds include corona, parainfluenza, influenza, respiratory syncytial, entero, and adeno. *See* ADENOVIRIDAE; RHINOVIRUS.

Cold viruses are spread from one person to another in either of two ways: by inhalation of infectious aerosols produced by the sneezing or coughing of ill individuals, or by inoculation with virus-containing secretions through direct contact with a person or a contaminated surface. Controlled experiments have not shown that chilling produces or increases susceptibility to colds. Infection in the nasopharynx induces symptoms, with the severity of the illness relating directly to the extent of the infection. Recovery after a few days of symptoms is likely, but some individuals may develop a complicating secondary bacterial infection of the sinuses, ear, or lung (pneumonia).

Colds are treated with medications designed to suppress major symptoms until natural defense mechanisms terminate the infection. Immunity to reinfection follows recovery and is most effective in relation to antibody in respiratory secretions. There is no established method for prevention of colds; however, personal hygiene is recommended to reduce contamination of environmental air and surfaces with virus that may be in respiratory secretions. *See* PNEUMONIA.   [R.B.C.]

Complement   A group of proteins in the blood and body fluids that play an important role in humoral immunity and the generation of inflammation. When activated by antigen-antibody complexes, or by other agents such as proteolytic enzymes (for example, plasmin), complement kills bacteria and other microorganisms. In addition, complement activation results in the release of peptides that enhance vascular permeability, release histamine, and attract white blood cells (chemotaxis). The binding of complement to target cells also enhances their phagocytosis by white blood cells. The most important step in complement system function is the activation of the third component of complement (C3), which is the most abundant of these proteins in the blood.

Genetic deficiencies of certain complement subcomponents have been found in humans, rabbits, guinea pigs, and mice. Certain deficiencies lead to immune-complex diseases, such as systemic lupus erythematosus; other deficiencies result in increased susceptibility to bacterial infections, particularly those of the genus *Neisseria* (for example, gonorrhea and meningococcal meningitis), and hereditary angioneurotic edema. *See* COMPLEMENT-FIXATION TEST; IMMUNITY.   [F.S.R.]

Complement-fixation test   A sensitive reaction used in serology for the detection of either antigen or antibody, as in the diagnosis of many bacterial, viral, and other diseases, including syphilis. It involves two stages: Stage 1 is the binding or fixation of complement if certain antigen-antibody reactions occur, and stage II is detection of residual unbound complement, if any, by its hemolytic action on the sensitized erythrocytes subsequently added (see illustration).

In the first stage either the antigen or the antibody must be supplied as a reagent, with the other of the pair as the test unknown. Fresh guinea pig serum is normally used as a complement source. Sheep erythrocytes which are coated with their corresponding antibody (amboceptor or hemolysin) are used in the second stage. *See* COMPLEMENT.

The controls A, B, and C in the diagram demonstrate that sufficient complement is present to effect hemolysis of the sensitized indicator cells and that neither antigen or antibody added alone will interfere with this by binding complement. In the test system the combination of a suitable antigen and antibody in the presence of complement will bind the complement to the complex so that the complement becomes unavailable for the hemolysis of the indicator cells added in stage II. If either antigen or antibody is added as a reagent in stage I, then the presence of the other in the test unknown added can be detected through its ability to complete the antigen-antibody system. A lack of

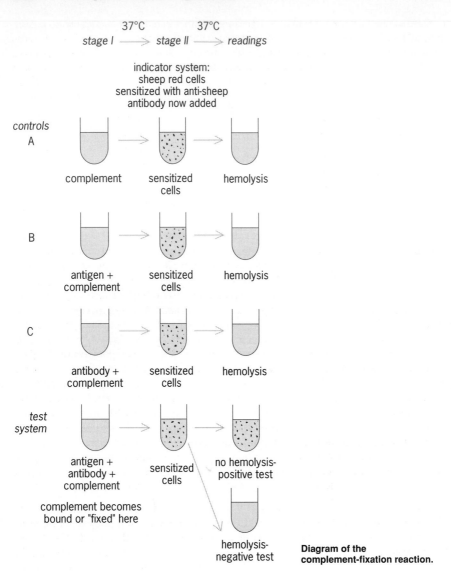

stage I $\xrightarrow{37°C}$ stage II $\xrightarrow{37°C}$ readings

indicator system:
sheep red cells
sensitized with anti-sheep
antibody now added

controls

A

complement → sensitized cells → hemolysis

B

antigen + complement → sensitized cells → hemolysis

C

antibody + complement → sensitized cells → hemolysis

test system

antigen + antibody + complement → sensitized cells → no hemolysis-positive test

complement becomes bound or "fixed" here

hemolysis-negative test

Diagram of the complement-fixation reaction.

hemolysis denotes that the complement is bound. *See* IMMUNOLOGY; LYTIC REACTION.

[H.P.T.]

Complementation (genetics)

The complementary action of different genetic factors. The term usually implies two homologous chromosomes or chromosome sets, each defective because of mutation and unable by itself to promote the normal development or metabolism of the organism, but able to do so jointly when brought together in the same cell. *See* CHROMOSOME; MUTATION.

S. Benzer proposed the term cistron for the unit within which mutants do not complement each other. The word gene is often used in the same sense. The usual biochemical function of a cistron, or gene, is to determine the structure of a specific polypeptide component of a protein. Full complementation between different genes is the rule except when, as sometimes in bacteria, the genes form part of a functionally coordinated complex (operon). Allelic mutants (mutants within one gene) show limited complementation in some cases, for example, when certain pairs of mutant polypeptides correct each other's defects through coaggregation in a complex protein. *See* GENETICS; OPERON.   [J.R.S.F.]

Conditioned reflex   A learned response performed by a trained animal to a signal that was previously associated with an event of consequence for that animal. Conditioned reflex (CR) was first used by the Russian physiologist I. P. Pavlov to denote the criterion measure of a behavioral element of learning, that is, a new association between the signal and the consequential event, referred to as the conditioned stimulus (CS) and unconditioned stimulus (US), respectively. In Pavlov's classic experiment, the conditioned stimulus was a bell and the unconditioned stimulus was sour fluid delivered into the mouth of a dog restrained by harness; the conditioned stimulus was followed by the unconditioned stimulus regardless of the dog's response. After training, the conditioned reflex is manifested when the dog salivates to the sound of the bell.

Ideally, certain conditions must be met to demonstrate the establishment of a conditioned reflex according to Pavlov's classical conditioning method. Before conditioning, the bell conditioned stimulus should attract the dog's attention or elicit the orienting reflex (OR), but it should not elicit salivation, the response to be conditioned. That response should be specifically and reflexively elicited by the sour unconditioned stimulus, thus establishing its unlearned or unconditioned status. After conditioned pairings of the conditioned stimulus and the unconditioned stimulus, salivation is manifested prior to the delivery of the sour unconditioned stimulus. Salivation in response to the auditory conditional stimulus is now a "psychic secretion" or the conditioned reflex.

To this day, Pavlov's methods provide important guidelines for basic research upon brain mechanisms in learning and memory. Scientists all over the world have paired a vast array of stimuli with an enormous repertoire of reflexes to test conditioned reflexes in representative species of almost all phyla, classes, and orders of animals. As a result, classical conditioning is now considered a general biological or psychobiological phenomenon which promotes adaptive functioning in a wide variety of physiological systems in various phylogenetic settings. *See* COGNITION; MEMORY.   [J.G.]

Connective tissue   One of the four primary tissues of the body. It differs from the other three tissues in that the extracellular components (fibers and intercellular substances) are abundant. It cannot be sharply delimited from the blood, whose cells may give rise to connective tissue cells, and whose plasma components continually interchange with and augment the ground substance of connective tissue. Bone and cartilage are special kinds of connective tissue.

The functions of connective tissues are varied. They are largely responsible for the cohesion of the body as an organism, of organs as functioning units, and of tissues as structural systems. The connective tissues are essential for the protection of the body both in the elaborate defense mechanisms against infection and in repair from chemical or physical injuries. Nutrition of nearly all cells of the body and the removal of their waste products are both mediated through the connective tissues. Connective tissues are important in the development and growth of many structures. Constituting the major environment of most cells, they are probably the major contributor to the homeostatic mechanisms of the body so far as salts and water are concerned. They act as the great storehouse for the body of salts and minerals, as well as of fat. The connective tissues determine in most cases the pigmentation of the body. Finally, the

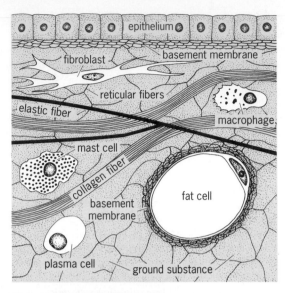

Components of connective tissue.

skeletal system (cartilage and bones) plus other kinds of connective tissue (tendons, ligaments, fasciae, and others) make motion possible.

The connective tissues consist of cells and extracellular or intercellular substance (see illustration). The cells include many varieties, of which the following are the most important: fibroblasts, macrophages (histiocytes), mast cells, plasma cells, melanocytes, and fat cells. Most of the cells of the connective tissue are developmentally related even in the adult; for example, fibroblasts may be developed from histiocytes or from undifferentiated mesenchymal cells.

The extracellular components of connective tissues may be fibrillar or nonfibrillar. The fibrillar components are reticular fibers, collagenous fibers, and elastic fibers. The nonfibrillar component of connective tissues appears amorphous with the light microscope and is the matrix in which cells and fibers are embedded. It consists of two groups of substances: (1) those probably derived from secretory activity of connective tissue cells including mucoproteins, protein-polysaccharide complexes, tropocollagen, and antibodies; and (2) those probably derived from the blood plasma, including albumin, globulins, inorganic and organic anions and cations, and water. In addition, the ground substance contains metabolites derived from, or destined for, the blood.

All the manifold varieties of connective tissue may contain all the cells and fibers discussed above in addition to ground substance. They differ from each other in the relative occurrence of one or another cell type, in the relative proportions of cells and fibers, in the preponderance and arrangement of one or another fiber, and in the relative amount and chemical composition of ground substance. They are classified as:

1. Irregularly arranged connective tissue—which may be loose (subcutaneous connective tissue) or dense (dermis). The dominant fiber type is collagen.

2. Regularly arranged connective tissue—primarily collagenous—with the fibers arranged in certain patterns depending on whether they occur in tendons or as membranes (dura mater, capsules, fasciae, aponeuroses, or ligaments).

3. Mucous connective tissue—ground substance especially prominent (umbilical cord).

4. Elastic connective tissue—predominance of elastic fibers or bands (ligamentum nuchae) or lamellae (aorta).

5. Reticular connective tissue—fibers mostly reticular, moderately rich in ground substance, frequently numerous undifferentiated mesenchymal cells.

6. Adipose connective tissue—yellow or brown fat cells constituting chief cell type, reticular fibers most numerous.

7. Pigment tissue—melanocytes numerous.

8. Cartilage—cells exclusively of one type, derived from mesenchymal cells.

9. Bone—cells are predominantly osteocytes, but also include fibroblasts, mesenchymal cells, endothelial cells, and osteoclasts.

See BLOOD; BONE; CARTILAGE; COLLAGEN; HISTOLOGY; LIGAMENT; TENDON.   [I.G.]

Conservation of resources   Management of the human use of natural resources to provide the maximum benefit to current generations while maintaining capacity to meet the needs of future generations. Conservation includes both the protection and rational use of natural resources.

Earth's natural resources are either nonrenewable, such as minerals, oil, gas, and coal, or renewable, such as water, timber, fisheries, and agricultural crops. The combination of growing populations and increasing levels of resource consumption is degrading and depleting the natural resource base. The world's population stood at 850 million at the onset of the industrial age. The global population has grown to nearly seven times as large (6 billion), and the level of consumption of resources is far greater. This human pressure now exceeds the carrying capacity of many natural resources.

Nonrenewable resources, such as fossil fuels, are replaced over geologic time scales of tens of millions of years. Human societies will eventually use up all of the economically available stock of many nonrenewable resources, such as oil. Conservation entails actions to use these resources most efficiently and thereby extend their life as long as possible. By recycling aluminum, for example, the same piece of material is reused in a series of products, reducing the amount of aluminum ore that must be mined. Similarly, energy-efficient products help to conserve fossil fuels since the same energy services, such as lighting or transportation, can be attained with smaller amounts of fuel. *See* HUMAN ECOLOGY.

It may be expected that the biggest challenge of resource conservation would involve nonrenewable resources, since renewable resources can replenish themselves after harvesting. In fact, the opposite is the case. Historically, when nonrenewable resources have been depleted, new technologies have been developed that effectively substitute for the depleted resources. Indeed, new technologies have often reduced pressure on these resources even before they are fully depleted. Fiber optics, for example, has substituted for copper in many electrical applications, and it is anticipated that renewable sources of energy, such as photovoltaic cells, wind power, and hydropower, will ultimately take the place of fossil fuels when stocks are depleted. Renewable resources, in contrast, can be seriously depleted if they are subjected to excessive harvest or otherwise degraded, and no substitutes are available for, say, clean water or food products such as fish or agricultural crops. Moreover, when the misuse of biological resources causes the complete extinction of a species or the loss of a particular habitat, there can be no substitute for that diversity of life.

"Conservation" is sometimes used synonymously with "protection." More appropriately, however, it refers to the protection and sustainable use of resources. Critical elements of the effective conservation of natural resources include sustainable resource management, establishment of protected areas, and ex situ (off-site) conservation.

Resource management. Some of the most pressing resource conservation problems stem directly from the mismanagement of important biological resources. Many marine fisheries are being depleted, for example, because of significant overcapacity of fishing vessels and a failure of resource managers to closely regulate the harvest. In theory, a renewable resource stock could be harvested at its maximum sustainable yield and maintain constant average annual productivity in perpetuity. In practice, however, fishery harvest levels are often set too high and, in many regions, enforcement is weak, with the result that fish stocks are driven to low levels. A similar problem occurs in relation to the management of timber resources. Short-term economic incentives encourage cutting as many trees as quickly as possible.

A number of steps are being taken to improve resource conservation in managed ecosystems. (1) Considerable scientific research has been undertaken to better understand the natural variability and productivity of economically important resources. (2) Many national and local governments have enacted regulations for resource management practices on public and private lands. (3) In some of regions, programs recently have been established either to involve local communities who have a greater incentive to manage for long-term production more directly in resource management decisions or to return to them resource ownership rights. (4) Efforts are under way to manage resources on a regional or ecosystem scale using methods that have come to be known as ecosystem management or bioregional management. Since the actions taken in one location often influence species and processes in other locations, traditional resource conservation strategies were often focused too narrowly to succeed.

Protected areas. One of the most effective strategies to protect species from extinction is the establishment of protected areas designed to maintain populations of a significant fraction of the native species in a region. Worldwide, 9832 protected areas, totaling more than 9.25 million square kilometers (24 million square miles), cover about 8% of land on Earth. Although these sites are not all managed exclusively for the conservation of species, they play an essential role in protecting species from extinction.

Many problems remain, however, in ensuring effective protected-area conservation networks. For example, several regions with important biodiversity still lack effective protected-area networks. In addition, where protected areas have been designated, human and financial resources are not always available to effectively manage the areas. Particularly in developing countries, the establishment of protected areas has resulted in conflicts with local communities that had been dependent upon the areas for their livelihood. These challenges are now being addressed through international efforts, such as the International Convention on Biological Diversity, which aims to increase the financing available for protected areas and to integrate conservation and development needs.

Ex situ conservation. The most effective and efficient means for conserving biological resources is to prevent the loss of important habitats and to manage resources for their long-term productivity of goods and services. In many cases, effective conservation in the field is no longer possible. For example, some species have been so depleted that only a few individuals remain in their natural habitat. In these cases, there is no alternative to the ex situ conservation of species and genetic resources in zoos, botanical gardens, and seed banks. Ex situ collections play important conservation roles as well as serving in public education and research. Worldwide, zoos contain more than 3000 species of birds, 1000 species of mammals, and 1200 species of reptiles, and botanic gardens are believed to hold nearly 80,000 species of plants. These collections hold many endangered species, some of which have breeding populations and thus could potentially be returned to the wild. Genebanks hold an important collection of the genetic diversity of crops and livestock.   [W.Re.]

Cortex (plant)   The mass of primary tissue in roots and stems extending inward from the epidermis to the phloem. The cortex may consist of one or a combination of three major tissues: parenchyma, collenchyma, and sclerenchyma. In roots the cortex almost always consists of parenchyma, and is bounded, more or less distinctly, by the hypodermis (exodermis) on the periphery and by the endodermis on the inside.

Cortical parenchyma is composed of loosely arranged thin-walled living cells. Prominent intercellular spaces usually occur in this tissue. In stems the cells of the outer parenchyma may appear green due to the presence of chloroplasts in the cells (see illustration). This green tissue is sometimes called chlorenchyma, and it is probable that photosynthesis takes place in it.

In some species the cells of the outer cortex are modified in aerial stems by deposition of hemicellulose as an additional wall substance, especially in the corners or angles of the cells. This tissue is called collenchyma, and the thickening of the cell walls gives mechanical support to the shoot.

The cortex makes up a considerable proportion of the volume of the root, particularly in young roots, where it functions in the transport of water and ions from the epidermis to the vascular (xylem and phloem) tissues. In older roots it functions primarily as a storage tissue.

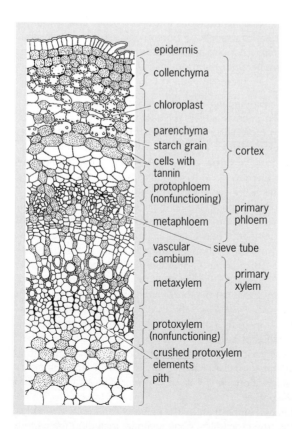

Transverse section of the *Prunus* stem showing the cortex which is composed of collenchyma and parenchyma. (*After K. Esau, Plant Anatomy, 2d ed., 1967*)

In addition to being supportive and protective, the cortex functions in the synthesis and localization of many chemical substances; it is one of the most fundamental storage tissues in the plant. The kinds of cortical cells specialized with regard to storage and synthesis are numerous.

Because the living protoplasts of the cortex are so highly specialized, patterns and gradients of many substances occur within the cortex, including starch, tannins, glucosides, organic acids, crystals of many kinds, and alkaloids. Oil cavities, resin ducts, and laticifers (latex ducts) are also common in the midcortex of many plants.   [D.S.V.F.]

Coxsackievirus   A large subgroup of the genus *Enterovirus* in the family Picornaviridae. The coxsackieviruses produce various human illnesses, including aseptic meningitis, herpangina, pleurodynia, and encephalomyocarditis of newborn infants. *See* PICORNAVIRIDAE.

Coxsackieviruses measure about 28 nanometers in diameter; they resemble other enteroviruses in many biological properties, but differ in their high pathogenicity for newborn mice. At least 23 antigenically distinct types in group A are now recognized, and 6 in group B.

After incubation for 2–9 days, during which the virus multiplies in the enteric tract, clinical manifestations appear which vary widely. Diagnosis is by isolation of virus in tissue culture or infant mice. Stools are the richest source of virus. Neutralizing and complement-fixing antibodies form during convalescence and are also useful in diagnosis. *See* ANTIBODY; COMPLEMENT-FIXATION TEST.

The coxsackieviruses have worldwide distribution. Infections occur chiefly during summer and early fall, often in epidemic proportions. Spread of virus, like that of other enteroviruses, is associated with family contact and contacts among young children. *See* ANIMAL VIRUS; VIRUS CLASSIFICATION.   [J.L.Me.; M.E.Re.]

Crocodylia   An order of the class Reptilia (subclass Archosauria) which is composed of large, voracious, aquatic species which include the alligators, caimans, crocodiles, and gavials. The group has a long fossil history from Late Triassic times and its members are the closest living relatives of the extinct dinosaurs and the birds. The 21 or 22 living species are found in tropic areas of Africa, Asia, Australia, and the Americas. One form, the salt-water crocodile (*Crocodylus porosus*), has traversed oceanic barriers from the East Indies as far east as the Fiji Islands.

The order is distinguished from other living reptiles in that it has two temporal foramina, an immovable quadrate, a bony secondary palate, no shell, a single median penis in males, socketed teeth, a four-chambered heart, and an oblique septum that completely separates the lung cavities from the peritoneal region. Certain of these unique features and other salient characteristics of the Crocodylia are intimately associated with their aquatic life. For example, there is a special pair of fleshy flaps at the posterior end of the mouth cavity which form a valvular mechanism which separates the mouth from the region where the air passage opens into the throat. This complex arrangement allows crocodilians to breathe even though most of the head is under water, or the mouth is open holding prey or full of water.

During the breeding season male crocodylians set up territories on land which they defend against intruders of the same species. Fertilization is internal and the hard-shelled eggs are deposited in excavations in the sand or in large nests of decaying vegetation, depending upon the species.

The living species are placed in two families and eight genera. The family Crocodylidae contains two subgroups: the true crocodiles, Crocodylinae, including the genera

Crocodylus found in all tropic areas, *Osteolaemus* in central Africa, and the false gavial (*Tomistoma*) in Malaya and the East Indies; the alligators and caimans, Alligatorinae, including the genera *Alligator* of the southeastern United States and near Shanghai, China, the *Caiman* from Central and South America, and *Melanosuchus* and *Paleosuchus* of South America. The gavial (*Gavialis gangeticus*) of India and north Burma is the only living member of the family Gavialidae. Crocodiles differ most obviously from alligators and caimans in head shape and in the position of the teeth, although other technical details also separate them.

Crocodylians first appear in deposits of Late Triassic or possibly Early Jurassic age in North America and South Africa. They formerly were much more widely distributed in temperate latitude than today; abundant paleobotanical evidence confirms a warmer climate in mid-latitudes at this time, It seems probable that the restriction of crocodilians to the tropics was a direct result of cooling climate in the late Cenozoic. *See* REPTILIA.

[J.T.G.]

Crossing-over (genetics) The process whereby one or more gene alleles present in one chromosome may be exchanged with their alternative alleles on a homologous chromosome to produce a recombinant (crossover) chromosome which contains a combination of the alleles originally present on the two parental chromosomes. Genes which occur on the same chromosome are said to be linked, and together they are said to compose a linkage group. In eukaryotes, crossing-over may occur during both meiosis and mitosis, but the frequency of meiotic crossing-over is much higher. *See* ALLELE; CHROMOSOME; GENE; LINKAGE (GENETICS).

Crossing-over is a reciprocal recombination event which involves breakage and exchange between two nonsister chromatids of the four homologous chromatids present at prophase I of meiosis; that is, crossing-over occurs after the replication of chromosomes which has occurred in premeiotic interphase. The result is that half of the meiotic products will be recombinants, and half will have the parental gene combinations. Using maize chromosomes which carried both cytological and genetical markers, H. Creighton and B. McClintock showed in 1931 that genetic crossing-over between linked genes was accompanied by exchange of microscopically visible chromosome markers. *See* RECOMBINATION (GENETICS).

In general, the closer two genes are on a chromosome, that is, the more closely linked they are, the less likely it is that crossing-over will occur between them. Thus, the frequency of crossing-over between different genes on a chromosome can be used to produce an estimate of their order and distances apart; this is known as a linkage map.

Since each chromatid is composed of a single deoxyribonucleic acid (DNA) duplex, the process of crossing-over involves the breakage and rejoining of DNA molecules. Although the precise molecular mechanisms have not been determined, it is generally agreed that the following events are necessary: (1) breaking (nicking) of one of the two strands of one or both nonsister DNA molecules; (2) heteroduplex (hybrid DNA) formation between single strands from the nonsister DNA molecules; (3) formation of a half chiasma, which is resolved by more single-strand breakages to result in either a reciprocal crossover, a noncrossover, or a nonreciprocal crossover (conversion event).

[C.B.G.]

Crossopterygii An infraclass of the bony fishes (class Osteichthyes), also known as fringe-finned fishes, that forms one of the two major divisions of the lobe-finned fishes (Sarcopterygii). The group first appeared as fossils in the Early Devonian; in the Paleozoic they were mostly small to medium-sized carnivorous fish living in shallow tropical seas, estuaries, and fresh waters. There were two principal groups: a diverse set of fishes termed Rhipidista and the Coelacanthini. Their principal radiations were in the Devonian, and by the Mississippian they were in sharp decline. The Rhipidista were wholly extinct by the Middle Permian, but the coelacanths underwent a second, smaller, Mesozoic radiation and managed to survive to the present day as the most famous lobe-fin of all, the living species *Latimeria chalumnae*. Crossopterygii are characterized by a unique hinge in the skull that allowed the front portion to be raised and lowered during feeding and respiratory movements.

Members of the order Rhipidistia were principally fusiform, fast-swimming carnivores that flourished in the rivers and lakes of the Late Devonian. They could breathe air, and the use of lungs as well as gills gave them an advantage in warm, shallow-water environments where dissolved oxygen was often low. Members of the order Coelacanthini are characterized by a special trifid tail and scales ornamented with tubercles. They are not thought to be close to the ancestors of tetrapods.   [K.T.]

Crown gall   A neoplastic disease of primarily woody plants, although the disease can be reproduced in species representing more than 90 plant families. The disease results from infection of wounds by the free-living soil bacterium *Agrobacterium tumefaciens* which is commonly associated with the roots of plants.

The first step in the infection process is the site-specific attachment of the bacteria to the plant host. Up to half of the bacteria become attached to host cells after 2 h. At 1 or 2

Crown gall on peach.

weeks after infection, swellings and overgrowths take place in tissue surrounding the site of infection, and with time these tissues proliferate into large tumors (see illustration). If infection takes place around the main stem or trunk of woody hosts, continued tumor proliferation will cause girdling and may eventually kill the host. Crown gall is therefore economically important, particularly in nurseries where plant material for commercial use is propagated and disseminated.

Unlike healthy normal cells, crown gall tumor cells do not require an exogenous source of phytohormones (auxins and cytokinin) for growth in culture because they readily synthesize more than sufficient quantities for their own growth. They also synthesize basic amino acids, each conjugated with an organic acid, called opines. The tumor cells also grow about four times faster and are more permeable to metabolites than normal cells.

These cellular alterations, such as the synthesis of opines and phytohormone regulation, result from bacterial genes introduced into host plant cells by *A. tumefaciens* during infection. Although it is not understood how these genes are introduced into the plant cell, the genes for the utilization of these opines and for regulating phytohormone production have been found to be situated on an extrachromosomal element called the pTi plasmid. This plasmid, harbored in all tumor-causing *Agrobacterium* species, also carries the necessary genetic information for conferring the tumor-inducing and host-recognition properties of the bacterium.

Crown gall is consequently a result of this unique bacteria-plant interaction, whereby *A. tumefaciens* genetically engineers its host to produce undifferentiated growth in the form of a large tumor, in which there is the synthesis of a unique food source in the form of an opine for specific use by the bacterial pathogen. *See* BACTERIAL GENETICS; GENETIC ENGINEERING; PLANT HORMONES; PLANT PATHOLOGY. [C.J.Ka.]

Crustacea A highly variable, species-rich group of arthropods that have inhabited marine environments since the beginning of the Cambrian Period. Within the marine realm the crustaceans occupy as diverse a spectrum of habitats as the insects inhabit on land.

The hierarchical rank of the Crustacea is a matter of continuing debate. The Crustacea are regarded as a phylum, distinct from other arthropods, by proponents of the concept of polyphyly in the Arthropoda. Alternatively, they are given the rank of subphylum or superclass by those who view the Arthropoda as a monophyletic taxon.

Species of Crustacea such as the shrimp, prawn, crab, or lobster are familiar. However, there are many more with less common vernacular names such as the water fleas, beach fleas, sand hoppers, fish lice, wood lice, sow bugs, pill bugs, barnacles, scuds, slaters, and krill or whale food. The Crustacea are one of the most difficult animal groups to define because of their great diversity of structure, habit, habitat, and development. No one character or generalization will apply equally well to all.

Crustaceans have segmented, chitin-encased bodies; articulated appendages; mouthparts known as mandibles during some stage of their life, however modified they may be for cutting, chewing, piercing, sucking, or licking; and two pairs of accessory feeding organs, the maxillules and maxillae. One or the other pair is sometimes vestigial or may be lacking. The Crustacea are unique in having two pairs of antennae: the first pair, or antennules, and the second pair, the antennae proper. The latter are almost always functional at some stage of every crustacean's life.

Taxonomy. Not only is there a lack of agreement on the rank of the Crustacea per se, but there is no consensus on hierarchial levels of subordinate taxa. The classification presented here is restricted to extant taxa and is, at best, a compromise among opposing opinions.

Superclass Crustacea
Class Cephalocarida
Class Branchiopoda
Order: Anostraca
Spinicaudata
Laevicaudata
Ctenopoda
Anomopoda
Onychopoda
Order: Haplopoda
Notostraca
Class Remipedia
Class Ostracoda
Subclass Myodocopa
Order: Myodocopida
Halocyprida
Subclass Podocopa
Order: Platyocopida
Podocopida
Class Maxillopoda
Subclass Mystacocarida
Subclass Cirripedia
Order: Ascothoracica
Thoracica
Acrothoracica
Rhizocephala
Subclass Copepoda
Order: Calanoida
Harpacticoida
Cyclopoida
Poecilostomatoida
Siphonostomatoida
Monstrilloida
Misophrioida
Mormonilloida
Subclass Branchiura
Subclass Tantulocarida
Class Malacostraca
Subclass Phyllocarida
Order: Leptostraca
Subclass Hoplocarida
Order: Stomatopoda
Subclass Eumalacostraca
Superorder Syncarida
Order: Bathynellacea
Anaspidacea
Superorder Peracarida
Order: Spelaeogriphacea
Mysidacea
Mictacea
Amphipoda

Isopoda
Tanaidacea
Cumacea

See BRANCHIOPODA; CEPHALOCARIDA; MALACOSTRACA; MAXILLOPODA; OSTRACODA; REMIPEDIA.

General morphology. The true body segments, the somites or metameres, are usually somewhat compressed or depressed. Each typically includes one pair of biramous appendages. The linear series of somites making up the body of a crustacean are more or less distinctly organized into three regions or tagmata: the head, thorax, and abdomen. Where regional organization of the postcephalic somites is not clearly marked, they collectively form the trunk. The somites are variously fused with one another in diagnostic combinations in different groups of the Crustacea.

Body. A dorsal shield or carapace of variable length arises from the dorsum of the third cephalic somite and covers the cephalon and cephalothorax to varying extent. The carapace reaches its greatest development in the malacostracan Decapoda (shrimps, lobsters, and crabs).

The chitinous cuticle covering the crustacean body is its external skeleton (exoskeleton). The chitin is flexible at the joints, in foliaceous appendages, and throughout the exoskeletons of many small and soft-bodied species, but it is often thickened and stiff in others. It becomes calcified in many species as a result of the deposition of lime salts.

The paired appendages are typically biramous and consist of two branches: the endopod and exopod. The endopod is definitely segmented in the higher Crustacea. The endopods are variously modified to serve a variety of functions and needs such as sensory perception, respiration, locomotion, prehension and comminution of food, cleansing, defense, offense, reproduction, and sex recognition and attraction. If retained in the adult, the exopod may remain leaf- or paddlelike, or become flagellated structures, facilitating swimming or aiding respiration.

Crustacea take up oxygen by means of gills, the general body surface, or special areas of it. Some of the few species that have become more or less terrestrial in their habits have developed modifications of their branchial mechanism such as water-retaining recesses which when sufficiently moist enable them to breathe air. Some sow or pill bugs have special tracheal developments in their abdominal appendages for the same purpose.

Reproductive system. The sexes are separate in most Crustacea and usually can be differentiated from each other by secondary sex characters. Chief among these characters are the size and shape of the body, appendages, or both, and placement of the genital apertures. Hermaphroditism is the rule in the Cephalocarida, Remipedia, some ostracods, sessile Cirripedia (barnacles), in isolated cases in other crustaceans, and in certain parasitic forms. Parthenogenesis (eggs developing and hatching without prior fertilization) occurs frequently in some of the lower crustaceans that have what might be called an alternation of generations. The parthenogenetic generations alternate with a generation produced by fertilized eggs. *See* CIRRIPEDIA.

The eggs of most crustaceans are carried attached to the female until hatched. Some females develop brood pouches in which the young are retained for a time. A nutrient secretion which sustains the young until they are released is produced in some species having a brood chamber. Penaeid shrimp and a few of the lower Crustacea deposit their eggs in the medium in which they live, in some cases attaching them to aquatic vegetation.

Development. The nauplius larva is characteristic of Crustacea. This first larval stage is common in the lower forms, but in many of the higher forms it occurs during development in the egg, and the young are hatched as a different and more advanced larva or, as in many Malacostraca, in a form similar to the adult. Life histories vary from the simple to the complex within the different groups of Crustacea.

Molting (ecdysis). This process involves several steps: (1) preparation, which includes some degree of resorption of the old cuticle; (2) the formation of a new, temporarily soft and thin one within it; (3) the accumulation and storing of calcium in the midgut gland or as lenticular deposits (gastroliths). The preparatory period is less complicated in the thinly chitinous forms. The actual molt follows. The old shell or cuticle splits at predetermined places, permitting the crustacean within, already enclosed in new but still soft exoskeleton, to withdraw. A temporary absorption of water enables the animal to split or crack its housing. Upon withdrawal of the entire animal, absorption of water again rapidly takes place with a pronounced increase in body size. The tender new cuticle is reinforced rapidly by the resorbed chitin, and hardened by whatever reserves of calcium the animal may have stored, supplemented and extended by the far more plentiful supplies in solution in the sea which may be absorbed or ingested by the growing crustacean. Molting takes place quite frequently in the larval stages when growth is rapid, but becomes less frequent as the animal ages. In many species there is a terminal molt at maturity.

Autotomy and regeneration. The mechanisms of autotomy and regeneration are developed in the crustaceans to minimize injury or loss to an enemy. When an appendage is broken, it is cast off or broken at the fracture or breaking plane. This sacrifice often enables the victim to escape. Even more remarkable is the fact that crustaceans, by voluntary muscular contraction, can part with a limb which may be injured. Crustacea also have the ability to regenerate lost parts. Although the regenerated parts are not always the same size as the original in the first molt after injury, increase in size in successive molts soon restores a lost limb to virtually its former appearance.

Bionomics and economics. Crustacea are ubiquitous. They live at almost all depths and levels of the sea, in fresh waters at elevations up to 12,000 ft (3658 m), in melted snow water, in the deepest of the sea's abysses more than 6 mi (9 km) down, and in waters of 0°C (32°F) temperature. Some species live on land, although most must descend to salt water areas again to spawn their young. Some live in strongly alkaline waters and others in salt water which is at the saturation point, still others in hot springs and hydrothermal vents with temperatures in excess of 55°C (131°F).

Crustacea are of all sizes, ranging from copepods 0.01 in. (0.25 mm) long to huge spider crabs of Japan, which span 12 ft (3.7 m) from tip to tip of the laterally extended legs. The American lobster, the heaviest so far known, tops all crustaceans at $44^1/_2$ lb (20 kg).

Most crustaceans are omnivorous and essentially scavengers. Many are filter feeders and screen particulate life, plankton, and organic detritus from the waters in which they live; others are largely carnivorous, still others vegetarian. Among the vegetarians are the grazers of the ocean meadows which convert the microscopic plant life (diatoms) into flesh and food for larger animals which in turn are harvested as food for humans.

[W.L.S.; P.A.McL.; R.M.Fe.]

Cryobiology The use of low-temperature environments in the study of living plants and animals. The principal effects of cold on living tissue are destruction of life and preservation of life at a reduced level of activity. Both of these effects are demonstrated in nature. Death by freezing is a relatively common occurrence in severe winter storms. Among cold-blooded animals winter weather usually results in a comalike sleep that may last for a considerable length of time.

In cryobiological applications much lower temperatures are used than are present in natural environments. The extreme cold of liquid nitrogen (boiling at $-320°F$ or $-196°C$) can cause living tissue to be destroyed in a matter of seconds or to be preserved for years and possibly for centuries with essentially no detectable biochemical activity. The result achieved when heat is withdrawn from living tissue depends on processes occurring in the individual cells. Basic knowledge of the causes of cell death, especially during the process of freezing, and the discovery of methods which circumvent these causes have led to practical applications both for long-term storage of living cells or tissue (cryopreservation) and for calculated and selective destruction of tissue (cryosurgery).

The biochemical constituents of a cell are either dissolved or suspended in water. During the physical process of freezing, water tends to crystallize in pure form, while the dissolved or suspended materials concentrate in the remaining liquid. In the living cell, this process is quite destructive. In a relatively slow freezing process ice first begins to form in the fluid surrounding the cells, and the concentration of dissolved materials in the remaining liquid increases. A concentration gradient is established across the cell wall, and water moves out of the cell in response to the osmotic force. As freezing continues, the cell becomes quite dehydrated. Salts may concentrate to extremely high levels. In a similar manner the acid-base ratio of the solution may be altered during the concentration process. Dehydration can affect the gross organization of the cell and also the molecular relationships, some of which depend on the presence of water at particular sites. Cellular collapse resulting from loss of water may bring in contact intracellular components normally separated to prevent destructive interaction. Finally, as the ice crystals grow in size, the cell walls may be ruptured by the ice crystals themselves or by the high concentration gradients which are imposed upon them.

By speeding the freezing process to the point that temperature drop is measured in degrees per second, some of these destructive events can be modified. However, most of the destructive processes will prevail. To prevent dehydration, steps must be taken to stop the separation of water in the form of pure ice so that all of the cell fluids can solidify together. The chief tools used to accomplish this are agents that lower the freezing point of the water. Glycerol, a polyalcohol which is compatible with other biochemical materials in living cells, is frequently used in cell preservation. Besides the antifreeze additive, refrigeration procedures are designed to control the rate of decline in temperature to the freezing point, through the liquid-solid transition, and below, to very low temperatures.

Cryopreservation. The earliest commercial application of cryopreservation was in the storage of animal sperm cells for use in artificial insemination. The microorganisms used in cheese production can be frozen, stored, and transported without loss of lactic acid–producing activity. Pollen from various plants can be frozen for storage and transport, facilitating plant-breeding experiments. Among the most valuable applications of cryopreservation is the storage of whole blood or separated blood cells.

Cryosurgery. Cellular destruction from freezing can be used to destroy tissue as a surgical procedure. One of the significant advantages of cryosurgery is that the apparatus can be employed to cool the tissue to the extent that the normal or the aberrant function is suppressed; yet at this stage the procedure can be reversed without permanent effect. When the surgeon is completely satisfied that he or she has located the exact spot to destroy, the temperature can be lowered enough to produce irreversible destruction. This procedure is of particular assistance in neurosurgery.

A second major advantage of cryosurgery is that the advancing front of reduced temperatures tends to cause the removal of blood and the constriction of blood vessels in the affected area. This means that little or no bleeding results from cryosurgical procedures.

A third major advantage of cryosurgery is that cryosurgery equipment currently employs a freezing apparatus that can be placed in contact with area to be destroyed with a minimum incision to expose the affected area.   [A.W.F.]

Cryptobiosis   A state of life in which the metabolic rate of an organism is reduced to an imperceptible level. The several kinds of cryptobiosis ("hidden life") include anhydrobiosis (life without water), cryobiosis (life at low temperatures), and anoxybiosis (life without oxygen). The most is known about anhydrobiosis.

States of anhydrobiosis occur in early developmental stages of various organisms, including seeds of plants, spores of bacteria and fungi, cysts of certain crustaceans, and larvae of certain insects; they occur in both developmental and adult stages of certain soil-dwelling micrometazoans (rotifers, tardigrades, and nematodes), mosses, lichens, and certain ferns.

A central question in the study of anhydrobiosis has been whether metabolism actually ceases. Available evidence strongly suggests that dry anhydrobiotes are ametabolic. In that case, a philosophical question immediately arises concerning the nature of life. This philosophical quandary can be avoided by applying the definition of life adopted by most students of anhydrobiosis: an organism is alive, provided its structural integrity is maintained. When that integrity is violated, it is dead. *See* METABOLISM.   [J.H.Cr.]

Ctenophora   A phylum of exclusively marine organisms, formerly included in the jellyfish and polyps as coelenterates. These animals, the so-called comb jellies, possess a biradial symmetry of organization and have eight rows of comblike plates as the main locomotory structures. Most are pelagic, but a few genera are creeping. Many are transparent and colorless; others are faintly to brightly colored. Almost all are luminescent. Many of these organisms are hermaphroditic. Development is biradially symmetrical, with a cydippid larval stage. Five orders constitute this phylum: Cydippida; Lobata; Cestida; Platyctenida; Beroida.

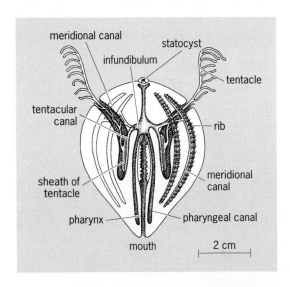

Structure of a cydippid ctenophore.

The body is gelatinous and extremely fragile; its form may be globular, pyriform, or bell- or helmet-shaped. Some species resemble a ribbon. Their size ranges from $\frac{1}{8}$ to 20 in. (3 mm to 50 cm). The axis of symmetry is determined by the mouth and the organ of equilibrium, or statocyst (see illustration). The mouth leads into the flattened, elongated pharynx. The sagittal plane is thus referred to as the stomodeal plane. The other plane of symmetry is perpendicular to the sagittal plane and is marked (Beroida excepted) by tentacles. Eight meridional comb-plate rows or ribs stretch from the aboral pole on the surface of the body. The comb plates, which are used as oars during locomotion, are the most characteristic structure of the ctenophores, possessed by all members of the phylum. Each plate consists of a great number of very long related cilia.

Fertilization usually occurs in seawater. Pelagic ctenophores are self-fertile, but cross-fertilization might also take place inside a swarm of ctenophores. Ctenophores have high powers of regeneration. Asexual reproduction (in a few platyctenid genera) is by regeneration of an entire organism from a small piece of the adult body.

The ctenophores feed on zooplankton. They are themselves important plankton organisms. They are quite common and have a worldwide distribution in all seas, where they can appear in enormous swarms. Some genera stand great changes in the seawater salinity. Because of their voracity as predators of zooplankton, they play an important role in plankton equilibrium and in fisheries. [J.M.F.]

Culture The cultivation of cells in the laboratory. Bacteria and yeasts may be grown suspended in a liquid medium or as colonies on a solid medium; molds grow on moist surfaces; and animal and plant cells (tissue cultures) usually adhere to the glass or plastic beneath a liquid medium. Cultures must provide sources of energy and raw material for biosynthesis, as well as a suitable physical environment.

The materials supplied determine which organisms can grow out from a mixed inoculum. Some bacteria (prototrophic) can produce all their constituents from a single organic carbon source; hence they can grow on a simple medium. Other cells (auxotrophic) lack various biosynthetic pathways and hence require various amino acids, nucleic acid bases, and vitamins. Obligatory or facultative anaerobes grow in the absence of O_2; many cells require elevated CO_2. Cultures isolated from nature are usually mixed; pure cultures are best obtained by subculturing single colonies. Viruses are often grown in cultures of a host cell, and may be isolated as plaques in a continuous lawn of those cells. In diagnostic bacteriology, species are ordinarily identified by their ability to grow on various selective media and by the characteristic appearance of their colonies on test media. *See* Bacterial growth.

Laboratory cultures are often made in small flasks, test tubes, or covered flat dishes (petri dishes). Industrial cultures for antibiotics or other microbial products are usually in fermentors of 10,000 gallons (37,850 liters) or more. The cells may be separated from the culture fluid by centrifugation or filtration.

Specific procedures are employed for isolation, cultivation, and manipulation of microorganisms, including viruses and rickettsia, and for propagation of plant and animal cells and tissues. A relatively minute number of cells, the inoculum, is introduced into a sterilized nutrient environment, the medium. The culture medium in a suitable vessel is protected by cotton plugs or loose-fitting covers with overlapping edges so as to allow diffusion of air, yet prevent access of contaminating organisms from the air or from unsterilized surfaces. The transfer, or inoculation, usually is done with the end of a flamed, then cooled, platinum wire. Sterile swabs may also be used and, in the case of liquid inoculum, sterile pipets.

The aqueous solution of nutrients may be left as a liquid medium or may be solidified by incorporation of a nutritionally inert substance, most commonly agar or silica gel. Special gas requirements may be provided in culture vessels closed to the atmosphere, as for anaerobic organisms. Inoculated vessels are held at a desired constant temperature in an incubator or water bath. Liquid culture media may be mechanically agitated during incubation. Maximal growth, which is visible as a turbidity or as masses of cells, is usually attained within a few days, although some organisms may require weeks to reach this stage. *See* CHEMOSTAT.   [B.D.D.]

Cutaneous sensation   The sensory quality of skin. The skin consists of two main layers, the epidermis and the dermis. Sensory receptors in or beneath the skin are peripheral nerve-fiber endings that are differentially sensitive to one or more forms of energy. The sensory endings can be loosely categorized into three morphological groups: endings with expanded tips, such as Merkel's disks found at the base of the epidermis; encapsulated endings, such as Meissner's corpuscles (particularly plentiful in the dermal papillae), and other organs located in the dermis or subcutaneous tissue, such as Ruffini endings, Pacinian corpuscles, Golgi-Mazzoni corpuscles, and Krause's end bulb; and bare nerve endings that are found in all layers of the skin (some of these nerve endings are found near or around the base of hair follicles).

There is a remarkable relationship between the response specificities of cutaneous receptors and five primary qualities of cutaneous sensation, the latter commonly described as touch-pressure (mechanoreceptors), cold and warmth (thermoreceptors), pain, and itch. Each quality is served by a specific set of cutaneous peripheral nerve fibers. More complex sensations must result from an integration within the central nervous system of information from these sets of nerve fibers. Exploration of the skin surface with a rounded metal point reveals that there exist local sensory spots on the skin, stimulation of which evokes only one of the five qualities of sensation. Thus, there may be plotted maps of pressure, warm, cold, pain, or itch spots. *See* MECHANORECEPTORS; SKIN; SOMESTHESIS.   [R.LaM.]

Cyanobacteria   A large and heterogeneous group of photosynthetic microorganisms, formerly referred to as blue-green algae. They had been classified with the algae because their mechanism of photosynthesis is similar to that of algal and plant chloroplasts; however, the cells are prokaryotic, whereas the cells of algae and plants are eukaryotic. The name cyanobacteria is now used to emphasize the similarity in cell structure to other prokaryotic organisms. *See* ALGAE; CELL PLASTIDS.

All cyanobacteria can grow with light as an energy source through oxygen-evolving photosynthesis; carbon dioxide (CO_2) is fixed into organic compounds via the Calvin cycle, the same mechanism used in green plants. Thus, all species will grow in the absence of organic nutrients. However, some species will assimilate organic compounds into cell material if light is available, and a few isolates are capable of growth in the dark by using organic compounds as carbon and energy sources. Some cyanobacteria can shift to a different mode of photosynthesis, in which hydrogen sulfide rather than water serves as the electron donor. Molecular oxygen is not evolved during this process, which is similar to that in purple and green photosynthetic sulfur bacteria. The photosynthetic pigments of cyanobacteria include chlorophyll *a* (also found in algae and plants) and phycobiliproteins. *See* CHLOROPHYLL; PHOTOSYNTHESIS.

Cyanobacteria are extremely diverse morphologically. Species may be unicellular or filamentous. Both types may aggregate to form macroscopically visible colonies. The cells range in size from those typical of bacteria (0.5–1 micrometer in diameter) to 60 μm.

When examined by electron microscopy, the cells of cyanobacteria appear similar to those of gram-negative bacteria. Many species produce extracellular mucilage or sheaths that promote the aggregation of cells or filaments into colonies.

The photosynthetic machinery is located on internal membrane foldings called thylakoids. Chlorophyll *a* and the electron transport proteins necessary for photosynthesis are located in these lipid membranes, whereas the water-soluble phycobiliprotein pigments are arranged in particles called phycobilisomes which are attached to the lipid membrane.

Several other types of intracellular structures are found in some cyanobacteria. Gas vesicles, which may confer buoyancy on the organisms, are often found in cyanobacteria that grow in the open waters of lakes. Polyhedral bodies, also known as carboxysomes, contain large amounts of ribulose bisphosphate carboxylase, the key enzyme of CO_2 fixation via the Calvin cycle. Several types of storage granules may be found.

Cyanobacteria can be found in a wide variety of fresh-water, marine, and soil environments. They are more tolerant of environmental extremes than are eukaryotic algae. For example, they are the dominant oxygenic phototrophs in hot springs (at temperatures up to 72°C or 176°F) and in hypersaline habitats such as may occur in marine intertidal zones.

Cyanobacteria are often the dominant members of the phytoplankton in fresh-water lakes that have been enriched with inorganic nutrients such as phosphate. It is now known that high population densities of small, single-celled cyanobacteria occur in the oceans, and that these are responsible for 30–50% of the CO_2 fixed into organic matter in these environments. About 8% of the lichens involve a cyanobacterium, which can provide both fixed nitrogen and fixed carbon to the fungal partner. *See* LICHENS; PHYTOPLANKTON.

Cyanobacteria are thought to be the first oxygen-evolving photosynthetic organisms to develop on the Earth, and hence responsible for the conversion of the Earth's atmosphere from anaerobic to aerobic about 2 billion years ago. This development permitted the evolution of aerobic bacteria, plants, and animals. *See* BACTERIA; PREBIOTIC ORGANIC SYNTHESIS. [A.Ko.]

Cyclic nucleotides   Derivatives of nucleic acids that control the activity of several proteins within cells to regulate and coordinate metabolism. They are members of a group of molecules known as intracellular second messengers; their levels are regulated by hormones and neurotransmitters, which are the extracellular first messengers in a regulatory pathway. Cyclic nucleotides are found naturally in all living cells.

Two major forms of cyclic nucleotides are characterized: 3′,5′-cyclic adenosine monophosphate (cyclic AMP or cAMP) and 3′,5′-cyclic guanosine monophosphate (cyclic GMP or cGMP). Like all nucleotides, cAMP and cGMP contain three functional groups: a nitrogenous aromatic base (adenine or guanine), a sugar (ribose), and a phosphate. Cyclic nucleotides differ from other nucleotides in that the phosphate group is linked to two different hydroxyl (3′ and 5′) groups of the ribose sugar and hence forms a cyclic ring. This cyclic conformation allows cAMP and cGMP to bind to proteins to which other nucleotides cannot.

An increase in cAMP or cGMP triggered by hormones and neurotransmitters can have many different effects on any individual cell. The type of effect is dependent to some extent on the cellular proteins to which the cyclic nucleotides may bind. Three types of effector proteins are able to bind cyclic nucleotides: protein kinases, ion channels, and cyclic nucleotide phosphodiesterases.

Protein kinases are enzymes which are able to transfer a phosphate group to (phosphorylate) individual amino acids of other proteins. This action often changes the function of the phosphorylated protein. Ion channels are proteins found in the outer plasma membrane of some cells; binding of cyclic nucleotides to them can alter the flow of sodium ions across the cell membranes. Cyclic nucleotide phosphodiesterases are enzymes responsible for the degradation of cyclic nucleotides.

In bacteria, cAMP can bind to a fourth type of protein, which can also bind to deoxyribonucleic acid (DNA). This catabolite gene activator protein (CAP) binds to specific bacterial DNA sequences, stimulating the rate at which DNA is copied into ribonucleic acid (RNA) and increasing the amount of key metabolic enzymes in the bacteria.

In humans, cyclic nucleotides acting as second messengers play a key role in many vital processes and some diseases. For example, in the brain, cAMP and possibly cGMP are critical in the formation of both long-term and short-term memory. In the liver, cAMP coordinates the function of many metabolic enzymes to control the level of glucose and other nutrients in the bloodstream. *See* ADENOSINE TRIPHOSPHATE (ATP); ENZYME; NUCLEIC ACID; NUCLEOPROTEIN; NUCLEOTIDE; PROTEIN.   [M.D.U.]

Cytochrome   Any of a group of proteins that carry as prosthetic groups various iron porphyrins called hemes. Hemes also constitute prosthetic groups for other proteins, but the function of prosthetic groups in the cytochromes is largely restricted to oxidation to the ferric heme, with the iron in the 3^+ valence state, and reduction to ferrous heme with a 2^+ iron. Thus, by alternate oxidation and reduction the cytochromes can transfer electrons to and from each other and other substances, and can operate in the oxidation of substrates. The energy released in their oxidation reactions is conserved by using it to drive the formation of the energy-rich compound adenosine triphosphate (ATP) from adenosine diphosphate (ADP) and inorganic phosphate. This process of coupling the oxidation of substrates to phosphorylation of ADP is called oxidative phosphorylation. In cells of eukaryotic organisms, the cytochromes have rather uniform properties; they are part of the respiratory chain and are located in the mitochondria. In contrast, prokaryotes exhibit much more varied cytochromes. Cytochromes are found even in metabolic pathways that employ oxidants other than oxygen. *See* ADENOSINE DIPHOSPHATE (ADP); ADENOSINE TRIPHOSPHATE (ATP); MITOCHONDRIA; PROTEIN.

Respiratory chain. There are four cytochromes in the respiratory chain of eukaryotes, termed respectively aa_3, b, c, and c_1. Cytochrome aa_3, also called cytochrome oxidase, functions by oxidizing reduced cytochrome c (ferrocytochrome c) to the ferric form. It then transfers the reducing equivalents acquired in this reaction to molecular oxygen, reducing it to water. The cytochrome oxidase reaction is probably the most important reaction in biology since it drives the entire respiratory chain and takes up over 95% of the oxygen employed by organisms, thus providing nearly all of the energy needed for living processes. *See* RESPIRATION.

The energy released during oxidation is utilized to actively pump protons (H^+) from the matrix of the mitochondrion through the inner membrane into the intermembrane space. This creates a proton gradient across the membrane, with the matrix space having a lower proton concentration and the outside having a higher proton concentration. This chemical and potential gradient can be released by allowing protons to flow down the gradient and back into the mitochondrial matrix, thereby driving the formation of ATP. A pair of electrons flowing down the respiratory chain yields three molecules of

ATP, a remarkable feat of energy conservation. This is called the chemiosmotic mechanism of oxidative phosphorylation, which is generally considered a true picture of respiratory chain function.

Cytochrome oxidase. The cytochrome oxidase of eukaryotes is a very complex protein assembly containing from 8 to 13 polypeptide subunits, two hemes, a and a_3, and two atoms of copper. The two hemes are chemically identical but are placed in different protein environments, so that heme a can accept an electron from cytochrome c and heme a_3 can react with oxygen. When cytochrome oxidase has accepted four electrons, one from each of four molecules of reduced cytochrome c, both its hemes and both its copper atoms are in reduced form, and it can transfer the electrons in a series of reactions to a molecule of oxygen to yield two molecules of water.

Cytochrome oxidase straddles the inner membrane of mitochondria, part of it on the matrix side, part within the membrane, and part on the outer surface or cytochrome c side of the inner membrane. *See* CELL MEMBRANES.

Cytochrome c. Cytochrome c is the only protein member of the respiratory chain that is freely mobile in the mitochondrial intermembrane space. It is a small protein consisting of a single polypeptide chain of 104 to 112 amino acid residues, wrapped around a single heme prosthetic group. The cytochromes c of eukaryotes are all positively charged proteins, with strong dipoles, while the systems from which cytochrome c accepts electrons, cytochrome reductase, and to which cytochrome c delivers electrons, cytochrome oxidase, are negatively charged. There is good evidence that this electrostatic arrangement correctly orients cytochrome c as it approaches the reductase or the oxidase, so that electron transfer can take place very efficiently, even though the surface area at which the reaction occurs is less than 1% of the total surface of the protein.

The amino acid sequences of the cytochromes c of eukaryotes have been determined for well over 100 different species, from yeast to humans, and have provided some very interesting correlations between protein structure and the evolutionary relatedness of different taxonomic groups. The extensive degree of similarity over the entire range of extant organisms has been taken as evidence that this is an ancient structure, developed long before the divergence of plants and animals, which in the course of its evolutionary descent has been adapted to serve a variety of electron transfer functions in different organisms. *See* PROTEINS, EVOLUTION OF.

Cytochrome reductase. Like cytochrome oxidase, the cytochrome reductase complex is an integral membrane protein system. There are numerous subunits, consisting of two molecules of cytochrome b, one molecule of a nonheme iron protein, and one molecule of cytochrome c_1. As in the case of the oxidase, the two cytochrome b hemes are chemically identical, but are present in somewhat different protein environments. The reductase complex is reduced by reaction with the reduced form of the fat-soluble coenzyme Q, dissolved within the inner mitochondrial membrane, which is itself reduced by the succinate dehydrogenase, the NADH dehydrogenase, and other systems. *See* COENZYME.

Other cytochromes. In addition to the mitochondrial respiratory chain cytochromes, animals have a heme protein, termed cytochrome P450, located in the liver and adrenal gland cortex. In the liver it is part of a mono-oxygenase system that can utilize oxygen and the reduced coenzyme NADPH, to hydroxylate a large variety of foreign substances and drugs and thus detoxify them; in the adrenal it functions in the hydroxylation of steroid precursors in the normal biosynthesis of adrenocortical hormones. *See* ADRENAL GLAND; LIVER.

Two varieties of cytochrome b, termed b_{563} and b_{559}, and one of cytochrome c, c_{552}, are involved in the photosynthetic systems of plants. Other plant cytochromes occur in specialized tissues and certain species. *See* PHOTOSYNTHESIS. [E.Ma.]

Cytokine Any of a group of soluble proteins that are released by a cell to send messages which are delivered to the same cell (autocrine), an adjacent cell (paracrine), or a distant cell (endocrine). The cytokine binds to a specific receptor and causes a change in function or in development (differentiation) of the target cell. Cytokines are involved in reproduction, growth and development, normal homeostatic regulation, response to injury and repair, blood clotting, and host resistance (immunity and tolerance). Unlike cells of the endocrine system, many different types of cells can produce the same cytokine, and a single cytokine may act on a wide variety of target cells. Further, several cytokines may produce the same effect on a target, so the loss of one type of cytokine may have few if any consequences for the organism; this situation is called redundancy. Finally, the response of a target cell may be altered by the context in which it receives a cytokine signal. The context includes other cytokines in the milieu, and extracellular matrix. Thus has developed the concept of cytokines as alphabet letters that combine to spell words which make up a molecular language.

Types of cytokines. Cytokines may be divided into six groups: interleukins, colony-stimulating factors, interferons, tumor necrosis factor, growth factors, and chemokines.

Interleukins are proteins that are produced by one type of lymphocyte or macrophage and act on other leukocytes. At least 18 types of this important class, with varying origin and function, exist. Production of interleukins is now known not to be confined to lymphocytes or macrophages.

Colony-stimulating factors are produced by lymphoid and nonlymphoid cells. These factors provide a mechanism whereby cells that are distant from bone marrow can call for different types of hemopoietic progeny. There are also growth-promoting actions of locally produced colony-stimulating factors within the bone marrow to stimulate progenitors to differentiate into macrophages, granulocytes, or colonies containing both cell types.

Interferons classically interfere with the virus replication mechanisms in cells. Interferon-α (produced by leukocytes) and interferon-β (produced by fibroblasts) activate cytotoxicity in natural killer cells. Interferon-γ also activates natural killer cells, and is a potent activator of macrophages as well.

Tumor necrosis factor-α (TNF-α) is produced by a variety of cell types, but activated macrophages represent the dominant source. TNF-α activates natural killer cell cytotoxicity, enhances generation of cytotoxic T-lymphocytes, and activates natural killer cells to produce interferon-γ. TNF-α also acts on vascular endothelium to promote inflammation and thrombosis. TNF-α may also induce apoptosis in cells such as trophoblasts. TNF-β is a product of Th1 T-cells; in addition to providing help in proinflammatory cell-mediated immune responses, these cells produce delayed-type hypersensitivity reactions where macrophages are locally recruited and activated to kill intracellular pathogens, such as certain bacteria. TNF-β has interferon-type activity and a narrower spectrum of action than TNF-α.

Transforming growth factors (TGFs) have the ability to promote unrestrained proliferation of cells which otherwise has a benign behavior phenotype. These factors have therefore been implicated in development of cancer. There are two groups of transforming growth factors. TGF-α is a 5-kilodalton peptide produced by a variety of cells and collaborates with TGF-β, a 25-kD peptide, in promoting unrestrained tumorlike growth. TGF-β has potent pleiotropic effects on a wide variety of tissues and is a potent fibrogenic and immunosuppressive agent.

Chemokines are chemoattractant cytokines of small (7–14 kD) heparin-binding proteins that are subdivided into four families: CXC, CC, C, and CX_3C. Chemokines are produced by macrophages stimulated by bacterial endotoxins, and control the nature and magnitude of cell infiltration in inflammation.

Wound healing. Wound healing is probably the most common phenomenon in which the importance of cytokines is seen. Cytokines ensure that the restorative sequences are carried out in the appropriate order by signaling blood cells and vascular endothelium to coagulate and fill in a wound opening, recruiting and signaling macrophages and neutrophils to engulf microbes, and guiding protective skin epidermal cells to grow over the wounded area. If the damage is more extensive, cytokines stimulate production of new skin cells, blood vessels (angiogenesis), connective tissue, and bone. *See* CELLULAR IMMUNOLOGY.   [D.A.C.]

Cytokinesis   The physical partitioning of a plant or animal cell into two daughter cells during cell reproduction. There are two modes of cytokinesis: by a constriction (the cleavage furrow in animal cells and some plant cells) or from within by an expanding cell plate (the phragmoplast of many plant cells). In either mode, cytokinesis requires only a few minutes, beginning at variable times after the segregation of chromosomes during mitosis (nuclear division). In the vast majority of cases the resulting daughter cells are completely separated. Since they are necessarily smaller cells as a result of cytokinesis, most cells grow in volume between divisions.

Occasionally, cytokinesis is only partial, permitting nutrients and metabolites to be shared between cells. Should cytokinesis fail to occur at all, mitosis may cause more than one nucleus to accumulate. Such a cell is a syncytium. Some tissues normally contain syncytia, for example, binucleate cells in the liver and multinucleate plant endosperm. Some whole organisms such as slime molds are syncytial.

Cytokinesis is precisely and indispensably linked to mitosis, yet the timing and actual mechanisms are distinct. The plane of cell partitioning is perpendicular to the axis of mitosis and coincides with the plane previously occupied by the chromosomes at metaphase. Despite the reliability of this correlation, the chromosomes themselves are not essential for cytokinesis. Experiments performed upon living cells have shown that it is the cell's machinery for chromosome separation, the mitotic apparatus, that provides the essential positional signal to other parts of the cytoplasm which initiates cytokinesis. Subsequently, the mitotic apparatus is no longer involved in cytokinesis and can be destroyed or even sucked out without affecting cytokinesis. *See* CHROMOSOME; MITOSIS.

A cleavage furrow develops by circumferential contraction of the peripheral cytoplasm, usually at the cell's equator. The mechanism of furrowing is very similar among a wide diversity of cell types in lower and higher animals and certain plants. The physical forces of contraction exhibited by a cleavage furrow are evidently greater than the forces of resistance elsewhere. Electron microscopic analysis of the peripheral cytoplasm beneath the cleavage furrow consistently reveals a specialization called the contractile ring. This transient cell organelle is composed of numerous long, thin protein fibers oriented circumferentially within the plane of furrowing. These microfilaments are about 5 nanometers in thickness, appear to attach to the cell membrane, and are known to be composed of actin intermixed with myosin. Both of these proteins are intimately involved in force generation in muscle cells. Thus, the present theory of cytokinesis by furrowing implicates the contractile ring as a transient, localized intracellular "muscle" that squeezes the cell in two. *See* MUSCLE PROTEINS.

In plant cells the dominant mode of cytokinesis involves a phragmoplast, a structure composed of fibrous and vesicular elements that resemble parts of the mitotic apparatus. Microtubules (the fibers) appear to convey a stream of small membranous vesicles toward the midline where they fuse into a pair of partitioning cell membranes. Cellulose cell walls are subsequently secreted between these membranes to solidify the separation between daughter cells. This mode of cytokinesis is well suited to plant cells whose stiff cell walls cannot participate in furrowing. Surprisingly, however, there are instances among the algae where cleavage furrows are the normal mode of cytokinesis. Occasionally, both cleavage furrows and phragmoplasts are employed in the same cell. *See* CELL WALLS (PLANT); PLANT CELL.   [T.E.S.]

Cytolysis   An important immune function involving the dissolution of certain cells. There are a number of different cytolytic cells within the immune system that are capable of lysing a broad range of cells. The most thoroughly studied of these cells are the cytotoxic lymphocytes, which appear to be derived from different cell lineages and may employ a variety of lytic mechanisms. Cytotoxic cells are believed to be essential for the elimination of oncogenically or virally altered cells, but they can also play a detrimental role by mediating graft rejection or autoimmune disease. There are two issues regarding cytotoxic lymphocytes that are of concern: one is the target structure that is being recognized on the target cell, that is, the cell that is killed, which triggers the response; and the other is the lytic mechanism. *See* CELLULAR IMMUNOLOGY.

When freshly isolated, large granular lymphocytes from peripheral blood are tested in cytotoxicity assays, they spontaneously lyse certain tumor cells. These cytotoxic cells are called natural killer cells, and they are important mediators of innate immunity as a first line of defense against invading pathogens. They are unique in that no previous sensitization is required for them to kill. It now appears that a number of different receptors on natural killer cells are capable of activating the lytic machinery. Recently, it has been found that these cells also express inhibitory receptors that actually inhibit cell lysis, thus adding another level of complexity to the regulation of cytolysis by these cells.

Another killer cell, called the lymphokine-activated killer cell can lyse any target cell, including cells from freshly isolated tumors, and are employed in cancer therapy. Lymphokine-activated killer cells may also be important in mounting a vigorous response under conditions of extreme immunological stress. Very little is known about the mechanisms by which these cells recognize and lyse the target cell.

The last group of cytotoxic cells is the cytotoxic T lymphocyte. These are T cells that can lyse any target cell in an antigen-specific fashion. That is, as a population they are capable of lysing a wide range of target cells, but an individual cytotoxic T lymphocyte is capable of lysing only those target cells which bear the appropriate antigen. These are truly immune cells in that they require prior sensitization in order to function. These cells are thought to mediate graft rejection, mount responses against viral infections and intracellular bacterial infections, and play a major role in tumor destruction.

Cytotoxic cell-mediated lysis is divided into three distinct steps. The first step is conjugation, when the killer cell determines if the target cell expresses the appropriate antigen and binds to it via a complex array of adhesion molecules. The second step involves the programming for lysis in which the lytic event is triggered. The third step is the destruction of the target cell.

Direct cell contact between the target cell and the killer cell is absolutely required for initiating the lytic mechanism. Killer cells remain unscathed during the lytic event, suggesting that the killer cell must either employ a unidirectional lytic mechanism or be resistant to the lytic mechanism. Also, when many, but not all, target cells die after cytotoxic T-lymphocyte interaction, nuclear damage with rapid DNA fragmentation precedes detectable plasma membrane damage. *See* ANTIGEN; HISTOCOMPATIBILITY.

It is becoming clear that cytotoxic lymphocytes employ multiple mechanisms designed to initiate target cell destruction. If cytolysis exists to protect the organism from invading pathogens, there should be redundancies in the system so that, if the pathogen has a mechanism for escaping one cytolytic pathway, alternative mechanisms would still be functional. Two mechanisms are the degranulation of cytolytic granules and the triggering of death receptors found on target cells. In the degranulation mechanism of killing, cytotoxic cells release the contents of cytotoxic granules after specific interaction with the target cell. This results in the leakage of salts, nucleotides, and proteins from the target cell, leading to cell death.

On virtually all cells of the body a number of receptors have been identified that are able to trigger apoptosis when engaged. These receptors are called death receptors. The most studied, and relevant to cytolytic cells, is a receptor called Fas. Fas, when engaged by its ligand (FasL), triggers the caspase cascade leading to the hallmark signs of apoptosis, which include membrane blebbing, chromosomal condensation, nuclear disintegration, DNA fragmentation, and cell death.   [H.L.O.; M.M.Ba.]

Cytomegalovirus infection   A common asymptomatic infection caused by cytomegalovirus, which can produce life-threatening illnesses in the immature fetus and in immunologically deficient subjects.

Cytomegalovirus is a member of the herpesvirus group, which asymptomatically infects 50–100% of the normal adult population. Such infections usually take place during the newborn period when the virus can be transmitted from the mother to the baby if the virus is present in the birth canal or in breast milk. Toddlers may also acquire the infection in nurseries. Later in life, the virus may be transmitted by heterosexual or male homosexual activity. After infection, cytomegalovirus remains latent in the body because it cannot be completely eradicated even by a competent immune system. It may be activated and cause illnesses when there is a breakdown of the immune system.

Congenital or transplacental cytomegalovirus infection is also a fairly common event. With rare exceptions, it too is usually asymptomatic. Congenital cytomegalovirus disease results from transplacental transmission of the virus, usually from a mother undergoing initial or primary cytomegalovirus infection, during pregnancy. Its manifestations range from subtle sensory neural hearing loss detectable only later in life, to a fulminating multisystem infection and eventual death of the newborn. This important congenital disease occurs in about 1 in 1000 pregnancies.

The only cytomegalovirus illness clearly described in mature, immunologically normal subjects is cytomegalovirus mononucleosis. This is a self-limited illness like infectious mononucleosis, the main manifestation of which is fever. *See* INFECTIOUS MONONUCLEOSIS.

Otherwise, cytomegalovirus illnesses are usually seen only when cellular immunity is deficient. They constitute the most important infection problem after bone marrow and organ transplantations. Manifestations vary from the self-limited cytomegalovirus mononucleosis to more serious organ involvement such as pneumonia, hepatitis, gastrointestinal ulcerations, and widespread dissemination. The virus causing these illnesses may come from activation of the patient's own latent infection, or it may be transmitted from an outside source, usually from latent cytomegalovirus infecting the graft from a donor. *See* IMMUNOLOGICAL DEFICIENCY; TRANSPLANTATION BIOLOGY.

Cytomegalovirus illnesses are also serious, fairly frequent complications of the acquired immunodeficiency syndrome (AIDS). One reason is that most individuals with human immunodeficiency virus (HIV) infection are already infected with cytomegalovirus. Disease manifestations are similar to what is seen in transplant cases, except they may be more severe. Cytomegalovirus retinitis is a typical problem associated with advanced AIDS. Without treatment, the retina is progressively destroyed such that blindness of one or both eyes is inevitable. *See* ACQUIRED IMMUNE DEFICIENCY SYNDROME (AIDS).

Cytomegalovirus diseases can be treated with two antivirals, ganciclovir or foscarnet, with varying degrees of success. Cytomegalovirus pneumonia in the bone marrow transplant recipient cannot be cured by antivirals alone because it probably has an immunopathologic component. Cytomegalovirus diseases in persons with AIDS can be contained but not cured by specific treatment. For example, ganciclovir treatment of cytomegalovirus retinitis is effective only as long as maintenance therapy is continued. *See* ANIMAL VIRUS.   [Mo.H.]

Cytoplasm   That portion of living cells bordered externally by the plasma membrane (cell membrane) and internally by the nuclear envelope. In the terminology of classical cytology, the substance in living cells and in living organisms not compartmentalized into cells was called protoplasm. It was assumed at the time that the protoplasm of various cells was similar in structure and chemistry. Results of research on cell chemistry and ultrastructure after about 1960 showed that each cell type had a recognizably different "protoplasm." Primarily for that reason, the term protoplasm gradually fell into disuse in contemporary biology. The terms cytoplasm and nucleoplasm have been retained and are used descriptively; they are used almost synonymously with the terms cytosome (body of cytoplasm) and nucleus, respectively.

Many cells, especially the single-celled organisms or protistans, have regional cytoplasmic differentiation. The outer region is the cortex or ectoplasm, and the inner region is the endoplasm. In many cases the cortical layer is a gel made up of a meshwork of cytoskeletal fibers.

Cytoplasm contains mostly water, from 80 to 97% in different cells, except for spores and other inactive forms of living material, in which water may be present in lesser amounts. The dry mass of cells consists mainly of macromolecules: proteins, carbohydrates, nucleic acids, and lipids associated with membranes. The small molecules present in cells are mainly metabolites or metabolic intermediates. The principal ions other than the hydrogen and hydroxyl ions of water are the cations of potassium, sodium, magnesium, and calcium, and the anions chloride and bicarbonate. Many other elements are present in cytoplasm in smaller amounts. Iron is found in cytochrome pigments in mitochondria; magnesium is present in chlorophyll in chloroplasts; copper, zinc, iodine, bromine, and several other elements are present in trace quantities.

Sedimentation of cells by centrifugation shows that organelles and inclusions can be separated from the ground cytoplasm, the fluid phase of the cytoplasm in which they are suspended. The ground cytoplasm in turn has been shown to consist of a cytoskeletal network and the cytosol, the fluid in which the cytoskeleton is bathed. The cytoskeleton consists of several biopolymers of wide distribution in cells. Microtubules have been observed in electron micrographs of a vast number of different cell types. They consist of the protein tubulin, and are frequently covered by a fuzzy layer of microtubule-associated proteins. *See* CYTOSKELETON.

In most cells the smaller particles exhibit Brownian motion due to thermal agitation. In some cells lacking extensive cytoskeletal structure, particles can be moved freely around the cell by Brownian motion. In others they are restricted by their surrounding cytoskeletal elements. Particles of various types may also undergo saltatory motions which carry them farther than Brownian motion possibly could. Such excursions result from the interaction of a particle with an element of the cytoskeleton such as one or more microtubules or microfilaments. *See* CELL (BIOLOGY).   [R.D.Al.]

Cytoskeleton   A system of filaments found in the cytoplasm of cells and responsible for the maintenance of and changes in cell shape, cell locomotion, movement of various elements in the cytoplasm, integration of the major cytoplasmic organelles, cell division, chromosome organization and movement, and the adhesion of a cell to a surface or to other cells.

Three major classes of filaments have been resolved on the basis of their diameter and cytoplasmic distribution: actin filaments (or microfilaments) each with an average diameter of 6 nanometers, microtubules with an average diameter of 25 nm, and intermediate filaments whose diameter of 10 nm is intermediate to that of the other two classes. The presence of this system of filaments in all cells, as well as their diversity in structure and cytoplasmic distribution, has been recognized only in the modern period of biology.

A technique that has greatly facilitated the visualization of these filaments, as well as the analysis of their chemical composition, is immunofluorescence applied to cells grown in tissue culture. See Immunofluorescence.

Actin is the main structural component of actin filaments in all cell types, both muscle and nonmuscle. Actin filaments assume a variety of configurations depending on the type of cell and the state it is in. They extend a considerable distance through the cytoplasm in the form of bundles, also known as stress fibers since they are important in determining the elongated shape of the cell and in enabling the cell to adhere to the substrate and spread out on it. Actin filaments can exist in forms other than straight bundles. In rounded cells that do not adhere strongly to the substrate (such as dividing cells and cancer cells), the filaments form an amorphous meshwork that is quite distinct from the highly organized bundles. The two filamentous states, actin filament bundles and actin filament meshworks, are interconvertible polymeric states of the same molecule. Bundles give the cell its tensile strength, adhesive capability, and structural support, while meshworks provide elastic support and force for cell locomotion.

Microtubules are slender cylindrical structures that exhibit a cytoplasmic distribution distinct from actin filaments. Microtubules originate in structures that are closely associated with the outside surface of the nucleus known as centrioles. The major structural protein of these filaments is known as tubulin. Unlike the other two classes of filaments, microtubules are highly unstable structures and appear to be in a constant state of polymerization-depolymerization. See Centriole.

Intermediate filaments function as the true cytoskeleton. Unlike microtubules and actin filaments, intermediate filaments are very stable structures. They have a cytoplasmic distribution independent of actin filaments and microtubules. In the intact cell, they anchor the nucleus, positioning it within the cytoplasmic space. During mitosis, they form a filamentous cage around the mitotic spindle which holds the spindle in a fixed place during chromosome movement.   [E.L.]

Deciduous plants   Plants that regularly lose their leaves at the end of each growing season. Dropping of the leaves occurs at the inception of an unfavorable season characterized by either cold or drought or both. Most woody plants of temperate climates have the deciduous habit, and it may also occur in those of tropical regions having alternating wet and dry seasons. Many deciduous trees and shrubs of regions with cold winters become evergreen when grown in a warm climate. Conversely, such trees as magnolias, evergreen in warm areas, become deciduous when grown in colder climates. *See* LEAF; PLANT PHYSIOLOGY; PLANT TAXONOMY.   [N.A.]

Deoxyribonucleic acid (DNA)   The material that carries genetic information in all organisms, except for some families of viruses that use ribonucleic acid (RNA). The set of DNA molecules that contains all genetic information for an organism is called its genome. DNA is found primarily in the nuclei of eukaryotic cells and in the nucleoid of bacteria. Small amounts of DNA are also found in mitochondria and chloroplasts and in autonomously maintained DNAs called plasmids. *See* NUCLEIC ACID.

DNA is composed of two long polymer strands of the sugar 2-deoxyribose, phosphate, and purine and pyrimidine bases. The backbone of each strand is composed

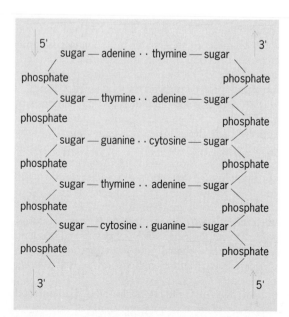

Fig. 1. **Diagram of the nucleic acid backbone, a repeating sugar-phosphate polymer chain with base side chains. The two chains are antiparallel, as shown by arrows. The dots between the bases represent hydrogen bonding. Although the chains are drawn flat, they are actually wound around each other in the molecule.**

of alternating 2-deoxyribose and phosphate linked together through phosphodiester bonds. A DNA strand has directionality; each phosphate is linked to the 3′ position of the preceding deoxyribose and to the 5′ position of the following deoxyribose (Fig. 1). The four bases found in DNA are adenine, thymine, guanine, and cytosine. Each 2-deoxyribose is linked to one of the four bases via a covalent glycosidic bond, forming a nucleotide. The sequence of these four bases allows DNA to carry genetic information. Bases can form hydrogen bonds with each other. Adenine forms two bonds with thiamine, and cytosine forms three bonds with guanine. These two sets of base pairs have the same geometry, allowing DNA to maintain the same structure regardless of the specific sequence of base pairs. See DEOXYRIBOSE; PURINE; PYRIMIDINE.

Structure. DNA is composed of two strands that wrap around each other to form a double helix. The two strands are held together by base pairing and are antiparallel. Thus if one strand is oriented in the 5′ to 3′ direction, the other strand will be 3′ to 5′. This double-helical structure of DNA was first proposed in 1954 by J. D. Watson and F. H. C. Crick. The most common form of DNA is the B-form, which is a right-handed double helix with 10.4 base pairs per turn. Less common forms of DNA include A-form, which is a right-handed double helix that has 11 base pairs per turn and has wider diameter than B-form, and Z-form, which is a narrow, irregular left-handed double helix.

For cells to live and grow, the genetic information in DNA must be (1) propagated and maintained from generation to generation, and (2) expressed to synthesize the components of a cell. These two functions are carried out by the processes of DNA replication and transcription, respectively. See GENETIC CODE.

Replication. Each of the two strands of a DNA double helix contains all of the information necessary to make a new double-stranded molecule (Fig. 2). During replication the two parental strands are separated, and each is used as a template for the synthesis of a new strand of DNA. Synthesis of the nascent DNA strands is carried out by a family of enzymes called DNA polymerases. Base incorporation is directed by the existing DNA strand; nucleotides that base-pair with the template are added to the nascent DNA strand. The product of replication is two complete double-stranded helices, each of which contains all of the genetic information (has the identical base sequence) of the parental DNA. Each progeny double helix is composed of one parental and one nascent strand. DNA replication is very accurate. In bacteria the mutation rate is about 1 error per 1000 bacteria per generation, or about 1 error in 10^9 base pairs replicated. This low error rate is due to a combination of the high accuracy of the replication process and cellular pathways which repair misincorporated bases. See MUTATION.

Transcription. In transcription, DNA acts as a template directing the synthesis of RNA. RNA is single-stranded polymer similar to DNA except that it contains the sugar ribose instead of 2-deoxyribose and the base uracil instead of thymidine. The two strands of DNA separate transiently, and one of the two single-stranded regions is used as a template to direct the synthesis of an RNA strand. As in DNA replication, base pairing between the incoming ribonucleotide and the template strand determines the sequence of bases incorporated into the nascent RNA. Thus, genetic information in the form of a specific sequence of bases is directly transferred from DNA to RNA in transcription. After the RNA is synthesized, the DNA reverts to double-stranded form. Transcription is carried out by a family of enzymes called RNA polymerases. Following transcription, newly synthesized RNA is often processed prior to being used to direct protein synthesis by ribosomes in a process called translation. See PROTEIN; RIBONUCLEIC ACID (RNA); RIBOSOMES.

Genetic variation. There is a great deal of variation in the DNA content and sequences in different organisms. Because of base pairing, the ratios of adenine to

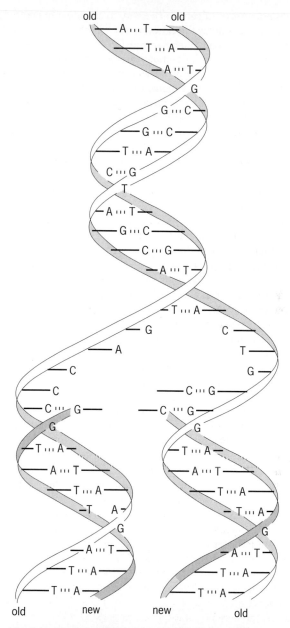

Fig. 2. Replication of DNA: A = adenine, C = cytosine, G = guanine, and T = thymine. (*After J. D. Watson, Molecular Biology of the Gene, W. J. Benjamin, 1965*)

thiamine and cytosine to guanine are always the same. However, the ratio of adenine and thymine to guanine and cytosine in different organisms ranges from 25 to 75%. There is also large variation in the amount of DNA in the genome of various organisms. The simplest viruses have genomes of only a few thousand base pairs, while complex eukaryotic organisms have genomes of billions of base pairs. This variation partially reflects the increasing number of genes necessary to encode more complex organisms, but mainly reflects an increase in the amount of DNA that does not encode proteins (known as introns). A large percentage of the DNA in multicellular eukaryotes is in introns or is repetitive DNA (sequences that are repeated many times). In most eukaryotes the DNA sequences that encode proteins (known as exons) are not continuous but have introns interspersed within them. The initial transcript synthesized by RNA polymerase contains both exons and introns and can be many times the length of the actual coding sequence. The RNA is then processed and the introns are removed through a mechanism called RNA splicing to yield messenger RNA (mRNA), which is translated to make protein.

Recombinant technology. Techniques have been developed to allow DNA to be manipulated in the laboratory. These techniques have led to a revolution in biotechnology. This revolution began when methods were developed to cleave DNA at specific sequences and to join pieces of DNA together. Another major component of this technology is the ability to determine the sequence of the bases in DNA. There are two general approaches for determining DNA sequence. Either chemical reactions are carried out which specifically cleave the sugar-phosphate bond at sites which contain a certain base, or DNA is synthesized in the presence of modified bases that cause termination of synthesis after the incorporation of a certain base. These methods can now be automated so that it is practical to determine the DNA sequences of the entire genome of an organism. Currently, the complete sequences of several bacterial and fungal genomes are known, drafts exist for the complete mouse and rat genomes, and 99% of the gene-containing part of the human sequence has been determined. *See* HUMAN GENOME PROJECT.   [M.C.Wo.]

In the cell. The full genome of DNA must be substantially compacted to fit into a cell. For example, the full human genome has a total length of about 3 m (10 ft). This DNA must fit into a nucleus with a diameter of 10^{-5} m. This immense reduction in length is accomplished in eukaryotes via multiple levels of compaction in a nucleoprotein structure termed chromatin. The first level involves spooling about 200 base pairs of DNA onto a complex of basic proteins called histones to form a nucleosome. Nucleosomes are connected like beads on a string (Fig. 3) to form a 10-nanometer diameter fiber, and this is further coiled to form a 30-nm fiber. The 30-nm fibers are further coiled and organized into loops formed by periodic attachments to a protein scaffold. This

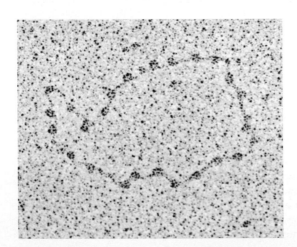

Fig. 3. Electron micrograph of the minichromosome of a virus that infects monkey cells. The circular viral DNA can be seen to be organized in nucleosome "beads." (*From L. Lutter et al., Mol. Cell. Biol., 12:5004–5014, 1992*)

scaffold organizes the complex into the shape of the metaphase chromosome seen at mitosis. *See* NUCLEOPROTEIN.

The nucleosome is the fundamental structural unit of DNA in all eukaryotes. Nucleosomes reduce the accessibility of the DNA to DNA-binding proteins such as polymerases and other protein factors essential for transcription and replication. Consequently, nucleosomes tend to act as general repressors of transcription. *See* NUCLEOSOME.   [L.C.L.]

Deoxyribose   A nucleic acid constituent (see illustration) of all animal, microbial, and plant cells; also known as 2-D-deoxyribose. Deoxyribose is enzymically formed in living cells by reduction of ribonucleoside di- or triphosphate. The four deoxyribose

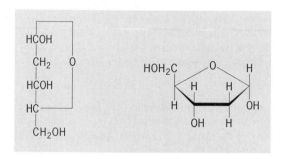

Formulas of 2-D-deoxyribose (α-D-2-deoxyribofuranose).

nucleotides, containing adenine, guanine, cytosine, and thymine, are the major constituents of the deoxyribonucleic acids (DNA), which control the hereditary characteristics of every living organism. *See* DEOXYRIBONUCLEIC ACID (DNA); NUCLEIC ACID; RIBOSE.
[W.Z.H.]

Desert   No precise definition of a desert exists. From an ecological viewpoint the scarcity of rainfall is all important, as it directly affects plant productivity which in turn affects the abundance, diversity, and activity of animals. It has become customary to describe deserts as extremely arid where the mean precipitation is less than 2.5–4 in. (60–100 mm), arid where it is 2.5–4 to 6–10 in. (60–100 to 150–250 mm), and semiarid where it is 6–10 to 10–20 in. (150–250 to 250–500 mm). However, mean figures tend to distort the true state of affairs because precipitation in deserts is unreliable and variable. In some areas, such as the Atacama in Chile and the Arabian Desert, there may be no rainfall for several years. It is the biological effectiveness of rainfall that matters and this may vary with wind and temperature, which affect evaporation rates. The vegetation cover also alters the evaporation rate and increases the effectiveness of rainfall. Rainfall, then, is the chief limiting factor to biological processes, but intense solar radiation, high temperatures, and a paucity of nutrients (especially of nitrogen) may also limit plant productivity, and hence animal abundance. Of the main desert regions of the world, most lie within the tropics and hence are hot as well as arid. The Namib and Atacama coastal deserts are kept cool by the Benguela and Humboldt ocean currents, and many desert areas of central Asia are cool because of high latitude and altitude.

The diversity of species of animals in a desert is generally correlated with the diversity of plant species, which to a considerable degree is correlated with the predictability and amount of rainfall. There is a rather weak latitudinal gradient of diversity with relatively more species nearer the Equator than at higher latitudes. This gradient is much more conspicuous in wetter ecosystems, such as forests, and in deserts appears to be overridden by the manifold effects of rainfall. Animals, too, may affect plant diversity: the burrowing activities of rodents create niches for plants which could not otherwise survive, and mound-building termites tend to concentrate decomposition and hence nutrients, which provide opportunities for plants to colonize.

Each desert has its own community of species, and these communities are repeated in different parts of the world. Very often the organisms that occupy similar niches in different deserts belong to unrelated taxa. The overall structural similarity between American cactus species and African euphorbias is an example of convergent evolution, in which separate and unrelated groups have evolved almost identical adaptations under similar environmental conditions in widely separated parts of the world. Convergent structural modification occurs in many organisms in all environments, but is especially noticeable in deserts where possibly the small number of ecological niches has necessitated greater specialization and restriction of way of life. The face and especially the large ears of desert foxes of the Sahara and of North America are remarkably similar, and there is an extraordinary resemblance between North American sidewinding rattlesnakes and Namib sidewinding adders. *See* ECOLOGY; PHYSIOLOGICAL ECOLOGY (PLANT).   [D.F.Ow.]

Deuteromycotina   A heterogeneous group of anamorphic (asexual or imperfect) fungi in which sporulation may occur on separate hyphae or composite fruit bodies (conidiomata). The diagnostic feature of the group is the lack of a teleomorphic (sexual or perfect) state. There are more than 2500 accepted genera containing 21,000 species.

Traditionally, Deuteromycotina are separated into two classes: Hyphomycetes, which are mycelial forms bearing conidia on separate hyphae or aggregations of hyphae; and Coelomycetes, which are forms that produce conidia in pycnidial, pycnothyrial, acervular, cupulate, or stromatic conidiomata. A third class is sometimes recognized, the Agonomycetes (Mycelia Sterilia); these fail to produce conidia and thus lack conidiomata, although they do form somatic survival propagules. Currently, no ranks are distinguished within the Deuteromycotina, and the subdivisional name itself is no longer in use, the preferred term being Mitotic Fungi or Fungi Anamorphici. *See* AGONOMYCETES; COELOMYCETES; HYPHOMYCETES.

Deuteromycetes are ubiquitous and occupy most conceivable ecological niches. Deuteromycetes such as *Penicillium*, *Aspergillus*, and *Saccharomyces* have been used extensively in manufacturing processes of different kinds. Increasingly important is the use of deuteromycetes in biological control of insects, nematodes, pathogenic fungi, and weeds.

Fungal infections (mycoses) are almost always the result of abnormal host immunity. Even before the association of the human immunodeficiency virus (HIV) with acquired immunedeficiency syndrome (AIDS), criteria used in defining the syndrome relied heavily on the existence of certain opportunistic infections in the absence of any of the established predisposing conditions. A significant number of these deep-seated infections are caused by deuteromycetes such as *Aspergillus, Candida, Cryptococcus*, and *Histoplasma*. *See* ACQUIRED IMMUNE DEFICIENCY SYNDROME (AIDS); MEDICAL MYCOLOGY; MYCOTOXIN; OPPORTUNISTIC INFECTIONS.   [B.C.S.]

Developmental biology   A large field of investigation that includes the study of all changes associated with an organism as it progresses through the life cycle. The life cycles of all multicellular organisms exhibit many similarities. That is, as an organism progresses from one generation to the next there is a series of common processes: for example, gametogenesis, fertilization, embryogenesis, cell differentiation, tissue differentiation, organogenesis, maturation, growth, reproduction, senescence, and death.   [D.Ru.]

Analysis of all of the events associated with an organism as it progresses through its life cycle employs a multiplicity of approaches. Tremendous strides have been made in describing at the molecular level the developmental process of cell differentiation. However, the molecular control mechanisms which regulate cell differentiation are not known. Tissue and organ differentiation, as well as morphogenesis, are processes which have been described in detail for many situations, but little is known about the physical and chemical nature of the mechanisms involved. A complete understanding of the development of an organism will require an appreciation and comprehension of the changes which occur at all levels of organization as an organism traverses its life cycle.

The major unifying theme in biology is evolution. Not only has evolution led to the wide variety of organisms now present on Earth, but also evolution has modified the initial processes and patterns of development to the diversity of types currently encountered. This evolution of developmental parameters in multicellular organisms began as single-celled organisms became multicellular. The development of a multicellular organism entails a host of problems not faced by a single-celled organism. For example, cells in one part of the aggregate must coordinate their activities with cells in other parts, nutrients and oxygen must be provided to all cells, and water balance must be maintained.

Developmental biologists have focused on two central areas: the processes and associated mechanisms by which cells become different, that is, cell differentiation; and the processes and associated mechanisms by which patterns are created, that is, morphogenesis.

Current theories state that cells become different by expressing different genes. Thus, a liver cell is different from a muscle cell, not because it contains different genes or genetic information, but because it expresses different sets of genes. This explanation of cell differences is based upon the results of three types of experimental analysis. (1) Some plant cells are totipotent; that is, for tobacco, carrot, and a few other plant species, it has been demonstrated that a single cell (not a gamete) can divide and undergo morphogenesis to form a fertile plant. (2) Nuclei from some differentiated animal cells are totipotent. That is, a nucleus from a differentiated cell can be injected into a mature egg which has had its nucleus removed or destroyed, and the injected nucleus can direct normal development of the organism. (3) The sequences of nucleotides in the DNA of all cells in an organism appear to be the same; that is, DNA-DNA hybridization of DNA from different cell types indicates that the different cell types do not have unique DNA base sequences. Since these results indicate that all cells contain the complete genome for an organism, different cell types appear to arise as a result of the expression of unique sets of genes in each cell type. *See* CELL DIFFERENTIATION; DEVELOPMENTAL GENETICS; GENE ACTION; SOMATIC CELL GENETICS.

Initially the cells of a developing embryo are not restricted in their developmental potential or fate, but as embryogenesis proceeds, a cell's developmental potential becomes restricted or fixed. Restriction of developmental fate is called determination. Two mechanisms have been identified that bring about determination. The first involves the presence of unique factors, called cytoplasmic determinants, which are products of the maternal genome and are located in specific areas of some animal eggs. The cells which come to contain these determinants differentiate along specific pathways. The second mechanism is induction, a process by which two tissues interact so that one or both differentiate along specific pathways. A classic example of induction is the action of mesoderm on the overlaying ectoderm in the frog embryo at the time of gastrulation. The mesoderm acts on the ectoderm, causing it to form the neural plate. Only ectoderm of a certain developmental age is capable of responding to the mesoderm, and this ectoderm is said to be competent. *See* EMBRYONIC INDUCTION.

Developmental biologists have gained substantial insights into the molecular bases for determination in model organisms such as *Drosophila*. At least three sets of cytoplasmic determinants (maternal gene products) are present in the fly egg: determinants for germ-cell formation, determinants controlling dorsal-ventral polarity, and determinants for the anterior-posterior polarity. Some of these determinants are messenger ribonucleic acids (mRNAs) coding for proteins which are transcriptional regulators (that is, proteins that regulate gene activity).

Morphogenesis involves the production of form and structure by integrating the differentiation of many different cells and cell types into specific spatial patterns. This higher level of organization has been difficult to investigate in terms of establishing mechanisms. The processes of determination, competence, and induction are involved. One of the greatest challenges faced by developmental biologists is to bridge the gap between genes and patterns. It is clear that patterns are a result of gene activity, but the relationship between genes and patterns in most organisms is not well understood. *See* ANIMAL MORPHOGENESIS; PLANT MORPHOGENESIS. [C.N.M.]

Developmental genetics The study of how genes control development. Advances in the field have emphasized the degree of conservation of the genes controlling development throughout evolution. Thus, such distant organisms as insects and vertebrates share a number of very homologous genes controlling early development. For example, homeobox genes (*Hox* genes) are used in both insects and mammals to provide information for anterior-posterior positioning. The conservation of the genes is so great that the human version of a *Hox* gene can sometimes substitute for the mutant *Drosophila* gene and correct abnormalities of early development.

Most genes involved in sex determination have not been conserved, but a gene has been cloned in the nematode *Caenorhabditis elegans* which is highly homologous to a gene involved in the *Drosphila* sex determination cascade and to a gene in mammals whose role in sex determination has yet to be fully elucidated. Another organism which is elucidating these genes and has become of great interest is the zebrafish. Its small size and clear embryo allow easy screening of many developmental mutations, and many of the above-mentioned evolutionary conservations have been confirmed in the zebrafish.

Determination is a stage during the developmental process when genes become committed to a particular expression pattern leading to a differentiated state. At the time of this stage, the differentiated state is not yet visible. This aspect can be confirmed by transplantation of determined but not yet differentiated tissues to ectopic sites and observing the transplant's development. Advances have shown that some cell types are not as highly determined as was previously thought. Brain cells have given rise to blood cells, and bone marrow cells have given rise to bone and muscle. This apparent lack of determination in cells previously believed to be determined suggests greater potential for plasticity and the possibility of manipulating cells to new fates to create organs for human transplantation, for example.

Another area of research has involved maternal inheritance. Many of the genes responsible for the determination of cell fate in *C. elegans* larva are laid down in the egg; that is, they are maternal-effect genes. In this case, it is not the genotype of the zygote which influences development but that of the mother. Thus, homozygosity for a recessive mutation in the mother leads to altered development, even though the sperm is from a homozygous wild-type male and the resulting zygote was heterozygous. The percentage of maternal-effect genes is also high in *Drosophila. See* GENE ACTION.

Another general phenomenon under genetic control during development is induction—the action of one cell or tissue on other cells in order to determine altered gene expression in them.

Homoeotic mutations change one paired structure to another of a more interior or posterior compartment (for example, a leg to an antenna). The study of their structure and function has provided a paradigm for the role of genes in conveying positional information during development. In *Drosophila*, seven homoeotic genes are grouped in two complexes. Their role in establishing segmental identities is well defined, and the DNA sequence of the genes shows a highly conserved element called the homeobox. This conserved sequence is also found in some pair-rule and polarity genes, and the search for genes homologous to these led to the identification of other genes that are highly conserved in animal evolution. Although *Drosophila* uses one set of homeobox genes (separated into two clusters on two different chromosomes), mammals have amplified the set of genes to a minimum of four clusters of the size of the single cluster in *Drosophila*. These genes maintain the same patterns of expression in both mammals and *Drosophila*. They are expressed 5' to 3' in order of transcription, and the 5'-to-3' order in the cluster is also reflected in the posterior-to-anterior limits of expression of the gene products. Most mutations in homeobox genes are recessive, and embryonic stem-cell knockouts have disclosed that, because there is sufficient redundancy in the mammalian homeobox clusters, the homozygous absence of one homeobox gene does not always result in an apparent phenotype. Paired box genes are another highly conserved family of genes, first identified for their important developmental roles in *Drosophila*. Mutations in these genes frequently cause dominantly inherited birth defects in mammals.

Imprinting, a developmentally important phenomenon that was first discovered in insects, is also important for mammalian development and human disease. In imprinting, genes transmitted through the testis sometimes function differently from those transmitted through the ovary. Many portions of the genome have been found to be imprinted, including the reciprocal imprinting of insulinlike growth factor and its receptor. Some major human diseases occur when both a paternal and a maternal copy of a gene are not present. The Prader-Willi syndrome, a disorder of mental retardation, poor appetite regulation, and mild dysmorphic features, is an example. Advances have strongly implicated gametogenesis-specific methylation of key controlling regions in the imprinting process. Such imprints seem to be erased from the migrating germ cells enroute to the developing gonad, and then are established differentially during ovigenesis and spermatogenesis, presumably by proteins uniquely expressed in the two different gonads and with specificity for the particular DNA sequences. The actual expression of imprinting differences frequently involves (1) competition between cis-linked genetic elements and (2) a nontranslated RNA species. *See* DEVELOPMENTAL BIOLOGY; GENETICS.

[R.P.E.]

Developmental psychology The study of age-related changes in behavior from birth to death. Developmental psychologists attempt to determine the causes of such changes. Most research has concentrated on the development of children, but there is increasing interest in the elderly, and to a lesser extent in other age groups. Although most developmental work examines humans, there has been some work on primates and other species that would be considered unethical with human beings. Thus the sensory deprivation of kittens and the separation of monkeys from their mothers have provided information about abnormal perceptual and emotional development, respectively.

Method. Developmental psychologists who study children rely more upon careful observation in natural settings than upon laboratory experiments. Under these circumstances, only partial conclusions can be drawn about the causes of development. The field has been dominated by descriptive research, with increasing attempts to explain developmental phenomena by the use of animal experiments or by statistical methods. In longitudinal research, a group of individuals is studied at regular intervals over a relatively long period of time. This contrasts with cross-sectional research, where individuals of different ages are studied at the same time. Conclusions from the two types of research may differ. Finally, case studies, that is, close and extensive observations of a few subjects, have been relied upon by important developmental theorists such as S. Freud and J. Piaget.

Theories. An explanation of developmental changes requires a judgment as to the relative importance of genetically programmed maturation and environmental influences. Although most developmentalists believe that genetic endowment and environmental experience interact to account for behavior, the degree to which either affects a particular behavior is still often debated. This issue has important implications for the success of environmental intervention in the face of genetic constraints. For example, the influence on children of parental speech versus genetic programming in language acquisition is much debated, as is the origin of gender differences in behavior. *See* BEHAVIOR GENETICS.

Developmental psychology is divided roughly between those who study personal–social (emotional) development and those who study intellectual and linguistic development, although there is a small but growing interest in the overlap between these two aspects of personality, known as social cognition. The study of personal-social development in childhood is dominated by the theory of attachment formulated by J. Bowlby and extended by M. Ainsworth. In adolescence and adulthood, E. Erikson's theory of psychosocial development is prominent. The study of intellectual development at all ages is dominated by Piaget's theory of cognitive constructivism.

Emotional development. Ainsworth defines attachment as "an affectional tie that one person forms to another specific person, binding them together in space, and enduring over time . . . [It] is discriminating and specific." It is not present at birth, but is developed. In a word, attachment means love. Attachment behaviors such as crying, smiling, physical contact, and vocalizing are the means by which attachment is forged but are not to be equated with the more abstract, underlying construct of attachment. Attachment theory is strongly based on ethological notions. Thus, attachment is seen as serving a biological function, that is, the protection of infants by ensuring their proximity to (attached) adults. The common goal of attached individuals is proximity. Bowlby was influenced by Freud's psychoanalytic theory of development, but argues that there is a primary biological need to become attached to at least one adult, whereas Freud argued that love for a mother was secondary to her satisfaction of an infant's hunger.

Intellectual development. For Piaget, intelligence is defined as the ability to adapt to the environment, an ability that depends upon physical and psychological (cognitive) organization. The adaptation process has two complementary components, assimilation and accommodation. Assimilation refers to the tendency to process new information, sometimes with distortion, in terms of existing cognitive structures. Accommodation refers to the opposite process, that is, the modification of existing cognitive structures in response to new information. An individual strives for equilibrium between assimilation and accommodation, with thought being neither unrealistic (excessive assimilation) nor excessively realistic and hence disorganized (excessive accommodation). *See* COGNITION; INTELLIGENCE.

For Piaget, cognition gradually becomes abstracted from perception over the course of 12 years. Infants begin cognitive exploration by actively perceiving and reflexively manipulating objects, giving the name sensorimotor period to the first phase of intellectual development. Perception is a key form of early cognitive activity, especially with newborns. The newborn infant can see, hear, smell, taste, and feel much better than previously thought, though sensitivity in these areas improves throughout the first year of life. Between the ages of 18 and 24 months, infants become capable of symbolic representation, occasionally solving problems just by thinking about them. The major accomplishment of the sensorimotor period is object permanence, the realization that objects continue to exist even when not observable. During the next 5 years, sometimes termed the preoperational period, children work on concrete operations such as classifying objects into categories, arranging things in serial order, figuring out causes and effects, or understanding a one-to-one correspondence of numbers to objects counted. They also eventually manipulate reality enough to overcome perceptual illusions such as that an amount of water changes when it is poured from a short wide glass into a tall narrow glass. From 7 to 11 years, children further consolidate their concrete mental operations. At about 12 years, many adolescents enter the final stage of intellectual development: formal operations. They become capable of abstract, logical thought. They understand reality as a subset of possible worlds, and are able to form multiple, systematic hypotheses, involving all possible combinations of relevant variables, in order to explain things.

Many quarrel with Piaget's age assessments of children, but most people accept his sequence of stages as useful for classifying children.

Moral development. L. Kohlberg's work on moral development spans the chasm between intellectual and emotional development. He studied reasoning about hypothetical moral dilemmas, such as whether a person should steal an unaffordable drug in order to save someone's life. He classified such reasoning in six stages. At birth children are considered to be premoral. By the age of 7, most children are in stage 1, chiefly characterized by the belief that people should act in certain ways in order to avoid physical or other punishment. In 2 or 3 years, children reason primarily in terms of doing things for rewards; this is stage 2. Stage 3 involves reasoning focused less on rewards than on maintaining the approval of others. Stage 4 involves reasoning that unquestioningly accepts conventional rules. Actions are judged by a rigid set of regulations, religious, legal, or both. Most individuals do not develop past this point. A few, however, do reach postconventional moral reasoning, stage 5. These individuals think in terms of moral principles. Rarely, a step higher to stage 6 is reached, governed by original abstract moral principles such as articulaton of the golden rule. Kohlberg argued that moral development is progressive, without regression to earlier stages.

Developmental psychopathology. Traditionally, child clinical psychology (abnormal development) and the study of normal development were separate. However, effort is being made to integrate them. Abnormal development is informative about normal processes. The serious disorders of childhood include autism, attention-deficit disorder with hyperactivity, and depression. Viewed another way, abnormal children are either overcontrolled (obsessive-compulsive) or undercontrolled (impulsive, aggressive). Developmental psychopathologists, however, are interested not just in disordered development in childhood, but in abnormal individuals over their lifetime. Such studies can shed light on the effectiveness of treatments and on the way in which disorders such as hyperactivity may be displayed differently at different ages.   [A.McC.]

Dicotyledons   A large group of flowering plants (angiosperms) that for many years has been considered one of the two main categories of plants, the other being monocotyledons. Dicotyledons have two seedling leaves as opposed to the single one in most monocotyledons. Several deoxyribonucleic acid (DNA) sequence studies subsequently demonstrated that there are two groups of angiosperms, but these correspond not to the number of seed leaves but to the two major pollen types. Thus, the term "dicotyledon" is no longer meaningful because some plants of this type are more closely related to monocotyledons. The group of former dicotyledons, which have pollen with a single aperture, includes magnolia, avocado, black pepper, and pipeworts; they are now termed magnoliids and include monocotyledons. The other category of dicotyledons, those with three (and often more) apertures in their pollen, are called eudicotyledons (true dicotyledons). *See* EUDICOTYLEDONS; FLOWER; MAGNO-LIOPHYTA; MONOCOTYLEDONS; PLANT KINGDOM.   [M.W.C.]

Digestive system   The vertebrate digestive system consists of the digestive tract and ancillary organs that serve for the acquisition of food and assimilation of nutrients required for energy, growth, maintenance, and reproduction. Food is ingested, reduced to particles, mixed with digestive fluids and enzymes, and propelled through the digestive tract. Enzymes produced by the host animal and microbes indigenous to the digestive tract destroy harmful agents and convert food into a limited number of nutrients, which are selectively absorbed. The digestive systems of vertebrates show numerous structural and functional adaptations to their diet, habitat, and other characteristics. Carnivores, which feed exclusively on other animals, and species that feed on plant concentrates (seeds, fruit, nectar, pollen) tend to have the shortest and simplest digestive tract. The digestive tract tends to be more complex in omnivores, which feed on both plants and animals, and most complex in herbivores, which feed principally on the fibrous portions of plants.

Gut structure and function can also vary with the habitat and other physiological characteristics of a species. The digestive tract of fish has adaptations for a marine or fresh-water environment. The basal metabolic rate per gram of body weight increases with a decrease in the body mass. Therefore, small animals must process larger amounts of food per gram of body weight, thus limiting their maximum gut capacity and digesta retention time.

Anatomy. Because of wide species variations, the digestive system of vertebrates is best described in terms of the headgut, foregut, midgut, pancreas, biliary system, and hindgut. The headgut consists of the mouthparts and pharynx, which serve for the procurement and the initial preparation and swallowing of food. The foregut consists of an esophagus for the swallowing of food and, in most species, a stomach that serves for its storage and initial stages of digestion. The esophagus of most vertebrates is lined with a multilayer of cells that are impermeable to absorption. In most birds it contains the crop, an outpocketing of its wall that provides for the temporary storage of food. A stomach is present in all but the cyclostomes and some species of advanced fish and in the larval amphibians. In most vertebrates it consists of a dilated segment of the gut that is separated from the esophagus and midgut by muscular sphincters or valves. This is often referred to as a simple stomach. However, in birds these functions are carried out by the crop (storage), proventriculus (secretion), and gizzard (grinding or mastication). In most vertebrates, a major portion of the stomach is lined with a proper gastric mucosa (epithelium), which secretes mucus, hydrochloric acid (HCl), and pepsinogen. The distal (pyloric) part of the stomach secretes mucus and bicarbonate ions (HCO_3^-), and its muscular contractions help reduce the size of food particles and transfer partially digested food into the midgut. The stomach of reptiles and most mammals has an additional area of cardiac mucosa near its entrance, which also secretes mucus and bicarbonate ions. *See* ESOPHAGUS.

The midgut or small intestine is the principal site for the digestion of food and the absorption of nutrients. It is lined with a single layer of cells that secrete mucus and fluids, contain enzymes that aid in the final stages of carbohydrate and protein digestion, and absorb nutrients from the lumen into the circulatory system. The surface area of the lumen can be increased by a variety of means, such as folds and pyloric ceca (blind sacs) in fish. In higher vertebrates the lumen surface is increased by the presence of villi, which are macroscopic projections of the epithelial and subepithelial tissue.

The lumen surface is also expanded by a brush border of microvilli on the lumen-facing (apical) surface of the midgut absorptive cells in all vertebrates. The brush border membranes contain enzymes that aid in the final digestion of food and mechanisms that provide for the selective absorption of nutrients. The lumenal surface area of the human small intestine is increased 10-fold by the presence of villi and an additional 20-fold by the microvilli, resulting in a total surface area of 310,000 in.^{2} (2,000,000 cm^2).

Digestion in the midgut is aided by secretions of digestive enzymes and fluid by pancreatic tissue, and secretion of bile by the liver. Pancreatic tissue is distributed along the intestinal wall, and even into the liver, of some species of fish. However, the pancreas is a compact organ in sharks, skates, rays, many teleosts, and all other vertebrates. The liver is a compact organ in all vertebrates. One of its many functions is the secretion of bile. In most vertebrates, the bile is stored in the gallbladder and released into the intestine as needed, but a gallbladder is absent in some species of fish and mammals. Bile salts serve to emulsify lipids and increase their surface area available for digestion by the water-soluble lipase. *See* GALLBLADDER; LIVER; PANCREAS.

The hindgut is the final site of digestion and absorption prior to defecation or evacuation of waste products. The hindgut of fish, amphibian larvae, and a few mammals is short and difficult to distinguish from the midgut. However, the hindgut of adult amphibians and reptiles, birds, and most mammals is a distinct segment, which is separated from the midgut by a muscular sphincter or valve. It also tends to be larger in diameter. Thus, the midgut and hindgut of these animals are often referred to as the small intestine and the large intestine. *See* INTESTINE.

The hindgut of some reptiles and many mammals includes a blind sac or cecum near its junction with the midgut. A pair of ceca are present in the hindgut of many birds and a few mammalian species. The remainder of the hindgut consists of the colon and a short, straight, terminal segment, which is called the rectum in mammals. The digestive and urinary tracts exit separately from the body of most species of fish and mammals. However, in adult amphibians and the reptiles, birds, and some mammals, this segment terminates in a chamber called the cloaca, which also serves as an exit for the urinary and reproductive systems. The hindgut or, where present, the cloaca terminates in the anus. *See* COLON; URINARY SYSTEM.

The hindgut is similarly lined with a single layer of absorptive and mucus-secreting cells. However, it lacks villi, and (with the exception of the cecum of birds) its absorptive cells lack digestive enzymes and the ability to absorb most nutrients. One major function of the hindgut is to reabsorb the fluids secreted into the upper digestive tract and (in animals that have a cloaca) excreted in the urine. It also serves as the principal site for the microbial production of nutrients in the herbivorous reptiles and birds and in most herbivorous mammals. Thus, the hindgut tends to be longest in animals that need to conserve water in an arid environment, and has a larger capacity in most herbivores.

Musculature. The digestion of food, absorption of nutrients, and excretion of waste products require the mixing of ingesta with digestive enzymes and the transit of ingesta and digesta through the digestive tract. In all vertebrates other than the cyclostome the contents are mixed and moved by an inner layer of circular muscle and an outer layer of muscle that runs longitudinally along the tract. The initial act of deglutition (swallowing) and the final act by which waste products are defecated from the digestive tract are effected by striated muscle. This type of muscle is characterized by rapid contraction and is controlled by extrinsic nerves. However, the esophagus of amphibians, reptiles, and birds, and the entire gastrointestinal tract of all vertebrates are enveloped by smooth muscle. This smooth muscle contracts more slowly, and its rate of contraction is partly independent of external stimulation. *See* MUSCLE.

Nerve and endocrine tissue. The initial act of deglutition and final act of defecation are under the voluntary control of the central nervous system. However, the remainder of the digestive system is subject to the involuntary control of nerves which release a variety of neurotransmitting or neuromodulating agents that either stimulate or inhibit muscular contractions and the secretions of glands and cells. The motor and secretory activities of the digestive system are also under the control of a wide range of other substances produced by endocrine cells that are released either distant from (hormones) or adjacent to (paracrine agents) their site of action. Although there are some major variations in the complement and activities of the neurotransmitters, neuromodulators, hormones, and paracrine agents, their basic patterns of control are similar.

The anatomy of the human digestive system is similar to that of other mammalian omnivores (see illustration). The teeth and salivary glands are those of a mammalian omnivore, and the initial two-thirds of the esophagus is enveloped by striated muscle. A simple stomach is followed by an intestine, whose length consists of approximately two-thirds small bowel and one-third large bowel. The structures of the pancreas and biliary system show no major differences from those of other mammals. During early fetal development, a distinct, conical cecum is present and continues to grow until the sixth month of gestation. However, unlike other primates, the cecum recedes to become little more than a bulge in the proximal colon by the time of birth. The colon continues to lengthen after the birth and is sacculated throughout its length like that of the apes and a few monkeys but few other mammals.

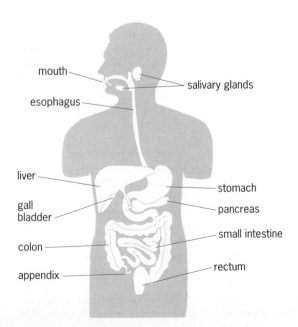

Human digestive system. (*After A. C. Guyton, Textbook of Medical Physiology, 8th ed., Saunders, 1991*)

Physiology. The major physiological activities of the digestive system are motility, secretion, digestion, and absorption. Each activity can be affected by diet and, in the cold-blooded species, is reduced with a decrease in body temperature.

Motility. The mastication of food and the movement of ingesta and digesta through the digestive tract are controlled by the motor activity of muscular contractions. Pressure of food against the palate and back of the mouth stimulates a nerve reflex that passes through a deglutition center in the brain. This reflex closes the entrance into the respiratory system and stops respiration, to prevent the inspiration of food into the lungs, and initiates muscular contractions that pass food into the esophagus. The food (bolus) is then passed down the esophagus and into the stomach by a moving wave of muscular contractions (peristalsis) accompanied by inhibition of the esophageal sphincters. The multicompartmental forestomach of ruminants undergoes a continuous series of complex, repetitive contractions that are controlled by the central nervous system. However, the gastric motility of most species and the intestinal motility of all vertebrates are controlled partially by the intrinsic characteristics of their smooth muscle cells. The result is production of either stationary (mixing) contractions of the stomach and intestine or a series of peristaltic contractions that carry digesta on through the tract.

Digestion. Digestion is accomplished by enzymes produced by the digestive system (endogenous enzymes) or by bacteria that are normal residents of the digestive tract. Plant and animal starches are converted to oligosaccharides (short-chain structures) and disaccharides by amylase, which is secreted by the salivary glands of some species and the pancreas of all vertebrates. The end products of starch digestion, plus the dietary disaccharides, are converted to monosaccharides by enzymes in the brush border of the absorptive epithelial cells lining the small intestine. Vertebrates do not produce enzymes capable of digesting the structural polysaccharides of plants.

Lipids are digested into alcohols, monoglycerides, and fatty acids by lipases and esterases, which are secreted predominantly by the pancreas. However, the lipases are water-soluble enzymes that can attack their substrate only at a lipid-water interface. Therefore, the lipids must be emulsified in order to provide the surface area required for efficient digestion. Emulsification is accomplished by the release of bile salts secreted by the liver and released into the midgut.

Dietary protein is first broken down into long chains of amino acids (polypeptides) by gastric pepsin and pancreatic trypsin. The polypeptides are then attacked by other pancreatic proteases (chymotrypsin, carboxypeptidase, elastase) to form tripeptides, dipeptides, and amino acids. All of these enzymes are secreted in an inactive form to prevent the self-digestion of the secretory cells prior to their release. Pepsin is activated by the acidity resulting from the secretion of hydrochloric acid (HCl) into the stomach, and trypsin is activated by an enzyme (enterokinase) that is secreted by intestinal epithelium. Tri- and dipeptides are digested into amino acids by enzymes in the brush border and contents of midgut absorptive cells. Nucleic acids are digested by pancreatic ribonucleases into pentose sugars, purines, and pyrimidines.

Substantial numbers of bacteria can be found in all segments of the gastrointestinal tract, but the highest numbers are present in those segments in which digesta are retained for prolonged periods of time at a relatively neutral pH. Indigenous bacteria help protect the animal from pathogenic microorganisms by stimulating immunity and competing for substrates. They also convert dietary and endogenous substances that are not digested by endogenous enzymes into absorbable nutrients. Many species of indigenous bacteria can ferment sugars, starches, and structural carbohydrates into short-chain fatty acids. The short-chain fatty acids, which are predominantly acetic, propionic, and butyric acids, are readily absorbed and serve as an additional source of energy. These bacteria also synthesize microbial protein and the B-complex vitamins that may be useful to their host. The contributions of indigenous bacteria to the production and conservation of nutrients are greatest in herbivores. Although it has been estimated that short-chain fatty acid absorption provides 4% of total maintenance energy requirement by dogs and 6–10% of the maintenance energy required by humans, they can account for 30% of the maintenance energy of rabbits and up to 70% of maintenance energy of horses and ruminants. *See* BACTERIAL PHYSIOLOGY AND METABOLISM.

Absorption. The epithelial cells that line the gastrointestinal tract are closely attached to one another at their lumen-facing border by tight junctions, which are relatively impermeable to most substances other than water. Therefore, the major restriction for the absorption of most substances from the lumen into the blood is the apical and basolateral membranes of these cells. Lipid-soluble substances can be transported across the apical cell membranes by passive diffusion down their concentration gradient. The short- and medium-chain fatty acids that result from lipid digestion in the small intestine pass directly into the blood. However, the monoglycerides and long-chain fatty acids are resynthesized into triglycerides by the epithelial cells in the midgut and incorporated into small spheres (chylomicrons), which are transported across the basolateral membrane into the lymphatic system. Fat-soluble vitamins, long-chain alcohols, and other lipids also appear to be incorporated into chylomicrons and to enter the lymphatic system.

The intestinal cell membranes are relatively impermeable to the passive diffusion of water-soluble monosaccharides, amino acids, vitamins, and minerals that constitute a major portion of the required nutrients. These nutrients are selectively transferred across the intestinal cell membranes by carrier-mediated transport. Membrane carriers combine with the nutrient at one membrane surface and pass it across the membrane for release at the opposing surface. Some simply facilitate the diffusion of a substance down its concentration gradient; others are capable of transporting a nutrient against its concentration gradient, which requires either a direct or indirect investment of cellular energy. *See* CELL MEMBRANES.

The metabolic processes of the body require a number of different minerals. Some such as iron, calcium, sodium, and chloride are required in relatively large quantities. Others such as manganese and zinc are labeled trace minerals because they are required in only minute amounts.

The nutrient that is required in largest quantity for digestion, absorption, metabolism, and excretion of waste products is water. Because it readily diffuses across cell membranes down its concentration gradient, the net secretion or absorption of water is determined by the net secretion or absorption of all other substances. Sodium, chloride, and bicarbonate are the principal ions that are present in the extracellular fluids that bathe the body cells of all vertebrates and that are transported across cell membranes. Therefore, the transport of these electrolytes is the major driving force for the secretion or absorption of water.   [C.E.St.]

Diphtheria   An acute infectious disease of humans caused by *Corynebacterium diphtheriae*. Classically, the disease is characterized by low-grade fever, sore throat, and a pseudomembrane covering the tonsils and pharynx. Complications such as inflammation of the heart, paralysis, and even death may occur due to exotoxins elaborated by toxigenic strains of the bacteria. The upper respiratory tract is the most common portal of entry for *C. diphtheriae*. It can also invade the skin and, more rarely, the genitalia, eye, or middle ear. The disease has an insidious onset after a usual incubation period of 2–5 days.

The only specific therapy is diphtheria antitoxin, administered in doses proportional to the severity of the disease. Antitoxin is produced by hyperimmunizing horses with diphtheria toxoid and toxin. It is effective only if administered prior to the binding of circulating toxin to target cells. Antibiotics do not alter the course, the incidence of complications, or the outcome of diphtheria, but are used to eliminate the organism from the patient.

Persons with protective antitoxin titers may become infected with diphtheria but do not develop severe disease. Since the 1920s, active immunization with diphtheria toxoid has proved safe and effective in preventing diphtheria in many countries. Diphtheria toxoid is produced by incubating the toxin with formalin. Active immunization requires a primary series of four doses, usually at 2, 4, 6, and 18 months of age, followed by a booster at school entry. *See* Immunity; Medical bacteriology; Toxin; Vaccination.

[R.Ch.; C.V.]

Dipnoi   The lungfishes, one of the three subclasses of Osteichthyes. In comparison with Devonian lungfishes, extant species have reduced the number of median fins, changed the shape of the tail, and decreased ossification of the braincase and other endochondral bones.

The recent family Lepidosirenidae includes five species from Africa and South America. Lepidosirenids have eellike bodies, filamentous paired fins, two lungs, tooth plates with three cutting blades, a greatly reduced skull roof, and an elongated ceratohyal important in suction feeding and respiration. Lepidosirenids are obligate air breathers, and the heart, arterial tree, and gills are highly specialized. To breathe air, the fish protrudes its snout from the water surface, gulps air into the mouth, and then forces it into the lung by closing the mouth and raising the floor of the oral cavity.

The family Ceratodontidae is represented by the single species *Neoceratodus forsteri* from Australia. They are stout-bodied with large scales, leaf-shaped paired fins, and tooth plates with flattened crushing surfaces. Adults reach more than 3 ft (1 m) in length. The diet includes plants, crustaceans, and soft-bodied invertebrates.   [W.Be.]

Early dipnoans were marine; fresh-water adaptations occur in Paleozoic and most post-Paleozoic dipnoans. Burrowing habits developed independently in late Paleozoic gnathorhizids and extant lepidosirenids. Dipnoans were common worldwide from the Early Devonian to the end of the Triassic, but are rare since. They are restricted to the southern continents in the Cenozoic.   [H.P.S.]

Disease ecology   The interaction of the behavior and ecology of hosts with the biology of pathogens, as it relates to the impact of diseases on populations.

Threshold theorem. For a disease to spread, on average it must be successfully transmitted to a new host before its current host dies or recovers. This observation lies at the core of the most important idea in epidemiology: the threshold theorem. The threshold theorem states that if the density of susceptible hosts is below some critical value, then on average the transmission of a disease will not occur rapidly enough to cause the number of infected individuals to increase. In other words, the reproductive rate of a disease must be greater than 1 for there to be an epidemic, with the reproductive rate being defined as the average number of new infections created per infected individual. Human immunization programs are based on applying the threshold theorem of epidemiology to public health; specifically, if enough individuals in a population can be vaccinated, then the density of susceptible individuals will be sufficiently lowered that epidemics are prevented. *See* Epidemiology; Vaccination.

In general, the rate of reproduction for diseases is proportional to their transmissibility and to the length of time that an individual is infectious. For this reason, extremely deadly diseases that kill their hosts too rapidly may require extremely high densities of hosts before they can spread. All diseases do not behave as simply as hypothesized by the threshold theorem, the most notable exceptions being sexually transmitted diseases. Because organisms actively seek reproduction, the rate at which a sexually transmitted disease is passed among hosts is generally much less dependent on host density.

Population effects. Cycles in many animal populations are thought to be driven by diseases. For example, the fluctuations of larch bud moths in Europe are hypothesized to be driven by a virus that infects and kills the caterpillars of this species. Cycles of red grouse in northern England are also thought to be driven by disease, in this case by parasitic nematodes. It is only when grouse are laden with heavy worm burdens that effects are seen, and those effects take the form of reduced breeding success or higher mortality during the winter. This example highlights a common feature of diseases: their effects may be obvious only when their hosts are assaulted by other stresses as well (such as harsh winters and starvation).

The introduction of novel diseases to wild populations has created massive disruptions of natural ecosystems. For example, the introduction of rinderpest virus into African buffalo and wildebeest populations decimated them in the Serengeti. African wild ungulates have recovered in recent years only because a massive vaccination program eliminated rinderpest from the primary reservoir for the disease, domestic cattle. But the consequences of the rinderpest epidemic among wild ungulates extended well beyond the ungulate populations. For example, human sleeping sickness increased following the rinderpest epidemic because the tsetse flies that transmit sleeping sickness suffered a shortage of game animals (the normal hosts for tsetse flies) and increasingly switched to humans to obtain meals.

It is widely appreciated that crop plants are attacked by a tremendous diversity of diseases, some of which may ruin an entire year's production. Diseases are equally prevalent among wild populations of plants, but their toll seems to be reduced because natural plant populations are so genetically variable that it is unlikely that any given pathogen strain can sweep through and kill all of the plants—there are always some resistant genotypes. But when agronomists have bred plants for uniformity, they have often depleted genetic diversity and created a situation in which a plant pathogen that evolves to attack the crop encounters plants with no resistance (all the plants are the same). For example, when leaf blight devastated the United States corn crop, 70% of that crop shared genetically identical cytoplasm, and the genetic uniformity of the host exacerbated the severity of the epidemic. *See* PLANT PATHOLOGY.

Disease emergence. Humans are dramatically altering habitats and ecosystems. Sometimes these changes can influence disease interactions in surprising ways. Lyme disease in the eastern United States provides a good example of the interplay of human habitat modifications and diseases. Lyme disease involves a spirochete bacterium transmitted to humans by ticks. However, humans are not the normal hosts for this disease; instead, both the ticks and the bacterium are maintained primarily on deer and mouse populations. Human activities influence both deer and mice populations, and in turn tick populations, affecting potential exposure of humans to the disease. Much less certain are the impacts of anticipated global warming on diseases. There is some cause for concern about the expansion of tropical diseases into what are now temperate regions in those cases where temperature sets limits to the activity or distribution of major disease vectors. *See* LYME DISEASE; POPULATION ECOLOGY.   [P.Ka.]

Dominance   The expression of a trait in both the homozygous and the heterozygous condition. In experiments with the garden pea, the Austrian botanist

Gregor Mendel crossed plants from true-breeding strains containing contrasting sets of characters. For seed shape, round and wrinkled strains were used. When plants with round seeds were crossed to plants with wrinkled seeds (P_1 generation), all offspring had round seeds. When the offspring (F_1 generation) were self-crossed, 5474 of the resulting F_2 offspring were round and 1850 were wrinkled. Thus, the round trait is expressed in both the F_1 and F_2 generations, while the wrinkled trait is not expressed in the F_1 but is reexpressed in the F_2 in about one-fourth of the offspring. In reporting these results in a paper published in 1866, Mendel called the trait which is expressed in the F_1 generation a dominant trait, while the trait which is unexpressed in the F_1 but reappears in the F_2 generation was called a recessive trait. See MENDELISM.

Traits such as round or wrinkled are visible expressions of genes. This visible expression of a gene is known as the phenotype, while the genetic constitution of an individual is known as its genotype. The alternate forms of a single gene such as round or wrinkled seed shape are known as alleles. In the P_1 round plants, both alleles are identical (since the plant is true-breeding), and the individual is said to be homozygous for this trait. The F_1 round plants are not true-breeding, since they give rise to both round and wrinkled offspring, and are said to be heterozygous. In this case, then, the round allele is dominant to the wrinkled, since it is expressed in both the homozygous and heterozygous condition. Dominance is not an inherent property of a gene or an allele, but instead is a term used to describe the relationship between phenotype and genotype. See ALLELE; GENE ACTION.

The production of phenotypes which are intermediate between those of the parents is an example of partial or incomplete dominance. The phenomenon of incomplete dominance which results in a clear-cut intermediate phenotype is relatively rare. However, even in cases where dominance appears to be complete, there is often evidence for intermediate gene expression.

The separate and distinct expression of both alleles of a gene is an example of codominance. This is a situation unlike that of incomplete dominance or complete dominance. In humans, the MN blood group is characterized by the presence of molecules called glycoproteins on the surface of red blood cells. These molecules or antigens contribute to the immunological identity of an individual. In the MN blood system, persons belong to blood groups M, MN, or N. These phenotypes are produced by two alleles, M and N, each of which controls the synthesis of a variant glycoprotein. In the heterozygote MN, there is separate and complete expression of each allele. This is in contrast to incomplete dominance, where there is an intermediate or blending effect in heterozygotes. Codominance usually results in the production of gene products of both alleles. See BLOOD GROUPS.

Individuals in which the phenotype of the heterozygote is more extreme than in either of the parents are said to exhibit overdominance. The concept of overdominance is important in understanding the genetic structure of populations and is usually related to characteristics associated with fitness, such as size and viability.

The production of superior hybrid offspring by crossing two different strains of an organism is known as heterosis. The hybrid superiority may take the form of increased resistance to disease or greater yield in grain production. The mechanism which results in heterosis has been widely debated but is still unknown. See BREEDING (PLANT); HETEROSIS.

A physiological explanation of dominance was put forward by S. Wright in 1934. He argued that variations in metabolic activity brought about by the heterozygous condition are likely to have little effect on the phenotype because enzymes are linked together in pathways so that the substrate of one enzyme is the product of another. Recessive mutations, when homozygous, may halt the activity of one enzyme and thus bring the entire pathway to a halt, producing a mutant phenotype. Heterozygotes, on the other hand, are likely to have only a reduction in activity of one enzyme which will be averaged out over the entire metabolic pathway, producing little phenotypic effect. Molecular studies of dominance have extended Wright's ideas by exploring the kinetic structure of metabolic pathways and enzyme systems. The results obtained thus far tend to support the thrust of his hypothesis, and have established that the dominant phenotype seen in heterozygotes for a recessive allele can be explained without the need to invoke the existence of modifiers. *See* GENETICS; MOLECULAR BIOLOGY; MUTATION.

[M.R.C.]

Dopamine A catecholamine neurotransmitter that is synthesized by certain neurons in the brain and interacts with specific receptor sites on target neurons.

Dopamine is manufactured inside dopamine neurons in a controlled manner from the amino acid precursor L-tyrosine, which mammals obtain through the normal diet. Dopamine is then stored in vesicles within the nerve terminals, which may fuse with the cell membrane to release dopamine into the synapse.

The release of neurotransmitter is controlled by a variety of factors, including the firing rate of the dopamine nerve cell (termed impulse-dependent release) and the release- and synthesis-modulating presynaptic dopamine receptors located on the dopamine nerve terminals. Since presynaptic dopamine receptors are sensitive to the cell's own neurotransmitter, they are called dopamine autoreceptors. Once released, dopamine also acts at postsynaptic receptors to influence behavior. The actions of dopamine in the synapse are terminated primarily by the reuptake of neurotransmitter into the presynaptic terminal by means of an active dopamine transporter. Dopamine may then be either repackaged into synaptic vesicles for rerelease or degraded by the enzyme monoamine oxidase. The dopamine transporter is an important site of action of the drugs cocaine and amphetamine. *See* SYNAPTIC TRANSMISSION.

Although it was first thought that dopamine occurred only as an intermediate product formed in the biosynthesis of two other catecholamine neurotransmitters, norepinephrine and epinephrine, dopamine is now recognized as a neurotransmitter in its own right. Several distinct dopamine neuronal systems have been identified in the brain. These include systems within the hypothalamus and the pituitary gland; systems within the midbrain that project to a variety of cortical and limbic regions and basal ganglia; the retinal system; and the olfactory system. *See* BRAIN; EPINEPHRINE; NORADRENERGIC SYSTEM.

The midbrain dopamine neurons which project to a variety of forebrain structures are critically involved in normal behavioral attention and arousal; abnormalities in the normal functioning of these systems have been implicated in a variety of disorders. For example, Parkinson's disease involves a degeneration of the midbrain dopamine neurons. This condition is often successfully treated by providing affected individuals with L-dopa, which is readily converted to dopamine in the brain. Attention deficit disorder, which is usually first diagnosed in childhood, is thought to involve dopamine systems, because the treatment of choice, methylphenidate, binds to the dopamine transporter and alters dopamine levels in the synapse. *See* PARKINSON'S DISEASE.

Drugs used to treat the major symptoms of schizophrenia are potent dopamine receptor antagonists. It is possible that certain schizophrenias are the result of increased activity in dopamine neuronal systems, but this has not as yet been conclusively demonstrated. A similar involvement of midbrain dopamine systems has been implicated in the multiple tic disorder Tourette's syndrome, which is treated, often successfully, with dopamine receptor antagonists. *See* NEUROBIOLOGY; SCHIZOPHRENIA.   [L.A.C.]

Dormancy   In the broadest sense, the state in which a living plant organ (seed, bud, tuber, bulb) fails to exhibit growth, even when environmental conditions are considered favorable. In a stricter context, dormancy pertains to a condition where the inhibition of growth is internally controlled by factors restricting water and nutrient absorption, gas exchange, cell division, and other metabolic processes necessary for growth. By utilizing the latter definition, dormancy can be distinguished from other terms such as rest and quiescence which reflect states of inhibited development due to an unfavorable environment.

Physically induced dormancy can be separated into two distinct classes, based on external conditions imposed by the environment (light, temperature, photoperiod) and restraints induced by structural morphology (seed-coat composition and embryo development).

The physical environment plays a key role in dormancy induction, maintenance, and release in several plant species.

1. *Temperature*. The onset of dormancy in many temperate-zone woody species coincides with decreasing temperature in the fall. However, it is the chilling temperature of the oncoming winter which is more crucial, particularly in regard to spring budbreak.

2. *Light duration and quality*. Possibly the single most important environmental variable affecting dormancy is day length or photoperiod. *See* PHOTOPERIODISM.

3. *Water and nutrient status*. Dormancy is affected by the availability of water and nutrients as demonstrated by many grasses, desert species, and subtropical fruits which go into dormancy when confronted by drought or lack of soil fertility. *See* PLANT MINERAL NUTRITION; PLANT-WATER RELATIONS.

4. *Environmental interactions*. Several of the factors previously discussed do not simply act independently, but combine to influence dormancy.

Examples of dormancy imposed by physical restrictions are most evident in the structural morphology of dormant seeds. These restrictions specifically pertain to the physical properties of the seed coat and developmental status of the embryo.

1. *Seed-coat factors*. The seed-coat material surrounding embryos of many plants consists of several layers of tissue, termed integuments, which are infiltrated with waxes and oils. In effect these waterproofing agents enable the seed coat to inhibit water absorption by the embryo. This results in a type of seed dormancy very characteristic of legume crops (clover and alfalfa). The environment itself can break this type of seed-coat dormancy through alternating temperature extremes of freezing and thawing. The extreme heat induced by forest fires is especially effective.

Seed-coat-induced dormancy can also result from mechanical resistance due to extremely hard, rigid integuments commonly found in conifer seeds and other tree species with hard nuts.

2. *Embryonic factors*. The morphological state of the embryo is yet another physical factor affecting dormancy. Often the embryo is in a rudimentary stage when the seed is shed from the maternal plant; dormancy will usually cease in these plants as the embryos reach an adequate state of maturation.

Studies dealing with dormancy have resulted in searches for endogenous plant hormones which regulate the process. Studies involving dormant buds of ash (*Fraxinus americana*) and birch (*Betula pubescens*) revealed the presence of high concentrations of a growth inhibitor or dormancy-inducing and -maintaining compound. This compound was later identified as abscisic acid. As buds of these trees began to grow and elongate, the levels of abscisic acid fell appreciably, supporting the role for abscisic acid in the regulation of dormancy. Abscisic acid is also important in the regulation of seed dormancy, as exemplified by seeds of ash in which abscisic acid levels are high during the phase of growth inhibition, but then decline rapidly during stratification, resulting in germination.

In conjunction with decreased levels of abscisic acid, the endogenous supply of many growth promoters, such as gibberellins, cytokinins, and auxins, have been reported to rise during budbreak in sycamore (*Acer pseudoplatanus*) as well as in Douglas fir (*Pseudotsuga menziesii*). Levels of these dormancy-releasing compounds also correlate well with the breaking of seed dormancy. The hormonal regulation of dormancy can best be perceived as a balance between dormancy inducers or maintainers and dormancy-releasing agents. *See* AUXIN; PLANT HORMONES.

In addition to endogenous hormones, there are a variety of compounds that can break dormancy in plant species when they are applied exogenously. Many of these substances are synthetic derivatives or analogs of naturally occurring, dormancy-releasing agents.

The physical environment exerts a marked influence on dormancy. The plant, however, needs a receptor system to perceive changes in the environment so it can translate them into physiological responses which in most cases are under hormonal control. In the case of changing day length or photoperiod, phytochrome may serve as a receptor pigment. Phytochrome essentially favors the production of either abscisic acid (short days) or gibberellic acid (long days). Stress conditions, such as limited water or nutrient availability, favor the production of abscisic acid, whereas a period of chilling often promotes synthesis of gibberellic acid and other compounds generally considered as growth promoters. *See* PHYTOCHROME.

The mode of action of endogenous growth regulators can only be postulated at this time. Whatever the specific mechanism, it probably involves the regulation of gene action at the level of deoxyribonucleic acid (DNA) and ribonucleic acid (RNA), which subsequently controls protein synthesis. In this framework, abscisic acid is believed to repress the functioning of nucleic acids responsible for triggering enzyme and protein synthesis needed for growth. Gibberellic acid, on the other hand, promotes synthesis of enzymes essential for germination as in the case of α-amylase production that is crucial for barley seed growth. *See* BUD; NUCLEIC ACID; PLANT GROWTH; SEED.   [C.S.M.]

Down syndrome   A developmental disability due to abnormal chromosome number or structure. It is characterized by physical and behavioral features and has been considered the most common form of genetic aberration. Incidence among the newborn is estimated at 3 in 1000, in the general population approximately 1 in 1000. The difference reflects the early mortality.

The most common type (trisomy 21) is due to a nondisjunction of chromosome 21 during the original cell division, resulting in an extra chromosome 21. These children have a total of 47 chromosomes instead of the usual 46. However, the extra material from chromosome 21 can also be attached to another chromosome through translocation; such children have Down syndrome but only 46 chromosomes. More rarely, the trisomy 21 breaks up, giving some cells with 47 chromosomes and some with 46 (mosaicism).

The characteristic physical features include almond-shaped eyes; a rounded, brachycephalic skull with flattened occipital region; a broad, flattened bridge of the nose; an enlarged fissured tongue; broad hands with stubby fingers; often a single "simian" palmar crease; hypotonic muscle development; thick, everted, and cracked lips; dry, rough skin; subnormal height; and infantile genitalia. Not all of these physical signs are present in every case, and some may be observed in individuals without Down syndrome. However, Down syndrome is diagnosed when most of the anomalies are present.

The degree of mental defect is not directly related to the number or gravity of the physical signs, but rather to a combination of those anomalies and the specific chromosomal defect. Few children with Down syndrome are classified today as severely retarded. Most are moderately to mildly retarded and are often educable and highly trainable. They tend to be curious, observant, skillful at mimicry, and usually, very affectionate. Aggression and hostility are rare; however, they are often stubborn and compulsive and are not easily frustrated. They are excellent candidates for vocational training.

Pathological research suggests nonspecific, generalized defective brain development. There is a tendency toward thyroid dysfunction and congenital heart defects. There may also be vision problems, but below-average dental caries. Medication has little effect on the physical condition or on the mental retardation. See ALZHEIMER'S DISEASE; CONGENITAL ANOMALIES.

Although there are some reports of more than one child with Down syndrome in a single family, it is not a classical hereditary disease. Incidence is increased if the mother is under 16 or over 35 years old or the father is of advanced age. Furthermore, the Down syndrome child may result from a late or problem pregnancy or the last of numerous pregnancies. Thyroid deficiency, hypopituitarism, and pathology of the ovary have been observed in the mothers, and the probability of upset in their endocrine balance may increase with age. However, the basic etiology is still very much in doubt.

Prenatal identification of Down syndrome in the fetus is possible through amniocentesis. See HUMAN GENETICS; MENTAL RETARDATION.   [H.Le.]

Drug resistance   The ability of an organism to resist the action of an inhibitory molecule or compound. Examples of drug resistance include disease-causing bacteria evading the activity of antibiotics, the human immunodeficiency virus resisting antiviral agents, and human cancer cells replicating despite the presence of chemotherapy agents. There are many ways in which cells or organisms become resistant to drugs, and some organisms have developed many resistance mechanisms, each specific to a different drug. Drug resistance is best understood as it applies to bacteria, and the increasing resistance of many common disease-causing bacteria to antibiotics is a global crisis.

Genetic basis. Some organisms or cells are innately or inherently resistant to the action of specific drugs. In other cases, the development of drug resistance involves a change in the genetic makeup of the organism. This change can be either a mutation in a chromosomal gene or the acquisition of new genetic material from another cell or the environment.

Organisms may acquire deoxyribonucleic acid (DNA) that codes for drug resistance by a number of mechanisms. Transformation involves the uptake of DNA from the environment. Once DNA is taken up into the bacterial cell, it can recombine with the recipient organism's chromosomal DNA. This process plays a role in the development and spread of antibiotic resistance, which can occur both within and between species.

Transduction, another mechanism by which new DNA is acquired by bacteria, is mediated by viruses that infect bacteria (bacteriophages). Bacteriophages can integrate their DNA into the bacterial chromosome.

Conjugation is the most common mechanism of acquisition and spread of resistance genes among bacteria. This process, which requires cell-to-cell contact, involves direct transfer of DNA from the donor cell to a recipient cell. While conjugation can involve cell-to-cell transfer of chromosomal genes, bacterial resistance genes are more commonly transferred on nonchromosomal genetic elements known as plasmids or transposons. See DEOXYRIBONUCLEIC ACID (DNA).

Mechanisms of resistance. The four most important antibiotic resistance mechanisms are alteration of the target site of the antibiotic, enzyme inactivation of the antibiotic, active transport of the antibiotic out of the bacterial cell, and decreased permeability of the bacterial cell wall to the antibiotic (see illustration).

By altering the target site to which an antibiotic must bind, an organism may decrease or eliminate the activity of the antibiotic. Alteration of the target site is the mechanism for one of the most problematic antibiotic resistances worldwide, methicillin resistance among *Staphylococcus aureus*. See BACTERIAL GENETICS.

The most common mechanism by which bacteria are resistant to antibiotics is by producing enzymes that inactivate the drugs. For example, β-lactam antibiotics (penicillins and cephalosporins) can be inactivated by enzymes known as β-lactamases.

Active transport systems (efflux pumps) have been described for the removal of some antibiotics (such as tetracyclines, macrolides, and quinolones) from bacterial cells. In these situations, even though the drug can enter the bacterial cell, active efflux of the agent prevents it from accumulating and interfering with bacterial metabolism or replication.

Bacteria are intrinsically resistant to many drugs based solely on the fact that the drugs cannot penetrate the bacterial cell wall or cell membrane. In addition, bacteria can acquire resistance to a drug by an alteration in the porin proteins that form channels in the cell membrane. The resistance that *Pseudomonas aeruginosa* exhibits to a variety of penicillins and cephalosporins is mediated by an alteration in porin proteins.

Promoters. In the hospital environment, many factors combine to promote the development of drug resistance among bacteria. Increasing use of powerful new antibiotics gives selective advantage to the most resistant bacteria. In addition, advances in medical technology allow for the survival of sicker patients who undergo frequent invasive procedures. Finally, poor infection control practices in hospitals allow for the unchecked spread of already resistant strains of bacteria.

Outside the hospital environment, other important factors promote antibiotic resistance. The overuse of antibiotics in outpatient medicine and the use of antibiotics in agriculture exert selective pressure for the emergence of resistant bacterial strains. The spread of these resistant strains is facilitated by increasing numbers of children in close contact at day care centers, and by more national and international travel.

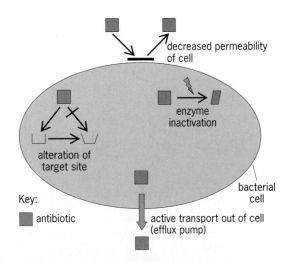

Key:

decreased permeability of cell

enzyme inactivation

alteration of target site

bacterial cell

antibiotic

active transport out of cell (efflux pump)

Four common mechanisms of antibiotics resistance.

Control. A multifaceted worldwide effort will be required to control drug resistance among disease-causing microorganisms. Ongoing programs to decrease the use of antibiotics, both in the clinics and in agriculture, will be necessary. The increased use of vaccines to prevent infection can help limit the need for antibiotics. Finally, the development of novel classes of antibiotics to fight emerging resistant bacteria will be required. *See* ANTIBIOTIC; BACTERIA.   [D.J.D.]

Ear (vertebrate) The organ which sends information about sound to the brain, constituting the sense of hearing, as well as vestibular information about the orientation of the head in space. The vertebrate ear is generally divided into three regions that have discrete functions: The inner ear is found in all vertebrates, and it subsumes both hearing and balance (functions). The external ear and the middle ear, not found in all vertebrates, enhance hearing. *See* HEARING (VERTEBRATE).

Ear structure. The inner ear is embedded in the ear (or otic) capsule and has a common embryological development in all vertebrate groups. In comparing the inner ears of different vertebrates, the major structural differences are associated with the auditory part of the ear. With few exceptions, the vestibular portion of the inner ear is developmentally, structurally, and functionally nearly the same in all vertebrates.

The middle ear and external ear are not found in the fishes. All tetrapods (amphibians, reptiles, birds, and mammals) have a middle ear with a tympanic membrane. Reptiles, birds, and mammals also have an external auditory meatus (or canal) which extends from the tympanic membrane to the external surface of the head. Mammals generally have an external structure, the pinna, that helps "collect"and carry the sound to the ear canal and then to the tympanum. The major difference in the middle ear among tetrapods is that it has a single ear bone, or ossicle (often called the columella or stapes), in amphibians, reptiles, and birds, while mammals have three middle-ear bones (malleus, incus, and stapes).

The basic sensory unit in the inner ear is the sensory hair cell. These specialized cells are morphologically similar in all of the epithelial structures of the ear in all vertebrates (and in the lateral line of fishes and amphibians), but they may have either auditory or vestibular functions depending upon the associated superstructure. The superstructure serves to facilitate the transmission of vibrations from the environment to the hair cells. For the vestibular apparatus, the superstructure blocks external vibratory energy, but sensitizes the sensory hair cells to the pull of gravity and to acceleratory and deceleratory movements of the head. *See* LATERAL LINE SYSTEM.

The sensory hair cell is a columnar, polarized structure from whose apex extend thin cilia that resemble hairs. Each hair cell has many such cilia, making up a ciliary bundle which bends in response to motional energy. The cilia in each bundle include many stereocilia and a single, eccentrically positioned kinocilium. The cilia extend into an extracellular fluid-filled space, with their tips embedded in a gelatinous membrane. *See* CILIA AND FLAGELLA.

The sensory hair cell is the detector of motion, either produced by compression and rarefaction of molecules due to sound waves, or imparted by movement of the head against gravity. This motion produces bending of the ciliary bundles, and this in turn results in a change in configuration of the membrane overlying the stereocilia and opening of channels in the membrane. It is generally thought that these channels admit

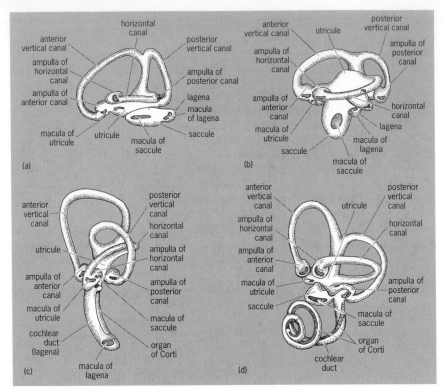

Fig. 1. Left-ear external view of the membranous labyrinths of (*a*) teleost, (*b*) frog, (*c*) bird, and (*d*) mammal. (*After A. S. Romer, The Vertebrate Body, 3d ed., Saunders, 1962*)

calcium into the cell, and this in turn interacts with other components of the cell. Ultimately, the energy generated by these interactions causes release of neurotransmitter at the base of the cell, and results in stimulation of afferent neurons which contact the cell. *See* Neurobiology; Synaptic transmission.

Fishes. In elasmobranchs and bony fishes the inner ear is located in the brain (cranial) cavity somewhat behind the eye. The inner ear has several regions, including three semicircular canals and otolith organs. Other than the very primitive jawless fishes which have one or two semicircular canals, all other vertebrates have three canals. All fishes, amphibians, reptiles, and birds have three otolith organs—the saccule, utricle, and lagena—while mammals do not have the lagena (Fig. 1).

At one end of each endolymph-filled semicircular canal is a widened area, the ampulla, which has a sensory area called the crista (or crista ampullaris). The crista contains large numbers of sensory hair cells, as well as other cells which provide support for the hair cells. At the base of the hair cells are nerve endings from the vestibular branch of the eighth cranial nerve. Each of the otolith organs also has a sensory area, called a macula, that contains hair cells and supporting cells. The cilia of the otolithic organs are embedded in a thin gelatinous membrane that also contains very dense calcium carbonate crystals. In elasmobranchs, primitive fishes, and all tetrapods, these crystals are called otoconia. In most bony fishes the crystals are fused into a single mass in each otolith organ called the otolith.

Fishes are able to detect a wide range of sound using their inner ear. Tetrapods detect sounds that impinge on the tympanic membrane and then are carried by the middle-ear bones to the inner ear, where the sounds set the fluids of the ear into motion and thus stimulate the sensory hair cells. In fishes, however, this kind of pathway is not needed since sound is already traveling through water. Indeed, since the fish's body is the same density as that of water, sound would travel right through the fish were it not for the otoconia or otoliths. Since these structures are much denser than the fish's body and the water, they stay still while the fish's body and the attached sensory hair cells move with the sound field. Since the stereocilia are attached to both the top of the hair cells and to the otoconia or otolith, they are bent as their base moves with the macula and their tops stand still with the otoliths. This bending sends signals to the nerves and then to the brain, indicating the presence of a sound. Most fishes detect sounds from 30 to 800 or 1000 Hz, with best hearing from 200 to 500 Hz. However, some fishes, called hearing specialists, have evolved special mechanisms to enhance hearing to 3000 or 4000 Hz. The hearing specialists use a secondary structure, the swim bladder, to enhance hearing capabilities. The swim bladder is a bubble of gas found in the abdominal cavity of most bony fishes, and it is used primarily for buoyancy control, though it may also be used in sound production in some species. Since the swim bladder is filled with gas, its density is different from that of the rest of the fish, and in a sound field the walls of the swim bladder are set into vibration and act as a small sound source to send sounds to the ear. *See* SWIM BLADDER.

Tetrapods. Many structural and functional features of the fish inner ear are also found in the tetrapod ear. The inner ear of tetrapods is embedded in the otic bones of the skull, with the membranous labyrinth attached to the bony labyrinth by connective tissue but suspended in perilymphatic fluid. There are three semicircular canals, with cristae, and, except in mammals which do not have a lagena, the three otolithic organs (Fig. 1b, c, d). In their morphology and physiology the vestibular parts of fish and tetrapod ears are nearly the same. For the most part, the tetrapod otolithic organs function only as vestibular organs rather than playing an auditory role as they do in fishes.

Amphibians. The tympanic membrane of frogs and toads is located on the lateral surface of the head. Attached to its inner aspect is a small rodlike bone, the stapes, or columella, which runs through the air space of the middle-ear cavity and plugs a small hole, the oval window, beyond which are the inner-ear fluids. The frog's tympanic membrane collects sound energy and transmits it through the columella to the inner-ear fluids. In the lagenar portion of the amphibian's membranous labyrinth are two areas of hair cells, the amphibian and basilar papillae, that are found in no other vertebrate group. The basilar papilla lies on the posterior wall of the saccule between the oval window and the round window, another membrane-covered opening between middle ear and inner ear. Vibratory energy enters the inner ear at the oval window, passes through the basilar and amphibian papillae causing them to vibrate, and then dissipates at the round window. *See* AMPHIBIA.

Birds and reptiles. In most reptiles and birds the tympanic membrane lies not on the surface of the head but internally, at the end of the tube called the external auditory meatus. A middle-ear cavity (with its eustachian tube to the mouth) lies medial to the tympanic membrane. A single ossicle, the columella, crosses this cavity from the tympanic membrane to the oval window at the inner ear. While both birds and reptiles have saccule, utricle, and lagena, as well as semicircular canals, they also have a newly evolved end organ, the basilar papilla, which is the part of the ear used for hearing in both groups of animals. (The avian and reptilian basilar papilla is thought to be a totally different structure, in terms of evolution and embryonic origin, than the basilar papilla found in amphibians.) The basilar papilla in birds and reptiles is often also called the cochlea, and there is some evidence to suggest that this end organ is directly related to

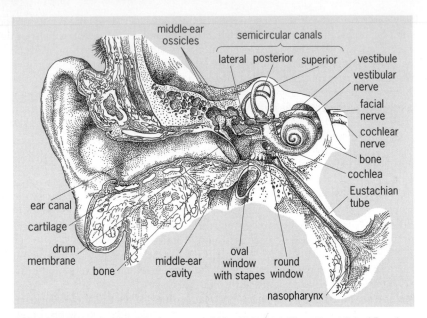

Fig. 2. Schematic drawing of the human ear. (*After M. Brödel, Three Unpublished Drawings of the Anatomy of the Human Ear, Saunders*)

the mammalian cochlea. The basilar papilla in reptiles is generally somewhat shorter than that found in birds, and there is considerable variation in the specific structure of this end organ in different species. The basilar papilla contains sensory hair cells. In birds, the basilar papilla sensory hair cells are differentiated into short and tall hair cells, which may have different functions in hearing. *See* AVES; REPTILIA.

Mammals. The mammalian ear consists of three parts: the external ear which receives the sound waves; the middle ear which transmits the vibrations by a series of three small bones; and the inner, or internal, ear, a complex bony chamber placed deep in the skull (Fig. 2). The external auditory meatus plus the newly evolved pinna, a cartilaginous structure projecting from the ear, compose the external ear. The shape and size of the pinna vary greatly. The auditory function of the pinna varies widely in different species. In some species the pinna is moved in the direction of a sound source and helps the animal focus sound to the external auditory meatus and then down the ear canal. In other species, such as humans, the pinna may have a lesser function, but even in humans the pinna helps to discriminate between sounds coming from the front and back of the head so that the person can better tell the direction of a sound source. *See* MAMMALIA.

As in other tetrapods, the first gill slit is modified as a middle-ear cavity, communicating with the pharynx by way of the eustachian tube. In other tetrapods this tube is permanently open, while in mammals it is usually closed. Instead of the single columella of other tetrapods, the mammalian middle ear has three bones, closely articulated with one another. The innermost is the stapes, which fits into the oval window of the inner ear and is homologous with the columella. Attached to the tympanic membrane is the malleus, and lying between the malleus and stapes is the incus. In spite of having additional bones, the mammalian middle ear functions basically as do those of amphibians, reptiles, and birds in transforming aerial vibrations into fluid vibrations within the inner ear.

In the mammalian inner ear the vestibular apparatus is much like that of other tetrapods. The auditory portion, however, is elongated and coiled into a snail shape. This structure is called the cochlea. The epithelium of the basilar papilla, called the organ of Corti, is more differentiated in mammals than in other tetrapods. The number of turns in the cochlea varies. At the base of the cochlea is the oval window, which carries sound energy into the inner ear, and the round window, where this energy is dissipated after traveling in the cochlea.

Running the length of the coiled cochlea are three channels; the uppermost, the scala vestibule, and the lowest, the scala tympani, are filled with perilymph. In the center is the scala media, or cochlear duct. The cochlear duct is filled with endolymph, and it is separated from the scala vestibule above by the thin Reissner's membrane and from the scala tympani below by the basilar membrane.

The basilar membrane is suspended on both sides by ligaments or bone. The basilar membrane varies regularly in width, being narrow at the base (where it is most responsive to high frequencies) and wide at the apex (where it is most responsive to low frequencies). Resting upon the basilar membrane is the organ of Corti. The organ of Corti contains several cell types in addition to the auditory hair cells. The hair cells lying on the internal side of the pillar cells are called the inner hair cells, and those lying on the external side are called the outer hair cells. There may be up to 20,000 sensory hair cells in a cochlea of a normal young human, although the number of hair cells declines with age as a result of normal cell death, damage due to some medications, and trauma caused by loud sounds. A healthy teenager may hear sounds from below 20 Hz to upward of 20,000 Hz, while an adult 40 or 50 years old may hear sounds only to 14,000 Hz (or even less). This loss of hearing is associated with death of sensory hair cells.

Sounds entering the mammalian inner ear at the oval window travel along the basilar membrane from basal to apical ends, causing vibrations of the membrane. Different frequencies maximally excite different regions of the basilar membrane based on differences in the stiffness of the membrane itself. The response of the different regions of the organ of Corti to specific frequencies is also thought to be enhanced by the sensory hair cells themselves. Whereas early investigations suggested that both inner and outer hair cells were involved in detection of sound per se, recent evidence suggests that the inner hair cells have the major role in hearing, while the outer hair cells modify the function of the ear and help to enhance the sensitivity of the inner hair cells. *See* HEARING (HUMAN).

[A.N.P.; D.B.W.]

Eating disorders　　Disorders characterized by abnormal eating behaviors and beliefs about eating, weight, and shape. The three major diagnoses are anorexia nervosa, bulimia nervosa, and binge eating disorder. In addition, there are many cases of abnormal eating that have only some of the features required for an eating disorder diagnosis; these cases are classified as eating disorders not otherwise specified. Obesity is classified as a general medical condition and not as an eating disorder (a psychiatric condition) because it is not consistently associated with psychological or behavioral problems.

There are also three childhood eating disorders: (1) Pica is a persistent pattern of eating nonnutritive substances in infants or young children. (2) Rumination disorder involves repeated regurgitation and rechewing of food. This behavior is not the result of a gastrointestinal or medical condition; the partially digested food comes back into the mouth without any observable nausea, disgust, or attempt to vomit. (3) Feeding disorder of infancy or early childhood is the persistent failure to eat adequately, as reflected in insufficient weight gain for age. Pica and rumination disorder are thought to be uncommon and frequently associated with developmental delays and mental retardation. Perhaps half of the pediatric hospitalizations for inadequate weight gain (which constitute 1–5% of all pediatric hospitalizations) may be due to feeding disorder of infancy or early childhood.

Anorexia nervosa. Anorexia nervosa is characterized by a refusal to maintain a minimal normal body weight (defined as 15% below average weight for height), an intense fear of becoming fat, and, if female, amenorrhea for at least 3 months. The majority of cases of anorexia nervosa are classified as restricting type; these individuals achieve abnormally low weight by severely dieting, fasting, and often by exercising compulsively. In severe cases, patients refuse to eat and can die of starvation or severe medical complications. Another subtype of anorexia nervosa is binge eating/purging type. Despite being emaciated or dangerously thin, persons with anorexia nervosa perceive themselves as overweight (distorted body image), deny the seriousness of their condition, and have an intense fear of becoming fat.

Anorexia nervosa occurs in roughly 1% of adolescent and young adult females. Most cases (90%) are female, and the majority are Caucasian and come from middle-class or higher socioeconomic groups. Anorexia nervosa is more prevalent in industrialized countries that share western views regarding thinness as an ideal. It develops most frequently during adolescence.

Persons with anorexia nervosa frequently manifest symptoms of depression and anxiety. The restricting type of anorexia nervosa is associated with obsessionality, rigidity, perfectionism, and overcontrol, whereas the binge/purge subtype is associated with greater mood instability and impulsivity across a wide range of areas, including substance abuse.

Although some cases of anorexia nervosa show no evidence of medical problems, prolonged starvation affects most organ systems, and a wide array of medical problems tend to be present. Long-term mortality from anorexia nervosa is estimated at 5–10% with most deaths resulting from starvation, cardiac events, or suicide.

The causes of anorexia nervosa are not yet understood but are likely to involve a complex combination of genetic, familial, psychological, and sociocultural factors. The onset of anorexia nervosa tends to follow a period of dieting and is frequently triggered by a stressful life events or transitions.

Since the starvation and weight loss can be life-threatening, initial treatment efforts need to focus on weight gain and the reestablishment of regular eating patterns. Inpatient hospitalization is frequently necessary. Although significant psychological issues tend to be present, it is generally ineffective to address these until weight has been stabilized. Once weight gain is achieved, psychotherapies can become useful. Relapse rates are high. *See* PSYCHOTHERAPY.

Bulimia nervosa. Bulimia nervosa is characterized by recurrent episodes of binge eating (eating large amounts of food while experiencing a subjective sense of lack of control over the eating), the regular use of extreme weight compensatory methods (for example, self-induced vomiting), and dysfunctional beliefs about weight and shape that unduly influence self-evaluation or self-worth.

Bulimia nervosa occurs in roughly 2% of adolescents and adults. It is most common in females (90% of cases), Caucasians, and middle-class or higher socioeconomic groups. The prevalence of bulimia has increased over the past few decades, and is also becoming more common in non-Caucasian groups.

Persons with bulimia nervosa have high rates of depression, anxiety, and substance abuse problems. Although this condition is less dangerous than anorexia nervosa, medical complications can occur. Dental erosion and periodontal problems are common. Electrolyte imbalance and dehydration can result in serious medical complications, including cardiac arrhythmias. In rare cases, esophageal bleeding and gastric ruptures occur.

Bulimia nervosa is likely to result from a combination of genetic, familial, psychological, and sociocultural factors. Although many persons have weight and diet concerns, the development of bulimia is thought to arise only in vulnerable individuals and usually after a stressful event. Bulimia nervosa is a self-maintaining vicious cycle.

Bulimia nervosa can often be treated successfully with outpatient therapies. Cognitive behavioral therapy and interpersonal psychotherapy have been found to be most effective for reducing binge eating and vomiting and improving associated concerns such as depression, self-esteem, and body image. These two therapies also have the best results over the long term. Certain types of pharmacotherapy, notably antidepressant medications, are also effective.

Binge eating disorder. Binge eating disorder is characterized by recurrent episodes of binge eating but, unlike bulimia nervosa, no extreme weight control behaviors (purging, laxatives, fasting) are present. Persons with binge eating disorder have chaotic eating patterns and frequently overeat as well as binge.

Although obesity is not required for the diagnosis, many people with binge eating disorder are overweight. Binge eating disorder is estimated to occur in 3% of the general population but in roughly 30% of obese persons. Binge eating disorder occurs most frequently in adulthood, affects men nearly as often as women, and occurs across different ethnic groups.

Obese binge eaters are characterized by higher levels of psychiatric problems (depression, anxiety, substance abuse) and psychological problems (poor self-esteem, body image dissatisfaction) than non-binge eaters and closely resemble persons with bulimia nervosa. Overweight persons with binge eating disorder are at high risk for further weight gain and weight fluctuations and associated medical complications. The etiology of binge eating disorder is unknown.

Cognitive behavioral therapy is effective for reducing binge eating and improving associated concerns such as depression, self-esteem, and body image, but does not seem to result in weight loss. There is some evidence that behavioral weight control treatment can reduce binge eating and facilitate weight loss. Antidepressant medications appear to reduce binge eating but do not produce weight loss; relapse is rapid after discontinuation of the medication. *See* AFFECTIVE DISORDERS. [C.M.G.]

Ebola virus Ebola viruses are a group of exotic viral agents that cause a severe hemorrhagic fever disease in humans and other primates. The four known subtypes or species of Ebola viruses are Zaire, Sudan, Reston, and Côte d'Ivoire (Ivory Coast), named for the geographic locations where these viruses were first determined to cause outbreaks of disease. Ebola viruses are very closely related to, but distinct from, Marburg viruses. Collectively, these pathogenic agents make up a family of viruses known as the Filoviridae.

Filoviruses have an unusual morphology, with the virus particle, or virion, appearing as long thin rods. A filovirus virion is composed of a single species of ribonucleic acid (RNA) molecule that is bound together with special viral proteins, and this RNA–protein complex is surrounded by a membrane derived from the outer membrane of infected cells. Infectious virions are formed when the virus buds from the surface of infected cells and is released. Spiked structures on the surface of virions project from the virion and serve to recognize and attach to specific receptor molecules on the surface of susceptible cells, allowing the virion to penetrate the cell. The genetic information contained in the RNA molecule directs production of new virus particles by using the cellular machinery to drive synthesis of new viral proteins and RNA. *See* RIBONUCLEIC ACID (RNA); VIRUS.

Although much is known about the agents of Ebola hemorrhagic fever disease, the ecology of Ebola viruses remains a mystery. The natural hosts of filoviruses remain unknown, and there has been little progress at unraveling the events leading to outbreaks or identifying sources of filoviruses in the wild. Fortunately, the incidence of human disease is relatively rare and has been limited to persons living in equatorial Africa or working with the infectious viruses. The virus is spread primarily through close contact with the body of an infected individual, his or her body fluids, or some other source of infectious material.

Ebola virus hemorrhagic fever disease in humans begins with an incubation period of 4–10 days, which is followed by abrupt onset of illness. Fever, headache, weakness, and other flulike symptoms lead to a rapid deterioration in the condition of the individual. In severe cases, bleeding and the appearance of small red spots or rashes over the body indicate that the disease has affected the integrity of the circulatory system. Individuals with Ebola virus die as a result of a shock syndrome that usually occurs 6–9 days after the onset of symptoms. This shock is due to the inability to control vascular functions and the massive injury to body tissues.

It appears that the immune response is impaired and that a strong cellular immune response is key to surviving infections. This immunosuppression may also be a factor in death, especially if secondary infections by normal bacterial flora ensue. *See* IMMUNOSUPPRESSION.

Outbreaks of Ebola virus disease in humans are controlled by the identification and isolation of infected individuals, implementation of barrier nursing techniques, and rapid disinfection of contaminated material. Diagnosis of Ebola virus cases is made by detecting virus proteins or RNA in blood or tissue specimens, or by detecting antibodies to the virus in the blood.

Dilute hypochlorite solutions (bleach), 3% phenolic solutions, or simple detergents (laundry or dish soap) can be used to destroy infectious virions. No known drugs have been shown to be effective in treating Ebola virus (or Marburg virus) infections, and protective vaccines against filoviruses have not been developed.　　　　　[A.San.]

Ecdysone　　The molting hormone of insects. It is a derivative of cholesterol. The most striking physiological activity of ecdysone is the induction of puffs (zones of gene activity) in giant chromosomes of the salivary glands and other organs of the midge *Chironomus*. The induction of puffs has been visualized as primary action of the hormone, indicating that ecdysone controls the activity of specific genes. It has been shown that ecdysone stimulates the synthesis of messenger RNA, among which is the messenger for dopa decarboxylase. This enzyme is involved in the biosynthesis of the sclerotizing agent *N*-acetyl-dopamine. *See* INSECTA.　　　　　[P.K.]

Echinodermata　　A unique group of exclusively marine animals with a peculiar body architecture. They are headless with a fivefold radial symmetry. The body wall contains the endoskeleton, made of numerous independent calcareous plates which frequently support spines. The plates may be tightly interlocked or loosely associated. The spines may protrude through the outer epithelium, and are often used for defense. The skeletal plates of the body wall, together with their associated muscles and connective tissue, form a tough and sometimes rigid test which encloses the large coelom. A unique water-vascular system is involved in locomotion, respiration, food gathering, and sensory perception. This shows outside the body as rows of fluid-filled tube feet in conspicuous double lines or ambulacra. Within the body wall lie the ducts and fluid reservoirs necessary to protract and retract the tube feet by hydrostatic pressure. The nervous system arises from the embryonic ectoderm and consists of a ring around the mouth with connecting nerve cords associated with each ambulacrum. There may also be diffuse nerve plexuses lying below the outer epithelium. The coelom houses the alimentary canal and associated organs and in most groups the reproductive organs.

The larvae are usually planktonic with a bilateral symmetry, but the adults are usually sedentary and benthic. They inhabit all seas and oceans, ranging from the shores to the ocean depths.

The phylum comprises about 6000 existing species and many fossils, providing a good fossil record. Echinoderms first appeared in the Early Cambrian and have been evolving over 600 million years. During this vast time several divergent patterns have arisen. The surviving groups show few resemblances to the original stock. The existing representatives fall into three subphyla: Crinozoa (class Crinoidea: sea lilies and feather stars); Asterozoa (class Asteroidea: starfishes, and class Ophiuroidea: brittle stars), and Echinozoa (class Echinoidea: sea urchins, sand dollars and heart urchins); and class Holothuroidea: sea cucumbers). The fourth subphylum, Homalozoa, has no living representatives.

Echinoderms evolved very rapidly near the beginning of the Paleozoic Era. During the Paleozoic, numerous well-marked evolutionary trends are discernible in nearly all echinoderm groups, including free-moving forms (especially echinoids) as well as crino-zoans. Many small classes of echinoderms became extinct during the Paleozoic, and the surviving groups, especially the crinoids, lost many members at the great Late Permian mass extinction. All groups of modern echinoderms have their origin in early Paleo-zoic stocks, and the lines of their phylogeny are mostly indicated by the fossil record. Echinoids predominate in Mesozoic and Cenozoic echinoderms.　　　　[R.C.Mo.; J.J.Se.]

Ecological communities　Assemblages of living organisms that occur to-gether in an area. The nature of the forces that knit these assemblages into organized systems and those properties of assemblages that manifest this organization have been topics of intense debate among ecologists since the beginning of the twentieth century. On the one hand, there are those who view a community as simply consisting of species with similar physical requirements, such as temperature, soil type, or light regime. The similarity of requirements dictates that these species be found together, but interactions between the species are of secondary importance and the level of organization is low. On the other hand, there are those who conceive of the community as a highly or-ganized, holistic entity, with species inextricably and complexly linked to one another and to the physical environment, so that characteristic patterns recur, and properties arise that one can neither understand nor predict from a knowledge of the component species. In this view, the ecosystem (physical environment plus its community) is as well organized as a living organism, and constitutes a superorganism. Between these extremes are those who perceive some community organization but not nearly enough to invoke images of holistic superorganisms. See ECOSYSTEM.

Every community comprises a given group of species, and their number and iden-tities are distinguishing traits. Most communities are so large that it is not possible to enumerate all species; microorganisms and small invertebrates are especially difficult to census. However, particularly in small, well-bounded sites such as lakes or islands, one can find all the most common species and estimate their relative abundances. The number of species is known as species richness, while species diversity refers to various statistics based on the relative numbers of individuals of each species in addition to the number of species. The rationale for such a diversity measure is that some commu-nities have many species, but most species are rare and almost all the individuals (or biomass) in such a community can be attributed to just a few species. Such a commu-nity is not diverse in the usual sense of the word. Patterns of species diversity abound in the ecological literature; for example, pollution often effects a decrease in species diversity.

The main patterns of species richness that have been detected are area and isolation effects, successional gradients, and latitudinal gradients. Larger sites tend to have more species than do small ones, and isolated communities (such as those on oceanic islands) tend to have fewer species than do less isolated ones of equal size. Later communities in a temporal succession tend to have more species than do earlier ones, except that the last (climax) community often has fewer species than the immediately preceding one. Tropical communities tend to be very species-rich, while those in arctic climates tend to be species-poor. This observation conforms to a larger but less precise rule that communities in particularly stressful environments tend to have few species.

Communities are usually denoted by the presence of species, known as dominants, that contain a large fraction of the community's biomass, or account for a large fraction of a community's productivity. Dominants are usually plants. Determining whether communities at two sites are truly representatives of the "same" community requires knowledge of more than just the dominants, however. "Characteristic" species, which are always found in combination with certain other species, are useful in deciding whether two communities are of the same type, though the designation of "same" is arbitrary, just as is the designation of "dominant" or "characteristic."

Communities often do not have clear spatial boundaries. Occasionally, very sharp limits to a physical environmental condition impose similarly sharp limits on a community. For example, serpentine soils are found sharply delimited from adjacent soils in many areas, and have mineral concentrations strikingly different from those of the neighboring soils. Thus they support plant species that are very different from those found in nearby nonserpentine areas, and these different plant species support animal species partially different from those of adjacent areas.

Here two different communities are sharply bounded from each other. Usually, however, communities grade into one another more gradually, through a broad intermediate region (an ecotone) that includes elements of both of the adjacent communities, and sometimes other species as well that are not found in either adjacent community.

The environment created by the dominant species, by their effects on temperature, light, humidity, and other physical factors, and by their biotic effects, such as allelopathy and competition, may entrain some other species so that these other species' spatial boundaries coincide with those of the dominants. See PHYSIOLOGICAL ECOLOGY (PLANT); POPULATION ECOLOGY.

More or less distinct communities tend to follow one another in rather stylized order. As with recognition of spatial boundaries, recognition of temporal boundaries of adjacent communities within a sere (a temporary community during a successional sequence at a site) is partly a function of the expectations that an observer brings to the endeavor. Those who view communities as superorganisms are inclined to see sharp temporal and spatial boundaries, and the perception that one community does not gradually become another community over an extended period of time confirms the impression that communities are highly organized entities, not random collections of species that happen to share physical requirements. However, this superorganismic conception of succession has been replaced by an individualistic succession. Data on which species are present at different times during a succession show that there is not abrupt wholesale extinction of most members of a community and concurrent simultaneous colonization by most species of the next community. Rather, most species within a community colonize at different times, and as the community is replaced most species drop out at different times. That succession is primarily an individualistic process does not mean that there are not characteristic changes in community properties as most successions proceed. Species richness usually increases through most of the succession, for example, and stratification becomes more highly organized and well defined. A number of patterns are manifest in aspects of energy flow and nutrient cycling. See ECOLOGICAL SUCCESSION.

Living organisms are characterized not only by spatial and temporal structure but by an apparent purpose or activity termed teleonomy. In the first place, the various species within a community have different trophic relationships with one another. One species may eat another, or be eaten by another. A species may be a decomposer, living on dead tissue of one or more other species. Some species are omnivores, eating many kinds of food; others are more specialized, eating only plants or only animals, or even just one other species. These trophic relationships unite the species in a community into a common endeavor, the transmission of energy through the community. This energy flow is analogous to an organism's mobilization and transmission of energy from the food it eats.

By virtue of differing rates of photosynthesis by the dominant plants, different communities have different primary productivities. Tropical forests are generally most productive, while extreme environments such as desert or alpine conditions harbor rather unproductive communities. Agricultural communities are intermediate. Algal communities in estuaries are the most productive marine communities, while open ocean communities are usually far less productive. The efficiency with which various animals ingest and assimilate the plants and the structure of the trophic web determine the secondary productivity (production of organic matter by animals) of a community. Marine secondary productivity generally exceeds that of terrestrial communities. See AGROECOSYSTEM; BIOLOGICAL PRODUCTIVITY.

A final property that any organism must have is the ability to reproduce itself. Communities may be seen as possessing this property, though the sense in which they do so does not support the superorganism metaphor. A climax community reproduces itself through time simply by virtue of the reproduction of its constituent species, and may also be seen as reproducing itself in space by virtue of the propagules that its species transmit to less mature communities. For example, when a climax forest abuts a cutover field, if no disturbance ensues, the field undergoes succession and eventually becomes a replica of the adjacent forest. Both temporally and spatially, then, community reproduction is a collective rather than an emergent property, deriving directly from the reproductive activities of the component species. See DESERT; ECOLOGY; GRASSLAND ECOSYSTEM; MANGROVE.   [D.Sim.]

Ecological competition

The interaction of two (or more) organisms (or species) such that, for each, the birth or growth rate is depressed and the death rate increased by the presence of the other organisms (or species). Competition is recognized as one of the more important forces structuring ecological communities, and interest in competition led to one of the first axioms of modern ecology, the competitive exclusion principle. The principle suggests that in situations where the growth and reproduction of two species are resource-limited, only one species can survive per resource.

The competitive exclusion principle was originally derived by mathematicians using the Lotka-Volterra competition equations. This model of competition predicts that if species differ substantially in competitive ability, the weaker competitor will be eliminated by the stronger competitor. However, a competitive equilibrium can occur if the negative effect of each species on itself (intraspecific competition) is greater than the negative effect of each species on the other species (interspecific competition). Because the competitive exclusion principle implies that competing species cannot coexist, it follows that high species diversity depends upon mechanisms through which species avoid competition.

In general, competitive exclusion can be prevented if the relative competitive abilities of species vary through time and space. Such variation occurs in two ways. First, dispersal rates into particular patches may fluctuate, causing fluctuations in the numerical advantage of a species in a particular patch. Second, competitive abilities of species may be environmentally dependent and, therefore, fluctuate with local environmental changes. Competitive exclusion can also be avoided if fluctuations in environmental factors reduce the densities of potentially competing species to levels where competition is weak and population growth is for a time insensitive to density.

Coexistence is not merely a result of environmental harshness or fluctuations but also involves the critical element of niche differentiation (that is, species must differ from one another if they are to coexist). However, the focus is not how species coexist by partitioning resources, but how species can coexist on the same resources by differing sufficiently in their responses to environmental conditions and fluctuations. See ECOLOGICAL COMMUNITIES; ECOLOGICAL SUCCESSION.

Competition theory has been applied to human-manipulated ecosystems used to produce food, fiber, and forage crops as well as in forestry and rangeland management. Although many characteristics of agricultural systems are similar to those of natural ecosystems, agricultural communities are unique because they are often managed for single-species (sometimes multispecies) production and they are usually characterized by frequent and intense disturbance. Studies of competition in agriculture have primarily examined crop loss from weed abundance under current cropping practices, and have evaluated various weed control tactics and intercropping systems. Factors that influence competition in agroecosystems include the timing of plant emergence, growth rates, spatial arrangements among neighbors, plant–plant-environment interactions, and herbivory. See ECOLOGY.   [P.C.M.]

Ecological energetics   The study of the flow of energy within an ecological system from the time the energy enters the living system until it is ultimately degraded to heat and irretrievably lost from the system. It is also referred to as production ecology, because ecologists use the word production to describe the process of energy input and storage in ecosystems.

Ecological energetics provides information on the energetic interdependence of organisms within ecological systems and the efficiency of energy transfer within and between organisms and trophic levels. Nearly all energy enters the biota by green plants' transformation of light energy into chemical energy through photosynthesis; this is referred to as primary production. This accumulation of potential energy is used by plants, and by the animals which eat them, for growth, reproduction, and the work necessary to sustain life. The energy put into growth and reproduction is termed secondary production. As energy passes along the food chain to higher trophic levels (from plants to herbivores to carnivores), the potential energy is used to do work and in the process is degraded to heat. The laws of thermodynamics require the light energy fixed by plants to equal the energy degraded to heat, assuming the system is closed with respect to matter. An energy budget quantifies the energy pools, the directions of energy flow, and the rates of energy transformations within ecological systems. See BIOLOGICAL PRODUCTIVITY; FOOD WEB; PHOTOSYNTHESIS.

The essentials of ecological energetics can be most readily appreciated by considering energy flowing through an individual; it is equally applicable to populations, communities, and ecosystems. Of the food energy available, only part is harvested in the process of foraging. Some is wasted, for example, by messy eaters, and the rest consumed. Part of the consumed food is transformed but is not utilized by the body, leaving as fecal material or as nitrogenous waste, the by-product of protein metabolism. The remaining energy is assimilated into the body, part of which is used to sustain the life functions and to do work—this is manifest as oxygen consumption. The remainder of the assimilated energy is used to produce new tissue, either as growth of the individual or as development of offspring. Hence production is also the potential energy (proteins, fats, and carbohydrates) on which other organisms feed. Production leads to an increase in biomass or is eliminated through death, migration, predation, or the shedding of, for example, hair, skin, and antlers.

Energy flows through the consumer food chain (from plants to herbivores to carnivores) or through the detritus food chain. The latter is fueled by the waste products of the consumer food chain, such as feces, shed skin, cadavers, and nitrogenous waste. Most detritus is consumed by microorganisms, although this food chain includes conspicuous carrion feeders like beetles and vultures. In terrestrial systems, more than 90% of all primary production may be consumed by detritus feeders. In aquatic systems, where the plants do not require tough supporting tissues, harvesting by herbivores may be efficient with little of the primary production passing to the detrivores.

Traditionally the calorie, a unit of heat energy, has been used in ecological energetics, but this has been largely replaced by the joule. Production is measured from individual growth rates and the reproductive rate of the population to determine the turnover time. The energy equivalent of food consumed, feces, and production can be determined by measuring the heat evolved on burning a sample in an oxygen bomb calorimeter, or by chemical analysis—determining the amount of carbon or of protein, carbohydrate, and lipid and applying empirically determined caloric equivalents to the values. The latter three contain, respectively, 16.3, 23.7, and 39.2 kilojoules per gram of dry weight. Maintenance costs are usually measured indirectly as respiration (normally the oxygen consumed) in the laboratory and extrapolated to the field conditions. Error is introduced by the fact that animals have different levels of activity in the field and are subject to different temperatures, and so uncertainty has surrounded these extrapolations. Oxygen consumption has been measured in animals living in the wild by using the turnover rates of doubly labeled water (D_2O).

Due to the loss of usable energy with each transformation, in an area more energy can be diverted into production by plants than by consumer populations. For humans this means that utilizing plants for food directly is energetically much more efficient than converting them to eggs or meat. See BIOMASS; ECOLOGICAL COMMUNITIES; ECOSYSTEM.

[W.F.H.]

Ecological modeling   The use of computer simulations or mathematical equations to address questions that cannot be answered solely by experiments or observations. Ecological models have two major aims: to provide general insight into how ecological systems or ecological interactions work; and to provide specific predictions about the likely futures of particular populations, communities, or ecosystems.

Models can be used to indicate general possibilities or to forecast the most likely outcomes of particular populations or ecosystems. Models differ in whether they are "basic" or are intended to address management decisions. As ecology has grown in its sophistication, models are increasingly used as decision support tools for policymakers. Models of virtually every possible type of ecological interaction have been developed (competition, parasitism, disease, mutualism, plant-herbivore interactions, and so forth). The models vary in their level of detail. Some models simply keep track of the density of organisms, treating all organisms of any species as identical (mass action models). At the other extreme, the movement and fate of each individual organism may be tracked in an elaborate computer simulation (individual behavior models). *See* POPULATION ECOLOGY.

Simple algebraic models are very useful for indicating general principles and possibilities. In order to be a management tool, the model must be more complicated and detailed to reflect the specific situation under examination. For example, instead of a few equations, ecologists have modeled spotted owl populations and old growth forests in Washington using a detailed computer simulation that keeps track of habitat in real maps at the scale of hectares. In these simulation models, owls are moved as individuals from one hectare to another, and their fate (survival, death, or reproduction) is recorded in the computer's memory. By tracking hundreds or even thousands of owls moving around in this computer world, different forestry practices corresponding to different logging scenarios can be examined. *See* SYSTEMS ECOLOGY.

A model is a formal way of examining the consequences of a series of assumptions about how nature works. Such models refine thinking and clarify what results are implied by any set of assumptions. As models become more complicated and specific, they can also be used to conduct experiments that are too expensive or impractical in the field.

One danger of ecological modeling is the uncertainty of the models and the shortage of supporting data. Properly used, models allow exploration of a wide range of uncertainty, pointing out the limits of current knowledge and identifying critical information required prior to management decision making. However, it would not be prudent to rely solely on the output of any model. *See* ECOLOGY.   [P.Ka.]

Ecological succession   A directional change in an ecological community. Populations of animals and plants are in a dynamic state. Through the continual turnover of individuals, a population may expand or decline depending on the success of its members in survival and reproduction. As a consequence, the species composition of communities typically does not remain static with time. Apart from the regular fluctuations in species abundance related to seasonal changes, a community may develop progressively with time through a recognizable sequence known as the sere. Pioneer populations are replaced by successive colonists along a more or less predictable path toward a relatively stable community. This process of succession results from interactions between different species, and between species and their environment, which govern the sequence and the rate with which species replace each other. The rate at which succession proceeds depends on the time scale of species' life histories as well as on the effects species may have on each other and on the environment which supports them. In some cases, seres may take hundreds of years to complete, and direct observation at a given site is not possible. Adjacent sites may be identified as successively older stages of the same sere, if it is assumed that conditions were similar when each seral stage was initiated. *See* ECOLOGICAL COMMUNITIES; POPULATION ECOLOGY.

The course of ecological succession depends on initial environmental conditions. Primary succession occurs on novel areas such as volcanic ash, glacial deposits, or bare rock, areas which have not previously supported a community. In such harsh, unstable environments, pioneer colonizing organisms must have wide ranges of ecological tolerance to survive. In contrast, secondary succession is initiated by disturbance such as fire, which removes a previous community from an area. Pioneer species are here constrained not by the physical environment but by their ability to enter and exploit the vacant area rapidly.

As succession proceeds, many environmental factors may change through the influence of the community. Especially in primary succession, this leads to more stable, less severe environments. At the same time interactions between species of plant tend to intensify competition for basic resources such as water, light, space, and nutrients. Successional change results from the normal complex interactions between organism and environment which lead to changes in overall species composition. Whether succession is promoted by changing environmental factors or competitive interactions, species composition alters in response to availability of niches. Populations occurring in the community at a point in succession are those able to provide propagules (such as seeds) to invade the area, being sufficiently tolerant of current environmental conditions, and able to withstand competition from members of other populations present at the same stage. Species lacking these qualities either become locally extinct or are unable to enter and survive in the community.

Early stages of succession tend to be relatively rapid, whereas the rates of species turnover and soil changes become slower as the community matures. Eventually an approximation to the steady state is established with a relatively stable community, the nature of which has aroused considerable debate. Earlier, the so-called climax vegetation was believed to be determined ultimately by regional climate and, given sufficient time, any community in a region would attain this universal condition. This unified concept of succession, the monoclimax hypothesis, implies the ability of organisms progressively to modify their environment until it can support the climatic climax community. Although plants and animals do sometimes ameliorate environmental conditions, evidence suggests overwhelmingly that succession has a variety of stable end points. This hypothesis, known as the polyclimax hypothesis, suggests that the end point of a succession depends on a complex of environmental factors that characterize the site, such as parent material, topography, local climate, and human influences.

Actions of the community on the environment, termed autogenic, provide an important driving force promoting successional change, and are typical of primary succession where initial environments are inhospitable. Alternatively, changes in species composition of a community may result from influences external to the community called allogenic.

Whereas intrinsic factors often result in progressive successional changes, that is, changes leading from simple to more complex communities, external (allogenic) forces may induce retrogressive succession, that is, toward a less mature community. For example, if a grassland is severely overgrazed by cattle, the most palatable species will disappear. As grazing continues, the grass cover is reduced, and in the open areas weeds characteristic of initial stages of succession may become established.

In some instances of succession, the food web is based on photosynthetic organisms, and there is a slow accumulation of organic matter, both living and dead. This is termed autotrophic succession. In other instances, however, addition of organic matter to an ecosystem initiates a succession of decomposer organisms which invade and degrade it. Such a succession is called heterotrophic. *See* BIOLOGICALS; FOOD WEB; PRODUCTIVITY.

Observed changes in the structure and function of seral communities result from natural selection of individuals within their current environment. Three mechanisms by which species may replace each other have been proposed; the relative importance of each apparently depends on the nature of the sere and stage of development.

1. The facilitation hypothesis states that invasion of later species depends on conditions created by earlier colonists. Earlier species modify the environment so as to increase the competitive ability of species which are then able to displace them. Succession thus proceeds because of the effects of species on their environment.

2. The tolerance hypothesis suggests that later successional species tolerate lower levels of resources than earlier occupants and can invade and replace them by reducing resource levels below those tolerated by earlier occupants. Succession proceeds despite the resistance of earlier colonists.

3. The inhibition hypothesis is that all species resist invasion of competitors and are displaced only by death or by damage from factors other than competition. Succession proceeds toward dominance by longer-lived species.

None of these models of succession is solely applicable in all instances; indeed most examples of succession appear to show elements of all three replacement mechanisms.

Succession has traditionally been regarded as following an orderly progression of changes toward a predictable end point, the climax community, in equilibrium with the prevailing environment. This essentially deterministic view implies that succession will always follow the same course from a given starting point and will pass through a recognizable series of intermediate states. In contrast, a more recent view of succession is based on adaptations of independent species. It is argued that succession is disorderly and unpredictable, resulting from probabilistic processes such as invasion of propagules and survival of individuals which make up the community. Such a stochastic view reflects the inherent variability observed in nature and the uncertainty of environmental conditions. In particular, it allows for succession to take alternative pathways and end points dependent on the chance outcome of interactions among species and between species and their environment.

Consideration of community properties such as energy flow supports the view of succession as an orderly process. The rate of gross primary productivity typically becomes limited also by the availability of nutrients, now incorporated within the community biomass, and declines to a level sustainable by release from decomposer organisms. Species diversity tends to rise rapidly at first as successive invasions occur, but declines again with the elimination of the pioneer species by the climax community.

Stochastic aspects of succession can be represented in the form of models which allow for transitions between a series of different "states." Such models, termed Markovian models, can apply at various levels: plant-by-plant replacement, changes in tree size categories, or transitions between whole communities. A matrix of replacement probabilities defines the direction, pathway, and likelihood of change, and the model can be used to predict the future composition of the community from its initial state.　　[P.Ran.]

Ecology　The subdiscipline of biology that concentrates on the relationships between organisms and their environments; it is also called environmental biology. Ecology is concerned with patterns of distribution (where organisms occur) and with patterns of abundance (how many organisms occur) in space and time. It seeks to explain the factors that determine the range of environments that organisms occupy and that determine how abundant organisms are within those ranges. It also emphasizes functional interactions between co-occurring organisms. In addition to being a unique component of the biological sciences, ecology is both a synthetic and an integrative science since it often draws upon information and concepts in other sciences, ranging from physiology to meteorology, to explain the complex organization of nature.

Environment is all of those factors external to an organism that affect its survival, growth, development, and reproduction. It can be subdivided into physical, or abiotic, factors, and biological, or biotic, factors. The physical components of the environment include all nonbiological constituents, such as temperature, wind, inorganic chemicals, and radiation. The biological components of the environment include the organisms. A somewhat more general term is habitat, which refers in a general way to where an organism occurs and the environmental factors present there. See ENVIRONMENT.

A recognition of the unitary coupling of an organism and its environment is fundamental to ecology; in fact, the definitions of organism and environment are not separate. Environment is organism-centered since the environmental properties of a habitat are determined by the requirements of the organisms that occupy that habitat. For example, the amount of inorganic nitrogen dissolved in lake water is of little immediate significance to zooplankton in the lake because they are incapable of utilizing inorganic nitrogen directly. However, because phytoplankton are capable of utilizing inorganic nitrogen directly, it is a component of their environment. Any effect of inorganic nitrogen upon the zooplankton, then, will occur indirectly through its effect on the abundance of the phytoplankton that the zooplankton feed upon. See PHYTOPLANKTON; ZOOPLANKTON.

Just as the environment affects the organism, so the organism affects its environment. Growth of phytoplankton may be nitrogen-limited if the number of individuals has become so great that there is no more nitrogen available in the environment. Zooplankton, not limited by inorganic nitrogen themselves, can promote the growth of additional phytoplankton by consuming some individuals, digesting them, and returning part of the nitrogen to the environment.

Ecology is concerned with the processes involved in the interactions between organisms and their environments, with the mechanisms responsible for those processes, and with the origin, through evolution, of those mechanisms. It is distinguished from such closely related biological subdisciplines as physiology and morphology because it is not intrinsically concerned with the operation of a physiological process or the function of a structure, but with how a process or structure interacts with the environment to influence survival, growth, development, and reproduction.

Major subdivisions of ecology by organism include plant ecology, animal ecology, and microbial ecology. Subdivisions by habitat include terrestrial ecology, the study of organisms on land; limnology, the study of fresh-water organisms and habitats; and oceanography, the study of marine organisms and habitats.

The levels of organization studied range from the individual organism to the whole complex of organisms in a large area. Autecology is the study of individuals, population ecology is the study of groups of individuals of a single species or a limited number of species, synecology is the study of communities of several populations, and ecosystem, or simply systems, ecology is the study of communities of organisms and their environments in a specific time and place. See POPULATION ECOLOGY; SYSTEMS ECOLOGY.

Higher levels of organization include biomes and the biosphere. Biomes are collections of ecosystems with similar organisms and environments and, therefore, similar ecological properties. All of Earth's coniferous forests are elements in the coniferous forest biome. Although united by similar dynamic relationships and structural properties, the biome itself is more abstract than a specific ecosystem. The biosphere is the most inclusive category possible, including all regions of Earth inhabited by living things. It extends from the lower reaches of the atmosphere to the depths of the oceans. See BIOME; BIOSPHERE.

The principal methodological approaches to ecology are descriptive, experimental, and theoretical. Descriptive ecology concentrates on the variety of populations, communities, and habitats throughout Earth. Experimental ecology involves manipulating organisms or their environments to discover the underlying mechanisms governing distribution and abundance. Theoretical ecology uses mathematical equations based on assumptions about the properties of organisms and environments to make predictions about patterns of distribution and abundance. See THEORETICAL ECOLOGY.

[S.J.McN.]

Ecosystem A functional system that includes an ecological community of organisms together with the physical environment, interacting as a unit. Ecosystems are characterized by flow of energy through food webs, production and degradation of organic matter, and transformation and cycling of nutrient elements. This production of organic molecules serves as the energy base for all biological activity within ecosystems. The consumption of plants by herbivores (organisms that consume living plants or algae) and detritivores (organisms that consume dead organic matter) serves to transfer energy stored in photosynthetically produced organic molecules to other organisms. Coupled to the production of organic matter and flow of energy is the cycling of elements. *See* ECOLOGICAL COMMUNITIES; ENVIRONMENT.

All biological activity within ecosystems is supported by the production of organic matter by autotrophs (organisms that can produce organic molecules such as glucose from inorganic carbon dioxide; see illustration). More than 99% of autotrophic production on Earth is through photosynthesis by plants, algae, and certain types of bacteria. Collectively these organisms are termed photoautotrophs (autotrophs that use energy from light to produce organic molecules). In addition to photosynthesis, some production is conducted by chemoautotrophic bacteria (autotrophs that use energy stored in the chemical bonds of inorganic molecules such as hydrogen sulfide to produce organic molecules). The organic molecules produced by autotrophs are used to support the organism's metabolism and reproduction, and to build new tissue. This new tissue is consumed by herbivores or detritivores, which in turn are ultimately consumed by predators or other detritivores.

Terrestrial ecosystems, which cover 30% of the Earth's surface, contribute a little over one-half of the total global photosynthetic production of organic matter—approximately 60×10^{15} grams of carbon per year. Oceans, which cover 70% of the Earth's surface, produce approximately 51×10^{15} g C y^{-1} of organic matter. *See* BIOMASS.

Food webs. Organisms are classified based upon the number of energy transfers through a food web (see illustration). Photoautotrophic production of organic matter represents the first energy transfer in ecosystems and is classified as primary production. Consumption of a plant by a herbivore is the second energy transfer, and thus herbivores occupy the second trophic level, also known as secondary production. Consumer organisms that are one, two, or three transfers from photoautotrophs are classified as

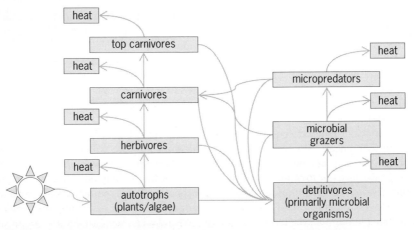

General model of energy flow through ecosystems.

primary, secondary, and tertiary consumers. Moving through a food web, energy is lost during each transfer as heat, as described by the second law of thermodynamics. Consequently, the total number of energy transfers rarely exceeds four or five; with energy loss during each transfer, little energy is available to support organisms at the highest levels of a food web. *See* ECOLOGICAL ENERGETICS; FOOD WEB.

Biogeochemical cycles. In contrast to energy, which is lost from ecosystems as heat, chemical elements (or nutrients) that compose molecules within organisms are not altered and may repeatedly cycle between organisms and their environment. Approximately 40 elements compose the bodies of organisms, with carbon, oxygen, hydrogen, nitrogen, and phosphorus being the most abundant. If one of these elements is in short supply in the environment, the growth of organisms can be limited, even if sufficient energy is available. In particular, nitrogen and phosphorus are the elements most commonly limiting organism growth. This limitation is illustrated by the widespread use of fertilizers, which are applied to agricultural fields to alleviate nutrient limitation. *See* BIOGEOCHEMISTRY; NITROGEN CYCLE.

Carbon cycles between the atmosphere and terrestrial and oceanic ecosystems. This cycling results, in part, from primary production and decomposition of organic matter. Rates of primary production and decomposition, in turn, are regulated by the supply of nitrogen, phosphorus, and iron. The combustion of fossil fuels is a recent change in the global cycle that releases carbon that has long been buried within the Earth's crust to the atmosphere. Carbon dioxide in the atmosphere traps heat on the Earth's surface and is a major factor regulating the climate. This alteration of the global carbon cycle along with the resulting impact on the climate is a major issue under investigation by ecosystem ecologists. *See* CONSERVATION OF RESOURCES; HUMAN ECOLOGY.   [J.B.Jo.]

Edentata   A group of mammals that encompasses several orders of unusual fossil and living animals characterized by reduced or strongly modified teeth. Usually included in this group are the order Pholidota, the pangolins or scaly anteaters of Africa and Southeast Asia; the order Xenarthra, the true anteaters, armadillos, sloths, and their relatives derived mainly from South and Central America; and the extinct Palaeanodonta, an early Cenozoic group of burrowing mammals from North America. The term "edentate" means toothless. Historically a wide range of toothless mammals and mammals with reduced dentition have been incorporated in this taxonomic group, among them aardvarks and echidnas. Modern systematists restrict the term to pholidotans, xenarthrans, and palaeanodonts based on several shared anatomical specializations found exclusively in these three taxa. Only the pangolins and the true anteaters lack teeth entirely, but all edentates are characterized by a reduced dentition. Typically the incisor teeth are lacking, the tooth enamel is strongly reduced or absent (although enamel is retained in a few of the early fossil forms and in the embryos of living armadillos), and tooth replacement is lost. All three groups share digging adaptations, and specializations for feeding on ants and termites. In addition, pangolins and some xenarthrans have a scaly external body covering. Some mammalian systematists have suggested that edentates represent one of the most primitive groups of living placental mammals, although the matter is somewhat controversial. *See* TOOTH.
          [T.J.G.]

Effector systems   Those organ systems of the animal body which mediate overt behavior. Injury to an effector system leads to loss or to subnormal execution of behavior patterns mediated by the system, conditions termed paralysis and paresis, respectively.

Overt behavior consists of either movement or secretion. Movement results from contraction of muscle. Secretion is a function of glands. Neither muscular contraction nor glandular secretion is autonomous but is regulated by an activating mechanism which may be either neural or humoral. In neurally activated systems the effector organ, whether muscle or gland, is supplied by nerve fibers originating from cell bodies situated in the central nervous system or in peripherally located aggregates of nerve cell bodies known as ganglia.

In other effector systems (humeromuscular and humeroglandular) the activating agent is normally a blood-borne chemical substance produced in an organ distant from the effector organ. For example, uterine smooth muscle is uninfluenced by the uterine nerve activity but contracts vigorously when the blood contains pitocin, a chemical substance elaborated by the posterior lobe of the hypophysis.

Finally, some effector systems are hybrid in the sense that both nerves and humors regulate their functions. The smooth muscle of arterioles contracts in response to either nerve stimulation or epinephrine. Secretion of hydrochloric acid by the gastric mucosa is increased by activation of the vagus nerve or by the presence in the blood of histamine. Effector systems with both neural and humoral regulation are never completely paralyzed by denervation but may be deficient in reaction patterns when the quick integrated activation provided by neural regulation is essential. *See* NERVOUS SYSTEM (VERTEBRATE). [T.C.R.; H.D.P.]

Egg (fowl)   A single, large, living, female sex cell enclosed in a porous, calcareous shell through which gases may pass. Although they vary in size, shape, and color, the eggs of chickens, ducks, geese, and turkeys are essentially the same in structure and content (see illustration). Inward from the shell are the outer and inner shell membranes which are also permeable to gases. The membranes are constructed to prevent rapid evaporation of moisture from the egg but to allow free entry of oxygen, which is necessary for life. Air begins to penetrate the shell soon after the egg is laid, and it tends to accumulate in a space between the two membranes at the large end of the egg. *See* CELL (BIOLOGY).

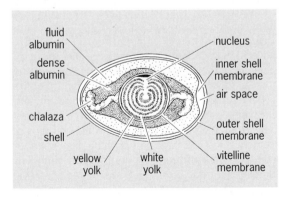

Egg of a bird. (*After L. P. Sayles, ed., Biology of the Vertebrates, 3d ed., Macmillan, 1949*)

The inner shell membrane surrounds a mass of fluid albumin which, in turn, encloses a body of dense albumin; these two types of protoplasm constitute the so-called egg white. The central part of the egg is occupied by the yolk, which contains the vital egg nucleus and its associated parts. The yolk consists of alternating layers of yellow and white yolk. The yolk, enclosed by the vitelline membrane, is held in place by the chalaza which is anchored at each end of the egg and prevents undue mechanical disturbance. *See* CELL NUCLEUS; YOLK SAC. [J.F.F.]

Eicosanoids   A family of naturally occurring, biologically active substances derived from 20 carbon polyunsaturated fatty acids such as arachidonic acid. Members of the family include prostaglandins, thromboxanes, leukotrienes, and epoxyeicosatrienoic acids (EETs). Functioning as local hormones, they are synthesized and exert their biological actions in the same tissue. Many have physiological and pathological effects on the cardiovascular, pulmonary, reproductive, and digestive systems.

Physiologically and pathologically, eicosanoids are local hormones. They are synthesized and exert their action in a tissue, and only certain eicosanoids are made by the cells of a tissue. As a result, the action of an eicosanoid is usually discrete and related to the physiological demands of the tissue.

The prostaglandins, leukotrienes, TXA_2, and anandamide act by binding to and activating membrane receptor proteins. Distinct receptors have been identified for many eicosanoids. The existence of receptor subgroups explains how some eicosanoids such as PGE_2 have multiple actions.

The prostaglandins and TXA_2 have several actions that are necessary for maintaining normal homeostasis and organ integrity. PGE_2 and PGI_2 are potent vasodilators. These prostaglandins are synthesized in the blood vessel in response to vasoconstrictors and antagonize their effects. This action protects the organ from intense vasoconstriction and maintains nutritive blood flow. They also inhibit gastric acid secretion and may exert other cellular protective effects. In their absence, gastric ulcers develop. TXA_2 is made principally by platelets. It causes vasoconstriction and promotes platelet aggregation. These actions prevent excessive blood loss when a blood vessel is damaged or severed. PGI_2 is made by the blood vessel wall and has the opposite effects. It prevents intravascular platelet aggregates from forming and obstructing blood flow. The balance between the proaggregatory or vasoconstrictor action of TXA_2 and the antiaggregatory or vasodilator action of PGI_2 is critical to cardiovascular homeostasis. $PGF_{2\alpha}$ contracts uterine smooth muscle. With menstruation and destruction of the uterine lining, arachidonic acid is released and metabolized to $PGF_{2\alpha}$. Contraction of the uterine smooth muscle by $PGF_{2\alpha}$ contributes to the pain associated with menstruation. In pregnancy, an increase in prostaglandin synthesis is a major determinant of the onset of labor.

Increased synthesis of PGE_2 and PGI_2 mediates the vasodilation and pain sensitization associated with inflammation and arthritic conditions. Inhibitors of cyclooxygenase-1 and -2 (important catalysts in the synthesis of prostaglandins) such as aspirin and ibuprofen relieve the signs and symptoms of inflammation. However, they also block the constitutive, homeostatic functions of the prostaglandins by blocking cyclooxygenase-1, which can result in renal failure and gastric ulcers. Selective cyclooxygenase-2 inhibitors such as celecoxib are anti-inflammatory without the deleterious effects on homeostatic functions of the prostaglandins.

The leukotrienes are synthesized by leukocytes, and they also serve as inflammatory mediators. LTB_4 is chemotactic and promotes leukocyte aggregation. Thus, it attracts other inflammatory cells to the site of inflammation and sequesters them. LTC_4, LTD_4, and LTB_4 increase capillary permeability, causing the leakage of fluid and protein from the vasculature into the tissue. This contributes to the swelling associated with inflammation. LTC_4 and LTD_4 also cause bronchiolar constriction and increase mucus formation in the airways. These actions are thought to contribute to bronchial asthma. Inhibitors of 5-lipoxygenase and leukotriene receptor antagonists are useful in treating inflammation and bronchial asthma.

The EETs and 20-HETE (hydroxyeicosatetraenoic acid) are involved in the regulation of vascular tone and organ blood flow. In the blood vessel, EETs are synthesized by the endothelial cells in response to vasodilator hormones. The EETs diffuse to the adjacent smooth muscle cells and exert their action. They open potassium channels and hyperpolarize the smooth muscle cell membrane. This results in vasodilation. Thus, EETs serve as mediators of vasodilation. 20-HETE is made by smooth muscle cells in response to increases in intravascular pressure. It is a mediator of myogenic tone in blood vessels. In the blood vessel wall, 20-HETE and the EETs are counterregulatory mechanisms that control blood flow.   [W.B.C.]

Electrodermal response   A transient change in certain electrical properties of the skin, associated with the sweat gland activity and elicited by any stimulus that evokes an arousal or orienting response. Originally termed the psychogalvanic reflex, this phenomenon became known as the galvanic skin response. Electrodermal response (EDR) has replaced galvanic skin response as the collective term.

The skin of a relaxed person has a low electrical conductance (high resistance), and the skin surface is some 40 mV negative with respect to interior tissues. Sweat gland activity changes these electrical properties by increasing skin conductance and by changing the balance of positive and negative ions in the secreted fluid.

Tonic skin conductance varies with psychological arousal, rising sharply when the subject awakens and rising further with activity, mental effort, or especially stress. Phasic skin conductance responses are wavelike increases in skin conductance that begin 1–2 s after stimulus onset and peak within about 5 s. The amplitude of the skin conductance response varies with the subjective impact of the eliciting stimulus, which in turn varies with the intensity of the stimulus, its novelty or unexpectedness for the subject, and its meaning or signal value. Aroused subjects display spontaneous skin conductance responses, generated apparently by mental events or other internal stimuli; their frequency, like the tonic skin conductance level, increases with the level of arousal.

Electrodermal responses are measured in studies of emotion and stress, conditioning, habituation, and cognitive processing, that is, when it is desired to assess the differential or changing impact of a series of stimuli. See ELECTROENCEPHALOGRAPHY; SYMPATHETIC NERVOUS SYSTEM.   [D.T.L.]

Electroencephalography   The biomedical technology and science of recording the minute electric currents produced by the brains of human beings and other animals. Electroencephalography (EEG) has important clinical significance for the diagnosis of brain disease. The interpretation of EEG records has become a clinical specialty for neurological diagnosis.

The recording machine, the electroencephalograph, usually produces a 16-channel ink-written record of brain waves, the electroencephalogram. It is interpreted by an electroencephalographer. The placement of about 20 equally spaced electrodes pasted to the surface of the scalp is in accordance with the standard positions adopted by the International Federation of EEG, and is called the 10/20 system. Electrode positions are carefully measured so that subsequent EEGs from the same person can be compared. About 10 patterns or montages of combinations of electrode pairs are selected for transforming the spatial location from the scalp to the channels which are traced on the EEG pen writer.

The aggregate of synchronized neuronal activity from hundreds of thousands or millions of neurons acting together form the electrical patterns on the surface of the brain (brain waves). The cellular basis of the EEG depends on the spontaneous fluctuations of postsynaptic membrane potentials between the inside and the outside of the dendritic processes of postsynaptic cells. See SYNAPTIC TRANSMISSION.

Electrical voltage is transduced from the scalp by differential input amplifiers and amplified about a million times in order to drive the pens for the paper record. The recording usually takes 30–60 min during a relaxed waking state, and also during sleep when possible. Often, activating procedures are used, such as a flickering light stimulator and hyperventilation or overbreathing for about 3 min.

EEG waves are defined by form and frequency. Various frequencies are given Greek letter designations. Alpha rhythm is defined as 8–12-Hz sinusoidal rhythmical waves. Alpha waves are normally present during the waking and relaxed state and enhanced by closing the eyes. They are suppressed or desynchronized when the eyes are open, or when the individual is emotionally aroused or doing mental work. They may be synchronized by bright light flashes and driven over a wide range of frequencies by repetitive visual stimulation (alpha driving). They are of highest amplitude in the posterior regions of the brain. The alpha rhythm develops with age, reaching maturity by about 12 years, stabilizes, and then declines in frequency and amplitude in old age (over 65).

Beta rhythms are faster, low-voltage sinusoidal waves, usually about 14–30 Hz. They are more prominent in the frontal areas. They are often synchronized and prevalent during sedation with phenobarbital or with the use of tranquilizers and some sedative drugs.

Slower rhythms are theta and delta waves. Theta waves of 4–7 Hz usually replace the alpha rhythm during drowsiness and light sleep. Delta waves of 0.5–4 Hz are present during deep sleep in normal people of all ages and they are the primary waves present in the records of normal infants. Delta waves are almost always pathological in the waking records of adults.

The EEG reveals functional abnormalities of the brain, whether caused by localized structural lesions, essential paroxysmal states such as epilepsy, or toxic and abnormal metabolic conditions. The three major classes of abnormalities are asymmetries between the hemispheres, slow rhythms, and very sharp waves or spikes. Slow waves represent a depression of cerebral cortical activity or injury in the projection pathways beneath the recording electrodes. Sharp waves or spikes often indicate a hyperexcitable or irritable state of the cortex. During a full epileptic seizure attack, spikes become repetitive and synchronized over the whole surface of the brain.

The EEG is frequently used for the evaluation of comatose states. The record is slowed in all areas in coma, with delta waves predominating. If the EEG becomes isoelectric or flat for several hours, brain function is not recoverable and the coma may be considered terminal. "Brain death" is indicated by a flat EEG, recorded at the highest gain with widely spaced electrode positions and the absence of cerebral reflexes and spontaneous respiration.

Computer advances in the analysis of EEG signals that are emitted by the brain during sensory stimulation and motor responses have led to the discovery and measurement of electrical waves known as event-related potentials or evoked potentials. These responses are averaged by a computer to enhance the small signals and increase the signal-to-noise ratio, so that they may be graphed and seen.

The complexity of evoked potential and EEG analysis makes interpretation difficult in relation to where various components originate and their pattern of spread through time along the neural transmission pathways. In the 1980s, with the development of minicomputers and color graphics screens, the presentation of topographic information could be analyzed in sophisticated statistical ways for research and clinical purposes by electroencephalographers and neurophysiologists. This method is best known as brain electrical activity mapping (BEAM) and is used in many research investigations of brain activity patterns in learning and language dysfunctions, psychiatric disorders, aging changes and dementia, and studies of normal and impaired child development. Difficult neurological diagnostic problems that do not show anatomical deformities by brain scan methods may often be clarified by these new electrographic procedures. *See* BRAIN; NEUROBIOLOGY.   [J.Co.]

Electromyography   The detection and recording of electrical activity generated by muscle fibers. The basic elements of motor control in the body are the motor units which comprise motor neurons in the brainstem or spinal cord, their axons, and from ten to several hundred muscle fibers supplied by each motor neuron. Motor units vary in the size and properties of their motoneurons, the sizes and conduction velocities of their axons, the morphology of their nerve muscle junctions, and the structure and physiological properties of the muscle fibers supplied by each motor neuron.

Impulses originating in single motoneurons in response to various command signals from the central nervous system conduct to the periphery of the unit, normally causing all the muscle fibers in the unit to discharge. The electrical activity generated by the more or less synchronous discharges of all the muscle fibers in the unit may be detected by recording electrodes on the skin surface or by needles inserted into the muscle. Such potentials reflect the electrical activity generated by the whole motor unit.

Diseases affecting motor neurons are sometimes accompanied by spontaneous discharges of the axons. Additionally, degeneration of motor axons may leave some muscle fibers deprived of their normal innervation, some of which spontaneously fire. Such single muscle-fiber discharges are called fibrillations and are readily detected for diagnostic purposes by needle electrodes inserted into the muscle.

Electromyography may also be used to study primary muscle diseases such as the muscular dystrophies, and a wide variety of other metabolic inflammatory and congenital myopathies affecting the muscle fibers rather than motor neurons or their axons. *See* BIOPOTENTIALS AND IONIC CURRENTS.   [W.F.Br.]

Embryobionta   One of the two plant subkingdoms, the other being the Thallobionta. The Embryobionta are here considered to include eight divisions, the Rhyniophyta, Bryophyta, Psilotophyta, Lycopodiophyta, Equisetophyta, Polypodiophyta, Pinophyta, and Magnoliophyta. The Rhyniophyta are represented only by Paleozoic fossils, but the other seven divisions have both modern and fossil representatives. See the separate articles on each division.

The Embryobionta differ from the green algae (Chlorophyta) and from most Thallobionta in that the normal life cycle of the Embryobionta shows a well-marked alternation of generations in which the sporophyte (spore-producing, typically diploid) generation always begins its development as a parasite on the gametophyte (gamete-producing, typically haploid) generation. The young sporophyte is called an embryo.

The more primitive divisions of Embryobionta have the gametes produced in multicellular sex organs (archegonia and antheridia), in contrast to the unicellular oogonia and antheridia of the Thallobionta in general. In the more advanced divisions (Pinophyta and Magnoliophyta) of Embryobionta, the antheridia and archegonia are highly modified or entirely suppressed, in conformity with the general reduction of the gametophyte generation.

All divisions of Embryobionta except the Bryophyta have specialized conducting tissues (xylem and phloem) in the sporophyte. With the exception of most bryophytes, they also commonly have a characteristic stomatal apparatus which controls the opening and closing of numerous tiny pores (stomates) in the leaves and stems in response to environmental conditions. These specializations, together with the progressive reduction of the gametophyte in the more advanced divisions, reflect the progressive evolutionary adaptation of the Embryobionta to life on dry land instead of in the ancestral water. The Embryobionta are therefore often called the land plants, in spite of the fact that many of them, such as the water lilies, have returned to an aquatic habitat. The seven divisions of Embryobionta which characteristically have xylem and phloem have sometimes been treated as a single comprehensive division under the name Tracheophyta. See PLANT KINGDOM; THALLOBIONTA. [A.Cr.]

Embryogenesis The formation of an embryo from a fertilized ovum, or zygote. Development begins when the zygote, originating from the fusion of male and female gametes, enters a period of cellular proliferation, or cleavage. Cells of the embryo subsequently give rise to the tissues and organs of the body in a temporal and spatial pattern that creates a functional, multicellular organism.

Following cleavage, the cells of the animal embryo rearrange into three germ layers: an outer ectoderm, a middle mesoderm, and an inner endoderm. Cells, responding to intrinsic and extrinsic factors, eventually segregate from the germ layers and organize into the rudiments of the tissues and organs of the body. These rudiments alter the size and the shape of the embryo, endowing the body with its axial symmetry. Cellular growth and differentiation are the principal processes that transform the rudiments into functional tissues and organs. Once the organs and organ systems are formed, further development consists primarily of growth. See GERM LAYERS. [M.J.Ca.]

Major features of embryogenesis in flowering plants include the formation of root and shoot apical meristems; differentiation of primary vascular tissue; the transition from a heterotrophic zygote to an embryo capable of independent growth and development; and preparations for desiccation, dormancy, and germination. See APICAL MERISTEM; CELL DIFFERENTIATION; DEVELOPMENTAL BIOLOGY; EMBRYOLOGY; EMBRYONIC DIFFERENTIATION; EMBRYONIC INDUCTION. [D.W.Me.]

Embryology The study of the development of an organism, commencing with the union of male and female gametes. Embryology literally means the study of embryos, but this definition is restrictive. An embryo is an immature organism contained within the coverings of an egg or within the body of the mother. Strictly speaking, the embryonic period ends at metamorphosis, hatching, or birth. Since developmental processes continue beyond these events, the scope of embryology is customarily broadened to encompass the entire life history of an organism. Embryology may, in this wider context, consider the mechanisms of both asexual reproduction and regeneration.

Animals. The production of male and female gametes is commonly considered to be the first phase in animal development. The differentiating gametes arise from diploid stem cells in the gonads. Cell division by meiosis reduces the number of chromosomes carried by a mature gamete to one-half that present in the stem cell. See GAMETOGENESIS.

The union of gametes (spermatozoon and ovum), representing the second phase of development, creates a diploid zygote with the potential to form an entire organism. Two events must occur for successful fertilization: the ovum must respond to contact with the spermatozoon by making preparations for further development, an event called activation, and the haploid nucleus of the spermatozoon must combine with the haploid nucleus of the ovum, an event called amphimixis.

Fertilization is the typical method to initiate development, but it is not the only method. In a few animals, the ovum develops independently by parthenogenesis, that is, without the participation of a spermatozoon.

A period of cell proliferation, converting the unicellular zygote into a multicellular embryo, represents the third phase of development. Cleavage is a modified form of cell division by mitosis, distinguished by little or no growth between the divisions. The cells of the embryo, or blastomeres, become progressively smaller at the end of each division, so the embryo maintains the relative size and shape of the zygote. Small, fluid-filled spaces form between the cleaving blastomeres, and these spaces eventually coalesce to create an internal cavity, or blastocoele. Upon the appearance of a blastocoele, the cells of an embryo are referred to collectively as the blastoderm. See BLASTULATION.

The fourth phase of development is poorly delineated from cleavage, because the cells of the embryo continue to divide. Gastrulation is distinguished from cleavage by extensive cell rearrangements that lead, in most animals, to the establishment of three germ layers: an outer ectoderm, a middle mesoderm, and an inner endoderm. Endodermal and mesodermal cells of the blastoderm migrate to the inside of the embryo, while ectodermal cells remain on the surface, where they spread to completely cover the body.

Control of development passes from the cytoplasm to the nucleus immediately prior to gastrulation. Responding to cytoplasmic cues, the nuclei begin to specify the production of proteins that make the cells qualitatively different from one another. In a few invertebrates, the transfer of control from cytoplasm to nucleus actually fixes the developmental fate of a cell. In most other organisms, and particularly in vertebrates, the determination of cell fate is not finalized until the blastoderm has rearranged into the three germ layers. See CELL LINEAGE; GASTRULATION; GERM LAYERS.

The organization of cells into the tissues and organs of the body, constituting the fifth phase of development, is closely allied with gastrulation. Blastodermal rearrangements during creation of the germ layers shift cells into new positions and bring about new intercellular relationships. The developmental fate of a cell can, to a considerable degree, be the consequence of its new position. The influence exerted by one group of cells over the developmental fate of a neighboring group is called induction. Induction occurs by the transmission of chemical substances, called inducing agents.

Differentiation, or the process by which a cell becomes specialized, correlates to a reduction in the amount of genetic information that is expressed. Determination, or the fixation of a developmental fate, occurs when a cell has such a limited amount of usable genetic information that it must commit to a terminal pathway of differentiation. See CELL DIFFERENTIATION.

Cellular differentiation is just one aspect of morphogenesis, or the development of form. Morphogenesis must be considered at all levels of organization, ranging from the individual cell to the whole organism. Such a broad perspective complicates the formulation of general theories of development. Presently, no comprehensive theory exists, but there are some embryologists who anticipate that a theory is possible once activities of the DNA molecule have been fully integrated into the topic of development. See ANIMAL MORPHOGENESIS; REPRODUCTION (ANIMAL).   [M.J.Ca.]

Plants. Reproductive development in multicellular plants is generally divided into three phases: gametogenesis, fertilization, and embryogenesis. The zygote produced by the fusion of male and female gametes divides to form a multicellular embryo with meristematic regions that ultimately produce the adult plant.

Development of the cell in flowering plants begins with a diploid megasporocyte located within the nucellar tissue of an immature ovule. This megasporocyte undergoes meiosis to form a tetrad of four haploid megaspores. In the most common pattern of development, three of these megaspores degenerate, leaving a single functional megaspore that undergoes several postmeiotic mitoses to form a mature megagametophyte (embryo sac) composed of seven cells and eight haploid nuclei. One of these haploid cells is the egg cell.

Development of the male gametes begins with numerous diploid cells (microsporocytes) located within the anthers of an immature flower. Each microsporocyte undergoes meiosis to form a tetrad of four haploid microspores, which then separate and enlarge to form mature pollen grains. Each microspore divides unequally to form a large vegetative cell, and a small generative cell located within the cytoplasm of the vegetative cell. The generative cell divides again, in either the maturing pollen grain or the elongating pollen tube, to form two genetically identical male gametes, the sperm cells.

The zygote is produced as part of a unique process known as double fertilization. One of the male gametes fuses with the egg cell to form the diploid zygote, while the other male gamete fuses with two polar nuclei, located near the center of the embryo sac, to form a triploid endosperm nucleus. Following double fertilization, the zygote develops into an embryo composed of two parts, the embryo proper and the suspensor. The embryo proper ultimately differentiates into the mature embryo, whereas the suspensor degenerates during later stages of development and is not usually present at maturity.

Flowering plants can be divided into two groups, monocots and dicots. In most dicots, the endosperm tissue is gradually absorbed by the developing embryo and is not present in the mature seed. Nutrients required for the germination of dicot seeds are generally stored in the embryonic leaves known as cotyledons. In contrast, most mature monocot seeds contain a significant amount of starchy endosperm tissue that serves as a source of nutrients for the germinating seedling.

Two important regions of the mature embryo are the root and the shoot apical meristems. The entire shoot system (stems, leaves, and flowers) of the adult plant forms from cells that are located in the shoot apical meristem of the mature embryo. The root apical meristem that is formed during embryogenesis becomes active during the early stages of germination and ultimately produces the entire root system of the adult plant. See APICAL MERISTEM; ROOT (BOTANY).

The final stages of embryogenesis in angiosperms include maturation, desiccation, and preparation for seed dormancy.

Different patterns of embryo development are found in gymnosperms and in the more primitive vascular and nonvascular plants. Double fertilization and the development of a nutritive endosperm tissue are features unique to the angiosperms. The haploid microgametophyte (germinating pollen grain) in most gymnosperms contains two male gametes, but only one of these participates in fertilization. The nutritive function served by the endosperm tissue in angiosperms is served in gymnosperms by the large haploid megagametophyte. Early divisions of the zygote are also different in gymnosperms; the zygote typically undergoes a series of free nuclear divisions during the earliest stages of embryogenesis, and multiple embryos often arise from a single zygote through a process known as polyembryony. Even more striking differences in embryogenesis are found in ferns and mosses, where the haploid or gametophytic phase of the life cycle is much more extensive.

Several major differences also exist between embryogenesis in plants and animals. Plant cells are surrounded by a cell wall that limits the contact and movement between adjacent cells. Embryogenesis in plants therefore proceeds without the morphogenetic movements that are characteristic of animal development. Morphogenesis in plants is also not limited to embryo development, but occurs throughout the life cycle. The mature plant embryo is therefore not simply a miniature version of the adult plant. See PLANT MORPHOGENESIS.   [D.W.Me.]

Embryonic differentiation   The process by which specialized and diversified structures arise during development of the embryo. The process involves (1) an increase in the number of cell types, and (2) an increase in morphological heterogeneity through the arrangement of cells into increasingly complex structural patterns in the form of tissues and organs.

Differentiation begins in most organisms with fertilization of an egg with a sperm, after which the relatively large egg divides into many smaller cells called blastomeres. The blastomeres receive unequal portions of the cytoplasmic materials of the egg and are therefore initially somewhat different from each other. At the end of cleavage, the blastomeres are organized into a blastula, commonly either a hollow ball of cells or a flattened two-layered disk of cells. The cells of the blastula lie in different relative positions from those that will be occupied by their descendants in the adult organism. By a process known as gastrulation, they move to their approximate final positions and are arranged into three basic layers, called germ layers. However, only two layers form in the simpler multicellular organisms. The outer layer is the ectoderm, from which arise the nervous system and the epidermal layer of the skin. The innermost germ layer, the entoderm, forms the epithelial lining of the digestive tract and contributes the essential tissue of associated organs. In all but the most primitive animals a third germ layer, the mesoderm, is formed by cells which come to lie in the area between the other two layers. In higher animals the mesoderm gives rise to most of the cells of the organism, such as those found in the muscles, skeleton, blood, connective tissue, kidneys, gonads, and certain other organs. The molding of groups of embryonic cells into such diverse tissues and organs proceeds through a variety of morphogenetic processes, such as migration, aggregation, dispersion, delamination, folding, and differential local growth of cells. *See* BLASTULATION; GASTRULATION; GERM LAYERS.

Underlying the visible structural diversification of the embryo is the more fundamental and concomitant process of cellular differentiation (chemodifferentiation), by which embryonic cells are transformed into the highly specialized cells of the adult.

The mechanisms by which the course of cellular differentiation is realized are not precisely known. The factors involved may, however, be divided into two classes: (1) intrinsic, those operating within the cell, and (2) extrinsic, those brought to bear upon the cell from outside. Both classes of factors play a role in the differentiation of every cell. However, the relative importance of these factors varies considerably from one cell strain to another and also within the same cell at different stages in its development.

The fertilized egg begins development with a rich endowment, consisting of a nucleus with a set of paternal and maternal chromosomes together with a complexly organized cytoplasm. The activation of the egg by the sperm sets off a chain of actions and reactions that progressively transform the physical and chemical constitution of each descendant cell. The emergence of new cell characteristics may be attributed to an oscillating interaction between the intrinsic gene makeup of the cell and the surrounding cytoplasm. The dynamic imbalance existing between these interacting components drives the cell along its path of differentiation. In certain kinds of invertebrate embryos, interactions within each separate cell seem sufficient for guiding differentiation to its terminal state. Such embryos exhibit mosaic development. By contrast, in the embryos of vertebrates and certain invertebrates such as echinoderms, influences from adjacent cells are an essential part of the differentiation process. These embryos show regulative development. *See* CELL LINEAGE; DEVELOPMENTAL BIOLOGY; EMBRYONIC INDUCTION.

[C.L.Ma.]

Embryonic induction   In the early development of many tissues and organs of complex, multicellular organisms, the action of one group of cells on another that leads to the establishment of the developmental pathway in the responding tissue. The groups of cells which influence the responding cells are termed the inducing tissue. Since specific inducing tissues cannot act on all types of cells, those cells which can respond are referred to as competent to react to the action of a specific inducer stimulus.

Embryonic induction is considered to play an important role in the development of tissues and organs in most animal embryos, from the lower chordates to the higher vertebrates.

Perhaps the first major induction phenomenon occurs during the final stages of gastrulation of most animal embryos. Following fertilization, the egg divides to form a multicellular blastula-stage embryo. The cells of the blastula then undergo a series of movements which generate a more complex embryo, the gastrula, which contains three major groups of cells: ectoderm, mesoderm, and endoderm. The mesoderm actually arises as cells move from the surface of the embryo to the inside. Once inside, they induce the cells which reside over them, the surface ectoderm cells, to develop into the neural tube. The neural tube eventually forms the central nervous system. The first induction event of early embryogenesis is called primary embryonic induction. The migratory cells which invaginate from the surface and induce the development of the neural tube are termed the embryonic organizer. The first step in the sequence of events termed primary embryonic induction is the acquisition by the mesoderm of neural inducing activity. Proteins such as fibro blast growth factor and activin, which belong to a category of so-called peptide growth factors, play key roles in programming the mesoderm cells to induce overlying ectoderm to differentiate into neural structures. *See* GASTRULATION.

The development of a large number of tissues and organs is influenced by embryonic inductions. Various eye structures (lens, optic cup, and so on), internal ear structures, as well as several tissues (for example, vertebral cartilage) emerge from cells which were acted upon by inducer tissues. *See* NERVOUS SYSTEM (VERTEBRATES).

Limbs, kidney, nasal structures, salivary glands, pancreas, teeth, feathers, and hair are organs which require inductive stimuli. It is not known whether a single common mechanism underlies each of those inductions. Many scientists believe that inductive interactions are mediated by cell-cell contacts; that is, the developmental information which is transferred from the inducing tissue is thought to reside at the cell surface of that tissue. Perhaps the surface of the responding tissue recognizes the signal molecules present on the surface of the inducing tissue. In other instances, a secreted protein might move among various cells or tissues and exert its effects on competent cells.

The principles of animal development also apply to plants. A greater role is, however, usually played by the diffusion of small-molecular-weight signal molecules rather than cell-cell contacts or protein growth factors. The earliest stages of plant embryo development involve groups of cells acquiring the competence to respond to inductive signals. Later in development, inductive signaling also becomes important. For example, in flowering plants the distance between nodes along the stem elongates, and lateral buds form below the shoot apex. The buds are believed to develop in response to a concentration gradient of signal molecules which exists along the stem. Thus, a process which is analogous to embryonic limb bud formation in animals is played out, and both plant and animal inductions can be conceptualized in similar terms. *See* CELL DIFFERENTIATION; DEVELOPMENTAL BIOLOGY; EMBRYOLOGY; PLANT MORPHOGENESIS.

[G.M.M.]

Emotion   An umbrella concept in the common language, typically defined by instantiation by reference to a variety of mental and behavioral states. These range from lust to a sense of liking, from joy to hostile aggression, and from esthetic appreciation to disgust. Emotions are usually considered to be accompanied by some degree of internal, frequently visceral, excitement, as well as strong evaluative components. Emotions are also often described as irrational, that is, not subject to deliberative cogitation, and as interfering with normal thought processes.

These latter qualities are often exacerbated in the emotional behavior and expression seen in clinical cases. The expression of strong emotions is typically considered to be symptomatic of some underlying conflict, and even the positive emotions are used as indices of unusually strong attachments and atypical earlier experiences. Sigmund Freud introduced the concept of repression to describe a defense mechanism against the occurrence of strong emotional experiences. From the psychoanalytic point of view, what is repressed is not the emotion itself, since the very concept of emotion implies conscious experience, but rather the memory of an event which, if it became conscious, would lead to strong conflicts and emotional consequences. Many other defense mechanisms, such as rationalization and compulsive or obsessive neurotic symptoms, are also seen as serving the purpose of avoiding conscious conflict and emotional sequelae. *See* PSYCHOANALYSIS.   [G.M.]

Endangered species   A species that is in danger of extinction throughout all or a significant portion of its range. "Threatened species" is a related term, referring to a species likely to become endangered within the foreseeable future. The main factors that cause species to become endangered are habitat destruction, invasive species, pollution, and overexploitation.

Habitat destruction is the single greatest threat to species around the globe. Natural habitat includes the breeding sites, nutrients, physical features, and processes such as periodic flooding or periodic fires that species need to survive. Humans have altered, degraded, and destroyed habitat in many different ways. Logging around the world has destroyed forests that are habitat to many species. This has a great impact in tropical areas, where species diversity is highest. Although cut forests often regrow, many species depend upon old-growth forests that are over 200 years old; these forests are destroyed much faster than they can regenerate. Agriculture has also resulted in habitat destruction. In the United States, tallgrass prairies that once were home to a variety of unique species have been almost entirely converted to agriculture. Housing development and human settlement have cleared large areas of natural habitat. Mining has destroyed habitat because the landscape often must be altered in order to access the minerals. Finally, water development, especially in arid regions, has fundamentally altered habitat for many species. Dams change the flow and temperature of rivers and block the movements of species up and down the river. Also, the depletion of water for human use (usually agriculture) has dried up vegetation along rivers and left many aquatic species with insufficient water.

The invasion of nonnative species is another major threat to species worldwide. Invasive species establish themselves and take over space and nutrients from native species; they are especially problematic for island species, which often do not have defensive mechanisms for the new predators or competitors. Habitat destruction and invasion of nonnative species can be connected in a positive feedback loop: when habitat is degraded or changed, the altered conditions which are no longer suitable for native species can be advantageous for invasive species. In the United States, approximately half of all endangered species are adversely affected by invasive species.

Pollution directly and indirectly causes species to become endangered. In some cases, pesticides and other harmful chemicals are ingested by animals low on the food chain. When these animals are eaten by others, the pollutants become more and more concentrated, until the concentration reaches dangerous levels in predators and omnivores. These high levels cause reproductive problems and sometimes death. In addition, direct harm often occurs when pollutants make water uninhabitable. Agriculture and industrial production cause chemicals such as fertilizers and pesticides to reach waterways. Lakes have become too acidic from acid rain. Other human activities such as logging, grazing, agriculture, and housing development cause siltation in waterways. Largely because of this water pollution, two out of three fresh-water mussel species in the United States are at risk of extinction.

Many species have become endangered or extinct from killing by humans throughout their ranges. For example, the passenger pigeon, formerly one of the most abundant birds in the United States, became extinct largely because of overexploitation. This overexploitation is especially a threat for species that reproduce slowly, such as large mammals and some bird species. Overfishing by large commercial fisheries is a threat to numerous marine and fresh-water species. See FISHERIES CONSERVATION.

Efforts to save species focus on ending exploitation, halting habitat destruction, restoring habitats, and breeding populations in captivity. In the United States, the Endangered Species Act of 1973 protects endangered species and the ecosystems upon which they depend. Internationally, endangered species are protected from trade which depletes populations in the wild, through the Convention on International Trade in Endangered Species (CITES). Over 140 member countries act by banning commercial international trade of endangered species and by regulating and monitoring trade of other species that might become endangered. For example, the international ivory trade was halted in order to protect elephant populations from further depletion.

Typically, the first step is identifying which species are in danger of extinction throughout all or part of their range and adding them to an endangered species list. In the United States, species are placed on the endangered species list if one or more factors puts it at risk, including habitat destruction or degradation, overutilization, disease, and predation. Florida and California contain the most endangered species of all the contiguous 48 states. Hawaii has more endangered species than any other state. Hawaii, like other islands, has a diversity of unique species that occur nowhere else in the world. These species are also highly susceptible to endangerment because they tend to have small population sizes, and because they are particularly vulnerable to introduced competitors, predators, and disease.

For many endangered species, a significant captive population exists in zoos and other facilities around the world. By breeding individuals in captivity, genetic variation of a species can be more easily sustained, even when the species' natural habitat is being destroyed. Some species exist only in captivity because the wild population became extinct. For a few species, captive individuals have been reintroduced into natural habitat in order to establish a population where it is missing or to augment a small population. Depending on the species, reintroduction can be very difficult and costly, because individual animals may not forage well or protect themselves from predators. See ECOLOGY.   [L.H.W.]

Endocrine system (invertebrate)   The chemical integrating system in animals that lack a vertebral (spinal) column. An endocrine system consists of those glandular cells, tissues, and organs whose products (hormones) supplement the rapid, short-term coordinating functions of the nervous system. Almost all of the information about invertebrates pertains to the more highly evolved groups that will be discussed below, the annelids, echinoderms, mollusks, and most particularly two classes of arthropods, the insects and crustaceans. Several of the hormones in invertebrates are neurohormones, that is, they are produced by nerve cells. See NEUROSECRETION.

Insects. Increase in linear dimensions of an insect can only occur at periodic intervals when the restricting exoskeleton is shed during a process known as molting. Once an insect becomes an adult, it ceases to molt. The orderly sequence of molts that leads from the newly hatched insect to the adult is controlled by three hormones. The brain produces a neurohormone which stimulates a pair of glands in the prothorax, the prothoracic glands, causing release of the molting hormone, ecdysone. A third hormone, the juvenile hormone, produced by a pair of glands near the brain, functions during the juvenile molts to suppress the differentiation of adult tissues. Juvenile hormone permits growth but prevents maturation. *See* ECDYSONE.

Two neurohormones with antagonistic actions are involved in regulating the water content of insects. One, the diuretic hormone, promotes water loss by increasing the volume of fluid secreted into the Malpighian tubules, the excretory organs. The second, the antidiuretic hormone, acts to conserve water by causing the wall of the rectum to increase the volume of water resorbed from its lumen while lowering the excretion rate from the Malpighian tubules.

Bursicon, a protein neurohormone, is responsible for the tanning and hardening of the newly formed cuticle. During the development of some insects, a period of arrested development occurs, termed the diapause. The mechanisms controlling the onset and the termination of diapause are largely unknown. However, in some insects there is evidence for a hormone, proctodone, that reinitiates development. A very few species of insects, most notably the stick insect (*Carausius morosus*), have the ability to change color. This insect becomes darker at night and lighter by day as a result of the rearrangement of pigment granules within the epidermal cells. Darkening is due to a hormone produced in the brain.

Crustaceans. Higher crustaceans have a structure, the sinus gland, which in most stalk-eyed species lies in the eyestalk and is the storage and release site of a molt-inhibiting hormone. The Y-organs, a pair of structures found in the anterior portion of the body near the excretory organs, are the source of the crustacean molting hormone, crustecdysone. Chemically, crustecdysone is very similar to the ecdysone from insects; both substances can cause molting in crustaceans and insects. The sinus gland is a neuroendocrine structure, but the Y-organs are nonneural.

Crustacean pigment cells (chromatophores) are under hormonal control, as in insects. The active substances are released from the sinus glands and the postcommissural organs, which lie near the esophagus. Substances have been found that cause dispersion of the pigment within the chromatophore, as well as substances with the opposite action. *See* CHROMATOPHORE.

The compound eye of crustaceans has three retinal pigments. The movements of these pigments with illumination level control the amount of light impinging on the photosensitive cells. A substance has been found that causes the migration of these pigments toward the light-adapted positions and another substance that causes migration toward dark-adapted positions.

The pericardial organs, which are found near the heart, are neuroendocrine organs that cause an increase in the amplitude of the heart beat. The sinus gland contains the hyperglycemic hormone, which causes a rise in blood glucose.

Annelids. Strong evidence for hormones in annelids has been obtained from studies of the reproductive system. One substance that has been found in some marine annelids inhibits maturation of the gametes. This substance was thought to have been produced by the brain, but studies show that another structure, the infracerebral gland, which lies ventral to the brain, may be involved.

Echinoderms. The radial nerves of starfishes contain two substances that are required for the maintenance of a normal reproductive cycle. One, the shedding substance, induces spawning. The second, shedhibin, inhibits the former.

Mollusks. The best-established endocrine organs in mollusks, the optic glands, occur in the octopus and squid. They are a pair of small structures, found near the brain, that produce a substance which causes gonadal maturation. The optic glands in turn are regulated by inhibitory nerves from the brain. There is also some evidence that a portion of the nervous system (the pleural ganglia) may secrete a hormone that affects water balance. Removal of the pleural ganglia from a freshwater snail results in swelling of the animal due to the influx of water.   [M.F.]

Endocrine system (vertebrate)   A system of chemical communication among cells. The classical vertebrate endocrine system consists of a group of discrete glands that secrete unique products (hormones) into the bloodstream. These products travel in the blood to distant sites or targets where they cause specific physiological responses. Thus endocrine glands differ from exocrine glands, in that they lack ducts and deliver their secretions in the bloodstream. The classical definition of an endocrine system has become harder to apply with the discovery of scattered cells rather than discrete glands that act as endocrine organs, of endocrine cells that affect themselves (autocrine effect) or nearby targets (paracrine effect) by diffusion through extracellular fluids rather than the bloodstream, and of neurons that secrete hormones (neurosecretion). All of these mechanisms, however, allow for chemical intercellular communication and can be considered part of the endocrine system. *See* Neurosecretion.

One important function of the endocrine system, along with the nervous system, is to maintain homeostasis, that is, a constancy of the internal environment of an organism. Thus an organism reacts and adjusts physiologically to changes in its external environment. The roles of the endocrine and nervous systems in maintaining homeostasis are many, complementary, and overlapping. *See* Homeostasis; Nervous system (vertebrate).

Nature of hormones. Hormones are the products of endocrine cells. They are either proteinlike or steroidal. Peptide hormones are produced by protein synthetic mechanisms directed by the genes of the endocrine cells. They are stored in endocrine cells in secretory granules that bud off the endoplasmic reticulum and Golgi membranes, where protein synthesis occurs. The granules leave the cell by endocytosis and enter the bloodstream. Steroid hormones, on the other hand, are produced from cholesterol by a number of well-characterized, enzyme-catalyzed steps. Cholesterol is thus converted stepwise to various steroid families: the hormones of the adrenal cortex (cortisol and aldosterone), the estrogens (estradiol) from the ovary, and the androgens (testosterone) from the testis. Steroid hormones diffuse across the endocrine cell plasma membrane to enter the circulation. *See* Hormone; Protein; Steroid.

Since in most cases the blood carries hormones throughout the body, there must be a system by which only certain tissues respond to each hormone. This is accomplished by receptors, which are binding sites either on the surface of the target cell or within its nucleus. Receptors are high-molecular-weight proteins; the structure of some, such as the insulin receptor, is known. In general, peptide hormones cannot cross the plasma membrane, so their receptors are located there, whereas steroid hormones do pass through the plasma membrane of their targets and bind to nuclear receptors, probably located in the deoxyribonucleic acid (DNA).

In order for peptide hormones to stimulate physiological changes within the target cell, the "message" must be passed from the hormone-receptor complex of the plasma membrane to the interior of the cell. This process of signaling across the plasma membrane is accomplished by so-called second messengers of which the best known is adenosine 3′,5′-cyclic monophosphate (cyclic AMP). Steroid hormones, of course, have no need for second messengers since they are lipid-soluble and pass readily through the plasma membrane and into the cell. *See* Cell membranes; Second messengers.

Once hormones are bound with their receptors and have stimulated their target cells, physiological responses occur. This may involve such biochemical processes as conversion of an inactive form of an enzyme into an active one, stimulation of critical enzymatic pathways, increase in transport of glucose or amino acids into cells, or synthesis of new proteins. These events may result in overall changes in cell or organ function, metabolism, growth, or even the behavior of the organism.

The endocrine system is regulated by control mechanisms, the means by which homeostasis is achieved. The most common relationship between the hormone and its target is one of negative feedback, whereby the response to the hormonal stimulus turns off the original stimulus. For example, the endocrine pancreatic beta cells produce insulin in response to high blood sugar levels. Insulin is released into the blood, where it causes its target cells to take up glucose, thus reducing blood sugar. When blood glucose concentration falls, the secretion of insulin is turned off. The system is turned back on when the blood glucose content gradually increases again. *See* CARBOHYDRATE METABOLISM; INSULIN.

Pituitary gland and hypothalamus. The pituitary gland, or hypophysis, is located near the base of the brain. It secretes many hormones and controls the function of other endocrine glands. The production and release of the various pituitary hormones are regulated in turn by small peptide-releasing hormones from the hypothalamus of the brain. These factors are produced by neurosecretory neurons and travel to the adenohypophysis (anterior lobe of the pituitary) by way of a portal blood system. The releasing hormones stimulate specific cells of the adenohypophysis to produce and release their hormones. Generally speaking, each of the adenohypophysial hormones is affected by a separate releasing hormone. Thus, the hypothalamic thyrotropin-releasing hormone stimulates the synthesis and release of thyroid-stimulating hormone (thyrotropin) by the adenohypophysis. Other adenohypophysial hormones include adrenocorticotropic hormone, which stimulates the production of steroid hormones by the adrenal cortex; growth hormone, which stimulates protein synthesis and growth in many cells; prolactin, which stimulates the production of milk by the mammary glands and is important in many other functions; follicle-stimulating hormone, which induces growth of the follicles of the ovary prior to ovulation; and luteinizing hormone, which induces ovulation. The release of both follicle-stimulating and luteinizing hormones is governed by gonadotropin-releasing hormone.

Other hypothalamic hormones do not reach the pituitary by way of the bloodstream; instead they travel down the long axons of the neurosecretory cells into the neurohypophysis (posterior lobe of the pituitary). Oxytocin acts upon the mammary glands of female mammals to cause milk release in response to suckling by the young, and stimulates the uterus to contract at the end of pregnancy to aid in expulsion of the offspring. Vasopressin (or antidiuretic hormone) is important in water conservation by the kidney tubules and also produces an increase in blood pressure. *See* PITUITARY GLAND.

Thyroid gland. The thyroid gland lies in the neck region of mammals. It produces two closely related hormones, triiodothyronine and thyroxine. These both increase the metabolic rate of an organism, and increase enzyme activity and protein synthesis. The thyroid hormones act along with growth hormone to promote cell growth and development. Thyroid hormones are peptides but their three-dimensional structures may be similar to those of steroid hormones. Thus they are unusual in their ability to pass through the plasma membrane of their target cells and bind to nuclear receptors.

The control of hormone secretion by the thyroid (as well as by the adrenal cortex and gonads) involves more complex feedback relationships. These endocrine glands are affected by the levels of hormones from the adenohypophysis. In the case of the thyroid gland, thyrotropin-releasing factor from the hypothalamus stimulates the release of thyroid-stimulating hormone by the adenohypophysis. In response, the thyroid secretes thyroxine and triiodothyronine. High blood levels of the thyroid hormones inhibit the secretion of both thyrotropin-releasing factor (long-loop feedback) and thyroid-stimulating hormone (short-loop feedback). *See* THYROID GLAND.

Calcium regulation. The parathyroid glands derive their name from the fact that in mammals they are embedded within the thyroids. These small glands are essential for life, as they regulate the concentration of calcium ion in blood and other extracellular fluids. If calcium is too low, the animal goes into tetanic convulsions and dies, whereas if calcium is too high, abnormal calcification and stone formation can occur. Parathyroid hormone is a protein hormone that raises the blood calcium levels (hypercalcemia). The hormone acts upon bone to cause the release of calcium and phosphate, and upon the kidney to increase the reabsorption (conservation) of calcium and excretion of phosphate.

Vitamin D is now recognized as a steroidlike hormone, although it does not originate from an endocrine gland. It is synthesized from precursors present in the diet or produced after exposure of skin lipids to ultraviolet light. Vitamin D plays roles in calcium conservation by the kidney and in bone mineralization, but its most important function is to enhance calcium transport across intestinal cells and thus conserve dietary calcium. *See* VITAMIN D.

Calcitonin is a newly recognized peptide hormone produced by thyroid cells in mammals (different cells from those that produce thyroid hormones) and from the ultimobranchial glands of nonmammalian vertebrates. Calcitonin is hypocalcemic and acts by inhibiting calcium loss from bone. Of the three calcium-regulating hormones, it appears to be the least important. *See* PARATHYROID GLAND.

Carbohydrate regulation. Insulin and glucagon are peptide hormones produced by endocrine cells of the pancreatic islets. Insulin is produced by the pancreatic beta cells and is the only hormone that decreases blood sugar (glucose) levels. It acts on its target cells (skeletal muscle, fat cells) to increase the uptake of glucose, amino acids, and fatty acids. Once taken into cells, glucose is used in metabolic reactions or stored as glycogen, a large carbohydrate. Insulin also causes the conversion of amino acids to proteins and fatty acids to fats in the target cells. In the absence of insulin, as in diabetes mellitus, the target cells cannot take up glucose, and thus the body must utilize amino acids and fats as energy sources. These processes result in the accumulation of toxic metabolic products which eventually disrupt the acid-base balance, leading to coma and death.

Glucagon, in contrast, is a hyperglycemic hormone. It is a small peptide from the pancreatic islet alpha cells that acts upon liver cells to cause the conversion of glycogen to glucose by activation of key enzymes in a complex metabolic pathway.

Many other hormones elevate blood sugar levels. For example, epinephrine (adrenalin), an amino acid derivative from the adrenal medulla, acts by the same pathway as glucagon to convert glycogen to glucose, except that the targets of epinephrine are skeletal and heart muscle. Epinephrine is secreted in times of stress and serves to prepare the body for an emergency by increasing the availability of energy in the form of glucose and by increasing the heart rate and blood pressure.

Growth hormone, a large protein hormone from the adenohypophysis, is secreted in response to low blood sugar levels. This hormone elevates blood sugar by blocking the uptake of glucose by cells and by favoring the utilization of fats rather than glucose as an energy source.

Many of the adrenal cortical hormones, such as cortisol, are known collectively as glucocorticoids, because they also elevate blood glucose levels. These steroid hormones favor the production of glucose from proteins and fats rather than glycogen (gluconeogenesis). Glucocorticoids also exert an anti-inflammatory action, which makes them useful for treatment of arthritis and other diseases. *See* ADRENAL GLAND.

Salt and water regulation. Several hormones affect the ability of the kidney to conserve or excrete salts and water. The antidiuretic hormone (vasopressin) promotes water reabsorption by the kidney tubules, so that the organism excretes less water. The secretion of vasopressin is regulated by hypothalamic neuro-secretory neurons that are sensitive to the concentration of salts in the extracellular fluids. In the absence of vasopressin, an individual excretes great volumes of dilute urine, leading to severe dehydration (diabetes insipidus).

Salt excretion is regulated mainly by two hormones that act in opposition. Aldosterone is an adrenal cortical steroid that promotes the reabsorption of sodium by the kidney tubules and thus decreases its excretion in the urine. In contrast, atriopeptin (atrial natriuretic factor), a peptide that originates in heart muscle, acts upon the kidney to increase the excretion of sodium in the urine. See OSMOREGULATORY MECHANISMS.

Reproductive hormones. Probably the best-studied endocrine glands are the gonads, the testes of the male and the ovaries of the female. The gonads are regulated by the follicle-stimulating hormone and luteinizing hormone from the adenohypophysis. In the male, follicle-stimulating hormone stimulates the initiation of sperm formation by the testis tubules, and luteinizing hormone acts on the nearby Leydig cells of the testis to produce testosterone, the principal male sex hormone. Testosterone acts by a paracrine mechanism to cause the final maturation of sperm, and by way of the blood to stimulate development of the male reproductive system and secondary sex characteristics. See TESTIS.

In the female, follicle-stimulating hormone stimulates the growth of the ovarian follicles at the beginning of each reproductive cycle. As the follicles grow, they produce estradiol. Increasing levels of estradiol cause feedback inhibition of gonadotropin-releasing hormone. High levels of estradiol also have an unusual positive feedback effect upon the hypothalamus and adenohypophysis to cause a surge in the secretion of luteinizing hormone, which results in ovulation. The corpus luteum, a remnant of the ovulated follicle, produces both estradiol and the second major female sex hormone, progesterone. Progesterone is necessary for the maintenance of a quiescent uterus during pregnancy, and both estrogen and progesterone are important in the regulation of the female reproductive cycle. Estradiol is also essential for the growth and maturation of the female reproductive system and secondary sex characteristics. In both males and females, the sex hormones affect reproductive behavior. See OVARY; REPRODUCTIVE BEHAVIOR.

Other hormones. There are many other factors that act in various ways to achieve homeostasis or intercellular communication, such as a large number of peptides found in both gastrointestinal cells and the brain. These were recognized for many years as gastrointestinal hormones which aid in secretion of digestive juices and motility of the gastrointestinal tract. Their function in the brain appears to be different, and there is evidence that they act in pain reception or analgesia, as factors that stimulate or curb appetite, or in memory or other functions. This field of neuropeptide hormones is in its infancy and serves to emphasize the close relationship between the endocrine and nervous systems in intercellular communication.   [N.B.C.]

Endocrinology   The study of the glands of internal secretion, the endocrine glands, and the hormones which they synthesize and secrete. These glands are ductless; the hormones are secreted directly into the blood to be carried to the target tissue or organ. The hormones, or chemical messengers, are highly specific and their action may be selective or generalized. See ENDOCRINE SYSTEM (VERTEBRATE); HORMONE.   [S.P.P.]

Endocytosis   The process by which animal cells internalize particulate material (such as cellular debris and microorganisms), macromolecules (such as proteins and complex sugars), and low-molecular-weight molecules (such as vitamins and simple sugars). Cells engage in at least three different types of endocytosis: phagocytosis where cells engulf particulate material, receptor-mediated-endocytosis of macromolecules, and potocytosis of small molecules.

Some of the essential nutrients that a cell needs are scarce in the environment. The cells overcome this problem by expressing high-affinity receptors, or binding sites, on the membrane surface. Each type of receptor is specific for either macromolecules or molecules. These endocytic receptors are capable of concentrating their ligand at the cell surface before carrying it into the cell, thus increasing the efficiency of uptake.

In all three endocytic pathways the internalization step begins with the invagination of plasma membrane and the conversion of this membrane into a closed vesicle called an endosome. Each of the pathways has its own set of molecules that control internalization. These molecules assemble at the cell surface and physically deform the membrane into the shape of a vesicle. The vesicle, the endosome, then detaches and migrates to other locations within the cell. The same cell-surface assemblage of molecules also attracts endocytic receptors that are moving around on the cell surface, causing them to cluster over the site of internalization. Receptor clustering, which is essential for efficient uptake, is sometimes stimulated by ligand binding.

Endosomes that are generated by the phagocytic and receptor-mediated endocytic pathways often fuse with lysosomes that contain many different hydrolytic enzymes. Small molecules, by contrast, do not need further processing, so during potocytosis they are delivered directly to the cytoplasm. *See* CELL MEMBRANES; LYSOSOME.

Phagocytosis. Phagocytosis is a receptor-mediated process where the receptors function as adhesive elements that bond the plasma membrane to the particle. The adhesive interaction of the phagocytic receptors with the membrane stimulates invagination. A critical molecule in this activity is actin, the same protein that provides power for muscle contraction. Surface membranes contain actin-binding proteins that link the phagocytic receptor to the actin cytoskeleton of the cell. Thus, when a particle binds to its endocytic receptor, a signal cascade is initiated that stimulates the recruitment of actin filaments to the site of phagocytosis. *See* CYTOSKELETON; PHAGOCYTOSIS; SIGNAL TRANSDUCTION.

Receptor-mediated endocytosis. The clathrin-coated pit is a segment of cell membrane that is specialized for receptor-mediated endocytosis. Each pit can be recognized by the presence of a polygonal lattice on the cytoplasmic surface of the membrane. This lattice shapes the plasma membrane into a coated vesicle that immediately uncoats and fuses with endosomes. The endosome functions as a switching area that directs membrane and content molecules to specific locations within the cell.

Potocytosis. Potocytosis uses membrane proteins that are anchored by lipid rather than protein as endocytic receptors. The lipid anchor causes the attached proteins to migrate in the plane of the membrane and cluster in a membrane specialization called a caveola. Clustering ensures that any ligand bound to these receptors will be concentrated in this location. When caveolae close, they create a tiny compartment of uniform size that is sealed off from the extracellular space. When the ligand dissociates from its receptor, it reaches such a high concentration that it naturally flows through water-filled membrane channels into the cell.

The closed caveolar compartment appears to be a unique space for the cell. It is transient, does not merge with other organelles, and can selectively concentrate extracellular molecules or ions and deliver them to the cytoplasm. In addition to importing molecules, cells can also use this space to store and process incoming or outgoing messengers that affect cell behavior. *See* CELL (BIOLOGY); CELL PERMEABILITY.   [R.G.W.A.]

Endodermis   The single layer of plant cells that is located between the cortex and the vascular (xylem and phloem) tissues. It has its most obvious development in roots and subaerial stems. The endodermis has many apparent functions: absorption of water, selection of solutes and ions, and production of oils, antibiotic phenols, and acetylenic acids.

The endodermis has been found to have extra sets of chromosomes as compared with cortical and other cells in the plant. In some plants the chromosome numbers may be so high in the endodermis that four sets of chromosomes may occur in each endodermal cell. The larger amount of nuclear material and nucleic acid in the cells of the endodermis may in part account for the great capacity of endodermal cells to produce large amounts of chemical substances, such as acetylenic oils, high in caloric energy. *See* CORTEX (PLANT).   [D.S.V.F.]

Endoplasmic reticulum   An intracellular membrane system that is present in all eukaryotic cells. In most cells the endoplasmic reticulum is thought to consist of only one continuous membrane enclosing only a single space. However, in protozoa, some unicellular algae, and possibly some fungi, the endoplasmic reticulum occurs as separate, multiple vesicles. *See* CELL MEMBRANES.

Several morphologically and functionally distinct domains of this continuous membrane system can be distinguished. At the level of the nuclear pores, the inner nuclear membrane is continuous with the outer nuclear membrane; both membranes together are referred to as the nuclear envelope. The outer nuclear membrane in turn is continuous with the rough endoplasmic reticulum, which contains specialized regions, termed transitional elements, and is continuous with the smooth endoplasmic reticulum. The two membranes of the nuclear envelope enclose the perinuclear space. The rough and smooth endoplasmic reticula and the transitional element enclose a space called the intracisternal space, or lumen. Both intracisternal and perinuclear spaces form a single compartment. All nucleated cells contain at least a nuclear envelope, but the amount of smooth and rough endoplasmic reticula varies greatly among different cell types. *See* CELL NUCLEUS.

The term rough endoplasmic reticulum is based on the morphologic appearance of attached ribosomes, which are absent from smooth endoplasmic reticulum. (Ribosomes are also associated with the outer nuclear membrane; in fact, the outer nuclear membrane and the rough endoplasmic reticulum appear to be functionally equivalent.)

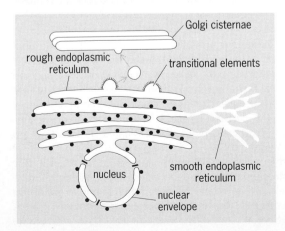

Nuclear envelope, connected to the rough and smooth endoplasmic reticulum. The rough endoplasmic reticulum is linked to the cis cisternae of the Golgi complex by vesicles that shuttle between the two compartments.

Another morphologic distinction is the organization of the rough endoplasmic reticulun in interconnected flattened sacs (called cisternae), whereas the smooth endoplasmic reticulum forms a tubular network (see illustration). *See* Ribosomes.

The rough endoplasmic reticulum is the site of translocation of secretory and lysosomal proteins from the cytosol to the intracisternal space, and of integration into the membrane of integral membrane proteins. Except for integral membrane proteins of chloroplast, mitochondria, and peroxisomes, essentially all other integral membrane proteins are integrated into the endoplasmic reticulum and either remain there (resident endoplasmic reticulum membrane proteins) or are subsequently distributed to other cellular membranes.

The signal hypothesis was formulated to explain how these proteins are targeted to and then translocated across or integrated into the endoplasmic reticulum membrane. Its tenets are that all polypeptides targeted to this membrane contain a discrete sequence (termed the signal sequence), that a complex machinery recognizes this sequence, and that recognition triggers the opening of a proteinaceous channel through which the polypeptide passes across the membrane. In the case of membrane proteins, the existence of an additional topogenic sequence, the so-called stop-transfer sequence, was postulated. This sequence is thought to trigger opening of the channel to the lipid bilayer to abort translocation and thus integrate the protein into the lipid bilayer.

The rough endoplasmic reticulum also contains numerous enzymes, most of which are involved in the modification of the nascent protein chain on the cisternal side. Thus the main function of the rough endoplasmic reticulum and the outer nuclear membrane is to serve as a port of entry of secretory, lysosomal, and integral membrane proteins and as the site of their initial modification.

Secretory and lysosomal proteins as well as those integral membrane proteins that are not residents of the endoplasmic reticulum are next transported to the cis Golgi cisternae. The transitional elements represent sites of transport from the rough endoplasmic reticulum. Coated vesicles carrying proteins to be transported form at these sites and, after uncoating, eventually fuse with the cis Golgi cisternae. *See* Golgi apparatus.

Smooth endoplasmic reticulum contains enzymes for phospholipid biosynthesis, steroid biosynthesis, and drug detoxification. *See* Cell (biology); Cell organization; Enzyme.

[G.B.B.]

Endorphins   A family of endogenous morphinelike peptides present within the central nervous system. The term endorphin is generic, referring to all the opioid peptides, while specific peptides are given individual names, such as the enkephalins and β-endorphin. Their discovery has greatly enhanced the understanding of the mechanism of action of opiate drugs and how the perception of pain is modulated within the central nervous system. *See* Opiates; Pain.

Morphine, codeine, and their many synthetic and semisynthetic analogs are effective pain killers that act through specific recognition sites, or receptors, localized on the surface of neurons within selected brain regions. These receptors have been extensively characterized, and a number of different subtypes have been identified which vary in their specificity for various opiates and opioid peptides and in the actions they mediate. The existence of these highly specific receptors implied that morphine was mimicking endogenous compounds within the brain with morphinelike actions, which have since been termed endorphins. *See* Morphine alkaloids.

The first endorphins to be isolated were the enkephalins, two pentapeptides differing only in their fifth amino acid, which is either methionine or leucine. Since the initial description of the enkephalins, a number of opioid peptides have been reported that all share either the structure of methionine (Met) enkephalin or leucine (Leu) enkephalin as their first five amino acids. The major genes for these peptides have been identified. β-Endorphin is perhaps the most interesting peptide; it is cogenerated with important, nonopioid hormones.

The enkephalins are distributed unevenly throughout the brain, with very high levels in the basal ganglia, the thalamus, and the periaqueductal gray. In addition, there are high concentrations of enkephalins in the adrenal medulla, where they are co-released with norepinephrine in response to stress, among other stimuli. The dynorphins and α-endorphin are located within the central nervous system with a distribution similar to that of the enkephalins. See STRESS (PSYCHOLOGY).

β-Endorphin has been identified in only a single group of cells within the hypothalamus. Its highest levels are in the pituitary gland. Within the pituitary, both ACTH and β-endorphin are derived from the same precursor protein and are located within the same cells. Stimuli that release ACTH, a stress hormone which in turn induces the adrenal gland to release steroids, also co-release β-endorphin at the same time. Thus, stressful stimuli that release ACTH and norepinephrine also release both β-endorphin from the pituitary and enkephalins from the adrenal into the blood. This is particularly intriguing in view of the decreased perception of pain reported under periods of stress, such as combat. See ENDOCRINE SYSTEM (VERTEBRATE).

All the endorphins can modulate the intensity of pain despite the fact that they act through different classes of opiate receptors. However, the presence of high concentrations of endorphins in brain regions unrelated to pain perception clearly demonstrates that the full range of actions of these compounds within the brain is not yet fully understood. Furthermore, their systemic hormonal role remains uncertain. See NERVOUS SYSTEM (VERTEBRATE). [G.Pas.]

Endotoxin A biologically active substance produced by bacteria and consisting of lipopolysaccharide, a complex macromolecule containing a polysaccharide covalently linked to a unique lipid structure, termed lipid A. All gram-negative bacteria synthesize lipopolysaccharide, which is a major constituent of their outer cell membrane. One major function of lipopolysaccharide is to serve as a selectively permeable barrier for organic molecules in the external environment. Different types of gram-negative bacteria synthesize lipopolysaccharide with very different polysaccharide structures. The biological activity of endotoxic lipopolysaccharide resides almost entirely in the lipid A component. See CELL MEMBRANES; LIPID; POLYSACCHARIDE.

When lipopolysaccharides are released from the outer membrane of the microorganism, significant host responses are initiated in humans and other mammals. It is generally accepted that lipopolysaccharides are among the most potent microbial products, known for their ability to induce pathophysiological changes, in particular fever and changes in circulating white blood cells. In humans as little as 4 nanograms of purified lipopolysaccharide per kilogram of body weight is sufficient to produce a rise in temperature of about 3.6°F (2°C) in several hours. This profound ability of the host to recognize endotoxin is thought to serve as an early warning system to signal the presence of gram-negative bacteria.

Unlike most microbial protein toxins (which have been termed bacterial exotoxins), endotoxin is unique in that its recognized mode of action does not result from direct damage to host cells and tissues. Rather, endotoxin stimulates cells of the immune system, particularly macrophages, and of the vascular system, primarily endothelial cells, to become activated and to synthesize and secrete a variety of effector molecules that cause an inflammatory response at the site of bacterial invasion. These mediator molecules promote the host response which results in elimination of the invading microbe. Thus, under these circumstances lipopolysaccharide is not a toxin at all, but serves an important function by helping to mobilize the host immune system to fight infection. *See* CYTOKINE; IMMUNOLOGY.

Even though endotoxin stimulation of host cells is important to host defense against infection, overstimulation due to excess production of endotoxin can lead to serious consequences. Endotoxin-induced multiple-organ failure continues to be a major health problem, particularly in intensive care; it has been estimated that as many as 50,000 deaths annually occur in the United States as the result of endotoxin-induced shock.

Immunization of humans with endotoxin vaccines to protect against endotoxin shock has not been considered practical. Efforts to provide immunologic protection against endotoxin-related diseases have focused upon development of antibodies that recognize the conserved lipid A structure of endotoxin as a means of passive protection against the lethal effects of this microbial product. *See* BACTERIA; MEDICAL BACTERIOLOGY; VACCINATION.   [D.C.M.]

Energy metabolism   Energy metabolism, or bioenergetics, is the study of energy changes that accompany biochemical reactions. Energy sustains the work of biosynthesis of cellular and extracellular components, the transport of ions and organic chemicals against concentration gradients (osmotic work), the conduction of electrical impulses in the nervous system, and the movement of cells and the whole organism. Sunlight is the ultimate source of energy for life. Photosynthetic cells use light energy to produce chemical energy and reducing compounds, used to convert carbon dioxide into organic chemicals such as glucose. The energy from the oxidation of carbohydrates, fats, and proteins sustains the biochemical reactions required for life.

The main sources of chemical energy for most organisms are carbohydrates, fats, and protein. Energy content is expressed in calories or joules. The nutritional calorie, or kilocalorie (kcal), in foodstuffs is equivalent to 1000 calories. The energy content per gram of carbohydrate is 4 kcal (16 J); protein, 4 kcal (16 J); and fat, 9 kcal (36 J). The metabolism of foodstuffs yields chemical energy and heat.

Energy is defined as the ability to do work, and metabolism represents the biochemical reactions that a cell can perform to produce energy. The most important thermodynamic parameter in bioenergetics is the free energy change, ΔG, occurring at constant temperature and pressure (the usual conditions for chemical reactions inside the cell). The Gibbs free energy change is defined as the free energy content of the final state minus the free energy content of the initial state.

All feasible reactions occur with a negative free energy change; the final state has less free energy than the initial state; that is, $\Delta G < 0$ (process is exergonic). If the free energy of the final state is more than that of the initial state, ΔG is positive and the reaction is not feasible without the input of energy; $\Delta G > 0$ (process is endergonic). When the free energy change is zero, the reaction or process is at equilibrium; $\Delta G = 0$ (process is isoergonic).

The complete oxidation of one mole of glucose to carbon dioxide and water is associated with the liberation of free energy. Energy is released in a stepwise fashion and is coupled to the biosynthesis of adenosine triphosphate (ATP) from adenosine diphosphate (ADP) and inorganic phosphate (P_i). The reaction of ATP with water to produce ADP and P_i results in the liberation of a large amount of energy (30 kJ, or 7 kcal per mole). Such compounds are said to be energy-rich and to possess a high-energy bond. Lipmann's law is the cornerstone of energy metabolism: ATP serves as the common currency of energy exchange in living systems (animals, plants, and bacteria). The ATP-ADP couple receives and distributes chemical energy in all living systems. Creatine phosphate is an energy-rich compound found in vertebrate muscle and brain; it is a storage form of chemical energy and can energize the regeneration of ATP from ADP. Such a reaction occurs in vigorously exercising skeletal muscle when ATP is expended to produce contraction. *See* ADENOSINE DIPHOSPHATE (ADP); ADENOSINE TRIPHOSPHATE (ATP). [R.Ros.]

Environment   The sum of all external factors, both biotic (living) and abiotic (non-living), to which an organism is exposed. Biotic factors include influences by members of the same and other species on the development and survival of the individual. Primary abiotic factors are light, temperature, water, atmospheric gases, and ionizing radiation, influencing the form and function of the individual.

For each environmental factor, an organism has a tolerance range, in which it is able to survive. The intercept of these ranges constitutes the ecological niche of the organism. Different individuals or species have different tolerance ranges for particular environmental factors—this variation represents the adaptation of the organism to its environment. The ability of an organism to modify its tolerance of certain environmental factors in response to a change in them represents the plasticity of that organism. Alterations in environmental tolerance are termed acclimation. Exposure to environmental conditions at the limit of an individual's tolerance range represents environmental stress. *See* ADAPTATION (BIOLOGY); ECOLOGY; PHYSIOLOGICAL ECOLOGY (ANIMAL); PHYSIOLOGICAL ECOLOGY (PLANT). [G.J.]

Enzyme   A catalytic protein produced by living cells. The chemical reactions involved in the digestion of foods, the biosynthesis of macromolecules, the controlled release and utilization of chemical energy, and other processes characteristic of life are all catalyzed by enzymes. In the absence of enzymes, these reactions would not take place at a significant rate. Several hundred different reactions can proceed simultaneously within a living cell, and the cell contains a comparable number of individual enzymes, each of which controls the rate of one or more of these reactions. The potentiality of a cell for growing, dividing, and performing specialized functions, such as contraction or transmission of nerve impulses, is determined by the complement of enzymes it possesses. Some representative enzymes, their sources, and reaction specificities are shown in the table.

Characteristics. Enzymes can be isolated and are active outside the living cell. They are such efficient catalysts that they accelerate chemical reactions measurably, even at concentrations so low that they cannot be detected by most chemical tests for protein. Like other chemical reactions, enzyme-catalyzed reactions proceed only when accompanied by a decrease in free energy; at equilibrium the concentrations of reactants and products are the same in the presence of an enzyme as in its absence. An enzyme can catalyze an indefinite amount of chemical change without itself being diminished or altered by the reaction. However, because most isolated enzymes are relatively unstable, they often gradually lose activity under the conditions employed for their study.

Chemical nature. All enzymes are proteins. Their molecular weights range from about 10,000 to more than 1,000,000. Like other proteins, enzymes consist of chains of amino acids linked together by peptide bonds. An enzyme molecule may contain one or more of these polypeptide chains. The sequence of amino acids within the polypeptide chains is characteristic for each enzyme and is believed to determine the unique three-dimensional conformation in which the chains are folded. This conformation, which is necessary for the activity of the enzyme, is stabilized by interactions of amino acids in different parts of the peptide chains with each other and with the surrounding medium. These interactions are relatively weak and may be disrupted readily by high temperatures, acid or alkaline conditions, or changes in the polarity of the medium.

Some representative enzymes, their sources, and reaction specificities

Enzyme	Some sources	Reaction catalyzed
Pepsin	Gastric juice	Hydrolysis of proteins to peptides and amino acids
Urease	Jackbean, bacteria	Hydrolysis of urea to ammonia and carbon dioxide
Amylase	Saliva, pancreatic juice	Hydrolysis of starch to maltose
Phosphorylase	Muscle, liver, plants	Reversible phosphorolysis of starch or glycogen to glucose-1-phosphate
Transaminases	Many animal and plant tissues	Transfer of an amino group from an amino acid to a keto acid
Phosphohexose isomerase	Muscle, yeast	Interconversion of glucose-6-phosphate and fructose-6-phosphate
Pyruvic carboxylase	Yeast, bacteria, plants	Decarboxylation of pyruvate to acetaldehyde and carbon dioxide
Catalase	Erythrocytes, liver	Decomposition of hydrogen peroxide to oxygen and water
Alcohol dehydrogenase	Liver	Oxidation of ethanol to acetaldehyde
Xanthine oxidase	Milk, liver	Oxidation of xanthine and hypoxanthine to uric acid

Such changes lead to an unfolding of the peptide chains (denaturation) and a concomitant loss of enzymatic activity, solubility, and other properties characteristic of the native enzyme. Enzyme denaturation is sometimes reversible. *See* AMINO ACIDS; PROTEIN.

Many enzymes contain an additional, nonprotein component, termed a coenzyme or prosthetic group. This may be an organic molecule, often a vitamin derivative, or a metal ion. The coenzyme, in most instances, participates directly in the catalytic reaction. For example, it may serve as an intermediate carrier of a group being transferred from one substrate to another. Some enzymes have coenzymes that are tightly bound to the protein and difficult to remove, while others have coenzymes that dissociate readily. When the protein moiety (the apoenzyme) and the coenzyme are separated from each other, neither possesses the catalytic properties of the original conjugated protein (the holoenzyme). By simply mixing the apoenzyme and the coenzyme together, the fully active holoenzyme can often be reconstituted. The same coenzyme may be associated with many enzymes which catalyze different reactions. It is thus primarily the nature of the apoenzyme rather than that of the coenzyme which determines the specificity of the reaction. *See* COENZYME.

The complete amino acid sequence of several enzymes has been determined by chemical methods. By x-ray crystallographic methods even the exact three-dimensional molecular structure of a few enzymes has been deduced. *See* X-RAY CRYSTALLOGRAPHY.

Classification and nomenclature. Enzymes are usually classified and named according to the reaction they catalyze. The principal classes are as follows.

Oxidoreductases catalyze reactions involving electron transfer, and play an important role in cellular respiration and energy production. Some of them participate in the process of oxidative phosphorylation, whereby the energy released by the oxidation of carbohydrates and fats is utilized for the synthesis of adenosine triphosphate (ATP) and thus made directly available for energy-requiring reactions.

Transferases catalyze the transfer of a particular chemical group from one substance to another. Thus, transaminases transfer amino groups, transmethylases transfer methyl groups, and so on. An important subclass of this group are the kinases, which catalyze the phosphorylation of their substrates by transferring a phosphate group, usually from ATP, thereby activating an otherwise metabolically inert compound for further transformations.

Hydrolases catalyze the hydrolysis of proteins (proteinases and peptidases), nucleic acids (nucleases), starch (amylases), fats (lipases), phosphate esters (phosphatases), and other substances. Many hydrolases are secreted by the stomach, pancreas, and intestine and are responsible for the digestion of foods. Others participate in more specialized cellular functions. For example, cholinesterase, which catalyzes the hydrolysis of acetylcholine, plays an important role in the transmission of nervous impulses. *See* ACETYLCHOLINE.

Lyases catalyze the nonhydrolytic cleavage of their substrate with the formation of a double bond. Examples are decarboxylases, which remove carboxyl groups as carbon dioxide, and dehydrases, which remove a molecule of water. The reverse reactions are catalyzed by the same enzymes.

Isomerases catalyze the interconversion of isomeric compounds.

Ligases, or synthetases, catalyze endergonic syntheses coupled with the exergonic hydrolysis of ATP. They allow the chemical energy stored in ATP to be utilized for driving reactions uphill.

Specificity. The majority of enzymes catalyze only one type of reaction and act on only one compound or on a group of closely related compounds. There must exist between an enzyme and its substrate a close fit, or complementarity. In many cases, a small structural change, even in a part of the molecule remote from that altered by the enzymatic reaction, abolishes the ability of a compound to serve as a substrate. An example of an enzyme highly specific for a single substrate is urease, which catalyzes the hydrolysis of urea to carbon dioxide and ammonia. On the other hand, some enzymes exhibit a less restricted specificity and act on a number of different compounds that possess a particular chemical group. This is termed group specificity.

A remarkable property of many enzymes is their high degree of stereospecificity, that is, their ability to discriminate between asymmetric molecules of the right-handed and left-handed configurations. An example of a stereospecific enzyme is L-amino acid oxidase. This enzyme catalyzes the oxidation of a variety of amino acids of the type $R—CH(NH_2)COOH$. The rate of oxidation varies greatly, depending on the nature of the R group, but only amino acids of the L configuration react.   [D.W.]

Enzyme inhibition   The prevention of an enzymic process as a result of the interaction of some substance with an enzyme so as to decrease the rate of the enzymic reaction. The substance causing such an effect is termed an inhibitor. Enzyme inhibitors are important as chemotherapeutic agents, as regulators in normal control of enzymic processes in living organisms, and as useful agents in the study of biochemistry. *See* ANTIBIOTIC; CHEMOTHERAPY; ENZYME.

Inhibitors have been classified as competitive, noncompetitive, and uncompetitive. The effect of a competitive inhibitor is to bind only free enzyme. This can be reversed by sufficiently increased substrate concentrations, so that essentially all of the enzyme is bound into an enzyme-substrate complex. Since both noncompetitive and uncompetitive inhibitors interact with the enzyme-substrate complex, their effects are not nullified by increased concentrations of substrate. An uncompetitive inhibitor exerts less effect (as percent of control) at low than at high substrate concentrations, since less of the enzyme is in the form of the enzyme-substrate complex, with which it interacts. A noncompetitive inhibitor, which reacts with both free enzyme and the enzyme-substrate complex, exerts comparable effects at all substrate concentrations.   [W.Sh.]

Epidemic   The occurrence of cases of disease in excess of what is usually expected for a given period of time. Epidemics are commonly thought to involve outbreaks of acute infectious disease, such as measles, polio, or streptococcal sore throat. More recently, other types of health-related events such as homicide, drownings, and even hysteria have been considered to occur as "epidemics."

Confusion sometimes arises because of overlap between the terms epidemic, outbreak, and cluster. Although they are closely related, epidemic may be used to suggest problems that are geographically widespread, while outbreak and cluster are reserved for problems that involve smaller numbers of people or are more sharply defined in terms of the area of occurrence. For example, an epidemic of influenza could involve an entire state or region, whereas an outbreak of gastroenteritis might be restricted to a nursing home, school, or day-care center. The term cluster may be used to refer to noncommunicable disease states.

In contrast to epidemics, endemic problems are distinguished by their consistently high levels over a long period of time. Lung cancer in males has been endemic in the United States, whereas the surge of lung cancer cases in women in the United States represents an epidemic problem that has resulted from increase in cigarette smoking among women in general. A pandemic is closely related to an epidemic, but it is a problem that has spread over a considerably larger geographic area; influenza pandemics are often global.

Disease and epidemics occur as a result of the interaction of three factors, agent, host, and environment. Agents cause the disease, hosts are susceptible to it, and environmental conditions permit host exposure to the agent. An understanding of the interaction between agent, host, and environment is crucial for the selection of the best approach to prevent or control the continuing spread of an epidemic.

For infectious diseases, epidemics can occur when large numbers of susceptible persons are exposed to infectious agents in settings or under circumstances that permit the spread of the agent. Spread of an infectious disease depends primarily on the chain of transmission of an agent: a source of the agent, a route of exit from the host, a suitable mode of transmission between the susceptible host and the source, and a route of entry into another susceptible host. Modes of spread may involve direct physical contact between the infected host and the new host, or airborne spread, such as coughing or sneezing. Indirect transmission takes place through vehicles such as contaminated water, food, or intravenous fluids; inanimate objects such as bedding, clothes, or surgical instruments; or a biological vector such as a mosquito or flea. *See* EPIDEMIOLOGY; INFECTIOUS DISEASE.   [R.A.Go.]

Epidemic viral gastroenteritis   A clinical syndrome characterized by acute infectious gastroenteritis with watery diarrhea, vomiting, malaise, and abdominal cramps with a relatively short incubation period (12–36 h) and duration (24–48 h). A viral etiology is suspected when bacterial and parasitic agents are not found. In the United States, no etiologic agent can be found in 70% of the outbreaks of gastroenteritis. Most of these may be due to viral agents, such as the Norwalk, Snow Mountain, and Hawaii agents, astroviruses, caliciviruses, adenoviruses, nongroup A rotaviruses, and paroviruses. Epidemics are common worldwide and have occurred following the consumption of fecally contaminated raw shellfish, food, or water, although the virus may be spread by airborne droplets as well. Epidemics are most frequent in residential homes, camps, institutions, and cruise ships. Many individual cases of mild diarrhea may in fact occur in epidemics for which the source of the infection cannot be found. Epidemic viral gastroenteritis is distinct from rotavirus diarrhea, a seasonal disease in winter that is the most common cause of diarrhea in young children, and affects virtually all children in the first 4 years of life. Since the diarrhea is often mild and of short duration, attention should be given to rehydration therapy and prevention by identification of the source. Fatalities have been associated with severe dehydration and loss of fluids and electrolytes in the stool. *See* ANIMAL VIRUS.   [R.G.]

Epidemiology   The study of the distribution of diseases in populations and of factors that influence the occurrence of disease. Epidemiology examines epidemic (excess) and endemic (always present) diseases; it is based on the observation that most diseases do not occur randomly, but are related to environmental and personal characteristics that vary by place, time, and subgroup of the population. The epidemiologist attempts to determine who is prone to a particular disease; where risk of the disease is highest; when the disease is most likely to occur and its trends over time; what exposure its victims have in common; how much the risk is increased through exposure; and how many cases of the disease could be avoided by eliminating the exposure.

In the course of history, the epidemiologic approach has helped to explain the transmission of communicable diseases, such as cholera and measles, by discovering what exposures or host factors were shared by individuals who became sick. Modern epidemiologists have contributed to an understanding of factors that influence the risk of chronic diseases, particularly cardiovascular diseases and cancer, which account for most deaths in developed countries today. Epidemiology has established the causal association of cigarette smoking with heart disease; shown that acquired immune deficiency syndrome (AIDS) is associated with certain sexual practices; linked menopausal estrogen use to increased risk of endometrial cancer but to decreased risk of osteoporosis; and demonstrated the value of mammography in reducing breast cancer mortality. By identifying personal characteristics and environmental exposures that increase the risk of disease, epidemiologists provide crucial input to risk assessments and contribute to the formulation of public health policy.

Epidemiologic studies, based mainly on human subjects, have the advantage of producing results relevant to people, but the disadvantage of not always allowing perfect control of study conditions. For ethical and practical reasons, many questions cannot be addressed by experimental studies in humans and for which observational studies (or experimental studies using laboratory animals or biomedical models) must suffice. Still, there are circumstances in which experimental studies on human subjects are appropriate, for example, when a new drug or surgical procedure appears promising and the potential benefits outweigh known or suspected risks. *See* DISEASE; EPIDEMIC.

Descriptive epidemiologic studies provide information about the occurrence of disease in a population or its subgroups and trends in the frequency of disease over time. Data sources include death certificates, special disease registries, surveys, and population censuses; the most common measures of disease occurrence are (1) mortality (number of deaths yearly per 1000 of population at risk); (2) incidence (number of new cases yearly per 100,000 of population at risk); and (3) prevalence (number of existing cases at a given time per 100 of population at risk). Descriptive measures are useful for identifying populations and subgroups at high and low risk of disease and for monitoring time trends for specific diseases. They provide the leads for analytic studies designed to investigate factors responsible for such disease profiles.

Analytic epidemiologic studies seek to identify specific factors that increase or decrease the risk of disease and to quantify the associated risk. In observational studies, the researcher does not alter the behavior or exposure of the study subjects, but observes them to learn whether those exposed to different factors differ in disease rates. Alternatively, the researcher attempts to learn what factors distinguish people who have developed a particular disease from those who have not. In experimental studies, the investigator alters the behavior, exposure, or treatment of people to determine the impact of the intervention on the disease. Usually two groups are studied, one that experiences the intervention (the experimental group) and one that does not (the control group). Outcome measures include incidence, mortality, and survival rates in both the intervention and control groups.   [V.L.E.]

Epidermis (plant)   The outermost layer (occasionally several layers) of cells on the primary plant body. Its structure is variable; this article singles out five structural components of the tissue: (1) cuticle; (2) stomatal apparatus (including guard cells and subsidiary cells); (3) bulliform (motor) cells; (4) trichomes; and (5) root hairs.

Leaves, herbaceous stems, and floral organs usually retain the epidermis through life. Most woody stems retain it for one to many years, after which it is replaced. In roots it is usually short-lived. See LEAF; PERIDERM.

Cutin is a mixture of fatty substances characteristically found in epidermal cells. It impregnates the outer cell walls and occurs as a continuous layer (cuticle) on the outer surface. The cuticle covers the surfaces of young stems, leaves, floral organs, and even apical meristems. Waxes appear as a deposit on the outside of the cuticle in many plants; the bloom on purple grapes and plums is an example. Most often the waxes are present in small quantity, but the leaves of some plants may be almost white with wax (*Echeveria subrigida*). The waxes of a few species are of great commercial value in the manufacture of polishes for floors, furniture, automobiles, and shoes. Other substances, such as gums, resins, and salts, usually in crystalline form, may be deposited on the outside of the cuticle.

The apertures in the epidermis which are surrounded by two specialized cells, the guard cells, are known as stomata. The singular form, stoma, is derived from the Greek word for mouth. However, some authorities prefer to include both aperture and guard cells within the concept of stoma. The apertures of stomata are contiguous with the intercellular space system of underlying tissues and thus permit gas exchange between internal cells and the external environment. The opening and closing of the stomatal aperture is caused by relative changes in turgor between the guard cells and surrounding epidermal cells.

Bulliform (motor) cells are large, highly vacuolated cells that occur on the leaves of many monocotyledons but are probably best known in grasses. They are thought to play a role in the unfolding of developing leaves and in the rolling and unrolling of mature leaves in response to alternating wet and dry periods.

Appendages derived from the protoderm are known as trichomes; the simplest are protrusions from single epidermal cells. Included in the concept, however, are such diverse structures as uniseriate hairs, multiseriate hairs (*Begonia, Saxifraga*), anchor hairs, stellate hairs, branched (candelabra) hairs, peltate scales, stinging hairs, and glandular hairs (see illustration). Cotton and kapok fibers are unicellular epidermal hairs.

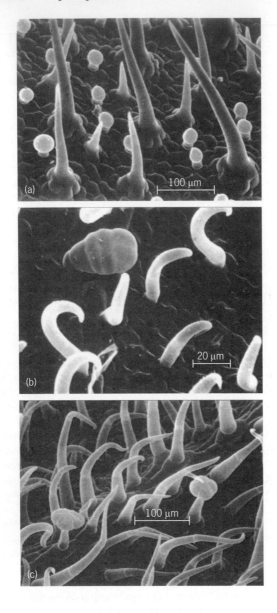

(a)

100 µm

(b)

20 µm

(c)

100 µm

Trichomes. (*a*) Unicellular and glandular (colleters) hairs of the geranium (*Pelargonium*), (*b*) Unicellular-hooked and uniseriate, club-shaped hairs of the bean (*Phaseolus*). (*c*) Uniseriate and glandular hairs of the tomato (*Lycopersicon*).

Root hairs are thin-walled extensions of certain root epidermal cells. They develop only on growing root tips and may arise from any epidermal cell, or from specialized cells known as trichoblasts. The life of a given root hair is usually numbered in days. *See* ROOT (BOTANY); SECRETORY STRUCTURES (PLANT).   [N.H.B.]

Epinephrine   A hormone which is the predominant secretion from the adrenal medulla; also known as adrenalin, it has the structure shown. Epinephrine is a sympathomimetic substance; that is, it acts on tissue supplied by sympathetic nerves,

OH

$$\text{CHOH}$$
$$|$$
$$\text{CH}_2\text{NHCH}_3$$

and generally the effects of its action are the same as those of other nerve stimuli. Conversely, the stimulation of the splanchnic or visceral nerves will cause the rapid release of the hormone from the medullary cells of the adrenal gland. Thus, epinephrine plays an important role in preparing the organism to meet conditions of physiologic emergency.

When injected intravenously, epinephrine causes an immediate and pronounced elevation in blood pressure, which is due to the coincident stimulation of the action of the heart and the constriction of peripheral blood vessels. The chief metabolic changes following the injection of epinephrine are a rise in the basal metabolic rate and an increase of blood sugar. These effects of epinephrine are transitory. See ADRENAL GLAND; CARBOHYDRATE METABOLISM.   [C.H.L.]

Epithelium   One of the four primary tissues of the body, which constitutes the epidermis and the lining of respiratory, digestive, and genitourinary passages. The major characteristic of epithelium is that the cells are close together, separated by a very small amount of intercellular substance. Epithelium may be derived from any of the three primary germ layers of the very early embryo—ectoderm, entoderm, or mesoderm. With very few exceptions, epithelium is free of blood vessels.

The functions of epithelium are varied and include (1) protective function, by completely covering the external surface (including the gastrointestinal surface—and the surface of the whole pulmonary tree including the alveoli); (2) secretory function, by secreting fluids and chemical substances necessary for digestion, lubrication, protection, excretion of waste products, reproduction, and the regulation of metabolic processes of the body; (3) absorptive function, by absorbing nutritive substances and preserving water and salts of the body; (4) sensory function, by constituting important parts of sense organs, especially of smell and taste; and (5) lubricating function, by lining all the internal cavities of the body, including the peritoneum, pleura, pericardium, and the tunica vaginalis of the testis.

The forces which hold the epithelial cells together are not satisfactorily understood. The intercellular substance between the cells, also called cement substance, is undoubtedly important. The interdigitation of adjacent cell surfaces and the occurrence of intercellular bridges in certain cells may also be important in holding the cells together. Finally, in certain cells local modifications of contiguous surfaces and the intervening intercellular substances, which together form the terminal bars, may be effective in the same way.

The outstanding property of the arrangement of most of the epithelium of the body is the economy of space achieved in the face of a broad exposure of the cell surfaces. The efficiency is achieved by the presence of numerous folds, which may be gross or microscopic and temporary or permanent. A part must also be attributed to the surface specialization of the epithelial cells themselves, such as their minute, fingerlike

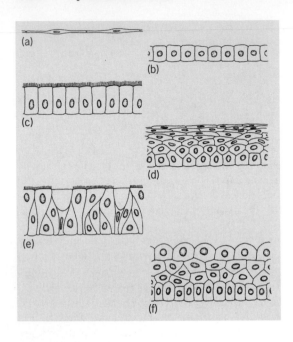

Cellular arrangements in epithelial tissues. (*a*) Squamous. (*b*) Cuboidal. (*c*) Columnar. (*d*) Stratified squamous. (*e*) Pseudostratified. (*f*) Transitional.

processes. Another specialization of the surface or epithelial cell is the occurrence of motile cilia. *See* CILIA AND FLAGELLA.

Classification of epithelia is based on morphology, that is, on the shape of the cells and their arrangement (see illustration):

I. Single-layered.
    A. Squamous (mesothelium, descending loop of Henle in the kidney)—thin, flat.
    B. Cuboidal (duct, thyroid, choroid plexus)—cubelike.
    C. Columnar (intestine), sometimes ciliated (Fallopian tube, or oviduct)—tall.
II. Multiple-layered or stratified.
    A. Squamous (skin, esophagus, vagina)—superficial cells thin and flat, deeper cells cuboidal and columnar.
    B. Columnar (pharynx, large ducts of salivary glands), sometimes ciliated (larynx)—two or more layers of tall cells.
III. Pseudostratified (male urethra), sometimes ciliated (respiratory passages)—all cells reach to basement membrane but some extend toward the surface only part of the way, while others reach the surface.
IV. Transitional (urinary bladder)—like stratified squamous in the fully distended bladder; in the empty bladder, superficial cells rounded, almost spherical.

An important property of epithelium is the ability of its cells to glide over surfaces. This allows replacement of dead cells to take place in the normal state, while presenting a closed surface to the external environment; replacement is especially important in wound repair. Gliding ability is also manifested normally in the movement of cells which slide over each other in transitional epithelium, for example, when the urinary bladder is being distended or contracted. *See* GLAND.   [I.G.]

Epstein-Barr virus   An antigenically distinct member of the herpesvirus group of viruses, whose genome is DNA. EB virus is the cause of one benign disease (infectious mononucleosis), and is associated with certain types of cancer; however, the great majority of EB virus infections are clinically inapparent. The virus was detected initially by electron microscopy in a small proportion of cells in continuous lymphoblastoid cell lines derived from Burkitt's lymphoma (but particles have not been seen in cells of the tumor itself). The virus also has been detected in cell lines derived from nasopharyngeal carcinomas, a type of cancer found with high frequency in persons from southern China. The virus is found in peripheral blood leukocytes from normal individuals and from patients with infectious mononucleosis. See INFECTIOUS MONONUCLEOSIS; LYMPHOMA.

If EB virus is indeed confirmed as having a role in the development of human malignancies, then one major question to be resolved is how a virus so ubiquitous can be involved in so wide a variety of responses. However, it should be recalled that many virus infections (for example, polio virus, hepatitis viruses, certain of the arboviral encephalitides) have a wide spectrum of outcomes, ranging from inapparent infection to severe syndromes. See ANIMAL VIRUS.   [J.L.Me.]

Ergot and ergotism   Ergot is the seedlike body of fungi (molds) of the genus *Claviceps*; ergotism is a complex disease of humans and certain domestic animals caused by ingestion of grains and cereals infested with ergot. Ingestion of these long, hard, purplish-black structures called sclerotia may lead to convulsions, abortion, hallucinations, or death. During the Middle Ages, hundreds of thousands of people are believed to have died from this disease, often referred to as holy fire, St. Anthony's fire, or St. Vitus' dance. Epidemics in humans, although less prevalent in modern times, last occurred in 1951, and the potential danger is always present, as shown by annual livestock losses due to ergot poisoning. There are 32 recognized species of *Claviceps*, most of which infect members of the grass family. Only three species are parasitic on the rushes and sedges. See PLANT PATHOLOGY.

Sclerotia have an unusual chemical makeup. They carry only 10% water by weight, and 50% of the dry weight is composed of fatty acids, sugars, and sugar alcohols, which make the ergot a storehouse of energy. Unfortunately, they also contain the poisonous alkaloids, ranging from 0 to 1.2% of the dry weight.

There are three types of ergotism (gangrenous, convulsive, and hallucinogenic). Their symptoms often overlap; the hallucinogenic form is usually observed in combination with one of the other two. The unusual combination of gangrenous and convulsive symptoms is sometimes observed in the Balkans and areas near the Rhine River.

The hallucinogenic form often includes symptoms of one of the other types. In its more pure form, it is referred to as choreomania, St. Vitus' dance, or St. John's dance. Vivid hallucinations are accompanied by psychic intoxication reminiscent of the effects of many of the modern psychedelic drugs. Early reports state that the disease usually manifested itself in the form of strange public dances that might last for days or weeks on end. Dancers made stiff jerky movements accompanied by wild hopping, leaping, screaming, and shouting. They were often heard conversing with devils or gods, and danced compulsively, as if possessed, until exhaustion caused them to fall unconscious or to lie twitching on the ground. High mortality rates were associated with severe epidemics involving any of the three forms of ergotism. The success with which the disease is controlled in humans has been brought about by (1) agricultural inspection, (2) use of wheat, potatoes, and maize instead of rye, (3) limited control of ergot, (4) reserves of sound grain, and (5) forecasting severe ergot years. The most recent and best-recorded epidemic was in southern France in 1951 when an unscrupulous miller used moldy grain to make flour.

In the early twentieth century two ergot alkaloids (ergotoxine and ergotamine) were isolated. Unfortunately, they caused significant side effects and were not as specific or active as some of the crude aqueous preparations. Shortly after its discovery, ergotamine was found to be effective in the treatment of migraines. Both ergotoxine and ergotamine cause vasoconstriction that can lead to gangrene with chronic use.

In 1935 a new water-soluble ergot alkaloid, ergonovine, was synthesized. Ergonovine is used to facilitate childbirth by stimulating uterine contractions. Many other important lysergic acid derivatives have been produced by means of semisynthesis. Of these derivatives, LSD-25 (d-lysergic acid diethylamide) is the most famous. LSD has been used experimentally, mainly in psychiatry and neurophysiology. See PSYCHOTOMIMETIC DRUG.

Through extensive research, many other uses for ergot alkaloids has been found. Ergotamine and dihydroergotamine are used to treat migraines, and methysergine is used in migraine prophylaxis. Dihydroergotoxine is prescribed for hypertension, cerebral diffuse sclerosis, and peripheral vascular disorders. Ergocorine and the less toxic agroclavine have been reported as unusual experimental birth-control agents. The drugs appear to inhibit implantation of the ovum. Several semisynthetic alkaloids are also active implantation inhibitors.   [R.L.M.]

Escherichia   A genus of bacteria named for Theodor Escherich, an Austrian pediatrician and bacteriologist, who first published on these bacteria in 1885. *Escherichia coli* is the most important of the six species which presently make up this genus, and it is among the most extensively scientifically characterized living organisms. *Escherichia coli* are gram-negative rod-shaped bacteria approximately 0.5×1–3 micrometers in size. Molecular taxonomic analysis based on the nucleotide sequences of ribosomal ribonucleic acid (RNA) has revealed that *Shigella*, a bacterial genus of medical importance previously thought to be distinct from *E. coli*, is actually the same species.

The natural habitat of *E. coli* is the colon of mammals, reptiles, and birds. In humans, *E. coli* is the predominant bacterial species inhabiting the colon that is capable of growing in the presence of oxygen. The presence of *E. coli* in the environment is taken to be an indication of fecal contamination.

Most strains of *E. coli* are harmless to the humans and other animals they colonize, but some strains can cause disease when given access to extraintestinal sites or the intestines of noncommensal hosts. *Escherichia coli* is the most important cause of urinary tract infections. Women are more susceptible than men; four out of ten women experience at least one urinary tract infection in their lifetime. Urinary tract infections may extend into the bloodstream, especially in hospitalized patients whose defenses are compromised by the underlying illness. This may lead to a type of whole-body inflammatory response known as sepsis, which is frequently fatal. Certain *E. coli* strains can invade the intestine of the newborn and cause sepsis and meningitis. These strains are acquired at birth from *E. coli* which have colonized the vagina of the mother.

Several different strains of *E. coli* cause intestinal infections. In the developing world, the most important of these are the enterotoxigenic *E. coli*, which produce enterotoxins that act on the epithelial cells lining the small intestine, causing the small intestine to reverse its normal absorptive function and secrete fluid. This leads to a dehydrating diarrhea which can be fatal, especially in poorly nourished infants. Therapy consists of oral or, in serious cases, intravenous rehydration. Enterotoxigenic *E. coli* are transmitted by ingestion of fecally contaminated water and food, and are a common cause of diarrheal disease in travelers in developing countries.

An important group of pathogenic *E. coli* in developed countries are the enterohemorrhagic strains, especially the serotype known as *E. coli* O157:H7. These strains are normal in cattle but cause bloody diarrhea in humans. A complication of approximately 10% of cases is a potentially fatal disease known as hemolytic uremic syndrome. The virulence of these strains involves the close attachment of bacteria to epithelial cells lining the colon, resulting in alteration of the epithelial cell structure, and the production of Shiga toxin. The toxin enters the bloodstream after being absorbed in the colon and damages the endothelial cells lining the blood vessels of the colon, resulting in bloody diarrhea. In cases of hemolytic uremic syndrome, the toxin circulating in the blood damages blood vessels in the kidney, resulting in kidney failure and anemia. Enterohemorrhagic *E. coli* are acquired by the ingestion of undercooked beef, uncooked vegetables, or unpasteurized juices from fruits which have been contaminated with the feces of infected cattle. An infection can also be acquired from contact with a human infected with the organism and from contaminated water. Children and the elderly are at greatest risk of developing hemolytic uremic syndrome.

Other strains which are pathogenic in the human colon include the enteroinvasive *E. coli* (including *Shigella*) and the enteropathogenic *E. coli*. Enteroinvasive *E. coli* cause a disease called bacillary dysentery characterized by bloody diarrhea. Enteropathogenic *E. coli* have been associated with protracted diarrhea in infants and can occasionally cause severe wasting. *See* TOXIN.   [S.L.M.]

Esophagus   A section of the alimentary canal that is interposed between the pharynx and the stomach. Because of divergent specializations in the various vertebrates, the esophagus cannot be described in general terms and is not always distinguishable.

In humans it is a tube running the full length of the neck and the thorax, held in its position ventral to the vertebral centra by a tunica adventitia of loose connective tissue. It has an inner lining of folded mucous membrane with an exceptionally thick lamina propria, a submucosa of elastic and collagenous connective tissue, and two layers of muscle. The musculature is striated in the anterior third of its length, unstriated in the posterior third, and variably intermixed in the middle. It is supplied with autonomic nerve fibers.

Although normally collapsed, the human esophagus is capable of considerable distension during the rapid passage of swallowed material, under which condition the folds of mucous membrane and lamina propria are temporarily smoothed out. Numerous microscopic esophageal glands open into the lumen, extending their compound tubules out into the submucosa.

In humans the transition from the esophagus to the stomach occurs quite abruptly at the diaphragm. The pharynx narrows posteriorly like a funnel and the foregut may thereupon enlarge, but much of what appears to be stomach may have an esophageal character histologically. *See* DIGESTIVE SYSTEM.   [W.W.B.]

Estrogen   A substance that maintains the secondary sex characters and organs, such as mammary glands, uterus, vagina, and fallopian tubes, of mammalian females. Naturally occurring substances with this activity are steroid hormones. The principal estrogenic hormone substances are 17(ß)-estradiol (with the structure shown), estrone, and estriol. They are produced and secreted directly into the bloodstream by the ovary, testis, adrenal, and placenta of pregnancy. Two other naturally occurring estrogenic hormones, equilin and equilenin, have been obtained only from the urine of pregnant mares and are apparently peculiar to that species. Stilbestrol, a synthetic compound with considerable estrogenic activity, has been used extensively in medical practice. *See* HORMONE; STEROID.   [R.I.D.]

Estrus   The period in mammals during which the female ovulates and is receptive to mating. It is commonly referred to as rut or heat. From one estrus period to the next there occurs a series of changes, particularly in the ovary, uterus, and vagina, termed the estrous cycle. With reference to the ovary, the cycle can be divided into a follicular phase, during which the Graafian follicles are ripening, and a luteal phase, during which the corpora lutea develop in the ovulated follicles. During these two phases, mainly estrogen and progesterone, respectively, are secreted, and these hormones control the uterine and vaginal changes. The beginning of the follicular phase is termed proestrus, and the luteal phase metestrus. Following the latter, there is a period of relatively little change, termed diestrus. In species in which the latter is prolonged, it is termed anestrus. *See* ESTROGEN; OVUM; REPRODUCTION (ANIMAL).   [A.T.; H.L.H.]

Ethology   The study of animal behavior. Modern ethology includes many different approaches, but the original emphasis, as expounded by Konrad Lorenz and Niko Tinbergen, was placed on the natural behavior of animals. This contrasted with the focus of comparative psychologists on behavior in artificial laboratory situations such as mazes and puzzle boxes. Ethologists view the naturalistic approach as crucial because it reveals the environmental and social circumstances in which the behavior originally evolved, and prepares the way for more realistically designed laboratory experiments. The approach goes back to the stress that Charles Darwin placed on hereditary contributions to behavior in all species, including humans. Viewing behavior as a product of evolutionary history has helped to elucidate many otherwise puzzling aspects of its biology and has paved the way for the new science of neuroethology, concerned with how the structure and functioning of the brain controls behavior and makes learning possible.

A central concept in classical ethology is that of the innate release mechanism. If a species has had a long history of experience with certain stimuli, especially those involving survival and reproduction, then to the extent that genes affect the ability to attend closely to such stimuli, natural selection leads to adaptations enhancing responsiveness to them. A common first step in the study of these adaptations was investigation of the development of responsiveness to such stimuli in infancy, focusing on situations that the ethologist knew to be especially relevant to survival. The term innate releasing mechanism, set forth by Tinbergen and Lorenz, eschews notions of innate mental imagery and has proved fertile in understanding how genes influence behavioral development, and in focusing attention of neuroethologists on inborn physiological mechanisms that permit learning while encouraging the infant to attend closely to very specific stimuli, the nature of which varies from species to species according to differences in ecology and social organization.

Modern research on the ethology of learning began when Lorenz discovered imprinting in geese. He found that if he led a flock of newly hatched goslings himself they became imprinted on him. When mature, they would court people as though confused about their own species identity. Learning occurred very rapidly and tended to be restricted to a short sensitive phase early in life. The learning is highly focused by genetically determined preferences both to follow a parent-object with particular appearance and emitting species-specific calls, and also to learn most quickly and ac-curately at a particular stage of development. The interplay between nature (genetic predisposition) and nurture (environmental influence) in learning is displayed especially clearly in imprinting, hence its special interest to biologists and psychiatrists. Indications are that it is not concerned so much with learning about species as with learning to recognize individual parents and kin, both to ensure mating with one's own kind and to avoid incestuous inbreeding.

There are many forms of imprinting. So-called filial imprinting, ensuring that duck-lings and goslings follow only their parent, is distinct from sexual imprinting, affecting mate choice in adulthood; the sensitive phases for learning are different in each case. Imprinting-like processes also shape the development of food preferences and abilities to use the Sun and stars in navigation.

Unlike psychological studies of animal learning in the laboratory, which have tended to favor the "blank-slate" view of the brain's contribution to learning, ethology empha-sizes the need to understand all aspects of the biology of a species under study before one can hope to understand how the animal learns to cope with the many complexities of individual existence and social living. Thus ethology may lead not only to an un-derstanding of how natural behavior evolves, but also to new insights into how brains help organisms learn to cope with social and environmental problems confronting them as individuals. *See* ANIMAL COMMUNICATION; BEHAVIOR GENETICS; INSTINCTIVE BEHAVIOR.
[P.R.M.]

Eudicotyledons   One of the two major types of flowering plants (angiosperms), characterized by possession of three apertures in their pollen; the other major type is magnoliids. Although this difference in pollen development and form has been known for a long time, it has become clear, as a result of several studies of deoxyribonucleic acid (DNA) sequences, that this difference is very significant. The high degree of coincidence of the genetic data with this pollen distinction means that it is more important to recognize this distinction than the number of seed leaves, as previously thought. *See* DICOTYLEDONS; FLOWER.
[M.W.C.; M.F.F.]

Eukaryotae   The vast array of living and fossil organisms comprising all taxo-nomic groups above the primitive unicellular prokaryotic level typified by the bacteria. The Eukaryotae thus include all plants and animals, the unicellular protists, and the fungi.

All organisms in this group possess an organized nucleus (or nuclei) in their cells, with a surrounding nuclear envelope and paired deoxyribonucleic acid–containing chro-mosomes; and elaborate cytoplasmic organelles, such as mitochondria, Golgi bodies, lysosomes, peroxisomes, endoplasmic reticulum, microfilaments and microtubules in various arrays, and, in photosynthetic forms, plastids or chloroplasts. Characteristically, centrioles, cilia, or flagelia are also present, the latter locomotory organelles composed mainly of tubulin with microtubules exhibiting a universal $9 + 2$ pattern. *See* CILIA AND FLAGELLA; PROKARYOTAE.

Organization at the organismal level ranges from solitary unicellular to colonial uni-cellular, mycelial, syncytial (coenocytic), and truly multicellular with extensive tissue dif-ferentiation. Modes of nutrition run the gamut: absorptive, ingestive, photoautotrophic, plus combinations of these three major kinds. Life cycles vary tremendously, with hap-loidy more characteristic of "lower" groups and diploidy of the "higher" taxa. Reproduc-tion, similarly, includes both asexual and sexual methods. In the "higher" multicellular forms, true embryos develop from the diploid zygote stage, which has resulted from fusion of sperm and egg cells.

Aerobic metabolism is commonly exhibited, especially by aquatic and terrestrial forms; anaerobic mechanisms exist, however, for numerous species found in poorly oxygenated habitats, including various sites within bodies of host organisms.

Size of species range from 1 micrometer (certain protozoa and algae) to many meters (whales, trees). Habitats cover all possible ecological niches: aquatic, terrestrial, and aerial, for free-living forms (many of which are motile, with the major exception of the trophic stage of various plants); and in or on all kinds of hosts, for symbiotic or parasitic forms (internal habitats, including cells, tissues, organs, or various body cavities). Dormant stages include cysts, spores, and seeds; these are often involved in dispersion or propagation of the species. *See* ANIMAL KINGDOM; FUNGI; PLANT KINGDOM; PROTOZOA.   [J.O.C.]

Eumycota   True fungi, a group of heterotrophic organisms with absorptive nutrition, capable of utilizing insoluble food from outside the cell by secretion of digestive enzymes and absorption. Glycogen is the primary storage product of fungi. Most fungi have a well-defined cell wall that is composed of chitin and glucans. Spindle pole bodies, rather than centrioles, are associated with the nuclear envelope during cell division in most species. Typically, the fungal body (thallus) is haploid and consists of microscopic, branched, threadlike hyphae (collectively called the mycelium), which develop into radiating, macroscopic colonies within a substrate or host. The filamentous hypha may be divided by cross walls (septa) into compartments. Hyphal growth is apical. Some species are coenocytic (without cross walls); others, including yeasts, are unicellular. Reproductive bodies are highly variable in morphology and size, and may be asexual or sexual.

Great changes in understanding the phylogenetic relationships of fungi have been brought about by the use of characters derived from deoxyribonucleic acid (DNA) sequences and the use of computer-assisted phylogenetic analysis; these changes are reflected in current classification schemes. A modern classification follows:

> Eumycota
>   Phylum: Chytridiomycota
>   Zygomycota
>   Class: Zygomycetes
>   Trichomycetes
>   Phylum: Ascomycota
>   Class: Archiascomycetes
>   Hemiascomycetes
>   Euascomycetes
>   Phylum: Basidiomycota
>   Class: Hymenomycetes
>   Urediniomycetes
>   Ustilaginomycetes

Fungi are found in practically every type of habitat. Most are strictly aerobic, although a few are anaerobes that live in the gut of herbivores. Some species are thermophilic. Many fungi form saprobic (including parasitic) relationships with animals and plants; the majority are saprobes. As now recognized, the Eumycota are a monophyletic group of the crown eukaryotes, presumed to have been present in the fossil record 900–570 million years ago. *See* FUNGI; MYXOMYCOTA; OOMYCETES.   [M.Bl.]

Eutheria A higher-level taxon that includes all mammals except monotremes and marsupials. Eutheria (Placentalia) is variously ranked as an infraclass or cohort within Mammalia. Eutheria includes over 4000 living species arranged in 18 orders; another 12 orders are known only from fossils. An ecologically diverse group, Eutheria includes primates, insectivores, bats, rodents, carnivores, elephants, ungulates, and whales. Like other mammals, eutherians are generally fur-covered and produce milk to nourish their young. In part because they can make their own body heat and regulate their body temperature, eutherians are widely distributed over most continents and occur in all oceans.

Eutherians, often called placental mammals, have a unique reproductive system in which unborn young are nourished for an extended period via a placenta. This system permits retention of the young in the protective environment of the uterus during most of early development. Fetal survival rates are high under most conditions. Young are born in a relatively advanced state of development and are never sheltered in a pouch after birth. Gestation time ranges from 20 days (for example, shrews and hamsters) to 22 months (elephants). Many eutherians have only one or two young per pregnancy, but as many as 20 offspring may be produced at a single birth in some species.

Eutherians range in size from insectivores and bats that weigh only a few grams to blue whales that can weigh over 190,000 kg (420,000 lb). All have a relatively large brain and exhibit complex behavior, with many living in social groups. Eutherians exhibit more variation in ecology than any other group of vertebrates, and these differences are reflected in their morphological specializations.

The fossil record of Eutheria extends back at least into the Cretaceous Period. Several differences in the skull and dentition distinguish fossil eutherians from early members of other mammal lineages (for example, marsupials). The earliest eutherians were apparently small, nocturnal mammals that may have resembled some modern insectivores. Although Cretaceous eutherians are known from most continents, diversification of the modern orders apparently did not occur until the Paleocene and Eocene. *See* CETACEA; CHIROPTERA; MAMMALIA; THERIA. [N.B.S.]

Evergreen plants Plants that retain their green foliage throughout the year. Popularly, needle-leaved trees (pine, fir, juniper, spruce) and certain broad-leaved shrubs (rhododendron, laurel) are called evergreens. In warm regions many broad-leaved trees (magnolia, live oak) are evergreen, and in the tropics most trees are evergreen and nearly all have broad leaves. Many herbaceous biennials and perennials have basal rosettes with leaves close to the ground that remain green throughout the winter. *See* FOREST AND FORESTRY; LEAF; PLANT TAXONOMY. [N.A.]

Exon In split genes, a portion that is included in the ribonucleic acid (RNA) transcript of a gene and survives processing of the RNA in the cell nucleus to become part of a spliced messenger RNA (mRNA) or structural RNA in the cell cytoplasm. Split genes are those in which regions that are represented in mature mRNAs or structural RNAs (exons) are separated by regions that are transcribed along with exons in the primary RNA products of genes, but are removed from within the primary RNA molecule during RNA processing steps (introns). *See* INTRON; RIBONUCLEIC ACID (RNA).

Exons comprise three distinct regions of a protein-coding gene. The first is a portion that is not translated into protein, but contains the signal for the beginning of RNA synthesis, and sequences that direct the mRNA to ribosomes for protein synthesis. The second is a set of exons containing information that is translated into the amino acid sequence of a protein. The third region of a gene that becomes part of an mRNA is an untranslated end portion that contains signals for transcription termination and for the addition of a polyadenylate tract at the end of a transcript.

The mechanism by which the exons are joined in RNA copies of genes is called RNA splicing, and it is part of the maturation of mRNAs and some transfer and ribosomal RNAs (tRNAs and rRNAs) from primary transcripts of genes. Three different RNA splicing processes have been identified. One involves mRNA precursors in nuclei, and specific sequences at exon-intron junctions that are recognized by certain nuclear ribonucleoprotein particles that facilitate the cleavage and ligation of RNA. Another applies to nuclear precursors of tRNA, where splice sites are determined by structural features of the folded RNA molecules. The third form of splicing was discovered in studies of protozoan rRNA synthesis, and has also been shown to be a part of the maturation of both rRNA and mRNA in yeast mitochondria; it is an autocatalytic process that requires neither an enzyme nor added energy such as from adenosine triphosphate. *See* GENE; GENETIC CODE; PROTEIN; RIBOSOMES.   [P.M.M.R.]

Exotic viral diseases   Viral diseases that occur only rarely in human populations of developed countries. However, many of these diseases cause significant human morbidity and mortality in underdeveloped areas, and have the proven capacity to be transported to population centers in developed countries and to cause explosive outbreaks or epidemics. Most of the exotic viruses are zoonotic, that is, they are transmitted to humans from an ongoing life cycle in animals or arthropods; the exception is smallpox.

Important diseases caused by exotic viruses include yellow fever, Venezuelan equine encephalitis, Rift Valley fever, tick-borne encephalitis, Crimean hemorrhagic fever, rabies, Lassa fever, hemorrhagic fever, and Marburg and Ebola hemorrhagic fevers. Control of these diseases is often very difficult because of the lack of detailed knowledge about the natural history of the viruses in their natural animal hosts, and because of the difficulty of controlling natural populations of alternative hosts such as insects or rodents.   [F.A.M.]

Eye (invertebrate)   An aggregation of photoreceptor cells together with any associated optical structures. Eyes occur almost universally among animals, and are possessed by some species of virtually every major animal phylum. However, the complexity of eyes varies greatly, and this sense organ undoubtedly evolved independently a number of times within the animal kingdom.

The simplest invertebrate organs that might be considered to be eyes are clusters of photoreceptor cells located on the surface of the body. Pigment cells are usually interspersed among the photoreceptors, giving the eye a red or black color. Accessory structures, such as the lens and cornea, are usually absent. Simple eyes of this type, called pigment spot ocelli, are found in such invertebrates as jellyfish, flatworms, and sea stars.

The most basic image-forming type of invertebrate eye probably arose from such patches of photoreceptor cells by an in-sinking of the sensory epithelium to form a cup, which may have become closed in conjunction with the evolution of a cornea and lens. Such an evolutionary history is clearly suggested by the embryology and comparative anatomy of many invertebrates.

In bilateral cephalic invertebrates, the eyes are typically paired and located at the anterior end of the body. Although one pair is usual, as in mollusks and many arthropods, multiple pairs are not uncommon. Some polychaete annelids have 4 eyes, and scorpions may have as many as 12. The greatest number of eyes is found in marine flatworms, where there may be over 100 ocelli scattered over the dorsal anterior surface and along the sides of the body. The occurrence of eyes on parts of the body other than the head is usually correlated with radial symmetry or unusual modes of existence.

The primitive function of animal eyes was merely to provide information regarding the intensity, direction, and duration of environmental light. The perception of objects is dependent upon several factors, namely, the number of photoreceptors in the retina, the quality of the optics, and central processing of visual information.

Image formation has evolved as an additional capacity of the eyes of some invertebrates. The number of photoreceptor cells composing the retinal surface is of primary importance, since each photoreceptor cell or group of cells acts as the detector for one point of light. An image is formed by the retina through the association of points of light of varying intensity, much as an image is produced by an array of pixels on a computer monitor. The ability of an eye to form an image and the coarseness or fineness of the image are, therefore, dependent upon the number of points of light that are distinguished which, in turn, is dependent upon the number of photoreceptor cells composing the retina. A large number of photoreceptor cells must be present to produce even a coarse image. The great majority of invertebrate eyes cannot form a detailed image because they do not possess a sufficient number of photoreceptor cells. The number of photoreceptor cells might be sufficient to detect movement of an object, but is inadequate to provide much information about the object's form. *See* PHOTORECEPTION.

The focusing mechanisms of invertebrate eyes vary considerably. The focus of arthropod eyes tends to be fixed, that is, the distance between the optical apparatus and the retina cannot be changed. Thus objects are in focus only at a certain distance from the eye, determined by the distance between the lens and the retina.

The oceanic family of swimming polychaete worms, Alciopidae, have eyes of that are focused hydrostatically. A bulb to one side of the eye injects fluid into the space between the retina and the lens, forcing the lens outward. Another mechanism is employed in octopods whereby lens movement is brought about by a ciliary muscle attached to the lens (as in aquatic vertebrates, like fish).

The compound eye of crustaceans, insects, centipedes, and horseshoe crabs has a sufficiently different construction from that of other invertebrates to warrant separate discussion. The structural unit of the compound eye is called an ommatidium (see illustration). The outer end of the ommatidium is composed of a cornea, which appears on the surface of the eye as a facet. Beneath the cornea is an elongated, tapered crystalline cone; in many compound eyes the cornea and cone together function as a lens. The receptor element at the inner end of the ommatidium is composed of one or more central translucent cylinders (rhabdome), around which are located several photoreceptor cells (typically 7 or 8).

The rhabdome is the initial photoreceptive element, and it in turn stimulates the adjacent photoreceptor cells to depolarize. The photoreceptor element of each ommatidium functions as a unit and can respond only to one point of light. Thus image formation is dependent upon the number of photoreceptor units present. The number of ommatidia composing a compound eye varies greatly.

Pigment granules surround the ommatidium proximally and distally, forming a light screen that separates one ommatidium from another. The pigment granules migrate, depending upon the amount of light. In bright light the ommatidium is adapted by funneling light directly down to the rhabdome, by extending the pigment screen, so that light received by one ommatidium is prevented from stimulating the rhabdome of another. Under these conditions the image produced is said to be appositional, or mosaic. The term mosaic has been misinterpreted to mean that a given ommatidium

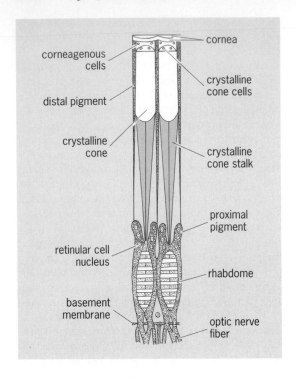

Two ommatidia from compound eye of crayfish *Astacus*. (*After R. D. Barnes, Invertebrate Zoology, 2d ed., W. B. Saunders, 1968*)

forms a separate image, even if only a part of the image. In general, however, the compound eyes function like any other eye—each photoreceptor unit represents one point in visual space. It is not obvious whether or not compound eyes have any special advantages over other eye designs, despite their universal occurrence in crustaceans and insects. However, in many arthropods the total corneal surface is greatly convex, resulting in a wide visual field.

Many invertebrate eyes are capable of seeing and analyzing patterns of polarized light in nature. This capacity reaches its apex in compound eyes, as well as in the simple eyes of cephalopods. Cuttlefish are known to communicate with each other with displays produced on their body surfaces that are visible only to animals that have polarization vision. Most invertebrates with polarization vision, however, use this ability to navigate with the assistance of patterns of polarization in the sky that occur naturally due to scattering of sunlight by the atmosphere. Bees and ants can find their way back to their nests or hives using only these celestial polarization cues. *See* EYE (VERTEBRATE).

[T.W.C.; R.D.B.]

Eye (vertebrate)   A sense organ that acts as a photoreceptor capable of image formation. The eye of vertebrates is constructed along a basic anatomical pattern which, in the diversification of animals, has undergone a variety of structural and functional modifications associated with different ecologies and modes of living. Often compared with a camera, the vertebrate eye is conveniently described in terms of its wall, cavities, and lens (see illustration).

Wall. The wall of the eye consists of three distinct layers or tunics which, from outward to inward, are termed the fibrous, vascular, and sensory tunics.

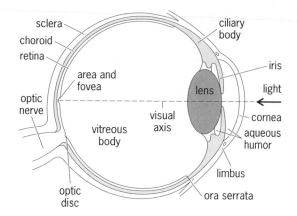

Horizontal section through human eye.

Fibrous tunic. This continuous, outermost fibrous tunic comprises a transparent anterior portion, the cornea, and a tough posterior portion, the sclera. In the human, the cornea represents about one-sixth of the fibrous tunic, the sclera five-sixths.

The vertebrate cornea exhibits very few modifications in structure regardless of environmental influences. Its major constituent is connective tissue (both cells and fibers), regularly arranged and bordered on both anterior and posterior surfaces by an epithelium. The anterior epithelium is stratified, ectodermal in origin, and continuous with the (conjunctival) epithelium lining the eyelids. The transparency of the cornea is attributed to the geometric organization of its connective tissue elements, its constant state of deturgescence, and its chemical composition. It is the first ocular component traversed by the incoming light.

The sclera, a touch connective tissue tunic, provides support for the eye and serves for the attachment (insertions) of the muscles that move it.

The limbus is located at the angle of the anterior chamber. This small, circular transitional zone between the cornea and the sclera houses the major route for the discharge of aqueous humor from the anterior chamber.

Vascular tunic. The vascular tunic or uvea makes up the middle layer of the wall of the eye. It does not form a continuous layer around the eye but is deficient anteriorly, where the opening is termed the pupil. Beginning at the pupil, three continuous components of the uvea can easily be recognized: the iris, ciliary body, and choroid.

The iris is a spongy, circular diaphragm of loose, pigmented connective tissue separating the anterior and posterior chambers and housing a hole, the pupil, in its center. When heavily pigmented, the human iris appears brown; when lightly pigmented, blue.

The ciliary body is continuous with the root of the iris. The posterior epithelium of the iris continues along the internal surface of the ciliary body as a double layer of cells (ciliary part of the retina) which assumes many folds for the attachment of the suspensory ligament of the lens. This ligament holds the lens in position and shape, and marks the posterior boundary of the posterior chamber. The inner layer of the ciliary epithelium contains no pigment. It produces aqueous humor which flows into the posterior chamber and thence into the anterior chamber (via the pupil). The continual production and removal of this fluid maintain the intraocular pressure of the eye (which is increased in glaucoma).

The choroid is the most posterior portion of the uvea. It is directly continuous with the subepithelial portion of the ciliary body and consists primarily of blood vessels embedded within deeply pigmented connective tissue.

Sensory tunic. The retina is the sensory tunic of the eye. It has the form of a cup closely applied to the inner portion of the choroid, and, internally, it is slightly adherent to the semisolid vitreous body. The vertebrate retina contains the light-sensitive receptors (visual cells) and a complex of well-organized impulse-carrying nerve cells (neurons), all arranged into discrete layers.

The pigment epithelium forms an important barrier between the light-sensitive receptors (visual cells) and their blood supply, the choroid. As in the choroid, the pigmentation serves to absorb light and prevent its reflection.

The rods and cones of vertebrates generally occur as single units, but combinations of each type are frequently encountered in several vertebrate classes. Cones appear to be adapted for photopic, or daylight, vision, based on correlations with the visual habits of the animals involved. Rods, which predominate in nocturnal vertebrates, are adapted for scotopic, or night, vision. Except for their external process, the structure of these cells does not reflect these differences. *See* PHOTORECEPTION; VISION.

An important adaptation for improving visual detail in vertebrates is the formation of circumscribed thickenings of the retina resulting from localized increases in the number of visual cells and the other retinal neurons associated synaptically with them. Such thickenings, termed areas of acute vision, appear in some members of all vertebrate classes and reach their greatest development in birds, in which one to three distinct areas may be found in the same retina. Only a single area occurs in humans; it is colored yellow and is called the macula. The macula is situated in the center of the fundus and contains only cones.

Cavities. Three cavities or chambers are present within the vertebrate eye: anterior, posterior, and vitreous. The anterior and posterior chambers are continuous with one another at the pupil and are filled with the aqueous humor. The eye is normally maintained in a distended state by the (intraocular) pressure created by this fluid. The vitreous cavity, on the other hand, is filled with a semisolid material, the vitreous body, which is fixed in amount and relatively permanent. Its consistency is not uniform in all vertebrates, however.

Lens. The lens is a transparent body, supported by thin suspensory fibers and by the vitreous body behind and by the iris in front. It is completely cellular, the anterior cells forming a thin epithelium, and the posterior cells, much elongated, forming the so-called lens fibers. The entire lens is surrounded by an elastic capsule which serves for the attachment of the ciliary zonule. In all vertebrates the lens functions in accommodation, either by moving backward and forward or by changing its shape. An opacity of the lens is termed a cataract.   [D.B.M.; R.O'Ra.]

Electrophysiology of rods and cones. Visual information perceived by the vertebrate eye is fed to the brain in the form of coded electrical impulses that are initiated by the light-sensitive, visual-pigment-containing outer segments of the rods and cones. Light striking the outer segments is absorbed by these pigments, resulting—in the case of rhodopsin, for example—in the isomerization of the 11-*cis*-retinal chromophore to all *trans*-retinal. The outcome of this photolytic process is a change in electrical activity at the plasma membrane enclosing the outer segments, and a sudden and drastic decrease in its permeability (particularly to Na^+). The net result is a hyperpolarization response, or increased negativity of membrane potential. Hyperpolarization generates a membrane current that spreads to the inner segment and finally to the synaptic terminal, where it regulates the release of neurotransmitter and thus controls the flow of information from the visual cells to other retinal cells (bipolars, horizontals, other photoreceptors).

Cyclic GMP is directly responsible for regulating the permeability of the plasma membrane by opening ionic channels (in the light). Its concentration is controlled by a peripheral membrane enzyme, phosphodiesterase, which in turn is activated by transducin, an intracellular messenger protein generated by a photolytic intermediate of rhodopsin. Since one molecule of photoactivated rhodopsin can react with many molecules of transducin, an amplification of the visual cells' response is produced, the final amplitude being enhanced by breakdown of cyclic GMP by phosphodiesterase and subsequent closure of outer segment ionic channels and hyperpolarization.

Since photoreceptors are depolarized in the dark, their axon terminals continually release a transmitter that hyperpolarizes (inhibits) the bipolar cell, and since this cell is hyperpolarized in the dark, it is prevented from releasing its excitatory transmitter at the ganglion cell synapse so that the synapse is not excited. In the light, hyperpolarization of the visual cells causes a decrease in the amount of inhibitory transmitter released at the bipolar synapse, leading to a depolarization of the latter, which in turn increases the amount of excitatory transmitter released at the bipolar-ganglion synapses and affecting the ganglion cells.

A change in the light energy taking place across the retina also initiates a transient complex of electrical waveforms, the electroretinogram, which is recorded as a difference in potential between the cornea and the back of the eye.   [D.B.M.]

F

Fallopian tube   The upper part of the female oviduct present in humans and other higher vertebrates. The Fallopian tube extends from the ovary to the uterus and transports ova from the ovary to the cavity of the uterus. Each tube is about 5 in. (12.5 cm) long; one lies on either side of the uterus and is attached at the upper portion. Each curves outward to end in a hoodlike opening, the infundibulum, with many fingerlike projections; the cavity of the Fallopian tube is continuous with the cavity of the coelom. The ovaries lie below and inside the tubal curve.

The ovum remains viable in the oviduct for about 1–3 days only. If fertilization occurs, the ovum moves into the cavity of the uterus and then implants on its wall. If fertilization fails to occur, the ovum degenerates in the uterus. Occasionally, a fertilized ovum fails to enter the uterus, or may be freed into the abdominal cavity, so that an ectopic pregnancy results if the ovum finds a site for implantation. See REPRODUCTIVE SYSTEM.

[W.B.]

Fate maps (embryology)   Diagrams of embryos showing the structures that the parts will become in the course of normal development. A series of fate maps for different developmental stages depicts the normal morphogenetic movements that the cells and tissues of an embryo undergo. However, a fate map for a given stage does not in itself include information about the developmental pathway to which different parts of the embryo are committed. States of commitment must be deduced by comparing the structures predicted by the fate map with those formed by tissue regions in isolation, or after grafting to unusual positions. An accurate fate map is thus a necessary tool for further studies in experimental embryology. See EMBRYOGENESIS; TRANSPLANTATION BIOLOGY.

For embryos in which there is no increase in size during development, and no random mixing of cells, it is possible in principle to project the fate map back into the fertilized egg. For example, in the nematode *Caenorhabditis elegans* the exact lineage of every cell has been determined. Where there is some local cell mixing, as in amphibian embryos, the fate map cannot be so precise, and represents the average behavior of a population of embryos. See CELL LINEAGE.

Clonal analysis, a special form of fate mapping in which a single cell is labeled, can give two pieces of information that a fate map of extended multicellular regions cannot. It allows for the detection of stem cells, which produce an entire structure by a sequence of unequal cell divisions. It also can set a lower bound to the time of developmental commitment. If a single cell can populate two structures, then clearly it cannot have been irreversibly committed to become either structure at the time of labeling.

In clonal analysis of plants, cells are labeled by exposing the seed or developing plant to ionizing irradiation or a chemical mutagen to produce chromosome mutations that result in distinct phenotypic alterations, usually deficiencies in the pigments chlorophyll or anthocyanin. The low frequency of mutations produced indicates that these are single-cell events. Because all of the progeny of a labeled cell will carry the same chromosome mutation, a shoot meristem cell labeled with a chlorophyll deficiency mutation, for example, will produce a sector, or clone, of white tissue in the developing plant. It is possible to deduce the number and fate of meristem cells labeled at one stage of development by examining the size and position of sectors present in the plant at a later stage of development. For example, a sector extending the entire length of the shoot would be generated by a permanent initial cell at the center of the meristem; if the width of that sector occupied one-third of the circumference of the shoot, then the shoot must have been formed by three such initial cells. *See* MUTATION; PLANT GROWTH.

[D.E.J.]

Feather   A specialized keratinous outgrowth of the skin, which is a unique characteristic of birds. Feathers are highly complex structures that provide insulation, protection against mechanical damage, and protective coloration, and also function significantly in behavior. One special functional role is in flight, where feathers provide propulsive surfaces and a body surface aerodynamically suitable for flight. Feathers are used in maintenance of balance and occasionally in the capture of prey and various specialized displays.

A representative definitive feather contains a single long central axis which supports a row of small branchlike structures along each side (barbs). Barbs form the vane, or web, of the feather. Individual barbs branch off at variable angles and point toward the outer tip of the feather. The barbules are small branches from the barbs. They lie in the same plane as the barbs and arise in rows from their anterior and posterior surfaces. The anterior barbules have a flattened base and a series of small hooklike projections which attach to the proximal ridge of the posterior barbules of the next barb, forming an interlocking structure characterized by its great strength and light weight. All feather types consist basically of these structural elements.

Most of the superficial feathers are contour feathers (pennae). These include the large flight feathers (remiges) of the wing and the long tail feathers (rectrices). Other common feather types include the down feathers (plumulae), intermediate types (semiplumes), and filoplumes (see illustration).

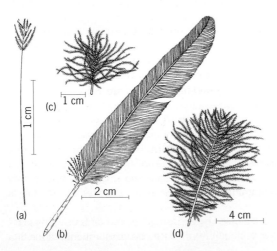

Types of feathers. (*a*) Filoplume. (*b*) Vane or contour. (*c*) Down. (*d*) Semiplume. (*After J. C. Welty, The Life of Birds, Saunders, 1962*)

Feathers normally undergo attrition because of the physical abuse attendant to the normal activity of birds. In most species, feathers are replaced completely at least annually, and many of the feathers are replaced more frequently. The sequence of feather molt is surprisingly orderly. Penguins, which shed large patches of feathers in an irregular pattern, are an exception. In most species the power of flight is retained during molt. The molt, that is, the normal shedding of feathers and their replacement by a new generation of feathers, is a single growth process which is actively concerned only with the production of the new generation of feathers. The old feathers are pushed out of the follicles passively.

A major physiological role of feathers is to provide insulation. This is accomplished by regulating the configuration of feather and skin in such a way that differing amounts of air are trapped in the dead space so formed. A second mechanism for control of heat dissipation is the balance of the exposure of feathered and unfeathered body parts.

Feathers act as a protective boundary in their role of providing waterproofing. Water repellency is a structural feature of feathers and is the result of precise geometric relationships between the diameter and spacing of barbs and barbules. Preening appears to be more important in the maintenance of this structure than it is for the application of oils or any other natural product, as was once thought.

A third function of the surface configuration and overall pattern of feathers is in the area of behavioral adaptations. These may be of two types. First is concealment, when the bird is cryptically marked to match its background and escape detection. The second type consists of various types of advertisement. See PROTECTIVE COLORATION.

[A.H.B.]

Fermentation   Decomposition of foodstuffs generally accompanied by the evolution of gas. The best-known example is alcoholic fermentation, in which sugar is converted into alcohol and carbon dioxide. During fermentation organic matter is decomposed in the absence of air (oxygen); hence, there is always an accumulation of reduction products, or incomplete oxidation products. Some of these products (for example, alcohol and lactic acid) are of importance to humans, and fermentation has therefore been used for their manufacture on an industrial scale. There are also many microbiological processes that go on in the presence of air while yielding incomplete oxidation products. Good examples are the formation of acetic acid (vinegar) from alcohol by vinegar bacteria, and of citric acid from sugar by certain molds (for example, *Aspergillus niger*). These microbial processes, too, have gained industrial importance, and are often referred to as fermentations, even though they do not conform to L. Pasteur's concept of fermentation as a decomposition in the absence of air. See INDUSTRIAL MICROBIOLOGY.

[C.B.V.N.]

Fetal membrane   One of the membranous structures which surround the embryo during its developmental period. Since such membranes are external to the embryo proper, they are called extraembryonic membranes. They function in the embryo's protection, nutrition, respiration, and excretion.

There are four fetal membranes—the amnion, chorion, yolk sac, and allantois. In the course of development, the chorion becomes the outermost, and the amnion the innermost, membrane surrounding the developing embryo. As the allantois increases in size, it expands and becomes closely associated, if not fused, with the chorion. The two membranes together are known as the chorioallantoic membrane.

The amniotic cavity within which the embryo is enclosed becomes filled with an aqueous fluid which gives osmotic and physical protection to the embryo during the remainder of its fetal existence. Smooth muscle fibers in the amnion spontaneously contract and gently rock the embryo before it develops the capacity for spontaneous movement.

As the stored nutrients of the yolk are depleted during development, the yolk sac gradually decreases in size and is eventually incorporated into the midgut of the embryo. The yolk sac in the nonyolky eggs of placental mammals is vestigial. It has evolutionary but essentially no functional significance.

At the time of birth or hatching, the embryo becomes completely separated from the amnion and chorion and from the major portion of the allantois. The proximal portion of the latter remains within the embryo, however, as the urinary bladder. *See* ALLANTOIS; AMNION; CHORION; YOLK SAC. [A.R.B.]

Fibrinogen The major clot-forming substrate in the blood plasma of vertebrates. Though fibrinogen represents a small fraction of plasma proteins (normal human plasma has a fibrinogen content of 2–4 mg/ml of a total of 70 mg protein/ml), its conversion to fibrin causes a gelation which blocks the flow of blood. Upon injury, sufficient amounts of the clotting enzyme, thrombin, are generated in about 5 min clotting time to produce a gel. Although clotting in the circulation (thrombosis) can be extremely dangerous, clotting is an essential and normal response for preventing the loss of blood. Individuals born with the hereditary absence of fibrinogen (afibrinogenemia) suffer from severe bleeding, which can be counteracted by transfusing normal plasma or purified fibrinogen.

Fibrinogen is synthesized by the hepatocytes in the liver, and the synthetic rate can be stimulated by hormones. Significant amounts of carbohydrates become attached to the protein before it is secreted into the circulation; alterations in its carbohydrate composition as found in some liver diseases can give rise to abnormal fibrinogens with defective clotting properties.

Clotting is regulated by two enzymes, thrombin and factor XIII$_a$ (fibrinoligase, activated fibrin-stabilizing factor, transglutaminase). Thrombin exerts a dual control by regulating the rate of fibrin formation as well as producing factor XIII$_a$. In the plasma milieu, the fibrin molecules readily aggregate into a clot. In order to obtain a clot structure of a strength sufficient to stem bleeding, however, it is necessary for the thrombin-modified factor XIII to be activated to XIII$_a$. Factor XIII$_a$ acts as a transamidating enzyme which strengthens the fibrin clot by creating cross-links between the molecules. Without such cross-links, a clot structure would be like a brick wall without mortar. Individuals with the hereditary absence of factor XIII often suffer from severe bleeding, even though their clotting times are in the normal range. *See* BLOOD; IMMUNOGLOBULIN. [L.Lo.]

Flavonoid A large category of natural plant products that derive from γ-pyrone. All flavonoid compounds, which are derived from either 2-phenylbenzopyrone (structure **1**) or 3-phenylbenzopyrone (**2**), can be classified into 10 groups: chalcones,

(1)   (2)

flavanones, flavones, flavonols, anthocyanidins (flavylium cations), flavan 3-ols (catechins), flavan 3,4-diols (proanthocyanidins), biflavonoids and oligomeric flavonoids, isoflavonoids, and the aurones. They differ in the oxidation level or substitution pattern of their heterocyclic ring (ring C).

More than 1300 different flavonoid compounds have been isolated from plants. Individual flavonoids in a group differ from each other by the number and position of the hydroxy, methoxy, and sugar substituents. As a rule, flavonoid compounds occur in plants as glycosides, with hexoses such as glucose, galactose, and rhamnose, and pentoses such as arabinose and xylose as the most commonly found sugars. The sugars can be attached singly or in combination with each other. Glycosylation renders these compounds water-soluble and permits their accumulation in the vacuoles of cells. *See* GLYCOSIDE.

The few reports available indicate that flavonoids accumulate in epidermal tissues, with approximately 70% in the upper and 30% in the lower epidermis. Vacuoles are probably the only site of flavonoid accumulation in the cells, but synthesis of flavonoids takes place in the cytoplasm.

Flavonoid compounds were once regarded as stray end products of metabolism, but some are now known to be physiologically active. For example, a number of flavonoid compounds were discovered to be the host-specific signal molecules in the formation of nitrogen-fixing root modules. In addition, flavonoids have been linked to protection from ultraviolet radiation. The enzymatic machinery for flavonoid production is induced by ultraviolet irradiation. Flavonoids accumulate in the vacuoles of epidermal cells and absorb light strongly in the critical range of 280–380 nm, where damage caused by ultraviolet radiation occurs. Finally, many plant species synthesize phytoalexins upon invasion by microorganisms. The majority of phytoalexins produced by legumes are isoflavonoids, and each plant species seems to produce a specific compound.

Because of their strikingly vivid color, ranging from deep red through purple to deep blue, anthocyanins represent the most visible class of flavonoid compounds. Anthocyanins are most obvious in flowers and fruits, but they are also present in roots, stems, leaves, seeds, and other parts of the plant. The accumulated anthocyanins, together with carotenes, provide the varied colors characteristic of autumn. Anthocyanins are also produced when plants are subjected to other stress, such as ultraviolet radiation, injury by insects, malnutrition, or unusual concentrations of metal. *See* PLANT METABOLISM.
[G.Hr.]

Flower   A higher plant's sexual apparatus in the aggregate, including the parts that produce sex cells and closely associated attractive and protective parts (Fig. 1). "Flower" as used in this article will be limited, as is usual, to the angiosperms, plants with enclosed seeds and the unique reproductive process called double fertilization. In its most familiar form a flower is made up of four kinds of units arranged concentrically. The green sepals (collectively termed the calyx) are outermost, showy petals (the corolla) next, then the pollen-bearing units (stamens, androecium), and finally the centrally placed seed-bearing units (carpels, gynoecium). This is the "complete" flower of early botanists, but it is only one of an almost overwhelming array of floral forms. One or more kinds of units may be lacking or hard to recognize depending on the species, and evolutionary modification has been so great in some groups of angiosperms that a flower cluster (inflorescence) can took like a single flower.

Flora diversity. Most botanical terms are descriptive, and a botanist must have a large store of them to impart the multiformity of flowers. The examples that follow are only a smattering. An extra series of appendages alternating with the sepals, as in purple

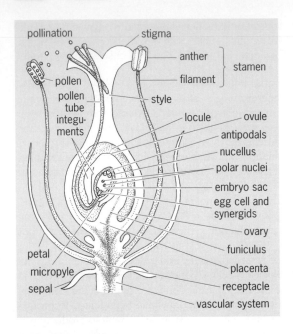

Fig. 1. Flower structure, median longitudinal section.

loosestrife, is an epicalyx. A petal with a broad distal region and a narrow proximal region is said to have a blade and claw: the crape myrtle has such petals. The term perianth, which embraces calyx and corolla and avoids the need to distinguish between them, is especially useful for a flower like the tulip, where the perianth parts are in two series but are alike in size, shape, and color. The members of such an undifferentiated perianth are tepals. When the perianth has only one series of parts, however, they are customarily called sepals even if they are petallike, as in the windflower.

A stamen commonly consists of a slender filament topped by a four-lobed anther, each lobe housing a pollen sac. In some plants one or more of the androecial parts are sterile rudiments called staminodes: a foxglove flower has four fertile stamens and a staminode. Carpellode is the corresponding term for an imperfectly formed gynoecial unit.

A gynoecium is apocarpous if the carpels are separate (magnolia, blackberry) and syncarpous if they are connate (tulip, poppy). Or the gynoecium may regularly consist of only one carpel (bean, cherry). A solitary carpel or a syncarpous gynoecium can often be divided into three regions: a terminal, pollen-receptive stigma; a swollen basal ovary enclosing the undeveloped seeds (ovules); and a constricted, elongate style between the two. The gynoecium can be apocarpous above and syncarpous below; that is, there can be separate styles and stigmas on one ovary (wood sorrel).

Every flower cited so far has a superior ovary: perianth and androecium diverge beneath it (hypogyny). If perianth and androecium diverge from the ovary's summit, the ovary is inferior and the flower is epigynous (apple, banana, pumpkin). A flower is perigynous if the ovary is superior within a cup and the other floral parts diverge from the cup's rim (cherry). A syncarpous ovary is unilocular if it has only one seed chamber, plurilocular if septa divide it into more than one. The ovules of a plurilocular ovary are usually attached to the angles where the septa meet; this is axile placentation, a placenta being a region of ovular attachment. There are other ways in which the ovules

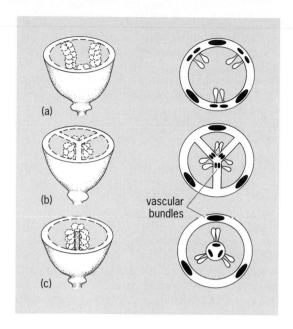

Fig. 2. Placentation: (*a*) parietal, (*b*) axile, and (*c*) free central. (*After P. H. Raven, R. F. Evert, and H. Curtis, Biology of Plants, Worth Publishers, 1976*)

can be attached—apically, basally, parietally, or on a free-standing central placenta—each characteristic of certain plant groups (Fig. 2).

The term bract can be applied to any leaflike part associated with one or more flowers but not part of a flower. Floral bracts are frequently small, even scalelike, but the flowering dogwood has four big petallike bracts below each flower cluster. The broad end of a flower stalk where the floral parts are attached is the receptacle. The same term is used, rather inconsistently, for the broad base bearing the many individual flowers (florets) that make up a composite flower like a dandelion or a sunflower.

Sexuality. A plant species is diclinous if its stamens and carpels are in separate flowers. A diclinous species is monoecious if each plant bears staminate and carpellate (pistillate) flowers, dioecious if the staminate and carpellate flowers are on different plants. The corn plant, with staminate inflorescences (tassels) on top and carpellate inflorescences (ears) along the stalk, is monoecious. Hemp is a well-known dioecious plant.

Nectaries. Flowers pollinated by insects or other animals commonly have one or more nectaries, regions that secrete a sugar solution. A nectary can be nothing more than a layer of tissue lining part of a floral tube or cup (cherry), or it can be as conspicuous as the secretory spur of a nasturtium or a larkspur. It can be a cushionlike outgrowth at the base of a superior ovary (orange blossom) or atop an inferior ovary (parsley family). Gladiolus and a number of other monocotyledons have septal nectaries, deep secretory crevices where the carpels come together. Substances that give off floral odors—essential oils for the most part—ordinarily originate close to the nectar-producing region but are not coincident with it. Production by the epidermis of perianth parts is most common, but in some species the odor emanates from a more restricted region and may even come from a special flap or brush. Most insect-pollinated plants have visual cues, some of them outside the human spectral range, as well as odor to bring the pollinators to the flowers and guide them to the nectar. *See* SECRETORY STRUCTURES (PLANT).

Inflorescence. Inflorescence structure, the way the flowers are clustered or arranged on a flowering branch, is almost as diverse as floral structure. To appreciate this, one need only contrast the drooping inflorescences (catkins) of a birch tree with the coiled flowers of a forget-me-not or with the solitary flower of a tulip. In some cases one kind of inflorescence characterizes a whole plant family. Queen Anne's lace and other members of the parsley family (Umbelliferae) have umbrellalike inflorescences with the flower stalks radiating from almost the same point in a cluster. The stalkless flowers (florets) of the grass family are grouped into clusters called spikelets, and these in turn are variously arranged in different grasses.

Flowers of the arum family (calla lily, jack-in-the-pulpit), also stalkless, are crowded on a thick, fleshy, elongate axis. In the composite family, florets are joined in a tight head at the end of the axis; the heads of some composites contain two kinds, centrally placed florets with small tubular corollas and peripheral ray florets with showy, strap-shaped corollas (the "petals" one plucks from a daisy). *See* INFLORESCENCE.

Anatomy. Some of the general anatomical features of leaves can be found in the floral appendages. A cuticle-covered epidermis overlies a core of parenchyma cells in which there are branching vascular bundles (solitary bundles in most stamens). Sepal parenchyma and petal parenchyma are often spongy, but palisade parenchyma occurs only rarely in flowers and then only in sepals. As in other parts of the plant, color comes mostly from plastids in the cytoplasm and from flavonoids in the cell sap. Cells of the petal epidermis may have folded side walls that interlock so as to strengthen the tissue. In some species the outer walls of the epidermis are raised as papillae; apparently, this is part of the means of attracting pollinators, for the papillae are light reflectors.

Stamen. As a stamen develops, periclinal divisions in the second cell layer of each of its four lobes start a sequence that will end with the shedding of pollen. The first division makes two cell layers. The outer daughter cells give rise to the wall of the pollen sac, and the inner ones are destined to become pollen after further divisions. When mature, a pollen sac typically has a prominent cell layer just below a less distinctive epidermis. The inner wall and the side walls of an endothecium cell carry marked thickenings, but the outer wall does not. Splitting of the ripe anther is due partly to the way in which these differentially thickened walls react to drying and shrinking and partly to the smaller size of the cells along the line of splitting. *See* POLLEN.

Carpel. Like other floral parts, a carpel is made up of epidermis, parenchyma, and vascular tissue. In addition, a carpel commonly has a special tissue system on which pollen germinates and through which, or along which, pollen tubes are transmitted to the ovules. Most angiosperms have solid styles, and the transmitting tissue is a column of elongate cells whose softened walls are the medium for tubal growth. The epidermis at the stigmatic end of a carpel usually changes to a dense covering of papillae or hairs; the hairs can be unicellular or pluricellular, branched or unbranched. In taxa with hollow styles, the transmitting tissue is a modified epidermis running down the stylar canal. There are two kinds of receptive surfaces, and they are distributed among the monocotyledons and the dicotyledons with taxonomic regularity. One kind has a fluid medium for germinating the pollen, and the other has a dry proteinaceous layer over the cuticle. The proteins of the dry stigmas have a role in the incompatibility reactions that encourage outbreeding.

Ovule. Ovule development usually takes place as the gynoecium forms, but it may be retarded when there is a long interval between pollination and fertilization (oaks, orchids). A typical ovule has a stalk (funiculus), a central bulbous body (nucellus), and one or two integuments (precursors of seed coats), which cover the nucellus except for a terminal pore (micropyle). Orientation of the ovule varies from group to group.

It can be erect on its stalk or bent one way or another to differing degrees. There are also taxonomic differences in the extent to which the ovule is vascularized by branches from the gynoecial vascular system. *See* FRUIT; REPRODUCTION (PLANT).   [R.H.E.]

Food poisoning   An acute gastrointestinal or neurologic disorder caused by bacteria or their toxic products, by viruses, or by harmful chemicals in foods.

Bacteria may produce food poisoning by three means: (1) they infect the individual following consumption of the contaminated food; (2) they produce a toxin in food before it is consumed; or (3) they produce toxin in the gastrointestinal tract after the individual consumes the contaminated food.

Infectious bacteria associated with food poisoning include *Brucella, Campylobacter jejuni*, enteroinvasive *Escherichia coli*, enterohemorrhagic *E. coli, Listeria monocytogenes, Salmonella, Shigella, Vibrio parahaemolyticus, V. vulnificus*, and *Yersinia enterocolitica*. These organisms must be ingested for poisoning to occur, and in many instances only a few cells need be consumed to initiate a gastrointestinal infection. *Salmonella* and *C. jejuni* are the most prevalent causes of food-borne bacterial infections. *See* YERSINIA.

Staphylococcus aureus and *Clostridium botulinum* are bacteria responsible for food poisonings resulting from ingestion of preformed toxin. *Staphylococcus aureus* produces heat-stable toxins that remain active in foods after cooking. *Clostridium botulinum* produces one of the most potent toxins known. Botulinal toxin causes neuromuscular paralysis, often resulting in respiratory failure and death. *See* BOTULISM; STAPHYLOCOCCUS; TOXIN.

Food-poisoning bacteria that produce toxin in the gastrointestinal tract following their ingestion include *Bacillus cereus, Clostridium perfringens*, enterotoxigenic *E. coli*, and *V. cholerae. Bacillus cereus* and *C. perfringens* are spore-forming bacteria that often survive cooking and grow to large numbers in improperly refrigerated foods. Following ingestion, their cells release enterotoxins in the intestinal tract. Enterotoxigenic *E. coli* is a leading cause of travelers' diarrhea. *See* ESCHERICHIA.

Viruses that cause food-borne disease generally emanate from the human intestine and contaminate food through mishandling by an infected individual, or by way of water or sewage contaminated with human feces. Hepatitis A virus and Norwalk-like virus are the preeminent viruses associated with food-borne illness. *See* HEPATITIS.

Chemical-induced food poisoning is generally characterized by a rapid onset of symptoms which include nausea and vomiting. Foods contaminated with high levels of heavy metals, insecticides, or pesticides have caused illness following ingestion. *See* MEDICAL BACTERIOLOGY.   [M.Do.]

Food web   A diagram depicting those organisms that eat other organisms in the same ecosystem. In some cases, the organisms may already be dead. Thus, a food web is a network of energy flows in and out of the ecosystem of interest. Such flows can be very large, and some ecosystems depend almost entirely on energy that is imported. A food chain is one particular route through a food web.

A food web helps depict how an ecosystem is structured and functions. Most published food webs omit predation on minor species, the quantities of food consumed, the temporal variation of the flows, and many other details.

Along a simple food chain, A eats B, B eats C, and so on. For example, the energy that plants capture from the sun during photosynthesis may end up in the tissues of a hawk. It gets there via a bird that the hawk has eaten, the insects that were eaten by the bird, and the plants on which the insects fed. Each stage of the food chain is called a trophic level. More generally, the trophic levels are separated into producers (the plants), herbivores or primary consumers (the insects), carnivores or secondary consumers (the bird), and top carnivores or tertiary consumers (the hawk).

Food chains may involve parasites as well as predators. The lice feeding in the feathers of the hawk are yet another trophic level. When decaying vegetation, dead animals, or both are the energy sources, the food chains are described as detrital. Food chains are usually short; the shortest have two levels. One way to describe and simplify various food chains is to count the most common number of levels from the top to the bottom of the web. Most food chains are three or four trophic levels long (if parasites are excluded), though there are longer ones.

There are several possible explanations for why food chains are generally short. Between each trophic level, much of the energy is lost as heat. As the energy passes up the food chain, there is less and less to go around. There may not be enough energy to support a viable population of a species at trophic level five or higher.

This energy flow hypothesis is widely supported, but it is also criticized because it predicts that food chains should be shorter in energetically poor ecosystems such as a bleak arctic tundra or extreme deserts. These systems often have food chains similar in length to energetically more productive systems. *See* ECOLOGICAL ENERGETICS.

Another hypothesis about the shortness of food chains has to do with how quickly particular species recover from environmental disasters. For example, in a lake with phytoplankton, zooplankton, and fish, when the phytoplankton decline the zooplankton will also decline, followed by the fish. The phytoplankton may recover but will remain at low levels, kept there by the zooplankton. At least transiently, the zooplankton may reach higher than normal levels because the fish, their predators, are still scarce. The phytoplankton will not completely recover until all the species in the food chain have recovered. Mathematical models can show that the longer the food chain, the longer it will take its constituent species to recover from perturbations. Species atop very long food chains may not recover before the next disaster. Such arguments predict that food chains will be longer when environmental disasters are rare, short when they are common, and will not necessarily be related to the amount of energy entering the system.

The number of trophic levels a food web contains will determine what happens when an ecosystem is subjected to a short, sharp shock—for example, when a large number of individuals of one species are killed by a natural disaster or an incident of human-made pollution and how quickly the system will recover. The food web will also influence what happens if the abundance of a species is permanently reduced (perhaps because of harvesting) or increased (perhaps by increasing an essential nutrient for a plant).

Some species have redundant roles in an ecosystem so that their loss will not seriously impair the system's dynamics. Therefore, the loss of such species from an ecosystem will not have a substantial effect on ecosystem function. The alternative hypothesis is that more diverse ecosystems could have a greater chance of containing species that survive or that can even thrive during a disturbance that kills off other species. Highly connected and simple food webs differ in their responses to disturbances, so once again the structure of food webs makes a difference. *See* ECOLOGICAL COMMUNITIES; ECOSYSTEM; POPULATION ECOLOGY.   [S.Pi.]

Foraminiferida   An order of Granuloreticulosia in the class Rhizopodea. Foraminiferans are dominantly marine protozoans, with a secreted or agglutinated shell, or test, enclosing the continually changing ameboid body (see illustration) that characterizes this and other orders of the superclass Sarcodina. Their unique combination of long geologic history, ubiquitous geographic distribution, and exceptional diversity

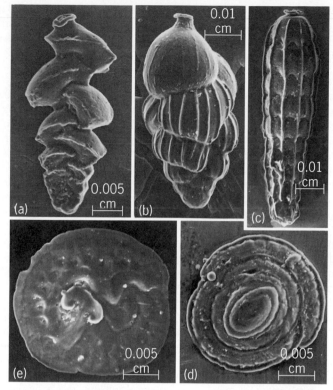

Scanning electron micrographs of foraminiferans of suborder Rotaliina. Superfamily Buliminacea: (*a*) *Eouvigerina*, elongate test. (*b*) *Uvigerina*, elongate triserial test. (*c*) *Siphogenerinoides*, reduced early biserial stage. **Superfamily Spirillinacea;** *Patellina*: (*d*) spiral view of low conical test; (*e*) umbilical view. (*R. B. MacAdam, Chevron Oil Field Research Co.*)

of test composition, form, and structure make the foraminiferans the most useful of all marine fossils for stratigraphic correlation, geologic age dating of sediments, and paleoecologic interpretation. Their tests accumulated in great numbers and are recoverable from small quantities of sediment, rock outcroppings, well cores or cuttings, or ocean dredging and submarine coring.

As is true of most protists with skeletons or tests, systematic differentiation and classification of foraminiferans is based on test composition, microstructure, and gross morphology. Information currently available concerning cytoplasmic characters, life cycles, and so on has shown good agreement with this classification, although the function and origin of many shell characters believed to be of systematic importance (canal systems, pores, septal doubling, and apertural tooth plates) are yet undetermined. There are 11 suborders.

Most foraminiferans are benthic, living upon the sea floor, within the upper few centimeters of ooze, or upon benthic algae or other organisms. They occur from the intertidal zone to oceanic depths, in brackish, normal marine, or hypersaline waters, and from the tropics to the poles. Some modern Lagynacea live in fresh water, but none are known as fossils. Assemblages vary widely in response to local conditions, with the greatest diversity occurring in warm, shallow water. A smaller number, the Globigerinina, are planktonic, living at various depths in the water column from the surface to the bottom, being most numerous between 18 and 90 ft (6 and 30 m). Vertical migration may be diurnal and may occur during ontogenetic development. The preferred depth range of a species may vary geographically in response to temperature differences or to changes in water density.   [H.T.L.]

Forest and forestry A plant community consisting predominantly of trees and other woody vegetation, growing closely together, is a forest. Forests cover about one-fourth of the land area on Earth. The trees can be large and densely packed, as they are in the coastal forests of the Pacific Northwest, or they can be relatively small and sparsely scattered, as they are in the dry tropical forests of sub-Saharan Africa.

Forests are complex ecosystems that also include soils and decaying organic matter, fungi and bacteria, herbs and shrubs, vines and lichens, ferns and mosses, insects and spiders, reptiles and amphibians, birds and mammals, and many other organisms. All of these components constitute an intricate web with many interconnections. *See* FOREST ECOSYSTEM.

Forests have important functions, such as cleansing the air, moderating the climate, filtering water, cycling nutrients, providing habitat, and performing a number of other vital environmental services. They also supply a variety of valuable products ranging from pharmaceuticals and greenery to lumber and paper products.

Forest types. There are many ways to classify forests, as by (1) location (for example, temperate zone forests, tropical zone forests); (2) ownership (for example, public forests, private forests); (3) age or origin (for example, old-growth forests, second-growth forests, plantation forests); (4) important species (such as Douglas-fir forests, redwood forests); (5) economic and social importance (for example, commercial forests, noncommercial forests, urban forests, wilderness); (6) wood properties (for example, hardwood forests, softwood forests); (7) botanical makeup (for example, broadleaf forests, evergreen forests); or (8) a combination of features (such as moist temperate coniferous forests, dry tropical deciduous forests). The last approach tends to be the most descriptive because it often integrates several dominant characteristics related to climate, geography, and botanical features.

Some examples of the major forest types are: Northern coniferous forests which span the cold, northern latitudes of Canada and Europe; Temperate mixed forests which occupy the eastern United States, southeastern Canada, central Europe, Japan, and East Asia, and parts of the Southern Hemisphere in Chile, Argentina, Australia, and New Zealand; Temperate rainforests which are situated along moist, coastal regions of the Pacific Northwest, southern Chile, southeastern Australia, and Tasmania; Tropical rainforests which are found in the equatorial regions of Central and South America (for example, Costa Rica, Brazil, and Ecuador); on the west coast of Africa (for example, Congo, Ivory Coast, and Nigeria); and Southeast Asia (for example, Thailand, Malaysia, and Indonesia); Dry forests which occur in the southwestern United States, the Mediterranean region, sub-Saharan Africa, and semiarid regions of Mexico, India, and Central and South America; and mountain forests which are characteristic of mountainous regions throughout the world.

Characteristics. Although forests take a variety of forms, they have several features in common that allow them to develop in their respective environments. Forests generally contain a broad array of species, each of which is well adapted to the environmental conditions of the region. This biodiversity and adaptability help the forests cope with natural (and in some cases human-caused) forces of destruction, including wildfire, windstorms, floods, and pests. This built-in resiliency also allows the periodic extraction of wood and other products without jeopardizing the long-term health and productivity of the ecosystems—provided such harvesting operations are performed with care. Forests are dynamic—they are constantly changing at both landscape and smaller scales of resolution. This natural propensity to change and develop over time is called forest succession. Forests have a mitigating influence on the environment. This characteristic not only facilitates their own survival and development but also moderates the surrounding climate.

Ecological processes and hydrologic cycle. Forests play a vital role in ecological processes. From a global perspective, they help convert carbon dioxide in the atmosphere to oxygen, thereby facilitating life for aerobic organisms. Forests can also capture, store, convert, and recycle a variety of nutrients such as nitrogen, phosphorus, and sulfur. Forests also play a critical role in the hydrologic cycle. Finally, forests play a crucial ecological role in the habitat that they provide for countless organisms. *See* ECOLOGICAL SUCCESSION.

Forestry and forest management. The Society of American Foresters defines forestry as the science, the art, and the practice of managing and using for human benefit the natural resources that occur on and in association with forest lands. Natural resources have traditionally entailed major commodities such as wood, forage, water, wildlife, and recreation. However, the concept of forestry has expanded to encompass consideration of the entire forest ecosystem, ranging from mushrooms to landscapes. The practice of forestry requires in-depth knowledge of the complex biological nature of the forest. It also requires an understanding of geology and soils, climate and weather, fish and wildlife, forest growth and development, and social and economic factors. Foresters, wildlife managers, park rangers, and other natural resource specialists are trained in biology, physics, chemistry, mathematics, statistics, computer science, communications, economics, and sociology.

Silviculture is the art, science, and practice of controlling the establishment, composition, and growth of a forest. It entails the use of both natural and induced processes to foster forest development. For example, reforestation of a harvested or burned-over area can be accomplished by natural seeding from nearby trees or by planting seedlings. *See* REFORESTATION.

Laws and policies. The management of forest land in the United States is regulated by numerous laws and policies. Federal agencies must comply with laws such as the National Forest Management Act (1976), the Forest and Rangeland Renewable Resources Planning Act (1974), and the National Environmental Policy Act (1969). Other public and private forest landowners generally must comply with state regulations or guidelines designed to promote sound forest stewardship in their respective regions. Policy makers in government, industry, environmental organizations, and the private sector strive to balance the multitude of interests surrounding forest resources. Input from the public as well as resource managers and specialists is a crucial ingredient in the process.

Utilization of forest resources. Forests are often focused on particular uses. For example, plantation forests are generally designed to produce wood and fiber products. Conversely, public forests are increasingly devoted to nonconsumptive purposes such as the preservation of biodiversity, natural conditions, and scenic vistas. However, all forests can provide multiple benefits, including harvestable products, watershed protection, recreation opportunities, wildlife habitat, and ecological services. *See* FOREST GENETICS.

[M.J.Cou.]

Forest ecosystem   The entire assemblage of organisms (trees, shrubs, herbs, bacteria, fungi, and animals, including people) together with their environmental sub-strate (the surrounding air, soil, water, organic debris, and rocks), interacting inside a defined boundary. Forests and woodlands occupy about 38% of the Earth's surface, and they are more productive and have greater biodiversity than other types of ter-restrial vegetation. Forests grow in a wide variety of climates, from steamy tropical rainforests to frigid arctic mountain slopes, and from arid interior mountains to windy rain-drenched coastlines. The type of forest in a given place results from a complex of factors, including frequency and type of disturbances, seed sources, soils, slope and aspect, climate, seasonal patterns of rainfall, insects and pathogens, and history of human influence.

Ecosystem concept. Often forest ecosystems are studied in watersheds draining to a monitored stream: the structure is then defined in vertical and horizontal dimen-sions. Usually the canopy of the tallest trees forms the upper ecosystem boundary, and plants with the deepest roots form the lower boundary. The horizontal structure is usually described by how individual trees, shrubs, herbs, and openings or gaps are distributed. Wildlife ecologists study the relation of stand and landscape patterns to habitat conditions for animals.

Woody trees and shrubs are unique in their ability to extend their branches and foliage skyward and to capture carbon dioxide and most of the incoming photosynthetically active solar radiation. Some light is reflected back to the atmosphere and some passes through leaves to the ground (infrared light). High rates of photosynthesis require lots of water, and many woody plants have deep and extensive root systems that tap stored ground water between rain storms. Root systems of most plants are greatly extended through a relation between plants and fungi, called mycorrhizal symbiosis. *See* PHOTOSYNTHESIS; ROOT (BOTANY).

The biomass of a forest is defined here as the mass of living plants, normally expressed as dry weight per unit area. Biomass production is the rate at which biomass is accrued per unit area over a fixed interval, usually one year. If the forest is used to grow timber crops, production measures focus on the biomass or volume of commercial trees. Likewise, if wildlife populations are the focus of management, managers may choose to measure biomass or numbers of individual animals. Ecologists interested in the general responses of forest ecosystems, however, try to measure net primary production (Npp), usually expressed as gross primary production (Gpp) minus the respiration of autotrophs (Ra).

Another response commonly of interest is net ecosystem production (NEP),

$$NEP = Gpp - (Ra + Rh) = Npp - Rh$$

usually expressed as where Rh is respiration of heterotrophs. *See* BIOMASS.

Productivity is the change in production over multiple years. Monitoring productiv-ity is especially important in managed forests. Changes in forest productivity can be detected only over very long periods. *See* BIOLOGICAL PRODUCTIVITY.

Forested ecosystems have great effect on the cycling of carbon, water, and nutri-ents, and these effects are important in understanding long-term productivity. Cycling of carbon, oxygen, and hydrogen are dominated by photosynthesis, respiration, and decomposition, but they are also affected by other processes. Forests control the hy-drologic cycle in important ways. Photosynthesis requires much more water than is required in its products. Water is lost back to the atmosphere (transpiration), and water on leaf and branch surfaces also evaporates under warm and windy conditions. Water not taken up or evaporated flows into the soil and eventually appears in streams, rivers, and oceans where it can be reevaporated and moved back over land, completing the cycle.

Forest plants and animals alter soil characteristics, for example, by adding organic matter, which generally increases the rate at which water infiltrates and is retained. Nutrient elements cycle differently from water and from each other.

Elements such as phosphorus, calcium, and magnesium are released from primary minerals in rocks through chemical weathering. Elements incorporated into biomass are returned to the soil with litterfall and root death; these elements become part of soil organic matter and are mineralized by decomposers or become a component of secondary minerals. All elements can leave ecosystems through erosion of particles and then be transported to the oceans and deposited as sediment. Deeply buried sediments undergo intense pressure and heat that reforms primary minerals. Volcanoes and plate tectonic movements eventually distribute these new minerals back to land.

Nitrogen is the most common gas in the atmosphere. Only certain bacteria can form a special enzyme (nitrogenase) which breaks apart N_2 and combines with photosynthates to form amino acids and proteins. In nature, free-living N_2-fixing microbes and a few plants that can harbor N_2-fixing bacteria in root nodules play important roles controlling the long-term productivity of forests limited by nitrogen supply. Bacteria that convert ammonium ion (NH_4^+) to NO_3^- (nitrifiers) and bacteria that convert NO_3^- back to N_2 (denitrifiers) are important in nitrogen cycling as well. *See* NITROGEN CYCLE.

Changes in the plant species of a forest over 10 to 100 years or more are referred to as succession. Changes in forest structure are called stand development; changes in composition, structure, and function are called ecosystem development. Simplified models of succession and development have been created and largely abandoned because the inherent complexity of the interacting forces makes model predictions inaccurate. *See* ECOLOGICAL SUCCESSION; FOREST FIRE.   [B.T.B.]

Streams. One of the products of an undisturbed forest is water of high quality flowing in streams. The ecological integrity of the stream is a reflection of the forested watershed that it drains. When the forest is disturbed (for example, by cutting or fire), the stream ecosystem will also be altered. Forest streams are altered by any practices or chemical input that alter forest vegetation, by the introduction of exotic species, and by the construction of roads that increase sediment delivery to streams.   [J.L.Mey.]

Vertebrates. Forest animals are the consumers in forest ecosystems. They influence the flow of energy and cycling of nutrients through systems, as well as the structure and composition of forests, through their feeding behavior and the disturbances that they create. In turn, their abundance and diversity is influenced by the structure and composition of the forest and the intensity, frequency, size, and pattern of disturbances that occur in forests. Forest vertebrates make up less than 1% of the biomass in most forests, yet they can play important functional roles in forest systems.

Invertebrates. Invertebrates are major components of forest ecosystems, affecting virtually all forest processes and uses. Many species are recognized as important pollinators and seed dispersers that ensure plant reproduction. Even so-called pests may be instrumental in maintaining ecosystem processes critical to soil fertility, plant productivity, and forest health.

Invertebrates affect forests primarily through the processes of herbivory and decomposition. They are also involved in the regulation of plant growth, survival, and reproduction; forest diversity; and nutrient cycling. Typically, invertebrate effects on ecosystem structure and function are modest compared to the more conspicuous effects of plants and fungi. However, invertebrates can have effects disproportionate to their numbers or biomass.

Changes in population size also affect the ecological roles of invertebrates. For example, small populations of invertebrates that feed on plants may maintain low rates of foliage turnover and nutrient cycling, with little effect on plant growth or survival, whereas large populations can defoliate entire trees, alter forest structure, and contribute a large amount of plant material and nutrients to the forest floor. Different life stages also may represent different roles. Immature butterflies and moths are defoliators, whereas the adults often are important pollinators.   [T.Sc.]

Microorganisms. Microorganisms, including bacteria, fungi, and protists, are the most numerous and the most diverse of the life forms that make up any forest ecosystem. The structure and functioning of forests are dependent on microbial interactions. Four processes are particularly important: nitrogen fixation, decomposition and nutrient cycling, pathogenesis, and mutalistic symbiosis.

Nitrogen fixation is crucial to forest function. While atmospheric nitrogen is abundant, it is unavailable to trees or other plants unless fixed, that is, converted to ammonia (NH_4), by either symbiotic or free-living soil bacteria.

Most microorganisms are saprophytic decomposers, gaining carbon from the dead remains of other plants or animals. In the process of their growth and death, they release nutrients from the forest litter, making them available once again for the growth of plants. Their roles in carbon, nitrogen, and phosphorus cycling are particularly important. Fungi are generally most important in acid soils beneath conifer forests, while bacteria are more important in soils with a higher pH. Bacteria often are the last scavengers in the food web and in turn serve as food to a host of microarthropods.

Microorganisms reduce the mass of forest litter and, in the process, contribute significantly to the structure and fertility of soils as the organic residue is incorporated.

Some bacteria and many fungi are plant pathogens, obtaining their nutrients from living plants. Some are opportunists, successful as saprophytes, but capable of killing weakened or wounded plant tissues. Others require a living host, often preferring the most vigorous trees in the forest. Pathogenic fungi usually specialize on roots or stems or leaves, on one species or genus of trees.

Pathogenic fungi are important parts of all natural forest ecosystems. The forest trees evolved with the fungi, and have effective means of defense and escape, reducing the frequency of infection and slowing the rates of tissue death and tree mortality. However, trees are killed, and the composition and structure of the forest is shaped in large part by pathogens.

Pathogens remove weak or poorly adapted organisms from the forest, thus maintaining the fitness of the population. Decay fungi that kill parts of trees or rot the heartwood of living trees create an essential habitat for cavity-nesting birds and the other animals dependent on hollow trees.

By killing trees, pathogens create light gaps in the forest canopy. The size and rate of light gap formation and the relative susceptibility of the tree species present on the site determine the ecological consequences of mortality. Forest succession is often advanced as shade-tolerant trees are released in small gaps. Gaps allow the growth of herbaceous plants in the island of light, creating habitat and food diversity for animals within the forest. In many forests, pathogens are the most important gap formers and the principal determinants of structure and succession in the long intervals between stand-replacing disturbances such as wildfires or hurricanes. *See* ECOLOGICAL SUCCESSION; PLANT PATHOLOGY.

The fungus roots of trees, and indeed most plants, represent an intimate physical and physiological association of particular fungi and their hosts. Mycorrhizae are the products of long coevolution between fungus and plant, resulting in mutual dependency. Mycorrhizae are particularly important to trees because they enhance the uptake of phosphorus from soils. Mycorrhizal fungi greatly extend the absorptive surface of roots through the network of external hyphae. *See* ECOSYSTEM; FOREST AND FORESTRY; MYCORRHIZAE.
[E.Ha.]

Forest fire   The term wildfire refers to all uncontrolled fires that burn surface vegetation (grass, weeds, grainfields, brush, chaparral, tundra, and forest and woodland); often these fires also involve structures. In addition to the wildfires, several million acres of forest land are intentionally burned each year under controlled conditions to accomplish some silvicultural or other land-use objective or for hazard reduction.

Most wildfires are caused by human beings, directly or indirectly. In the United States less than 10% of all such fires are caused by lightning, the only truly natural cause. In the West (the 17 Pacific and Rocky Mountain states) lightning is the primary cause, with smoking (cigarettes, matches, and such) the second most frequent. Combined they account for 50 to 75% of all wildfires. In the 13 southern states (Virginia to Texas) the primary cause is incendiary. This combined with smoking and debris burning make up 75% of the causes. The 20 eastern states have smoking and debris burning as causing close to 50% of all wildfires. Miscellaneous causes of wildfires are next in importance in most regions. The other causes of wildfires are machine use and campfires. Machine use includes railroads, logging, sawmills, and other operations using equipment.

The manner in which fuel ignites, flame develops, and fire spreads and exhibits other phenomena constitutes the field of fire behavior. Factors determining forest fire behavior may be considered under four headings: attributes of the fuel, the atmosphere, topography, and ignition. A forest fire may burn primarily in the crowns of trees and shrubs (a crown fire); primarily in the surface litter and loose debris of the forest floor and small vegetation (a surface fire); or in the organic material beneath the surface litter (a ground fire). The most common type is a surface fire.

The U.S. Forest Service has developed a National Fire Danger Rating System (NFDRS) to provide fire-control personnel with numerical ratings to help them with the tasks of fire-control planning and the suppression of specific fires. The system includes three basic indexes: an occurrence index, a burning index, and a fire load index. Each of these is related to a specific part of the fire-control job. These indexes are used by dispatchers in making decisions on setting up firefighting forces, lookout systems, and so forth.
[W.S.Br.]

Forest genetics   The subdiscipline of genetics concerned with genetic variation and inheritance in forest trees. The study of forest genetics is important because of the unique biological nature of forest trees (large, long-lived plants covering 30% of the Earth's surface) and because of the trees' social and economic importance. Forest genetics is the basis for conservation, maintenance, and management of healthy forest ecosystems; and development of programs which breed high-yielding varieties of commercially important tree species.

Variation in natural forests.   The outward appearance of a tree is called its phenotype. The phenotype is any characteristic of the tree that can be measured or observed such as its height or leaf color. The phenotype is influenced by (1) the tree's genetic potential (its genotype); and (2) the environment in which the tree grows as determined by climate, soil, diseases, pests, and competition with other plants.

No two trees of the same species have exactly the same phenotype, and in most forests there is tremendous phenotypic variation among trees of the same species. Forest geneticists often question whether the observed phenotypic variation among trees in forests is caused mostly by genetic differences or by differences in environmental effects. Common garden tests are often used to hold the environment constant and therefore isolate the genetic and environmental effects on phenotypic variability.

Geographic variation. The term "provenance" refers to a specific geographical location within the natural range of a tree species. Natural selection during the course of evolution has adapted each provenance to its particular local environment. This means that there are large genetic differences among provenances growing in different environments. Provenances originating from colder regions, for example, tend to have narrower crowns with flatter branches better adapted to the dry snow and types of frosts in colder climates. To demonstrate that these differences are genetic in origin, common garden tests called provenance tests have been planted. That is, seed has been collected from several provenances and planted for comparison in randomized, replicated studies in various forest locations. The study of geographic variation through provenance tests should be a first step in the genetic research of any tree species.

Genetic variation. In addition to genetic differences among provenances, there is usually substantial genetic variation among trees within the same provenance and even within the same forest stand. There are two reasons for this genetic diversity: (1) Different trees have different genotypes in most natural stands. (2) Each tree is heterozygous for many genes, meaning that a given tree has multiple forms (different alleles) of many genes. Population genetics studies patterns of genetic diversity in populations (such as forest stands). Results of many studies have shown that most forest tree species maintain very high levels of genetic diversity within populations. *See* POPULATION GENETICS.

Forest tree breeding. Beginning with the natural genetic variation that exists in an undomesticated tree species, tree breeding programs use selection, breeding, and other techniques to change gene frequencies for a few key traits of the chosen species. As with agricultural crops, tree breeders produce genetically improved, commercial varieties that are healthier, grow faster, and yield better wood products. After an existing forest stand is harvested, a new stand of trees is planted to replace the previous stand in the process called reforestation. Use of a genetically improved variety for this reforestation means that the new plantation will grow faster and produce wood products sooner than did the previous stand.

Several laboratory techniques promise to make major contributions to forest genetics and tree breeding: (1) Somatic embryogenesis is a technique to duplicate (or propagate) selected trees asexually from their vegetative (somatic) cells, and this allows the best trees to be immediately propagated commercially as clones without sexual reproduction (that is, no seed is involved). (2) Genetic mapping of some important tree species is well under way, and these maps will be useful in many ways to understand the genetic control of important traits, such as disease resistance. (3) Marker-assisted selection is the use of some kinds of genetic maps to help select excellent trees at very early ages based on their deoxyribonucleic acid (DNA) genotype as assessed in a laboratory (instead of growing trees in the field and selecting based on performance in the forest). (4) Functional genomic analysis is an exciting new field of genetics that aims to understand the function, controlled expression, and interaction of genes in complex traits such as tree growth. (5) Genetic engineering or genetic modification is the insertion of new genes into trees from other species.

Conservation of genetic resources. For commercially important species of forest trees, gene conservation is practiced by tree breeding programs to sustain the genetic diversity needed by the program. However, conservation of genetic diversity is a major global concern and is important for all forest species to maintain the health and function of forest ecosystems, and to sustain the genetic diversity of noncommercial species that may eventually have economic value. There are two broad categories of gene conservation programs. In-situ programs conserve entire forest ecosystems in forest reserves, national parks, wilderness areas, or other areas set aside for conservation purposes. Ex-situ programs obtain a sample of the genotypes from different provenances of a single tree species and collect seed or vegetative plant material from each genotype to store in a separate location (such as a seed bank in a refrigerated room). Both types of programs are important for conserving the world's forest resources. *See* BREEDING (PLANT); FOREST AND FORESTRY; FOREST ECOSYSTEM; GENETIC ENGINEERING; PLANT PROPAGATION. [T.L.W.]

Fresh-water ecosystem   Fresh water is best defined, in contrast to the oceans, as water that contains a relatively small amount of dissolved chemical compounds. Some studies of fresh-water ecosystems focus on water bodies themselves, while others include the surrounding land that interacts with a lake or stream. *See* ECOLOGY; ECOSYSTEM.

Fresh-water ecosystems are often categorized by two basic criteria: water movement and size. In lotic or flowing-water ecosystems the water moves steadily in a uniform direction, while in lentic or standing-water systems the water tends to remain in the same general area for a longer period of time. Size varies dramatically in each category. Lotic systems range from a tiny rivulet dripping off a rock to large rivers. Lentic systems range from the water borne within a cup formed by small plants or tree holes to very large water bodies such as the Laurentian Great Lakes. Fresh-water studies also consider the interactions of the geological, physical, and chemical features along with the biota, the organisms that occur in an area.

Physical environment. The quantity and spectral quality of light have major influences on the distribution of the biota and also play a central role in the thermal structure of lakes. The light that reaches the surface of a lake or stream is controlled by latitude, season, time of day, weather, and the conditions that surround a water body. Light penetration is controlled by the nature of water itself and by dissolved and particulate material in a water column.

Water exhibits a number of unusual thermal properties, including its existence in liquid state at normal earth surface temperatures, a remarkable ability to absorb heat, and a maximum density at $39.09°F$ ($3.94°C$), which leads to a complex annual cycle in the temperature structure of fresh-water ecosystems.

As water is warmed at the surface of a lake, a stable condition is reached in which a physically distinct upper layer of water, the epilimnion, is maintained over a deeper, cooler stratum, the hypolimnion. The region of sharp temperature changes between these two layers is called the metalimnion. The characteristic establishment of two layers is of major importance in the chemical cycling within lakes and consequently for the biota.

As the surface waters of a lake cool, the density of epilimnetic waters increases, which decreases their resistance to mixing with the hypolimnion. If cooling continues, the entire water column will mix, an event known as turnover. At temperatures below $39.09°F$ ($3.94°C$), water again becomes less dense; ice and very cold water float above slightly warmer water, maintaining liquid water below ice cover even in lakes in the Antarctic. Many lakes in the temperate zones undergo two distinct periods of mixing annually, one in the spring and the other in the fall, that separate periods of stratification in the summer and winter.

Water movement is more extensive in lotic than in standing-water ecosystems, but water motion has important effects in both types. Turbulence occurs ubiquitously and affects the distribution of organisms, particles, dissolved substances, and heat. Turbulence increases with the velocity of flowing water, and the amount of material transported by water increases with turbulence. Flowing-water ecosystems are characterized by large fluctuations in the velocity and amount of water. Aside from surface waves on large lakes, most water movement in lentic systems is not conspicuous.

Chemical environment. For an element, three basic parameters are of importance: the forms in which it occurs, its source, and its concentration in water relative to its biological demand or effect. Most elements are derived from dissolved gases in the atmosphere or from minerals in geological materials surrounding a lake. In some cases the presence of elements is strongly mediated by biological activities. *See* BIO-GEOCHEMISTRY.

Oxygen occurs as dissolved O_2 and in combination with other elements resulting from chemical or biological reactions. It enters water primarily from the atmosphere through a combination of diffusion and turbulent mixing. When biological demands for oxygen exceed supply rates, it can be depleted from fresh-water ecosystems. Anoxic conditions occur in hypolimnia during summer and under ice cover in winter when lake strata are isolated from the atmosphere. Oxygen depletion may also occur in rivers that receive heavy organic loading. Aside from specialized bacteria, few organisms can occur under anoxic conditions.

Carbon dioxide is derived primarily from the atmosphere, with additional sources from plant and animal respiration and carbonate minerals. Its chemical species exert a major control on the hydrogen ion concentration of water (the acidity or pH). *See* PH.

Phosphorus occurs primarily as a phosphate ion or in a number of complex organic forms. It is the element which is most commonly in the shortest supply relative to biological demand. Phosphorus is thus a limiting nutrient, and its addition to fresh-water ecosystems through human activities can lead to major problems due to increased growth of aquatic plants.

Nitrogen occurs in water as N_2, NO_2, NO_3, NH_4, and in diverse organic forms. It may be derived from precipitation and soils, but its availability is usually regulated by bacterial processes. Nitrogen occurs in relatively short supply relative to biological demand. It may also limit growth in some fresh-water systems, particularly when phosphorus levels have been increased because of human activity.

A variety of other elements also help determine the occurrence of fresh-water organisms either directly or by the elements' effects on water chemistry.

Biota. In addition to taxonomy, fresh-water organisms are classified by the areas in which they occur, the manner in which they move, and the roles that they occupy in trophic webs. Major distinctions are made between organisms that occur in bottom areas and those within the water column, the limnetic zone. Production is the most difficult variable to measure, but it provides the greatest information on the role of organisms in an ecosystem. *See* BIOLOGICAL PRODUCTIVITY; BIOMASS.

Plankton organisms occur in open water and move primarily with general water motion. Planktonic communities occur in all lentic ecosystems. In lotic systems they are important only in slow-moving areas.

Phytoplankton (plant plankton) comprise at least eight major taxonomic groups of algae, most of which are microscopic. They exhibit a diversity of forms ranging from one-celled organisms to complex colonies. *See* ALGAE; PHYTOPLANKTON.

Zooplankton (animal plankton) comprise protozoans and three major groups of eukaryotic organisms: rotifers, cladocerans, and copepods. Most are microscopic but some are clearly visible to the naked eye. *See* COPEPODA; POPULATION ECOLOGY; ROTIFERA; ZOOPLANKTON.

Animals, such as fishes and swimming insects, that occur in the water column and can control their position independently of water movement are termed nekton. In addition to their importance as a human food source, fishes may affect zooplankton, benthic invertebrates, vegetation, and lake sediments.

Benthic organisms are a diverse group associated with the bottoms of lakes and streams. The phytobenthos ranges from microscopic algae to higher plants. Benthic animals range from microscopic protozoans and crustaceans to large aquatic insects and fishes. *See* FOOD WEB.

Bacteria occur throughout fresh-water ecosystems in planktonic and benthic areas and play a major role in biogeochemical cycling. Most bacteria are heterotrophic, using reduced carbon as an energy source; others are photosynthetic or derive energy from reduced compounds other than carbon. *See* BACTERIAL PHYSIOLOGY AND METABOLISM.

Interactions. Ultimately the conditions in a fresh-water ecosystem are controlled by numerous interactions among biotic and abiotic components. Primary production in a fresh-water ecosystem is controlled by light and nutrient availability. As light diminishes with depth in a column or water, a point is reached where energy for photosynthesis balances respiratory energy demands. In benthic areas, the region where light is sufficient for plant growth is termed the littoral zone; deeper areas are labeled profundal.

Nutrient availability generally controls the total amount of primary production that occurs in fresh-water ecosystems. One classification scheme for lakes ranks them according to total production, ranging from oligotrophic lakes, where water is clear and production is low, to eutrophic systems, characterized by high nutrient concentrations, high standing algal biomass, high production, low water clarity, and low concentrations of oxygen in the hypolimnion. Eutrophic conditions are more likely to occur as a lake ages. This aging process, termed eutrophication, occurs naturally but can be greatly accelerated by anthropogenic additions of nutrients. A third major lake category, termed dystrophy, occurs when large amounts of organic materials that are resistant to decomposition wash into a lake basin. These organic materials stain the lake water and have a major influence on water chemistry which results in low production.   [T.M.F.]

Fructose   A sugar that is the commonest of ketoses and the sweetest of the sugars. It is also known as D-fructose, D-fructopyranose, and levulose fruit sugar. It is found in free state, usually accompanied by D-glucose and sucrose in fruit juices, honey, and nectar of plant glands. D-Fructose is the principal sugar in seminal fluid. *See* CARBOHYDRATE.

Fructose is readily utilized by diabetic animals. In persons with diabetes mellitus or parenchymal hepatic disease, the impairment of fructose tolerance is relatively small and not at all comparable to the diminution in their tolerance to glucose. *See* MONOSACCHARIDE.   [W.Z.H.]

Fruit   A matured carpel or group of carpels (the basic units of the gynoecium or female part of the flower) with or without seeds, and with or without other floral or shoot parts (accessory structures) united to the carpel or carpels. Carpology is the study of the morphology and anatomy of fruits. The ovary develops into a fruit after fertilization and usually contains one or more seeds, which have developed from the fertilized ovules. Parthenocarpic fruits usually lack seeds. Fruitlets are the small fruits or subunits of aggregate or multiple fruits. Flowers, carpels, ovaries, and fruits are, by definition, restricted to the flowering plants (angiosperms), although fruitlike structures may enclose seeds in certain other groups of seed plants. The fruit is of ecological significance because of seed dispersal. *See* SEED.

Morphology. A fruit develops from one or more carpels. Usually only part of the gynoecium, the ovary, develops into a fruit; the style and stigma wither. Accessory (extracarpellary or noncarpellary) structures may be closely associated with the carpel or carpels and display various degrees of adnation (fusion) to them, thus becoming part of the fruit. Such accessory parts include sepals (as in the mulberry), the bases of sepals, petals, and stamens united into a floral tube (apple, banana, pear, and other species with inferior ovaries), the receptacle (strawberry), the pedicel and receptacle (cashew), the peduncle (fleshy part of the fig), the involucre composed of bracts and bracteoles (walnut and pineapple), and the inflorescence axis (pineapple). *See* FLOWER.

A fruit derived from only carpellary structures is called a true fruit, or, because it develops from a superior ovary (one inserted above the other floral parts), a superior fruit (corn, date, grape, plum, and tomato). Fruits with accessory structures are called accessory (or inaptly, false or spurious) fruits (pseudocarps), or, because of their frequent derivation from inferior ovaries (inserted below the other floral parts), inferior fruits (banana, pear, squash, and walnut).

Fruits can be characterized by the number of ovaries and flowers forming the fruit. A simple fruit is derived form one ovary, an aggregate fruit from several ovaries of one flower (magnolia, rose, and strawberry). A multiple (collective) fruit is derived from the ovaries and accessory structures of several flowers consolidated into one mass (fig, pandan, pineapple, and sweet gum).

The fruit wall at maturity may be fleshy or, more commonly, dry. Fleshy fruits range from soft and juicy to hard and tough. Dry fruits may be dehiscent, opening to release seeds, or indehiscent, remaining closed and containing usually one seed per fruit. Fleshy fruits are rarely dehiscent.

The pericarp is the fruit wall developed from the ovary. In true fruits, the fruit wall and pericarp are synonymous, but in accessory fruits the fruit wall includes the pericarp plus one or more accessory tissues of various derivation. Besides the fruit wall, a fruit contains one or more seed-bearing regions (placentae) and often partitions (septa).

Anatomy. Anatomically or histologically, a fruit consists of dermal, ground (fundamental), and vascular systems and, if present, one or more seeds. After fertilization the ovary and sometimes accessory parts develop into the fruit; parthenocarpy is fruit production without fertilization. The fruit generally increases in size and undergoes various anatomical changes that usually relate to its manner of dehiscence, its mode of dispersal, or protection of its seeds. The economically important, mainly fleshy fruits have received the most histological and developmental study.

Size increase of fruits is hormonally controlled and results from cell division and especially from cell enlargement. Cell number, volume, and weight thus control fruit weight. Cell division generally is more pronounced before anthesis (full bloom); cell enlargement is more pronounced after.

Functional aspects. Large fruits generally require additional anatomical modifications for nutrition or support or both. The extra phloem in fruit vascular bundles and the often increased amount of vascular tissue in the fruit wall and septa supply nutrients to the developing seeds and, especially in fleshy fruits, to the developing walls. Large, especially fleshy fruits (apple, gourd, and kiwi) usually contain proportionally more vascular tissue than small fruits. Vascular tissue also serves for support and in lightweight fruits may be the chief means of support.

Crystals, tannins, and oils commonly occur in fruits and may protect against pathogens and predators. The astringency of tannins, for example, may be repellent to organisms. With fruit maturation, tannin content ordinarily decreases, so the tannin repellency operative in early stages is superseded in fleshy fruits by features (tenderness, succulence, sweetness through odor and increased sugar content, and so on) attractive to animal dispersal agents. Many fruits are dispersed by hairs, hooks, barbs, spines, and sticky mucilage adhering the fruit to the surface of the dispersal agent. Lightweight fruits with many air spaces or with wings or plumes may be dispersed by wind or water. Gravity is always a factor in dispersal of fruits and seeds.   [R.S.]

Fungal biotechnology   All aspects of cultivating fungi together with products and processes derived from such cultures. Fungi exhibit a wide range of biosynthetic and biodegradative activities. Since fungi can bring about chemical change in almost any natural or synthetic organic molecule, many species have been selected and propagated in pure culture specifically for applications in biotechnology and industry, for example in food and beverage production.

While the fermentation industry remains the largest and economically most important user of fungal cultures, fungi are also utilized by the pharmaceutical, cosmetic, chemical, agricultural, food, enzyme, wood product, and waste treatment industries. In the United States, two prominent examples of fungal products are citric acid, with an annual production of 350,000 tons (160,000 kg), and beta-lactam antibiotics. Yeasts are the most commercially exploited microorganisms. They have been used extensively in baking, brewing, winemaking, and distilling, and in making various metabolic products. Several million tons of fresh yeast are produced each year, mostly for the baking industry. See FERMENTATION.

Because they are capable of secreting large quantities of certain proteins in liquid culture, fungi have proven to be useful as cloning hosts for the production of recombinant proteins of fungal and human origin. Technologies have been developed to scale up the production of new or novel products. *Aspergillus nidulans* has been designed to produce many human therapeutic proteins, including growth factors and protein hormones. The yeasts *Sac. cerevisiae* and *P. pastoris* have been utilized for the expression of human interferon and serum albumin. Yeast chromosomes are also being employed in the mapping of the human genome. See GENETIC ENGINEERING.   [S.C.J.]

Manufactured products which contain living fungi and are used to control pests are called mycopesticides. They are utilized to control weeds, harmful insects, nematodes (roundworms), or even other fungi. Although formerly confined to experimental settings, mycopesticides are increasingly available as commercial products, especially for the agricultural market. They may impact pest populations through direct parasitism, secretion of antibiotics, competition for nutrients, or a combination of these effects, and may be used alone or in combination with chemical pesticides.   [F.M.D.]

Fungal ecology   The subdiscipline in mycology and ecology that examines community composition and structure; responses, activities, and interactions of single species; and the functions of fungi in ecosystems. These organisms display an extraordinary diversity of ecological interactions and life history strategies, but are alike in being efficient heterotrophs. Fungi, along with bacteria, are the primary decomposers, facilitating the flow of energy and the cycling of materials through ecosystems. See ECOLOGICAL ENERGETICS; FUNGI.

Fungi occur in many different habitat types—on plant surfaces; inside plant tissues; in decaying plant foliage, bark and wood; and in soil—generally changing in abundance and species composition through successional stages of decomposition. Fungi are also found in marine and aquatic habitats; in association with other fungi, lichens, bacteria, and algae; and in the digestive tracts and waste of animals. Some fungi grow in extreme environments: rock can harbor free-living endolithic fungi or the fungal mutualists of lichens; thermotolerant and thermophilic fungi can grow at temperatures above 45°C (113°F); psychrophilic fungi can grow at temperatures to below −3°C (27°F). Xerotolerant fungi are able to grow in extremely dry habitats, and osmotolerant fungi grow on subtrates with high solute concentrations. Most fungi are strict aerobes, but species of the chytrid *Neocallimastix*, which inhabit the rumen of herbivorous mammals, are obligate anaerobes. Several aquatic fungi are facultative anaerobes. Many fungi occur as free-living saprobes, but fungi are particularly successful as mutualistic, commensal, or antagonistic symbionts with other organisms. *See* POPULATION ECOLOGY.

Fungi possess unique features that affect their capacity to adapt and to function in ecosystems:

1. Fungi are composed of a vegetative body (hyphae or single cells) capable of rapid growth. Hyphae are linear strands composed of tubular cells that are in direct contact with the substrate. The cells secrete extracellular enzymes that degrade complex polymers, such as cellulose, into low-molecular-weight units that are then absorbed and catabolized. Many fungi also produce secondary metabolites such as mycotoxins and plant growth regulators that affect the outcomes of their interactions with other organisms.

2. Filamentous fungi are able to mechanically penetrate and permeate the substrate.

3. Fungi have an enormous capacity for metabolic variety. Fungal enzymes are able to decompose highly complex organic substances such as lignin, and to synthesize structurally diverse, biologically active secondary metabolites. Saprotrophic fungi are very versatile; some are able to grow on tree resins and even in jet fuel.

4. Structural and physiological features of fungi facilitate absorption and accumulation of mineral nutrients as well as toxic elements. The capacity of fungi to absorb, accumulate, and translocate is especially significant ecologically where hyphal networks permeate soil and function as a link between microhabitats.

5. Fungi have the capacity for indeterminate growth, longevity, resilience, and asexual reproduction. The vegetative cells of Eumycota are often multinucleate, containing dissimilar haploid nuclei. This combination of features gives the fungi an unparalleled capacity for adaptation to varying physiological and ecological circumstances and ensures a high level of genetic diversity.

6. Many species of fungi have a capacity to shift their mode of nutrition. The principal modes are saprotrophy (the utilization of dead organic matter) and biotrophy, which is characteristic of parasitic, predacious, and mutualistic fungi (including mycorrhizae and lichen fungi). *See* BIODEGRADATION; FUNGAL GENETICS; MYCORRHIZAE.

Fungi interact with all organisms in ecosystems, directly or indirectly, and are key components in ecosystem processes. As decomposers, fungi are crucial in the process of nutrient cycling, including carbon cycling as well as the mineralization or immobilization of other elemental constituents. As parasites, pathogens, predators, mutualists, or food sources, fungi can directly influence the species composition and population dynamics of other organisms with which they coexist. Fungi may act both as agents of successional change or as factors contributing to resilience and stability. Mycorrhizal fungi function as an interface between plant and soil, and are essential to the survival of most plants in natural habitats.

There are several economically important areas that benefit from application of the principles of fungal ecology: biotechnology, biological control, bioremediation, agriculture, forestry, and land reclamation. With only a small fraction of the total species known, the fungi offer a rich potential for bioprospecting, the search for novel genetic resources with unique, useful biochemical properties. *See* ECOLOGY; ECOSYSTEM; FUNGI; FUNGAL BIOTECHNOLOGY.   [M.Ch.; J.K.St.]

Fungal genetics   The study of gene structure and function in fungi. Genetic research has provided important knowledge about genes, heredity, genetic mechanisms, metabolism, physiology, and development in fungi, and in higher organisms in general, because in certain respects the fungal life cycle and cellular attributes are ideally suited to both mendelian and molecular genetic analysis.

Fungal nuclei are predominantly haploid; that is, they contain only one set of chromosomes. This characteristic is useful in the study of mutations, which are usually recessive and therefore masked in diploid organisms. Mutational dissection is an important technique for the study of biological processes, and the use of haploid organisms conveniently allows for the immediate expression of mutant genes. *See* MUTATION.

Reproduction in fungi can be asexual, sexual, or parasexual (see illustration). Asexual reproduction involves mitotic nuclear division during the growth of hyphae, cell division, or the production of asexual spores. Sexual reproduction is based on meiotic nuclear divisions fairly typical of eukaryotes in general. In ascomycetes and basidiomycetes, the spores, containing nuclei that are the four products of a single meiosis, remain together in a group called a tetrad. The isolation and testing of the phenotypes of cultures arising from the members of a tetrad (tetrad analysis) permit the study of the genetic events occurring in individual meioses; this possibility is offered by virtually no other eukaryotic group. In other groups, genetic analysis is limited to products recovered randomly from different meioses. Since a great deal of genetic analysis is based on meiosis, fungal tetrads have proved to be pivotal in shaping current ideas on this key process of eukaryotic biology. *See* EUKARYOTAE; MEIOSIS.

Because their preparation in large numbers is simple, fungal cells are useful in the study of rare events (such as mutations and recombinations) with frequencies as little as one in a million or less. In such cases, selective procedures must be used to identify cells derived from the rare events. The concepts and techniques of fungal asexual and parasexual genetics have been applied to the genetic manipulation of cultured cells of higher eukaryotes such as humans and green plants. However, the techniques remain much easier to perform with fungi.

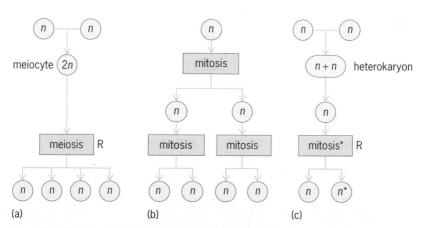

Three different kinds of reproduction occurring in fungi, each of which provides opportunities for genetic analysis. (*a*) Sexual reproduction leads to recombination (R) of genes at meiosis. (*b*) Asexual reproduction (shown here in a typical haploid fungal cell) usually reproduces the gene set faithfully. (*c*) Parasexual reproduction derives from an atypical mitotic division of an unstable cell that produces haploid cells and other aneuploid (deviating from normal chromosome complement) unstable intermediates.

The fact that each enzyme is coded by its own specific gene was first recognized in fungi and was of paramount importance because it showed how the many chemical reactions that take place in a living cell could be controlled by the genetic apparatus. The discovery arose from a biochemical study of nutritional mutants in *Neurospora*. *See* ENZYME.

In genetically transformed organisms, the genome has been modified by the addition of DNA, a key technique in genetic engineering. The cell wall is temporarily removed; exogenous DNA is then taken up by cells and the cell wall is restored. The incorporation of DNA must be detected by a suitable novel genetic marker included on the assimilated molecule in order to distinguish transformed from nontransformed cells. The fate of the DNA inside the cell depends largely on the nature of the vector or carrier. Some vectors can insert randomly throughout the genome. Others can be directed to specific sites, either inactivating a gene for some purpose or replacing a resident gene with an engineered version present on the vector. A third kind of vector remains uninserted as an autonomously replicating plasmid. The ability to transform fungal cells has permitted the engineering of fungi with modified metabolic properties for making products of utility in industry. *See* GENETIC ENGINEERING.

A surprising development in the molecular biology of eukaryotes was the discovery of transposons, pieces of DNA that can move to new locations in the chromosomes. Although transposons were once known only in bacteria, they are now recognized in many eukaryotes. The transposons found in fungi mobilize by either of two processes: one type via a ribonucleic acid (RNA) intermediate that is subsequently reverse-transcribed to DNA, and the other type via DNA directly. In either case, a DNA copy of the transposed segment is inserted into the new site and may contain, in addition to the transposon itself, segments of contagious DNA mobilized from the original chromosomal site. Because of the rearrangements which transposons may produce, they have been important in the evolution of the eukaryotic genome. *See* FUNGI; GENETICS; TRANSPOSONS.   [A.J.F.G.; R.U.]

Fungal infections   Several thousand species of fungi have been described, but fewer than 100 are routinely associated with invasive diseases of humans. In general, healthy humans have a very high level of natural immunity to fungi, and most fungal infections are mild and self-limiting. Intact skin and mucosal surfaces and a functional immune system serve as the primary barriers to colonization by these ubiquitous organisms, but these barriers are sometimes breached.

Unlike viruses, protozoan parasites, and some bacterial species, fungi do not require human or animal tissues to perpetuate or preserve the species. Virtually all fungi that have been implicated in human disease are free-living in nature. However, there are exceptions, including various *Candida* spp., which are frequently found on mucosal surfaces of the body such as the mouth and vagina, and *Malassezia furfur*, which is usually found on skin surfaces that are rich in sebaceous glands. These organisms are often cultured from healthy tissues, but under certain conditions they cause disease. Only a handful of fungi cause significant disease in healthy individuals. Once established, these diseases can be classified according to the tissues that are initially colonized.

Superficial mycoses. Four infections are classified in the superficial mycoses. Black piedra, caused by *Piedraia hortai*, and white piedra, caused by *Trichosporn beigleii*, are infections of the hair. The skin infections include tinea nigra, caused by *Exophiala werneckii*, and tinea versicolor, caused by *M. furfur*. Where the skin is involved, the infections are limited to the outermost layers of the stratum corneum; in the case of hairs, the infection is limited to the cuticle. In general, these infections cause no physical discomfort to the patient, and the disease is brought to the attention of the physician for cosmetic reasons.

Cutaneous mycoses. The cutaneous mycoses are caused by a homogeneous group of keratinophilic fungi termed the dermatophytes. Species within this group are capable of colonizing the integument and its appendages (the hair and the nails). In general, the infections are limited to the nonliving keratinized layers of skin, hair, and nails, but a variety of pathologic changes can occur depending on the etiologic agent, site of infection, and immune status of the host. The diseases are collectively called the dermatophytoses, ringworms, or tineas. They account for most of the fungal infections of humans.

Subcutaneous mycoses. The subcutaneous mycoses include a wide spectrum of infections caused by a heterogeneous group of fungi. The infections are characterized by the development of lesions at sites of inoculation, commonly as a result of traumatic implantation of the etiologic agent. The infections initially involve the deeper layers of the dermis and subcutaneous tissues, but they eventually extend into the epidermis. The lesions usually remain localized or spread slowly by direct extension via the lymphatics, for example, subcutaneous sporotrichosis.

Systemic mycoses. The initial focus of the systemic mycoses is the lung. The vast majority of cases in healthy, immunologically competent individuals are asymptomatic or of short duration and resolve rapidly, accompanied in the host by a high degree of specific resistance. However, in immunosuppressed patients the infection can lead to life-threatening disease. See FUNGI; MEDICAL MYCOLOGY.   [G.S.K.]

Fungal virus   Any of the viruses that infect fungi (mycoviruses). In general these viruses are spheres of 30–45-nanometer diameter composed of multiple units of a single protein arranged in an icosahedral structure enclosing a genome of segmented double-stranded ribonucleic acid (dsRNA). Viruses are found in most species of fungi, where they usually multiply without apparent harm to the host. Most fungal viruses are confined to closely related species in which they are transmitted only through sexual or asexual spores to progeny or by fusion of fungal hyphae (filamentous cells). Some fungal strains are infected with multiple virus species. Although hundreds of virus-containing fungi have been reported, very few have been studied in significant detail. Three families of mycoviruses are recognized by the International Committee on Taxonomy of Viruses. The most thoroughly studied mycoviruses are in the family Totiviridae. See FUNGI; MYCOLOGY; PLANT PATHOLOGY; VIRUS; VIRUS CLASSIFICATION.
                                                                    [R.F.Bo.]

Fungi   Nucleated, usually filamentous, sporebearing organisms devoid of chlorophyll; typically reproducing both sexually and asexually; living as parasites in plants, animals, or other fungi, or as saprobes on plant or animal remains, in aquatic, marine, terrestrial, or subaerial habitats. Yeasts, mildews, rusts, mushrooms, and truffles are examples of fungi.

Some fungal classifications were constructed to facilitate identification, whereas others emphasize phylogeny. The more widely used classifications reflect a series of compromises between identification and phylogeny, and tend to conserve the vocabulary and nomenclature familiar to broad groups of users. The following is a conventional classification, in which all organisms are treated as members of the kingdom Fungi:

> Division: Eumycota
> Subdivision: Mastigomycotina
> Class: Chytridiomycetes

Class: Hyphochytriomycetes
Oomycetes
Subdivision: Zygomycotina
Class: Zygomycetes
Trichomycetes
Subdivision: Ascomycotina
Class: Hemiascomycetes
Plectomycetes
Pyrenomycetes
Discomycetes
Loculoascomycetes
Subdivision: Basidiomycotina
Class: Hymenomycetes
Gasteromycetes
Urediniomycetes
Ustilaginomycetes
Subdivision: Deuteromycotina
Class: Blastomycetes
Hyphomycetes
Coelomycetes
Agonomycetes
Division: Myxomycota   [F.M.D.]

Organisms in the kingdom Fungi are mostly haploid, use chitin as a structural cell-wall polysaccharide, and synthesize lysine by the alpha amino adipic acid pathway; and their body is made of branching filaments (hyphae). The fungi arose about 1 billion years ago along with plants (including green algae), animals plus choanoflagellates, red algae, and stramenopiles. Ribosomal comparison indicates that the closest relatives to the fungi are the animals plus choanoflagellates. *See* CHOANOFLAGELLIDA.

Ascomycetes are the most numerous fungi (75% of all described species), and include lichen-forming symbionts. The group has traditionally been divided into unicellular yeasts and allies with naked asci, and hyphal forms with protected asci. However, ribosomal gene sequences indicate that some traditional yeasts and allied forms diverged early (early ascomycetes), at about the time ascomycetes were diverging from basidiomycetes. Hyphal ascomycetes protect their asci with a variety of fruiting bodies; the earliest fruiting bodies may have been open cups (Discomycetes), while in more recent groups they are flask shaped (Pyrenomycetes and Loculoascomycetes) or are completely closed (Plectomycetes). Ascomycetes lacking sexual structures have been classified in the Fungi Imperfecti, but molecular comparisons now allow their integration with the ascomycetes. *See* ASCOMYCOTA; DEUTEROMYCOTINA.   [J.W.T.]

The mycelium, generally the vegetative body of fungi, is extremely variable. Unicellular forms, thought to be primitive or derived, grade into restricted mycelial forms; in most species, however, the mycelium is extensive and capable of indefinite growth. Some are typically perennial though most are ephemeral. The mycelium may be nonseptate, that is, coenocytic, with myriad scattered nuclei lying in a common cytoplasm, or septate, with each cell containing one to a very few nuclei or an indefinite number of nuclei. Septa may be either perforate or solid. Cell walls are composed largely of chitinlike materials except in one group of aquatic forms that have cellulose walls. Most mycelia are white, but a wide variety of pigments can be synthesized by specific forms and may be secreted into the medium or deposited in cell walls and protoplasm.

Mycelial consistency varies from loose, soft wefts of hyphae to compact, hardened masses that resemble leather. Each cell is usually able to regenerate the entire mycelium, and vegetative propagation commonly results from mechanical fragmentation of the mycelium.

Asexual reproduction, propagation by specialized elements that originate without sexual fusion, occurs in most species and is extremely diverse. The most common and important means of asexual reproduction are unicellular or multicellular spores of various types that swim, fall, blow, or are forcibly discharged from the parent mycelium.

Sexual reproduction occurs in a majority of species of all classes. Juxtaposition and fusion of compatible sexual cells are achieved by four distinct sexual mechanisms, involving various combinations of differentiated sexual cells (gametes), undifferentiated sexual cells (gametangia), and undifferentiated vegetative cells.   [J.R.Ra.]

Fungi obtain organic substances (food) from their environment which have been produced through the (photosynthetic) activities of green plants, since fungi do not contain chlorophyll and are unable to manufacture their own food. Fungi are able to digest food externally by releasing enzymes into their environment. These smaller molecules can be absorbed into the fungal body and transported to various locations where they can be used for energy or converted into different chemicals to make new cells or to serve other purposes. Some of the by-products of fungal metabolism may be useful to humans. Most fungi use nonliving plant material for food, but a few use nonliving animal material and therefore are called saprophytic organisms. In nature the decomposition of dead plant material is an important function of fungi, as the process releases nutrients back into the surrounding ecosystem where they can be reused by other organisms, including humans. See BIODEGRADATION; FUNGAL ECOLOGY.

A few fungi have the physiological capability to grow on living plants and may cause diseases such as wheat rust or corn smut on these economically important plants. Some fungi can grow on grains and may produce substances known as aflatoxins which can be detrimental to animals or humans. A few species of fungi have the ability to grow and acquire their food from skin or hair on living animals such as cats, horses, and humans. The disease known as ringworm may result. It is not caused by a worm but by an expanding circular growth of a fungus which has the physiological capability to use the components of skin or hair as the food source. The most frequently encountered fungal disease in humans is candidiasis, which is caused by one of the few fungi that is normally found associated with humans (*Candida albicans*). See AFLATOXIN; MEDICAL MYCOLOGY; PLANT PATHOLOGY; YEAST INFECTION.

A number of fungal species are able to enter plant roots and develop an association that may be beneficial to the plant under natural field conditions. This association of a higher plant root and a fungus that does not produce a disease is called a mycorrhiza. This fungal association with the plant root may permit the plant to live under soil conditions where it may not otherwise survive because of an excess of acid in the soil or a lack or excess of certain nutrients. See MYCORRHIZAE.

Certain species of fungi have been used by humans since early times in the preparation of foods such as leavened bread, cheeses, and beverages. Additional by-products of fungal physiology are used in industrial applications such as antibiotics, solvents, and pharmaceuticals. See FUNGAL BIOTECHNOLOGY; INDUSTRIAL MICROBIOLOGY; YEAST.

[M.C.W.]

Galactose   A monosaccharide and a constituent of oligosaccharides, notably lactose, melibiose, raffinose, and stachyose. It is also known as D-galactose and cerebrose (see illustration). Agar, gum arabic, mesquite gum, larch arabo galactan, and a variety of other gums and mucilages contain D-galactose. See AGAR; MONOSACCHARIDE.

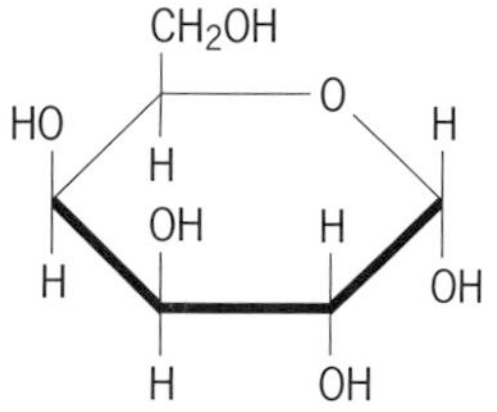

CH$_2$OH

HO   O   H

H

OH   H

H   OH

H   OH

**Structural formula for
α-D-galactose.**

L-Galactose (enantiomorph of D-galactose) occurs in several polysaccharides, including agar, flaxseed mucilage, snail galactogen, and chagual gum. Since D-galactose is usually also present, hydrolysis of these polysaccharides produces DL-galactose. See CARBOHYDRATE.   [W.Z.H.]

Gallbladder   A hollow muscular organ, present in humans and most vertebrates, which receives dilute bile from the liver, concentrates it, and discharges it into the duodenum. It also participates in the entero-hepatic (re)circulation of bile, and in secretion and removal of conjugated xenobiotics, including radiopaque substances taken orally or intravenously for diagnostic purposes. Although not a vital organ, it stores bile, regulates biliary tract pressures, and, when diseased, enhances precipitation of various constituents of the bile as gallstones.

The system of bile ducts lying outside the liver is known as the extrahepatic biliary tract. In humans (Illus.) right and left hepatic ducts empty into the common hepatic duct, which continues to the duodenum as the common bile duct, or ductus choledochus. The gallbladder and cystic duct thus appear to be accessory organs and therefore are removable. However, they are converted into main-line structures by the presence of a sphincter (sphincter of Oddi) at the choledochoduodenal junction. Tonic contraction of this sphincter between meals forces the bile to back up into the gallbladder.

In most other vertebrates essentially similar relations exist except when the gallbladder is absent, but there is considerable variation in proportion and arrangement of ducts, including the pancreatic ducts. See LIVER; PANCREAS.

In humans, evacuation of the gallbladder is accomplished by a trigger mechanism which is set off by the presence of fatty foods, meat, and hydragogue cathartics in the duodenum and upper jejunum. Absorption of these substances by the mucous membrane results in the release of cholecystokinin (CCK), a hormone which rapidly

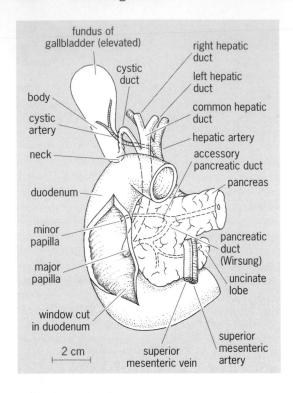

fundus of gallbladder (elevated)

right hepatic duct

cystic duct

left hepatic duct

body

common hepatic duct

cystic artery

hepatic artery

neck

accessory pancreatic duct

duodenum

pancreas

minor papilla

pancreatic duct (Wirsung)

major papilla

uncinate lobe

window cut in duodenum

2 cm

superior mesenteric vein

superior mesenteric artery

Extrahepatic biliary tract in humans.

circulates in the bloodstream and simultaneously produces contraction of the gallbladder and relaxation of the sphincter of Oddi. The most effective food is egg yolk, which contains certain *l*-amino acids. Resorption of bile salts by the intestine stimulates secretion of bile for hours after a meal. *See* Digestive system. [E.A.B.; J.Gi.]

Gametogenesis The production of gametes, either eggs by the female or sperm by the male, through a process involving meiosis. In animals, the cells which will ultimately differentiate into eggs and sperm arise from primordial germ cells set aside from the potential somatic cells very early in the formation of the embryo.

The final products of gametogenesis are the large, sedentary egg cells, and the smaller, motile sperm cells. Each type of gamete is haploid; that is, it contains half the chromosomal complement and thus half as much deoxyribonucleic acid (DNA) as the somatic cells, which are diploid. Reduction of the DNA content is accomplished by meiosis, which is characterized by one cycle of DNA replication followed by two cycles of cell division. *See* Chromosome; Meiosis.

The production of sperm differs from that of oocytes in that each primary spermatocyte divides twice to produce four equivalent spermatozoa which differ only in the content of sex chromosomes (in XY sex determination, characteristic of mammals, two of the sperm contain an X chromosome and two contain a Y). The morphology of sperm is highly specialized, with distinctive organelles forming both the posterior motile apparatus and the anterior acrosome, which assists in penetration of the oocyte at fertilization. *See* Spermatogenesis.

The cytoplasm of the primary oocyte increases greatly during the meiotic prophase and often contains large quantities of yolk accumulated from the blood. Meiotic divisions in the oocyte are often set in motion by sperm entry, and result in the production of one large egg and three polar bodies. The polar bodies play no role, or a very subordinate one, in the formation of the embryo. *See* OOGENESIS.

After fertilization and the formation of the polar bodies, the haploid sperm and egg nuclei (pronuclei) fuse, thus restoring the normal diploid complement of chromosomes. *See* REPRODUCTION (ANIMAL). [S.J.B.]

Meiosis in flowering plants, or angiosperms, is essentially similar to that in animals. However, the cells produced after meiosis are spores, and these do not develop directly into gametes. Female spores (megaspores) and male spores (microspores) develop into gametophytes, that is, female and male haploid plants that bear within them the egg and sperm, respectively. There is a wide range in the details of development and structure of gametes among the different groups of plants other than angiosperms. *See* REPRODUCTION (PLANT). [J.P.M.]

Gastropoda   The largest and most varied class in the phylum Mollusca, possibly numbering over 74,000 species and commonly known as snails.

General characteristics. The shell is in one piece which, in the majority of forms, grows along a turbinate (equiangular) spiral (see illustration), but which is modified into an open cone in various limpets or is secondarily lost in various slugs.

All gastropods, at some time in their phylogeny and at some stage in their development, have undergone torsion. The process does not occur in any other mollusks. It implies that the visceral mass and the mantle shell covering it have become twisted through 180° in relation to the head and foot. As a result of torsion, all internal organs are twisted into a loop. Similarly in gastropods, the mantle cavity (the semi-internal space enclosed by the pallium or mantle) containing the characteristic molluscan gills (ctenidia) has become anterior and placed immediately above and behind the head. The most primitive gastropods retain a pair of aspidobranch (bipectinate or featherlike)

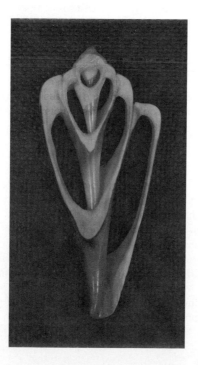

Longitudinal section ground through the shell of a specimen of *Conus spurius* to reveal the central columella and spiral of whorls expanding to the aperture. (*From W. D. Russell-Hunter, A Life of Invertebrates, Macmillan, 1979*)

gills, each with alternating ctenidial leaflets on either side of a ctenidial axis in which run afferent and efferent blood vessels. Lateral cilia on the faces of the leaflets create a respiratory water current (toward the midline and anteriorly) in the direction opposite to the flow of blood through the gills, to create the physiological efficiency of a countercurrent exchange system.

Classification and diversity. The usual systematic arrangement of the class Gastropoda involves three somewhat unequal subclasses. The first, the largest and most diverse, is the subclass Prosobranchia, which is made up largely of marine snails all retaining internal evidence of torsion. Prosobranchs are divided into at least four orders: Archaegastropoda, Caenogastropoda, Neritida, and Patellogastropoda; three superfamilies remain to be assigned to one of the four orders, and may each comprise a distinct order. The other two subclasses (Opisthobranchia and Pulmonata) are each considerably more uniform than the subclass Prosobranchia and, in both, the effects of torsion are reduced or obscured by secondary processes of development and growth.

More than half of all molluscan species are gastropods, and they encompass a range from marine zygobranchs, which can be numbered among the most primitive of all living mollusks, to the highly evolved terrestrial air-breathing slugs and snails. Pulmonates and certain mesogastropod families are the only successful molluscan colonizers of land and fresh waters.   [W.D.R.H.]

Fossils. Fossil gastropods have a long geologic history, being common throughout the Paleozoic and increasingly abundant in the Mesozoic and Cenozoic. All three subclasses are known in the fossil record; many superfamilies, particularly prosobranchs, are extinct. Average duration of a genus has been estimated to range from 30,000,000 to 90,000,000 years.

Marine gastropods are important stratigraphic indicators in Cenozoic strata and locally are abundant in Cretaceous rocks. They are less common and less useful in the Jurassic and Triassic. Although individual genera have stratigraphic utility within the Paleozoic, it is only in the Ordovician that they are significant for correlation. *See* Mollusca.   [E.L.Y.]

Gastrotricha   A phylum of minute metazoan animals (formerly placed in the aschelminth group) numbering 500 described species worldwide. Some 300 species have been reported from the marine habitat, with new ones being described every year.

Gatrotrichs comprise two orders, the Macrodasyida and the Chaetonotida. The term Gastrotricha refers to the ventral locomotor cilia by which the animals glide gracefully over the substratum or through its interstices; unlike many other ciliated animals, they cannot move in reverse. Gastrotrichs have a complete digestive tract, with a sucking pharynx, a simple intestine with a wall only a single cell thick, and an anus. They appear to be selective feeders on bacteria, very small protozoa, and yeasts. Most have protonephridia, accounting in part for their broad salinity tolerances.

Gastrotrichs appear to be regionally cosmopolitan, with 20–30% having broad distributions within continents, and 10–15% between continents; endemism probably does not exceed 20%.

The phylum Gastrotricha is the most primitive in the aschelminth group of phyla. Gastrotrichs and nematodes probably share a common ancestor, which in turn was descended from a stock that included gnathostomulids and turbellarianoid animals. *See* Nemata.   [W.D.Hu.]

Gastrulation The formation of the primordial gut, the archenteron, or digestive cavity of an early animal embryo. More generally, and originally, the term gastrulation referred to the process by which the gastrula stage of the embryo is formed. Thus to nineteenth-century embryologists, gastrulation was the process by which the single-layered blastula, a hollow ball of cells, is converted into the double-layered gastrula. The term has now come to have a still more general meaning, namely, the process by which the three germ layers, or primordial tissues of the embryo, are brought into the positions and relations characteristic of the late gastrula stage, with ectoderm (outer skin), mesoderm (middle skin), and endoderm (inner skin) from the outside to the inside. The terms epiblast, mesoblast, and hypoblast are also used to denote ectoderm, mesoderm, and endoderm, respectively. *See* BLASTULATION.

Two general but not mutually exclusive methods of gastrulation have been recognized: epiboly and emboly. Epiboly is the growing or extending of one part, such as the upper hemisphere of a spherical blastula, over and around another part, such as the lower hemisphere. Emboly is the pushing or growing of one part into another. In many embryos, both types of cell movement may occur; in certain invertebrate embryos, one type may predominate almost to the exclusion of the other. Generally speaking, epiboly tends to be the major, but not the only, method of gastrulation in forms with large, yolky eggs. *See* GERM LAYERS. [N.T.S.]

Gene The basic unit in inheritance. There is no general agreement as to the exact usage of the term, since several criteria that have been used for its definition have been shown not to be equivalent.

The facts of mendelian inheritance indicate the presence of discrete hereditary units that replicate at each cell division, producing remarkably exact copies of themselves, and that in some highly specific way determine the characteristics of the individuals that bear them. The evidence also shows that each of these units may at times mutate to give a new equally stable unit (called an allele), which has more or less similar but not identical effects on the characters of its bearers. These hereditary units are the genes, and the criteria for the recognition that certain genes are alleles have been that they (1) arise from one another by a single mutation, (2) have similar effects on the characters of the organism, and (3) occupy the same locus in the chromosome. It has long been known that there were a few cases where these criteria did not give consistent results, but these were explained by special hypotheses in the individual cases. However, such cases have been found to be so numerous that they appear to be the rule rather than the exception. *See* ALLELE; GENE ACTION; MENDELISM; MUTATION; RECOMBINATION (GENETICS).

The term gene, or cistron, may be used to indicate a unit of function. The term is used to designate an area in a chromosome made up of subunits present in an unbroken unit to give their characteristic effect. *See* CHROMOSOME.

Every gene consists of a linear sequence of bases in a nucleic acid molecule. Genes are specified by the sequence of bases in DNA in prokaryotic, archaeal, and eukaryotic cells, and in DNA or ribonucleic acid (RNA) in prokaryotic or eukaryotic viruses. The ultimate expressions of gene function are the formation of structural and regulatory RNA molecules and proteins. These macromolecules carry out the biochemical reactions and provide the structural elements that make up cells. *See* DEOXYRIBONUCLEIC ACID (DNA); NUCLEIC ACID; RIBONUCLEIC ACID (RNA); VIRUS.

One goal of molecular biology is to understand the function, expression, and regulation of a gene in terms of its DNA or RNA sequence. The genetic information in genes that encode proteins is first transcribed from one strand of DNA into a complementary messenger RNA (mRNA) molecule by the action of the RNA polymerase enzyme. Many kinds of eukaryotic and a limited number of prokaryotic mRNA molecules are further processed by splicing, which removes intervening sequences called introns. In some eukaryotic mRNA molecules, certain bases are also changed posttranscriptionally by a process called RNA editing. The genetic code in the resulting mRNA molecules is translated into proteins with specific amino acid sequences by the action of the translation apparatus, consisting of transfer RNA (tRNA) molecules, ribosomes, and many other proteins. The genetic code in an mRNA molecule is the correspondence of three contiguous (triplet) bases, called a codon, to the common amino acids and translation stop signals; the bases are adenine (A), uracil (U), guanine (G), and cytosine (C). There are 61 codons that specify the 20 common amino acids, and 3 codons that lead to translation stopping. *See* GENETIC CODE; INTRON.   [A.H.St.]

In many cases, the genes that mediate a specific cellular or viral function can be isolated. The recombinant DNA methods used to isolate a gene vary widely depending on the experimental system, and genes from RNA genomes must be converted into a corresponding DNA molecule by biochemical manipulation using the enzyme reverse transcriptase. The isolation of the gene is referred to as cloning, and allows large quantities of DNA corresponding to a gene of interest to be isolated and manipulated.

After the gene is isolated, the sequence of the nucleotide bases can be determined. The goal of the large-scale Human Genome Project is to sequence all the genes of several model organisms and humans. The sequence of the region containing the gene can reveal numerous features. If a gene is thought to encode a protein molecule, the genetic code can be applied to the sequence of bases determined from the cloned DNA. The application of the genetic code is done automatically by computer programs, which can identify the sequence of contiguous amino acids of the protein molecule encoded by the gene. If the function of a gene is unknown, comparisons of its nucleic acid or predicted amino acid sequence with the contents of huge international databases can often identify genes or proteins with analogous or related functions. These databases contain all the known sequences from many prokaryotic, archaeal, and eukaryotic organisms. Putative regulatory and transcript-processing sites can also be identified by computer. These putative sites, called consensus sequences, have been shown to play roles in the regulation and expression of groups of prokaryotic, archaeal, or eukaryotic genes. However, computer predictions are just a guide and not a substitute for analyzing expression and regulation by direct experimentation. *See* GENETIC ENGINEERING; HUMAN GENOME PROJECT; MOLECULAR BIOLOGY.   [M.E.Wi.]

Gene action   The functioning of genes (hereditary units) in determining the structural and functional characteristics of an individual, that is, its phenotype. Gene action is studied by two somewhat different, but complementary, approaches: (1) the analysis of changes which occur in the phenotype when a gene mutates, or is changed in dosage, or in position relative to other genes; this is frequently called the study of phenogenetics; and (2) the more direct approach, which attempts to determine the actual means by which genes exert their control over metabolism and the processes of development in multicellular, differentiated organisms. The more direct approach is best described as study of primary gene action, but includes study of the interaction of primary or secondary products of gene action. *See* GENE.

All genes, with the exception of those in ribonucleic acid (RNA) viruses, are constituted of deoxyribonucleic acid (DNA), and the primary action of the great majority of them is to initiate a series of events leading directly or indirectly to the determination of the amino acid sequences of specific polypeptides. *See* DEOXYRIBONUCLEIC ACID (DNA); PROTEIN; VIRUS.

The base sequence of one of the chains of the DNA double helix constituting the gene is transcribed into an RNA molecule with a chain of complementary bases in the presence of RNA polymerases. This RNA molecule may then frequently become a messenger RNA (mRNA) by some alteration of the original transcript, or it may become a transfer RNA (tRNA) or a ribosomal RNA (rRNA). *See* RIBONUCLEIC ACID (RNA).

The primary action of a gene is transcription, but the expression of this action lies in the next step—translation—for many genes. The mRNAs are translated into polypeptides in what may be considered the culmination of the primary process of gene action. The proteins so formed may act as enzymes, structural units, regulators of various metabolic processes by interacting with other proteins and genes, and essential agents in guiding and directing the processes of development.

The actual effects of gene action are recognized for the most part by noting the effects of gene mutation on the phenotype, but in complex multicellular organisms the final phenotypic effect observed superficially may be far removed from the initial action of the gene itself, for example, a change in shape of the ear or a change in eye color. Studies of a wide variety of different genetic strains of organisms ranging over phages and bacteria, plants and animals, including humans, have shown that the mutations of some genes are reflected in the qualitative alteration of the proteins they code for. These kinds of genes are called structural genes. Frequently the protein changes resulting from their mutation are simple substitutions of a single amino acid in the chain by another. The cause for this substitution can be traced back to a change in the genetic code. If a codon in the DNA of a gene coding for a specific polypeptide is altered by a base, for example, AAA → CAA, this mutation will result in the substitution of valine for the phenylalanine originally present at the specific site in the polypeptide chain coded for by this codon. A protein so changed, even though it may involve only one amino acid residue out of more than 100, may have no noticeable effects on the phenotype, or it may have drastic effects. *See* GENETIC CODE.

If there is no noticeable effect of mutation on a protein's action in forming the phenotype, the mutant allele may be called a neutral allele. However, even a single amino acid substitution may cause a protein to be completely inactive and, if the protein is an enzyme, create a genetic metabolic block. Over 100 different inherited blocks are known in humans, including phenylketonuria. The mutant protein may also be active, but its activity is altered so that it is less active than the wild type, or more active, or only active at certain temperatures or pH, or may be inhibited by substances not inhibitory to the wild-type enzyme. The range of possible effects is considerable, and by no means are all recognized and cataloged.

Some genes code for RNA that is not translated. The obvious ones are those that code for tRNA and rRNA, but other RNAs are also transcribed that do not appear to be transcribed and may have a role in the regulation of the activity of other genes. Finally, some genes code for proteins that act as regulators of the processes of metabolism and development. As yet, little is known about this class of genes in the eukaryotes, but they have been studied intensively in bacteria and phages. Mutations of genes coding for regulators may have profound effects on the course of development and, if they do not cause early lethality, they may result in the birth of a malformed individual. *See* BACTERIAL GENETICS; OPERON.

Under certain conditions, an increase in the number of times a particular gene is present has a direct quantitative effect on one or more aspects of the phenotype. This effect is considered to be a manifestation of quantitative gene activity or gene dosage. It means that the gene does something, and that the higher the dose with which it is present, the greater the physiological or chemical end result. The best examples of this are found in the genetics of polyploid plants. In these plants, it is possible to increase the dosage of a particular allele from zero to four or more, when this is done, for example, with certain genes which control the production of the flower pigments of

Dahlia, there is a demonstrable increase in the amount of pigment in the petals. *See* POLYPLOIDY.

An increase in the dose of an active allele of a gene does not always cause an increase in the manifestation of a particular aspect of the phenotype. It may have quite the opposite effect, and cause a decrease. Plants and animals are also subject to aneuploidy, in which not all of the chromosomes of the genome are increased in number proportionately. Instead, only one of the chromosomes of the diploid set may be increased or decreased in number. In humans these conditions usually lead to the early death of the embryo. If the fetus reaches term and is born, it is always abnormal. A relatively common occurrence in humans is trisomy-21, which leads to Down syndrome. *See* DOWN SYNDROME.

Some heterozygous combinations of mutant alleles do not produce the phenotype expected from the phenotypes of the homozygotes. This is defined as a manifestation of allelic interaction. It is in contrast to those situations in which one allele is dominant over the other, so that the phenotype of the heterozygote is very similar or identical to that of the homozygous dominant. Also, it is different from those situations in which the two alleles show an additive effect, and the phenotype of the heterozygote is intermediate between those expected from the homozygotes. Diploid organisms heterozygous for two mutant alleles will produce two polypeptide species, one for each allele. The two proteins may interact and form hybrid multimers, which may be more or less active than the homomultimers formed by the polypeptides of each of the two genes alone. *See* DOMINANCE.

The final phenotype of an organism is the resultant of the action of all the active genes in its cell or cells. These genes may act independently in producing their respective primary products, but the primary products, and the products of their activity, that is, enzymes and other macromolecules, interact at the level of extragenic metabolism to give the final phenotype. Thus, there is really no one gene determining the shape of an organ, or even the production of a certain pigment. These end products are determined by many genes acting together through their respective immediate and then succeeding interrelated products. The manifestation of these interactions, as determined initially by the results from breeding experiments and in a few cases from biochemical analysis, is called gene interaction. This term does not necessarily imply that the genes themselves interact. In general, the term is applied to apparent interactions between genes. Examples include: complementary genes, in which nonallelic genes are so directly involved in the formation of the same end product, or phenotype, that the mutation of any one of them to an inactive state will result in no end product or type effect; epistasis, in which one gene masks the effects of other genes that may be present; and suppressor genes, which cause a wild-type or normal phenotype despite the presence of nonallelic mutant genes.

The environment must be considered in any analysis of gene action, if it is desired to arrive at an understanding of how genes act toward the production of the phenotype. Practically, this is best done by keeping the environment as constant as possible while making studies of gene action. However, much also can be learned by varying the environmental conditions and keeping the genotype as constant as possible. *See* GENETICS.

The environment of genes is a complex one. For convenience, two areas can be defined: (1) that immediately around the genes, the intracellular environment of the rest of the cell; and (2) the extracellular and extraorganismal environment. The intracellular environment can be changed by the mutation of other genes, which may then modify the action of a gene under study. Gene interaction is thus seen to be in part an aspect of the study of the internal environment of the cell. Extracellular environmental factors, such as light and heat, may also influence the action of genes greatly.

Changes in phenotype which occur against a constant genetic background are in reality responses to the environment by the extragenic part of the living system. The genes themselves are not changed, as can be readily demonstrated by changing the environment back to the original condition, or by breeding the individual and showing that the offspring inherit the original parental genotype. See DEVELOPMENTAL GENETICS; GENE.   [R.P.W.]

Gene amplification

Gene amplification   The process by which a cell specifically increases the copy number of a particular gene to a greater extent than it increases the copy number of genes composing the remainder of the genome (all the genes which make up the genetic machinery of an organism). It is therefore distinguished from duplication, which is a precise doubling of the genome preparatory to cell division, and endoreduplication, which leads to endopolyploidy.

Gene amplification results from the repeated replication of the deoxyribonucleic acid (DNA) in a limited portion of the genome, in the absence of or to a much greater extent than replication of DNA composing the remainder of the genome. Thus is formed a cell in which the genes composing a limited portion of the genome are present in relatively high copy number, while the genes composing the remainder of the genome are present in approximately normal copy number. See DEOXYRIBONUCLEIC ACID (DNA).

Since gene amplification increases the copy number of a specific region of the genome without altering the copy number of genes composing the remainder of the genome, it would appear to offer an alternative method for developmental control of gene expression. By increasing the number of copies of a particular gene, the number of gene copies available for transcription could thereby be increased.

In a number of instances of gene amplification, the amplification phenomenon appears to be developmentally regulated, and the amplified copies of the gene are subsequently lost from the cell. Studies on cells in culture have demonstrated "amplification" of genes involved in resistance to specific drugs. See GENE; GENE ACTION.   [M.D.C.]

Genetic code

Genetic code   The rules by which the base sequences of deoxyribonucleic acid (DNA) are translated into the amino acid sequences of proteins. Each sequence of DNA that codes for a protein is transcribed or copied into messenger ribonucleic acid (mRNA). Following the rules of the code, discrete elements in the mRNA, known as codons, specify each of the 20 different amino acids that are the constituents of proteins. During translation, another class of RNAs, called transfer RNAs (tRNAs), are coupled to amino acids, bind to the mRNA, and, in a step-by-step fashion provide the amino acids that are linked together in the order called for by the mRNA sequence. The specific attachment of each amino acid to the appropriate tRNA, and the precise pairing of tRNAs via their anticodons to the correct codons in the mRNA, form the basis of the genetic code. See DEOXYRIBONUCLEIC ACID (DNA); PROTEIN; RIBONUCLEIC ACID (RNA).

The genetic information in DNA is found in the sequence or order of four bases that are linked together to form each strand of the two-stranded DNA molecule. The bases of DNA are adenine, guanine, thymine, and cytosine, which are abbreviated as A, G, T, and C. Chemically, A and G are purines, and C and T are pyrimidines. The two strands of DNA are wound about each other in a double helix that looks like a twisted ladder. Each rung of the ladder is formed by two bases, one from each strand, that pair with each other by means of hydrogen bonds. For a good fit, a pyrimidine must pair with a purine; in DNA, A bonds with T, and G bonds with C. See PURINE; PYRIMIDINE.

	U	C	A	G	
U	UUU ⌐ Phe UUC ⌐ UUA ⌐ Leu UUG ⌐	UCU ⌐ UCC UCA Ser UCG ⌐	UAU ⌐ Tyr UAC ⌐ UAA ⌐ Stop UAG ⌐	UGU ⌐ Cys UGC ⌐ UGA – Stop UGG – Trp	
C	CUU ⌐ CUC CUA Leu CUG ⌐	CCU ⌐ CCC CCA Pro CCG ⌐	CAU ⌐ His CAC ⌐ CAA ⌐ Gln CAG ⌐	CGU ⌐ CGC CGA Arg CGG ⌐	
A	AUU ⌐ AUC Ile AUA ⌐ AUG – Met	ACU ⌐ ACC ACA Thr ACG ⌐	AAU ⌐ Asn AAC ⌐ AAA ⌐ Lys AAG ⌐	AGU ⌐ Ser AGC ⌐ AGA ⌐ Arg AGG ⌐	
G	GUU ⌐ GUC GUA Val GUG ⌐	GCU ⌐ GCC GCA Ala GCG ⌐	GAU ⌐ Asp GAC ⌐ GAA ⌐ Glu GAG ⌐	GGU ⌐ GGC GGA Gly GGG ⌐	

Universal (standard) genetic code. Each of the 64 codons found in mRNA specifies an amino acid (indicated by the common three-letter abbreviation) or the end of the protein chain (*stop*). The amino acids are phenylalanine (Phe), leucine (Leu), isoleucine (Ile), methionine (Met), valine (Val), serine (Ser), proline (Pro), threonine (Thr), alanine (Ala), tyrosine (Tyr), histidine (His), glutamine (Gln), asparagine (Asn), lysine (Lys), aspartic acid (Asp), glutamic acid (Glu), cysteine (Cys), tryptophan (Trp), arginine (Arg), and glycine (Gly).

Ribonucleic acids such as mRNA or tRNA also comprise four bases, except that in RNA the pyrimidine uracil (U) replaces thymine. During transcription a single-stranded mRNA copy of one strand of the DNA is made.

If two bases at a time are grouped together, then only 4 × 4 or 16 different combinations are possible, a number that is insufficient to code for all 20 amino acids that are found in proteins. However, if the four bases are grouped together in threes, then there are 4 × 4 × 4 or 64 different combinations. Read sequentially without overlapping, those groups of three bases constitute a codon, the unit that codes for a single amino acid.

The 64 codons can be divided into 16 families of four (see illustration), in which each codon begins with the same two bases. With the number of codons exceeding the number of amino acids, several codons can code for the same amino acid. Thus, the code is degenerate. In eight instances, all four codons in a family specify the same amino acid. In the remaining families, the two codons that end with the pyrimidines U and C often specify one amino acid, whereas the two codons that end with the purines A and G specify another. Furthermore, three of the codons, UAA, UAG, and UGA, do not code for any amino acid but instead signal the end of the protein chain.

On the ribosome, the nucleic acid code of an mRNA is converted into an amino acid sequence with the aid of tRNAs. These RNAs are relatively small nucleic acids, varying from 75 to 93 bases in length, that are folded in three dimensions to form an L-shaped molecule to which an amino acid can be attached. At the other end of the tRNA molecule, three bases are free to pair with a codon in the mRNA. These three bases of a tRNA constitute the anticodon. Each amino acid has one or more tRNAs, and because of the degeneracy of the code, many of the tRNAs for a specific amino acid have different anticodon sequences. However, the tRNAs for one amino acid are capable of pairing their anticodons only with the codon or codons in the mRNA that specify that amino acid. The tRNAs act as interpreters of the code, providing the correct amino acid in response to each codon by virtue of precise codon-anticodon pairing. The tRNAs pair with the codons and sequentially insert their amino acids in the exact order specified by the sequence of codons in the mRNA. *See* RIBOSOMES.

The rules of the genetic code are virtually the same for all organisms, but there are some interesting exceptions. In the microorganism *Mycoplasma capricolum*, UGA is not a stop codon; instead it codes for tryptophan. This alteration in the code is also found in the mitochondria of some organisms. In addition to changes in the meanings of codons, a modified system for reading codons that requires fewer tRNAs is found in mitochondria. *See* GENE; GENE ACTION; GENETICS.   [P.Sc.; H.E.We.]

Genetic engineering   The artificial recombination of nucleic acid molecules in the test tube, their insertion into a virus, bacterial plasmid, or other vector system, and the subsequent incorporation of the chimeric molecules into a host organism in which they are capable of continued propagation. The construction of such molecules has also been termed gene manipulation because it usually involves the production of novel genetic combinations by biochemical means. *See* NUCLEIC ACID.

Genetic engineering provides the ability to propagate and grow in bulk a line of genetically identical organisms, all containing the same artificially recombinant molecule. Any genetic segment as well as the gene product encoded by it can therefore potentially be amplified. For these reasons the process has also been termed molecular cloning or gene cloning. *See* GENE.

Basic techniques.   The central techniques of such gene manipulation involve (1) the isolation of a specific deoxyribonucleic acid (DNA) molecule or molecules to be replicated (the passenger DNA); (2) the joining of this DNA with a DNA vector (also known as a vehicle or a replicon) capable of autonomous replication in a living cell after foreign DNA has been inserted into it; and (3) the transfer, via transformation or transfection, of the recombinant molecule into a suitable host.

Isolation of passenger DNA.   Passenger DNA may be isolated in a number of ways; the most common of these involves DNA restriction. Restriction endonucleases make possible the cleavage of high-molecular-weight DNA. Although three different classes of these enzymes have been described, only type II restriction endonucleases have been used extensively in the manipulation of DNA. Type II restriction endonucleases are DNAases that recognize specific short nucleotide sequences (usually 4 to 6 base pairs in length), and then cleave both strands of the DNA duplex, generating discrete DNA fragments of defined length and sequence. A number of restriction enzymes make staggered cuts in the two DNA strands, generating single-stranded termini. *See* RESTRICTION ENZYME.

The various fragments generated when a specific DNA is cut by a restriction enzyme can be easily resolved as bands of distinct molecular weights by agarose gel electrophoresis. Specific sequences of these bands can be identified by a technique known as Southern blotting. In this technique, DNA restriction fragments resolved on a gel are denatured and blotted onto a nitrocellulose filter. The filter is incubated together with a radioactively labeled DNA or RNA probe specific for the gene under study. The labeled probe hybridizes to its complement in the restricted DNA, and the regions of hybridization are detected autoradiographically. Fragments of interest can then be eluted out of these gels and used for cloning. Purification of particular DNA segments prior to cloning reduces the number of recombinants that must later be screened.

Another method that has been used to generate small DNA fragments is mechanical shearing. Intense sonification of high-molecular-weight DNA with ultrasound, or high-speed stirring in a blender, can both be used to produce DNA fragments of a certain size range. Shearing results in random breakage of DNA, producing termini consisting of short, single-stranded regions. Other sources include DNA complementary to poly(A)

RNA, or cDNA, which is synthesized in the test tube, and short oligonucleotides that are synthesized chemically. See OLIGONUCLEOTIDE.

Joining DNA molecules. Once the proper DNA fragments have been obtained, they must be joined. When cleavage with a restriction endonuclease creates cohesive ends, these can be annealed with a similarly cleaved DNA from another source, including a vector molecule. When such molecules associate, the joint has nicks a few base pairs apart in opposite strands. The enzyme DNA ligase can then repair these nicks to form an intact, duplex recombinant molecule, which can be used for transformation and the subsequent selection of cells containing the recombinant molecule. Cohesive ends can also be created by the addition of synthetic DNA linkers to blunt-ended DNA molecules.

Another method for joining DNA molecules involves the addition of homopolymer extensions to different DNA populations followed by an annealing of complementary homopolymer sequences. For example, short nucleotide sequences of pure adenine can be added to the 3′ ends of one population of DNA molecules and short thymine blocks to the 3′ ends of another population. The two types of molecules can then anneal to form mixed dimeric circles that can be used directly for transformation.

The enzyme T4 DNA ligase carries out the intermolecular joining of DNA substrates at completely base-paired ends; such blunt ends can be produced by cleavage with a restriction enzyme or by mechanical shearing followed by enzyme treatment.

Transformation. The desired DNA sequence, once attached to a DNA vector, must be transferred to a suitable host. Transformation is defined as the introduction of foreign DNA into a recipient cell. Transformation of a cell with DNA from a virus is usually referred to as transfection.

Transformation in any organism involves (1) a method that allows the introduction of DNA into the cell and (2) the stable integration of DNA into a chromosome, or maintenance of the DNA as a self-replicating entity. See TRANSFORMATION (BACTERIA).

Escherichia coli is usually the host of choice for cloning experiments, and transformation of *E. coli* is an essential step in these experiments. *Escherichia coli* treated with calcium chloride are able to take up DNA from bacteriophage lambda as well as plasmid DNA. Calcium chloride is thought to effect some structural alterations in the bacterial cell wall. An efficient method for transformation in *Bacillus* species involves polyethylene glycol-induced DNA uptake in bacterial protoplasts and subsequent regeneration of the bacterial cell wall. Actinomycetes can be similarly transformed. Transformation can also be achieved by first entrapping the DNA with liposomes followed by their fusion with the host cell membrane. Similar transformation methods have been developed for lower eukaryotes such as the yeast *Saccharomyces cerevisiae* and the filamentous fungus *Neurospora crassa*. See LIPOSOMES.

Several methods are available for the transfer of DNA into cells of higher eukaryotes. Specific genes or entire viral genomes can be introduced into cultured mammalian cells in the form of a coprecipitate with calcium phosphate. DNA complexed with calcium phosphate is readily taken up and expressed by mammalian cells. DNA complexed with diethylamino-ethyl-dextran (DEAE-dextran) or DNA trapped in liposomes or erythrocyte ghosts may also be used in mammalian transformation. Alternatively, bacterial protoplasts containing plasmids can be fused to intact animal cells with the aid of chemical agents such as polyethylene glycol (PEG). Finally, DNA can be directly introduced into cells by microinjection. The efficiency of transfer by each of these methods is quite variable.

Introduction of DNA sequences by insertion into the transforming (T)-DNA region of the tumor-inducing (Ti) plasmid of *Agrobacterium tumefaciens* is a method of introducing DNA into plant cells and ensuring its integration. Because of the limitations of the host range of *A. tumefaciens*, however, alternative transformation systems are being developed for gene transfer in plants. They include the use of liposomes, as well as induction of DNA uptake in plant protoplasts. Foreign DNA has been introduced into plant cells by a technique called electroporation. This technique involves the use of electric pulses to make plant plasma membranes permeable to plasmid DNA molecules. Plasmid DNA taken up in this way has been shown to be stably inherited and expressed.

Cloning vectors. There is a large variety of potential vectors for cloned genes. The vectors differ in different classes of organisms.

Prokaryotes and lower eukaryotes. Three types of vectors have been used in these organisms: plasmids, bacteriophages, and cosmids. Plasmids are extrachromosomal DNA sequences that are stably inherited. *Escherichia coli* and its plasmids constitute the most versatile type of host-vector system known for DNA cloning. Several natural plasmids, such as ColE1, have been used as cloning vehicles in *E. coli*. In addition, a variety of derivatives of natural plasmids have been constructed by combining DNA segments and desirable qualities of older cloning vehicles. The most versatile and widely used of these plasmids is pBR322. Transformation in yeast has been demonstrated using a number of plasmids, including vectors derived from the naturally occurring 2μ plasmid of yeast.

Bacteriophage lambda is a virus of *E. coli*. Several lambda-derived vectors have been developed for cloning in *E. coli*, and for the isolation of particular genes from eukaryotic genomes. These lambda derivatives have several advantages over plasmids: (1) Thousands of recombinant phage plaques can easily be screened for a particular DNA sequence on a single petri dish by molecular hybridization. (2) Packaging of recombinant DNA in laboratory cultures provides a very efficient means of DNA uptake by the bacteria. (3) Thousands of independently packaged recombinant phages can be easily replicated and stored in a single solution as a "library" of genomic sequences. *See* BACTERIOPHAGE.

Plasmids have also been constructed that contain the phage *cos* DNA site, required for packaging into the phage particles, and ColE1 DNA segments, required for plasmid replication. These plasmids have been termed cosmids. The recombinant cosmid DNA is injected into a host and circularizes like phage DNA but replicates as a plasmid. Transformed cells are selected on the basis of a vector drug resistance marker.

Animal cells. In contrast to the wide variety of plasmid and phage vectors available for cloning in prokaryotic cells, relatively few vectors are available for introducing foreign genes into animal cells. The most commonly used are derived from simian virus 40 (SV40). Normal SV40 cannot be used as a vector, since there is a physical limit to the amount of DNA that can be packaged into the virus capsid, and the addition of foreign DNA would generate a DNA molecule too large to be packaged. However, SV40 mutants lacking portions of the genome can be propagated in mixed infections in which a "helper" virus supplies the missing function. *See* ADENO-SV40 HYBRID VIRUS.

Plant cells. Two systems for the delivery and integration of foreign genes into the plant genome are the Ti plasmid of the soil bacterium *Agrobacterium* and the DNA plant virion cauliflower mosaic virus. The Ti plasmid is a natural gene transfer vector carried by *A. tumefaciens*, a pathogenic bacterium that causes crown gall tumor formation in dicotyledonous plants. A T-DNA segment present in the Ti plasmid becomes stably integrated into the plant cell genome during infection. This property of the Ti plasmid has been exploited to show that DNA segments inserted in the T-DNA region can be cotransferred to plant DNA. *See* CROWN GALL.

Applications. Recombinant DNA technology has permitted the isolation and detailed structural analysis of a large number of prokaryotic and eukaryotic genes. This contribution is especially significant in the eukaryotes because of their large genomes. The methods outlined above provide a means of fractionating and isolating individual genes, since each clone contains a single sequence or a few DNA sequences from a very large genome. Isolation of a particular sequence of interest has been facilitated by the ability to generate a large number of clones and to screen them with the appropriate "probe" (radioactively labeled RNA or DNA) molecules.

Genetic engineering techniques provide pure DNAs in amounts sufficient for mapping, sequencing, and direct structural analyses. Furthermore, gene structure-function relationships can be studied by reintroducing the cloned gene into a eukaryotic nucleus and assaying for transcriptional and translational activities. The DNA sequences can be altered by mutagenesis before their reintroduction in order to define precise functional regions.

Genetic engineering methodology has provided means for the large-scale production of polypeptides and proteins. It is now possible to produce a wide variety of foreign proteins in E. coli. These range from enzymes useful in molecular biology to a vast range of polypeptides with potential human therapeutic applications, such as insulin, interferon, growth hormone, immunoglobins, and enzymes involved in the dynamics of blood coagulation. See BIOTECHNOLOGY.

Finally, experiments showing the successful transfer and expression of foreign DNA in plant cells using the Ti plasmid, as well as the demonstration that whole plants can be regenerated from cells containing mutated regions of T-DNA, indicate that the Ti plasmid system may be an important tool in the genetic engineering of plants. Such a system will help in the identification and characterization of plant genes as well as provide basic knowledge about gene organization and regulation in higher plants. Once genes useful for crop improvement have been identified, cloned, and stably inserted into the plant genome, it will be possible to engineer plants to be resistant to environmental stress, to pests, and to pathogens. See BREEDING (PLANT); GENE; GENE ACTION; SOMATIC CELL GENETICS.   [P.K.M.]

Genetics   The science of biological inheritance, that is, the causes of the resemblances and differences among related individuals.

Genetics occupies a central position in biology, for essentially the same principles apply to all animals and plants, and understanding of inheritance is basic for the study of evolution and for the improvement of cultivated plants and domestic animals. It has also been found that genetics has much to contribute to the study of embryology, biochemistry, pathology, anthropology, and other subjects. See BIOCHEMISTRY; EMBRYOLOGY.

Genetics may also be defined as the science that deals with the nature and behavior of the genes, the fundamental hereditary units. From this point of view, evolution is seen as the study of changes in the gene composition of populations, whereas embryology is the study of the effects of the genes on the development of the organism. See GENE ACTION; POPULATION GENETICS.   [A.H.St.]

The field of molecular genetics describes the basis of inheritance at the molecular level. It focuses on two general questions: how do genes specify the structure and function of organisms, and how are genes replicated and transmitted to successive generations? Both questions have been answered. Genes specify organismal structure and function according to a process described by the central dogma of molecular biology: DNA is made into messenger ribonucleic acid (mRNA), which specifies the structure of a protein; the mRNA molecule then serves as a template for protein synthesis, which is carried out by complex machinery that comprises a particle called a ribosome and special adapter RNA molecules called transfer RNA. *See* DEOXYRIBONUCLEIC ACID (DNA); RIBONUCLEIC ACID (RNA); RIBOSOMES.

The structure of DNA provides a simple mechanism for genes to be faithfully reproduced: the specific interaction between the nucleotides means that each strand of the double helix carries the information for producing the other strand. *See* GENETIC CODE; GENETIC ENGINEERING; MOLECULAR BIOLOGY; MUTATION. [M.J.]

Germ layers The primitive cell layers, or first tissues, which appear early in the development of animals and from which the embryo body and its auxiliary membranes, when present, are constructed. These are more or less distinct anatomically, but do not necessarily have sharp boundaries of demarcation. Germ layers are almost universal among animal embryos and appear to establish discontinuities of architectural importance without complete loss of continuity. Three kinds of germ layers are recognizable: (1) the ectoderm or outer skin, (2) the endoderm or inner skin, and (3) the mesoderm or middle skin. The layers have been named in accordance with their positions in the spherical type of gastrula such as that of the sea urchin or amphibian. The terms epiblast, mesoblast, and hypoblast are sometimes used as synonyms for ectoderm, mesoderm, and endoderm, respectively. The three primary germ layers are present as a basic structural plan in all Metazoa with the exception of the coelenterates and the Porifera, in which a distinct mesodermal layer is absent. *See* GASTRULATION. [N.T.S.]

Gestation period In mammals, the interval between fertilization and birth. It covers the total period of development of the offspring, which consists of a preimplantation phase (from fertilization to implantation in the mother's womb), an embryonic phase (from implantation to the formation of recognizable organs), and a fetal phase (from organ formation to birth).

There is widespread confusion over the duration of the gestation period in humans because of the way in which it is defined medically. The time of ovulation, and hence the time of fertilization, is difficult to determine in humans, so for purely practical reasons doctors measure the duration of pregnancy as the interval between the last menstrual period and birth, which is typically about 40 weeks or 280 days. For comparison with other mammals, however, the true gestation period between fertilization and birth in humans is about 267 days.

The length of the gestation period in mammals depends primarily on body size and the state of development of the offspring at birth. Large-bodied mothers have big offspring that take longer to develop, and development is also prolonged for offspring that are born at an advanced stage of development. Compared to all other mammals, human beings are found to have one of the longest gestation periods relative to body size.

One remarkable feature of mammalian gestation periods is that they show very little variability within a species. After excluding exceptional cases, departures from the average usually lie in a range of no more than ±4%. This is one of the smallest degrees of variability found in any biological dimension. *See* REPRODUCTIVE SYSTEM. [R.D.Ma.]

Gland A structure which produces a substance or substances essential and vital to the existence of the organism and species. Glands are classified according to (1) the nature of the product; (2) the structure; (3) the manner by which the secretion is delivered to the area of use; and (4) the manner of cell activity in forming secretion. A commonly used scheme for the classification of glands follows.

I. Morphological criteria
    A. Unicellular (mucous goblet cells)
    B. Multicellular
        1. Sheets of gland cells (choroid plexus)
        2. Restricted nests of gland cells (urethral glands)
        3. Invaginations of varying degrees of complexity
            a. Simple or branched tubular (intestinal and gas-tric glands)—no duct inter-posed between surface and glandular portion
            b. Simple coiled (sweat gland)—duct interposed between glandular portion and surface
            c. Simple, branched, acinous (sebaceous gland)—glandular portion spheri-cal or ovoid, connected to surface by duct
            d. Compound, tubular glands (gastric cardia, renal tubules)—branched ducts between surface and glandular portion
            e. Compound tubular-acinous glands (pancreas, parotid gland)—branched ducts, terminating in secretory portion which may be tubular or acinar

II. Mode of secretion
    A. Exocrine—the secretion is passed directly or by ducts to the exterior surface (sweat glands) or to another surface which is continuous with the external surface (intestinal glands, liver, pancreas, submaxillary gland)
    B. Endocrine—the secretion is passed into adjacent tissue or area and then into the bloodstream directly or by way of the lymphatics; these organs are usually circumscribed, highly vascularized, and usually have no connection to an ex-ternal surface (adrenal, thyroid, parathyroid, islets of Langerhans, parts of the ovary and testis, anterior lobe of the hypophysis, intermediate lobe of the hy-pophysis, groups of nerve cells of the hypothalamus, and the neural portion of the hypophysis)
    C. Mixed exocrine and endocrine glands (liver, testis, pancreas)
    D. Cytocrine—passage of a secretion from one cell directly to another (melanin granules from melanocytes in the connective tissue of the skin to epithelial cells of the skin)

III. Nature of secretion
    A. Cytogenous (testis, perhaps spleen, lymph node, and bone marrow)—gland "secretes" cells
    B. Acellular (intestinal glands, pancreas, parotid gland)—gland secretes noncellular product

IV. Cytological changes of glandular portion during secretion
    A. Merocrine (sweat glands, choroid plexus)—no loss of cytoplasm
    B. Holocrine (sebaceous glands)—gland cells undergo dissolution and are entirely extruded, together with the secretory product
    C. Apocrine (mammary gland, axillary sweat gland)—only part of the cytoplasm is extruded with the secretory product

V. Chemical nature of the product
    A. Mucous goblet cells (submaxillary glands, urethral glands)—the secretion con-tains mucin
    B. Serous (parotid gland, pancreas)—the secretion does not contain mucin

[O.E.N.]

Global climate change   The periodic fluctuations in global temperatures and precipitation, such as the glacial (cold) and interglacial (warm) cycles of the Pleistocene (a geological period from 1.8 million to 10,000 years ago). Presently, the increase in global temperatures since 1900 is of great interest. Many atmospheric scientists and meteorologists believe it is linked to human-produced carbon dioxide (CO_2) in the atmosphere.

Greenhouse effect. The greenhouse effect is a process by which certain gases (water vapor, carbon dioxide, methane, nitrous oxide) trap heat within the Earth's atmosphere and thereby produce warmer air temperatures. These gases act like the glass of a greenhouse: they allow short (ultraviolet; UV) energy waves from the Sun to penetrate into the atmosphere, but prevent the escape of long (infrared) energy waves that are emitted from the Earth's surface.

Human-induced changes in global climate caused by release of greenhouse gases into the atmosphere, largely from the burning of fossil fuels, have been correlated with global warming. Since 1900, the amount of two main greenhouse gases (carbon dioxide and methane) in the Earth's atmosphere has increased by 25%. Over the same period, mean global temperatures have increased by about 0.5°C (0.9°F). The most concern centers on carbon dioxide. Not only is carbon dioxide produced in much greater quantities than any other pollutant, but it remains stable in the atmosphere for over 100 years. Methane, produced in the low-oxygen conditions of rice fields and as a by-product of coal mining and natural gas use, is 100 times stronger than carbon dioxide in its greenhouse effects but is broken down within 10 years.

Chloroflurocarbon (CFC) pollution, from aerosol propellants and coolant systems, affects the Earth's climate because CFCs act as greenhouse gases and they break down the protective ozone (O_3) layer. Other pollutants released into the atmosphere are also likely to influence global climate. Sulfur dioxide (SO_2) from car exhaust and industrial processes, such as electrical generation from coal, cool the Earth's surface air temperatures and counteract the effect of greenhouse gases. Nevertheless, there have been attempts in industrialized nations to reduce sulfur dioxide pollution because it also causes acid rain.

Possible impact. A rise in mean global temperatures is expected to cause changes in global air and ocean circulation patterns, which in turn will alter climates in different regions. Changes in temperature and precipitation have already been detected. In the United States, total precipitation has increased, but it is being delivered in fewer, more extreme events, making floods (and possibly droughts) more likely.

Global warming has caused changes in the distribution of a species throughout the world. By analyzing preserved remains of plants, insects, mammals, and other organisms which were deposited during the most recent glacial and interglacial cycles, scientists have been able to track where different species lived at times when global temperatures were either much warmer or much cooler than today's climate. Several studies have documented poleward and upward shifts of many plant and insect species during the current warming trend.

Changes in the timing of growth and breeding events in the life of an individual organism, called phenological shifts, have resulted from global warming. For example, almost one-third of British birds are nesting earlier (by 9 days) than they did 25 years ago, and five out of six species of British frog are laying eggs 2–3 weeks earlier.

Community reassembly, changes in the species composition of communities, has resulted from climate change because not all species have the same response to environmental change.

To date, there have been no extinctions of species directly attributable to climate change. However, there is mounting evidence for drastic regional declines. For example, the abundance of zooplankton (microscopic animals and immature stages of many species) has declined by 80% off the California coast. This decline has been related to gradual warming of sea surface temperatures. [C.Pa.]

Globulin A general name for any member of a heterogeneous group of serum proteins precipitated by 50% saturated ammonium sulfate. *See* PROTEIN; SERUM.

The introduction of electrophoresis during the 1930s permitted subdivision of the globulins into alpha, beta, and gamma globulins on the basis of relative mobility at alkaline pH (8.6). However, each of these subgroups, though electrophoretically homogeneous, consists of a great variety of proteins with different biological properties and markedly different sizes and chemical properties other than net charge. Thus the α_2-globulins, for example, as defined by moving boundary or paper electrophoresis, contain proteins ranging in molecular weight from approximately 50,000 to approximately 1,000,000 (α_2-macroglobulin), each with differing functions. *See* IMMUNOGLOBULIN. [H.H.F.]

Glucagon The protein hormone secreted by the pancreas which is known to influence a wide variety of metabolic reactions. Glucagon, along with insulin and other hormones, plays a role in the complex and dynamic process of maintaining adequate supplies of sugar in the blood. Glucagon has often been called the hyperglycemic-glycogenolytic factor because it causes the breakdown of liver glycogen to sugar (a process known as glycogenolysis) and thereby increases the concentration of sugar in the bloodstream (a condition known as hyperglycemia). Glucagon may also be involved in the regulation of protein and fat metabolism, gastric acid secretion and gut motility, excretion of electrolytes (such as sodium, potassium and chloride) by the kidney, contractility of heart muscle, and release of insulin from the pancreas. Glucagon is used in human medicine chiefly in certain diabetic conditions when a dangerously low blood sugar must be rapidly raised. *See* CARBOHYDRATE METABOLISM; GLYCOGEN; HORMONE; INSULIN; PANCREAS. [W.W.Bro.]

Glucose A monosaccharide also known as D-glucose, D-glucopyranose, grape sugar, corn sugar, dextrose, and cerelose. The structure of glucose is shown in the illustration.

Structural formula for α-D-glucose.

Glucose in free or combined form is not only the most common of the sugars but is probably the most abundant organic compound in nature. It occurs in free state in practically all higher plants. It is found in considerable concentrations in grapes, figs, and other sweet fruits and in honey. In lesser concentrations, it occurs in the animal body fluids, for example, in blood and lymph. Urine of diabetic patents usually contains 3–5%.

Cellulose, starch, and glycogen are composed entirely of glucose units. Glucose is also a major constituent of many oligosaccharides, notably sucrose, and of many glycosides. It is produced commercially from cornstarch by hydrolysis with dilute mineral acid. The commercial glucose so obtained is used largely in the manufacture of confections and in the wine and canning industries. *See* GLYCOGEN.

D-Glucose is the principal carbohydrate metabolite in animal nutrition; it is utilized by the tissues, and it is absorbed from the alimentary tract in greater amounts than any other monosaccharide. Glucose could serve satisfactorily in meeting at least 50% of the entire energy needs of humans and various animals.

Glucose enters the bloodstream by absorption from the small intestine. It is carried via the portal vein to the liver, where part is stored as glycogen, the remainder reentering the circulatory system. Another site of glycogen storage is muscle tissue.

Glucose is readily fermented by yeast, producing ethyl alcohol and carbon dioxide. It is also metabolized by many bacteria, resulting in the formation of various degradation products, such as hydrogen, acetic and butyric acids, butyl alcohol, acetone, and many others. *See* CARBOHYDRATE; MONOSACCHARIDE.

Glycogen   The primary reserve polysaccharide of the animal kingdom. It is found in the muscles and livers of all higher animals, as well as in the cells of lower animals. Because of its close relationship to starch, it is often called animal starch, although glycogen is found in some lower plants, fungi, yeast, and bacteria. *See* STARCH.

Glycogen is a nonreducing, white, amorphous polysaccharide which dissolves readily in cold water, forming an opalescent, colloidal solution. The molecular weight of glycogen is usually very high, and it varies with the source and the method of preparation; molecular weights of the order of $1-20 \times 10^6$ have been reported. Chemical studies show glycogen to possess a branched structure similar to the amylopectin starch fraction.

In its biochemical reactions, glycogen is similar to starch. It is attacked by the same plant amylases that attack starch, and like starch, it is degraded to maltose and dextrins. Both glycogen and starch are broken down by animal or plant phosphorylase enzyme in the presence of inorganic phosphate with the production of α-D-glucose-1-phosphate. *See* CARBOHYDRATE METABOLISM.

The metabolic formation of glycogen from glucose in the liver is frequently termed glycogenesis. In fasted animals, glycogen formation can be induced by the feeding, not only of materials that can be hydrolyzed to glucose and other monosaccharides, such as fructose, but also of various other materials. A number of L-amino acids, such as alanine, serine, and glutamic acid, upon deamination in the liver give rise to substances, such as pyruvic acid and α-ketoglutaric acid, that can be converted in the liver to glucose units which are subsequently converted to glycogen. Furthermore, substances such as glycerol derived from fats, dihydroxyacetone, or lactic acid can all be utilized for glycogen synthesis in the liver. Such noncarbohydrate precursors are termed glycogenic compounds. The process of glycogen formation from these precursors is known as glyconeogenesis. The term glycogenolysis is used to connote glycogen breakdown. *See* POLYSACCHARIDE.   [W.Z.H.]

Glycolipid   One of a class of compounds having solubility properties of a lipid and containing one or more molecules of a covalently attached sugar.

Glycosphingolipids, the most abundant and structurally diverse type of glycolipids in animals, are glycosides of ceramide, a fatty acid amide of the amino alcohol sphingosine. Galactosyl ceramide is enriched in brain tissue and is a major component of the myelin sheaths around nerves. Glucosyl ceramide is present in the cell membranes of many cell types and is abundant in serum.

Larger, neutral glycosphingolipids containing more than one sugar include lactosyl ceramide, abundant in leukocyte membranes; globosides; and other oligosaccharyl ceramides, some of which are important antigens defining blood groups. Gangliosides are oligosaccharyl ceramides, abundant in brain, spleen, erythrocytes, liver, and kidney, that contain glucose, galactose, N-acetylglucosamine, and sialic acids.

Glycosphingolipids carry blood group antigens and define tumor-specific or developmental antigens. In addition, they serve as receptors for many microorganisms and toxins, as modulators of cell surface receptors that mediate cell growth, and as mediators of cell adhesion. *See* ANTIGEN; CELLULAR ADHESION.

Glycosyl phosphatidylinositols are a class of glycolipids that serve as membrane anchors for a multitude of proteins in organisms ranging from yeast to protozoa to humans. Glycosyl phosphatidylinositol–core structures can have many different modifications, depending upon the protein and cell type. Lipophosphoglycans are glycosyl phosphatidylinositols attached to large polysaccharide structures that coat the surfaces of many parasitic protozoa, such as *Leishmania donovani*, the causative agent of visceral leishmaniasis (kala azar). Lipophosphoglycans appear to protect these organisms from host defenses.

Mannosylphosphoryl dolichol, glucosylphophoryl dolichol, and oligosaccharyl phosphoryl dolichols are glycolipids with sugars attached to large polyisoprenoids by phosphate esters. Dolichols are structurally related to cholesterol. Saccharylphosphoryl dolichols serve as important biosynthetic intermediates in the assembly of both asparagine-linked glycoproteins and glycosyl phosphatidylinositols. *See* GLYCOPROTEIN.

Glycosyl glycerides are glycolipids that have a structure analogous to phospholipids. They are the major glycolipids of plants and microorganisms but are rare in animals.

Bacteria produce a wide variety of glycolipids not easily categorized. Examples include fatty acid esters of carbohydrates, such as cord factor. Cord factor is a toxic component of the waxy capsular material of virulent strains of *Mycobacterium tuberculosis*, the causative agent of tuberculosis. Mycosides, glycolipids that are also found in tubercle bacilli, comprise long-chain, highly branched, hydroxylated hydrocarbon terminated by a phenol group, with the sugar glycosidically attached to the phenolic hydroxyl. *See* LIPID; SPHINGOLIPID; TUBERCULOSIS.   [G.W.Ha.]

Glycoprotein   A compound in which carbohydrate (sugar) is covalently linked to protein. The carbohydrate may be in the form of monosaccharides, disaccharides, oligosaccharides, or polysaccharides, and is sometimes referred to as glycan. The sugar may be linked to sulfate or phosphate groups. In different glycoproteins, 100–200 glycan units may be present. Therefore, the carbohydrate content of these compounds varies markedly, from 1% (as in the collagens), to 60% (in certain mucins), to >99% (in glycogen). *See* COLLAGEN; GLYCOGEN.

Glycoproteins are ubiquitous in nature, although they are relatively rare in bacteria. They occur in cells, in both soluble and membrane-bound forms, as well as in the intercellular matrix and in extracellular fluids, and include numerous biologically active macromolecules. A number of glycoproteins are produced industrially by genetic engineering techniques for use as drugs; among them are erythropoietin, interferons, colony stimulating factors, and blood-clotting factors. *See* GENETIC ENGINEERING.

In most glycoproteins, the carbohydrate is linked to the polypeptide backbone by either N- or O-glycosidic bonds. A different kind of bond is found in glycoproteins that are anchored in cell membranes by a special carbohydrate-containing compound, glycosylphosphatidylinositol, which is attached to the C-terminal amino acid of the protein. A single glycoprotein may contain more than one type of carbohydrate-peptide linkage. N-linked units are typically found in plasma glycoproteins, in ovalbumin, in many enzymes (for example, the ribonucleases), and in immunoglobulins. O-linked units are found in mucins; collagens; and proteoglycans (typical constituents of connective tissues), including chondroitin sulfates, dermatan sulfate, and heparin. *See* AL-BUMIN; CARBOHYDRATE; ENZYME; IMMUNOGLOBULIN; MONOSACCHARIDE; OLIGOSACCHARIDE; POLYSACCHARIDE; PROTEIN.

Within any organism, all molecules of a particular protein are identical. In contrast, a variety of structurally distinct carbohydrate units are found not only at different attachment sites of a glycoprotein but even at each single attachment site—a phenomenon known as microheterogeneity. For instance, ovalbumin contains one glycosylated amino acid, but over a dozen different oligosaccharides have been identified at that site, even in a preparation isolated from a single egg of a purebred hen.   [N.Sh.]

Glycoside   A large important class of sugar derivatives in which the sugar is combined with a nonsugar. In their cyclic forms, monosaccharides (simple sugars) possess one carbon (C) atom (the anomeric carbon) that is bonded to two oxygen (O) atoms; one oxygen atom forms a part of the ring, whereas the other is outside the ring (exocyclic) and is part of a hydroxyl (OH) group. If the oxygen atom of the anomeric hydroxyl group becomes bonded to a carbon atom, other than that of a carbonyl (C$=$O) group, the resulting compound is a glycoside. A glycoside thus consists of two parts (see illustration): the sugar (glycosyl) unit, which provides the anomeric carbon, and the moiety (the aglycon), which is the source of the exocyclic oxygen and carbon atoms of the glycosidic linkage. Such compounds frequently are referred to as O-glycosides to distinguish them from analogs having a sulfur (thio- or S-glycosides), nitrogen (amino- or N-glycosides), or carbon (anomalously called C-glycosides) as the exocyclic atom on the anomeric carbon. *See* MONOSACCHARIDE.

The formation of glycosides is the principal manner in which monosaccharides are incorporated into more complex molecules. For example, lactose (illus. *b*), the most abundant disaccharide in mammalian milk, has a glycosidic bond involving the anomeric

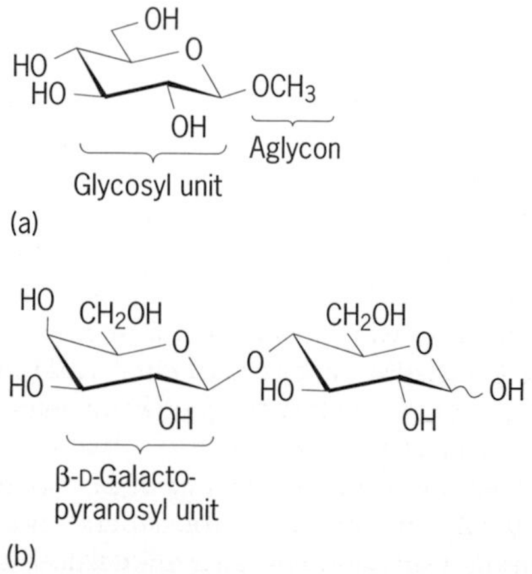

(a)

(b)

Glycosyl unit

Aglycon

β-D-Galacto-pyranosyl unit

Structural formulas of two glycosides. (*a*) Methyl β-D-glucopyranoside. (*b*) Lactose, 4-*O*-β-D-galactopyranosyl-D-glucopyranose; the wavy bond indicates that the group may have various orientations in space.

carbon of D-galactose and the C-4 hydroxyl of D-glucose. The anomeric carbon atom can exist in either of two stereoisomeric configurations, a fact which is of immense importance to the chemistry and biochemistry of glycosides. For example, the principal structural difference between cellulose and amylose is that cellulose is β-glycosidically linked whereas amylose is α-linked. Humans are able to digest amylose but are unable to utilize cellulose for food. *See* CELLULOSE; LACTOSE.

A very large number of glycosides exist in nature, many of which possess important biological functions. In many of these biologically important compounds the carbohydrate portion is essential for cell recognition, the terminal sugar units being able to interact with specific receptor sites on the cell surface.

One class of naturally occurring glycosides is called the cardiac glycosides because they exhibit the ability to strengthen the contraction of heart muscles. These cardiotonic agents are found in both plants and animals and contain complex aglycons, which are responsible for most of the drug action; however, the glycoside may modify the biological activity. The best-known cardiac glycosides come from digitalis and include the drug digoxin.

Glycosidic units frequently are found in antibiotics. For example, the important drug erythromycin A possesses two glycosidically linked sugar units. *See* ANTIBIOTIC.

Perhaps the most ubiquitous group of glycosides in nature is the glycoproteins; in many of them carbohydrates are linked to a protein by *O*-glycosidic bonds. These glycoproteins include many enzymes, hormones, such antiviral compounds as interleukin-2, and the so-called antifreeze glycoproteins found in the sera of fish from very cold marine environments. *See* AMINO ACIDS; CARBOHYDRATE; ENZYME; GLYCOPROTEIN; HORMONE.

Glycolipids are a very large class of natural glycosides having a lipid aglycon. These complex glycosides are present in the cell membranes of microbes, plants, and animals. *See* GLYCOLIPID; LIPID.   [G.W.Hay.]

Gnathostomulida

Gnathostomulida Microscopic marine worms of uncertain systematic relationship, mainly characterized by cuticular structures in the pharynx and a monociliated skin epithelium. It is the most recently described phylum of the animal kingdom. The total number of species probably exceeds 1000.

Gnathostomulids are worm-shaped, cylindrical or slightly depressed, and semitransparent (or bright red), and sometimes have the external division of head and tail. The skin is a one-layered epithelium that is completely monociliated; that is, each of the polygonal epidermal cells bears only one cilium. The sensory system usually consists of 1–2 pairs of simple and 3–4 pairs of compound bristles (frontally and laterally), and a bundle of stiff cilia (dorsally on the head). The reproductive system consists of a dorsal ovarium and in most cases two caudolateral groups of testes follicles in the same specimen. Fertilization is internal.

The distribution of gnathostomulids is worldwide, the majority of localities being known from European coasts, some from the North American east coast, and some scattered over the western Pacific.   [R.J.R.; W.E.S.]

Gnotobiotics

Gnotobiotics The science involved with maintaining a microbiologically controlled environment, and with the knowledge necessary to obtain and use biological specimens in this environment. The roots of the word are *gnotos*, meaning well known, and *biota*, the combined flora and fauna of a region.

All exposed surfaces of an animal are teeming with microbes. For example, the contents of the large intestine may contain 3 trillion microbes per ounce (100 billion per gram), belonging to several hundred species. Even if the animal itself is the primary interest of a researcher, there is no direct way to determine how many of an animal's normal characteristics are truly its own, and how many involve interaction with or reaction against resident microbiota. The only way to determine this is comparison with animals that have no microbiota. If differences are found, then the role of individual microbial species can be studied by inoculating pure cultures of these species into the animals without a microbiota.

Thus, gnotobiotics evolved initially to answer questions about what difference the resident microbiota makes, and which members of the microbiota make the difference. Answers become more and more essential in going beyond the effects of pathogenic microbes to the harmful or helpful long-term effects of environmental chemicals, compounds produced in the host's own metabolism, and therapeutic drugs being tested for efficacy, toxicity, or carcinogenicity. The activity of the microbiota is proportionately much greater in laboratory animals than it is in humans, and could have a decisive effect on such chemicals, especially since the chemicals are often received in small doses. For example, intestinal microbes turn a minor component of the cycad bean, a South Pacific foodstuff, into a carcinogen. One of the best drugs against parasitic schistosomes in humans is turned into a carcinogen by a single species of intestinal streptococcus. Gnotobiotic studies are designed to detect such possibilities.

Gnotobiote is the term applied to an animal (or plant) with a defined microbiota. The most simple of gnotobiotes is the animal with no microbiota. Invertebrate animals of this type are most frequently called axenic. Vertebrate animals may also be called axenic, but are more frequently called germfree. Gnotobiology is a term sometimes used to designate studies involving gnotobiotes, although it tends to suggest that there is a unified body of knowledge which results from studying gnotobiotes. In fact, the gnotobiote is a more precisely defined laboratory animal which helps elucidate biological phenomena in immunology, nutrition, physiology, oncology, gastroenterology, microbial ecology, gerontology, pathogenic microbiology, parasitology, and so on.

[J.R.P.]

Golgi apparatus   An organelle, named after the Italian histologist Camillo Golgi, found in all eukaryotic cells but absent from prokaryotes such as bacteria. It consists of flattened membrane-bounded compartments known as cisternae. In most cells, the Golgi cisternae are organized into stacks. Different cell types contain from one to several thousand Golgi stacks. The Golgi apparatus sorts newly synthesized proteins for delivery to various destinations, and modifies the oligosaccharide chains found on glycoproteins and glycolipids. *See* CELL ORGANIZATION.

The Golgi apparatus acts at an intermediate stage in the secretory pathway. A subset of the proteins synthesized by the cell are inserted into the endoplasmic reticulum. Most such proteins are then delivered to the Golgi apparatus by means of coat protein II (COPII) transport vesicles, which form at endoplasmic reticulum exit sites. Newly synthesized proteins traverse the Golgi stack until they reach the trans-most Golgi compartment, which is termed the trans-Golgi network to connote its extensive tubulation. The trans-Golgi network sorts the proteins into several types of vesicles. Clathrin-coated vesicles carry certain proteins to lysosomes. Other proteins are packaged into secretory vesicles for immediate delivery to the cell surface. Still other proteins are packaged into secretory granules, which undergo regulated secretion in response to specific signals. This sorting function of the Golgi apparatus allows the various organelles to grow while maintaining their distinct identities. *See* CELL MEMBRANES; ENDOPLASMIC RETICULUM; LYSOSOME.

The best understood of the processing reactions carried out by the Golgi apparatus is the remodeling of oligosaccharides (chains of six-carbon sugars) that are attached to glycoproteins. During insertion of a newly synthesized protein into the endoplasmic reticulum, one or more copies of a 14-sugar oligosaccharide may be attached to the amino acid asparagine at specific locations in the polypeptide chain. As the protein passes through the Golgi stack, the asparagine-linked oligosaccharides are modified to generate a diverse range of structures. Additional oligosaccharides may become linked to the amino acids serine and threonine. Although the particular oligosaccharide modifications are quite different in animal, plant, and fungal cells, the Golgi apparatus always functions as a "carbohydrate factory." *See* OLIGOSACCHARIDE.

The Golgi apparatus also carries out other processing events, including the addition of sulfate groups to the amino acid tyrosine in some proteins, the cleavage of protein precursors to yield mature hormones and neurotransmitters, and the synthesis of certain membrane lipids such as sphingomyelin and glycosphingolipids. *See* LIPID; PROTEIN.

[B.S.Gl.]

Gonorrhea   A common sexually transmitted disease caused by the bacterium *Neisseria gonorrhoeae*. Humans are the only natural hosts for *N. gonorrhoeae*, which directly infects the epithelium of the mucous membranes of the human genital tract, pharynx, rectum, or conjunctiva. Local epithelial cell destruction usually occurs, but the organisms may spread to adjacent organs or disseminate via the bloodstream. In women, local complications include inflammation of the uterine lining (endometritis), inflammation of the fallopian tube (salpingitis), inflammation of the abdominal wall (peritonitis), and inflammation of Bartholin's glands (bartholinitis); in men, periurethral abscess and inflammation of a duct connected to the testes (epididymitis). Systemic manifestations such as arthritis or dermatitis may develop, and rarely endocarditis or meningitis.

Women are disproportionately affected by the complications of gonorrhea. Acute pelvic inflammatory disease and salpingitis, the most serious complications of gonorrhea, result in ectopic pregnancy and infertility. Gonococcal infection during pregnancy may also predispose women to premature rupture of membranes, delivery in less than full term, and postpartum endometritis. During childbirth, the gonococcus may infect the conjunctiva of the infant and result in the infection ophthalmia neonatorum. This infection is a serious complication that remains common in less developed countries and can lead to permanent damage to the eye and blindness.

Gonorrhea continues to be the most commonly reported communicable disease in the United States, although incidence has declined since 1984. Risk factors that may influence the probability of infection include number of sexual partners, lack of barrier contraceptives, and young age.

Gonorrhea is an infection spread by physical contact with the mucosal surfaces of an infected person, usually a sexual partner. The risk of infection depends on the anatomic site, the amount of substance containing bacteria, and the number of exposures. Variations in host susceptibility have not been well defined. In a small but significant proportion of infections, there are no symptoms. These individuals are important in the epidemiology of this disease because gonorrhea is usually spread by carriers who have no symptoms or have ignored symptoms.

Control of gonorrhea depends on early diagnosis, effective treatment, and identification of asymptomatic individuals. The last has been accomplished, in part, through screening programs. However, complete control has not been possible because of the emergence and spread of strains that are resistant to less-expensive antimicrobial treatments such as penicillin and tetracycline.

There is no evidence that infected individuals develop long-lasting immunity to re-infection, and vaccination is not available. Thus, the prevention of gonorrhea relies on behavior modification and risk reduction, use of appropriate screening and diagnostic tests, routine use of highly effective antibiotics, early identification and treatment of sexual partners of individuals with gonorrhea, and the appropriate use of barrier methods such as condoms.

An increasing proportion of infections are due to antibiotic-resistant strains of *N. gonorrhoeae*. Chromosomally mediated resistance to multiple antibiotics as well as plasmid-mediated resistance to beta-lactam antibiotics and tetracycline occurs in strains from both developed and developing countries. Nevertheless, infections can be effectively treated with third-generation cephalosporins (for example, ceftriaxone) or fluoroquinolones (for example, ciprofloxacin or ofloxacin). *See* SEXUALLY TRANSMITTED DISEASES.   [S.A.L.; S.A.Mo.]

Grassland ecosystem   A biological community that contains few trees or shrubs, is characterized by mixed herbaceous (nonwoody) vegetation cover, and is dominated by grasses or grasslike plants. Mixtures of trees and grasslands occur as savannas at transition zones with forests or where rainfall is marginal for trees. About $1.2 \times 10^8 \text{ mi}^2$ ($4.6 \times 10^7 \text{ km}^2$) of the Earth's surface is covered with grasslands, which make up about 32% of the plant cover of the world. In North America, grasslands include the Great Plains, which extend from southern Texas into Canada. The European meadows cross the subcontinent, and the Eurasian steppe ranges from Hungary eastward through Russia to Mongolia; the pampas cover much of the interior of Argentina and Uruguay. Vast and varied savannas and velds can be found in central and southern Africa and throughout much of Australia. *See* SAVANNA.

Grasslands occur in regions that are too dry for forests but that have sufficient soil water to support a closed herbaceous plant canopy that is lacking in deserts. Thus, temperate grasslands usually develop in areas with 10–40 in. (25–100 cm) of annual precipitation, although tropical grasslands may receive up to 60 in. (150 cm). Grasslands are found primarily on plains or rolling topography in the interiors of great land masses, and from sea level to elevations of nearly 16,400 ft (5000 m) in the Andes. Because of their continental location they experience large differences in seasonal climate and wide ranges in diurnal conditions. In general, there is at least one dry season during the year, and drought conditions occur periodically.

Significant portions of the world's grasslands have been modified by grazing or tillage or have been converted to other uses. The most fertile and productive soils in the world have developed under grassland, and in many cases the natural species have been replaced by cultivated grasses (cereals).

Different kinds of grasslands develop within continents, and their classification is based on similarity of dominant vegetation, presence or absence of specific dominant species, or prevailing climate conditions.

The climate of grasslands is one of daily and seasonal extremes. Deep winter cold does not preclude grasslands since they occur in some of the coldest regions of the world. However, the success of grasslands in the Mediterranean climate shows that marked summer drought is not prohibitive either. In North America, the rainfall gradient decreases from an annual precipitation of about 40 in. (100 cm) along the eastern border of the tallgrass prairie at the deciduous forest to only about 8 in. (20 cm) in the shortgrass prairies at the foothills of the Rocky Mountains. A similar pattern exists in Europe. Growing-season length is determined by temperature in the north latitudes and by available soil moisture in many regions, especially those adjacent to deserts.

Plants are frequently subjected to hot and dry weather conditions, which are often exacerbated by windy conditions that increase transpirational water loss from the plant leaves.

Soils of mesic temperate grasslands are usually deep, about 3 ft (1 m), are neutral to basic, have high amounts of organic matter, contain large amounts of exchangeable bases, and are highly fertile, with well-developed profiles. The soils are rich because rainfall is inadequate for excessive leaching of minerals and because plant roots produce large amounts of organic material. With less rainfall, grassland soils are shallow, contain less organic matter, frequently are lighter colored, and may be more basic. Tropical and subtropical soils are highly leached, have lower amounts of organic material because of rapid decomposition and more leaching from higher rainfall, and are frequently red to yellow.

Grassland soils are dry throughout the profile for a portion of the year. Because of their dense fibrous root system in the upper layers of the soil, grasses are better adapted than trees to make use of light rainfall showers during the growing season. When compared with forest soils, grassland soils are generally subjected to higher temperatures, greater evaporation, periodic drought, and more transpiration per unit of total plant biomass. *See* BIOMASS.

Throughout the year, flowering plants bloom in the grasslands with moderate precipitation, and flowers bloom after rainfall in the drier grasslands. With increasing aridity and temperature, grasslands tend to become less diverse in the number of species; they support more warm-season species; the complexity of the vegetation decreases; the total above-ground and below-ground production decreases; but the ratio of above-ground to below-ground biomass becomes smaller.

There are many more invertebrate species than any other taxonomic group in the grassland ecosystem. Invertebrates play several roles in the ecosystem. For example, many are herbivorous, and eat leaves and stems, whereas others feed on the roots of plants. Earthworms process organic matter into small fragments that decompose rapidly, scarab beetles process animal dung on the soil surface, flies feed on plants and are pests to cattle, and many species of invertebrates are predaceous and feed on other invertebrates. Soil nematodes, small nonarthropod invertebrates, include forms that are herbivorous, predaceous, or saprophagous, feeding on decaying organic matter. *See* SOIL ECOLOGY.

Most of the reptiles and amphibians in grassland ecosystems are predators. Relatively few bird species inhabit the grassland ecosystem, although many more species are found in the flooding pampas of Argentina than in the dry grasslands of the western United States. Their role in the grassland ecosystem involves consumption of seeds, invertebrates, and vertebrates; seed dispersal; and scavenging of dead animals.

Small mammals of the North American grassland include moles, shrews, gophers, ground squirrels, and various species of mice. Among intermediate-size animals are the opossum, fox, coyote, badger, skunk, rabbit, and prairie dog; large animals include various types of deer and elk. The most characteristic large mammal species of the North American grassland is the bison, although many of these animals were eliminated in the late 1800s. Mammals include both ruminant (pronghorns) and nonruminant (prairie dogs) herbivores, omnivores (opossum), and predators (wolves).

Except for large mammals and birds, the animals found in the grassland ecosystem undergo relatively large population variations from year to year. These variations, some of which are cyclical and others more episodic, are not entirely understood and may extend over several years. Many depend upon predator–prey relationships, parasite or disease dynamics, or weather conditions that influence the organisms themselves or the availability of food, water, and shelter. *See* POPULATION ECOLOGY.

Within the grassland ecosystem are enormous numbers of very small organisms, including bacteria, fungi, algae, and viruses. From a systems perspective, the hundreds of species of bacteria and fungi are particularly important because they decompose organic material, releasing carbon dioxide and other gases into the atmosphere and making nutrients available for recycling. Bacteria and some algae also capture nitrogen from the atmosphere and fix it into forms available to plants.

Much of the grassland ecosystem has been burned naturally, probably from fires sparked by lightning. Human inhabitants have also routinely started fires intentionally to remove predators and undesirable insects, to improve the condition of the rangeland, and to reduce cover for predators and enemies; or unintentionally. Thus, grasslands have evolved under the influences of grazing and periodic burning, and the species have adapted to withstand these conditions. If burning or grazing is coupled with drought, however, the grassland will sustain damage that may require long periods of time for recovery by successional processes. *See* ECOLOGICAL SUCCESSION; ECOSYSTEM.

[P.G.Ri.]

Growth factor   Any of a group of biologically active poly-peptides which function as hormonelike regulatory signals, controlling the growth and differentiation of responsive cells. Indeed, the distinction between growth factors and hormones is frequently arbitrary and stems more from the manner of their discovery than from a clear difference in function. *See* CELL DIFFERENTIATION; HORMONE.

The sequence of amino acids has been determined for several growth-factor polypeptides. This information permits a number of growth factors to be placed into families, members of which have related amino acid sequences, suggesting that they evolved from a single ancestral protein. The insulin family comprises somatemedins A and C, insulin, insulinlike growth factor (IGF), and multiplication-stimulating factor (MSF). A second family consists of sarcoma growth factor (SGF), transforming growth factors (TGFs), and epidermal growth factor (EGF). In addition, there are growth factors, such as nerve growth factor (NGF), fibroblast growth factor (FGF), and platelet-derived growth factor (PDGF), for which structural homologs have not been identified. *See* INSULIN; PROTEIN.

The stimulation of cell proliferation by several growth factors is similar in some ways to the rapid cell proliferation characteristic of tumor cells. Furthermore, the growth factor receptors are similar to the tumor-causing proteins produced by several RNA tumor viruses. It has been demonstrated that platelet-derived growth factor is virtually identical to the tumor-causing protein of the RNA tumor virus, simian sarcoma virus. Some forms of cancer involve improper function of growth factors.   [M.Bo.]

Guild   A group of species that utilize the same kinds of resources, such as food, nesting sites, or places to live, in a similar manner. Emphasis is on ecologically associated groups that are most likely to compete because of similarity in ecological niches, even though species can be taxonomically unrelated. The term was derived from the guild in human society composed of people engaged in an activity or trade held in common.

The guild concept focuses attention on the ways in which ecologically related species differ enough to permit coexistence, or avoid competitive displacement. For example, new places to live for some plants are provided by badger mounds in dense tall-grass prairie vegetation.

The guild is also commonly used as the smallest unit in an ecosystem in studies relating to environmental impact, wildlife management, and habitat classification. A representative species of a guild may be selected for study involving the uncertain assumption that environmental impact will influence this species in the same way as other guild members. *See* ECOSYSTEM.   [P.W.P.]

H

Haemophilus A genus of gram-negative, pleomorphic bacteria that are facultative anaerobes and are nonmotile and non-spore-forming.

Haemophilus influenzae was the first of the species to be isolated and is considered the type species. It was originally recovered during the influenza pandemic of 1889 and for a time was believed to be the causative agent of influenza; thus it was called the influenza bacillus. However, when this fallacy became apparent, the organism was renamed, still reflecting the historical association with influenza.

Haemophilus species are distinguished by a number of criteria. Strains of *H. influenzae* can be separated into encapsulated and nonencapsulated forms. Encapsulated strains express one of six biochemically and antigenically distinct capsular polysaccharides that are designated serotypes a through f. Nonencapsulated strains are referred to as nontypable. *See* INFLUENZA; MENINGITIS.

Haemophilus influenzae is a human-specific pathogen that inhabits the upper respiratory tract and is acquired by exposure to airborne droplets or contact with respiratory secretions. Nontypable strains can be isolated from the nasopharynx of up to 80% of normal children and adults at any given time, usually in association with asymptomatic colonization. Overall, these organisms are the leading cause of exacerbations of chronic bronchitis, and the second most common etiology of acute otitis media and sinusitis. On occasion, nontypable *H. influenzae* causes invasive disease such as meningitis, septicemia, endocarditis, epiglottitis, or septic arthritis. Invasive disease occurs most often in neonates and in patients with underlying immunodeficiency, especially when abnormalities in humoral immunity are present.

Encapsulated strains of *H. influenzae* are present in the nasopharynx of only 2–5% of children and an even smaller percentage of adults. Historically, *H. influenzae* type b strains were the primary cause of childhood bacterial meningitis and a majority of other bacteremic diseases in children. However, in recent years the incidence of disease due to *H. influenzae* type b has plummeted in the United States and other developed countries, reflecting the routine use of *H. influenzae* conjugate vaccines. These vaccines provide effective protection against disease due to *H. influenzae* type b but fail to protect against non-type b strains.

Haemophilus aphrophilus, *H. haemolyticus*, *H. parahaemolyticus*, *H. parainfluenzae*, and *H. segnis* are members of the normal flora in the human oral cavity and oropharynx and have low pathogenic potential. Among these species, *H. parainfluenzae* is the most common pathogen and has been reported in association with a variety of diseases.

Strains of *H. influenzae* are increasingly resistant to a wide variety of antibiotics. Accordingly, an extended-spectrum cephalosporin is generally recommended for empiric treatment of serious disease. *See* ANTIBIOTIC; DRUG RESISTANCE; MEDICAL BACTERIOLOGY.

[G.P.Kr.; J.W.St.G.]

Haemosporina A relatively small and generally rather compact group of protozoans in the subphylum Sporozoa. Authorities differ as to the group's taxonomic status; that assigned it by the Committee on Taxonomy and Taxonomic Problems of the Society of Protozoologists is followed here: a suborder of the order Eucoccida, subclass Coccidia, class Telosporea, subphylum Sporozoa. The Haemosporina are common protozoan parasites of vertebrates, and some of them are important as causes of illness and death. The best known of the group are the four species (genus *Plasmodium*) of malarial parasites of humans.

Transmission of these parasites is probably always effected in nature by the bite of some bloodsucking invertebrate. In the vertebrate host they reproduce asexually; sometimes this occurs in the tissues of certain internal organs, such as the lungs, liver, spleen, and brain; sometimes in the red blood cells (erythrocytes), or even in other types of blood and blood-forming cells; and often in both tissues and blood cells. The immature sex cells, gametocytes, always occur in erythrocytes or leukocytes (white blood cells). Gametocytes mature into gametes after ingestion by an intermediate host (arthropod). Fertilization ensues, with a subsequent period of development culminating in the production of numerous sporozoites. These tiny filamentous forms are infective for the vertebrate host. Since they can develop no further in the arthropod, infection in this host is self-limited, in the sense that no further buildup is possible; the insect is seldom harmed by the parasite. However, sporozoites may remain infective for a long time in the invertebrate host, perhaps as long as the insect lives. *See* SPOROZOA.

[R.D.M.]

Hair Nonliving, specialized epidermal derivatives characteristic only of modern mammals. However, it is now thought that hair was present in at least some therapsid reptiles. It consists of keratinized cells, tightly cemented together, which arise from the matrix at the base of a follicle. A follicle is a tubular epidermal downgrowth that penetrates into the dermis and widens into a bulb (the hair root) at its deep end. The follicle, together with a lateral outgrowth called the sebaceous gland, forms the pilosebaceous system. Rapid cell production in the matrix, and differentiation in the regions immediately above, produces a hair shaft which protrudes from the follicle mouth at the skin surface. *See* GLAND.

Hairs are not permanent structures but are continually replaced throughout the life of a mammal. In some species, for example, the rat, hamster, mouse, chinchilla, and rabbit, the replacement pattern is undulant, and waves of follicular activity can be traced across the body. In other species, for example, humans, cats, and guinea pigs, each follicle appears to cycle independently of others in the immediate area. [P.F.M.]

Hallucination A perceptual experience in the absence of external stimulation. Hallucinations differ from illusions, which are changes in the perception of a real object. Hallucinations tend to fade with fixation or with attention to the content. Except for afterimages, which lie like a film over objects, hallucinations replace objects and object space. A hallucination is not objectlike in its realness. The conviction of reality is due to the loss of an object for comparison and the inability to disprove the image through other sensory modalities.

Hallucinations that are recognized as such by the experiencer include those resulting from sensory deprivation, drug use, and the phantom limb state. *See* SCHIZOPHRENIA.

Hallucinations may occur in a range of neurologic and psychiatric conditions, although they are usually considered hallmarks of schizophrenia. Delusional misidentification syndromes are a subtype of hallucinations and may also occur in neurological and psychiatric disease. For example, Capgras syndrome, which is commonly seen in schizophrenia, causes the individual to replace a familiar person (usually the spouse) with an imposter with the same or similar physical appearance. Frégoli syndrome is the delusional confusion of an individual as a familiar person in disguise.

Neurotransmitters are directly involved in the regulation of drug-induced and schizophrenic hallucinations, with many accounts pointing to the involvement of serotonin and dopamine. Therefore, it is possible to treat individuals with antipsychotic drugs that stabilize the chemical systems involved.

With localized damage to the brain, hallucinations are usually brief and intermittent, though in some cases, especially neurologic damage involving the brainstem, hallucinations can be chronic and sustained.

Physical input to the eyes and ears constrains and guides the construction of mental images, but the final result—the perception of an object or sound as a meaningful event occurring in the external world—also reflects very complex physiological processes. They begin in the brainstem, pass to the limbic system of the brain, and finally involve the temporal, parietal, and occipital areas of the cerebral cortex. Various types of hallucination are caused by disruptions that occur at different levels along that sequence of brain processes. *See* COGNITION.

At its earliest phase, damage to the upper brainstem produces peduncular (crepuscular) hallucinations of faces, torsos, and occasionally geometric patterns or landscapes near the viewer at the close of day. The images may be static and immobile or may change in content and affective tonality while being viewed. A smiling young boy, for example, may change into a scowling old woman. The hallucinations are often vivid and chromatic, and tend to be multimodal: they are seen, heard, and even touched, and occur over the entire visual field. Olfactory and gustatory images have also been described. Peduncular hallucinations are similar to the hypnagogic hallucinations that are experienced when falling asleep. *See* SLEEP AND DREAMING.

Neurologic damage involving limbic and temporal-lobe structures yields hallucinations of faces or formed scenes laden with meaning and affect. Changes in size (micropsia, macropsia) and shape (metamorphopsia) may occur. Déjà vu, derealization, and dreamy states are common. Auditory hallucinations are usually of speech or music. Microscopic (Lilliputian) and autoscopic (out-of-the-body) hallucinations also occur with temporal-lobe lesions. Exposure to a wide range of drugs and many psychiatric disorders, especially schizophrenia, can lead to hallucinations whose form suggests dysfunction involving limbic or temporal-lobe structures. *See* PSYCHOTOMIMETIC DRUG.

Damage to the parietal lobe leads to illusory distortions of shape, size, and motion, whereas occipital lesions or stimulation—or migraine—gives elementary hallucinations of sparks, flames, lines, or simple patterns. These hallucinations share features with afterimages. Palinopsia, the hallucinatory persistence of an object after the viewer has turned away, is a form of pathological afterimagery. *See* PERCEPTION.

[J.W.Br.; K.L.C.]

Halophilism (microbiology)   The requirement of high salt (NaCl) concentrations for growth of microorganisms. Microorganisms (mainly bacteria) can be classified by their physiological tolerance to salt. Most normal eubacteria, such as *Escherichia coli* and *Pseudomonas fluorescens*, and most fresh-water microorganisms, are nonhalophiles (best growth at less than 1.2% NaCl). Slight halophiles (1.2–3% NaCl) include many marine microorganisms. Moderate halophiles (3–15% NaCl) include *Vibrio costicola*, *Paracoccus halodenitrificans*, and many others. Borderline extreme halophiles (9–25% NaCl) include the photosynthetic bacterium *Ectothiorhodospira halophila*, the actinomycete *Actinopolyspora halophila*, and the halophylic archaebacteria

Halobacterium volcanii and *H. mediterranei.* Extreme halophiles (require at least 10% NaCl; optima 15–30% NaCl) are *Halobacterium salinarium* and *Halococcus morrhuae.* See METHANOGENESIS (BACTERIA).

The halophilic aerobic archaebacteria give a striking red color to hypersaline waters. They are found in the Dead Sea, the Great Salt Lake, Lake Magadi in Kenya, and other alkaline salt lakes, and in solar salterns where salt is prepared by evaporating seawater. Their red color is due to carotenoid pigments (bacterioruberins), which seem to protect them from strong sunlight in their natural environments. See CAROTENOID.

Microorganisms that live in high concentrations of salt or other solutes do not exclude solutes from the interior of the cell. However, the internal solute composition is quite different from the outside composition. *Dunaliella* species have internal glycerol concentrations corresponding to the external concentration of NaCl. Other salt-tolerant algae and yeasts also have high internal concentrations of glycerol, or other polyols. Solutes which maintain osmotic equilibrium between inside and outside of the cell without interfering with the cell's physiological processes are called compatible solutes. See OSMOREGULATORY MECHANISMS.

Mechanisms of adaptation to a highly saline environment have been best characterized in aerobic halophilic bacteria whose enzymes are able to function in high salt concentrations; indeed, most of them require such salt concentrations for activity, stability, or both. For a number of enzyme systems, KCl rather than NaCl is required. Other parts of the cells of these bacteria also require high salt concentrations for function or stability. Halobacteria lyse and their cell walls may completely dissolve unless salt concentrations are high. NaCl is specifically required for active transport of ions and nutrients in all halophilic bacteria. [D.J.K.]

Haplosporida   A group of Protozoa usually regarded as an order within the class Haplosporea. The chief distinguishing characteristic of the Haplosporida, and the one from which their name is derived, is the production of uninucleate spores that lack polar capsules and polar filaments.

Haplosporida are mainly parasites of invertebrates, such as rotifers, annelids, crustacea, insects, and mollusks, but they also occur in the bodies of Ascidia (tunicates), which are primitive chordates. If the genus *Icthyosporidium* is properly included in the order, Haplosporida also parasitize fish. One species causes "neon" fish disease.

It is of considerable biological interest that some species of Haplosporida are hyperparasites, that is, parasitic on other parasites. They have been found in gregarines parasitizing annelids, and also in flukes. See SPOROZOA. [R.D.M.]

Hearing (human)   The general perceptual behavior and the specific responses that are made in relation to sound stimuli. The auditory system consists of the ear and the auditory nervous system. The ear comprises outer, middle, and inner ear. The outer ear, visible on the surface of the body, directs sounds to the middle ear, which converts sounds into vibrations of the fluid that fills the inner ear. The inner ear contains the vestibular and the auditory sensory organs. See EAR (VERTEBRATE).

The auditory part of the inner ear, known as the cochlea because of its snaillike shape, analyzes sound in a way that resembles spectral analysis. It contains the sensory cells that convert sounds into nerve signals to be conducted through the auditory portion of the eighth cranial nerve to higher brain centers. The neural code in the auditory nerve is transformed as the information travels through a complex system of nuclei connected by fiber tracts, known as the ascending auditory pathways. They carry auditory information to the auditory cortex, which is the part of the sensory cortex where perception and interpretation of sounds are believed to take place. Interaction between the neural pathways of the two ears makes it possible for a person to determine the direction of a sound's source. *See* BRAIN.

Role of the ear. The pinna, the projecting part of the outer ear, collects sound, but because it is small in relation to the wavelengths of sound that are important for human hearing, the pinna plays only a minor role in hearing. The ear canal acts as a resonator: it increases the sound pressure at the tympanic membrane in the frequency range between 1500 and 5000 Hz. The difference between the arrival time of a sound at each of the two ears and the difference in the intensity of the sound that reaches each ear are used by the auditory nervous system to determine the location of the sound source.

Sound that reaches the tympanic membrane causes the membrane to vibrate, and these vibrations set in motion the three small bones of the middle ear: the malleus, the incus, and the stapes. The footplate of the stapes is located in an opening of the cochlear bone—the oval window. Moving in a pistonlike fashion, the stapes sets the cochlear fluid into motion and thereby converts sound (pressure fluctuations in the air) into motion of the cochlear fluid. Motion of the fluid in the cochlea begins the neural process known as hearing.

There are two small muscles in the middle ear: the tensor tympani and the stapedius muscles. The former pulls the manubrium of the malleus inward, while the latter is attached to the stapes and pulls the stapes in a direction that is perpendicular to its pistonlike motion. The stapedius muscle is the smallest striated muscle in the body, and it contracts in response to an intense sound. This is known as the acoustic middle-ear reflex. The muscle's contraction reduces sound transmission through the middle ear and thus acts as a regulator of input to the cochlea. Perhaps a more important function of the stapedius muscle is that it contracts immediately before and during a person's own vocalization, reducing the sensitivity of the speaker's ears to his or her own voice and possibly reducing the masking effect of an individual's own voice. The role of the tensor tympani muscle is less well understood, but it is thought that contraction of the tensor tympani muscle facilitates proper ventilation of the middle-ear cavity. These two muscles are innervated by the facial (VIIth) nerve for the stapedius and the trigeminal (Vth) nerve for the tensor tympani. The acoustic stapedius reflex plays an important role in the clinical diagnosis of disorders affecting the middle ear, the cochlea, and the auditory nerve.

Vibrations in the cochlear fluid set up a traveling wave on the basilar membrane of the cochlea. When tones are used to set the cochlear fluid into vibration, one specific point on the basilar membrane will vibrate with a higher amplitude than any other. Therefore, a frequency scale can be laid out along the basilar membrane, with low frequencies near the apex and high frequencies near the base of the cochlea.

The sensory cells that convert the motion of the basilar membrane into a neural code in individual auditory nerve fibers are located along the basilar membrane. They are also known as hair cells, because they have hairlike structures on their surfaces. The hair cells in the mammalian cochlea function as mechanoreceptors: motion of the basilar membrane causes deflection of the hairs, starting a process that eventually results in a change in the discharge rate of the nerve fiber connected to each hair cell. This process includes the release of a chemical transmitter substance at the base of the hair cells that controls the discharge rate of the nerve fiber (see illustration).

The frequency selectivity of the basilar membrane provides the central nervous system with information about the frequency or spectrum of a sound, because each auditory nerve fiber is "tuned" to a specific frequency. The frequency of a sound is also

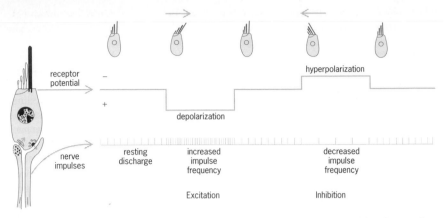

Schematic illustration of the excitation in hair cells. A deflection of hairs in one direction results in an increase in the neural discharge rate in the nerve fiber associated with the hair cell, whereas a deflection in the opposite direction causes inhibition, or slowing, of this discharge rate. (*After A. Fiock, Transducing mechanisms in lateral line canal organ receptors, Proceedings of the Cold Spring Harbor Symposia on Quantitative Biology, 30:133–146, 1965*)

represented in the time pattern of the neural code, at least for frequencies up to 5 kHz. Thus, the frequency or spectrum of a sound can be coded for place and time in the neural activity in the auditory nervous system. *See* AUDIOMETRY.

Auditory nervous system. The ascending auditory nervous system consists of a complex chain of clusters of nerve cells (nuclei), connected by nerve fibers (nerve tracts). The chain of nuclei relays and transforms auditory information from the periphery of the auditory system, the ear, to the central structures, or auditory cortex, which is believed to be associated with the ability to interpret different sounds. Neurons in the entire auditory nervous system are, in general, organized anatomically according to the frequency of a tone to which they respond best, which suggests a tonotopical organization in the auditory nervous system and underscores the importance of representations of frequency in that system. However, when more complex sounds were used to study the auditory system, qualities of sounds other than frequency or spectrum were found to be represented differently in different neurons in the ascending auditory pathway, with more complex representation in the more centrally located nuclei. Thus, the response patterns of the cells in each division of the cochlear nucleus are different, which indicates that extensive signal processing is taking place. Although the details of that processing remain to be determined, the cells appear to sort the information and then relay different aspects of it through different channels to more centrally located parts of the ascending auditory pathway. As a result, some neurons seem to respond only if more than one sound is presented at the same time, others respond best if the frequency or intensity of a sound changes rapidly, and so on.

Another important feature of the ascending auditory pathway is the ability of particular neurons to signal the direction of sound origination, which is based on the physical differences in the sound reaching the two ears. Certain centers in the ascending auditory pathway seem to have the ability to compute the direction to the sound source on the basis of such differences in the sounds that reach the ears.

Knowledge of the descending auditory pathway is limited to the fact that the most peripheral portion can control the sensitivity of the hair cells.   [A.R.Mø.]

Hearing (vertebrate)   The ability to perceive sound arriving from distant vibrating sources through the environmental medium (such as air, water, or ground). The primary function of hearing is to detect the presence, identity, location, and activity of distant sound sources. Sound detection is accomplished using structures that collect sound from the environment (outer ears), transmit sound efficiently to the inner ears (via middle ears), transform mechanical motion to electrical and chemical processes in the inner ears (hair cells), and then transmit the coded information to various specialized areas within the brain. These processes lead to perception and other behaviors appropriate to sound sources, and probably arose early in vertebrate evolution.

Sound is gathered from the environment by structures that are variable among species. In many fishes, sound pressure reaching the swim bladder or another gas-filled chamber in the abdomen or head causes fluctuations in volume that reach the inner ears as movements. In addition, the vibration of water particles that normally accompany underwater sound reaches the inner ears to cause direct, inertial stimulation. In land animals, sound causes motion of the tympanic membrane (eardrum). In amphibians, reptiles, and birds, a single bone (the columella) transmits tympanic membrane motion to the inner ears. In mammals, there are three interlinked bones (malleus, incus, and stapes). Mammals that live underground may detect ground-borne sound via bone conduction. In whales and other sea mammals, sound reaches the inner ears via tissue and bone conduction.

The inner ears of all vertebrates contain hair-cell mechanoreceptors that transform motion of their cilia to electrochemical events resulting in action potentials in cells of the eighth cranial nerve. Patterns of action potentials reaching the brain represent sound wave features in all vertebrates. All vertebrates have an analogous set of auditory brain centers. *See* EAR (VERTEBRATE).

Experiments show that vertebrates have more commonalities than differences in their sense of hearing. The major difference between species is in the frequency range of hearing, from below 1 Hz to over 100,000 Hz. In other fundamental hearing functions (such as best sensitivity, sound intensity and frequency discrimination acuity, time and frequency analysis, and source localization), vertebrates have much in common. All detect sound within a restricted frequency range. All species are able to detect sounds in the presence of interfering sounds (noise), discriminate between different sound features, and locate the sources of sound with varying degrees of accuracy.

The sensitivity range is similar among all groups, with some species in all groups having a best sensitivity in the region of −20 to 0 dB. Fishes, amphibians, reptiles, and birds hear best between 100 and 5000 Hz. Only mammals hear at frequencies above 10,000 Hz. Humans and elephants have the poorest high-frequency hearing.   [R.R.F.]

Heart (invertebrate)   Hearts of invertebrates can be categorized according to the source of the electrical rhythmicity that underlies their beat. Rhythmic electrical activity can arise in the muscle itself (myogenic hearts) or in neurons that drive the heart muscle (neurogenic hearts). Most mollusks and some insects appear to have purely myogenic hearts; these hearts beat normally when isolated from neural inputs. Conversely, the hearts of the higher crustaceans and the xiphosuran *Limulus* are usually considered to be purely neurogenic: motor neurons impose their rhythmic electrical activity on heart muscle fibers by means of direct excitatory synapses. Without neural input, the heart ceases to beat. Other invertebrates, including gnathobdellid leeches and some insects, have hearts that can produce a myogenic beat but require rhythmic neural input to coordinate that beat and maintain the proper rate.

In the marine snail *Aplysia*, an organism with a myogenic heart, a muscular heart consisting of an auricle and a ventricle is located in a dorsal pericardial cavity. The rhythmic contractions of the auricle fill the ventricle with hemolymph, which is then pumped through the open circulatory system by the rhythmic contractions of the ventricle. The normal heartbeat period lasts about 3 s. A pair of semilunar valves prevents backflow of hemolymph into the auricle during ventricular contraction. Three arteries issue from the ventricle toward the anterior, and a single semilunar valve prevents backflow from them during ventricular expansion. The arteries carry the hemolymph to the various body organs, where they end in tissue spaces. The hemolymph then collects in the hemocoel and returns to the heart by two parallel veins, one through the kidney and one through the gill. Although the Aplysia heart is innervated, its normal beat persists after denervation.

The lobster is an example of an organism with a neurogenic heart. A muscular heart pumps hemolymph through the open circulatory system. This heart is located dorsally along the thoracic midline and is suspended within a pericardial cavity by ligaments. The heartbeat period lasts about 2 s. Large anterior- and posterior-going arteries, which branch extensively to supply various body organs, issue from the heart. Semilunar valves, located at the juncture of each artery with the heart, prevent backflow of blood into the heart when it relaxes. Hemolymph enters the heart from the pericardial sinus through six ostia, which have valves to ensure unidirectional flow. The rhythmic discharge of motor neurons innervating the heart by way of excitatory chemical synapses produces the heartbeat. These motor neurons are located in the cardiac ganglion on the inner dorsal surface of the heart. The cardiac ganglion contains only nine neurons, which generate a simple two-phased rhythm of electrical activity. The four posterior small cells (cells 6–9) are interneurons, and the five anterior large cells (cells 1–5) are the motor neurons. See NERVOUS SYSTEM (INVERTEBRATE).   [R.L.Ca.; C.S.Co.]

Heart (vertebrate)   The muscular pumping organ of the cardiovascular system. The heart typically lies ventrally, near the anterior end of the trunk; it is ventral and medial to the gills in fish and at the base of the neck or in the chest region of tetrapods. In humans it is located behind the breastbone and ribs between the third and fifth costal cartilages. Its anterior portion or base is directed to the right and dorsally and is the area where the great vessels enter and leave the heart. The lower muscular portion ends in a blunt apex which lies behind the fifth costal cartilage on the left.

The muscular wall of the heart, the myocardium, is lined by an inner endocardium and is covered externally by membranous visceral pericardium. There are coronary arteries and veins to and from the heart, which has a specialized neuromuscular conducting system and autonomic nerve supply.

In fishes the heart is basically a simple tube which becomes subdivided into four successive chambers, the sinus venosus, atrium, ventricle, and conus arteriosus. Blood from the body enters the sinus and leaves the conus to go to the gills to be oxygenated. The ventricle supplies the main pumping force.

When lungs are introduced into the system in lungfish and tetrapods, the mixing of oxygenated and nonoxygenated blood becomes a problem. In brief, the sinus venosus and conus arteriosus disappear, becoming incorporated into the other chambers or the bases of the great vessels. At the same time the atrium and later the ventricle become divided into right and left chambers by a median septum.

In birds and mammals including humans (see illustration) the medial fibromuscular septum divides the heart into two lateral halves, each consisting of a thin-walled receiving chamber or atrium and a thicker, muscular pumping chamber or ventricle. Blood enters the right atrium from the superior and inferior venae cavae which drain most of the body. It passes through the tricuspid valve to the right ventricle and is pumped to

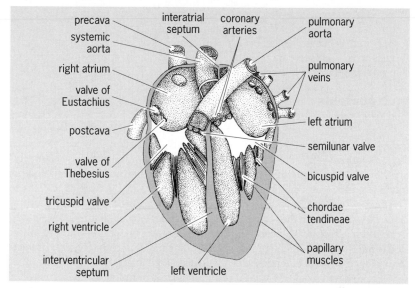

precava

systemic aorta

right atrium

valve of Eustachius

postcava

valve of Thebesius

tricuspid valve

right ventricle

interventricular septum

interatrial septum

coronary arteries

left ventricle

pulmonary aorta

pulmonary veins

left atrium

semilunar valve

bicuspid valve

chordae tendineae

papillary muscles

Internal structure of four-chambered mammalian heart, ventral view. (*After C. K. Weichert, Anatomy of the Chordates, 2d ed., McGraw-Hill, 1958*)

the lungs during systole, or contraction of the heart. Blood returns from the lungs by way of the pulmonary veins to the left atrium, passes into the left ventricle through the mitral valve, and during contraction is pumped out into the aorta. *See* Cardiovascular System.   [T.S.P.]

Helicobacter   A genus of gram-negative bacilli whose members are spiral shaped, showing corkscrewlike motility generated by multiple, usually polar flagella. *Helicobacter* species require low concentrations of oxygen for maximum growth and produce the enzymes oxidase, catalase, and urease.

Different species of *Helicobacter* are found in the stomachs of different animals: *H. felis* in cats and dogs, *H. mustelae* in the domestic ferret, *H. nemestrinae* in the pigtailed macaque, and *H. acinonyx* in captive cheetahs with gastritis. *Helicobacter pylori*, found in the human stomach, is extremely common. In the United States and similarly developed countries, its prevalence increases at about 1% per year of age so that the majority of adults above age 50 are infected. In less developed countries, infection rates are dramatically higher, with up to 80% of children infected.

Helicobacter pylori is present in virtually all cases of chronic gastritis, which progresses slowly (years or decades) from asymptomatic to atrophic gastritis with impaired acid secretion. Virtually all individuals with duodenal ulcers are infected with *H. pylori*, which colonizes sites in the duodenum. The termination of treatment for duodenal ulcers leads to a high rate of recurrence of the ulcers, but ulcer treatment plus eradication of *H. pylori* from the stomach usually leads to a permanent cure. A significant proportion of individuals with *H. pylori*-associated atrophic gastritis develop intestinal-cell metaplasia in the stomach, a condition which is known to represent a precancerous state.

Helicobacter pylori virulence factors include its shape and its ability to rapidly move into and through the gastric mucous coating, which protects the organism from stomach acid; its surface-associated urease enzyme which neutralizes stomach acid near the organism; a cytotoxin; and a fibrillar adhesin which binds the organism to the surface of gastric epithelial cells. *Helicobacter pylori* can survive in large numbers in spite of antibodies which are secreted into the stomach and the host immune cell response (inflammatory response) characteristic of gastritis.   [D.J.Ev.]

Hematopoiesis   The process by which the cellular elements of the blood are formed. The three main types of cells are the red cells (erythrocytes), which serve to carry oxygen, the white cells (leukocytes), which function in the prevention of and recovery from disease, and the thrombocytes, which function in blood clotting. The formation of these cells is one of the most active and important processes in the body. Most of the circulating cells live only for a short time and must be replaced in order to maintain life. For instance, in the human adult a red blood cell has a life of 120 days; 250 billion new red cells have to be produced daily to replace those that are destroyed.

Blood cells originate in the reticuloendothelial tissue, which is a loose, fibrous, highly vascularized mesh of fibers, endothelial cells, and macrophages. Within the spaces of the tissue are found the precursor (blast) cells of the definitive adult types. For the sake of convenience, the reticuloendothelial tissue is divided into two general but imprecise types: lymphoid and myeloid tissue. Lymphoid tissue is primarily localized in the lymph nodes of the lymphatic system and is also in the spleen, thymus, and bone marrow. Several classes of white cells are produced, including the lymphocytes, macrophages, and monocytes. *See* CELLULAR IMMUNOLOGY; LYMPHATIC SYSTEM.

Myeloid tissue is normally limited in humans to the red bone marrow of the ribs, sternum, vertebrae, and proximal ends of the long bones of the body. It is concerned with the production of the erythrocytes and certain types of leukocytes. The latter are the granular leukocytes (called eosinophils, basophils, and neutrophils on the basis of the affinity of granules in their cytoplasm for certain dyes) and megakaryocytes. Fragments of megakaryocytes form the blood platelets (thrombocytes), which are necessary for blood clotting. *See* BLOOD.   [F.Wi.]

Hemiascomycetes   A class of the phylum Ascomycota that includes the yeasts and yeastlike fungi. These are morphologically simple fungi; no ascoma is formed, and the asci are produced free on the host or substrate. Asexual reproduction occurs by the formation of blastospores (budding) or, less frequently, by fission arthrospores. Two main orders are recognized, the Saccharomycetales and the Taphrinales. *See* YEAST.

The vegetative body (thallus) of the Saccharomycetales may be either unicellular (true yeasts) or mycelial. In unicellular species, asci form when two vegetative cells fuse, and then the fused cell undergoes meiosis to form ascospores. In mycelial species, the hyphae are not very extensive. Sexual reproduction occurs when adjacent cells extend short lateral branches that fuse to form the asci. Variations on these modes of ascus formation, however, are common among the yeasts.

The Saccharomycetales are common on substrates high in sugars, such as plant exudates, ripe fruits, and flower parts. Because they are microscopic, they are recognized mainly from cultures that have a homogeneous appearance and a characteristic odor. The most important genus is *Saccharomyces*; *S. cerevisiae* is the common bakery and brewery yeast, and *S. ellipsoideus* is used in winemaking. An important mycelial species is *Nematospora coryli*, which causes yeast spot disease of various crops.

The order Taphrinales includes the leaf curl disease fungi. The most widely recognized species are *Taphrina deformans*, cause of leaf curl of peach and almond trees, and *T. caerulescens*, cause of leaf blister of oaks. These fungi produce a well-developed mycelium in the host tissue but, when grown in culture, form only a yeastlike colony of single cells. Asci are produced when special binucleate hyphal cells beneath the host cuticle undergo nuclear fusion and the resulting diploid cell elongates to form an ascus on the leaf surface. The nucleus undergoes meiosis, and ascospores are formed. *See* ASCOMYCOTA; EUMYCOTA; FUNGI.

On the basis of molecular data, some workers now propose separating the Taphrinales and the fission yeast, *Schizosaccharomyces*, into a new class, Archiascomycetes. These fungi are considered to be more primitive and phylogenetically basal to the rest of the ascomycetes.   [R.T.Ha.]

Hemispheric laterality

Hemispheric laterality   The human brain is a bilaterally symmetrical structure which is for the most part richly interconnected by two main bridges of neurons called the corpus callosum and anterior commissure. These structures can be surgically sectioned in humans in an effort to control the spread of epileptic seizures. Although there is no apparent change in everyday behavior of these patients, dramatic differences in cognitive function can be demonstrated under specialized testing conditions. In normal humans these cerebral commissures are largely responsible for behavioral unity; the neural mechanism keeps the left side of the body up to date with the activities of the right side, and vice versa.

Changes in behavioral responses of persons whose cerebral commissures have been sectioned are almost undetectable. The person walks, talks, and behaves in a normal fashion. Dramatic effects are observed only under testing conditions which utilize stimuli that are lateralized exclusively to one hemisphere or the other. For example, if a picture of an apple is flashed in the right visual field, the person describes the object normally. However, if the same picture is flashed in the left visual field, in the early days of postoperative testing the person denies that the stimulus was presented at all. After many test sessions the person may have the impression that something was flashed, but is unable to say what. This disparity of recognition in the two sides of the visual field occurs because the information is projected to the right hemisphere, which is incapable of speech. Because the right hemisphere is now disconnected from the left, information arriving in the right hemisphere cannot be communicated by means of speech.

When tests are used which do not require a spoken response, numerous mental abilities are observed to be present in the "disconnected" right hemisphere. For example, even though the person is unable to describe a picture of an orange flashed to the left field, when the left hand searches through a field of objects placed out of view, it correctly retrieves the orange. If asked what the object is, the person would say he does not know. Here again the left hemisphere controls speech but cannot solve the problem. The right hemisphere solves the problem but cannot elicit speech.

Despite its linguistic superiority, the left hemisphere does not excel over the right in all tasks. Tests have demonstrated that in some specialized functions the right hemisphere is decidedly superior to the left. In the area of emotional reactions there appears to be equal reactivity in the two hemispheres.

Tests have been conducted on subjects in which the cerebral commissure had not been entirely sectioned (because it is now believed total commissure section is not necessary to stop the interhemispheric spread of some kinds of seizure activity). These persons showed dramatic breakdown in interhemispheric transfer. When the posterior part of the callosum is sectioned, visual aspects of the syndrome appear. When it is spared and more interior regions are cut, tactile and auditory communications are blocked, but not visual ones. It also appears that no fundamental reorganization of the interhemispheric transfer system takes place, since years after surgery these same deficits are present and are not compensated for in any way.

There appears to be a large variation in the lateralized talents of each half-brain. While the right hemisphere frequently appears to have some language talent, not all split-brain persons have language skills in the right hemisphere. Similarly, visual spatial skills, which are usually present exclusively in the right hemisphere, are frequently bilaterally represented and sometimes represented only in the left speech hemisphere. There is even some evidence that the commissure system itself varies in what is transferred where. *See* BRAIN; PSYCHOLOGY.   [M.S.G.]

Hemoglobin   The oxygen-carrying molecule of the red blood cells of vertebrates. This protein represents more than 95% of the solid constituents of the red cell. It is responsible for the transport of oxygen from the lungs to the other tissues of the body and participates in the transport of carbon dioxide in the reverse direction.

Each molecule of hemoglobin comprises four smaller subunits, called polypeptide chains. These are the protein or globin parts of hemoglobin. A heme group, which is an iron-protoporphyrin complex, is associated with each polypeptide subunit and is responsible for the reversible binding of one molecule of oxygen. The polypeptide chains and the heme are synthesized and combine together in nucleated red cells of the bone marrow. As these cells mature, the nuclei fragment and the cells, now called reticulocytes, begin to circulate in the blood. After sufficient hemoglobin has been formed in the reticulocyte, all nuclear material disappears and the cell is then called an erythrocyte, or red blood cell. Each hemoglobin molecule lasts as long as the red cell, which has an average life of 120 days. *See* PORPHYRIN.

Normal adult males and females have about 16 and 14 g, respectively, of hemoglobin per 100 ml of blood; each red cell contains about 29×10^{-12} g of hemoglobin. Red cells normally comprise 40–45% of the volume of whole blood.

The reversible combination of hemoglobin and oxygen can be represented by the reaction shown below. The equilibrium constants for each step are not the same because

$$Hb + 4O_2 \overset{K_1}{\rightleftharpoons} HbO_2 + 3O_2 \overset{K_2}{\rightleftharpoons} Hb(O_2)_2 + 2O_2 \overset{K_3}{\rightleftharpoons} Hb(O_2)_3 + O_2 \overset{K_4}{\rightleftharpoons} Hb(O_2)_4$$

an oxygen molecule on one heme group changes the affinity of the other hemes for additional oxygen molecules. This alteration in binding affinity during oxygenation is called heme-heme interaction and is due to small changes in the three-dimensional structure of the molecule.

Hemoglobin combines reversibly with carbon monoxide about 210 times more strongly than with oxygen. This strong affinity for carbon monoxide accounts for the poisoning effects of this gas.

Hemoglobin binds carbon dioxide by means of free amino groups of the protein but not by the heme group. The reversible combination with carbon dioxide provides part of the normal blood transport of this gas. Hemoglobin serves also as a buffer by reversible reactions with hydrogen ions. The acidic property of oxyhemoglobin is greater than deoxygenated hemoglobin. The extra binding of hydrogen ion by deoxy-hemoglobin promotes the conversion of tissue carbon dioxide into bicarbonate ion and thus increases the amount of total carbon dioxide which can be transported by blood. *See* BLOOD; RESPIRATION.   [R.T.J.]

Hepatitis   An inflammation of the liver caused by a number of etiologic agents, including viruses, bacteria, fungi, parasites, drugs, and chemicals. The most common infectious hepatitis is of viral etiology. All types of hepatitis are characterized by distortion of the normal hepatic lobular architecture due to varying degrees of necrosis of individual liver cells or groups of liver cells, acute and chronic inflammation, and

Kupffer cell enlargement and proliferation. There is usually some degree of disruption of normal bile flow, which causes jaundice. The severity of the disease is highly variable and often unpredictable. *See* LIVER.

A frequently occurring form of hepatitis is caused by excessive ethyl alcohol intake and is referred to as alcoholic hepatitis. It usually occurs in chronic alcoholics and is characterized by fever, high white blood cell count, and jaundice. Some drugs are capable of damaging the liver and can occasionally cause enough damage to produce clinical signs and symptoms. Among these drugs are tetracycline, methotrexate, anabolic and contraceptive steroids, phenacetin, halothane, chlorpromazine, and phenylbutazone.

Clinical features of hepatitis include malaise, fever, jaundice, and serum chemical tests revealing evidence of abnormal liver function. In most mild cases of hepatitis, treatment consists of bedrest and analgesic drugs. In those individuals who develop a great deal of liver cell necrosis and subsequently progress into a condition known as hepatic encephalopathy, exchange blood transfusions are often used. This is done with the hope of removing or diluting the toxic chemicals thought to be the cause of this condition. Chronic hepatitis is a condition defined clinically by evidence of liver disease for at least 6 consecutive months.   [S.P.H.]

Hepatitis C is a disease of the liver caused by the hepatitis C virus (HCV). The prevalence of HCV infection worldwide is 3% (170 million people), with infection rates in North America ranging from 1 to 2% of the population. A simulation analysis estimated that in the period from 1998 to 2008 there will be an increase of 92% in the incidence of cirrhosis of the liver, resulting in a 126% increase in the incidence of liver, failures and a 102% increase in the incidence of hepatocellular carcinoma (HCC), all attributed to HCV.

Hepatitis C virus can be transmitted only by blood-to-blood contact. With the institution of screening of blood, intravenous drug use has become the major source of transmission in North America. Approximately 89% of people who use intravenous drugs for one year become infected with HCV.

Management strategies can be divided into three main areas: surveillance of patients with chronic HCV infection who have not developed cirrhosis; surveillance of patients with established cirrhosis; and strategies to eradicate HCV.   [N.Ar.; N.G.; G.L.]

Herbivory   The consumption of living plant tissue by animals. Herbivorous species occur in most of the major taxonomic groups of animals. Herbivorous insects alone may account for one-quarter of all species. The fraction of all plant biomass that is eaten by herbivores varies widely among plants and ecosystems, ranging from less than 1% to nearly 90%. In terms of both the number of species involved and the role that herbivory plays in the flow of energy and nutrients in ecosystems, herbivory is a key ecological interaction between species.

Herbivory usually does not kill the plant outright, although there are striking exceptions (such as bark beetle outbreaks that decimate conifer trees over thousands of square kilometers). Nevertheless, chronic attack by herbivores can have dramatic cumulative effects on the size, longevity, or reproductive output of individual plants. As a consequence, plants have evolved several means to reduce the level of damage from herbivores and to ameliorate the impact of damage.

Many plants possess physical defenses that interfere mechanically with herbivore feeding on or attachment to the plant. In addition, plant tissues may contain chemical compounds that render them less digestible or even toxic to herbivores. Many plant compounds even can cause death if consumed by unadapted herbivores. While natural selection imposed by herbivores was the likely force driving the elaboration of these plant chemicals, humans have subsequently found many uses for the chemicals as active components of spices, stimulants, relaxants, hallucinogens, poisons, and drugs. An exciting recent finding is that some plants possess induced resistance, elevated levels of physical or chemical defenses that are brought on by herbivore damage and confer enhanced resistance to further damage.

Herbivores can either avoid or counteract plant defenses. Many herbivores avoid consuming the plant tissues that contain the highest concentrations of toxic or antinutritive chemicals. Herbivores have also evolved an elaborate array of enzymes to detoxify otherwise lethal plant chemicals. Because few herbivores have the ability to detoxify the chemical compounds produced by all the plant species they encounter, many herbivores have restricted diets; the larvae of more than half of all species of butterflies and moths include only a single genus of plants in their diets. Some insect species that have evolved the means to tolerate toxic plant chemicals have also evolved ways to use them in their own defense. Larvae of willow beetles store plant compounds in glands along their back. When the larvae are disturbed, the glands exude droplets of the foul-smelling compounds, which deter many potential predators.

If a plant evolved the ability to produce a novel chemical compound that its herbivores could not detoxify, the plant and its descendants would be freed for a time from the negative effects of herbivory. A herbivore that then evolved the means to detoxify the new compound would enjoy an abundance of food and would increase until the level of herbivory on the plant was once again high, favoring plants that acquire yet another novel antiherbivore compound. These repeated rounds of evolution of plant defenses and herbivore countermeasures (coevolution) over long periods of time help to explain similar patterns of evolutionary relatedness between groups of plant species and the herbivorous insect species that feed on them.

Plants and their herbivores seldom occur in isolation, and other species can influence the interaction between plants and herbivores. For example, mammalian herbivores often rely on gut microorganisms to digest cellulose in the plant material they consume. Thus, herbivory occurs against a backdrop of multiple interactions involving the plants, the herbivores, and other species in the ecological community.   [W.F.Mo.]

Herpes   Any virus of the herpesvirus group, which comprises a family of 70 species, 5 of which are pathogenic to humans; the term also refers to any infection caused by these viruses. Since these pathogens are ubiquitous in nature, most individuals of all populations are exposed to and thus immunized to these viruses. The five pathogenic groups include herpes simplex I and II, varicella-zoster, cytomegalovirus, and the Epstein-Barr virus.

In nonimmunized hosts, the vast majority of all herpes infections present symptoms of nonspecific viral illnesses which resolve spontaneously. However, the infections that cause clinical disease in fact may cause serious morbidity and mortality in afflicted individuals. Reactivation of herpes infection, characteristic of the immunocompromised host, is an important cause of mortality in the treatment of patients with advanced cancer, and is a potential complication of an otherwise possibly curable systemic disease.

Herpesviruses have a deoxyribonucleic acid (DNA) core and are 150 to 200 nanometers in size with icosahedral symmetry, and are coated by a protein barrier, the capsid, derived from the infected host cells. The surface of the virions in general contains protein-carbohydrate structures which allow cellular attachment and thus cellular penetration. All viruses require living cells for their replication; the virus may replicate and destroy the cell, or replicate and allow cell survival, or incorporate its viral gene structure into the host gene structure. This incorporation phenomenon is designated as latency. For example, herpes simplex virus exhibits the phenomenon of latency within nerve cells in the area of previous infection. The Epstein-Barr virus characteristically causes latent infection in lymphocytes (white blood cells in the circulating blood), and the cytomegalic virus also causes latent infection within lymphocytes and possibly within nerve cells. Once the viral genome is incorporated into the host cell, antiviral drugs are of no use, since therapeutic agents cannot selectively destroy or inhibit the viral genome. Factors which are possibly involved in the reactivation of latent virus generally revolve around some depression of the host immune response system. Viral genome incorporation into host cells is of great interest as several herpesvirus types are implicated in the development of cancer.

The foundation of therapeutic intervention for all herpesviruses involves a series of chemicals with structures similar to the base pairs which compose the viral DNA structure. The base analogs compete with or inhibit viral enzymes necessary for the assembly of DNA. See VIRUS.

Herpes simplex I and II infections are spread by intimate contact of mucocutaneous surfaces during the period of virus shedding from active lesions. They usually affect the genitalia, but may affect the oral mucosa, causing painful ulcerations which crust and heal. Upon healing, the virus resides in latent form within local nerve cells. Viral reactivation is poorly understood, but may relate in part to the host immune system. The type II virus has been linked to the development of uterine cervical carcinoma, however its precise role remains a question.

Herpes simplex virus I (cold sores, fever blisters) afflicts 20–40% of the population in the United States and usually affects the oropharynx, causing pharyngitis, tonsillitis, gingivostomatitis, or keratitis (eye inflammation) as primary infections. Inflammation of the mouth, eye, or brain may occur as a secondary infection.

Primary infection (airborne) due to herpes varicella-zoster usually affects preschool children, causing chickenpox, with rare complications usually affecting the immuno-compromised host. Secondary infection usually afflicts the elderly when latent viral reactivation occurs, presumably due to an immune imbalance in the host, and involves the spread of virus along the skin in the anatomic distribution of nerve (this disorder is known as shingles).

Cytomegalovirus is ubiquitous, with the majority of infections remaining subclinical. Adult syndromes include a mononucleosislike syndrome and hepatitis, both of which are self-limited diseases in the normal host. However, reactivation of latent infection is a major source of morbidity and especially mortality in the compromised host, for example, the patient being treated with chemoradiotherapy for advanced malignant disease. See CYTOMEGALOVIRUS INFECTION; HEPATITIS.

The characteristic clinical syndrome caused by Epstein-Barr virus infection includes generalized lymphadenopathy, hepatosplenomegaly, pharyngitis, tonsillitis, and general fatigue and fever. This disorder affects individuals of all ages, but predominantly adolescents. The majority of children are subclinically infected. This mononucleosis syndrome is usually a self-limited disorder, and investigational drugs in use for prophylaxis of high-risk individuals include interferons and acyclovir. Epstein-Barr virus is suspected to be of etiologic importance in Burkitt's African lymphoma. See ANIMAL VIRUS; EPSTEIN-BARR VIRUS.   [D.J.D.]

Heterochrony   An evolutionary phenomenon that involves changes in the rate and timing of development. As animals and plants grow from their earliest embryonic stages to the adult, they undergo changes in shape and size. This life history of an individual organism is known as its ontogeny. The amount of growth that an organism experiences during its ontogeny can be more or less than its ancestor. This can apply to the organism as a whole or to specific parts.

Evolution can be viewed as a branching tree of modified ontogenies. Heterochrony that produces these changes in size and shape may be the link between genetics at one extreme and natural selection at the other.

If a character of one species in an evolutionary sequence undergoes less growth than its ancestor, the process is known as pedomorphosis. If it undergoes more growth, the process is known as peramorphosis. Each state can be achieved by varying the timing of onset, offset, or rate of development.

If development is stopped at an earlier growth stage in the descendant than in the ancestor (for example, by earlier onset of sexual maturity), ancestral juvenile features will be retained by the descendant adult (progenesis). If the onset of development of a particular structure is delayed in a descendant, the structure will develop less than in the ancestor (postdisplacement). The third process that produces pedomorphosis is neoteny, whereby the rate of growth is reduced.

For peramorphosis, development can start earlier in the descendant than in the ancestor (predisplacement); or the rate of development can be increased, thus increasing the allometric coefficient (acceleration); or development can be extended by a delay in the onset of sexual maturity (hypermorphosis).

As an organism grows, the number of cells that it produces increases. Ultimately, changes to rate and timing of growth are reflections of changes to the timing of onset and rate of cell development, and the balance between cell growth and cell death. Morphogens and growth hormones play a major role in controlling development in terms of initiation, rate of division, and migration. Therefore, changes to the timing of their expression affect the shape and size of the final adult structure. Inception of hormonal activity is under the control of genes that regulate the timing of its production.

[K.J.McN.]

Heterosis   Hybrid vigor or increase in size, yield, and performance found in hybrids, especially if the parents have previously been inbred. The application of heterosis has been one of the most important contributions of genetics to scientific agriculture in providing hybrid corn, and vigorous, high-yielding hybrids in other plants and in livestock. *See* BREEDING (ANIMAL); BREEDING (PLANT); GENETICS; MENDELISM.

There are two principal hypotheses to account for the association of size and vigor with heterozygosity, dominance and overdominance. The dominance hypothesis notes that any noninbred population carries a number of recessive genes that are harmful to a greater or lesser extent, but which are rendered ineffective by their dominant alleles. As they become homozygous through inbreeding, they exert their harmful effect. With hybridization, some of the detrimental recessives contributed to the hybrid by one parent are masked by dominant alleles from the other, and an increase in vigor is the result. The alternative hypothesis is that there are loci at which the heterozygote is superior in vigor to either homozygote. This, the overdominance hypothesis, also has the consequence that vigor is proportional to heterozygosity. The dominance hypothesis has been more widely accepted, but the two are very difficult to distinguish experimentally, and it is likely that overdominant loci are playing an appreciable role in heterosis, particularly in determining why one hybrid is better than another. *See* DOMINANCE.

[J.F.Cr.]

Hibernation   A term generally applied to a condition of dormancy and torpor found in cold-blooded (poikilotherm) vertebrates and invertebrates. (The term is also applied to relatively few species of mammals and birds, which are warm-blooded vertebrates.) This rather universal phenomenon can be readily seen when body temperatures of poikilotherm animals drop in a parallel relation to ambient environmental temperatures.

Poikilotherm animals. Hibernation occurs with exposure to low temperatures and, under normal conditions, occurs principally during winter seasons when there are lengthy periods of low environmental temperatures. A related form of dormancy is known as estivation. Many animals estivate when they are exposed to prolonged periods of drought or during hot, dry summers. For all practical purposes, hibernation and estivation in animals are indistinguishable, except for the nature of the stimulus, which is either cold or an arid environment.

There is no complete list of animals that hibernate; however, many examples can be found among the poikilotherms, both vertebrate and invertebrate. The poikilotherms are sometimes referred to as ectothermic, because their body temperatures are not internally regulated but follow the rise and fall of environmental temperatures. During hibernation and winter torpor, body temperatures reflect the environmental temperature, often to within a fraction of a degree. Among the classic examples of hibernators or estivators are reptiles, amphibians, and fishes among the vertebrates, and insects, mollusks, and many other invertebrates.

For many ectothermic vertebrates (fishes, amphibians, and reptiles) the ability to avoid seasonal and periodic environmental rigors by entering a state of metabolic inactivity is a crucial element in their survival. Specifically, winter dormancy and summer estivation—the usual context in which these terms are applied to ectotherms—permit these animals to survive and flourish, first, by reducing the impact of seasonal extremes and, second, by significantly lowering the ectotherm's energetic costs during times that would not be favorable for activity (that is, when food is available).

Many terrestrial reptiles, such as lizards, snakes, and turtles, become dormant and hibernate by burrowing in crevices under rocks, logs, and in the ground below the frost line. Terraqueous turtles also become cold-torpid and may often be found completely submerged in mud and in ponds under ice.

Since the hibernating reptile is subject to the caprices of duration of seasonal low temperature, there is no well-defined period of dormancy. The period of hibernation may often be related to latitudinal positions as evidenced by the turtle family Emydae. Species that inhabit the northern climes will hibernate longer than their southern relatives, thus showing hibernation periods which are proportional to the length of the winter period. Hibernating reptiles show a loss of appetite and discontinue the ingestion of food. Although the metabolic rate is reduced as much as 95% in hibernating turtles, there is some utilization of stored food products. There are two principal types of reserve food: lipids and glycogen, the animal starch, which is less stable and more rapidly used than fats. Glycogen is generally localized in tissues such as liver and muscle. There is evidence that these reserve foods are selectively utilized. In hibernating turtles, the tissue glycogen is used during the initial days and weeks of hibernation; later, the lipids are utilized.

A major hazard to hibernating poikilotherms is death from freezing; ice crystals form in free protoplasmic water and ultimately destroy the cells and tissues, causing the death of the animal. Frogs, salamanders, and turtles are able to survive, despite the reduction in body temperatures to about 32 to 31°F (0 to −1°C). As winter approaches, the water content of the tissues becomes reduced and the blood more concentrated.

Hibernation in fishes does not occur. Many fishes do, however, spend much of the winter in a state of quiescence while partially frozen in mud and ice.

The phenomenon of estivation is best known in the dipnoans, that is, the lungfishes. These fishes are restricted to tropical regions marked by repeated seasons of drought. They survive the dry seasons by becoming dormant and torpid. The lungfishes are among the more primitive air-breathing animals possessing a lung which utilizes atmospheric oxygen. This lung becomes the primary organ of respiration during the torpidity of estivation. In general, the lungfishes follow a similar behavioral pattern as the dry seasons approach. *Protopterus*, for example, burrows in the bottom mud as the water begins to diminish during the dry season. A lifeline of air is provided by the tunnel from the burrow to the surface. In preparation for estivation, *Protopterus* secretes a slimy mucus around itself which hardens in a tight cocoonlike chamber, preventing the desiccation of the fish. There is but one opening, formed around the mouth. Thus the air from the tunnel enters the mouth and passes to the lung apparatus. At the termination of the dry season, water slowly enters the burrow, softens the contents, and awakens the lungfish. The metabolism of the lungfish is at a low ebb during estivation, with the energy for its modest life processes provided by the utilization of tissue protein.

In some snails estivation may be extended for years at a time, and among the insects and spiders the period of hibernation becomes intimately associated with a phase in the life cycle. During the winter months and during a hot dry summer, the soil contains a remarkable variety of torpid invertebrates, for example, earthworms, snails and slugs, nematodes, insects and spiders, grubs, larvae, and pupae of many insects, egg cases, and cocoons.

Insects overwinter, for the most part, in the egg or larval stage of metamorphosis. Hibernation frequently becomes integrated with the diapause, or arrested development, of the egg or larva which occurs during the winter. The familiar cocoon of the butterfly is the hibernaculum of the larva and pupa. *See also* INSECT PHYSIOLOGY.

The phenomenon of encystment is commonplace in the protozoa, or single-celled animals. Encystment is remarkably similar to estivation and hibernation, and an encysted protozoon is extremely quiescent and almost nonmetabolizing. *See* PROTOZOA.

The hibernacula of poikilotherm vertebrates and invertebrates are as varied as the animals themselves (see illustration). The minute cysts in protozoa, the cocoon and egg case of insects and spiders, the burrows and crevices of reptiles, and the dried mucous case of the lungfish, in all instances, protect the animal from evaporation or desiccation and freezing.   [X.J.M.]

Warm-blooded vertebrates. Many mammals and some birds spend at least part of the winter in hiding, but remain no more drowsy than in normal sleep. On the other hand, some mammals undergo a profound decrease in metabolic rate and physiological

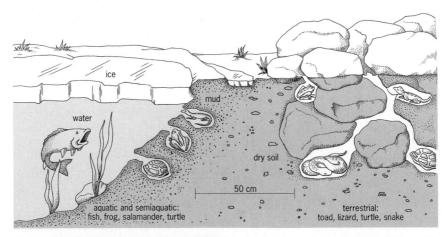

Hibernacula of various cold-blooded vertebrates.

function during the winter, with a body temperature near 32°F (0°C). This condition, sometimes known as deep hibernation, is the only state in which the warm-blooded vertebrate, with its complex mechanisms for temperature control, abandons its warm-blooded state and chills to the temperature of the environment. Between the drowsy condition and deep hibernation are gradations about which little is known. The bear, skunk, raccoon, and badger are animals which become drowsy in winter. Although usually considered the typical hibernator, the bear's body temperature does not drop more than a few degrees.

The deep hibernators are confined to five orders of mammals: the marsupials, the Chiroptera or bats, the insectivores, the rodents, and, probably, the primates. Most, if not all, of the insect-eating bats of temperate climates not only hibernate in the winter, but also drop their body temperature when they roost and sleep. The advantage of this for a small mammal with a disproportionately large heat-losing surface is obvious when conservation of energy is considered. Many rodents are deep hibernators, including ground squirrels, woodchucks, dormice, and hamster. The fat-tailed and mouse lemurs are primates that hibernate or estivate. Among birds, the poorwill (*Phalaenoptilus*) and some hummingbirds and swifts undergo a lowering of body temperature and metabolic rate in cold periods.

With all deep hibernators, except the bats, hibernation is seasonal, usually occurring during the cold winter months. In all cases, it occurs in animals which would face extremely difficult conditions if they had to remain active and search for food. During a preparation period for hibernation, the animals either become fat, like the woodchuck, or store food in their winter quarters, like the chipmunk and hamster. Prior to hibernation, there is a general involution of the endocrine glands, but at least part of this occurs soon after the breeding season and is not directly concerned with hibernation. Animals such as ground squirrels become more torpid during the fall, even when kept in a warm environment, indicating a profound metabolic change which may be controlled by the endocrine glands. In most hibernators lack of food has little if any effect, and the stimulus for hibernation is not known. It has been reported that an extract from the blood of an animal in hibernation will induce hibernation when infused into an active potential hibernator, indicating that the factor which produces hibernation may be bloodborne.

Hibernation in mammals is not caused by an inability to remain warm when exposed to cold, for hibernators are capable of very high metabolic rates and sometimes do not enter hibernation if exposed to cold for months at a time. When the animal is entering hibernation, heart rate and oxygen consumption decline before body temperature, indicating that the animal is actively damping its heat-generating mechanisms. The autonomic nervous system is involved in this process. As normal hibernation deepens, the heart rate, blood pressure, metabolic rate, and body temperature slowly drop, but in some animals periodic bouts of shivering and increased oxygen consumption occur, elevating the body temperature temporarily and causing a stepwise entrance into hibernation. *See* AUTONOMIC NERVOUS SYSTEM.

In deep hibernation at a steady state the body temperature is 33–35.5°F (0.5–2°C) above that of the environment, and it is a peculiarity of hibernators that the vital processes can function at lower temperatures than those of nonhibernators. The heart rate varies between 3 and 15 beats per minute. The metabolic rate is less than one-thirtieth of the warm-blooded rate at rest, and the main source of energy is fat. In spite of its low body temperature, the hibernating animal retains a remarkably rigid control of its internal environment. If the environmental temperature drops to 32°F (0°C), the hibernating animal may respond either by increasing its metabolic rate and remaining in hibernation or by a complete arousal from the hibernating state.

A hibernating mammal reduces its metabolic rate by nearly 30-fold and shifts from glycogen to lipid (that is, fat stores) as the major fuel source for metabolism. The magnitude of metabolic rate reduction is far in excess of what would be expected solely as a result of a hibernator's lowered body temperature. Moreover, suppression of glycogen metabolism during hibernation must be poised for regular and rapid relaxation during periods of arousal (which are fueled by glycolysis) as well as at the end of the hibernation period.

Mechanisms controlling these aspects of hibernation metabolism appear to be the relative acidification of the intracellular fluids of the hibernator. This is a consequence of the hibernator's tendency to continuously regulate its blood pH (at about pH 7.4, termed pH stat), and of the adoption of a modified breathing pattern that, although variable among species, is typified by periods of apnea lasting up to 2 h that are interspersed between 3–30 min intervals of rapid ventilation.   [J.B.G.]

The hibernator is capable of waking at any time, using self-generated heat, and this characteristic clearly separates the hibernating state from any condition of induced hypothermia. During the total period of hibernation, the hibernator spontaneously wakes from time to time, usually at least once a week. In the period of wakefulness the stored food is evidently eaten, but animals which do not store food rely on their fat for the extra energy during the whole winter. The cause of the periodic arousals has not been definitely determined, but it is theorized that the arousal is due to the effect of the accumulation of a metabolite or other substance which can be neutralized only in the warm-blooded state.   [C.P.L.]

As in hibernating endotherms (birds and mammals), a key factor regulating seasonal torpor in ectotherms is the continuous internal monitoring of environmental cues, such as day length, which in turn triggers temporally precise seasonally adaptive changes in systemic function, metabolism, and behavior. A second important factor is the presence in ectotherms of a bioenergetic metabolic system that, when compared to mammals and birds, operates at a much lower intensity and has less absolute dependence on molecular oxygen. The metabolic energy adaptations for seasonal torpor in ectothermic vertebrates are to a large extent similar to those required by vigorous activity or prolonged diving, and thus involve the processing or storage of intermediate metabolitics such as lactic acid, the regulation of intra- and extracellular pH, and enduring periods without access to oxygen. *See* ENERGY METABOLISM; METABOLISM.   [J.B.G.]

Hirudinea   A class of the annelid worms commonly known as leeches. These organisms are parasitic or predatory and have terminal suckers for attachment and locomotion. Most inhabit inland waters, but some are marine and a few live on land in damp places. The majority feed by sucking the blood of other animals, including humans.

Leeches differ from other annelids in having the number of segments in the body fixed at 34, chaetae or bristles lacking, and the coelomic space between the gut and the body wall filled with packing tissue (see illustration). In a typical leech the first six segments of the body are modified to form a head, bearing eyes, and a sucker, and the last seven segments are incorporated into a posterior sucker.

The mouth of a leech opens within the anterior sucker, and there are two main methods of piercing the skin of the host to obtain blood: an eversible proboscis or three jaws, each shaped like half a circular saw, placed just inside the mouth. The process of digestion is very slow, and a meal may last a leech for 9 months. The carnivorous forms have lost most or all of their gut diverticula and resemble earthworms in having

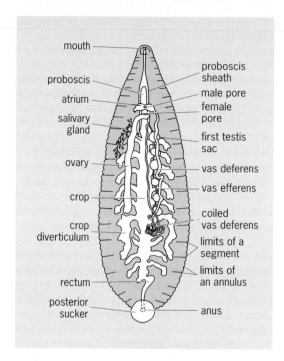

mouth

proboscis

atrium

salivary gland

ovary

crop

crop diverticulum

rectum

posterior sucker

proboscis sheath

male pore

female pore

first testis sac

vas deferens

vas efferens

coiled vas deferens

limits of a segment

limits of an annulus

anus

General structure of a leech. Male reproductive system Is shown on the right, the female on the left. (*After K. H. Mann, A key to the British freshwater leeches, Freshwater Blol. Ass. Scl. Publ., 14:3–21, 1954*)

a straight, tubular gut. Leeches are hermaphroditic, having a single pair of ovaries and several pairs of testes.

The importance of leeches as a means of making incisions for the letting of blood or the relief of inflammation is declining, and in developed countries the bloodsucking parasites of mammals are declining, because of lack of opportunity for contact with the hosts. In other countries they are still serious pests.   [K.H.M.]

Histamine   A biologically active amine that is formed by the decarboxylation of the amino acid histidine. It is widely distributed in nature and is found in plant and animal tissues as well as in insect venoms. In humans, histamine is a mediator of inflammatory reactions, and it functions as a stimulant of hydrochloric acid secretion in the stomach.

Most tissue histamine is found stored in mast cells, where it can be released by a variety of stimuli. Once released, it can cause many effects, including constriction of bronchiolar, gastrointestinal, uterine smooth muscle, and lowering of blood pressure. If histamine is released in the skin, itching, a flare (area of redness) due to vasodilation, and a wheal due to leaking of fluid into the tissue are observed. The increase in vascular permeability that permits this leakage is due to an action on the endothelial cells of postcapillary venules.

All of these actions of histamine are mediated by the activation of histamine receptors, designated either H-1 or H-2. Antihistamine drugs exert their effects by blocking the combination of histamine with these receptors. *See* ANTIHISTAMINE.

Histamine release can be caused by tissue injury, by physical stimuli such as cold or pressure, by drugs such as heroin, and most importantly by immunologic mechanisms.

Mast cells in the skin, the lung, the nasal passages, or other sites may become sensitized to antigens such as ragweed or other pollens, and then release histamine and other biologically active substances upon exposure to them. The released histamine may then cause the effects commonly associated with allergic responses. If the allergic reaction becomes generalized and severe, life-threatening anaphylactic shock may ensue. The prompt administration of epinephrine, which exerts effects opposite to those of histamine, can be life-saving in such cases. *See* ALLERGY; ANTIGEN; EPINEPHRINE; HYPERSENSITIVITY; IMMUNOLOGY.   [A.Bu.]

Histocompatibility   A term used to describe the genes that influence acceptance or rejection of grafts. When grafts of tissue are exchanged between genetically dissimilar individuals, profound immunological rejection generally takes place. In contrast, grafts between genetically similar individuals, such as identical twins, are normally tolerated; they are histocompatible. Most known examples of histocompatibility (or H) genes encode polymorphic (that is, tending to differ between individuals) cell-surface proteins.

The major histocompatibility complex (MHC) contains a set of histocompatibility genes, termed major because mismatching at these genes invokes rapid rejection. The main function of MHC genes involves distinguishing self from nonself in the immune system, as part of preventing the spread of infectious disease. The body employs special mechanisms to avoid rejection of the fetus, which is effectively an allograft, that is, a graft from a donor to a genetically dissimilar recipient of the same species; in this case, the mechanisms include a diminution of MHC gene expression.

The MHC contains a spectrum of genes, many of which influence processing and presentation of antigens to the immune system. In mice, the MHC is designated the H-2 complex; in humans, it is referred to as the HLA complex (for human leukocyte A system). Mice and other mammals seem to have a similar arrangement of genes in their MHCs. *See* ANTIGEN; CELLULAR IMMUNOLOGY; MENDELISM; TRANSPLANTATION BIOLOGY.
                                                                        [J.Tr.]

Histology   The study of the structure and chemical composition of tissues of animals and plants as related to their function. The primary aim is to understand how tissues are organized at all structural levels, including the molecular and macromolecular, the entire cell and intercellular substances, and the tissues and organs.

The four tissues of the animal body include cells and intercellular substances. They are (1) epithelium, in which the cells are generally closely applied to each other and separated by very little intercellular substance; (2) connective tissue, in which the cells are usually separated by greater amounts of intercellular substance, which may indeed form the great bulk of the tissue; (3) muscular tissue, whose cells are primarily concerned with contractility; and (4) nervous tissue, whose components are concerned primarily with rapid conduction of impulses. *See* CONNECTIVE TISSUE; EPITHELIUM; MUSCULAR SYSTEM; NERVOUS SYSTEM (VERTEBRATE).

The major fields of histological studies are morphological descriptions; developmental studies; histo- and cytophysiology; histo- and cytochemistry; and (5) fine (or submicroscopic) structure.   [I.G.]

Historadiography   The technique for taking x-ray pictures of cells, tissues, or sometimes the whole animal or plant, if it is a small one. Soft x-rays, those with low penetrating power and relatively long wavelengths, are required for this type of picture. The best pictures are obtained when the tissues contain deposits of metallic elements which have a high absorption capacity for x-rays.

In applying the technique to tissues, a relatively thin section is placed against an x-ray film and irradiated with a beam of x-rays. When the film is developed, a picture of the object or section of tissue shows on the film. Another method attempts to focus the x-rays after they pass through the specimen.   [J.H.T.]

Homeosis   The formation of a normal plant or animal body structure or organ in place of another at an abnormal site. Examples of homeosis (also called homeotic transformation) are most obvious in insect appendages, where an appendage that is characteristic of one segment, for example the antennae on an insect head segment, are transformed into insect legs that normally develop only on trunk segments. Similar examples of homeotic transformations can also occasionally be found in vertebrates where lumbar vertebrae are transformed into thoracic vertebrae which then extend into rib processes, or in floral organs where petals are transformed into sepals. Homeotic transformations rarely occur in nature in living organisms, and are due to genetic defects in a class of proteins called homeotic proteins, the products of homeotic genes. Homeotic transformations may also be induced in the laboratory by the accidental or deliberate manipulation of homeotic gene expression so that homeotic proteins are produced in the wrong place or at the wrong time in developing plants and animals. *See* CELL DIFFERENTIATION; DEVELOPMENTAL BIOLOGY; DEVELOPMENTAL GENETICS; GENE ACTION; MUTATION.   [W.McG.]

Homeostasis   The relatively constant conditions within organisms, or the physiological processes by which such conditions are maintained in the face of external variation.

Similar homeostatic controls are used to keep factors such as temperature and blood pressure nearly constant despite changes in an organism's activity level or surroundings. Such systems operate by detecting changes in the variable that the system is designed to hold constant and initiating some action that offsets any change. All incorporate a sensor within the system that responds when the actual condition differs from the desired one, a device to ensure that any action taken will reduce the difference between actual and desired, and an effector to take the needed action as directed. The crucial aspect is that information is fed back from effector to sensor and action is taken to reduce any imbalance—hence the term negative feedback.

Blood pressure is, at least on a moment-to-moment basis, regulated by a system for which the sensors are stretch-sensitive cells located in the neck arteries that carry blood from heart to brain. An increase in blood pressure triggers sensor activity; their signal passes to the brain; and, in turn, the nerve supplying the heart (the vagus) is stimulated to release a chemical (acetylcholine) that causes the heart to beat more slowly—which decreases blood pressure.

The volume of the blood is subject to similar regulation. Fluid (mainly plasma) moves between the capillaries and the intercellular fluid in response to changes in pressure in the capillaries. A decrease in blood volume is detected by sensors at the base of the brain; the brain stimulates secretion of substances that cause contraction of tiny muscles surrounding the blood vessels that lead into the capillaries. The resulting arteriolar constriction reduces the flow of blood to, and the pressure within, the capillaries, so fluid moves from intercellular space into capillaries, thus restoring overall blood volume.

Body temperature in mammals is regulated by a sensor that consists of cells within the hypothalamus of the brain. Several effectors are involved, which vary among animals. These include increasing heat production through nonspecific muscle activity such as shivering; increasing heat loss through sweating, panting, and opening more blood vessels in the skin (vasodilation); and decreasing heat loss through thickening of fur (piloerection) and curling up. Humans sweat, but they retain only a vestige of piloerection ("goose flesh"). *See* THERMOREGULATION.

While the homeostatic mechanisms described involve the neural and endocrine systems of mammals, it is clear that such arrangements pervade systems from genes to biological communities, and that they are used by the simplest and the most complex organisms.

Organisms of every kind develop, mature, and even shift physiological states periodically—between day and night, with seasons, or as internal rhythms. Thus organisms cannot be considered constant except over short periods. However, all such changes appear to involve the same basic sensing of the results of the past activity of the system and the adjusting of future activity in response to that information. Development of an organism from a fertilized egg is far from a direct implementation of a genetic program; probably no program could anticipate all the variation in the external context in which an organism must somehow successfully develop. *See* BIOLOGICAL CLOCKS; NERVOUS SYSTEM (VERTEBRATE).   [S.V.]

Hormone   One of the chemical messengers produced by endocrine glands, whose secretions are liberated directly into the bloodstream and transported to a distant part or parts of the body, where they exert a specific effect for the benefit of the body as a whole. The endocrine glands involved in the maintenance of normal body conditions are pituitary, thyroid, parathyroid, adrenal, pancreas, ovary, and testis. However, these organs are not the only tissues concerned in the hormonal regulation of body processes. For example, the duodenal mucosa, which is not organized as an endocrine gland, elaborates a substance called secretin which stimulates the pancreas to produce its digestive juices. The placenta is also a very important hormone-producing tissue. See separate articles on the individual glands.

The hormones obtained from extracts of the endocrine glands may be classified into four groups according to their chemical constitution: (1) phenol derivatives, such as epinephrine, norepinephrine, thyroxine, and triiodothyronine; (2) proteins, such as the anterior pituitary hormones, with the exception of adrenocorticotropic hormone (ACTH), human chorionic gonadotropin, pregnant-mare-serum gonadotropin, and thyroglobulin; (3) peptides, such as insulin, glucagon, ACTH, vasopressin, oxytocin, and secretin; and (4) steroids, such as estrogens, androgens, progesterone, and corticoids. Hormones, with a few exceptions like pituitary growth hormone and insulin, may also be classified as either tropic hormones or target-organ hormones. The former work indirectly through the organs or glands which they stimulate, whereas the latter exert a direct effect on peripheral tissues. *See* ENDOCRINE SYSTEM (VERTEBRATE).   [C.H.L.]

Human ecology   The study of how the distributions and numbers of humans are determined by interactions with conspecific individuals, with members of other species, and with the abiotic environment. Human ecology encompasses both the responses of humans to, and the effects of humans on, the environment. Human ecology today is the combined result of humans' evolutionary nature and cultural developments. *See* ECOLOGICAL COMMUNITIES; ECOSYSTEM.

Humans' strong positive and negative emotional responses to components of the environment evolved because our ancestors' responses to environmental information affected survival and reproductive success. Early humans needed to interpret signals from other organisms and the abiotic environment, and they needed to evaluate and select habitats and the resources there. These choices were emotionally driven. For example, food is one of the most important resources provided by the environment. Gathering food requires decisions of where to forage and what items to select. Anthropologists often use the theory of optimal foraging to interpret how these decisions are made. The theory postulates that as long as foragers have other valuable ways to spend their time or there are risks associated with seeking food, efficient foraging will be favored even when food is not scarce. This approach has facilitated development of simple foraging models and more elaborate models of food sharing and gender division of labor, symbolic communication, long-term subsistence change, and cross-cultural variation in subsistence practices.

Significant modification of the environment by people was initiated by the domestication of fire, used to change vegetation structure and influence populations of food plants and animals. Vegetation burning is still common in the world, particularly in tropic regions. The arrival of humans with sophisticated tools precipitated the next major transformation of Earth, the extinction of large vertebrates. Agriculture drove the third major human modification of environments. Today about 35–40% of terrestrial primary production is appropriated by people, and the percentage is rising.

Humans will continue to exert powerful influences on the functioning of the Earth's ecological systems. The human population is destined to increase for many years. Rising affluence will be accompanied by increased consumption of resources and, hence, greater appropriation of the Earth's primary production. Nevertheless, many future human ecology scenarios are possible, depending on how much the human population grows and how growth is accommodated, the efficiency with which humans use and recycle resources, and the value that people give to preservation of biodiversity. *See* ECOLOGY; ENVIRONMENT.   [G.H.O.]

Human genetics   A discipline concerned with genetically determined resemblances and differences among human beings. Technological advances in the visualization of human chromosomes have shown that abnormalities of chromosome number or structure are surprisingly common and of many different kinds, and that they account for birth defects or mental impairment in many individuals as well as for numerous early spontaneous abortions. Progress in molecular biology has clarified the molecular structure of chromosomes and their constituent genes and the ways in which change in the molecular structure of a gene can lead to a disease. Concern about possible genetic damage through environmental agents and the possible harmful effects of hazardous substances in the environment on prenatal development has also stimulated research in human genetics. The medical aspects of human genetics have become prominent as nonhereditary causes of ill health or early death, such as infectious disease or nutritional deficiency, have declined, at least in developed countries.

In normal humans, the nucleus of each normal cell contains 46 chromosomes, which comprise 23 different pairs. Of each chromosome pair, one is paternal and the other maternal in origin. In turn, only one member of each pair is handed on through the reproductive cell (egg or sperm) to each child. Thus, each egg or sperm has only 23 chromosomes, the haploid number; fusion of egg and sperm at fertilization will restore the double, or diploid, chromosome number of 46. *See* CHROMOSOME; FERTILIZATION.

The segregation of chromosome pairs during meiosis allows for a large amount of "shuffling" of genetic material as it is passed down the generation. Two parents can provide $2^{23} \times 2^{23}$ different chromosome combinations. This enormous source of variation is multiplied still further by the mechanism of crossing over, in which homologous chromosomes exchange segments during meiosis. *See* CROSSING-OVER (GENETICS); MEIOSIS.

Twenty-two of the 23 chromosome pairs, the autosomes, are alike in both sexes; the other pair comprises the sex chromosomes. A female has a pair of X chromosomes; a male has a single X, paired with a Y chromosome which he has inherited from his father and will transmit to each of his sons. Sex is determined at fertilization, and depends on whether the egg (which has a single X chromosome) is fertilized by an X-bearing or a Y-bearing sperm. *See* SEX DETERMINATION.

Any gene occupies a specific chromosomal position, or locus. The alternative genes at a particular locus are said to be alleles. If a pair of alleles are identical, the individual is homozygous; if they are different, the individual is heterozygous. *See* ALLELE.

Genetic variation has its origin in mutation. The term is usually applied to stable changes in DNA that alter the genetic code and thus lead to synthesis of an altered protein. The genetically significant mutations occur in reproductive cells and can therefore be transmitted to future generations. Natural selection acts upon the genetic diversity generated by mutation to preserve beneficial mutations and eliminate deleterious ones.

A very large amount of genetic variation exists in the human population. Everyone carries many mutations, some newly acquired but others inherited through innumerable generations. Though the exact number is unknown, it is likely that everyone is heterozygous at numerous loci, perhaps as many as 20%. *See* MUTATION.

The patterns of inheritance of characteristics determined by single genes or gene pairs depend on two conditions: (1) whether the gene concerned is on an autosome (autosomal) or on the X chromosome (X-linked); (2) whether the gene is dominant, that is, expressed in heterozygotes (when it is present on only one member of a chromosomal pair and has a normal allele) or is recessive (expressed only in homozygotes, when it is present at both chromosomes). *See* DOMINANCE.   [M.W.T.]

A quantitative trait is one that is under the control of many factors, both genetic and environmental, each of which contributes only a small amount to the total variability of the trait. The phenotype may show continuous variation (for example, height and skin color), quasicontinuous variation (taking only integer values—such as the number of ridges in a fingerprint), or it may be discontinuous (a presence/absence trait, such as diabetes or mental retardation). With discontinuous traits, it is assumed that there exists an underlying continuous variable and that individuals having a value of this variable above (or below) a threshold possess the trait.

A trait that "runs in families" is said to be familial. However, not all familial traits are hereditary because relatives tend to share common environments as well as common genes.

The variability of almost any trait is partly genetic and partly environmental. A rough measure of the relative importance of heredity and environment is an index called heritability. For example, in humans, the heritability of height is about 0.75. That is, about 75% of the total variance in height is due to variability in genes that affect height and 25% is due to exposure to different environments.   [C.De.]

Hereditary diseases. Medical genetics has become an integral part of preventive medicine (that is, genetic counseling, including prenatal diagnostics). Hereditary diseases may be subdivided into three classes: chromosomal diseases; hereditary diseases with simple, mendelian modes of inheritance; and multifactorial diseases.

One out of 200 newborns suffers from an abnormality that is caused by a microscopically visible deviation in the number or structure of chromosomes. The most important clinical abnormality is Down syndrome—a condition due to trisomy of chromosome 21, one of the smallest human chromosomes. This chromosome is present not twice but three times; the entire chromosome complement therefore comprises 47, not 46, chromosomes. Down syndrome occurs one to two times in every 1000 births; its pattern of abnormalities derives from an imbalance of gene action during embryonic development. Down syndrome is a good example of a characteristic pattern of abnormalities that is produced by a single genetic defect. *See* DOWN SYNDROME.

Other autosomal aberrations observed in living newborns that lead to characteristic syndromes include trisomies 13 and 18 (both very rare), and a variety of structural aberrations such as translocations (exchanges of chromosomal segments between different chromosomes) and deletions (losses of chromosome segments). Translocations normally have no influence on the health status of the individual if there is no gain or loss of chromosomal material (these are called balanced translocations). However, carriers of balanced translocations usually run a high risk of having children in whom the same translocation causes gain or loss of genetic material, and who suffer from a characteristic malformation syndrome.

Clinical syndromes caused by specific aberrations vary, but certain clinical signs are common: low birth weights (small for date); a peculiar face; delayed general, and especially mental, development, often leading to severe mental deficiency; and multiple malformations, including abnormal development of limbs, heart, and kidneys.

Less severe signs than those caused by autosomal aberrations are found in individuals with abnormalities in number (and, sometimes, structure) of sex chromosomes. This is because in individuals having more than one X chromosome, the additional X chromosomes are inactivated early in pregnancy. For example, in women, one of the two X chromosomes is always inactivated. Inactivation occurs at random so that every normal woman is a mosaic of cells in which either one or the other X chromosome is active. Additional X chromosomes that an individual may have received will also be inactivated; in trisomies, genetic imbalance is thus avoided to a certain degree. However, inactivation is not complete; therefore, individuals with trisomies—for example, XXY (Klinefelter syndrome), XXX (triple-X syndrome), or XYY—or monosomies (XO; Turner syndrome) often show abnormal sexual development, intelligence, or behavior.

In contrast to chromosomal aberrations, the genetic defects in hereditary diseases with simple, mendelian modes of inheritance cannot be recognized by microscopic examination; as a rule, they must be inferred more indirectly from the phenotype and the pattern of inheritance in pedigrees. The defects are found in the molecular structure of the DNA. Often, one base pair only is altered, although sometimes more complex molecular changes, such as deletions of some bases or abnormal recombination, are involved. Approximately 1% of all newborns have, or will develop during their lives, a hereditary disease showing a simple mendelian mode of inheritance.

In medical genetics, a condition is called dominant if the heterozygotes deviate in a clearly recognizable way from the normal homozygotes, in most cases by showing an abnormality. Since such dominant mutations are usually rare, almost no homozygotes are observed.

In some dominant conditions, the harmful phenotype may not be expressed in a gene carrier (this is called incomplete penetrance), or clinical signs may vary in severeness between carriers (called variable expressivity). Penetrance and expressivity may be influenced by other genetic factors; sometimes, for example, by the sex of the affected person, whereas in other instances, the constitution of the "normal" allele has been implicated. Environmental conditions may occasionally be important. In most cases, however, the reasons are unknown.

X-linked modes of inheritance occur when the mutant allele is located on the X chromosome. The most important X-linked mode of inheritance is the recessive one. Here, the males (referred to as hemizygotes since they have only one allele) are affected, since they have no normal allele. The female heterozygotes, on the other hand, will be unaffected, since the one normal allele is sufficient for maintaining function. A classical example is hemophilia A, in which one of the serum factors necessary for normal blood clotting is inactive or lacking. (The disease can now be controlled by repeated substitution of the deficient blood factor—a good example for phenotypic therapy of a hereditary disease by substitution of a deficient gene product.) Male family members are affected whereas their sisters and daughters, while being unaffected themselves, transmit the mutant gene to half their sons. Only in very rare instances, when a hemophilic patient marries a heterozygous carrier, are homozygous females observed. See SEX-LINKED INHERITANCE.

There are thousands of hereditary diseases with simple mendelian modes of inheritance, but most common anomalies and diseases are influenced by genetic variability at more than one gene locus. Most congenital malformations, such as congenital heart disease, cleft lip and palate, neural tube defects and many others, fall into this category, as do the constitutional diseases, such as diabetes mellitus, coronary heart disease, anomalies of the immune response and many mental diseases, such as schizophrenia or affective disorders. All of these conditions are common and often increase in frequency with advanced age. [F.V.]

Biochemical genetics. Biochemical genetics began with the study of inborn errors of metabolism. These are diseases of the body chemistry in which a small molecule such as a sugar or amino acid accumulates in body fluids because an enzyme responsible for its metabolic breakdown is deficient. This molecular defect is the result of mutation in the gene coding for the enzyme protein. The accumulated molecule, dependent on its nature, is responsible for the causation of a highly specific pattern of disease.

The field of biochemical genetics expanded with the recognition that similar heritable defective enzymes interfere with the breakdown of very large molecules, such as mucopolysaccharides and the complex lipids that are such prominent components of brain substance. The resultant storage disorders present with extreme alterations in morphology and bony structure and with neurodegenerative disease.

The majority of hereditary disorders of metabolism are inherited in an autosomal recessive fashion. In these families, each parent carries a single mutant gene on one chromosome and a normal gene on the other. Most of these mutations are rare. In populations with genetic diversity, most affected individuals carry two different mutations in the same gene. Some metabolic diseases are coded for by genes on the X chromosome. Most of these disorders are fully recessive, and so affected individuals are all males, while females carrying the gene are clinically normal. The disorders that result from mutations in the mitochondrial genome are inherited in nonmendelian fashion because mitochondrial DNA is inherited only from the mother. Those that carry a mutation are heteroplasmic; that is, each carries a mixed population of mitochondria, some with the mutation and some without.

Phenylketonuria (PKU) is a prototypic biochemical genetic disorder. It is an autosomally recessive disorder in which mutations demonstrated in a sizable number of families lead, when present in the genes on both chromosomes, to defective activity of the enzyme that catalyzes the first step in the metabolism of phenylalanine. This results in accumulation of phenylalanine and a recognizable clinical disease whose most prominent feature is severe retardation of mental development.

The diseases that result from mutation in mitochondrial DNA have been recognized as such only since the 1990s. They result from point mutations, deletions, and other rearrangements. A majority of these disorders express themselves chemically in elevated concentrations of lactic acid in the blood or cerebrospinal fluid. Many of the disorders are known as mitochondrial myopathies (diseases of muscles) because skeletal myopathy or cardiomyopathy are characteristic features. [W.L.Ny.]

Human Genome Project   An organized international scientific endeavor to determine the complete structure of the human genetic material deoxyribonucleic acid (DNA) and understand its function. *See* HUMAN GENETICS.

History. The idea for the Human Genome Project (HGP) first arose in the mid-1980s. Several scientific groups met to discuss the feasibility, and various reports were published. The most influential report was prepared by the National Research Council (NRC) of the U.S. National Academy of Sciences. It proposed a detailed scientific strategy that persuaded many scientists that the project was possible. October 1, 1990, was declared the official start time for the HGP in the United States; significant funding had become available and research groups were starting their work. Major contributions to the HGP have been made by the United Kingdom, France, Japan, and Germany, with smaller contributions from many other quarters. Coordination among the countries has been informal, relying largely on scientist-to-scientist collaborations, but has proved to be very effective.

Scientific strategy. First, markers are placed on the chromosomes by genetic mapping, that is, observing how the markers are inherited in families. Second, a physical map is created from overlapping cloned pieces of the DNA. Third, the sequence of each piece is determined, and the sequences are lined up by computer until a continuous sequence along the whole chromosome is obtained. The second and third steps can be reversed or done in parallel. As the pieces are sequenced, the sequences at the overlapping ends can be used to help order the pieces. If the sequencing is done before the pieces are mapped, the process is called whole-genome shotgun sequencing. *See* DEOXYRIBONUCLEIC ACID (DNA); GENE.

Because the human genome is so big (human DNA consists of about 3 billion nucleotides connected end to end in a linear array), it was necessary to break the task down into manageable chunks (see illustration).

Model organisms. An important element of the overall strategy was to include the study of model organisms in the HGP. There were two reasons for this: (1) Simpler

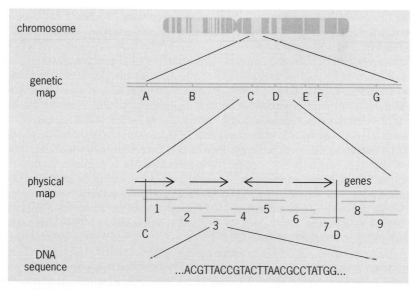

Steps in analyzing a genome.

organisms provide good practice material. (2) Comparisons between model organisms and humans yield very valuable scientific information. The HGP initially adopted five model organisms to have their DNA sequenced: the bacterium *Escherichia coli*, the yeast *Saccharomyces cerevisiae*, the roundworm *Caenorhabditis elegans*, the fruitfly *Drosophila melanogaster*, and the laboratory mouse *Mus musculus*. The mouse genome is just as complex as the human genome, but the mouse offers the advantages that it can be bred and other experiments can be conducted that are not possible on humans.

Findings. How many genes are there is probably the most common question regarding the human genome. The first two human chromosomes to be sequenced, chromosomes 22 and 21, provided some interesting observations. Although the two chromosomes are approximately the same length, chromosome 22 has more than twice as many genes as chromosome 21. Extrapolation of the number of genes found on chromosomes 22 and 21 led to the estimate that the whole human genome contains about 36,000 genes. This is quite a surprise because previous estimates were 80,000 to 100,000 genes. Preliminary examination of the draft sequence of the entire human genome confirmed that the number of genes is much lower than previously thought. This does not necessarily mean that the human genome is less complex, because many genes can produce more than one protein by alternate splicing of their exons (protein-encoding regions of the gene) during translation into the constituents of proteins. *See* CHROMOSOME; GENETIC CODE.

Another fascinating feature of the human genome sequence is the large fraction that consists of repeated sequence elements; 40% of chromosome 21 and 42% of chromosome 22 are composed of repeats. The function of any of these repeats is not yet known, but elucidating their distribution in the genome may help to reveal it.

Another statistic that is of interest is the base composition, the percent of the DNA that is made of guanine-cytosine (GC) base pairs as opposed to adenine-thymine (AT) base pairs. Chromosome 22 has a 48% GC content, whereas chromosome 21 has 41% and the average over the genome is 42%. Again, the significance of this is not yet known, but higher GC content seems to correlate with higher gene density.

The type of analysis performed initially on chromosomes 21 and 22 has been extended to the entire human sequence. However, a full understanding will take decades to achieve.

Future research. With the complete sets of genes of organisms available, how genes are turned on and off and how genes interact with each other can be studied. What the different genes do and how they affect human health must also be learned. Consequently, much effort is now directed to studying the regulation of gene expression and annotating the sequence with useful biological information about function.

Another key challenge is to understand how DNA function varies with differences in the DNA sequence. Each human being has a unique DNA sequence which differs from that of any other human being by about 0.1%, regardless of ethnic origin. Yet this small difference affects characteristics such as how humans look and to what diseases they are susceptible. The differences also provide clues about the evolution of the human species and the historical migration patterns of people across the world. *See* MOLECULAR BIOLOGY; NUCLEIC ACID.   [F.Co.; E.Jor.]

Hunger   A term most commonly used to refer to the subjective feelings that accompany the need for food; however, the study of this topic has come to include consideration of the overall control of food intake. More specifically, experimental work on the problem of hunger has been concerned with the sensory cues that give rise to feelings of hunger, the physiological mechanisms that determine when and how much food will be ingested, and the mechanism governing the selection of the food to be eaten.

Food consumption is basically controlled by the organism's nutritional status. Food deprivation leads to eating, and the ingestion of food materials terminates hunger sensations. The issues are to determine which physiological processes vary quantitatively with nutritional status, and to find out if these changes can be detected by the nervous system in a manner that would instigate and terminate food consumption.

Blood-sugar level, which has received more attention than any other factor, can be used as a case in point. The concentration of blood sugar does indeed vary appropriately in a general way with the periodicity of the food cycle. Detailed analyses of normal life variations of blood sugar, however, reveal that the relation between the concentration of blood sugar and hunger is not sufficiently close for this single humoral factor to be able to control hunger in any simple and direct manner. The evaluation of more local tissue utilization of food has proved a more promising approach to this problem. There is now some evidence suggesting that the status of the liver is pivotal in the control of feeding. Depletion of liver glycogen stimulates feeding; its repletion terminates feeding in rats and rabbits. *See* CARBOHYDRATE METABOLISM; LIVER.

Many stimuli that terminate feeding have been identified. Eating in food-deprived animals is inhibited by the reduction of either cellular water or of plasma fluid. It is also reduced by gastric distension and by infusing nutrients into the intestine and into the systemic, especially venous hepatic, circulation. Satiation produced by nutrient absorption from the intestine may be mediated, in part, by the gut hormone cholecystokinin. It is likely that cholecystokinin is effective because it reduces the rate at which food passes through the stomach. The previously held notions of discrete neural centers for the onset and termination of feeding have been abandoned, as the complexity of the feeding act and its corresponding neural complexity have become more widely appreciated.

Deprivation of certain, specific food substances precipitates an increased appetite for the needed substance. This so-called specific hunger behavior has been demonstrated experimentally with many substances, such as salt, calcium, fats, proteins, and certain vitamins in children and in the lower animals studied. It is now clear that only the hunger for salt in salt-deprived animals appears before the animal has learned about the beneficial consequences of salt ingestion. Specific hungers for other minerals, proteins, and vitamins appear only gradually and reflect the animal's learning that certain foods are no longer beneficial and, in fact, may be harmful. *See* THIRST AND SODIUM APPETITE.

[E.M.B.]

Hyaluronic acid　A polysaccharide which is an integral part of the gel-like substance of animal connective tissue; it supposedly serves as a lubricant and shock absorbent in the joints. Hyaluronic acid has also been isolated from umbilical cord, synovial fluid, skin, certain fowl tumors, and other sources. Treatment of this polysaccharide with the enzyme hyaluronidase, followed by acid hydrolysis, yields a disaccharide consisting of N-acetyl-D-glucosamine and D-glucuronic acid. This disaccharide appears to be the basic repeating structural unit that constitutes the hyaluronic acid molecule. *See* HYALURONIDASE; POLYSACCHARIDE.

[W.Z.H.]

Hyaluronidase　Any one of a family of enzymes, also known as hyaluronate lyases or spreading factors, produced by mammals, reptiles, insects, and bacteria, which catalyze the breakdown of hyaluronic acid. Some hyaluronidases also attack other similar polysaccharides. Since all liquefy the polysaccharide gel which fills the tissue spaces, they effectively accelerate diffusion so that injected, dissolved, or particulate matter (bacteria, viruses, toxins, or pigments) can diffuse through a larger volume of tissue. *See* HYALURONIC ACID.

The biological importance of the enzyme depends upon its source. That found in the culture filtrates of many strains of virulent bacteria permits the microorganisms to gain access to a larger volume of the host's tissue and, hence, to additional nutriment. That found in the venom of certain snakes and bees permits the toxin to produce more extensive damage to the victim. *See* ENZYME.   [R.H.P.]

Hydrothermal vent   A hot spring on the ocean floor, where heated fluids exit from cracks in the Earth's crust. Most hydrothermal vents occur along the central axes of mid-oceanic ridges, which are underwater mountain ranges that wind through all of the deep oceans. The best-studied vents are at tectonic spreading centers on the East Pacific Rise and at the Mid-Atlantic Ridge. However, vents are also found over hot spots such as the Hawaiian Islands and Iceland, in back-arc basins such as those in the western Pacific, in shallow geothermal systems such as those off the Kamchatka Peninsula, and on the flanks of some underwater volcanoes and seamounts. Hydrothermal vent sites, or closely grouped clusters of vent deposits and exit ports, may cover areas from hundreds to thousands of square feet (tens to hundreds of square meters). Individual vent sites may be separated along mid-ocean ridges by more than 1000 mi (1600 km).

All of the hydrothermal vent sites occur in areas where quantities of magma exist below the sea floor. Cold seawater is drawn down into the oceanic crust toward the heat source. As the seawater is heated and reacts with surrounding rock, its composition changes. Sulfate and magnesium are major components of seawater lost during the reactions; sulfide, metals, and gases such as helium and methane are major components gained. This modified seawater is known as hydrothermal fluid. Buoyant, hot hydrothermal fluid rises toward the sea floor in a concentrated zone of upflow to exit from the sea floor at temperatures ranging from 50°F (10°C) to greater than 750°F (400°C), depending on the degree of cooling and of mixing with seawater during the ascent. If the sea floor is shallow enough and the fluid hot enough, the solution may boil; but it usually does not because of the pressure of overlying seawater.

Hydrothermal fluid that mixes extensively with seawater below the sea floor surface may reach the sea floor as warm springs, with temperatures of 50–86°F (10–30°C). This outflow is usually detectable as cloudy or milky water, but the flow is slow and no mineral deposits accumulate except for some hydrothermal staining or oxidation of sea floor basalts. When hotter, relatively undiluted hydrothermal fluid reaches the sea floor, it is still buoyant with respect to seawater, so that the hot solution rises out of cracks in the sea floor at velocities up to about 6 ft (2 m) per second, mixing turbulently with seawater as it rises. Mixing of hydrothermal fluid with seawater leads to precipitation of minerals from solution, forming mineral deposits at the exit from the sea floor and so-called smoke, tiny mineral particles suspended in the rising plume of fluid. Black smoker vents are distinguished by the presence of such large quantities of minute mineral particles that the plumes become virtually opaque.

Perhaps the most striking feature of sea-floor hydrothermal vents is their dense biologic communities. Vent faunas tend to be dominated by mollusks, annelids, and crustaceans, whereas faunas on nonvent hard-bottom habitats consist predominantly of cnidarians, sponges, and echinoderms. Biologically, vents are among the most productive ecosystems on Earth. Sulfide from hydrothermal fluids provides the energy to drive these productive systems. Whereas most animal life depends on food of photosynthetic origin (inorganic carbon converted to useful sugars by plants using energy from the Sun), the animals at hydrothermal vents obtain most or all of their food by a process of chemosynthesis. Chemosynthesis is accomplished by specialized bacteria residing in hydrothermal fluids, in mats on the sea floor, or in symbiotic relationships with other organisms. The bacteria convert inorganic carbon to sugars by mediating the oxidation of hydrogen sulfide, thereby exploiting the energy stored in chemical bonds. A few vent animals are also known to use methane gas as a source of energy and carbon. The physical and chemical conditions at hydrothermal vents would be lethal to most marine animals, but vent species have adapted to the conditions there.

In a remarkable discovery, it was shown that chemosynthetic microbes known as Archaea are flushed from cavities deep within the Earth's crust by hydrothermal and volcanic activity. These microbes are hyperthermophilic (hot-water-loving) and thrive at temperatures exceeding 90°C (194°F). It is now suspected that an entire community of such microbes inhabits the rocks deep within the water-saturated portions of the Earth's crust. [M.Go.]

Hydrozoa   A class of the phylum Coelenterata which includes the fresh-water hydras, the marine hydroids, many of the smaller jellyfish, a few special corals, and the Portuguese man-of-war. The Hydrozoa may be divided into six orders: the Hydroida, Milleporina, Stylasterina, Trachylina, Siphonophora, and Spongiomorphida. See separate article on each order.

The form of the body varies greatly among the hydrozoans. This diversity is due in part to the existence of two body types, the polyp and the medusa. A specimen may be a polyp, a medusa, a colony of polyps, or even a composite of the first two. Polyps are somewhat cylindrical, attached at one end, and have a mouth surrounded by tentacles at the free end. Medusae are free-swimming jellyfish with tentacles around the margin of the discoidal body.

In a representative life cycle, the fertilized egg develops into a swimming larva which soon attaches itself and transforms into a polyp. The polyp develops stolons (which fasten to substrates), stems, and other polyps to make up a colony of interconnected polyps. Medusae are produced by budding and liberated to feed, grow, and produce eggs and sperm.

Most hydrozoans are carnivorous and capture animals which come in contact with their tentacles. The prey is immobilized by poison injected by stinging capsules, the nematocysts. Most animals of appropriate size can be captured, but small crustaceans are probably the most common food. See COELENTERATA. [S.C.]

Hypersensitivity   Heightened reactivity to antigens (molecules capable of stimulating an immune response). Many different examples of hypersensitivity have been recognized in animals and humans. These are often referred to collectively as allergies, and clinically may take such forms as asthma, hives, hay fever, anaphylactic reactions to certain foods or insect venoms, some forms of eczema and kidney diseases, and skin reactions to poison ivy antigens and many other substances. See ANTIGEN.

Because molecules foreign to the body are often antigenic, the various forms of hypersensitivity are most commonly induced either by exposure to foreign antigens derived from microorganisms during infections, or by contact with certain noninfectious agents (some plant pollens, some drugs, and certain simple chemicals such as components of poison ivy). However, under certain circumstances, molecules of the body itself can induce an immune response. In these cases, hypersensitivity reactions can be directed against antigens of the body's own organs or tissues. Whether foreign or derived from the body itself, antigenic substances often produce little or no tissue reaction in unsensitized individuals. But once hypersensitivity develops, additional exposure to antigen can give rise to clinically obvious symptoms (hives, sneezing, runny nose), tissue damage, or even (in certain extreme cases) death. *See* AUTOIMMUNITY.

The development of hypersensitivity in animals or humans may be divided into two phases. During the first phase, induction of hypersensitivity, exposure of the organism to antigen results in (1) recognition of the antigen by cells of the immune system; (2) proliferation (multiplication) of the types of immune cells that recognize and respond to that antigen; and (3) long-term storage of the information required to recognize and respond to the antigen in immune "memory" cells. Although a variety of cell types assist in these processes, all of the three functions are primarily dependent on various types of lymphocytes.

Once the state of hypersensitivity has been induced, reexposure of the organism to the antigen that induced the response usually leads to the second phase, expression of a hypersensitivity reaction. Hypersensitivity reactions historically have been classified according to two characteristics: the delay between the exposure of a previously sensitized (hypersensitive) individual to antigen and the development of a clinically recognizable reaction; and the types of cells and humoral substances thought to be responsible for the induction and expression of the reaction. According to this scheme, classical delayed hypersensitivity reactions differ from other forms of hypersensitivity in first becoming clinically prominent in sensitized individuals approximately 1 day after exposure to the specific antigen against which the individual expresses hypersensitivity; and depending for their expression on the activity of certain lymphocytes (thymic-dependent lymphocytes, or T cells) rather than soluble antibodies. By contrast, immediate hypersensitivity reactions may develop within seconds or minutes of exposure to specific antigen, and require the participation of antibodies. *See* ANTIBODY.

In addition to its association with certain infections, delayed hypersensitivity has been implicated in a variety of noninfectious disease processes. These include the annoying reactions induced in some individuals by contact with certain plants (for example, poison ivy), detergents, or drugs, as well as certain of the immune responses resulting in the rejection of transplanted tissues such as skin, kidneys, and hearts. In many of these processes, the immunological reactions are thought largely to reflect the activity of T lymphocytes (as in classical delayed hypersensitivity), whereas in others soluble antibodies may also have a role. *See* CELLULAR IMMUNOLOGY; TRANSPLANTATION BIOLOGY. [S.J.Ga.]

Immediate hypersensitivity reactions, collectively known as allergies, occur usually within minutes or up to a few hours after inhalation, ingestion, or injection of an antigen. Such reactions may be severe, even life-threatening, such as anaphylactic shock and asthma, or relatively minor but uncomfortable, such as hay fever or urticaria (hives). They may be of short duration—hours for anaphylaxis—or prolonged for several days or even weeks, as in immune complex-induced vasculitis. *See* ALLERGY.

Hypersensitivities have been classified into four main types with different mechanisms: type I, anaphylaxis or atopy; type II, cytotoxic or cytolytic; type III, immune complex or Arthus reaction; and type IV, delayed or cellular-immune; the last type has been described above.

In type I the antigen is recognized immunologically upon first exposure and initiates antibody formation, usually of immunoglobulin E (IgE) or IgG class. IgE-mediated allergy, known as atopy, has a strong hereditary component, and occurs commonly in humans and dogs, while IgG-mediated anaphylaxis can occur in most vertebrates. The antibodies (IgE or IgG) attach or fix to target cells, such as tissue mast cells and blood basophils. Upon subsequent exposure to the antigen, the target cell–fixed antibodies react with antigen to cause degranulation and release of chemical mediators, such as histamine. *See* HISTAMINE; IMMUNOGLOBULIN.

In cytotoxic or cytolytic (type II) reactions, the antigen may be certain altered body cells themselves; they may be altered physically or by chemicals and drugs attached to the cells. These are usually circulating cells, such as red blood cells coated with penicillin, platelets coated with a drug, or white blood cells coated with sulfonamides. Altered cells are recognized by the body's immune system as foreign or altered self, and IgG or IgM antibodies are formed which react with the altered cells and activate the serum complement enzymatic cascade that culminates in the lysis of the altered cells. Thus, cytotoxic hypersensitivity leads to anemia, bleeding due to low platelet levels, and increased infections from loss of white blood cells (agranulocytosis).

In immune complex or Arthus (Type III) reaction, neither antibody nor antigen is fixed to cells. Rather, they combine in various ratios in blood and tissues. If they are in the proper ratio, they form microprecipitates, or immune complexes, in capillaries and venules. The immune complexes activate complement to form chemoattractants for neutrophils and monocytes. Microprecipitates and phagocytosing neutrophils block the small vessels, resulting in a typical Arthus reaction—lack of blood to the tissue and subsequent tissue necrosis and death.   [O.L.F.]

Hyphomycetes   A class of mitosporic or anamorphic (asexual or imperfect) fungi belonging to the Deuteromycotina. They lack locular fruit bodies (conidiomata), and so sporulation occurs on separate or aggregated hyphae, which may or may not be differentiated; the thallus consists of septate hyphae. About 1400 genera comprising more than 11,500 species are recognized.

The Hyphomycetes, like other groups of Deuteromycetes, is an artificial one composed almost entirely of anamorphic fungi of ascomycete affinity. The majority are known anamorphs of Ascomycetes, although some have basidiomycete affinities. Several of the latter are aquatic or aero-aquatic. Taxa are referred to as form genera and form species, because the absence of a sexual or perfect teleomorph state forces classification and identification by artificial rather than phylogenetic means. The unifying feature of the group is the production of conidia from superficial, exposed conidiogenous cells arising separately from vegetative hyphae or cells (mononematous), or incorporated on conidiophores that may be entirely separate or aggregated in cushion-like sporodochia or stalk-like synnemata. Differences in insertion and arrangement of conidiogenous cells and conidiophores traditionally have been used to separate three orders. In the Hyphomycetales they are solitary or at most fasciculate and tufted; in the Tuberculariales they are produced over the outer surface of a cushion-shaped-to-flattened conidioma (sporodochium), and in the Stilbellales they are united into a stipitate conidioma (synnema). An alternative means of classifying hyphomycetes is based on differences in the ways that conidia are produced and conidiogenous cells grow before, during, and after conidiogenesis. *See* ASCOMYCOTA; BASIDIOMYCOTA; COELOMYCETES.

To the naked eye, hyphomycete colonies are conspicuous as black, brown, green, gray, and white growths on substrata. In size, hyphomycete conidia vary from the minute to extremely long or wide. Shapes vary markedly within and between genera. Many hyphomycetes produce conidia in mucilaginous matrices. As in the Coelomycetes, the matrix inhibits or retards germination until the conidia become dispersed, and maintains germinability during periods of environmental stress. Other genera produce conidia in powdery masses, such hydrophobic conidia being more suited for air dispersal. Sterile elements in the form of simple or branched setae are commonly present among conidiophores or on conidiomata, and since they are particularly common among leaf-litter fungi they are thought to function as a form of predator defense.

The Hyphomycetes draw nourishment from living or dead organic matter and are adapted to grow, reproduce, and survive in a wide range of ecological situations. They can also be either stress-tolerant or combative. Some species grow among rubbish, and because their thin-walled, hyaline vegetative and reproductive structures make them more prone to attack and decay, they are ephemeral. Their ability to colonize, decompose, and use substrates and to interact with or parasitize other organisms is a result of the enzymes, antibiotics, toxins, and other metabolites they produce, coupled with wide genetic diversity. They are extremely common in soils of all types and on leaf litter and other organic debris of both natural and manufactured origin. They also cause extensive problems in food spoilage and occur in saline, stagnant, and fresh water.

Some hyphomycetes are found on or associated with fungi, including pathogens such as *Verticillium*, *Mycogone*, and *Cladobotryum*, and on lichens. Several are of medical importance, being associated with superficial, cutaneous, subcutaneous, and systemic infections. They are often opportunistic organisms that cause infections in immunocompromised patients. Toxic metabolites, or mycotoxins, are formed by many hyphomycetes, notably *Aspergillus*, *Fusarium*, and *Penicillium*. Others are nematophagous, capturing or consuming nematodes and other microfauna. *Beauveria*, *Metarhizium*, *Hirsutella*, and *Entomophthora*, for example, have been exploited for insect control. Many also cause economically important diseases in all types of vascular plants, especially agricultural and forestry crops. Hyphomycetes are primary pathogens of plants and weeds, causing root, stem, and leaf necrosis; diebacks; cankers; wilts; and blights. By infesting or contaminating seed, they can transmit seed-borne defects or reduce seed viability. *See* MEDICAL MYCOLOGY; MYCOTOXIN; PLANT PATHOLOGY.

Hyphomycetes produce a wide variety of primary and secondary metabolites and are capable of effecting many different chemical and biochemical changes. By harnessing that capability in industrial processes, organic acids, enzymes, antibiotics, growth substances, alcohol, and cheese, among others, can be produced and steroid transformation can take place. *See* DEUTEROMYCOTINA; FUNGI.   [B.C.S.]

Hypnosis   A presumed altered state of consciousness in which the hypnotized individual is usually more susceptible to suggestion than in his or her normal state. In this context, a suggestion is understood to be an idea or a communication carrying an idea that elicits a covert or overt response not mediated by the higher critical faculties (that is, the volitional apparatus).

Hypnosis cannot be physiologically distinguished from the normal awake state of an individual, and for this reason its existence has been questioned by some investigators. There are few phenomena observed in association with hypnosis, if any, that are specific to the hypnotic state. Most are directly or indirectly produced by suggestions. Through suggestions given to hypnotized individuals, it is possible to induce alterations in memory, perception, sensation, emotions, feelings, attitudes, beliefs, and muscular state. Such changes can be, and usually are, incorporated into the complex behavior of the individual, resulting in amnesias and paramnesias, fuguelike conditions, paralysis, loss of sensory functions, changes in attention, personality alterations, hallucinatory and delusional behavior, and even physiological changes. Enhanced recall is sometimes possible. Although sometimes remarkable, the effects produced through hypnosis with the majority of individuals are much less spectacular than popularly believed.   [A.M.W.]

Hypothermia   A condition in which the internal temperature of the (human) body is at least $3.6°F$ ($2.0°C$) below an internal temperature of $98.6°F$ ($37°C$). Hypothermia represents a continuum of effects that vary with the severity of cold on physiological systems. The human body needs a specific internal temperature that is regulated on a minute-by-minute basis to maintain all normal body functions. The many physiological and behavioral processes involved in maintaining the internal temperature constant are called thermoregulation. *See* THERMOREGULATION.

Various environmental situations predispose humans to hypothermia, which can occur even in the absence of cold. In fact, hypothermia is more common in temperate regions than in the colder climates. Because of the uniqueness of the situations in which hypothermia can occur, various kinds of hypothermia have been classified, all of which can prove fatal.

Primary hypothermia. Primary hypothermia is a decrease in internal temperature that is caused by environmental factors in which the body's physiological processes are normal but thermoregulation capability is overwhelmed by environmental stress.

Air (formerly exposure) hypothermia is thought to be the most common form. A person exposed to cold air experiences the same processes as a person in cold water, but air hypothermia occurs more slowly. The induction of air hypothermia is more subtle and therefore more dangerous since it can occur over a number of weeks. The degree to which a person reacts to a cold air stress is dependent on such factors as age, physical stamina, the intensity of the cold stress, and the responsiveness of the thermoregulatory system. One of the most convenient ways to determine whether someone is suffering from hypothermia is a noted change in personality: Complaints of fatigue, sluggish speech, and confusion are common, and in some cases the behavior resembles that of intoxication.

Initially, skin temperature falls rapidly, blood vessels to the skin constrict, and shivering begins. After 5–10 min, shivering ceases for about 10–15 min, but this is followed by uncontrollable shivering. In a cold situation, the nervous system causes blood to be redistributed away from the skin as the blood vessels of the skin close down to minimize heat transfer to the cold environment. The decrease in skin temperature coupled with vasoconstriction makes the person feel cold, and sometimes the fingers and toes can become painful. Internally, there is an increase in the levels of hormones that control metabolism, and blood is shunted primarily to the lungs, heart, and brain. The person becomes dehydrated as the inspired air is warmed and humidified. If the tense and shivering muscles do not generate enough heat, the hypothermic process begins and progresses for at least 3–5 h. As hypothermia continues, the arms become rigid, and the person loses the ability to make fine movements. During this period of time the heart rate initially increases, then stabilizes and as the person's internal temperature becomes progressively colder, the heart rate and respiration slow. In severely hypothermic persons, it is very difficult to detect a slow heart rate or determine if the person is breathing. A temperature of 95°F (35°C) is only the beginning of mild hypothermia and shivering can continue for hours, depending on the muscle and fat supplies available. Eventually, the environment becomes overwhelming. At 86°F (30°C), the person loses consciousness and shivering ceases. Death does not occur until the internal temperature drops further: Death results at 68–77°F (20–35°C) because of cardiac standstill.

When a person falls into cold water, a gasping response is triggered by the thermal receptors on the skin. For some individuals, the cold stress may trigger a heart attack. Although as much of the body as possible should be kept out of the water, many victims of immersion hypothermia stay in the cold water because they cannot tell how cold they are. Shivering becomes generalized and, unlike its effect in cold air, may cause a faster drop in internal temperature since the water layer closest to the body is stirred and convective heat loss is promoted. Although the greater conductive property of water relative to air is a major heat sink, physiological and behavioral responses act to minimize the heat loss. Survival in 50°F (10°C) water is possible for several hours at most if the person is dressed in street clothes and a life jacket.

The cooling of the body in submersion hypothermia allows the brain and heart to withstand approximately 45 min of oxygen debt. This is most operative for young children. A child can survive for an extended period of time while completely submerged because the body is undergoing both internal and external cooling. As the child is drowning, cold water is swallowed and enters the lungs, which cools the core. At the same time, the cold water that bathes the skin rapidly cools the periphery. The multiple effects of the internal and external cooling decrease the metabolic rate and give the child a window of safety of approximately 45 min. In warm water, survival is possible for only 5–7 min.

Secondary hypothermia. A decrease in core temperature caused by an underlying pathology that prevents the body from generating enough core heat is referred to as secondary hypothermia. If any of the thermoregulatory systems are altered, the body's ability to generate heat decreases and hypothermia can then develop without warning. Insufficient muscle mass to generate heat, medications that interfere with metabolism, an underlying systemic infection, decreased thyroid hormone production, and paralysis predispose to hypothermia. Premature infants with low body fat and a large surface-to-volume ratio lose heat rapidly and are at risk for becoming hypothermic. The elderly are perhaps the most susceptible to secondary hypothermia. However, whether the process of aging with no associated debility also alters the thermoregulatory system in the elderly remains to be determined.

Clinical hypothermia. Some cardiac surgical procedures require clinically induced cooling to stop the heart from beating. Induced hypothermia lowers the oxygen demand of the body tissues, so that oxygenated blood need not circulate. In the case of coronary bypass surgery, the entire body is cooled, enabling the surgeons to work for an extended period of time on the cold heart.

Frostbite. In hypothermia, the body's internal temperature decreases, but no solid freezing takes place. In frostbite, which is freezing of the digits or the limbs, there is actual formation of ice crystals. Basically the digits go through various stages of cooling. Initially, in the prefreeze phase, the finger temperature is 37.4–50°F (3–10°C). Next, at 24.8°F (−4°C) ice crystals form outside the cells of the digits, circulation is limited, and cell death takes place if the process is allowed to continue. The cells of the digits and limbs can tolerate low temperatures that would be lethal to brain or nerve cells. However, once they are rewarmed and thawed, they develop an increased sensitivity to the cold and become more susceptible to frostbite. Any part of the body can become frostbitten, but the fingers, toes, ears, nose, and cheeks are most often affected. *See* HOMEOSTASIS.   [R.W.Po.; L.E.W.; J.Ho.]

Immune complex disease   Local or systemic tissue injury caused by the vascular deposition of products of antigen-antibody interaction, termed immune complexes. Immune complex formation with specific antibodies causes the inactivation or elimination of potentially harmful consequences only when immune complexes deposit in tissues, inciting various mediators of inflammation. When the reaction takes place in the extravascular fluids near the site of origin of the antigen (by injection, secretion, and such), focal injury can occur, as exemplified by the Arthus reaction or such conditions as experimental immune thyroiditis. Systemic disease may occur when soluble antigens combine with antibodies in the vascular compartment, forming circulating immune complexes that are trapped nonspecifically in the vascular beds of various organs, causing such clinical diseases as serum sickness or systemic lupus erythematosus with vasculitis and glomerulonephritis. The term immune complex disease usually signifies this systemic immune complex formation and vascular deposition. *See* ANTIGEN-ANTIBODY REACTION.

Circulating immune complex disease occurs when the host's antibody production, relative to the amount of antigens, is inadequate for prompt elimination of antigen. Normally, excess amounts of antibody are formed which generate large immune complexes that are removed very rapidly from the circulation and are disposed of by the mononuclear phagocytic system. If the antibody response is very poor, only a few very small complexes are formed which are not prone to vascular deposition. When the relative antibody production is such that complexes of intermediate size form, vascular trapping can occur and injury results from the effects of inflammation. In addition to immune complex size, other factors influence vessel deposition, including the efficiency of systemic clearance of immune complexes, the hemodynamics of blood flow, and vasoactive amine-influenced changes in vascular permeability. Through dynamic equilibrium, continual modification of the deposits occurs as antigen and antibody fluctuate in the body fluids.

Treatment of immune complex disease can be divided into nonspecific and more specific modalities. Primary among the specific measures is the identification and elimination of the offending antigen. This may be possible with some infections when specific therapies are available, and in certain instances where the antigenic source can be removed, such as a neoplasm. More frequently, nonspecific anti-inflammatory (corticosteroids) and immunosuppressive agents (such as cyclophosphamide and azathioprine) are used to attempt to blunt the person's immune response, thereby lessening the amount of immune complexes produced. *See* AUTOIMMUNITY; IMMUNOLOGY.

[E.H.C.; C.B.W.]

Immunity   A state of resistance to an agent, the pathogen, that normally produces an infection. Pathogens include microorganisms such as bacteria and viruses, as well as larger parasites. The immune response that generates immunity is also responsible in some situations for allergies, delayed hypersensitivity states, autoimmune disease, and transplant rejection. *See* ALLERGY; AUTOIMMUNITY; TRANSPLANTATION BIOLOGY.

Immunity is engendered by the host immune system, reacting in very specific ways to foreign components (such as proteins) of particular parasites or infective agents. It is influenced by many factors, including the environment, inherited genes, and acquired characteristics. Reaction to a pathogen is through a nonadaptive or innate response as well as an adaptive immune response. The innate response is not improved by repeated encounters with the pathogen. An adaptive response is characterized by specificity and memory: if reinfection occurs, the host will mount an enhanced response.

The components of the pathogen that give rise to an immune response, to which antibodies are generated, are called antigens. There are two types of specific responses to an antigen, antibodies and the cellular response. Antibodies help to neutralize the infectious agent by specifically binding it. A series of proteins in the blood (called complement) act in conjunction with antibodies to destroy pathogenic bacteria. In the cellular response, cytotoxic T cells are recruited to kill cells infected with intracellular agents such as viruses. Helper T cells may also be generated, which influence B cells to produce appropriate antibodies. Inflammatory responses and activation of other kinds of cells, such as macrophages, in conjunction with lymphocytes, is another important aspect of the immune response, as in delayed hypersensitivity. This kind of response seems to be common in certain chronic infections. *See* ANTIBODY; ANTIGEN; COMPLEMENT.

Complex immune systems (antibody and specific cellular responses) have been demonstrated in mammals, birds, amphibians, and fish, and are probably restricted to vertebrates.

Natural or innate immunity. There are natural barriers to infection, both physical and physiological, which are known collectively as innate immunity, and include the effects of certain cells (macrophages, neutrophils and natural killer cells) and substances such as serum proteins, cytokines, complement, lectins, and lipid-binding proteins. The skin or mucous membranes of the respiratory tract are obvious barriers and may contain bacteriostatic or bactericidal agents (such as lysozyme and spermine) that delay widespread infection until other defenses can be mobilized.

If organisms manage to enter tissues, they are often recognized by molecules present in serum and by receptors on cells. Bacterial cell walls, for example, contain substances such as lipopolysaccharides that activate the complement pathway or trigger phagocytic cells. Host range is dramatic in its specificity. Animals and plants are generally not susceptible to each other's pathogens. Within each kingdom, infectious agents are usually adapted to affect a restricted range of species. For example, mice are not known to be susceptible to pneumococcal pneumonia under natural conditions. The health of the host and environmental conditions may also make a difference to susceptibility. This is readily apparent in fish that succumb to fungal infections if their environment deteriorates. Genetic factors have an influence on susceptibility. Some of these genes have been identified, in particular the genes of the major histocompatibility complex which are involved in susceptibility to autoimmune diseases as well as some infectious disorders. *See* HISTOCOMPATIBILITY.

Once parasites gain entry, phagocytic cells attack them. They may engulf and destroy organisms directly, or they may need other factors such as antibody, complement, or lymphokines, secreted by lymphocytes, which enhance the ability of the phagocytes to take up antigenic material. In many cases these cells are responsible for alerting cells involved in active immunity so there is two-way communication between the innate and adaptive responses. *See* PHAGOCYTOSIS.

Adaptive immune response. Adaptive immunity is effected in part by lymphocytes. Lymphocytes are of two types: B cells, which develop in the bone marrow or fetal liver and may mature into antibody-producing plasma cells, and T cells, which develop in the thymus. T cells have a number of functions, which include helping B cells to produce antibody, killing virus-infected cells, regulating the level of immune response, and controlling the activities of other effector cells such as macrophages.

Each lymphocyte carries a different surface receptor that can recognize a particular antigen. The antigen receptor expressed by B cells consists of membrane-bound antibody of the specificity that it will eventually secrete; B cells can recognize unmodified antigen. However, T cells recognize antigen only when parts of it are complexed with a molecule of the major histocompatibility complex. The principle of the adaptive immune response is clonal recognition: each lymphocyte recognizes only one antigenic structure, and only those cells stimulated by antigen respond. Initially, in the primary response, there are few lymphocytes with the appropriate receptor for an antigen, but these cells proliferate. If the antigen is encountered again, there will be a proportionally amplified and more rapid response. Primed lymphocytes either differentiate into immune effector cells or form an expanded pool of memory cells that respond to a secondary challenge with the same antigen.

The acquired or adaptive immune response is characterized by exquisite specificity such that even small pieces of foreign proteins can be recognized. This specificity is achieved by the receptors on T cells and B cells as well as antibodies that are secreted by activated B cells. The genes for the receptors are arranged in multiple small pieces that come together to make novel combinations, by somatic recombination. Each T or B cell makes receptors specific to a single antigen. Those cells with receptors that bind to the foreign protein and not to self tissues are selected out of a large pool of cells. For T cells, this process takes place in the thymus. The extreme diversity of T- and B-cell receptors means that an almost infinite number of antigens can be recognized. It has been calculated that potentially about 3×10^{22} different T-cell receptors are made in an individual. Even if 99% of these are eliminated because they bind to self tissues, 3×10^{20} would still be available.

Inflammation takes place to activate immune mechanisms and to eliminate thoroughly the source of infection. Of prime importance is the complement system, which consists of tens of serum proteins. A variety of cells are activated, including mast cells and macrophages. Inflammation results in local attraction of immune cells, increased blood supply, and increased vascular permeability. *See* CELLULAR IMMUNOLOGY.

Autoimmunity. The immune system is primed to react against foreign antigens while avoiding responses to self tissue by immunological tolerance. Although most T cells which might activate against host proteins are deleted in the thymus, these self-reactive cells are not always destroyed. These exceptions to self tolerance are frequently associated with disease, the autoimmune diseases, which are widespread pathological conditions, including Addison's disease, celiac disease, Goodpasture's syndrome, Hashimoto's thyroiditis, juvenile-onset diabetes mellitus, multiple sclerosis, myasthenia gravis, pemphigus vulgaris, rheumatoid arthritis, Sjögren's disease, and systemic lupus erythematosus. In these diseases, antibodies or T cells activate against self components. *See* AUTOIMMUNITY.

Immunization. Adaptive immunity is characterized by the ability to respond more rapidly and more intensely when encountering a pathogen for a second time, a feature known as immunological memory. This permits successful vaccination and prevents reinfection with pathogens that have been successfully repelled by an adaptive immune response. Mass immunization programs have led to the virtual eradication of several very serious diseases, although not always on a worldwide scale. Living attenuated vaccines against a variety of agents, including poliomyelitis, tuberculosis, yellow fever, and bubonic plague, have been used effectively. Nonliving vaccines are commonly used for prevention of bacterial diseases such as pertussis, typhoid, and cholera as well as some viral diseases such as influenza and bacterial toxins such as diphtheria and tetanus. *See* VACCINATION.

Passive immunization. Protective levels of antibody are not formed until some time after birth, and to compensate for this there is passive transfer of antibody across the placenta. Alternatively, in some animals antibody is transferred in the first milk (colostrum). Antibody may also be passively transferred artificially, for example, with a concentrated preparation of human serum gamma globulin containing antibodies against hepatitis. Protection is temporary. Horse serum is used for passive protection against snake venom. Serum from the same (homologous) species is tolerated, but heterologous serum is rapidly eliminated and may produce serum sickness. On repeated administration, a sensitized individual may experience anaphylactic shock, which in some cases is fatal. Cellular immunity can also be transferred, particularly in experimental animal situations when graft and host reactions to foreign tissue invariably occur unless strain tissue types are identical.   [J.Tr.]

Immunoassay   An assay that quantifies antigen or antibody by immunochemical means. The antigen can be a relatively simple substance such as a drug, or a complex one such as a protein or a virus. *See* ANTIBODY; ANTIGEN.

The reactants are first mixed so that a varying quantity of one (A) is added to a constant amount of the other (B). The formation of an immune (antigen-antibody) complex is measured as a function of the varied reactant (A). The result is represented by a "standard curve" for reactant A. An unknown sample is tested by adding it to reactant B. The extent of the measured change is referred to the standard curve, and thereby is obtained the amount of reactant A which produces a comparable change. The amount is represented as the content of reactant A in the unknown sample. *See* IMMUNOFLUORESCENCE; IMMUNOLOGY; RADIOIMMUNOASSAY.   [A.B.]

Immunochemistry   A discipline concerned both with the structure of antibody (immunoglobulin) molecules and with their ability to bind an apparently limitless number of diverse chemical structures (antigens); with the structure, organization, and rearrangement of the genes coding for the immunoglobulin molecules; and with the structure and function of molecules on the surface of animal cells, such as the transplantation (histocompatibility) antigens, which recognize antibodies and the thymus-derived lymphocytes mediating the cellular immune response. *See* ANTIGEN; IMMUNOASSAY; IMMUNOGLOBULIN; RADIOIMMUNOASSAY; TRANSPLANTATION BIOLOGY.   [W.H.K.; F.F.R.]

Immunoelectrophoresis   A combination of the techniques of electrophoresis and immunodiffusion used to separate the components of a mixture of antigens and make them visible by reaction with specific antibodies.

A medium such as agar is deposited on a convenient base, for example, a microscopic slide. A small well is cut in the medium. A test solution is deposited in the well, and the contained substances are separated by electrophoresis along one axis of the plate. A trough is then cut in the medium parallel to, but at some distance from, the line of the separated substances. The trough is filled with antiserum which contains antibodies to one or more of the separated substances. The antiserum and substances diffuse toward one another and, where they meet, form curvilinear patterns of precipitation. These can be seen directly in clear media or can be visualized after washing out unreacted materials and staining in opaque media. *See* IMMUNOASSAY.   [A.B.]

Immunofluorescence A technique that uses a fluorochrome to indicate the occurrence of a specific antigen-antibody reaction. The fluorochrome labels either an antigen or an antibody. The labeled reactant is then used to detect the presence of the unlabeled reactant. The use of a labeled reactant (such as an antibody which both detects and indicates the antigen) to reveal the presence of an unlabeled one is termed direct immunofluorescence. The use of a labeled indicator antibody, which reacts with an unlabeled detector antibody that has previously reacted with an antigen, is termed indirect immunofluorescence. Substitution of a light meter for the human eye permits a quantitative measurement in immunofluorometry. See IMMUNOASSAY. [A.B.]

Immunogenetics A scientific discipline that uses immunological methods to study the inheritance of traits. Traditionally, immunogenetics has been concerned with moieties that elicit immune response, that is, with antigens (antigenic determinants). It has now broadened its scope to study also the genetic control of the individual's ability to respond to an antigen. See ANTIGEN.

The immunological methods used in immunogenetics are of two principal kinds, serological and histogenetical. In serological methods, antibodies are used to detect antigens, either in solution or on a cell surface. In histogenetical methods, immune cells (lymphocytes) are used to detect antigens on the surface of other cells. In modern immunogenetics research, the serological and histogenetical methods are combined with molecular methods in which the researcher isolates and works with the genes that code for the traits. This approach of going back and forth from classical to molecular methods has proved to be very successful and has led to the elucidation of several complex genetic systems. See ANTIBODY.

Animal immunogenetics relies heavily on the use of inbred, congenic, and recombinant inbred strains. Inbred lines result when individuals that are more closely related to each other than randomly chosen individuals mate together, for many generations. The advantage in working with inbred strains rather than outbred animals is that inbred strains restrict the variability of the conditions of an experiment. However, when two strains are compared and it is found that they respond differently to a treatment, it is not known to what gene this difference should be attributed. The strains may differ at as many genetic loci as two unrelated individuals in an outbred population do. To study the effect of single, defined genes, immunogeneticists have developed congenic lines. These lines always come in groups, the smallest group being a pair, which consists of a congenic line and its inbred partner strain. The two are homozygous at more than 97% of their loci (that is, they are inbred) and are identical except, ideally, at one locus—the locus that is to be studied. To find out whether two loci are on the same or on different chromosomes, two individuals that differ in the traits controlled by these loci are mated and then the F_1 hybrids are intercrossed. In the F_2 generation that results from this intercross, the genes assort either independently, if they are on different chromosomes, or nonrandomly, if they are the same chromosome—that is, when they are linked. Each time the strains are tested for linkage, this laborious procedure must be repeated. To avoid this repetition, immunogeneticists have prepared a "frozen" F_2 generation by establishing separate inbred lines from the different F_2 individuals. Such lines are called the recombinant inbred strains.

Contemporary immunogenetic research concentrates on two main categories of antigenic substances—those present in body fluids, primarily blood serum or plasma, and those expressed on surfaces of various cells. In the body-fluid antigens category, a prominent position is occupied by immunoglobulins. Although antibodies are usually used to detect antigens, they themselves may also serve as antigens, and antibodies can be produced against them. These antibodies against antibodies detect three principal kinds of antigenic determinants: isotypic, allotypic, and idiotypic. The main categories of cell-surface molecules studied by immunogenetical methods are blood-group antigens, histocompatibility antigens, tissue-restricted antigens, and receptors. Blood-group antigens are alloantigens found on erythrocytes. Histocompatibility antigens are antigens capable of inducing cellular immune responses and hence are detectable by histogenetical methods. Tissue-restricted antigens are expressed on some tissues but not on others and therefore serve as markers for cell sorting. Receptors are molecules that are capable of specifically interacting with certain other molecules. The interaction often leads to activation or inhibition of the receptor-bearing cell. *See* BLOOD GROUPS; GENETICS; HISTOCOMPATIBILITY; IMMUNOGLOBULIN; IMMUNOLOGY.   [J.K.]

Immunoglobulin   Any of the glycoproteins in the blood serum that are induced in response to invasion by foreign antigens and that protect the host by eradicating pathogens. Antibodies belong to this group of proteins. An antigen is any substance capable of inducing an immune response. Intact antigens are able to specifically interact with the induced immunoglobulins. Normally, the immune system operates in a state known as self-tolerance, and does not attack the host's own tissues, but occasionally the immune system targets host-specific antigens, resulting in autoimmune disease. *See* AUTOIMMUNITY.

Immunoglobulins are composed of two identical heavy (H) and two identical light (L) polypeptide chains. Each H and L chain has an amino-terminal variable (V) region and a carboxyl-terminal constant (C) region. Although V regions from different antibodies exhibit considerable sequence variation, there is a large degree of sequence similarity among C regions of different antibodies. In the living animal, antibodies first bind to antigen at the antigen combining site and then, ideally, eliminate it as a threat to the host.

Immunoglobulins are heterogeneous with respect to charge, size, antigenicity, and function. There are three categories of antigenic determinants present on immunoglobulins: isotypes are found in all individuals, allotypes are found in some individuals, and idiotypes are associated with the amino-terminal variable region. Isotypic determinants are located on the carboxyl-terminal constant region and are used to group immunoglobulin H and L chains into isotypes or classes. In total, there are five human H-chain classes. IgM contains mu (μ) H chains, IgG contains gamma (γ) H chains, IgA contains alpha (α) H chains, IgD contains delta (δ) H chains, and IgE contains epsilon (ϵ) H chains. IgG has four subclasses, IgG1, IgG2, IgG3, and IgG4, while IgA has two subclasses, IgA1 and IgA2. There are two L-chain isotypes named kappa (κ) and lambda (λ). Kappa and lambda chains may be associated with H chains of any isotype, and a complete description of an immunoglobulin molecule requires identification of both H and L chains.

IgG is the most abundant immunoglobulin class in the serum. IgG isotypes are associated with complement fixation, opsonization (that is, rendering more susceptible to phagocytosis), fixation to macrophages, and membrane transport. Of the two IgA subclasses, IgA1 is the predominant subclass of IgA in human serum. IgA1 is the dominant subclass in all external secretions, including milk, saliva, tears, and bronchial fluids. The percentage of subclass IgA2 is higher in these fluids than in serum. IgM is the first immunoglobulin to appear during the primary immune response. IgD and IgE are present in minute amounts in normal human serum. No function has been clearly attributed to IgD. IgE is active against parasites and acts as a mediator of immediate hypersensitivity. *See* ANAPHYLAXIS; ANTIBODY; ANTIGEN; ANTIGEN-ANTIBODY REACTION; HYPERSENSITIVITY; IMMUNOLOGY; PROTEIN.   [J.D.C.; K.N.P.]

Immunologic cytotoxicity The mechanism by which the immune system destroys or damages foreign or abnormal cells. Immunologic cytotoxicity may lead to complete loss of viability of the target cells (cytolysis) or an inhibition of the ability of the cells to continue growing (cytostasis). Immunologic cytotoxicity can be manifested against a wide variety of target cells, including malignant cells, normal cells from individuals unrelated to the responding host, and normal cells of the host that are infected with viruses or other microorganisms. In addition, the immune system can cause direct cytotoxic effects on some microorganisms, including bacteria, parasites, and fungi.

Immunologic cytotoxicity is a principal mechanism by which the immune response copes with, and often eliminates, foreign materials or abnormal cells. Cytotoxic reactions are frequently observed as a major component of an immune response that develops following exposure to foreign cells or microorganisms. In addition, there is increasing evidence that cytotoxic reactions represent a major mechanism for natural immunity and resistance to such materials. In most instances, cytotoxicity by immune components involves the recognition of particular structures on the target cells; also, the targets need to be susceptible to attack by the immune components. Some cells are quite resistant to immunologic cytotoxicity, and this appears to represent a major mechanism by which they can escape control by the immune system.

There are a variety of mechanisms for immunologic cytotoxicity. The two main categories are antibody- and cell-mediated cytotoxicity. Within cell-mediated cytotoxicity, there is a multiplicity of effector cell types and mechanisms that can be involved, including cytotoxic T lymphocytes, macrophage-mediated cytotoxicity, natural killer cells, granulocyte cytoxicity, and antibody-dependent cell-mediated cytotoxicity. *See* IMMUNOLOGY. [R.B.He.]

Immunological deficiency A state wherein the immune mechanisms are inadequate in their ability to perform their normal function, that is, the elimination of foreign materials (usually infectious agents such as bacteria, viruses, and fungi). Immune mechanisms are also responsible for the rejection of transplanted organs. These processes are accomplished by white blood cells known as lymphocytes, of which there are two major types, T lymphocytes (thymus-derived) and B lymphocytes (bone marrow-derived). *See* CELLULAR IMMUNOLOGY, TRANSPLANTATION BIOLOGY.

Immunological deficiency states result from a failure at any point in the complex set of interactions involving lymphocytes and immunoglobulins. In general, the diseases are due to absence of cell populations; failure of cells to mature; failure to secrete the products necessary for effective cell interactions; or failure of accessory cell populations or protein systems (for example, complement) which are necessary for the complete competence of B-cell immune function. Some of the diseases are carried on the X-chromosome and affect only males, being carried by females. *See* COMPLEMENT; SEX-LINKED INHERITANCE.

The prime symptom of immunodeficiency is an increased suceptibility to infections. Many of the organisms to which people are constantly exposed do not ordinarily have the capability to cause infections in immunocompetent individuals because these organisms are so weak that they cannot establish themselves in normals. In immunodeficients, however, they can cause fatal infections.

In general, immunodeficiency states are inherited. Immunodeficiency can also be acquired as a complication of other disease processes. One of the most common forms of deficiency is caused by aggressive treatment of leukemia. Another cause of induced immunodeficiency is seen with transplant rejection therapy. To prevent organ rejection, drugs which destroy lymphocytes must be administered. Certain viruses, such as the Epstein-Barr virus (EBV), which causes infectious mononucleosis, infect lymphocytes.

Involvement of the lymphoid system is nearly always only temporary, but in a small number of individuals the virus cannot be eliminated, and a chronic infection of B cells leads to the loss of normal lymphocyte function. Another immunodeficiency disorder caused by virus infection is acquired immune deficiency syndrome (AIDS). Immunodeficiency can also be observed secondary to dietary deficiency. Two main varieties are seen. In protein-calorie malnutrition, serious deficiency primarily involving the T-cell system predisposes affected individuals to overwhelming infection by the agents of measles or tuberculosis. In the second variety, deficiency of single substances is the cause; the two most commonly observed deficiencies are those of zinc and biotin. *See* ACQUIRED IMMUNE DEFICIENCY SYNDROME (AIDS); TRANSPLANTATION BIOLOGY.

[Ri.H.]

Immunological ontogeny The origin and development (ontogeny) of the lymphocyte system, from its earliest stages to the two major populations of mature lymphocytes: the thymus-dependent or T lymphocytes, and the thymus-independent or B lymphocytes. The T lymphocytes carry out those aspects of function which are called cell-mediated immunity, including graft rejection, elimination of tumor cells, and delayed hypersensitivity. B cells are responsible for humoral or antibody-mediated immunity. *See* CELLULAR IMMUNOLOGY; IMMUNITY.

For both systems, development or differentiation proceeds in discrete stages. In the first stage, pluripotent hematopoietic stem cells, which originate in the yolk sac in the embryo and then successively in fetal liver and fetal bone marrow, develop into precursor cells committed to becoming T or B cells. Hematopoiesis in human fetal liver begins at about 4 weeks of gestational age and in fetal bone marrow after 20 weeks. *See* HEMATOPOIESIS.

The thymus plays a strategic role in the development of T lymphocytes. Precursor cells are attracted into the thymus where, under the influence of this microenvironment, they undergo rapid proliferation and maturation. These maturing T cells also begin to express a variety of cell-surface markers, which parallels developing immunocompetence. From the thymus, the maturing T cells are exported to the peripheral lymphoid tissues. *See* THYMUS GLAND.

The earliest B cells identified in fetal liver are pre-B cells. As the cells mature, they express immunoglobulin M (IgM) and subsequently IgD on their surface. At this stage, the cell is a specific, competent B cell ready to interact with an antigen. In the course of B-lymphocyte differentiation, diversity of immunoglobulin classes is generated by an orderly switch from IgM to IgG to IgA with expression of the respective immunoglobulin on the cell surface. *See* ANTIGEN; IMMUNOGLOBULIN. [E.W.Ge.]

Immunological phylogeny The study of immunology and the immune system in evolution. All vertebrates can recognize and respond to nonself-molecular configurations on microorganisms, cells, or organic molecules by utilizing a complex recognition system termed the immune response. The presence of lymphocytes and circulating antibodies has been documented in all extant vertebrate species. However, the existence of induced, specific reactions directly homologous to the immune repertoire of vertebrates has not been clearly established in invertebrates.

The role of phagocytic cells in engulfing foreign pathogens has been documented in virtually all metazoan organisms. Phagocytic cells possess a limited capacity to discriminate self from nonself, and this is due in part to the presence of lectins (molecules capable of binding specifically to various sugars) on their surface. Although there is no evidence to suggest that invertebrate lectins and vertebrate immunoglobulins are homologous structures, sufficient diversity exists within lectins of certain species to indicate that these types of molecules and their cellular expression on phagocytes might serve as a primitive and universal recognition mechanism. *See* IMMUNOGLOBULIN; LECTINS.

All true vertebrates possess cells clearly recognizable as lymphocytes and can carry out T-cell functions, such as graft rejection, and show the capacity of B cells to synthesize and secrete immunoglobulins. True lymph nodes are not present in vertebrate species more primitive than mammals, but birds possess aggregates of lymphoid tissue probably serving a similar function. *See* CELLULAR IMMUNOLOGY; LYMPHATIC SYSTEM.

Humans possess five major classes or isotypes of immunoglobulin: IgG, IgM, IgA, IgE, and IgD. The IgM molecule is the first immunoglobulin to appear in ontogeny, and the first to appear in phylogeny. Immunoglobulins of cyclostomes, elasmobranchs (sharks and rays), and many teleost fishes consist only of IgM polymers. Immunoglobulins possessing heavy chains distinct from the μ-like heavy chains of those groups are present in some lungfish (Dipnoi) and in anuran amphibians (frogs and toads). Dipnoi have a low-molecular-weight non-IgM immunoglobulin (termed IgN). Birds possess IgM and IgA immunoglobutins, but also possess a non-IgM immunoglobulin similar to that of amphibians as their major immunoglobulin class. This immunoglobulin has been termed IgY. IgG immunoglobulins containing gamma chains clearly homologous to those of the humans and of true mammals are found only within the three subclasses of living mammals, namely, eutherians, metatherians (marsupials), and monotremes (for example, the echidna). *See* IMMUNOLOGICAL ONTOGENY.

Although the precise nature of the precursors of the specific elements of the immune system in evolution remains to be determined, the genetic and cellular events which lead to the capacity for specific immune recognition, diversification, and reactivity occurred early in vertebrate evolution. *See* IMMUNITY; IMMUNOLOGY.   [J.J.Ma.]

Immunology   The division of biological science concerned with the native or acquired response of complex living organisms to the intrusion of other organisms or foreign substances. The immune system allows the host organism to distinguish between self and nonself and to respond to a target (termed an antigen).

It was not until the germ theory of infectious disease was established that the full implication of immunology was realized. First came the recognition that certain bacteria caused corresponding diseases. Second came the recognition that it was a specific resistance to that bacterium or its toxins that prevented recurrence of the same disease. Third came the discovery that after recovery from an infectious disease, protective substances called antibodies could be found in the blood of animals and humans. Antigens, such as bacteria and their products, triggered the production of antibodies and indeed all kinds of chemical and biological molecules. The action of these effector mechanisms, however, has come to be recognized as being not always protective or conferring immunity, but sometimes becoming grossly exaggerated or inappropriate, or capable of turning upon the host in a destructive fashion that causes disease. These responses are classified as allergies. Illnesses associated with a misguided response of the immune system that is directed against the self and results from a breakdown in the normal immunological tolerance of, or unresponsiveness to, self antigens are termed autoimmune. The mechanisms responsible for these disorders are unknown but probably include the intervention of factors such as viruses that either modify or naturally resemble self molecules. Subsequently, the immune response, in seeking out what is foreign, proceeds to attack the self. *See* ALLERGY; AUTOIMMUNITY.

Immunology is also concerned with assaying the immune status of the host through a variety of serological procedures, and in devising methods of increasing host resistance through prophylactic vaccination. There has also been much important investigation of induced resistance and tolerance to transplants of skin and organs, including tumors.

See BLOOD GROUPS; HYPERSENSITIVITY; IMMUNITY; IMMUNOASSAY; ISOANTIGEN; PHAGOCY-
TOSIS; SEROLOGY; TRANSPLANTATION BIOLOGY; VACCINATION.   [A.B.; M.J.Po.]

Immunosuppression   The natural or induced active suppression of the immune response, as contrasted with deficiency or absence of components of the immune system. Like many other complex biological processes, the immune response
is controlled by a series of regulatory factors. A variety of suppressor cells play a
role in essentially all of the known immunoregulatory mechanisms, such as maintenance of immunological tolerance; limitation of antibody response to antigens of both
thymic-dependent and thymic-independent types, as well as to antigens that stimulate reaginic antibody (antibodies involved in allergic reactions); genetic control of the
immune response; idiotype suppression; control of contact and delayed hypersensitivity; and antigenic competition. All of the major cell types involved in the positive side
of cellular interactions required for an immune response have also been found capable of functioning as suppressors in different regulatory systems. *See* IMMUNOLOGICAL
DEFICIENCY.

Suppressor cells. Some suppressor functions are antigen- or carrier-specific. (A
carrier is a molecule that can be chemically bound to another small molecule, called a
hapten, in such a way that the combination induces an immune response that the hapten alone would not induce.) Others may not be carrier-specific, but may be specific for
the type of response, such as immunoglobulin production but not delayed hypersensitivity. In the case of immunoglobulin production, the suppressor T cell may regulate
the production of all immunoglobulin classes, a single class of immunoglobulins, or
molecules that bind only a given antigen. Other suppressors may affect only cellular
immunity and not humoral immunity. *See* CELLULAR IMMUNOLOGY; IMMUNOGLOBULIN.

Suppressor cells are critical in the regulation of the normal immune response. Immunological tolerance refers to the ability of an individual's immune system to distinguish between its own and foreign antigens and to mount a response only to foreign
antigens. A major role has been established for suppressor T lymphocytes in this phenomenon. Suppressor cells also play a role in regulating the magnitude and duration
of the specific antibody response to an antigenic challenge.

Reagin, or IgE, is the class of immunoglobulin that mediates allergic reactions such as
asthma and urticaria. The reaginic antibody response depends heavily on nonspecific
cooperator T cells and specific helper T cells as well as the B cells that produce the
antibody. In a negative direction, IgG-blocking antibodies regulate the response, but
antigen-specific and antigen-nonspecific suppressor T cells also play a critical role in
regulating this response. *See* ALLERGY.

T cells are the major cells involved in immunosuppression, although activated phagocytic mononuclear cells are also significant as nonspecific suppressors in many systems.
Helper T cells and suppressor T cells are different cell populations that are distinguished
to a considerable extent by surface antigens that react with monoclonal antibodies or
receptors for specific substances such as histamine.

No single model explains the entire array of cellular suppressor phenomena. In different systems, other T cells, macrophages, or even B cells may be the immediate targets
of the suppressor cells and their secretions. Some suppression requires direct cell-cell
interaction, whereas other suppression may be mediated by suppressor lymphokines.
Both antigen-specific and antigen-nonspecific factors are known, and they may be secreted to act upon other cells, or especially in the case of antigen-specific factors, they
may be integral parts of the cell membrane. The soluble immune-response suppressor
factor, produced by activated T cells and then activated by monocytes, inhibits B-cell
proliferation and immunoglobulin production in response to antigens. Macrophages

also secrete suppressor factors, including prostaglandins that act on T cells and other soluble factors that are B-cell-specific.

There is a variety of disorders of immunoglobulin production in humans. In many cases these involve intrinsic defects in the bone marrow stem cells that normally mature into immunoglobulin-producing plasma cells. Defects in cell-mediated immunity occur in individuals who are infected with various fungal organisms. Suppressor T cells have been implicated, although it is not clear whether the appearance of suppressor cells is the initial event allowing development of the fungal infection or whether they develop secondarily after infection. Those individuals found to have suppressor T cells are at high risk for dissemination of the fungal infection and relapse following therapy. Although probably only one of many mechanisms, suppressor cells interfere with the host tumor-growth-inhibiting immune response to the foreign tumor-specific transplantation antigens that occur on malignant cells, thus allowing the tumors to progress. Both animal and human studies indicate a major role for both an activation of immunoglobulin-producing B cells as well as the absence or reduced numbers or function of suppressor T cells in autoimmune disorders such as Coombs-positive hemolytic anemia, systemic lupus erythematosus, rheumatoid disorders, and thyroid disorders in which antithyroid antibodies appear in the serum. *See* AUTOIMMUNITY.

[K.S.W.; T.A.Wa.]

Immunosuppressors. Suppression of the immune response may be specific to a particular antigen or may be a response to a wide range of antigens encountered. The whole immune response may be depressed, or a particular population of immunologically active lymphocytes may be selectively affected. In some cases, the effect may be preferentially on T cells rather than B cells. If B cells are affected, it may be on a specific subclass of antibody-producing cells. Antigen-specific immunosuppression may be the result of deletion or suppression of a particular clone of antigen-specific cells, or the result of enhanced regulation of the immune response by antigen-specific suppressor cells. It can also be the result of increased production of antiidiotypic antibody.

Nonspecific suppression of the immune response occurs in a number of rare immunological deficiency diseases of childhood. Acquired deficiency states affecting mainly T-cell function occur in states of malnutrition and in the presence of tumors, particularly those of the lymphoreticular system. Acquired deficiencies may also occur secondary to a number of infectious diseases. The acquired immune deficiency syndrome (AIDS) is probably of similar origin; its manifestations are similar although more severe and more dramatic. *See* ACQUIRED IMMUNE DEFICIENCY SYNDROME (AIDS); IMMUNE COMPLEX DISEASE.

There are a number of compounds capable of suppressing the immune response. The main stimulus for studies designed to identify these substances has been to devise means for controlling organ graft rejection. However, there has also been considerable activity in looking for compounds that will suppress the immune response and reduce the inflammatory process in experimental models of rheumatoid arthritis. The ideal immunosuppressive drug should fulfill five main requirements: (1) There should be a wide margin of safety between a toxic and a therapeutic dose. (2) The drug should have a selective effect on lymphoid cells and not cause damage to the rest of the body. (3) If possible, this effect should be only on those cells which are involved in the specific immune process to be suppressed. (4) The drug should need to be administered for only a limited period until the immunological processes become familiar with the foreign antigen and begin to recognize it as part of "self." (5) The drug should be effective against immune processes once they have developed. *See* TRANSPLANTATION BIOLOGY.

The result of any immune response is a balance between the action of effector cells mediating the phenomenon and suppressor cells regulating the response. Anything that reduces the regulatory function of suppressor cells will functionally increase the immune response. As suppressor cells are derived from rapidly turning-over precursor cells, and effector cells of T-cell-mediated immunity are derived from slowly dividing precursors, it is possible preferentially to depress the action of suppressor cells without affecting effector cells. This may be done by the use of alkylating agents such as cyclophosphamide given before immunization. Cyclophosphamide used in this way can increase a normal cell-mediated immune response, reverse immunological tolerance caused by increased regulatory activity of suppressor cells, and even reverse antigenic competition. It is likely that the chemotherapeutic effect of alkylating agents which are used extensively in the treatment of cancer in humans is partially due to these agents modifying the biological response to the tumor, producing an immunopotentiating action. *See* IMMUNITY; IMMUNOLOGY.   [J.L.T.]

Immunotherapy   The treatment of cancer by improving the ability of a tumor-bearing individual (the host) to reject the tumor immunologically. There are molecules on the surface of tumor cells, and perhaps in their interior, that are recognized as different from normal structures by the immune system and thus generate an immune response. The two components of the immune response are cell-mediated and antibody-mediated immunity, which must work in concert to overcome tumor cells. One type of thymus-derived lymphocyte (also called a cytotoxic T cell) can destroy tumor cells directly, while another recruits other white blood cells, the macrophages, that do the killing. Natural killer cells and perhaps other white blood cells may also participate. However, elements that normally regulate immunity, such as suppressor T cells, are stimulated excessively by the tumor, which leads to an immune response that is deficient and unable to reject the growing tumor. Thus the strategy of immunotherapy is to stimulate within or transfer to the tumor-bearing individual the appropriate antitumor elements while avoiding further stimulation of suppressor elements. *See* CELLULAR IMMUNOLOGY; IMMUNOLOGIC CYTOTOXICITY; IMMUNOSUPPRESSION.

There are four broad categories of immunotherapy: active, adoptive, restorative, and passive. Active immunotherapy attempts to stimulate the host's intrinsic immune response to the tumor, either nonspecifically or specifically. Nonspecific active immunotherapy utilizes materials that have no apparent antigenic relationship to the tumor, but have modulatory effects on the immune system, stimulating macrophages, lymphocytes, and natural killer cells. Specific active immunotherapy attempts to stimulate specific antitumor responses with tumor-associated antigens as the immunizing materials. Adoptive immunotherapy involves the transfer of immunologically competent white blood cells or their precursors into the host. Bone marrow transplantation, while performed principally for the replacement of hematopoietic stem cells, can also be viewed as adoptive immunotherapy. Restorative immunotherapy comprises the direct and indirect restoration of deficient immunological function through any means other than the direct transfer of cells. Passive immunotherapy means the transfer of antibodies to tumor-bearing recipients. This approach has been made feasible by the development of hybridoma technology, which now permits the production of large quantities of monoclonal antibodies specific for an antigenic determinant on tumor cells. *See* GENETIC ENGINEERING; IMMUNOLOGY; MONOCLONAL ANTIBODIES.   [J.K.M.; M.S.Mi.]

Industrial microbiology   A field concerned with the development of technologies to control and manipulate the growth and activities of selected biological agents to create desirable products and economic gain or to prevent economic loss. In addition to bacteria and yeasts, animal and plant cell cultures are now used to produce sophisticated products such as monoclonal antibodies, immunomodulating compounds, and complex plant metabolites.

Although fermented products have been consumed for thousands of years, only in the nineteenth century was microbial activity associated with the fermentation process. Soon after that discovery, microorganisms, especially bacteria, were selectively introduced on the commercial level. Techniques were developed gradually for pure-culture fermentation and strain improvement, but the major advance in industrial microbiology occurred during World War II with the large-scale production of penicillin by submerged-culture fermentation. In the 1950s, industrial microbiology shifted its focus to the production of therapeutic agents, especially antibiotics. Advances in molecular biology have greatly increased the potential applications of industrial microbiology in areas such as therapeutics, diagnostics, environmental protection, and agriculture. The techniques of genetic engineering, along with technology developments in bioprocessing, make possible large-scale production of complex natural compounds that would otherwise be very difficult to obtain.

With the exception of the food industry, few commercial fermentation processes use wild strains of microorganisms. Of the many thousands of microbial species, few are used commercially, and fewer still are used as hosts for genetically engineering genes. Process development occurs in large part by strain improvement directed at increasing product yield, enhancing growth on cheaper substrates, and simplifying purification.

Strain development is achieved by either a traditional mutation and selection program or direct genetic manipulation. The recombinant DNA approach has succeeded in introducing new genetic material into a convenient host microorganism and amplifying genetic material. About 20% of the synthesizing capacity of a bacterium can be devoted to a single polypeptide or protein. *See* RECOMBINATION (GENETICS).

Commercial microbial compounds are produced in two distinct phases: fermentation and product recovery. Production usually occurs in a batch fermentor, where gas of controlled composition and flow is bubbled through a stirred pure microbial culture suspended in a liquid medium of optimum nutrient composition. Product recovery and purification involves a series of operations. The first steps usually involve cell disruption or the separation of the cell or cellular debris from the fluid medium, typically through centrifugation and filtration. Later stages of purification include finer membrane filtration, extraction, precipitation, and chromatography. *See* FERMENTATION; STERILIZATION.

The production of certain foods and beverages was an early application of industrial microbiology. Now, the fields of mineral recovery, medicine, environmental protection, and food and agriculture are using similar techniques.

Bacterial leaching reactions have been used to alter metal-bearing minerals, usually converting them to more soluble forms before the metals are extracted. Such operations can result in improved extraction rates in comparison to those of conventional processes, which are usually conducted on ore waste dumps and heaps. Large-scale commercial applications of biochemical mining and extraction have been limited mainly to copper and uranium. Besides enhancing or inhibiting the recovery of metal values from ores, bacteria are being used to precipitate or accumulate metal. The process, known as bioaccumulation, normally involves the adsorption of metal ions on the bacteria, which are then chemically transformed to an insoluble precipitate.

The most visible products of industrial microbiology are therapeutics for human health. Microbial synthesis is the preferred method of production for most health care drugs with complex chemistry. Microorganisms still have a remarkable ability for producing new commercial antibiotics, the largest class of drugs, and for continued yield improvement. With recombinant DNA technology, many proteins and polypeptides that are present naturally in the human body in trace amounts can be produced in large amounts during fermentation of recombinant microorganisms. See ANTIBIOTIC; INSULIN.

Microbial activities have long been the basis for sewage treatment facilities, and industrial and hazardous waste cleanup, or bioremediation, has become important. Bioremediation successes have been achieved by using native bacteria to degrade petroleum products, toxic chlorinated herbicides, and toxic biocides. See HAZARDOUS WASTE; SEWAGE.

Some of the oldest and most established areas of industrial microbiology concern food and beverage products, such as the production and use of brewer's yeast and baker's yeast. The food industry and the detergent industry are the major users of industrial enzymes produced by microbial fermentation. Detergents, especially in Europe, often contain protein-degrading enzymes (proteases). In the food industry, amylases convert starch to glucose, and glucose isomerase converts glucose to fructose.   [R.Kor.]

Infection   A term considered by some to mean the entrance, growth, and multiplication of a microorganism (pathogen) in the body of a host, resulting in the establishment of a disease process. Others define infection as the presence of a microorganism in host tissues whether or not it evolves into detectable pathologic effects. The host may be a bacterium, plant, animal, or human being, and the infecting agent may be viral, rickettsial, bacterial, fungal, or protozoan.

A differentiation is made between infection and infestation. Infestation is the invasion of a host by higher organisms such as parasitic worms. See EPIDEMIOLOGY; MEDICAL BACTERIOLOGY; MEDICAL MYCOLOGY; MEDICAL PARASITOLOGY; OPPORTUNISTIC INFECTIONS; PATHOGEN; VIRUS.   [D.N.La.]

Infectious disease   A pathological condition spread among biological species. Infectious diseases, although varied in their effects, are always associated with viruses, bacteria, fungi, protozoa, multicellular parasites and aberrant proteins known as prions. A complex series of steps, mediated by factors contributed by both the infectious agent and the host, is required for microorganisms or prions to establish an infection or disease. Worldwide, infectious diseases are the third leading cause of human death.

The most common relationship between a host and a microorganism is a commensal one, in which advantages exist for both organisms. For example, hundreds of billions of bacteria of many genera live in the human gastrointestinal tract, coexisting in ecological balance without causing disease. These bacteria help prevent the invasion of the host by more virulent organisms. In exchange, the host provides an environment in which harmless bacteria can readily receive nutrients. There are very few microorganisms that cause disease every time they encounter a host. Instead, many factors of both host and microbial origin are involved in infectious disease. These factors include the general health of the host, previous exposure of the host to the microorganism, and the complement of molecules produced by the bacteria.

Spread of a pathogenic microorganism among individual hosts is the hallmark of an infectious disease. This process, known as transmission, may occur through four major pathways: contact with the microorganism, airborne inhalation, through a common vehicle such as blood, or by vector-borne spread.

The manner in which an infectious disease develops, or its pathogenesis, usually follows a consistent pattern. To initiate an infection, there must be a physical encounter as which the microorganism enters the host. The most frequent portals of entry are the respiratory, gastrointestinal, and genitourinary tracts as well as breaks in the skin.

Surface components on the invading organism determine its ability to adhere and establish a primary site of infection. The cellular specificity of adherence of microorganisms often limits the range of susceptible hosts. For example, although measles and distemper viruses are closely related, dogs do not get measles and humans do not get distemper. From the initial site of infection, microorganisms may directly invade further into tissues or travel through the blood or lymphatic system to other organs.

Microorganisms produce toxins that can cause tissue destruction at the site of infection, can damage cells throughout the host, or can interfere with the normal metabolism of the host. The damage that microorganisms cause is directly related to the toxins they produce. Toxins are varied in their mechanism of action and host targets. See CHOLERA; STAPHYLOCOCCUS.

The host's reaction to an infecting organism is the inflammatory response, the body's most important internal defense mechanism. Although the inflammatory response is also seen as secondary to physical injury and nonspecific immune reactions, it is a reliable indicator of the presence of pathogenic microorganisms. Immune cells known as lymphocytes and granulocytes are carried by the blood to the site of infection. These cells either engulf and kill, or secrete substances which inhibit and neutralize, microorganisms. Other white blood cells, primarily monocytes, recognize foreign organisms and transmit chemical signals to other cells of the host's immune system, triggering the production of specific antibodies or specialized killer cells, both of which are lethal to the infecting microorganism. Any influence that reduces the immune system's ability to respond to foreign invasion, such as radiation therapy, chemotherapy, or destruction of immune cells by an immunodeficiency virus such as HIV, increases the likelihood that a organism will cause disease within the host.

Chemical compounds that are more toxic to microorganisms than to the host are commonly employed in the prevention and treatment of infectious disease; however, the emergence of drug-resistant organisms has led to increases in the morbidity and mortality associated with some infections. Other methods for controlling the spread of infectious diseases are accomplished by breaking a link in the chain of transmission between the host, microorganism, and mode of spread by altering the defensive capability of the host. Overall, the three most important advances to extend human life are clean water, vaccination, and antibiotics (in that order of importance).

Water-borne infections are controlled by filtration and chlorination of municipal water supplies. Checking food handlers for disease, refrigeration, proper cooking, and eliminating rodent and insect infestation have markedly reduced the level of food poisonings. The transmission of vector-borne diseases can be controlled by eradication of the vector. Blood-borne infections are reduced by screening donated blood for antibodies specific for HIV and other viruses and by rejecting donations from high-risk donors. For diseases such as tuberculosis, the airborne spread of the causative agent, *Mycobacterium tuberculosis*, can be reduced by quarantining infected individuals. The spread of sexually transmitted diseases, including AIDS, syphilis, and herpes simplex, can be prevented by inhibiting direct contact between the pathogenic microorganism and uninfected hosts. See ACQUIRED IMMUNE DEFICIENCY SYNDROME (AIDS); FOOD POISONING; VACCINATION; WATER-BORNE DISEASE.   [P.J.McN.]

Infectious mononucleosis   A disease of children and young adults, characterized by fever and enlarged lymph nodes and spleen. EB (Epstein-Barr) herpesvirus is the causative agent.

Onset of the disease is slow and nonspecific with variable fever and malaise; later, cervical lymph nodes enlarge, and in about 50% of cases the spleen also becomes enlarged. The disease lasts 4–20 days or longer. Epidemics are common in institutions where young people live. EB virus infections occurring in early childhood are usually asymptomatic. In later childhood and adolescence, the disease more often accompanies infection—although even at these ages inapparent infections are common. *See* Epstein-Barr virus.   [J.L.Me.]

Inflorescence   A flower cluster segregated from any other flowers on the same plant, together with the stems and bracts (reduced leaves) associated with it. Certain plants produce inflorescences, whereas others produce only solitary flowers. *See* Flower.   [G.J.W.]

Influenza   An acute respiratory viral infection characterized by fever, chills, sore throat, headache, body aches, and severe cough. The term flu, which is frequently used incorrectly for various respiratory and even intestinal illnesses (such as stomach flu), should be used only for illness with these classic symptoms. The onset is typically abrupt, in contrast to common colds which begin slowly and progress over a period of days. Influenza is usually epidemic in occurrence. The first documented pandemic, or global epidemic, of influenza is considered to have been in 1580. The influenza pandemic of 1918, the most famous occurrence, was responsible for at least 20 million deaths worldwide.

The three types of influenza viruses, types A, B, and C, are classified in the virus family Orthomyxoviridae, and they are similar, but not identical, in structure and morphology. Types A and B are more similar in physical and biologic characteristics to each other than they are to type C. Influenza viruses may be spherical or filamentous in shape, and they are of medium size among common viruses of humans. *See* Animal virus.

When a cell is infected by two similar but different viruses of one type, especially type A, various combinations of the original parental viruses may be packaged or assembled into the new progeny; thus, a progeny virus may be a mixture of gene segments from each parental virus and therefore may gain a new characteristic, for example, a new surface protein. This phenomenon is called genetic reassortment, and the frequency with which it occurs and leads to viruses with new features is a significant cause of the constant appearance of new variants of the virus. In the laboratory, reassortment occurs between animal and human strains as well as between human strains. It probably occurs in nature also, and is thought to contribute to the appearance of new strains that infect humans. Generally, if a new variant is sufficiently different from the vaccine currently in use, the vaccine will provide limited or no protection.

The influenza virus has a short incubation period; that is, there is only a period of 1–3 days between infection and symptoms, and this leads to the abrupt development of symptoms that is a hallmark of influenza infections. The virus is typically shed in the throat for 5–7 days. Complete recovery from uncomplicated influenza usually takes several days, and the individual may feel weak and exhausted for a week or more after the major symptoms disappear. The two main complications of influenza are primary influenza virus pneumonia and secondary bacterial pneumonia. Primary influenza pneumonia is relatively infrequent, occurring in less than 1% of cases during an epidemic, although mortality may be 25–30%. The damage to epithelial cells and subsequent loss of the ability to clear particles from the respiratory tract can lead to secondary bacterial pneumonia. This problem commonly occurs in elderly individuals or those with underlying chronic lung disease or similar problems. Influenza-induced pneumonia may cause as many as 20,000 deaths in a typical influenza season. Another complication, known as Reye's syndrome, may follow influenza, and is more common in children. This disease of the brain develops within 2–12 days of a systemic viral infection, and can result in vomiting, liver damage, coma, and sometimes death.

All three types of influenza viruses can cause disease in humans, but there are significant differences in severity of the disease and the range of hosts. In contrast to the large number of animal species infected by type A virus, types B and C are only rarely isolated from animals and infect predominantly humans.

The presence or absence of antibodies is very important in the epidemiology of influenza. In individuals with no immunity, attack rates may reach 70% and severe illness may result. Even low levels of antibody may provide partial protection in an individual and decrease the severity of the illness to only coldlike symptoms.

During an epidemic, one strain of influenza is predominant, but it is not unusual for two or more other strains to be present as minor infections in a population. Outbreaks of influenza occur during cold-weather months in temperate climates, and typically most cases cluster on a period of 1–2 months, in contrast to broader periods of illness with many other respiratory viruses. An increased death rate due to primary pneumonia and bacterial superinfection is common and is one of the ways that public health authorities monitor an epidemic.

Control and prevention of influenza are attempted through the use of drugs and vaccines. Inactivated viral vaccines are used to prevent influenza, although use of attenuated live strains of the virus may better stimulate the cell-mediated immune response and provide higher-quality and longer-lasting immunity. The makeup of the vaccine is modified annually, based upon predictions of the expected prevalent strain for each flu season, but usually contains antigens of two type A viruses and one type B virus. These vaccines take advantage of the natural ability of the viral nucleic acid to reassort and form new strains. The vaccines utilize strains that are not virulent and will replicate at lower temperatures, as found in the nasopharynx, but not at higher temperatures as found in the lower respiratory tract. The techniques of modern biotechnology are employed to clone copies of parts of the virus or to provide oligonucleotides corresponding to crucial functional areas of the virus, to obtain improved protection and reduced side effects. See BIOTECHNOLOGY; VACCINATION.   [J.M.Q.]

Inoculation   The process of introducing a microorganism or suspension of microorganism into a culture medium. The medium may be (1) a solution of nutrients required by the organism or a solution of nutrients plus agar; (2) a cell suspension (tissue culture); (3) embryonated egg culture; or (4) animals, for example, rat, mouse, guinea pig, hamster, monkey, birds, or human being. When animals are used, the purpose usually is the activation of the immunological defenses against the organism. This is a form of vaccination, and quite often the two terms are used interchangeably. Both constitute a means of producing an artificial but active immunity against specific organisms, although the length of time given by such protection may vary widely with different organisms. See IMMUNITY; VACCINATION.   [E.G.St./N.K.M.]

Inositol   The generic name for hexahydroxycyclohexanes, which are classified as carbohydrates. The inositols have exceptional chemical stability and are easily crystallized. Of the forms common in nature, the most ubiquitous and biologically important is myoinositol, a water-soluble crystalline compound. Many biological functions require myoinositol, and thus it is identified as an essential metabolite. Although originally classified as a vitamin, myoinositol is now known to be a cellular precursor of phospholipids that serve as a source of metabolic regulators and as membrane anchors for certain proteins. Some microorganisms require exogenous myoinositol for growth. See CARBOHYDRATE; LIPID.   [C.E.Ba.]

Insecta   A class of the phylum Arthropoda, sometimes called the Hexapoda. In fact, Hexapoda is a superclass consisting of both Insecta and the related class Parainsecta (containing the springtails and proturans). Class Insecta is the most diverse group of organisms, containing about 900,000 described species, but there are possibly as many as 5 million to perhaps 20 million actual species of insects. Like other arthropods, they have an external, chitinous covering. Fossil insects dating as early as the Early Devonian have been found.

Classification. The class Insecta is divided into orders on the basis of the structure of the wings and the mouthparts, on the type of metamorphosis, and on various other characteristics. There are differences of opinion among entomologists as to the limits of some of the orders. The orders of insects (and their relatives the parainsects) are shown below.

```
        Superclass Hexapoda
          Class Parainsecta
                Order: Protura: proturans
                       Collembola: springtails
          Class Insecta
            Subclass Monocondylia
                Order: Diplura: telsontails
                       Archaeognatha: bristletails
            Subclass Dicondylia
              Infraclass Apterygota
                Order: Zygentoma: silverfish, firebrats
              Infraclass Pterygota
               Section Palaeoptera
                Order: Ephemeroptera: mayflies
                       Odonata: damselflies and dragonflies
               Section Neoptera
               Hemimetabola
                Order: Plecoptera: stoneflies
                       Grylloblattodea: rockcrawlers
                       Orthoptera: grasshoppers, katy-dids, crickets
                       Phasmatodea: walkingsticks
                       Mantodea: mantises
                       Blattodea: cockroaches
                       Isoptera: termites
                       Dermaptera: earwigs
                       Embioptera: webspinners
                       Zoraptera: zorapterans
                       Psocoptera: psocids, booklice
                       Phthiraptera: lice
                       Thysanoptera: thrips
                       Hemiptera: cicadas, hoppers, aphids, white-
                          flies, scales
               Holometabola
                Order: Megaloptera: dobsonflies, alderflies
                       Raphidioidea: snakeflies
                       Neuroptera: lacewings, antlions
                       Coleoptera: beetles
                       Strepsiptera: twisted-wing parasites
```

Mecoptera: scorpionflies
Siphonaptera: fleas
Diptera: true flies
Trichoptera: caddisflies
Lepidoptera: moths, butterflies
Hymenoptera: sawflies, wasps, ants, bees

Morphology. Insects are usually elongate and cylindrical in form, and are bilaterally symmetrical. The body is segmented, and the ringlike segments are grouped into three distinct regions: the head, thorax, and abdomen. The head bears the eyes, antennae, and mouthparts; the thorax bears the legs and wings, when wings are present; the abdomen usually bears no locomotor appendages but often bears some appendages at its apex. Most of the appendages of an insect are segmented.

The skeleton is primarily on the outside of the body and is called an exoskeleton. However, important endoskeletal structures occur, particularly in the head. The body wall of an insect serves not only as a covering, but also as a supporting structure to which many important muscles are attached. The body wall of an insect is composed of three principal layers: the outer cuticula, which contains, among other chemicals, chitin; a cellular layer, the epidermis, which secretes the chitin; and a thin noncellular layer beneath the epidermis, the basement membrane. The surface of an insect's body consists of a number of hardened plates, or sclerites, separated by sutures or membranous areas, which permit bending or movement. *See* CHITIN.

A pair of compound eyes usually cover a large part of the head surface. In addition most insects also possess two or three simple eyes, the ocelli, usually located on the upper part of the head between the compound eyes; each of these has a single lens. *See* EYE (INVERTEBRATE).

Insect mouthparts typically consist of a labrum, or upper lip; a pair each of mandibles and maxillae; a labium, or lower lip; and a tonguelike structure, the hypopharynx. These structures are variously modified in different insect groups and are often used in classification and identification. The type of mouthparts an insect has determines how it feeds and what type of damage it is capable of causing.

Several forms of antennae are recognized, to which various names are applied; they are used extensively in classification. The antennae are usually located between or below the compound eyes and are often reduced to a very small size. They are sensory in function and act as tactile organs, organs of smell, and in some cases organs of hearing.

Insects are the only winged invertebrates, and their dominance as a group is probably due to their wings. Immature insects do not have fully developed wings, except in the mayflies. The wings may be likened to the two sides of a cellophane bag that have been pressed tightly together. The form and rigidity of the wing are due to the stiff chitinous veins which support and strengthen the membranous portion. At the base are small sclerites which serve as muscle attachments and produce consequent wing movement. The wings vary in number, placement, size, shape, texture, and venation, and in the position at which they are held at rest. Adult insects may be wingless or may have one pair of wings on the mesothorax, or, more often two pairs. There is a common basic pattern of wing venation in insects which is variously modified and in general quite specific for different large groups of insects. Much of insect classification depends upon these variations. A knowledge of fossil insects depends largely upon the wings, because they are among the more readily fossilized parts of the insect body.

Internal anatomy. The intake of oxygen, its distribution to the tissues, and the removal of carbon dioxide are accomplished by means of an intricate system of tubes called the tracheal system. The principal tubes of this system, the tracheae, open externally at the spiracles. Internally they branch extensively, extend to all parts of the body, and terminate in simple cells, the tracheoles. Many adaptations for carrying on respiration are known.

Insects possess an alimentary tract consisting of a tube, usually coiled, which extends from the mouth to the anus. It is differentiated into three main regions: the foregut, midgut, and hindgut. Valves between the three main divisions of the alimentary canal regulate the passage of food from one region to another.

The excretory system consists of a group of tubes with closed distal ends, the Malpighian tubules, which arise as evaginations of the anterior end of the hindgut. They vary in number from 1 to over 100, and extend into the body cavity. Various waste products are taken up from the blood by these tubules and passed out via the hindgut and anus.

The circulatory system of an insect is an open one. The only blood vessel is a tube located dorsal to the alimentary tract and extending through the thorax and abdomen. The posterior portion of this tube, the heart, is divided into a series of chambers, each of which has a pair of lateral openings called ostia. The anterior part of the tube is called the dorsal aorta.

The nervous system consists of a brain, often called the supraesophageal ganglion, located in the head above the esophagus; a subesophageal ganglion, connected to the brain by two commissures that extend around each side of the esophagus; and a ventral nerve cord, typically double, extending posteriorly through the thorax and abdomen from the subesophageal ganglion. In the nerve cords there are enlargements, called ganglia. Typically, there is a pair to each body segment. From each ganglion of the chain, nerves extend to each adjacent segment of the body, and also extend from the brain to part of the alimentary canal.

Reproduction in insects is nearly always sexual, and the sexes are separate. Variations from the usual reproductive pattern occur occasionally. In many social insects, such as the ants and bees, certain females, the workers, may be unable to reproduce because their sex organs are undeveloped; in some insects, individuals occasionally occur that have characters of both sexes, called gynandromorphs. Also, parthenogenesis—the process of females giving rise to females—is known in some species.

Metamorphosis. After insects hatch from an egg, they begin to increase in size and will also usually change, to some degree at least, in form and often in appearance. This developmental process is metamorphosis. The growth of an insect is accompanied by a series of molts, or ecdyses, in which the cuticle is shed and renewed.

The molt involves not only the external layers of the body wall, the cuticula, but also the cuticular linings of the tracheae, foregut, and hindgut; the cast skins often retain the shape of the insects from which they were shed. The shedding process begins with a splitting of the old cuticle. This split grows and the insect eventually wriggles out of the old cuticle. The new skin, remains soft and pliable long enough for the body to expand to its fullest capacity before hardening.

Insects differ regarding the number of molts during their growing period. Many have as few as four molts; a few species have 40 or more, and the latter continue to molt throughout life.

Insects have been grouped or classified on the basis of the type of metamorphosis they undergo. Although all entomologists do not agree upon the same classification, the following outline is presented:

1. Ametabolous or primitive: No distinct external changes are evident with an increase in size.

2. Hemimetabolous: Direct metamorphosis that is simple and gradual; immature forms resemble the adults except in size, wings, and genitalia. Immatures are referred to as nymphs or naiads if aquatic.

3. Holometabolous: Complete, or indirect, metamorphosis; stages in this developmental type are: egg→larva→pupa→adult (or imago). [D.M.DeL.]

Fossils. Insects and parainsects have a rich fossil record that extends to 415 million years, representing all taxonomic orders and 70% of all families that occur today. Insect deposits are characterized by an abundance of exceptionally well-preserved deposits known as Lagerstätten. Lagerstätten refer not only to the familiar amber deposits that entomb insects in hardened tree resin, but more importantly to a broad variety of typically laminar, sedimentary deposits. These deposits, formed in lake basins, are the most persistent of insect-bearing deposits and document the evolution of insect biotas during the past 300 million years. By contrast, the oldest amber is approximately 120 million years old and extends modern lineages and associated taxa to the Early Cretaceous. Other major types of insect deposits include terrestrial shales and fine-grained sandstones marginal to marine deposits during the Early and Middle Devonian, a proliferation of nodular ironstone-bearing strata of late Carboniferous age from the equatorial lowlands of the paleocontinent Euramerica, and distinctive lithographic limestones worldwide from the Middle Jurassic to Early Cretaceous. More modern deposits are Miocene to Recent sinter deposits created by hydrothermal zones with mineral-rich waters, and similarly aged asphaltum, representing the surface accumulation of tar. Lastly, insects are abundant in many Pleistocene glacial deposits of outwash and stranded lake sediments, formed by the waxing and waning of alpine and continental glaciers. [C.C.La]

Insectivora An order of placental mammals including shrews, moles, and hedgehogs. The tree shrews (Tupaiidae) and elephant shrews (Macroscelididae) are now recognized as unrelated, and they are placed in separate orders (Scandentia and Macroscelidea). Formerly thought to be the basal placental order, from which other orders were derived, the Insectivora is now restricted to members of the former suborder Lipotyphla. It evolved side by side with the other placental orders, with a fossil record going back to the Paleocene. A number of fossil families from the Cretaceous and early Tertiary, formerly included in the Insectivora, are classified as Proteutheria.

Living lipotyphlous insectivores are small animals: the largest (*Potamogale*) weighs about 1 kg (2 lb). Most eat insects, worms, and other invertebrates, for which they search in ground litter and vegetation, using their highly developed olfactory sense and their mobile, sensitive snouts. Some burrow, such as moles; some are aquatic, such as the desman. Anatomically, they are distinguished by the absense of a cecum on the intestine, reduction of the pubic symphysis (fibrocartilaginous union of bones), and characters of the skull. The cheek teeth typically have sharp cusps and crests, and the incisors are often enlarged to act as forceps. Insectivores are found on all continents except Australia and Antarctica, but only one genus (*Cryptotis*, a shrew) has reached South America.

Three suborders can be distinguished: Erinaceomorpha, Soricomorpha, and Chrysochloromorpha. Living erinaceomorphs belong to the family Erinaceidae, comprising the spiny hedgehogs (Erinaceinae) of Eurasia and Africa and the hairy moonrats (Echinosoricinae) of Southeast Asia.

Four living families are included in the Soricomorpha: Soricidae (shrews), Talpidae (moles, desman), Tenrecidae (Madagascan tenrecs and African otter shrews), and

Solenodontidae (*Solenodon*, confined to Cuba and Hispaniola). Among the talpids, the subfamily Talpinae is the most advanced in modification of the forelimbs for burrowing, the Desmaninae have aquatic adaptations, and the Uropsilinae (represented by the Chinese shrew mole) retained shrewlike limbs. True moles did not reach North America until the Miocene; they were preceded in the Oligocene by the Proscalopidae, which burrowed in a different way, with the hands moving longitudinally beneath the body, instead of laterally as in true moles. The living *Solenodon*, in the West Indies, is one of the largest insectivores, but nevertheless shrewlike. The Tenrecidae are far removed geographically from other soricomorphs. They probably evolved in Africa, where their fossil history goes back to the early Miocene, and the otter shrews (Potamogalinae) survive on the continent of Africa today. The remainder are in Madagascar where, like the lemurs, they have evolved in diverse directions during a long time of isolation. In some ways, for example brain size, they have remained more primitive than other insectivores.

The golden moles (Chrysochloridae) are put into a separate suborder, Chrysochloromorpha. They are highly specialized burrowers, using large claws on the forefoot. They are confined to Africa, where fossils show that they were already specialized in the early Miocene. *See* MAMMALIA. [P.M.B.; M.C.McK.]

Instinctive behavior   A relatively complex response pattern which is usually present in one or both sexes of a given species. These responses have a genetic basis, are essentially unlearned, and are generally adaptive.

Instinctive behavior occurs when an animal has a particular internal state while it is in the presence of a specific external stimulation called a releaser or a sign stimulus. Neither the internal state nor the external stimulus alone is adequate for the elicitation of the response. Many animals show particular instinctive behaviors only during the mating season, when hormonal changes associated with sexual behavior sensitize specific portions of the central nervous system, which will then be active in the presence of the releaser. The external stimulus may be relatively simple or incredibly complex.

Within limits, the instinctive behaviors can be modified by learning. There is evidence, for example, that some predators learn to attack their prey at the back of the neck because when held in that position the prey cannot counterattack. *See* MIGRATORY BEHAVIOR; REPRODUCTIVE BEHAVIOR. [K.E.M.]

Instrumental conditioning   Learning based upon the consequences of behavior. For example, a rat may learn to press a lever when this action produces food. Instrumental or operant behavior is the behavior by which an organism changes its environment. The particular instances of behavior that produce consequences are called responses. Classes of responses having characteristic consequences are called operant classes; responses in an operant class operate on (act upon) the environment. For example, a rat's lever-press responses may include pressing with the left paw or with the right paw, sitting on the lever, or other activities, but all of these taken together constitute the operant class called lever pressing.

Consequences of responding that produce increases in behavior are called reinforcers. For example, if an animal has not eaten recently, food is likely to reinforce many of its responses. Whether a particular event will reinforce a response or not depends on the relation between the response and the behavior for which its consequences provide an opportunity. Some consequences of responding called punishers produce decreases in behavior. The properties of punishment are similar to those of reinforcement, except for the difference in direction.

The consequences of its behavior are perhaps the most important properties of the world about which an organism can learn, but few consequences are independent of other circumstances. Organisms learn that their responses have one consequence in one setting and different consequences in another. Stimuli that set the occasion on which responses have different consequences are called discriminative stimuli (these stimuli do not elicit responses; their functions are different from those that are simply followed by other stimuli). When organisms learn that responses have consequences in the presence of one but not another stimulus, their responses are said to be under stimulus control. For example, if a rat's lever presses produce food when a light is on but not when it is off and the rat comes to press only when the light is on, the rat's presses are said to be under the stimulus control of the light. *See* CONDITIONED REFLEX.

[A.C.Ca.]

Insulin Produced and secreted by the beta cells of the islets (insulae) of Langerhans of the pancreas, the hormone which regulates the use and storage of foodstuffs, especially the carbohydrates. Chemically insulin is a small, simple protein. Insulins from various species differ in the composition; these differences account for the fact that diabetics treated with animal insulins develop antibodies which may sometimes interfere with the action of the hormone. The structure has been verified by synthesis of insulin from pure amino acids in the laboratory. *See* CARBOHYDRATE METABOLISM; IMMUNOLOGY; PANCREAS.

Insulin, being a polypeptide, can also be broken down by many proteolytic enzymes to its constituent amino acids. Because of these breakdown systems, the turnover of insulin in the body is rapid; its "half-life" has been estimated to be 10–30 min. The liver alone is capable of destroying about 50% of the insulin passing through it on its way from the pancreas to the bodily tissues.

The role played by insulin in the body is most clearly approached by considering the abnormalities resulting from removing insulin from an organism by surgical excision of the pancreas or by the chemical destruction of the insulin-producing cells: A state of severe diabetes is produced. Normally the blood glucose level is about 100 mg/100 ml. A carbohydrate meal raises the blood sugar to about 150 mg and the premeal value is reached again within 1.5 h. The normal organism manages to dispose of food by storage and oxidation within this period because insulin is present. When food (carbohydrate and protein) reaches the upper intestine, a substance is liberated which in turn stimulates the beta cells to secrete extra insulin. Insulin acts on most tissues to speed the uptake of glucose. In the cells the glucose is burned for energy, stored as glycogen, or transformed to and stored as fat. The human pancreas probably produces 1–2 mg of the hormone per day. This is sufficient to regulate the metabolism of more than 250 g of carbohydrate, 70 g of protein, and 75 g of fat, the usual composition of an ordinary 2000-calorie diet.

In diabetes the rate of glucose uptake is slowed, the level of circulating blood sugar rises, and sugar spills over into the excreted urine. Calories are wasted, more water is excreted, and there is muscular weakness and weight loss; hence urinary frequency, hunger, thirst, and fatigue. Whenever glucose metabolism is defective, stored fat is broken down to fatty acids because of the actions of adrenaline and the pituitary growth hormone. Insulin is able to reverse all these phenomena by favoring storage and swift intake of glucose into the tissues, by decreasing the breakdown of stored fat, and by promoting protein synthesis.

When insulin is secreted or given in excess, it may lower the blood sugar level much below its normal value, causing hypoglycemia. Hypoglycemia is dangerous because the metabolism in the brain cells depends primarily upon an adequate supply of glucose.

The precise molecular mechanisms of insulin action are still not known. The initial step is the binding of the hormone to a specific receptor on the cell membrane. This event somehow activates a set of transport molecules, so that glucose, potassium, and amino acids enter cells more freely. At the same time, fat breakdown is slowed and glycogen storage increased. All these actions depend upon the integrity of the outer cell membrane. *See* CELL PERMEABILITY.

Not all the cells of the body require or respond to insulin. The insulin-responsive tissues are the liver, skeletal muscle, the heart, and the adipose tissue. Sensitivity to insulin is affected by many conditions. Obesity, antibodies to the hormone or its receptor, oversecretion of growth hormone or adrenal steroids, ketosis, and unknown genetic factors all cause insulin resistance. Muscular exercise, correction of obesity, and a deficiency of pituitary or adrenal hormones are associated with an increased sensitivity to the hormone.   [R.Lev.; B.F.]

Intelligence   General mental ability due to the integrative and adaptive functions of the brain that permit complex, unstereotyped, purposive responses to novel or changing situations, involving discrimination, generalization, learning, concept formation, inference, mental manipulation of memories, images, words and abstract symbols, eduction of relations and correlates, reasoning, and problem solving.

Intelligence tests are diverse collections of tasks (or items), graded in difficulty. The person's performance on each item can be objectively scored (for example, pass or fail); the total number of items passed is called the raw score. Raw scores are converted to some form of scaled scores which can be given a statistical interpretation.

The first practical intelligence test for children, devised in 1905 by the French psychologist Alfred Binet, converted raw scores to a scale of "mental age," defined as the raw score obtained by the average of all children of a given age. Mental age (MA) divided by chronological age (CA) yields the well known intelligence quotient or IQ. When multiplied by 100 (to get rid of the decimal), the average IQ at every age is therefore 100, with a standard deviation of approximately 15 or 16. Because raw scores on mental tests increase linearly with age only up to about 16 years, the conversion of raw scores to a mental-age scale beyond age 16 must resort to statistical artifices. Because of this problem and the difficulty of constructing mental-age scales which preserve exactly the same standard deviation of IQs at every age, all modern tests have abandoned the mental-age concept and the calculation of IQ from the ratio of MA to CA. Nowadays the IQ is simply a standardized score with a population mean of 100 and a standard deviation (σ) of 15 at every age from early childhood into adulthood. The middle 50%, considered "average," fall between IQs of 90 and 110. IQs below 70 generally indicate "mental retardation," and above 130, "giftedness."
                                                                                    [A.R.J.]

Intestine   The tubular portion of the digestive tract, usually between the stomach and the cloaca or anus. The detailed functions vary with the region, but are primarily digestion and absorption of food.

The structure of the intestine varies greatly in different vertebrates, but there are several common modifications, mainly associated with increasing the internal surface area. One, seen in many fishes, is the development of a spiral valve; this turns the intestine into a structure resembling a spiral staircase. Another, seen in some fish and most tetrapods, is simply elongating and then coiling the intestine. This can reach extremes in large herbivores: Oxen have intestinal lengths of over 150 ft (45 m). In numerous forms there are blind pouches, or ceca, off part of the intestine. In fish these are commonly at the anterior end; in tetrapods they generally lie at the junc-

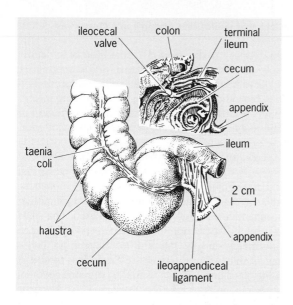

ileocecal valve

colon

terminal ileum

cecum

appendix

ileum

taenia coli

2 cm

haustra

appendix

cecum

ileoappendiceal ligament

Junction of ileum with large intestine in humans.

tion between the large and small intestines. In all vertebrates the inner surface of the intestine is irregular, with ridges and projections of various sorts; these reach their maximum development in the extremely fine and numerous finger-shaped villi found in mammals.

In humans the intestine consists of the small and large intestines. The small intestine is further divided into three major parts: the duodenum, the jejunum, and the ileum. The duodenum, 10–12 in. (25–30 cm) long, begins at the pyloric sphincter of the stomach and curves around the head of the pancreas on the right side of the anterior part of the abdomen. It receives the ducts of the biliary system and the pancreas. The jejunum and ileum are about 19 ft (6 m) long and form a much-coiled tube that empties at right angles into the large intestine through the ileocolic valve (see illustration). The large intestine, or colon, consists of five parts: the ascending, transverse, descending, and sigmoid regions, and the terminal rectum which empties into the anal canal.

The microscopic structure of the intestine comprises an inner glandular mucosa, a muscular coat, and an outer serosa of connective tissues which is covered in most areas by peritoneum.

The intestine is supported by dorsal mesenteries of varying extent, which contain an extensive system of arteries, veins, lymphatics, and nerves to the various regions. *See* Digestive system.

[T.S.P.]

Intron   In split genes, a portion that is included in ribonucleic acid (RNA) transcripts but is removed from within a transcript during RNA processing and is rapidly degraded. Split genes are those in which portions appearing in messenger RNAs (mRNAs) or in structural RNAs, termed exons, are not contiguous in a gene but are separated by lengths of deoxyribonucleic acid (DNA) encoding parts of transcripts that do not survive the maturation of RNA (introns). Most genes in eukaryotes, and a few in prokaryotes, are split. These include not just a large number of different protein-coding genes but also genes encoding transfer RNAs (tRNAs) in such diverse eukaryotes as yeast and frogs, and genes encoding structural RNAs of ribosomes in some protozoa. Introns are also found in mitochondrial genes of lower eukaryotes and in some chloroplast genes. *See* EXON.

The number of introns in a gene varies greatly, from 1 in the case of structural RNA genes to more than 50 in collagen. The lengths, locations, and compositions of introns also vary greatly among genes. However, in general, sizes and locations—but not DNA sequence—are comparable in homologous genes in different organisms. The implication is that introns became established in genes early in the evolution of eukaryotes, and while their nucleotide sequence is not very important, their existence, positions, and sizes are significant.

Speculation on the roles and the evolution of introns is mostly based on correlations that have been seen between domains of protein structure and the exons of genes that are defined by intervening introns. For example, the enzyme alcohol dehydrogenase (ADH) has two domains, one portion of the protein that binds alcohol, and another that binds the enzyme cofactor nicotinamide adenine dinucleotide (NAD). The ADH gene has an intron that cleanly separates the nucleotide sequences which encode each domain, and gene-sequence arrangements such as this are not uncommon. It has been suggested that introns became established in the genes of eukaryotes (and to a limited extent in bacteria) because they facilitate a genetic shuffling or rearrangement of portions of genes which encode various units of function, thus creating new genes with new combinations of properties. The introns allow genetic recombination to occur between the coding units rather than within them, thus providing a means of genetic evolution via wholesale reassortments of functional subunits or building blocks, rather than by fortuitous recombinations of actual protein-coding DNA sequences. *See* GENE; GENETIC CODE; RECOMBINATION (GENETICS).   [P.M.M.R.]

Invasion ecology   The study of the establishment, spread, and ecological impact of species translocated from one region or continent to another by humans. Biological invasions have gained attention as a tool for basic research, used to study the ecology and evolution of populations and of novel biotic interactions; and as a conservation issue tied to the preservation of biodiversity. The invasion of nonindigenous (also called exotic, alien, or nonnative) species is a serious concern for those charged with managing and protecting natural as well as managed ecosystems. *See* ECOLOGY; POPULATION ECOLOGY.

Ecologists make a distinction between introduced species, meaning any species growing outside its natural habitat including cultivated or domesticated organisms, and invasive species, meaning the subset of introduced species that establish free-living populations in the wild. The great majority of introduced species (approximately 90% as estimated from some studies) do not become invasive. While certain problem invaders, such as the zebra mussel (*Dreissena polymorpha*), exact enormous economic and ecological costs, other introduced species are generally accepted as beneficial additions, such as most major food crops.

Intentional plant introductions have been promoted primarily by the horticulture industry to satisfy the public's desire for novel landscaping. However, plants have also been introduced for agriculture, for silviculture, and for control of soil erosion. Intentional animal introductions include game species brought in for sport hunting or fishing. Unlike these examples, intentional introductions can also include species that are not necessarily intended to form self-sustaining populations, such as those promoted by the aquarium or pet trade.

Species introduced accidentally are "hitchhikers." Shipping ballast has been a major vector, first in the form of soil carrying terrestrial invertebrates and plant seeds or rhizomes, and more recently in the form of ballast water carrying planktonic larvae from foreign ports. While many species are introduced in ballast or by similar means, hitchhikers can also be unwanted parasites that bypass importation and quarantine precautions. For example, many nonindigenous agricultural weeds have been imported in contaminated seed lots.

Certain types of habitats seem to have higher numbers of established nonindigenous species than others. The characteristics that make a site open to invasion must be determined. For example, islands are notably vulnerable to invasions. Islands usually have fewer resident species to begin with, leading to the conjecture that simpler systems have less biotic resistance to invaders. That is, an introduced species is less likely to be met by a resident competitor, predator, or pathogen capable of excluding it. The idea of biotic resistance is also consistent with the idea that complexity confers stability in natural systems. *See* INVASION ECOLOGY.

A second generalization about invasibility is that ecosystems with high levels of anthropogenic disturbance, such as agricultural fields or roadsides, seem to be more invaded. Increased turnover of open space in these sites could provide more opportunities for the establishment of new species. An alternative explanation is that many species that adapted to anthropogenic habitats in Europe simply tagged along as humans re-created those habitats in new places. Those species would naturally have an advantage over native species at exploiting human disturbances. A final suggestion by proponents of ecosystem management is that disturbance (including, in this context, a disruption of natural disturbance regimes, for example, fire suppression) weakens the inherent resistance of ecosystems and promotes invasion.

Invasive species can have several different types of impacts. First, they can affect the traits and behavior of resident organisms (for example, causing a shift in diet, size, or shape of the native species they encounter). Second, impacts can occur at the level of the population, either by changing the abundance of a native population or by changing its genetic composition. Hybridization between an invader and a closely related native can result in introgression and genetic pollution. The endpoint can be the de facto extinction of the native species when the unique aspects of its genome are overwhelmed. Third, impacts can occur at the level of ecological communities. When individual populations are reduced or even driven extinct by competition or predation by an invasive species, the result is a decrease in the overall biodiversity of the invaded site. Finally, invaders can impact not only other species but the physical characteristics of an ecosystem as well.

There are two main contributing factors in determining which species have the biggest impacts: abundance and special characteristics. Invaders that reach extremely high density simply overwhelm all other organisms. Other species have special traits that result in an impact out of proportion to their numbers.

Because of the economic and conservation importance of nonindigenous species, much of invasion ecology focuses on the prevention, eradication, and control of invaders, and the restoration of sites after control. Research has emphasized the importance of early detection and eradication of problem species. Biological control has been touted as an environmentally friendly alternative to herbicides and pesticides. *See* ALLELOPATHY; ECOLOGICAL COMMUNITIES; ECOLOGICAL SUCCESSION; SPECIATION; SPECIES CONCEPT.   [I.M.P.]

Invertebrate pathology   The study of diseases affecting invertebrate animals, including etiology, pathogenesis, symptomatology, pathology, histopathology, physiopathology, and epizootiology. Interactions between invertebrates and their diverse pathogens, such as bacteria, viruses, and protozoa, range from obligate parasitism to various associations that may result in disease. Disease is usually described as a disturbance of the equilibrium between the invertebrate animal and the environment, and it should be understood as a process and not a thing. The disease process represents the response of an invertebrate organism to injury. Its occurrence is a normal biological phenomenon, and it has been recognized as a balancing factor in nature. Understanding invertebrate pathology is essential to understanding invertebrate life and behavior.

Infectious diseases of invertebrates have been thoroughly studied, while less attention has been devoted to noninfectious diseases. The latter involve mechanical and physiological injuries caused by chemicals, nutritional disturbances, inherited abnormalities (genetic diseases), tumors, predation, and the actions of other invertebrates.

Numerous diseases and pathogens of invertebrate animals have been described throughout the world. By 1999, in Mollusca as many as 46 diseases of oysters, 20 of clams and cockles, 19 of scallops, and 9 of abalone had been described. Diseases of Crustacea included 17 lobster diseases, 35 diseases of shrimp and prawns, 17 of crabs, and 13 of crayfish.

Immune reactions of invertebrates can be cellular or humoral. In cellular immunity, several types of hemocytes have been demonstrated. Three defense reactions have been recognized: phagocytosis, encapsulation, and hemostasis (coagulation and wound healing). Phagocytosis is localized in the plasma membrane and the cytoskeleton. Encapsulation occurs when bacteria, fungi, nematodes, or protozoa, as well as nonliving objects that are too large to be phagocytyzed, are encapsulated by plasmatocytes or granulocytes. Wound healing and coagulation in invertebrates differs from hemostasis in vertebrate animals.

All types of hemocytes involved in invertebrate immunity are called immunocytes. The recognition of foreign antigens is affected by surface receptors and molecules located on the plasma membrane of immunocytes. Parasitoids and parasites of invertebrates often possess defensive mechanisms that can overcome immunological reactions of their hosts. Humoral immunity of invertebrates provides the second line of defense against massive invasion, when immunocytes become depleted.

The immune system of invertebrate animals produces antimicrobial proteins in immunocytes or in the fat body. Arthropods do not possess antibodies, but they synthesize lectins that can agglutinate microorganisms. Cytokine-like molecules have been found in mollusks, worms, echinoderms, and arthropods. In many invertebrate animals, a prophenoloxidase-activating system can contribute to humoral immunity. Neuropeptides and opiates mediate phagocytosis in the earthworm, mollusks, arthropods, starfishes, and sea urchins. Complement-like molecules have been detected in all invertebrates, and in some the C-reactive protein has been reported. Obviously the immune system of invertebrates is very sophisticated, sharing many fundamental mechanisms with vertebrates.

Invertebrate pathology has applications in agriculture, medicine, general biology, and biotechnology. In agriculture the prevention of diseases affecting honeybees and silkworm, and the use of bacterial toxins and baculoviruses for microbial control of insect pests, constitute the most important applications of invertebrate pathology. *See* Annelida; Antibody; Arthropoda; Echinodermata; Immunity; Insecta; Mollusca; Nemata; Porifera.   [K.M.]

Ion transport   Movement of salts and other electrolytes in the form of ions from place to place within living systems.

Ion transport may occur by any of several different mechanisms: electrochemical diffusion, active-transport requiring energy, or bulk flow as in the flow of blood in the circulatory system of animals or the transpiration stream in the xylem tissue of plants.

The best-known system for transporting ions actively is the sodium/potassium (Na/K) exchange pump, which occurs in plasma membranes of virtually all cells.

Experimental studies revealed that many transport processes, such as in bacterial cells and in the mitochondria of eukaryotic cells, are associated with a transport of protons (hydrogen ions, H^+). This fact led to the concept of proton pumps, in which the coupling or transfer of energy between oxidation processes and synthesis of adenosine triphosphate (ATP) and between hydrolysis of ATP and transport or other cellular work is explained in terms of a flow of protons as the means of energy transfer.

The processes of oxidation in the citric acid cycle of reactions in mitochondria are known to be coupled with the synthesis of ATP, which is formed from adenosine diphosphate (ADP) and inorganic orthophosphate (P_i), through the system of enzymes and cytochromes known as the electron transfer chain or electron transport system. This system transports electrons, removed in dehydrogenation from the organic molecules of the citric acid cycle on one side of the mitochondrial membrane, to the site of their incorporation into water, formed from two hydrogen ions and an atom of oxygen on the other side of the membrane. The flow of electrons from a relatively high potential level in the organic substrate to a level of lower potential in water constitutes, in effect, a current of negative electricity, and it was proposed that the flow drives a flow of protons in the opposite direction, as a current of positive electricity. This proton flow in turn is proposed as the force that drives the synthesis of three molecules of ATP for every two electrons flowing through the electron transport system. In effect, this is the machinery of the cellular power plant.

The Na/K ATPase pump then provides an example of a way in which a proton pump may transfer energy between the hydrolysis of ATP and a process of cellular work. The enzyme which is the basis of the pump is known to be bound to the lipid bilayer of the plasma membrane through phosphatides and to function only when so bound. The binding of Na^+, K^+, H^+, and ATP to active sites on the enzyme presumably has an allosteric effect, changing the shape of the enzyme molecule, activating the hydrolysis of ATP, and opening pathways of exchange of Na^+ and K^+.   [B.T.S.]

Transport processes are involved in uptake and release of inorganic ions by plants and in distribution of ions within plants, and thus determine ionic relations of plants. The cell wall and the external lipid-protein membrane (plasmalemma) have to be passed by the ions. Intracellular distribution and compartmentation are determined by transport across other membranes within the cells. The most important one is the tonoplast separating the cell vacuole from the cytoplasm.

Within tissues the continuous cell walls of adjacent cells form an apoplastic pathway for ion transport. A symplastic pathway is constituted by the cytoplasm extending from cell to cell via small channels of about 40 nanometers diameter (plasmodesmata) crossing the cell walls. Transport over longer distances is important in organs (roots, shoots, leaves, fruits), which are composed of different kinds of tissues, and in the whole plant. Xylem and phloem serve as pathways for long-distance transport. Roots take up ions from the soil and must supply other plant organs. The nutritional status of roots and shoots regarding both inorganic anions and organic substrates plays a large role in regulation of ionic relations of whole plants. Phytohormones affect transport mechanisms; they are produced in particular tissues, are distributed via the transport pathways, and thus exert a signaling function. *See* PHLOEM; PLANT HORMONES; PLANT TISSUE SYSTEMS; XYLEM.

The pipe system of the xylem in its mature transporting state is composed of rows of dead cells (tracheids, tracheary elements) whose cross-walls are perforated or removed entirely. The driving force for long-distance transport in the xylem is very largely passive. Transport is caused by transpiration, the loss of water from the aerial parts of the plant, driven by the water potential gradient directed from soil to roots, leaves, and atmosphere. A normally much smaller component driving the ascent of sap in the xylem is osmotic root pressure due to the pumping mechanisms concentrating ions in the root xylem, with water following passively. In a simplifying way the xylem can be considered as pathway for long-distance transport of ions from root to shoot, and the phloem for metabolite transport from photosynthesizing source leaves to various sinks in the plant. The long-distance transport pathways of the phloem are the sieve tubes, pipe systems with porous structures in the cross-walls (sieve plates) but, in contrast to vessels of the xylem, having living cytoplasm. Concentration and pressure gradients built up by active loading and unloading of sieve tubes in the source and sink regions, respectively, are the driving forces for transport.   [U.L.]

Island biogeography   The distribution of plants and animals on islands. Islands harbor the greatest number of endemic species. The relative isolation of many islands has allowed populations to evolve in the absence of competitors and predators, leading to the evolution of unique species that can differ dramatically from their mainland ancestors.

Plant species produce seeds, spores, and fruits that are carried by wind or water currents, or by the feet, feathers, and digestive tracts of birds and other animals. The dispersal of animal species is more improbable, but animals can also be carried long distances by wind and water currents, or rafted on vegetation and oceanic debris. Long-distance dispersal acts as a selective filter that determines the initial composition of an island community. Many species of continental origin may never reach islands unless humans accidentally or deliberately introduce them. Consequently, although islands harbor the greatest number of unique species, the density of species on islands (number of species per area) is typically lower than the density of species in mainland areas of comparable habitat. See POPULATION DISPERSAL.

Once a species reaches an island and establishes a viable population, it may undergo evolutionary change because of genetic drift, climatic differences between the mainland and the island, or the absence of predators and competitors from the mainland. Consequently, body size, coloration, and morphology of island species often evolve rapidly, producing forms unlike any related species elsewhere. Examples include the giant land tortoises of the Galápagos, and the Komodo dragon, a species of monitor lizard from Indonesia. See POLYMORPHISM (GENETICS); POPULATION GENETICS; SQUAMATA.

If enough morphological change occurs, the island population becomes reproductively isolated from its mainland ancestor, and it is recognized as a unique species. Because long-distance dispersal is relatively infrequent, repeated speciation may occur as populations of the same species successively colonize an island and differentiate. The most celebrated example is Darwin's finches, a group of related species that inhabit the Galápagos Islands and were derived from South American ancestors. The island species have evolved different body and bill sizes, and in some cases occupy unique ecological niches that are normally filled by mainland bird species. The morphology of these finches was first studied by Charles Darwin and constituted important evidence for his theory of natural selection. See ANIMAL EVOLUTION; SPECIATION.

Island biogeography theory has been extended to describe the persistence of single-species metapopulations. A metapopulation is a set of connected local populations in a fragmented landscape that does not include a persistent source pool region. Instead, the fragments themselves serve as stepping stones for local colonization and extinction. The most successful application of the metapopulation model has been to spotted owl populations of old-growth forest fragments in the northwestern United States. *See* BIOGEOGRAPHY; ECOLOGICAL COMMUNITIES; ECOSYSTEM.   [N.J.Go.]

Isoantigen   An immunologically active protein or polysaccharide present in some but not all individuals in a particular species. These substances initiate the formation of antibodies when introduced into other individuals of the species that genetically lack the isoantigen. Like all antigens, they are also active in stimulating antibody production in heterologous species. The ABO, MN, and Rh blood factors in humans constitute important examples. Consequently, elaborate precautions for typing are required in blood transfusion. *See* ANTIBODY; ANTIGEN; BLOOD GROUPS.   [M.J.Po.]

Joint (anatomy)   The structural component of an animal skeleton where two or more skeletal elements meet, including the supporting structures within and surrounding it. The relative range of motion between the skeletal elements of a joint depends on the type of material between these elements, the shapes of the contacting surfaces, and the configuration of the supporting structures.

In bony skeletal systems, there are three general classes of joints: synarthroses, amphiarthroses, and diarthroses. Synarthroses are joints where bony surfaces are directly connected with fibrous tissue, allowing very little if any motion. Synarthroses may be further classified as sutures, syndesmoses, and gomphoses. Sutures are joined with fibrous tissue, as in the coronal suture where the parietal and frontal bones of the human skull meet. Syndesmoses are connected with ligaments, as are the shafts of the tibia and fibula. The roots of a tooth that are anchored in the jaw bone with fibrous tissue form a gomphosis. Amphiarthroses are joints where bones are directly connected with fibrocartilage or hyaline cartilage and allow only limited motion. An amphiarthrosis joined with fibrocartilage, as found between the two pubic bones of the pelvis, is known as a symphysis; but when hyaline cartilage joins the bones, a synchondrosis is formed, an example being the first sternocostal joint. The greatest range of motion is found in diarthrodial joints, where the articulating surfaces slide and to varying degrees roll against each other. *See* LIGAMENT.

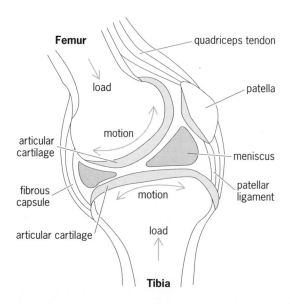

Cross section of the human knee showing its major components. This diarthrodial joint contains contacting surfaces on the tibia, femur, meniscus, and patella (knee cap). The patella protects the joint and also serves to redirect the force exerted by the quadriceps muscles to the tibia. (*After R. Skalak and S. Chien, eds., Handbook of Bioengineering, McGraw-Hill, 1987*)

The contacting surfaces of the bones of a diarthrodial joint are covered with articular cartilage, an avascular, highly durable hydrated soft tissue that provides shock absorption and lubrication functions to the joint (see illustration). Articular cartilage is composed mainly of water, proteoglycans, and collagen. The joint is surrounded by a fibrous joint capsule lined with synovium, which produces lubricating synovial fluid and nutrients required by the tissues within the joint. Joint motion is provided by the muscles that are attached to the bone with tendons. Strong flexible ligaments connected across the bones stabilize the joint and may constrain its motion. Different ranges of motion result from several basic types of diarthrodial joints: pivot, gliding, hinge, saddle, condyloid, and ball-and-socket. *See* COLLAGEN.   [V.C.M.; R.J.F.]

K

Kidney An organ involved with the elimination of water and waste products from the body. In vertebrates the kidneys are paired organs located close to the spine dorsally in the body cavity. They consist of a number of smaller functional units called urinary tubules or nephrons. The nephrons open to large ducts, the collecting ducts, which open into a ureter. The two ureters run backward to open into the cloaca or into a urinary bladder. In mammals, the kidneys are bean-shaped and found between the thorax and the pelvis. The number, structure, and function of the nephrons vary with evolution and, in certain significant ways, with the adaptation of the animals to their various habitats.

In its most primitive form, found only in invertebrates, the nephron has a funnel opening into the coelomic cavity followed by a urinary tubule leading to an excretory pore. In amphibians, some of the tubules have this funnel, but most of the tubules have a Bowman capsule (see illustration). In all higher vertebrates, the nephron has the Bowman capsule, which surrounds a tuft of capillary loops, called the glomerulus, constituting the closed end of the nephron. The inner epithelial wall of the Bowman capsule is in intimate contact with the endothelial wall of the capillaries. The wall of the capillaries, together with the inner wall of the Bowman capsule, forms a membrane ideally suited for filtration of the blood.

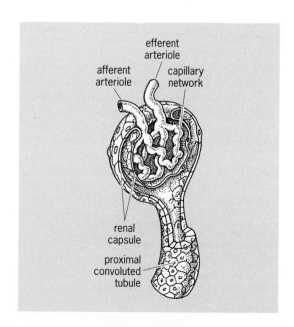

Nephron from frog kidney, dissected to show glomerulus within Bowman capsule.

The blood pressure in the capillaries of the glomerulus causes filtering of blood by forcing fluid, small molecules, and ions through the membrane into the lumen of Bowman's capsule. This filtrate contains some of the proteins and all of the smaller molecules in the blood. As the filtrate passes down through the tubule, the walls of the tubule extract those substances not destined for excretion and return them to the blood in adjacent capillaries. Many substances which are toxic to the organism are moved in the opposite direction from the blood into the tubules. The urine thus produced by each nephron is conveyed by the collecting duct and ureter to the cloaca or bladder from which it can be eliminated.

In all classes of vertebrates the renal arteries deliver blood to the glomeruli and through a second capillary net to the tubules. The major blood supply to the kidney tubules comes, however, from the renal portal vein, which is found in all vertebrates except mammals and cyclostomes. Waste products from the venous blood can thus be secreted directly into the urinary tubules. *See* URINARY SYSTEM.   [B.S.N.]

Kinetoplastida   An order of the class Zoomastigophorea in the phylum Protozoa, also known as Protomastigida, containing a heterogeneous group of colorless flagellates possessing one or two flagella in some stage of their life cycle. These small organisms (5–89 μm in length) typically have pliable bodies. Some species are holozoic and ingest solid particles, while others are saprozoic and obtain their nutrition by absorption.

There is disagreement on the division of the order into families. However, the five or more families can be divided into two general groups (see illustration). The first group contains simple organisms with no distinctive features save one or two flagella of equal or unequal length (includes the families Oikomonadidae, Amphimonadidae, Monadidae, and Bodonidae). The second group contains organisms which have an undulating membrane in addition to one or two flagella (includes Trypanosomatidae

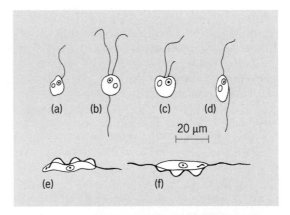

Representative genera of families of order Kinetoplastida. (*a*) *Oikomonas* (family Oikomonadidae), one anterior flagellum. (*b*) *Amphimonas* (family Amphimonadidae), two equally long anterior flagella. (*c*) *Monas* (family Monadidae), two unequally long anterior flagella. (*d*) *Bodo* (family Bodonidae), two unequally long flagella, one of them trailing. (*e*) *Trypanosoma* (family Trypanosomatidae), one flagellum with undulating membrane. (*f*) *Cryptobia* (family Cryptobiidae), two flagella, one free and one with undulating membrane.

and Cryptobiidae). The most important family is the Trypanosomatidae, since it includes several species that infect humans and domestic animals with serious diseases, such as African sleeping sickness. *See* CILIA AND FLAGELLA.   [M.M.B.]

Kinorhyncha   A phylum of free-living marine invertebrates less than 0.04 in. (1 mm) long. They are segmented and lack external ciliation (see illustration). Kinorhynchs are benthonic, so-called because they generally dwell in mud or sand from intertidal to deep-sea habitats. Two orders are generally recognized, Cyclorhagida and Homalorhagida.

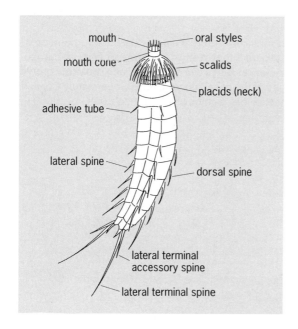

Echinoderes sp., a cyclorhagid kinorhynch (ventrolateral view).

The body is covered by a transparent cuticle secreted by an underlying epidermis. The cuticle is molted only in the process of juvenile growth. Three body regions are recognized: a head segment, a neck segment and an 11-segment trunk. The head is completely retractable. When everted, it extends its five to seven circles of recurved spines called scalids. The neck consists of plates called placids which function to close the anterior opening of the trunk when the head is retracted. Most kinorhynchs have a pair of adhesive tubes on the ventral surface of the third or fourth segment.   [R.P.Hi.]

Klebsiella   A genus of gram-negative, nonmotile bacteria. Characteristic large mucoid colonies are due to production of a large amount of capsular material. Species of *Klebsiella* are commonly found in soil and water, on plants, and in animals and humans. Harmless strains of *Klebsiella* are beneficial because they fix nitrogen in soil. Pathogenic species include *K. pneumoniae, K. rhinoscleromatis*, and *K. ozaenae*, also known as *K. pneumoniae* subspecies *pneumoniae, rhinoscleromatis*, and *ozaenae*.

Klebsiella pneumoniae is the second most frequently isolated colon-related bacterium in clinical laboratories. The carbohydrate-containing capsule of *Klebsiella* promotes virulence by protecting the encased bacteria from ingestion by leukocytes; nonencapsulated variants of *Klebsiella* do not cause disease. Capsular types 1 and 2 cause pneumonia; types 8, 9, 10, and 24 are commonly associated with urinary tract infections. *See* ESCHERICHIA; PNEUMONIA.

Klebsiella accounts for a large percentage of hospital-acquired infections, mostly skin infections (in immunocompromised burn patients), bacteremia, and urinary tract infections. It is also the most common contaminant of intravenous fluids such as glucose solutions and other medical devices.

Klebsiella may produce *E. coli*-like enterotoxins and cause acute gastroenteritis in infants and young children. Enteric illnesses due to *Klebsiella* are more predominant where populations are more crowded and conditions less sanitary. Other virulence factors of *Klebsiella* include a relatively high ability to survive and multiply outside the host in a variety of environments, and its relatively simple growth requirements. *See* ENDOTOXIN.

Klebsiella rhinoscleromatis causes rhinoscleroma, a chronic destructive granulomatous disease of the upper respiratory tract that is most common in eastern Europe, central Africa, and tropical South America. *Klebsiella ozaenae* is one cause of chronic rhinitis (ozena), a destructive atrophy of the nasal mucosa, and is infrequently isolated from urinary tract infections and bacteremia. *See* MEDICAL BACTERIOLOGY.   [D.J.Ev.]

Lactate A salt or ester of lactic acid ($CH_3CHOHCOOH$). In lactates, the acidic hydrogen of the carboxyl group has been replaced by a metal or an organic radical. Lactates are optically active, with a chiral center at carbon 2. Commercial fermentation produces either the dextrorotatory (R) or the levorotatory (S) form, depending on the organism involved. *See* OPTICAL ACTIVITY.

The R form of lactate occurs in blood and muscle as a product of glycolysis. Lack of sufficient oxygen during strenuous exercise causes enzymatic (lactate dehydrogenase) reduction of pyruvic acid to lactate, which causes tiredness, sore muscles, and even muscle cramps. During renewed oxygen supply (rest) the lactate is reoxidized to pyruvic acid and the fragments enter the Krebs (citric acid) cycle. The plasma membranes of muscle and liver are permeable to pyruvates and lactates, permitting the blood to transport them to the liver (Cori cycle). Lactates also increase during fasting and in diabetics. *See* BIOLOGICAL OXIDATION; CARBOHYDRATE METABOLISM; CITRIC ACID CYCLE.

Lactates are found in certain foods (sauerkraut), and may be used for flour conditioning and in food emulsification. Alkali-metal salts act as blood coagulants and are used in calcium therapy, while esters are used as plasticizers and as solvents for lacquers. *See* ESTER; SALT (CHEMISTRY). [E.H.H.]

Lactation The function of the mammary gland providing milk nourishment to the newborn mammal. This process is under the control of the endocrine and nervous systems. It involves transformation of an inactive duct system to a lobuloalveolar glandular structure during pregnancy, cellular production of the components of milk (galactopoiesis), secretion into the ducts, and ejection under the stimulus of milking or suckling.

Lactation makes demands on the maternal regulation of calcium metabolism. Resorption of bone increases in lactating rats and women, and there is a marked increase in the absorption of calcium from the intestine. The elevated need for calcium results in an increased role for parathyroid hormone, calcitonin, and vitamin D in the regulation of the absorption and utilization of calcium. In humans a concomitant phenomenon frequently associated with lactation is amenorrhea. Consequently in some societies prolonged nursing is used as a birth control technique. *See* MAMMARY GLAND; MILK. [H.J.L.]

Lactose Milk sugar or 4-*O*-β-D-galactopyranosyl-D-glucose. This reducing disaccharide is obtained as the α-D anomer (see formula, where the asterisk indicates a reducing group); the melting point is 202°C (396°F). Lactose is found in the milk of mammals to the extent of approximately 2–8%. It is usually prepared from whey, which is obtained by a by-product in the manufacture of cheese. Upon concentration of the whey, crystalline lactose is deposited.   [W.Z.H.]

Lagomorpha   The order of mammals including rabbits, hares, and pikas. Lagomorphs have two pairs of upper incisors (the second pair minute), and enamel surrounds the tooth, which does not form a sharp chisel. Motion of the jaw is vertical or transverse. Lagomorphs have three upper and two lower premolars, the earliest fossil rodents have one less of each. The tibia and fibula are fused, the fibula articulating with the calcaneum as in artiodactyls. There is a spiral valve in the cecum, and the scrotum is prepenial.

The order includes three families: Leporidae (rabbits and hares); Ochotonidae (pikas, whistling hares, or American coneys); and Eurymylidae, an extinct family from the Paleocene of Mongolia. *See* MAMMALIA.

Leporidae are the most familiar members of the order. There are, in general, two kinds: rabbits (such as the American cottontail), which are relatively small, with shorter hindlegs, shorter ears, and short tails; and hares, larger forms with longer legs, ears, and tails. Rapid locomotion is by leaps, using the hindlegs, combined (especially in rabbits) with abrupt changes of direction. Both types occur in the same region, with rabbits inhabiting brush, scrub, or woods and hares living in open grassland. In North America, hares are usually called jackrabbits.   [A.E.Wo.]

Landscape ecology   The study of the distribution and abundance of elements within landscapes, the origins of these elements, and their impacts on organisms and processes. A landscape may be thought of as a heterogeneous assemblage or mosaic of internally uniform elements or patches, such as blocks of forest, agricultural fields, and housing subdivisions. Biogeographers, land-use planners, hydrologists, and ecosystem ecologists are concerned with patterns and processes at large scale. Landscape ecologists bridge these disciplines in order to understand the interplay between the natural and human factors that influence the development of landscapes, and the impacts of landscape patterns on humans, other organisms, and the flows of materials and energy among patches. Much of landscape ecology is founded on the notion that many observations, such as the persistence of a small mammal population within a forest patch, may be fully understood only by accounting for regional as well as local factors.

Factors that lead to the development of a landscape pattern include a combination of human and nonhuman agents. The geology of a region, including the topography and soils along with the regional climate, is strongly linked to the distribution of surface water and the types of vegetation that can exist on a site. These factors influence the pattern of human settlement and the array of past and present uses of land and water. One prevalent effect of humans is habitat fragmentation, which arises because humans tend to reduce the size and increase the isolation among patches of native habitat.

The pattern of patches on a landscape can in turn can have direct effects on many different processes. The structure and arrangement of patches can affect the physical movement of materials such as nutrients or pollutants and the fate of populations of plants and animals. Many of these impacts can be traced to two factors, the role of patch edges and the connectedness among patches.

The boundary between two patches often act as filters or barriers to the transport of biological and physical elements. As an example, leaving buffer strips of native vegetation along stream courses during logging activities can greatly reduce the amount of sediment and nutrients that reach the stream from the logged area. Edge effects can result when forests are logged and there is a flux of light and wind into areas formerly located in the interior of a forest. In this example, edges can be a less suitable habitat for plants and animals not able to cope with drier, high-light conditions. When habitats are fragmented, patches eventually can become so small that they are all edge. When this happens, forest interior dwellers may become extinct. When patch boundaries act as barriers to movement, they can have pronounced effects on the dynamics of populations within and among patches. In the extreme, low connectivity can result in regional extinction even when a suitable habitat remains. This can occur if populations depend on dispersal from neighboring populations. When a population becomes extinct within a patch, there is no way for a colonist to reach the vacant habitat and reestablish the population. This process is repeated until all of the populations within a region disappear. Landscape ecologists have promoted the use of corridors of native habitat between patches to preserve connectivity despite the fragmentation of a landscape.   [D.Sk.]

Larynx   The complex of cartilages and related structures at the opening of the trachea, or windpipe, into the pharynx, or throat. In humans and most other mammals, the signet-shaped cricoid cartilage forms the base of the larynx and rests upon the trachea. The thyroid cartilage, which forms the prominent Adam's apple ventrally, lies anterior to the cricoid. Dorsally there are paired pivoting cartilages, the arytenoids. Each is pyramid-shaped and acts as the movable posterior attachment for the vocal cords and the laryngeal muscles that regulate the cords. Two other small paired cartilages, the cuneiform and the corniculate, also lie dorsal to the thyroid cartilage. The epiglottis, a leaf-shaped elastic cartilage with its stem inserted into the thyroid notch, forms a lid to the larynx.   [T.S.P.]

Laser photobiology   The interaction of laser light with biological molecules, and the applications to biology and medicine. *See* LASER.

Microirradiation is a useful technique for the study of cell function by alteration of a specific organelle or part of a cell. The laser beam is focused through the objective of a microscope onto the cell. Practically speaking, it is easy to obtain spots of about 1 micrometer in diameter. Ruby, neodymium, and argon lasers are used for this purpose.

Laser spectroscopy is used to probe biological processes in which very fast reactions are involved or to study structural changes of complex molecules. The two techniques used are flash photolysis (in the nanosecond and picosecond range) and Raman spectroscopy.

Continuous-wave lasers have been employed as a "light knife," that is as a surgical cutting and coagulation tool. Generally, CO_2 lasers, emitting in the infrared, are used for this purpose. When the laser energy is focused onto a tissue surface, a small volume of tissue is heated, and thus only this area is "cut off." An advantage of this procedure is that small capillaries are coagulated, preventing hemorrhage resulting from cut blood vessels. Argon lasers are the most commonly used for treating retinopathies, but also for glaucoma and cataract. Laser irradiation is used for removal of foreign pigments in the skin (tattoos), for treatment of vascular disorders ("wine marks"), and for removal of various pigmented skin lesions.   [G.Mo.]

Lateral line system   A primitive vertebrate sensory system that is present in all larval and adult fishes, in larval amphibians (such as tadpoles), and in some adult amphibians that retain an aquatic lifestyle. The lateral line system consists of 100 or more sensory organs (neuromasts) that are typically arranged in lines on or just under the skin of the head and body. Neuromasts are composed of sensory hair cells, which are also found in the auditory system of all vertebrates. The lateral line system responds to water flowing past the skin surface and uses different flow patterns over the body to form hydrodynamic images of the animal's nearby surroundings, just as the visual system forms visual images of the environment using different light patterns on the retina.

Neuromasts are found just under the skin in fluid-filled canals that communicate with the skin surface through a series of pores (canal neuromasts, found in fishes only), or on the skin surface (superficial neuromasts, found in fishes and amphibians). A prominent canal that often forms a visible line along the trunk of most fishes is probably the origin of the term "lateral line," but in reality the lateral line system includes neuromasts that are distributed all over the head and body of the animal.

A neuromast contains up to hundreds of mechanosensory hair cells that are surrounded by support cells. Hair cells function as directional sensors that convey information to the brain about both the strength and direction of water currents. The ciliary bundle of each hair cell contains one long cilium (kinocilium) and a cluster of shorter cilia (stereocilia). The ciliary bundles of the hair cells are embedded in a gelatinous cupula. Hair cells are activated when water flows past the skin surface, causing the cupula to move, thus causing the cilia to bend. The neural response of each hair cell is proportional to both the degree of cilia displacement and the direction in which the stereocilia are displaced relative to the eccentrically placed kinocilium of each hair cell.

Information from neuromasts is transmitted to the brain by sensory (afferent) nerve fibers, which form five cranial nerves (the lateral line nerves) that terminate in distinct medullary regions of the brainstem (medulla oblongata). Distinct regions and pathways in the brain are dedicated to processing information from the lateral line system. These are similar in overall organization, and in proximity to regions of the brain dedicated to processing information from two other closely allied sensory systems, the auditory system and the electrosensory system. Information is also carried from the brain to the sense organs by efferent nerve fibers, which can modulate the sensitivity of the organs to certain stimuli (for example, to reduce sensitivity when water flows are produced by the animal's own movements). *See* AMPHIBIA.

The lateral line system is thought to have a function that is intermediate between touch and hearing, and is best described as a sense of touch-at-a-distance. In general, large-scale water movements such as oceanic currents, tides, and river flows that are strong enough to carry a fish with them are not by themselves very effective lateral line stimuli. Smaller-scale movements, such as those produced by a slowly moving (less than 8 cm or 0.25 ft/s) stream or by nearby animals (less than one or two body lengths away), can be effective lateral line stimuli.

Fishes can use different types of water flows to form hydrodynamic images of their surroundings. They can form images passively by remaining still and simply detecting the water currents created by other moving animals, or by detecting current distortions or turbulent wakes created by a stationary obstacle in moving water. Alternatively, fishes can actively form images by swimming past a stationary obstacle and then detecting the distortions in their own self-generated flows due to the presence of the obstacle.

Fishes and amphibians can also use their lateral line system to orient themselves relative to a water current (rheotaxis), hold a stationary position in a stream, capture prey, avoid predators, and communicate with intraspecifics. Many stream-dwelling fishes (such as trout and salmon) show rheotactic and station-holding behaviors by orienting their bodies upstream and holding positions behind stationary rocks or boulders. These behaviors are important for the upstream spawning migrations of these fishes and for capturing prey that are being carried downstream. *See* ELASMOBRANCHII; NERVOUS SYSTEM (VERTEBRATE).   [S.Co.; J.F.Web.]

Lateral meristem Strips or cylinders of dividing cells located parallel to the long axis of the organ in which they occur. Radial enlargement of the cells derived from these meristems increases the diameter of the organ. The lateral meristem is concerned with secondary growth in the sense that its meristematic activity adds cells to the primary body which was derived from the apical meristems. *See* APICAL MERISTEM.

[V.I.C.]

Leaf A lateral appendage which is borne on a plant stem at a node (joint) and which usually has a bud in its axil. In most plants, leaves are flattened in form, although they may be nearly cylindrical with a sheathing base as in onion. Leaves usually contain chlorophyll and are the principal organs in which the important processes of photosynthesis and transpiration occur.

Morphology. A complete dicotyledon leaf consists of three parts: the expanded portion or blade; the petiole which supports the blades; and the leaf base. Stipules are small appendages that arise as outgrowths of the leaf base and are attached at the base of the petiole. The leaves of monocotyledons may have a petiole and a blade, or they may be linear in shape without differentiation into these parts; in either case the leaf base usually encircles the stem. The leaves of grasses consist of a linear blade attached to the stem by an encircling sheath.

Leaves are borne on a stem in a definite fixed order, or phyllotaxy, according to species (Fig. 1). For identification purposes, leaves are classified according to type (Fig. 2) and shape (Fig. 3), and types of margins (Fig. 4), tips, and bases (Fig. 5). The arrangement of the veins, or vascular bundles, of a leaf is called venation (Fig. 6). The main longitudinal veins are usually interconnected with small veins. Reticulate venation is most common in dicotyledons, parallel venation in monocotyledons.

Surfaces of leaves provide many characteristics that are used in identification. A surface is glabrous if it is smooth or free from hairs; glaucous if covered with a whitish, waxy material, or "bloom"; scabrous if rough or harsh to the touch; pubescent, a general term for surfaces that are hairy; puberulent if covered with very fine, downlike hairs; villous if covered with long, soft, shaggy hairs; hirsute if the hairs are short, erect, and stiff; and hispid if they are dense, bristly, and harshly stiff.

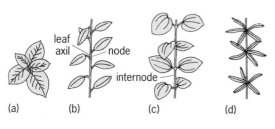

Fig. 1. Leaf arrangement. (*a*) Helical (top view). (*b*) Helical with elongated internodes (alternate). (*c*) Opposite (decussate). (*d*) Whorled (verticillate).

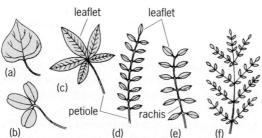

Fig. 2. Leaf types. (*a*) Simple. (*b*) Trifoliate. (*c*) Palmately compound. (*d*) Odd-pinnately compound. (*e*) Even-pinnately compound. (*f*) Decompound.

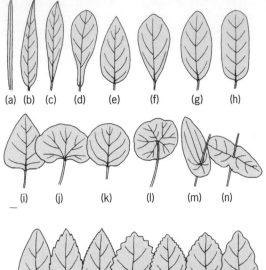

(a) (b) (c)   (d)   (e)   (f)   (g)   (h)

Fig. 3. Leaf shapes. (*a*) Linear.
(*b*) Lanceolate. (*c*) Oblanceolate.
(*d*) Spatulate. (*e*) Ovate.
(*f*) Obovate. (*g*) Elliptic.
(*h*) Oblong. (*i*) Deltold.
(*j*) Reniform. (*k*) Orbicular.
(*l*) Peltate. (*m*) Perfoliate.
(*n*) Connate.

(i)   (j)   (k)   (l)   (m)   (n)

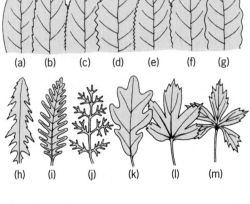

(a)   (b)   (c)   (d)   (e)   (f)   (g)

**Fig. 4. Leaf margins of various
types.** (*a*) Entire. (*b*) Serrate.
(*c*) Serrulate. (*d*) Dentate.
(*e*) Denticulate. (*f*) Crenate.
(*g*) Undulate. (*h*) Incised.
(*i*) Pinnatifid. (*j*) Dissected.
(*k*) Lobed. (*l*) Cleft. (*m*) Parted.

(h)   (i)   (j)   (k)   (l)   (m)

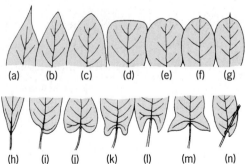

(a)   (b)   (c)   (d)   (e)   (f)   (g)

Fig. 5. Leaf tips and bases.
(*a*) Acuminate. (*b*) Acute.
(*c*) Obtuse. (*d*) Truncate.
(*e*) Emarginate. (*f*) Mucronate.
(*g*) Cuspidate. (*h*) Cuneate.
(*i*) Oblique. (*j*) Cordate.
(*k*) Auriculate. (*l*) Sagittate.
(*m*) Hastate. (*n*) Clasping.

(h)   (i)   (j)   (k)   (l)   (m)   (n)

The texture may be described as succulent when the leaf is fleshy and juicy; hyaline if it is thin and almost wholly transparent; chartaceous if papery and opaque but thin; scarious if thin and dry, appearing shriveled; and coriaceous if tough, thickish, and leathery.

Leaves may be fugacious, failing nearly as soon as formed; deciduous, failing at the end of the growing season; marcescent, withering at the end of the growing season but

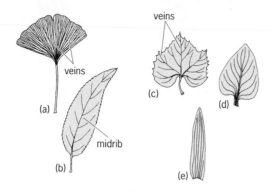

Fig. 6. Leaf venation.
(*a*) Dichotomous. (*b*) Pinnate reticulate. (*c*) Palmate reticulate. (*d*) Parallel (expanded leaf). (*e*) Parallel (linear leaf).

not falling until toward spring; or persistent, remaining on the stem for more than one season, the plant thus being evergreen. *See* DECIDUOUS PLANTS; EVERGREEN PLANTS.

Anatomy. The foliage leaf is the chief photosynthetic organ of most vascular plants. Although leaves vary greatly in size and form, they share the same basic organization of internal tissues and have similar developmental pathways. Like the stem and root, leaves consist of three basic tissue systems: the dermal tissue system, the vascular tissue system, and the ground tissue system. However, unlike stems and roots which usually have radial symmetry, the leaf blade usually shows dorsiventral symmetry, with vascular and other tissues being arranged in a flat plane.

Stems and roots have apical meristems and are thus characterized by indeterminate growth; leaves lack apical meristems, and therefore have determinate growth. Because leaves are more or less ephemeral organs and do not function in the structural support

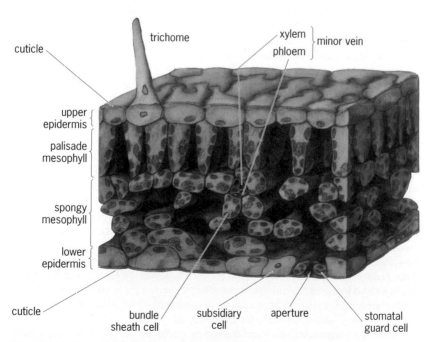

Fig. 7. Three-dimensional diagram of internal structure of a typical dicotyledon leaf.

of the plant, they usually lack secondary growth and are composed largely of primary tissue only. *See* APICAL MERISTEM; ROOT (BOTANY); STEM.

The internal organization of the leaf is well adapted for its major functions of photosynthesis, gas exchange, and transpiration. The photosynthetic cells, or chlorenchyma tissue, are normally arranged in horizontal layers, which facilitates maximum interception of the Sun's radiation. The vascular tissues form an extensive network throughout the leaf so that no photosynthetic cell is far from a source of water, and carbohydrates produced by the chlorenchyma cells need travel only a short distance to reach the phloem in order to be transported out of the leaf (Fig. 7). The epidermal tissue forms a continuous covering over the leaf so that undue water loss is reduced, while at the same time the exchange of carbon dioxide and oxygen is controlled. *See* EPIDERMIS (PLANT); PARENCHYMA; PHLOEM; XYLEM.   [N.G.D.]

Lectins   A class of proteins of nonimmune origin that bind carbohydrates reversibly and noncovalently without inducing any change in the carbohydrate. Lectins bind a variety of cells having cell-surface glycoproteins (carbohydrate bound proteins) or glycolipids (carbohydrate bound lipids). The presence of two or more binding sites for each lectin molecule allows the agglutination of many cell types, and the agglutination reaction has been used extensively to detect the presence of lectins in extracts from different organisms. Although lectins are ubiquitous in nature, their biological role is not well understood. *See* CARBOHYDRATE.

Hemagglutinating activity has been found in more than 1000 plant taxa. However, knowledge on distribution of well-characterized lectins covers only 4–5% of flowering plant families. Moreover, most of the best-characterized lectins come from a single family, Leguminosae.

Animal lectins have also been characterized in only a small number of species, but they have been found in almost all of the invertebrate and vertebrate phyla. Invertebrate lectins occur in body fluids or secretions, such as fish serum, snake venom, seminal and coelomic fluids, and hemolymph. Vertebrate lectins occur as soluble or integral membrane proteins in embryonic and adult fluids, organs, and tissues.

Microbial lectins have been isolated mainly from bacteria, but they are also found in viruses, slime molds, protozoa, green algae, and fungi.

From the few known examples, it seems clear that lectins are involved in recognition phenomena and their ability to bind particular carbohydrate structures is the key to their biological functions. These recognition functions include their involvement in interactions with cells or extracellular materials from the same organism (self-recognition) and interactions with foreign particles or cells (non-self recognition). Among the best-known examples of self-recognition mediated by lectins are the hepatic lectins involved in the recognition of glycoproteins that must be cleared from circulation. Specific lectins recognize and internalize the target proteins into lysosomes, where they are destroyed. *See* LYSOSOME.

Examples of lectin-mediated non-self-recognition are seen in the involvement of bacterial surface lectins in infection. Numerous bacterial strains produce surface lectins that recognize specific sugars in the surface of host cells and thus initiate the infection process. Another example is the symbiotic interaction between nitrogen-fixing bacteria and plant roots. The lectins present in the roots of legumes are localized at the surface of root hairs and in the root exudates, where they recognize the appropriate *Rhizobium* strain and account for part of the specificity in the initiation of nodulation.

Lectins are very useful reagents for the study of complex carbohydrates and cell surfaces, for the separation and identification of particular cells, and for the stimulation of cell proliferation. Lectins covalently attached to insoluble matrices are used to separate glycoproteins or glycopeptides that contain different carbohydrates. Labeled lectins are also used in histochemical and cytochemical studies to localize glyconjugates that carry particular sugars. This technique is particularly interesting, since changes in lectin-binding patterns occur during embryonic differentiation, malignant transformation, aging, and some pathological conditions. *See* PROTEIN.   [R.P.Le.]

Legionnaires' disease   A type of pneumonia usually caused by infection with the bacterium *Legionella pneumophila*, but occasionally with a related species (such as *L. micdadei* or *L. dumoffii*). The disease was first observed in an epidemic among those attending an American Legion convention in Philadelphia, Pennsylvania, in 1976. The initial symptoms are headache, fever, muscle aches, and a generalized feeling of discomfort. The fever rises rapidly, reaching 102–105°F (32–41°C), and is usually accompanied by cough, shortness of breath, and chest pains. Abdominal pain and diarrhea are often present. The mortality rate can be as high as 15% in untreated or improperly diagnosed cases. Erythromycin, new-generation fluroquinolones, and rifampicin are considered highly effective medications, whereas the penicillins and cephalosporins are ineffective.

While epidemics of Legionnaires' disease (also referred to as legionellosis) can often be traced to a common source (cooling tower, potable water, or hot tub), most cases seem to occur sporadically. It is estimated that *Legionella* spp. account for approximately 4% of all community- and hospital-acquired pneumonia. Legionnaires' disease is most fequently associated with persons of impaired immune status. *Legionella* bacteria are commonly found in fresh water and moist soils worldwide and are often spread to humans through inhalation of aerosols containing the bacteria. Legionnaires' disease is not a communicable disease, indicating that human infection is not part of the survival strategy of these bacteria. Therefore, the legionellae are considered opportunistic pathogens of humans. It is technology (air conditioning) and the ability to extend life through medical advances (such as transplantation and treatments for terminal diseases) that have brought these bacteria into proximity with a susceptible population.

For most humans exposed to *L. pneumophila*, infection is asymptomatic or short-lived. This is attributed to a potent cellular immune response in healthy individuals. Recovery from Legionnaires' disease often affords immunity against future infection. However, no vaccine exists at the present time. *See* MEDICAL BACTERIOLOGY; PNEUMONIA.
[P.S.H.]

Leprosy   A chronic infectious disease caused by *Mycobacterium leprae* that primarily affects the skin and peripheral nerves and, to a lesser extent, the eyes and mucous membranes. Leprosy, or Hansen's disease, has been known for more than 2000 years. It afflicts at least 3 million people worldwide and is most common in developing countries. There are about 200 new cases yearly in the United States. Its epidemiology is not fully understood, but transmission probably takes place by the respiratory route. The bacillus is very slow-growing, and the incubation period is usually 3–5 years. Less than 5% of any population is susceptible, and these individuals have a deficient cell-mediated immune response specifically to *M. leprae*, which may be genetic in origin. Epidemics have occurred, but are rare. *See* MYCOBACTERIAL DISEASES.

A skin rash and loss of feeling due to nerve damage by *M. leprae* are the hallmarks of leprosy. Usually the nerve damage is mild, but when severe the inability to feel, particularly in the hands and feet, predisposes the individuals to frequent injuries. Nerve involvement may also lead to a loss of muscle function that produces clawing of the fingers and toes as well as other neuromuscular dysfunctions. Manifestations of the disease depend upon the degree of the immune defect. Initially, most patients develop one or several depigmented areas of skin that may have decreased sensation, a stage referred to as indeterminate disease. The condition may self-heal. If treatment or self-healing does not halt the disease, it may progress to one of three advanced types. The mildest of these, tuberculoid disease, is usually manifested as a single large depigmented, scaly, numb area. The most severe type, lepromatous leprosy, usually involves most of the skin to varying degrees, with variously sized nodules or other changes. Between the two extremes immunologically is borderline disease, with skin changes of both types. The World Health Organization's simplified classification labels indeterminate and tuberculoid patients paucibacillary (few bacilli) and borderline and lepromatous patients multibacillary.

Paucibacillary disease is treated with dapsone plus rifampin for 6–12 months. Clofazimine is added for multibacillary individuals and the treatment continued for 2 or more years. Isolation is unnecessary, since patients become noninfectious within days of starting treatment. See INFECTIOUS DISEASE. [R.R.J.]

Leptospirosis An acute febrile disease of humans produced by spirochetes of many species of *Leptospira*. The incubation period is 6–15 days. Among the prominent features of the disease are fever, jaundice, muscle pains, headaches, hepatitis, albuminuria, and multiple small hemorrhages in the conjunctiva or skin. Meningeal involvement often occurs. The febrile illness subsides after 3–10 days. Fatal cases show hemorrhagic lesions in the kidney, liver, skin, muscles, and central nervous system.

Wild rodents are the principal reservoirs, although natural infection occurs in swine, cattle, horses, and dogs and may be transmitted to humans through these animals. Humans are infected either through contact with the urine or flesh of diseased animals, or indirectly by way of contaminated water or soil, the organisms entering the body through small breaks in the skin or mucous membrane. [T.B.T.]

Lichens Symbiotic associations of fungi (mycobionts) and photosynthetic partners (photobionts). These associations always result in a distinct morphological body termed a thallus that may adhere tightly to the substrate or be leafy, stalked, or hanging. A thallus consists of layers, that is, a cortex and medulla made up of the fungus, and a photosynthetic layer of algal or cyanobacterial cells that are closely associated with fungal hyphae. Rhizoids anchor thalli to their substrates. See CYANOBACTERIA.

Lichens are formed from specialized groups of parasitic fungi; this association is one of a controlled parasitism rather than mutualism. Thus, the photobionts that lichen fungi slowly parasitize should be considered victims and not partners. Lichen-forming fungi share two characteristics with fungi that parasitize plants: concentric bodies and specialized branches of hyphae (haustoria) that penetrate host cells and absorb nutrients from them.

Lichens have a worldwide distribution and grow on almost any inanimate object. They are among the hardiest of organisms and thrive in some of the Earth's harshest environments, such as polar regions, deserts, and high mountains.

The name given to a lichen applies only to the mycobiont, while the photobiont has a separate name. Most of the 15,000 lichen-forming fungi are in the fungal class Ascomycotina (ascolichens). Approximately a dozen species of basidiomycetes form lichens. Lichens that do not have sexual reproduction (*Lepraria*) are placed in the Lichenes Imperfecti.

Photobionts of lichens are either green algae or cyanobacteria. The most common photobiont is *Trebouxia*. This unicellular green algae has never been found in the free-living state. It is believed that *Trebouxia* is a lichenized and highly modified form of the filamentous alga *Pleurastrum terrestre*.

The basic metabolic processes of lichens are photosynthesis, respiration, and nitrogen fixation. Lichens have adapted these processes to different conditions of light, temperature, day length, and water. The mycobiont causes the photobiont to excrete most of the carbon that it fixes during photosynthesis. Only a single type of compound is excreted. The mycobiont absorbs these compounds and converts them to mannitol, its own storage compound. *See* PLANT RESPIRATION.

Nitrogen-fixing lichens are common and contribute nitrogen to different ecosystems when they decay. In cyanolichens the mycobiont inhibits the nitrogen-assimilating enzymes of the cyanobiont, causing it to release most of the ammonia it produces. The ammonia is absorbed by the mycobiont and used to make proteins and nucleic acids. *See* NITROGEN FIXATION.

Lichens produce several hundred secondary compounds that accumulate as crystals in the thalli, often at high concentrations. These compounds may protect the slow-growing thalli from harmful bacteria, fungi, and insects and may play a regulatory role in the interactions between bionts. Lichen secondary compounds represent a new class of antibiotics in an age where standard antibiotics such as penicillin are becoming ineffective against antibiotic-resistant microbes. Secondary compounds are used extensively by taxonomists to characterize new taxa of lichens (chemotaxonomy).   [V.Ah.]

Ligament   A strong, flexible connective tissue band usually found between two bony prominences. Most ligaments are composed of dense fibrous tissue formed by parallel bundles of collagen fibers. They have a shining white appearance and are pliable, strong, and noncompliant. A second kind of ligament, composed either partly or almost entirely of yellow elastic fibers, is extensible or compliant, thereby allowing the connected bones to move apart. *See* CONNECTIVE TISSUE; JOINT (ANATOMY).   [W.J.B.]

Linguistics   The science, that is, the general and universal properties, of language. The middle of the twentieth century saw a shift in the principal direction of linguistic inquiry from one of data collection and classification to the formulation of a theory of generative grammar, which focuses on the biological basis for the acquisition and use of human language and the universal principles that constrain the class of all languages. Generative grammar distinguishes between the knowledge of language (linguistic competence), which is represented by mental grammar, and the production and comprehension of speech (linguistic performance).

If grammar is defined as the mental representation of linguistic knowledge, then a general theory of language is a theory of grammar. A grammar includes everything one knows about a language; its phonetics and phonology (the sounds and the sound system), its morphology (the structure of words), its lexicon (the words or vocabulary), its syntax (the structure of sentences and the constraints on well-formed sentences), and its semantics (the meaning of words and sentences). *See* PSYCHOACOUSTICS; SPEECH; SPEECH PERCEPTION.

Linguistics is not limited to grammatical theory. Descriptive linguistics analyzes the grammars of individual languages; anthropological linguistics, or ethnolinguistics, and sociolinguistics focus on languages in relation to culture, social class, race, and gender; dialectologists investigate how these factors fragment one language into many. In addition, sociolinguists and applied linguists examine language planning, literacy, bilingualism, and second-language acquisition. Computational linguistics encompasses automatic parsing, machine processing, and computer simulation of grammatical models for the generation and parsing of sentences. If viewed as a branch of artificial intelligence, computational linguistics has as its goal the modeling of human language as a cognitive system. A branch of linguistics concerned with the biological basis of language development is neurolinguistics. The form of language representation in the mind, that is, linguistic competence and the structure and components of the mental grammar, is the concern of theoretical linguistics. The branch of linguistics concerned with linguistic performance, that is, the production and comprehension of speech (or of sign language by the deaf), is called psycholinguistics. Psycholinguists also investigate how children acquire the complex grammar that underlies language use. *See* INFORMATION PROCESSING; PSYCHOLINGUISTICS.   [V.A.F.]

Linkage (genetics)   Failure of two or more genes to recombine at random as a result of their location on the same chromosome pair. Among the haploid products of a cell which has gone through meiosis, two genes located in the same chromosome pair remain in their two original combinations of alleles ("parental") unless an odd number of exchanges of homologous segments occurred within the interval bounded by their loci. The incidence of exchanges of homologous segments at meiosis is roughly proportional to the length of the chromosome segment between two loci. The percentage of recombinants thus provides an estimate of this length and a basis for constructing gene maps on which linked loci are arranged in linear order and spaced out in proportion to the recombination percentages between them. *See* MEIOSIS.   [G.Po.]

Lipid   One of a class of compounds which contains long-chain aliphatic hydrocarbons (cyclic or acyclic) and their derivatives, such as acids (fatty acids), alcohols, amines, amino alcohols, and aldehydes. The presence of the long aliphatic chain as the characteristic component of lipids confers distinct solubility properties on the simpler members of this class of naturally occurring compounds.

The lipids are generally classified into the following groups:

A. Simple lipids

  1. Triglycerides or fats and oils are fatty acid esters of glycerol. Examples are lard, corn oil, cottonseed oil, and butter.
  2. Waxes are fatty acid esters of long-chain alcohols. Examples are beeswax, spermaceti, and carnauba wax.
  3. Steroids are lipids derived from partially or completely hydrogenated phenanthrene. Examples are cholesterol and ergosterol.

B. Complex lipids

  1. Phosphatides or phospholipids are lipids which contain phosphorus and, in many instances, nitrogen. Examples are lecithin, cephalin, and phosphatidyl inositol.
  2. Glycolipids are lipids which contain carbohydrate residues. Examples are sterol glycosides, cerebrosides, and plant phytoglycolipids.
  3. Sphingolipids are lipids containing the long-chain amino alcohol sphingosine and its derivatives. Examples are sphingomyelins, ceramides, and cerebrosides.

Lipids are present in all living cells, but the proportion varies from tissue to tissue. The triglycerides accumulate in certain areas, such as adipose tissue in the human being and in the seeds of plants, where they represent a form of energy storage. The more complex lipids occur closely linked with protein in the membranes of cells and of subcellular particles. More active tissues generally have a higher complex lipid content; for example, the brain, liver, kidney, lung, and blood contain the highest concentration of phosphatides in the mammal. *See* FAT AND OIL; FAT AND OIL (FOOD); GLYCOLIPID;

SPHINGOLIPID; STEROID; TERPENE; TRIGLYCERIDE; VITAMIN; WAX, ANIMAL AND VEGETABLE.

[R.H.G.]

Lipid metabolism   The assimilation of dietary lipids and the synthesis and degradation of lipids; this article is restricted to mammals.

The principal dietary fat is triglyceride. This substance is not digested in the stomach and passes into the duodenum, where it causes the release of enterogastrone, a hormone which inhibits stomach motility. The amount of fat in the diet, therefore, regulates the rate at which enterogastrone is released into the intestinal tract. Fat, together with other partially digested foodstuffs, causes the release of hormones, secretin, pancreozymin, and cholecystokinin from the wall of the duodenum into the bloodstream.

Secretin causes the secretion of an alkaline pancreatic juice rich in bicarbonate ions, while pancreozymin causes secretion of pancreatic enzymes. One of these enzymes, important in the digestion of fat, is lipase. Cholecystokinin, which is a protein substance chemically inseparable from pancreozymin, stimulates the gallbladder to release bile into the duodenum. Bile is secreted by the liver and concentrated in the gallbladder and contains two bile salts, both derived from cholesterol: taurocholic and glycocholic acids. These act as detergents by emulsifying the triglycerides in the intestinal tract, thus making the fats more susceptible to attack by pancreatic lipase. In this reaction, which works best in the alkaline medium provided by the pancreatic juice, each triglyceride is split into three fatty acid chains, forming monoglycerides. The fatty acids pass across the membranes of the intestinal mucosal (lining) cells. Enzymes in the membranes split monoglyceride to glycerol and fatty acid, but triglycerides are reformed within the mucosal cells from glycerol and those fatty acids with a chain length greater than eight carbons: Short- and medium-chain fatty acids are absorbed directly into the bloodstream once they pass through the intestinal mucosa. See CHOLESTEROL; DIGESTIVE SYSTEM; GALLBLADDER; LIVER; PANCREAS; TRIGLYCERIDE.

Obesity is a condition in which excessive fat accumulates in the adipose tissue. One factor responsible for this condition is excessive caloric intake. In starvation, uncontrolled diabetes, and many generalized illnesses the opposite occurs and the adipose tissue becomes markedly depleted of lipid. See ADIPOSE TISSUE; DIABETES; LIPID; METABOLIC DISORDERS; OBESITY.

[M.A.R.]

Lipoprotein   Classes of conjugated proteins consisting of a protein combined with a lipid. The normal functioning of higher organisms requires movement of insoluble lipids, such as cholesterol, steroid hormones, bile, and triglycerides, between tissues. To accomplish this movement, lipids are incorporated into macromolecular complexes called lipoproteins.

All major types of lipoproteins share a general structure. The core of these spherical particles contains primarily cholesteryl ester and triglyceride. These insoluble molecules are surrounded by a coating of proteins and phospholipids that are amphipathic; that is, they have both polar and nonpolar regions. Lipoproteins vary by size and density. The largest lipoproteins, chylomicrons, are up to 500 nanometers in diameter, and since they contain primarily triglyceride they are so buoyant that they float in plasma. Very low density lipoproteins (VLDL) also primarily transport triglyceride. Low-density lipoproteins (LDL) and the smallest, most dense lipoproteins, high-density lipoproteins (HDL), transport cholesterol. The interactions of these particles with cell surface receptors and with metabolic enzymes are mediated by the protein components of the particles, termed apolipoproteins. See CHOLESTEROL; TRIGLYCERIDE.

Chylomicrons contain triglyceride (fat) from the diet. In addition, they carry fat-soluble vitamins, such as vitamin A and E, into the circulation. Chylomicrons are produced in the intestine, enter the body via the lymphatic system, and then enter the bloodstream.

Very low density lipoproteins are made in the liver and contain triglyceride that is synthesized either from excess carbohydrate sources of calories or from fatty acids that enter the liver and are reassembled into triglyceride. Lipoprotein lipase (LpL) is an enzyme found on the surface of blood vessels that is responsible for the breakdown of triglyceride in lipoproteins. The partially degraded lipoproteins are termed remnants. They are ultimately removed from the circulation by the liver.

Low-density lipoproteins result after triglyceride is removed from very low density lipoproteins. This leaves a smaller, denser particle that primarily contains cholesteryl ester as its core lipid and a single protein called apoB. Cells throughout the body contain an LDL receptor that recognizes apoB. This allows the uptake of low-density lipoproteins into cells, supplying them with cholesterol. When sufficient low-density lipoproteins and cholesterol are available, cells use them in preference to synthesizing new cholesterol from precursors. In contrast, high-density lipoproteins both deliver and remove cholesterol from tissues.

Blood levels of lipoproteins are major factors regulating risk for development of coronary artery atherosclerosis. Via unknown mechanisms, low-density lipoproteins and remnant lipoproteins infiltrate and then become attached to extracellular matrix molecules within the artery. Some of the lipoproteins are internalized by macrophages and smooth muscle cells. This might first require chemical modification such as oxidation of the lipids. The resulting pathological findings are deposition of cholesterol in cells and matrix within the vessel wall, leading to a decrease in the diameter of the artery.

In contrast, high-density lipoproteins appear to prevent atherosclerosis formation. The reasons are not entirely understood. Most likely, high-density lipoproteins remove excess cholesterol that accumulates in the artery, or prevent the oxidation of low-density lipoproteins. See ARTERIOSCLEROSIS.   [I.J.Go.]

Liposomes   Aqueous compartments enclosed by lipid bilayer membranes; liposomes are also known as lipid vesicles. Phospholipid molecules consist of an elongated nonpolar (hydrophobic) structure with a polar (hydrophilic) structure at one end. When dispersed in water, they spontaneously form bilayer membranes, also called lamellae, which are composed of two monolayer layer sheets of lipid molecules with their nonpolar (hydrophobic) surfaces facing each other and their polar (hydrophilic) surfaces facing the aqueous medium. The membranes enclose a portion of the aqueous phase much like the cell membrane which encloses the cell; in fact, the bilayer membrane is essentially a cell membrane without its protein components.

Liposomes are often used to study the characteristics of the lipid bilayer. Properties of liposomes have been characterized by a variety of techniques: molecular organization by x-ray diffraction, nuclear magnetic resonance, electron paramagnetic resonance, and Raman spectroscopy; melting behavior (that is, crystal to liquid-crystal transition) by calorimetry; net electric surface charge by microelectrophoresis; size by light scattering and electron microscopy. See LIPID.

Liposomes have numerous uses as biochemical and biophysical tools: (1) as vehicles for the delivery of both water- and of oil-soluble materials to the cell; (2) as immunological adjuvants; (3) as substrates for the study of membrane properties such as rotational or translational diffusion in the plane of the membrane; and (4) as intermediates in the construction of bilayers large enough for the study of electrical properties of membranes. See CELL MEMBRANES.   [R.C.MacD.; R.I.MacD.]

Lissamphibia The subclass of Amphibia including all living amphibians (frogs, toads, salamanders, and apodans). The other two subclasses are the Labyrinthodontia and the Lepospondyli. *See* LABYRINTHODONTIA; LEPOSPONDYLI.

Living amphibians are grouped together by possession of a unique series of characters, the most important of which are (1) pedicellate teeth, consisting of two segments, a crown and a pedicel; (2) an operculum-plectrum complex of the middle ear; (3) the papilla amphibiorum, a special sensory area of the inner ear; (4) green rods in the retina of the eye; (5) similar skin glands; and (6) a highly vascular skin used in respiration (cutaneous respiration). *See* AMPHIBIA; ANURA; URODELA. [R.E.]

Liver A large gland found in all vertebrates. It consists of a continuous parenchymal mass arranged to form a system of walls through which venous blood emanating from the gut must pass. This strategic localization between nutrient-laden capillary beds and the general circulation is associated with hepatic regulation of metabolite levels in the blood through storage and mobilization mechanisms controlled by liver enzymes.

Function. The large size of the liver is matched by its functional complexity and involvement in a diverse array of regulatory mechanisms. The liver plays a key role in assuring carbohydrate homeostasis (dynamic steady-state conditions) by removing simple sugars from the general circulation after ingestion of food and storing them as glycogen. In the intervals between ingestion of food, liver glycogen is broken down. This process tends to maintain blood sugar levels between 80 and 100 mg per 100 ml of blood. Under conditions of prolonged fast, where glycogen stores are exhausted, the liver is capable of converting noncarbohydrate metabolites such as amino acids and fats into glucose to maintain blood sugar levels. The complex steps involved in maintaining carbohydrate metabolism are subject to endocrine control, with the liver serving as a particularly sensitive target organ of hormone regulators such as insulin. *See* CARBOHYDRATE METABOLISM; GLUCOSE; GLYCOGEN; INSULIN.

The liver is key in the interconversion of many metabolites. It is a major site of production of fatty acids, triglycerides, phospholipids, ketone bodies, and cholesterol. Steroid hormones are degraded in the liver. *See* CHOLESTEROL; KETONE; LIPID; STEROID.

The liver is the sole source of such necessary constituents of the blood as fibrinogen, serum albumin, and cholinesterase. In the embryonic stage of most vertebrates the liver serves as the major manufacturing site of erythrocytes, a process known as erythropoiesis. The liver also removes toxins from the systemic circulation and degrades them, as well as excess hormones. Particulate material may be removed through a phagocytic action of specialized cells (Kupffer cells) lining the lumen of the hepatic "capillary spaces," or sinusoids. In addition to the products which the liver delivers directly to the general circulation (endocrine function), it secretes bile through a duct system which, involving the gallbladder as a storage chamber, eventually passes into the duodenum (exocrine function). Bile functions as an emulsifier of fats to facilitate their digestion by fat-splitting lipases, and may also activate the lipase directly. *See* GALLBLADDER.

Anatomy. The human liver is a massive wedge-shaped organ divided into a large right lobe and a smaller left lobe. Its anterior surface underlies the diaphragm. The upper portion of the liver is partially covered ventrally by the lungs, whereas the lower portion overhangs the stomach and intestine. The entire liver is covered by Glisson's capsule, an adherent membranous sheet of collagenous and elastic fibers.

Venous blood from the intestine, and to a lesser extent from spleen and stomach, converges upon a short broad vessel, called the hepatic portal vein, which enters the liver through a depression in the dorsocaudal surface termed the porta hepatis. There the hepatic portal vein divides into a short right branch and a longer left branch. These vessels then ramify into the small branches which actually penetrate the functional parenchymal mass as the inner tubes of the portal canals.

The hepatic artery also enters at the porta hepatis and ramifies into smaller branches, which flank the portal venules within the portal canals. The branches of the portal vein and hepatic artery then empty into sinusoids, which are major regions of hepatovascular exchange. They communicate with small branches of the hepatic veins and, through the hepatic vein, the blood is returned to the heart by way of the vena cava.

The tiny bile canaliculi, which lie between grooves in adjacent parenchymal cells, communicate with tiny intralobular bile ducts. These intralobular bile ducts empty into increasingly larger interlobular bile ducts which lie within the portal canals and make up the third element of the so-called portal triad.   [G.H.F.]

Lophophore   The crown of tentacles which surrounds the mouth in the Bryozoa, Phoronida, and Brachiopoda. The numerous ciliated tentacles arise from a circular or horseshoe-shaped fold of the body wall. The tentacles are hollow outgrowths of the body wall, each containing fluid-filled extensions of the body cavity and extended hydraulically. The primary function of the lophophore is to gather food. On the tentacles are ciliary tracts which drive a current of food-particle-bearing water through the lophophore. While the lophophore is primarily a feeding organ, it may also play a role in reproduction, respiration, and larval locomotion. *See* BRACHIOPODA; BRYOZOA; PHORONIDA.   [J.E.Wi.]

Loricifera   A phylum of multicellular invertebrates. These marine organisms are entirely meiobenthic; that is, they never exceed a maximum dimension of 400 micrometers and live in sediments ranging from deep-sea red clay to coarse sand or shell hash. They have some of the smallest known cells in the animal kingdom.

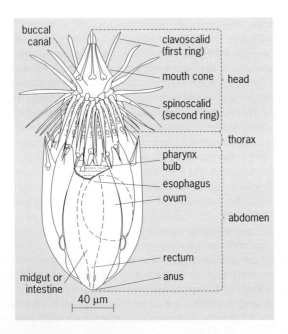

Ventral view of adult female loriciferan (*Nannaloricus mysticus*). (*After R. M. Kristensen, Loricifera, a new phylum with Aschelminthes characters from the meiobenthus, Z. Zool. Syst. Evolutionsforsch., 21(3):163–180, 1983*)

Although they have been found throughout the world, only 10 species representing three genera and two families have been described. Well over 50 species thought to represent several additional genera are known but remain undescribed.

Adult loriciferans are bilaterally symmetrical. The body is regionated into a mouth cone which telescopically protrudes anteriorly from the center of a spherical, appendage-ringed (up to 400 rings may be present) head; a short, usually plated neck region; and a distinctively loricated (thick-cuticled) thorax-abdomen (see illustration). The head, along with its withdrawn mouth cone, may be inverted into the thorax-abdomen, which is then closed anteriorly by the cuticle of the neck region.

Loriciferans appear to be closely related to the Priapulida and perhaps less so to the Kinorhyncha. Certain structures of the mouth cone suggest affinities to the Tardigrada. Their presence may support the idea that proarthropods could have been developed from aschelminth ancestral stock. *See* ANIMAL KINGDOM; ARTHROPODA; KINORHYNCHA; PRIAPULIDA; TARDIGRADA. [R.P.H.]

Lung Paired, air-filled respiratory sacs, usually in the anterior or anteroventral part of the trunk of most tetrapods. They lie within the coelom and are covered by peritoneum. In mammals they are within special chambers of the coelom known as pleural cavities and the peritoneum is termed pleura.

Amphibian lungs are often simple sacs, with only small ridges on the internal walls. In higher forms the lungs become more and more subdivided internally, thus increasing greatly the surface areas across which the respiratory exchange takes place. However, even in many reptiles the lungs may be quite simple. Birds have especially complex lungs with a highly differentiated system of tubes leading into and through them to the air sacs which are contained in many parts of the bird's body. Mammalian lungs are simpler, but in them the internal subdivision into tiny sacs or alveoli is extreme; there may be over 350,000,000 of them in one human lung.

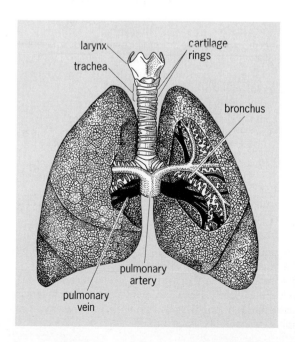

The human lung. (*After T. I. Storer and R. L. Usinger, General Zoology, 4th ed., McGraw-Hill, 1965*)

In humans the two lungs lie within the chest, separated by the heart and mediastinum. The right lung has three lobes and the left lung two. A bronchus, an artery, and a vein enter each lung medially at the hilum; each branches again and again as it enters the lobules and smaller divisions of the lungs (see illustration). The terminal airways or bronchioles expand into small clusters of grapelike air cells, the alveoli. The alveolar walls consist of a single layer of epithelium and collectively present a huge surface. A small network of blood capillaries in the walls of the alveoli affords surfaces for the actual exchange of gases. See RESPIRATION; RESPIRATORY SYSTEM.   [T.S.P.]

Lyme disease   A multisystem illness caused by the tick-borne spirochete *Borrelia burgdorferi*. The disease, also known as Lyme borreliosis, generally begins with a unique expanding skin lesion, erythema migrans, which is often accompanied by symptoms resembling those of influenza or meningitis. During the weeks or months following the tick bite, some individuals may develop cardiac and neurological abnormalities, particularly meningitis or inflammation of the cranial or peripheral nerves. If the disease is untreated, intermittent or chronic arthritis and progressive encephalomyelitis may develop months or years after primary infection. See NERVOUS SYSTEM DISORDERS.

The causative agent, *B. burgdorferi*, is a helically shaped bacterium with dimensions of 0.18–0.25 by 4–30 micrometers. Once thought to be limited to the European continent, Lyme borreliosis and related disorders are now known to occur also in North America, Russia, Japan, China, Australia, and Africa, where *B. burgdorferi* is maintained and transmitted by ticks of the genus *Ixodes*, namely *I. dammini, I. pacificus*, and possibly *I. scapularis* in the United States, *I. ricinus* in Europe, and *I. persulcatus* in Asia. Reports of Lyme disease in areas where neither *I. dammini* nor *I. pacificus* is present suggest that other species of ticks or possibly other bloodsucking arthropods such as biting flies or fleas may be involved in maintaining and transmitting the spirochetes. See IXODIDES.

All stages of Lyme borreliosis may respond to antibiotic therapy. Early treatment with oral tetracycline, doxycycline, penicillin, amoxicillin, or erythromycin can shorten the duration of symptoms and prevent later disease. See ANTIBIOTIC.

Prevention and control of Lyme borreliosis must be directed toward reduction of the tick population. This can be accomplished through reducing the population of animals that serve as hosts for the adult ticks, elimination of rodents that are not only the preferred hosts but also the source for infecting immature ticks with *B. burgdorferi*, and application of tick-killing agents to vegetation in infested areas. Personal use of effective tick repellents and toxins is also recommended. See INFECTIOUS DISEASE; INSECTICIDE.

Lyme disease affects not only humans but also domestic animals such as dogs, horses, and cattle that serve as hosts for the tick vectors. Animals affected show migratory, intermittent arthritis in some joints similar to that observed in humans.   [W.Ba.; J.J.Ka.]

Lymphatic system   A system of vessels in the vertebrate body, beginning in a network of exceedingly thin-walled capillaries in almost all the organs and tissues except the brain and bones. This network is drained by larger channels, mostly coursing along the veins and eventually joining to form a large vessel, the thoracic duct, which runs beside the spinal column to enter the left subclavian vein at the base of the neck. The lymph fluid originates in the tissue spaces by filtration from the blood capillaries. While in the lymphatic capillaries it is clear and watery. However, at intervals along the larger lymphatic vessels, the lymph passes through spongelike lymph nodes, where it receives great numbers of cells, the lymphocytes, and becomes turbid.

The lymph nodes of mammals vary in number, size, form, and structure in different species. The amount of connective tissue of the lymph nodes, that is, the degree of development of the capsule and trabeculae, also varies in different mammals. Other lymphoid organs include the tonsils, thymus gland, and spleen, and in certain classes and groups of animals, structures which are confined to such groups, for instance, the bursa of Fabricius in the birds, a diverticulum from the lower end of the alimentary canal. *See* SPLEEN; THYMUS GLAND; TONSIL.

The functions of the lymphatics are to remove particulate materials such as molecular proteins and bacteria from the tissues; to transport fat from the intestine to the blood; to supply the blood with lymphocytes; to remove excess fluid; also to return to the bloodstream the protein which has escaped from the blood capillaries. Basically, the composition of lymph closely resembles that of the plasma; lymph contains all of the types of protein found in plasma, but in lower concentration. The composition of lymph varies to some extent from one part of the body to another. Thus, the lymph from the liver contains more protein than that from the skin.

The lymph nodes serve as filtering-out places for foreign particles, including microorganisms, because the lymph comes into intimate contact with the many phagocytic cells of the sinusoids. These macrophages are of both the fixed and free wandering types. In addition to the phagocytic function, lymphoid tissue produces antibodies, although the actual process of antibody formation is not well understood. *See* CELLULAR IMMUNOLOGY; PHAGOCYTOSIS.   [W.An.]

Lysin   A term used to describe substances that will disrupt a cell, with the release of some of its constituents. Unless the damage is minor, this action leads to the death of the cell. Lysins vary in the range of host species whose cells they will attack and in their requirements for accessory factors for lysis; the immune lysins are strictest in their requirements. Erythrocytes are lysed by a wide variety of chemicals, including water and hypertonic salt solutions, which displace the osmotic pressure from that of isotonicity. They are also susceptible to surface-active substances, such as saponin. Many bacteria, such as the staphylococcus and the streptococcus, elaborate one or more hemolysins that will lyse erythrocytes from certain, although not all, species of animals. *See* LYTIC REACTION.   [H.P.T.]

Lysogeny   Almost all strains of bacteria are lysogenic; that is, they have the capacity on rare occasions to lyse with the liberation of particles of bacteriophage (see illustration). Such particles can be detected by their ability to form plaques (colonies of bacteriophage) on lawns of sensitive (indicator) bacteria. The genetic determinant of the capacity of lysogenic bacteria to produce bacteriophage is a repressed phage genome (provirus) which exists in the bacterium in one of two states: (1) integrated into the bacterial chromosome (most cases), or (2) occupying some extra-chromosomal location (rare cases).

Bacteriophages which have the potential to exist as provirus are called temperate phages. When the provirus is integrated into the bacterial genome, it is called prophage. When the germinal substance (deoxyribonucleic acid or deoxyribonucleoprotein) of certain temperate phages enters a sensitive bacterium, the outcome may be death (lysis) for the bacterium as a result of phage multiplication, or it may result in the integration of the phage nucleic acid into the host genome (as a prophage), with the formation of a stable lysogenic bacterium. The lysogenic strain is designated by the name of the sensitive strain followed, in parentheses, by the strain of lysogenizing phage, for

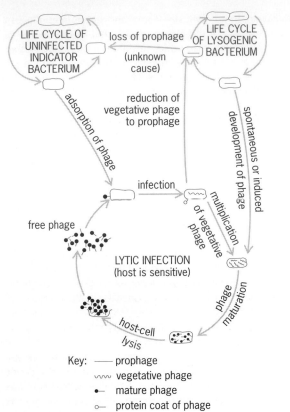

Key: —— prophage
         ∿∿ vegetative phage
         •— mature phage
         ○— protein coat of phage

Life cycles of phage and bacterial host. (*After E. Jawetz, J. L. Melnick, and E. A. Adelberg, Review of Medical Microbiology, 2d ed., Lange, 1956*)

example, *Escherichia coli* (λ). Such a bacterium differs from its nonlysogenic ancestor in one very special way: It is immune to lysis by phage homologous to its carried prophage. *See* BACTERIOPHAGE.   [L.B.]

Lysosome   A digestive structure found within virtually all types of animal cells. Lysosome sizes, microscopic appearances, and other properties vary among different cell types and circumstances owing, in part, to differences in their functions and states. Typical lysosomes are roughly spherical or elongate bodies with largest dimensions of 0.1–1 micrometer or greater; tens to hundreds are present in a single cell.

Each lysosome is bounded by a membrane and contains several dozen different species of digestive enzymes, each of which can sever particular chemical bonds found in natural materials. Most lysosomal enzymes function best in an acid environment. This acidification is accomplished by a proton pump, built into the membrane surrounding the lysosome, which effects the transport of hydrogen ions into the lysosomes. *See* CELL MEMBRANES; ENZYME; ION TRANSPORT.

Lysosomes digest materials taken into the cell from the outside (a process known as heterophagy) as well as other materials that originate in the cell's own cytoplasm (autophagy). The materials to be digested are ultimately incorporated into the same membrane-bounded compartments as the lysosomal enzymes. Selective degradative products can pass out of the lysosome by crossing the membrane, but the enzymes cannot. This sequestration, which protects the cell, persists because the admixture of the enzymes and the materials to digest takes place through fusion of membrane-bounded compartments.

In heterophagy, the cell takes up particles or molecules by the process of endocytosis, engulfing them in membrane-bounded vesicles or vacuoles that are formed at the cell surface. The endocytosed material enters lysosomes via intermediate membrane-bounded compartments known as endosomes. In higher animals, heterophagy is most prominently used by leukocytes and macrophages. These specialized cells endocytose invasive microorganisms and use endocytosis in clearing debris and disposing of dead or senescent cells. *See* CELL SENESCENCE AND DEATH; ENDOCYTOSIS; PHAGOCYTOSIS.

In autophagy, cells segregate regions of their own cytoplasm within compartments that come to be bounded by single membranes and to receive lysosomal enzymes. Autophagic lysosomes take part in the remodeling of cells as part of the processes of development and during stressful circumstances. They also participate, along with nonlysosomal enzymes and heterophagic lysosomes, in normal turnover of the body's constituents—the balanced synthesis and destruction through which most molecules of most cells are replaced by new molecules.

Genetic defects in lysosomal enzymes and related proteins are known to be associated with a large number of rare disorders in humans and animals (such as Tay-Sachs disease and Niemann-Pick disease type C). Defective lysosomal function leads to storage of particular classes of molecules that cannot be degraded and, in long-lived cells such as neurons, to complex pathogenic cascades with widespread impact on endosomal-lysosomal function, membrane trafficking, and signal transduction. Such disorders are most often fatal. Lysosomes or prelysosomal structures also have been "adopted" as intracellular homes by certain pathogenic microorganisms that avoid or survive the attacks of the lysosomal system. Some strains of viruses, and toxins such as the one responsible for diphtheria, may use endosomes as their route of entry into the cell, penetrating through the endosomal membrane into the surrounding cytoplasm.   [E.Ho.; S.U.W.]

Lysozyme   An enyme that was first identified and named by Alexander Fleming, who recognized its bacteriolytic properties. It has been designated muramidase, since it is known to facilitate the hydrolysis of a β-1-4-glycosidic bond between N-acetylglucosamine and N-acetylmuramic acid in bacterial cell walls; it also hydrolyzes similar glycosidic bonds in fragments of chitin. The most detailed studies have been performed on hen egg-white lysozyme, because this product is readily available. However, enzymes possessing lysozyme activity have been found in bacteria, bacteriophages, and plants and in human leukocytes, nasal secretions, saliva, and tears. The three-dimensional structure of the protein has been defined by x-ray crystallography. Additional data are available for the amino acid sequence of human lysozyme and also for a bacteriophage lysozyme. These results have given rise to speculation concerning the origin of the lysozyme gene during evolution.

Certain enzyme functions appear to be widely distributed in nature. The amino acid sequences of proteins possessing these functions reflect changes that have occurred in the course of evolution. The structures of lysozymes from three sources, distant in evolution, have been carefully examined. Hen egg lysozyme has no structural elements in common with bacteriophage lysozyme. Thus it must be concluded that these two enzymes emerged in evolution completely independent of each other. Preliminary studies of the structure of human lysozyme reveal considerable similarity to the structure of hen egg lysozyme. In fact, the resemblance is so great that it can be concluded that these proteins evolved from the same gene and have an essentially identical mechanism of action.

The amino acid composition of α-lactalbumin, a protein in cow's milk, is quite similar to that of hen egg lysozyme; nearly half of the amino acid positions in these two proteins are identical. It is postulated from a comparison of the amino acid sequences of hen egg lysozyme, human lysozyme, and α-lactalbumin that a "deletion" occurred during evolution in the α-lactalbumin gene with a resulting loss of information for two amino acids near position 13. In addition, positions 10, 12, and 19 in human lysozyme and α-lactalbumin are identical, so it is possible to see remnants of a common ancestral gene in all three proteins. These data illustrate the manner in which amino acid sequence information is being used as a molecular reflection of the paths of evolution. *See* ENZYME; PROTEINS, EVOLUTION OF.   [R.E.Ca.]

Lytic infection   Infection of a bacterium by a bacteriophage with subsequent production of more phage particles and lysis, or dissolution, of the cell. The viruses responsible are commonly called virulent phages. Lytic infection is one of the two major bacteriophage-bacterium relationships, the other being lysogenic infection. *See* BACTERIOPHAGE; LYSOGENY.   [P.B.C.]

Lytic reaction   A term used in serology to describe a reaction that leads to the disruption or lysis of a cell. The best example is the lysis of sheep red blood cells by specific antibody and complement in the presence of Ca^{2+} by (calcium ion) and Mg^{2+} (magnesium ion), a reaction that forms the indicator system of the standard Wassermann test for syphilis, as well as other complement-fixation reactions. In this example lysis results in the release of cellular hemoglobin into the medium; the reaction may be followed by visual or instrumental estimation of the decreased cell turbidity or the increased color of the medium due to the free hemoglobin. The initiation of lysis by complement can apparently proceed after the attachment of only one molecule of IgM or two molecules of IgG antibody to the red blood cell. IgM and IgG are both immunoglobulins. *See* ANTIBODY; COMPLEMENT; COMPLEMENT-FIXATION TEST; SEROLOGY.
                                           [H.P.T.]

M

Macroevolution   Large-scale patterns and processes in the history of life, including the origins of novel organismal designs, evolutionary trends, adaptive radiations, and extinctions. Macroevolutionary research is based on phylogeny, the history of common descent among species. The formation of species and branching of evolutionary lineages mark the interface between macroevolution and microevolution, which addresses the dynamics of genetic variation within populations. Phylogenetic reconstruction, the developmental basis of evolutionary change, and long-term trends in patterns of speciation and extinction among lineages constitute major foci of macroevolutionary studies.

Phylogenetic reconstruction. Phylogenetic relationships are revealed by the sharing of evolutionarily derived characteristics among species, which provides evidence for common ancestry. Shared derived characteristics are termed synapomorphies, and are equated by many systematists with the older concept of homology. Characteristics of different organisms are homologous if they descend, with some modification, from an equivalent characteristic of their most recent common ancestor. Closely related species share more homologous characteristics than do species whose common ancestry is more distant. Species are grouped into clades according to patterns of shared homologies. The clades form a nested hierarchy in which large clades are subdivided into smaller, less inclusive ones, and are depicted by a branching diagram called a cladogram. A phylogenetic tree is a branching diagram, congruent with the cladogram, that represents real lineages of past evolutionary history.

A cladogram or phylogenetic tree is necessary for constructing a taxonomy, but the principles by which higher taxa are recognized remain controversial. The traditional evolutionary taxonomy of G. G. Simpson recognizes higher taxa as units of adaptive evolution called adaptive zones. Species of an adaptive zone share common ancestry, and distinctive morphological or behavioral characteristics associated with use of environmental resources. Higher taxa receive Linnean categorical ranks (genus, family, order, and so forth) reflecting the breadth and distinctness of their adaptive zones. All taxa must have a single evolutionary origin, which means that the taxon must include the most recent common ancestor of all included species. A taxon is monophyletic if it contains all descendants of the group's most recent common ancestor, or paraphyletic if some descendants of the group's most recent common ancestor are excluded because they have evolved a new adaptive zone. For example, evolutionary taxonomy of the anthropoid primates groups the orangutan, gorilla, and chimpanzee in the paraphyletic family Pongidae and the humans in the monophyletic family Hominidae. Although the humans and chimpanzees share more recent common ancestry than either does with the gorilla or orangutan, the chimpanzees are grouped with the latter species at the family level and the humans are placed in a different family because they are considered to have evolved a new adaptive zone. The Hominidae and

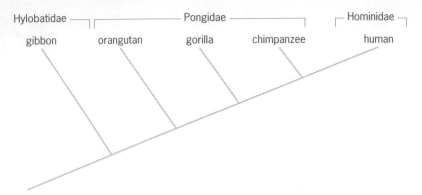

Phylogenetic relationships of anthropoid primates showing traditional family-level taxa. All apes and humans together form a monophyletic group. The family Pongidae is paraphyletic, and therefore considered invalid by cladistic taxonomists. (*After C. P. Hickman, Jr., L. S. Roberts, and A. Larson, Integrated Principles of Zoology, 9th ed., 1993*)

Pongidae together form a monophyletic group at a higher level (see illustration). *See* ANIMAL SYSTEMATICS.

Cladistic taxonomy or phylogenetic systematics accepts only monophyletic taxa because these alone are considered natural units of common descent. Linnean rankings are considered unimportant. Taxa recognized using both the Simpsonian and cladistic taxonomies are standardly used in macroevolutionary analyses of extinction and patterns of diversity through time. The Simpsonian versus cladistic taxonomies often lead to fundamentally different interpretations, however. For example, extinction of a paraphyletic group, such as dinosaurs, would be considered pseudoextinction by cladists because some descendants of the group's most recent common ancestor survive. Birds are living descendants of the most recent common ancestor of all dinosaurs. The dinosaurs as traditionally recognized, therefore, do not form a valid cladistic taxon. *See* AVES; DINOSAUR; PHYLOGENY.

Developmental processes. Comparative studies of organismal ontogeny are used to find where in development the key features of higher taxa appear and how developmental processes differ between taxa. Evolutionary developmental biologists denote the characteristic body plans of taxa by the term Bauplan. The major characteristics of animal phyla and their developmental and molecular attributes appear to have arisen and stabilized early in the history of life, during the Cambrian Period. Subsequent evolutionary diversification builds upon the Bauplan established early in animal evolution. *See* CAMBRIAN.

Particularly important to the evolutionary diversification of life are historical processes that generate change by altering the timing of organismal development, a phenomenon called heterochrony. Heterochronic changes can produce either paedomorphic or paeramorphic results. Paedomorphosis denotes the retention of preadult characteristics of ancestors in the adult stages of descendants; peramorphosis is the opposite outcome, in which the descendant ontogeny transcends that of the ancestor, adding new features at the final stages. Heterochronic changes can be produced by changing the rates of developmental processes or the times of their onset or termination.

Developmental dissociation occurs when different kinds of heterochronic change alter the development of different parts of the organism independently. Extensive dissociation can fundamentally restructure organismal ontogeny, producing ontogenetic repatterning. However, it is rare that a single heterochronic transformation affects all parts of the organism simultaneously. For most taxa, novel morphologies are produced by a mosaic of different heterochronic processes and by changes in the physical location of developmental events within the organism.

Long-term trends. Traditional Darwinian theory emphasizes natural selection acting on varying organisms within populations as the main causal factor of evolutionary change. Over many generations, the accumulation of favorable variants by natural selection produces new adaptations and new species. Macroevolutionary theory postulates two additional processes analogous to natural selection that act above the species level and on much longer time scales. An evolving lineage ultimately experiences one of two fates, branching speciation or extinction. Lineages that have a high propensity to produce new species and an ability to withstand extinction will dominate evolutionary history.

The higher-level process of differential speciation and extinction caused by the varying characteristics of species or lineages has been called species selection. Because the precise meaning of the term species is controversial, the more neutral terms lineage selection and clade selection are sometimes substituted for species selection. Most species show an evolutionary duration from a few million to approximately 10 million years in the fossil record between geologically instantaneous events of branching speciation. Species selection therefore generally occurs on a time scale of millions of years, rather than the generational time scale of natural selection. Species selection may be the primary factor underlying morphological evolutionary trends at this scale if lineages evolve by punctuated equilibrium, in which most morphological evolutionary change accompanies branching speciation, and species remain morphologically stable between speciational events. *See* SPECIATION.

The fossil record reveals mass extinctions in which enormous numbers of species from many different taxa are lost within a relatively short interval of geological time. Some lineages may be better able to survive mass extinction events than others, and the characteristics that make a lineage prone to survive mass extinction may be very different from those that influence species selection between events of mass extinction. Catastrophic species selection denotes differential survival and extinction of lineages during events of mass extinction as determined by character variation among lineages. Prior to the Cretaceous mass extinction, dinosaur taxa dominated mammalian taxa, whereas mammals survived the mass extinction and then diversified extensively. The characteristics of the ancestral mammals may have permitted them to survive environmental challenges to which dinosaurs were susceptible. *See* EXTINCTION (BIOLOGY); FOSSIL; MAMMALIA; PALEONTOLOGY; PERMIAN.

Because natural selection, species selection, and catastrophic species selection can differ in the biological characteristics they promote, higher-level processes may undo or reverse evolutionary trends arising from lower-level processes. *See* ORGANIC EVOLUTION.

[A.Lar.]

Magnetic reception (biology)   Sensitivity to magnetic stimuli, especially the very weak ones occurring naturally in the environment.

Evidence of magnetic detection has been found in a variety of invertebrates, including protozoa, flatworms, snails, and insects. In 1968 Martin Lindauer and Herman Martin first published extensive data showing that the Earth's geomagnetic field influences the orientation of the waggle-run dance by which a scout honeybee communicates the distance and direction of a food source to the forager bees. Later, Lindauer and Martin showed that fluctuations of less than 10^{-4} gauss (roughly 1/10,000 of the Earth's field) can influence these bees' behavior. Other investigators found evidence of magnetic detection in other kinds of insects, including termites, beetles, and fruit flies (*Drosophila*).

Most of the evidence for magnetic detection by birds has come from studies of their migratory and, homing behavior. Results strongly suggest that birds possess a magnetic compass, that is, they can determine compass bearings from the geomagnetic field. Evidence indicates that birds' sensitivity to magnetic stimuli is roughly similar to the honeybees'. It appears that the tiny fluctuations in the Earth's magnetic field caused by solar flares and other solar disturbances have a detectable effect on birds' navigation. The detection system probably has a narrow range of sensitivity; magnetic fields much stronger or weaker than the Earth's probably cannot be detected. *See* MIGRATORY BEHAVIOR.

Although behavioral effects of magnetic stimuli have been found in many kinds of animals, no one has yet succeeded in conditioning an animal to a magnetic stimulus in the laboratory. There is abundant evidence that the detection process is not quick, usually taking 15 min or more; hence, the flash stimuli presented in most classical conditioning attempts may be undetectable.

The physical mechanism for magnetic detection by living organisms is unknown, though a variety of possibilities have been put forward.   [W.T.K.]

Magnoliidae   A subclass of the class Magnoliopsida (dicotyledons) in the division Magnoliophyta (Angiospermae), the flowering plants. The subclass consists of 8 orders, 39 families, and more than 12,000 species. The Magnoliidae are the most primitive subclass of flowering plants. In general, they have a well-developed perianth, which may or may not be numerous, centripetal stamens, and they are apocarpous. *See* ARISTOLOCHIALES; ILLICIALES; LAURALES; MAGNOLIALES; MAGNOLIOPHYTA; MAGNOLIOPSIDA; NYMPHAEALES; PAPAVERALES; PIPERALES; PLANT KINGDOM; RANUNCULALES.   [A.Cr.; T.M.Ba.]

Magnoliophyta   A division of seed plants consisting of about 250,000 species, which form the bulk and most conspicuous element of the land plants. Often called flowering plants or angiosperms, they have several unique characteristics, the most prominent of which are their reproductive structure, flowers, and covered seeds. The other obvious woody land plants are the gymnosperms, which have cones instead of flowers and have naked seeds. Another trait distinguishing the angiosperms is the presence of double fertilization, which results in the production of stored food (starch or oils) within their seeds. *See* FLOWER.

Angiosperms range from some of the smallest plants known to large forest trees, and they occur in all habitats, including the oceans, where they are only a minor element in most marine ecosystems. Some are capable of growing directly on rock surfaces as well as on the limbs of trees. The angiosperms are usually considered to be the most highly evolved division of the subkingdom Embryobionta. Their highly specialized and relatively efficient conducting tissues, combined with the protection of their ovules in an ovary, give them a competitive advantage over most other groups of land plants in most regions. *See* EMBRYOBIONTA.

The angiosperms may be characterized as vascular plants with roots, stems, and leaves, usually with well-developed vessels in the xylem and with companion cells in the phloem. The central cylinder has leaf gaps or scattered vascular bundles; the ovules are enclosed in an ovary; and the female gametophyte is reduced to a few-nucleate embryo sac without an archegonium. The male gametophyte is reduced to a tiny pollen grain that gives rise to a pollen tube containing a tube nucleus and two sperms; one sperm fuses with the egg in the embryo sac to form a zygote, and the other fuses with two nuclei of the embryo sac to form a triple fusion nucleus that is typically the forerunner of the endosperm of the seed. *See* LEAF; PHLOEM; POLLEN; REPRODUCTION (PLANT); ROOT (BOTANY); SEED; STEM; XYLEM.   [M.W.C.]

Among plants with alternation of sporophyte and gametophyte generations, the angiosperms represent the most extreme stage in reduction of the gametophyte, which in effect is reduced to a mere stage in the reproduction of the sporophyte. The pollen grain, with its associated pollen tube, and the embryo sac represent the male and female gametophyte generations; the endosperm is a new structure not referable to either generation; and the remainder of the plant throughout its life cycle is the sporophyte. Many angiosperms can also propagate asexually by means of creeping stems or roots or by other specialized vegetative structures such as bulbils.

It is obvious to biologists that the angiosperms must have evolved from gymnosperms, but beyond this the facts are obscure. They appear in the fossil record early in the Cretaceous Period as obvious angiosperms, without any hint of a connection to any particular group of gymnosperms. Many believe that among the gymnosperms the seed ferns provide the most likely ancestors. *See* PALEOBOTANY; PINOPHYTA.

The Magnoliophyta consist of two large groups that have not been formally named: the eudicots and the magnoliids. The eudicots are characterized by flowers that are highly organized in terms of the number and orientation of parts whereas the magnoliids have many parts without any particular fixed patterns among the parts— except for the monocots, in which the most developed groups, like the eudicots, exhibit developed flowers with highly organized patterns. *See* LILIOPSIDA; MAGNOLIOPSIDA.

[A.Cr.; T.M.Ba.; M.W.C.]

Maltose   An oligosaccharide, known as malt sugar, a reducing disaccharide (see illustration). It is fermentable by yeast in the presence of D-glucose.

Formula for maltose (α form; * indicates reducing group).

The action of animal (salivary and pancreatic) as well as plant (germinating cereals, sweet potato) amylases on starch, dextrin, and glycogen produces maltose as the main end product. Maltose is hydrolyzed by acids and the enzyme maltase to two molecules of D-glucose. *See* GLUCOSE; MALTASE; OLIGOSACCHARIDE.   [W.Z.H.]

Mammalia   The class Mammalia has been the dominant group of vertebrates since the extinction of the dinosaurs 65 million years ago. There are over 4200 living species, classified into over 1000 genera, 140 families, and 18 orders. The number of extinct mammals is at least five times that. Most living mammals are terrestrial. However, many groups of mammals moved to the water from land-dwelling ancestors. These included manatees and dugongs (which are distantly related to elephants), otters (which are related to weasels), seals, sea lions, and walruses (which are distantly related to bears), and whales (which are distantly related to even-toed hoofed mammals), as well as numerous extinct groups. Mammals have also taken to the air, with over 920 living species of bats, as well as numerous gliding forms such as the flying squirrels, phalangerid marsupials, and flying lemurs or colugos. Mammals are even more successful at small body sizes, with hundreds of small species of rodents, rabbits, and insectivores.

Mammals are distinguished from all other animals by a number of unique characteristics. These include a body covered with hair or fur (secondarily reduced in some mammals, particularly aquatic forms); mammary glands in the female for nursing the young; a jaw composed of a single bone, the dentary; and three middle ear bones, the incus, malleus, and stapes. All mammals maintain a constant body temperature through metabolic heat. Their four-chambered heart (two ventricles and two atria) keeps the circulation of the lungs separate from that of the rest of the body, resulting in more efficient oxygen transport to the body tissues. They have many other adaptations for their active life-style, including specialized teeth (incisors, canines, molars, and premolars) for biting, tearing, and grinding up food for more efficient digestion. These teeth are replaced only once in the lifetime of the animal (rather than continuous replacement, found in other toothed vertebrates). Mammals have a unique set of muscles that allow the jaw to move in many directions for chewing and for stronger bite force. Their secondary palate encloses the internal nasal passage and allows breathing while they have food in the mouth. Ribs (found only in the thoracic region) are firmly attached to the breastbone (sternum), so that expansion of the lung cavity is accomplished by a muscular wall in the abdominal cavity called the diaphragm. *See* CARDIOVASCULAR SYSTEM; DENTITION; EAR (VERTEBRATE); HAIR; LACTATION; MAMMARY GLAND; THERMOREGULATION; TOOTH.

All mammals have large brains relative to their body size. Most mammals have excellent senses, and some have extraordinary senses of sight, smell, and hearing. To accommodate their large brains and more sophisticated development, mammals are born alive (except for the platypus and echidnas, which lay eggs), and may require considerable parental care before they are ready to fend for themselves. Juvenile mammals have separate bony caps (epiphyses) on the long bones, separated from the shaft of the bone by a layer of cartilage. This allows the long bones to grow rapidly while still having a strong, bony articulation at the end. When a mammal reaches maturity, these epiphyses fuse to the shaft, and the mammal stops growing (in contrast to other vertebrates, which grow continuously through their lives). *See* BRAIN; NERVOUS SYSTEM (VERTEBRATE); SKELETAL SYSTEM.

The living mammals are divided into three major groups: the monotremes (platypus and echidnas), which still lay eggs, retain a number of reptilian bones in their skeletons, and have other primitive features of their anatomy and physiology; the marsupials (opossums, kangaroos, koalas, wombats, and their relatives), which give birth to an immature embryo that must crawl into the mother's pouch (marsupium), where it finishes development; and the placentals (the rest of the living mammals), which carry the young through a long gestation until they give birth to relatively well-developed progeny. In addition to these three living groups, there were many other major groups, such as the rodentlike multituberculates, now extinct. The most recent classification of the mammals can be summarized as follows:

> Class Mammalia
> > Subclass Prototheria (monotremes)
> > Subclass Theriiformes
> > > Infraclass Holotheria
> > > > Cohort Marsupialia (marsupials or pouched mammals)
> > > > Cohort Placentalia (placentals)
> > > > Magnorder Xenarthra (sloths, anteaters, armadillos)
> > > > Magnorder Epitheria
> > > > > Grandorder Anagalida (= Glires) (rodents, rabbits,

elephant shrews)
Grandorder Ferae (carnivores, pangolins, many extinct
groups)
Grandorder Lipotyphla (hedgehogs, shrews, moles,
tenreces, and kin)
Grandorder Archonta
Order Chiroptera (bats)
Order Primates (lemurs, monkeys, apes, humans)
Order Scandentia (tree shrews)
Grandorder Ungulata (hoofed mammals)
Order Tubulidentata (aardvarks)
Order Artiodactyla (even-toed hoofed mammals:
pigs, hippos, camels, deer, antelopes, cattle,
giraffes, pronghorns, and relatives)
Order Cete (whales and their extinct land relatives)
Order Perissodactyla (odd-toed hoofed mammals:
horses, rhinos, tapirs, and extinct relatives)
Order Hyracoidea (hyraxes)
Order Tethytheria (elephants, manatees, and extinct
relatives)

This classification does not list all the extinct groups, which include at least a dozen more ordinal-level taxa. See separate articles on each group. See REPRODUCTIVE SYSTEM.

Mammals evolved from the Synapsida, an early branch of the terrestrial amniotes that has been erroneously called the mammallike reptiles. (This name is inappropriate because synapsids were never related to reptiles.) The first undoubted mammals appeared in the Late Triassic (about 210 million years ago), and were tiny insectivorous forms much like living shrews. Through the rest of the age of dinosaurs, a number of different groups evolved over the next 145 million years of the Jurassic and Cretaceous. Most remained tiny, shrewlike animals, hiding from the dinosaurs in the underbrush and coming out mostly at night. The first two-thirds of mammalian history had passed before the dinosaurs became extinct 65 million years ago, and this allowed mammals to emerge from their shadow. Between 65 and 55 million years ago, a rapid adaptive radiation yielded all the living orders of placental mammals and many extinct forms as well.   [D.R.Pr.]

Mammary gland   A unique anatomical structure of mammals that secretes milk for the nourishment of the newborn. The mammary gland contains thousands of milk-producing units called alveoli, each of which consists of a unicellular layer of epithelial cells arranged in a spheroid structure. The alveolar epithelial cells take up a variety of nutrients from the blood that perfuses the outer surface of the alveolar structures. Some of the nutrients are then secreted directly into the alveolar lumen; other nutrients are used to synthesize the unique constituents of milk which are then secreted. Each alveolus is connected to a duct through which milk flows. The ducts from many alveoli are connected via a converging ductal system which opens externally by way of the lactiferous pore.

Surrounding each alveolus and its associated small ducts are smooth muscle cells called myoepithelial cells. These cells contract in response to the posterior pituitary hormone oxytocin; milk is thus forced out of the alveoli, through the ductal system, and out the lactiferous pore for the nourishment of the newborn. The release of oxytocin is a neuroendocrine reflex triggered by the stimulation of sensory receptors by the suckling of the newborn. *See* ENDOCRINE MECHANISMS.

Mammary glands are basically highly modified and specialized sebaceous glands which derive from ectoderm. In the embryo, mammary lines, formed on both sides of the midventral line, mark the location of future mammary glands. Along the mammary lines discrete ectodermal ingrowths, called mammary buds, produce a rudimentary branched system of ducts at birth. In all species (except the monotremes) a nipple or teat develops in concert with the mammary buds. In the most primitive mammal (the duckbill or platypus), which lacks nipples or teats, milk simply oozes out of the two mammary gland areas and is lapped up by the young.

From birth to sexual maturity the mammary gland consists of a nipple and a rudimentary ductal system in both males and females. At the onset of puberty in the female, the enhanced secretion of estrogen causes a further development of the mammary ductal system and an accumulation of lipids in fat cells. After puberty in women, the mammary gland consists of about 85% fat cells and a partially developed ductal system. *See* ESTROGEN.

During pregnancy the mammary gland comes under the influence of estrogen and progesterone which are derived from both the ovary and placenta. These hormones cause a further branching of the ductal system and the development of milk-secreting structures, the alveoli. In humans, approximately 200 alveoli are surrounded by a connective tissue sheath forming a structure called a lobule. About 26 lobules are packaged via another connective tissue sheath into a larger structure called a lobe. Each of 15–20 lobes is exteriorized into the nipple via separate lactiferous pores. *See* PROGESTERONE.

A complement of hormones maximizes the development of the ductal and lobuloalveolar elements in the mammary gland. Optimal ductal growth is attained with estrogen, a glucocorticoid, prolactin, and insulin. Maximal lobuloalveolar growth is obtained with estrogen, progesterone, growth hormone, prolactin, a glucocorticoid, and insulin. During pregnancy estrogen and progesterone stimulate mammary development but inhibit milk production.

During the final third of pregnancy, the alveolar epithelial cells begin secreting a fluid called colostrum. This fluid fills the alveoli and causes a gradual enlargement of the breast or udder. At parturition, the inhibitory influence of estrogen and progesterone is removed, and the gland can secrete milk under the influence of a further complement of hormones including prolactin, a glucocorticoid, insulin, and the thyroid hormones. *See* GLAND; LACTATION; MAMMALIA; MILK; PREGNANCY.   [J.A.Ri.]

Mangrove   A taxonomically diverse assemblage of trees and shrubs that form the dominant plant communities in tidal, saline wetlands along sheltered tropical and subtropical coasts. The development and composition of mangrove communities depend largely on temperature, soil type and salinity, duration and frequency of inundation, accretion of silt, tidal and wave energy, and cyclone or flood frequencies. Extensive mangrove communities seem to correlate with areas in which the water temperature of the warmest month exceeds 75°F (24°C), and they are absent from waters that never exceed 75°F (24°C) during the year. Intertidal, sheltered, low-energy, muddy sediments are the most suitable habitats for mangrove communities, and under optimal conditions, forests up to 148 ft (45 m) in height can develop. Where less favorable conditions are found, mangrove communities may reach maturity at heights of only 3 ft (1 m). *See* ECOSYSTEM.

At the generic level, *Avicennia* and *Rhizophora* are the dominant plants of mangrove communities throughout the world, with each genus having several closely related species in both hemispheres. At the species level, however, only a few species, such as the portia tree (*Thespesia populnea*), the mangrove fern (*Acrostichum aureum*), and the swamp hibiscus (*Hibiscus tiliaceus*), occur in both hemispheres.

Most plants of the mangrove community are halophytes, well adapted to salt water and fluctuations of tide level. Many species show modified root structures such as stilt or prop roots, which offer support on the semiliquid or shifting sediments, whereas others have erect root structures (pneumatophores) that facilitate oxygen penetration to the roots in a hypoxic environment. Salt glands, which allow excess salt to be extruded through the leaves, occur in several species; others show a range of physiological mechanisms that either exclude salt from the plants or minimize the damage excess salts can cause by separating the salt from the sensitive enzyme systems of the plant. Several species have well-developed vivipary of their seeds, whereby the hypocotyl develops while the fruit is still attached to the tree. The seedlings are generally buoyant, able to float over long distances in the sea and rapidly establish themselves once stranded in a suitable habitat. *See* PLANTS, SALINE ENVIRONMENTS OF.

A mangrove may be considered either a sheltered, muddy, intertidal habitat or a forest community. The sediment surface of mangrove communities abounds with species that have marine affinities, including brightly colored fiddler crabs, mound-building mud lobsters, and a variety of mollusks and worms, as well as specialized gobiid fish (mudskippers). The waterways among the mangroves are important feeding and nursery areas for a variety of juvenile finfish as well as crustaceans. Animals with forest affinities that are associated with mangroves include snakes, lizards, deer, tigers, crab-eating monkeys, bats, and many species of birds.

Economically, mangroves are a major source of timber, poles, thatch, and fuel. The bark of some trees is used for tanning materials, whereas other species have food or medicinal value. *See* ECOLOGICAL COMMUNITIES; FOREST MANAGEMENT.   [P.Sae.]

Marine ecology   An integrative science that studies the basic structural and functional relationships within and among living populations and their physical-chemical environments in marine ecosystems. Marine ecology draws on all the major fields within the biological sciences as well as oceanography, physics, geology, and chemistry. Emphasis has evolved toward understanding the rates and controls on ecological processes that govern both short- and long-term events, including population growth and survival, primary and secondary productivity, and community dynamics and stability. Marine ecology focuses on specific organisms as well as on particular environments or physical settings. *See* ENVIRONMENT.

Marine environments. Classification of marine environments for ecological purposes is based very generally on two criteria, the dominant community or ecosystem type and the physical-geological setting. Those ecosystems identified by their dominant community type include mangrove forests, coastal salt marshes, submersed seagrasses and seaweeds, and tropical coral reefs. Marine environments identified by their physical-geological setting include estuaries, coastal marine and nearshore zones, and open-ocean-deep-sea regions. *See* DEEP-SEA FAUNA; ECOLOGICAL COMMUNITIES; HYDROTHERMAL VENT; PHYTOPLANKTON; ZOOPLANKTON.

An estuary is a semienclosed area or basin with an open outlet to the sea where fresh water from the land mixes with seawater. The ecological consequences of freshwater input and mixing create strong gradients in physical-chemical characteristics, biological activity and diversity, and the potential for major adverse impacts associated with human activities. Because of the physical forces of tides, wind, waves, and freshwater input, estuaries are perhaps the most ecologically complex marine environment.

They are also the most productive of all marine ecosystems on an area basis and contain within their physical boundaries many of the principal marine ecosystems defined by community type. *See* ESTUARINE OCEANOGRAPHY; MANGROVE; SALT MARSH.

Coastal and nearshore marine ecosystems are generally considered to be marine environments bounded by the coastal land margin (seashore) and the continental shelf 300–600 ft (100– 200 m) below sea level. The continental shelf, which occupies the greater area of the two and varies in width from a few to several hundred kilometers, is strongly influenced by physical oceanographic processes that govern general patterns of circulation and the energy associated with waves and currents. Ecologically, the coastal and nearshore zones grade from shallow water depths, influenced by the adjacent landmass and input from coastal rivers and estuaries, to the continental shelf break, where oceanic processes predominate. Biological productivity and species diversity and abundance tend to decrease in an offshore direction as the food web becomes supported only by planktonic production. Among the unique marine ecosystems associated with coastal and nearshore water bodies are seaweed-dominated communities (for example, kelp "forests"), coral reefs, and upwellings. *See* CONTINENTAL MARGIN; REEF; UPWELLING.

Approximately 70% of the Earth's surface is covered by oceans, and more than 80% of the ocean's surface overlies water depths greater than 600 ft (200 m), making open-ocean–deep-sea environments the largest, yet the least ecologically studied and understood, of all marine environments. The major oceans of the world differ in their extent of landmass influence, circulation patterns, and other physical-chemical properties. Other major water bodies included in open-ocean–deep-sea environments are the areas of the oceans that are referred to as seas. A sea is a water body that is smaller than an ocean and has unique physical oceanographic features defined by basin morphology. Because of their circulation patterns and geomorphology, seas are more strongly influenced by the continental landmass and island chain structures than are oceanic environments.

Within the major oceans, as well as seas, various oceanographic environments can be defined. A simple classification would include water column depths receiving sufficient light to support photosynthesis (photic zone); water depths at which light penetration cannot support photosynthesis and which for all ecological purposes are without light (aphotic zone); and the benthos or bottom-dwelling organisms. Classical oceanography defines four depth zones; epipelagic, 0–450 ft (0–150 m), which is variable; mesopelagic, 450–3000 ft (150–1000 m); bathypelagic, 3000–12,000 ft (1000–4000 m); and abyssopelagic, greater than 12,000 ft (4000 m). These depth strata correspond approximately to the depth of sufficient light penetration to support photosynthesis; the zone in which all light is attenuated; the truly aphotic zone; and the deepest oceanic environments.

Marine ecological processes. Fundamental to marine ecology is the discovery and understanding of the principles that underlie the organization of marine communities and govern their behavior, such as controls on population growth and stability, quantifying interactions among populations that lead to persistent communities, and coupling of communities to form viable ecosystems. The basis of this organization is the flow of energy and cycling of materials, beginning with the capture of radiant solar energy through the processes of photosynthesis and ending with the remineralization of organic matter and nutrients.

Photosynthesis in seawater is carried out by various marine organisms that range in size from the microscopic, single-celled marine algae to multicellular vascular plants. The rate of photosynthesis, and thus the growth and primary production of marine plants, is dependent on a number of factors, the more important of which are availability and uptake of nutrients, temperature, and intensity and quality of light. Of these three, the last probably is the single most important in governing primary production and the distribution and abundance of marine plants. Considering the high attenuation of light in water and the relationships between light intensity and photosynthesis, net autotrophic production is confined to relatively shallow water depths. The major primary producers in marine environments are intertidal salt marshes and mangroves, submersed seagrasses and seaweeds, phytoplankton, benthic and attached microalgae, and—for coral reefs—symbiotic algae (zooxanthellae). On an areal basis, estuaries and nearshore marine ecosystems have the highest annual rates of primary production. From a global perspective, the open oceans are the greatest contributors to total marine primary production because of their overwhelming size.

The two other principal factors that influence photosynthesis and primary production are temperature and nutrient supply. Temperature affects the rate of metabolic reactions, and marine plants show specific optima and tolerance ranges relative to photosynthesis. Nutrients, particularly nitrogen, phosphorus, and silica, are essential for marine plants and influence both the rate of photosynthesis and plant growth. For many phytoplankton-based marine ecosystems, dissolved inorganic nitrogen is considered the principal limiting nutrient for autotrophic production, both in its limiting behavior and in its role in the eutrophication of estuarine and coastal waters. *See* PHOTOSYNTHESIS.

Marine food webs and the processes leading to secondary production of marine populations can be divided into plankton-based and detritus-based food webs. They approximate phytoplankton-based systems and macrophyte-based systems. For planktonic food webs, current evidence suggests that primary production is partitioned among groups of variously sized organisms, with small organisms, such as cyanobacteria, playing an equal if not dominant role at times in aquatic productivity. The smaller autotrophs—both through excretion of dissolved organic compounds to provide a substrate for bacterial growth and by direct grazing by protozoa (microflagellates and ciliates)—create a microbially based food web in aquatic ecosystems, the major portion of autotrophic production and secondary utilization in marine food webs may be controlled, not by the larger organisms typically described as supporting marine food webs, but by microscopic populations.

Macrophyte-based food webs, such as those associated with salt marsh, mangrove, and seagrass ecosystems, are not supported by direct grazing of the dominant vascular plant but by the production of detrital matter through plant mortality. The classic example is the detritus-based food webs of coastal salt marsh ecosystems. These ecosystems, which have very high rates of primary production, enter the marine food web as decomposed and fragmented particulate organics. The particulate organics of vascular plant origin support a diverse microbial community that includes bacteria, flagellates, ciliates, and other protozoa. These organisms in turn support higher-level consumers.

Both pelagic (water column) and benthic food webs in deep ocean environments depend on primary production in the overlying water column. For benthic communities, organic matter must reach the bottom by sinking through a deep water column, a process that further reduces its energy content. Thus, in the open ocean, high rates of secondary production, such as fish yields, are associated with areas in which physical-chemical conditions permit and sustain high rates of primary production over long periods of time, as is found in upwelling regions.

Regardless of specific marine environment, microbial processes provide fundamental links in marine food webs that directly or indirectly govern flows of organic matter and nutrients that in turn control ecosystem productivity and stability. *See* BIOLOGICAL PRODUCTIVITY; ECOLOGY; ECOSYSTEM; SEAWATER FERTILITY.   [R.We.]

Marine microbiology An independent discipline applying the principles and methods of general microbiology to research in marine biology and biogeochemistry. Marine microbiology focuses primarily on prokaryotic organisms, mainly bacteria. Because of their small size and easy dispersability, bacteria are virtually ubiquitous in the marine environment. Furthermore, natural populations of marine bacteria comprise a large variety of physiological types, can survive long periods of starvation, and are able to start their metabolic activity as soon as a substrate becomes available. As a result, the marine environment, similar to soil, possesses the potential of a large variety of microbial processes that degrade (heterotrophy) but also produce (autotrophy) organic matter. Considering the fact that the marine environment represents about 99% of the biosphere, marine microbial transformations are of tremendous global importance. *See* BIOSPHERE.

Heterotrophic transformations. Quantitatively, the most important role of microorganisms in the marine environment is heterotrophic decomposition and remineralization of organic matter. It is estimated that about 95% of the photosynthetically produced organic matter is recycled in the upper 300–400 m (1000–1300 ft) of water, while the remaining 5%, largely particulate matter, is further decomposed during sedimentation. Only about 1% of the total organic matter produced in surface waters arrives at the deep-sea floor in particulate form. In other words, the major source of energy and carbon for all marine heterotrophic organisms is distributed over the huge volume of pelagic water mass with an average depth of about 3800 m (2.5 mi). In this highly dilute medium, particulate organic matter is partly replenished from dissolved organic carbon by microbial growth, the so-called microbial loop.

Of the large variety of organic material decomposed by marine heterotrophic bacteria, oil and related hydrocarbons are of special interest. Other environmentally detrimental pollutants that are directly dumped or reach the ocean as the ultimate sink by land runoff are microbiologically degraded at varying rates. Techniques of molecular genetics are aimed at encoding genes of desirable enzymes into organisms for use as degraders of particular pollutants.

A specifically marine microbiological phenomenon is bacterial bioluminescence, which may function as a respiratory bypass of the electron transport chain. Free-living luminescent bacteria are distinguished from those that live in symbiotic fashion in light organelles of fishes or invertebrates. *See* BIOLUMINESCENCE.

Photoautotrophs and chemoautotrophs. The type of photosynthesis carried out by purple sulfur bacteria uses hydrogen sulfide (instead of water) as a source of electrons and thus produces sulfur, not oxygen. Photoautotrophic bacteria are therefore limited to environments where light and hydrogen sulfide occur simultaneously, mostly in lagoons and estuaries. In the presence of sufficient amounts of organic substrates, heterotrophic sulfate-reducing bacteria provide the necessary hydrogen sulfide where oxygen is depleted by decomposition processes. Anoxygenic photosynthesis is also carried out by some blue-green algae, which are now classified as cyanobacteria. *See* CYANOBACTERIA; PHOTOSYNTHESIS.

Chemoautotrophic bacteria are able to reduce inorganic carbon to organic carbon (chemosynthesis) by using the chemical energy liberated during the oxidation of inorganic compounds. Their occurrence, therefore, is not light-limited but depends on the availability of oxygen and the suitable inorganic electron source. Their role as producers of organic carbon is insignificant in comparison with that of photosynthetic producers (exempting the processes found at deep-sea hydrothermal vents). The oxidation of ammonia and nitrite to nitrate (nitrification) furnishes the chemically stable and biologically most available form of inorganic nitrogen for photosynthesis. *See* NITROGEN CYCLE.

The generation of methane and acetic acid from hydrogen and carbon dioxide stems from anaerobic bacterial chemosynthesis, and is common in anoxic marine sediments. *See* METHANOGENESIS (BACTERIA).

Marine microbial sulfur cycle. Sulfate is quantitatively the most prominent anion in seawater. Since it can be used by a number of heterotrophic bacteria as an electron acceptor in respiration following the depletion of dissolved oxygen, the resulting sulfate reduction and the further recycling of the reduced sulfur compounds make the marine environment microbiologically distinctly different from fresh water and most soils. The marine anaerobic, heterotrophic sulfate-reducing bacteria are classified in three genera; *Desulfovibrio, Desulfotomaculum*, and *Clostridium*.

The marine aerobic sulfur-oxidizing bacteria fall into two groups: the thiobacilli and the filamentous or unicellular organisms. While the former comprise a wide range from obligately to facultatively chemoautotrophic species (requiring none or some organic compounds), few of the latter have been isolated in pure culture, and chemoautotrophy has been demonstrated in only a few.

Hydrothermal vent bacteria. Two types of hydrothermal vents have been investigated: warm vents (8–25°C or 46–77°F) with flow rates of 1–2 cm (0.4–0.8 in.) per second, and hot vents (260–360°C or 500–600°F) with flow rates of 2 m (6.5 ft) per second. In their immediate vicinity, dense communities of benthic invertebrates are found with a biomass that is orders of magnitude higher than that normally found at these depths and dependent on photosynthetic food sources. This phenomenon has been explained by the bacterial primary production of organic carbon through the chemosynthetic oxidation of reduced inorganic compounds. The chemical energy required for this process is analogous to the light energy used in photosynthesis and is provided by the geothermal reduction of inorganic chemical species. The specific compounds contained in the emitted vent waters and suitable for bacterial chemosynthesis are mainly hydrogen sulfide, hydrogen, methane, and reduced iron and manganese. The extremely thermophilic microorganisms isolated from hydrothermal vents belong, with the exception of the genus *Thermotoga*, to the Archaebacteria. Of eight archaeal genera, growing within a temperature range of about 75–110°C (165–230°F), three are able to grow beyond the boiling point of water, if the necessary pressure is applied to prevent boiling. These organisms are strictly anaerobic. However, unlike mesophilic bacteria, hyperthermophilic marine isolates tolerate oxygen when cooled below their minimum growth temperature. *See* ARCHAEBACTERIA; HYDROTHERMAL VENT.   [H.W.J.]

Marsupialia   An order of animals, long considered the only order of the mammalian infraclass Metatheria.

The marsupials are characterized by the presence of a pouch (marsupium) in the female, a skin pocket whose teat-bearing abdominal wall is supported by epipubic bones. The young are born in the embryonic state and crawl unaided to the marsupium, where they attach themselves to the teats and continue their development. In a few species the pouch is vestigial or has disappeared completely.

A wide variety of terrestrial adaptations are found among the 82 genera of living marsupials. Some spectacular examples of evolution convergent upon placental modes of life are exemplified by the Australian marsupial "moles" (*Notoryctes*), "wolves" (*Thylacinus*), and "flying squirrels" (*Petaurus*). For the most part, the adaptive radiation of the marsupials has paralleled that of the placentals, yielding many ecological analogs, such as kangaroos and wallabies, which are the counterparts of the placental deer and antelopes, although these groups differ widely in structure. *See* ANTEATER; EUTHERIA; KANGAROO; KOALA; MAMMALIA; METATHERIA; OPOSSUM.   [R.H.T.]

Mathematical biology   The application of mathematics to biological systems. Mathematical biology spans all levels of biological organization and biological function, from the configuration of biological macromolecules to the entire ecosphere over the course of evolutionary time.

The influence of physics on mathematical biology has been twofold. On the one hand, organisms simply are material systems, and presumably can be analyzed in the same terms as any other material system. Reductionism, the theory that biological processes find their resolution in the particularities of physics, finds its practical embodiment in biophysics. Thus, one of the roots of mathematical biology is what was originally called mathematical biophysics. On the other hand, other early investigations in mathematical biology, such as population dynamics (mathematical ecology), exploited the form of such analyses, such as using differential rate equations, but they expressed their analyses in strictly biological terms. Such approaches were guided by analogy with mathematical physics rather than by reduction to physics and so rest on the form rather than the substance of physics. *See* BIOPHYSICS.

Both of these approaches are important, especially since organisms possess characteristics that have no obvious counterpart in inorganic systems. As a result, mathematical biology has acquired an independent and unique character. In several important cases, these characteristics have required a reconsideration of physics itself, as in the impact of open systems on classical thermodynamics.

Surrogacy and models.   The idea that something can be learned about a system by studying a different system, or surrogate, is central to all science. The relation between a system and its surrogates is embodied in the concept of a model. The basic idea of mathematical biology is that an appropriate formal or mathematical system may similarly be used as a surrogate for a biological system. The use of mathematical models offers possibilities that transcend what can be done on the basis of observation and experiment alone.

For example, morphological differences between related species can be made to disappear by means of relatively simple coordinate transformations of the space in which the forms are embedded. Surrogacy explicitly becomes a matter of intertransformability, or similarity, and what is true for morphology also holds true for other functional relationships that are characteristic of organisms, whether they be chemical, physical, or evolutionary. These assertions of surrogacy and modeling can be restated: closely related implies similar. This is a nontrivial assertion: "closely related" is a metric relation pertaining to genotypes, whereas "similar" is an equivalence relation based on phenotypes. It is the similarity relation between phenotypes that provides the basis for surrogacy. Thus the question immediately arises: given a genotype, how far can it be varied or changed or mutated, and still preserve similarity?

Such questions fall mathematically into the province of stability theory, particularly structural stability. Under very general conditions, there exist many genomes that are unstable (bifurcation points) in the sense that however high a degree of metric approximation is chosen, the associated phenotypes may be dissimilar, that is, not intertransformable. That observation by R. Thom provides the basis for his theory of catastrophes and demonstrates the complexity of the surrogacy relationship. The fundamental importance of such ideas for phenomena of development, for evolution (particularly for macroevolution), and for the extrapolation of data from one species to another, or the relation between health and disease, is evident.

Metaphor.   A closely related group of ideas that are characteristic of mathematical biology may be described as metaphoric. One example of a metaphoric approach is the study of brain activities through the application of the properties of neural networks, that is, networks of interconnected boolean (binary-state) switches. Appropriately configured switching networks are known to exhibit behaviors that are analogous to those that characterize the brain, such as learning, memory, and discrimination. That is, networks of neuronlike units can automatically manifest brainlike behaviors and can be regarded as metaphorical brains. Such boolean neural nets also underlie digital computation, a relationship which is explored in the hybrid area of artificial intelligence. The same mathematical formulation of switching networks arises in genetic and developmental phenomena, such as the concept of operon, and in other physiological systems, such as the immune system.

Another important example of metaphor in biology is morphogenesis, or pattern generation, through the coupling of chemical reactions with physical diffusion. Chemical reactions tend to make systems heterogeneous, diffusion tends to smooth them out, and combining the two can lead to highly complex behaviors. Since reactions and diffusions typically occur together in biological systems, exploring the general properties of such systems can illuminate pattern generation in general.

Such ideas turn out to be closely related to those of bifurcation and catastrophe and have a profound impact on physics itself, since they are inherently associated with systems that are thermodynamically open and hence completely outside the realm of classical thermodynamics. The behavior of such open systems can be infinitely more complicated than those that are commonly explored in physics. Open systems may possess large numbers of stable and unstable steady states of various types, as well as more complicated oscillatory steady-state behaviors (limit cycles) and still more general behaviors collectively called chaotic. Changes in initial conditions or in environmental circumstances can result in dramatic switching (bifurcations) between these modes of behavior. *See* CHAOS.

Applications. Perhaps the biotechnology that has affected everyone most directly is medicine. Medicine can be regarded as a branch of control theory, geared to the maintenance or restoration of a state of health. It is unique in that the systems needed for control are themselves control systems that are far more intricate and complex than any that can be fabricated. In addition to the light it sheds on the processes needed for control, mathematical biology is indispensable for designing the controls themselves and for assessing their costs, benefits, safety, and efficacy.

In general, the object of any theory of control is to produce an algorithm, or protocol, that will achieve optimal results. Mathematical biology allows one to relate systems of different characters through the exploitation of their mathematical commonalities. Biology has many optimal designs and optimal controls, which are the products of biological evolution through natural selection. The design of optimal therapies in medicine is analogous to the generation of optimal organisms. Thus the mathematical theory appropriate for analyzing one discipline of biology, such as evolution, itself becomes transmuted into a theory of control in an entirely different realm. The same holds true for other biotechnologies, such as the efficient exploitation of biological populations.

[R.Ro.]

Measles   An acute, highly infectious viral disease with cough, fever, and maculopapular rash. It is of worldwide endemicity.

The virus enters the body via the respiratory system, multiplies there, and circulates in the blood. Cough, sneezing, conjunctivitis, photophobia, and fever occur, with Koplik's spots (small red spots containing a bluish-white speck in the center) in the mouth.

A rash appears after 14 days' incubation and persists 5–10 days. Serious complications may occur in 1 out of 15 persons; these are mostly respiratory (bronchitis, pneumonia), but neurological complications are also found. Encephalomyelitis occurs rarely. Permanent disabilities may ensue for a significant number of persons. Measles is one of the leading causes of death among children in the world, particularly in the developing countries.

In unvaccinated populations, immunizing infections occur in early childhood during epidemics which recur after 2–3 years' accumulation of susceptible children. Transmission is by coughing or sneezing. Measles is infectious from the onset of symptoms until a few days after the rash has appeared. Second attacks of measles are very rare. Treatment is symptomatic.

Killed virus vaccine should not be used, as certain vaccinees become sensitized and develop local reactions when revaccinated with live attenuated virus, or develop a severe illness upon contracting natural measles. Live attenuated virus vaccine effectively prevents measles; vaccine-induced antibodies persist for years. See BIOLOGICALS; HYPERSENSITIVITY; SKIN TEST.   [J.L.Me.]

Mechanoreceptors   Sensory receptors that provide the organism with information about such mechanical changes in the environment as movement, tension, and pressure. In higher animals receptors are actually the only means by which information of the surroundings is gained and by which reactions to environmental changes are started. See SENSATION.

Mechanoreceptors are excited by mechanical disturbances of their surroundings through deformation of their structure, through pressure or tension, or through a combination of these. In general, little energy is required for mechanical stimuli to cause a detectable excitation in mechanoreceptors.

From a physical point of view, mechanoreceptors are energy transducers; they convert mechanical into electrical energy, which in turn triggers the nerve impulse. Deformation leads to a sequence of events which may be summarized by the following scheme:

$$\begin{array}{ccc} \text{Mechanical} & & \text{Generator} & & \text{Nerve impulse} \\ \text{stimulus} & \rightarrow & \text{current} & \rightarrow & \text{(action potential)} \end{array}$$

The generator current is the earliest detectable sign of excitation. The most salient characteristic of the generator current is its graded nature; its amplitude increases continuously, without visible steps, if the stimulus strength is progressively increased. When the generator current reaches a certain critical amplitude, an all-or-nothing potential is discharged in the sense organ which may then propagate as an all-or-nothing nerve impulse along the afferent axon of the receptor. See NERVOUS SYSTEM (INVERTEBRATE); NERVOUS SYSTEM (VERTEBRATE).   [W.R.L.]

Medical bacteriology   The study of bacteria that cause human disease. The field encompasses the detection and identification of bacterial pathogens, determination of the sensitivity and mechanisms of resistance of bacteria to antibiotics, the mechanisms of virulence, and some aspects of immunity to infection. See VIRULENCE.

The clinical bacteriology laboratory identifies bacterial pathogens present in specimens such as sputum, pus, blood, and spinal fluid, or from swabs of skin, throat, rectal, or urogenital surfaces. Identification involves direct staining and microscopic examination of these materials, and isolation of bacteria present in the material by growth in appropriate media. The laboratory must differentiate bacterial pathogens from harmless bacteria that colonize humans. Species and virulent strains of bacteria can be identified on the basis of growth properties, metabolic and biochemical tests, and reactivity with specific antibodies.

Recent advances in the field of diagnostic bacteriology have involved automation of biochemical testing; the development of rapid antibody-based detection methods; and the application of molecular biology techniques. Once a bacterial pathogen has been identified, a major responsibility of the diagnostic bacteriology laboratory is the determination of the sensitivity of the pathogen to antibiotics. This involves observation of the growth of the bacteria in the presence of various concentrations of antibiotics. The process has been made more efficient by the development of automated instrumentation.

An increasingly serious problem in the therapy of infectious diseases is the emergence of antibiotic-resistant strains of bacteria. An important area of research is the mechanisms of acquisition of antibiotic resistance and the application of this knowledge to the development of more effective antibiotics. See ANTIBIOTIC; ANTIGEN-ANTIBODY REACTION; BACTERIAL PHYSIOLOGY AND METABOLISM; BACTERIAL TAXONOMY; IMMUNOCHEMISTRY.

The study of bacterial pathogenesis involves the fields of molecular genetics, biochemistry, cell biology, and immunology. In cases where the disease is not serious and easily treated, research may involve the deliberate infection of human volunteers. Otherwise, various models of human disease must be utilized. These involve experimental infection of animals and the use of tissue cell culture systems. Modern molecular approaches to the study of bacterial pathogenesis frequently involve the specific mutation or elimination of a bacterial gene thought to encode a virulence property, followed by observation of the mutant bacteria in a model system of human disease. In this way, relative contributions of specific bacterial traits to different stages of the disease process can be determined. This knowledge permits the design of effective strategies for intervention that will prevent or cure the disease. See BACTERIAL GENETICS.

The presence of specific antibodies is frequently useful in the diagnosis of bacterial diseases in which the pathogen is otherwise difficult to detect. An example is the sexually transmitted disease syphilis; the diagnosis must be confirmed by the demonstration of antibodies specific for *T. pallidum*. See ANTIBODY; BIOLOGICALS.

Immunity to some bacteria that survive intracellularly is not mediated by antibodies but by immune effector cells, known as T cells, that activate infected cells to kill the bacteria that they contain. An active area of research is how bacterial components are presented to the immune system in a way that will induce effective cell-mediated immunity. This research may lead to the development of T-cell vaccines effective against intracellular bacterial pathogens.

For disease entities caused by specific bacteria see ANTHRAX; BOTULISM; BRUCELLOSIS; CHOLERA; DIPHTHERIA; GONORRHEA; LEPROSY; PLAGUE; TUBERCULOSIS. For disease entities caused by more than one microorganism see FOOD POISONING; MENINGITIS; PNEUMONIA. For groups of disease-producing bacteria see HAEMOPHILUS; IMMUNOLOGY; MEDICAL BACTERIOLOGY; PNEUMOCOCCUS; STREPTOCOCCUS.   [S.L.M.]

Medical mycology   The study of fungi (molds and yeasts) that cause human disease. Fungal infections are classified according to the site of infection on the body or whether an opportunistic setting is necessary to establish disease. Fungal infections that occur in an opportunistic setting have become more common due to conditions that compromise host defenses, especially cell-mediated immunity. Such conditions include acquired immunodeficiency syndrome (AIDS), cancer, and immunosuppressive therapy to prevent transplant rejection or to control inflammatory syndromes. Additionally, opportunistic fungal infections have become more significant as severely debilitated individuals live longer because of advances in modern medicine, and nosocomial (hospital-acquired) fungal infections are an increasing problem. Early diagnosis with treatment of the fungal infection and control of the predisposing cause are essential. *See* OPPORTUNISTIC INFECTIONS.

Antifungal drug therapy is extremely challenging since fungi are eukaryotes, as are their human hosts, leading to problems with toxicity or cross-reactivity with host molecules. Most antifungal drugs target the fungal cell membrane or wall. The "gold standard" for therapy of most severe fungal infections is amphotericin B, which binds to ergosterol, a membrane lipid found in most fungi and some other organisms but not in mammals. Unfortunately, minor cross-reactive binding of amphotericin B to cholesterol in mammalian cell membranes can lead to serious toxicity, especially in the kidney where the drug is concentrated. Recent advances in antifungal therapy include the use of liposomal amphotericin B and newer azoles such as fluconazole and itra-conazole, which show reduced toxicity or greater specificity. Conversely, drug resistance in pathogenic fungi is an increasing problem, as it is in bacteria.

Candidiasis is the most common opportunistic fungal infection, and it has also be-come a major nosocomial infection in hospitalized patients. *Candida albicans* is a dimorphic fungus with a yeast form that is a member of the normal flora of the surface of mucous membranes. In an opportunistic setting, the fungus may proliferate and convert to a hyphal form that invades these tissues, the blood, and other organs. The disease may extend to the blood or other organs from various infected sites in patients who are suffering from a grave underlying disease or who are immunocompromised. Other important opportunistic fungal diseases include aspergillosis, mucormycosis, and cryptococcus.

Healthy persons can acquire disease from certain pathogenic fungi following inhala-tion of their fungal spores. The so-called deep or systemic mycoses are all caused by different species of soil molds; most infections are unrecognized and produce no or few symptoms. However, in some individuals infection may spread to all parts of the body from the lung, and treatment with amphotericin B or an antifungal azole drug is essential.

Other fungal infections develop when certain species of soil molds are inoculated deep into the subcutaneous tissue, such as by a deep thorn prick or other trauma. A specific type of lesion develops with each fungus as it grows within the tissue. Proper wound hygiene will prevent these infections.

Ringworm, also known as dermatophytosis or tinea, is the most common of all fungal infections. Some species of pathogenic molds can grow in the stratum corneum, the dead outermost layer of the skin. Disease results from host hypersensitivity to the metabolic products of the infecting mold as well as from the actual fungal invasion. Tinea corporis, ringworm of the body, appears as a lesion on smooth skin and has a red, circular margin that contains vesicles. The lesion heals with central clearing as the margin advances. On thick stratum corneum, such as the interdigital spaces of the feet, the red, itching lesions, known as athlete's foot or tinea pedis, become more serious if secondary bacterial infection develops. The ringworm fungi may also invade the hair shaft (tinea capitis) or the nail (onychomycosis). Many pharmaceutical agents are available to treat or arrest such infections, but control of transmission to others is important. *See* FUNGAL INFECTIONS; FUNGI; YEAST.   [C.Ha.; J.P.W.]

Medical parasitology   The study of diseases of humans caused by parasitic agents. It is commonly limited to parasitic worms (helminths) and the protozoa. Current usage places the various nonprotozoan microbes in distinct disciplines, such as virology, rickettsiology, and bacteriology.

Nematodes. The roundworms form an extremely large yet fairly homogeneous assemblage, most of which are free-living (nonparasitic). Some parasitic nematodes, however, may cause disease in humans (zoonosis), and others cause disease limited to human hosts (anthroponosis). Among the latter, several are enormously abundant and widespread. See NEMATA.

The giant roundworm (*Ascaris lumbricoides*) parasitizes the small intestine, probably affecting over a billion people; and the whipworm (*Trichuris trichiura*) infects the human colon, probably affecting a half billion people throughout the tropics. Similarly, the hookworms of humans, *Necator americanus* in the Americas and the tropical regions of Africa and Asia, and *Ancylostoma duodenale* in temperate Asia, the Mediterranean, and Middle East, suck blood from the small intestine and cause major debilitation, especially among the undernourished. The human pinworm (*Enterobius vermicularis*) infects the large intestine of millions of urban dwellers. Most intestinal nematodes, which require a period of egg maturation outside the human host before they are infective, are associated with fecal contamination of soil or food crops and are primarily rural in distribution.

The nonintestinal nematodes are spread by complex life cycles that usually involve bloodsucking insects. One exception is the guinea worm (*Dracunculus medinensis*), a skin-infecting 2–3-ft (0.6–1-m) worm transmitted by aquatic microcrustaceans that are ingested in drinking water that has been contaminated by larvae that escape from the skin sores of infected humans. Such bizarre life cycles are typical of many helminths. Other nematodes of humans include (1) the filarial worms, which are transmitted by mosquitoes and may induce enormously enlarged fibrous masses in legs, arms, or genitalia (elephantiasis), and (2) *Onchocerca volvulus*, which is transmitted by blackflies (genus *Simulium*) and forms microscopic embryos (microfilariae) in the eyes causing high incidence of blindness in Africa and parts of central and northern South America.

A more familiar tissue-infecting nematode of temperate regions is *Trichinella spiralis*, the pork or trichina worm, which is the agent of trichinosis. The tiny spiraled larvae encyst in muscle and can carry the infection to humans and other carnivorous mammals who eat raw or undercooked infected meat.

Trematodes. Parasites of the class Trematoda vary greatly in size, form, location in the human host, and disease produced, but all go through an initial developmental period in specific kinds of fresh-water snails, where they multiply as highly modified larvae of different types. Ultimately, an infective larval stage (cercaria) escapes in large numbers from the snail and continues the life cycle. Each trematode species follows a highly specific pathway from snail to human host, usually by means of another host or transport mechanism. These include the intestinal, liver, blood, and lung flukes. See SCHISTOSOMIASIS; TREMATODA.

Cestodes. Tapeworms, the other great assemblage of parasitic flatworms, parasitize most vertebrates, with eight or more species found in humans. Their flat ribbonlike body form consists of a chain of hermaphroditic segments. Like the trematodes, their life cycles are complex, although not dependent on a snail host. The enormous beef tapeworm of humans, *Taenia saginata*, is transmitted by infected beef ("measly beef") from cattle that grazed where human feces containing egg-filled tapeworm segments contaminated the soil. Other tapeworms include the pork, dog, and broad (or fish) tapeworms. See CESTODA.

Protozoa. Of the many protozoa that can reside in the human gut, only the invasive strain of *Entamoeba histolytica* causes serious disease. This parasite, ingested in water contaminated with human feces containing viable cysts of *E. histolytica*, can cause the disease amebiasis, which in its most severe form is known as amebic dysentery. Another common waterborne intestinal protozoon is the flagellate *Giardia lamblia*, which causes giardiasis, a mild to occasionally serious or long-lasting diarrhea. *See* PROTOZOA.

Other flagellate parasites infect the human skin, bloodstream, brain, and viscera. The tsetse fly of Africa carries to humans the blood-infecting agents of trypanosomiasis, or African sleeping sickness, *Trypanosoma brucei gambiense* and *T. brucei rhodesiense*. The infection can be fatal if the parasites cross the blood-brain barrier. In Latin America, the flagellate *T. cruzi* is the agent of Chagas' disease, a major cause of debilitation and premature heart disease among those who are poorly housed. The infection is transmitted in the liquid feces of a conenose bug (genus *Triatoma*) and related insects. The infective material is thought to be scratched into the skin or rubbed in the eye, especially by sleeping children. *See* TRYPANOSOMATIDAE.

Another group of parasitic flagellates includes the macrophage-infecting members of the genus *Leishmania*, which are transmitted by blood-sucking midges or sand flies. Cutaneous leishmaniasis is characterized by masses of infected macrophages in the skin, which induce long-lasting dermal lesions of varying form and severity. The broad spectrum of host-parasite interactions is well exemplified by leishmaniases. The various manifestations of the disease are the result of the particular species of agent and vector, the immunological status of the host, the presence or absence of reservoir hosts, and the pattern of exposure.

Two remaining major groups of protozoa are the ciliates and the sporozoans. The former group is largely free-living, with only a single species, *Balantidium coli*, parasitic in humans (and pigs). This large protozoon is found in the large intestine, where it can cause balantidiasis, an ulcerative disease. The sporozoans, on the other hand, are all parasitic and include many parasites of humans. The most important are the agents of malaria. Other disease agents are included in the genera *Isospora, Sarcocystis, Cryptosporidium*, and *Toxoplasma. Pneumocystis*, a major cause of death among persons with acquired immune deficiency syndrome (AIDS), was formerly considered a protozoon of uncertain relationship, but now it is thought to be a member of the Fungi. *See* ACQUIRED IMMUNE DEFICIENCY SYNDROME (AIDS); MALARIA; SPOROZOA.

Toxoplasma gondii, the agent of toxoplasmosis, infects as many as 20% of the world's population. It can penetrate the placenta and infect the fetus if the mother has not been previously infected and has no antibodies. As with most medically important parasites, the great majority of *Toxoplasma* infections remain undetected and nonpathogenic. The parasite primarily affects individuals lacking immune competence—the very young, the very old, and the immunosuppressed. *See* MEDICAL BACTERIOLOGY; MEDICAL MYCOLOGY; PARASITOLOGY; ZOONOSES.   [D.He.]

Meiosis   The set of two successive cell divisions that serve to separate homologous chromosome pairs prior to the formation of gametes (sperm and eggs). The major purpose of meiosis is the precise reduction in the number of chromosomes by one-half, so that a diploid cell can create haploid gametes. Meiosis is therefore a critical component of sexual reproduction. *See* GAMETOGENESIS.

The basic events of meiosis are actually quite simple. As the cell begins meiosis, each chromosome has already duplicated its deoxyribonucleic acid (DNA) and carries two identical copies of the DNA molecule. These are visible as two lateral parts, called sister chromatids, which are connected by a centromere. Homologous pairs of chromosomes are first identified and matched. This process, which occurs only in the first of the two meiotic divisions, is called pairing. The matched pairs are then physically interlocked by recombination, which is also known as exchange or crossing-over. After recombination, the homologous chromosomes separate from each other, and at the first meiotic division are partitioned into different nuclei. As a consequence, the second meiotic division begins with half of the original number of chromosomes. During this second meiotic division, the sister chromatids of each chromosome separate and migrate to different daughter cells. *See* CHROMOSOME.

The patterns by which genes are inherited are determined by the movement of the chromosomes during the two meiotic divisions. It is a fundamental tenet of mendelian inheritance that each individual carries two copies of each gene, one derived from its father and one derived from its mother. Moreover, each of that individual's gametes will carry only one copy of that gene, which is chosen at random. The process by which the two copies of a given gene are distributed into separate gametes is referred to as segregation. Thus, if an individual is heterozygous at the A gene for two different alleles, A and a, his or her gametes will be equally likely to carry the A allele or the a allele, but never both or neither. The fact that homologous chromosomes, and thus homologous genes, segregate to opposite poles at the first meiotic division explains this principle of inheritance. *See* CELL CYCLE.

Meiotic divisions. The two meiotic divisions may be divided into a number of distinct stages. Meiotic prophase refers to the period after the last cycle of DNA replication, during which time homologous chromosomes pair and recombine. The end of prophase is signaled by the breakdown of the nuclear envelope, and the association of the paired chromosomes with the meiotic spindle. The spindle is made up of microtubules that, with associated motor proteins, mediate chromosome movement. In some cases (such as human sperm formation), the spindle is already formed at the point of nuclear envelope breakdown, and the chromosomes then attach to it. In other systems (such as human female meiosis), the chromosomes themselves organize the spindle.

Metaphase I is the period before the first division during which pairs of interlocked homologous chromosomes, called bivalents, line up on the middle of the meiotic spindle. The chromosomes are primarily (but not exclusively) attached to the spindle by their centromeres such that the centromere of one homolog is attached to spindle fibers emanating from one pole, and the centromere of its partner is attached to spindle fibers from the other pole (see illustration). The bivalents are physically held together by structures referred to as chiasmata that are the result of meiotic recombination events. In most meiotic systems, meiosis will not continue until all of the homolog pairs are

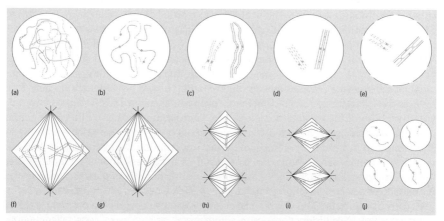

Stages of meiosis. (*a*) **Pre-meiotic interphase.** (*b*) **Leptotene.** (*c*) **Zygotene.** (*d*) **Pachytene.** (*e*) **Diplotene/ diakinesis.** (*f*) **Metaphase I.** (*g*) **Anaphase I.** (*h*) **Metaphase II.** (*i*) **Anaphase II.** (*j*) **Telophase II.**

properly oriented at the middle of the spindle, the metaphase plate. The orientation of each pair of homologs on the spindle occurs in a random fashion, such that the paternally derived homolog of one bivalent may point toward one pole of the spindle, while in the adjacent bivalent the maternally derived homolog is oriented toward the same pole.

Anaphase I refers to the point at which homologous chromosome pairs separate and move to opposite poles. Depending on the organism, there may or may not be a true telophase, or a time in which nuclei reform. In most organisms, the first cell division occurs after the completion of anaphase I.

Following the completion of the first meiotic division, the chromosomes recondense and align themselves on a new pair of spindles, with their sister chromatids oriented toward opposite poles. The stage at which each chromosome is so aligned is referred to as metaphase II. In some, but not all, organisms, metaphase II is preceded by a brief prophase II. DNA replication does not occur during prophase II; each chromosome still consists of the two sister chromatids. Nor are there opportunities for pairing or recombination at this stage due to the prior separation of homologs at anaphase I.

The start of anaphase II is signaled by the separation of sister centromeres, and the movement of the two sister chromatids to opposite poles. At telophase II, the sisters have reached opposite poles and the nuclei begin to reform. The second cell division usually occurs at this time. Thus, at the end of the second meiotic division, there will be four daughter cells, each with a single copy of each chromosome.

Details of meiotic prophase. Because pairing and recombination occur during the first meiotic prophase, much attention has been focused on this stage of the process. The prophase of the first meiotic division is subdivided into five stages: leptotene, zygotene, pachytene, diplotene, and diakinesis (see illustration). Homolog recognition, alignment, and synapsis occur during leptotene and zygotene. In the leptotene, initial homolog alignments are made. By zygotene, homologous chromosomes have become associated at various points along their length. These associations facilitate a more intimate pairing that results in the homologous chromosomes lying abreast of a tracklike structure called the synaptonemal complex. The beginning of pachytene is signaled by the completion of a continuous synaptonemal complex running the full length of each bivalent. During diplotene, the attractive forces that mediated homologous pairing disappear, and the homologs begin to repel each other. However, homologs virtually always recombine, and those recombination events can be seen as chiasmata that tether the homologs together. The final stage in meiotic prophase is diakinesis, during which the homologs shorten and condense in preparation for nuclear division.

Recombination. Meiotic recombination involves the physical interchange of DNA molecules between the two homologous chromosomes, thus allowing the creation of new combinations of alleles for genes located on that pair of chromosomes. Recombination involves the precise breakage and rejoining of two nonsister chromatids. The result is the formation of two recombinant chromatids, each of which carries information from both of the original homologs. The number and position of recombination events is very precisely controlled. Exchange occurs only in the gene-rich euchromatin that makes up most of the chromosome arms, never in the heterochromatin that surrounds the centromeres. Moreover, as a result of a process known as interference, the occurrence of one exchange in a given chromosomal region greatly decreases the probability of a second exchange in that region. See RECOMBINATION (GENETICS).

Errors of meiosis. The failure of two chromosomes to segregate properly is called nondisjunction. Nondisjunction occurs either because two homologs failed to pair and/or recombine or because of a failure of the cell to properly move the segregating chromosomes on the meiotic spindle. The result of nondisjunction is the production of gametes that are aneuploid, carrying the wrong number of chromosomes. When such a gamete is involved in a fertilization event, the resulting zygote is also aneuploid. Those cases where the embryo carries an extra copy of a given chromosome are said to be trisomic, while those that carry but one copy are said to be monosomic for that chromosome. Most aneuploid zygotes are not viable and result in early spontaneous abortion. There are no viable monosomies for the human autosomes; however, a few types of trisomic zygotes are capable of survival. These are trisomies for the sex chromosomes (XXX, XXY, XYY), trisomy 21 (Down syndrome), trisomy 18, and trisomy 13. *See* CROSSING-OVER (GENETICS).

Meiosis versus mitosis. The fundamental difference between meiosis and mitosis is that at the first meiotic division, sister chromatids do not separate; rather, homologous chromosomes separate from each other with their sister chromatids still attached to each other. Recombination is frequent in most meiotic cells; however, it occurs only rarely in mitotic cells, usually as part of DNA repair events. Most critically, DNA synthesis occurs only once within the two meiotic divisions, while there is a complete replication before every mitotic division. This allows mitosis to produce two genetically identical daughter cells, while meiosis produces four daughter cells, each of which have only one-half the number of chromosomes present prior to meiosis. *See* CELL DIVISION; GENE; MITOSIS.

[M.Y.W.; R.S.H.]

Memory   The ability to store and access information that has been acquired through experience. Memory is a critical component of practically all aspects of human thinking, including perception, learning, language, and problem solving. *See* PERCEPTION.

Stages. The information-processing approach divides memory into three general stages: sensory memory, short-term memory, and long-term memory. Sensory memory refers to the sensations that briefly continue after something has been perceived. Short-term memory includes all of the information that is currently being processed in a person's mind, and is generally thought to have a very limited capacity. Long-term memory is where all the information that may be used at a later time is kept.

A number of interesting facts are known about sensory memory, including the following: (1) sensory memories appear to be associated with mechanisms in the central nervous system rather than at the sensory receptor level, and (2) the amount of attention that a person pays to a stimulus can affect the duration of the sensory memory. Although all of the functions of sensory memory are not understood, one of its most important purposes is to provide people with additional time to determine what should be transferred to the next stage in the memory system, that is, short-term memory.

Information obtained from either sensory memory or long-term memory is processed in short-term memory in order for a person to achieve current goals. In some situations, short-term memory processing simply involves the temporary maintenance of a piece of information, such as remembering a phone number long enough to dial it. Other times, short-term memory can involve elaborate manipulations of information in order to generate new forms. For example, when someone reads 27 + 15, the person manipulates the symbols in short-term memory in order to come up with the solution. One useful manipulation that can be done in short-term memory is to reorganize items into meaningful chunks. For example, it is a difficult task to keep the letters S K C A U Q K C U D E H T in mind all at once. However, if they are rearranged in short-term memory, in this case reversing them, they can be reduced to a single simple chunk: THE DUCK QUACKS. Short-term memory can accommodate only five to seven chunks at any one time. However, the amount of information contained in each chunk is constrained only by one's practice and ingenuity. In order to increase the amount of information that can be kept in short-term memory at one time, people need to develop specific strategies for organizing that information into meaningful chunks. In addition, many studies have also demonstrated that the transfer of information from short-term to long-term memory is much greater when the information is manipulated rather than simply maintained.

One can keep massive amounts of information in long-term memory. In general, recall from long-term memory simply involves figuring out the heading under which a memory has been filed. Many tricks for effective retrieval of long-term memories involve associating the memory with another more familiar memory that can serve as an identification tag. This trick of using associations to facilitate remembering is called mnemonics. Long-term memory stores related concepts and incidents in close range of one another. This logical association of memories is indicated by subjects' reaction times for identifying various memories. Generally, people are faster at recalling memories if they have recently recalled a related memory. One good way to locate a long-term memory is to remember the general situation under which it was stored. Accordingly, techniques that reinstate the context of a memory tend to facilitate remembering.

Sometimes information may not have been filed in long-term memory in the first place, or if it has, is inaccessible. In these situations, the long-term memory system often fills in the gaps by using various constructive processes. One common component to memory constructions is a person's expectations. Countless studies have also indicated that memories tend to systematically change in the direction of a prior expectation or inference about what is likely to have occurred.

Physiology. A number of physiological mechanisms appear to be involved in the formation of memories, and the mechanisms may differ for short-term and long-term memory. There is both direct and indirect evidence suggesting that short-term memory involves the temporary circulation of electrical impulses around complex loops of interconnected neurons. A number of indirect lines of research indicate that short-term memories are eradicated by any event that either suppresses neural activity (for example, a blow to the head or heavy anesthesia) or causes neurons to fire incoherently (for example, electroconvulsive shock). More direct support for the electric circuit model of short-term memory comes from observing electrical brain activity. By implanting electrodes in the brain of experimental animals, researchers have observed that changes in what an animal is watching are associated with different patterns of circulating electrical activity in the brain. These results suggest that different short-term memories may be represented by different electrical patterns. However, the nature of these patterns is not well understood. *See* ELECTROENCEPHALOGRAPHY.

Long-term memories appear to involve some type of permanent structural or chemical change in the composition of the brain. This conclusion is derived both from general observations of the imperviousness of long-term memories and from physiological studies indicating specific changes in brain composition. Even in acute cases of amnesia where massive deficits in long-term memory are reported, often, with time, all long-term memories return. Similarly, although electroconvulsive therapy is known to eliminate recent short-term memories, it has practically no effect on memories for events occurring more than an hour prior to shocking. Thus the transfer from a fragile short-term memory to a relatively solid long-term memory occurs within an hour. This process is sometimes called consolidation.

The nature of the "solid" changes associated with long-term memories appears to involve alterations in both the structural (neural connections) and chemical composition of the brain. One study compared the brains of rats that had lived either in enriched environments with lots of toys or in impoverished environments with only an empty cage. The cerebral cortices of the brains of the rats from the enriched environment were thicker, heavier, endowed with more blood vessels, and contained significantly greater amounts of certain brain chemicals (such as the neurotransmitter acetylcholine). Other researchers have observed that brief, high-frequency stimulation of a neuron can produce long-lasting changes in the neuron's communications across synapses.

Researchers believe that different brain structures may be involved in the formation and storage of long-term memories. The hippocampus, thalamus, and amygdala are believed to be critical in the formation of long-term memories. Individuals who have had damage to these structures are able to recall memories prior to the damage, indicating that long-term memory storage is intact; however, they are unable to form new long-term memories, indicating that the long-term memory formation process has been disrupted. It is not known where long-term memories are stored, but they may be localized in the same areas of the brain that participated in the actual learning. *See* BRAIN.

[J.Sc.; E.F.Lo.]

Mendelism   Fundamental principles governing the transmission of genetic traits, discovered by an Augustinian monk Gregor Mendel in 1856. Mendel performed his first set of hybridization experiments with pea plants. Although the pea plant is normally self-fertilizing, it can be easily crossbred, and grows to maturity in a single season. True breeding strains, each with distinct characteristics, were available from local seed merchants. For his experiments, Mendel chose seven sets of contrasting characters or traits. For stem height, the true breeding strains tall (7 ft or 2.1 m) and dwarf (18 in. or 45 cm) were used. He also selected six other sets of traits, involving the shape and color of seeds, pod shape and color, and the location of flowers on the plant stem.

The most simple crosses performed by Mendel involved only one pair of traits; each such experiment is known as a monohybrid cross. The plants used as parents in these crosses are known as the P_1 (first parental) generation. When tall and dwarf plants were crossed, the resulting offspring (called the F_1 or first filial generation) were all tall. When members of the F_1 generation were self-crossed, 787 of the resulting 1064 F_2 (second filial generation) plants were tall and 277 were dwarf. The tall trait is expressed in both the F_1 and F_2 generations, while the dwarf trait disappears in the F_1 and reappears in the F_2 generation. The trait expressed in the F_1 generation Mendel called the dominant trait, while the recessive trait is unexpressed in the F_1 but reappears in the F_2. In the F_2, about three-fourths of the offspring are tall and one-fourth are dwarf (a 3:1 ratio). Mendel made similar crosses with plants exhibiting each of the other pairs of traits, and in each case all of the F_1 offspring showed only one of the parental traits and, in the F_2, three-fourths of the plants showed the dominant trait and one-fourth exhibited the recessive trait. In subsequent experiments, Mendel found that the F_2 recessive plants bred true, while among the dominant plants one-third bred true and two-thirds behaved like the F_1 plants. *See* DOMINANCE.

Law of segregation. To explain the results of his monohybrid crosses, Mendel derived several postulates. First, he proposed that each of the traits is controlled by a factor (now called a gene). Since the F_1 tall plants produce both tall and dwarf offspring, they must contain a factor for each, and thus he proposed that each plant contains a pair of factors for each trait. Second, the trait which is expressed in the F_1 generation is controlled by a dominant factor, while the unexpressed trait is controlled by a recessive factor. To prevent the number of factors from being doubled in each generation, Mendel postulated that factors must separate or segregate from each other during gamete formation. Therefore, the F_1 plants can produce two types of gametes, one type containing a factor for tall plants, the other a factor for dwarf plants. At fertilization, the random combination of these gametes can explain the types and ratios of offspring in the F_2 generation (see illustration). *See* FERTILIZATION; GENE.

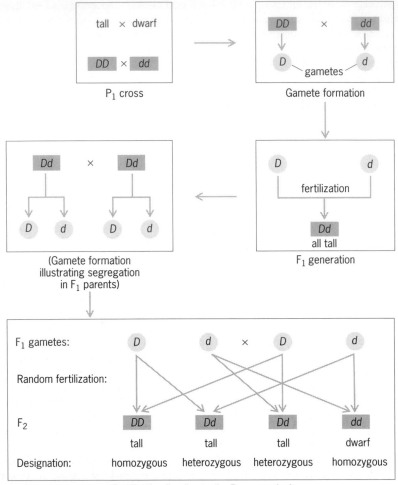

Schematic representation of a monohybrid cross. Pure-bred tall and dwarf strains are crossed, and yield typical 3:1 ratio in the F_2 generation. *D* and *d* represent the tall and dwarf factors (genes), respectively. (*After W. S. Klug and M. R. Cummings, Concepts of Genetics, Charles E. Merrill, 1983*)

Independent assortment. Mendel extended his experiments to examine the inheritance of two characters simultaneously. Such a cross, involving two pairs of contrasting traits, is known as a dihybrid cross. For example, Mendel crossed plants with tall stems and round seeds with plants having dwarf stems and wrinkled seeds. The F_1 offspring were all tall and had round seeds. When the F_1 individuals were self-crossed, four types of offspring were produced in the following proportions: 9/16 were tall, round; 3/16 were tall, wrinkled; 3/16 were dwarf, round; and 1/16 were dwarf, wrinkled. On the basis of similar results in other dihybrid crosses, Mendel proposed that during gamete formation, segregating pairs of factors assort independently of one another. As a result of segregation, each gamete receives one member of every pair of factors [this assumes that the factors (genes) are located on different chromosomes]. As a result of independent assortment, all possible combinations of gametes will be found in equal frequency. In other words, during gamete formation, round and wrinkled factors segregate into gametes independently of whether they also contain tall or dwarf factors. *See* GAMETOGENESIS; MEIOSIS.

It might be useful to consider the dihybrid cross as two simultaneous and independent monohybrid crosses. In this case, the predicted F_2 results are 3/4 tall, 1/4 dwarf, and 3/4 round, 1/4 wrinkled. Since the two sets of traits are inherited independently, the number and frequency of phenotypes can be predicted by combining the two events:

$$3/4\,\text{tall}\begin{cases}3/4\,\text{round} & (3/4)(3/4) = 9/16\,\text{tall, round}\\ 1/4\,\text{wrinkled} & (3/4)(1/4) = 3/16\,\text{tall, wrinkled}\end{cases}$$

$$1/4\,\text{dwarf}\begin{cases}3/4\,\text{round} & (1/4)(3/4) = 3/16\,\text{dwarf, round}\\ 1/4\,\text{wrinkled} & (1/4)(1/4) = 1/16\,\text{dwarf, wrinkled}\end{cases}$$

This 9:3:3:1 ratio is known as a dihybrid ratio and is the result of segregation, independent assortment, and random fertilization. *See* GENETICS.   [M.R.C.]

Meningitis   Inflammation of the meninges. Certain types of meningitis are associated with distinctive abnormalities in the cerebrospinal fluid. With certain types of meningitis, especially bacterial, the causative organism can usually be recovered from the fluid. *See* CENTRAL NERVOUS SYSTEM.

Meningeal inflammation in most cases is caused by invasion of the cerebrospinal fluid by an infectious organism. Noninfectious causes also occur. For example, in immune-mediated disorders antigen-antibody reactions can cause meningeal inflammation. Other noninfectious causes of meningitis are the introduction into the cerebrospinal fluid of foreign substances such as alcohol, detergents, chemotherapeutic agents, or contrast agents used in some radiologic imaging procedures. Meningeal inflammation brought about by such foreign irritants is called chemical meningitis. Inflammation also can occur when cholesterol-containing fluid or lipid-laden material leaks into the cerebrospinal fluid from some intracranial tumors.

Bacterial meningitis is among the most feared of human infectious diseases because of its possible seriousness, its rapid progression, its potential for causing severe brain damage, and its frequency of occurrence. Most cases of bacterial meningitis have an acute onset. Common clinical manifestations are fever, headache, vomiting, stiffness of the neck, confusion, seizures, lethargy, and coma. Symptoms of brain dysfunction are caused by transmission of toxic materials from the infected cerebrospinal fluid into brain tissue and the disruption of arterial perfusion and venous drainage from the brain because of blood vessel inflammation. These factors also provoke cerebral swelling, which increases intracranial pressure. Before antibiotics became available, bacterial meningitis was almost invariably fatal. *See* ANTIBIOTIC.

Most types of acute bacterial meningitis are septic-borne in that they originate when bacteria in the bloodstream (bacteremia, septicemia) gain entrance into the cerebrospinal fluid. Meningitis arising by this route is called primary bacterial meningitis. Secondary meningitis is that which develops following direct entry of bacteria into the central nervous system, which can occur at the time of neurosurgery, in association with trauma, or through an abnormal communication between the external environment and the cerebrospinal fluid.

Many viruses can cause meningeal inflammation, a condition referred to as viral aseptic meningitis. The most common viral causes include the enteroviruses, the various herpesviruses, viruses transmitted by arthropods, the human immunodeficiency virus type I (HIV-1), and formerly, the mumps virus. If the virus attacks mainly the brain rather than the spinal cord, the disorder is termed viral encephalitis. *See* ANIMAL VIRUS; ARBOVIRAL ENCEPHALITIDES; ENTEROVIRUS; HERPES.

Fungal, parasitic, and rickettsial meningitis are less common in the United States than are bacterial and viral. These infections are more likely to be subacute or chronic than those caused by bacteria or viruses; in most cases, the meningeal inflammation is associated with brain involvement. An acute form of aseptic meningitis can occur in the spirochetal diseases, syphilis and Lyme disease. *See* LYME DISEASE; MEDICAL MYCOLOGY; MEDICAL PARASITOLOGY; RICKETTSIOSES; SYPHILIS.   [W.E.B.]

Meningococcus   A major human pathogen belonging to the bacterial genus *Neisseria*, and the cause of meningococcal meningitis and meningococcemia. The official designation is *N. meningitidis*. The meningococcus is a gram-negative, aerobic, nonmotile diplococcus. It is fastidious in its growth requirements and is very susceptible to adverse physical and chemical conditions.

Humans are the only known natural host of the meningococcus. Transmission occurs by droplets directly from person to person. Fomites and aerosols are probably unimportant in the spread of the organism. The most frequent form of host-parasite relationship is asymptomatic carriage in the nasopharynx.

The most common clinical syndrome caused by the meningococcus is meningitis, which is characterized by fever, headache, nausea, vomiting, and neck stiffness and has a fatality rate of 15% (higher in infants and adults over 60). Disturbance of the state of consciousness quickly occurs, leading to stupor and coma. Many cases also have a typical skin rash consisting of petechiae or purpura. *See* MENINGITIS.
                                                                                     [R.Go.]

Menstruation   Periodic sloughing of the uterine lining in women of reproductive age. Menstrual bleeding indicates the first day of the menstrual cycle, which lasts an average of 27–30 days, although ranges of 21–60 days have been recorded. Menarche, the onset of menstruation, occurs between the ages of 9 and 16. The majority of females begin menstruating at ages 12–14. During the first few years, the duration and intensity of menstrual flow and the total cycle length may be quite variable, but regularity is gradually established. Cessation of menses, or menopause, occurs at an average age of 51, with a range of 42–60 years.

The menstrual cycle consists of cyclic changes in both the ovary and the uterus. These changes are controlled by the interaction of several hormones including follicle-stimulating hormone (FSH) and luteinizing hormone (LH), which are secreted by the anterior pituitary, and the steroid hormones estrogen and progesterone, which are secreted by follicles in the ovary. At the beginning of the cycle, the follicle is stimulated by FSH. In response, it grows and secretes estrogen. The amount of estrogen secretion increases rapidly near the middle of the cycle. Estrogen, in turn, stimulates growth of the uterine lining (mucosa), which becomes thicker and fills with blood vessels. In midcycle, the rapid increase in estrogen causes a massive surge of LH release and a smaller release of FSH from the pituitary. This surge causes ovulation, which is the release of the ovum from the follicle. After ovulation, the follicle undergoes rapid changes and is then called a corpus luteum, which secretes progesterone in response to LH stimulation. Progesterone and estrogen together cause a further thickening of the uterine mucosa, preparing the uterus for pregnancy. If pregnancy does not occur, the corpus luteum degenerates, the uterine mucosa sloughs off, and the cycle begins again.

There is no menstrual bleeding during pregnancy, as the uterine mucosa is needed for the maintenance of pregnancy. This amenorrhea, or lack of normal ovarian function, sometimes continues during nursing.   [J.M.Ba.]

Mental retardation   A developmental disability characterized by significantly subaverage general intellectual functioning, with concurrent deficits in adaptive behavior. The causes are many and include both genetic and environmental factors as well as interactions between the two. In most cases the diagnosis is not formally made until children have entered into school settings. In the preschool years, the diagnosis is more likely to be established by evidence of delayed maturation in the areas of sensory-motor, adaptive, cognitive, social, and verbal behaviors. By definition, evidence of mental retardation must exist prior to adulthood, where vocational limitation may be evident, but the need for supervision or support may persist beyond the usual age of social emancipation.

From the aspect of etiology, mental retardation can be classified by prenatal, perinatal, or postnatal onset. Prenatal causes include genetic disorders, syndromal disorders, and developmental disorders of brain formation. Upward of 700 genetic causes have been suggested as associated with the development of mental retardation. Many environmental influences on the developing fetus, for example, infection, and other unknown errors of development may account for mental retardation.

Perinatal causes include complications at birth, extreme prematurity, infections, and other neonatal disorders. Postnatal causes include trauma, infections, demyelinating and degenerative disorders, consequences of seizure disorders, toxic-metabolic disorders, malnutrition, and environmental deprivation. Often no specific cause can be identified for the mental retardation of a particular individual.

Individuals with mental retardation are typically subclassified in terms of the manifest severity of cognitive disability as reflected by the ratio of mental age to chronological age, or intelligence quotient (IQ). Subaverage intellectual functioning is defined as an IQ score of at least two standard deviations below the mean, or approximately 70 to 75 or below. Mild, moderate, severe, and profound degrees of mental retardation refer to two, three, four, or five standard deviations below the normal IQ for the general population.

Limitations in adaptive behavior must also be demonstrable in order to satisfy diagnostic criteria for mental retardation. This criterion is important because certain artistic or other gifts may not be revealed by formal IQ testing, and different levels of learning difficulty may be accentuated by the demands of specific environments. Outside such environments, an individual may navigate a normal course in life.

A specific genetic or other cause of mental retardation may also predispose to other medical or neurologic conditions. In these circumstances, the comorbid medical conditions may increase the likelihood of emotional or behavioral problems, or contribute to the challenges with which a given child must contend. Thus, the identification of cause can be important in planning for the medical, educational, and treatment needs of a particular individual.

Considerable progress has been made in both prevention and treatment. Diet is a method of treatment following early detection of phenylketonuria; warnings regarding alcohol consumption during pregnancy, lead exposure in infancy, and disease immunization and therapy are measures for prevention of retardation. Advances in prenatal, obstetrical, and neonatal care and genetic counseling have had the effect of reducing the incidence or the severity of various conditions. Energetic training and the application of psychosocial techniques have resulted in improved social performance and adaptive behavior in many persons with mental retardation.   [B.H.Ki.]

Mesozoa A division of the animal kingdom sometimes ranked as intermediate between the Protozoa and the Metazoa. These animals are unassignable to any of the better-known phyla, as usually defined. In the absence of proof concerning their relationships, and in view of the disagreement among zoologists relative to their affinities and even with respect to the facts and interpretation of their structure and life cycle, they are treated as a small phylum somewhere between Protozoa and Platyhelminthes. No particular phylogenetic interpretation should be attached to this placement.

The Mesozoa comprise two orders of small, wormlike organisms, the Dicyemida and the Orthonectida. Both are parasitic in marine invertebrates. The body consists of a single layer of ciliated cells enclosing one or more reproductive cells. These body cells are rather constant in number and arrangement for any given species. The internal cells do not correspond to the entoderm of other animals, as they have no digestive function. The life cycles are complex, involving both sexual and asexual generations (metagenesis). [B.H.McC.]

Metabolism All the physical and chemical processes by which living, organized substance is produced and maintained and the transformations by which energy is made available for use by an organism.

In defining metabolism, it is customary to distinguish between energy metabolism and intermediary metabolism, although the two are, in fact, inseparable. Energy metabolism is primarily concerned with overall heat production in an organism, while intermediary metabolism deals with chemical reactions within cells and tissues. In general, the term metabolism is interpreted to mean intermediary metabolism. See ENERGY METABOLISM.

Metabolism thus includes all biochemical processes within cells and tissues which are concerned with their building up, breaking down, and functioning. The synthesis and maintenance of tissue structure generally involves the union of smaller into larger molecules. This part of metabolism, the building of tissues, is termed anabolism. The process of breaking down tissue, of splitting larger protoplasmic molecules into smaller ones, is termed catabolism. Growth or weight gain occurs when anabolism exceeds catabolism. On the other hand, weight loss results if catabolism proceeds more rapidly than anabolism, as in periods of starvation, serious injury, or disease. When the two processes are balanced, tissue mass remains the same.

The metabolism of the three major foodstuffs, carbohydrates, fats, and proteins, is intimately interrelated, so any clearcut division of the three is arbitrary and inaccurate. Thus the metabolism of protoplasm is concerned with all three of these foodstuffs. The metabolic pathways of carbohydrates, fats, and proteins cross at many points; thus certain pathways of metabolism are shared in common by fragments of these different classes of foodstuffs.

Some of the metabolic processes of the protoplasm of both plant and animal cells occur along common pathways; carbohydrate metabolism in plants is similar in many details to carbohydrate metabolism in animals. Therefore the study of metabolism in any organism is, in a sense, the study of metabolism in all protoplasm. See CARBOHYDRATE METABOLISM; LIPID METABOLISM; PROTEIN METABOLISM. [M.B.McC.]

Metallochaperones A family of proteins that shuttle metal ions to specific sites within a cell. The target sites for metal delivery include a number of metalloenzymes, or proteins that bind metal ions, such as copper, zinc, or iron, and use these ions as cofactors to carry out essential biochemical reactions. Metallochaperones escort the ion to a specific intracellular location and facilitate incorporation of the metal into designated metalloenzymes. See CELL (BIOLOGY).

The bulk of current knowledge on metallochaperones is restricted to copper, although it is reasonable to assume that a distinct class of proteins is responsible for the incorporation of other metal ion cofactors into metalloenzymes. Among the metallochaperones that have been studied in detail are a family of three copper chaperones. These molecules operate in eukaryotic (nucleated) cells to direct copper to distinct intracellular locations: the mitochondria, the secretory pathway, and the cytosol.

Intracellular copper is normally present at exquisitely low levels, and activation of copper enzymes is wholly dependent upon copper chaperones. Copper not only is an essential nutrient but also is quite toxic to living cells, and elaborate detoxification mechanisms prevent the free metal ion from accumulating to any substantial degree. The copper-requiring metalloenzymes cannot compete for these vanishingly low levels of available metal, explaining the requirement for the copper metallochaperones. [V.C.C.]

Metameres   The serial repetition of parts along the length of the body axis in bilaterally symmetrical animals. The successive subdivisions are called metameres, somites, or segments, hence the synonym, segmentation. Common examples are the muscles and spinal nerves in the human body and in the body and tail of many mammals, snakes and lizards, salamanders, and fishes. It also occurs in other chordates, and in arthropods and annelid worms. It never involves reproductive organs, and thus differs from strobilization in tapeworms and certain jellyfish. Metamerism arises either from a bilateral series of coelomic pouches which form the segmental muscles, kidneys, and body cavities of lower forms, or from mesoblastic somites which form the skeletal and muscular segments of vertebrates. Repetitive features of the nervous system are acquired secondarily through the influence of mesodermal metameres upon adjoining ectodermal tissues. Several primitive embryonic somites become fused in the heads of adult arthropods and vertebrates. See COELOM; MUSCULAR SYSTEM; NEURULATION.
[H.L.Ha.]

Metamorphosis   A pronounced change in both the internal and external morphology of an animal that takes place in a short amount of time, triggered by some combination of external and internal cues. The extent of morphological change varies considerably among species. Even when morphological changes are relatively slight, metamorphosis typically brings about a pronounced shift in habitat and lifestyle. The precise morphological, physiological, and biochemical changes that constitute metamorphosis; the neural, hormonal, and genetic mechanisms through which those changes are controlled; and the ecological consequences of those changes and when they take place continue to be studied in a wide variety of animals. The hormonal and genetic control of metamorphosis has been best examined in a few species of insect, amphibian, and fish (such as flounder), but other aspects of metamorphosis have been investigated for other insect, amphibian, and fish species as well as for marine invertebrates and, indeed, representatives of essentially every animal phylum.

Amphibians exhibit extensive tissue remodeling during metamorphosis, including resorption of the tail musculature and skeletal system; major reconstruction of the digestive tract; degeneration of larval skin and pronounced alteration in skin chemical composition; growth of the hind and fore limbs; degeneration of the gills and associated support structures; shifts in mode of nitrogen excretion, from ammonia to urea; alteration in visual system biochemistry; replacement of larval hemoglobin with adult hemoglobin; and differential growth of the cerebellum. See AMPHIBIA.

Metamorphosis among insects is associated primarily with wing development. Bristletails and other species that do not develop wings and are not descended from winged ancestors exhibit no pronounced metamorphosis. Metamorphosis is most dramatic among holometabolous species, which pass through a distinctive and largely inactive pupal stage; in such species, all of the transformations separating the larval morphology and physiology from that of the adult take place in the pupa. Wings, compound eyes, external reproductive parts, and thoracic walking legs develop from discrete infolded pockets of tissue (imaginal discs) that form during larval development. *See* INSECTA.

The most dramatic metamorphic changes in fish are seen among flounder and other flatfish: in such species, during metamorphosis a symmetrical fish larva becomes an asymmetrical adult, with both eyes displaced to the dorsal surface. The transformation of leptocephalus larvae into juvenile eels is also dramatic; such transformation includes a shift in the position of the urinary and digestive tracts from posterior to anterior.

The control of metamorphosis among crabs, barnacles, gastropods, bivalves, bryozoans, echinoderms, sea squirts, and other marine invertebrates is poorly understood, partly due to the very small size of the larvae—they rarely exceed 1 mm in length, and most are less than 0.5 mm. The larvae of some marine invertebrate species are triggered to metamorphose by specific substances associated with adults of the same species, or with the algae or animals on which they prey. *See* ANNELIDA; BIVALVIA; ECHINODERMATA; GASTROPODA; MOLLUSCA.

Among insects, the timing of metamorphosis is influenced by environmental factors such as temperature, humidity, photoperiod, pheromone production by neighboring individuals, and the nutritional quality of the diet. In a number of species, larvae can undergo developmental arrest (a diapause) in response to unfavorable environmental conditions, so that metamorphosis can be delayed for many months or even years. The hormonal basis for such effects has been at least partly worked out for a number of insect species.

Among marine invertebrates and in at least some fish species, there is also considerable flexibility in the timing of metamorphosis. At some point in the development of marine invertebrates and apparently also in the development of some coral reef fishes, individual larvae become "competent" to metamorphose. It is not yet clear what makes larvae competent; the development of external receptor cells, or the completion of specific neural pathways, or the activation of hormonal systems or their receptors are likely possibilities. *See* ENDOCRINE SYSTEM (INVERTEBRATE).   [J.A.Pe.]

Metazoa   The kingdom (or subkingdom) comprising all many-celled animals, whether constructed of simple tissue layers or of complex organs. In some five-kingdom systems and in the six-kingdom systems of classification for living organisms, metazoans constitute a separate kingdom, while in the older two-kingdom and some three-kingdom systems the subphylum Metazoa made up the greater part of the kingdom Animalia. Most usual classifications subdivide the Metazoa into about 30 phyla of many-celled animals (such as Arthropoda or Mollusca), each representing a major kind of body design. In all classifications, the only animal forms not included in the Metazoa are the single-celled protozoa (Protista) and the independently evolved sponges (Parazoa). *See* ANIMAL KINGDOM; EUKARYOTAE; PORIFERA; PROTISTA.

Metazoans are made up of eukaryotic cells, each with a membrane surrounding the nuclear material and with the mechanics of cell multiplication always involving the mitotic division of chromosomes. Cellular specialization is common. In addition to increasing functional interdependence and specialization of cells, the evolution of the higher phyla of Metazoa has involved the potentialities and penalties of increasing size, particularly those associated with the surface-mass ratio. Despite differing grades of structural and functional complexity, interdependence of organs, tissues, and cell types is diagnostic of the phyla of animals making up the kingdom (or subkingdom) Metazoa. *See* CLASSIFICATION, BIOLOGICAL; HOMEOSTASIS. [W.D.R.H.]

Methanogenesis (bacteria) The microbial formation of methane, which is confined to anaerobic habitats where occurs the production of hydrogen, carbon dioxide, formic acid, methanol, methylamines, or acetate—the major substrates used by methanogenic microbes (methanogens). In fresh-water or marine sediments, in the intestinal tracts of animals, or in habitats engineered by humans such as sewage sludge or biomass digesters, these substrates are the products of anaerobic bacterial metabolism. Methanogens are terminal organisms in the anaerobic microbial food chain—the final product, methane, being poorly soluble, anaerobically inert, and not in equilibrium with the reaction which produces it.

Two highly specialized digestive organs, the rumen and the cecum, have been evolved by herbivores to delay the passage of cellulose fibers so that microbial fermentation may be complete. In these organs, large quantities of methane are produced from hydrogen and carbon dioxide or formic acid by methanogens. From the rumen, an average cow may belch 26 gallons (100 liters) of methane per day.

Methanogens are the only living organisms that produce methane as a way of life. The biochemistry of their metabolism is unique and definitively delineates the group. Two reductive biochemical strategies are employed: an eight-electron reduction of carbon dioxide to methane or a two-electron reduction of a methyl group to methane. All methogens form methane by reducing a methyl group. The major energy-yielding reactions used by methanogens utilize substrates such as hydrogen, formic acid, methanol, acetic acid, and methylamine. Dimethyl sulfide, carbon monoxide, and alcohols such as ethanol and propanol are substrates that are used less frequently. *See* ARCHAEBACTERIA; BACTERIAL PHYSIOLOGY AND METABOLISM. [R.S.W.]

Microbial ecology The study of interrelationships between microorganisms and their living and nonliving environments. Microbial populations are able to tolerate and to grow under varying environmental conditions, including habitats with extreme environmental conditions such as hot springs and salt lakes. Understanding the environmental factors controlling microbial growth and survival offers insight into the distribution of microorganisms in nature, and many studies in microbial ecology are concerned with examining the adaptive features that permit particular microbial species to function in particular habitats.

Within habitats some microorganisms are autochthonous (indigenous), filling the functional niches of the ecosystem, and others are allochthonous (foreign), surviving in the habitat for a period of time but not filling the ecological niches. Because of their diversity and wide distribution, microorganisms are extremely important in ecological processes. The dynamic interactions between microbial populations and their surroundings and the metabolic activities of microorganisms are essential for supporting productivity and maintaining environmental quality of ecosystems. Microorganisms are crucial for the environmental degradation of liquid and solid wastes and various pollutants and for maintaining the ecological balance of ecosystems—essential for preventing environmental problems such as acid mine drainage and eutrophication. *See* ECOSYSTEM.

The various interactions among microbial populations and between microbes, plants, and animals provide stability within the biological community of a given habitat and ensure conservation of the available resources and ecological balance. Interactions between microbial populations can have positive or negative effects, either enhancing the ability of populations to survive or limiting population densities. Sometimes they result in the elimination of a population from a habitat.

The transfer of carbon and energy stored in organic compounds between the organisms in the community forms an integrated feeding structure called a food web. Microbial decomposition of dead plants and animals and partially digested organic matter in the decay portion of a food web is largely responsible for the conversion of organic matter to carbon dioxide. *See* BIOMASS; FOOD WEB.

Only a few bacterial species are capable of biological nitrogen fixation. In terrestrial habitats, the microbial fixation of atmospheric nitrogen is carried out by free-living bacteria, such as *Azotobacter*, and by bacteria living in symbiotic association with plants, such as *Rhizobium* or *Bradyrhizobium* living in mutualistic association within nodules on the roots of leguminous plants. In aquatic habitats, cyanobacteria, such as *Anabaena* and *Nostoc*, fix atmospheric nitrogen. The incorporation of the bacterial genes controlling nitrogen fixation into agricultural crops through genetic engineering may help improve yields. Microorganisms also carry out other processes essential for the biogeochemical cycling of nitrogen. *See* NITROGEN CYCLE.

The biodegradation (microbial decomposition) of waste is a practical application of microbial metabolism for solving ecological problems. Solid wastes are decomposed by microorganisms in landfills and by composting. Liquid waste (sewage) treatment uses microbes to degrade organic matter, thereby reducing the biochemical oxygen demand (BOD). *See* ESCHERICHIA.   [R.M.A.]

Microbiology   The multidisciplinary science of microorganisms. The prefix micro generally refers to an object sufficiently small that a microscope is required for visualization. In the seventeenth century, Anton van Leeuwenhoek first documented observations of bacteria by using finely ground lenses. Bacteriology, as a precursor science to microbiology, was based on Louis Pasteur's pioneering studies in the nineteenth century, when it was demonstrated that microbes as minute simple living organisms were an integral part of the biosphere involved in fermentation and disease. Microbiology matured into a scientific discipline when students of Pasteur, Robert Koch, and others sustained microbes on various organic substrates and determined that microbes caused chemical changes in the basal nutrients to derive energy for growth. Modern microbiology continued to evolve from bacteriology by encompassing the identification, classification, and study of the structure and function of a wide range of microorganisms including protozoa, algae, fungi, viruses, rickettsia, and parasites as well as bacteria. The comprehensive range of organisms is reflected in the major subdivisions of microbiology, which include medical, industrial, agricultural, food, and dairy. *See* ALGAE; BACTERIOLOGY; BIOTECHNOLOGY; FUNGI; IMMUNOLOGY; INDUSTRIAL MICROBIOLOGY; MEDICAL BACTERIOLOGY; MEDICAL MYCOLOGY; MEDICAL PARASITOLOGY; PROTOZOA; RICKETTSIOSES; VIRUS.   [E.W.V.]

Microbiota (human)   Microbial flora harbored by normal, healthy individuals. A number of microorganisms have become adapted to a particular site or ecologic niche in or on their host. Some are normal residents that are regularly found, and if disturbed will rapidly reestablish themselves; others are transient microorganisms that may colonize the host for short periods but are unable to permanently colonize. The normal fetus is sterile, but during and after birth the infant is exposed to an increasing number of microorganisms. Subsequently, those organisms best adapted to survive and colonize particular sites establish themselves and become predominant. Physiologic factors such as the availability of nutrients, temperature, moisture, pH, oxidation-reduction potential, and resistance to local antibacterial substances play an important role in determining the ability of a microorganism to become established at a particular site. The normal indigenous microbial flora is exceedingly complex, consisting of many different species of bacteria, fungi, viruses, and protozoa. The great majority of these commensal and symbiotic organisms are bacteria and fungi.

The indigenous microorganisms play an important role by protecting the normal host from invasion by microorganisms with a greater potential for causing disease. They compete with the pathogens for essential nutrients and for receptors on host cells by producing bacteriocins and other inhibitory substances, making the environment inimical to colonization by pathogens.

In the healthy individual the morphologic integrity of the body surface provides a very effective first line of defense. The intact skin is an efficient physical barrier that can be penetrated by very few microorganisms. The secretion of specific antimicrobial substances and bactericidal fatty acids by the sebaceous glands also retards microbial invasion.

Mucosal surfaces also provide a mechanical barrier in the respiratory, gastrointestinal, and genitourinary tracts. These surfaces are bathed in secretions with antimicrobial activity. In the respiratory tract, mechanical cleansing is accomplished by the cough and mucociliary action. Recurrent infections of the sinuses, middle ear, bronchial tract, and lungs occur in individuals who have an impairment of ciliary activity. These infections are usually caused by *Staphylococcus pneumoniae* and *Haemophilus influenzae*, the more virulent pus-forming organisms found in the nasopharynx. Defects in ciliary activity also cause bacterial respiratory infections in cigarette smokers and heavy alcohol drinkers. *See* STAPHYLOCOCCUS.

Once the natural barriers of the skin and mucous membranes are breached, the next major line of defense is the polymorphonuclear leukocytes. Individuals with disorders of these phagocytic cells have an increased incidence of serious infections with their indigenous microflora.

The complement system is another nonspecific mechanism of the body for the elimination of invading microorganisms. Complement proteins in conjunction with organs of the reticuloendothelial system (spleen, liver, and bone marrow) play a key role in the removal of encapsulated bacteria from the bloodstream. Splenectomized individuals and those with a nonfunctioning spleen because of sickle cell disease have an increased incidence of fulminating infections caused by *S. pneumoniae*, *H. influenzae*, *Neisseria meningitidis*, and recently recognized unusual organisms. *See* COMPLEMENT.   [H.P.W.]

Migratory behavior   Regularly occurring, oriented seasonal movements of individuals of many animal species. The term migration is used to refer to a diversity of animal movements, ranging from short-distance dispersal and one-way migration to round-trip migrations occurring on time scales from hours (the vertical movements of aquatic plankton) to years (the return of salmon to their natal streams following several years and thousands of kilometers of travel in the open sea).

Many temperate zone species, including many migrants, are known to respond physiologically to changes in the day length with season (photoperiodism). For example, many north temperate organisms are triggered to come into breeding condition by the interaction between the lengthening days in spring and their biological clocks (circadian rhythms). Similar processes, acting through the endocrine system, bring animals into migratory condition.

To perform regular oriented migrations, animals need some mechanism for determining and maintaining compass bearings. Animals use many environmental cues as sources of directional information. Work with birds has shown that species use several compasses.

Many species of vertebrates and invertebrates possess a time-compensated Sun compass. With such a system, the animal can determine absolute compass directions at any time of day; that is, its internal biological clock automatically compensates for the changing position of the Sun as the Earth rotates during the day. Many arthropods, fish, salamanders, and pigeons can perceive the plane of polarization of sunlight, and may use that information to help localize the Sun even on partly cloudy days.

Only birds that migrate at night have been shown to have a star compass. Unlike the Sun compass, it appears not to be linked to the internal clock. Rather, directions are determined by reference to star patterns which seem to be learned early in life.

Evidence indicates that several insects, fish, a salamander, certain bacteria, and birds may derive directional information from the weak magnetic field of the Earth. *See* MAGNETIC RECEPTION (BIOLOGY).

Many kinds of animals show the ability to return to specific sites following a displacement. The phenomenon can usually be explained by familiarity with landmarks near "home" or sensory contact with the goal. For example, salmon are well known for their ability to return to their natal streams after spending several years at sea. Little is known about their orientation at sea, but they recognize the home stream by chemical (olfactory) cues in the water. The young salmon apparently imprint on the odor of the stream in which they were hatched. Current evidence indicates that birds imprint on or learn some feature of their birthplace, a prerequisite for them to be able to return to that area following migration. On its first migration, a young bird appears to fly in a given direction for a programmed distance. Upon settling in a wintering area, it will also imprint on that locale and will thereafter show a strong tendency to return to specific sites at both ends of the migratory route.

Only in birds can an unequivocal case be made for the existence of true navigation, that is, the ability to return to a goal from an unfamiliar locality in the absence of direct sensory contact with the goal. This process requires both a compass and the analog of a map. Present evidence suggests that the map is not based on information from the Sun, stars, landmarks, or magnetic field. Other possibilities such as olfactory, acoustic, or gravitational cues are being investigated, but the nature of the navigational component of bird homing remains the most intriguing mystery in this field.   [K.P.A.]

Mitochondria   Specialized organelles of all eukaryotic cells that use oxygen (see illustration). Often called the powerhouses of the cell, mitochondria are responsible for energy generation by the process of oxidative phosphorylation. In this process, electrons produced during the oxidation of simple organic compounds are passed along a chain of four membrane-bound enzymes (the electron transport or respiratory chain), finally reacting with and reducing molecular oxygen to water. The movement of the electrons releases energy that is used to build a gradient of protons across the membrane in which the electron transport chain is situated. Like a stream of water that drives the turbines in a hydroelectric plant, these protons flow back through adenosine triphosphate (ATP) synthase, a membrane-bound enzyme that acts as a molecular turbine. Rotation of part of ATP synthase results in storage of energy in the form of ATP, the universal energy currency of the cell.

Besides their role in energy generation, mitochondria house numerous enzymes that carry out steps essential to metabolism. Defects in mitochondrial assembly or function generally have serious consequences for survival of the cell. In humans, mitochondrial dysfunction is the underlying cause of a wide range of degenerative diseases, with

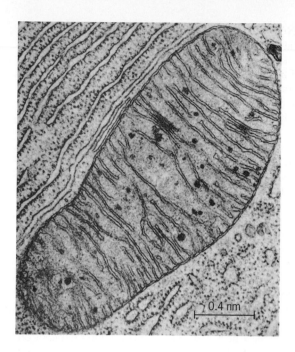

Electron micrograph of a thin section through the pancreas of a bat, showing a typical mitochondrion in profile. Note how the cristae are formed by extensive folding of the inner membrane. (*Courtesy of K. R. Porter*)

0.4 nm

energy-demanding cells such as those of the central nervous and endocrine systems, heart, muscle, and kidney being most severely affected.

Mitochondria are bounded by two concentric membranes referred to as the outer and the inner. This creates two distinct compartments, the matrix and the intermembrane space. The outer membrane consists of a bilayer containing about 80% lipid. It is freely permeable to molecules smaller than about 5000 daltons. The inner membrane is also a lipid bilayer. It is extremely rich in protein (about 75%) and is impermeable to even the smallest of ions. The inner membrane contains the enzymes of the electron transport chain and the ATP synthase, together with a set of transporter proteins that regulate the movement of metabolites in and out of the matrix space. Mitochondria of cells that depend on a high level of ATP production are usually extensively folded to produce structures called cristae (see illustration). These greatly increase the surface area of the inner membrane, allowing many more copies of the enzymes of oxidative phosphorylation.

The intermembrane space contains enzymes capable of using some of the ATP that is transported out of the matrix to phosphorylate other nucleotides. The matrix space is packed with a hundred or so water-soluble proteins that form a sort of semisolid gel. They include enzymes of the tricarboxylic acid (Krebs) cycle and enzymes required for the oxidation of pyruvate and fatty acids, comprising steps in the biosynthesis or degradation of amino acids, nucleotides, and steroids.

Both mitochondria and chloroplasts contain DNA and the machinery necessary to express the information stored there. In both cases, the DNAs are relatively small and simple compared with DNA in the nucleus. While chloroplast DNA tends to be very similar in size in all organisms examined, mtDNA varies widely in complexity, from 16–18 kilobases in metazoa to upward of 2000 kilobases in some higher plants. In the case of higher-plant mtDNAs, some extra sequences appear to have been picked up from chloroplast and nuclear DNAs. MtDNA is generally circular, although some linear exceptions are known among the yeasts, algae, and protozoa.

The information content of most mtDNA is limited. This means that most of the several hundred proteins found in these organelles are encoded by genes located in nuclear DNA. These proteins are synthesized in the cytosol and subsequently transported specifically to the respective organelles. The contributions of the two genetic systems are usually closely coordinated, so that cells synthesize organelles of more or less constant composition.

Many organisms, including humans, show uniparental inheritance of mitochondrial genes because one parent contributes more cytoplasm to the zygote than the other. In humans, it is the egg cell provided by the mother that contributes the cytoplasm. Human mitochondrial genes are thus inherited maternally.

Recent years have seen a growing interest in human diseases that result from mitochondrial dysfunction. A number of these result from mutations in mtDNA. Others are linked to nuclear genes, whose mutation disturbs oxidative phosphorylation or impairs mitochondrial assembly. Mutations in mtDNA are remarkably frequent and lead to a wide range of degenerative, mainly neuromuscular diseases. Most of these diseases are maternally inherited, but some appear to be spontaneous, possibly resulting from error-prone replication of mtDNA. A striking feature of mtDNA-related diseases is the enormous diversity in clinical presentation. This diversity is attributable to two main factors: (1) Heterogeneity in the mtDNA population. Most human tissues contain many thousands of mtDNA molecules per cell. The severity of clinical symptoms depends on the number of mutated molecules present. (2) Dependence of a particular cell type on mitochondrial function (mainly ATP production). Cells with a high requirement for mitochondrially generated ATP are more severely affected than cells with alternative sources of ATP.

Besides their role in metabolism and energy-linked processes, mitochondria have recently been identified as important players in the initiation of apoptosis (programmed cell death). On one hand, the mitochondrial outer membrane houses a number of members of the Bcl-2 family of apoptosis regulatory proteins. On the other hand, release of certain mitochondrial proteins from the intermembrane space is instrumental in activating specialized proteases called caspases. These catalyze a degradative cascade in the cytoplasm that eventually ends in cell death.

Mammalian mtDNAs accumulate mutations at high rates and evolve correspondingly fast (up to 12–15 times faster than single-copy genes in nuclear DNA and up to 100 times faster for rRNA and tRNA genes). This behavior reflects both a high incidence of mutations and a high probability of their fixation. The first is probably related to oxidative damage to mtDNA by oxygen free radicals produced as by-products of electron transfer through the respiratory chain. The second has been attributed to the lack of efficient DNA repair (mitochondria lack nucleotide-excision repair) and to a relatively high tolerance of many mitochondrial gene products to mutational change.

The rapid rate of sequence evolution of mammalian mtDNAs makes these genomes highly sensitive indicators of recent evolutionary relationships. Unlike their nuclear counterparts, mtDNAs do not undergo recombination during sexual transmission and are strictly maternally inherited. Sequence changes in mtDNA therefore provide a clear record of the history of the female lineages through which this DNA has been transmitted.   [L.A.Gr.]

Mitosis   The series of visible changes that occur in the nucleus and chromosomes of non-gamete-producing plant and animal cells as they divide. During mitosis the replicated genes, packaged within the nucleus as chromosomes, are precisely distributed

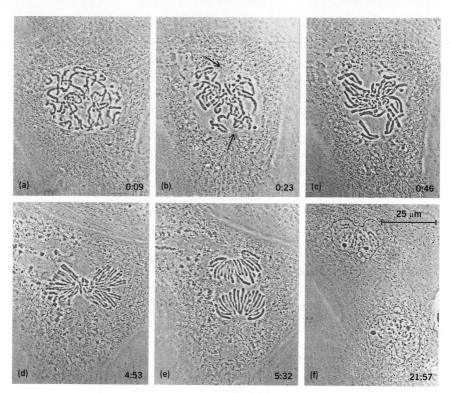

Selected phase-contrast light micrographs showing changes in chromosome position during mitosis in a living newt lung epithelial cell. (*a*) **Late prophase.** (*b*) **Prometaphase.** (*c*) **Mid-prometaphase.** (*d*) **Metaphase.** (*e*) **Anaphase.** (*f*) **Telophase.**

into two genetically identical daughter nuclei (see illustration). The series of events that prepare the cell for mitosis is known as the cell cycle. When viewed in the context of the cell cycle, the definition of mitosis is often expanded to include cytokinesis, the process by which the cell cytoplasm is partitioned during cell division.

Chromosome segregation is mediated in all nonbacterial cells (that is, eukaryotes) by the transient formation of a complex structure known as the mitotic spindle. During mitosis in most higher plants and animals, the nuclear membrane surrounding the replicated chromosomes breaks down, and the spindle is formed in the region previously occupied by the nucleus (open mitosis). In lower organisms, including some protozoa and fungi, the spindle is formed and functions entirely within the nucleus which remains intact throughout the process (closed mitosis).

All spindles are bipolar structures, having two ends or poles. In animal cells, each spindle pole contains an organelle, the centrosome, onto which the spindle focuses and terminates. The polar regions of plant spindles lack centrosomes and, as a result, are much broader. In animals the bipolar nature of the spindle is established by the separation of the centrosomes, which is critical for successful mitosis; the presence of only one pole produces a monopolar spindle in which chromosome segregation is inhibited. The presence of more than two poles produces multipolar spindles which distribute the chromosomes unequally among three or more nuclei. Centrosomes are duplicated during interphase near the time that the DNA is replicated, but then act as a single functional unit until the onset of mitosis. In plants, and during meiosis in some animals, the two spindle poles are organized by the chromosomes and by molecular motors that order randomly nucleated microtubules into parallel bundles. *See* CENTROSOME; PLANT CELL.

Microtubules are the primary structural components of the mitotic spindle and are required for chromosome motion. These are 25-nanometer-diameter, hollow, tubelike structures. During interphase, microtubules are distributed throughout the cytoplasm, where they serve to maintain cell shape and also function as polarized roadways for transporting organelles and cell products. As the cell enters mitosis, the cytoplasmic microtubule network is disassembled and replaced by the mitotic spindle. The microtubules in animal cells originate from the centrosome which, like the chromosomes, was inherited during the previous mitosis where it functioned as a spindle pole. The motion associated with microtubules is mediated by several families of molecular motors which bind to and move along the wall of the microtubule. *See* CYTOSKELETON.

As mitosis begins, each replicated chromosome consists of two identical sister chromatids that are joined along their length. In most cells, chromosomes possess a unique region of highly condensed chromatin (DNA plus protein), known as the centromere, which forms an obvious constriction on the chromosome, referred to as the primary constriction. Spindle microtubules attach to a small specialized structure on the surface of the centromere known as the kinetochore. Fragments of chromosomes lacking a kinetochore do not move poleward; it is always the kinetochore that leads in the poleward motion of the chromosome. The centromere region of each replicated chromosome contains two sister kinetochores, one attached to each chromatid, that lie on opposite sides of the primary constriction.

Once initiated, mitosis is a continuous process that, depending on the temperature and organism, requires several minutes to many hours to complete. Traditionally it has been subdivided into five consecutive stages that are distinguished primarily by chromosome structure, position, and behavior. These stages are prophase, prometaphase, metaphase, anaphase, and telophase. In prophase, cell chromosomes condense within the nucleus. By late prophase/early prometaphase, the nuclear envelope breaks down; kinetochore-containing primary constrictions are sometimes visible; the cytoplasmic microtubule complex is replaced by two radial astral microtubule arrays; centrosomes separate; and microtubules in each aster grow and shorten at their ends away from the centrosome. By mid-prometaphase, the kinetochores on the chromosomes interact with the asters to form the spindle. In metaphase, all of the chromosomes are aligned on the spindle equator; sister kinetochores are attached to opposite poles by kinetochore fibers. In anaphase, the sister chromatids separate and move toward their respective spindle poles; at the same time the spindle poles move farther apart. In telophase, the two groups of sister chromosomes become two well-separated sister nuclei, and the cytoplasm of the cell divides (cytokinesis). *See* CELL (BIOLOGY); CELL NUCLEUS.

[C.L.R.]

Molecular biology   The study of structural and functional properties of biological systems, pursued within the context of understanding the roles of the various molecules in living cells and the relationship between them. Molecular biology has its roots in biophysics, genetics, and biochemistry. A prime focus of the field has been the molecular basis of genetics, and with the demonstration in the mid-1940s that deoxyribonucleic acid (DNA) is the genetic material, emphasis has been on structure, organization, and regulation of genes. Initially, molecular biologists restricted their studies to bacterial and viral systems, largely because of their genetic and biochemical simplicity. *Escherichia coli* has been extensively examined because of its limited number of cellular functions and the corresponding restricted amount of genetic information encoded in the bacterial chromosome. Simple eukaryotic cells, such as protozoa and yeast, offer similar advantages and also have been studied. For these same reasons, bacteriophage and animal viruses have provided molecular biologists with the ability to study the structural and functional properties of molecules in intact cells. However, a series of conceptual and technological developments occurred rapidly during the late 1970s that permitted molecular biologists to approach a broad spectrum of plant and animal cells with experimental techniques. One of the major factors has been the development and applications of genetic engineering. Recombinant DNA technology allowed the isolation and selective modification of specific genes, thereby reducing both their structural and functional complexity and facilitating the study of gene expression in higher cells. The concepts and techniques used by molecular biologists have been rapidly and effectively employed to resolve numerous cellular, biological, and biochemical problems—becoming routine at both the basic and applied levels.

The recognition of DNA as the genetic material coupled with the discovery that genes reside in chromosomes resulted in an intensive effort to map genes to specific chromosomes. Initially genes were assigned to chromosomes on the basis of correlations between modifications in cellular function, particularly biochemical defects, and the addition, loss, or modification of specific chromosomes. *See* CHROMOSOME ABERRATION; MUTATION.

A major breakthrough was the development of somatic cell genetics. This is an approach in which, for example, human and hamster cells are fused, resulting in a hybrid cell initially containing the complement of human and hamster chromosomes. As the cells grow and divide in culture, the hamster chromosomes are retained while there is a progressive loss of human chromosomes. By correlating the loss of human biological or biochemical traits with the loss of specific human chromosomes, a number of human genes have been successfully mapped. *See* SOMATIC CELL GENETICS.

The development of methods for isolating genes and for determining the genetic sequences of the DNA in which the genes are encoded, led to rapid advances in gene mapping at several levels of resolution. Localization of specific genes to chromosomes is routinely carried out with cloned genes as probes. Further information about the segment of a chromosome in which a specific gene resides can be obtained by directly determining the DNA sequences of both the gene itself and the surrounding region.

Chromosome localization of specific genes has numerous applications at both the basic and clinical levels. At the basic level, knowledge of the positions of various genes provides insight into potentially functional relationships. At the clinical level, chromosome aberrations are now routinely used in prenatal diagnosis of an extensive series of human genetic disorders, and several chromosomal modifications have been linked to specific types of cancer. Knowledge of genetic defects at the molecular level has permitted the development of diagnostic procedures that in some instances, such as sickle cell anemia, are based on a single nucleotide change in the DNA.

Recombinant DNA. Recombinant DNA technology has provided molecular biology with an extremely powerful tool. In broad terms, applications of recombinant DNA technology can be divided into four areas—biomedical, basic biological, agricultural, and industrial. Biomedical applications include the elucidation of the cellular and molecular bases of a broad spectrum of diseases, as well as both diagnostic and therapeutic applications in clinical medicine.

In a strictly formal sense, the term recombinant DNA designates the joining or recombination of DNA segments. However, in practice, recombinant DNA has been applied to a series of molecular manipulations whereby segments of DNA are rearranged, added, deleted, or introduced into the genomes of other cells.

The ability to manipulate or "engineer" genetic sequences is based on several developments.

1. *Methods for breaking and rejoining DNA*. The precise breaking and rejoining of DNA has been made possible by the discovery of restriction endonucleases, enzymes that have the ability to recognize specific DNA sequences and to cleave the double helix precisely at these sites. Also important are the ability to join fragments of DNA together with the enzyme DNA ligase, and the techniques to determine the nucleotide sequence of genes and thereby confirm the identity and location of structural and regulatory sequences.

2. *Carriers for genetic sequences*. Bacterial plasmids, that is, circular double-stranded DNA molecules that replicate extrachromosomally, have been modified so that they can serve as efficient carriers for segments of DNA, complete genes, regions of genes, or sequences contained within several different genes. Bacteriophage and animal viruses, retroviruses, and bovine papilloma virus have also been successfully utilized as DNA carriers. These carriers are referred to as cloning vectors. Host cells in which vectors containing cloned genes can replicate range from bacteria to numerous other cells, including normal, transformed, and malignant human cells.

3. *Introduction of recombinant DNA molecules*. Genetic sequences in the form of isolated DNA fragments, or chromosomes, or of DNA molecules cloned in plasmid vectors can be introduced into host cells by a procedure referred to as transfection or DNA-mediated gene transfer—a technique that renders the cell membrane permeable by a brief treatment with calcium phosphate, thereby facilitating DNA uptake. Genes cloned in viruses can also be introduced by infection of host cells.

4. *Selection of cells containing cloned sequences*. Bacterial cells containing plasmids with cloned genes can be detected by selective resistance or sensitivity to antibiotics. In addition, the presence of introduced genes in bacterial, plant, or animal cells can be assayed by a procedure known as nucleic acid hybridization.

5. *Amplification*. Amplification of genetic sequences cloned in bacterial plasmids is efficiently achieved by treatment of host cells with antibiotics which suppress replication of the bacterial chromosome, yet do not interfere with replication of the plasmid with its cloned gene. Sequences cloned in bacterial or animal viruses are often amplified by virtue of the ability of the virus to replicate preferentially. *See* GENE AMPLIFICATION.

6. *Expression*. Expression of cloned human genes can be mediated by regulatory sequences derived from the natural gene, from exogenous genes, or by host cell sequences.

Two clinically important genes, human insulin and human growth hormone, have been cloned and introduced into bacteria under conditions where biologically active hormones can be produced.

Progress has been made in applications of recombinant DNA technology to the resolution of agricultural problems, especially for the improvement of both crops and livestock. *See* ADENOHYPOPHYSIS HORMONE; BREEDING (ANIMAL); BREEDING (PLANT); GENETIC ENGINEERING; INSULIN.

Biophysical analysis. Understanding of the structural properties of molecules and the interaction between molecules that constitute biologically important complexes has been facilitated by biophysical analysis. For example, developments in the resolution offered by techniques such as electron microscopy, x-ray diffraction, and neutron scattering have provided valuable insight into the structure of chromatin, the protein-DNA complex which constitutes the genome of eukaryotic cells. These techniques have also provided clues about modifications in chromatin structure that accompany functional changes. One possible application of biophysical analysis is the diagnosis of human disorders by adaptation of nuclear magnetic resonance for tissue and whole body evaluation of soft tissue tumors, blood flow, and cardiac function.

Flow of molecular information. Information for all cellular activities is encoded in DNA; selective elaboration of this information is prerequisite to meeting both structural and biochemical requirements of the cell. In this regard, there are three major areas of investigations by molecular biologists: (1) the composition, structure, and organization of chromatin, the protein-DNA molecular complex in which genetic information is encoded and packaged; (2) the molecular events associated with the expression of genetically encoded information so that specific cellular biochemical requirements can be met; and (3) the molecular signals that trigger the expression of specific genes and the types of communication and feedback operative to monitor and mediate gene control. See CHROMOSOME; DEOXYRIBONUCLEIC ACID (DNA); GENE; GENETIC CODE; NUCLEIC ACID.

[G.S.S.; J.L.St.]

Molecular recognition   The ability of biological and chemical systems to distinguish between molecules and regulate behavior accordingly. How molecules fit together is fundamental in disciplines such as biochemistry, medicinal chemistry, materials science, and separation science. A good deal of effort has been expended in trying to evaluate the underlying inter-molecular forces. The weak forces that act over short distances (hydrogen bonds, van der Waals interactions, and aryl stacking) provide most of the selectivity observed in biological chemistry and permit molecular recognition. The recognition event initiates behavior such as replication in nucleic acids, immune response in antibodies, signal transduction in receptors, and regulation in enzymes. Most studies of recognition in organic chemistry have been inspired by these biological phenomena. It has been the task of bioorganic chemistry to develop systems capable of such complex behavior with molecules that are comprehensible and manageable in size, that is, with model systems. See ANTIBODY; CHEMORECEPTION; ENZYME; NUCLEIC ACID; SYNAPTIC TRANSMISSION.

[J.Reb.]

Mollusca   A major phylum of the animal kingdom comprising an extreme diversity of external body forms (oysters, clams, chitons, snails, slugs, squid, and octopuses among others), all based on a remarkably uniform basic plan of structure and function. The phylum name is derived from *mollis*, meaning soft, referring to the soft body within a hard calcareous shell, which is usually diagnostic. Soft-bodied mollusks make extensive use of ciliary and mucous mechanisms in feeding, locomotion, and reproduction. Most molluscan species are readily recognizable as such.

The Mollusca constitute a successful phylum; there are probably over 110,000 living species of mollusks, a number second only to that of the phylum Arthropoda, and more than double the number of vertebrate species. More than 99% of living molluscan species belong to two classes: Gastropoda (snails) and Bivalvia. Ecologically, these two classes can make up a dominant fraction of the animal biomass in many natural communities, both marine and fresh-water.

Classification. The phylum Mollusca is divided into seven distinct extant classes, three of which (Gastropoda, Bivalvia, and Cephalopoda) are of major significance in terms both of species numbers and of ecological bioenergetics, and one extinct class. An outline of their classification follows.

> Class Monoplacophora (mainly fossil; but
>   one living genus *Neopilina*)
> Class Aplacophora
>   Subclass Neomeniomorpha

Subclass Chaetodermomorpha
Class Polyplacophora
Class Scaphopoda
Class Rostroconchia (fossil only)
Class Gastropoda
  Subclass Prosobranchia
    Order: Archaeogastropoda
          Mesogastropoda
          Neogastropoda
  Subclass Opisthobranchia
    Order: Bullomorpha (or Cephalaspidea)
          Aplysiomorpha (or Anaspidea)
          Thecosomata
          Gymnosomata
          Pleurobranchomorpha
            (or Notaspidea)
          Acochlidiacea
          Sacoglossa
          Nudibranchia (or Acoela)
  Subclass Pulmonata
    Order: Systellommatophora
          Basommatophora
          Stylommatophora
Class Bivalvia (or Pelecypoda)
  Subclass Protobranchia
  Subclass Lamellibranchia
    Order: Taxodonta
          Anisomyaria
          Heterodonta
          Schizodonta
          Adapedonta
          Anomalodesmata
  Subclass Septibranchia
Class Cephalopoda
  Subclass Nautiloidea
  Subclass Ammonoidea (fossil only)
  Subclass Coleoidea
    Order: Belemnoidea
          Sepioidea
          Teuthoidea
          Vampyromorpha
          Octopoda

Functional morphology. The unique basic plan of the Mollusca involves the different modes of growth and of functioning of the three distinct regions of the molluscan body (see illustration). These are the head-foot with some nerve concentrations, most of the sense organs, and all the locomotory organs; the visceral mass (or hump) containing organs of digestion, reproduction, and excretion; and the mantle (or pallium) hanging from the visceral mass and enfolding it and secreting the shell. In its development and growth, the head-foot shows a bilateral symmetry with an anterioposterior axis of growth. Over and around the visceral mass, however, the mantle-shell shows

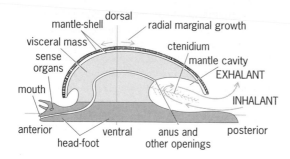

dorsal
mantle-shell — radial marginal growth
visceral mass
sense organs
ctenidium
mantle cavity
EXHALANT
mouth
INHALANT
anterior — ventral — anus and other openings — posterior
head-foot

Generalized model of a stem mollusk (or archetype) in side view. There are three distinct regions in the molluscan body: head-foot, visceral mass, and mantle-shell. Water circulation through the mantle cavity, gills (ctenidia), and pallial complex is from ventral inhalant to dorsal exhalant. (*After W. D. Russell-Hunter, A Life of Invertebrates, Macmillan, 1979*)

a biradial symmetry, and always grows by marginal increment around a dorsoventral axis. It is of considerable functional importance that a space is left between the mantle-shell and the visceral mass forming a semi-internal cavity; this is the mantle cavity or pallial chamber within which the typical gills of the mollusk, the ctenidia, develop. This mantle cavity is almost diagnostic of the phylum; it is primarily a respiratory chamber housing the ctenidia, but with alimentary, excretory, and genital systems all discharging into it.

In looking at any mollusk, it is important to realize that whatever the shape of the shell, it is always underlain by the mantle, a fleshy fold of tissues which has secreted it. The detailed structure of the shell and of the mantle edge (with three functionally distinct lobes) is also consistent throughout the Mollusca. The shell is made up of calcium carbonate crystals enclosed in a meshwork of tanned proteins. It is always in three layers: the outer periostracum, the prismatic layer and the innermost or nacreous layer.

Each of the eight classes of the Mollusca has a characteristic body form and shell shape. Two classes are enormous (Gastropoda and Bivalvia), one of moderate extent (Cephalopoda), the others being minor by comparison. The Gastropoda constitute a diverse group with the shell usually in one piece. This shell may be coiled as in typical snails—that is, helicoid or turbinate—or it may form a flattened spiral, or a short cone as in the limpets, or it may be secondarily absent as in the slugs. Most gastropods are marine, but many are found in fresh waters and on land; in fact, they are the only successful nonmarine mollusks.

The Bivalvia are a more uniform group, with the shell in the form of two calcareous valves united by an elastic hinge ligament. Mussels, clams, and oysters are familiar bivalves. The group is mainly marine with a few genera in estuaries and in fresh waters. There can be no land bivalves since their basic functional organization is as filter feeders. The third major group, the Cephalopoda, includes the most active and most specialized mollusks. There is a chambered, coiled shell in *Nautilus* and in many fossil forms; this becomes an internal structure in cuttlefish and squids, and is usually entirely absent in octopods.

A diversity of gill patterns have evolved in the major molluscan groups, paralleling the evolution of the mantle-shell patterns. The more advanced gastropods show reduction from a pair of aspidobranch ctenidia to a single one, and from that to a one-sided pectinibranch ctenidium (or comb gill), and subsequently to no gill at all in the pulmonate snails. The bivalves show enlargement of gill leaflets to longer filaments and their subsequent folding into the true lamellibranch condition, used in filter feeding. The gills in the cephalopods, while still structurally homologous, are modified with new skeletal elements to resist the stresses of water pumping by muscles.

Besides the gills, the other organs of the mantle cavity (termed collectively the pallial complex) again show morphological and functional consistency throughout the main groups of the Mollusca. The ctenidia form a curtain functionally dividing the mantle cavity into an inhalant part (usually ventral) containing the osphradia (pallial sense organs which sample the incoming water), and an exhalant part (usually dorsal) containing hypobranchial glands and both the anus and the openings of the kidney and genital ducts.

The cardiac structures of mollusks are also closely linked to the pallial complex. If there is a symmetrical pair of ctenidia, there will be a symmetrical pair of auricles on either side of the muscular ventricle of the heart; if one ctenidium, one auricle; if four ctenidia, four auricles. Note that body fluids in mollusks are almost all blood, just as body cavities are almost all hemocoel.

The respiratory pigment is usually hemocyanin in solution, so that neither circulatory efficiency nor blood oxygen-carrying capacity is high. However, mollusks are mostly sluggish animals with low metabolic (and hence respiratory) rates.

Uniquely molluscan is the use of cilia in "sorting surfaces," which can segregate particles into different size categories and send them to be disposed of in different ways in several parts of the organism. In a simpler type of sorting surface, the epithelium is thrown into a series of ridges and grooves, the cilia in the grooves beating along them and the cilia on the crests of the ridges beating across them. Thus, fine particles impinging on the surface can be carried in the direction of the grooves, while larger particles are carried at right angles. Such sorting surfaces occur both externally on the feeding organs and internally in the gut of many mollusks. For example, on the labial palps of bivalves, they are used to separate the larger sand grains (which are rejected) from the smaller microorganisms which then pass to the mouth.

The range in levels of complexity of molluscan nervous systems is comparable to that found in the phylum Chordata. The four-strand nervous system with one pair of tiny ganglia found in chitons is not dissimilar to the neural plan in turbellarian flatworms. In contrast, the nervous system and sense organs of a cephalopod like an octopus are equaled and exceeded only by those of some birds and mammals. In the majority of mollusks the nervous system is in an intermediate condition. In mollusks other than cephalopods, the main effectors controlled by the nervous system are cilia and mucous glands. In fact, apart from the muscles which withdraw it into its shell, the typical mollusk is a slow-working animal with little fast nervous control or quick reflexes. In the brain of modern cephalopods, paired ganglia have been fused into a massive structure, with over 300 million neurons and extensive "association" centers providing considerable mnemic and learning capacities.

In all primitive mollusks, the sexes are separate, and external fertilization follows the spawning of eggs and sperm into the sea.

In more advanced mollusks, eggs are larger (and fewer), fertilization may become internal (with complex courtship and copulatory procedures), and larval stages may be sequentially suppressed. A remarkably large number of mollusks (including many higher snails) are hermaphroditic. Although some are truly simultaneous hermaphrodites, many more show various kinds of consecutive sexuality. Most often the male phase occurs first, and these species are said to show protandric hermaphroditism.

Distributional ecology. Mollusks are largely marine. The extensive use of ciliary and mucous mechanisms in feeding, locomotion, reproduction, and other functions demands a marine environment for the majority of molluscan stocks. Apart from a small number of bivalve genera living in brackish and fresh waters, all nonmarine mollusks are gastropods.

Despite the soft, hydraulically moved bodies and relatively permeable skins typical of all mollusks, some snails are relatively successful as land animals, although they are largely limited to more humid habitats. The primary physiological requirements for life on land concern water control, conversion to air breathing, and temperature regulation.

In the sea, all classes of mollusks are found, and all habitats have mollusks. Protobranchiate bivalves are found at depths of over 30,000 ft (9000 m). Although ecologically cephalopod mollusks are limited to the sea, there are sound reasons for claiming modern cephalopods as the most highly organized invertebrate animals. The functional efficiencies of jet propulsion and of massive brains in squid, cuttlefish, and octopuses have not been paralleled in their other physiological systems.

In addition to the extreme diversity of external body form exhibited by different mollusks, they show a remarkable diversity in their ecological distribution and life styles. However, the basic molluscan plan of structure and function always remains recognizable. *See* BIVALVIA; CEPHALOPODA; GASTROPODA.   [W.D.R.H.]

Monoamine oxidase
Either of two enzymes found in the outer membrane of mitochondria that degrade biogenic amines and are thus responsible for the destruction of transmitter substances at neuronal synapses. Nerve cells release neurotransmitter into the synapse in response to stimulation. The neuron must then dispose of this neurotransmitter to stop the signal or a new signal cannot get through. This is accomplished by one of three mechanisms: diffusion; reuptake into the presynaptic area; and degradation by a number of enzymes, including monoamine oxidase. *See* SYNAPTIC TRANSMISSION.

Monoamine oxidase inhibitors are drugs that block degradation of amine transmitters within the cell; however, not all of their effects can be attributed directly to monoamine oxidase inhibition, since a number of different neuronal effects have been described. The most prominent consequence of monoamine oxidase inhibition is a rapid increase in the intracellular concentrations of monoamines. In addition, the level of serotonin in the brain is raised to a greater extent than that of norepinephrine and dopamine. After these amine concentrations rise, secondary adaptive consequences occur, including a reduction in amine synthesis via an apparent feedback mechanism, which has been most clearly demonstrated for the noradrenergic system. *See* NEUROBIOLOGY; SEROTONIN.

Two types of monoamine oxidase have been identified. These are designated A and B and are distinguished by having different substrate specificity. Type A preferentially deaminates norepinephrine, cortical dopamine, and serotonin, and is selectively inhibited by clorgyline. Type B degrades phenylethylamine, dopamine, and benzylamine, and is sensitive to deprenyl or pargyline inhibition. Commonly used monoamine oxidase inhibitors are nonselective inhibitors that affect types A and B. Seventy-five percent of monoamine oxidase in the human is type B.

Monoamine oxidase inhibitors are used in medicine for controlling hypertension and for treating depression and other disorders. Other psychiatric disorders, such as obsessive-compulsive disorder, bulimia, somatoform pain disorder, panic disorder, and schizophrenia, have been reported to occasionally respond to treatment with monoamine oxidase inhibitors. There is also some evidence that patients with so-called atypical depression preferentially respond to monoamine oxidase inhibitors. *See* AFFECTIVE DISORDERS.   [M.A.Je.]

Monoclonal antibodies
Antibody proteins that bind to a specific target molecule (antigen) at one specific site (antigenic site). In response to either infection of immunization with a foreign agent, the immune system generates many different

antibodies that bind to the foreign molecules. Individual antibodies within this polyclonal antibody pool bind to specific sites on a target molecule known as epitopes. Isolation of an individual antibody within the polyclonal antibody pool would allow biochemical and biological characterization of a highly specific molecular entity targeting only a single epitope. Realization of the therapeutic potential of such specificity launched research into the development of methods to isolate and continuously generate a supply of a single lineage of antibody, a monoclonal antibody (mAb).

In 1974, W. Köhler and C. Milstein developed a process for the generation of monoclonal antibodies. In their process, fusion of an individual B cell (or B lymphocyte), which produces an antibody with a single specificity but has a finite life span, with a myeloma (B cell tumor) cell, which can be grown indefinitely in culture, results in a hybridoma cell. This hybridoma retains desirable characteristics of both parental cells, producing an antibody of a single specificity that can grow in culture indefinitely.

Generation of monoclonal antibodies through the hybridoma process worked well with B cells from rodents but not with B cells from humans. Consequently, the majority of the first monoclonal antibodies were from mice. When administered into humans as therapeutic agents in experimental tests, the human immune system recognized the mouse monoclonal antibodies as foreign agents, causing an immune response, which was sometimes severe. Although encouraging improvements in disease were sometimes seen, this response made murine (mouse) antibodies unacceptable for use in humans with a functional immune system.

Fueled by advances in molecular biology and genetic engineering in the late 1980s, efforts to engineer new generations of monoclonal antibodies with reduced human immunogenicity have come to fruition. Today there are a number of clonal antibodies approved for human therapeutic use in the United States.

Characterization of the structure of antibodies and their genes laid the foundation for antibody engineering. In most mammals, each antibody is composed of two different polypeptides, the immunoglobulin heavy chain (IgH) and the immunoglobulin light chain (IgL). Comparison of the protein sequences of either heavy of light antibody chain reveals a portion that typically varies from one antibody to the next, the variable region, and a portion that is conserved, the constant region. A heavy and a light chain are folded together in an antibody to align their respective variable and constant regions. The unique shape of the cofolded heavy- and light-chain variable domains creates the variable domain of the antibody, which fits around the shape of the target epitope and confers the binding specificity of the antibody.

Mice genetically engineered to produce fully human antibodies allow the use of established hybridoma technology to generate fully human antibodies directly, without the need for additional engineering. These transgenic mice contain a large portion of human DNA encoding the antibody heavy and light chains. Inactivation of the mouse's own heavy- and light-chain genes forces the mouse to use the human genes to make antibodies. Current versions of these mice generate a diverse polyclonal antibody response, thereby enabling the generation and recovery of optimal monoclonal antibodies using hybridoma technology.

Disease areas that currently are especially amenable to antibody-based treatments include cancer, immune dysregulation, and infection. Depending upon the disease and the biology of the target, therapeutic monoclonal antibodies can have different mechanisms of action. A therapeutic monoclonal antibody may bind and neutralize the normal function of a target. For example, a monoclonal antibody that blocks the activity of the of protein needed for the survival of a cancer cell causes the cell's death. Another therapeutic monoclonal antibody may bind and activate the normal function of a target. For example, a monoclonal antibody can bind to a protein on a cell and trigger an apoptosis signal. Finally, if a monoclonal antibody binds to a target expressed only on diseased tissue, conjugation of a toxic payload (effective agent), such as a chemotherapeutic or radioactive agent, to the monoclonal antibody can create a guided missile for specific delivery of the toxic payload to the diseased tissue, reducing harm to healthy tissue. *See* ANTIBODY; ANTIGEN; GENETIC ENGINEERING; IMMUNOLOGY.

[L.Gre.]

Monocotyledons   This group of flowering plants (angiosperms), with one seed leaf, was previously thought to be one of the two major categories of flowering plants (the other group is dicotyledons). However, deoxyribonucleic acid (DNA) studies have revealed that, although they do constitute a group of closely related families, they are closely related to the magnoliids, with which they share a pollen type with a single aperture. The eudicots are much more distantly related. In general, monocots can also be recognized by their parallel-veined leaves and three-part flowers. Their roots have disorganized vascular bundles, and if they are treelike (yuccas, aloes, dracaenas) their wood is unusually structured. Among the important monocots are grasses (including corn, rice, and wheat), lilies, orchids, palms, and sedges. *See* DICOTYLEDONS; EUDICOTYLEDONS; FLOWER; MAGNOLIOPHYTA.

[M.W.C.; M.F.F.]

Monosaccharide   A class of simple sugars containing a chain of 3–10 carbon atoms in the molecule, known as polyhydroxy aldehydes (aldoses) or ketones (ketoses). They are very soluble in water, sparingly soluble in ethanol, and insoluble in ether. The number of monosaccharides known is approximately 70, of which about 20 occur in nature. The remainder are synthetic. The existence of such a large number of compounds is due to the presence of asymmetric carbon atoms in the molecules. Aldohexoses, for example, which include the important sugar glucose, contain no less than four asymmetric atoms, each of which may be present in either D or L configuration. The number of stereoisomers rapidly increases with each additional asymmetric carbon atom.

A list of the best-known monosaccharides is given below:

Trioses:	$CH_2OH \cdot CHOH \cdot CHO$, glycerose (glyceric aldehyde)
	$CH_2OH \cdot CO \cdot CH_2OH$, dihydroxy acetone
Tetroses:	$CH_2OH \cdot (CHOH)_2 \cdot CHO$, erythrose
	$CH_2OH \cdot CHOH \cdot CO \cdot CHO$, erythrulose
Pentoses:	$CH_2OH \cdot (CHOH)_3 \cdot CHO$, xylose, arabinose, ribose
	$CH_2OH \cdot (CHOH)_2 \cdot CO \cdot CH_2OH$, xylulose, ribulose
Methyl pentoses (6-deoxyhexoses):	
	$CH_3(CHOH)_4 \cdot CHO$, rhamnose, fucose
Hexoses:	$CH_2OH \cdot (CHOH)_4 \cdot CHO$, glucose, mannose, galactose
	$CH_2OH \cdot (CHOH)_3 \cdot CO \cdot CHOH$, fructose, sorbose
Heptoses:	$CH_2OH \cdot (CHOH)_5 \cdot CHO$, glucoheptose, galamannoheptose
	$CH_2OH \cdot (CHOH)_4 \cdot CO \cdot CH_2OH$, sedoheptulose, mannoheptulose

Aldose monosaccharides having 8, 9, and 10 carbon atoms in their chains have been synthesized. *See* CARBOHYDRATE.

[W.Z.H.]

Monotremata The single order of the mammalian subclass Prototheria. Two living families, the Tachyglossidae and the Ornithorhynchidae, make up this unusual order of quasimammals, or mammallike reptiles.

The Tachyglossidae comprise the echidnas (spiny anteaters), which have relatively large brains with convoluted cerebral hemispheres. The known genera, *Tachyglossus* and *Zaglossus*, are terrestrial, feeding on termites, ants, and other insects. They are capable diggers, both to obtain food and to escape enemies. Like hedgehogs, they can erect their spines and withdraw their limbs when predators threaten. Commonly one egg, but occasionally two or even three, is laid directly into the marsupium (pouch) of the mother where it is incubated for up to 10 days. Species of *Tachyglossus* live in rocky areas, semideserts, open forests, and scrublands. They are found in Australia, Tasmania, New Guinea, and Salawati Island. Species of *Zaglossus* are found in mountainous, forested areas.

The duck-billed platypus, constituting the Ornithorhynchidae, has a relatively small brain with smooth cerebral hemispheres. The young have calcified teeth, but in the adult these are replaced by horny plates which form around the teeth in the gums. The snout is duck-billed. The semiaquatic platypus is a capable swimmer, diver, and digger. Two eggs are usually laid by the female into a nest of damp vegetation. After incubating the eggs for about 10 days the female leaves, returning only when the eggs are hatched. The platypus is found in Australia and Tasmania in almost all aquatic habitats. *See* MAMMALIA; PROTOTHERIA. [F.S.S.]

Mosaicism The coexistence of two or more genetically distinct cell populations derived originally from a single zygote. Mosaics may arise at any stage of development, from the two-cell stage onward, or in any tissue which actively proliferates thereafter. The phenomenon is commonly observed in many species of animals and plants and may be caused by somatic mutation or chromosomal nondisjunction. An individual animal or plant may exhibit mosaicism, or it may occur in a culture of a single cell- or tissue-type obtained from an individual.

Chromosome nondisjunction is probably the principal cause of chromosomal aberration, which in turn may lead to the development of mosaicism. During cell division, the two sister chromatids usually separate completely, each chromatid going to opposite

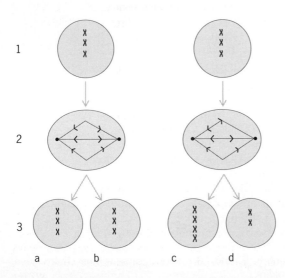

Fig. 1. Mosaicism caused by chromosome nondisjunction. (1) Two cells with an identical chromosome complement are in the process of cellular division. (2) In the cell on the left, the sister chromatids have separated normally, whereas in the other cell, one chromatid has remained in the equatorial zone. (3) Two normal daughter cells (a and b) are produced as a result of a normal mitotic division. Two aneuploid cells (c and d) result from the abnormal division. If c and d are viable, a tissue mosaicism may result with a mixture of normal cells and some aneuploid cells (c, d, or c and d).

Fig. 2. Bilateral gynandromorphism in the moth *Abraxas
grossulariata*. The left side
shows the typical male wing
patterning, whereas the right
side shows a female form.

poles of the cell guided by the spindle apparatus. In some cases, one chromatid will fail to completely separate, or it may lag behind. This nondisjunction will lead to the presence of both sister chromatids in the same daughter cell instead of one in each of the daughter cells (Fig. 1). Somatic crossing-over leads to the production of a recombinant mosaic where chromosome segments, with their corresponding blocks of genes, are exchanged between homologous chromosomes during mitosis. The occurrence of this process leads to mosaicism, mostly manifested as spots (clones of variant cells) on the cuticle of insects or on leaves, petals, or stamen hairs. *See* CHROMOSOME.

Sex chromosome mosaicism, the presence of a mixture of cell populations with different X and Y chromosome constitutions, is not uncommon and is often seen in individuals with ovarian dysgenesis. The presence of a significant proportion of chromosomally abnormal cells in any such mosaic will tend to lead to a clinically expressed syndrome. The proportion of each constituent clone may vary from tissue to tissue, but is relatively stable in each individual site throughout adult life. Sex mosaics (gynandromorphs) are particularly striking where a difference in the secondary sexual characteristics exists between the normal sexes. For example, in a butterfly with bilateral gynandromorphism, the left side may show the characteristic wing color and pattern of the male, and the light wing, typical female patterning (Fig. 2). *See* CHIMERA; GENETICS; SEX-LINKED INHERITANCE.   [A.W.W.]

Motivation   The intentions, desires, goals, and needs that determine human and animal behavior. An inquiry is made into a person's motives in order to explain that person's actions.

Different roles have been assigned to motivational factors in the causation of behavior. Some have defined motivation as a nonspecific energizing of all behavior. Others define it as recruiting and directing behavior, selecting which of many possible actions the organism will perform. The likely answer is that both aspects exist. More specific determinants of action may be superimposed on a dimension of activation or arousal that affects a variety of actions nonselectively. The situation determines what the animal does; arousal level affects the vigor, promptness, or persistence with which the animal does it.

There is a question as to how behavior can be guided by a state or event (goal attainment) that does not yet exist. Modern approaches to this question lean heavily on cognitive concepts. Mammals, birds, and even some insects can represent to themselves a nonexistent state of affairs. They can represent what a goal object is (search images): a chimpanzee may show behavioral signs of surprise if a different food is substituted for the usual one. They can represent where it is (cognitive maps): a digger wasp remembers the location of its nest relative to arbitrary landmarks, and will fly to the wrong place if the landmarks are moved. If this idea is generalized, motivated behavior can be thought of as guided by a feedback control system with a set point. A set point establishes a goal state which the control system seeks to bring about. Behavior is controlled, not by present external or internal stimuli alone, but by a comparison between the existing state of affairs and a desired state of affairs, that is, the set point or goal, registered or specified within the brain. The animal then acts to reduce the difference between the existing and the desired state of affairs. This way of looking at motivation helps bridge the gap between simple motives in animals and complex ones in humans. If to be motivated is to do whatever is necessary to bring about an imagined state of affairs, then human motives can literally be as complex, and be projected as far into the future, as human imaginations permit. See COGNITION.

Motivation and emotion are closely related. Indeed, it has been argued that emotions are the true motivators and that other factors internal, situational, and cognitive take hold of behavior by way of the emotions they evoke. In the simplest case, pleasure and displeasure have been recognized for centuries as having motivational force. In more complex cases, the role of cognitive operations, such as how an individual feels about an event, as well as what is done about it, can depend heavily on how an individual thinks about it.

The culture in which an individual is raised has a powerful effect on how the individual behaves. It has been argued that culture teaches its members what to believe are the consequences of a specific action (cognitive), and how the individuals should feel about those consequences or about the actions themselves (emotional/motivational).

[D.G.M.]

Motor systems   Those portions of nervous systems that regulate and control the contractile activity of muscle and the secretory activity of glands. Muscles and glands are the two types of organ by which an organism reacts to its environment; together they constitute the machinery of behavior. Cardiac muscle and some smooth muscle and glandular structures can function independently of the nervous system but in a poorly coordinated fashion. Skeletal muscle activity, however, is entirely dependent on neural control. Destruction of the nerves supplying skeletal muscles results in paralysis, an inability to move. The somatic motor system includes those regions of the central nervous system involved in controlling the contraction of skeletal muscles in a manner appropriate to environmental conditions and internal states. See GLAND; MUSCLE.

Skeletal muscle. The nerve supply to skeletal muscles of the limbs and trunk is derived from large nerve cells called motoneurons, whose cell bodies are located in the ventral horn of the spinal cord. Muscles of the face and head are innervated by motoneurons in the brainstem. The axons of the motoneurons traverse the ventral spinal roots (or the appropriate cranial nerve roots) and reach the muscles via peripheral nerve trunks. In the muscle, the axon of every motoneuron divides repeatedly into many terminal branches, each of which innervates a single muscle fiber. The region of innervation, called the neuromuscular junction or motor end plate, is a secure synaptic contact between the motoneuron terminal and the muscle fiber membrane. See SYNAPTIC TRANSMISSION.

Since synaptic transmission at the neuromuscular junction is very secure, an action potential in the motoneuron will produce contraction of every muscle fiber that it contacts. For this reason, the motoneuron and all the fibers it innervates form a functional

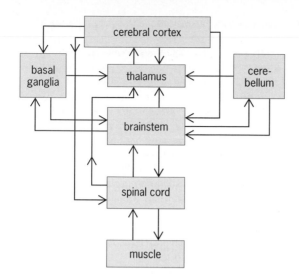

Schematic diagram of the major components of the vertebrate motor systems. Arrows indicate the main neural connections between regions.

unit called the motor unit. The number of muscle fibers in a single motor unit may be as small as six (for intrinsic eye muscles) or over 700 (for motor units of large limb muscles). In general, muscles involved in delicate rapid movements have fewer muscle fibers per motor unit than large muscles concerned with gross movements.

Components of skeletal motor system. Motoneurons are activated by nerve impulses arriving through many different neural pathways. Some of their neural input originates in peripheral receptor organs located in the muscles themselves, or in receptors in skin or joints. Many muscle receptors discharge in proportion to muscle length or tension; such receptors have relatively potent connections to motoneurons, either direct monosynaptic connections or relays via one or more interneurons. Similarly, stimulation of skin and joints, particularly painful stimulation, can strongly affect motoneurons. Such simple segmental pathways constitute the basis for spinal reflexes. The other major source of input to motoneurons arises from supraspinal centers. The illustration shows the main nervous system centers involved in controlling the input to motoneurons.

Segmental circuits. At the spinal level, the motoneurons and muscles have a close reciprocal connection. Afferent connections from receptors in the muscles return sensory feedback to the same motoneurons which contract the muscle. Connections to motoneurons of synergist and antagonist muscles are sufficiently potent and appropriately arranged to subserve a variety of reflexes. In animals with all higher centers removed, these segmental circuits may function by themselves to produce simple reflex responses. Under normal conditions, however, the activity of segmental circuits is largely controlled by supraspinal centers. Descending tracts arise from two major supraspinal centers: the cerebral cortex and the brainstem.

Brainstem. The brainstem, which includes the medulla and pons, is a major and complex integrating center which combines signals descending from other higher centers, as well as afferent input arising from peripheral receptors. The descending output from brainstem neurons affects motor and sensory cells in the spinal cord. Brainstem centers considerably extend the motor capacity of an animal beyond the stereotyped reflex reactions mediated by the spinal cord. In contrast to segmental reflexes, these motor responses involve coordination of muscles over the whole body. Another major motor function of the brainstem is postural control, exerted via the vestibular nuclei of the ear.

Besides neurons controlling limb muscles, the brainstem also contains a number of important neural centers involved in regulating eye movements. These include motor neurons of the eye muscles and various types of interneurons that mediate the effects of vestibular and visual input on eye movement.

Cerebellum. Another important coordinating center in the motor system is the cerebellum, an intricately organized network of cells closely interconnected with the brainstem. The cerebellum receives a massive inflow of sensory signals from peripheral receptors in muscles, tendons, joints, and skin, as well as from visual, auditory, and vestibular receptors. Higher centers, particularly the cerebral cortex, also provide extensive input to the cerebellum via pontine brainstem relays. The integration of this massive amount of neural input in the cerebellum somehow serves to smooth out the intended movements and coordinate the activity of muscles. Without the cerebellum, voluntary movements become erratic, and the animal has difficulty accurately terminating and initiating responses. The output of the cerebellum affects primarily brainstem nuclei, but it also provides important signals to the cerebral cortex.

Basal ganglia. At another level of motor system are the basal ganglia. These massive subcortical nuclei receive descending input connections from all parts of the cerebral cortex. Their output projections send recurrent information to the cerebral cortex via the thalamus, and their other major output is to brainstem cells.

Cerebral cortex. At the highest level of the nervous system is the cerebral cortex, which exerts control over the entire motor system. The cerebral cortex performs two kinds of motor function: certain motor areas exert relatively direct control over segmental motoneurons, via a direct corticospinal pathway, the pyramidal tract, and also through extrapyramidal connections via supraspinal motor centers. The second function, performed in various cortical association areas, involves the programming of movements appropriate in the context of sensory information, and the initiation of voluntary movements on the basis of central states. Cortical language areas, for example, contain the circuitry essential to generate the intricate motor patterns of speech. Limb movements to targets in extrapersonal space appear to be programmed in parietal association cortex. Such cortical areas involved in motor programming exert their effects via corticocortical connections to the motor cortex, and by descending connections to subcortical centers, principally basal ganglia and brainstem.

As indicated in the illustration, the motor centers are all heavily interconnected, so none really functions in isolation. In fact, some of these connections are so massive that they may form functional loops, acting as subsystems within the motor system. For example, most regions of the cerebral cortex have close reciprocal interconnections with underlying thalamic nuclei, and the corticothalamic system may be considered to form a functional unit. Another example is extensive connection from cerebral cortex to pontine regions of the brainstem, controlling cells that project to the cerebellum, which in turn projects back via the thalamus to the cerebral cortex. Such functional loops are at least as important in understanding motor coordination as the individual centers themselves. *See* BRAIN; NERVOUS SYSTEM (VERTEBRATE).   [E.E.F.]

Mumps   An acute contagious viral disease, characterized chiefly by enlargement of the parotid glands (parotitis).

Besides fever, the chief signs and symptoms are the direct mechanical effect of swelling on glands or organs where the virus localizes. One or both parotids may swell rapidly, producing severe pain when the mouth is opened. In orchitis, the testicle is inflamed but is enclosed by an inelastic membrane and cannot swell; pressure necrosis produces atrophy, and if both testicles are affected, sterility may result. The ovary may enlarge, without sequelae.

An attenuated live virus vaccine can induce immunity without parotitis. It is recommended particularly for adults exposed to infected children, for students in boarding schools and colleges, and for military troops.   [J.L.Me.]

Muscle   The tissue in the body in which cellular contractility has become most apparent. Almost all forms of protoplasm exhibit some degree of contractility, but in muscle fibers specialization has led to the preeminence of this property. In vertebrates three major types of muscle are recognized: smooth, cardiac, and skeletal.

Smooth muscle. Smooth muscle, also designated visceral and sometimes involuntary, is the simplest type. These muscles consist of elongated fusiform cells which contain a central oval nucleus. The size of such fibers varies greatly, from a few micrometers up to 0.02 in. (0.5 mm) in length. These fibers contract relatively slowly and have the ability to maintain contraction for a long time. Smooth muscle forms the major contractile elements of the viscera, especially those of the respiratory and digestive tracts, and the blood vessels. Smooth muscle fibers in the skin regulate heat loss from the body. Those in the walls of various ducts and tubes in the body act to move the contents to their destinations, as in the biliary system, ureters, and reproductive tubes.

Smooth muscle is usually arranged in sheets or layers, commonly oriented in different directions. The major physiological properties of these muscles are their intrinsic ability to contract spontaneously and their dual regulation by the autonomic nerves of the sympathetic and parasympathetic systems. See AUTONOMIC NERVOUS SYSTEM.

Cardiac muscle. Cardiac muscle has many properties in common with smooth muscle; for example, it is innervated by the autonomic system and retains the ability to contract spontaneously. Presumably, cardiac muscle evolved as a specialized type from the general smooth muscle of the circulatory vessels. Its rhythmic contraction begins early in embryonic development and continues until death. Variations in the rate of contraction are induced by autonomic regulation and by many other local and systemic factors.

The cardiac fiber, like smooth muscle, has a central nucleus, but the cell is elongated and not symmetrical. It is a syncytium, a multinuclear cell or a multicellular structure without cell walls. Histologically, cardiac muscle has cross-striations very similar to those of skeletal muscle, and dense transverse bands, the intercalated disks, which occur at short intervals. See HEART (VERTEBRATE).

Skeletal muscle. Skeletal muscle is also called striated, somatic, and voluntary muscle, depending on whether the description is based on the appearance, the location, or the innervation. The individual cells or fibers are distinct from one another and vary greatly in size from over 6 in. (15 cm) in length to less than 0.04 in. (1 mm). These fibers do not ordinarily branch, and they are surrounded by a complex membrane, the sarcolemma. Within each fiber are many nuclei; thus it is actually a syncytium formed by the fusion of many precursor cells.

The transverse striations of skeletal muscle form a characteristic pattern of light and dark bands within which are narrower bands. These bands are dependent upon the arrangement of the two sets of sliding filaments and the connections between them. See MUSCLE PROTEINS; MUSCULAR SYSTEM.   [W.J.B.]

Muscle proteins   Specialized proteins in muscle cells are the building blocks of the structures constituting the moving machinery of muscle. They are disposed in

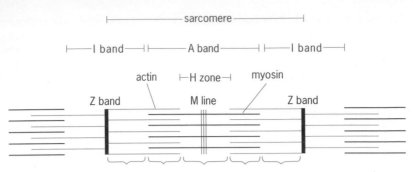

Banding pattern of a sarcomere, showing arrangement of myosin and actin molecules. A, I, and Z indicate bands.

myofilaments which are discernible by electron microscopy. These myofilaments are of two kinds, and their regular arrangement within the cell gives the striated pattern to skeletal muscle fibers (see illustration). It is recognized that the sliding of the two sets of filaments relative to each other is the molecular basis of muscle contraction. To understand the ultimate mechanism that causes the movement of these filaments (relative to each other), it is necessary to consider the features of the individual molecules making up these filaments. Evidence has been accumulating that practically all nonmuscle cells, although lacking the filaments of muscle, contain proteins similar to those found in muscle; these proteins are likely to be involved in cell motility and in determining properties of cell membranes.

Molecules of myosin, amounting to about 60% of the total muscle protein, are arranged in filaments occupying the central zone of each segment (sarcomere) or the fibril, the A band. Myosin is an elongated molecule made up of two intertwined heavy peptide chains (molecular weight of about 200,000) whose ends form two separate globular structures. The intertwined portion forms a rigid rod; each of the two globular portions (heads) contains a center capable of combining with, and splitting off, the terminal phosphate of adenosine triphosphate (ATP); ATP is the ultimate source of energy for muscle contraction. Each globular head can combine with actin.

The chief constituent of the filaments originating in the Z band of each sarcomere is actin. Actin filaments are made up of globular units in a double helix; there are 13 to 15 of these units in each strand for every complete turn of this helix.

These two proteins, or rather protein complexes, are associated with the actin filaments. Tropomyosin is an α-helical protein containing two intertwined polypeptide chains that extend over about seven globular actin units. Each tropomyosin molecule is associated with one troponin molecule, which in turn consists of three different types of subunits. In contrast to the tropomyosin molecule, the troponin complex and its subunits are thought to be essentially spherical in shape. Both tropomyosin and troponin are required to make the interaction of actin and myosin sensitive to calcium ions.

A great deal of information has come to light concerning the process by which the interaction between actin and myosin is regulated in the living cell. In higher organisms troponin and tropomyosin participate in this regulation. In the presence of these proteins the combination of actin and myosin cannot take place. However, if a small amount of ionized calcium is present, the inhibitory effect of the tropomyosin-troponin system is reversed, and the interaction with actin and myosin becomes fully effective. *See* MOTOR SYSTEMS; MUSCLE.   [J.Ge.]

Muscular system The muscular system consists of muscular cells, the contractile elements with the specialized property of exerting tension during contraction, and associated connective tissues. The three morphologic types of muscles are voluntary muscle, involuntary muscle, and cardiac muscle. The voluntary, striated, or skeletal muscles are involved with general posture and movements of the head, body, and limbs. The involuntary, nonstriated, or smooth muscles are the muscles of the walls of hollow organs of the digestive, circulatory, respiratory, and reproductive systems, and other visceral structures. Cardiac muscle is the intrinsic muscle tissue of the heart. *See* MUSCLE.

Anatomy. Muscle groups are particularly distinct in elasmobranchs and other primitive fishes, and they are generally defined on the basis of their embryonic origin in these animals. Two major groups of skeletal muscles are recognized, somatic (parietal) muscles, which develop from the myotomes, and branchiomeric muscles, which develop in the pharyngeal wall from lateral plate mesoderm. The somatic musculature is subdivided into axial muscles, which develop directly from the myotomes and lie along the longitudinal axis of the body, and appendicular muscles, which develop within the limb bud from mesoderm derived phylogenetically as buds from the myotomes.

The vertebrate muscular system is the largest of the organ systems, making up 35–40% of the body weight in humans. The movement of vertebrates is accomplished exclusively by muscular action, and muscles play the major role in transporting materials within the body. Muscles also help to tie the bones of the skeleton together and supplement the skeleton in supporting the body against gravity. *See* SKELETAL SYSTEM.

Most of the axial musculature is located along the back and flanks of the body, and this part is referred to as trunk musculature. But anteriorly the axial musculature is modified and assigned to other subgroups. Certain of the occipital and neck myotomes form the hypobranchial muscles, and the most anterior myotomes form the extrinsic ocular muscles.

The hypaxial musculature of tetrapods can be subdivided into three groups: (1) a subvertebral (hyposkeletal) group located ventral to the transverse processes and lateral to the centra of the vertebrae, (2) the flank muscles forming the lateral part of the body wall, and (3) the ventral abdominal muscles located on each side of the midventral line. The subvertebral musculature assists the epaxial muscles in the support and movement of the vertebral column. Most of the flank musculature takes the form of broad, thin sheets of muscle that form much of the body wall and support the viscera. The midventral hypaxial musculature in all tetrapods consists of the rectus abdominis, a longitudinal muscle on each side of the midline that extends from the pelvic region to the anterior part of the trunk.

The hypobranchial musculature extends from the pectoral girdle forward along the ventral surface of the neck and pharynx to the hyoid arch, chin, and into the tongue. It is regarded as a continuation of part of the hypaxial trunk musculature.

Limb muscles are often classified as intrinsic if they lie entirely within the confines of the appendage and girdle, and extrinsic if they extend from the girdle or appendage to other parts of the body. In fishes, movements of the paired fins are not complex or powerful and the appendicular muscles in the strictest sense are morphologically simple. In terrestrial vertebrates, the limbs become the main organs for support and locomotion, and the appendicular muscles become correspondingly powerful and complex. The muscles are too numerous to describe individually, but they can be sorted into dorsal and ventral groups, because tetrapod muscles originate embryonically in piscine fashion from a dorsal and a ventral premuscular mass within the limb bud. In general, the ventral muscles, which also spread onto the anterior surface of the girdle and appendage, act to protract and adduct the limb and to flex its distal segments; the dorsal

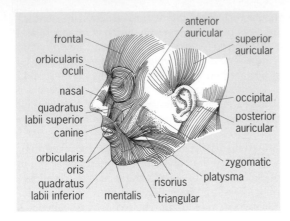

Fig. 1. Human facial muscles. (*After H. W. Rand, The Chordates, Blakiston, 1950*)

muscles, which also extend onto the posterior surface of the girdle and appendage, have the opposite effects (retraction, abduction, and extension). The limb muscles also serve as flexible ties or braces that can fix the bones at a joint and support the body.

Flight in birds has entailed a considerable modification of the musculature of the pectoral region. As one example, the ventral adductor muscles are exceedingly large and powerful, and the area from which they arise is increased by the enlargement of the sternum and the evolution of a large sternal keel. Not only does a ventral muscle, the pectoralis, play a major role in the downstroke of the humerus, but a ventral muscle, the supracoracoideus, is active in the upstroke as well.

In a number of terrestrial vertebrates, particularly amniotes, certain of the more superficial skeletal muscles of the body have spread out beneath the skin and inserted into it. These may be described as integumentary muscles. Integumentary muscles are particularly well developed in mammals and include the facial muscles (Fig. 1) and platysma, derived from the hyoid musculature, and often a large cutaneous trunci. The last is derived from the pectoralis and latissimus dorsi and fans out beneath the skin of the trunk. The twitching of the skin of an ungulate is caused by this muscle.

Muscle mechanics. Many of the bones serve as lever arms, and the contractions of muscles are forces acting on these arms (Fig. 2). The joint, of course, is the fulcrum and it is at one end of the lever. The length of the force arm is the perpendicular distance from the fulcrum to the line of action of the muscle; the length of the work arm is the perpendicular distance from the fulcrum to the point of application of the power generated in the lever. Compactness of the body and physiological properties of the muscle necessitates that a muscle attach close to the fulcrum; therefore, the force arm is considerably shorter than the work arm. Most muscles are at a mechanical disadvantage, for they must generate forces greater than the work to be done, but an advantage of this is that a small muscular excursion can induce a much greater movement at the end of the lever.

Slight shifts in the attachments of a muscle that bring it toward or away from the fulcrum, and changes in the length of the work arm, can alter the relationship between force and amount or speed of movement.

In general, the force of a muscle is inversely related to the amount and speed of movement that it can cause. Certain patterns of the skeleton and muscles are adapted for extensive, fast movement at the expense of force, whereas others are adapted for force at the expense of speed. In the limb of a horse, which is adapted for long strides and speed, the muscles that move the limb insert close to the fulcrum and the

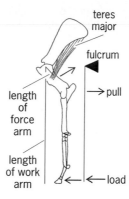

teres
major

fulcrum

pull

length
of
force
arm

length
of work
arm

load

Fig. 2. A typical vertebrate lever system.

appendage is long. This provides a short force arm but a very long work arm to the lever system (Fig. 2). In the front leg of a mole, which is adapted for powerful digging, the distance from the fulcrum to the insertion of the muscles is relatively greater and the length of the appendage is less, with the result that the length of the force arm is increased relative to the length of the work arm.   [W.F.W.]

Mushroom   A macroscopic fungus with a fruiting body (also known as a sporocarp). Approximately 14% (10,000) described species of fungi are considered mushrooms. Mushrooms grow aboveground or underground. They have a fleshy or non-fleshy texture. Many are edible, and only a small percentage are poisonous.

Mushrooms reproduce via microscopic spheres (spores) that are roughly comparable to the seeds of higher plants. Spores are produced in large numbers on specialized structures in or on the fruiting body. Spores that land on a suitable medium absorb moisture, germinate, and produce hyphae that grow and absorb nutrients from the substratum. If suitable mating types are present and the mycelium (the threadlike filaments or hyphae that become interwoven) develops sufficiently to allow fruiting, the life cycle will continue. In nature, completion of the life cycle is dependent on many factors, including temperature, moisture and nutritional status of the substratum, and gas exchange capacity of the medium.

Fewer than 20 species of edible mushrooms are cultivated commercially. The most common cultivated mushroom is *Agaricus bisporus*, followed by the oyster mushroom (*Pleurotus* spp.). China is the leading mushroom-producing country; Japan leads the world in number of edible species cultivated commercially.

Mushrooms may be cultivated on a wide variety of substrates. They are grown from mycelium propagated on a base of steam-sterilized cereal grain. This grain and mycelium mixture is called spawn, which is used to seed mushroom substrata.

Mushrooms contain digestible crude protein, all essential amino acids, vitamins (especially provitamin D-2), and minerals; they are high in potassium and low in sodium, saturated fats, and calories. Although they cannot totally replace meat and other high-protein food in the diet, they can be considered an important dietary supplement and a health food.

Fungi have been used for their medicinal properties for over 2000 years. Although there remains an element of folklore in the use of mushrooms in health and medicine, several important drugs have been isolated from mushroom fruiting bodies and mycelium. The best-known drugs obtained are lentinan from *L. edodes*, grifolin from *Grifola frondosa*, and krestin from *Coriolus versicolor*. These compounds are protein-bound polysaccharides or long chains of glucose, found in the cell walls, and function as antitumor immunomodulatory drugs. *See* FUNGI; MEDICAL MYCOLOGY.

[D.M.C.]

Mutagens and carcinogens   A mutagen is a substance or agent that induces heritable change in cells or organisms. A carcinogen is a substance that induces unregulated growth processes in cells or tissues of multicellular animals, leading to cancer. Although mutagen and carcinogen are not synonymous terms, the ability of a substance to induce mutations and its ability to induce cancer are strongly correlated. Mutagenesis refers to processes that result in genetic change, and carcinogenesis (the processes of tumor development) may result from mutagenic events. *See* MUTATION; RADIATION BIOLOGY.

A mutation is any change in a cell or in an organism that is transmitted to subsequent generations. Mutations can occur spontaneously or be induced by chemical or physical agents. The cause of mutations is usually some form of damage to DNA or chromosomes that results in some change that can be seen or measured. However, damage can occur in a segment of DNA that is a noncoding region and thus will not result in a mutation. Mutations may or may not be harmful, depending upon which function is affected. They may occur in either somatic or germ cells. Mutations that occur in germ cells may be transmitted to subsequent generations, whereas mutations in somatic cells are generally of consequence only to the affected individual.

Not all heritable changes result from damage to DNA. For example, in growth and differentiation of normal cells, major changes in gene expression occur and are transmitted to progeny cells through changes in the signals that control genes that are transcribed into ribonucleic acid (RNA). It is possible that chemicals and radiation alter these processes as well. When such an effect is seen in newborns, it is called teratogenic and results in birth defects that are not transmitted to the next generation. However, if the change is transmissible to progeny, it is a mutation, even though it might have arisen from an effect on the way in which the gene is expressed. Thus, chemicals can have somatic effects involving genes regulating cell growth that could lead to the development of cancer, without damaging DNA.

Cancer arises because of the loss of growth control by dearrangement of regulatory signals. Included in the phenotypic consequences of mutations are alterations in gene regulation brought about by changes either in the regulatory region or in proteins involved with coordinated cellular functions. Altered proteins may exhibit novel interactions with target substrates and thereby lose the ability to provide a regulatory function for the cell or impose altered functions on associated molecules. Through such a complex series of molecular interactions, changes occur in the growth properties of normal cells leading to cancer cells that are not responsive to normal regulatory controls and can eventually give rise to a visible neoplasm or tumor. While mutagens can give rise to neoplasms by a process similar to that described above, not all mutagens induce cancer and not all mutational events result in tumors.

The identification of certain specific types of genes, termed oncogenes, that appear to be causally involved in the neoplastic process has helped to focus mechanistic studies on carcinogenesis. Oncogenes can be classified into a few functionally different groups, and specific mutations in some of the genes have been identified and are believed to be critical in tumorigenesis. Tumor suppressor genes or antioncogenes provide a normal regulatory function; by mutation or other events, the loss of the function of these genes may release cells from normal growth-control processes, allowing them to begin the neoplastic process.

There are a number of methods and systems for identifying chemical mutagens. Mutations can be detected at a variety of genetic loci in very diverse organisms, including bacteria, insects, cultured mammalian cells, rodents, and humans. Spontaneous and induced mutations occur very infrequently, the estimated rate being less than 1 in 10,000 per gene per cell generation. This low mutation rate is probably the result of a combination of factors that include the relative inaccessibility of DNA to damaging agents and the ability of cellular processes to repair damage to DNA.

Factors that contribute to the difficulty in recognizing substances that may be carcinogenic to humans include the prevalence of cancer, the diversity of types of cancer, the generally late-life onset of most cancers, and the multifactorial nature of the disease process. Approximately 50 substances have been identified as causes of cancer in humans, but they probably account for only a small portion of the disease incidence. *See* CANCER (MEDICINE); HUMAN GENETICS; MUTATION; RADIATION BIOLOGY.   [R.W.T.]

Mutation   Any alteration capable of being replicated in the genetic material of an organism. When the alteration is in the nucleotide sequence of a single gene, it is referred to as gene mutation; when it involves the structures or number of the chromosomes, it is referred to as chromosome mutation, or rearrangement. Mutations may be recognizable by their effects on the phenotype of the organism (mutant).

Gene mutations. Two classes of gene mutations are recognized: point mutations and intragenic deletions. Two different types of point mutation have been described. In the first of these, one nucleic acid base is substituted for another. The second type of change results from the insertion of a base into, or its deletion from, the polynucleotide sequence. These mutations are all called sign mutations or frame-shift mutations because of their effect on the translation of the information of the gene. *See* NUCLEIC ACID.

More extensive deletions can occur within the gene which are sometimes difficult to distinguish from mutants which involve only one or two bases. In the most extreme case, all the informational material of the gene is lost.

A single-base alteration, whether a transition or a transversion, affects only the codon or triplet in which it occurs. Because of code redundancy, the altered triplet may still insert the same amino acid as before into the polypeptide chain, which in many cases is the product specified by the gene. Such DNA changes pass undetected. However, many base substitutions do lead to the insertion of a different amino acid, and the effect of this on the function of the gene product depends upon the amino acid and its importance in controlling the folding and shape of the enzyme molecule. Some substitutions have little or no effect, while others destroy the function of the molecule completely.

Single-base substitutions may sometimes lead not to a triplet which codes for a different amino acid but to the creation of a chain termination signal. Premature termination of translation at this point will lead to an incomplete and generally inactive polypeptide.

Sign mutations (adding or subtracting one or two bases to the nucleic acid base sequence of the gene) have a uniformly drastic effect on gene function. Because the bases of each triplet encode the information for each amino acid in the polypeptide product, and because they are read in sequence from one end of the gene to the other without any punctuation between triplets, insertion of an extra base or two bases will lead to translation out of register of the whole sequence distal to the insertion or deletion point. The polypeptide formed is at best drastically modified and usually fails to function at all. This sometimes is hard to distinguish from the effects of intragenic deletions. However, whereas extensive intragenic deletions cannot revert, the deletion of a single base can be compensated for by the insertion of another base at, or near, the site of the original change. *See* GENE; GENETIC CODE.

Chromosomal changes. Some chromosomal changes involve alterations in the quantity of genetic material in the cell nuclei, while others simply lead to the rearrangement of chromosomal material without altering its total amount. *See* CHROMOSOME.

Origins of mutations. Mutations can be induced by various physical and chemical agents or can occur spontaneously without any artificial treatment with known mutagenic agents.

Until the discovery of x-rays as mutagens, all the mutants studied were spontaneous in origin; that is, they were obtained without the deliberate application of any mutagen. Spontaneous mutations occur unpredictably, and among the possible factors responsible for them are tautomeric changes occurring in the DNA bases which alter their pairing characteristics, ionizing radiation from various natural sources, naturally occurring chemical mutagens, and errors in the action of the DNA-polymerizing and correcting enzymes.

Spontaneous chromosomal aberrations are also found infrequently. One way in which deficiencies and duplications may be generated is by way of the breakage-fusion-bridge cycle. During a cell division one divided chromosome suffers a break near its tip, and the sticky ends of the daughter chromatids fuse. When the centromere divides and the halves begin to move to opposite poles, a chromosome bridge is formed, and breakage may occur again along this strand. Since new broken ends are produced, this sequence of events can be repeated. Unequal crossing over is sometimes cited as a source of duplications and deficiencies, but it is probably less important than often suggested.

In the absence of mutagenic treatment, mutations are very rare. In 1927 H. J. Muller discovered that x-rays significantly increased the frequency of mutation in *Drosophila*. Subsequently, other forms of ionizing radiation, for example, gamma rays, beta particles, fast and thermal neutrons, and alpha particles, were also found to be effective. Ultraviolet light is also an effective mutagen. The wavelength most employed experimentally is 253.7 nm, which corresponds to the peak of absorption of nucleic acids.

Some of the chemicals which have been found to be effective as mutagens are the alkylating agents which attack guanine principally although not exclusively. The N7 portion appears to be a major target in the guanine molecule, although the O^6 alkylation product is probably more important mutagenically. Base analogs are incorporated into DNA in place of normal bases and produce mutations probably because there is a higher chance that they will mispair at replication. Nitrous acid, on the other hand, alters DNA bases in place. Adenine becomes hypoxanthine and cytosine becomes uracil. In both cases the deaminated base pairs differently from the parent base. A third deamination product, xanthine, produced by the deamination of guanine, appears to be lethal in its effect and not mutagenic. Chemicals which react with DNA to generate mutations produce a range of chemical reaction products not all of which have significance for mutagenesis.

Significance of mutations. Mutations are the source of genetic variability, upon which natural selection has worked to produce organisms adapted to their present environments. It is likely, therefore, that most new mutations will now be disadvantageous, reducing the degree of adaptation. Harmful mutations will be eliminated after being made homozygous or because the heterozygous effects reduce the fitness of carriers. This may take some generations, depending on the severity of their effects. Chromosome alterations may also have great significance in evolutionary advance. Duplications are, for example, believed to permit the accumulation of new mutational changes, some of which may prove useful at a later stage in an altered environment.

Rarely, mutations may occur which are beneficial: Drug yields may be enhanced in microorganisms; the characteristics of cereals can be improved. However, for the few mutations which are beneficial, many deleterious mutations must be discarded. Evidence suggests that the metabolic conditions in the treated cell and the specific activities of repair enzymes may sometimes promote the expression of some types of mutation rather than others. *See* DEOXYRIBONUCLEIC ACID (DNA). [B.J.K.]

Mutualism An interaction between two species that benefits both. Individuals that interact with mutualists experience higher sucess than those that do not. Hence, behaving mutualistically is advantageous to the individual, and it does not require any concern for the well-being of the partner. At one time, mutualisms were thought to be rare curiosities primarily of interest to natural historians. However, it is now believed that every species is involved in one or more mutualisms. Mutualisms are thought to lie at the root of phenomena as diverse as the origin of the eukaryotic cell, the diversification of flowering plants, and the pattern of elevated species diversity in tropical forests.

Mutualisms generally involve an exchange of substances or services that organisms would find difficult or impossible to obtain for themselves. For instance, *Rhizobium* bacteria found in nodules on the roots of many legume (bean) species fix atmospheric nitrogen into a form (NH_3) that can be taken up by plants. The plant provides the bacteria with carbon in the form of dicarboxylic acids. The carbon is utilized by the bacteria as energy for nitrogen fixation. Consequently, leguminous plants often thrive in nitrogen-poor environments where other plants cannot persist. Another well-known example is lichens, in which fungi take up carbon fixed during photosynthesis of their algae associates.

A second benefit offered within some mutualisms is transportation. Prominent among these mutualisms is biotic pollination, in which certain animals visit flowers to obtain resources and return a benefit by transporting pollen between the flowers they visit. A final benefit is protection from one's enemies. For example, ants attack the predators and parasites of certain aphids in exchange for access to the aphids' carbohydrate-rich excretions (honeydew).

Another consideration about mutualisms is whether they are symbiotic. Two species found in intimate physical association for most or all of their lifetimes are considered to be in symbiosis. Not all symbioses are mutualistic; symbioses may benefit both, one, or neither of the partners.

Mutualisms can also be characterized as obligate or facultative (depending on whether or not the partners can survive without each other), and as specialized or generalized (depending on how many species can confer the benefit in question).

Two features are common to most mutualisms. First, mutualisms are highly variable in time and space. Second, mutualisms are susceptible to cheating. Cheaters can be individuals of the mutualist species that profit from their partners' actions without offering anything in return, or else other species that invade the mutualism for their own gain.

Mutualism has considerable practical significance. Certain mutualisms play central roles in humans' ability to feed the growing population. It has been estimated that half the food consumed is the product of biotic pollination. *See* ECOLOGY; PLANT PATHOLOGY.

[J.L.Br.]

Mycobacterial diseases Diseases caused by mycobacteria, a diffuse group of acid-fast, rod-shaped bacteria in the genus *Mycobacterium*. The two most important species are *M. tuberculosis* (the cause of tuberculosis) and *M. leprae* (the cause of leprosy); other species have been called by several names, particularly the atypical mycobacteria or the nontuberculous mycobacteria. *See* LEPROSY; TUBERCULOSIS.

These bacteria are classified according to their pigment formation, rate of growth, and colony morphology. The most commonly involved disease site is the lungs. Nontuberculous mycobacteria are transmitted from natural sources in the environment, rather than from person to person, and thus are not a public health hazard. The diagnosis of disease caused by nontuberculous mycobacteria can be difficult, since colonization or contamination of specimens may be present rather than true infection. Pulmonary disease resembling tuberculosis is a most important manifestation of disease caused by nontuberculous mycobacteria. The symptoms and chest x-ray findings are similar to those seen in tuberculosis. *Mycobacterium kansasii* and *M. avium intracellulare* are the most common pathogens. The disease usually occurs in middle-aged men and women with some type of chronic coexisting lung disease. The pathogenic mechanisms are obscure. Pulmonary infections due to *M. kansasii* can be treated successfully with chemotherapy. The treatment of pulmonary infections due to *M. avium intracellulare* complex is difficult.

Chronic infection involving joints and bones, bursae, synovia, and tendon sheaths can be caused by various species.

Localized abscesses due to *M. fortuitum* or *M. chelonei* can occur after trauma, after surgical incision, or at injection sites. The usual treatment is surgical incision. The most common soft tissue infection is caused by *M. marinum*, which may be introduced, following an abrasion or trauma, from handling fish or fish tanks, or around a swimming pool. Treatment is surgical. *Mycobacterium ulcerans* causes a destructive skin infection in tropical areas of the world. It is treated by wide excision and skin grafting.

Disseminated *M. avium intracellulare* is one of the opportunistic infections seen in the acquired immune deficiency syndrome (AIDS). In individuals with AIDS, the organism has been cultured from lung, brain, cerebrospinal fluid, liver, spleen, intestinal mucosa, and bone marrow. No treatment has yet been effective in this setting. *See* ACQUIRED IMMUNE DEFICIENCY SYNDROME (AIDS).   [G.M.L.; L.B.R.]

Mycology   The study of organisms classified under the kingdom Fungi. Common names for some of these organisms are mushrooms, boletes, bracket or shelf fungi, powdery mildew, bread molds, yeasts, puffballs, morels, stinkhorns, truffles, smuts, and rusts. Fungi are found in every ecological niche. Mycologists estimate that there are 1.5 million species of fungi, with only 70,000 species now described. Fungi typically have a filamentous-branched somatic structure surrounded by thick cell walls known as hyphae. The phyla considered to be true fungi are Chytridiomycota, Zygomycota, Ascomycota, and Basidiomycota. Other phyla that sometimes are included as true fungi are Myxomycota, Dictyosteliomycota, Acrasiomycota, and Plasmodiophoromycota. *See* FUNGAL BIOTECHNOLOGY; FUNGAL ECOLOGY; FUNGAL GENETICS; FUNGI; MEDICAL MYCOLOGY; PLANT PATHOLOGY.   [S.C.Jo.]

Mycoplasmas   The smallest prokaryotic microorganisms that are able to grow on cell-free artificial media. Their genome size is also among the smallest recorded in prokaryotes, about 5×10^8 to 10^9 daltons. The mycoplasmas differ from almost all other prokaryotes in lacking a rigid cell wall and in their incapability to synthesize peptidoglycan, an essential component of the bacterial cell wall.

Taxonomically, the mycoplasmas are assigned to a distinct class, the Mollicutes, containing two orders, Mycoplasmatales and Acholeplasmatales. The distinction between the orders is based primarily on differences in nutritional criteria: members of the Mycoplasmatales require cholesterol or other sterols for growth whereas those of the second order do not. The term mycoplasmas is generally used as the vernacular or trivial name for all members of the class Mollicutes, irrespective of the classification in a particular genus.

The mycoplasmas are almost ubiquitous in nature. Several species are important pathogens of humans, animals and plants, while others constitute part of the normal microbial flora of, for example, the upper respiratory and lower urogenital tracts of humans. *Mycoplasma pneumoniae* was found to be the cause of cold agglutinin-associated primary atypical pneumonia. This disease is particularly frequent in the 5–15-year age group; it is probably endemic almost all over the world and often reaches epidemic proportions at intervals of 4 to 5 years.

Mycoplasmas are generally highly resistant to benzyl penicillin and other antibiotics which act by interfering with the biosynthesis of peptidoglycan. They are usually susceptible to antibiotics that specifically inhibit protein synthesis in prokaryotes, such as tetracyclines and chloramphenicol. Susceptibility to other antibiotics, such as erythromycin and other macrolides, is variable. *See* ANTIBIOTIC; BACTERIAL PHYSIOLOGY AND METABOLISM; PLANT PATHOLOGY; PNEUMONIA.   [E.A.F.]

Mycorrhizae   Dual organs of absorption that are formed when symbiotic fungi inhabit healthy absorbing organs (roots, rhizomes, or thalli) of most terrestrial plants and many aquatics and epiphytes.

Mycorrhizae appear in the earliest fossil record of terrestrial plant roots. Roughly 80% of the nearly 10,000 plant species that have been examined are mycorrhizal. Present-day plants that normally lack mycorrhizae are generally evolutionarily advanced. It has been inferred that primitive plants evolved with a symbiosis between fungi and rhizoids or roots as a means to extract nutrients and water from soil. The degree of dependence varies between species or groups of plants. In absolute dependence, characteristic of perennial, terrestrial plants, the host requires mycorrhizae to survive. Some plants are facultative; they may form mycorrhizae but do not always require them. This group includes many of the world's more troublesome weeds. A minority of plant species characteristically lack mycorrhizae, so far as is known, including many aquatics, epiphytes, and annual weeds.

The three major types of mycorrhizae differ in structural details but have many functions in common. The fungus colonizes the cortex of the host root and grows its filaments (hyphae) into surrounding soil from a few centimeters to a meter or more. The hyphae absorb nutrients and water and transport them to host roots. The fungi thus tap far greater volumes of soil at a relatively lower energy cost than the roots could on their own. Moreover, many, if not all, mycorrhizal fungi produce extracellular enzymes and organic acids that release immobile elements such as phosphorus and zinc from clay particles, or phosphorus and nitrogen bound in organic matter. The fungi are far more physiologically capable in extracting or recycling nutrients in this way than the rootlets themselves.

Mycorrhizal fungi are relatively poorly competent in extracting carbon from organic matter. They derive energy from host-photosynthesized carbohydrates. Hosts also provide vitamins and other growth regulators that the fungi need.

The major types are ectomycorrhizae, vesicular-arbuscular mycorrhizae, and ericoid mycorrhizae. Ectomycorrhizae are the most readily observed type. Ectomycorrhizal hosts strongly depend on mycorrhizae to survive. Relatively few in number of species, they nonetheless dominate most forests outside the tropics. Vesicular-arbuscular mycorrhizae (sometimes simply termed arbuscular mycorrhizae) form with the great majority of terrestrial herbaceous plant species plus nearly all woody perennials that are not ectomycorrhizal. Vesicular-arbuscular mycorrhizal hosts range from strongly mycorrhiza-dependent, especially the woody perennials, to faculative, as are many grasses.

Ericoid mycorrhizae are restricted to the Ericales, the heath order. The hosts are strongly mycorrhiza-dependent. Though relatively few in number, heath species dominate large areas around the world and are common understory plants in many forests. Other mycorrhiza types include those special for the Orchidaceae (orchids) and Gentianaceae (gentians). *See* ASCOMYCOTA.

The succession of plants from pioneering through seral to climax communities is governed by availability of mycorrhizal propagules. When catastrophic fire, erosion, or clearcutting reduce the availability of mycorrhizal fungi in the soil, plants dependent on those fungi will have difficulty becoming established. Each mycorrhizal fungus has its own array of physiological characteristics. Some are especially proficient at releasing nutrients bound in organic matter, some produce more effective antibiotics or growth regulators than others, and some are more active in cool, hot, wet, or dry times of year than others. Healthy plant communities or crops typically harbor diverse populations of mycorrhizal fungal species. This diversity, evolved over a great expanse of time, is a hallmark of thriving ecosystems. Factors that reduce this diversity also reduce the resilience of ecosystems.

Mycorrhizal inoculation of plants in nurseries, orchards, and fields has succeeded in many circumstances, resulting in improved survival and productivity of the inoculated plants. Inoculation with selected fungi is especially important for restoring degraded sites or introducing exotics. Because ectomycorrhizal fungi include many premier edibles such as truffles, seedlings can also be inoculated to establish orchards for production of edible fungi. *See* FUNGI.   [J.M.Tr.]

Mycotoxin   Any of the mold-produced substances that may be injurious to vertebrates upon ingestion, inhalation, or skin contact. The diseases they cause, known as mycotoxicoses, need not involve the toxin-producing fungus. Diagnostic features characterizing mycotoxicoses are the following: the disease is not transmissible; drug and antibiotic treatments have little or no effect; in field outbreaks the disease is often seasonal; the outbreak is usually associated with a specific foodstuff; and examination of the suspected food or foodstuff reveals signs of fungal activity.

The earliest recognized mycotoxicoses were human diseases. Ergotism, or St. Anthony's fire, results from eating rye infected with *Claviceps purpurea*. Yellow rice disease, a complex of human toxicoses, is caused by several *Penicillium islandicum* mycotoxins. World attention was directed toward the mycotoxin problem with the discovery of the aflatoxins in England in 1961. The aflatoxins, a family of mycotoxins produced by *Aspergillus flavus* and *A. parasiticus*, can induce both acute and chronic toxicological effects in vertebrates. Aflatoxin B_1, the most potent of the group, is toxic, carcinogenic, mutagenic, and teratogenic. Major agricultural commodities that are often contaminated by aflatoxins include corn, peanuts, rice, cottonseed, and various tree nuts. *See* AFLATOXIN; ERGOT AND ERGOTISM.   [A.Ci.; M.Kl.]

Myxomycota   Organisms that are classified in the kingdom Fungi and given the class name Myxomycetes, following the rules of botanical nomenclature; or classified in the kingdom Protista at various taxonomic ranks, as class Mycetozoa, following the rules of zoological nomenclature. Evolutionary origins are controversial, but many now believe, based on DNA sequencing techniques, that the Myxomycetes diverge early on the tree of life in the region where other protists are found.

The class consists of 3 subclasses, 6 orders, approximately 57 genera, and 600 species. Subclasses Ceratiomyxomycetidae, Myxogastromycetidae, and Stemonitomycetidae are distinguished by the type of sporophore development, type of plasmodium, and method of bearing spores. The various orders, families, genera, and species are distinguished by characteristics of the fruiting bodies such as spore color, peridium, capillitium, calcium carbonate, or columella.

Myxomycetes begin to appear in May and fruit throughout the summer until October in the north temperate regions. Many species are universally distributed and live in moist and dark places on decaying organic matter. Some species are restricted to more specialized habitats.

Spores are released from the fruiting bodies when disturbed and fall onto the substratum where, when water is present, they germinate and release protoplasts. The protoplasts may develop into either a myxamoeba or a flagellated swarm cell, both of which are haploid and behave like gametes (sex cells). The haploid (monoploid) gametes fuse in pairs forming diploid zygotes, which then divide mitotically without subsequent cell division, resulting in the formation of a multinucleated, free-living mass of unwalled protoplasm called the plasmodium. The diploid plasmodium is representative of the slime stage, and hence the common names sometimes used for this group of organisms include plasmodial, acellular, or true slime molds. The plasmodia ingest food as particulate matter (usually bacteria) by engulfment and are capable of growing to over 70 cm in diameter.

The separate stages in their life cycle make myxomycetes ideal organisms to study basic biological problems, ranging through protoplasmic streaming, the mitotic cycle, morphogenesis, aging, and cell division in cancerous cells. *See* EUMYCOTA.   [H.W.K.]

N

Nemata   A phylum of unsegmented or pseudosegmented (any superficial annulation limited to the cuticle) bilaterally symmetrical worms with a basically circular cross section. The body is covered by a noncellular cuticle. The cylindrical body is usually bluntly rounded anteriorly and tapering posteriorly. The body cannot be easily divided into head, neck, and trunk or tail, although a region posterior to the anus is generally referred to as the tail. The oral opening is terminal (rarely subterminal) and followed by the stoma, esophagus, intestine, and rectum which opens through a subterminal anus. Females have separate genital and digestive tract openings. In males the tubular reproductive system joins posteriorly with the digestive tract to form a cloaca. The sexes are separate and the gonads may be paired or unpaired. Females may be oviparous or ovoviviporous.

Adult nematodes are extremely variable in size, ranging from less than 0.012 in. (0.3 mm) to over 26 ft (8 m). Nematodes are generally colorless except for food in the intestinal tract or for those few species which have eyespots.

Reproduction among nematodes is either amphimictic or parthenogenetic (rarely hermaphroditic). After the completion of oogenesis the chitinous egg shell is formed and a waxy vitelline membrane forms within the egg shell; in some nematodes the uterine cells deposit an additional outermost albuminoid coating. Upon deposition or within the female body, the egg proceeds through embryonation to the eellike first- or second-stage larva, but following eclosion the larva proceeds through four molts to adulthood. This represents a direct life cycle, but among parasites more diversity occurs.

Nemata comprise the third largest phylum of invertebrates, being exceeded only by Mollusca and Arthropoda. In sheer numbers of individuals they exceed all other metazoa. As parasites of animals they exceed all other helminths combined. Nematodes have been recovered from the deepest ocean floors to the highest mountains, from the Arctic to the Antarctic, and in soils as deep as roots can penetrate.   [A.R.M.]

Nematomorpha   A phylum of worms that was formerly considered to be a class of the phylum Aschelminthes; commonly called the hairworms, and closely allied to the nematodes. The adults are free-living in aquatic habitats, while the juveniles are parasitic in arthropods. The nematomorphs are found all over the world. They are divided into two classes, the Nectonematoidea and Gordioidea, with a total of 225 species. See NEMATA.

The body is long and slender with a maximum length of 5 ft (1.5 m) and a diameter of 0.02–0.12 in. (0.5–3 mm). The females are longer than the males. The posterior end may be rounded with a terminal cloaca, or it may form two or three lobes in a forklike structure. The body color is yellowish, brown, or almost black. The body wall consists of three layers: an outer, rather thick fibrous cuticle; an epidermis consisting of a single layer of cells; and innermost, a muscle layer with longitudinal fibers only.

The sexes are always separate, and the gonads are paired and stringlike extending the length of the body. The eggs are laid in water in strings, and the adults die after egg laying. When hatched, the larvae swim to an aquatic arthropod. They penetrate the body wall of the host by means of their characteristic proboscis, which is armed with hooks and three long stylets. The gradual development in the host lasts some months without any metamorphosis. When they are mature, the worms leave the host. [B.J.Mu.]

Neornithes   The subclass of Aves that contains all of the known birds other than those placed in the Archaeornithes. Comprising more than 30 orders, both fossil and living, its members are characterized by a bony, keeled sternum with fully developed powers of flapping flight (secondarily lost in a number of groups); a short tail with the caudal vertebrae fused into a single platelike pygostyle to which all tail feathers attach; a large fused pelvic girdle with a reversed pubis which is fused to a large synsacrum; and a large brain and eyes contained within a fused braincase. The jaws are specialized into a beak covered with a horny rhamphotheca; the upper jaw is kinetic, being either prokinetic or rhynchokinetic. Prokinesis refers to a bending zone at the base of the upper jaw, and rhynchokinesis to one within the upper jaw. A few fossil groups still possess teeth, but most fossil and all Recent birds have lost teeth. See ARCHAEORNITHES.

The Neornithes contains two superorders, the Odontognathae and the Neognathae. The Odontognathae, alternately known as the Odontornithes, may be an artificial group. Its members, which include the Cretaceous fossil orders Hesperornithiformes and Ichthyornithiformes, are united only by the presence of teeth in all species. The Neognathae contains the remaining modern birds, which have lost the teeth, and includes 26 orders. See AVES. [W.J.B.]

Nervous system (invertebrate)   All multicellular organisms have a nervous system, which may be defined as assemblages of cells specialized by their shape and function to act as the major coordinating organ of the body. Nervous tissue underlies the ability to sense the environment, to move and react to stimuli, and to generate and control all behavior of the organism. Compared to vertebrate nervous systems, invertebrate systems are somewhat simpler and can be more easily analyzed. Invertebrate nerve cells tend to be much larger and fewer in number than those of vertebrates. They are also easily accessible and less complexly organized; and they are hardy and amenable to revealing experimental manipulations. However, the rules governing the structure, chemistry, organization, and function of nervous tissue have been strongly conserved phylogenetically. Therefore, although humans and the higher vertebrates have unique behavioral and intellectual capabilities, the underlying physical-chemical principles of nerve cell activity and the strategies for organizing higher nervous systems are already present in the lower forms. Thus neuroscientists have taken advantage of the simpler nervous systems of invertebrates to acquire further understanding of those processes by which all brains function. See NERVOUS SYSTEM (VERTEBRATE).

Invertebrate and vertebrate nerve cells differ more in quantity, or degree, than in qualitative features. Aside from differences in size and numbers, the most striking difference is that invertebrate neurons have a unipolar shape, whereas most vertebrate neurons are multipolar. An additional general contrast between invertebrate and vertebrate nervous systems is that invertebrates tend to have more neurons displaced to the periphery (outside the central nervous system) and to perform more integrative and processing functions in the periphery. Vertebrates perform almost all their integration within the central nervous system, using interneurons. Invertebrate nervous systems also seem to have a greater potential for regrowth, regeneration, or repair after damage than do vertebrate nerve cells. Many invertebrates continue to add new nerve cells to their ganglia with age; vertebrates, in general, do not. Only vertebrate neurons have myelin sheaths, a specialized wrapping of glial membrane around axons, increasing their conduction speed. Invertebrates tend to enhance conduction velocity by using giant axons, particularly for certain escape responses.   [J.E.Bla.]

Nervous system (vertebrate)   A coordinating and integrating system which functions in the adaptation of an organism to its environment. An environmental stimulus causes a response in an organism when specialized structures, receptors, are excited. Excitations are conducted by nerves to effectors which act to adapt the organism to the changed conditions of the environment.

Comparative morphology. The brain of all vertebrates, including humans, consists of three basic divisions: prosencephalon, mesencephalon, and rhombencephalon (Fig. 1). The individual divisions or patterns of the brain do not function separately to bring about a final response; rather, each pattern acts on a common set of connections in the spinal cord.

Spinal patterns are the final common patterns used by all higher brain pathways to influence all organs of the body. These reflexes are divided into two basic patterns: the monosynaptic arc and the multisynaptic arc. The monosynaptic arc, or myotatic reflex, maintains tonus and posture in vertebrates and consists of two neurons, a sensory and a motor neuron.

The multisynaptic arc, or flexor reflex, is the pattern by which an animal withdraws a part of its body from a noxious stimulus. Both sensory neurons and internuncial neurons send information to brain centers. Coordinated limb movement is based on a connective pattern of neurons at the spinal level.

The structure of the spinal cord and its connections are basically similar among all vertebrates. The major evolutionary changes in the spinal cord have been the increased segregation of cells and fibers of a common function from cells and fibers of other

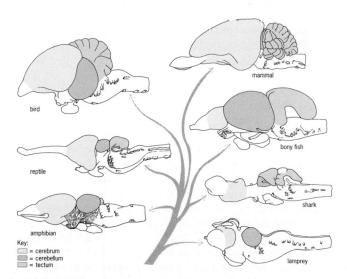

Fig. 1. Lateral views of several vertebrate brains showing evolutionary relationships.

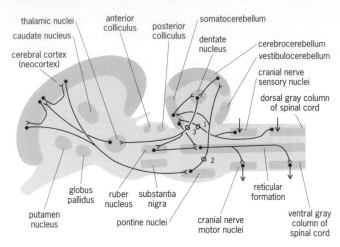

Fig. 2. Mammalian brain in sagittal section. Cerebellar patterns: tract 1, posterior cerebellar peduncle; 2, middle cerebellar peduncle; 3, anterior cerebellar peduncle.

functions and the increase in the length of fibers which connect brain centers with spinal centers. *See* POSTURAL EQUILIBRIUM.

The rhombencephalon of the brain is subdivided into a roof, or cerebellum, and a floor, or medulla oblongata. The medulla is similar to the spinal cord and is divided into a dorsal sensory region and a ventral motor region. It is an integrating and relay area between higher brain centers and the spinal cord. In addition to these nuclei and their connections, the medulla consists of both ascending and descending pathways to and from higher brain centers. The same basic connections occur throughout vertebrates.

In mammals, the cerebellum does not initiate movement; it only times the length of muscle contractions and orders the sequence in which muscles should contract to bring about a movement. The command to initiate a movement is received from the cerebral cortex (Fig. 2). Similarly, the cerebral cortex receives information regarding limb position and state of muscular contraction to ensure that its commands can be carried out by the cerebellum.

The mesencephalon is divided into a roof or optic tectum and a floor or tegmentum. The tegmentum contains the nuclei of the oculomotor and trochlear cranial nerves and a rostral continuation of the sensory nucleus of the trigeminal cranial nerve.

In the evolution of vertebrates, the prosencephalon develops as two major divisions, the diencephalon and the telencephalon. The diencephalon retains the tubular form and serves as a relay and integrating center for information passing to and from the telencephalon and lower centers. The telencephalon is divided into a pair of cerebral hemispheres and an unpaired telencephalon medium.

There are three divisions of the diencephalon in all vertebrates: an epithalamus which forms the roof of the neural tube, a thalamus which forms the walls of the neural tube, and a hypothalamus which forms the floor of the neural tube. The epithalamus and hypothalamus are primarily concerned with autonomic functions such as homeostasis. The thalamus is subdivided into dorsal and ventral regions. The dorsal region relays and integrates sensory information, and the ventral thalamus relays and integrates motor information. *See* HOMEOSTASIS; INSTINCTIVE BEHAVIOR.

The telencephalon is the most complex brain division in vertebrates. It is divided into a roof, or pallium, and a floor, or basal region. The pallium is divided into three primary divisions: a medial PI or hippocampal division, a dorsal PII or general pallial division, and a lateral PII division, often called the pyriform pallium.

The most striking change in the telencephalon of land vertebrates involves the PIIIa component. In mammals, it has proliferated with the PIIb component of the dorsal pallium to produce the mammalian neocortex. In all land vertebrates except amphibians, the PIIb and the PIIIa components, along with the corpus striatum (BI and BII), are the highest centers for the analysis of sensory information and motor coordination. The PI, PIIa, PIIIb, BIII, and posterior parts of BI and BII form part of the limbic system which is concerned with behavioral regulation. [R.G.No.]

Comparative histology. The nervous system is composed of several basic cell types, including nerve cells called neurons, interstitial cells called neurolemma (cells of Schwann), satellite cells, oligodendroglia, and astroglia; and several connective-tissue cell types, including fibroblasts and microglia, blood vessels, and extracellular fluids.

Each neuron possesses three fundamental properties, involving specialized capacity to react to stimuli, to transmit the resulting excitation rapidly to other portions of the cell, and to influence other neurons, muscle, or glandular cells. Each neuron consists of a cell body (soma), one to several cytoplasmic processes called dendrites, and one process called an axon. Cell bodies vary from about 7 to more than 70 micrometers in diameter; each contains a nucleus and several cytoplasmic structures, including Nissl (chromophil) granules, mitochondria, and neurofibrils. The cell body is continuously synthesizing new cytoplasm, especially protein, which flows down the cell processes. The dendrites range from a fraction of a millimeter to a few millimeters in length. An axon may range from about a millimeter up to many feet in length. The site where two neurons come into contact with each other and where influences of one neuron are transmitted to the other neuron is called a synapse. Neurotransmitters are secreted across the presynaptic membrane into the synaptic cleft where they may excite (excitatory synapse) or inhibit (inhibitory synapse) the postsynaptic membrane. *See* BIOPOTENTIALS AND IONIC CURRENTS; SENSATION; SYNAPTIC TRANSMISSION.

There are three layers of connective tissue membranes, the meninges, covering the brain and spinal cord: the inner, pia mater; the middle layer, the arachnoid; and the outermost, the dura mater. Between the pia mater and the arachnoid is the subarachnoid space; this space and the ventricular cavities within the brain are filled with an extracellular fluid, the cerebrospinal fluid. [C.No.]

Comparative embryology. The anlage of the nervous system is formed in the outer germ layer, the ectoderm, although some later contributions are also obtained from the middle germ layer, the mesoderm. In most vertebrates a neural plate is formed, which later folds into a neural groove, then closes to form a neural tube. The formation of neural tissue within the ectoderm is due to inductive influences from underlying chordomesodermal structures. *See* DEVELOPMENTAL BIOLOGY; EMBRYONIC INDUCTION; NEURAL CREST.

When the neural tube is developing, a segmentation of the central nervous system occurs by the formation of transverse bulges, neuromeres. At the time of neuromeric segmentation, the brain is subdivided into the so-called brain vesicles by local widenings of its lumen. In the rostral end more or less well-developed hemispheres are formed; in the middle of the brain anlage the mesencephalic bulge develops; and behind the latter the walls of the tube thicken into cerebellar folds. In this way the brain anlage is divided into five sections: the telencephalon, diencephalon, mesencephalon, metencephalon, and myelencephalon, and its cavity is divided into the rudiments of the adult ventricles.

In spite of the extraordinary variation in adult morphology of the vertebrate brain in different species, the early phases of development are essentially similar. The spinal cord remains as a comparatively slightly differentiated tube.

The cranial or cerebral nerves are the peripheral nerves of the head that are related to the brain. Twelve pairs of cranial nerves have been distinguished in human anatomy and these nerves have been numbered rostrally to caudally as follows:

> I. Olfactory nerve, fila olfactoria
> II. Optic nerve, fasciculus opticus
> III. Oculomotor nerve
> IV. Trochlear nerve
> V. Trigeminal nerve, in most vertebrates divided
> into three branches: ophthalmic, maxillary,
> and mandibular
> VI. Abducens nerve
> VII. Facial nerve
> VIII. Statoacoustic nerve
> IX. Glossopharyngeal nerve
> X. Vagus nerve
> XI. Accessory nerve
> XII. Hypoglossal nerve

The spinal ganglia are formed from the neural crest which grows out like a continuous sheet from the dorsal margin of the neural tube and is secondarily split up into cell groups, the ganglia, by a segmentating influence from the somites. Fibers grow out from the ganglionic cells and form the sensory fibers of the spinal nerves. Motor nerve fibers emerge from cells situated in the ventral horns of the spinal cord. The ventral motor fibers and the dorsal sensory fibers fuse to form a common stem, which is again laterally divided into branches, innervating the corresponding segment of the body.

The ganglia of the sympathetic nervous system develop ventrolateral to the spinal cord as neural crest derivatives. At first a continual column of sympathetic nerve cells is formed; it later subdivides into segmental ganglia.

The parasympathetic system is made up of preganglionic fibers emanating as general visceromotor fibers from the brain and from the sacral cord segments. Cells migrate to form the peripheral ganglia along them. See AUTONOMIC NERVOUS SYSTEM.   [B.Kal.]

Nervous system disorders   A satisfactory classification of diseases of the nervous system should include not only the type of reaction (congenital malformation, infection, trauma, neoplasm, vascular diseases, and degenerative, metabolic, toxic, or deficiency states) but also the site of involvement (meninges, peripheral nerves or gray or white matter of the spinal cord, brainstem, cerebellum, and cerebrum). To these may be added various other correlates, such as age and sex. The nerve cell may be damaged primarily, as in certain infections, but much more commonly the nerve cell is damaged secondarily as the result of metabolic or vascular diseases affecting other important organs, such as the heart, lungs, liver, and kidneys.

Malformation. The central nervous system develops as a hollow neural tube by the fusion of the crests of the neural groove, beginning in the cervical area and progressing rostrally and caudally, the last points to close being termed the anterior and posterior neuropores. If the anterior neuropore fails to close (about 24 days of fetal age), anencephaly develops. The poorly organized brain is exposed to amniotic fluid and becomes necrotic and hemorrhagic, with death usually within hours after birth. *See* CONGENITAL ANOMALIES.

If the posterior neuropore fails to close (about 26 days of fetal age), the lumbosacral neural groove is exposed to amniotic fluid. The nervous tissue becomes partially necrotic and incorporated in a scar. Such a meningomyelocele is readily infected unless buried surgically within a few hours after birth. In addition, in about 95% of such infants hydrocephalus occurs, which usually can be adequately treated by shunting the ventricular fluid into the venous system or peritoneal cavity.

Other developmental disorders of the nervous system may appear as hypoplasia or hyperplasia (decrease or increase in growth of cells, respectively) or as a destruction of otherwise normally developing tissues. Rapidly growing tissues such as the embryonic nervous system are generally rather easily damaged by many toxic agents. The time of onset and the extent of repair rather than the nature of the agent determine the resulting pattern of abnormal development.

Infection. Infections of the nervous system may occur through a defect in the normal protective coverings caused by certain congenital malformations, as mentioned above, but also through other defects as the result of trauma, especially penetrating wounds or fractures opening into the paranasal sinuses or mastoid air cells. Subsequent infection of the nervous system may be the major complication of such "open head" injuries.

Infections may also spread directly from adjacent structures, as from mastoiditis, sinusitis, osteomyelitis, or subcutaneous abscesses. Such infections usually spread along venous channels producing epidural abscess, subdural empyema, leptomeningitis, and brain abscess. All of these infections are characteristically caused by pyogenic (pusforming) bacteria. Other pyogenic bacteria may metastasize by way of the bloodstream from more distant infections, such as bacterial endocarditis, pneumonia, and enteritis.

Infections of the nervous system must be treated promptly as medical emergencies. The diagnosis is easily established by spinal puncture; the microorganisms can be visualized with special stains.

Many other microorganisms can infect the nervous system: *Mycobacterium tuberculosis* (the organism causing tuberculosis), *Treponema pallidum* (the organism causing syphilis), several fungi and rickettsiae, and many viruses.

Viral infections vary widely geographically, generally related to the necessity for intermediate hosts and vectors (animal reservoirs) by which the virus is spread. Poliomyelitis, now largely prevented by effective vaccination of most children, is primarily an intestinal infection which occasionally spreads to the nervous system, infecting and destroying motor nerve cells, thereby producing weakness of certain muscles. Herpes zoster has a similar preference for infecting sensory nerve cells and producing an acute skin eruption in the distribution of the affected sensory cells. Herpes simplex is closely related to herpes zoster, resides in the trigeminal or sacral sensory nerve cells, and intermittently produces eruptions in the distribution of these cells: "fever blisters" in and around the mouth in type I herpes, or similar blisters in the genital area in type II herpes. The latter is increasingly being recognized as a venereal disease. Rabies virus also affects certain nerve cells in the temporal lobe of the brain, as well as in the cerebellum, and is transmitted through the saliva of animals that bite other animals or humans; rabies is the single exception to the rule that immunization must precede infection to be effective, and the immunization must begin promptly after the bite. *See* ANIMAL VIRUS; HERPES; POLIOMYELITIS.

Inflammation. Certain viruses frequently produce a meningitis in humans from whose cerebrospinal fluid the virus is relatively easily grown. Other viruses, such as measles and varicella, occasionally produce meningitis or encephalomyelitis, but the cerebrospinal fluid does not contain the virus. *See* MENINGITIS.

Allergy to one's own tissue elements is an interesting possibility that has evoked many experimental approaches. Two human diseases, multiple sclerosis, a demyelinating disease affecting the central nervous system, and the Landry-Guillain-Barré syndrome, a demyelinating disease affecting the peripheral nervous system, are considered likely candidates to be related to experimental allergic encephalomyelitis and experimental allergic neuritis, respectively. *See* AUTOIMMUNITY.

Vascular disease. Vascular diseases of the nervous system are commonly called strokes, a term which emphasizes the suddenness of onset of neurological disability. Such a cataclysmic onset is characteristic of vascular diseases, since the nerve cell can function without nutrients for only a matter of seconds and will die if not renourished within several minutes.

Two main types of hemorrhage occur: hemorrhage into the subarachnoid space from rupture of an aneurysm (a focal weakening and dilatation) of a large artery; and hemorrhage into the brain from rupture of an aneurysm of a small artery or arteriole. Both types of hemorrhage occur more commonly in hypertensive adults.

Nerve cells require oxygen and glucose for functional activity, and can withstand only brief periods of hypoxia or hypoglycemia. Even a few seconds of hypoxia can block the nerve cell's function, and more than 10 min is almost certainly fatal to most nerve cells. Transient ischemic attacks may result, with temporary impairment of blood flow to a part of the brain and consequent focal neurological dysfunction. These attacks may also be successfully treated with drugs or surgery and the disastrous major stroke prevented. Myocardial infarction, postural hypotension, and stenosis or narrowing of the carotid or vertebral arteries greater than 60% are common causes of cerebral ischemia. If the ischemia is not rapidly reversed, the neurons undergo selective necrosis; if the ischemia is more severe or prolonged, the glia and blood vessels in the gray matter also undergo necrosis; and if the ischemia is still more severe or prolonged, all the gray and white matter in the ischemic zone becomes necrotic, a condition known as cerebral infarction or encephalomalacia. One of the common ways the brain reacts to small or large hemorrhages or ischemic episodes is by swelling. Such swelling itself may be fatal within a few days to a week or so by a process known as transtentorial herniation, compressing the brainstem, where there are important neural circuits for vital functions, such as breathing and maintenance of blood pressure.

Degenerative and other diseases. Degenerative, metabolic, toxic, and deficiency states include the largest numbers of both common and rare diseases of the nervous system. Since neurons in the brain may be destroyed after birth and cannot be replaced, mental deterioration, deafness and blindness, incoordination and adventitious movements, and other neurologic signs that are so typical of these disorders are generally not reversible even if the basic metabolic defect can be corrected. Advances have been made in the early diagnosis and treatment of several diseases usually manifest in infancy with mental retardation. Three examples are phenylpyruvic oligophrenia (phenylketonuria or PKU), which is treatable with a phenylalanine-deficient diet; galactosemia, requiring a galactose-free diet also as early as possible to avoid cataracts and mental retardation; and cretinism, which requires treatment with thyroid.

Neoplasm. Neoplasms of the nervous system can be divided into primary and metastatic, the primary into gliomas and others, and the metastatic into bronchogenic and others. These four groups each account for about 25% of all intracranial neoplasms.

[E.C.A.; C.M.S.]

Neural crest   A strip of ectodermal material in the early vertebrate embryo inserted between the prospective neural plate and epidermis. After closure of the neural tube the crest cells migrate into the body and give rise to parts of the neural system: the main part of the visceral cranium, the mesenchyme, the chromaffin cells, and pigment cells. The true nature of the neural crest eluded recognition for many years because this primary organ has a temporary existence; its cells and derivatives are difficult to analyze when dispersed throughout the body. The fact that mesenchyme arises from this ectodermal organ was directly contrary to the doctrine of the specificity of the germ layers.

Neural crest no doubt exists, with similar qualities, in all vertebrate groups, including the cyclostomes. It has been most thoroughly studied in amphibians and the chick. *See* GERM LAYERS.
[S.H.]

Neurobiology   Study of the development and function of the nervous system, with emphasis on how nerve cells generate and control behavior. The major goal of neurobiology is to explain at the molecular level how nerve cells differentiate and develop their specific connections and how nerve networks store and recall information. Ancillary studies on disease processes and drug effects in the nervous system also provide useful approaches for understanding the normal state by comparison with perturbed or abnormal systems. The functions of the nervous system may be studied at several levels: molecular, subcellular (organelle), cellular, simple multicellular interacting systems, complex systems, and higher functions (whole animal behavior). *See* BIOPOTENTIALS AND IONIC CURRENTS; MEMORY; MOTOR SYSTEMS; NERVOUS SYSTEM (INVERTEBRATE); NERVOUS SYSTEM (VERTEBRATE); NERVOUS SYSTEM DISORDERS; NEURON; SENSE ORGAN; SYNAPTIC TRANSMISSION.
[J.R.B.; M.D.Br.]

Neurohypophysis hormone   Either of two peptide hormones secreted by the neurohypophysis, or posterior lobe of the pituitary gland, in humans. These hormones, oxytocin and vasopressin, each comprise nine amino acid residues. Vasopressin is responsible for arterial vasoconstriction (pressor action) and inhibition of water excretion through the kidneys (antidiuretic action), and has a weak effect on contraction of smooth muscle including that of the uterus. The principal action of oxytocin is stimulation of smooth muscle contraction, specifically that of the uterine muscle, and milk ejection from the mammary gland.

Oxytocin and vasopressin are synthesized in neurons in the hypothalamus and subsequently packaged into neurosecretory granules, which migrate down the axon of the neuron and are stored in the posterior lobe of the pituitary gland, from where they are secreted into the systemic circulation. These hormones are also secreted directly from the hypothalamus into the third ventricle and into the hypothalamo-hypophysial portal circulation of the anterior pituitary gland. *See* NEUROSECRETION.

Major stimuli controlling the release of vasopressin include changes in osmolality of the blood, alterations in blood volume, and psychogenic stimuli such as pain, fear, and apprehension. Stimuli evoking release of oxytocin include nipple stimulation or suckling, and stretching of the cervix and vagina (Ferguson reflex).

Oxytocin probably plays an important role in the onset of labor and delivery (parturition) in primates. During lactation, significant amounts of oxytocin are released by the mother during suckling. When there is total destruction of the pituitary or the neurohypophysis, diabetes insipidus may occur. *See* HORMONE; PITUITARY GLAND.   [M.Y.D.]

Neuroimmunology The study of basic interactions among the nervous, endocrine, and immune systems during development, homeostasis, and host defense responses to injury. In its clinical aspects, neuroimmunology focuses on diseases of the nervous system, such as myasthenia gravis and multiple sclerosis, which are caused by pathogenic autoimmune processes, and on nervous system manifestations of immunological diseases, such as primary and acquired immunodeficiencies. *See* AUTOIMMUNITY; IMMUNOLOGICAL DEFICIENCY.

Neuroimmune interactions are dependent on the expression of at least two structural components: immunocytes must display receptors for nervous system-derived mediators, and the mediators must be able to reach immune cells in concentrations sufficient to alter migration, proliferation, phenotype, or secretory or effector functions. More than 20 neuropeptide receptors have been identified on immunocompetent cells.

It has been found that stimuli derived from the nervous system could affect the course of human disease. The onset or progression of tumor growth, infections, or chronic inflammatory diseases, for example, could be associated with traumatic life events or other psychosocial variables such as personality types and coping mechanisms. More direct indications of the influence of psychosocial factors on immune function have been provided by findings that cellular immunity can be impaired in individuals who are exposed to unusually stressful situations, such as the loss of a close relative. *See* CELLULAR IMMUNOLOGY.

During responses to infection, trauma, or malignancies, cells of the immune system produce some cytokines in sufficiently high quantities to reach organs that are distant from the site of production. These cytokines are known to act on the nervous system. Fever is the classic example of changes in nervous system function induced by products of the immune system; interleukin 1, which is produced by monocytes after stimulation by certain bacterial products, binds to receptors in the hypothalamus and evokes changes via the induction of prostaglandins. Interleukin 1 also induces slow-wave sleep. Both fever and sleep may be regarded as protective behavioral changes. *See* ENDOCRINE SYSTEM (VERTEBRATE); IMMUNOLOGY; NERVOUS SYSTEM (VERTEBRATE); NEUROSECRETION. [M.L.; W.Ku.; P.V.]

Neurosecretion The synthesis and release of hormones by neurons. Such neurons are called neurosecretory cells, and their products are often called neurohormones. Like conventional (that is, nonglandular or ordinary) neurons, neurosecretory cells are able to receive signals from other neurons. But unlike ordinary neurons that have cell-to-cell communication over short distances at synapses, neurosecretory cells release their product into an extracellular space that may be at some distance from the target cells. In an organism with a circulatory system, the neurohormones are typically sent by the vascular route to their target, whereas in lower invertebrates that lack an organized circulatory system the neurohormones apparently simply diffuse from the release site to the target. It is now clear that the nervous and endocrine systems interact in many ways, as in the suckling reflex of mammals (where the hormone oxytocin, a neurohormone, elicits milk ejection and is reflexly released in response to nerve impulses generated by stimulation of the nipples), and neurosecretory cells form a major link between them. *See* ENDOCRINE SYSTEM (INVERTEBRATE); ENDOCRINE SYSTEM (VERTEBRATE).

It has been shown that peptides or low-molecular-weight proteins as well as amines, such as octopamine and dopamine, are released from neurosecretory cells into the circulatory systems of various animals, where they function as neurohormones. In classical neurosecretory cells, the secreted material is synthesized in the cell body by the rough-surfaced endoplasmic reticulum and subsequently packaged in the form of membrane-bounded granules by the Golgi apparatus, and is then typically transported along the axon to the axonal terminals, where it is stored until released. The release of neurohormones from axonal terminals into an extracellular space is triggered when the electrical activity (action potential) that is propagated by the axon enters the neurosecretory terminals. Calcium ions are essential for neurohormone release. *See* BIOPOTENTIALS AND IONIC CURRENTS; ENDOPLASMIC RETICULUM; GOLGI APPARATUS.

Neurohormones have a wide variety of functions. The role of the vertebrate hypothalamo-neurohypophysial system has been especially well elucidated. The pars nervosa is the site of release of vasopressin (also called the antidiuretic hormone) and oxytocin, and the median eminence is the release site for several hypothalamic neurohormones that regulate the adenohypophysis, the nonneural portion of the pituitary gland. *See* ADENOHYPOPHYSIS HORMONE; NERVOUS SYSTEM (VERTEBRATE); NEUROHYPOPHYSIS HORMONE; PITUITARY GLAND.   [M.F.]

Neurulation   The process by which the vertebrate neural tube is formed. The primordium of the central nervous system is the neural plate, which arises at the close of gastrulation by inductive action of the chorda-mesoderm on the overlying ectoderm. The axial mesodermal substratum causes the neural ectoderm to thicken into a distinct plate across the dorsal midline and influences both its size and shape. Its shieldlike appearance, broader anteriorly and narrower posteriorly, presages the areas of brain and spinal cord, respectively. The lateral edges of the neural plate then rise as neural folds which meet first at the level of the future midbrain, above the dorsal midline, then fuse anteriorly and posteriorly to form the neural tube. The body ectoderm becomes confluent above the closing neural tube and separates from it. Upon closure, the cells (known as neural crest cells) which occupied the crest of the neural folds leave the roof of the tube and migrate through the mesenchyme to all parts of the embryo, forming diverse structures. The neural tube thus formed gives rise to the brain and about half of the spinal cord. The remainder of the neural tube is added by the tail bud, which proliferates a solid nerve cord that secondarily hollows into a tube. *See* NERVOUS SYSTEM (VERTEBRATE); NEURAL CREST.   [H.L.H.]

Neutralization reaction (immunology)   A procedure in which the chemical or biological activity of a reagent or a living organism is inhibited, usually by a specific neutralizing antibody. As an example, the lethal or the dermonecrotic actions of diphtheria toxin on animals may be completely neutralized by an equivalent amount of diphtheria antitoxin.

Antibodies to bacterial, snake-venom, and other enzyme preparations regularly precipitate them from solution so that the supernates are devoid of enzyme activity; however, the neutralization of activity in the precipitate may range from complete to negligible. *See* IMMUNOLOGY; SEROLOGY.   [H.P.T.]

Nicotinamide adenine dinucleotide (NAD)   An organic coenzyme and one of the most important components of the enzymatic systems concerned with biological oxidation-reduction reactions. It is also known as NAD, diphosphopyridine nucleotide (DPN) coenzyme I, and codehydrogenase I. NAD is found in the tissues of all living organisms. *See* COENZYME.

The nicotinamide, or pyridine, portion of NAD can be reduced chemically or enzymatically with the formation of reduced or hydrogenated NAD (NADH). NAD functions as the immediate oxidizing agent for the oxidation, or dehydrogenation, of various organic compounds in the presence of appropriate dehydrogenases, which are specific apoenzymes, or protein portions of the enzyme. In the dehydrogenase reactions one hydrogen atom is transferred from the substrate to NAD, while another is liberated as hydrogen ion.

NAD and its reduced form, NADH, serve to couple oxidative and reductive processes and are constantly regenerated during metabolism. Hence, they serve as catalysts and NAD is referred to as a coenzyme. In some enzymatic reactions a different coenzyme, triphosphopyridine nucleotide is required. Dehydrogenases are generally quite specific with respect to the coenzyme which they can utilize. *See* ENZYME; NICOTINAMIDE ADENINE DINUCLEOTIDE PHOSPHATE (NADP).   [M.D.]

Nicotinamide adenine dinucleotide phosphate (NADP) A coenzyme and an important component of the enzymatic systems concerned with biological oxidation-reduction systems. It is also known as NAD, triphosphopyridine nucleotide (TPN), coenzyme II, and codehydrogenase II. The compound is similar in structure and function to nicotinamide adenine dinucleotide (NAD). It differs structurally from NAD in having an additional phosphoric acid group esterified at the 2' position of the ribose moiety of the adenylic acid portion. In biological oxidation-reduction reactions the NADP molecule becomes alternately reduced to its

Triphosphopyridine nucleotide. (*a*) Reduced form of the nicotinamide portion of TPNH. (*b*) Oxidized form of the molecule (TPN).

hydrogenated form (NADPH) and reoxidized to its initial state (see illustration). *See* CARBOHYDRATE METABOLISM; COENZYME; ENZYME.   [M.D.]

Nitric oxide   An important messenger molecule in mammals and other animals. It can be toxic or beneficial, depending on the amount and where in the body it is released. Initial research into the chemistry of nitric oxide (NO) was motivated by its production in car engines, which results in photochemical smog and acid rain. In the late 1980s, researchers in immunology, cardiovascular pharmacology, neurobiology, and toxicology discovered that nitric oxide is a crucial physiological messenger molecule. Nitric oxide is now thought to play a role in blood pressure regulation, control of blood clotting, immune defense, digestion, the senses of sight and smell, and possibly learning and memory. Nitric oxide may also participate in disease processes such as diabetes, stroke, hypertension, impotence, septic shock, and long-term depression. *See* IMMUNOLOGY; NEUROBIOLOGY.

Most cellular messengers are large, unreactive biomolecules that make specific contacts with their targets. In contrast, nitric oxide is a small molecule that contains a free radical—that is, an unpaired electron—making it very reactive. Nitric oxide can freely diffuse through aqueous solutions or membranes, reacting rapidly with metal centers in cellular proteins and with reactive groups in other cellular molecules.

Nitric oxide is produced in the body by an enzyme called nitric oxide synthase, which converts the amino acid L-arginine to nitric oxide and L-citrulline. There are three types of nitric oxide synthase: brain, endothelial, and inducible. Both brain and endothelial enzymes are constitutive, that is, they are always present in cells, while the production of inducible nitric oxide synthase can be turned on or off when a system needs nitric oxide. After nitric oxide is produced in specific areas of the body by nitric oxide synthase, it diffuses to nearby cells. Nitric oxide then reacts preferentially in the interior of these cells with the metal centers of proteins. Nitric oxide binds specifically to the iron (Fe) atom of the heme group in proteins; it can also interact with other metal sites in proteins as well as with the thiol group (SH) of the amino acid cysteine. The interaction of nitric oxide with these proteins causes a cascade of intracellular events that leads to specific physiological changes within cells. For example, nitric oxide causes the smooth muscle cells surrounding blood vessels to relax, decreasing blood pressure. Nitric oxide plays an important role in the central and peripheral nervous systems; the overproduction of nitric oxide in brain tissues has been implicated in stroke and other neurological problems.

Nitric oxide also functions as an important agent in the immune system by killing invading bacterial cells. Nitric oxide released by macrophages can inhibit important cellular processes in the bacteria, including deoxyribonucleic acid (DNA) synthesis and respiration, by binding to and destroying iron-sulfur centers in key enzymes in these pathways.

Although nitric oxide production in the immune system serves a crucial biological function, there can be adverse effects when too much nitric oxide is produced. During a massive bacterial infection, excess nitric oxide can go into the vascular system, causing a dramatic decrease in blood pressure, which may lead to possibly fatal septic shock. Thus, scientists are working on drugs that can selectively inhibit the inducible form of nitric oxide synthase in order to avoid the harmful effects produced by excess nitric oxide without interfering with useful nitric oxide pathways.   [J.N.Bu.; M.F.R.]

Nitrogen cycle   The collective term given to the natural biological and chemical processes through which inorganic and organic nitrogen are interconverted. It includes the process of ammonification, ammonia assimilation, nitrification, nitrate assimilation, nitrogen fixation, and denitrification.

Nitrogen exists in nature in several inorganic compounds, namely N_2, N_2O, NH_3, NO_2^-, and NO_3^-, and in several organic compounds such as amino acids, nucleotides,

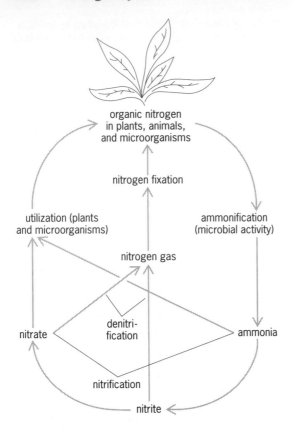

organic nitrogen
in plants, animals,
and microorganisms

nitrogen fixation

utilization (plants
and microorganisms)

ammonification
(microbial activity)

nitrogen gas

denitri-
fication

nitrate

ammonia

nitrification

nitrite

Diagram of the nitrogen cycle.

amino sugars, and vitamins. In the biosphere, biological and chemical reactions continually occur in which these nitrogenous compounds are converted from one form to another. These interconversions are of great importance in maintaining soil fertility and in preventing pollution of soil and water.

An outline showing the general interconversions of nitrogenous compounds in the soil-water pool is presented in the illustration. There are three primary reasons why organisms metabolize nitrogen compounds: (1) to use them as a nitrogen source, which means first converting them to NH_3, (2) to use certain nitrogen compounds as an energy source such as in the oxidation of NH_3 to NO_2^- and of NO_2^- to NO_3^-, and (3) to use certain nitrogen compounds (NO_3^-) as terminal electron acceptors under conditions where oxygen is either absent or in limited supply. The reactions and products involved in these three metabolically different pathways collectively make up the nitrogen cycle.

There are two ways in which organisms obtain ammonia. One is to use nitrogen already in a form easily metabolized to ammonia. Thus, nonviable plant, animal, and microbial residues in soil are enzymatically decomposed by a series of hydrolytic and other reactions to yield biosynthetic monomers such as amino acids and other small-molecular-weight nitrogenous compounds. These amino acids, purines, and pyrimidines are decomposed further to produce NH_3 which is then used by plants and bacteria for biosynthesis, or these biosynthetic monomers can be used directly by some microorganisms. The decomposition process is called ammonification.

The second way in which inorganic nitrogen is made available to biological agents is by nitrogen fixation (this term is maintained even though N_2 is now called dinitrogen), a process in which N_2 is reduced to NH_3. Since the vast majority of nitrogen is in the form of N_2, nitrogen fixation obviously is essential to life. The N_2-fixing process is confined to prokaryotes (certain photosynthetic and nonphotosynthetic bacteria). The major nitrogen fixers (called diazotrophs) are members of the genus *Rhizobium*, bacteria that are found in root nodules of leguminous plants, and of the cyanobacteria (originally called blue-green algae).   [L.E.Mo.]

Noradrenergic system   A neuronal system that is responsible for the synthesis, storage, and release of the neurotransmitter norepinephrine. Norepinephrine, also known as noradrenalin, consists of a single amine group and a catechol nucleus (a benzene ring with two hydroxyl groups) and is therefore referred to as a monoamine or catecholamine. It exists in both the central and peripheral nervous systems. Norepinephrine is the primary neurotransmitter released by the sympathetic nervous system, which mediates the "fight or flight" reaction, preparing the body for action by affecting cardiovascular function, gastrointestinal motility and secretion, bronchiole dilation, glucose metabolism, and so on. Within the central nervous system, norepinephrine has been associated with several brain functions, including sleep, memory, learning, and emotions.

After synthesis, the majority of norepinephrine is transported into synaptic vesicles in the nerve terminals, where it remains until needed. When the nerve terminal is activated by depolarization, calcium flows into it, leading to the release of norepinephrine into the synaptic cleft. Once released into the synaptic cleft, norepinephrine is free to bind to specific receptors located on the presynaptic or postsynaptic terminal, which initiates a chain of events (the effector system) in the target cell that can be mediated by a number of different second messenger systems. The exact effect is determined by the identity of the receptor activated. See EPINEPHRINE; SECOND MESSENGER; SYMPATHETIC NERVOUS SYSTEM; SYNAPTIC TRANSMISSION.

Termination of norepinephrine occurs by a reuptake mechanism in the presynaptic membrane. Once transported back into the presynaptic terminal, norepinephrine can be stored in vesicles for future use or enzymatically degraded by monoamine oxidase.

Certain medications achieve their effect by altering various stages of synthesis, storage, release, and inactivation of norepinephrine. The behavioral manifestations of these alterations have led to a better understanding of norepinephrine's role in various psychiatric disorders. See AFFECTIVE DISORDERS; MONOAMINE OXIDASE; PSYCHOPHARMACOLOGY; SCHIZOPHRENIA; STRESS.   [M.My.; D.S.C.; A.Bre.; S.So.]

Nucleic acid   An acidic, chainlike biological macromolecule consisting of multiply repeated units of phosphoric acid, sugar, and purine and pyrimidine bases. Nucleic acids as a class are involved in the preservation, replication, and expression of hereditary information in every living cell. There are two types of nucleic acid; deoxyribonucleic acid (DNA) and ribonucleic acid (RNA). See DEOXYRIBONUCLEIC ACID (DNA); RIBONUCLEIC ACID (RNA).   [E.Jo.]

Nucleoprotein   A generic term for any member of a large class of proteins associated with nucleic acid molecules. Nucleoprotein complexes occur in all living cells and in viruses, where they play vital roles in reproduction and protein synthesis.

Classification of the nucleoproteins depends primarily upon the type of nucleic acid involved—deoxyribonucleic acid (DNA) or ribonucleic acid (RNA)—and on the biological function of the complex. Deoxyribonucleoproteins (complexes of DNA and proteins) constitute the genetic material of all organisms and of many viruses. They function as the chemical basis of heredity and are the primary means of its expression and control. Most of the mass of chromosomes is made up of DNA and proteins whose structural and enzymatic activities are required for the proper assembly and expression of the genetic information encoded in the molecular structure of the nucleic acid. *See* DEOXYRIBONUCLEIC ACID (DNA).

Ribonucleoproteins (complexes of RNA and proteins) occur in all cells as part of the machinery for protein synthesis. This complex operation requires the participation of messenger RNAs (mRNAs), amino acyl transfer RNAs (tRNAs), and ribosomal RNAs (rRNAs), each of which interacts with specific proteins to form functional complexes called polysomes, on which the synthesis of new proteins occurs. *See* RIBONUCLEIC ACID (RNA).

In simpler life forms, such as viruses which infect animal and plant cells and bacteriophages which infect bacteria, most of the mass of the viral particle is due to its nucleoprotein content. The material responsible for the hereditary continuity of the virus may be DNA or RNA, depending on the type of virus, and it is usually enveloped by one or more proteins which protect the nucleic acid and facilitate infections. *See* BACTERIOPHAGE; CHROMOSOME; NUCLEIC ACID; VIRUS.

A typical human diploid nucleus contains 5.6×10^{-12} g of DNA. This DNA is arranged in 23 pairs of chromosomes differing in size and DNA content. The large number 1 chromosome, for example, contains 0.235×10^{-12} g of DNA, while the much smaller chromosome number 22 contains only 0.046×10^{-12} g. The DNA double-helix of chromosome 1 is actually 7.3 cm long, but this thin filamentous molecule is packaged to form a chromosome less than 10 micrometers long. The enormity of the packing problem can be appreciated from the fact that the average human contains about 100 g of DNA, and 0.5 g would reach from the Earth to the Sun! The reduction in size is largely due to interactions between the DNA and sets of small basic proteins called histones. All somatic cells of higher organisms contain five major histone classes, all of which are characterized by a high content of basic (positively charged) amino acids.   [V.G.A.]

Nucleosome   The fundamental histone-containing structural subunit of eukaryotic chromosomes. In most eukaryotic organisms, nuclear deoxyribonucleic acid (DNA) is complexed with an approximately equal mass of histone protein. The nucleosome is organized so that the DNA is exterior and the histones interior. The DNA makes two turns around a core of eight histone molecules, thus forming a squat cylinder 11 nanometers in diameter and 5.5 nm in height. A short length of linker or spacer DNA connects one nucleosome to the next, forming a nucleosomal chain that has been likened to a beaded string. This basic structure is found in all forms of chromatin. Nucleosomes have been found in all eukaryotic organisms examined, the only exceptions being some sperm nuclei and the dinoflagellate algae.

A chain of adjacent nucleosomes is approximately sixfold shorter than the DNA it contains. Moreover, chains of nucleosomes have the property of self-assembling into thicker fibers in which the DNA packing ratio approaches 35:1. These observations, and the lack of any obvious catalytic activity, have led to the assumption that the primary function of the nucleosome consists of organizing and packing DNA. *See* CHROMOSOME; DEOXYRIBONUCLEIC ACID (DNA); GENE.   [C.L.F.W.]

Nucleotide   A cellular constituent that is one of the building blocks of ribonucleic acids (RNA) and deoxyribonucleic acid (DNA). In biological systems, nucleotides are linked by enzymes in order to make long, chainlike polynucleotides of defined sequence. The order or sequence of the nucleotide units along a polynucleotide chain plays an important role in the storage and transfer of genetic information. Many nucleotides also perform other important functions in biological systems. Some, such as adenosine triphosphate (ATP), serve as energy sources that are used to fuel important biological reactions. Others, such as nicotinamide adenine dinucleotide (NAD) and coenzyme A (CoA), are important cofactors that are needed to complete a variety of enzymatic reactions. Cyclic nucleotides such as cyclic adenosine monophosphate (cAMP) are often used to regulate complex metabolic systems. Chemically modified nucleotides such as fluoro-deoxyridine monophosphate (Fl-dUMP) contain special chemical groups that are useful for inactivating the normal function of important enzymes. These and other such compounds are widely used as drugs and therapeutic agents to treat cancer and a variety of other serious illnesses. See COENZYME; CYCLIC NUCLEOTIDES; NICOTINAMIDE ADENINE DINUCLEOTIDE (NAD).

Nucleotides are generally classified as either ribonucleotides or deoxyribonucleotides. Both classes consist of a phosphorylated pentose sugar that is linked via an N-glycosidic bond to a purine or pyrimidine base. The combination of the pentose sugar and the purine or pyrimidine base without the phosphate moiety is called a nucleoside. See PURINE; PYRIMIDINE.

Ribonucleosides contain the sugar D-ribose, whereas deoxyribonucleosides contain the sugar 2-deoxyribose. The four most common ribonucleosides are adenosine, guanosine, cytidine, and uridine. The purine ribonucleosides, adenosine and guanosine, contain the nitrogenous bases adenine and guanine, respectively. The pyrimidine ribonucleosides, cytidine and uridine, contain the bases cytosine and uracil, respectively. Similarly, the most common deoxyribonucleosides include deoxyadenosine, deoxyguanosine, deoxycytidine, and thymidine, which contains the pyrimidine base thymine. Phosphorylation of the ribonucleosides or deoxyribonucleosides yields the corresponding ribonucleotide or deoxyribonucleotide. See DEOXYRIBONUCLEIC ACID (DNA); ENZYME; NUCLEIC ACID; RIBONUCLEIC ACID (RNA).   [E.P.G.]

Numerical taxonomy   The grouping by numerical methods of taxonomic units based on their character states. The application of numerical methods to taxonomy, dating back to the rise of biometrics in the late nineteenth century, has received a great deal of attention with the development of the computer and computer technology. Numerical taxonomy provides methods that are objective, explicit, and repeatable, and is based on the ideas first put forward by M. Adanson in 1963. These ideas, or principles, are that the ideal taxonomy is composed of information-rich taxa based on as many features as possible, that a priori every character is of equal weight, that overall similarity between any two entities is a function of the similarity of the many characters on which the comparison is based, and that taxa are constructed on the basis of diverse character correlations in the groups studied.

In the early stages of development of numerical taxonomy, phylogenetic relationships were not considered. However, numerical methods have made possible exact measurement of evolutionary rates and phylogenetic analysis. Furthermore, rapid developments in the techniques of direct measurement of the homologies of deoxyribonucleic acid (DNA), and ribonucleic acid (RNA) between different organisms now provide an estimation of "hybridization" between the DNAs of different taxa and, therefore, possible evolutionary relationships. Thus, research in numerical taxonomy often includes analyses of the chemical and physical properties of the nucleic acids of the organisms the data from which are correlated with phenetic groupings established by numerical techniques. See PHYLOGENY; TAXONOMIC CATEGORIES.   [R.R.C.]

Olfaction   One of the chemical senses, specifically the sense of smell. Olfaction registers chemical information in organisms ranging from insects to humans, including marine organisms. For terrestrial animals, its stimuli comprise airborne molecules. The typical stimulus is an organic chemical with molecular weight below 300 daltons. A few inorganic chemicals can also stimulate olfaction, notably hydrogen sulfide, ozone, ammonia, and the halogens.

The anatomy of olfactory structures and the neurophysiology of olfaction differ significantly among different animal groups. For examples, insect olfactory receptors exist within sensory hairs on the antennae. The olfactory organ of fishes resides typically in tubular chambers on either side of the mouth. In terrestrial vertebrates, the olfactory receptors reside within a sac or cavity more or less similar to the human nasal cavity. The olfactory mucosa patch in the cavity characteristically contains millions of receptor cells, though in some olfactory-dominated mammals, such as the dog and rabbit, it contains tens of millions. The location of the olfactory mucosa relative to air currents in the cavity plays some role in the ongoing olfactory vigilance of the organism. In the human the mucosa sits out of the main airstream. During quiet breathing eddy currents may carry just enough stimulus to evoke a sensation, whereupon sniffing will occur. Sniffing amplifies the amount of stimulus reaching the receptors by as much as tenfold.

Reception of the chemical stimulus and transduction into a neural signal apparently occur on the olfactory receptor cilia. The ciliary membrane contains receptor protein molecules that interact with stimulating molecules through reversible binding. Vertebrate receptor cells show broad tuning, that is, they respond to many odorants.

Adjacent points in the mucosa generally project to adjacent points in the olfactory bulb of the brain (see illustration). The synapses between the incoming olfactory

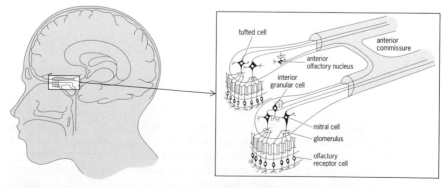

Location of the olfactory bulbs at the interior surface of the human brain and their connections via the anterior commissure. (*After D. Ottoson, Physiology of the Nervous System, Oxford University Press, 1983*)

nerve fibers and the second-order cells, mitral cells, occur in basketlike structures called glomeruli. On average, a glomerulus receives about 1000 receptor cell fibers for each mitral cell. The location of cells within the bulb seems to play a role in encoding odor quality: each odorant stimulates a more or less unique spatial array.

The central neural pathways of the olfactory system have a complexity unmatched among the sensory systems. One pathway carries information to the pyriform cortex (paleocortex of the temporal lobe), to a sensory relay in the thalamus (dorsomedial nucleus), and to the frontal cortex (orbitofrontal region). This pathway seems rather strictly sensory. Another pathway carries information to the pyriform cortex, the hypothalamus, and other structures of the limbic system. The latter have much to do with the control of emotions, feeding, and sex. The strong affective and motivational consequences of olfactory stimulation seem compatible with projections to the limbic system and with the role of olfaction in certain types of physiological regulation. In many vertebrate species, reception of pheromones occurs via an important accessory olfactory organ, known as the vomeronasal organ, which characteristically resides in the hard palate of the mouth or floor of the nasal cavity. *See* PHEROMONE.

Human olfactory sensitivity varies from odorant to odorant over several orders of magnitude. A common range of thresholds for materials used in fragrances and flavors is 1 to 100 parts per 10^9 parts of air. Thresholds gathered from various groups of human subjects permit certain generalities about how the state of the organism affects olfaction. For instance, persons aged 70 and above are about tenfold less sensitive than young adults. Males and females have about equal sensitivity, except perhaps in old age, where females are more sensitive. Persons with certain medical disorders, such as multiple sclerosis, Parkinson's disease, paranasal sinus disease, Kallmann's syndrome, and olfactory tumors, exhibit decreased sensitivity (hyposmia) or complete absence of sensitivity (anosmia).

Above its threshold, the perceived magnitude of an odor changes by relatively small amounts as concentration increases. A tenfold increment in concentration will cause, on average, about a twofold change in perceived magnitude. The perceived magnitude of an odor is often greatly influenced by olfactory adaptation, a process whereby during continuous short-term exposure to a stimulus its perceived magnitude falls to about one-third of its initial value.

The stimuli for olfaction are commonly complex, that is, they are mixtures. Such products as coffee, wine, cigarettes, and perfumes contain at least hundreds of odor-relevant constituents. Only rarely does the distinctive quality of a natural product, such as a vegetable, arise from only a single constituent. A chemical analysis of most products will not usually allow a simple prediction of odor intensity or quality. One general rule, however, is that the perceived intensity of the mixture falls well below the sum of the intensities of the unmixed components.

General notions about the properties that endow a molecule with its quality have spawned more than two dozen theories of olfaction, including various chemical and vibrational theories. Most modern theories hold that the key to quality lies in the size and shape of molecules, with some influence of chemical functionality. For molecules below about 100 daltons, functional group has obvious importance: for example, thiols smell skunky, esters fruity, amines fishy-uriny, and carboxylic acids rancid. For larger molecules, the size and shape of the molecule seem more important. Shape detection is subtle enough to enable easy discrimination of some optical isomers. Progressive changes in molecular architecture along one or another dimension often lead to large changes in odor quality. No current theory makes testable predictions about such changes. *See* CHEMICAL SENSES; CHEMORECEPTION.   [W.Ca.]

Oligochaeta   A class of the phylum Annelida including worms such as the earthworms. There are 21 families with over 3000 species. These animals exhibit both external and internal segmentation. They usually possess setae which are not borne on parapodia. Oligochaetes are hermaphroditic. The gonads are few in number and situated in the anterior part of the body, the male gonads being anterior to the female gonads. The gametes are discharged through special ducts, the oviducts and sperm ducts. A clitellum is present at maturity. There is no larval stage during development.

The oligochaetes are primarily fresh-water and burrowing terrestrial animals. A few are marine and several species occur in the intertidal zone.

Oligochaetes are cylindrical, elongated animals with the anterior mouth usually overhung by a fleshy lobe, the prostomium, and the anus terminal. The body plan is that of a tube within a tube. Externally, the segments are marked by furrows. The setae or bristles are borne on most segments. Other external features are the pores of the reproductive systems opening on certain segments, the openings of the nephridia, and in many earthworms dorsal pores which open externally from the coelom. Some aquatic species have extensions of the posterior part of the body which function as gills.

The oligochaetes have been used in studies of physiology, regeneration, and metabolic gradients. Some aquatic forms are important in studies of stream pollution as indicators of organic contamination. Earthworms are important in turning over the soil and reducing vegetable material into humus. It is likely that fertile soil furnishes a suitable habitat for earthworms, rather than being a result of their activity. *See* ANNELIDA.   [P.C.H.]

Oligonucleotide   A deoxyribonucleic acid (DNA) or ribonucleic acid (RNA) sequence composed of two or more covalently linked nucleotides. Oligonucleotides are classified as deoxyribooligonucleotides or ribooligonucleotides. Fragments containing up to 50 nucleotides are generally termed oligonucleotides, and longer fragments are called polynucleotides. *See* DEOXYRIBONUCLEIC ACID (DNA); RIBONUCLEIC ACID (RNA).

A deoxyribooligonucleotide consists of a 5-carbon sugar called deoxyribose joined covalently to phosphate at the 5′ and 3′ carbons of this sugar to form an alternating, unbranched polymer. A ribooligonucleotide consists of a similar repeating structure where the 5-carbon sugar is ribose. Chemically synthesized oligonucleotides of predetermined sequence have proven to be very useful for studying a large number of biochemical processes. In the 1960s, these compounds were used to decipher the genetic code. Later, chemically prepared deoxyoligonucleotides were joined to form genes for transfer RNAs. Gene synthesis from synthetic deoxyoligonucleotides is now routinely used to prepare genes and modified genes for proteins having potential clinical applications. Oligonucleotides have also been used to diagnose genetic disorders and bacterial or viral infections. *See* GENE; GENETIC CODE; GENETIC ENGINEERING; NUCLEIC ACID.   [M.H.C.]

Oligosaccharide   A carbohydrate molecule composed of 3–20 monosaccharides (simple sugars). Generally, free oligosaccharides do not constitute a significant proportion of naturally occurring carbohydrates. Most carbohydrates that occur in nature are in the form of monosaccharides (such as blood sugar, or glucose), disaccharides (such as table sugar, or sucrose, and milk sugar, or lactose), and polysaccharides (such as starch and glycogen, polyglucose molecules, or chitin). *See* GLUCOSE; LACTOSE; MONOSACCHARIDE; POLYSACCHARIDE.

The monosaccharides of multiple sugar units such as oligosaccharides are connected with each other through bonds called glycosidic linkages. They are linked primarily to other sugars and to other molecules through aldehyde or ketone reducing groups.

Most naturally occurring oligosaccharides are linked either to proteins (glycoproteins) or to lipids (glycolipids). Glycoconjugates are present in essentially all life forms and particularly in cell membranes and cell secretions. Many hormones are glycoproteins, and an increasing number of enzymes have been shown to have sugars attached. Antigenic properties of the human red blood cell ABO blood group system are determined by glycolipid oligosaccharides. In fact, all the major protein components of blood serum, with the exception of serum albumin, are glycoproteins. *See* BLOOD GROUPS; CELL MEMBRANES; GLYCOLIPID; GLYCOPROTEIN.

Many changes in the structures of oligosaccharides of glycoconjugates have been detected in cancer cells. Changes or differences in oligosaccharide structures are generally the result of differences in biosynthetic pathways or of degradative pathways. An understanding of glycoconjugates in normal biological systems and in certain disease states is currently of great importance.   [D.M.Ca.]

Oncofetal antigens   Antigens that are commonly present both in fetal tissue during early development of life and in adult tissue when cancer occurs. These antigens, primarily glycoprotein in nature, are the products of one or more genes that normally are expressed only during fetal development and then are repressed in adult life. Their production in adults is a result of activation of the controlled genes by a yet unknown mechanism in association with cancer. Minute but significant changes of these fetal antigens in body fluids can serve in detecting the early oncogenic process and in monitoring the efficacy of, and in developing new modalities of, cancer treatment. *See* ANTIGEN.

Several oncofetal antigens have been investigated extensively, including alpha fetoprotein, carcinoembryonic antigen, and prostate specific antigen.

Alpha fetoprotein is a normal embryonic product during fetal development. After birth the serum alpha fetoprotein decreases to only trace amounts by 2–5 weeks, and to normal adult levels (less than 20 nanograms per milliliter) within 1 year. Alpha fetoprotein in the serum is elevated in individuals with primary hepatocellular carcinoma and with teratocarcinomas of the ovary or testes. Nonhepatic primary cancer generally exhibits an elevation of serum alpha fetoprotein only after spread to the liver.

The carcinoembryonic antigen of human digestive cancer has been the most studied oncofetal antigen. Although it is generally accepted that the carcinoembryonic antigen assay should not be used as a screening test for cancer in the general population, it does have an adjunctive role in diagnostic procedures. One of the more significant results in clinical applications of carcinoembryonic antigen is the use of radioactive-labeled antibodies for localization of carcinoembryonic antigen–producing tumors. Although carcinoembryonic antigen is not specific for malignant disease, it is found in association with a variety of epithelially derived cancers.

Prostate specific antigen is expressed exclusively by human prostate epithelial cells. An elevated level of this antigen in the blood is detected in individuals with prostate cancer, although a slightly elevated antigen also can be detected in individuals with benign prostatic hypertrophy, that is, older men with an enlarged prostate. Prostate specific antigen is the most effective parameter for monitoring the treatment response and detecting the early disease recurrence in individuals with an established diagnosis of prostate cancer. Moreover, prostate specific antigen is of clinical value as a reliable aid in the screening of the high-risk or older population for early detection of prostate cancer.   [T.M.Ch.]

Ontogeny   The developmental history of an organism from its origin to maturity. It starts with fertilization and ends with the attainment of an adult state, usually expressed in terms of both maximal body size and sexual maturity. Fertilization is the joining of haploid gametes (a spermatozoon and an ovum, each bearing half the number of chromosomes typical for the species) to form a diploid zygote (with a full chromosome number), a new unicellular living being which will grow through a series of asexual reproductions. The gametes are the link between one generation and the next: the fusion of male and female gametes is the onset of a new ontogenetic cycle. Many organisms die shortly after sexual reproduction, whereas others live longer and generations are overlapped. Species are usually conceived as adults, but in most cases the majority of their representation in the environment is as intermediate ontogenetic stages. *See* REPRODUCTION (ANIMAL).

In unicellular organisms, each asexual reproduction leads to the formation of new individuals, the cells deriving from a first sexually derived individual forming a clone of genetically identical individuals. In multicellular organisms, the products of the asexual reproductions starting with the first division of the zygote remain connected, and the clone they form is a single individual. Clonation of individuals occurs even in humans, when the first results of asexual reproduction of the zygote separate from each other, leading to twin formation.

The ontogeny of a multicellular organism involves segmentation (or cleavage): the zygote divides into two, four, etc., cells which continue to divide. These cells are initially similar to the zygote, although smaller in size. They soon start to differentiate from their ancestors, acquiring special features, and forming specific tissue layers and, eventually, organs. These processes lead to the formation and growth of an embryo. Embryos can develop freely, within egg shells, or within the body of one parent; they can grow directly into juveniles (as in humans) or into larvae (with an indirect development, as in insects).

Juveniles are similar to adults but are smaller in size and not sexually mature. Their ontogeny continues until they reach a maximal size and reproductive ability. Larvae have different morphology, physiology, and ecology from adults; they become juveniles through a metamorphosis (that is, an abrupt change). Usually ontogeny is interrupted at adulthood, but some organisms can grow throughout their life, so that ontogeny ends with their death. *See* ECOLOGY.   [F.V.B.]

Onychophora   The only living animal phylum with true lobopods (annulate, saclike legs with internal musculature). There are about 70 known living species in two families, Peripatopsidae and Peripatidae. These terrestrial animals are frequently referred to as Peripatus. Onychophora comprise a single class or order of the same name. They were once considered a missing link between annelid worms and arthropods, but are best considered to be aligned with the arthropods.

They have a cylindrical body, 0.5–6 in. (1.4–15 cm) long, with one antennal pair, an anterior ventral mouth, and 14–43 pairs of stubby, unsegmented legs ending in walking pads and paired claws. Mandibles are present as modified tips of the first appendage pair. The body surface has a flexible chitinous cuticle. The body wall has three layers of smooth muscle, as in annelids, but the coelom is reduced to gonadal and nephridial cavities; the body cavity has an arthropodlike partitioned hemocoel; the heart is tubular with metameric ostia; and the nephridia are segmental. Gas exchange takes place by means of tracheae; spiracles are minute and numerous, located between skin folds. Slow locomotion is effected by legs and body contractions; the animals can squeeze into very tight spaces. The eyes, located at the antennal base, are the direct type with a chitinous lens and retinal layer. The sexes are separate; the testes and ovaries are paired; and the genital tracts open though the posterior ventral pore. Onychophora are oviparous, ovoviviparous, or viviparous.

The Onychophora are predatory, feeding on small invertebrates. They are largely nocturnal, occurring in humid habitats in forests.   [S.B.P.]

Oogenesis   The generation of ova or eggs, the female gametes. Primordial germ cells, once they have populated the gonads, proliferate and differentiate into sperm (in the testis) or ova (in the ovary). The decision to produce either spermatocytes or oocytes is based primarily on the genotype of the embryo. In rare cases, this decision can be reversed by the hormonal environment of the embryo, so that the sexual phenotype may differ from the genotype. Formation of the ovum most often involves substantial increases in cell volume as well as the acquisition of organellar structures that adapt the egg for reception of the sperm nucleus, and support of the early embryo. In histological sections, the structure of the oocyte often appears random but as the understanding of its chemical and structural organization increases, an order begins to emerge. *See* Ovum; Spermatogenesis.

Among lower vertebrates and invertebrates, mitotic divisions of the precursor cells, the oogonia, continue throughout the reproductive life of the adult; thus extremely large numbers of ova are produced. In the fetal ovary of mammals, the oogonia undergo mitotic divisions until the birth of the fetus, but a process involving the destruction of the majority of the developing ova by the seventh month of gestation reduces the number of oocytes from millions to a few hundred. Around the time of birth, the mitotic divisions cease altogether, and the infant female ovary contains its full complement of potential ova. At puberty, the pituitary hormones, follicle stimulating hormone (FSH), and luteinizing hormone (LH) stimulate the growth and differentiation of the ova and surrounding cells (see illustration). *See* Mitosis.

One important feature of oocyte differentiation is the reduction of the chromosome complement from the diploid state of the somatic cells to the haploid state of gametes. Fusion with the haploid genome of the sperm will restore the normal diploid number of chromosomes to the zygote. The meiotic divisions which reduce the chromosome content of the oocyte occur after the structural differentiation of the oocyte is complete, often only after fertilization. Unlike the formation of sperm, in which the two divisions of meiosis produce four equivalent daughter cells, the cytoplasm of the oocyte is divided unequally, so that three polar bodies with reduced cytoplasm and one oocyte are the final products. Generally, each fertilized oocyte produces a single embryo, but there are exceptions. Identical twins, for example, arise from the same fertilized egg. *See* Meiosis.

The provision of nutrients for the embryo is a major function of the egg, and this is accomplished by the storage of yolk in the cytoplasm. Yolk consists of complex mixtures of proteins (vitellins), lipids, and carbohydrates in platelets, which are membrane-surrounded packets dispersed throughout the egg cytoplasm (ooplasm). The amount of yolk in an egg correlates with the nutritional needs of the embryo. Although the eggs of mammals are extremely small as compared to the fetus, the bulk of the nutrition is supplied by the placenta; yolk is required only until implantation in the uterine wall.

Egg cytoplasm also contains large stores of ribonucleic acid (RNA) in the form of ribosomal, messenger, and transfer RNA. These RNAs direct the synthesis of proteins in the early embryo, and may have a decisive influence on the course of development. The mechanism by which the RNA is supplied to the egg is the basis for a major classification of ovary types. Panoistic ovaries, in which the egg nucleus is responsible for the production of all the stored RNA in the ooplasm, are typical of vertebrates, primitive insects, and a number of invertebrates. The amounts of RNA produced during

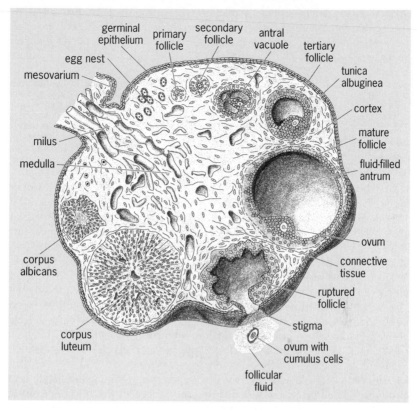

germinal epithelium
primary follicle
secondary follicle
antral vacuole
tertiary follicle
egg nest
mesovarium
tunica albuginea
cortex
milus
mature follicle
medulla
fluid-filled antrum
corpus albicans
ovum
connective tissue
ruptured follicle
corpus luteum
stigma
ovum with cumulus cells
follicular fluid

Three-dimensional view of the cyclic changes in the mammalian ovary.

the meiotic prophase in such ovaries are much larger than those produced by a somatic cell, and thus special mechanisms seem to be involved in the synthetic process. *See* DEOXYRIBONUCLEIC ACID (DNA); RIBONUCLEIC ACID (RNA). [S.J.B.]

Oomycetes A class of fungi in the subdivision Mastigomycotina. They comprise a group of heterotropic, funguslike organisms that are classified with the zoosporic fungi (Mastigomycotina) but in reality are related to the heterokont algae. They are distinguished from other zoosporic fungi by the presence of biflagellate zoospores. Some taxa are nonzoosporic. Asexual reproduction involves the release of zoospores from sporangia; in some taxa the sporangium germinates with outgrowth of a germ tube. Sexual reproduction occurs when an oogonial cell is fertilized by contact with an antheridium, resulting in one or more oospores.

Oomycetes are cosmopolitan, occurring in fresh and salt water, in soil, and as terrestrial parasites of plants. Many species can be grown in pure culture on defined media. There are four orders: The Saprolegniales and Leptomitales are popularly known as water molds. Some species are destructive fish parasites. Many Lagenidiales are parasites of invertebrates and algae. The Peronosporales are primarily plant parasites attacking the root, stem, or leaf, and include some of the more destructive plant pathogens. *See* EUMYCOTA; FUNGI. [D.J.S.B.]

Operon A group of distinct genes that are expressed and regulated as a unit. Each operon is a deoxyribonucleic acid (DNA) sequence that contains at least two regulatory sites, the promoter and the operator, and the structural genes that code for specific proteins (see illustration). The promoter (*p*) site is the location at which ribonucleic

DNA — *i* | *p* | *o* | *z* | *y* | *a* |

mRNA ———————————————————→

The lactose (*lac*) operon from *Escherichia coli*: *z*, *y*, and *a* are structural genes; *i* is the *lac* repressor gene; *p* is the promoter site; and *o* is the operator site. The arrow indicates length and direction of mRNA synthesis.

acid (RNA) polymerase binds to the operon. RNA polymerase moves down the operon catalyzing the synthesis of a messenger RNA (mRNA) molecule with a sequence that is complementary to DNA. This process is called transcription. The mRNA is used as a template by ribosomes to synthesize the proteins coded for by the structural genes (in the original DNA) in a process called translation. This mRNA is referred to as polycistronic because its sequence directs the synthesis of more than one protein. The operator (*o*) site is located between the *p* site and the beginning of the coding region for the first structural gene. It is at this site that molecules called repressors can bind to the DNA and block RNA polymerase from transcribing the DNA, thus shutting off the operon. Some systems can be derepressed by the addition of small molecules called effectors, which bind to the repressor protein and cause a conformational (shape) change that makes it no longer able to bind to the DNA at the operator site. *See* DEOXYRIBONUCLEIC ACID (DNA); RIBONUCLEIC ACID (RNA).

Activation is believed to arise from the binding of a protein immediately adjacent to the promoter. The protein provides additional locations with which RNA polymerase can interact; the extra interactions result in an increased amount of polymerase binding to the promoter. Activators are more frequently involved in the regulation of genes in eukaryotes than in prokaryotes.

Once RNA polymerase begins transcribing a gene, it continues making RNA until a termination site is reached. Antiterminators are proteins that prevent termination at certain sites. In the presence of these antiterminators, RNA polymerase continues along the genome and transcribes the genes following the termination site until a different class of termination site is encountered.

Attenuation is the premature termination of the mRNA translation. Although the exact mechanism of attenuation has not been determined, it is thought that attenuation is due to the formation of a translation termination site in mRNA. *See* GENE; GENE ACTION.

[D.H.O.]

Opportunistic infections Infections that cause a disease only when the host's immune system is impaired. The classic opportunistic infection never leads to disease in the normal host. The protozoon *Pneumocystis carinii* infects nearly everyone at some point in life but never causes disease unless the immune system is severely depressed. The most common immunologic defect associated with pneumocystosis is acquired immune deficiency syndrome (AIDS). *See* ACQUIRED IMMUNE DEFICIENCY SYNDROME (AIDS).

A compromised host is an individual with an abnormality or defect in any of the host defense mechanisms that predisposes that person to an infection. The altered defense mechanisms or immunity can be either congenital, that is, occurring at birth and genetically determined, or acquired. Congenital immune deficiencies are relatively rare.

Acquired immunodeficiencies are associated with a wide variety of conditions such as (1) the concomitant presence of certain underlying diseases such as cancer, diabetes, cystic fibrosis, sickle cell anemia, chronic obstructive lung disease, severe burns, and cirrhosis of the liver; (2) side effects of certain medical therapies and drugs such as corticosteroids, prolonged antibiotic usage, anticancer agents, alcohol, and nonprescribed recreational drugs; (3) infection with immunity-destroying microorganisms such as the human immunodeficiency virus that leads to AIDS; (4) age, both old and young; and (5) foreign-body exposure, such as occurs in individuals with prosthetic heart valves, intravenous catheters, and other indwelling prosthetic devices.

Virtually any microorganism can become an opportunist. The typical ones fall into a number of categories and may be more likely to be associated with a specific immunologic defect. Examples include (1) gram-positive bacteria: both *Staphylococcus aureus* and the coagulase-negative *S. epidermidis* have a propensity for invading the skin and as well as catheters and other foreign implanted devices; (2) gram-negative bacteria: the most common is *Escherichia coli* and the most lethal is *Pseudomonas aeruginosa*; these pathogens are more likely to occur in cases of granulocytopenia (granulocyte deficiency, as occurs in leukemia or chemotheraphy; (3) acid-fast bacteria: *Mycotuberculum tuberculosis* is more likely to reactivate in the elderly and in those individuals with underlying malignancies and AIDS; (4) protozoa: defects in cell-mediated immunity, such as AIDS, are associated with reactivated infection with *Toxoplasma gondii* and *Cryptosporidium*; (5) fungi: *Cryptococcus neoformans* is a fungus that causes meningitis in individuals with impaired cell-mediated immunity such as AIDS, cancer, and diabetes; *Candida albicans* typically causes blood and organ infection in individuals with granulocytopenia. *See* CELLULAR IMMUNOLOGY; ESCHERICHIA; MEDICAL MYCOLOGY; STAPHYLOCOCCUS; TUBERCULOSIS.

The first step in treatment of opportunistic infections involves making the correct diagnosis, which is often difficult as many of the pathogens can mistakenly be thought of as benign. The second step involves administration of appropriate antimicrobial agents. As a third step, if possible, the underlying immune defect needs to be corrected. *See* IMMUNOLOGICAL DEFICIENCY; INFECTION; MEDICAL BACTERIOLOGY.   [R.Mur.]

Organic evolution   The modification of living organisms during their descent, generation by generation, from common ancestors. Organic, or biological, evolution is to be distinguished from other phenomena to which the term evolution is often applied, such as chemical evolution, cultural evolution, or the origin of life from nonliving matter. Organic evolution includes two major processes: anagenesis, the alteration of the genetic properties of a single lineage over time; and cladogenesis, or branching, whereby a single lineage splits into two or more distinct lineages that continue to change anagenetically.

Anagenesis consists of change in the genetic basis of the features of the organisms that constitute a single species. Populations in different geographic localities are considered members of the same species if they can exchange members at some rate and hence interbreed with each other, but unless the level of interchange (gene flow) is very high, some degree of genetic difference among different populations is likely to develop. The changes that transpire in a single population may be spread to other populations of the species by gene flow. *See* SPECIES CONCEPT.

Almost every population harbors several different alleles at each of a great many of the gene loci; hence many characteristics of a species are genetically variable. All genetic variations ultimately arise by mutation of the genetic material. Broadly defined, mutations include changes in the number or structure of the chromosomes and changes in individual genes, including substitutions of individual nucleotide pairs, insertion and deletion of nucleotides, and duplication of genes. Many such mutations alter the properties of the gene products (ribonucleic acid and proteins) or the timing or tissue localization of gene action, and consequently affect various aspects of the phenotype (that is, the morphological and physiological characteristics of an organism). Whether and how a mutation is phenotypically expressed often depends on developmental (epigenetic) events. *See* GENE; GENETIC CODE; MUTATION; RIBONUCLEIC ACID (RNA).

Natural selection is a consistent difference in the average rate at which genetically different entities leave descendants to subsequent generations; such a difference arises from differences in fitness (that is, in the rate of survival, reproduction, or both). In fact, a good approximate measure of the strength of natural selection is the difference between two such entities in their rate of increase. The entities referred to are usually different alleles at a locus, or phenotypically different classes of individuals in the population that differ in genotype. Thus selection may occur at the level of the gene, as in the phenomenon of meiotic drive, whereby one allele predominates among the gametes produced by a heterozygote. Selection at the level of the individual organism, the more usual case, entails a difference in the survival and reproductive success of phenotypes that may differ at one locus or at more than one locus. As a consequence of the difference in fitness, the proportion of one or the other allele increases in subsequent generations. The relative fitness of different genotypes usually depends on environmental conditions.

Different alleles of a gene that provides an important function do not necessarily differ in their effect on survival and reproduction; such alleles are said to be neutral. The proportion of two neutral alleles in a population fluctuates randomly from generation to generation by chance, because not all individuals in the population have the same number of surviving offspring. Random fluctuations of this kind are termed random genetic drift. If different alleles do indeed differ in their effects on fitness, both genetic drift and natural selection operate simultaneously. The deterministic force of natural selection drives allele frequencies toward an equilibrium, while the stochastic (random) force of genetic drift brings them away from that equilibrium. The outcome for any given population depends on the relative strength of natural selection (the magnitude of differences in fitness) and of genetic drift (which depends on population size).

The great diversity of organisms has come about because individual lineages (species) branch into separate species, which continue to diverge. This splitting process, speciation, occurs when genetic differences develop between two populations that prevent them from interbreeding and forming a common gene pool. The genetically based characteristics that cause such reproductive isolation are usually termed isolating mechanisms. Reproductive isolation seems to develop usually as a fortuitous by-product of genetic divergence that occurs for other reasons (either by natural selection or by genetic drift). *See* SPECIATION.

A frequent consequence of natural selection is that a species comes to be dominated by individuals whose features equip them better for the environment or way of life of the species. Such features are termed adaptations. Although many features of organisms are adaptive, not all are, and it is a serious error to suppose that species are capable of attaining ideal states of adaptation. Some characteristics are likely to have developed by genetic drift rather than natural selection, and so are not adaptations; others are side effects of adaptive features, which exist because of pleiotropy or developmental correlations.

Higher taxa are those above the species level, such as genera and families. A taxon such as a genus is typically a group of species, derived from a common ancestor, that share one or more features so distinctive that they merit recognition as a separate taxon. The degree of difference necessary for such recognition, however, is entirely arbitrary:

there are often no sharp limits between related genera, families, or other higher taxa, and very often the diagnostic character exists in graded steps among a group of species that may be arbitrarily divided into different higher taxa. Moreover, a character that in some groups is used to distinguish higher taxa sometimes varies among closely related species or even within species. In addition, the fossil record of many groups shows that a trait that takes on very different forms in two living taxa has developed by intermediate steps along divergent lines from their common ancestor; thus the inner ear bones of mammals may be traced to jaw elements in reptiles that in turn are homologous to gill arch elements in Paleozoic fishes.

The characteristics of a species evolve individually or in concert with certain other traits that are developmentally or functionally correlated. Because of this mosaic pattern of evolution, it is meaningful to speak of the rate of evolution of characters, but not of species or lineages as total entities. Thus in some lineages, such as the so-called living fossils, many aspects of morphology have evolved slowly since the groups first came into existence, but evolution of their deoxyribonucleic acid and amino acid sequences has proceeded at much the same rate as in other lineages. Every species, including the living fossils, is a mixture of traits that have changed little since the species' remote ancestors, and traits that have undergone some evolutionary change in the recent past. The history of life is not one of progress in any one direction, but of adaptive radiation on a grand scale: the descendants of any one lineage diverge as they adapt to different resources, habitats, or ways of life, acquiring their own specialized features as they do so. There is no evidence that evolution has any goal, nor does the mechanistic theory of evolutionary processes admit of any way in which genetic change can have a goal or be directed toward the future. However, for life taken as a whole, the only clearly discernible trend is toward ever-increasing diversity. [D.J.Fu.]

Osmoregulatory mechanisms Physiological mechanisms for the maintenance of an optimal and constant level of osmotic activity of the fluid within and around the cells, considered to be most favorable for the initiation and maintenance of vital reactions in the cell and for maximal survival and efficient functioning of the entire organism.

The actions of osmoregulatory mechanisms are, first, to impose constraints upon the passage of water and solute between the organism and its surroundings and, second, to accelerate passage of water and solute between organism and surroundings. The first effect requires a change of architecture of membranes in that they become selectively permeable and achieve their purpose without expenditure of energy. The accelerating effect, apart from requiring a change of architecture of cell membranes, requires expenditure of energy and performance of useful osmotic work. Thus substances may be moved from a region of low to a region of higher chemical activity. Such movement can occur in opposition to the forces of diffusion of an electric field and of a pressure gradient, all of which may act across the cell membrane. It follows that there must be an energy source which is derived from the chemical reactions of cellular metabolism and that part of the free energy so generated must be stored in molecules which are driven across the membrane barrier. Active transport is the modern term for such processes. *See* CELL MEMBRANES. [W.A.B.; T.P.S.]

Ovary A part of the reproductive system of all female vertebrates. Although not vital to individual survival, the ovary is vital to perpetuation of the species. The function of the ovary is to produce the female germ cells or ova, and in some species to elaborate hormones that assist in regulating the reproductive cycle.

The ovaries develop as bilateral structures in all vertebrates, but adult asymmetry is found in certain species of all vertebrates from the elasmobranchs to the mammals.

The ovary of all vertebrates functions in essentially the same manner. However, ovarian histology of the various groups differs considerably. Even such a fundamental element as the ovum exhibits differences in various groups. *See* Ovum.

The mammalian ovary is attached to the dorsal body wall. The free surface of the ovary is covered by a modified peritoneum called the germinal epithelium. Just beneath the germinal epithelium is a layer of fibrous connective tissue. Most of the rest of the ovary is made up of a more cellular and more loosely arranged connective tissue (stroma) in which are embedded the germinal, endocrine, vascular, and nervous elements.

The most obvious ovarian structures are the follicles and the corpora lutea. The smallest, or primary, follicle consists of an oocyte surrounded by a layer of follicle (nurse) cells. Follicular growth results from an increase in oocyte size, multiplication of the follicle cells, and differentiation of the perifollicular stroma to form a fibrocellular envelope called the theca interna. Finally, a fluid-filled antrum develops in the granulosa layer, resulting in a vesicular follicle.

The cells of the theca interna hypertrophy during follicular growth and many capillaries invade the layer, thus forming the endocrine element that is thought to secrete estrogen. The other known endocrine structure is the corpus luteum, which is primarily the product of hypertrophy of the granulosa cells remaining after the follicular wall ruptures to release the ovum. Ingrowths of connective tissue from the theca interna deliver capillaries to vascularize the hypertrophied follicle cells of this new corpus luteum; progesterone is secreted here. *See* ESTROGEN; ESTRUS; MENSTRUATION; PROGESTERONE.

[K.L.D.]

Ovum   The egg or female sex cell. Strictly speaking, the term refers to this cell when it is ready for fertilization, but it is often applied to earlier or later stages. Confusion is avoided by using qualifying adjectives such as immature, ripe, mature, fertilized, or developing ova. The mature ova are generally spheroidal and large. The number of ova produced at one time varies in different animals, from millions in many marine animals that spawn into the surrounding sea water to about a dozen or less in mammals in which adaptations for internal nourishment of the developing embryo and care of the young are highly developed.

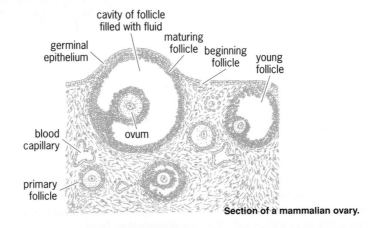

Section of a mammalian ovary.

In the ovary the immature ovum is associated with follicle cells through which it receives material for growth. In mammals, as the egg matures, these cells arrange themselves into a structure known as the Graafian, or vesicular, follicle, consisting of a large fluid-filled cavity into which the ovum, surrounded by several layers of cells, projects from the layer of follicle cells that constitutes the inner wall (see illustration). The fluid contains estrogenic female sex hormone secreted by cells in an intermediate layer of the follicular wall.

Yolk, or deutoplasm, is essentially a food reserve in the form of small spherules, present to a greater or lesser extent in all eggs. It accounts largely for the differences in size of eggs. Eggs are classified according to the distribution of yolk. In the isolecithal type there is a nearly uniform distribution through the cytoplasm, as in most small eggs. The yolk in telolecithal eggs is increasingly concentrated toward one pole, as in the large eggs of fish, amphibians, reptiles, and birds. Centrolecithal, or centrally located, yolk occurs in eggs of insects and cephalopod mollusks. See GAMETOGENESIS; OOGENESIS.

[A.T./I.I.L.I I.]

Oxygen toxicity   A toxic effect in a living organism caused by a species of oxygen. Oxygen has two aspects, one benign and the other malignant. Those organisms that avail themselves of the enormous metabolic advantages provided by dioxygen (O_2) must defend themselves against its toxicity. The complete reduction of one molecule of O_2 to two of water (H_2O) requires four electrons; therefore, intermediates must be encountered during the reduction of O_2 by the univalent pathway. The intermediates of O_2 reduction, in the order of their production, are the superoxide radical (O_2^-), hydrogen peroxide (H_2O_2), and the hydroxyl radical (HO·).

The intermediates of oxygen reduction, rather than O_2, itself, are probably the primary cause of oxygen toxicity. It follows that defensive measures must deal with these intermediates. The superoxide radical is eliminated by enzymes that catalyze the following reaction.

$$O_2^- + O_2^- + 2H^+ \leftrightharpoons H_2O_2 + O_2$$

These enzymes, known as superoxide dismutases, have been isolated from a wide variety of living things.

Hydrogen peroxide (H_2O_2) must also be eliminated, and this is achieved by two enzymatic mechanisms. The first of these is the dismutation of H_2O_2 into water and oxygen, a process catalyzed by catalases. The second is the reduction of H_2O_2 into two molecules of water at the expense of a variety of reductants, a process catalyzed by peroxidases. See ENZYME.

The multiplicity of superoxide dismutases, catalases, and peroxidases, and the great catalytic efficiency of these enzymes, provides a formidable defense against O_2^- and H_2O_2. If these first two intermediates of O_2 reduction are eliminated, the third (HO·) will not be produced. No defense is perfect, however, and some HO· is produced; therefore its deleterious effects must be minimized. This is achieved to a large extent by antioxidants, which prevent free-radical chain reactions from propagating. See ANTIOXIDANT; PEPTIDE.

The apparent comfort in which aerobic organisms live in the presence of an atmosphere that is 20% O_2 is due to a complex and effective system of defenses against this peculiar gas. Indeed, these defenses are easily overwhelmed, and overt symptoms of oxygen toxicity become apparent when organisms are exposed to 100% O_2. For example, a rat maintained in 100% O_2 will die in 2 to 3 days.   [I.Fr.]

P

Pancreas A composite gland in most vertebrates, containing both exocrine cells—which produce and secrete enzymes involved in digestion—and endocrine cells, arranged in separate islets which elaborate at least two distinct hormones, insulin and glucagon, both of which play a role in the regulation of metabolism, and particularly of carbohydrate metabolism. *See* CARBOHYDRATE METABOLISM.

Anatomy. The pancreas of mammals shows large variations. The extremes are the unique, massive pancreas of humans, and the richly branched organ of the rabbit. Usually, the main duct, the duct of Wirsung, opens into the duodenum very close to the hepatic duct. In humans, the pancreas weighs about 2.5 oz (70 g). It can be divided into head, body, and tail. Accessory pancreases are frequently found anywhere along the small intestine, in the wall of the stomach, and in Meckel's diverticulum.

The exocrine portion of the pancreas shows tubuloalveolar glands. Each terminal alveolus is called an acinus. The various acini have central cavities, which open into intralobular ducts through narrow intercalated tubes. The interlobular ducts anastomose and ultimately form the main duct of Wirsung. The activity of the acini is stimulated by secretin as well as by pilocarpine.

The endocrine portion shows cellular masses called islands or islets of Langerhans, in which the cellular cords or masses are more or less isolated by irregular spaces filled with connective tissue and blood capillaries. The two main types of cells are the alpha and the beta cells.

Between the grapelike exocrine portion with its ducts and the islands of Langerhans, it is possible to observe connective tissue septa, numerous blood vessels, and nerves.

Physiology. The pancreatic juice carried to the duodenum is a slightly alkaline liquid containing trypsinogen, which, when activated, causes the hydrolysis of the proteins into amino acids, amylase, and maltase, which act on the glucides, and lipase, which causes the hydrolysis of fatty substances. The intense stimulation of the pancreatic secretion after ingestion of food is considered to be the result of a nervous reflex originating in the mouth, and also of direct introduction of acids and fats into the duodenum, causing the liberation of a hormone called secretin into the bloodstream to stimulate the exocrine secretion.

F. Banting and C. Best (1922) prepared pancreatic extracts which were able to prevent the lethal effects of pancreatectomy. The same effect was obtained with extracts from pancreas in which, after ligature of the duct of Wirsung, the exocrine portion of the gland had disappeared.

The alpha cells and beta cells in the islets are the sources of two hormones, insulin from the beta, and glucagon, also known as the hyperglycemic factor, from the alpha. The former is a hormone which influences carbohydrate metabolism, enabling the organism to utilize sugar. The latter accelerates the conversion of liver glycogen into glucose. Glucagon elevates the blood sugar level, and its effects are the opposite of those of insulin, so that the two hormones together maintain the sugar metabolism of the body in balance. When the level of sugar in the blood becomes too low, the secretion of glucagon is stimulated. *See* GLUCAGON; INSULIN.   [E.L.V.C.]

Paramyxovirus   A subgroup of myxoviruses that includes the viruses of mumps, measles, parainfluenza, respiratory syncytial (RS) disease, and Newcastle disease. Like influenza viruses, the paramyxoviruses are ribonucleic acid (RNA)-containing viruses and possess an ether-sensitive lipoprotein envelope. *See* ANIMAL VIRUS; MEASLES; MUMPS.   [J.L.Me.]

Paranoia   A mode of thought, feeling, and behavior characterized centrally by false persecutory beliefs, more specifically referred to as paranoidness. Commonly associated with these core persecutory beliefs are properties of suspiciousness, fearfulness, hostility, hypersensitivity, rigidity of conviction, and an exaggerated sense of self-reference. These properties are evident with varying degrees of intensity and duration.

The paranoid mode can be triggered at either biological or psychological levels. Common precipitating biological causes are brain trauma or tumor, thyroid disorder, cerebral arteriosclerosis, and intoxication with certain drugs, including alcohol, amphetamines, cocaine, other psychostimulants, and hallucinogens such as mescaline or lysergic acid diethylamide (LSD). They can produce disordered activity of central dopaminergic and noradrenergic pathways. At the psychological level, triggering causes include false arrest, birth of a deformed child, social isolation, deafness, and intensely humiliating experiences. *See* NORADRENERGIC SYSTEM.

The paranoid mode is resistant to modification by psychotherapeutic or pharmacological methods. Acute psychotic states of paranoidness accompanied by high levels of anxiety are usually responsive to neuroleptic medication. *See* PSYCHOPHARMACOLOGY.
                                                                                      [K.M.C.]

Parasitology   The scientific study of parasites and of parasitism. Parasitism is a subdivision of symbiosis and is defined as an intimate association between an organism (parasite) and another, larger species of organism (host) upon which the parasite is metabolically dependent. Implicit in this definition is the concept that the host is harmed, while the parasite benefits from the association. Although technically parasites, pathogenic bacteria and viruses and nematode, fungal, and insect parasites of plants are traditionally outside the field of parasitology.

Parasites often cause important diseases of humans and animals. For this reason, parasitology is an active field of study; advances in biotechnology have raised expectations for the development of new drugs, vaccines, and other control measures. However, these expectations are dampened by the inherent complexity of parasites and host-parasite relationships, the entrenchment of parasites and vectors in their environments, and the vast socioeconomic problems in the geographical areas where parasites are most prevalent.

The ecological and physiological relationships between parasites and their hosts constitute some of the most impressive examples of biological adaptation known. Much of classical parasitology has been devoted to the elucidation of one of the most important aspects of host-parasite ecological relationships, namely, the dispersion and the transmission of parasites to new hosts.

Parasite life cycles range from simple to highly complex. Simple life cycles (transmission from animal to animal) are direct and horizontal with adaptations that include high reproduction rates, and the production of relatively inactive stages (cysts or eggs) that are resistant to environmental factors such as desiccation, ultraviolet radiation, and extreme temperatures. The infective stages are passively consumed when food or water is contaminated with feces that contain cysts. The cysts are then activated in the gut by cues such as acidity to continue their development. Other direct-transmission parasites, such as hookworms, actively invade new hosts by penetrating the skin. Physiologically more complicated are those life cycles that are direct and vertical, with transmission being from mother to offspring. The main adaptation of the parasite for this type of life cycle is the ability to gain access to the fetus or young animal through the ovaries, placenta, or mammary glands of the mother.

Many parasites have taken advantage of the food chain of free-living animals for transmission to new hosts. During their life cycle, these parasites have intermediate hosts that are the normal prey of their final hosts. Parasites may ascend the food chain by utilizing a succession of progressively larger hosts, a process called paratenesis. *See* FOOD WEB.

Vectors are intermediate hosts that are not eaten by the final host, but rather serve as factories for the production of more parasites and may even carry them to new hosts or to new environments frequented by potential hosts. Blood-sucking athropods such as mosquitoes and tsetse flies are well-known examples. After acquiring the parasite from an infected host, they move to another host, which they bite and infect. Snails are important vectors for two-host trematodes (flukes), which increase their numbers greatly in the snail by asexual reproduction. The stages that leave the snail may either infect second intermediate hosts that are eaten by carnivorous final hosts, may encyst on vegetation that is eaten by herbivorous hosts, or in the case of the blood flukes (schistosomes) may swim to and directly penetrate the final host.

Metabolic dependency is the key to parasitism, and parasites employ many ways to feed off their hosts. The simplest is exhibited by the common intestinal round-worm, *Ascaris*, which consumes the host's intestinal contents. Parasites require from their hosts not only energy-yielding molecules but also basic monomers for macro-molecular synthesis and essential cofactors for these synthetic processes. Many examples of the specific absence of key parts of energy-yielding or biosynthetic pathways in parasites are known, and these missing enzymes, cofactors, or intermediates are supplied by the host. Tapeworms are more complex than *Ascaris* in nutritional require-ments from the host. They lack a gut, but their surface actively takes up, by facili-tated diffusion or active transport, small molecules such as amino acids and simple sugars.

Parasites, by coevolving with their hosts, have the ability to evade the immune response. The best-known evasive tactic is antigenic variation, as found in African trypanosomes, which have a complicated genetic mechanism for producing alternative forms of a glycoprotein that virtually cover the entire parasite. By going through a genetically programmed sequence of variant surface glycoproteins, the trypanosome population in a host stays one step ahead of immunity and is not eliminated. Other possible immune escape mechanisms in parasites have been discovered and probably cooperate to prolong parasite survival.

Parasites are not altogether exempt from the effects of immunity. Rather than com-pletely eliminating parasites, the immune system more often functions to control their populations in the host. Thus a balance is achieved between hosts and parasites that have lived in long evolutionary association, with both surviving through compromise. Enhancing these particular antiparasite mechanisms and neutralizing the parasite's eva-sion mechanisms would tip the balance in favor of the host. *See* MEDICAL PARASITOLOGY; POPULATION ECOLOGY.

[R.T.D.]

Parasympathetic nervous system A portion of the autonomic system. It consists of two neuron chains, but differs from the sympathetic nervous system in that the first neuron has a long axon and synapses with the second neuron near or in the organ innervated. In general, its action is in opposition to that of the sympathetic nervous system, which is the other part of the autonomic system. It cannot be said that one system, the sympathetic, always has a excitatory role and the other, the parasympathetic, an inhibitory role; the situation depends on the organ in question. However, it may be said that the sympathetic system, by altering the level at which various organs function, enables the body to rise to emergency demands encountered in flight, combat, pursuit, and pain. The parasympathetic system appears to be in control during such pleasant periods as digestion and rest. The alkaloid pilocarpine excites parasympathetic activity while atropine inhibits it. *See* AUTONOMIC NERVOUS SYSTEM; SYMPATHETIC NERVOUS SYSTEM.   [D.B.W.]

Parathyroid gland An endocrine organ usually associated with the thyroid gland and possessed by all vertebrates except the fishes. In response to lowered serum calcium concentration, a hormone is produced which promotes bone destruction and inhibits the phosphorus-conserving activity of the kidneys. *See* THYROID GLAND.

In humans, there are typically four glands situated as shown in the illustration; however, the number varies between three and six, with four appearing about 80% of the time. Variations in the positioning of the glands along the craniocaudal axis occur but, excepting parathyroid III which may occasionally be found upon the anterior surface of the trachea, the relation to the posterior surface of the thyroid is rarely lost. [W.E.D.]

The parathyroid glands are essential for the regulation of calcium and phosphate concentrations in the extracellular fluids of amphibians and higher vertebrates. Parathyroid hormone has two major target organs, bone and kidney. It acts on bone in several ways.

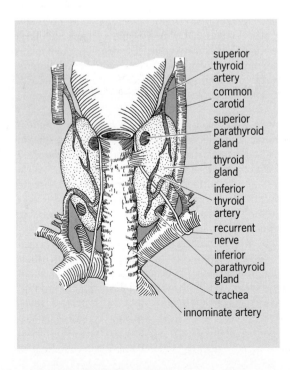

Common positions of human parathyroid glands on the posterior aspect of the thyroid. (*After W. H. Hollinshead, Anatomy of the endocrine glands, Surg. Clin, N. Amer., 21(4):1115–1140, 1952*)

Short-term changes include a rapid uptake of bone fluid calcium into osteoblast cells, which in turn pump the calcium into the extracellular fluids. Long-term effects include increased activity and number of osteoclasts, bone cells which act to break down bone matrix and release calcium from bone. All of these effects result in increased blood calcium values. *See* BONE; CALCIUM METABOLISM.

Parathyroid hormone inhibits the renal reabsorption of phosphate, thus increasing the urinary output of phosphate. Phosphate reabsorption across the renal tubule is dependent upon sodium transport, and parathyroid hormone interferes with this sodium-dependent phosphate transport in the proximal tubule. Another important effect of parathyroid hormone on the kidney is to increase the renal reabsorption of calcium, thus reducing the loss of calcium in the urine and conserving calcium in the body. *See* KIDNEY.

Finally, there are reports that parathyroid hormone indirectly stimulates calcium uptake into the body across the intestine. Parathyroid hormone stimulates the production of the most active metabolite of vitamin D, 1,25-dihydroxycholecalciferol, during vitamin D synthesis. This metabolite of vitamin D directly stimulates the intestinal absorption of calcium. *See* ENDOCRINE SYSTEM (VERTEBRATE); PARATHYROID HORMONE.

[N.B.C.]

Parathyroid hormone   The secretory product of the parathyroid glands. Parathyroid hormone (PTH) is a single-chain polypeptide composed of 84 amino acids. The sequences of human, bovine, and porcine parathyroid hormone are known, and the gene for human parathyroid hormone has been cloned and sequenced.

The major regulator of parathyroid hormone secretion is the serum concentration of calcium ions, to which the parathyroid cells are exquisitely sensitive. Only a limited amount of parathyroid hormone is stored in secretory granules, so that a hypocalcemic stimulus must ultimately influence biosynthesis as well as secretion of the hormone. Parathyroid secretory protein is a large, acidic glycoprotein which is stored and cosecreted with parathyroid hormone in roughly equimolar amounts; the biological function of parathyroid secretory protein is unknown.

Parathyroid hormone is responsible for the fine regulation of serum calcium concentration on a minute-to-minute basis. This is achieved by the acute effects of the hormone on calcium resorption in bone and calcium reabsorption in the kidney. The phosphate mobilized from bone is excreted into the urine by means of the hormone's influence on renal phosphate handling. Parathyroid hormone also stimulates calcium absorption in the intestine, this being mediated indirectly by 1,25-dihydroxyvitamin D. Thus, a hypocalcemic stimulus of parathyroid hormone secretion results in an increased influx of calcium from three sources (bone, kidney, and intestine), resulting in a normalization of the serum calcium concentration without change in the serum phosphate concentration. *See* PARATHYROID GLAND; THYROCALCITONIN.   [A.E.Bro.]

Parazoa   A name proposed for a subkingdom of animals which includes the sponges. Erection of a separate subkingdom for the sponges implies that they originated from protozoan ancestors independently of all other Metazoa. This theory is supported by the uniqueness of the sponge body plan and by peculiarities of fertilization and development. Much importance is given to the fact that during the development of sponges with parenchymella larvae, the flagellated external cells of the larva take up an internal position as choanocytes after metamorphosis, whereas the epidermal and mesenchymal cells arise from what was an internal mass of cells in the larva. These facts suggest that either the germ layers of sponges are reversed in comparison with those of other Metazoa or the choanocytes cannot be homologized with the endoderm of other animals. Either interpretation supports the wide separation of sponges from all other Metazoa to form the subkingdom Parazoa or Enantiozoa. On the other hand, there are cogent arguments in favor of the basic similarity of the development of sponges and other Metazoa. *See* METAZOA; PORIFERA.   [W.D.H.]

Parenchyma   A ground tissue of plants chiefly concerned with the manufacture and storage of food. The primary functions of plants, such as photosynthesis, assimilation, respiration, storage, secretion, and excretion—those associated with living protoplasm—proceed mainly in parenchymal cells. Parenchyma is frequently found as a homogeneous tissue in stems, roots, leaves, and flower parts. Other tissues, such as sclerenchyma, xylem, and phloem, seem to be embedded in a matrix of parenchyma; hence the use of the term ground tissue with regard to parenchyma is derived. The parenchymal cell is one of the most frequently occurring cell types in the plant kingdom. *See* PLANT ANATOMY; PLANT PHYSIOLOGY.

Typical parenchyma occurs in pith and cortex of roots and stems as a relatively undifferentiated tissue composed of polyhedral cells that may be more or less compactly arranged and show little variation in size or shape. The mesophyll, that is, the tissue located between the upper and lower epidermis of leaves, is a specially differentiated parenchyma called chlorenchyma because its cells contain chlorophyll in distinct chloroplastids.

This chlorenchymatous tissue is the major locus of photosynthetic activity and consequently is one of the more important variants of parenchyma. Specialized secretory parenchymal cells are found lining resin ducts and other secretory structures. *See* PHOTOSYNTHESIS; SECRETORY STRUCTURES (PLANT).   [R.L.Hu.]

Pasteurella   A genus of gram-negative, nonmotile, nonsporulating, facultatively anaerobic coccobacillary to rod-shaped bacteria which are parasitic and often pathogens in many species of mammals, birds, and reptiles. It was named to honor Louis Pasteur in 1887. Genetic studies have shown that *Pasteurella*, together with *Haemophilus* and *Actinobacillus*, constitute a family, Pasteurellaceae.

The genus contains at least 10 species. *Pasteurella multocida* causes hemorrhagic septicemia in various mammals and fowl cholera, and is occasionally transmitted to humans, mainly in rural areas. Human pasteurellosis may include inflammation in bite and scratch lesions, infections of the lower respiratory tract and of the small intestine, and generalized infections with septicemia and meningitis. *Pasteurella canis* and *P. stomatis* may cause similar, though generally less severe, infections in humans after contact with domestic or wild animals. Although drug-resistant *Pasteurella* strains have been encountered, human *Pasteurella* infections are as a rule readily sensitive to the penicillins and a variety of other chemotherapeutic agents. *See* ANTIBIOTIC; DRUG RESISTANCE.   [W.Ma.]

Pasteurellosis   A variety of infectious diseases caused by the coccobacilli *Pasteurella multocida* and *P. haemolytica*; the term also applies to diseases caused by any *Pasteurella* species. All *Pasteurella* species occur as commensals in the upper respiratory and alimentary tracts of their various hosts. Although varieties of some species cause primary disease, many of the infections are secondary to other infections or result from various environmental stresses. *Pasteurella* species are generally extracellular parasites that elicit mainly a humoral immune response. Several virulence factors have been identified. *See* VIRULENCE.

Pasteurella multocida is the most prevalent species of the genus causing a wide variety of infections in many domestic and wild animals, and humans. It is a primary or, more frequently, a secondary pathogen of cattle, swine, sheep, goats, and other animals. As a secondary invader, it is often involved in pneumonic pasteurellosis of cattle (shipping fever) and in enzootic or mycoplasmal pneumonia of swine. It is responsible for a variety of sporadic infections in many animals, including abortion, encephalitis, and meningitis. It produces severe mastitis in cattle and sheep, and toxin-producing strains are involved in atrophic rhinitis, an economically important disease of swine. Hemorrhagic septicemia, caused by capsular type B strains, has been reported in elk and deer in the United States.

All strains of *P. haemolytica* produce a soluble cytotoxin (leukotoxin) that kills various leukocytes of ruminants, thus lowering the primary pulmonary defense. It is the principal cause of the widespread pneumonic pasteurellosis of cattle. Other important diseases caused by certain serotypes of *P. haemolytica* are mastitis of ewes and septicemia of lambs.

All of the *Pasteurella* species can be isolated by culturing appropriate clinical specimens on blood agar. Multiple drug resistance is frequently encountered. Treatment is effective if initiated early. Among the drugs used are penicillin and streptomycin, tetracyclines, chloramphenicol, sulphonamides, and some cephalosporins. Sound sanitary practices and segregation of affected animals may help limit the spread of the major pasteurelloses. Live vaccines and bacterins (killed bacteria) are used for the prevention of some. *See* PASTEURELLA.   [G.R.Ca.]

Pathogen Any agent capable of causing disease. The term pathogen is usually restricted to living agents, which include viruses, rickettsia, bacteria, fungi, yeasts, protozoa, helminths, and certain insect larval stages. *See* DISEASE.

Pathogenicity is the ability of an organism to enter a host and cause disease. The degree of pathogenicity, that is, the comparative ability to cause disease, is known as virulence. The terms pathogenic and nonpathogenic refer to the relative virulence of the organism or its ability to cause disease under certain conditions. This ability depends not only upon the properties of the organism but also upon the ability of the host to defend itself (its immunity) and prevent injury. The concept of pathogenicity and virulence has no meaning without reference to a specific host. For example, gonococcus is capable of causing gonorrhea in humans but not in lower animals. *See* MEDICAL MYCOLOGY; MEDICAL PARASITOLOGY; PLANT PATHOLOGY; PLANT VIRUSES AND VIROIDS; VIRULENCE.
                                                                              [D.N.La.]

Pathotoxin A chemical of biological origin, other than an enzyme, that plays an important causal role in a plant disease. Most pathotoxins are produced by plant pathogenic fungi or bacteria, but some are produced by higher plants, and one has been reported to be the product of an interaction between a plant and a bacterial pathogen. Some pathogen-produced pathotoxins are highly selective in that they cause severe damage and typical disease symptoms only on plants susceptible to the pathogens that produce them. Others are nonselective and are equally toxic to plants susceptible or resistant to the pathogen involved. A few pathotoxins are species-selective, and are damaging to many but not all plant species. In these instances, some plants resistant to the pathogen are sensitive to its toxic product. *See* PLANT PATHOLOGY.   [H.Wh.]

Pattern formation (biology) The mechanisms that ensure that particular cell types differentiate in the correct location within the embryo and that the layers of cells bend and grow in the correct relative positions. Pattern formation is one of four processes that underlie development, the others being growth, cell diversification, and morphogenesis. *See* ANIMAL MORPHOGENESIS; CELL DIFFERENTIATION; PLANT GROWTH.

Pattern formation is the creation of a predictable arrangement of cell types in space during embryonic development. The types of patterns of cell types found in animals and plants can be conveniently described as simple or complex. Simple patterns involve the spatial arrangement of identical or equivalent structures such as bristles on the leg of a fly, hairs on a person's head, or leaves on a plant. Such equivalent patterns are thought to be produced by mechanisms that are the same or very similar in the fly and the plant. Complex patterns are those that are made up of parts that are not equivalent to one another. In the vertebrate limb, for example, the structure of the arm is different at each level, with one bone (humerus) in the upper arm, two bones (radius and ulna) in the lower arm, and a complex set of bones making up the wrist and the hand. How are such nonequivalent parts patterned during development? The theoretical framework that allows a basis for understanding how such patterns arise is called positional information. Two stages exist in the positional information framework. First, a cell must become aware of its position within a developing group, or field, of cells. This specification of cellular position requires a mechanism by which each cell within a field can obtain a unique value or address. The second component is the interpretation of the positional address by a cell to manifest a particular cell type by the expression of a particular set of genes. *See* DEVELOPMENTAL BIOLOGY; EMBRYONIC DIFFERENTIATION.   [N.Ho.]

Penis   The male organ of copulation, or phallus. In mammals the penis consists basically of three elongated masses of erectile tissue. The central corpus spongiosum (corpus urethrae) lies ventral to the paired corpora cavernosa. The urethra runs along the underside of the spongiosum and then normally rises to open at the expanded, cone-shaped tip, the glans penis, which fits like a cap over the end of the penis. Loose skin encloses the penis and also forms the retractable foreskin, or prepuce.

Erection of the penis is caused by nervous stimulation resulting in engorgement of the spiral helicine arteries and the plentiful venous sinuses of the organ. In most mammals other than Primates the penis is retracted into a sheath when not in use.

In submammalian forms the penis is not as well developed. Crocodilians, turtles, and some birds have a penis basically like that of mammals, lying in the floor of the cloaca. When erected, it protrudes from the cloaca and functions in copulation. Other vertebrates lack a penis, although various functionally comparable organs may be developed such as the claspers on the pelvic fins of sharks and the gonopodia on the anal fins of certain teleost fishes.   [T.S.P.]

Peptide   A compound that is made up of two or more amino acids joined by covalent bonds which are formed by the elimination of a molecule of H_2O from the amino group of one amino acid and the carboxyl group of the next amino acid. Peptides larger than about 50 amino acid residues are usually classified as proteins. Glutathione is the most abundant peptide in mammalian tissue. Hormones such as oxytocin (8), vasopressin (8), glucagon (29), and adrenocorticotropic hormone (39) are peptides whose structures have been deduced; in parentheses are the numbers of amino acid residues for each peptide.

For each step in the biological synthesis of a peptide or protein there is a specific enzyme or enzyme complex that catalyzes each reaction in an ordered fashion along the biosynthetic route. However, it is noteworthy that, although the biological synthesis of proteins is directed by messenger RNA on cellular structures called ribosomes, the biological synthesis of peptides does not require either messenger RNA or ribosomes. *See* AMINO ACIDS; PROTEIN; RIBONUCLEIC ACID (RNA); RIBOSOMES. [J.M.M.]

Perception Those subjective experiences of objects or events that ordinarily result from stimulation of the receptor organs of the body. This stimulation is transformed or encoded into neural activity (by specialized receptor mechanisms) and is relayed to more central regions of the nervous system where further neural processing occurs. Most likely, it is the final neural processing in the brain that underlies or causes perceptual experience, and so perceptionlike experiences can sometimes occur without external stimulation of the receptor organs, as in dreams.

In contemporary psychology, interest generally focuses on perception or the apprehension of objects or events, rather than simply on sensation or sensory process. While no sharp line of demarcation between these topics exists, it is fair to say that sensory qualities are generally explicable on the basis of mechanisms within the receptor organ, whereas object and event perception entails higher-level activity of the brain. *See* HEARING (HUMAN); SENSATION; VISION.

Since objects or events are not experienced only through vision, the term perception obviously applies to other sense modalities as well. Certainly things and their movement may be experienced through the sense of touch. Such experiences derive from receptors in the skin (tactile perception), but more importantly, from the positioning of the fingers with respect to one another when an object is grasped, the latter information arising from receptors in the muscles and joints (haptic or tactual perception). The position of the parts of the body are also perceived with respect to one another whether they are stationary (proprioception) or in motion (kinesthesis), and the position of the body is experienced with respect to the environment through receptors sensitive to gravity such as those in the vestibular apparatus in the inner ear. Auditory perception yields recognition of the location of sound sources and of structures such as melodies and speech. Other sense modalities such as taste (gustation), smell (olfaction), pain, and temperature provide sensory qualities but not perceptual structures as do vision, audition, and touch, and thus are usually dealt with as sensory processes. *See* OLFACTION; PAIN; PROPRIOCEPTION.

Constancy. By and large, these perceptual properties of objects remain remarkably constant despite variations in distance, slant, and retinal locus caused by movements of the observer. This fact, referred to as perceptual constancy, is perhaps the hallmark of perception and more than any other, serves to characterize the field of perception.

Examples of perceptual constancy are: size (except at very great distances, an object appears the same size whether seen nearby or far away, although the size of its image on the retina can be very different); shape (a circle seen from the side is perceived as a circle, although it appears as an ellipse on the retina); orientation (objects appear to keep the same orientation in space, independently of the orientation of the observer's head); and position (a fixed object remains perceived as stationary even when its image on the retina moves because of eye or head movements).

A central problem is whether the perception of properties such as form and depth is innately determined or is based on past experience. By "innate" it is meant that the perception is the result of evolutionary adaptation and thus is present at birth or when the necessary neural maturation has occurred. By "past experience" it is meant that the perception in question is the end result of prior exposure to certain relevant patterns or conditions, a kind of learning process. Despite centuries of discussion of this problem, and considerable experimental work, there is still no final answer to the question. It now seems clear that certain kinds of perception are innate, but equally clear that past experience also is a determining factor. *See* INTELLIGENCE. [I.R.]

Periderm   A group of tissues which replaces the epidermis in the plant body. Its main function is to protect the underlying tissues from desiccation, freezing, heat injury, mechanical destruction, and disease. Although periderm may develop in leaves and fruits, its main function is to protect stems and roots. The fundamental tissues which compose the periderm are the phellogen, phelloderm, and phellem.

The phellogen is the meristematic portion of the periderm and consists of one layer of initials. These exhibit little variation in form, appearing rectangular and somewhat flat in cross and radial sections, and polygonal in tangential sections.

The phelloderm cells are phellogen derivatives formed inward. The number of phelloderm layers varies with species, season, and age of the periderm. In some species, the periderm lacks the phelloderm altogether. The phelloderm consists of living cells with photosynthesizing chloroplasts and cellulosic walls.

The phellem, or cork, cells are phellogen derivatives formed outward. These cells are arranged in tiers with almost no intercellular spaces except in the lenticel regions. After completion of their differentiation, the phellem cells die and their protoplasts disintegrate. The cell lumens remain empty, excluding a few species in which various crystals can be found. The remarkable impermeability of the suberized cell walls is largely due to their impregnation with waxes, tannins, cerin, friedelin, and phellonic and phellogenic acids.

Lenticels are loose-structured openings that develop usually beneath the stomata and that facilitate gas transport through the otherwise impermeable layers of phellem. *See* SCLERENCHYMA.   [Y.W.; H.Wi.]

Perissodactyla   An order of herbivorous, odd-toed, hoofed mammals, including the living horses, zebras, asses, tapirs, rhinoceroses, and their extinct relatives. They are defined by a number of unique specializations, but the most diagnostic feature is their feet. Most perissodactyls have either one or three toes on each foot, and the axis of symmetry of the foot runs through the middle digit.

The perissodactyls are divided into three groups: the Hippomorpha (horses and their extinct relatives); the Titanotheriomorpha (the extinct brontotheres); and the Moropomorpha (tapirs, rhinoceroses, and their extinct relatives). *See* RHINOCEROS; TAPIR.

Perissodactyls originated in Asia some time before 57 million years ago (Ma). By 55 Ma, the major groups of perissodactyls had differentiated, and migrated to Europe and North America. Before 34 Ma, the brontotheres and the archaic tapirs were the largest and most abundant hoofed mammals in Eurasia and North America. After these groups became extinct, horses and rhinoceroses were the most common perissodactyls, with a great diversity of species and body forms. Both groups were decimated during another mass extinction about 5 Ma, and today only five species of rhinoceros, four species of tapir, and a few species of horses, zebras, and asses cling to survival in the wild. The niches of large hoofed herbivores have been taken over by the ruminant artiodactyls, such as cattle, antelopes, deer, and their relatives. *See* MAMMALIA.   [D.R.Pr.]

Peroxisome   An intracellular organelle found in all eukaryotes except the archezoa (original lifeforms). In electron micrographs, peroxisomes appear round with a diameter of 0.1–1.0 micrometer, although there is evidence that in some mammalian tissues peroxisomes form an extensive reticulum (network). They contain more than 50 characterized enzymes and perform many biochemical functions, including detoxification. *See* CELL ORGANIZATION; ENZYME.

Peroxisomes are important for lipid metabolism. In humans, the β-oxidation of fatty acids greater than 18 carbons in length occurs in peroxisomes. In yeast, all fatty acid β-oxidation occurs in peroxisomes. Peroxisomes contain the first two enzymes required for the synthesis of plasmalogens. Peroxisomes also play important roles in cholesterol and bile acid synthesis, purine and polyamine catabolism, and prostaglandin metabolism. In plants, peroxisomes are required for photorespiration. See LIPID METABOLISM; PHOTORESPIRATION.

A number of recessively inherited peroxisomal disorders have been described and grouped into three categories. Group I is the most severe and is characterized by a general loss of peroxisomal function. Many of the enzymes normally localized to the peroxisome are instead found in the cytosol. Among the diseases found in group I are Zellweger syndrome, neonatal adrenoleukodystrophy, and infantile Refsum disease. Patients with these disorders usually die within the first years after birth and exhibit neurological and hepatic (liver) dysfunction, along with craniofacial dysmorphism (malformation of the cranium and the face). Groups II and III peroxisomal disorders are characterized by a loss of peroxisomal function less severe than in group I. [R.A.Ra.]

Personality theory   A branch of psychology concerned with developing a scientifically defensible model or view of human nature—in the modern parlance, a general theory of behavior.

Most personality theories can be classified in terms of two broad categories, depending on their underlying assumptions about human nature. On the one hand, there are a group of theories that see human nature as fixed, unchanging, deeply perverse, and self-defeating. These theories emphasize self-understanding and resignation; in the cases of Freudian psychoanalysis and existentialism, they also reflect a distinctly tragic view of life—the sources of human misery are so various that the best that can be hoped for is to control some of the causes of suffering. On the other hand, there are a group of theories that see human nature as plastic, flexible, and always capable of growth, change, and development. Human nature is basically benevolent; therefore bad societies are the source of personal misery. Social reform will produce human happiness if not actual perfection. These theories emphasize self-expression and self-actualization—in the cases of Carl Rogers and Abraham Maslow, they reflect a distinctly optimistic and romantic view of life.   [R.Hog.]

pH regulation (biology)   The processes operating in living organisms to preserve a viable acid-base state. In higher animals, much of the body substance (60–70%) consists of complex solutions of inorganic and organic solutes. For convenience, these body fluids can be subdivided into the cellular fluid (some two-thirds of the total) and the extracellular fluid. The latter includes blood plasma and interstitial fluid, the film of fluid that bathes all the cells of the body. For normal function, the distinctive compositions of these various fluids are maintained within narrow limits by a process called homeostasis. A crucial characteristic of these solutions is pH, an expression representing the concentration (or preferably the activity) of hydrogen ions, $[H^+]$, in solution. The pH is defined as $- \log [H^+]$, so that in the usual physiological pH range of 7 to 8, $[H^+]$ is exceedingly low, between 10^{-7} and 10^{-8} M. Organisms use a variety of means to keep pH under careful control, because even small deviations from normal pH can disrupt living processes. See HOMEOSTASIS.

The most accessible and commonly studied body fluid is blood, and it, therefore, provides the most information on pH regulation. Blood pH in humans, and in mammals generally, is about 7.4. This value indicates that blood is slightly alkaline, because neutrality, the condition in which the concentration of hydrogen ions $[H^+]$ equals the concentration of hydroxyl ions $[OH^-]$, is pH 6.8 at mammalian body temperature of 98°F (37°C). The pH within cells, including the red blood cells, is typically lower by 0.2–0.6 unit, and is thus close to neutrality. In most animals other than warm-blooded mammals, blood pH deviates from the familiar value of 7.4. The major reason is that body temperature has an important influence on pH regulation. Consequently, animals that experience significant changes in body temperature have no single normal pH at which they regulate, but rather a series of values depending on body temperature.

Blood pH regulation is necessary because metabolic and ingestive processes add acidic or basic substances to the body and can displace pH from its proper value. For true regulation, active physiological mechanisms are required that can alter the acid-base composition of the blood in a controlled fashion. It is conventional to identify these control mechanisms with their effects on the principal buffer of the extracellular fluid, carbon dioxide (CO_2). Carbon dioxide is produced by cellular metabolism and distributes readily throughout the body because of its high solubility and rapid diffusion. In solution, CO_2 is hydrated to carbonic acid (H_2CO_3) which dissociates almost completely to H^+ and bicarbonate ions [HCO_3^-]. Dissolved CO_2 can be identified with a particular partial pressure of CO_2 (PCO_2). To regulate blood pH, organisms have mechanisms to independently control PCO_2 and [HCO_3^-].

The cells, while benefitting from the stability afforded by whole body mechanisms (respiratory and ionic), also have local means for their own pH regulations. An acute acid load on a cell, whether from its intrinsic metabolism or from an external source, is dealt with first by the cell's chemical buffering capacity, a capacity that exceeds that of the blood by severalfold. Other cellular mechanisms include the conversion of organic acids to neutral compounds through metabolic transformations, and the transfer of acid equivalents from the primary cell fluid, the cytoplasm, into cellular organelles. *See* BIOPOTENTIALS AND IONIC CURRENTS; CHEMIOSMOSIS; ENZYME.   [D.C.J.]

Phagocytosis A mechanism by which single cells of the animal kingdom, such as smaller protozoa, engulf and carry particles into the cytoplasm. It differs from endocytosis primarily in the size of the particle rather than in the mechanism; as particles approach the dimensions and solubility of macromolecules, cells take them up by the process of endocytosis.

Cells such as the free-living amebas or the wandering cells of the metazoa often can "sense" the direction of a potential food source and move toward it (chemotaxis). If, when the cell contacts the particle, the particle has the appropriate chemical composition, or surface charge, it adheres to the cell. The cell responds by forming a hollow, conelike cytoplasmic process around the particle, eventually surrounding it completely. Although the particle is internalized by this sequence of events, it is still enclosed in a portion of the cell's surface membrane and thus isolated from the cell's cytoplasm. The combined particle and membrane package is referred to as a food or phagocytic vacuole. *See* VACUOLE.

Ameboid cells of the metazoa also selectively remove foreign particles, bacteria, and other pathogens by phagocytosis. After the foreign particle or microorganism is trapped in a vacuole inside the macrophage, it is usually digested. To accomplish this, small packets (lysosomes) of lytic proenzymes are introduced into the phagocytic vacuole, where the enzymes are then dissolved and activated. *See* LYSOSOME.   [P.W.B.]

Pharynx A chamber at the oral end of the vertebrate alimentary canal, leading to the esophagus. In adult humans it is divided anteriorly by the soft palate into a nasopharynx and an oropharynx, lying behind the tongue but anterior to the epiglottis; there is also a retropharyngeal compartment, posterior to both epiglottis and soft palate. The nasopharynx receives the nasal passages and communicates with the two middle ears through auditory tubes. The retropharynx leads to the esophagus and to the larynx, and the paths of breathing and swallowing cross within it. *See* ESOPHAGUS; LARYNX.   [W.W.B.]

Pheromone   A substance that acts as a molecular messenger, transmitting information from one member of a species to another member of the same species. A distinction is made between releaser pheromones, which elicit a rapid, behavioral response, and primer pheromones, which elicit a slower, developmental response and may pave the way for a future behavior.

Communication via pheromones is common throughout nature, including some eukaryotic microorganisms such as fungi that exchange vital chemical signals. The cellular slime molds form large aggregations of amebas which unite to form a sorocarp made up of a long, slender stalk that supports a spore-containing fruiting body. A pheromone is responsible for the aggregation. In several species of algae, relatively simple hydrocarbons act as sperm attractants.

By far the largest number of characterized pheromones come from insect species. In social insects, such as termites and ants, there may be as many as a dozen different types of messages that are used to coordinate the complex activities which must be carried out to maintain a healthy colony. These activities might require specialized pheromones such as trail pheromones (to lead to a food source), alarm pheromones (recruiting soldiers to the site of an enemy attack), or pheromones connected with reproductive behavior. Much less is known about mammalian pheromones because mammalian behavior is more difficult to study. There are, however, a small number of well-characterized mammalian pheromones from pigs, dogs, hamsters, mice, and marmosets.

There is great potential for controlling the behavior of a given species by manipulating its natural chemical signals. For example, pheromones have been used to disrupt the reproduction of certain insect pests. This approach can lead to reduced use of pesticides as well as advances in the control of both agricultural pests and disease vectors. *See* CHEMICAL ECOLOGY; CHEMORECEPTION; SOCIAL INSECTS.   [J.Mein.]

Phloem   The principal food-conducting tissue in vascular plants. Its conducting cells are known as sieve elements, but phloem may also include companion cells, parenchyma cells, fibers, sclereids, rays, and certain other cells. As a vascular tissue, phloem is spatially associated with xylem, and the two together form the vascular system. *See* XYLEM.

Sieve elements differ from phloem parenchyma cells in the structure of their walls and to some extent in the character of their protoplasts. Sieve areas, distinctive structures in sieve element walls, are specialized primary pit fields in which there may be numerous modified plasmodesmata. Plasmodesmata are strands of cytoplasm connecting the protoplasts of two contiguous cells. These strands are often surrounded by callose, a carbohydrate material, that appears to form rapidly in plants when they are placed under stress.

Typical sieve cells are long elements in which all the sieve areas are of equal specialization, though sieve areas may be more numerous in some walls than in others. In contrast, a sieve-tube member has some sieve areas more specialized than others; that is, the pores, or modified plasmodesmata, are larger in some sieve areas. Parts of the walls containing such sieve areas are called sieve plates.

Companion cells are specialized parenchyma cells that occur in close ontogenetic and physiologic association with sieve tube members. Some sieve-tube members lack companion cells. The precise functional relationship between these two kinds of cells is unknown.

Parenchyma cells in the phloem occur singly or in strands of two or more cells. They store starch, frequently contain tannins or crystals, commonly enlarge as the sieve elements become obliterated, or may be transformed into sclereids or cork cambium cells.

Phloem fibers vary greatly in length (from less than 0.04 in. or 1 mm in some plants to 20 in. or 50 cm in the ramie plant). The secondary walls are commonly thick and typically have simple pits, but may or may not be lignified.   [M.A.W.]

Phobia   An intense irrational fear that often leads to avoidance of an object or situation. Phobias (or phobic disorders) are common (for example, fear of spiders, or arachnophobia; fear of heights, or acrophobia) and usually begin in childhood or adolescence. Psychiatric nomenclature refers to phobias of specific places, objects, or situations as specific phobias. Fear of public speaking, in very severe cases, is considered a form of social phobia. Social phobias also include other kinds of performance fears (such as playing a musical instrument in front of others; signing a check while observed) and social interactional fears (for example, talking to people in authority; asking someone out for a date; returning items to a store). Individuals who suffer from social phobia often fear a number of social situations. Although loosely regarded as a fear of open spaces, agoraphobia is actually a phobia that results when people experience panic attacks (unexpected, paroxysmal episodes of anxiety and accompanying physical sensations such as racing heart, shortness of breath).

The origin of phobias is varied and incompletely understood. Most individuals with specific phobias have never had anything bad happen to them in the past in relation to the phobia. In a minority of cases, however, some traumatic event occurred that likely led to the phobia. It is probable that some common phobias, such as a fear of snakes or a fear of heights, may actually be instinctual, or inborn. Both social phobia and agoraphobia run in families, suggesting that heredity plays a role. However, it is also possible that some phobias are passed on through learning and modeling.

Phobias occur in over 10% of the general population. Social phobia may be the most common kind, affecting approximately 7% of individuals. When persons encounter the phobic situation or phobic object, they typically experience a phobic reaction consisting of extreme fearfulness, physical symptoms (such as racing heart, shaking, hot or cold flashes, or nausea), and cognitive symptoms (particularly thoughts such as "I'm going to die" or "I'm going to make a fool of myself"). These usually subside quickly when the individual is removed from the situation. The tremendous relief that escape from the phobic situation provides is believed to reinforce the phobia and to fortify the individual's tendency to avoid the situation in the future.

Many phobias can be treated by exposure therapy: the individual is gradually encouraged to approach the feared object and to successively spend longer periods of time in proximity to it. Cognitive therapy is also used (often in conjunction with exposure therapy) to treat phobias. It involves helping individuals to recognize that their beliefs and thoughts can have a profound effect on their anxiety, that the outcome they fear will not necessarily occur, and that they have more control over the situation than they realize.

Medications are sometimes used to augment cognitive and exposure therapies. For example, beta-adrenergic blocking agents, such as propranolol, lower heart rate and reduce tremulousness, and lead to reduced anxiety. Certain kinds of antidepressants and anxiolytic medications are often helpful. It is not entirely clear how these medications exert their antiphobic effects, although it is believed that they affect levels of

neurotransmitters in regions of the brain that are thought to be important in mediating emotions such as fear.
[M.B.St.]

Phonoreception The perception of sound by animals through specialized sense organs. A sense of hearing is possessed by animals belonging to two divisions of the animal kingdom: the vertebrates and the insects. The sense is mediated by the ear, a specialized organ for the reception of vibratory stimuli. Such an organ is found in all except the most primitive vertebrates, but only in some of the many species of insects. The vertebrate and insect types of ear differ in evolutionary origin and in their modes of operation, but both have attained high levels of performance in the reception and discrimination of sounds.

The vertebrate ear is a part of the labyrinth, located deep in the bone or cartilage of the head, one ear on either side of the brain. A complex assembly of tubes and chambers contains a membranous structure which bears within it a number of sensory endings of different kinds. Beginning with the amphibians, which are the earliest vertebrates to spend a considerable portion of their lives on land, there appears a special mechanism, the middle ear, whose function is the transmission of aerial vibrations to the sensory endings of the inner ear. All the vertebrates above the fishes, and certain of the fishes as well, have some type of sound-facilitative mechanism. *See* EAR (VERTEBRATE); HEARING (VERTEBRATE).

The group of invertebrates which has received the most attention has been the insects. Other arthropods, such as certain crustaceans and spiders, have also been found to be sensitive to sound waves. The insect ear consists of a superficial membrane of thin chitin with an associated group of sensilla called scolophores. These ears are found in most species of katydids, crickets, grasshoppers, cicadas, waterboatmen, mosquitoes, and nocturnal and spinner moths. The occur in different places in the body: on the antennae of mosquitoes, on the forelegs of katydids and crickets, on the metathorax of cicadas and waterboatmen, and on the abdomen of grasshoppers. Probably these differently situated organs represent separate evolutionary developments, through the association of a thinned-out region of the body wall with sensilla that are found extensively in the bodies of insects and that by themselves seem to serve for movement perception.

The insects mentioned above are noted for their production of stridulatory sounds made by rubbing the edges of the wings together, or a leg against a wing, or by other means. These sounds are produced by the males and serve for enticing the females in mating. A striking adaptation is that shown by mosquitoes: The ear of the male mosquito is sensitive only to a narrow range of frequencies around 380 Hz, and this frequency is the one which is produced by the wings of the female in flight. If the ear of the male mosquito is made nonfunctional, the mosquito fails to find a mate.
[E.G.W.]

Phoresy A relationship between two different species of organisms in which the larger, or host, organism transports a smaller organism, the guest. It is regarded as a type of commensalism in which the relationship is limited to transportation of the guest.
[C.B.C.]

Phoronida A small, relatively homogeneous group of animals now generally considered to constitute a separate animal phylum. Two genera, *Phoronis* and *Phoronopsis*, and about 16 species are recognized.

Phoronids may occur in vertical tubes placed just below the surface in intertidal or subtidal mud flats, or as feltlike masses of intertwined tubes attached to rocks, pilings, or old logs in shallow water. In both cases the tubes, composed basically of a secreted,

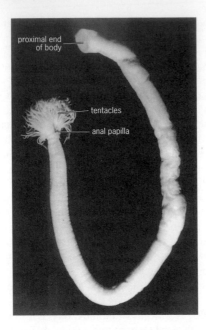

Phoronopsis harmeri removed from its tube.

parchmentlike material, are encrusted with small particles of sand or shell. A third living habit concerns those phoronids found inside channels, probably self-made, in limestone rock or the shells of dead pelecypod mollusks.

The geographical distribution of phoronids appears to be worldwide in temperate and tropical seas. There are no records of phoronids from the polar regions.

The body is more or less elongate, ranging in length from about 1.6 to 8 in. (4 to 20 cm), and bears a crown of tentacles arranged in a double row surrounding the mouth which is usually crescent-shaped (see illustration). The anus occurs at the level of the mouth and is borne on a papilla immediately outside the double row of tentacles. The digestive tract is therefore U-shaped, the mouth and anus opening close together at one end of the animal. The tentacles rest on a connective tissue base known as the lophophore. Associated with the mouth is a ciliated flap of tissue known as the epistome. *See* LOPHOPHORE.

The phylum includes both dioecious animals and hermaphrodites. All phoronids may reproduce sexually, and in most cases the life history includes the pelagic actinotroch larva. Some species reproduce asexually by transverse fission.   [J.R.M.]

Phospholipid   A lipid that contains one or more phosphate groups. Phospholipids are amphipathic in nature; that is, each molecule consists of a hydrophilic (water-loving) portion and a hydrophobic (water-hating) portion. Due to the amphipathic nature and insolubility in water, phospholipids are ideal compounds for forming the biological membrane. *See* LIPID.

There are two classes of phospholipids: those that have a glycerol backbone and those that contain sphingosine. Both classes are present in the biological membrane. Phospholipids that contain a glycerol backbone are called phosphoglycerides (or glycerophospholipids), which are the most abundant class of phospholipid found in nature. The most abundant types of naturally occurring phosphoglyceride are phosphatidylcholine (lecithin), phosphatidylethanolamine, phosphatidylserine, phosphatidylinositol, phosphatidylglycerol, and cardiolipin. The structural diversity within each type of phosphoglyceride is due to the variability of the chain length and degree of saturation of the fatty acid ester groups.

Sphingomyelin is the major sphingosine-containing phospholipid. Its general structure consists of a fatty acid attached to sphingosine by an amide linkage.

A bilayer membrane is formed spontaneously when phospholipids are dispersed in an aqueous solution. In this bilayer structure, phospholipids are arranged in two leaflets with the hydrophobic tails facing each other, and the hydrophilic ends exposed to the aqueous medium. Differences in the head group, the chain length, and the degree of saturation of fatty acids in the hydrophobic end are important factors in determining the shape of the bilayer. Individual phospholipid molecules are able to move freely in the lateral plane of the bilayer but not in the transverse plane (flip-flop). Small uncharged molecules are able to diffuse through the bilayer structure, but the permeability of larger or charged molecules is restricted. The arrangement of phospholipid molecules into a bilayer in an aqueous medium follows the laws of thermodynamics and represents the structural basis for the formation of all biological membranes. *See* CELL MEMBRANES.

For a long time, phospholipids were regarded as merely building blocks for the biological membrane. It was discovered in the mid-1970s, however, that phospholipids participate in the transduction of biological signals across the membrane. For example, when the hormone vasopressin is bound to its receptor on the plasma membrane of a liver cell, the binding sets off a cascade of reactions which result in enhanced breakdown of glycogen in the liver cell, thus producing more glucose. *See* SECOND MESSENGERS.

A special form of phosphoglyceride, 1-alkyl-2-acetyl-glycero-3-phosphocholine, acts as a very powerful biological mediator. It causes the aggregation and degranulation of blood platelets, and is known as platelet-activating factor (PAF).

Phospholipases are responsible for the degradation of phosphoglycerides. These enzymes are found in all tissues and in the pancreatic juice. A number of toxins and venoms have very high phospholipase activity, and several pathogenic bacteria produce phospholipases that dissolve cell membrane and allow the spread of infection. There are very few inherited diseases associated with the metabolism of phosphoglycerides; presumably, such genetic defects would be lethal during the early stage of cellular development.

Sphingomyelinase, a lysosomal enzyme, hydrolytically degrades sphingomyelin. A genetic disorder caused by a defect in the production of sphingomyelinase, called Niemann-Pick disease, leaves the cell with no or limited or ability to degrade sphingomyelin. In a severe form (type A) of this disease, the liver and spleen are sites of lipid deposits and are therefore tremendously enlarged. The lipid deposits consist primarily of the sphingomyelin that cannot be degraded. *See* LIPID METABOLISM.   [P.Ch.]

Photomorphogenesis   The regulatory effect of light on plant form, involving growth, development, and differentiation of cells, tissues, and organs. Morphogenic influences of light on plant form are quite different from light effects that nourish the plant through photosynthesis, since the former usually occur at much lower energy levels than are necessary for photosynthesis. Light serves as a trigger in photomorphogenesis, frequently resulting in energy expenditure orders of magnitude larger than the amount required to induce a given response. Photomorphogenic processes determine the nature and direction of a plant's growth and thus play a key role in its ecological adaptations to various environmental changes. *See* PHOTOSYNTHESIS.

Morphogenically active radiation is known to control seed and spore germination, growth and development of stems and leaves, lateral root initiation, opening of the hypocotyl or epicotyl hook in seedlings, differentiation of the epidermis, formation of epidermal hairs, onset of flowering, formation of tracheary elements in the stem, and form changes in the gametophytic phase of ferns, to mention but a few of such known phenomena. Many nonmorphogenic processes in plants are also basically controlled by light independent of photosynthesis. Among these are chloroplast movement, biochemical reactions involved in the synthesis of flavonoids, anthocyanins, chlorophyll, and carotenoids, and leaf movements in certain legumes.   [W.R.Br.]

Photoperiodism The growth, development, or other responses of organisms to the length of night or day or both. Photoperiodism has been observed in plants and animals, but not in bacteria (prokaryotic organisms), other single-celled organisms, or fungi.

A true photoperiodism response is a response to the changing day or night. Some species respond to increasing day lengths and decreasing night lengths (for example, by forming flowers or developing larger gonads); this is called a long-day response. Other species may exhibit the same response, or the same species may respond in some different way, to decreasing days and increasing nights; this is a short-day response. Sometimes a response is independent or nearly independent of day length, and is said to be day-neutral. There are many plant responses to photoperiod. These include development of reproductive structures in lower plants (mosses) and in flowering plants; rate of flower and fruit development; stem elongation in many herbaceous species as well as coniferous and deciduous trees (usually a long-day response and possibly the most widespread photoperiodism response in higher plants); autumn leaf drop and formation of winter dormant buds (short days); development of frost hardiness (short days); formation of roots on cuttings; formation of many underground storage organs such as bulbs (onions, long days), tubers (potato, short days), and storage roots (radish, short days); runner development (strawberry, short day); balance of male to female flowers or flower parts (especially in cucumbers); aging of leaves and other plant parts; and even such obscure responses as the formation of foliar plantlets (such as the minute plants formed on edges of *Bryophyllum* leaves), and the quality and quantity of essential oils (such as those produced by jasmine plants). Note that a single plant, for example, the strawberry, might be a short-day plant for one response and a long-day plant for another response.

Animal responses. There are also many responses to photoperiod in animals, including control of several stages in the life cycle of insects (for example, diapause) and the long-day promotion in birds of molting, development of gonads, deposition of body fat, and migratory behavior. Even feather color may be influenced by photoperiod (as in the ptarmigan). In several mammals the induction of estrus and spermatogenic activity is controlled by photoperiod (sheep, goat, snowshoe hare), as is fur color in certain species (snowshoe hare). Growth of antlers in American elk and deer can be controlled by controlling day length. Increasing day length causes antlers to grow, whereas decreasing day length causes them to fall off. By changing day lengths rapidly, a cycle of antler growth can be completed in as little as 4 months; slow changes can extend the cycle to as long as 2 years. When attempts are made to shorten or extend these limits even more, the cycle slips out of photoperiodic control and reverts to a 10–12-month cycle, apparently controlled by an internal annual "clock."

Seasonal responses. Response to photoperiod means that a given manifestation will occur at some specific time during the year. Response to long days (shortening nights) normally occurs during the spring, and response to short days (lengthening nights) usually occurs in late summer or autumn. Since day length is accurately determined by the Earth's rotation on its tilted axis as it revolves in its orbit around the Sun, detection of day length provides an extremely accurate means of determining the season at a given latitude. Such other environmental factors as temperature and light levels also vary with the seasons but are clearly much less dependable from year to year.

Mechanisms. It has long been the goal of researchers on photoperiodism to understand the plant or animal mechanisms that account for the responses. Light must be detected, the duration of light or darkness must be measured, and this time measurement must be metabolically translated into the observed response: flowering, stem elongation, gonad development, fur color, and so forth. Basic mechanisms differ not only between plants and animals but among different species as well. The roles (synchronization, anticipation, and so on) are similar in all organisms that exhibit photoperiodism, but the mechanisms through which these roles are achieved are apparently quite varied.

Strongest inhibition of flowering in short-day plants comes when the light interruption occurs around the time of the critical night (about 7–9 h for cocklebur plants), but actual effectiveness also depends on the length of the dark period. With short-day cockleburs, the shorter the night, the less the flowering and the longer the time that light inhibits flowering.

Orange-red wavelengths used as a night interruption are by far the most effective part of the spectrum in inhibition of short-day responses and promotion of long-day responses (flowering in most studies), and effects of orange-red light can be completely reversed by subsequent exposure of plants to light of somewhat longer wavelengths, called far-red light. These observations led in the early 1950s to discovery of the phytochrome pigment system, which is apparently the molecular machinery that detects the light effective in photoperiodism of higher plants. *See* PHYTOCHROME.

In photoperiodism of short-day plants, an optimum response is usually obtained when phytochrome is in the far-red receptive form during the day and the red-receptive form during the night. Although normal daylight contains a balance of red and far-red wavelengths, the red-receptive form is most sensitive, so the pigment under normal daylight conditions is driven mostly to the far-red receptive form. At dusk this form is changed metabolically, and the red-receptive form builds up. It is apparently this shift in the form of phytochrome that initiates measurement of the dark period. This is how a plant "sees": when the far-red-sensitive form of the pigment is abundant, the plant "knows" it is in the light; the red-sensitive form (or lack of far-red form) indicates to the plant's biochemistry that it is in the dark.

The measurement of time—the durations of the day or night—is the very essence of photoperiodism. The discovery of a biological clock in living organisms was made in the late 1920s. It was shown that the movement of leaves on a bean plant (from horizontal at noon to vertical at midnight) continued uninterruptedly for several days, even when plants were placed in total darkness and at a constant temperature, and that the time between given points in the cycle (such as the most vertical leaf position) was almost but not exactly 24 h. In the case of bean leaves, it was about 25.4 h. Many other cycles have now been found with similar characteristics in virtually all groups of plants and animals. There is strong evidence that the clocks are internal and not driven by some daily change in the environment. Such rhythms are called circadian.

Circadian rhythms usually have period lengths that are remarkably temperature-insensitive, which is also true of time measurement in photoperiodism. Furthermore, the rhythms are normally highly sensitive to light, which may shift the cycle to some extent. Thus, daily rhythms in nature are normally synchronized with the daily cycle as the Sun rises and sets each day. Their circadian nature appears only when they are allowed to manifest themselves under constant conditions of light (or darkness) and temperature, so that their free-running periods can appear. [F.B.S.]

Photoreception   The process of absorption of light energy by plants and animals and its utilization for biologically important purposes. In plants photoreception plays an essential role in photosynthesis and an important role in orientation. Photoreception in animals is the initial process in vision. *See* PHOTOSYNTHESIS; TAXIS; VISION.

The photoreceptors of animals are highly specialized cells or cell groups which are light-sensitive because they contain pigments which are unstable in the presence of light of appropriate wavelengths. These light-sensitive receptor pigments absorb radiant energy and then undergo physicochemical changes, which lead to the initiation of nerve impulses that are conducted to the central nervous system. *See* EYE (INVERTEBRATE); EYE (VERTEBRATE).   [V.J.W.]

Photorespiration   Light-dependent carbon dioxide release and oxygen uptake in photosynthetic organisms caused by the fixation of oxygen instead of carbon dioxide during photosynthesis. This oxygenation reaction forms phosphoglycolate, which represents carbon lost from the photosynthetic pathway. Phosphoglycolate also inhibits photosynthesis if it is allowed to accumulate in the plant. The reactions of photorespiration break down phosphoglycolate and recover 75% of the carbon to the photosynthetic reaction sequence. The remaining 25% of the carbon is released as carbon dioxide. Photorespiration reduces the rate of photosynthesis in plants in three ways: carbon dioxide is released; energy is diverted from photosynthetic reactions to photorespiratory reactions; and competition between oxygen and carbon dioxide reduces the efficiency of the important photosynthetic enzyme ribulose-bisphosphate (RuBP) carboxylase. There is no known function of the oxygenation reaction; most scientists believe it is an unavoidable side reaction of photosynthesis. *See* PHOTOSYNTHESIS.

The rate of photosynthesis can be stimulated as much as 50% by reducing photorespiration. Since photosynthesis provides the material necessary for plant growth, photorespiration inhibits plant growth by reducing the net rate of carbon dioxide assimilation (photosynthesis). Plants grow faster and larger under nonphotorespiratory conditions, in either low oxygen or high carbon dioxide atmospheres. Most of the beneficial effects on plant growth achieved by increasing CO_2 may result from the reduced rate of photorespiration. *See* PLANT GROWTH.

There are some plants that avoid photorespiration under certain conditions by actively accumulating carbon dioxide inside the cells that have ribulose-bisphosphate carboxylase/oxygenase. Many cacti do this by taking up carbon dioxide at night and then releasing it during the day to allow normal photosynthesis. These plants are said to have crassulacean acid metabolism (CAM). Another group of plants, including corn (*Zea mays*), take up carbon dioxide by a special accumulating mechanism in one part of the leaf, then transport it to another part of the leaf for release and fixation by normal photosynthesis. The compound used to transport the carbon dioxide has four carbon atoms, and so these plants are called C_4 plants. Plants that have no mechanism for accumulating carbon dioxide produce the three-carbon compound phosphoglycerate directly and are therefore called C_3 plants. Most species of plants are C_3 plants. *See* PLANT RESPIRATION.   [T.D.S.]

Photosynthesis   The manufacture in light of organic compounds (primarily certain carbohydrates) from inorganic materials by chlorophyll- or bacteriochlorophyll-containing cells. This process requires a supply of energy in the form of light. In chlorophyll-containing plant cells and in cyanobacteria, photosynthesis involves oxidation of water (H_2O) to oxygen molecules, which are released into the environment. In contrast, bacterial photosynthesis does not involve O_2 evolution—instead of H_2O, other electron donors, such as H_2S, are used. This article will focus on photosynthesis in plants. *See* BACTERIAL PHYSIOLOGY AND METABOLISM; CHLOROPHYLL; PLANT RESPIRATION.

The light energy absorbed by the pigments of photosynthesizing cells, especially by the pigment chlorophyll or bacteriochlorophyll, is efficiently converted into stored chemical energy. Together, the two aspects of photosynthesis—the conversion of inorganic into organic matter, and the conversion of light energy into chemical energy—make it the fundamental process of life on Earth: it is the ultimate source of all living matter and of all life energy.

The net overall chemical reaction of plant photosynthesis is shown in the equation below, where $\{CH_2O\}$ stands for a carbohydrate (sugar).

$$H_2O + CO_2 + \text{light energy} \xrightarrow[\text{enzymes}]{\text{chlorophyll}} \{CH_2O\} + O_2$$

The photochemical reaction in photosynthesis belongs to the type known as oxidation-reduction, with CO_2 acting as the oxidant (hydrogen or electron acceptor) and water as the reductant (hydrogen or electron donor). The unique characteristic of this particular oxidation-reduction is that it goes "in the wrong direction" energetically; that is, it converts chemically stable materials into chemically unstable products. Light energy is used to make this "uphill" reaction possible.

Photosynthesis is a complex, multistage process. Its main parts are (1) the primary photochemical process in which light energy absorbed by chlorophyll is converted into chemical energy, in the form of some energy-rich intermediate products; and (2) the enzyme-catalyzed "dark" (that is, not photochemical) reactions by which these intermediates are converted into the final products—carbohydrates and free oxygen.

Experiments suggest that plants contain two pigment systems. One (called photosystem I, or PS I, sensitizing reaction I) contains the major part of chlorophyll *a*; the other (called photosystem II, or PS II, sensitizing reaction II) contains some chlorophyll *a* and the major part of chlorophyll *b* or other auxiliary pigments (for example, the red and blue pigments, called phycobilins, in red and blue-green algae, and the brown pigment fucoxanthol in brown algae and diatoms). It appears that efficient photosynthesis requires the absorption of an equal number of light quanta in PS I and in PS II; and that within both systems excitation energy undergoes resonance migration from one pigment to another until it ends in special molecules of chlorophyll *a* called the reaction centers. The latter molecules then enter into a series of chemical reactions that result in the oxidation of water to produce O_2 and the reduction of nicotinamide adenine dinucleotide phosphate ($NADP^+$). Chromatophores from photosynthetic bacteria and chloroplasts from green plants, when illuminated in the presence of adenosine diphosphate (ADP) and inorganic phosphate, also use light energy to synthesize adenosine triphosphate (ATP); this photophosphorylation could be associated with some energy-releasing step in photosynthesis.   [G.; R.Gov.]

The light-dependent conversion of radiant energy into chemical energy as ATP and reduced nicotinamide adenine dinucleotide phosphate (NADPH) serves as a prelude to the utilization of these compounds for the reductive fixation of CO_2 into organic molecules. Such molecules, broadly designated as photosynthates, are usually but not invariably in the form of carbohydrates such as glucose polymers or sucrose, and form the base for the nutrition of all living things. Collectively, the biochemical processes by which CO_2 is assimilated into organic molecules are known as the photosynthetic dark reactions, not because they must occur in darkness, but because light—in contrast to the photosynthetic light reactions—is not required.

C₃ photosynthesis. The essential details of C_3 photosynthesis can be seen in Fig. 1. Three molecules of CO_2 combine with three molecules of the five-carbon compound

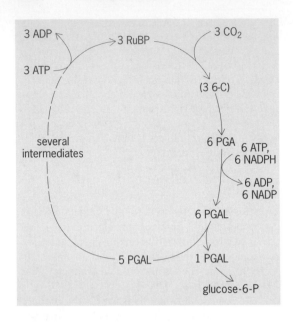

Fig. 1. Schematic outline of the Calvin (C_3) carbon dioxide assimilation cycle.

ribulose bisphosphate (RuBP) in a reaction catalyzed by RuBP carboxylase to form three molecules of an enzyme-bound six-carbon compound. These are hydrolyzed into six molecules of the three-carbon compound phosphoglyceric acid (PGA), which are phosphorylated by the conversion of six molecules of ATP (releasing ADP for photophosphorylation via the light reactions). The resulting compounds are reduced by the NADPH formed in photosynthetic light reactions to form six molecules of the three-carbon compound phosphoglyceraldehyde (PGAL). One molecule of PGAL is made available for combination with another three-carbon compound, dihydroxyacetone phosphate, which is isomerized from a second PGAL (requiring a second "turn" of the Calvin-cycle wheel) to form a six-carbon sugar. The other five PGAL molecules, through a complex series of enzymatic reactions, are rearranged into three molecules of RuBP, which can again be carboxylated with CO_2 to start the cycle turning again. The net product of two "turns" of the cycle, a six-carbon sugar (glucose-6-phosphate) is formed either within the chloroplast in a pathway leading to starch (a polymer of many glucose molecules), or externally in the cytoplasm in a pathway leading to sucrose (condensed from two six-carbon sugars, glucose and fructose).

C_4 photosynthesis. Initially, the C_3 cycle was thought to be the only route for CO_2 assimilation, although it was recognized by plant anatomists that some rapidly growing plants (such as maize, sugarcane, and sorghum) possessed an unusual organization of the photosynthetic tissues in their leaves (Kranz morphology). It was then demonstrated that plants having the Kranz anatomy utilized an additional CO_2 assimilation route now known as the C_4-dicarboxylic acid pathway (Fig. 2). Carbon dioxide enters a mesophyll cell, where it combines with the three-carbon compound phosphoenolpyruvate (PEP) to form a four-carbon acid, oxaloacetic acid, which is reduced to malic acid or transaminated to aspartic acid. The four-carbon acid moves into bundle sheath cells, where the acid is decarboxylated, the CO_2 assimilated via the C_3 cycle, and the resulting three-carbon compound, pyruvic acid, moves back into the mesophyll cell and is transformed into PEP, which can be carboxylated again. The two cell types, mesophyll and bundle sheath, are not necessarily adjacent, but in all documented cases of C_4

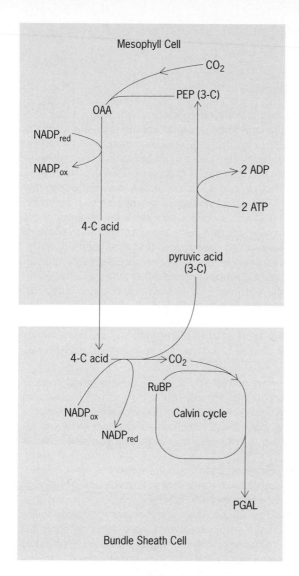

Fig. 2. Schematic outline of the Hatch-Slack (C_4) carbon dioxide assimilation route in two cell types of a NADP-ME-type plant.

photosynthesis the organism had two distinct types of green cells. C_4 metabolism is classified into three types, depending on the decarboxylation reaction used with the four-carbon acid in the bundle sheath cells:

1. NADP-ME type (sorghum):

$$NADP^+ + \text{malic acid} \xrightarrow[\text{enzyme}]{\text{NADP-malic}} \text{pyruvic acid} + CO_2 + NADPH$$

2. NAD-ME type (*Atriplex* species):

$$NAD^+ + \text{malic acid} \xrightarrow[\text{enzyme}]{\text{NAD-malic}} \text{pyruvic acid} + CO_2 + NADH$$

3. PCK type (*Panicum* species):

$$\text{Oxaloacetic acid} + \text{ATP} \xrightarrow{\text{phosphoenol pyruvate carboxykinase}} \text{PEP} + \text{CO}_2 + \text{ADP}$$

CAM photosynthesis. Under arid and desert conditions, where soil water is in short supply, transpiration during the day when temperatures are high and humidity is low may rapidly deplete the plant of water, leading to desiccation and death. By keeping stomata closed during the day, water can be conserved, but the uptake of CO_2, which occurs entirely through the stomata, is prevented. Desert plants in the Crassulaceae, Cactaceae, Euphorbiaceae, and 15 other families evolved, apparently independently of C_4 plants, an almost identical strategy of assimilating CO_2 by which the CO_2 is taken in at night when the stomata open; water loss is low because of the reduced temperatures and correspondingly higher humidities. First studied in plants of the Crassulaceae, the process has been called crassulacean acid metabolism (CAM).

In contrast to C_4, where two cell types cooperate, the entire process occurs within an individual cell; the separation of C_4 and C_3 is thus temporal rather than spatial. At night, CO_2 combines with PEP through the action of PEP carboxylase, resulting in the formation of oxaloacetic acid and its conversion into malic acid. The PEP is formed from starch or sugar via the glycolytic route of respiration. Thus, there is a daily reciprocal relationship between starch (a storage product of C_3 photosynthesis) and the accumulation of malic acid (the terminal product of nighttime CO_2 assimilation).   [M.G.; G.A.B.]

Phycobilin   Any member of a class of intensely colored pigments found in some algae that absorb light for photosynthesis. Phycobilins are structurally related to mammalian bile pigments, and they are unique among photosynthetic pigments in being covalently bound to proteins (phycobiliproteins). In at least two groups of algae, phycobiliproteins are aggregated in a highly ordered protein complex called a phycobilisome.

Phycobilins occur only in three groups of algae: cyanobacteria (blue-green algae), Rhodophyta (red algae), and Cryptophyceae (cryptophytes), and are largely responsible for their distinctive colors, including blue-green, yellow, and red. Five different phycobilins have been identified to date, but the two most common are phycocyanobilin, a blue pigment, and phycoerythrobilin, a red pigment. In the cell, these pigments absorb light maximally in the orange (620-nanometers) and green (550-nm) portion of the visible light spectrum, respectively. A blue-green light (495-nm) absorbing pigment, phycourobilin, is found in some cyanobacteria and red algae. A yellow light (575-nm) absorbing pigment, phycobiliviolin (also called cryptoviolin) is apparently found in all cryptophytes but in only a few cyanobacteria. A fifth phycobilin, which absorbs deep-red light (697 nm), has been identified spectrally in some cryptophytes, but its chemical properties are unknown.

Phycobilins are associated with the photosynthetic light-harvesting system in chloroplasts of red algae and cryptophytes and with the photosynthetic membranes of cyanobacteria, which lack chloroplasts. Phycobilins are covalently bound to a water-soluble protein that aggregates on the surface of the photosynthetic membrane. All other photosynthetic pigments (for example, chlorophylls and carotenoids) are bound to photosynthetic membrane proteins by hydrophobic attraction. Phycobiliprotein can constitute a major fraction of an alga. In some cyanobacteria, phycobiliproteins can account for more than 50% of the soluble protein and one-quarter of the dry weight of the cell. *See* CELL PLASTIDS.

Phycobilins are photosynthetic accessory pigments that absorb light efficiently in the yellow, green, orange, or red portion of the light spectrum, where chlorophyll *a* only weakly absorbs. Light energy absorbed by phycobilins is transferred with greater than 90% efficiency to chlorophyll *a*, where it is used for photosynthesis. *See* CHLOROPHYLL; PHOTOSYNTHESIS.

[T.M.K.]

Phylogeny   The genealogical history of organisms, both living and extinct. Phylogeny represents the historical pattern of relationships among organisms which has resulted from the actions of many different evolutionary processes. Phylogenetic relationships are depicted by branching diagrams called cladograms, or phylogenetic trees. Cladograms show relative affinities of groups of organisms called taxa. Such groups of organisms have some genealogical unity, and are given a taxonomic rank such as species, genera, families, or orders. For example, two species of cats—say, the lion (*Panthera leo*) and the tiger (*Panthera tigris*)—are more closely related to each other than either is to the gray wolf (*Canis latrans*). The family including all cats, Felidae, is more closely related to the family including all dogs, Canidae, than either is to the family that includes giraffes, Giraffidae. The lion and tiger, and the Felidae and Canidae, are called sister taxa because of their close relationship relative to the gray wolf, or to the Giraffidae, respectively.

Cladograms thus depict a hierarchy of relationships among a group of taxa (illus. *a*). Branch points, or nodes, of a cladogram represent hypothetical common ancestors (not specific real ancestors), and the branches connect descendant sister taxa. If the taxa being considered are species, nodes are taken to signify speciation events. The goal of the science of cladistics, or phylogenetic analysis, is to discover these sister-group (cladistic) relationships and to identify what are termed monophyletic groups—two or more taxa postulated to have a single, common origin.

The acceptance of a cladogram depends on the empirical evidence that supports it relative to alternative hypotheses of relationship for those same taxa. Evidence for or against alternative phylogenetic hypotheses comes from the comparative study of the characteristics of those taxa. Similarities and differences are determined by comparison of the anatomical, behavioral, physiological, or molecular [such as deoxyribonucleic acid (DNA) sequences] attributes among the taxa. A statement that two features in two or more taxa are similar and thus constitute a shared character is, in essence, a preliminary hypothesis that they are homologous; that is, the taxa inherited the specific form of the feature from their common ancestor. However, not all similarities are homologs; some are developed independently through convergent or parallel evolution, and although they may be similar in appearance, they had different histories and thus are not really the same feature. In cladistic theory, shared homologous similarities are either primitive (plesiomorphic condition) or derived (apomorphic con-

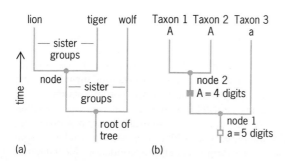

Phylogenetic trees. (*a*) A tree representing a hierarchical pattern of sister-group relationships (those taxa descended from a common ancestor). (*b*) Relationships are determined by identifying derived characters; in this case the condition of five digits is primitive, whereas the loss of a digit is derived and unites taxa 1 and 2.

dition), whereas nonhomologous similarities are termed homoplasies (or sometimes, parallelisms or convergences). This distinction over concepts and terminology is important because only derived characters constitute evidence that groups are actually related.

As evolutionary lineages diversify, some characters will become modified. Examples include the enlargement of forelimbs or the loss of digits on the hand. Thus, during evolution the foot of a mammal might transform from a primitive condition of having five digits to a derived form with only four digits (illus. b). Following branching at node 1, the foot in one lineage undergoes an evolutionary modification involving the loss of a digit (expressed as character state A). A subsequent branching event then produced taxa 1 and 2, which inherited that derived character. The lineage leading to taxon 3, however, retained the primitive condition of five digits (character state a). The presence of the shared derived character, A, is called a synapomorphy, and identifies taxa 1 and 2 as being more closely related to each other than either is to taxon 3. Distinguishing between the primitive and derived conditions of a character within a group of taxa (the ingroup) is usually accomplished by comparisons to groups postulated to have more distant relationships (outgroups). Character states that are present in ingroups but not outgroups are postulated to be derived. Systematists have developed computer programs that attempt to identify shared derived characters (synapomorphies) and, at the same time, use them to construct the best phylogenetic trees for the available data.

Knowledge of phylogenetic relationships provides the basis for classifying organisms. A major task of the science of systematics is to search for monophyletic groups. Some groups, such as birds and mammals, are monophyletic; that is, phylogenetic analysis suggests they are all more closely related to each other than to other vertebrates. However, other traditional groups, such as reptiles, have been demonstrated to be nonmonophyletic (some so-called reptiles, such as dinosaurs and their relatives, are more closely related to birds than they are to other reptiles such as snakes). Classifications based on monophyletic groups are termed natural classifications. Phylogenies are also essential for understanding the distributional history, or biogeography, of organisms. Knowing how organisms are related to one another helps the biogeographer to decipher relationships among areas and to reconstruct the spatial histories of groups and their biotas. See ANIMAL EVOLUTION; ANIMAL SYSTEMATICS; BIOGEOGRAPHY; TAXONOMIC CATEGORIES.   [J.Cr.]

Physiological ecology (animal)

Physiological ecology (animal)   A discipline that combines the study of physiological processes, the functions of living organisms and their parts, with ecological processes that connect the individual organism with population dynamics and community structure. See POPULATION ECOLOGY.

Physiological ecologists focus on whole-animal function and adjustments to ever-changing environments, in both laboratory and field. Short-term behavioral adjustments and longer-term physiological adjustments tend to maximize the fitness of animals, that is, their capacity to survive and reproduce successfully. Among the processes that physiological ecologists study are temperature regulation, energy metabolism and energetics, nutrition, respiratory gas exchange, water and osmotic balance, and responses to environmental stresses. These environmental stresses may include climate variation, nutrition, disease, and toxic exposure. For instance, climate affects animal heat and mass balances, and such changes affect body temperature regulation. Behavioral temperature regulation (typically, avoidance of temperature extremes) modifies mass and energy intake and expenditure, and the difference between intake and expenditure provides the discretionary mass for growth and reproduction. Mortality risk (survivorship) also depends on temperature-dependent behavior, which determines daily activity. Activity time constrains the time for foraging and habitat selection, which in turn influence not only mortality risk but also community composition. Animals are similarly constrained in their discretionary mass and energy by reduction in nutrition, which decreases absorbed food, and by disease and toxins, which may elevate the costs to maintain a higher body temperature (fever). See BEHAVIORAL ECOLOGY; HOMEOSTASIS.

[W.Po.]

Physiological ecology (plant)   The branch of plant science that seeks physiological (mechanistic) explanations for ecological observations. Emphasis is placed on understanding how plants cope with environmental variation at the physiological level, and on the influence of resource limitations on growth, metabolism, and reproduction of individuals within and among plant populations, along environmental gradients, and across different communities and ecosystems. The responses of plants to natural, controlled, or manipulated conditions above and below ground provide a basis for understanding how the features of plants enable their survival, persistence, and spread. Information gathered is often used to identify the physiological and morphological features of a plant that permit adaptation to different sets of environmental conditions.

The environments that plants occupy are often subject to variation or change. The ecophysiological characteristics of these plants must be able to accommodate this or the plants face extinction. Given the right conditions, ample time, and genetic variation among a group of interbreeding individuals, plant populations and species can evolve to accommodate marked ecological change or habitat heterogeneity. If evolutionary changes in physiology or morphology occur on a local or regional scale, populations within a single species may diverge in their characteristics. Separate ecological races (ecotypes) arise in response to an identifiable, set of environmental conditions. Ecotypes are genetically distinct and are particularly well suited to the local or regional environment they occupy. Such ecotypes can often increase the geographical range and amplitude of environmental conditions that the species occupies or tolerates. Ecotypes may also occur as a series of populations arrayed over a well-defined environmental gradient called an ecocline. In contrast, if ecotypes are not present, some plant species may still be able to accommodate a wide range of growth conditions through morphological and physiological adjustments, by acclimation to a single factor (such as light) or acclimatization to a complex suite of factors which define the entire habitat. Acclimatization can occur when individuals from several different regions or populations are grown in a common location and adjust, physiologically or morphologically, to this location. Acclimation and acclimatization can therefore be defined as the ability of a single genotype (individual) to express multiple phenotypes (outward appearances) in response to variable growing conditions. Neither requires underlying genetic changes, though some genetic change might occur which could mean that the response seen may itself evolve. Acclimation and acclimatization may also be called phenotypic plasticity. See PLANT EVOLUTION.

Studies of metabolic rates in relation to environmental conditions within populations, ecotypes, or species provide a way to measure the tolerance limits expressed at different scales. These data in turn help identify the scales at which different adaptations are expressed, and enhance an understanding of the evolution of physiological processes. Combining observations and measurements from the field with those obtained in laboratory and controlled environment experiments can help identify which conditions may be most influential on plant processes and therefore what may have shaped the physiological responses seen. Laboratory and controlled environment (common garden) experiments also assist in helping identify how much of the variation expressed in a particular metabolic process can be assigned to a particular environmental factor and how much to the plants themselves and the genetic and developmental plasticity they possess. *See* ECOLOGY; ECOSYSTEM; PLANT PHYSIOLOGY.   [T.E.D.]

Phytoalexin   Any antibiotic produced by plants in response to microorganisms. Plants use physical and chemical barriers as a first line of defense. When these barriers are breached, however, the plant must actively protect itself by employing a variety of strategies. Plant cell walls are strengthened, and special cell layers are produced to block further penetration of the pathogen. These defenses can permanently stop a pathogen when fully implemented, but the pathogen must be slowed to gain time.

The rapid defenses available to plants include phytoalexin accumulation, which takes a few hours, and the hypersensitive reaction, which can occur in minutes. The hypersensitive reaction is the rapid death of plant cells in the immediate vicinity of the pathogen. Death of these cells is thought to create a toxic environment of released plant components that may in themselves interfere with pathogen growth, but more importantly, damaged cells probably release signals to surrounding cells and trigger a more comprehensive defense effort. Thus, phytoalexin accumulation is just one part of an integrated series of plant responses leading from early detection to eventual neutralization of a potentially lethal invading microorganism.

The tremendous capacity of plants to produce complex chemical compounds is reflected in the structural diversity of phytoalexins. Each plant species produces one or several phytoalexins, and the types of phytoalexins produced are similar in related species. The diversity, complexity, and toxicity of phytoalexins may provide clues about their function. The diversity of phytoalexins may reflect a plant survival strategy. That is, if a plant produces different phytoalexins from its neighbors, it is less likely to be successfully attacked by pathogens adapted to its neighbor's phytoalexins. Diversity and complexity, therefore, may reflect the benefits of using different deterrents from those found in other plants. *See* PLANT PATHOLOGY.   [A.R.A.]

Phytochrome   A pigment that controls most photomorphogenic responses in higher plants. Mechanisms have evolved in plants that allow them to adapt their growth and development to more efficiently seek and capture light and to tailor their life cycle to the climatic seasons. These mechanisms enable the plant to sense not only the presence of light but also its intensity, direction, duration, and spectral quality. Plants thus regulate important developmental processes such as seed germination, growth direction, growth rate, chloroplast development, pigmentation, flowering, and senescence, collectively termed photomorphogenesis.

To perceive light signals, plants use several receptor systems that convert light absorbed by specific pigments into chemical or electrical signals to which the plants respond. This signal conversion is called photosensory transduction. Pigments used include cryptochrome, a blue light-absorbing pigment; an ultraviolet light-absorbing pigment; and phytochrome, a red/far-red light-absorbing pigment.

Phytochrome consists of a compound that absorbs visible light (chromophore) bound to a protein. The chromophore is an open-chain tetrapyrrole closely related to the photosynthetic pigments found in the cyanobacteria and similar in structure to the circular tetrapyrroles of chlorophyll and hemoglobin. Phytochrome is one of the most intensely colored pigments found in nature, enabling phytochrome in seeds to sense even the dim light present well beneath the surface of the soil and allowing leaves to perceive moonlight. *See* CHLOROPHYLL; HEMOGLOBIN.

Phytochrome can exist in two stable photointerconvertible forms, P_r or P_{fr}, with only P_{fr} being biologically active. Absorption of red light (near 666 nanometers) by inactive P_r converts it to active P_{fr}, while absorption of far-red light (near 730 nm) by active P_{fr} converts phytochrome back to inactive P_r. Plants frequently respond quantitatively to light by detecting the amount of P_{fr} produced. As a result, the amount of P_{fr} must be strictly regulated nonphotochemically by precisely controlling both the synthesis and degradation of the pigment.

Phytochrome has a variety of functions in plants. Initially, production of P_{fr} is required for many seeds to begin germination. This requirement prevents germination of seeds that are buried too deep in the soil to successfully reach the surface. In etiolated (dark-grown) seedlings, phytochrome can measure an increase in light intensity and duration through the increased formation of P_{fr}. Light direction also can be deduced from the asymmetry of P_{fr} levels from one side of the plant to the other. Different phytochrome responses vary in their sensitivity to P_{fr}; some require very low levels of P_{fr} (less than 1% of total phytochrome) to elicit a maximal response, while others require almost all of the pigment to be converted to P_{fr}. Thus, as the seedling grows toward the soil surface, a cascade of photomorphogenic responses are induced, with the more sensitive responses occurring first. This chain of events produces a plant that is mature and photosynthetically competent by the time it finally reaches the surface. Production of P_{fr} also makes the plant aware of gravity, inducing shoots to grow up and roots to grow down into the soil. See PLANT MOVEMENTS; SEED.

In light-grown plants, phytochrome allows for the perception of daylight intensity, day length, and spectral quality. Intensity is detected through a measurement of phytochrome shuttling between P_r and P_{fr}; the more intense the light, the more interconversion. This signal initiates changes in chloroplast morphology to allow shaded leaves to capture light more efficiently. If the light is too intense, phytochrome will also elicit the production of pigments to protect plants from photodamage.

Temperate plants use day length to tailor their development, a process called photoperiodism. How the plant measures day length is unknown, but it involves phytochrome and actually measures the length of night. See PHOTOPERIODISM.

Finally, phytochrome allows plants to detect the spectral quality of light, a form of color vision, by measuring the ratio of P_r to P_{fr}. When a plant is grown under direct sun, the amounts of red and far-red light are approximately equal, and the ratio of P_r to P_{fr} in the plant is about 1:1. Should the plant become shaded by another plant, the P_r/P_{fr} ratio changes dramatically to 5:1 or greater. This is because the shading plant's chlorophyll absorbs much of the red light needed to produce P_{fr} and absorbs almost none of the far-red light used to produce P_r. For a shade-intolerant plant, this change in P_r/P_{fr} ratio induces the plant to grow taller, allowing it to grow above the canopy.

It is not known how phytochrome elicits the diverse array of photomorphogenic responses, but the regulatory action must result from discrete changes in the molecule following photoconversion of P_r to P_{fr}. These changes must then start a chain of events in the photosensory transduction chain leading to the photomorphogenic response. Many photosensory transduction chains probably begin by responding to P_{fr} or the P_r/P_{fr} ratio and branch off toward discrete end points. See PHOTOMORPHOGENESIS.   [R.D.V.]

Phytoplankton   Mostly autotrophic microscopic algae which inhabit the illuminated surface waters of the sea, estuaries, lakes, and ponds. Many are motile. Some perform diel (diurnal) vertical migrations, others do not. Some nonmotile forms regulate their buoyancy. However, their locomotor abilities are limited, and they are largely transported by horizontal and vertical water motions.

A great variety of algae make up the phytoplankton. Diatoms (class Bacillario-phyceae) are often conspicuous members of marine, estuarine, and fresh-water plankton. Dinoflagellates (class Dinophyceae) occur in both marine and fresh-water environments and are important primary producers in marine and estuarine environments. Coccolithophorids (class Haptophyceae) are also marine primary producers of some importance. They do not occur in fresh water.

Even though marine and fresh-water phytoplankton communities contain a number of algal classes in common, phytoplankton samples from these two environments will appear quite different. These habitats support different genera and species and groups of higher rank in these classes. Furthermore, fresh-water plankton contains algae belonging to additional algal classes either absent or rarely common in open ocean environments. These include the green algae (class Chlorophyceae), the euglenoid flagellates (class Euglenophyceae), and members of the Prasinophyceae.

The phytoplankton in aquatic environments which have not been too drastically affected by human activity exhibit rather regular and predictable seasonal cycles. Coastal upwelling and divergences, zones where deeper water rises to the surface, are examples of naturally occurring phenomena which enrich the mixed layer with needed nutrients and greatly increase phytoplankton production. In the ocean these are the sites of the world's most productive fisheries.   [R.W.H.]

Picornaviridae   A viral family made up of the small (18–30 nanometer) ether-sensitive viruses that lack an envelope and have a ribonucleic acid (RNA) genome. The name is derived from "pico" meaning very small, and RNA for the nucleic acid type. Picornaviruses of human origin include the following subgroups: enteroviruses (polioviruses, coxsackieviruses, and echoviruses) and rhinoviruses. There are also picornaviruses of lower animals (for example, bovine foot-and-mouth disease, a rhinovirus). See ANIMAL VIRUS; COXSACKIEVIRUS; POLIOMYELITIS; RHINOVIRUS.   [J.L.Me.]

Pigmentation   A property of biological materials that imparts coloration. Hence, pigmentation determines the quantity and quality of reflected visible light. The characteristics of light returning from living matter are a function of its chemical and physical properties and, therefore, are not only due to pigments proper but can be of structural origin (for example, due to reflection, scattering, or interference) as well.

Pigments are essential constituents of the living world. Their contribution to the evolution and maintenance of life, and its manifold expressions, is most evident in the role of chlorophylls and the associated carotenoids of certain bacteria and most plants. These pigments harvest solar light energy for utilization in the photosynthesis of organic material from inorganic precursors. See CHLOROPHYLL; PHOTOSYNTHESIS.

The outermost structures on the animal skin are pigmented for many reasons, for example, to reduce the animal's visibility against a colored background or to provide optical signals to the other sex or to other species. Conspicuously pigmented flowers attract pollinators, and colored fruits are easily found by animals, which eat them and then disperse the undigested seeds.

The role of pigments in communication depends on the ability of organisms to discriminate between different regions of the solar spectrum. In animals with eyes, this is accomplished by differently colored visual pigments contained in specialized receptor cells. Microorganisms, fungi, and plants also have special pigment systems that permit these organisms to move or grow toward, or away from, light (positive and negative phototaxis and phototropism, respectively). See PLANT MOVEMENTS.

Since most organisms are totally dependent on light—at least indirectly—elaborate pigment systems have evolved which tune metabolic and activity patterns to the daily pattern of light and dark, and to the changes in the relative lengths of day and night in the course of a year. The phytochrome of plants and the pigments of the eye or of extraretinal photoreceptor organs of many vertebrates and invertebrates are typical representatives of pigments that correlate biological activity with light-dark cycles (photoperiodism). *See* COLOR VISION; PHOTOPERIODISM; PHOTORECEPTION.

In the examples listed above, pigments mediate, in various ways, the beneficial actions of light. Absorbed solar light energy may, however, also have detrimental effects by causing undesirable or even destructive reactions. Pigmentations can provide a light-absorbing shield that protects the tissue below from such potentially damaging radiation of the Sun. *See* SKIN.   [P.H.Ho.]

Pineal gland   An endocrine gland located in the brain which secretes melatonin, is strongly regulated by light stimuli, and is an important component of the circadian timing system. The pineal gland is virtually ubiquitous throughout the vertebrate animal kingdom. In nonmammalian vertebrates, it functions as a photoreceptive third eye and an endocrine organ. In mammals, it serves as an endocrine organ that is regulated by light entering the body via the eyes. Despite extensive species variation in anatomy and physiology, the pineal gland generally serves as an essential component of the circadian system which allows animals to internally measure time and coordinate physiological time-keeping with the external environment. *See* BIOLOGICAL CLOCKS; BRAIN.

The pineal gland is an unpaired organ attached by a stalk to the roof of the diencephalon. In frogs and lizards, one component of the pineal complex (the frontal organ or parietal eye) projects upward through the skull to lie under the skin; in all other vertebrates the pineal is located beneath the roof of the skull. Across evolution, cells within the pineal gland have progressed from classic photoreceptor cells in the earliest vertebrates, to rudimentary photoreceptors in birds, to classic endocrine cells in mammals. *See* PHOTORECEPTION; SENSE ORGAN.

In mammals, nerve fibers extend from a variety of sources in the brain to the pineal gland. The best studied of these neural inputs is through the retinohypothalamic tract, which extends from the eyes to the pineal gland in mammals. Originating in the retina, the majority of the retinohypothalamic fibers project to or around the bilateral suprachiasmatic nuclei in the hypothalamus. These nuclei serve as endogenous oscillators with period lengths close to 24 h. Thus, the suprachiasmatic nuclei function as pacemakers for the circadian system, which regulates daily physiological and behavioral rhythms. From the suprachiasmatic nuclei there are short projections to the paired paraventricular hypothalamic nuclei, and then long descending axons project from these nuclei to synapse on preganglionic sympathetic neurons in the upper thoracic spinal cord. These sympathetic neurons then extend out of the central nervous system to the superior cervical ganglia in the neck region. From there, postganglionic sympathetic axons reenter the cranium and ultimately innervate the pineal gland.

In mammals, information about environmental light and darkness is relayed from the eye to entrain circadian neural activity of the suprachiasmatic nuclei. In turn, the suprachiasmatic nuclei synchronize circadian rhythms in the pineal gland through its sympathetic innervation. One of the best-studied rhythms in the pineal gland is the biosynthesis of the hormone melatonin. Pinealocytes also have the necessary enzymes for converting tryptophan into a larger family of indole compounds, and numerous polypeptides have been localized in the pineal gland. The biological functions of these other pineal indole and peptide constituents are currently unknown.

In all vertebrate species studied, high levels of melatonin are produced and secreted during the night, while low levels are released during the day. The melatonin circadian rhythm is produced by the endogenous pacemaking activity of the suprachiasmatic nuclei, while the entrainment of this rhythm is coordinated by signals of light and darkness relayed from the eyes. Day length or photoperiod can influence the duration that melatonin production is elevated during the night. This represents a seasonal effect of light on the pineal gland. Specifically, in the summer when days are longer and nights are shorter, the duration of increased nocturnal melatonin secretion is shorter than during the winter when nights are longer. This effect of photoperiod length influencing the duration of nighttime melatonin rise has been documented in many species, including humans.

There is extensive species diversity in the capacity of melatonin to regulate physiology. Numerous species, ranging from insects to mammals, have yearly cycles of activity, morphology, reproduction, or development which are responsive to seasonal changes in day length (photoperiodism). Among many species that breed seasonally, melatonin has been shown to be a potent regulator of the reproductive axis in both males and females. The effects of melatonin on the regulation of circadian physiology has been elucidated in many vertebrate species, including humans. In addition, melatonin has been studied in different species for its influence on retinal physiology, sleep, body temperature regulation, immune function, and cardiovascular regulation.   [G.C.B.]

Pinnipeds   Carnivorous mammals of the suborder Pinnipedia, which includes 32 species of seals, sea lions, and walrus in 3 families. All species of the order are found along coastal areas, from the Antarctic to the Arctic regions. Although many species have restricted distribution, the group as a whole has worldwide distribution.

Pinnipeds are less modified both anatomically and behaviorally for marine life than are other marine mammals: Each year they return to land to breed, and they have retained their hindlimbs. They are primarily carnivorous mammals, with fish supplying the basic diet. They also eat crustaceans, mollusks, and, in some instances, sea birds. Their body is covered with a heavy coat of fur, the limbs are modified as flippers, the eyes are large, the external ear is small or lacking, and the tail is absent or very short.

The single species of the family Odobenidae is the walrus (*Odobenus rosmarus*); it grows to 10 ft (3 m) and weighs 3000 lb (1350 kg). It has no external ears but does have a distinct neck region. The upper canines of both sexes are prolonged as tusks which can be used defensively (illus. *a*). The walrus feeds on marine invertebrates and fish.

The family Otariidae, the eared seals, includes the sea lions and fur seals (illus. *b*), which are characterized by an external ear. The neck is longer and more clearly defined than that of true seals, and the digits lack nails. The California sea lion (*Zalophus californianus*) occurs along the Pacific coast, and is commonly seen in zoos and performing in circuses. The southern sea lion (*Otaria byronia*) is found around the Galapagos Islands and along the South American coast. Stellar's sea lion (*Eumetopias jubatus*) is a large species found along the Pacific coast. Minor species are the Australian sea lion (*Neophoca cinerea*) and the New Zealand species (*Phocarctos hookeri*).

Phocidae is the largest family of pinnipeds, the true seals. It includes the monk seals, elephant seals, common seals, and other less well-known forms. The family is unique in that the digits have nails, the soles and palms are covered with hair, and the necks are very short. Most species live in marine habitats; however, the Caspian seal (*Pusa caspica*) lives in brackish water. The only fresh-water seal is the Baikal seal (*P. sibirica*). It is estimated that there are between 40,000 and 100,000 Baikal seals in Lake Baikal. One of the best-known species is the Atlantic gray seal (*Halichoerus grypus*), a species

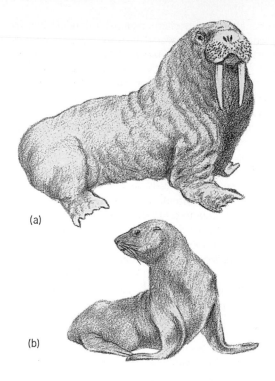

Pinnipeds. (*a*) **Walrus** (*Odobenus rosmarus*). (*b*) **Alaska fur seal** (*Callorhinus ursinus*).

(a)

(b)

fround in the North Atlantic along the coasts of Europe, Iceland, and Greenland. *See* CARNIVORA; MAMMALIA. [C.B.C.]

Pinophyta   One of the two divisions of the seed plants, comprising about 600 to 700 species extant on all continents except Antarctica. The most familiar and common representatives are the evergreen, cone-bearing trees of the Pinales. Because the ovules (young seeds) are exposed directly to the air at the time of pollination, the Pinophyta are commonly known as the gymnosperms, in contrast to the other division of flowering plants, the angiosperms (division Magnoliophyta), which have the ovules enclosed in an ovary. The division Pinophyta consists of three classes: Ginkgoopsida, Cycadopsida, and Pinopsida. *See* MAGNOLIOPHYTA; PLANT KINGDOM. [T.A.Z.]

Pisces (zoology)   A term that embraces all fishes and fishlike vertebrates. The Pisces include four well-defined groups that merit recognition as classes: the Agnatha or jawless fishes, the most primitive; the Placodermi or armored fishes, known only as Paleozoic fossils; the Chondrichthyes or cartilaginous fishes; and the Osteichthyes or bony fishes. *See* CHONDRICHTHYES. [R.M.B.]

Pith   The central zone of tissue of an axis in which the vascular tissue is arranged as a hollow cylinder. Pith is present in most stems and in some roots. Stems without pith rarely occur in angiosperms but are characteristic of psilopsids, lycopsids, *Sphenophyllum*, and some ferns. Roots of some ferns, many monocotyledons, and some dicotyledons include a pith, although most roots have xylem tissue in the center.

Pith is composed usually of parenchyma cells often arranged in longitudinal files. This arrangement results from predominantly transverse division of pith mother cells near the apical meristem. *See* Parenchyma; Root (botany); Stem.   [H.W.Bl.]

Pituitary gland   The most structurally and functionally complex organ of the endocrine system. Through its hormones, the pituitary, also known as the hypophysis, affects every physiological process of the body. All vertebrates have a pituitary gland with a common basic structure and function. In addition to its endocrine functions, the pituitary may play a role in the immune response.

The hypophysis of all vertebrates has two major segments—the neurohypophysis (a neural component) and the adenohypophysis (an epithelial component)—each with a different embryological origin. The neurohypophysis develops from a downward process of the diencephalon (the base of the brain), whereas the adenohypophysis originates as an outpocketing of the primitive buccal epithelium, known as Rathke's pouch. The adenohypophysis has three distinct subdivisions: the pars tuberalis, the pars distalis, and the pars intermedia. The neurohypophysis comprises the pars nervosa and the infundibulum. The latter consists of the infundibular stalk and the median eminence of the tuber cinereum.

The structural intimacy of neurohypophysis and adenohypophysis that is established early during embryogenesis reflects the direct functional interaction between the central nervous system and endocrine system. The extent of this anatomical intimacy varies considerably among the vertebrate classes, from limited contact to intimate interdigitation. Vascular or neuronal pathways, or both, provide the means of exchanging chemical signals, thus enabling centers in the brain to exert control over the synthesis and release of adenohypophysial hormones.

Neurohormones, which are synthesized in specific regions of the brain, are conveyed to the neurohypophysis by way of axonal tracts, where they may be stored in distended axonal endings. Axons may also contact blood vessels and discharge their neurosecretory products into the systemic circulation or into a portal system leading to the adenohypophysis, or they may directly innervate pituitary gland cells. *See* Neurosecretion.

In most animals, the vascular link is the prime route of information transfer between brain and pituitary gland. This link begins in the tuber cinereum, the portion of the third ventricle floor that extends toward the infundibulum. The lower tuber cinereum, which is known as the median eminence, is well endowed with blood vessels that drain down into the pituitary stalk and ultimately empty into the anterior pituitary. The vascular link between the median eminence and the pituitary gland is known as the hypothalamo-hypophysial portal system. The median eminence in humans is vascularized by the paired superior hypophysial arteries. The pituitary gland is believed to have the highest blood flow rate of any organ in the body. However, its blood is received indirectly via the median eminence and the hypothalamo-hypophysial portal system. Most of the blood flow is from the brain to the pituitary gland, with retrograde flow from the adenohypophysis to the hypothalamus, suggesting a two-way communication between nervous and endocrine systems. Although the brain is protected from the chemical substances in the circulatory system by the blood–brain barrier, the median eminence lies outside that protective mechanism and is therefore permeable to intravascular substances. *See* Brain.

The hormones of the adenohypophysis may be grouped into three categories based on chemical and functional similarities. The first category consists of growth hormone (also known as somatotropin) and prolactin, both of which are large, single, polypeptide chains; the second category consists of the glycoprotein hormones; this family of hormones contains the gonadotropins and thyrotropin. The gonadotropins in many species, including humans, can be segregated into two distinct hormones, follicle-stimulating hormone and luteinizing hormone. The third group comprises adrenocortiotropic hormone and melanotropin (MSH; melanocyte-stimulating hormone). See ADENOHYPOPHYSIS HORMONE.

The regulation of the release of pituitary hormones is determined by precise monitoring of circulating hormone levels in the blood and by genetic and environmental factors that manifest their effect through the releasing and release-inhibiting factors of the hypothalamus. The hypothalamus is located at the base of the brain (the diencephalon) below the thalamus and above the pituitary gland, forming the walls and the lower portion of the third ventricle. It receives major neuronal inputs from the sense organs, hippocampus, thalamus, and lower brainstem structures, including the reticular formation and the spinal cord. Thus, the hypothalamus is designed and anatomically positioned to receive a diversity of messages from external and internal sources that can be transmitted by way of hypothalamic releasing factors to the pituitary gland, where they are translated into endocrine action. See NERVOUS SYSTEM (VERTEBRATE).

The neurohypophysis hormones, oxytocin and vasopressin, are synthesized in different neurons of the paraventricular and supraoptic nuclei of the hypothalamus and travel by axonal flow to the terminals in the neurohypophysis for storage and ultimate release into the vascular system. Oxytocin is important in stimulating milk release through its contractile action on muscle elements in the mammary gland. It also stimulates uterine smooth muscle contraction at parturition. Vasopressin affects water retention by its action on certain kidney tubules. Thus, it also affects blood pressure. See LACTATION; NEUROHYPOPHYSIS HORMONE.

The better-known neurotransmitters of the central nervous system include the catecholamines (dopamine, epinephrine, and norepinephrine), serotonin, acetylcholine, gamma-amino butyric acid (GABA), histamine, and the opioid peptides (enkephalins, endorphins, dynorphin, neoendorphin, rimorphin, and leumorphin). These substances are distributed widely in the central nervous system and, for most, also in the pituitary gland. If a particular amine or neurotransmitter is present in nerve fibers leading to the median eminence, it probably will influence pituitary gland activity via the portal system. Dopamine, serotonin, gamma-amino butyric acid, and acetylcholine are best known for such activity. These neurotransmitters play an important, but poorly understood, role in regulating pituitary function, either directly or by their action on neuropeptide-producing neurons. Understanding the pharmacology of neurotransmitters holds promise for the treatment of basic disorders of the hypothalamic-pituitary axis. See ACETYLCHOLINE; ENDOCRINE SYSTEM (VERTEBRATE); ENDORPHINS; HISTAMINE; HORMONE; NEUROBIOLOGY; NEUROIMMUNOLOGY; SEROTONIN.   [M.P.S.]

Placentation   The intimate association or fusion of a tissue or organ of the embryonic stage of an animal to its parent for physiological exchange to promote the growth and development of the young. It enables the young, retained within the body or tissues of the mother, to respire, acquire nourishment, and eliminate wastes by bringing the bloodstreams of mother and young into close association but never into direct connection. Placentation characterizes the early development of all mammals except the egg-laying duckbill platypus and spiny anteater. It occurs in some species of all other orders of vertebrates except the birds. In fact, in certain sharks and reptiles it is almost as well developed as in mammals. A few examples are also known among invertebrates (*Peripatus*, certain tunicates, and insects). See FETAL MEMBRANE.

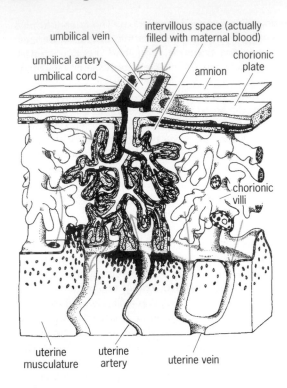

uterine musculature · uterine artery · uterine vein

Block removed from center of human placenta.

Efficient interchange depends on close proximity of large areas of fetal tissues to maternal blood and glandular areas. This is provided in mammals by a remarkable regulatory cooperation between the developing outer layer (trophoblast) of the chorion, together with the vascular yolk sac or allantois or both, and the mother's uterine lining (endometrium). In the typical mammalian placenta, which is always formed by the chorion and the allantoic vessels, the fetal and maternal bloodstreams are as close as a few thousandths of a millimeter from each other (see illustration). The surface area of the fetal villi which contain the functional fetal capillaries is probably several times larger than the body surface of the female. In humans this ratio is known to be about 8:1.   [H.W.Mo.]

Plague   An infectious disease of humans and rodents caused by the bacterium *Yersinia pestis*. The sylvatic (wild-animal) form persists today in more than 200 species of rodents throughout the world. The explosive urban epidemics of the Middle Ages, known as the Black Death, resulted when the infection of dense populations of city rats living closely with humans introduced disease from the Near East. The disease then was spread both by rat fleas and by transmission between humans. During these outbreaks, as much as 50% of the European population died. At present, contact with wild rodents and their fleas, sometimes via domestic cats and dogs, leads to sporadic human disease. *See* INFECTIOUS DISEASE.

After infection by *Y. pestis*, fleas develop obstruction of the foregut, causing regurgitation of plague bacilli during the next blood meal. The rat flea, *Xenopsylla cheopsis*, is an especially efficient plague vector, both between rats and from rats to humans. Human (bubonic) plague is transmitted by the bite of an infected flea; after several days, a painful swelling (the bubo) of local lymph nodes occurs. Bacteria can then spread to other organ systems, especially the lung; fever, chills, prostration, and death may occur. Plague pneumonia develops in 10–20% of all bubonic infections. In some individuals, the skin may develop hemorrhages and necrosis (tissue death), probably the origin of the ancient name, the Black Death. The last primary pneumonic plague outbreak in the United States occurred in 1919, when 13 cases resulting in 12 deaths developed before the disease was recognized and halted by isolation of cases.

Bubonic plaque is suspected when the characteristic painful, swollen glands develop in the groin, armpit, or neck of an individual who has possibly been exposed to wild-animal fleas in an area where the disease is endemic. Immediate identification is possible by microscopic evaluation of bubo aspirate stained with fluorescent-tagged antibody. Antibiotics should be given if plague is suspected or confirmed. Such treatment is very effective if started early. The current overall death rate, approximately 15%, is reduced to less than 5% among patients treated at the onset of symptoms. *See* IMMUNOFLUORESCENCE; MEDICAL BACTERIOLOGY.   [D.L.Pa.]

Plant   An organism that belongs to the Kingdom Plantae (plant kingdom) in biological classification. The study of plants is called botany. *See* BOTANY; CLASSIFICATION, BIOLOGICAL.

The Plantae share the characteristics of multicellularity, cellulose cell walls, and photosynthesis using chlorophylls *a* and *b* (except for a few plants that are secondarily heterotrophic). Most plants are also structurally differentiated, usually having organs specialized for anchorage, support, and photosynthesis. Tissue specialization for photosynthetic, conducting, and covering functions is also characteristic. Plants have a sporic (rather than gametic or zygotic) life cycle that involves both sporophytic and gametophytic phases, although the latter is evolutionarily reduced in the majority of species. Reproduction is sexual, but diversification of breeding systems is a prominent feature of many plant groups. *See* PHOTOSYNTHESIS; REPRODUCTION (PLANT).

A conservative estimate of the number of described species of plants is 250,000. There are possibly two or three times that many species as yet undiscovered, primarily in the Southern Hemisphere. Plants are categorized into nonvascular and vascular groups, and the latter into seedless vascular plants and seed plants. The nonvascular plants include the liverworts, hornworts, and mosses. The vascular plants without seeds are the ground pines, horsetails, ferns, and whisk ferns; seed plants include cycads, ginkgos, conifers, gnetophytes, and flowering plants. Each of these groups constitutes a division in botanical nomenclature, which is equivalent to a phylum in the zoological system. *See* PLANT TAXONOMY.   [M.La.]

Plant anatomy   The area of plant science concerned with the internal structure of plants. It deals both with mature structures and with their origin and development.

The plant anatomist dissects the plant and studies it from different planes and at various levels of magnification. At the level of the cell, anatomy overlaps plant cytology, which deals exclusively with the cell and its contents. Sometimes the name plant histology is applied to the area of plant anatomy directed toward the study of cellular details of tissues. *See* PLANT CELL; PLANT ORGANS.   [K.E.]

Plant-animal interactions   The examination of the ecology of interacting plants and animals by using an evolutionary, holistic perspective. For example, the chemistry of defensive compounds of a plant species may have been altered by natural-selection pressures resulting from the long-term impacts of herbivores. Also, the physiology of modern herbivores may be modified from that ofthousands of years ago as

Effects of interaction types for each species*

Interaction	Effect on species A	Effect on species B
Mutualism	+	+
Commensalism	+	0
Antagonism	+	−
Competition	−	−
Amensalism	0	−
Neutralism	0	0

*+ = beneficial, − = harmful, 0 = neutral.

adaptations for the detoxification or avoidance of plant defensive chemicals have arisen.

The application of the theories based on an understanding of plant-animal interactions provides an understanding of problems in modern agricultural ecosystems. In addition, plant-animal interactions have practical applications in medicine. For example, a number of plant chemicals, such as digitalin from the foxglove plant, that evolved as herbivore-defensive compounds have useful therapeutic effects on humans.

The evolutionary consequences of plant-animal interactions vary, depending on the effects on each participant. Interaction types range from mutualisms, that is, relationships which are beneficial to both participating species, to antagonisms, in which the interaction benefits only one of the participating species and negatively impacts the other. Interaction types are defined on the basis of whether the impacts of the interaction are beneficial, harmful, or neutral for each interacting species (see table).   [W.G.A.]

Fossil record. Plants and animals interact in a variety of ways within modern ecosystems. These interactions may range from simple examples of herbivory (animals eating plants) to more complex interactions such as pollination or seed and fruit dispersal. Animals also rely on plants for food and shelter. The complex interactions between these organisms over geologic time not only have resulted in an abundance and diversity of organisms in time and space but also have contributed to many of the evolutionary adaptations found in the biological world.

Paleobiologists have attempted to decipher some of the interrelationships that existed between plants and animals throughout geologic time. The ecological setting in which the organisms lived in the geologic past is being analyzed in association with the fossils. Thus, as paleobiologists have increased their understanding of certain fossil organisms, it has become possible to consider some aspects of the ecosystems in which they lived, and in turn, how various types of organisms interacted.

Herbivory. Perhaps the most widespread interaction between plants and animals is herbivory, in which plants are utilized as food. One method of determining the extent of herbivory in the fossil record is by analyzing the plant material that has passed through the digestive gut of the herbivore.

The stems of some fossil plants show tissue disruption similar to various types of wounds occurring in plant parts that have been pierced by animal feeding structures. As plants developed defense systems in the form of fibrous layers covering inner, succulent tissues, some animals evolved piercing mouthparts that allowed them to penetrate these thick-walled layers. In some fossil plants, it is also possible to see evidence of wound tissue that has grown over these penetration sites. See HERBIVORY.

Mimicry. Another example of the interactions between plants and animals that can be determined from the fossil record is mimicry. Certain fossil insects have wings that are morphologically identical to plant leaves, thus providing camouflage from predators as the insect rested on a seed fern frond.

Pollination. The transfer of pollen from the pollen sacs to the receptive stigma in angiosperms or to the seed in gymnosperms is an example of an ancient interaction between plants and animals. It has been suggested that pollination in some groups initially occurred as a result of indiscriminate foraging behavior by certain animals, and later evolved specifically as a method to effect pollination. The size, shape, and organization of fossil pollen grains provide insight into potential pollination vectors. *See* POLLINATION.

[T.N.T.]

Plant cell   The basic unit of structure and function in nearly all plants. Although plant cells are variously modified in structure and function, they have many common features. The most distinctive feature of all plant cells is the rigid cell wall, which is absent in animal cells. The range of specialization and the character of association of plant cells is very wide. In the simplest plant forms a single cell constitutes a whole organism and carries out all the life functions. In just slightly more complex forms, cells are associated structurally, but each cell appears to carry out the fundamental life functions, although certain ones may be specialized for participation in reproductive processes. In the most advanced plants, cells are associated in functionally specialized tissues, and associated tissues make up organs such as the leaves, stem, and root. *See* CELL WALLS (PLANT).

Plant and animal cells are composed of the same fundamental constituents—nucleic acids, proteins, carbohydrates, lipids, and various inorganic substances—and are organized in the same fundamental manner. A characteristic of their organization is the presence of unit membranes composed of phospholipids and associated proteins and in some instances nucleic acids.

Perhaps the most conspicuous and certainly the most studied of the features peculiar to plant cells is the presence of plastids. The plastids are membrane-bound organelles with an inner membrane system. Chlorophylls and other pigments are associated with the inner membrane system. *See* CELL (BIOLOGY); CELL PLASTIDS; CHLOROPHYLL.

[W.G.W.]

Plant communication   Movement of signals or cues, presumably chemical, among individual plants or plant parts. These chemical cues are a consequence of damage to plant tissues and stimulate physiological changes in the undamaged "receiving" plant or tissue. There are very few studies of this phenomenon, and so theories of its action and significance are fairly speculative.

Plants produce a wealth of secondary metabolites that do not function in the main, or primary, metabolism of the plant, which includes photosynthesis, nutrient acquisition, and growth. Since many of these chemicals have very specific negative effects on animals or pathogens, ecologists speculate that they may be produced by plants as defenses. Plant chemical defenses either may be present all of the time (constitutive) or may be stimulated in response to attack (induced). Those produced in response to attack by pathogens are called phytoalexins. In order to demonstrate the presence of an induced defense, the chemistry of plant tissues or their suitability to some "enemy" (via a bioassay) must be compared before and after real or simulated attack. Changes found in the chemistry and suitability of control or unattacked plants when nearby experimental plants are damaged imply that some signal or cue has passed from damaged to undamaged plants. Controlled studies have shown that responses in undamaged plants are related to the proximity of a damaged neighbor. *See* ALLELOPATHY; PHYTOALEXIN; PLANT METABOLISM.

[J.C.Sc.]

Plant evolution   The process of biological and organic change within the plant kingdom by which the characteristics of plants differ from generation to generation. The main levels (grades) of evolution have long been clear from comparisons among living plants, but the fossil record has been critical in dating evolutionary events and revealing extinct intermediates between modern groups, which are separated from each other by great morphological gaps. Plant evolution has been clarified by cladistic methods for estimating relationships among both living and fossil groups. These methods attempt to reconstruct the branching of evolutionary lines (phylogeny) by using shared evolutionary innovations (for example, presence of a structure not found in other groups) as evidence that particular organisms are descendants of the same ancestral lineage (a monophyletic group, or clade). Many traditional groups are actually grades rather than clades; these are indicated below by names in quotes.

Most botanists restrict the term plants to land plants, which invaded the land after 90% of Earth history. There is abundant evidence of photosynthetic life extending back 3.5 billion years to the early Precambrian, in the form of microfossils resembling cyanobacteria (prokaryotic blue-green algae) and limestone reefs (stromatolites) made by these organisms. Larger cells representing eukaryotic "algae" appear in the late Precambrian, followed by macroscopic "algae" and animals just before the Cambrian. *See* ALGAE; EUKARYOTAE.

Origin of land plants. Cellular, biochemical, and molecular data place the land plants among the "green algae," specifically the "charophytes," which resemble land plants in their mode of cell division and differentiated male and female gametes (oogamy). Land plants themselves are united by a series of innovations not seen in "charophytes," many of them key adaptations required for life on land. They have an alternation of generations, with a haploid, gamete-forming (gametophyte) and diploid, spore-forming (sporophyte) phase. Their reproductive organs (egg-producing archegonia, sperm-producing antheridia, and spore-producing sporangia) have a protective layer of sterile cells. The sporophyte, which develops from the zygote, begins its life inside the archegonium. The spores, produced in fours by meiosis, are air-dispersed, with a resistant outer wall that prevents desiccation. *See* REPRODUCTION (PLANT).

Land plants have been traditionally divided into "bryophytes" and vascular plants (tracheophytes). These differ in the relative role of the sporophyte, which is subordinate and permanently attached to the gametophyte in "bryophytes" but dominant and independent in vascular plants. In vascular plants, tissues are differentiated into an epidermis with a waxy cuticle that retards water loss and stomates for gas exchange, parenchyma for photosynthesis and storage, and water- and nutrient-conducting cells (xylem, phloem). However, cladistic analyses imply that some "bryophytes" are closer to vascular plants than others. This implies that the land-plant life cycle originated before the full suite of vegetative adaptations to land life, and that the sporophyte began small and underwent a trend toward elaboration and tissue specialization. *See* EPIDERMIS (PLANT); PHOTOSYNTHESIS; PRIMARY VASCULAR SYSTEM (PLANT).

In the fossil record, the first recognizable macroscopic remains of land plants are Middle Silurian vascular forms with a branched sporophyte, known as "rhyniophytes." These differed from modern plants in having no leaves or roots, only dichotomously branching stems with terminal sporangia. However, spore tetrads formed by meiosis are known from older beds (Middle Ordovician); these may represent more primitive, bryophytic plants. *See* BRYOPHYTA.

In one of the most spectacular adaptive radiations in the history of life, vascular plants diversified through the Devonian. At the beginning of this period, vegetation was low and probably confined to wet areas, but by the Late Devonian, size had increased in many lines, resulting in large trees and forests with shaded understory habitats. Of the living groups of primitive vascular plants, the lycopsids (club mosses) branched off first, along with the extinct "zosterophyllopsids." A second line, the "trimerophytes," gave rise to sphenopsids (horsetails) and ferns (filicopsids). This radiation culminated in the coal swamp forests of the Late Carboniferous, with tree lycopsids (Lepidodendrales), sphenopsids (*Calamites*), and ferns (Marattiales). Remains of these plants make up much of the coal of Europe and eastern North America, which were then located on the Equator.

Seed plants. Perhaps the most significant event after the origin of land plants was evolution of the seed. Primitive seed plants ("gymnosperms") differ from earlier groups in their reproduction, which is heterosporous (producing two sizes of spores), with separate male and female gametophytes packaged inside the pollen grain (microspore), and the ovule (a sporangium with one functional megaspore, surrounded by an integument, which develops into the seed). The transfer of sperm (two per pollen grain) from one sporophyte to another through the air, rather than by swimming, represents a step toward independence from water for reproduction. This step must have helped plants invade drier areas than they had previously occupied. In addition, seed plants have new vegetative features, particularly secondary growth, which allows production of a thick trunk made up of secondary xylem (wood) surrounded by secondary phloem and periderm (bark). Together, these innovations have made seed plants the dominant organisms in most terrestrial ecosystems ever since the disappearance of the Carboniferous coal swamps. *See* ECOSYSTEM; SEED.

A major breakthrough in understanding the origin of seed plants was recognition of the "progymnosperms" in the Middle and Late Devonian. These plants, which were the first forest-forming trees, had secondary xylem, phloem, and periderm, but they still reproduced by spores, implying that the anatomical advances of seed plants arose before the seed. Like sphenopsids and ferns, they were apparently derived from "trimerophytes." The earliest seed plants of the Late Devonian and Carboniferous, called "seed ferns" because of their frondlike leaves, show steps in origin of the seed. Origin of the typical mode of branching in seed plants, from buds in the axils of the leaves, occurred at about the same time.

Seed plants became dominant in the Permian during a shift to drier climate and extinction of the coal swamp flora in the European-American tropical belt, and glaciation in the Southern Hemisphere Gondwana continents. Early conifers predominated in the tropics; extinct glossopterids inhabited Gondwana. Moderation of climate in the Triassic coincided with the appearance of new seed plant groups as well as more modern ferns. Many Mesozoic groups show adaptations for protection of seeds against animal predation, while flowers of the Bennettitales constitute the first evidence for attraction of insects for cross-pollination, rather than transport of pollen by wind.

Angiosperms. The last major event in plant evolution was the origin of angiosperms (flowering plants), the seed plant group that dominates the modern flora. The flower, typically made up of protective sepals, attractive petals, pollen-producing stamens, and ovule-producing carpels (all considered modified leaves), favors more efficient pollen transfer by insects. The ovules are enclosed in the carpel, so that pollen germinates on the sticky stigma of the carpel rather than in the pollen chamber of the ovule. The carpels (separate or fused) develop into fruits, which often show special adaptations for seed dispersal. Other advances include an extreme reduction of the gametophytes, and double fertilization whereby one sperm fuses with the egg, and the second sperm with two other gametophyte nuclei to produce a triploid, nourishing tissue called the endosperm. Angiosperms also developed improved vegetative features, such as more efficient water-conducting vessels in the wood and leaves with several orders of reticulate venation. These features may have contributed to their present dominance in tropical forests, previously occupied by conifers with scale leaves. *See* RAINFOREST.

Most botanists believed that the most primitive living angiosperms are "magnoliid dicots," based on their "gymnosperm"-like pollen, wood anatomy, and flower structure. Studies of Cretaceous fossil pollen, leaves, and flowers confirm this view by showing a rapid but orderly radiation beginning with "magnoliid"-like and monocotlike types, followed by primitive eudicots (with three pollen apertures), some related to sycamores and lotuses. *See* MAGNOLIOPHYTA.

Both morphological and molecular data imply that angiosperms are monophyletic and most closely related to Bennettitales and Gnetales, a seed plant group that also radiated in the Early Cretaceous but later declined to three living genera. Since all three groups have flowerlike structures, suggesting that the flower and insect pollination arose before the closed carpel, they have been called anthophytes. These relationships, plus problematical Triassic pollen grains and macrofossils with a mixture of angiospermlike and more primitive features, suggest that the angiosperm line goes back to the Triassic, although perhaps not as fully developed angiosperms. Within angiosperms, it is believed that "magnoliids" are relatively primitive, monocots and eudicots are derived clades, and wind-pollinated temperate trees such as oaks, birches, and walnuts (Amentiferae) are advanced eudicots. However, "magnoliids" include both woody plants, and herbs, and their flowers range from large, complex, and insect-pollinated to minute, simple, and wind-pollinated. These extremes are present among the earliest Cretaceous angiosperms, and cladistic analyses disagree on which is most primitive.

Although plant extinctions at the end of the Cretaceous have been linked with radiation of deciduous trees and proliferation of fruits dispersed by mammals and birds, they were less dramatic than extinctions in the animal kingdom. Mid-Tertiary cooling led to contraction of the tropical belt and expansion of seasonal temperate and arid zones. These changes led to the diversification of herbaceous angiosperms and the origin of open grassland vegetation, which stimulated the radiation of hoofed mammals, and ultimately the invention of human agriculture. *See* AGRICULTURE; FLOWER; PLANT KINGDOM. [J.A.Do.]

Plant geography The study of the spatial distributions of plants and vegetation and of the environmental relationships which may influence these distributions. Plant geography (or certain aspects of it) is also known as phytogeography, phytochorology, geobotany, geographical botany, or vegetation science.

A flora is the collection of all plant species in an area, or in a period of time, independent of their relative abundances and relationships to one another. The species can be grouped and regrouped into various kinds of floral elements based on some common feature. For example, a genetic element is a group of species with a common evolutionary origin; a migration element has a common route of entry into the territory; a historical element is distinct in terms of some past event; and an ecological element is related to an environmental preference. An endemic species is restricted to a particular area, which is usually small and of some special interest. The collection of all interacting individuals of a given species, in an area, is called a population.

An area is the entire region of distribution or occurrence of any species, element, or even an entire flora. The description of areas is the subject of areography, while chorology studies their development. The local distribution within the area as a whole, as that of a swamp shrub, is the topography of that area. Areas are of interest in regard to their general size and shape, the nature of their margin, whether they are continuous or disjunct, and their relationships to other areas. Closely related plants that are mutually exclusive are said to be vicarious (areas containing such plants are also called vicarious). A relict area is one surviving from an earlier and more extensive occurrence. On the basis of areas and their floristic relationships, the Earth's surface is divided into floristic regions, each with a distinctive flora.

Floras and their distribution have been interpreted mainly in terms of their history and ecology. Historical factors, in addition to the evolution of the species themselves, include consideration of theories of shifting continental masses, changing sea levels, and orographic and climatic variations in geologic time, as well as theories of island biogeography, all of which have affected migration and perpetuation of floras. The main ecological factors include the immediate and contemporary roles played by climate, soil, animals, and humans. *See* ISLAND BIOGEOGRAPHY.

Vegetation refers to the mosaic of plant life found on the landscape. The vegetation of a region has developed from the numerous elements of the local flora but is shaped also by nonfloristic physiological and environmental influences. Vegetation is an organized whole, at a higher level of integration than the separate species, composed of those species and their populations. Vegetation may possess emergent properties not necessarily found in the species themselves. Sometimes vegetation is very weakly integrated, as pioneer plants of an abandoned field. Sometimes it is highly integrated, as in an undisturbed tropical rainforest. Vegetation provides the main structural and functional framework of ecosystems. *See* ECOSYSTEM.

Plant communities are an important part of vegetation. No definition has gained universal acceptance, in part because of the high degree of independence of the species themselves. Thus, the community is often only a relative social continuity in nature, bounded by a relative discontinuity, as judged by competent botanists. *See* ECOLOGICAL COMMUNITIES.

In looking at vegetation patterns over larger areas, it is the basic physiognomic distinctions between grassland, forest, and desert, with such variants as woodland (open forest), savanna (scattered trees in grassland), and scrubland (dominantly shrubs), which are most often emphasized. These general classes of vegetation structure can be broken down further by reference to leaf types and seasonal habits (such as evergreen or deciduous). Geographic considerations may complete the names of the main vegetation formation types, also called biomes (such as tropical rainforest, boreal coniferous forest, or temperate grasslands). Such natural vegetation regions are most closely related to climatic patterns and secondarily to soil or other environmental factors.

Vegetational plant geography has emphasized the mapping of such vegetation regions and the interpretation of these in terms of environmental (ecological) influences. Distinction has been made between potential and actual vegetation, the latter becoming more important due to human influence. *See* VEGETATION AND ECOSYSTEM MAPPING.

Some plant geographers point to the effects of ancient human populations, natural disturbances, and the large-herbivore extinctions and climatic shifts of the Pleistocene on the species composition and dynamics of so-called virgin vegetation. On the other hand, it has been shown that the site occurrence and geographic distributions of plant and vegetation types can be predicted surprisingly well from general climatic and other environmental patterns. Unlike floristic botany, where evolution provides a single unifying principle for taxonomic classification, vegetation structure and dynamics have no single dominant influence.

Basic plant growth forms (such as broad-leaved trees, stem-succulents, or forbs) have long represented convenient groups of species based on obvious similarities. When these forms are interpreted as ecologically significant adaptations to environmental factors, they are generally called life forms and may be interpreted as basic ecological types.

In general, basic plant types may be seen as groups of plant taxa with similar form and ecological requirements, resulting from similar morphological responses to similar environmental conditions. When similar morphological or physiognomic responses occur in unrelated taxa in similar but widely separated environments, they may be called convergent characteristics. *See* PLANTS, LIFE FORMS OF.

As human populations alter or destroy more and more of the world's natural vegetation, problems of species preservation, substitute vegetation, and succession have increased in importance. This is especially true in the tropics, where deforestation is proceeding rapidly. Probably over half the species in tropical rainforests have not yet even been identified. Because nutrients are quickly washed out of tropical rainforest soils, cleared areas can be used for only a few years before they must be abandoned to erosion and much degraded substitute vegetation. Perhaps the greatest current challenge in plant geography is to understand tropical vegetation and succession sufficiently well to design self-sustaining preserves of the great diversity of tropical vegetation. *See* BIOGEOGRAPHY; ECOLOGY; RAINFOREST.   [E.O.B.]

Plant growth   An irreversible increase in the size of the plant. As plants, like other organisms, are made up of cells, growth involves an increase in cell numbers by cell division and an increase in cell size. Cell division itself is not growth, as each new cell is exactly half the size of the cell from which it was formed. Only when it grows to the same size as its progenitor has growth been realized. Nonetheless, as each cell has a maximum size, cell division is considered as providing the potential for growth. *See* CELL (BIOLOGY).

While growth in plants consists of an increase in both cell number and cell size, animal growth is almost wholly the result of an increase in cell numbers. Another important difference in growth between plants and animals is that animals are determinate in growth and reach a final size before they are mature and start to reproduce. Plants have indeterminate growth and, as long as they live, continue to add new organs and tissues. In a plant new cells are produced all the time, and some parts such as leaves and flowers may die, while the main body of the plant persists and continues to grow. The basic processes of cell division are similar in plants and animals, though the presence of a cell wall and vacuole in plant cells means that there are certain important differences. This is particularly true in plant cell enlargement, as plant cells, being restrained in size by a cellulose cell wall, cannot grow without an increase in the wall. Plant cell growth is thus largely a property of the cell wall. *See* CELL WALLS (PLANT).

Sites of cell division. Cell division in plants takes place in discrete zones called meristems. The stem and root apical meristems produce all the primary (or initial) tissues of the stem and root. The cylindrical vascular cambium produces more conducting cells at the time when secondary thickening (the acquisition of a woody nature) begins. The vascular cambium is a sheet of elongated cells which divide to produce xylem or water-conducting cells on the inside, and phloem or sugar-conducting cells on the outside. Unlike the apical meristems whose cell division eventually leads to an increase in length of the stem and root, divisions of the vascular cambium occur when that part of the plant has reached a fixed length, and lead only to an increase in girth, not in length. The final meristematic zone, the cork cambium, is another cylindrical sheet of cells on the outer edge of older stems and roots of woody plants. It produces new outer cells only, and these cells differentiate into the corky layers of the bark so that new protective layers are produced as the tree increases in circumference. *See* APICAL MERISTEM; BUD; LATERAL MERISTEM; PERIDERM; ROOT (BOTANY); STEM.

Controls. Plant growth is affected by internal and external factors. The internal controls are all the product of the genetic instructions carried in the plant. These influence the extent and timing of growth and are mediated by signals of various types transmitted within the cell, between cells, or all around the plant. Intercellular communication in plants may take place via hormones (or chemical messengers) or by other forms of communication not well understood. There are several hormones (or groups of hormones), each of which may be produced in a different location, that have a different target tissue and act in a different manner. *See* PLANT HORMONES.

The external environments of the root and shoot place constraints on the extent to which the internal controls can permit the plant to grow and develop. Prime among these are the water and nutrient supplies available in the soil. Because cell expansion is controlled by cell turgor, which depends on water, any deficit in the water supply of the plant reduces cell turgor and limits cell elongation, resulting in a smaller plant. *See* PLANT-WATER RELATIONS.

Mineral nutrients are needed for the biochemical processes of the plant. When these are in insufficient supply, growth will be less vigorous, or in extreme cases it will cease altogether. *See* PLANT MINERAL NUTRITION.

An optimal temperature is needed for plant growth. The actual temperature range depends on the species. In general, metabolic reactions and growth increase with temperature, though high temperature becomes damaging. Most plants grow slowly at low temperatures, 32–50°F (0–10°C), and some tropical plants are damaged or even killed at low but above-freezing temperatures.

Light is important in the control of plant growth. It drives the process of photosynthesis which produces the carbohydrates that are needed to osmotically retain water in the cell for growth. *See* PHOTOSYNTHESIS.

Fruits and seeds. Fruits and seeds are rich sources of hormones. Initial hormone production starts upon pollination and is further promoted by ovule fertilization. These hormones promote the growth of both seed and fruit tissue. Fruits grow initially by cell division, then by cell enlargement, and finally sometimes by an increase in air spaces.

The growth of a seed starts at fertilization. A small undifferentiated cell mass is produced from the single-celled zygote. This proceeds to form a small embryo consisting of a stem tip bearing two or more leaf primordia at one end and a root primordium at the other. Either the endosperm or the cotyledons enlarge as a food store. *See* FRUIT; SEED.

Flowering. At a certain time a vegetative plant ceases producing leaves and instead produces flowers. This often occurs at a particular season of the year. The determining factor for this event is day length (or photoperiod). Different species of plants respond to different photoperiods. *See* FLOWER; PHOTOPERIODISM.

The light signal for flowering is received by the leaves, but it is the stem apex that responds. Exposing even a single leaf to the correct photoperiod can induce flowering. Clearly, then, a signal must travel from the leaf to the apex. Grafting a plant that has been photoinduced to flower to one not so induced can cause the noninduced plant to flower. It has been proposed that a flower-inducing hormone travels from the leaf to the stem apex and there induces changes in the development of the cells such that the floral morphology results.

Dormancy. At certain stages of the life cycle, most perennial plants cease growth and become dormant. Plants may cease growth at any time if the environmental conditions are unfavorable. When dormant, however, a plant will not grow even if the conditions are favorable. *See* DORMANCY.

Leaf abscission. As a perennial plant grows, new leaves are continuously or seasonally produced. At the same time the older leaves are shed because newer leaves are metabolically more efficient in the production of photosynthates. A total shedding of tender leaves may enable the plant to withstand a cold period or drought. In temperate deciduous trees, leaf abscission is brought about by declining photoperiods and temperatures. *See* ABSCISSION; PLANT MORPHOGENESIS.   [P.J.D.]

Plant hormones   Organic compounds other than nutrients that regulate plant development and growth. Plant hormones, which are active in very low concentrations, are produced in certain parts of the plants and are usually transported to other parts where they elicit specific biochemical, physiological, or morphological responses. They are also active in tissues where they are produced. Each plant hormone evokes many different responses. Also, the effects of different hormones overlap and may be stimulatory or inhibitory. The commonly recognized classes of plant hormones are the auxins, gibberellins, cytokinins, abscisic acid, and ethylene. Circumstantial evidence suggests that flower initiation is controlled by hypothetical hormones called florigens, but these substances remain to be identified. A number of natural or synthetic substances such as brassin, morphactin, and other growth regulators not considered to be hormones nevertheless influence plant growth and development. Each hormone performs its specific functions; however, nearly all of the measurable responses of plants to heredity or environment are controlled by interaction between two or more hormones. Such interactions may occur at various levels, including the synthesis of hormones, hormone receptors, and second messengers, as well as at the level of ultimate hormone action. Furthermore, hormonal interactions may be cooperative, antagonistic, or in balance.

The term plant growth regulator is usually used to denote a synthetic plant hormone, but most of the synthetic compounds with structures similar to those of the natural hormones have also been called hormones. For instance, the synthetic cytokinin kinetin is considered a hormone. *See* ABSCISSION.

There are a number of applications of plant hormones in agriculture, horticulture, and biotechnology. Synthetic auxins are used as weed killers. Auxins are also used to counteract the effects of hormones that promote the dropping of fruit from trees. Gibberellins are used extensively to increase the size of seedless grapes: when applied at the appropriate time and with the proper concentration, gibberellins cause fruits to elongate so that they are less tightly packed and less susceptible to fungal infections. Gibberellins are also used by some breweries to increase the rate of malting because they enhance starch digestion. They have also been sprayed on fruits and leaves of navel orange trees to prevent several rind disorders that appear during storage. They are used commercially to increase sugarcane growth and sugar yields. Cytokinins and auxins are used in plant cell culture, particularly in cultivating genetically engineered plants. The ability of cytokinins to retard senescence also applies to certain cut flowers and fresh vegetables. Ethylene has been used widely in promoting pineapple flowering; flowering occurs more rapidly and mature fruits appear uniformly, so that a one-harvest mechanical operation is possible. Because carbon dioxide in high concentrations inhibits ethylene production, it is often used to prevent overripening of picked fruits. Ethylene is also used for accelerating fruit ripening. *See* HORMONE; PLANT GROWTH; PLANT PHYSIOLOGY.   [Cm.C.]

Plant kingdom   The worldwide array of plant life, including plants that have roots in the soil, plants that live on or within other plants and animals, plants that float on or swim in water, and plants that are carried in the air. Fungi used to be included in the plant kindom because they looked more like plants than animals and did not move about. It is now known that fungi are probably closer to animals in terms of their evolutionary relationships. Also once included in plants were the "blue-green algae," which are now clearly seen to be bacteria, although they are photosynthetic (and presumably the group of organisms from which the chloroplasts present in true plants were derived). The advent of modern methods of phylogenetic DNA analysis has allowed such distinctions, but even so, what remains of the plantlike organisms is still remarkably divergent and difficult to classify.

Plants range in size from unicellular algae to giant redwoods. Some plants complete their life cycles in a matter of hours, whereas the bristlecone pines are known to be over 4000 years old. Plants collectively are among the most poorly understood of all forms of life, with even their most basic functions still inadequately known, including how they sense gravity and protect themselves from infection by bacteria, viruses, and fungi. Furthermore, new species are being recorded every year.

Within the land plants, a great deal of progress has been made in sorting out phylogenetic (evolutionary) relationships of extant taxa based on DNA studies, and the system of classification listed below includes these changes. The angiosperms or flowering plants (Division Magnoliophyta) have recently been reclassified based on phylogenetic studies of DNA sequences. Within the angiosperms, several informal names are indicated in parentheses; these names may at some future point be formalized, but for the present they are indicated in lowercase letters because they have not been formally recognized under the Code of Botanical Nomenclature.

It is known that the bryophytes (Division Bryophyta) are not closely related to each other, but which of the three major groups is closest to the other land plants is not yet clear. Among the extant vascular plants, Lycophyta are the sister group to all the rest, with all of the fernlike groups forming a single monophyletic (natural) group, which is reflected here in the classification by putting them all under Polypodiophyta. This group is the sister to the extant seed plants, within which all gymnosperms form a group that is sister to the angiosperms. Therefore, if Division is taken as the highest category within Embryobionta (the embryo-forming plants), then the following scheme would reflect the present state of knowledge of relationships (an asterisk indicates that a group is known only from fossils).

Subkingdom Thallobionta (thallophytes)
  Division Rhodophycota (red algae)
    Class Rhodophyceae
  Division Chromophycota
    Class: Chrysophyceae (golden or
      golden-brown algae)
        Prymnesiophyceae
        Xanthophyceae (yellow-green
          algae)
        Eustigmatophyceae
        Bacillariophyceae (diatoms)
        Dinophyceae (dinoflagellates)
        Phaeophyceae (brown algae)
        Raphidophyceae
          (chloromonads)
        Cryptophyceae
          (cryptomonads)
  Division Euglenophycota (euglenoids)
    Class Euglenophyceae
  Division Chlorophycota (green algae)
    Class: Chlorophyceae
        Charophyceae
        Prasinophyceae
Subkingdom Embryobionta
  (embryophytes)
  Division Rhyniophyta*
    Class Rhyniopsida
  Division Bryophyta
    Class Hepaticopsida (liverworts)
      Subclass Jungermanniidae

Order: Takakiales
    Calobryales
    Jungermanniales
    Metzgeriales
Subclass Marchantiidae
Order: Sphaerocarpales
    Monocleales
    Marchantiales
Class: Anthocerotopsida (hornworts)
    Sphagnopsida (peatmosses)
    Andreaeopsida (granite
      mosses)
    Bryopsida (mosses)
Subclass: Archidiidae
    Bryidae
Order: Fissidentales
    Bryoxiphiales
    Schistostegales
    Dicranales
    Pottiales
    Grimmiales
    Seligeriales
    Encalyptales
    Funariales
    Splachnales
Order: Bryales
    Mitteniales
    Orthotrichales
    Isobryales
    Hookeriales
    Hypnales
Subclass: Buxbaumiidae
    Tetraphididae
    Dawsoniidae
    Polytrichidae
Division Lycophyta
Class Lycopsida
Order: Lycopodiales
    Asteroxylales*
    Protolepidodendrales*
    Selaginellales*
    Lepidedendrales*
    Isoetales
Class Zosterophyllopsida*
Division Polypodiophyta
Class Polypodopsida
Order: Equisetales
    Marattiales
    Sphenophyllales*
    Pseudoborniales*
    Psilotales

Ophioglossales
Noeggerathiales*
Protopteridales*
Polypodiales
Class Progymnospermopsida*
Division Pinopsida
Class Ginkgoopsida
Order: Calamopityales*
    Callistophytales*
    Peltaspermales*
    Ginkgoales
    Leptostrobales*
    Caytoniales
    Arberiales*
    Pentoxylales*
Class Cycadopsida
Order: Lagenostomales*
    Trigonocarpales*
    Cycadales
    Bennettiales*
Class Pinopsida
Order: Cordaitales*
    Pinales
    Podocarpales
    Gnetales
Division Magnoliophyta (angiosperms,
  flowering plants)
Class Magnoliopsida
unplaced groups: Amborellaceae,
  Ceratophyllaceae, Chloranthaceae,
  Nymphaeaceae, etc.
eumagnoliids
Order: Magnoliales
    Laurales
    Piperales
    Winterales
monocotyledons
Order: Acorales
    Alismatales
    Asparagales
    Dioscoreales
    Liliales
    Pandanales
commelinids
    Arecales
    Commelinales
    Poales
    Zingiberales
eudicotyledons
(basal eudicots)

Order: Ranunculales
  Proteales
  Buxales
  Trochodendrales
(core eudicots)
  Order: Berberidopsidales
    Gunnerales
    Dilleniales
    Santalales
    Caryophyllales
    Saxifragales
Rosidae
  Order: Vitales
    Myrtales
    Geraniales
    Crossosomatales
(eurosid I)
  Order: Celastrales
    Cucurbitales
    Fabales
    Fagales

Malpighiales
Oxalidales
Rosales
Zygophyllales
(eurosid II)
  Order: Brassicales
    Malvales
    Sapindales
Asteridae
  Order: Cornales
    Ericales
(euasterid I)
  Order: Garryales
    Gentianales
    Lamiales
    Solanales
(euasterid II)
  Order: Apiales
    Aquifoliales
    Asterales
    Dipsacales

See DEOXYRIBONUCLEIC ACID (DNA); PLANT EVOLUTION; PLANT PHYLOGENY; PLANT TAXON-OMY.   [M.W.C.; M.F.F.]

Plant metabolism   The complex of physical and chemical events of photosynthesis, respiration, and the synthesis and degradation of organic compounds. Photosynthesis produces the substrates for respiration and the starting organic compounds used as building blocks for subsequent biosyntheses of nucleic acids, amino acids, and proteins, carbohydrates and organic acids, lipids, and natural products. *See* PHOTORESPIRATION; PHOTOSYNTHESIS; PLANT RESPIRATION.   [I.P.T.]

Plant mineral nutrition   The relationship between plants and all chemical elements other than carbon, hydrogen, and oxygen in the environment. Plants obtain most of their mineral nutrients by extracting them from solution in the soil or the aquatic environment. Mineral nutrients are so called because most have been derived from the weathering of minerals of the Earth's crust. Nitrogen is exceptional in that little occurs in minerals: the primary source is gaseous nitrogen of the atmosphere.

Some of the mineral nutrients are essential for plant growth; others are toxic, and some absorbed by plants may play no role in metabolism. Many are also essential or toxic for the health and growth of animals using plants as food. Six basic facts have been established: (1) plants do not need any of the solid materials in the soil—they cannot even take them up; (2) plants do not need soil microorganisms; (3) plant roots must have a supply of oxygen; (4) all plants require at least 14 mineral nutrients; (5) all of the essential mineral nutrients may be supplied to plants as simple ions of inorganic salts in solution; and (6) all of the essential nutrients must be supplied in adequate but nontoxic quantities. These facts provide a conceptually simple definition of and test for an essential mineral nutrient. A mineral nutrient is regarded as essential if, in its absence, a plant cannot complete its life cycle.

Nutrients which plants require in relatively large amounts, that is, the essential macronutrients, are nitrogen, sulfur, phosphorus, calcium, potassium, and magnesium.

Iron is not required in large amounts and hence is regarded as an essential micronutrient or trace element. With the progressive development of better techniques for purifying water and salts, the list of essential nutrients for all plants has expanded to include boron, manganese, zinc, copper, molybdenum, and chlorine. Evidence has accumulated in support of nickel being essential. In addition, sodium and silicon have been shown to be essential for some plants, beneficial to some, and possibly of no benefit to others. Cobalt has also been shown to be essential for the growth of legumes when relying upon atmospheric nitrogen. Claims that two other chemical elements (vanadium and selenium) may be essential micronutrients have still to be firmly established.

Mineral nutrients may be toxic to plants either because the specific nutrient interferes with plant metabolism or because its concentration in combination with others in solution is excessive and interferes with the plant's water relations. Other chemical elements in the environment may also be toxic. High concentrations of salts in soil solutions or aquatic environments may depress their water potential to such an extent that plants cannot obtain sufficient water to germinate or grow. Some desert plants growing in saline soils can accumulate salt concentrations of 20–50% dry weight in their leaves without damage, but salt concentrations of only 1–2% can damage the leaves of many species. *See* PLANT-WATER RELATIONS.

A number of elements interfere directly with other aspects of plant metabolism. Sodium is thought to become toxic when it reaches concentrations in the cytoplasm that depress enzyme activity or damage the structure of organelles, while the toxicity of selenium is probably due to its interference in metabolism of amino acids and proteins. The ions of the heavy metals, cobalt, nickel, chromium, manganese, copper, and zinc are particularly toxic in low concentrations, especially when the concentration of calcium in solution is low; increasing calcium increases the plant's tolerance. Aluminum is toxic only in acid soils. Boron may be toxic in soils over a wide pH range, and is a serious problem for sensitive crops in regions where irrigation waters contain excessive boron or where the soils contain unusually high levels of boron.

All plants grow poorly on very acid soils (pH $\leq$ 3.5); some plants may grow reasonably well on somewhat less acid soils. Several factors may be involved, and their interactions with plant species are complex. The harmful effects of soil acidity in some areas have been exacerbated by industrial emissions resulting in acid rain and in deposition of substances which increase the acidity on further reaction in the soil, with consequent damage to plants and animals in these ecosystems.

The elemental composition of plants is important to the health and productivity of animals which graze them. With the exception of boron, all elements which are essential for plant growth are also essential for herbivorous mammals. Animals also require sodium, iodine, and selenium and, in the case of ruminant herbivores, cobalt. As a result, animals may suffer deficiencies of any one of this latter group of elements when ingesting plants which are quite healthy but contain low concentrations of these elements. In addition, nutrients in forage may be rendered unavailable to animals through a variety of factors that prevent their absorption from the gut. Plants and animals differ also in their tolerance of high levels of nutrients, sometimes with deleterious results for grazing animals. For example, the toxicity of high concentrations of selenium in plants to animals grazing them, known as selenosis, was recognized when the puzzling and long-known "alkali disease" and "blind staggers" in grazing livestock in parts of the Great Plains of North America were shown to be symptoms of chronic and acute selenium toxicity. *See* ABSORPTION (BIOLOGY); NITROGEN CYCLE; PLANT TRANSPORT OF SOLUTES; ROOT (BOTANY).   [J.F.L.]

Plant morphogenesis   The origin and development of plant form and structure. Morphogenesis may be concerned with the whole plant, with a plant part, or with the subcomponents of a structure.

The establishment of differences at the two ends of a structure is called polarity. In plants, polar differences can be recognized very early in development. In the zygote, cytological differences at the two ends of the cell establish the position of the first cell division, and thus the fate of structures produced from the two newly formed cells. During the development of a plant, polarity is also exhibited in the plant axis (in the shoot and root tips). If a portion of a shoot or root is excised and allowed to regenerate, the end toward the shoot tip always regenerates shoots whereas the opposite end forms roots. Polarity is also evident on the two sides of a plant organ, such as the upper and lower surface of a leaf, sepal, or petal.

The diversity in plant form is produced mainly because different parts of the plant grow at different rates. Furthermore, the growth of an individual structure is different in various dimensions. Thus the rate of cell division and cell elongation as well as the orientation of the plane of division and of the axis of cell elongation ultimately establish the form of a structure. Such differential growth rates are very well orchestrated by genetic factors. Although the absolute growth rates of various parts of a plant may be different, their relative growth rates, or the ratio of their growth rates, are always constant. This phenomenon is called allometry (or heterogony), and it supports the concept that there is an interrelationship between the growth of various organs of a plant body. *See* PLANT GROWTH.

During development, either the removal of or changes in one part of the plant may drastically affect the morphogenesis of one or more other parts of the plant. This phenomenon is called correlation and is mediated primarily through chemical substances, such as nutrients and hormones.

The ultimate factors controlling the form of a plant and its various organs are the genes. In general, several genes interact during the development of a structure, although each gene plays a significant role. Thus, a mutation in a single gene may affect the shape or size of a leaf, flower, or fruit, or the color of flower petals, or the type of hairs produced on stems and leaves. There are at least two classes of genes involved in plant morphogenesis: regulatory genes that control the activity of other genes, and effector genes that are directly involved in a developmental process. The effector genes may affect morphogenesis through a network of processes, including the synthesis and activity of proteins and enzymes, the metabolism of plant growth substances, changes in the cytoskeleton and the rates and planes of cell division, and cell enlargement. *See* GENE ACTION; PLANT HORMONES.

Plant form is also known to be affected by nutritional factors, such as sugars or nitrogen levels. For example, leaf shape can be affected by different concentrations of sucrose, and the sexuality of flowers is related to the nitrogen levels in the soil in some species. Inorganic ions (such as silver and cobalt) have also been known to affect the type of flower produced. *See* PLANT MINERAL NUTRITION.

Although genes are the ultimate controlling factors, they do not act alone, but interact with the existing environmental factors during plant development. Environmental factors, including light, temperature, moisture, and pressure, affect plant form. *See* PHYSIOLOGICAL ECOLOGY (PLANT); PLANT-WATER RELATIONS.   [V.K.S.]

Plant movements   The wide range of movements that allow plants to reorient themselves in relation to changed surroundings, to facilitate spore or seed dispersal, or, in the case of small free-floating aquatic plants, to migrate to regions optimal for their activities. There are two types of plant movement: abiogenic movements, which arise purely from the physical properties of the cells and therefore take place in nonliving tissues or organs; and biogenic movements, which occur in living cells or organs and require an energy input from metabolism.

Abiogenic movements. Drying or moistening of certain structures causes differential contractions or expansions on the two sides of cells and hence causes movements of curvature. Such movements are called hygroscopic and are usually associated with seed and spore liberation and dispersal. Examples of such movement occur in the "parachute" hairs of the fruit of dandelion (*Taraxacum officinale*), which are closed when damp but open when the air is dry to induce release from the heads and give buoyancy for wind dispersal.

Another type of abiogenic movement is due to changes in volume of dead water-containing cells. In the absence of a gas phase, water will adhere to lignocellulose cell walls. As water is lost by evaporation from the surface of these cells, considerable tensions can build up inside, causing them to decrease in volume while remaining full of water. The effect is most commonly seen in some grasses of dry habitats, such as sand dunes, where longitudinal rows of cells on one side of the leaf act as spring hinges, contracting in a dry atmosphere and causing the leaf to roll up into a tight cylinder, thus minimizing water loss by transpiration.

Biogenic movements. There are two types of biogenic movement. One of these is locomotion of the whole organism and is thus confined to small, simply organized units in an aqueous environment. The other involves the change in shape and orientation of whole organs of complex plants, usually in response to specific stimuli.

Locomotion. In most live plant cells the cytoplasm can move by a streaming process known as cyclosis. Energy for cyclosis is derived from the respiratory metabolism of the cell. The mechanism probably involves contractile proteins very similar to the actomyosin of animal muscles.

Cell locomotion is a characteristic of many simple plants and of the gametes of more highly organized ones. Motility in such cells is produced by cilia anchored in the peripheral layers of the cell and projecting into the surrounding medium. *See* CILIA AND FLAGELLA.

Cell locomotion is usually not random but is directed by some environmental gradient. Thus locomotion may be in response to specific chemicals, in which case it is called chemotaxis. Light gradients induce phototaxis; temperature gradients induce thermotaxis; and gravity induces geotaxis. One or more of these environmental factors may operate to control movement to optimal living conditions.

Movement of organs. In higher plants, organs may change shape and position in relation to the plant body. When bending or twisting of the organ is evoked spontaneously by some internal stimulus, it is termed autonomous movement. The most common movements, however, are those initiated by external stimuli such as light and the force of gravity. Of these there are two kinds. In nastic movements (nasties), the stimulus usually has no directional qualities (such as a change in temperature), and the movement is therefore not related to the direction from which the stimulus comes. In tropisms, the stimulus has a direction (for instance, gravitational pull), and the plant movement direction is related to it.

The most common autonomous movement is circumnutation, a slow, circular, sometimes waving movement of the tips of shoots, roots, and tendrils as they grow; one complete cycle usually takes from 1 to 3 h. These movements are due to differential growth, but some may be caused by turgor changes in the cells of special hinge organs and are thus reversible.

1. *Nastic movements.* There are two kinds of nastic movements, due either to differential growth or to differential changes in the turgidity of cells. They can be triggered by a wide variety of external stimuli.

Photonastic (light/dark trigger) movements are characteristic of many flowers and inflorescences, which usually open in the light and close in the dark. Thermonasty (temperature-change trigger) is seen in the tulip and crocus flowers, which open in a warm room and close again when cooled. The most striking nastic movements are seen in the sensitive plant (*Mimosa pudica*). Its multipinnate leaves are very sensitive to touch or slight injury. Leaflets fold together, pinnae collapse downward, and the whole leaf sinks to hang limply.

Epinasty and hyponasty occur in leaves as upward and downward curvatures respectively. They arise either spontaneously or as the result of an external stimulus, such as exposure to the gas ethylene in the case of epinasty; they are not induced by gravity.

2. *Tropisms.* Of these the most universal and important are geotropism (or more properly gravitropism) and phototropism; others include thigmotropism and chemotropism.

In geotropism, the stimulus is gravity. The main axes of most plants grow in the direction of the plumb line with shoots upward (negative geotropism) and roots downward (positive geotropism).

In phototropism the stimulus is a light gradient, and unilateral light induces similar curvatures; those toward the source are positively phototropic; those away from the source are negatively phototropic. Main axes of shoots are usually positively phototropic, while the vast majority of roots are insensitive.

In thigmotropism (sometimes called haptotropism), the stimulus is touch; it occurs in climbing organs and is responsible for tendrils curling around a support. In many tendrils the response may spread from the contact area, causing the tight coiling of the basal part of the tendril into an elaborate and elastic spring.

Chemotropism is induced by a chemical substance. Examples are the incurling of the stalked digestive glands of the insectivorous plant *Drosera* and incurling of the whole leaf of *Pinguicula* in response to the nitrogenous compounds in the insect prey. A special case of chemotropism concerns response to moisture gradients; for example, under artificial conditions in air, the primary roots of some plants will curve toward and grow along a moist surface. This is called hydrotropism and may be of importance under natural soil conditions in directing roots toward water sources. *See* PLANT HORMONES; PLANT PHYSIOLOGY.   [L.J.A.]

Plant organs   Plant parts having rather distinct form, structure, and function. Organs, however, are interrelated through both evolution and development and are similar in many ways.

Roots, stems, and leaves are vegetative, or asexual, plant organs. They do not produce sex cells or play a direct role in sexual reproduction. In many species, nevertheless, these organs or parts of them (cuttings), may produce new plants asexually (vegetative reproduction). Sex organs are formed during the reproductive stage of plant development. In flowering plants, sex cells are produced in certain floral organs. The flower as a whole is sometimes called an organ, although it is more appropriate to consider it an assemblage of organs. *See* FLOWER; FRUIT; LEAF; REPRODUCTION (PLANT); ROOT (BOTANY); STEM.   [K.E.]

Plant pathology   The study of disease in plants; it is an integration of many biological disciplines and bridges the basic and applied sciences. As a science, plant pathology encompasses the theory and general concepts of the nature and cause of disease, and yet it also involves disease control strategies, with the ultimate goal being reduction of damage to the quantity and quality of food and fiber essential for human existence.

Kinds of plant diseases. Diseases were first classified on the basis of symptoms. Three major categories of symptoms were recognized long before the causes of disease were known; necroses, destruction of cell protoplasts (rots, spots, wilts); hypoplases, failure in plant development (chlorosis, stunting); and hyperplases, overdevelopment in cell number and size (witches'-brooms, galls). This scheme remains useful for recognition and diagnosis.

When fungi, and then bacteria, nematodes, and viruses, were recognized as causes of disease, it became convenient to classify diseases according to the responsible agent. If the agents were infectious (biotic), the diseases were classified as being "caused by bacteria," "caused by nematodes," or "caused by viruses." To this list were added phanerogams and protozoans, and later mollicutes (mycoplasmas, spiroplasmas), rickettsias, and viroids. In a second group were those diseases caused by such noninfectious (abiotic) agents as air pollutants, inadequate oxygen, and nutrient excesses and deficiencies.

Other classifications of disease have been proposed, such as diseases of specific plant organs, diseases involving physiological processes, and diseases of specific crops or crop groups (for example, field crops, fruit crops, vegetable crops).

Symptoms of plant diseases. Symptoms are expressions of pathological activity in plants. They are visible manifestations of changes in color, form, and structure: leaves may become spotted, turn yellow, and die; fruits may rot on the plants or in storage; cankers may form on stems; and plants may blight and wilt. Diagnosticians learn how to associate certain symptoms with specific diseases, and they use this knowledge in the identification and control of pathogens responsible for the diseases.

Those symptoms that are external and readily visible are considered morphological. Others are internal and primarily histological, for example, vascular discoloration of the xylem of wilting plants. Microscopic examination of diseased plants may reveal additional symptoms at the cytological level, such as the formation of tyloses (extrusion of living parenchyma cells of the xylem of wilted tissues into vessel elements).

It is important to make a distinction between the visible expression of the diseased condition in the plant, the symptom, and the visible manifestation of the agent which is responsible for that condition, the sign. The sign is the structure of the pathogen, and when present it is most helpful in diagnosis of the disease.

All symptoms may be conveniently classified into three major types because of the manner in which pathogens affect plants. Most pathogens produce dead and dying tissues, and the symptoms expressed are categorized as necroses. Early stages of necrosis are evident in such conditions as hydrosis, wilting, and yellowing. As cells and tissues die, the appearance of the plant or plant part is changed, and is recognizable in such common conditions as blight, canker, rot, and spot.

Many pathogens do not cause necrosis, but interfere with cell growth or development. Plants thus affected may eventually become necrotic, but the activity of the pathogen is primarily inhibitory or stimulatory. If there is a decrease in cell number or size, the expressions of pathological activity are classified as hypoplases; if cell number or size is increased, the symptoms are grouped as hyperplases. These activities are very specific and most helpful in diagnosis. In the former group are such symptoms as mosaic, rosetting, and stunting, with obvious reduction in plant color, structure, and size. In the latter group are gall, scab, and witches'-broom, all visible evidence of stimulation of growth and development of plant tissues. *See* CROWN GALL.

The primary agents of plant disease are fungi, bacteria, viruses and viroids, nematodes, parasitic seed plants, and a variety of noninfectious agents. *See* BACTERIA; FUNGI; NEMATA; PLANT VIRUSES AND VIROIDS.   [C.W.B.]

Epidemiology of plant disease. Epidemiology is the study of the intensification of disease over time and the spread of disease in space. The botanical epidemiologist is concerned with the interrelationships of the host plant (suscept), the pathogen, and the environment, which are the components of the disease triangle. With a thorough knowledge of these components, the outbreak of disease may be forecast in advance, the speed at which the epidemic will intensify may be determined, control measures can be applied at critical periods, and any yield loss to disease can be projected. The maximum amount of disease occurs when the host plant is susceptible, the pathogen is aggressive, and the environment is favorable.

Epidemiologically, there are two main types of diseases: monocyclic, those that have but a single infection cycle (with the rare possibility of a second or even third cycle) per crop season; and polycyclic, those that have many, overlapping, concatenated cycles of infection per crop season. For both epidemiological types, the increase of disease slows as the proportion of disease approaches saturation or 100%.   [R.D.Ber.]

Control of plant disease is defined as the maintenance of disease severity below a certain threshold, which is determined by economic losses. Diseases may be high in incidence but low in severity, or low in incidence but high in severity, and are kept in check by preventing the development of epidemics. The principles of plant disease control form the basis for preventing epidemics. However, the practicing agriculturist uses three approaches to the control of plant disease: cultural practices affecting the environmental requirement of the suscept-pathogen-environment triangle necessary for disease development, disease resistance, and chemical pesticides.   [R.E.St.]

Plant phylogeny   The evolutionary chronicle of plant life on the Earth. Understanding of this history is largely based on knowledge of extant plants, but the fossil record is playing an increasingly important role in refining and illuminating this picture. Study of deoxyribonucleic acid (DNA) sequences has also been revolutionizing this process in recent years. The molecular data (largely in the form of DNA sequences from several genes) have been demonstrated to be highly correlated with other information. *See* PHYLOGENY.

"Algae" was once a taxonomic designation uniting the lower photosynthetic organisms, but ultrastructural and molecular data have uncovered a bewildering diversity of species. Algae are now recognized as 10 divergent lineages on the tree of life that join organisms as distinct as bacteria and eukaryotic protozoans, ciliates, fungi, and embryophytes (including the land plants). In a biochemical context, the term "algae" defines species characterized by chlorophyll *a* photosynthesis (except Embryophyta); some of their descendants are heterotrophic (secondary chloroplast loss). Despite the variety of species it encompasses, the term "algae" also retains phylogenetic relevance. *See* ALGAE; CHLOROPHYLL; PHOTOSYNTHESIS.   [G.W.Sa.]

Embryobionta, or embryophytes, are largely composed of the land plants that appear to have emerged 475 million years ago. The evidence indicates that land plants have not evolved from different groups of green algae (Chlorophyta) as suggested in the past, but instead share a common ancestor, which was a green alga. Land plants all have adaptations to the terrestrial environment, including an alternation of generations (sporophyte or diploid and gametophyte or haploid) with the sporophyte generation producing haploid spores that are capable of resisting desiccation and dispersing widely, a cuticle covering their outside surfaces, and separate male and female reproductive organs in the gametophyte stage. The life history strategies of land plants fall into two categories that do not reflect their phylogenetic relationships. The mosses, hornworts, and liverworts represent the first type, and they have expanded the haploid generation, upon which the sporophyte is dependent. Several recent analyses of DNA data as well as evidence from mitochondrial DNA structure have demonstrated that the liverworts alone are the remnants of the earliest land plants and that the mosses and hornworts are closer to the vascular plants (tracheophytes). The tracheophytes include a large number of extinct and relatively simple taxa, such as the rhiniophytes and horneophytes known only as Silurian and Devonian fossils. All tracheophytes are of the second category, and they have expanded the sporophyte generation. Among extant tracheophytes, the earliest branching are the lycopods or club mosses (*Lycopodium* and *Selaginella*), and there are still a diversity of other forms, including sphenophytes (horsetails, *Equisetum*) and ferns (a large and diverse group in which the positions of several families still are not clear). *See* EMBRYOBIONTA.

All seeds plants take the reduction of the gametophyte generation a step further and make it dependent on the sporophyte, typically hiding it within reproductive structures, which are either cones or flowers. The first seed plants originated at least by the Devonian, and they are known to have a great diversity of extinct forms, including the seed ferns. There are two groups of extant seed-bearing plants, gymnosperms and angiosperms. In the gymnosperms, the seeds are not enclosed within tissue derived from the parent plant. There are four distinct groups of extant gymnosperms, often recognized as classes: Cycadopsida, Gnetopsida, Ginkgoopsida, and Pinopsida.

The angiosperms (also flowering plants or Magnoliopsida) are the dominant terrestrial plants, although the algae collectively must still be acknowledged as the most important in the maintenance of the Earth's ecological balance (fixation of carbon dioxide and production of oxygen). In angiosperms the seeds are covered by protective tissues derived from the parental plant. There are no generally accepted angiospermous fossils older than 120 million years, but the lineage is clearly much older based on DNA clocks and other circumstantial lines of evidence such as their current geographic distributions.

Traditionally the angiosperms have been divided into two groups, monocotyledons (monocots) and dicotyledons (dicots), based on the number of seed leaves. However, DNA sequence data have demonstrated that, although there are two groups, these are characterized by fundamentally different pollen organization, such that the monocots share with a group of dicots pollen with one pore whereas the rest of the dicots have pollen with three (or more) pores.   [M.W.C.]

Plant physiology   That branch of plant sciences that aims to understand how plants live and function. Its ultimate objective is to explain all life processes of plants by a minimal number of comprehensive principles founded in chemistry, physics, and mathematics.

Plant physiology seeks to understand all the aspects and manifestations of plant life. In agreement with the major characteristics of organisms, it is usually divided into three major parts: (1) the physiology of nutrition and metabolism, which deals with the uptake, transformations, and release of materials, and also their movement within and between the cells and organs of the plant; (2) the physiology of growth, development, and reproduction, which is concerned with these aspects of plant function; and (3) environmental physiology, which seeks to understand the manifold responses of plants to the environment. The part of environmental physiology which deals with effects of and adaptations to adverse conditions—and which is receiving increasing attention—is called stress physiology.

Plant physiological research is carried out at various levels of organization and by using various methods. The main organizational levels are the molecular or subcellular, the cellular, the organismal or whole-plant, and the population level. Work at the molecular level is aimed at understanding metabolic processes and their regulation, and also the localization of molecules in particular structures of the cell but with little if any consideration of other processes and other structures of the same cell. Work at the cellular level often deals with the same processes but is concerned with their integration in the cell as a whole. Research at the organismal level is concerned with the function of the plant as a whole and its different organs, and with the relationships between the latter.

Research at the population level, which merges with experimental ecology, deals with physiological phenomena in plant associations which may consist either of one dominant species (like a field of corn) or of numerous diverse species (like a forest). Work at the organismal and to some extent the population level is carried out in facilities permitting maintenance of controlled environmental conditions (light, temperature, water and nutrient supply, and so on). See PLANT METABOLISM; PLANT RESPIRATION; PHYSIOLOGICAL ECOLOGY (PLANT).　　　　　　　　　　　　　　　　　　　　　　　　　　[A.L.]

Plant propagation　The deliberate, directed reproduction of plants using plant cells, tissues, or organs. Asexual propagation, also called vegetative propagation, is accomplished by taking cuttings, by grafting or budding, by layering, by division of plants, or by separation of specialized structures such as tubers, rhizomes, or bulbs. This method of propagation is used in agriculture, in scientific research, and in professional and recreational gardening. It has a number of advantages over seed propagation: it retains the genetic constitution of the plant type almost completely; it is faster than seed propagation; it may allow elimination of the nonfruiting, juvenile phase of the plant's life; it preserves unique, especially productive, or esthetically desirable plant forms; and it allows plants with roots well adapted for growth on poor soils to be combined with tops that produce superior fruits, nuts, or other products. See BREEDING (PLANT); REPRODUCTION (PLANT).　　　　　　　　　　　　　　　　　　　　　　　　　　[C.E.LaM.]

Tissue cultures and protoplast cultures are among the techniques that have been investigated for plant propagation; the success of a specific technique depends on a number of factors. Practical applications of such methods include the clonal propagation of desirable phenotypes and the commercial production of virus-free plants.

Plant tissue cultures are initiated by excising tissue containing nucleated cells and placing it on an enriched sterile culture medium. The response of a plant tissue to a culture medium depends on a number of factors: plant species, source of tissue, chronological age and physiological state of the tissue, ingredients of the culture medium, and physical culturing conditions, such as temperature, photoperiod, and aeration.

Though technically more demanding, successful culture of plant protoplasts involves the same basic principles as plant tissue culture. Empirical methods are used to determine detailed techniques for individual species; such factors as plant species, tissue source, age, culture medium, and physical culture conditions have to be considered. See PLANT CELL.　　　　　　　　　　　　　　　　　　　　　　　　　　[K.G.F.]

Plant respiration　A biochemical process whereby specific substrates are oxidized with a subsequent release of carbon dioxide, CO_2. There is usually conservation of energy accompanying the oxidation which is coupled to the synthesis of energy-rich compounds, such as adenosine triphosphate (ATP), whose free energy is then used to drive otherwise unfavorable reactions that are essential for physiological processes such as growth. Respiration is carried out by specific proteins, called enzymes, and it is necessary for the synthesis of essential metabolites, including carbohydrates, amino acids, and fatty acids, and for the transport of minerals and other solutes between cells. Thus respiration is an essential characteristic of life itself in plants as well as in other organisms.

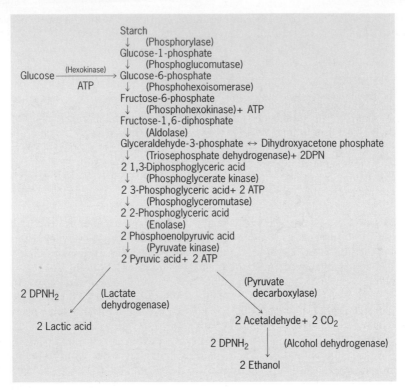

Reaction sequence for anaerobic glycolysis. The soluble enzymes are shown in parentheses.

Overall aerobic respiration is the end result of a sequence of many biochemical reactions that ultimately lead to O_2 uptake and CO_2 evolution. In the absence of O_2, as may occur in bulky plant tissues such as the potato tuber and carrot root and in submerged plants such as germinating rice seedlings, the breakdown of hexose does not go to completion. The end products are either lactic acid or ethanol, which are produced by anaerobic glycolysis or fermentation.

The sequence of reactions of anaerobic glycolysis or fermentation is shown in the illustration. The enzymes associated with anerobic glycolysis have been isolated from many plant tissues, but more often ethanol and not lactic acid is the final product.

In aerobic tissues, pyruvic acid produced during glycolysis is completely oxidized with the accompanying synthesis of much more ATP than in anaerobic glycolysis. Pyruvic acid oxidation takes place in the mitochondria by means of a cyclic sequence of reactions, the Krebs cycle (also known as the citric acid cycle) which begins when the first product of pyruvate oxidation, acetyl coenzyme A, reacts with oxaloacetic acid to produce citric acid. Oxaloacetic acid is eventually regenerated. Thus the cycle can be repeated. In terms of conservation of chemical energy, the Krebs cycle is about 12 times more efficient than anaerobic glycolysis per mole of glucose oxidized. *See* CITRIC ACID CYCLE.

In addition to anaerobic glycolysis and the Krebs cycle, there are two other sequences of biochemical reactions related to respiration that are important in plant tissues: (1) The pentose phosphate pathway permits an alternate mechanism for converting hexose phosphate to pyruvate, and (2) in germinating fatty seeds the reactions of the Krebs cycle are modified so that acetyl coenzyme A is converted to succinic acid and then to hexose by a pathway called the glyoxylate cycle. *See* PHOTORESPIRATION; PHOTOSYNTHESIS; PLANT GROWTH; PLANT METABOLISM. [I.Z.]

Plant taxonomy   The area of study focusing on the development of a classification system, or taxonomy, for plants based on their evolutionary relationships (phylogeny). The assumption is that if classification reflects phylogeny, reference to the classification will help researchers focus their work in a more accurate manner. The task is to make phylogeny reconstruction as accurate as possible. The basic unit of classification is generally accepted to be the species, but how a species should be recognized has been intensely debated. *See* PLANT KINGDOM; PLANT PHYLOGENY.

The earliest classifications of plants were those of the Greek philosophers such as Aristotle (384–322 B.C.) and Theophrastus (372–287 B.C.). The latter is often called the father of botany largely because he listed the names of over 500 species, some of which are still used as scientific names today. In the next 1600 years little progress occurred in plant taxonomy. It was not until the fifteenth century that there was renewed interest in botany, much of which was propelled by the medical use of plants. In 1753 Carolus Linnaeus, a Swedish botanist, published his *Species Plantarum*, a classification of all plants known to Europeans at that time. Linnaeus's system was based on the arrangement and numbers of parts in flowers, and was intended to be used strictly for identification (a system now referred to as an artificial classification as opposed to a natural classification, based on how closely related the species are).

In *Species Plantarum*, Linnaeus made popular a system of binomial nomenclature developed by the French botanist Gaspard Bauhin (1560–1624), which is still in use. Each species has a two-part name, the first being the genus and the second being the species epithet. For example, *Rosa alba* (italicized because it is Latin) is the scientific name of one species of rose; the genus is *Rosa* and the species epithet is *alba*, meaning white (it is not a requirement that scientific names be similar to common names or have real meaning, although such relevance is often the case). The genus name *Rosa* is shared by all species of roses, reflecting that they are thought to be more closely related to each other than to species in any other group.

Today, we understand that the best classification system is one that reflects the patterns of the evolutionary processes that produced these plants. The rules of botanical nomenclature (and those of zoology as well, although they are not identical) are part of an internationally accepted Code that is revised (minimally) at an international congress every 5 years. *See* PLANT EVOLUTION.

Use of common names in science and horticulture is not practical. Scientific names are internationally agreed upon so that a consistent taxonomic name is used everywhere for a given organism. In addition to genus and species, plants are classified by belonging to a family; related families are grouped into orders, and these are typically grouped into a number of yet higher and more encompassing categories. In general, higher categories are composed of many members of lower types—for example, a family may contain 350 genera, but some may be composed of a single genus with perhaps a single species if that species is distantly related to all others.

Many botanists use a number of intermediate categories between the level of genus and family, such as subfamilies, tribes, and subtribes, as well as some between species and genus, such as subgenera and sections, but none of these categories is formally mandated. They are useful nonetheless to reflect intermediate levels of relatedness, particularly in large families (composed of several hundreds or even thousands of species). Below the level of species, some botanists use the concept of subspecies (which is generally taken to mean a geographically distinct form of a species) and variety (which is often a genetic form or genotype, for example a white-flowered form of a typically blue-flowered species, or a form that is ecologically distinct).

The basic idea that plant classification should reflect evolutionary (genetic) relationships has been well accepted for some time, but the degree to which this could be assessed by the various means available differed. It has only recently become possible to assess genetic patterns of relatedness directly by analyzing DNA sequences. In the 1990s, DNA technology became much more efficient and less costly, resulting in a dramatic upsurge in the availability of DNA sequence data for various genes from each of the three genetic compartments present in plants (nuclear, mitochondrial, and plastid or chloroplast). In 1998 a number of botanists collectively proposed the first DNA-based classification of a major group of organisms, the angiosperms or flowering plants. For the first time, a classification was directly founded on assessments of the degree of relatedness made with objective, computerized methods of phylogeny reconstruction. Other data, such as chemistry and morphology, were also incorporated into these analyses, but by far the largest percentage of information came from DNA sequences—that is, relatedness was determined mostly on the basis of similarities in plants' genetic codes. The advantages of such a classification were immediately obvious: (1) it was not based on intuition about which category of information best reflected natural relationships; (2) it ended competition between systems based on differing emphases; (3) the analysis could be repeated by other researchers using either the same or different data (other genes or categories of information); and (4) it could be updated as new data emerged, particularly from studies of how chromosomes are organized and how morphology and other traits are determined by the genes that code for them. *See* DEOXYRIBONUCLEIC ACID (DNA).

At the same time that DNA data became more widely available as the basis for establishing a classification, a more explicit methodology for turning the results of a phylogenetic analysis into a formal classification became popular. This methodology, called cladistics, allowed a large number of botanists to share ideas of how the various taxonomic categories could be better defined. Although there remain a number of dissenting opinions about some minor matters of classification, it is now impossible for scientists to propose alternative ideas based solely on opinion. *See* PHYLOGENY; TAXONOMY.   [M.W.C.; M.F.F.]

Plant tissue systems   Most plants are composed of coherent masses of cells called tissues. Large units of tissues having some features in common are called tissue systems. In actual usage, however, the terms tissue and tissue system are not strictly separated. A given tissue or a combination of tissues may be continuous throughout the plant or large parts of it.

Plant tissues are primary or secondary in origin. The primary arise from apical meristems, the perennially embryonic tissues at the tips of roots and shoots. The primary tissues include the surface layer, or epidermis; the primary vascular tissues, xylem and phloem, which conduct water and food, respectively; and the ground tissues. The ground tissues are parenchyma (chiefly concerned with manufacture and storage of food) and collenchyma and sclerenchyma (the two supporting tissues). In the stem and root, the vascular tissues and some associated ground tissue are often treated as a unit, the stele. Ground tissue may be present in the center of the stele (pith) and on its periphery (pericycle). The ground tissue system enclosing the stele on the outside is the cortex. It may have a hypodermis peripherally and an endodermis next to the stele.

The secondary tissues arise from lateral meristems, and their formation is mainly responsible for the growth in thickness of stems and roots. They comprise secondary vascular tissues and the protective tissue called periderm. Secondary growth may build up a massive core of wood, but the outer tissue system, the bark, remains relatively thin because its outer or older part becomes compressed and, in many species, is continuously sloughed off.

The production of flowers instead of vegetative shoots results from physiological and morphological changes in the apical meristem, which then becomes the flower meristem. The latter, however, produces tissue systems fundamentally similar to those in the vegetative body of the plant.   [K.E.]

Plant transport of solutes   The movement of organic and inorganic compounds through plant vascular tissues. Transport can take place over considerable distances; in tree species transport distances are often 100–300 ft (30–100 m).

This long-distance transport is necessary for survival in higher land plants in which specialized organs of uptake or synthesis are separated by a considerable distance from the organs of utilization. Diffusion is not rapid enough to account for the amount of material moved over such long distances. Rather, transport depends on a flowing stream of liquid in vascular tissues (phloem and xylem) that are highly developed structurally.

The movement of organic solutes occurs mainly in the phloem, where it is also known as translocation and where the direction of transport is from places of production, such as mature leaves, to places of utilization or storage, such as the shoot apex or developing storage roots. Organic materials translocated in the phloem include the direct products of photosynthesis (sugars) as well as compounds derived from them (nitrogenous compounds and plant hormones, for example). Some movement of organic solutes does occur in the xylem of certain species. Inorganic solutes or mineral elements, however, generally move with water in the xylem from sites of uptake in the roots to sites where water is lost from the plant, primarily the leaves. Some redistribution of the ions throughout the plant may then occur in the phloem.

The mechanism of phloem translocation is not known with certainty. Proposed mechanisms fall into two classes: one stresses the role of the conducting tissues in generating the moving force, and the other views the regions of supply and utilization as the source of this force. In the former group are mechanisms that depend on cytoplasmic streaming, electroosmosis, and activated diffusion in the sieve elements. The second group of theories, which has received more general acceptance in spite of a number of admitted limitations, includes a variety of mass-flow mechanisms. Theories of translocation must account for the important observations: polarity, bidirectional movement, velocity, energy requirement, turgor pressure, and phloem structure.

The model for the ascent of sap in the xylem which is correct according to all present evidence is called the cohesion hypothesis. According to this hypothesis, water is lost in the leaves by evaporation from cell-wall surfaces; water vapor then diffuses into the atmosphere by way of small pores between two specialized cells (guard cells). The guard cells and the pore are collectively called a stomate. This loss of water from the leaf causes movement of water out of the xylem in the leaf to the surfaces where evaporation is occurring. Water has a high internal cohesive force, especially in small tubes with wettable walls. In addition, the xylem elements and the cell walls provide a continuous water-filled system in the plant. Thus the loss of water from the xylem elements in the leaves causes a tension or negative pressure in the xylem sap. This tension is transmitted all the way down the stem to the roots, so that a flow of water occurs up the plant from the roots and eventually from the soil. The velocity of this sap flow in tree species ranges from 3 to approximately 165 ft/h (1 to 50 m/h), depending on the diameter of the xylem vessels.   [S.S.D.]

Plant viruses and viroids   Plant viruses are pathogens which are composed mainly of a nucleic acid (genome) normally surrounded by a protein shell (coat); they replicate only in compatible cells, usually with the induction of symptoms in the affected plant. Viroids are among the smallest infections agents known. Their circular, single-stranded riboncleic acid (RNA) molecule is less than one-tenth the size of the smallest viruses.

Viruses. Viruses can be seen only with an electron microscope (see illustration). Isometric (spherical) viruses range from 25 to 50 nanometers in diameter, whereas most anisometric (tubular) viruses are 12 to 25 nm in diameter and of various lengths (200–2000 nm), depending on the virus. The coat of a few viruses is covered by a membrane which is derived from its host.

Over 800 plant viruses have been recognized and characterized. The genomes of most of them, such as the tobacco mosaic virus (TMV), are infective single-stranded RNAs; some RNA viruses have double-stranded RNA genomes. Cauliflower mosaic virus and bean golden mosaic virus are examples of viruses having double-stranded and single-stranded deoxyribonucleic acid (DNA), respectively. The genome of many plant viruses is a single polynucleotide and is contained in a single particle, whereas the genomes of brome mosaic and some other viruses are segmented and distributed between several particles. There are also several low-molecular-weight RNAs (satellite RNAs) which depend on helper viruses for their replication. *See* DEOXYRIBONUCLEIC ACID (DNA); RIBONUCLEIC ACID (RNA).

The natural hosts of plant viruses are widely distributed throughout the higher-plant kingdom. Some viruses (TMV and cucumber mosaic virus) are capable of infecting over a hundred species in many families, whereas others, such as wheat streak mosaic virus,

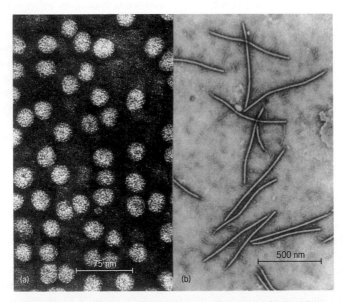

Representative plant viruses in purified virus preparation obtained from infected leaves. (*a*) Tobacco streak virus (isometric). (*b*) Pea seed-borne mosaic virus (anisometric).

are restricted to a few species in the grass family. The replication of single-stranded RNA viruses involves release of the virus genome from the coat protein; the association of the RNA with the ribosomes of the cell; translation of the genetic information of the RNA into specific proteins, including subunits of the coat protein and possibly viral RNA-synthesizing enzymes (replicases); transmission by vectors and diseases induction; synthesis of noninfective RNA using parental RNA as the template; and assembly of the protein subunits and viral RNA to form complete virus particles.

In other RNA viruses, such as lettuce necrotic yellows virus, an enzyme which is contained in the virus must first make a complementary (infective) copy of the RNA; this is then translated into enzymes and coat protein subunits. The replication of double-stranded RNA viruses is similar to that of lettuce necrotic yellows virus.

With double-stranded DNA viruses, viral DNA is uncoated in a newly infected cell and transported to the nucleus, where it associates with histones to form a closed circular minichromosome. Two major RNA species (35S and 19S) are transcribed from the minichromosome by a host-encoded enzyme and are translated in the cytoplasm to produce virus-associated proteins. The 35S RNA serves as the template for a viral enzyme which transcribes it to viral DNA, which is then encapsidated to form virus particles.

Symptoms are the result of an alteration in cellular metabolism and are most obvious in newly developing tissues. In some plants, depending on the virus, the initial infection does not spread because cells surrounding the infected cells die, resulting in the formation of necrotic lesions. Such plants are termed hypersensitive. The size and shape of leaves and fruit may be adversely affected, and in some instances plants may be killed. Not all virus infections produce distinctive symptoms.

The most common mode of transmission for many viruses is by means of vectors, mainly insects (predominantly aphids and leafhoppers), and to a lesser extent mites, soil-inhabiting fungi, and nematodes which acquire viruses by feeding on infected plants. Viruses transmitted by one class of vector are rarely transmitted by another, and there is often considerable specificity between strains of a virus and their vectors.

Some viruses are transmitted to succeeding generations mainly by embryos in seeds produced by infected plants; over 200 viruses are transmitted in this way.

Viroids. Only about 30 viroids are known, but they cause very serious diseases in such diverse plants as chrysanthemum, citrus, coconut, and potato. They can also be isolated from plants that do not exhibit symptoms. Viroids are mainly transmitted by vegetative propagation, but some, such as potato spindle tuber viroid, are transmitted by seed or by contact between infected and healthy plants. Tomato planta macho viroid is efficiently transmitted by aphids. See PLANT PATHOLOGY; VIROIDS; VIRUS.   [R.I.H.]

Plant-water relations   Water is the most abundant constituent of all physiologically active plant cells. Leaves, for example, have water contents which lie mostly within a range of 55–85% of their fresh weight. Other relatively succulent parts of plants contain approximately the same proportion of water, and even such largely nonliving tissues as wood may be 30–60% water on a fresh-weight basis. The smallest water contents in living parts of plants occur mostly in dormant structures, such as mature seeds and spores. The great bulk of the water in any plant constitutes a unit system. This water is not in a static condition. Rather it is part of a hydrodynamic system, which in terrestrial plants involves absorption of water from the soil, its translocation throughout the plant, and its loss to the environment, principally in the process known as transpiration.

Cellular water relations. The typical mature, vacuolate plant cell constitutes a tiny osmotic system, and this idea is central to any concept of cellular water dynamics.

Although the cell walls of most living plant cells are quite freely permeable to water and solutes, the cytoplasmic layer that lines the cell wall is more permeable to some substances than to others.

If a plant cell in a flaccid condition—one in which the cell sap exerts no pressure against the encompassing cytoplasm and cell wall—is immersed in pure water, inward osmosis of water into the cell sap ensues. This gain of water results in the exertion of a turgor pressure against the protoplasm, which in turn is transmitted to the cell wall. This pressure also prevails throughout the mass of solution within the cell. If the cell wall is elastic, some expansion in the volume of the cell occurs as a result of this pressure, although in many kinds of cells this is relatively small.

If a turgid or partially turgid plant cell is immersed in a solution with a greater osmotic pressure than the cell sap, a gradual shrinkage in the volume of the cell ensues; the amount of shrinkage depends upon the kind of cell and its initial degree of turgidity. When the lower limit of cell wall elasticity is reached and there is continued loss of water from the cell sap, the protoplasmic layer begins to recede from the inner surface of the cell wall. Retreat of the protoplasm from the cell wall often continues until it has shrunk toward the center of the cell, the space between the protoplasm and the cell wall becoming occupied by the bathing solution. This phenomenon is called plasmolysis. *See* OSMOREGULATORY MECHANISMS.

In some kinds of plant cells movement of water occurs principally by the process of imbibition rather than osmosis. The swelling of dry seeds when immersed in water is a familiar example of this process.

Stomatal mechanism. Various gases diffuse into and out of physiologically active plants. Those gases of greatest physiological significance are carbon dioxide, oxygen, and water vapor. The great bulk of the gaseous exchanges between a plant and its environment occurs through tiny pores in the epidermis that are called stomates. Although stomates occur on many aerial parts of plants, they are most characteristic of, and occur in greatest abundance in, leaves. *See* EPIDERMIS (PLANT); LEAF.

Transpiration process. The term transpiration is used to designate the process whereby water vapor is lost from plants. Although basically an evaporation process, transpiration is complicated by other physical and physiological conditions prevailing in the plant. Whereas loss of water vapor can occur from any part of the plant which is exposed to the atmosphere, the great bulk of all transpiration occurs from the leaves. There are two kinds of foliar transpiration: (1) stomatal transpiration, in which water vapor loss occurs through the stomates, and (2) cuticular transpiration, which occurs directly from the outside surface of epidermal walls through the cuticle. In most species 90% or more of all foliar transpiration is of the stomatal type.

Transpiration is a necessary consequence of the relation of water to the anatomy of the plant, and especially to the anatomy of the leaves. Terrestrial green plants are dependent upon atmospheric carbon dioxide for their survival. In terrestrial vascular plants the principal carbon dioxide–absorbing surfaces are the moist mesophyll cells walls which bound the intercellular spaces in leaves. Ingress of carbon dioxide into these spaces occurs mostly by diffusion through open stomates. When the stomates are open, outward diffusion of water vapor unavoidably occurs, and such stomatal transpiration accounts for most of the water vapor loss from plants. Although transpiration is thus, in effect, an incidental phenomenon, it frequently has marked indirect effects on other physiological processes which occur in the plant because of its effects on the internal water relations of the plant.

Water translocation. In terrestrial rooted plants practically all of the water which enters a plant is absorbed from the soil by the roots. The water thus absorbed is translocated to all parts of the plant. The mechanism of the "ascent of sap" (all translocated water contains at least traces of solutes) in plants, especially tall trees, was one of the first processes to excite the interest of plant physiologists.

The upward movement of water in plants occurs in the xylem, which, in the larger roots, trunks, and branches of trees and shrubs, is identical with the wood. In the trunks or larger branches of most kinds of trees, however, sap movement is restricted to a few of the outermost annual layers of wood. *See* XYLEM.

Root pressure is generally considered to be one of the mechanisms of upward transport of water in plants. While it is undoubtedly true that root pressure does account for some upward movement of water in certain species of plants at some seasons, various considerations indicate that it can be only a secondary mechanism of water transport.

Upward translocation of water (actually a very dilute sap) is engendered by an increase in the negativity of water potential in the cells of apical organs of plants. Such increases in the negativity of water potentials occur most commonly in the mesophyll cells of leaves as a result of transpiration.

Water absorption. The successively smaller branches of the root system of any plant terminate ultimately in the root tips, of which there may be thousands and often millions on a single plant. Most absorption of water occurs in the root tip regions, and especially in the root hair zone. Older portions of most roots become covered with cutinized or suberized layers through which only very limited quantities of water can pass. *See* ROOT (BOTANY).

Whenever the water potential in the peripheral root cells is less than that of the soil water, movement of water from the soil into the root cells occurs. There is some evidence that, under conditions of marked internal water stress, the tension generated in the xylem ducts will be propagated across the root to the peripheral cells. If this occurs, water potentials of greater negativity could develop in peripheral root cells than would otherwise be possible. The absorption mechanism would operate in fundamentally the same way whether or not the water in the root cells passed into a state of tension. The process just described, often called passive absorption, accounts for most of the absorption of water by terrestrial plants.

The phenomenon of root pressure represents another mechanism of the absorption of water. This mechanism is localized in the roots and is often called active absorption. Water absorption of this type only occurs when the rate of transpiration is low and the soil is relatively moist. Although the xylem sap is a relatively dilute solution, its osmotic pressure is usually great enough to engender a more negative water potential than usually exists in the soil water when the soil is relatively moist. A gradient of water potentials can thus be established, increasing in negativity across the epidermis, cortex, and other root tissues, along which the water can move laterally from the soil to the xylem. *See* PLANT MINERAL NUTRITION.   [B.S.M.]

Plants, life forms of   A term for the vegetative (morphological) form of the plant body. Life-form systems are based on differences in gross morphological features, and the categories bear no necessary relationship to reproductive structures, which form the basis for taxonomic classification. Features used in establishing life-form classes include deciduous versus evergreen leaves, broad versus needle leaves, size of leaves, degree of protection afforded the perennating tissue, succulence, and duration of life cycle (annual, biennial, or perennial).

There is a clear correlation between life forms and climates. For example, broad-leaved evergreen trees clearly dominate in the hot humid tropics, whereas broad-leaved deciduous trees prevail in temperature climates with cold winters and warm summers, and succulent cacti dominate American deserts. Although cacti are virtually absent from

African deserts, members of the family Euphorbiaceae have evolved similar succulent life forms. Such adaptations are genetic, having arisen by natural selection.

Many life-form systems have been developed. The most successful and widely used system is that of C. Raunkiaer, proposed in 1905. Reasoning that it was the perennating buds (the tips of shoots which renew growth after a dormant season, either of cold or drought) which permit a plant to survive in a specific climate, Raunkiaer's classes were based on the degree of protection afforded the bud and the position of the bud relative to the soil surface. They applied to autotrophic, vascular, self-supporting plants. Raunkiaer's classificatory system is:

Phanerophytes: bud-bearing shoots in the air, predominantly woody trees and shrubs; subclasses based on height and on presence or absence of bud scales

Chamaephytes: bud within 10 in. (25 cm) of the surface, mostly prostrate or creeping shrubs

Hemicryptophytes: buds at the soil surface, protected by scales, snow, and litter

Cryptophytes: buds underneath the soil surface or under water

Therophytes: annuals, the seed representing the only perennating tissue

By determining the life forms of a sample of 1000 species from the world's floras, Raunkiaer showed a correlation between the percentage of species in each life-form class present in an area and the climate of the area. Raunkiaer concluded that there were four main phytoclimates: phanerophyte-dominated flora of the hot humid tropics, hemicryptophyte-dominated flora in moist to humid temperate areas, therophyte-dominated flora in arid areas, and a chamaephyte-dominated flora of high latitudes and altitudes.

Subsequent studies modified Raunkiaer's views. (1) Phanerophytes dominate, to the virtual exclusion of other life forms, in true tropical rainforest floras, whereas other life forms become proportionately more important in tropical climates with a dry season. (2) Therophytes are most abundant in arid climates and are prominent in temperate areas with an extended dry season, such as regions with Mediterranean climate. (3) Other temperate floras have a predominance of hemicryptophytes with the percentage of phanerophytes decreasing from summer-green deciduous forest to grassland. (4) Arctic and alpine tundra are characterized by a flora which is often more than three-quarters chamaephytes and hemicryptophytes, the percentage of chamaephytes increasing with latitude and altitude.

There has been interest in developing systems which describe important morphologic features of plants and which permit mapping and diagramming vegetation. Descriptive systems incorporate essential structural features of plants, such as stem architecture and height; deciduousness; leaf texture, shape, and size; and mechanisms for dispersal. These systems are important in mapping vegetation because structural features generally provide the best criteria for recognition of major vegetation units.   [A.W.C.]

Plasmid A circular extrachromosomal genetic element that is ubiquitous in prokaryotes and has also been identified in a number of eukaryotes. In general, bacterial plasmids can be classified into two groups on the basis of the number of genes and functions they carry. The larger plasmids are deoxyribonucleic acid (DNA) molecules of around 100 kilobase (kb) pairs, which is sufficient to code for approximately 100 genes. There is usually a small number of copies of these plasmids per host chromosome, so that their replication must be precisely coordinated with the cell division cycle. The plasmids in the second group are smaller in size, about 6–10 kb. These plasmids may harbor 6–10 genes and are usually present in multiple copies (10–20 per chromosome). *See* GENE.

Plasmids have been identified in a large number of bacterial genera. Some bacterial species harbor plasmids with no known functions (cryptic plasmids) which have been identified as small circular molecules present in the bacterial DNA. The host range of a particular plasmid is usually limited to closely related genera. Some plasmids, however, are much more promiscuous and have a much broader host range.

The functions specified by different bacterial plasmids are usually quite specialized in nature. Moreover, they are not essential for cell growth since the host bacteria are viable without a plasmid when the cells are cultured under conditions that do not select for plasmid-specified gene products. Plasmids thus introduce specialized functions to host cells which provide versatility and adaptability for growth and survival. Plasmids which confer antibiotic resistance (R plasmids) have been extensively characterized because of their medical importance. Plasmids have played a seminal role in the spectacular advances in the area of genetic engineering. Individual genes can be inserted into specific sites on plasmids in cell cultures and the recombinant plasmid thus formed introduced into a living cell by the process of bacterial transformation. *See* GENETIC ENGINEERING. [R.H.R.]

Platyhelminthes A phylum of the invertebrates, commonly called the flat-worms. They are bilaterally symmetrical, nonsegmented, dorsoventrally flattened worms characterized by lack of coelom, anus, circulatory and respiratory systems, and exo- or endoskeleton. They possess a protonephridial excretory system, a complicated

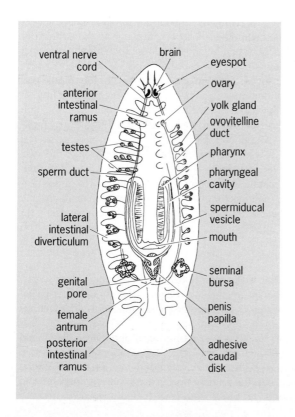

Bdelloura candida (Tricladida), ectocommensal on the king crab, *Limulus*. Complete digestive and male systems are shown on left, female systems on right.

hermaphroditic reproductive system, and a solid mesenchyme which fills the interior of the body (see illustration). Three classes occur in the phylum: (1) the Turbellaria, mainly free-living, predacious worms; (2) the Trematoda, or flukes, holozoic ecto- or endoparasites; and (3) the Cestoda, or tapeworms, saprozoic endoparasites in the enteron of vertebrates, whose larvae are found in the tissues of invertebrates or vertebrates.

Turbellaria are widespread in fresh water and the littoral zones of the sea, while one group of triclads occurs on land in moist habitats. Adult trematodes occur on, or in, practically all tissues and cavities of the vertebrates on which they feed. They are responsible for troublesome diseases in humans and animals. Larval flukes are frequent in mollusks, mainly gastropods, and occasionally occur in pelecypods. Vector hosts, such as insects and fish, are often interpolated between mollusk and vertebrate. Adult tapeworms, living in the enteron or the biliary ducts, compete with the host for food and accessory food factors such as vitamins. Larval tapeworms reside chiefly in arthropods, but larvae of one group, the Cyclophyllidea, develop in mammals, which may be severely impaired, or even killed, by the infection.   [C.G.G.]

Pneumococcus   The major causative microorganism (*Streptococcus pneumoniae*) of lobar pneumonia. Pneumococci occur singly or as pairs or short chains of oval or lancet-shaped cocci, 0.05–1.25 micrometers each, flattened at proximal sides and pointed at distal ends. A capsule of polysaccharide envelops each cell or pair of cells. The organism is nonmotile and stains gram-positive unless degenerating.

Pneumococci have been isolated from the upper respiratory tract of healthy humans, monkeys, calves, horses, and dogs. Epizootics of pneumococcal infection have been described in monkeys, guinea pigs, and rats but are not the source of human infection. In humans, pneumococci may be found in the upper respiratory tract of nearly all individuals at one time or another. Following damage to the epithelium lining the respiratory tract, pneumococci may invade the lungs. They are the principal cause of lobar pneumonia in humans and may cause also pleural empyema, pericarditis, endocarditis, meningitis, arthritis, peritonitis, and infection of the middle ear. Approximately one of four cases of pneumococcal pneumonia is accompanied by invasion of the bloodstream by pneumococci, producing bacteremia. Although the high mortality of untreated pneumococcal infection has been reduced significantly by treatment with antibiotics, one of every six patients with bacteremic lobar pneumonia still succumbs despite optimal therapy. In addition, the number of isolates of pneumococci resistant to one or more antimicrobial drugs has been gradually but steadily increasing. For these reasons, prophylactic vaccination is recommended, especially for those segments of the population that are at high risk for fatal infection. The polyvalent vaccine contains the purified capsular polysaccharides of the 23 types that are responsible for 85% of bacteremic pneumococcal infection and has an aggregate efficacy of 65–70% in preventing infection with any of the types represented in it.   [R.Au.]

Pneumonia   An acute or chronic inflammatory disease of the lungs. More specifically when inflammation is caused by an infectious agent, the condition is called pneumonia; when the inflammatory process in the lung is not related to an infectious organism, it is called pneumonitis.

An estimated 45 million cases of infectious pneumonia occur annually in the United States, with up to 50,000 deaths directly attributable to it. Pneumonia is a common immediate cause of death in persons with a variety of underlying diseases. With the use of immunosuppressive and chemotherapeutic agents for treating transplant and cancer patients, pneumonia caused by infectious agents that usually do not cause infections in healthy persons (that is, pneumonia as an opportunistic infection) has become commonplace. Moreover, individuals with acquired immune deficiency syndrome (AIDS) usually die from an opportunistic infection, such as pneumocystis pneumonia or cytomegalovirus pneumonia. Concurrent with the variable and expanding etiology of pneumonia and the more frequent occurrence of opportunistic infections is the development of new antibiotics and other drugs used in the treatment of pneumonia. See ACQUIRED IMMUNE DEFICIENCY SYNDROME (AIDS); OPPORTUNISTIC INFECTIONS.

Bacteria, as a group, are the most common cause of infectious pneumonia, although influenza virus has replaced *Streptococcus pneumoniae* (*Diplococcus pneumoniae*) as the most common single agent. Some of the bacteria are normal inhabitants of the body and proliferate to cause disease only under certain conditions. Other bacteria are contaminants of food or water.

Most bacteria cause one of two main morphologic forms of inflammation in the lung. *Streptococcus pneumoniae* causes lobar pneumonia, in which an entire lobe of a lung or a large portion of a lobe becomes consolidated (firm, dense) and nonfunctional secondary to an influx of fluid and acute inflammatory cells that represent a reaction to the bacteria. This type of pneumonia is uncommon today, usually occurring in people who have poor hygiene and are debilitated. If lobar pneumonia is treated adequately, the inflammatory process may entirely disappear, although in some instances it undergoes a process called organization, in which the inflammatory tissue changes into fibrous tissue, usually rendering that portion of the lung nonfunctional.

The other morphologic form of pneumonia, which is caused by the majority of bacteria, is called bronchopneumonia. In this form there is patchy consolidation of lung tissue, usually around the small bronchi and bronchioles, again most frequently in the lower lobes. This type of pneumonia may also undergo complete resolution if there is adequate treatment, although rarely it organizes.

Viral pneumonia is usually a diffuse process throughout the lung and produces a different type of inflammatory reaction than is seen in bronchopneumonia or lobar pneumonia. Mycoplasma pneumonia, caused by *Mycoplasma pneumoniae*, is referred to as primary atypical pneumonia and causes an inflammatory reaction similar to that of viral pneumonia.

Pneumonia can be caused by a variety of other fungal organisms, especially in debilitated persons such as those with cancer or AIDS. *Mycobacterium tuberculosis*, the causative agent of pulmonary tuberculosis, produces an inflammatory reaction similar to fungal organisms. See MYCOBACTERIAL DISEASES; TUBERCULOSIS.

Legionella pneumonia, initially called Legionnaire's disease, is caused by bacteria of the genus *Legionella*. The condition is frequently referred to under the broader name of legionellosis. See LEGIONNAIRES' DISEASE.

The signs and symptoms of pneumonia and pneumonitis are usually nonspecific, consisting of fever, chills, shortness of breath, and chest pain. Fever and chills are more frequently associated with infectious pneumonias but may also be seen in pneumonitis. The physical examination of a person with pneumonia or pneumonitis may reveal abnormal lung sounds indicative of regions of consolidation of lung tissue. A chest x-ray also shows the consolidation, which appears as an area of increased opacity (white area). Cultures of sputum or bronchial secretions may identify an infectious organism capable of causing the pneumonia.

The treatment of pneumonia and pneumonitis depends on the cause. Bacterial pneumonias are treated with antimicrobial agents. If the organisms can be cultured, the sensitivity of the organism to a specific antibiotic can be determined. Viral pneumonia is difficult to treat, as most drugs only help control the symptoms. The treatment of pneumonitis depends on identifying its cause; many cases are treated with cortisone-type medicines.   [S.P.H.]

Pogonophora   The beard worms—a phylum of sedentary marine worms living in cool waters of all the world's oceans, generally at depths between 330 and 13,200 ft (100 and 4000 m), shallower at higher latitudes and deeper in trenches. They were first dredged late in the nineteenth century but first investigated in the 1950s. Pogonophorans construct a tube, and are the only nonparasitic metazoans to have no mouth, gut, or anus in their postembryonic anatomy. These are long, slender worms, the diameter in most being less than 1 mm and the length being over 100 times the diameter. Superficially the tubes remind one of corn silk or coarse thread, but most have a characteristic banding pattern with annuli of brown or yellow pigments. The larger tubes are sometimes rigid, thicker, and darkcolored.

The evidence now suggests that these worms absorb their nutrients, such as amino acids, glucose, and fatty acids, through the pinnules and microvilli of the tentacles without the aid of digestive enzymes. This is accomplished against concentration gradients and may be supplemented by limited pinocytosis and phagocytosis by tentacular surfaces in a few species. The presence of internal symbiotic bacteria was demonstrated in several genera. These chemosynthetic organisms also play an important role in providing nutrients to these worms.

The sexes are separate, with the gonopore location being the only sexual dimorphism. Spermatophores with long tail filaments are released by the male. Fertilization has not been observed but must occur within the maternal tube, as fertilized eggs and developing larvae have been found there.

The Pogonophora consist of two orders: Athecanephria and Thecanephria.   [E.B.Cu.]

Poison gland   The specialized gland of certain fishes, as well as the granular glands and some mucous glands of many aquatic and terrestrial Amphibia. The poison glands of fishes are simple or slightly branched acinous structures which use the holocrine method of secreting a mucuslike substance. The poison glands of snakes are modified oral or salivary glands. Amphibian glands are simple, acinous, holocrine, with granular secretion. In some cases these amphibian poison glands produce mucus by a merocrine method of secretion. These glands function as protective devices. *See* GLAND.   [O.E.N.]

Poliomyelitis   An acute infectious viral disease which in its serious form affects the central nervous system and, by destruction of motor neurons in the spinal cord, produces flaccid paralysis. However, about 99% of infections are either inapparent or very mild. *See* ANIMAL VIRUS; CENTRAL NERVOUS SYSTEM.

The virus probably enters the body through the mouth; primary multiplication occurs in the throat and intestine. Transitory viremia occurs; the blood seems to be the most likely route to the central nervous system. The severity of the infection may range from a completely inapparent through minor influenzalike illness, or an aseptic meningitis syndrome (nonparalytic poliomyelitis) with stiff and painful back and neck, to the severe forms of paralytic and bulbar poliomyelitis. In all clinical types, virus is regularly present in the enteric tract. In paralytic poliomyelitis the usual course begins as a minor illness but progresses, sometimes with an intervening recession of symptoms (hence biphasic), to flaccid paralysis of varying degree and persistence. When the motor neurons affected are those of the diaphragm or of the intercostal muscles, respiratory paralysis occurs. Bulbar poliomyelitis results from viral attack on the medulla (bulb of the brain) or higher brain centers, with respiratory, vasomotor, facial, palatal, or pharyngeal disturbances.

Poliomyelitis occurs throughout the world. In temperate zones it appears chiefly in summer and fall, although winter outbreaks have been known. It occurs in all age groups, but less frequently in adults because of their acquired immunity. The virus is spread by human contact; the nature of the contact is not clear, but it appears to be associated with familial contact and with interfamily contact among young children. The virus may be present in flies.

Inactivated poliovirus vaccine (Salk; IPV), prepared from virus grown in monkey kidney cultures, was developed and first used in the United States, but oral poliovirus vaccine (Sabin; OPV) is now generally used throughout the world. The oral vaccine is a living, attenuated virus.   [J.L.Me.]

Pollen   The small male reproductive bodies produced in the pollen sacs of seed plants (gymnosperms and angiosperms).

On maturation in the pollen sac, a pollen grain may reach 0.00007 mg as in spruce, or less than 1/20 of this weight. A grain usually has two waxy, durable outer walls, the exine, and an inner fragile wall, the intine. These walls surround the contents with their nuclei and reserves of starch and oil.

Pollen identification depends on interpretation of morphological features. Exine and aperture patterns are especially varied in the more highly evolved dicots, so that recognition at family, genus, or even species level may be possible despite the small surface area available on a grain (Figs. 1 and 2). Since the morphological characters are conservative in the extreme, usually changing very slowly through geologic time, studies of fine detail serve to establish the lineal descent of many plants living today. *See* PALYNOLOGY.

Extreme variations in size may occur within a family, but pollen grains range mainly from 24 to 50 micrometers, with the dicot range being from 2 μm in *Myosotis* to 250 μm in *Mirabilis*; the monocots range from about 15 to 150 μm or more in the ginger family, with eelgrass (*Zostera*) having pollen measuring 2550 $\times$ 3.7 μm in a class of its own; living gymnosperms range from 15 μm in *Gnetum* to about 180 μm in *Abies* (including sacs), while fossil types range from about 11 μm (one-furrowed) to 300 μm.

Most grains are free (monads) though often loosely grouped because of the spines or sticky oils and viscin threads. Compound grains (polyads) are richly developed in

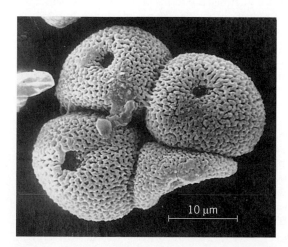

10 μm

Fig. 1. Tetrad of cattail (*Typha latifolia*), with grains cohering, one-pored, exine reticulate. (*Scanning electron micrograph by C. M. Drew, U.S. Naval Weapons Center, Cina Lake, California*).

Fig. 2. Young tetrad of *Lavatera* (mallow family), with grains free in callose of pollen mother cell. (*Photomicrograph by Luc Waterkeyn*)

25 µm

some angiosperm families, commonly occurring in four (tetrads), or in multiples of four up to 64 or more.

In most microspores (pollen and spore) the polar axis runs from the inner (proximal) face to the outer (distal) face, as oriented during tetrad formation. The equator crosses it at right angles. Bilateral grains dominate in the gymnosperms and monocots, the polar axis usually being the shorter one, with the single aperture on the distal side. On the other hand, almost all dicot pollen is symmetrical around the polar axis (usually the long axis), with shapes ranging mainly from spheroidal to ellipsoidal, with rounded equatorial outlines, and sometimes "waisted" as in the Umbelliferae. Three-pored grains often have strikingly triangular outlines in polar view.

Rarely lacking, the flexible membranes of apertures are sometimes covered only by endexine. They allow for sudden volume changes, as for the emergence of the germ tube. They are classified as furrows, with elongate outlines, and pores usually more or less circular in shape. Short slitlike intermediate forms occur. A few families have no apertures, some as a result of reduction of exine as an adaptation to wind- or water-pollination. Gymnosperms may also lack openings, or have one small papilla; most have one furrow, or a long weak area.

Few pollen grains are completely smooth (psilate) at ordinary magnifications; most have sculpture both on the surface and the structure below it. *See* FLOWER; POLLINATION; REPRODUCTION (PLANT).   [L.M.C.]

Pollination   The transport of pollen grains from the plant parts that produce them to the ovule-bearing organs, or to the ovules (seed precursors) themselves. In gymnosperms, the pollen, usually dispersed by the wind, is simply caught by a drop of fluid excreted by each freely exposed ovule. In angiosperms, where the ovules are contained in the pistil, the pollen is deposited on the pistil's receptive end (the stigma), where it germinates. *See* FLOWER.

Without pollination, there would be no fertilization; it is thus of crucial importance for the production of fruit crops and seed crops. Pollination also plays an important part in plant breeding experiments aimed at increasing crop production through the creation of genetically superior types. *See* BREEDING (PLANT); REPRODUCTION (PLANT).

Self- and cross-pollination. In most plants, self-pollination is difficult or impossible, and there are various mechanisms which are responsible. For example, in dichogamous flowers, the pistils and stamens reach maturity at different times; in protogyny, the pistils mature first, and in protandry, the stamens mature before the pistils. Selfing is also impossible in dioecious species, where some plants bear flowers that have only pistils (pistillate or female flowers), while other individuals have flowers that produce only pollen (staminate or male flowers). In monoecious species, where pistillate and staminate flowers are found in the same plant, self-breeding is at least reduced. Heterostyly is another device that promotes outbreeding. Here some flowers (pins) possess a long pistil and short stamens, while others (thrums) exhibit the reverse condition; each plant individual bears only pins or only thrums.

Flower attractants. As immobile organisms, plants normally need external agents for pollen transport. These can be insects, wind, birds, mammals, or water, roughly in that order of importance. In some plants the pollinators are simply trapped; in the large majority of cases, however, the flowers offer one or more rewards, such as sugary nectar, oil, solid food bodies, perfume, sex, an opportunity to breed, a place to sleep, or some of the pollen itself. For the attraction of pollinators, flowers provide either visual or olfactory signals. Color includes ultraviolet, which is perceived as a color by most insects and at least some hummingbird species. Fragrance is characteristic of flowers pollinated by bees, butterflies, or hawkmoths, while carrion or dung odors are produced by flowers catering to certain beetles and flies. A few orchids, using a combination of olfactory and visual signals, mimic the females of certain bees or wasps so successfully that the corresponding male insects will try to mate with them, thus achieving pollination (pseudocopulation).

While some flowers are "generalists," catering to a whole array of different animals, others are highly specialized, being pollinated by a single species of insect only. Extreme pollinator specificity is an important factor in maintaining the purity of plant species in the field, even in those cases where hybridization can easily be achieved artificially in a greenhouse or laboratory, as in most orchids. The almost incredible mutual adaptation between pollinating animal and flower which can frequently be observed exemplifies the idea of coevolution. *See* POLLEN.   [B.J.D.M.]

Polychaeta   The largest class of the phylum Annelida, containing 68–70 families. About 1600 genera and 10,000 species have been named from worldwide areas; about one-fourth of this number may be synonymous. Polychaeta (meaning "many setae") is conveniently though not clearly divisible into the Errantia, or free-moving annelids, and Sedentaria, or tubicolous families.

The body may be long, cylindrical, and multisegmented, or short and compact, with a limited number of segments. It consists of prostomium (Fig. 1), or head; peristomium, or first segment around the mouth; trunk, or body proper; and tail region, or pygidium. Most segments have highly diagnostic paired, lateral fleshy appendages called parapodia. These are provided with secreted supporting rods and spreading fascicles of setae, or hooks, which display remarkable specificity.

The anterior end, or prostomium, may be a simple lobe derived from the larval trochophore, modified as a pseudoannulated cone, or covered by peristomial structures so as to be invisible. Oral tentacles for food gathering may be eversible from the buccal cavity; they may be long, slender, or thick and their surface smooth or papillated.

The anterior, preoral end may be developed as a thick, fleshy papillated, nonretractile proboscis (Fig. 2), or the prostomium may be completely retractile into the

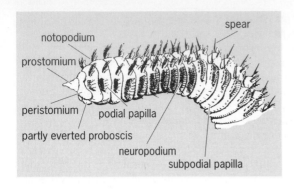

Fig. 1. Terminology of the anterior parts of the body, based on *Phylo* (Orbiniidae).

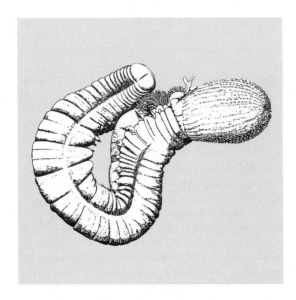

Fig. 2. Nonretractile proboscis organ preceding prostomium in *Artacama* (Terebellidae).

first several segments and protected by a cage formed of setae directed forward, or concealed by a compact operculum formed of setae of the first several segments. The anterior end of the alimentary tract is muscular or epithelial; it may be covered with soft papillae or hard structures. These structures function for secretion, food gathering, and maintaining traction; they are named for their form or function.

The trunk is the main body region and is composed of metameres numbering few to many. They may be similar to one another (homonomous) as in Errantia, or different (heteronomous) resulting in anterior thoracic and posterior abdominal regions.

Reproduction is highly evolved and diversified; it can be sexual or asexual. Sexual reproduction is usually dioecious, with the two sexes similar. In rare cases it is dimorphic.

Polychaetes range in length from a fraction of 0.04 in. (1 mm) to more than 144 in. (360 cm). Colors and patterns are varied and specific, due to pigment and refraction of light. Littoral, warm-water species may be brilliant and multicolored, whereas polar and deep-water species tend to be drab or sometimes melanistic to almost black.

Most polychaetes are free-living; some of the remaining members are commensal with another animal for attachment surface, for food, or for protection. Polychaetes are distributed in all marine habitats and show remarkable specificity according to latitude, depth, and kinds of substrata. Most of the families tend to be represented in any major geographic area, although taxa may differ with place. *See* ANNELIDA.   [O.H.]

Polymorphism (genetics)

A form of genetic variation, specifically a discontinuous variation, occurring within plant and animal species in which distinct forms exist together in the same population, even the rarest of them being too common to be maintained solely by mutation. Thus the human blood groups are examples of polymorphism, while geographical races are not; nor is the diversity of height among humans, because height is "continuous" and does not fall into distinct tall, medium, and short types. *See* MUTATION.

Distinct forms must be controlled by some switch which can produce one form or the other without intermediates such as those arising from environmental differences. This clear-cut control is provided by the recombination of the genes. Each gene may have numerous effects and, in consequence, all genes are nearly always of importance to the organism by possessing an overall advantage or disadvantage. They are very seldom of neutral survival value, as minor individual variations in appearance often are. Thus a minute extra spot on the hindwings of a tiger moth is in itself unlikely to be of importance to the survival of the insect, but the gene controlling this spot is far from negligible since it also affects fertility. *See* RECOMBINATION (GENETICS).

Genes having considerable and discontinuous effects tend to be eliminated if harmful, and each gene of this kind is therefore rare. On the other hand, those that are advantageous and retain their advantage spread through the population so that the population becomes uniform with respect to these genes. Evidently, neither of these types of genes can provide the switch mechanism necessary to maintain a polymorphism. That can be achieved only by a gene which has an advantage when rare, yet loses that advantage as it becomes commoner.

Occasionally there is an environmental need for diversity within a species, as in butterfly mimicry. Mimicry is the resemblance of different species to one another for protective purposes, chiefly to avoid predation by birds. Sexual dimorphism falls within the definition of genetic polymorphism. In any species, males and females are balanced at optimum proportions which are generally near equality. Any tendency for one sex to increase relative to the other would be opposed by selection.

In general, a gene having both advantageous and disadvantageous effects may gain some overall advantage and begin to spread because one of the features it controls becomes useful in a new environment. A balance is then struck between the advantages and disadvantages of such a gene, ensuring that a proportion of the species carry it, thus giving rise to permanent discontinuous variation, that is, to polymorphism. *See* PROTECTIVE COLORATION.

Polymorphism is increasingly known to be a very common situation. Its existence is apparent whenever a single gene having a distinct recognizable effect occurs in a population too frequently to be due merely to mutation. Even if recognized by some trivial effect on the phenotype, it must in addition have important other effects. About 30% of the people in western Europe cannot taste as bitter the substance phenylthiourea. This is truly an insignificant matter; indeed, no one even had the opportunity of tasting it until the twentieth century. Yet this variation is important since it is already known that it can affect disease of the thyroid gland. *See* GENETICS; POPULATION GENETICS.

[E.B.F.; J.R.Po.]

Polyploidy

The occurrence of related forms possessing chromosome numbers which are multiples of a basic number (n), the haploid number. Forms having $3n$ chromosomes are triploids; $4n$, tetraploids; $5n$, pentaploids; and so on. Autopolyploids are forms derived by the multiplication of chromosomes from a single diploid organism. As a result the homologous chromosomes come from the same source. These are distinguished from allopolyploids, which are forms derived from a hybrid between two diploid organisms. As a result, the homologous chromosomes come from different sources. About one-third of the species of vascular plants have originated at least partly by polyploidy, and as many more appear to have ancestries which involve ancient occurrences of polyploidy. The condition can be induced artificially with the drug colchicine and the production of polyploid individuals has become a valuable tool for plant breeding.

In animals, most examples of polyploidy occur in groups which are parthenogenetic, or in species which reproduce asexually by fission. See BREEDING (PLANT); CHROMOSOME ABERRATION; GENE; GENETICS; PLANT EVOLUTION; SPECIATION.   [G.L.St.]

In addition to polyploid organisms in which all of the body cells contain multiples of the basic chromosome number, most plants and animals contain particular tissues that are polyploid or polytene. Both polyploid and polytene cells contain extra copies of DNA, but they differ in the physical appearance of the chromosomes. In polytene cells the replicated copies of the DNA remain physically associated to produce giant chromosomes that are continuously visible and have a banded pattern. The term polyploid has been applied to several types of cells: multinucleate cells; cells in which the chromosomes cyclically condense but do not undergo nuclear or cellular division (this process is termed endomitosis); and cells in which the chromosomes appear to be continually in interphase, yet the replicated chromosomes are not associated in visible polytene chromosomes. See CHROMOSOME; CHROMOSOME ABERRATION; GENETICS; MITOSIS.   [T.L.O.W.]

Polypodiophyta   A division of the plant kingdom, commonly called the ferns, which is widely distributed throughout the world but is most abundant and varied in moist, tropical regions, The Polypodiophyta are sometimes treated as a class Polypodiopsida of a broadly defined division Tracheophyta (vascular plants). The group consists of five living orders (Ophioglossales, Marattiales, Polypodiales, Marsileales, and Salviniales), plus several orders represented only by Paleozoic fossils. The vast majority of the nearly 10,000 species belong to the single order Polypodiales, sometimes also called Filicales.

The Polypodiophyta ordinarily have well-developed roots, stems, and leaves that contain xylem and phloem as conducting tissues. The central cylinder of vascular tissue in the stem usually has well-defined parenchymatous leaf gaps where the leaf traces depart from it. The leaves are spirally arranged on the stem and are usually relatively large, with an evidently branching vascular system. In most kinds of ferns the leaves, called fronds, are compound or dissected. See LEAF; PHLOEM; ROOT (BOTANY); STEM; XYLEM.

The Polypodiophyta show a well-developed alternation of generations, both the sporophyte and the gametophyte generation being detached and physiologically independent of each other at maturity. The sporophyte is much the more conspicuous, and is the generally recognized fern plant. On some or all of its leaves it produces tiny sporangia which in turn contain spores. See REPRODUCTION (PLANT).   [A.Cr.]

Polysaccharide   A class of high-molecular-weight carbohydrates, colloidal complexes, which break down on hydrolysis to monosaccharides containing five or six carbon atoms. The polysaccharides are considered to be polymers in which monosaccharides have been glycosidically joined with the elimination of water. A polysaccharide consisting of hexose mono-saccharide units may be represented by the reaction below.

$$nC_6H_{12}O_2 \rightarrow (C_6H_{10}O_5)_n + (n-1)H_2O$$

The term polysaccharide is limited to those polymers which contain 10 or more monosaccharide residues. Polysaccharides such as starch, glycogen, and dextran consist of several thousand D-glucose units. Polymers of relatively low molecular weight, consisting of two to nine monosaccharide residues, are referred to as oligosaccharides. *See* DEXTRAN; GLUCOSE; GLYCOGEN; MONOSACCHARIDE; STARCH.

Polysaccharides are often classified on the basis of the number of monosaccharide types present in the molecule. Polysaccharides, such as cellulose or starch, that produce only one monosaccharide type (D-glucose) on complete hydrolysis are termed homopolysaccharides. On the other hand, polysaccharides, such as hyaluronic acid, which produce on hydrolysis more than one monosaccharide type (N-acetylglucosamine and D-glucuronic acid) are named heteropolysaccharides. *See* CARBOHYDRATE.

[W.Z.H.]

Population dispersal   The process by which groups of living organisms expand the space or range within which they live. Dispersal operates when individual organisms leave the space that they have occupied previously, or in which they were born, and settle in new areas. Natal dispersal is the first movement of an organism from its birth site to the site in which it first attempts to breed. Adult dispersal is a subsequent movement when an adult organism changes its location in space. As individuals move across space and settle into new locations, the population to which they belong expands or contracts its overall distribution. Thus, dispersal is the process by which populations change the area they occupy.

Migration is the regular movement of organisms during different seasons. Many species migrate between wintering and breeding ranges. Such migratory movement is marked by a regular return in future seasons to previously occupied regions, and so usually does not involve an expansion of population range. Some migratory species show astounding abilities to return to the exact locations used in previous seasons. Other species show no regular movements, but wander aimlessly without settling permanently into a new space. Wandering (called nomadism) is typical of species in regions where the availibility of food resources are unpredictable from year to year. Neither migration nor nomadism is considered an example of true dispersal. *See* MIGRATORY BEHAVIOR.

Virtually all forms of animals and plants disperse. In most higher vertebrates, the dispersal unit is an entire organism, often a juvenile or a member of another young age class. In other vertebrates and many plants, especially those that are sessile (permanently attached to a surface), the dispersal unit is a specialized structure (disseminule). Seeds, spores, and fruits are disseminules of plants and fungi; trochophores and planula larvae are disseminules of sea worms and corals, respectively. Many disseminules are highly evolved structures specialized for movement by specific dispersal agents such as wind, water, or other animals.

A special case of zoochory (dispersal using animal agents) involves transport by humans. The movement of people and cargo by cart, car, train, plane, and boat has increased the potential dispersal of weedy species worldwide. Many foreign aquatic species have been introduced to coastal areas by accidental dispersal of disseminules in ship ballast water. The zebra mussel is one exotic species that arrive in this manner and is now a major economic problem throughout the Great Lakes region of North America. Some organisms have been deliberately introduced by humans into new areas. Domestic animals and plants have been released throughout the world by farmers. A few pest species were deliberately released by humans; European starlings, for example.

Some of the most highly coevolved dispersal systems are those in which the disseminule must be eaten by an animal. Such systems have often evolved a complex series of signals and investments by both the plant and the animal to ensure that the seeds are dispersed at an appropriate time and that the animal is a dependable dispersal agent. Such highly evolved systems are common in fruiting plants and their dispersal agents, which are animals called frugivores. Fruiting plants cover their seeds with an attractive, edible package (the fruit) to get the frugivore to eat the seed. To ensure that fruits are not eaten until the seeds are mature, plants change the color of their fruits as a signal to show that the fruits are ready for eating.

Many plants in the tropical rainforests are coevolved to have their seeds dispersed by specific animal vectors, including birds, mammals, and ants. Many tropical trees, shrubs, and herbaceous plants are specialized to have their seeds dispersed by a single animal species. Temperate forest trees, in contrast, often depend on wind dispersal of both pollen and seeds.

Dispersal barriers are physical structures that prevent organisms from crossing into new space. Oceans, rivers, roads, and mountains are examples of barriers for species whose disseminules cannot cross such features. It is believed that the creation of physical barriers is the primary factor responsible for the evolution of new species. A widespread species can be broken into isolated fragments by the creation of a new physical barrier. With no dispersal linking the newly isolated populations, genetic differences that evolve in each population cannot be shared between populations. Eventually, the populations may become so different that no interbreeding occurs even if dispersal pathways are reconnected. The populations are then considered separate species. *See* SPECIATION.

Dispersal is of major concern for scientists who work with rare and endangered animals. Extinction is known to be more prevalent in small, isolated populations. Conservation biologists believe that many species exist as a metapopulation, that is, a group of populations interconnected by the dispersal of individuals or disseminules between subpopulations. The interruption of dispersal in this system of isolated populations can increase the possibility of extinction of the whole metapopulation. Conservation plans sometimes propose the creation of corridors to link isolated patches of habitat as a way of increasing the probability of successful dispersal. *See* POPULATION DISPERSION.

[J.B.D.]

Population ecology   The study of spatial and temporal patterns in the abundance and distribution of organisms and of the mechanisms that produce those patterns. Species differ dramatically in their average abundance and geographical distributions, and they display a remarkable range of dynamical patterns of abundance over time, including relative constancy, cycles, irregular fluctuations, violent outbreaks, and extinctions. The aims of population ecology are threefold: (1) to elucidate general principles explaining these dynamic patterns; (2) to integrate these principles with mechanistic models and evolutionary interpretations of individual life-history tactics, physiology, and behavior as well as with theories of community and ecosystem dynamics; and (3) to apply these principles to the management and conservation of natural populations.

In addition to its intrinsic conceptual appeal, population ecology has great practical utility. Control programs for agricultural pests or human diseases ideally attempt to reduce the intrinsic rate of increase of those organisms to very low values. Analyses of the population dynamics of infectious diseases have successfully guided the development of vaccination programs. In the exploitation of renewable resources, such as in forestry or fisheries biology, population models are required in order to devise sensible harvesting strategies that maximize the sustainable yield extracted from exploited populations. Conservation biology is increasingly concerned with the consequences of habitat fragmentation for species preservation. Population models can help characterize minimum viable population sizes below which a species is vulnerable to rapid extinction, and can help guide the development of interventionist policies to save endangered species. Finally, population ecology must be an integral part of any attempt to bring the world's burgeoning human population into harmonious balance with the environment. *See* ECOLOGY; THEORETICAL ECOLOGY. [R.Hol.]

Population genetics The study of both experimental and theoretical consequences of mendelian heredity on the population level, in contradistinction to classical genetics which deals with the offspring of specified parents on the familial level. The genetics of populations studies the frequencies of genes, genotypes, and phenotypes, and the mating systems. It also studies the forces that may alter the genetic composition of a population in time, such as recurrent mutation, migration, and intermixture between groups, selection resulting from genotypic differential fertility, and the random changes incurred by the sampling process in reproduction from generation to generation. This type of study contributes to an understanding of the elementary step in biological evolution. The principles of population genetics may be applied to plants and to other animals as well as humans. *See* GENETICS; MENDELISM. [C.C.L.]

Population viability The ability of a population to persist and to avoid extinction. The viability of a population will increase or decrease in response to changes in the rates of birth, death, and growth of individuals. In natural populations, these rates are not stable, but undergo fluctuations due to external forces such as hurricanes and introduced species, and internal forces such as competition and genetic composition. Such factors can drive populations to extinction if they are severe or if several detrimental events occur before the population can recover. *See* ECOLOGY; POPULATION ECOLOGY.

One of the most important uses of population viability models comes from modern conservation biology, which uses these models to determine whether a population is in danger of extinction. This is called population viability analysis (PVA) and consists of demographic and genetic models that are used to make decisions on how to manage populations of threatened or endangered species. The National Research Council has called population viability analysis "the cornerstone, the obligatory tool by which recovery objectives and criteria [for endangered species] are identified." *See* ECOLOGICAL MODELING. [G.LeB.; T.E.M.]

Porifera The sponges, a phylum of the animal kingdom which includes about 5000 described species. The body plan of sponges is unique among animals. Currents of water are drawn through small pores, or ostia, in the sponge body and leave by way of larger openings called oscula. The beating of flagella on collar cells or choanocytes, localized in chambers on the interior of the sponge, maintains the water current. Support for the sponge tissues is provided by calcareous or siliceous spicules, or by organic fibers, or by a combination of organic fibers and siliceous spicules. Some species have a compound skeleton of organic fibers, siliceous spicules, and a basal mass of aragonite or calcite. The skeletons of species with supporting networks of organic fibers have long been used for bathing and cleaning purposes. Because of their primitive organization, sponges are of interest to zoologists as an aid in understanding the origin of multicellular animals. *See* ANIMAL KINGDOM; PARAZOA.

The Porifera have a fossil record extending from the Precambrian to Recent times. More than 1000 genera of fossil sponges have been described from the Paleozoic, Mesozoic, and Cenozoic eras. The living Porifera are divided into four classes on the basis of their skeletal structures: Hexactinellida; Calcarea; Demospongiae; and Sclerospongiae.   [J.K.Ri.]

Porphyrin   One of a class of cyclic compounds in which the parent macrocycle consists of four pyrrole-type units linked together by single carbon bridges. Several porphyrins with selected peripheral substitution and metal coordination carry out vital biochemical processes in living organisms. Chlorins, bacteriochlorins, and corrins are related tetrapyrrolic macrocycles that are also observed in biologically important compounds.

The complexity of porphyrin nomenclature parallels the complex structures of the naturally occurring derivatives. Hans Fischer used a simple numbering system for the porphyrin nucleus and a set of common names to identify the different porphyrins and their isomers. A systematic naming based on the 1–24 numbering system for the porphyrin nucleus was later developed by the International Union of Pure and Applied Chemistry (IUPAC) and the International Union of Biochemistry (IUB), and this system has gained general acceptance. The need for common names is clear after examination of the systematic names; for example, protoporphyrin IX has the systematic name 2,7,12,18-tetramethyl-3,8-divinyl-13,17-dipropanoic acid.

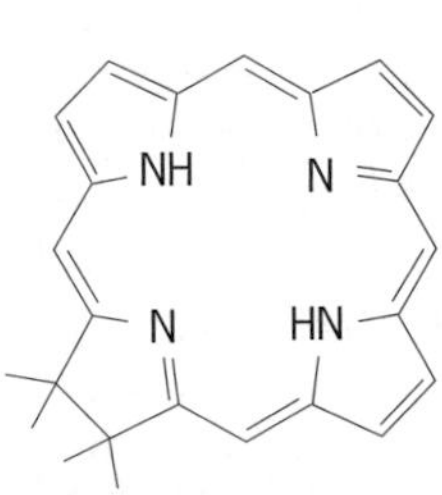

Chlorin

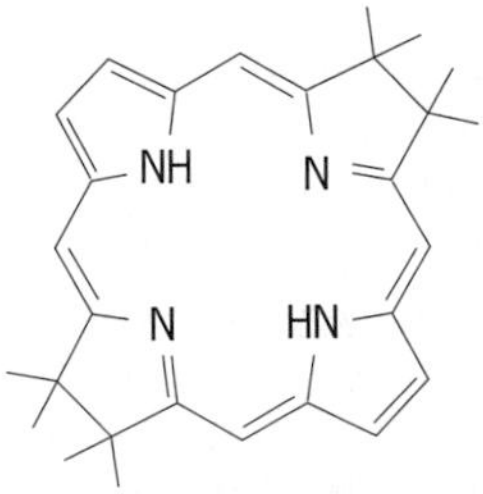

Bacteriochlorin

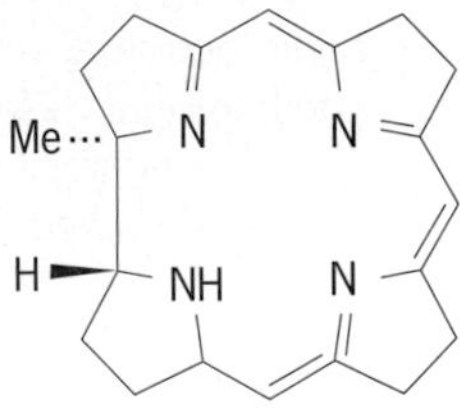

Corrin
Me = CH$_3$

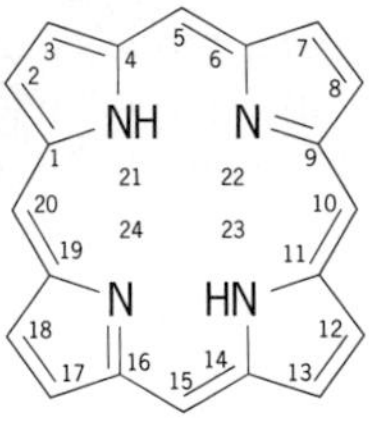

Porphyrin nucleus

The aromatic character (hence stability) of porphyrins has been confirmed by measurements of their heats of combustion. In addition, x-ray crystallographic studies have established planarity of the porphyrin macrocycle which is a basic requirement for aromatic character.

Most metals and metalloids have been inserted into the central hole of the porphyrin macrocycle. The resulting metalloporphyrins are usually very stable and can bind a variety of small molecules (known as ligands) to the central metal atom. Heme, the iron complex of protoporphyrin IX, is the prosthetic group of a number of major proteins and enzymes that carry out diverse biological functions. These include binding, transport, and storage of oxygen (hemoglobin and myoglobin), electron-transfer processes (cytochromes), activation and transfer of oxygen to substrates (cytochromes P450), and managing and using hydrogen peroxide (peroxidases and catalases). *See* CYTOCHROME; HEMOGLOBIN.

Chlorophylls and bacteriochlorophylls are magnesium complexes of porphyrin derivatives known as chlorins and bacteriochlorins, respectively. They are the pigments responsible for photosynthesis. Several chlorophylls have been identified, the most common being chlorophyll *a*, which is found in all oxygen-evolving photosynthetic plants. Bacteriochlorophyll *a* is found in many photosynthetic bacteria. *See* CHLORO-PHYLL; PHOTOSYNTHESIS.

Porphyrins and metalloporphyrins exhibit many potentially important medicinal and industrial properties. Metalloporphyrins are being examined as potential catalysts for a variety of processes, including catalytic oxidations. They are also being examined as possible blood substitutes and as electrocatalysts for fuel cells and for the electrochemical generation of hydrogen peroxide. The unique optical properties of porphyrins make them likely candidates for photovoltaic devices and in photocopying and other optical devices. A major area where porphyrins are showing significant potential is in the treatment of a wide range of diseases, including cancer, using photodynamic therapy.

[T.W.D.]

Posttraumatic stress disorder
An anxiety disorder in some individuals who have experienced an event that poses a direct threat to the individual's or another person's life. The characteristic features of anxiety disorders are fear, particularly in the absence of a real-life threat to safety, and avoidance behavior.

A diagnosis of posttraumatic stress disorder requires that four criteria be met. First, the individual must have been exposed to an extremely stressful and traumatic event beyond the range of normal human experience. Second, the individual must periodically and persistently reexperience the event. This reexperiencing can take different forms, such as recurrent dreams and nightmares, an inability to stop thinking about the event, flashbacks during which the individual relives the trauma, and auditory hallucinations. Third, there is persistent avoidance of events related to the trauma, and psychological numbing that was not present prior to the trauma. Fourth, enduring symptoms of anxiety and arousal are present. These symptoms can be manifested in different forms, including anger, irritability, a very sensitive startle response, an inability to sleep well, and physiological evidence of fear when the individual is reexposed to a traumatic event.

Posttraumatic stress disorder symptoms appear to range over a continuum of severity, and it is unlikely that the disorder is an all-or-nothing phenomenon. The degree of the posttraumatic stress response is likely to be influenced by a complex interaction of personality, nature of the trauma, and posttraumatic events.

Physiological arousal responses in individuals with posttraumatic stress disorder include increases in heart rate, respiration rate, and skin conductivity upon reexposure to traumatic stimuli. Posttraumatic stress disorder may also be associated with structural and physiological changes in the brain. Stressful events also affect the activity level of the pituitary and adrenal glands. All these physiological changes are probably complexly related to the persistence and waxing and waning of symptoms in posttraumatic stress disorder. In addition, extreme and prolonged stress is associated with a variety of physical ailments, including heart attacks, ulcers, colitis, and decreases in immunological functioning. *See* NEUROBIOLOGY.

When an individual is diagnosed as having this disorder, particularly after it has been present for a number of years, it is common to also find significant depression, generalized anxiety, substance abuse and dependence, marital problems, and intense, almost debilitating anger. Although the primary symptoms of posttraumatic stress disorder are quite amenable to psychological treatment efforts, these secondary problems commonly associated with the chronic disorder are more difficult to treat.

Posttraumatic stress disorder can be treated by pharmacological means and with psychotherapy. Most psychological treatments for the disorder involve reexposure to the traumatic event. This reexposure is typically imaginal and can range from simply talking about the trauma to having the person vividly imagine reliving the traumatic event. This latter behavioral procedure is called implosion therapy or flooding. While flooding is not appropriate for all posttraumatic stress disorder cases, the procedure can dramatically decrease anxiety and arousal, intrusive thoughts, avoidance behavior, and emotional numbing. Along with specific behavior interventions, individuals with posttraumatic stress disorder should become involved in psychotherapeutic treatment for secondary problems. *See* NORADRENERGIC SYSTEM; PSYCHOPHARMACOLOGY; STRESS (PSYCHOLOGY).   [R.W.But.]

Postural equilibrium   A lifeless object is said to be in equilibrium, or in a state of balance, when all forces acting upon it cancel. The result is a state of rest. In an actively moving animal, internal as well as external forces have to be considered, and the maintenance of a balanced attitude in a body consisting of a number of parts that are loosely connected by movable joints is complex.

The maintenance of equilibrium is relatively easy in limbless animals. When the animal is turned on its back, the lack of contact pressure on the creeping surface and the tactile stimulation of the back initiate movements which return the animal to its normal position. This is known as the righting reflex. Free-swimming and flying animals are often in a precariously poised state of equilibrium, so that the normal attitude can be maintained only by the continuous operation of corrective equilibrating mechanisms. The same applies to a lesser degree to long-legged quadrupeds, such as many mammals, and to bipeds, such as birds and some primates (including humans).

For most species, there is a specific orientation of the whole body or of body segments (such as the head) with respect to gravity. This orientation is based on multisensory inputs and on a set of inborn reflexes acting on the musculature. These postural reflexes also stabilize the genetically defined body orientation against external disturbances. The sensory information relies on a number of sources: (1) static and dynamic information from the eyes; (2) static and dynamic mechanoreceptors incorporated in the various types of statocysts in invertebrate animals and in the vestibular organ or labyrinth of vertebrates; (3) proprioceptor organs such as muscle spindles, Golgi endings in tendons, Pacinian corpuscles and similar encapsulated endings associated with tendons and joints, and other pressure receptors in supporting surfaces (for example, the soles of feet); and (4) sensory endings in the viscera, capable of being differentially stimulated by changes in the direction of visceral pull on mesenteries, and on other structures. *See* SENSATION; SENSE ORGAN.

In higher terrestrial vertebrates, during stance the center of mass is usually situated high above the ground due to the support of the body by the limbs. A critical aspect of posture in quadrupedal and bipedal stance is equilibrium maintenance which is preserved only when under static conditions the projection of the center of mass remains inside the support base. This positioning of the center of mass is based on two main controls. A "bottom up" control is based on the afferent nerve impulses, cutaneous and proprioceptive, from the feet and the ankle joint muscles. These nerve impulse serve in building up posture from the feet to the head. A "top down" control starts from the head, and is predominant during dynamic activities such as locomotion. Due to labyrinthine afferent nerve impulses, the head axis orientation remains stable with respect to space. The movement-related visual afferents recorded by the retina monitor the head displacements with respect to space and adjust the body posture as a function of these inputs.

Two levels of control are involved in maintaining balance. A first level includes the spinal cord and the brainstem, where a set of inborn reflexes are organized for stance regulation and head orientation. Most postural reflexes rely on networks at that level. The cerebellum is involved in the adaptation of these reflexes to the external constraints. *See* REFLEX.

A second level of control includes cortical areas involved in multisensory integration and control as well as the basal ganglia. The postural body schema and the body orientation with respect to the external world are organized mainly at that level, with a predominant role in the right hemisphere. Coordination between balance control and locomotion or movements also depends on these higher levels.   [J.Mas.]

Prebiotic organic synthesis   The plausible pathways by which the molecular precursors of life may have formed on the primitive Earth. Amino acids, the nitrogenous bases, and ribose phosphates can be prepared under conditions that might have prevailed on the primitive Earth. The linking together of amino acids to form polypeptides, and of nucleotides to form polynucleotides, has in principle been established.

Harold C. Urey's model of the primordial Earth postulates an atmosphere rich in methane, ammonia, water, and hydrogen. When this gas mixture is subjected to an electrical spark, analogous to the way that lightning may have initiated such syntheses 4 billion years ago, the identified products included several amino acids (glycine, alanine, and aspartic acid), the building blocks of proteins. This novel result lent credibility to a theory in which the origin of life was viewed as a cumulative, stepwise process, beginning with the gaseous synthesis of small molecules, which rained down into oceans, lagoons, and lakes. With water as a ubiquitous solvent, organic molecules could then react with one another to form larger molecules (biopolymers) and finally to assemble into primitive cells. This general scenario has guided the design of prebiotic simulations.

However, an accumulation of geophysical data and computational models has cast doubt on the relevance of the synthesis of amino acids to the primordial Earth. Hydrogen probably escaped rapidly as the Earth cooled, leaving an atmosphere in which methane and ammonia were virtually absent. As the input of hydrogen is diminished, the formation of biomolecules is inhibited. This problem has led some scientists to look for extraterrestrial sources of organic matter. For example, meteorites are known to contain a rich source of amino acids and other small biomolecules, and perhaps the infall of such cosmic bodies onto the young Earth gave life its start. Alternatively, there may have been localized environments on the Earth where methane and other hydrogen-rich precursors were abundant, such as deep-ocean hydrothermal vents, which would have been favorable for the formation of life. *See* AMINO ACIDS; HYDROTHERMAL VENT.
                                                                              [W.J.Hag.]

Predator-prey interactions   Predation occurs when one animal (the predator) eats another living animal (the prey) to utilize the energy and nutrients from the body of the prey for growth, maintenance, or reproduction. In the special case in

which both predator and prey are from the same species, predation is called canni-
balism. Sometimes the prey is actually consumed by the predator's offspring. This is
particularly prevalent in the insect world. Insect predators that follow this type of lifestyle
are called parasitoids, since the offspring grow parasitically on the prey provided by
their mother.

Predation is often distinguished from herbivory by requiring that the prey be an
animal rather than a plant or other type of organism (bacteria). To distinguish predation
from decomposition, the prey animal must be killed by the predator. Some organisms
occupy a gray area between predator and parasite. Finally, the requirement that both
energy and nutrients be assimilated by the predator excludes carnivorous plants from
being predators, since they assimilate only nutrients from the animals they consume.
See FOOD WEB.

Population dynamics refers to changes in the sizes of populations of organisms
through time, and predator-prey interactions may play an important role in explaining
the population dynamics of many species. They are a type of antagonistic interaction, in
which the population of one species (predators) has a negative effect on the population
of a second (prey), while the second has a positive effect on the first. For population dynamics, predator-prey interactions are similar to other types of antagonistic interactions,
such as pathogen-host and herbivore-plant interactions.

Community structure refers generally to how species within an ecological community
interact. The simplest conception of a community is as a food chain, with plants or
other photosynthetic organisms at the bottom, followed by herbivores, predators that
eat herbivores, and predators that eat other predators. This simple conception works
well for some communities. Nonetheless, the role of predator species in communities is
often not clear. Many predators change their ecological roles over their lifetime. Many
insect predators that share the same prey species are also quite likely to kill and devour
each other. This is called intraguild predation, since it is predation within the guild
of predators. Furthermore, many species are omnivores, feeding at different times as
either predators or herbivores. Therefore, the role of particular predator species in a
community is often complex.

Predator-prey interactions may have a large impact on the overall properties of a
community. For example, most terrestrial communities are green, suggesting that predation on herbivores is great enough to stop them from consuming the majority of
plant material. In contrast, the biomass of herbivorous zooplankton in many aquatic
communities is greater than the biomass of the photosynthetic phytoplankton, suggesting that predation on zooplankton is not enough to keep these communities green. *See*
POPULATION ECOLOGY.   [A.R.I.]

Priapulida   One of the minor groups of wormlike marine animals, now regarded
as a separate phylum of the animal kingdom with uncertain zoological affinities. The
phylum is a small one with only two genera, *Priapulus* and *Halicryptus*.

Priapulida inhabit the colder waters of both hemispheres. They burrow in mud and
sand of the sea floor, from the intertidal region to depths of 14,850 ft (4500 m).

Priapulids are small to medium-sized animals, the largest specimen attaining 6 in.
(15 cm) in length. The body of *Priapulus* is made up of three distinct portions: proboscis,
trunk, and caudal appendage (see illustration). Separated by a constriction from the
trunk, the bulbous, introversible proboscis usually constitutes the anterior third of the
body and is marked by 25 longitudinal ridges of papillae or spines. The mouth is
located at the anterior end of the proboscis and is surrounded by concentric rows of
teeth. The cylindrical trunk is annulated, but not segmented, and is often covered with

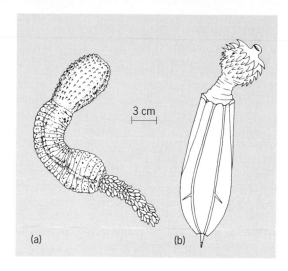

(a)   (b)

**Priapulida. (a) *Priapulus* adult
and (b) larva.**

irregularly dispersed spines and tubercles. At the posterior end of the trunk there are
three openings: the anus and two urogenital apertures.   [M.E.Ri.]

Primary vascular system (plant)   The arrangement of conducting elements which serves for two-way transportation of substances between different parts
of a plant. The conducting elements are of two principal kinds: xylem, which is mainly
responsible for the conduction of water together with dissolved inorganic substances
upward from the root to other plant organs; and phloem, which is mainly responsible
for the conduction of food materials (assimilates), a flow which may take place in either
direction. In the shoot region of the plant, xylem and phloem are usually associated
into vascular bundles. In the root, however, they usually alternate with one another on
different radii. *See* PHLOEM; XYLEM.   [W.R.P.]

Primates   The mammalian order to which humans belong. Primates are generally
arboreal mammals with a geographic distribution largely restricted to the Tropics. Unlike
most other mammalian orders, the primates cannot be defined by a diagnostic suite
of specializations, but are characterized by a combination of primitive features and
progressive trends. These include:

1. Increased dominance of vision over olfaction, with eyes more frontally directed,
development of stereoscopic vision, and reduction in the length of the snout.

2. Eye sockets of the skull completely encircled by bone.

3. Loss of an incisor and premolar from each half of the upper and lower jaws with
respect to primitive placental mammals.

4. Increased size and complexity of the brain, especially those centers involving
vision, memory, and learning.

5. Development of grasping hands and feet, with a tendency to use the hands rather
than the snout as the primary exploratory and manipulative organ.

6. Progressive elaboration of the placenta in conjunction with longer gestation period, small litter size (only one or two infants), and precocial young.

7. Increased period of infant dependency and more intensive parenting.

8. A tendency to live in complex, long-lasting social groups.

It has been recognized for a long time that many of these features are adaptations for living in trees. However, it has been proposed more recently that primates may have developed their specializations as a consequence of being visually directed predators, living among the smaller branches of the forest canopy or undergrowth, that captured insects with their hands.

Classification of the primates is as follows:

Order Primates
  Suborder Strepsirhini
    Infraorder Lorisiformes
      Superfamily Lorisoidea
        Family: Lorisidae (lorises)
            Galagidae (bushbabies)
    Infraorder Lemuriformes
    Superfamily Lemuroidea
        Family: Cheirogaleidae (dwarf lemurs)
            Lepilemuridae (sportive lemur)
            Lemuridae (true lemurs)
            Indriidae (sifakas, indri, woolly lemur)
            Daubentoniidae (aye-aye)
  Suborder Haplorhini
    Hyporder Tarsiiformes
      Superfamily Tarsioidea
      Family Tarsiidae (tarsiers)
    Hyporder Anthropoidea
      Infraorder Platyrrhini
        Superfamily Ceboidea
        Family: Callitrichidae (marmosets, tamarins)
            Cebidae (capuchins, squirrel monkeys, douroucoulis, titis)
            Atelidae (sakis, uakaris, howler monkeys, spider monkeys, woolly monkeys)
    Infraorder Catarrhini
      Superfamily Cercopithecoidea
      Family Cercopithecidae (Old World monkeys)
      Superfamily Hominoidea
      Family: Hylobatidae (gibbons, siamang)
            Hominidae (orangutan, gorilla, chimpanzees, humans)

There are two major groups of primates: the strepsirhines or "lower" primates, and the haplorhines or "higher" primates. Strepsirhines have elongated and forwardly projecting lower front teeth that form a toothcomb, used for grooming the fur and for obtaining resins and gums from trees as a source of food. The digits of the hands and feet bear flattened nails, rather than claws, except for the second toe, which retains a sharp toilet claw for grooming. They also have a moist, naked rhinarium and cleft upper lip (similar to the wet noses of dogs). Most strepsirhines are nocturnal, with large eyes and a special reflective layer (the tapetum lucidum) behind the retina that intensifies images in low light. Compared with haplorhines, the brain size is relatively small and the snout tends to be longer.

The strepsirhines are subdivided into two major groups: the lorisoids, which are found throughout tropical Africa and Asia, and the lemuroids, which are restricted to Madagascar.

The lorisoids include the galagids or bushbabies (*Galago, Otolemur, Euoticus,* and *Galagoides*) and the lorisids or lorises (*Loris, Nycticebus, Perodicticus, Pseudopotto,* and *Arctocebus*). They are small nocturnal primates, in which the largest species, the greater bushbaby, weighs only about 1 kg (2 lb). Their diet consists mainly of a combination of insects, fruits, and gums. Lorisoids are semisolitary, living in small, dispersed social groups.

The greatest diversity of strepsirhines is found on Madagascar, where more than 30 species are represented, belonging to five different families.

Tarsiers, tiny primates (weighing only about 120 g) from the islands of Southeast Asia, all belong to a single genus, *Tarsius*. They are nocturnal with the largest eyes of any primate, and other adaptations for a specialized lifestyle as vertical clingers and leapers. In the past, tarsiers have been grouped together with the strepsirhines as prosimians, because they retain many primitive features lost in higher primates. However, tarsiers share a number of distinctive specializations with anthropoids that suggest that they are more closely related to each other than either is to the strepsirhines. For this reason, tarsiers and anthropoids are classified together as haplorhines.

The anthropoids include the platyrrhines or New World monkeys and the catarrhines or Old World monkeys, apes, and humans. Anthropoids are distinguished from strepsirhines and tarsiers in having a larger brain, relatively small eyes (all anthropoids are diurnal, active by day, except for the nocturnal douroucouli from South America), eye sockets almost completely enclosed by a bony septum, the two halves of the lower jaw fused in the midline rather than separated by a cartilage, small and immobile ears, the hands and feet bearing nails with no toilet claws (except for the callitrichids that have secondarily evolved claws on all fingers and toes), a single-chambered uterus rather than two-horned, and a more advanced placenta.

The platyrrhines from South and Central America are a diverse group of primates comprising more than 50 species and 16 genera. Primatologists have had a difficult time establishing a classification of platyrrhines that reflects their evolutionary interrelationships, and no consensus has been reached. There is agreement, however, that three distinct clusters can be defined: the callitrichids, the pithecines, and the atelines. The last two groups appear to be closely related and are commonly included together in the family Atelidae. The relationships of the remaining platyrrhines are uncertain, and they are often placed together for convenience in the Cebidae.

All platyrrhines are arboreal, and they are widely distributed throughout tropical forests extending from Mexico to northern Argentina. They are small to medium-sized primates ranging from 100 g to 15 kg (0.2 to 33 lb). Platyrrhines exhibit a variety of quadrupedal locomotor types ranging from squirrellike scrambling, to leaping and forelimb suspension. Atelines and capuchin monkeys are unique among primates in having a specialized prehensile tail that can grasp around branches for extra support.

The catarrhines include all anthropoid primates from Africa, Asia, and Europe. There are two main groups: the cercopithecids or Old World monkeys, and the hominoids or apes and humans. Catarrhines are distinguished from platyrrhines by a reduction in the number of premolars from three to two in each half of the upper and lower jaw, and the development of a tubelike (rather than ringlike) tympanic bone to supports the eardrum.

Old World monkeys are widely distributed throughout sub-Saharan Africa and tropical Asia, and also occur in the extreme southwestern tip of the Arabian Peninsula, northwest Africa, Gibraltar (their only European record), and East Asia. They are a highly successful group comprising more than 80 species. They are distinguished from other anthropoids in having bilophodont molar teeth that bear a pair of transverse crests. They also have naked, roughened sitting pads on their rumps, called ischial callosities—a feature that they share with hylobatids. In addition, most Old World monkeys are highly sexually dimorphic, with males considerably larger than females.

Hominoidea is the superfamily to which apes and humans belong. Hominoids are distinguished from cercopithecoids in having primitive nonbilophodont molars, larger brains, longer arms than legs (except in humans), a broader chest, a shorter and less flexible lower back, and no tail. Many of these specializations relate to a more upright posture in apes, associated with a greater emphasis on vertical climbing and forelimb suspension.

Hominoids can be classified into two families: the Hylobatidae, which includes the gibbons and siamang, and the Hominidae, which includes the great apes and humans. The gibbons and siamang (*Hylobates*) are the smallest of the hominoids (4–11 kg or 9–24 lb), and for this reason they are sometimes referred to as the lesser apes. The nine or so species are common throughout the tropical forests of Asia. They are remarkable in having the longest arms of any primates, which are 30–50% longer than their legs. This is related to their highly specialized mode of locomotion, called brachiation, in which they swing below branches using only their forelimbs. Gibbons are fruit eaters, while the larger siamang incorporates a higher proportion of leaves in its diet. Hylobatids live in monogamous family groups in which males and females are similar in size.

The great apes include the orangutan (*Pongo*) from Asia and the gorilla (*Gorilla*) and chimpanzees (*Pan*) from Africa. These were formerly included together in their own family, the Pongidae, to distinguish them from humans, who were placed in the Hominidae. However, recent anatomical, molecular, and behavioral evidence has confirmed that humans are closely related to the great apes, especially to the African apes, and for this reason most scientists now classify them together in a single family, the Hominidae. The orangutan is restricted to the tropical rainforests of Borneo and northern Sumatra. They are large, arboreal primates that climb cautiously through the trees using all four limbs for support. Orangutans subsist mainly on fruits.

The gorilla, the largest of the hominoids, has a disjunct distribution in tropical Africa. Because of their great size, gorillas are almost entirely terrestrial, although females and young individuals frequently climb trees. Nests are often built on the ground. Gorillas move quadrupedally, and like chimpanzees, the hands are specialized for knuckle walking in which the weight of the animal is borne on the upper surface of the middle joints of the fingers. Mountain gorillas eat a variety of leaves, stems, and roots, while lowland gorillas eat a greater proportion of fruits. Groups consist of a dominant male, called a silverback, as well as several adult females, subadults, and infants.

There are two species of chimpanzees, the common chimpanzee (*Pan troglodytes*) and the bonobo or pygmy chimpanzee (*Pan panicus*). The common chimpanzee is widely distributed in the forests and woodlands stretching across equatorial Africa, while the pygmy chimpanzee is restricted to the tropical rainforests of the Congo. Both species nest and feed in trees, but they mostly travel on the ground. Common chimpanzees have eclectic diets, including meat, which they obtain by hunting small to medium-sized mammals. Tool-using behaviors are common, and more than a dozen simple tool types have been identified. Chimpanzees are gregarious and sociable, and they live in large multimale communities that divide into smaller subgroups for foraging.
See MAMMALIA.   [T.Ha.]

Primitive gut   The tubular structure in embryos which differentiates into the alimentary canal. The method by which the primitive gut arises depends chiefly on the yolk content of the egg.

Eggs with small or moderate amounts of yolk usually develop into spherical blastulae which invaginate at the vegetative pole to form double-walled gastrulae. The invaginated sac extends in length to become the primitive gut.

Animals such as fish, reptiles, and birds, having more yolk than can be cleaved, form flattened gastrulae consisting of three-layered blastoderms surmounting the yolk. Mammals also belong in this group, although the yolk has been lost secondarily in all except the monotremes. The head is formed by a folding of the blastoderm upon itself. The entodermal layer within the head fold becomes the pharynx. This foregut is extended by an anterior growth of the whole head and by the union of lateral entodermal folds at its posterior boundary. In most forms, the hindgut arises by a similar folding in the opposite direction, the tail fold, at the posterior end of the blastoderm. *See* CLEAVAGE (EMBRYOLOGY); GASTRULATION; OVUM   [H.L.Ha.]

Prion disease   Transmissible spongiform encephalopathies in both humans and animals. Scrapie is the most common form in animals, while in humans the most prevalent form is Creutzfeldt-Jakob disease. This group of disorders is characterized at a neuropathological level by vacuolation of the brain's gray matter (spongiform change). They were initially considered to be examples of slow virus infections. Experimental work has consistently failed to demonstrate detectable nucleic acids—both ribonucleic acid (RNA) and deoxyribonucleic acid (DNA)—as constituting part of the infectious agent. Contemporary understanding suggests that the infectious particles are composed predominantly, or perhaps even solely, of protein, and from this concept was derived the acronym prion (proteinaceous infectious particles). Also of interest is the apparent paradox of how these disorders can be simultaneously infectious and yet inherited in an autosomal dominant fashion (from a gene on a chromosome other than a sex chromosome).

Disorders. Scrapie, which occurs naturally in sheep and goats, was the first of the spongiform encephalopathies to be described. An increasing range of animal species have been recognized as occasional natural hosts of this type of disease. Bovine spongioform encephalopathy, commonly known as mad cow disease, has been epidemic in British cattle. The first confirmed cases were reported in late 1986. By early 1995 it had been identified in almost 150,000 cattle and more than half of all British herds. Its exact origin is not known, but claims that it came from sheep are now discredited.

So far, animal models have indicated that only central nervous system tissue has been shown to transmit the disease after oral ingestion—a diverse range of other organs, including udder, skeletal muscle, lymph nodes, liver, and buffy coat of blood (white blood cells) proving noninfectious.

The currently recognized spectrum of human disorders encompasses kuru, Creutzfeldt-Jakob disease, Gerstmann-Straussler-Scheinker disease, and fatal familial insomnia. All, including familial cases, have been shown to be transmissible to animals and hence potentially infectious; all are invariably fatal with no effective treatments currently available.

Human-to-human transmission. A variety of mechanisms of human-to-human transmission have been described. Transmission is due in part to the ineffectiveness of conventional sterilization and disinfection procedures to control the infectivity of transmissible spongiform encephalopathies. Numerically, pituitary hormone–related

Creutzfeldt-Jakob disease is the most important form of human-to-human transmission of disease. However, epidemiological evidence suggests that there is no increased risk of contracting Creutzfeldt-Jakob disease from exposure in the form of close personal contact during domestic and occupational activities. Incubation periods in cases involving human-to-human transmission appear to vary enormously, depending upon the mechanism of inoculation. Current evidence suggests that transmission of Creutzfeldt-Jakob disease from mother to child does not occur. Two important factors pertaining to transmissibility are the method of inoculation and the dose of infectious material administered. A high dose of infectious material administered by direct intracerebral inoculation is clearly the most effective method of transmissibility and generally provides the shortest incubation time. *See* BRAIN; MUTATION; NERVOUS SYSTEM DISORDERS.

[C.L.Mas.; S.J.Co.]

Progesterone   A steroid hormone produced in the corpus luteum and placenta. The hormone has an important physiological role in the luteal phase of the menstrual cycle and in the maintenance of pregnancy. In addition, progesterone produced in the testis and adrenals has a key role as an intermediate in the biosynthesis of androgens, estrogens, and the corticoids (adrenal cortex steroids). *See* ANDROGEN; CHOLESTEROL; ESTROGEN; MENSTRUATION; STEROID; STEROL.   [R.I.D.]

Proprioception   The sense of position and movement of the limbs and the sense of muscular tension. The awareness of the orientation of the body in space and the direction, extent, and rate of movement of the limbs depend in part upon information derived from sensory receptors in the joints, tendons, and muscles. Information from these receptors, called proprioceptors, is normally integrated with that arising from vestibular receptors (which signal gravitational acceleration and changes in velocity of movements of the head), as well as from visual, auditory, and tactile receptors. Sensory information from certain proprioceptors, particularly those in muscles and tendons, need not reach consciousness, but can be used by the motor system as feedback to guide postural adjustments and control of well-practiced or semiautomatic movements such as those involved in walking.

Receptors for proprioception are the endings of peripheral nerve fibers within the capsule or ligaments of the joints or within muscle. These endings are associated with specialized end organs such as Pacinian corpuscles, Ruffini's cylinders, and Golgi organs (the latter resembling histologic Golgi structures in the skin), and muscle spindles. *See* CUTANEOUS SENSATION; SENSATION; SOMESTHESIS.   [R.LaM.]

Prostate gland   A triangular body in men, the size and shape of a chestnut, that lies immediately in front of the bladder with its apex directed down and forward. It is found only in the male, having no female counterpart. The prostatic portion of the urethra extends through it, passing from the bladder to the penis. This organ contains 15–20 branched, tubular glands which form lobules. The gland ducts open into the urethra. Between the gland clusters, or alveoli, there is a dense, fibrous, connecting tissue, the stroma, which also forms a tough capsule around the gland, continuous with the bladder wall. Penetrating the prostate to empty into the urethra are the ejaculatory ducts from the seminal vesicles which are located above and behind the organ (see illustration). The prostatic gland secretes a viscid, alkaline fluid which aids in sperm motility and in neutralizing the acidity of the vagina, thus enhancing fertilization. After

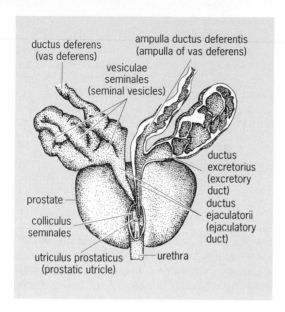

ductus deferens
(vas deferens)

ampulla ductus deferentis
(ampulla of vas deferens)

vesiculae
seminales
(seminal vesicles)

ductus
excretorius
(excretory
duct)

prostate

ductus
ejaculatorii
(ejaculatory
duct)

colliculus
seminales

utriculus prostaticus
(prostatic utricle)

urethra

**Prostate gland and seminal
vesicles. (*After Eycleshymer
and Jones, in W. A. N. Darland,
ed., American Illustrated
Medical Dictionary, 19th ed.,
Saunders, 1942*)**

middle age, the prostate is sometimes subject to new tissue growth, usually benign, that may result in interference with urine flow through the compressed urethra.   [W.J.B.]

Protective coloration   A strategy that organisms use to avoid or deflect the attacks of predators by misleading the latter's visual senses.

Protective coloration can be classified according to whether the functioning or malfunctioning of the vertebrate visual system is exploited. Exploiting the malfunction of the system means simply "not being seen": the prey fails to attract the attention of the predator, usually because it is the same color as the general background or because it fails to cast a shadow. The organism avoids producing shadow by flattening itself against the substrate, or by countershading, in which the lower parts of a cylindrical prey such as a caterpillar are more lightly colored than the upper parts. As shadows normally form on the underside of cylinders, the shading cancels the shadow and makes the caterpillar optically flat. Animals that match their background often have an ability to select the appropriate background to rest on, or much less frequently can change their own color to match (as in the case of the chameleon).

Exploiting the functioning of the vertebrate perceptual system takes many forms. The vertebrate visual cortex decodes the image on the retina in a hierarchical process starting with the detection of edges. A moth may counter this by possessing strikingly contrasted patches of color on its wings, arranged in a random way. The outline of the moth is thus broken up, and the predator cannot decode it as a significant shape. The prey may also exploit the learning capacity of the predator. For example, insectivorous birds see leaves but do not attack them because they have learned (or perhaps know innately) that these are not edible. Resemblances to leaves, twigs, thorns, flowers, parts of flowers, and more bizarre objects like fresh turds (usually bird droppings) are very widespread. This type of camouflage is termed mimetic camouflage. Camouflage in general is often termed cryptic coloration.

Coloration may be considered mimetic if protection is achieved by a resemblance to some other existing object, which is recognized by the predator but not associated in its mind with feeding. Usually this negative or neutral association is learned, but in a minority of instances it is almost certainly innate. Small birds have an innate flight response to large eyes in close-up (which normally indicate that a cat or a predatory bird is dangerously close). This reaction is exploited by many moths and other insects, which have eyelike markings, sometimes very convincing in their shading and highlighting, on concealed parts of the wings. Attack by a bird causes such a moth to change its posture rapidly to reveal the fake eyes, thus frightening away the attacker. Motmots (birds which habitually prey on snakes) have a similar innate fear of the red, black, and yellow striping patterns of the deadly coral snakes. These patterns are mimicked by various nonvenomous snakes, and even some caterpillars.

Flash coloration describes the phenomenon in which the prey is cryptic when at rest, but reveals brilliantly colored parts while escaping. This behavior seems to function simply by startling the predator. Very small eye marks at the tips of the wings, or a false head at the wrong end of the body (shown by some coral reef fish, for example) may cause the predator to misdirect its attack.

Protection through the possession of a chemical or physical defense that is dangerous to one's potential predator, accompanied by a strikingly conspicuous pattern known as warning coloration (often black, red, yellow, and white), is widespread—the ensemble of defense and color is termed aposematic. The actual defense ranges from toxic venoms through stings (in wasps, for example), to the oozing of noxious foams or hemolymph (as in ladybirds), to the possession of toxic chemicals (cyanides, cardiac glycosides, alkaloids) that will poison the predator or simply produce a revolting taste. The function of the warning color is to remind the predator of its previous unpleasant experience.

Sometimes the term mimicry is restricted to resemblances between edible species and actively defended and warningly colored models (as opposed to inedible objects such as thorns). Much is known about the evolution of this kind of mimicry in butterflies (and to a lesser extent, in bees and flies). If the mimic is entirely edible, the relationship is parasitic; the mimic benefits from the resemblance, but as every encounter with a mimic reduces the predator's aversion, the model suffers some increase in the rate of attack. Such mimicry has traditionally been termed Batesian mimicry. Alternatively, the mimic may be almost or fully as defended as the model, leading to a mutualistic relationship known as Müllerian mimicry, in which both the model and the mimic species suffer a decreased rate of predation.   [J.R.G.T.]

Protein   A biological macromolecule made up of various α-amino acids that are joined by peptide bonds. A peptide bond is an amide bond formed by the reaction of an α-amino group ($-NH_2$) of one amino acid with the carboxyl group ($-COOH$) of another, as shown below. Proteins generally contain from 50 to 1000 amino acid residues per polypeptide chain. See PEPTIDE.

Occurrence.   Proteins are of importance in all biological systems, playing a wide variety of structural and functional roles. They form the primary organic basis of structures such as hair, tendons, muscle, skin, and cartilage. All of the enzymes, the catalysts in biochemical transformations, are protein in nature. Many hormones, such as insulin and growth hormone, are proteins. The substances responsible for oxygen and electron transport (hemoglobin and the cytochromes, respectively) are conjugated proteins that contain a metalloporphyrin as the prosthetic group. Chromosomes are highly complex nucleoproteins, that is, proteins conjugated with nucleic acid. Viruses are also nucleoprotein in nature. Of the more than 200 amino acids that have been discovered either in the free state or in small peptides, only 20 amino acids are present in mammalian

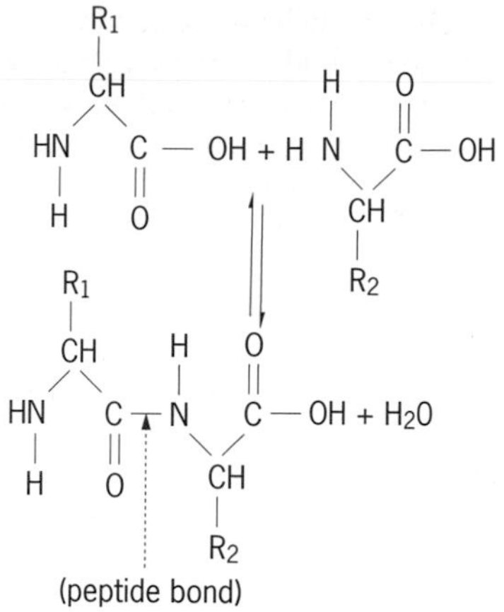

proteins. Thus, proteins play a fundamental role in the processes of life. *See* AMINO ACIDS.

Specificity. The linear arrangement of the amino acid residues in a protein is termed its sequence (primary structure). The sequence in which the different amino acids are linked in any given protein is highly specific and characteristic for that particular protein.

This specificity of sequence is one of the most remarkable aspects of protein chemistry. The number of possible permutations of sequence in even so small a protein as insulin, of molecular weight 5732 and with 51 amino acid residues, is astronomic: 1051 permutations. Yet it has been established that the pancreatic cell of a given species has only one of these possible sequences. The elucidation of the mechanism conferring such a high degree of specificity on the biosynthetic reactions by which proteins are built up from free amino acids has been one of the key problems of modern biochemistry. *See* MOLECULAR BIOLOGY.

Proteins are not stretched polymers; rather, the polypeptide backbone of the molecule can fold in several ways by means of hydrogen bonds between the carbonyl oxygen and the amide nitrogen. The folding of each protein is determined by its particular sequence of amino acids. The long polypeptide chains of proteins, particularly those of the fibrous proteins, are held together in a rather well-defined configuration. The backbone is coiled in a regular fashion, forming an extended helix. As a result of this coiling, peptide bonds separated from one another by several amino acid residues are brought into close spatial approximation. The stability of the helical configuration can be attributed to hydrogen bonds between these peptide bonds.

In addition to hydrogen bonds, there are electrostatic interactions, such as those between COO^- and NH_3^+ groups of the side chains, and van der Waals forces, that is, hydrophobic interactions, which help to determine the configuration of the polypeptide chain. The term secondary structure is used to refer to all those structural features of the polypeptide chain determined by noncovalent bonding interactions.

In addition to the α-helical sections of proteins, there are segments that contain β-structures in which there are hydrogen bonds between two polypeptide chains that run in parallel or antiparallel fashion.

The tertiary structure (third level of folding) of a protein comes about through various interactions between different parts of the molecule. Disulfide bridges formed between cysteine residues at different locations in the molecule can stabilize parts of a three-dimensional structure by introducing a primary valence bond as a cross-link. Hydrogen bonds between different segments of the protein, hydrophobic bonds between nonpolar side chains of amino acids such a phenylalanine and leucine, and salt bridges such as those between positively charged lysyl side chains and negatively charged aspartyl side chains all contribute to the individual tertiary structure of a protein.

Finally, for those proteins that contain more than one polypeptide chain per molecule, there is usually a high degree of interaction between each subunit, for example, between the α- and β-polypeptide chains of hemoglobin. This feature of the protein structure is termed its quarternary structure.

Properties. The properties of proteins are determined in part by their amino acid composition. As macromolecules that contain many side chains that can be protonated and unprotonated depending upon the pH of the medium, proteins are excellent buffers. The fact that the pH of blood varies only very slightly in spite of the numerous metabolic processes in which it participates is due to the very large buffering capacity of the blood proteins.

Biosynthesis. The processes by which proteins are synthesized biologically have become one of the central themes of molecular biology. The sequence of amino acid residues in a protein is controlled by the sequence of the DNA as expressed in messenger RNA at ribosomes. See DEOXYRIBONUCLEIC ACID (DNA); RIBONUCLEIC ACID (RNA); RIBOSOMES. [G.E.Pe.; J.M.Ma.]

Degradation. As with many other macromolecular components of the organism, most body proteins are in a dynamic state of synthesis and degradation (proteolysis). During proteolysis, the peptide bond that links the amino acids to each other is hydrolyzed, and free amino acids are released. The process is carried out by a diverse group of enzymes called proteases. During proteolysis, the energy invested in generation of the proteins is released. See ENZYME.

Distinct proteolytic mechanisms serve different physiological requirements. Proteins can be divided into extracellular and intracellular, and the two groups are degraded by two distinct mechanisms. Extracellular proteins such as the plasma immunoglobulins and albumin are degraded in a process known as receptor-mediated endocytosis. Ubiquitin-mediated proteolysis of a variety of cellular proteins plays an important role in many basic cellular processes such as the regulation of cell cycle and division, differentiation, and development; DNA repair; regulation of the immune and inflammatory responses; and biogenesis of organelles. [A.J.Ci.]

Molecular chaperones. Molecular chaperones are specialized cellular proteins that bind nonnative forms of other proteins and assist them to reach a functional conformation. The role of chaperone proteins under conditions of stress, such as heat shock, is to protect proteins by binding to misfolded conformations when they are just starting to form, preventing aggregation; then, following return of normal conditions, they allow refolding to occur. Chaperones also play essential roles in folding under normal conditions, providing kinetic assistance to the folding process, and thus improving the overall rate and extent of productive folding. [A.Ho.]

Protein engineering. The amino acid sequences, sizes, and three-dimensional conformations of protein molecules can be manipulated by protein engineering, in which the basic techniques of genetic engineering are used to alter the genes that encode proteins. These manipulations are used to generate proteins with novel activities or properties for specific applications, to discover structure-function relationships, and to generate biologically active minimalist proteins (containing only those sequences necessary for biological activity) that are smaller than their naturally occurring counterparts.

Many subtle variations in a particular protein can be generated by making amino acid replacements at specific positions in the polypeptide sequence. For example, at any specific position an amino acid can be replaced by another to generate a mutant protein that may have different characteristics by virtue of the single replaced amino acid. Amino acids can also be deleted from a protein sequence, either individually or in groups. These proteins are referred to as deletion mutants. Deletion mutants may or may not be missing one or more functions or properties of the full, naturally occurring protein. Moreover, part or all of a protein sequence can be joined or fused to that of another protein. The resulting protein is called a hybrid or fusion protein, which generally has characteristics that combine those of each of the joined partners.   [P.Sc.]

Protein metabolism   The transformation and fate of food proteins from their ingestion to the elimination of their excretion products. Proteins are of exceptional importance to organisms because they are the chief constituents, aside from water, of all the soft tissue of the body. Special proteins have unique roles as structural and functional elements of cells and tissues. Examples are keratin of skin, collagen of tendons, actin and myosin of muscle, the blood proteins, enzymes in all tissues, and protein hormones of the hypophysis. *See* BLOOD; ENZYME; HORMONE; MUSCLE.

Isotopic labeling experiments have established that body proteins are in a dynamic state, constantly being broken down and replaced. This is a rapid process in organs active in metabolism, such as liver, kidney, intestinal mucosa, and pancreas, much slower in skeletal muscle, and extremely slow in connective tissue elements and skin.

Protein is digested to amino acids in the gastrointestinal tract. These are absorbed and distributed among the different tissues, where they form a series of amino acid pools that are kept equilibrated with each other through the medium of the circulating blood. The needs for protein synthesis of the different organs are supplied from these pools. Excess amino acids in the tissue pools lose their nitrogen by a combination of transamination and deamination. The nitrogen is largely converted to urea and excreted in the urine. The residual carbon products are then further metabolized by pathways common to the other major foodstuffs—carbohydrates and fats. *See* CARBOHYDRATE; LIPID.

Ingestion of protein is needed primarily to supply amino acids for the formation of new and depleted body protein and as a source of various other body constituents derived from the amino acids. The amino acids of proteins fall into two nutritional categories: essential or indispensable, and nonessential or dispensable. For a number of amino acids, the category to which they belong changes between the periods of body growth and adulthood and changes also in different animal species. Eight essential amino acids are needed for maintenance of nitrogen equilibrium in healthy young men. The remaining amino acids can be formed in the body from other materials. *See* AMINO ACIDS.

Protein digestion occurs to a limited extent in the stomach and is completed in the duodenum of the small intestine. The main proteolytic enzyme of the stomach is pepsin, which is secreted in an inactive form, pepsinogen. Its transformation to the active pepsin, initiated by the acidity of the gastric juice, involves liberation of a portion of the pepsinogen molecule as a peptide. Pepsin preferentially hydrolyzes peptide bonds containing an aromatic amino acid, and it requires an acid medium to function. *See* DIGESTIVE SYSTEM.

The acid chyme is discharged from the stomach, containing partially degraded proteins, into a slightly alkaline fluid in the small intestine. This fluid is composed of pancreatic juice and succus entericus, the intestinal secretion. The pancreas secretes three known proteinases, trypsin, chymotrypsin, and carboxypeptidase. All three are secreted as inactive zymogens. Activation starts with the transformation of the inactive trypsinogen into the active trypsin. Trypsin, in turn, activates chymotrypsin and carboxypeptidase. *See* PEPTIDE.

Trypsin and chymotrypsin are endopeptidases; that is, they cleave internal peptide bonds. The so-called peptidases are exopeptidases; they cleave terminal peptide bonds. Trypsin has a predilection for those containing the basic amino acid residues of lysine and arginine. These two proteinases perform the major share in hydrolyzing proteins to small peptides. Digestion to amino acids is completed by the exopeptidases. Carboxypeptidase acts on peptides from the free carboxyl end; aminopeptidases from the free amino end. Other peptidases act on di- or tripeptides, or peptides containing such special amino acids as proline.

The amino acid digestion products of the proteins are absorbed by the small intestine as rapidly as they are liberated. The absorbed amino acids are carried by the portal blood system to the liver, from which they are distributed to the rest of the body. Small amounts of the peptides formed during digestion escape further hydrolysis and may also enter the circulation from the intestine. This is shown by a rise in the peptide nitrogen in the blood.

The unabsorbed food residue in the small intestine is passed into the cecum, then the colon, and finally is eliminated as feces.

The absorbed amino acids that escape decomposition become part of the amino acid pools of the body. From these amino acids, new tissue proteins are synthesized to meet body needs. The rate of tissue replacement varies greatly for different tissues. In humans, it has been estimated that the average half-life of the total body protein is 80 days; that of lung, brain, bone, skin, and most muscle combined is 158 days; while that of liver and serum proteins combined is only 10 days.

The major organ of plasma protein synthesis is the liver. It forms all of the plasma albumin and fibrinogen and a considerable proportion of the globulins. (A portion of the total plasma globulin is synthesized in other tissues containing reticuloendothelial cells. The hormones and enzymes present in blood plasma are derived in the main from nonhepatic sources.) *See* ALBUMIN; FIBRINOGEN; LIVER.

The plasma proteins have numerous important physiological functions. The albumin is the major factor in the regulation of the blood volume through its osmotic action, which counteracts the fluid expulsion effect of the hydrostatic pressure resulting from the contractions of the heart. Fibrinogen is one component of a sequential process essential for coagulation of the blood. Other plasma components include the blood platelets and prothrombin. The globulins include fractions that are carriers of phospholipids and sterols and certain essential metal ions, iron, and copper. Other fractions, chiefly γ-globulin, contain the antibodies that are the defenses against numerous diseases.

Synthesis and utilization of the plasma proteins is a rapid process. There is a complete turnover of the major plasma proteins in a period of a few days. The difference from normal in the turnover times in a variety of diseases provides an insight into the nature of the disease processes.   [D.M.G.]

Proteins, evolution of Proteins are large organic molecules that are involved in all aspects of cell structure and function. They are made up of polypeptide chains, each constructed from a basic set of 20 amino acids, covalently linked in specific sequences. Each amino acid is coded by three successive nucleotide residues in deoxyribonucleic acid (DNA); the sequence of amino acids in a polypeptide chain, which determines the structure and function of the protein molecule, is thus specified by a sequence of nucleotide residues in DNA. *See* GENE; PROTEIN.

Sequence analyses of polypeptides which are shared by diverse taxonomic groups have provided considerable information regarding the genetic events that have accompanied speciation. Interspecies comparison of the amino acid sequences of functionally similar proteins has been used to estimate the amount of genetic similarity between species; species that are genetically more similar to each other are considered to be evolutionarily more closely related than those that are genetically less similar.

The study of functionally related proteins from different animal species has suggested that single amino acid substitutions are the predominant type of change during evolution of such proteins. Insertions or deletions of one or more amino acids have also been reported. In proteins that serve the same function in dissimilar species small differences in the amino acid sequence will often not affect overall functioning of the protein molecule.

In taxonomic protein sequence analysis, the amino acid sequence of a protein from one species is compared with the amino acid sequence of the protein from another species, and the minimum number of nucleotide replacements (in DNA) required to shift from one amino acid to another is calculated. Peptide "genealogies" can be constructed from many such comparisons in a related group of organisms.

Classical versus protein-derived phylogenies. It has been recognized for a long time that the amino acid sequences of a protein are species-specific. Protein sequencing has been used widely since the mid-1960s to examine taxonomic relationships. Results indicate that, in general, genealogical relationships (phylogenies) based on sequence analyses correspond fairly well with the phylogeny of organisms as deduced from more classical methods involving morphological and paleontological data.

Evolutionary biologists are turning increasingly to the new nucleic acid sequencing technology as an alternative to determining the amino acid sequence of proteins. Knowing the actual nucleotide sequences of genes rather than having to infer them from protein sequence data allows more accurate data to be used in determining genealogical relationships of organisms. For example, silent nucleotide substitutions (that is, base changes in DNA codons that do not result in amino acid changes) can be detected.

Orthologous and paralogous sequences. The reconstruction of phylogenies from analysis of protein sequences is based on the assumption that the genes coding for the proteins are homologous, that is, descendants of a common ancestor. Those sequences whose evolutionary history reflects that of the species in which they are found are referred to as orthologous. The cytochrome c molecules (present in all eukaryotes) are an example of an orthologous gene family. Organisms as diverse as humans and yeast have a large proportion of the amino acids in these molecules in common; they derive from a single ancestral gene present in a species ancestral to both these organisms and to numerous others.

Sequences which are descendants of an ancestral gene that has duplicated are referred to as paralogous. Paralogous genes evolve independently within each species. The genes coding for the human α, β, γ, δ, ϵ, and ζ hemoglobin chains are paralogous. Their evolution reflects the changes that have accumulated since these genes duplicated. Analysis of paralogous genes in a species serves to construct gene phylogenies, that is, the evolutionary history of duplicated genes within a given lineage.

Rate of evolution. Sequence data from numerous proteins have shown that different proteins evolve at different rates. Some proteins show fewer amino acid substitutions, or more conservation, than others. Proteins such as immunoglobulins, snake venom toxins, and albumins have changed extensively. Their function apparently requires relatively less specificity of structure and therefore has relatively greater tolerance for variance. By contrast, certain proteins, such as various histones, have changed relatively little over long periods of time. Histone H4 shows extreme conservation; it has essentially the same sequence in all eukaryotes examined. Such extensive sequence conservation is generally interpreted to indicate that the functions of H4 are extremely dependent on its entire structure; thus little or no change is tolerated in its structure.

The rates at which different proteins evolve are therefore thought to be due to different functional constraints on the structure of the proteins—the more stringent the conditions that determine the function of a protein molecule, the smaller the chance that a random change will be tolerated in its structure.

Each protein generally has a nearly constant evolutionary rate (the rate of acceptance of mutations) in each line of descent. Exceptions to this rule have been reported, however, and much effort has been spent on determining whether these anomalies are genuine. Some anomalies have been shown to be due to comparison of nonhomologous proteins, and others due to sequencing errors. Other deviations from constant rate of sequence evolution remain to be explained; once uncovered, these may provide useful information about the mechanisms of evolution at the molecular level.

[P.K.M.]

Protista   The kingdom comprising all single-celled forms of living organisms in both the five-kingdom and six-kingdom systems of classification. Kingdom Protista encompasses both Protozoa and Protophyta, allowing considerable integration in the classification of both these animallike and plantlike organisms, all of whose living functions as individuals are carried out within a single cell membrane. Among the kingdoms of cellular organisms, this definition can be used to distinguish the Protista from the Metazoa (sometimes named Animalia) for many-celled animals, or from the Fungi and from the Metaphyta (or Plantae) for many-celled green plants. See METAZOA.

The most significant biological distinction is that which separates the bacteria and certain other simply organized organisms, including blue-green algae (collectively, often designated Kingdom Monera), from both Protista and all many-celled organisms. The bacteria are described as prokaryotic; both the Protista and the cells of higher plants and animals are eukaryotic. Structurally, a distinguishing feature is the presence of a membrane, closely similar to the bounding cell membrane, surrounding the nuclear material in eukaryotic cells, but not in prokaryotic ones. See EUKARYOTAE; PROTOZOA.

The definition that can separate the Protista from many-celled animals is that the protistan body never has any specialized parts of the cytoplasm under the sole control of a nucleus. In some protozoa, there can be two, a few, or even many nuclei, rather than one, but no single nucleus ever has separate control over any part of the protistan cytoplasm which is specialized for a particular function. In contrast, in metazoans there are always many cases of nuclei, each in control of cells of specialized function.

Most authorities would agree that the higher plants, the Metazoa, and the Parazoa (or sponges) almost certainly evolved (each independently) from certain flagellate stocks of protistans.

[W.D.R.H.]

Prototheria   One of the four subclasses of the class Mammalia. Prototheria contains a single order, the Monotremata. No ancestral genera of fossil monotremes are known, and the structure of the living monotremes is so specialized that the affinities of the Prototheria are largely conjectural. Most mammalogists believe that the prototheres arose from a different stock of therapsid reptiles than the one that gave rise to the Theria.

No fossils earlier than the Pleistocene are known, and these come from Australia. The duckbilled platypus and several species of the echidnas are living representatives of this group. Everything indicates that the Prototheria represent a very small and relatively unsuccessful group that has miraculously survived in an isolated corner of the Earth. See MAMMALIA; MONOTREMATA.

[D.D.D.; F.S.S.]

Protozoa   A group of eukaryotic microorganisms traditionally classified in the animal kingdom. Although the name signifies primitive animals, some Protozoa (phytoflagellates and slime molds) show enough plantlike characteristics to justify claims that they are plants.

Protozoa are almost as widely distributed as bacteria. Free-living types occur in soil, wet sand, and in fresh, brackish, and salt waters. Protozoa of the soil and sand live in films of moisture on the particles. Habitats of endoparasites vary. Some are intracellular, such as malarial parasites in vertebrates, which are typical Coccidia in most of the cycle. Other parasites, such as *Entamoeba histolytica*, invade tissues but not individual cells. Most trypanosomes live in the blood plasma of vertebrate hosts. Many other parasites live in the lumen of the digestive tract or sometimes in coelomic cavities of invertebrates, as do certain gregarines.

Many Protozoa are uninucleate, others are binucleate or multinucleate, and the number of nuclei also may vary at different stages in a life cycle. Protozoa range in size from 1 to 10^6 micrometers. Colonies are known in flagellates, ciliates, and Sarcodina. Although marked differentiation of the reproductive and somatic zooids characterizes certain colonies, such as *Volvox*, Protozoa have not developed tissues and organs.

Morphology. A protozoan may be a plastic organism (ameboid type), but changes in form are often restricted by the pellicle. A protective layer is often secreted outside the pellicle, although the pellicle itself may be strengthened by incorporation of minerals. Secreted coverings may fit closely, for example, the cellulose-containing theca of Phytomonadida and Dinoflagellida, analogous to the cell wall in higher plants. The dinoflagellate theca (Fig. 1*a*) may be composed of plates arranged in a specific pattern. Tests, as seen in Rhizopodea (Arcellinida, Gromiida, Foraminiferida), may be composed mostly of inorganic material, although organic (chitinous) tests occur in certain species. Siliceous skeletons, often elaborate, characterize the Radiolaria (Figs. 1*d* and 2*c*). A vase-shaped lorica, from which the anterior part of the organism or its appendages may be extended, occurs in certain flagellates (Fig. 1*b*) and ciliates (Fig. 1*c*). Certain marine ciliates (Tintinnida) are actively swimming loricate forms.

Flagella occur in active stages of Mastigophora and flagellated stages of certain Sarcodina and Sporozoa. A flagellum consists of a sheath enclosing a matrix in which an axoneme extends from the cytoplasm to the flagellar tip. In certain groups the sheath shows lateral fibrils (mastigonemes) which increase the surface area and also may modify direction of the thrust effecting locomotion. Although typically shorter than flagella, cilia are similar in structure. *See* CILIA AND FLAGELLA.

Two major types of pseudopodia have been described, the contraction-hydraulic and the two-way flow types. The first are lobopodia with rounded tips and ectoplasm denser than endoplasm. The larger ones commonly contain granular endoplasm and clear ectoplasm. Two-way flow pseudopodia include reticulopodia of Foraminiferida and related types, filoreticulopodia of Radiolaria, and axopodia of certain Heliozoia.

In addition to nuclei, food vacuoles (gastrioles) in phagotrophs, chromatophores and stigma in many phytoflagellates, water-elimination vesicles in many Protozoa, and sometimes other organelles, the cytoplasm may contain mitochondria, Golgi material, pinocytotic vacuoles, stored food materials, endoplasmic reticulum, and sometimes pigments of various kinds.

Nutrition. In protozoan feeding, either phagotrophic (holozoic) or saprozoic (osmotrophic) methods predominate in particular species. In addition, chlorophyll-bearing flagellates profit from photosynthesis; in fact, certain species have not been grown in darkness and may be obligate phototrophs.

Phagotrophic ingestion of food, followed by digestion in vacuoles, is characteristic of Sarcodina, ciliates, and many flagellates. Digestion follows synthesis of appropriate

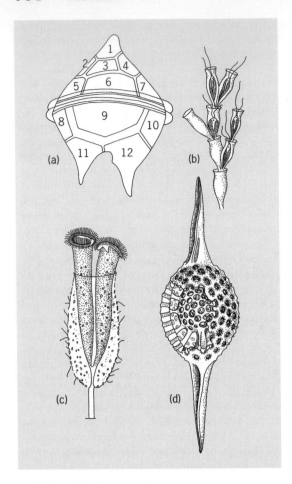

Fig. 1. External coverings of Protozoa. (*a*) Theca of dinoflagellate (*Peridinium*), showing separate plates. (*b*) Lorica of a colonial chrysomonad, *Dinobryon*. (*c*) Two zooids within a lorica of a peritrich, *Cothurnia*. (*d*) A radiolarian skeleton, siliceous type. (*After L. H. Hyman, The Invertebrates, vol. 1, McGraw-Hill, 1940*)

enzymes and their transportation to the food vacuole. Details of ingestion vary. Formation of food cups, or gulletlike invaginations to enclose prey, is common in more or less ameboid organisms, such as various Sarcodina, many flagellates, and at least a few Sporozoa. Entrapment in a sticky reticulopodial net occurs in Foraminiferida and certain other Sarcodina. A persistent cytostome and gullet are involved in phagotrophic ciliates and a few flagellates. Many ciliates have buccal organelles (membranes, membranelies, and closely set rows of cilia) arranged to drive particles to the cytostome. Particles pass through the cytostome into the cytopharynx (gullet), at the base of which food vacuoles (gastrioles) are formed. Digestion occurs in such vacuoles.

By definition saprozoic feeding involves passage of dissolved foods through the cortex. It is uncertain to what extent diffusion is responsible, but enzymatic activities presumably are involved in uptake of various simple sugars, acetate and butyrate. In addition, external factors, for example, the pH of the medium, may strongly influence uptake of fatty acids and phosphates.

Reproduction. Reproduction occurs after a period of growth which ranges, in different species, from less than half a day to several months (certain Foraminiferida). General methods include binary fission, budding, plasmotomy, and schizogony. Fission, involving nuclear division and replication of organelles, yields two organisms

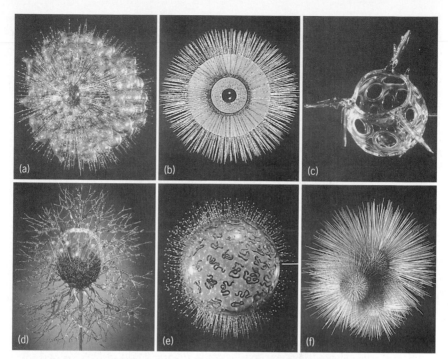

Fig. 2. Glass models of marine Protozoa. Radiolarian types: (*a*) *Trypanosphaera transformata* Haeckel (Indian Ocean); (*b*) *Actissa princeps* Haeckel (Indian and Pacific oceans); (*c*) *Peridium spinipes* Haeckel (Pacific Ocean); (*d*) *Lithocircus magnificus* Haeckel (Atlantic Ocean); (*e*) *Collozoum serpentinum* Haeckel (Atlantic Ocean). (*f*) Foraminiferan type: the pelagic *Globigerina bulloides* d'Orbigny (which is found in all seas). (*American Museum of Natural History*)

similar in size. Budding produces two organisms, one smaller than the other. In plasmotomy, a multinucleate organism divides into several, each containing a number of nuclei. Schizogony, characteristic of Sporozoa, follows repeated nuclear division, yielding many uninucleate buds.

Simple life cycles include a cyst and an active (trophic) stage undergoing growth and reproduction. In certain free-living and parasitic species, no cyst is developed. Dimorphic cycles show two active stages; polymorphic show several. The former include adult and larva (Suctoria); flagellate and ameba (certain Mastigophora and Sarcodina); flagellate and palmella (nonflagellated; certain Phytomonadida); and ameba and plasmodium (Mycetozoia especially).

Parasitic protozoa. Parasites occur in all major groups. Sporozoa are exclusively parasitic, as are some flagellate orders (Trichomonadida, Hypermastigida, and Oxymonadida), the Opalinata, Piroplasmea, and several ciliate orders (Apostomatida, Astomatida, and Entodiniomorphida). Various other groups contain both parasitic and free-living types. Protozoa also serve as hosts of other protozoa, certain bacteria, fungi, and algae.

Relatively few parasites are distinctly pathogenic, causing amebiasis, visceral leishmaniasis (kala azar), sleeping sickness, Chagas' disease, malaria, tick fever of cattle, dourine of horses, and other diseases. *See* CILIOPHORA; SARCOMASTIGOPHORA; SPOROZOA.   [R.P.H.]

Pseudomonas   A genus of gram-negative, nonsporeforming, rod-shaped bacteria. Motile species possess polar flagella. They are strictly aerobic, but some members do respire anaerobically in the presence of nitrate. Some species produce acids oxidatively from carbohydrates; none is fermentative and none photosynthetic.

Members of the genus *Pseudomonas* cause a variety of infective diseases; some species cause disease of plants. One species, *P. mallei*, is a mammalian parasite, and is the causative agent of glanders, an infectious disease of horses that occasionally is transmitted to humans by direct contact. *Pseudomonas aeruginosa* is the most significant cause of hospital-acquired infections, particularly in predisposed patients with metabolic, hematologic, and malignant diseases. The spectrum of clinical disease ranges from urinary tract infections to septicemia, pneumonia, meningitis, and infections of postsurgical and posttraumatic wounds. *See* MENINGITIS; PNEUMONIA.

[G.L.Gi.]

Psychoacoustics   All of the psychological interactions between humans (and animals) and the world of sound. It encompasses all studies of the perception of sound, as well as the production of speech. *See* HEARING (HUMAN); SPEECH.   [L.E.M.]

Psychoanalysis   Psychoanalysis may be defined as (1) a psychological theory; (2) a form of psychotherapy, especially for the treatment of neurotic and character or personality disorders; and (3) a method for investigating psychological phenomena. Psychoanalysis was created and developed by Sigmund Freud, who presented his method, clinical observations, and theory in *Interpretation of Dreams* and other major works, including *The Psychopathology of Everyday Life* and *Three Essays on the Theory of Sexuality*, as well as in many of his case studies.

Psychoanalytic theory. Generally, psychoanalysis is concerned with the causal role of wishes and beliefs in human life. More specifically, it attempts to explain mental or behavioral phenomena that do not appear to make sense as the effects of unconscious wishes and beliefs. Such phenomena include dreams, disturbances in functioning such as slips of the tongue or pen and transient forgetting, and neurotic symptoms. Typically, unconscious wishes and beliefs are constituents of conflicts.

The term unconscious in psychoanalysis does not mean simply that mental contents are out of awareness. Its psychodynamic meaning is that the person does not want to be aware of these contents, and takes active steps to avoid being aware of them. A fundamental hypothesis of psychoanalysis is that because a mental entity is dynamically unconscious it has the causal power to produce the phenomena that are of interest to psychoanalysis.

At first, the dynamic unconscious was thought to consist of traumatic memories. Later, it was believed to consist of impulses or wishes—especially sexual (and aggressive) impulses or wishes. Psychoanalysis now emphasizes that the dynamic unconscious consists of fantasies, which have a history reaching back to childhood. These fantasies are internal scenarios in which sexual (and aggressive) wishes are imagined as fulfilled.

Psychoanalysis is distinct in attributing causal powers to unconscious sexual wishes. Such attribution depends on extending the meaning of sexual to encompass the quest for sensual pleasure in childhood (so-called infantile sexuality) and choices of objects and aims. One theme that is thought to have particular importance is the Oedipus complex, in which the child rivals one parent in seeking sensual gratifications of various kinds from the other parent.

When an unconscious fantasy is activated, it manifests itself in conscious mental states or in actions—importantly, in emotions; in interpretations of the significance of events or states of affairs; in attributions of motives to others; and in daydreams, dreams, and neurotic symptoms.

Unconscious fantasies, as distinct from both conscious reality-oriented imagining and conscious day-dreaming, are constructed when imagination functions under very special conditions.

This emphasis on fantasy underscores the fact that psychoanalysis gives priority to the relation between wishes (including wishes a person knows could not conceivably be gratified in reality) and imagination (functioning under very special conditions).

Psychotherapy. Free association is the method of psychoanalysis. Patients are encouraged not to talk about some particular problem or aspect of their lives but rather to suspend any conscious purposive organization of what they say, speaking freely. Both psychoanalyst and patient follow the patient's productions: conscious purposes are replaced by unconscious purposes, which, under these conditions, can determine the direction of the patient's mental processes with less interference.

Interventions are predominantly interpretative; psychoanalysts do not seek primarily to tell their patients what to do, to educate them about the world, to influence their values, or to reassure them in one way or another that everything is or will be all right. Psychoanalysts look for patterns in what each patient says and for signs of feelings of which the patient is more or less unaware. They then engage their patients (who are increasingly aware of these patterns and able to experience and articulate these feelings) in an inquiry about the reasons for them or motives behind them. The focus is on what the patients do not know—and do not want to know—about themselves and their inner life, including strategies for avoiding such knowledge and the consequences of these strategies.

The goal of psychoanalytic psychotherapy is to extend the realm of what patients permit themselves to experience. It tries to mitigate the misery that patients with a neurotic, character, or personality disorder inflict on themselves.

The case-study method is characteristic of psychoanalytic research. The arguments that can be used in case studies are analogy (the use of familiar or homely models in which postulated causes and mechanisms can be shown to exist); consilience (the convergence of inferences from different kinds of information on a common cause); and abduction (inference to the best explanation). *See* PSYCHOTHERAPY.   [M.Ed.]

Psycholinguistics   An area of study which draws from linguistics and psychology and focuses upon the comprehension and production of language. Although psychologists have long been interested in language, and the field of linguistics is an older science than psychology, scientists in the two fields have had little contact until the work of Noam Chomsky was published in the late 1950s. Chomsky's writing had the effect of making psychologists acutely aware of their lack of knowledge about the structure of language, and the futility of focusing attention exclusively upon the surface structure of language. As a result, psycholinguists, who have a background of training in both linguistics and psychology, have been attempting since the early 1960s to gain a better understanding of how the abstract rules which determine human language are acquired and used to communicate appropriately created meaningful messages from one person to another via the vocal-auditory medium. Research has been directed to the evolutionary development of language, the biological bases of language, the nature of the sound system, the rules of syntax, the nature of meaning, and the process of language acquisition.   [D.S.P.]

Psychology   The study of human behavior and mental processes. Psychology is sharply divided into applied and experimental areas. However, many fields are represented in both research and applied psychology.

Researchers in psychology study a wide range of areas. Cognitive research is often included as part of subdiscipline called cognitive science. This area examines central issues such as how mental process work, the relation between mind and brain, and the way in which biological transducing systems can convert physical regularities into perceptions of the world. Cognitive science is carved from the common ground shared by computer science, cognitive psychology, philosophy of mind, linguistics, neuropsychology, and cognitive anthropology. The study of human attention is a cognitive area that is central in the field. *See* COGNITION.

The study of consciousness involves such basic questions as the physiological basis of mental activity, the freedom of will, and the conscious and unconscious uses of memory. The latter topic can be classified under the rubric of implicit memory. *See* INSTINCTIVE BEHAVIOR; MEMORY; PSYCHOLINGUISTICS; SENSATION.

Social psychology includes the study of interactions between individuals and groups, as well as the effects of groups on the attitudes, opinions, and behavior of individuals. The field covers such topics as persuasion, conformity, obedience to authority, stereotyping, prejudice, and decision making in social contexts. *See* MOTIVATION; PERSONALITY THEORY.

Developmental psychology has three subfields: life-span development, child development, and aging. Most research in the area concentrates on child development, which examines the development of abilities, personality, social relations, and, essentially, every attribute and ability seen in adults. *See* INTELLIGENCE.

A clinical psychologist is usually known by the term psychologist, which in some states is a term that can be used only by a registered practitioner. A psychiatrist is a physician with a specialty in psychiatric treatment and, in most states, with certification as a psychiatrist by a board of medical examiners. A psychoanalyst is typically trained by a psychoanalytic institute in a version of the Freudian method of psychoanalysis. A large number of practitioners qualify both as psychoanalysts and psychiatrists. *See* PSYCHOANALYSIS.

Neuropsychologists are usually psychologists, who may come from an experimental or a clinical background but who must go through certification as psychologists. They treat individuals who have psychological disorders with a clear neurological etiology, such as stroke.

Clinical practice includes individual consultation with clients, group therapy, and work in clinics or with teams of health professionals. Psychological therapists work in many settings and on problems ranging from short-term crises and substance abuse, to psychosis and major disorders. While there are definite biases within each field, it is possible for a practitioner with any background to prefer behavior therapy, a humanistic approach, a Freudian (dynamic) approach, or an eclectic approach derived from these and other areas.

Nonclinical professional work in psychology includes the human-factors element, which traditionally is applied to the design of the interface between a machine and its human operator. Cognitive engineering is a branch of applied psychology that deals mainly with software and hardware computer design. Industrial psychology also includes personnel selection and management and organizational planning and consulting.

The use of psychology in forensic matters is a natural result of the fact that much of law is based on psychology. Psychologists have been involved in jury selection, organization of evidence, evaluation of eyewitness testimony, and presentation of material in court cases. Psychiatrists and psychologists are also called on to diagnose potential defendants for mental disorders and the ability to stand trial. [W.P.B.]

Psychoneuroimmunology   The study of the interactions among behavioral, neural and endocrine, and immune functions. This convergence of disciplines has evolved to achieve a more complete understanding of adaptive processes. At one time, the immune system was considered an independent agency of defense that protected the organism against foreign material (that is, proteins that were not part of one's "self"). Indeed, the immune system is capable of considerable self-regulation. However, converging data from the behavioral and brain sciences indicate that the brain plays a critical role in the regulation or modulation of immunity. Thus, psychoneuroimmunology emphasizes the study of the functional significance of the relationship between these systems—not in place of, but in addition to, the more traditional analysis of the mechanisms governing the functions within a single system—and the significance of these interactions for health and disease. See NEUROIMMUNOLOGY.

Brain–immune system interactions. Evidence for nervous system–immune system interactions exists at several biological levels. Primary and secondary lymphoid organs are innervated by the sympathetic nervous system, and lymphoid cells bear receptors for many hormones and neurotransmitters. These substances, secreted by the pituitary gland, are thus able to influence lymphocyte function. Moreover, lymphocytes themselves can produce neuropeptide substances. Thus, there are anatomical and neurochemical channels of communication that provide a structural foundation for the several observations of functional relationships between the nervous and immune systems.

Stress and immunity. The link between behavior and immune function is suggested by experimental and clinical observations of a relationship between psychosocial factors, including stress, and susceptibility to or progression of disease processes that involve immunologic mechanisms. Abundant data document an association between stressful life experiences and changes in immunologic reactivity. The death of a family member and other, less severe, stressful experiences (such as taking examinations) result in transient impairments in several parameters of immune function. See STRESS (PSYCHOLOGY).

In animals, a variety of stressors can influence a variety of immune responses. Since immune responses are themselves capable of altering levels of circulating hormones and neurotransmitters, these interactions probably include complex feedback and feedforward mechanisms. See ENDOCRINOLOGY.

The direction, magnitude, and duration of stress-induced alterations of immunity are influenced by (1) the quality and quantity of stressful stimulation; (2) the capacity of the individual to cope effectively with stressful events; (3) the quality and quantity of immunogenic stimulation; (4) the temporal relationship between stressful stimulation and immunogenic stimulation; (5) the sampling times and the particular aspect of immune function chosen for measurement; (6) the experiential history of the individual and the existing social and environmental conditions upon which stressful and immunogenic stimulation are superimposed; (7) a variety of host factors such as species, strain, age, sex, and nutritional state; and (8) interactions among these variables.

Conditioning. Central nervous system involvement in the modulation of immunity is dramatically illustrated by the classical (Pavlovian) conditioning of the acquisition and extinction of suppressed and enhanced antibody- and cell-mediated immune responses. In a one-trial taste-aversion conditioning situation, a distinctively flavored drinking solution (the conditioned stimulus) was paired with an injection of the immunosuppressive drug cyclophosphamide (the unconditioned stimulus). When subsequently immunized with sheep red blood cells, conditioned animals reexposed to the conditioned stimulus showed a reduced antibody response compared to nonconditioned animals and conditioned animals that were not reexposed to the conditioned stimulus. *See* CONDITIONED REFLEX.

The acquisition and the extinction (elimination of the conditioned response by exposures to the conditioned stimulus without the unconditioned stimulus) of the conditioned enhancement and suppression of both antibody- and cell-mediated immune responses—and nonimmunologically specific host defense responses as well—have been demonstrated under a variety of experimental conditions.

Prospects. An elaboration of the integrative nature of neural, endocrine, and immune processes and the mechanisms underlying behaviorally induced alterations of immune function is likely to have clinical and therapeutic implications that will not be fully appreciated until more is known about the extent of these interrelationships in normal and pathophysiological states. *See* ENDOCRINE SYSTEM (VERTEBRATE); IMMUNOLOGY; NERVOUS SYSTEM (VERTEBRATE). [R.Ad.]

Psychopharmacology   A discipline that merges the subject matter of psychology, which studies cognition, emotion, and behavior, and pharmacology, which characterizes different drugs. Thus, psychopharmacology focuses on characterizing drugs that affect thinking, feeling, and action. In addition, psychopharmacology places particular emphasis on those drugs that affect abnormalities in thought, affect, and behavior, and thus has a relationship to psychiatry. Psychopharmacology is predominantly, but not exclusively, concerned with four major classes of drugs that are of clinical significance in controlling four major categories of psychiatric disorder: anxiety, depression, mania, and schizophrenia.

Anxiety is an emotional state that can range in intensity from mild apprehension and nervousness to intense fear and even terror. It has been estimated that 2–4% of the general population suffer from an anxiety disorder at some time. Although anxiety in some form is a common experience, it can become so intense and pervasive as to be debilitating; it may therefore require psychiatric attention and treatment with an anxiolytic drug. There are three major groups of anxiolytics. Members of the first group are called propanediols; meprobamate is the most widely used. The second group is the barbiturates, of which phenobarbital is the most generally prescribed. The third group, most frequently prescribed, is the benzodiazepines, the best known of which is diazepam.

A major advance in understanding the benzodiazepines was the identification of the cellular sites at which these drugs act (so-called benzodiazepine receptors). The distribution of these receptors in the brain has also been found to have a striking parallel to the distribution of the receptors for a naturally occurring substance called gamma-amino butyric acid (GABA). Furthermore, it is known that GABA has a ubiquitous inhibitory role in modulating brain function. Most importantly, it is now clear that benzodiazepines share a biochemical property in that all augment the activity of GABA. *See* ANXIETY DISORDERS; SEROTONIN.

The symptoms of depression can include a sense of sadness, hopelessness, despair, and irritability, as well as suicidal thoughts and attempts, which are sometimes successful. In addition, physical symptoms such as loss of appetite, sleep disturbances, and psychomotor agitation are often associated with depression. When depression becomes so pervasive and intense that normal functioning is impaired, antidepressant medication may be indicated. It has been estimated that as much as 6% of the population will require antidepressant medication at some time in their lives.

There are two major groups of antidepressant drugs. Members of the first group are called heterocyclics because of their characteristic chemical structures. Members of the second group, which are less often prescribed, are called monoamine oxidase inhibitors. *See* MONOAMINE OXIDASE.

The antidepressants typically require at least several weeks of chronic administration before they become effective in alleviating depression. This contrasts with the anxiolytics, which are effective in reducing anxiety in hours and even minutes. Another difference between these two classes of drugs is that the anxiolytics are more likely to be efficacious: anxiolytics are effective in the vast majority of nonphobic, anxious patients, whereas the antidepressants are effective in only about 65–70% of depressed patients. *See* AFFECTIVE DISORDERS.

Manic episodes are characterized by hyperactivity, grandiosity, flight of ideas, and belligerence; affected patients appear to be euphoric, have racing thoughts, delusions of grandeur, and poor if not self-destructive judgment. Periods of depression follow these episodes of mania in the majority of patients. The cycles of this bipolar disorder are typically interspersed among periods of normality that are, in most cases, relatively protracted.

Mania can usually be managed by chronic treatment with lithium salts and can be expected to be effective in 70–80% of the individuals treated. Furthermore, the period of depression that typically follows the manic episode can usually be prevented, or at least attenuated, if lithium treatment is maintained after the manic phase has subsided. Any periods of depression that do occur can be managed by antidepressant drugs. Lithium is no longer the only drug used in the management of mania. Carbamazepine, an anticonvulsant that is used in the treatment of epilepsy, is also useful in the treatment of periods of mania.

Schizophrenia is a form of psychosis; it incorporates a broad range of symptoms that can include bizarre delusions, hallucinations, incoherence of thought processes, inappropriate affect, and grossly disorganized movements. It affects 1–2% of the population. The symptoms of schizophrenia can be controlled, in varying degrees, by a large group of drugs called antipsychotics. Symptom management requires chronic medication and can be expected in about 80% or more of the schizophrenics treated. However, management is only partially successful in that normal functioning is not completely restored in most patients.

The antipsychotics have a broad range of side effects among which are disturbances of movement that fall into two general classes. The first class includes an array of symptoms very like those characteristic of Parkinson's disease. The second class of movement disorder is called tardive dyskinesia. Signs of this disturbance typically include involuntary movements that most often affect the tongue and facial and neck muscles but can also include the digits and trunk.

Although different antipsychotic drugs have different kinds and degrees of side effects, all share a single biochemical action: they all attenuate the activity of dopamine, a naturally occurring substance in the brain. The reduction in dopamine activity produced by the antipsychotics directly accounts for their effects on motor behavior. It is to be expected, therefore, that disrupted dopamine activity in this system would produce disturbances of movement. It is less clear, however, whether reduced dopamine function is also a factor in the process by which these drugs control psychotic (including schizophrenic) symptoms. *See* SCHIZOPHRENIA.   [PL.C.]

Psychophysical methods   Methods for the quantitative study of the relations between physical stimulus magnitudes and the corresponding magnitudes of sensation, for example, between the physical intensity of a light and its perceived brightness or the concentration of a sugar solution and its observed sweetness. To establish these relations, measurement scales are needed, not only for physical magnitudes but also for subjective magnitudes. Subjective scales are not obtained directly from observation but are theoretical models which summarize observed relations between stimuli and responses. *See* SENSATION.

The term psychophysical methods is sometimes extended to include certain scaling techniques which are most often used with subjective dimensions to which there correspond no simple physical dimensions, for example, food preferences.

In 1860, G. Fechner designed psychophysical methods to measure the absolute threshold, defined as the minimum stimulus energy that an organism can detect, and the differential threshold, defined as the minimum detectable change in a stimulus. Both quantities had to be defined as statistical averages. To obtain reliable measurements for these averages, Fechner devised the method of limits (also called the method of minimal changes) and the method of constant stimuli.

In the method of limits, the experimenter begins with a stimulus which is too weak for the subject to detect. In successive presentations, the stimulus intensity is increased in small, equal steps, the subject reporting after each presentation whether the stimulus was perceived until it has been detected. The descending series is then begun, the stimulus intensity beginning at an above-threshold value and decreasing in steps until the subject signals the disappearance of the stimulus. Many such series are given.

In measuring the difference threshold, essentially the same procedure is involved, except that the subject now signals the relation of a comparison stimulus to a standard stimulus. After a large number of such trials, the average of each of these four threshold values is computed.

To measure the absolute threshold by the method of constant stimuli, the experimenter selects a small number of stimulus values in the neighborhood of the absolute threshold (previously roughly located by informal use of the method of limits) and presents them to the subject a large number of times each, in an irregular order unknown to the subject. Each time a stimulus is presented, the subject reports the presence or absence of sensation.

The data provide the proportion of times that each stimulus resulted in a report of sensation by the subject. One can then estimate the stimulus value that has a probability of .50 of producing sensation, this value being defined as the absolute threshold. An analogous procedure is followed in obtaining difference thresholds.

Fechner proposed to use the results of threshold measurement in developing a subjective metric or scale. He defined the difference threshold, or just noticeable difference (jnd), as the subjective unit and the absolute threshold as the zero point of the subjective scale. Thus the subjective intensity of a particular brightness of light, for example, would be specified when it was given as 100 jnd's above threshold. The subjective scale so defined is not a linear function of the physical stimulus scale since jnd's, though defined as subjectively equal units, are not of physically equal magnitude throughout the intensity scale. The size of the jnd is approximately proportional to physical stimulus intensity. To the extent that this relation holds, Fechner deduced that subjective intensity should be proportional to the logarithm of the stimulus intensity.

Rather than requiring of the subject merely either yes-no or ordinal judgments, some methods require the subject to make direct-ratio discriminations. For instance, he or she may be presented with a moderately loud tone, and then required, by turning a knob, to adjust the loudness of a comparison tone until it is half as loud, or twice as loud, as the first. The first case illustrates the method of fractionation, the second the method of multiplication. In the method of magnitude estimation, the subject is given a stimulus, such as the brightness of a light, to serve as a modulus with a value assigned to it, for example, 10. The task, as other lights of different intensities are presented, is to assign them numbers which shall stand in the same ratio to 10 as their brightness stands to that of the modulus. One twice as bright is given the designation 20; one half as bright is 5. In these and other similar methods, whether the subject's task is to estimate or to produce the prescribed ratio or the prescribed fraction, there are certain common characteristics. Direct-ratio assessments are obtained from the subject; there can be experimental checks on internal consistency of the results, and since the individual judgments are not of high precision, repetition is required if stable averages are to be obtained.

The empirical results obtained by the various methods are in fairly good agreement. They agree in that, to at least a first approximation, subjective magnitudes on a variety of dimensions are found to be power functions of suprathreshold stimulus intensity; that is to say, subjective magnitude is proportional to the suprathreshold stimulus magnitude raised to a power. The powers have a range from 0.3 for auditory loudness to 3.5 for subjective intensity of alternating current that is applied to the skin.

In direct-matching methods the subject is not required to produce or assess the ratio of one subjective magnitude to another, but only to adjust a comparison stimulus until some attribute appears to match that of a standard stimulus. For example, the subject might be asked to adjust the physical intensities of tones of various frequencies until their loudness matched that of a 1000-Hz tone of fixed intensity. The result would be an equal-loudness contour, showing the intensities to which tones of various frequencies must be set to produce sensations of equal loudness. These data are of use in acoustics. *See* LOUDNESS.

The method of average error, the third of the three methods devised by Fechner, is a special application of direct-matching methods to cases in which the point of interest is in discrepancies between perception and stimulation. The subject adjusts a comparison stimulus to match a standard stimulus; the average of a number of such settings gives the point of subjective equality, and the difference between this point and the standard stimulus is the average error. Two illustrative uses of the method are the measurement of accuracy of distance perception and the measurement of the magnitude of so-called optical illusions. *See* HEARING (HUMAN); PSYCHOLOGY. [J.F.H.]

Psychosis Any disorder of higher mental processes of such severity that judgments pertaining to the reality of external events are significantly impaired. A wide range of conditions can bring about a psychotic state. They include schizophrenia, mania, depression, ingestion of drugs, withdrawal from drugs, liver or kidney failure, endocrine disorders, metabolic disorders, and Alzheimer's disease, epilepsy, and other neurologic dysfunctions. The dreams of normal sleep are a form of psychosis.

Psychotic alterations of beliefs are called delusions. Psychotic alterations of perception are referred to as hallucinations. Psychotic states that are due to alcoholism, metabolic diseases, or other medical conditions are frequently accompanied by general mental confusion. On the other hand, psychiatric illnesses and drugs can produce hallucinations and delusions in the absence of general confusion. Few of those symptoms are unique to a particular illness, which can make proper diagnosis difficult and challenging. Correct diagnosis, however, is critical so that appropriate treatment can be provided. *See* ADDICTIVE DISORDERS; AFFECTIVE DISORDERS; ALZHEIMER'S DISEASE; PARANOIA; SCHIZOPHRENIA. [R.E.Ho.]

Psychosomatic disorders Disorders characterized by physiological changes that originate, at least in part, from emotional factors. The classical psychosomatic symptoms and their theorized causes are shown in the table.

Theorized psychological factors in classical psychosomatic disorders

Symptom (disease)	Psychological factors	Presumed psychosomatic mechanism
Hyperacidity (peptic ulcer)	Inhibited dependence; general stress	Increased acid secretion
Essential hypertension	Conflict over hostility; general stress	Vasoconstriction
Bronchial asthma	Conflict over wish for protection or separation; anxiety; general stress	Bronchospasm Bronchospasm
Migraine	Conflict over control; general stress	Vasoconstriction and vasodilatation
Thyrotoxicosis (Graves' disease)	Conflict over premature self-sufficiency	Increased thyroid-stimulating hormone secretion
Diarrhea (ulcerative colitis)	Conflict over an obligation	Gastrointestinal cholinergic activation

Psychological states influence body organs through a combination of three inter-related mechanisms: neural, hormonal, and immunologic. Voluntary movements (for example, clenching the teeth) are mediated through the motor neurons by the conscious command of the brain. In stress, clenching of the teeth, mediated by the same motor neurons, may also occur, but the act may not be voluntary and conscious. Stress usually causes an activation of the sympathetic nervous system and the hypothalamo-pituitary-adrenal axis followed by a decrease in immunocompetence. Immune mechanisms may be suppressed in part through corticosteroid activation, but a decrease in T-lymphocyte activity in stress may not be mediated by hormones. Individual specific, but inadvertent, conditioning of specific conflict or stress to specific bodily malfunction may be an important psychosomatic mechanism. *See* CONDITIONED REFLEX; NEUROIMMUNOLOGY.

Conversion disorders refer to physical symptoms referrable to the somatosensory nervous system or special sensory organs that cannot be explained on the basis of a medical or neurologic disease. Common symptoms include paralysis, blindness, ataxia, aphonia, and numbness of the feet (stocking anesthesia). The symptoms may represent a psychological conflict or may be a form of body-language communication. The treatment of choice is psychotherapy.

In somatization disorder (also known as Briquet's syndrome), the patient recurrently complains of multiple somatic symptoms that are referrable to practically every organ system in the body and which, upon medical investigation, turn out not to be a diagnosable physical disease. This disorder is distinguished from conversion disorder by the chronicity and multiplicity of its symptoms. The symptoms do not usually symbolize psychological conflicts but may represent general dysphoria and distorted illness behavior. There is no definitive treatment; patients should be managed by one physician who coordinates all diagnostic and treatment plans and who provides ongoing support and follow-up without unnecessary invasive procedures.

Specific psychological conflicts often characterize patients with classical psychosomatic symptoms or disorders they represent; however, only one aspect of a multifactorial or heterogeneous disorder is not considered to be etiologic. Genetic factors are known to play important roles in the pathogenesis of most of these diseases. Some of the psychological difficulties demonstrated by these patients may in fact be a result of the disease. Psychotherapy is often helpful in resolving the conflicts when they are severe enough to warrant it, but it does not necessarily ameliorate the physical symptoms or the course of disease. *See* PSYCHOTHERAPY.   [H.Lei.]

Psychotherapy   Any treatment or therapy that is primarily psychological in nature. In recent years, counseling also has been included in this categorization.

Psychodynamic therapies. Historically, psychoanalysis—created by Sigmund Freud—has played an important role in the growth and development of psychotherapy. Central to Freud's theories was the importance of unconscious conflicts in producing the symptoms and defenses of the patient. The goal of therapy is to help the patient attain insight into the repressed conflicts which are the source of difficulty. Since patients resist these attempts bring to consciousness the painful repressed material, therapy must proceed slowly. Consequently, psychoanalysis is a long-term therapy requiring several years for completion and almost daily visits. Since Freud's time, there have been important modifications associated with former disciples such as Alfred Adler and Carl Jung. Self psychology and ego psychology are among more recent emphases. However, the popularity of psychoanalysis has waned. *See* PSYCHOANALYSIS.

Experiential therapies. A number of related therapies are included in this group. Probably best known was the patient-centered therapy of Carl Rogers appearing in the 1940s. In Rogers' therapy, a major emphasis is placed on the ability of the patient to change when the therapist is empathic and genuine and conveys nonpossessive warmth. The therapist is nondirective in the interaction with the patient and attempts to facilitate the growth potential of the patient. Other therapeutic approaches considered as experiential include Gestalt therapy, existential approaches, and transpersonal approaches. The facilitation of experiencing is emphasized as the basic therapeutic task, and the therapeutic relationship is viewed as a significant potentially curative factor.

Cognitive, behavioral, and interpersonal therapies. In behavioral therapies, therapists play a more directive role. The emphasis is on changing the patient's behavior, using positive reinforcement, and increasing self-efficacy. More recently, cognitive therapies such as those of A. T. Beck have tended to be combined with behavioral emphases. The cognitive-behavioral therapies have focused on changing dysfunctional attitudes into more realistic and positive ones and providing new information-processing skills. *See* COGNITION.

Most of the developments in interpersonal therapy have occurred in work with depressed patients. The goal of interpersonal therapy (a brief form of therapy) is centered on increasing the quality of the patient's interpersonal interactions. Emphasis is placed on enhancing the patient's ability to cope with stresses, improving interpersonal communications, increasing morale, and helping the patient deal with the effects of the depressive disorder. *See* PERSONALITY THEORY.

Eclectic and integrative therapies. The largest number of psychotherapists consider themselves to be eclectics. They do not adhere strictly to one theoretical orientation or school but use any procedures that they believe will be helpful for the individual patient. Eclecticism has been linked with the development of a movement for integration in psychotherapy. The emphasis in this new development is on openness to the views of other approaches, a less doctrinaire approach to psychotherapy, and an attempt to integrate two or more different theoretical views or systems of psychotherapy.

Group, family, and marital therapy. Most psychotherapy is conducted on a one-to-one basis—one therapist for one patient—and the confidentiality of these sessions is extremely important. However, there are other instances where more than one patient is involved because of particular goals. These include marital, family, and group therapy. Outpatient groups have been used for smoking cessation, weight loss, binge eating, and similar problems as well as for what were traditionally viewed as psychoneurotic problems. Inpatient group therapy was frequently employed in mental hospital settings.

There has been research on the combined use of medication and psychotherapy. In general, where two highly successful treatments are combined in cases with depressive or anxiety disorders, there appears to be little gain in effectiveness. However, in several studies of hospitalized patients with schizophrenia where individual psychotherapy has been ineffective, a combination of psychotherapy and medication has produced better results than medication alone. *See* AFFECTIVE DISORDERS; PSYCHOPHARMACOLOGY; SCHIZOPHRENIA.   [S.L.G]

Psychotomimetic drug   A class of drugs reliably inducing temporary states of altered perception, often with symptoms similar to those of psychosis. The drug experiences are clearly perceived, vivid, and remembered. Sensory input is heightened and subjective experience is intensified, but control is diminished. The subject's feelings and momentary perceptions gain an independence from the normal corrections of logic; whatever stray item occupies the attention (a sensation or an unguarded and unevaluated memory or thought) becomes at the moment compellingly significant. Thinking and perceiving of this order coexist with the capacity for, but not an interest in, normal thought and function.

These drugs have been called psychedelic (or mind-manifesting) because of the convincing clarity with which a normally suppressed, more sensory, plastic, and primitive part of the mind is revealed to the drugged subject, contrasting sharply with the capacity to focus, discriminate, and judge.

The two drugs of chief interest, mescaline and LSD-25 (lysergic acid diethylamide), are of ancient lineage. Mescaline, used in highly structured Amerindian tribal religious rituals, is derived from peyote buttons, which are the dried tops of a cactus found in the southwestern United States. LSD has been synthesized with compounds derived from ergot, which infests such grasses as rye. (Some ergot derivatives are useful in the treatment of migraine and in obstetrics for the postpartum constriction of the uterus and blood vessels.) *See* ERGOT AND EROTISM.

There are a number of other psychotomimetics (less potent than LSD but similar), such as those from mushrooms (psilocybin and psilocin) and those synthesized in the laboratory. Ring-substituted amphetamines resembling mescaline's structure (for example, "STP") have been produced in profusion. There are subtle differences among these newer compounds, some producing more or less euphoria and more or less dyscontrol and anxiety.   [D.X.F]

Purine   A heterocyclic organic compound (**1**) containing fused pyrimidine and

(**1**)

imidazole rings. A number of substituted purine derivatives occur in nature; some, as components of nucleic acids and coenzymes, play vital roles in the genetic and metabolic processes of all living organisms. *See* COENZYME; NUCLEIC ACID.

Purines are generally white solids of amphoteric character. They can form salts with both acids and bases. Conjugated double bonds in purines results in aromatic chemical properties, that confers considerable stability, and accounts for their strong ultraviolet absorption spectra. With the exception of the parent compound, most substituted purines have low solubilities in water and organic solvents.

The purine bases, adenine (**2**) and guanine (**3**), together with pyrimidines, are fundamental components of all nucleic acids. Certain methylated derivatives of adenine and guanine are also present in some nucleic acids in low amounts. In biological systems, hypoxanthine (**4**), adenine, and guanine occur mainly as their 9-glycosides, the sugar

(2)   (3)   (4)

being either ribose or 2-deoxyribose. Such compounds are termed nucleosides generically, and inosine (hypoxanthine nucleoside), adenosine, or guanosine specifically. The principal nucleotides contain 5'-phosphate groups, as in guanosine 5'-phosphate (GTP) and adenosine 5'-triphosphate (ATP).

Most living organisms are capable of synthesizing purine compounds. The sequence of enzymatic reactions by which the initial purine product, inosine 5'-phosphate, is formed utilizes glycine, carbon dioxide, formic acid, and amino groups derived from glutamine and aspartic acid. Adenosine 5'-phosphate and guanosine 5'-phosphate are formed from inosine 5'-phosphate.

Metabolic degradation of purine derivatives may also occur by hydrolysis of nucleotides and nucleosides to the related free bases. Deamination of adenine and guanine produces hypoxanthine and xanthine (**5**), both of which may be oxidized to uric acid (**6**).

(5)   (6)

See URIC ACID.

Purine-related compounds have been investigated as potential chemotherapeutic agents. In particular, 6-mercaptopurine, in the form of its nucleoside phosphate, inhibits several enzymes required for synthesis of adenosine and guanosine nucleotides, and thus proves useful in selectively arresting the growth of tumors. The pyrazolopyrimidine has been used in gout therapy. As a purine analog, this agent serves to block the biosynthesis of inosine phosphate, as well as the oxidation of hypoxanthine and xanthine to uric acid. As a result of its use, overproduction of uric acid is prevented and the primary cause of gout is removed. *See* CHEMOTHERAPY; PYRIMIDINE.   [S.C.H.]

Pyrimidine   A heterocyclic organic compound (**1**) containing nitrogen atoms at

(**1**)

positions 1 and 3. Naturally occurring derivatives of the parent compound are of considerable biological importance as components of nucleic acids and coenzymes and, in addition, synthetic members of this group have found use as pharmaceuticals. *See* COENZYME; NUCLEIC ACID.

Pyrimidine compounds which are found universally in living organisms include uracil (**2**), cytosine (**3**), and thymine (**4**). Together with purines these substances make up

(2)   (3)   (4)

the "bases" of nucleic acids, uracil and cytosine being found characteristically in ribonucleic acids, with thymine replacing uracil in deoxyribonucleic acids. A number of related pyrimidines also occur in lesser amounts in certain nucleic acids. Other pyrimidines of general natural occurrence are orotic acid and thiamine (vitamin B_1). *See* DEOXYRIBONUCLEIC ACID (DNA); PURINE; RIBONUCLEIC ACID (RNA).

Among the sulfa drugs, the pyrimidine derivatives, sulfadi-azine, sulfamerazine, and sulfamethazine, have general formula (**5**). These agents are inhibitors of folic acid

(5)

biosynthesis in microorganisms. The barbiturates are pyrimidine derivatives which possess potent depressant action on the central nervous system.   [S.C.H.]

Pyroelectricity (biology)

Electrical polarity in a biological material produced by a change in temperature. Pyroelectricity is probably a basic physical property of all living organisms. First discovered in 1966 in tendon and bone, it has since been shown to exist in most animal and plant tissues and in individual cells. Pyroelectricity appears to play a fundamental part in the growth processes (morphogenesis) and in physiological functions (such as sensory perception) of organisms.

The elementary components (for example, molecules) of biological (as well as of nonbiological) pyroelectric structures have a permanent electric dipole moment, and are arranged so that all positive dipole ends point in one direction and all negative dipole ends in the opposite direction. This parallel alignment of elementary dipoles is termed spontaneous polarization because it occurs spontaneously without the action of external fields or forces. In this state of molecular order, the structure concerned has a permanent electric dipole moment on a microscopic and macroscopic level.

Spontaneous polarization is temperature-dependent; thus any change in temperature causes a change of the dipole moments, measurable as a change of electric charges at both ends of the polar axis. This is the pyroelectric effect. All pyroelectric structures are also piezoelectric, but the reverse is not true.

Prerequisites for the development of spontaneous polarization and pyroelectric activity in biological structures are (1) the presence of a permanent dipole moment in the molecules or molecular aggregates and (2) a molecular shape that favors a parallel alignment as much as possible (or at least does not impede it). Both these conditions are ideally fulfilled in bar- or board-shaped molecules with a permanent dipole moment along the longitudinal molecular axis. Several important organic substances have these molecular properties, and therefore behave pyroelectrically in biological structures. Examples include the epidermis of animals and plants, sensory receptors in animals, and tissues of the nervous and skeletal systems.

Living organisms are able to detect and discriminate between different stimuli in the environment, such as rapid changes of temperature, of illumination, and of hydrostatic and uniaxial pressure. These stimuli represent different forms of energy and are transduced, or converted, into the nearly uniform type of electrical signals whose voltage-time course frequently depends on dX/dt (X = external stimulus, t = time). Such electrical signals have been recorded on cutaneous sensory receptors, on external nerve endings, on epidermal structures, and even on the cell wall of single-cell organisms. The mechanisms of detection and transduction in these biological systems, still little understood, may lie in the pyroelectric behavior of the structures. Pyroelectric (and thus piezoelectric) behavior has been proved to exist in most biological systems, which means that these systems should in principle be able to function as pyroelectric detectors and transducers.   [H.A.]

R

Rabies   An acute, encephalitic viral infection. Human beings are infected from the bite of a rabid animal, usually a dog. Canine rabies can infect all warm-blooded animals, and death usually results. *See* ANIMAL VIRUS.

The virus is believed to move from the saliva-infected wound through sensory nerves to the central nervous system, multiply there with destruction of brain cells, and thus produce encephalitis, with severe excitement, throat spasm upon swallowing (hence hydrophobia, or fear of water), convulsions, and death—with paralysis sometimes intervening before death.

All bites should immediately be cleaned thoroughly with soap and water, and a tetanus shot should be considered. The decision to administer rabies antibody, rabies vaccine, or both depends on four factors: the nature of the biting animal; the existence of rabies in the area; the manner of attack (provoked or unprovoked) and the severity of the bite and contamination by saliva of the animal; and recommendations by local public health officials.

Diagnosis in the human is made by observation of Negri bodies (cytoplasmic inclusion bodies) in brains of animals inoculated with the person's saliva, or in the person's brain after death. A dog which has bitten a person is isolated and watched for 10 days for signs of rabies; if none occur, rabies was absent. If signs do appear, the animal is killed and the brain examined for Negri bodies, or for rabies antigen by testing with fluorescent antibodies. *See* VIRAL INCLUSION BODIES.

Individuals at high risk, such as veterinarians, must receive preventive immunization. If exposure is believed to have been dangerous, postexposure prophylaxis should be undertaken. If antibody or immunogenic vaccine is administered promptly, the virus can be prevented from invading the central nervous system. An inactivated rabies virus vaccine is available in the United States. It is made from virus grown in human or monkey cell cultures and is free from brain proteins that were present in earlier Pasteur-type vaccines. This material is sufficiently antigenic that only four to six doses of virus need be given to obtain a substantial antibody response. *See* VACCINATION.   [J.L.Me.]

Radiation biology   The study of the action of ionizing and nonionizing radiation on biological systems. Ionizing radiation includes highly energetic electromagnetic radiation (x-rays, gamma rays, or cosmic rays) and particulate radiation (alpha particles, beta particles, neutrons, or heavy charged ions). Nonionizing radiation includes ultraviolet radiation, microwaves, and extralow-frequency (ELF) electromagnetic radiation. These two types of radiation have different modes of action on biological material: ionizing radiation is sufficiently energetic to cause ionizations, whereas nonionizing radiation causes molecular excitations. In both cases, the result is that chemical bonds of molecules may be altered, causing mutations, cell death, or other biological changes.

Ionizing radiation originates from external sources (medical x-ray equipment, cathode-ray tubes in television sets or computer video displays) or from internal sources (ingested or inhaled radioisotopes, such as radon-222, strontium-90, and iodine-131), and is either anthropogenic or natural.

Nonionizing radiation originates from natural sources (sunlight, Earth's magnetic field, lightning, static electricity, endogenous body currents) and technological sources (computer video displays and television sets, microwave ovens, communications equipment, electric equipment and appliances, and high-voltage transmission lines).

Ionizing radiation. The absorbed dose of ionizing radiation is measured as the gray (Gy, 1 joule of energy absorbed by 1 kilogram of material). Because of the very localized absorption of ionizing radiation, an amount of ionizing radiation energy equivalent to 1/100 the heat energy in a cup of coffee will result in a 50% chance that the person absorbing the radiation will die in 30 days.

The most important biological targets for damage from ionizing radiation are probably the plasma membrane and DNA, because there is only one copy, or a few copies, in the cell; because they serve critical roles for the survival and propagation of cells; and because they are large. The last factor is important because ionizing radiation releases its energy in a random manner; thus the larger the target, the more likely that it will be damaged by radiation. Consequences of radiation damage in membranes are changes in ion permeability, with leakage of potassium ions; changes in active transport; and cell lysis. Lesions in DNA include single-strand breaks, double-strand breaks, base damage, interstrand cross-links, and DNA-protein cross-links. *See* CELL MEMBRANES; DEOXYRIBONUCLEIC ACID (DNA).

Various biological effects can result from the actions of ionizing radiation. Reproductive death is most pronounced in mammalian cells that are actively dividing and in nondifferentiated tissue. Thus, dividing tissues (bone marrow and the germinal cells of the ovary and testis) are radiosensitive, and nondividing tissues (liver, kidney, brain, muscle, cartilage, and connective tissue) are radioresistant. Developing embryos are quite radiosensitive. The radiosensitivity of organisms varies greatly, being related to their intrinsic sensitivity to radiobiological damage and to their ability to repair the damage. Radiation doses resulting in 10% survival range from 3 Gy (mouse and human cells), to greater than 1000 Gy (the bacterium *Deinococcus radiodurans*).

The three organ systems that generally contribute to the death of mammals following a single dose of whole-body irradiation are, in decreasing order of radiosensitivity, the hematopoietic system, the gastrointestinal system, and the cerebrovascular system. Late somatic effects may take years or decades to appear and include genetic mutations transmitted to subsequent generations, tumor development and carcinogenesis, and shortening of life span. *See* MUTAGENS AND CARCINOGENS; MUTATION.

Nonionizing radiation. Of all the nonionizing radiations, only ultraviolet radiation, microwaves, and high-voltage electromagnetic radiation are considered in the study of radiation biology.

Ultraviolet radiation. Since it can penetrate only several layers of cells, the effects of ultraviolet (UV) radiation on humans are restricted to the skin and the eyes. Ultraviolet radiation is divided into UV-C (wavelength of 200–280 nanometers), UV-B (280–320 nm), and UV-A (320–400 nm). The most biologically damaging is UV-C, and the least damaging is UV-A. The solar spectrum at the Earth's surface contains only the UV-B and UV-A radiations.

Biological effects can arise only when absorption of ultraviolet radiation occurs. Absorption is dependent on the chemical bonds of the material, and it is highly specific. Sunburn is a form of erythema produced by overexposure to the UV-B portion of the solar spectrum. A rare but deadly form of skin cancer in humans, malignant melanoma, is induced by exposure to sunlight, with occurrences localized on those regions of the body that are most frequently exposed. Ultraviolet light can also cause photochemical damage. Cyclobutane pyrimidine dimers are the main photoproduct following exposure to UV-C and UV-B, and they can lead to cell death and precarcinogenic lesions.

Microwaves. Microwaves are electromagnetic radiation in the region from 30 MHz to 300 GHz. They originate from devices such as telecommunications equipment and microwave ovens. Thermal effects of microwaves occur at exposure rates greater than 10 mW/cm^2 (70 mW/in.^{2}), while nonthermal effects are associated with exposure rates less than 10 mW/cm^2. Material with a high water content will have a higher absorption coefficient for microwaves, and thus a greater thermal response to microwave action. Microwave absorption is high in skin, muscle, and internal organs, and lower in bone and fat tissue.

Cultured mammalian cells exposed to microwaves at a high power density show chromosome abnormalities after 15 min of exposure. Progression through the cell cycle is also temporarily interrupted, which interrupts DNA synthesis. Chromosome aberrations in peripheral blood lymphocytes are significantly greater for persons who are occupationally exposed to microwaves. Microwaves can be lethal when the power intensity and exposure time are sufficient to cause a rise in temperature that exceeds an organism's homeostatic capabilities.

There are also some nonthermal effects associated with microwaves. A list of clinical symptoms includes increased fatigue, periodic or constant headaches, extreme irritability, decreased hearing acuity, and drowsiness during work. Laboratory studies involving exposure of animals to microwaves have produced changes in the electroencephalogram, blood-brain barrier, central nervous system, hematology, and behavior. Cell membrane permeability is also altered.

Extremely low frequency electromagnetic fields. This type of radiation is generated by the electric and magnetic fields associated with high-voltage current in power transmission lines, and also some household and industrial electrical equipment. Biological effects from ELF radiation are the least understood, and the potential consequences are the most controversial. The issue of potential biological damage from this type of radiation has arisen only since the introduction of very high voltage electric power transmission lines (440 kV and above) and the occurrence of widespread use of various electrical and electronic equipment.

Biological studies on ELF electromagnetic fields have been performed on cells and whole animals; and epidemiological studies have been carried out on populations exposed occupationally. Some of the reported effects are subjective, and may be related to normal physiological adaptation to environmental changes. In humans, qualitative biological effects of low-frequency radiation (0 to 300 Hz) include headaches, lethargy, and decreased sex drive. Humans have been noted to perceive the presence of a 60-Hz electric field when the intensity is in the range of 2 to 12 kV/m (0.6 to 3.6 kV/ft), and animals were observed to avoid entering an area where the electric field was greater than 4 kV/m (1.2 kV/ft).   [P.M.Ac.]

Radioecology The study of the fate and effects of radioactive materials in the environment. It derives its principles from basic ecology and radiation biology.

Responses to radiation stress have consequences for both the individual organism and for the population, community, or ecosystem of which it is a part. When populations or individuals of different species differ in their sensitivities to radiation stress, for example, the species composition of the entire biotic community may be altered as the more radiation-sensitive species are removed or reduced in abundance and are replaced in turn by more resistant species. Such changes have been documented by studies in which natural ecological systems, including grasslands, deserts, and forests, were exposed to varying levels of controlled gamma radiation stress. *See* POPULATION ECOLOGY.

Techniques of laboratory toxicology are also available for assessing the responses of free-living animals to exposure to low levels of radioactive contamination in natural environments. This approach uses sentinel animals, which are either tamed, imprinted on the investigator, or equipped with miniature radio transmitters, to permit their periodic relocation and recapture as they forage freely in the food chains of contaminated habitats. When the animals are brought back to the laboratory, their level of radioisotope uptake can be determined and blood or tissue samples taken for analysis. In this way, even subtle changes in deoxyribonucleic acid (DNA) structure can be evaluated over time. These changes may be suggestive of genetic damage by radiation exposure. In some cases, damage caused by a radioactive contaminant may be worsened by the synergestic effects of other forms of environmental contaminants such as heavy metals.

Because of the ease with which they can be detected and quantified in living organisms and their tissues, radioactive materials are often used as tracers. Radioactive tracers can be used to trace food chain pathways or determine the rates at which various processes take place in natural ecological systems. Although most tracer experiments were performed in the past by deliberately introducing a small amount of radioactive tracer into the organism or ecological system to be studied, they now take advantage of naturally tagged environments where trace amounts of various radioactive contaminants were inadvertently released from operating nuclear facilities such as power or production reactors or waste burial grounds.

An important component of radioecology, and one that is closely related to the study of radioactive tracers, is concerned with the assessment and prediction of the movement and concentration of radioactive contaminants in the environment in general, and particularly in food chains that may lead to humans. *See* ECOLOGY; FOOD WEB; RADIATION BIOLOGY.   [I.L.B.]

Radioimmunoassay   A general method employing the reaction of antigen with specific antibody, permitting measurement of the concentration of virtually any substance of biologic interest, often with unparalleled sensitivity. The basis of the method is summarized in the competing reactions shown in the illustration. The unknown concentration of the antigenic substance in a sample is obtained by comparing its inhibitory effect on the binding of radioactively labeled antigen to a limited amount of specific antibody with the inhibitory effect of known standards.

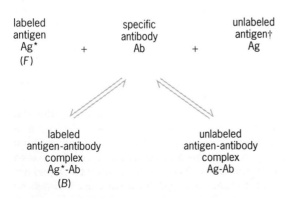

Competing reactions that form basis of radioimmunoassay; * indicates the labeled antigen, and † "in known standard solutions or unknown samples."

A typical radioimmunoassay is performed by the simultaneous preparation of a series of standard and unknown mixtures in test tubes, each containing identical concentrations of labeled antigen and specific antibody. After an appropriate reaction time the antibody- bound (B) and free (F) fractions of the labeled antigen are separated by one of a variety of techniques. The B/F ratios in the standards are plotted as a function of the concentration of unlabeled antigen (standard curve), and the unknown concentration of antigen is determined by comparing the observed B/F ratio with the standard curve.

The radioimmunoassay principle has found wide application in the measurement of a large and diverse group of substances in a variety of problems of clinical and biological interest. It is therefore not unexpected that there are differences in the specific methods employed for the assay of a particular substance. The full potential of the method has yet to be exploited. It seems that virtually any substance of biologic interest can be measured, the method being modified according to the characteristics of the particular substance. *See* ANTIBODY; ANTIGEN; IMMUNOLOGY. [R.S.Y.]

Radioisotope (biology) A radioactive isotope used in studying living systems, such as in the investigation of metabolic processes. The usefulness of radioisotopes as tracers arises chiefly from three properties: (1) At the molecular level the physical and chemical behavior of a radioisotope is practically identical with that of the stable isotopes of the same element. (2) Radioisotopes are detectable in extremely minute concentrations. (3) Analysis for radioisotopic content often can be achieved without alteration of the sample or system. In some applications, principally those in which reaction rates and transfer rates are studied, isotopes, particularly radioisotopes, have unique advantages as tracers.

The amount of isotope to be used and the path by which it is introduced into the system are governed by many factors. Sufficient tracer to be detectable must be used, but the amounts of material which are introduced must be small enough not to disturb the system by their mass, pharmacological effects, or the effects of radiation. The mass of 1 curie, the unit of disintegration rate, depends inversely upon the half-life and directly upon the atomic weight of the particular radioisotope; it is 1 gram for ^{226}Ra (half-life 1620 years), but only 8 micrograms for ^{131}I (half-life 8.0 days). In tracer experiments with small animals, microcurie quantities are usually adequate.

There are many methods for detecting the presence of radioactive material. The Geiger counter has largely been displaced by thallium-activated sodium iodide scintillation crystals for counting gamma rays, but Geiger counters and proportional counters are still useful for counting alpha and beta particles. In histological and cytological studies the method of autoradiography, in which photographic film is exposed through contact with the specimen, is very useful. The autoradiographic method is also used extensively in conjunction with paper or column chromatography, particularly in studies of metabolic pathways.

One of the outstanding achievements in which radioisotopes have played a role has been the use of carbon-14 in the elucidation of the metabolic path of carbon in photosynthesis. The products produced in the first few seconds following exposure to light have been identified by combinations of paper chromatography and autoradiography. The extrathyroidal metabolism of iodine, the path of iodine in the thyroid gland, and other problems of intermediary metabolism have been studied intensively. The concept of the dynamic state of cell constituents is largely attributable to discoveries made with isotopic tracers. At one time it was thought that concentration gradients across cell membranes depended upon their being impermeable, but the use of isotopes has refuted this hypothesis by proving that in many such cases the substances involved are normally transported in both directions across the membrane. In physiology, radioisotopes have been used in a wide variety of permeability, absorption, and distribution studies. *See* ABSORPTION (BIOLOGY); CELL MEMBRANE; PHOTOSYNTHESIS.

The kinetics of cellular proliferation has provided a rich vein for application of radioisotopic methods. For example, the lifetime of human red blood cells (about 120 days) was established with the use of ^{59}Fe-labeled cells. Some applications, such as the intake of ^{131}I by the thyroid, the measurement of the red-cell mass with ^{51}Cr-labeled red cells, and the absorption of ^{60}Co-labeled vitamin B$_{12}$, are of practical clinical importance in the diagnosis and treatment of disease, and knowledge of the rates of distribution and disposal of a wide variety of radioactive substances is basic to the problem of evaluating the hazard from fallout radiation.   [J.S.Ro.]

Radiolaria   A group of marine protozoa, regarded as a subclass of Actinopodea in older classifications, but not recognized as a natural group in some modern systems owing to its heterogeneity. In certain modern systems, the Radiolaria are subdivided into two classes, Polycystinea and Phaeodarea. Radiolarians occur almost exclusively in the open ocean as part of the plankton community, and are widely recognized for their ornate siliceous skeletons produced by most of the groups (illus. *a–c*). Their skeletons occur abundantly in ocean sediments and are used in analyzing the layers of the sedimentary record (biostratigraphy).

A characteristic feature of the group is the capsule, a central mass of cytoplasm bearing one or more nuclei, food reserves, and metabolic organelles. This is surrounded by a perforated wall and a frothy layer of cytoplasm known as the extracapsulum, where food digestion generally occurs and where numerous axopodia (stiffened strands of cytoplasm) and rhizopodia radiate toward the surrounding environment. Algal symbionts including dinoflagellates, green algae, and golden-brown pigmented algae occur profusely in the extracapsulum. The algal symbionts living within the protection of the extracapsulum provide photosynthetically derived food for the radiolarian host.

In the order Spumellarida (class Polycystinea) the central capsule is perforated by numerous pores distributed evenly on the surface of the capsular wall. These pores, containing strands of cytoplasm, provide continuity between the cytoplasm in the central capsule and the surrounding extracapsulum. The skeletons of the Spumellarida are characteristically developed on a spherical organizational plan, but some are spiral-shaped (resembling snail shells) or produce elongate skeletons composed of numerous chambers built one upon another. In some genera, such as *Thalassicolla* (illus. *e*), there is no skeleton; in others there are rods or spicules, or often a single or multiple concentric latticework skeleton (illus. *c*).

Multicellular aggregates (colonies of spumellaridans), measuring several centimeters in diameter (or even several meters in some rare elongate forms), consist of numerous radiolarian central capsules enclosed within a gelatinous envelope and interconnected by a web of rhizopodia that bears abundant algal symbionts. A thin halo of feeding rhizopodia protrudes from the surface of the colony and is used to capture prey. Reproduction is poorly understood. In some colonial forms, daughter colonies are produced by asexual reproduction (fission). Flagellated swarmers (illus. *f*) released from mature central capsules of some species are possibly gametes and contain a large crystal inclusion of strontium sulfate.

In the Nasselarida (Polycystinea), the central capsule is often ovate and the pores are localized at one pole (illus. *d*). The axopodia and rhizopodia emerge from this pore field and are supplied by a conelike array of microtubules within the central capsule. The skeleton, when present, is often shaped like a dome or helmet.

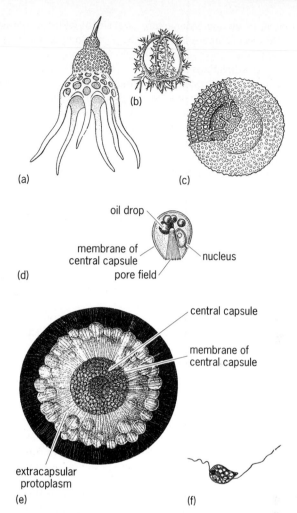

Radiolaria. Skeletons representing (*a, b*) certain Nasselarida
(or Monopylina) and (*c*) certain Spumellarida (or Peripylina).
(*d*) Central capsule, one of the Nasselarida showing one
group of pores. (*e*) *Thalassicolla*, one of the Spumellarida
without skeletal elements. (*f*) Biflagellate gametes. (*After
L. H. Hyman, The Invertebrates, vol. 1, McGraw-Hill*, 1940)

Radiolarians in the class Phaeodarea possess a central capsule with two types of
pore areas, a larger one (astropyle) that serves as a kind of cytopharynx where food is
carried into the central capsule, and two accessory openings (parapylae) where smaller
strands of cytoplasm emerge. The skeleton exhibits a wide range of shapes, including
geodesic-like lattice spheres and small porous clam-shaped shells.

Radiolarians have a fossil record that extends back to early Paleozoic time, about a
half billion years ago. Compared to other groups of shell-bearing marine microplankton, they are highly diverse, several hundred species having inhabited the oceans at
any given time. Because they are planktonic and have undergone continuous evolutionary change, radiolarians are particularly useful for determining time equivalence

(and geological ages) of marine sedimentary deposits at widely separated localities. The Cenozoic record of radiolarians in sediments, particularly on the deep-sea floor, is sufficiently complete to show the course of evolutionary change in considerable detail.

Assemblages of fossil radiolarians also provide clues to oceanic conditions during the geological past. Each of the major oceanic water masses has its characteristic radiolarian fauna, and so changes in the distribution or composition of these assemblages can be interpreted in terms of changes in the pattern of water masses, or in their oceanographic properties. *See* PROTOZOA.   [O.R.A.; W.R.R.]

Raffinose   The best-known trisaccharide (oligosaccharide), widely distributed in higher plants. The best-known sources are cottonseed meal and the manna of *Eucalyptus*. It is also known as melitose, melitriose, gossypose, and *O*-α-D-galactopyranosyl-(1→6)-*O*-α-D-glucopyranosyl-(1→2)-β-D-fructofuranoside. *See* OLIGOSACCHARIDE.

Complete acid hydrolysis gives 1 mole each of D-galactose, D-glucose, and D-fructose. In structure, it comprises melibiose and sucrose with the central D-glucose in common. *See* FRUCTOSE; GALACTOSE; GLUCOSE.

Raffinose can be hydrolyzed by enzymes in two ways. Invertase (β-D-fructofuranoside) hydrolyzes the sucrose part of the molecule to give melibiose and D-fructose. Almond emulsin, which contains an α-D-galactosidase, hydrolyzes the melibiose residue to yield D-galactose and sucrose.

Raffinose was found to be enzymically synthesized in plants from uridine diphosphate D-galactose and sucrose by an enzyme which transfers the D-galactose moiety of this sugar nucleotide to sucrose, resulting in the formation of raffinose.   [W.Z.H.]

Rainforest   Forests that occur in continually wet climates with no dry season. There are relatively small areas of temperate rainforests in the Americas and Australasia, but most occur in the tropics and subtropics.

The most extensive tropical rainforests are in the Americas. These were originally 1.54×10^6 mi^2 (4×10^6 km^2) in extent, about half the global total, and mainly in the Amazon basin. A narrow belt also occurs along the Atlantic coast of Brazil, and a third block lies on the Pacific coast of South America, extending from northern Peru to southern Mexico.

Tropical rainforests have a continuous canopy (commonly 100–120 ft or 30–36 m tall) above which stand huge emergent trees, reaching 200 ft (60 m) or taller. Within the rainforest canopy are trees of many different sizes, including pygmies, that reach only a few feet. Trees are the main life form and are often, for purposes of description and analysis, divided into strata or layers. Trees form the framework of the forest and support an abundance of climbers, orchids, and other epiphytes, adapted to the microclimatic conditions of the different zones of the canopy, from shade lovers in the gloomy, humid lower levels, to sun lovers in the brightly lit, hotter, and drier upper levels. Most trees have evergreen leaves, many of which are pinnate or palmate. These features of forest structure and appearance are found throughout the world's lowland tropical rainforests. There are other equally distinctive kinds of rainforest in the lower and upper parts of perhumid tropical mountains, and additional types on wetlands.

Rainforests occur where the monthly rainfall exceeds 4 in. (100 mm) for 9–12 months. They merge into other seasonal or monsoon forests where there is a stronger dry season (3 months or more with 2.5 in. or 60 mm of rainfall). The annual mean temperature in the lowlands is approximately 64°F (18°C). There is no season unfavorable for growth.

Primary rainforests are exceedingly rich in species of both plants and animals. There are usually over 100 species of trees 2.5 in. (10 cm) in diameter or bigger per 2.4 acres (1 ha). There are also numerous species of climbers and epiphytes. Flowering and fruiting occur year-round, but commonly there is a peak season; animal breeding may be linked to this. Secondary rainforests are much simpler. There are fewer tree species, less variety from location to location, and fewer epiphytes and climbers; the animals are also somewhat different. *See* ECOLOGICAL SUCCESSION.

Tropical rainforests are a source of resins, dyes, drugs, latex, wild meat, honey, rattan canes, and innumerable other products essential to rural life and trade. Modern technology for extraction and for processing has given timber of numerous species monetary value, and timber has come to eclipse other forest products in importance. The industrial nations use much tropical hardwood for furniture, construction, and plywood. Rainforest timbers, however, represent only 11% of world annual industrial wood usage, a proportion that has doubled since 1950. West Africa was the first main modern source, but by the 1960s was eclipsed by Asia, where Indonesia and Malaysia are the main producers of internationally traded tropical hardwoods. Substantial logging has also developed in the neotropics. *See* FOREST ECOSYSTEM.   [T.C.Wh.]

Recombination (genetics)   The formation of new genetic sequences by piecing together segments of previously existing ones. Recombination often follows deoxyribonucleic acid (DNA) transfer in bacteria and, in higher organisms, is a regular feature of sexual reproduction. *See* DEOXYRIBONUCLEIC ACID (DNA); REPRODUCTION (ANIMAL); REPRODUCTION (PLANT).

The fact that recombinants occur in sexual reproduction is due to reciprocal exchanges between chromosomes (crossing over) that take place in the first meiotic division. *See* CROSSING-OVER (GENETICS).

Crossing-over between homologous chromosome pairs can also occur during the prophase of mitotic nuclear division. The frequency is very much lower than in meiosis, presumably because the mitotic cell does not form the synaptic apparatus for efficient pairing of homologs. *See* MITOSIS.

Recombination was once thought to occur only between genes, never within them. Indeed, the supposed indivisibility of the gene was regarded as one of its defining features, the other being that it was a single unit of function. However, examination of very large progenies shows that, in all organisms studied, nearly all functionally allelic mutations of independent origin can recombine with each other to give nonmutant products, generally at frequencies ranging from a few percent (the exceptionally high frequency found in *Saccharomyces*) down to 0.001% or less. Recombination within genes is most frequently nonreciprocal.

Bacteria have no sexual reproduction in the true sense, but many or most of them are capable of transferring fragments of DNA from cell to cell by one of three mechanisms. (1) Fragments of the bacterial genome can become joined to plasmid DNA and transferred by cell conjugation. (2) Genomic fragments can be carried from cell to cell in the infective coats of bacterial viruses (phages), a process called transduction. (3) Many bacteria have the capacity to assimilate fragments of DNA from solution and so may acquire genes from disrupted cells. Fragments of DNA acquired by any of these methods can be integrated into the DNA of the genome in place of homologous sequences previously present. Homologous integration in bacteria is similar in its nonreciprocal nature to recombination within genes of eukaryotic organisms. *See* BACTERIAL GENETICS; BACTERIOPHAGE; TRANSDUCTION (BACTERIA).

Bacteriophages, plasmids, bacteria, and unicellular eukaryotes provide many examples of differentiation through controlled and site-specific recombination of DNA segments. In vertebrates, a controlled series of deletions leads to the generation of the great diversity of gene sequences encoding the antibodies and T-cell receptors necessary for immune defense against pathogens. All these processes depend upon interaction and recombination between specific DNA sequences, catalyzed by site-specific recombinase enzymes. The molecular mechanisms may have some similarities with those responsible for general meiotic recombination, except that the latter does not depend on any specific sequence, only on similarity (homology) of the sequence recombined.

Techniques have been devised for the artificial transfer of DNA fragments from any source into cells of many different species, thus conferring new properties upon them (transformation). In bacteria and the yeast *S. cerevisiae*, integration of such DNA into the genome requires substantial sequence similarity between incoming DNA and the recipient site. However, cells of other fungi, higher plants, and animals are able to integrate foreign DNA into their chromosomes with little or no sequence similarity. These organisms appear to have some system that recombines the free ends of DNA fragments into chromosomes regardless of their sequences. It may have something in common with the mechanism, equally obscure, whereby broken ends of chromosomes can heal by nonspecific mutual joining. *See* TRANSFORMATION (BACTERIA).

The science of genetics has been revolutionized by the development of techniques using isolated cells for specific cleaving and rejoining of DNA segments and the introduction of the reconstructed molecules into living cells. This artificial recombination depends on the use of site-specific endonucleases (restriction enzymes) and DNA ligase. *See* GENE; GENE ACTION; GENETIC ENGINEERING; GENETICS; RESTRICTION ENZYME.   [J.R.S.F.]

Reflex   A simple, unlearned, yet specific behavioral response to a specific stimulus. Reflexes are exhibited by virtually all animals from protozoa to primates. Along with other, more complex stimulus-bound responses such as fixed action patterns, they constitute much of the behavioral repertoire of invertebrates. In higher animals, such as primates, where learned behavior dominates, reflexes nevertheless persist as an important component of total behavior.

The simplest known reflexes require only one neuron or, in the strictest sense, none. For example, ciliated protozoa, which are single cells and have no neurons, nevertheless exhibit apparently reflexive behaviors. However, most reflexes require activity in a large sequence of neurons. The neurons involved in most reflexes are connected by specific synapses to form functional units in the nervous system. Such a sequence begins with sensory neurons and ends with effector cells such as skeletal muscles, smooth muscles, and glands, which are controlled by motor neurons. The central neurons which are often interposed between the sensory and motor neurons are called interneurons. The sensory side of the reflex arc conveys specificity as to which reflex will be activated. The remainder of the reflex response is governed by the specific synaptic connections that lead to the effector neurons. A familiar reflex is the knee-jerk or stretch reflex. It involves the patellar (kneecap) tendon and a group of upper leg muscles. Other muscle groups show similar reflexes.   [J.L.La.]

Reforestation   The reestablishment of forest cover either naturally or artificially. Given enough time, natural regeneration will usually occur in areas where temperatures and rainfall are adequate and when grazing and wildfires are not too frequent.

Reforestation occurs on land where trees have been recently removed due to harvesting or to natural disasters such as a fire, landslide, flooding, or volcanic eruption. When abandoned cropland, pastureland, or grasslands are converted to tree cover, the practice is termed afforestation (where no forest has existed in recent memory). Afforestation is common in countries such as Australia, South Africa, Brazil, India, and New Zealand. Although natural regeneration can occur on abandoned cropland, planting trees will decrease the length of time required until the first harvest of wood.

Planting also has an advantage in that both tree spacing and tree species can be prescribed. The selection of tree species can be very important since it affects both wood quality and growth rates. Direct seeding is also used for both afforestation and reforestation, although it often is less successful and requires more seed than tree planting. Unprotected seed are often eaten by birds and rodents, and weeds can suppress growth of newly germinated seed. For these reasons, direct seeding accounts for only about 5% and 1% of artificial reforestation in Canada and the United States, respectively.

[D.B.So.]

Regeneration (biology)   The process by which an animal restores a lost part of its body. Broadly defined, the term can include wound healing, tissue repair, and many kinds of restorative activities. Within the field of developmental biology, however, most research in regeneration involves systems in which removing a complex structure or major part of an organism initiates a chain of events that produces a structure that duplicates the missing part both functionally and anatomically.

The best-known and most widely studied examples of regeneration are those involving epimorphosis, in which the lost structure is reproduced directly by a combination of cell proliferation and redifferentiation of new tissue. Examples can be found throughout the animal kingdom. Research on regenerating systems yields information regarding basic mechanisms of animal development. Noteworthy has been the progress in understanding the factors that control pattern formation in the development of complex structures, such as vertebrate limbs.

Mammals, birds, and reptiles have a much more poorly developed ability than amphibians and fish to regenerate complete organs, but nevertheless can reform missing tissue and restore function after partial removal of certain organs. For example, if part of the liver is cut away, the remaining portions increase in size to compensate for the missing tissue and to restore the normal functional capacity of the organ. The process of liver regeneration involves the triggering of active growth in the remaining liver cells, in cells of bile ductules, and in unspecialized cells called stem cells, all of which are usually quiescent in the normal liver. Proliferation of these cells and their subsequent differentiation are key events in the process by which the missing liver mass is replaced and adequate hepatic function restored. In the musculoskeletal system, different populations of quiescent stem cells allow efficient replacement of damaged or partially removed bones and muscles. *See* BONE; LIVER; MUSCLE.

Of all vertebrates, amphibians have the most highly developed capacity for regeneration. Certain species have the ability to regenerate not only limbs and tails but also parts of the eye, lower jaw, intestine, and heart. Complete regeneration of amputated limbs can occur throughout the lifetime of most salamanders and newts. In frogs and toads, the ability to regenerate limbs is lost during metamorphosis to the adult form.

Protozoa and simple multicellular animals, including sponges, coelenterates, and flatworms, display remarkable capacities for regeneration following various experimental manipulations. Regenerative ability in such organisms correlates closely with their capacity to reproduce asexually, most commonly by fission or by budding, and the mechanisms of growth involved in regeneration are often very similar to those of asexual propagation. For example, just as complete ciliated protozoa will develop after fission, which divides the nucleus and organelles between daughter cells, intact individuals will also be reconstituted from fragments of a single organism if the fragment contains a complete set of the genetic material and a portion of the original cell's cortical cytoplasm. Similar rules regarding the importance of the nucleus apply to regenerative processes in all protozoa.

Most annelids, such as the earthworm, can readily regenerate segments after their removal: some species can regenerate whole organisms from any fragment. Like more primitive invertebrates, certain annelids can reproduce asexually by transverse fission. The capacities for fission and for reconstitution from fragments in annelids are remarkable, considering the anatomical complexity of animals in this phylum. When an earthworm is cut transversely into two parts, the anterior part can regenerate several posterior segments. The ability of the posterior half to regenerate anterior segments is, however, more limited and is absent altogether in some species. Experiments in which components of the nervous system are removed surgically have revealed the importance of a neural influence for segment regeneration, presumably mediated by a growth-stimulating hormone secreted from neural cells. *See* ANNELIDA.

The ability of certain echinoderms, such as starfish, to regenerate missing arms is well known. Cutting such an animal into several pieces results in each piece forming a new organism, a phenomenon that usually requires the presence of at least some of the central portion of the body. Equally remarkable is a regenerative response shown by another echinoderm, the sea cucumber. When this animal is strongly irritated, it eviscerates itself through its anus or through a rupture of its body wall. This phenomenon produces a nearly empty sack of skin and muscle, which then proceeds to regenerate all the internal organs, beginning with the digestive tract. *See* ECHINODERMATA.

The capacity for appendage regeneration is widespread among the many diverse members of the phylum *Arthropoda*. In these complex animals with well-developed exoskeletons and no asexual mode of reproduction, regeneration shows a close correlation with the molting process. *See* ARTHROPODA; DEVELOPMENTAL BIOLOGY.   [A.Me.]

Reproduction (animal)   The formation of new individuals, which may occur by asexual or sexual methods. In the asexual methods, which occur mainly among the lower animals, the offspring are derived from a single individual. Sexual methods are general throughout the animal kingdom, with offspring ordinarily derived from the paired union of special cells, the gametes, from two individuals. Basic to all processes of reproduction is the origin of the new individual from one or more living cells of the parent or parents.

Asexual reproduction. Asexual processes of reproduction include binary fission, multiple fission, fragmentation, budding, and polyembryony. Among the protozoa and lower metazoa, these are common methods of reproduction. However, the last-mentioned process can occur in mammals, including humans.

Binary fission involves an equal, or nearly equal, longitudinal or transverse splitting of the body of the parent into two parts, each of which grows to parental size and form. This method of reproduction occurs regularly among protozoans.

Multiple fission, schizogony, or sporulation produces several new individuals from a single parent. It is common among the Sporozoa, such as the malarial parasite, which form cystlike structures containing many cells, each of which gives rise to a new individual.

Fragmentation is a form of fission occurring in some metazoans, especially the Platyhelminthes, or flatworms; the Nemertinea, or ribbon worms; and the Annelida, or segmented worms. The parent worm breaks up into a number of parts, each of which regenerates missing structures to form a whole organism.

Budding is a form of asexual reproduction in which the new individual arises from a relatively small mass of cells that initially forms a growth or bud on the parental body. The bud may assume parental form either before separation from the body of the parent as in external budding, or afterward, as in internal budding. External budding is common among sponges, coelenterates, bryozoans, flatworms, and tunicates. Internal budding occurs among fresh-water sponges and bryozoans. In the sponges the internal buds, termed gemmules, consist of groups of primitive cells surrounded by a dense capsule formed by the body wall. If the parent animal dies as a result of desiccation or low temperature, the cells of the gemmules can later be released and form new sponges. In the bryozoans the similarly functioning buds are known as statoblasts.

Polyembryony is a form of asexual reproduction, occurring at an early developmental stage of a sexually produced embryo, in which two or more offspring are derived from a single egg. Examples are found scattered throughout the animal kingdom, including humans; in humans it is represented by identical twins, triplets, or quadruplets.

Sexual reproduction. Sexual reproduction in animals assumes various forms which may be classified under conjugation, autogamy, fertilization (syngamy), and parthenogenesis. Basically, the various processes all involve the occurrence of certain special nuclear changes, termed meiotic divisions, preliminary to the production of the new individual. *See* GAMETOGENESIS; MEIOSIS.

Conjugation occurs principally among the ciliate protozoans, such as *Paramecium*, and involves a temporary union of two individuals during which each is "fertilized" by a micronucleus from the other.

In autogamy the nuclear changes described for conjugation take place, but since there is no mating, there is no transfer of micronuclei. Instead, the prospective migratory micronucleus reunites with the stationary one. The process may be considered related to parthenogenesis.

Fertilization, or syngamy, comprises a series of events in which two cells, the gametes, fuse and their nuclei, which had previously undergone meiotic divisions, fuse. In metazoans, the gametes are of two morphologically distinct types: spermatozoa, or microgametes, and eggs, also called ova or macrogametes. These types are produced by male and female animals, respectively, but in some cases both may be produced by a single, hermaphroditic individual. The nucleus of the spermatozoon has half the number of chromosomes characteristic of the ordinary (somatic) cells of the animal. The nucleus of the ripe egg in some animals, for instance, coelenterates and echinoderms, also has attained this haploid condition, but in most species of animals it is at an early stage of the meiotic divisions when ready for fertilization. In the latter situation, the meiotic divisions of the egg, characterized by formation of small, nonfunctional cells termed polar bodies, are completed after the sperm enters, whereupon the haploid egg nucleus fuses with the haploid sperm nucleus. Fertilization thus produces a zygote with the diploid chromosome number typical of the somatic cells of the species (23 pairs in humans), and this is maintained during the ensuing cell divisions.

Parthenogenesis is the development of the egg without fertilization by a spermatozoon. It is listed as a form of sexual reproduction because it involves development from a gamete. Rotifers, crustaceans, and insects are the principal groups in which it occurs naturally. It has also been induced (artificial parthenogenesis) in species from all the major phyla by various kinds of chemical or physical treatment of the unfertilized egg. Even in mammals, several adult rabbits have reportedly been thus produced. *See* ESTRUS; OOGENESIS; OVUM; SPERM CELL; SPERMATOGENESIS.   [A.T.; H.L.H.]

Reproduction (plant)   The formation by a plant of offspring that are either exact copies or reasonable likenesses. When the process is accomplished by a single individual without fusion of cells, it is referred to as asexual; when fusion of cells is involved, whether from an individual or from different donors, the process is sexual.

Asexual reproduction. Using the technique of tissue culture, higher green plants can be regenerated from a single cell and can usually flower and set seed normally when removed and placed in soil. This experiment shows that each cell of the plant body carries all the information required for formation of the entire organism. The culture of isolated cells or bits of tissue thus constitutes a means of vegetative propagation of the plant and can provide unlimited copies identical to the organism from which the cells were derived.

All other vegetative reproductive devices of higher plants are elaborations of this basic ability and tendency of plant cells to produce tissue masses that can organize into growing points (meristems) to yield the typical patterns of differentiated plant organs. For example, a stem severed at ground level may produce adventitious roots. Similarly, the lateral buds formed along stems can, if excised, give rise to entire plants. The "eyes" of the potato tuber, a specialized fleshy stem, are simply buds used in vegetative propagation of the crop. In many plants, cuttings made from fleshy roots can similarly form organized buds and reconstitute the plant by vegetative propagation. Thus, each of the vegetative organs of the plant (leaf, stem, and root) can give rise to new plants by asexual reproduction. *See* PLANT PROPAGATION.

Sexual reproduction. While in asexual reproduction, the genetic makeup of the progeny rarely differs greatly from that of the parent, the fusion of cells in sexual reproduction can give rise to new genetic combinations, resulting in new types of plants. The life cycle of higher green plants consists of two distinct generations, based on the chromosomal complement of their cells. The sporophyte generation is independent and dominant in the flowering plants and ferns, but small, nongreen, and dependent in the mosses, and contains the $2n$ number of chromosomes. The diploidy results in each case from the fusion of sperm and egg to form the zygote, which then develops into an embryo and finally into the mature sporophyte. The sporophyte generation ends with the formation of $1n$ spores by reduction division, or meiosis, in a spore mother cell. The spore then develops into the gametophyte generation, which in turn produces the sex cells, or gametes. The gametophyte generation ends when gametes fuse to form the zygote, restoring the $2n$ situation typical of sporophytes. *See* MEIOSIS.

In flowering plants, the gametophyte or $1n$ generation is reduced to just a few cells (generally three for the male and eight for the female). The male gametophyte is formed after meiosis occurs in the microspore mother cells of the anther, yielding a tetrad of $1n$ microspores. Each of these microspores then divides mitotically at least twice. The first division produces the tube nucleus and the generative nucleus. The generative nucleus then divides again to produce two sperms. These nuclei are generally not separated by cell walls, but at this stage the outer wall of the spore becomes thickened and distinctively patterned—a stage typical of the mature male gametophyte, the pollen grain. *See* FLOWER; MITOSIS; POLLEN; POLLINATION.

Each pollen grain has a weak pore in its wall, through which the pollen tube emerges at the time of germination. Pollen germinates preferentially in the viscous secretion on the surface of the stigma, and its progress down the style to the ovary is guided through specific cell-to-cell recognition processes. Throughout its growth, which occurs through the deposition of new cell wall material at the advancing tip, the pollen tube is controlled by the tube nucleus, usually found at or near the tip. When the pollen tube, responding to chemical signals, enters the micropyle of the ovule, its growth ceases and the tip bursts, discharging the two sperms into the embryo sac, the female gametophyte of the ovary.

The female gametophyte generation, like the male, arises through meiotic division of a $2n$ megaspore mother cell. This division forms four $1n$ megaspores, of which three usually disintegrate, the fourth developing into an eight-nucleate embryo sac by means of three successive mitotic divisions. The eight nuclei arrange themselves into two groups of four, one at each pole of the embryo sac. Then one nucleus from each pole moves to the center of the embryo sac. One of the three nuclei at the micropylar end of the embryo sac is the female gamete, the egg, which fuses with one of the sperm nuclei to form the zygote, the first cell of the sporophyte generation, which produces the embryo. The second sperm fuses with the two polar nuclei at the center of the embryo sac to form a $3n$ cell that gives rise to the endosperm of the seed, the tissue in which food is stored. The entire ovule ripens into the seed, with the integuments forming the protective seed coat. The entire ovary ripens into a fruit, whose color, odor, and taste are attractive to animals, leading to dispersal of the seeds. The life cycle is completed when the seed germinates and grows into a mature sporophyte with flowers, in which meiotic divisions will once again produce $1n$ microspores and megaspores.

Nonflowering higher plants such as the ferns and mosses also show a distinct alternation of generations. The familiar fern plant of the field is the sporophyte generation. Meiosis occurs in sporangia located in special places on the leaves, generally the undersides or margins. A spore mother cell produces a tetrad of $1n$ spores, each of which can germinate to produce a free-living, green gametophyte called a prothallus. On the prothallus are produced male and female sex organs called antheridia and archegonia, which give rise to sperms and eggs, respectively. Sperms, motile because of their whiplike flagella, swim to the archegonium, where they fertilize the egg to produce the zygote that gives rise to the sporophyte generation again.

In mosses, by contrast, the dominant green generation is the gametophyte. Antheridia or archegonia are borne at the tips of these gametophytes, where they produce sperms and eggs, respectively. When suitably wetted, sperms leave the antheridium, swim to a nearby archegonium, and fertilize the egg to produce a $2n$ zygote that gives rise to a nongreen, simple, dependent sporophyte. The moss sporophyte consists mainly of a sporangium at the end of a long stalk, at the base of which is a mass of tissue called the foot, which absorbs nutrients from the green, photosynthetic gametophyte. Meiosis occurs in the sporangium when a spore mother cell gives rise to four reduced spores. Each spore can germinate, giving rise to a filamentous structure from which leafy gametophytic branches arise, completing the life cycle.

Various members of the algae that reproduce sexually also display alternation of generations, producing sperms and eggs in antheridia and oogonia. Sporophyte and gametophyte generations may each be free-living and independent, or one may be partially or totally dependent on the other. *See* Fruit; Plant physiology; Population dispersal; Seed.   [A.W.G.]

Reproductive behavior   Behavior related to the production of offspring; it includes such patterns as the establishment of mating systems, courtship, sexual behavior, parturition, and the care of young. Successful reproductive efforts require the establishment of a situation favorable for reproduction, often require behavior leading to the union of male and female gametes, and often require behavior that facilitates or ensures the survival and development of the young; the mere union of gametes is not generally sufficient for successful reproduction. For each species, there is a complex set of behavioral adaptations that coordinate the timing and patterning of reproductive activity. Typically, this entails integration of both overt behavioral and internal physiological events in both male and female, all of which are intricately enmeshed in manners adapted to the environment in which the animals live. The behavioral patterns related to reproduction tend to be relatively stereotyped within a species, but diverse among different species—especially distantly related species. The end products of cycles of reproductive activity are viable, fertile offspring which, in turn, will reproduce and thus perpetuate the species. *See* Animal communication; Behavioral ecology; Ethology; Reproduction (animal).   [D.A.D.]

Reproductive system   The structures concerned with the production of sex cells (gametes) and perpetuation of the species. The reproductive function constitutes the only vertebrate physiological function that necessitates the existence of two morphologically different kinds of individuals in each animal species, the males and the females (sexual dimorphism). The purpose of the reproductive function is fertilization, that is, the fusion of a male and a female sex cell produced by two distinct individuals.

Anatomy. Egg cells, or ova, and sperm cells, or spermatozoa, are formed in the primary reproductive organs, which are collectively known as gonads. Those of the male are called testes; those of the female are ovaries. The gonads are paired structures, although in some forms what appears to be an unpaired gonad is the result either of fusion of paired structures or of unilateral degeneration.

The reproductive elements formed in the gonads must be transported to the outside of the body. In most vertebrates, ducts are utilized for this purpose. These ducts, together with the structures that serve to bring the gametes of both sexes together, are known as accessory sex organs. The structures used to transport the reproductive cells in the male are known as deferent ducts and those of the female as oviducts. In a few forms no ducts are present in either sex, and eggs and sperm escape from the body cavity through genital or abdominal pores.

Oviducts, except in teleosts and a few other fishes, are modifications of Möllerian ducts formed during early embryonic development. In all mammals, each differentiates into an anterior, nondistensible Fallopian tube and a posterior, expanded uterus. In all mammals except monotremes the uterus leads to a terminal vagina which serves for the reception of the penis of the male during copulation. The lower part, or neck, of the uterus is usually telescoped into the vagina to a slight degree. This portion is referred to as the cervix.

In most vertebrates the reproductive ducts in both sexes open posteriorly into the cloaca. In some, modifications of the cloacal region occur and the ducts open separately to the outside or, in the male, join the excretory ducts to emerge by a common orifice. *See* OVARY; REPRODUCTION (ANIMAL); TESTIS.   [C.K.W.]

Physiology. The physiological process by which a living being gives rise to another of its kind is considered one of the outstanding characteristics of plants and animals. It is one of the two great drives of all animals; self-preservation and racial perpetuation.

Estrous and menstrual cycles. The cyclic changes of reproductive activities in mammalian females are known as estrous or menstrual cycles.

Most mammalian females accept males only at estrus (heat). Estrus in mammals can occur several times in one breeding season; the mare, ewe, and rat come to estrus every 21, 16, and 5 days respectively if breeding does not take place. This condition is called poly estrus. The bitch is monestrous; she has only one heat, or estrus, to the breeding season and if not served then, she does not come into heat again for a prolonged interval, 4–6 months according to different breeds. In monestrous and seasonally polyestrous species the period of sexual quiescence between seasons is called anestrus. *See* ESTRUS.

The reproductive cycle of the female in the primate and human is well marked by menstruation, the period of vaginal blood flow. Menstruation does not correspond to estrus but occurs between the periods of ovulation at the time the corpus luteum declines precipitously. *See* MENSTRUATION.

Mating. Mating, also called copulation or coitus, is the synchronized bodily activity of the two sexes which enables them to deposit their gametes in close contact. It is essential for successful fertilization because sperm and ovum have a very limited life span.

The logistics of sperm transport to the site of fertilization in the oviduct present many interesting features in mammals, but it is important to distinguish between passive transport of sperm cells in the female genital tract, and sperm migration, which clearly attributes significance to the intrinsic motility of the cell. Viable spermatozoa are actively motile, and although myometrial contractions play a major role in sperm transport through the uterus, progressive motility does contribute to migration into and within the oviducts. Even though a specific attractant substance for spermatozoa has not yet been demonstrated to be released from mammalian eggs or their investments, some form of chemotaxis may contribute to the final phase of sperm transport and orientation toward the egg surface.

Although in most mammalian species the oocyte is shed from the Graafian follicle in a condition suitable for fertilization, ejaculated spermatozoa must undergo some form of physiological change in the female reproductive tract before they can penetrate the egg membranes. The interval required for this change varies according to species, and the process is referred to as capacitation. The precise changes that constitute capacitation remain unknown, although there is strong evidence that they are—at least in part—membrane-associated phenomena, particularly in the region of the sperm head, that permit release of the lytic acrosomal enzymes with which the spermatozoon gains access to the vitelline surface of the egg.

Fertilization takes place in the oviducts of mammals and the fertilized eggs or embryos do not descend to the uterus for some 3 to 4 days in most species. During this interval, the embryo undergoes a series of mitotic divisions until it comprises a sphere of 8 or 16 cells and is termed a morula. Formation of a blastocyst occurs when the cells of the morula rearrange themselves around a central, fluid-filled cavity, the blastocoele. As the blactocyst develops within the uterine environment, it sheds its protective coat and undergoes further differentiation before developing an intimate association with the endometrium, which represents the commencement of implantation or nidation.

Association of the embryo with the uterine epithelium, either by superficial attachment or specific embedding in or beneath the endometrium, leads in due course to the formation of a placenta and complete dependence of the differentiating embryo upon metabolic support from the mother. Implantation and placentation exhibit a variety of forms, but in all instances the hormonal status of the mother is of great importance in determining whether or not implantation can proceed.

Endocrine function. The endocrine glands secrete certain substances (hormones) which are necessary for growth, metabolism, reproduction, response to stress, and various other physiological processes. The endocrine glands most concerned with the process of reproduction are the pituitary and the gonads.

The posterior lobe of the pituitary gland secretes two neuro-humoral agents, vasopressin and oxytocin. These are involved in reproduction only indirectly, through their effect on uterine contractility in labor and on the release of milk from the mammary gland when a suckling stimulus is applied. The anterior lobe secretes a variety of trophic hormones, including two gonadotrophic hormones, the follicle-stimulating hormone (FSH) and the luteinizing or interstitial-cell stimulating hormone (LH or ICSH). These hormones act directly on both ovaries and testes. *See* PITUITARY GLAND.

The gonadal (steroidal) hormones control the secretion of gonadotrophins by acting on the hypothalamus. It has been suggested that steroids act by means of a "negative feedback"; that is, high levels of circulating gonadal hormones stop further release of gonadotropins. However, although this is true for experiments involving pharmacological doses of such hormones, it may not be the case with endogenous physiological levels. It is certainly true that less steroid is required to inhibit pituitary function in the female than in the male. Under certain circumstances small doses of gonadal hormones can stimulate release of gonadotropic hormones from the pituitary. Estrogen can simulate the release of LH; hence the occurrence of ovulation in rats, rabbits, sheep, and women. Progesterone can also facilitate ovulation in persistently estrous rats, in chickens, and in estrous sheep and monkeys. *See* ESTROGEN; PROGES-TERONE.

The formation of gametes (spermatogenesis and oogenesis) is controlled by anterior pituitary hormones. The differentiation of male and female reproductive tracts is influenced, and mating behavior and estrous cycles are controlled, by male or female hormones. The occurrence of the breeding season is mainly dependent upon the activity of the anterior lobe of the pituitary, which is influenced through the nervous system by external factors, such as light and temperature. The transportation of ova from the ovary to the Fallopian tube and their subsequent transportation, development, and implantation in the uterus are controlled by a balanced ratio between estrogen and progesterone. Furthermore, it is known that estrogens, androgens, and progesterone can all have the effect of inhibiting the production or the secretion, or both, of gonadotrophic hormones, permitting the cyclic changes of reproductive activity among different animals.

Mammary glands are essential for the nursing of young. Their growth, differentiation, and secretion of milk, and in fact the whole process of lactation, are controlled by pituitary hormones as well as by estrogen and progesterone. Other glands and physiological activities also influence lactation, although this is largely via the trophic support of other pituitary hormones.   [M.C.C.; M.J.K.H.; R.H.F.H.]

Reptilia   A class of vertebrates composed of four living orders, the turtles or Chelonia, the tuatara or Sphenodonta, the lizards and snakes or Squamata, and the crocodylians or Crocodylia. Numerous extinct orders are also known. The group first appeared in the Carboniferous and underwent a culminating evolutionary radiation in the Mesozoic, often called the age of reptiles. Although the major portion of the class is now extinct, several Recent groups, particularly the Squamata, are very successful, and there are approximately 5000 living species of reptiles as compared to about 4000 living mammals.

The reptiles are the most primitive of the completely terrestrial vertebrates and are consequently the first to exhibit amniote features. Reptile eggs are covered by a complex series of protective layers, including a leathery or calcareous shell. A rich supply of food material in the form of yolk is deposited inside the ovum to furnish food for the developing embryo. A series of protective extraembryonic membranes, the serosa and amnion, appears later in embryogenesis to protect the embryo from water loss and shock. A third such membrane, the allantois, functions as a storage sac for nitrogenous wastes. The serosa and allantois usually fuse to form a respiratory structure. Gaseous exchanges take place across the shell and seroallantoic membrane between the outside air and the blood vessels of the allantois. These adaptations allowed the reptile egg to be deposited on land, undergo its development there, and hatch into a fully developed form without a gilled larval stage. Most reptilian eggs are buried in the soil or in rotting vegetation out of direct sunlight. *See* AMNIOTA.

Paleoherpetology, the study of fossil reptiles, is especially important for two reasons. First, the class Reptilia lies at the center of vertebrate history; the reptiles evolved from the amphibians (which themselves had originated from the fishes), and both birds and mammals evolved from the reptiles. Thus reptiles are concerned in three of the four major "jumps" (the class-to-class transitions) in vertebrate evolution. The distinction between the living representatives of two successive classes is always very clear, being based on a number of features of their anatomy, physiology, and embryology; the distinction between their fossil members, however, is inevitably less clear, not only because the distinction must be based almost entirely upon characters of the skeleton but also because there must have been animals with a mixture of the characters of both classes during the transitional period. These help elucidate the reasons for the jumps and the precise mechanism by which each occurred. *See* AMPHIBIA; ANIMAL EVOLUTION.

Second, the Reptilia were the dominant class of land vertebrates (and were also important in the sea and in the air) during a very long period of the Earth's history. Knowledge of the extinct reptiles, their morphology and their habits, is vital to an understanding of the life of those times, of how the animals and plants and the physical environment reacted upon each other (paleoecology).   [A.J.C.]

Respiration The various processes associated with the biochemical transformation of the energy available in the organic substrates derived from foodstuffs, to energy usable for synthetic and transport processes, external work, and, eventually, heat. This transformation, generally identified as metabolism, most commonly requires the presence of oxygen and involves the complete oxidation of organic substrates to carbon dioxide and water (aerobic respiration). If the oxidation is incomplete, resulting in organic compounds as end products, oxygen is typically not involved, and the process is then identified as anaerobic respiration. *See* METABOLISM.

The term "external respiration" is more appropriate for describing the exchange of O_2 and CO_2 between the organism and its environment. In most multicellular organisms, and nearly all vertebrates (with the exception of a few salamanders lacking both lungs and gills), external respiration takes place in specialized structures termed respiratory organs, such as gills and lungs. *See* LUNG; RESPIRATORY SYSTEM.

The ultimate physical process causing movement of gases across living tissues is simple passive diffusion. Respiratory gas exchange also depends on two convective fluid movements. The first is the bulk transport of the external medium, air or water, to and across the external respiratory exchange surfaces. The second is the transport of coelomic fluid or blood across the internal surfaces of the respiratory organ. These two convective transports are referred to as ventilation and circulation (or perfusion). They are active processes, powered by ciliary or muscular pumps.

In all vertebrates and many invertebrates, the circulating internal medium (coelomic fluid, hemolymph, or blood) contains a respiratory pigment, for example, hemocyanin or hemoglobin, which binds reversibly with O_2, CO_2, and protons. Respiratory pigments augment respiratory gas exchange, both by increasing the capacity for bulk transport of the gases, and by influencing gas partial pressure (concentration) gradients across tissue exchange surfaces. *See* BLOOD; HEMOGLOBIN; RESPIRATORY PIGMENTS (INVERTEBRATE).

The physiological adjustment of organisms to variations in their need for aerobic energy production involves regulated changes in the exchange and transport of respiratory gases. The adjustments are effected by rapid alterations in the ventilatory and circulatory pumps and by longer-term modifications in the respiratory properties of blood.   [K.J.]

Respiratory system The system of organs involved in the acquisition of oxygen and the elimination of carbon dioxide by an organism. The lungs and gills are the two most important structures of vertebrates involved in the phase known as external respiration, or gaseous exchanges, between the blood and environment. Internal respiration refers to the gaseous exchanges which occur between the blood and cells. Certain other structures in some species of vertebrates serve as respiratory organs; among these are the integument or skin of fishes and amphibians. The moist, highly vascular skin of anuran amphibians is important in respiration. Certain species of fish have a vascular rectum which is utilized as a respiratory structure, water being taken in and ejected regularly by the animal. Saclike cloacal structures occur in some aquatic species of turtles. These are vascular and are intermittently filled with, and emptied of, water. It is thought that they may function in respiration. During embryonic life the yolk sac and allantois are important respiratory organs in certain vertebrates. *See* YOLK SAC.

Structurally, respiratory organs usually present a vascular surface that is sufficiently extensive to provide an adequate area of absorption for gaseous exchange. This surface is moist and thin enough to allow for the passage of gases.   [R.S.McE./T.S.P.]

The shape and volume of the lung, because of its pliability, conforms almost completely to that of its cavity. The lungs are conical; each has an apex and a base, two surfaces, two borders, and a hilum. The apex extends into the superior limit of the thoracic cavity. The base is the diaphragmatic surface. The costal surface may show bulgings into the intercostal spaces. The medial surface has a part lying in the space beside the vertebral column and a part imprinted by the form of structures bulging outward beneath the mediastinal pleura. The cardiac impression is deeper on the left lung because of the position of the heart.

For convenience the lung may be divided into anatomical areas. The bronchial tree branches mainly by dichotomy. The ultimate generations, that is, the respiratory bronchioles, alveolar ducts, and alveoli constitute all of the respiratory portion of the lung. The trachea and extrapulmonary bronchi are kept open by C-shaped bars of hyaline cartilage. When in their branching the bronchi and bronchioles are reduced to a diameter of 1 mm or less, they are then free of cartilage and are called terminal bronchioles. One of the terminal bronchioles enters the apex of a secondary lobule of the lung. These secondary lobules are anatomic units of the lung, whose hexagonal bases rest on the pleura or next to a bronchiole or blood vessel. Finer lines divide the bases of the secondary lobules into smaller areas. These are the bases of primary lobules, each served by a respiratory bronchiole. *See* LUNG; RESPIRATION.

The blood supply to the lung is provided by the pulmonary and the bronchial arteries. The nerves which supply the lung are branches of the vagus and of the thoracic sympathetic ganglia 2, 3, and 4. Efferent vagal fibers are bronchoconstrictor and secretory, whereas the afferents are part of the arc for the breathing reflex. Efferent sympathetic fibers are bronchodilators; hence, the use of adrenalin for relief of bronchial spasm resulting from asthma. *See* NERVOUS SYSTEM (VERTEBRATE).   [L.P.C.]

Restoration ecology   A field in the science of conservation that is concerned with the application of ecological principles to restoring degraded, derelict, or fragmented ecosystems. The primary goal of restoration ecology (also known as ecological restoration) is to return a community or ecosystem to a condition similar in ecological structure, function, or both, to that existing prior to site disturbance or degradation.

A reference framework is needed to guide any restoration attempt—that is, to form the basis of the design (for example, desired species composition and density) and monitoring plan (for example, setting milestones and success criteria for restoration projects). Such a reference system is derived from ecological data collected from a suite of similar ecosystems in similar geomorphic settings within an appropriate biogeographic region. Typically, many sites representing a range of conditions (for example, pristine to highly degraded) are sampled, and statistical analyses of these data reveal what is possible given the initial conditions at the restoration site. *See* ECOSYSTEM.
                 [P.L.Fi.]

Restriction enzyme An enzyme, specifically an endode-oxyribonuclease, that recognizes a short specific sequence within a deoxyribonucleic acid (DNA) molecule and then catalyzes double-strand cleavage of that molecule. Restriction enzymes have been found only in bacteria, where they serve to protect the bacterium from the deleterious effects of foreign DNA. *See* DEOXYRIBONUCLEIC ACID (DNA).

There are three known types of restriction enzymes. Type I enzymes recognize a specific sequence on DNA, but cleave the DNA chain at random locations with respect to this sequence. They have an absolute requirement for the cofactors adenosine triphosphate (ATP) and S-adenosylmethionine. Because of the random nature of the cleavage, the products are a heterogeneous array of DNA fragments. Type II enzymes also recognize a specific nucleotide sequence but differ from the type I enzymes in that they do not require cofactors and they cleave specifically within or close to the recognition sequence, thus generating a specific set of fragments. It is this exquisite specificity which has made these enzymes of great importance in DNA research, especially in the production of recombinant DNAs. Type III enzymes have properties intermediate between those of the type I and type II enzymes. They recognize a specific sequence and cleave specifically a short distance away from the recognition sequence. They have an absolute requirement for the ATP cofactor, but they do not hydrolyze it.

A key feature of the fragments produced by restriction enzymes is that when mixed in the presence of the enzyme DNA ligase, the fragments can be rejoined. Should the new fragment carry genetic information that can be interpreted by the bacterial cell containing the recombinant molecule, then the information will be expressed as a protein and the bacterial cell will serve as an ideal source from which to obtain that protein. For instance, if the DNA fragment carries the genetic information encoding the hormone insulin, the bacterial cell carrying that fragment will produce insulin. By using this method, the human gene for insulin has been cloned into bacterial cells and used for the commercial production of human insulin. The potential impact of this technology forms the basis of the genetic engineering industry. *See* ENZYME; GENETIC ENGINEERING.

[R.Ro.]

Retrovirus A family of viruses distinguished by three characteristics: (1) genetic information in ribonucleic acid (RNA); (2) virions possess the enzyme reverse transcriptase; and (3) virion morphology consists of two proteinaceous structures, a dense core and an envelope that surrounds the core. Some viruses outside the retrovirus family have some of these characteristics, but none has all three. Numerous retroviruses have been described; they are found in all families of vertebrates. *See* ANIMAL VIRUS; REVERSE TRANSCRIPTASE; RIBONUCLEIC ACID (RNA).

The genome is composed of two identical molecules of single-stranded RNA, which are similar in structure and function to cellular messenger RNA. Deoxyribonucleic acid (DNA) is not present in the virions of retroviruses. The reverse transcriptase in each virus makes a DNA copy of the RNA genome shortly after entry of the virus into the host cell. The discovery of this enzyme changed thinking in biology. Previously, the only known direction for the flow of genetic information was from DNA to RNA, yet retroviruses make DNA copies of their genome by using an RNA template. This reversal of genetic information was considered backward and hence the family name retrovirus, meaning backward virus.

Once the DNA copy of the RNA genome is made, it is inserted directly into one of the chromosomes of the host cell. This results in new genetic information being acquired by the host species. The study of reverse transcriptase has led to other discoveries of how retroviruses add a variety of new genetic information into the host. One such class of genes carried by retroviruses is oncogenes, meaning tumor genes. Retroviral oncogenes appear to be responsible for tumors in animals. *See* ONCOGENES; VIRUS CLASSIFICATION.

Two distinct retroviruses have been discovered in humans. One is human T-cell lymphotropic virus type 1 (HTLV-1), a type C-like virus associated with adult T-cell leukemia. The other is the human acquired immune deficiency syndrome (AIDS) virus, a type E lentivirus. *See* ACQUIRED IMMUNE DEFICIENCY SYNDROME (AIDS).   [P.A.Ma.]

Reverse transcriptase   Any of the deoxyribonucleic acid (DNA) polymerases present in particles of retroviruses which are able to carry out DNA synthesis using an RNA template. This reaction is called reverse transcription since it is the opposite of the usual transcription reaction, which involves RNA synthesis using a DNA template. *See* RETROVIRUS.

The transfer of genetic information from RNA to DNA in retrovirus replication was proposed in 1964 by H. M. Temin in the DNA provirus hypothesis for the replication of Rous sarcoma virus, an avian retrovirus which causes tumors in chickens and transformation of cells in culture, and reverse transcriptase has since been purified from virions of many retroviruses. The avian, murine, and human retrovirus DNA polymerases have been extensively studied.

Studies indicate that reverse transcriptase is widely distributed in living organisms and that all reverse transcriptases are evolutionarily related. For example, the organization of the nucleotide sequence of integrated retroviral DNA has a remarkable resemblance to the structure of bacterial transposable elements, in particular, transposons.

Reverse transcriptase genes are present in the eukaryotic organisms in retrotransposons and in retroposons or long interspersed (LINE) elements. Both of these types of elements can transpose in cells. *See* DEOXYRIBONUCLEIC ACID (DNA); RIBONUCLEIC ACID (RNA); TRANSPOSONS.   [H.M.T.]

Rheumatic fever   An illness that follows an upper respiratory infection with the group A streptococcus (*Streptococcus pyogenes*) and is characterized by inflammation of the joints (arthritis) and the heart (carditis). Arthritis typically involves multiple joints and may migrate from one joint to another. The carditis may involve the outer lining of the heart, the heart muscle itself, or the inner lining of the heart. A minority of affected individuals also develop a rash (erythema marginatum), nodules under the skin, or Sydenham's chorea (a neurologic disorder characterized by involuntary, uncoordinated movements of the legs, arms, and face). Damage to heart valves may be permanent and progressive, leading to severe disability or death from rheumatic heart disease years after the initial attack. The disease occurs an average of 19 days after the infection and is thought to be the result of an abnormal immunologic reaction to the group A streptococcus. Initial attacks of rheumatic fever generally occur among individuals aged 5 to 15. Those who have had one attack are highly susceptible to recurrences after future streptococcal infections.

Initial attacks of rheumatic fever can be prevented by treatment of strep throat with penicillin for at least 10 days. Patients who have had an episode of rheumatic fever should continue taking antibiotics for many years to prevent group A streptococcal infections that may trigger a recurrence of rheumatic fever. *See* STREPTOCOCCUS.   [A.L.Bi.; J.B.Da.]

Rhinovirus   A genus of the family Picornaviridae. Members of the human rhinovirus group include at least 113 antigenically distinct types. Like the enteroviruses, the rhinoviruses are small (17–30 nanometers), contain ribonucleic acid (RNA), and are not inactivated by ether. Unlike the enteroviruses, they are isolated from the nose and throat rather than from the enteric tract, and are unstable if kept under acid conditions (pH 3–5) for 1–3 h. Rhinoviruses have been recovered chiefly from adults with colds and only rarely from patients with more severe respiratory diseases. See COMMON COLD.

In a single community, different rhinovirus types predominate during different seasons and during different outbreaks in a single season, but more than one type may be present at the same time.

Although efforts have been made to develop vaccines, none is available. Problems that hinder development of a useful rhinovirus vaccine include the short duration of natural immunity even to the specific infecting type, the large number of different antigenic types of rhinovirus, and the variation of types present in a community from one year to the next. See ANIMAL VIRUS; PICORNAVIRIDAE; VIRUS CLASSIFICATION.   [J.L.Me.; M.E.Re.]

Rhynchocoela   A phylum of bilaterally symmetrical, un-segmented, ribbonlike worms, frequently referred to as the Nemertinea. They have an eversible proboscis and a complete digestive tract with an anus. There is no coelom or body cavity, and the mesenchyme or parenchyma and the muscle fibers fill the area between the ciliated epidermis and the cellular lining of the digestive tract. Many species are brightly colored, sometimes having stripes or transverse bars.

The nemertineans are the simplest animals with a circulatory system. There are two lateral blood vessels and in some a third, unpaired dorsal vessel. The blood consists of a colorless fluid which may contain blood cells of several types. In species in which the blood is colored, the pigment is present in the cells. There is no heart, but the walls of the principal vessels may be contractile.

The nervous system has a pair of cerebral ganglia forming the brain as well as two longitudinal nerve cords and many smaller nerves. The ganglia and lateral cords may contain unusually large neurochord cells. In the epidermis there are scattered sensory nerve cells, probably tactile. A few to many simple eyes, or ocelli, may be present in front of the cerebral ganglia. There are no special respiratory organs; respiration occurs through the body surface. Nemertineans are usually either male or female, but a few individuals have both sex organs. Fertilization occurs outside the body in many species but may be internal in certain forms.

The nemertineans are mostly marine, bottom-dwelling worms, found in greatest numbers along the coasts of northern temperate regions. They live under stones, among the tangled masses of plants, in sand, mud, or gravel, and sometimes form mucus-lined tubes. A few are pelagic, fresh-water, or terrestrial. Certain species are commensal with other animals, but none can be regarded as parasitic in a strict sense.

That the Rhynchocoela represent the most highly organized acoelomate animals is indicated by the circulatory system, the presence of an anus, and the specialization of the epidermis. All groups of animals more, complex than the nemertineans have some kind of cavity, a pseudocoele or coelom, between the body wall and the gut, instead of solid mesenchyme. See COELOM.

The phylum Rhynchocoela, containing about 550 known species, is divided into two classes, Anopla and Enopla.   [A.G.Hu.: J.B.J.]

Ribonuclease   A group of enzymes, widely distributed in nature, which catalyze hydrolysis of the internucleotide phosphodiester bonds in ribonucleic acid (RNA). The sites of hydrolysis may vary considerably, depending upon the specificity of the particular enzyme. Differences in specificity for the site of cleavage have led to the use of these various ribonucleases as tools in determining the structure and chemistry of RNA. *See* Enzyme; Nucleic acid.

Research on ribonuclease has played a prime role in advancing the understanding of protein structure and function; also, it was the first protein to be totally synthesized from its component amino acids. Since the elucidation of the amino acid sequence of ribonuclease, much information has been compiled with regard to the three-dimensional structure of the enzyme and to specific regions of the molecule which are catalytically important. *See* Protein.   [R.L.He.]

Ribonucleic acid (RNA)   One of the two major classes of nucleic acid, mainly involved in translating into proteins the genetic information that is carried in deoxyribonucleic acid (DNA). Ribonucleic acids serve two functions in protein synthesis: transfer RNAs (tRNAs) and ribosomal RNAs (rRNAs) function in the synthesis of all proteins, while messenger RNAs (mRNAs) are a diverse set, each member of which acts specifically in the synthesis of one protein. Messenger RNA is the intermediate in the usual biological pathway DNA → RNA → protein. Ribonucleic acid is a very versatile molecule, however. In addition to the roles in protein synthesis, other types of RNA serve other important functions for cells and viruses, such as the involvement of small nuclear RNAs (snRNAs) in mRNA splicing. In some cases, RNA performs functions typically considered DNA-like, such as serving as the genetic material for certain viruses, or roles typically carried out by proteins, such as RNA enzymes or ribozymes. *See* Deoxyribonucleic acid (DNA).

Structure. RNA is a linear polymer of four different nucleotides. Each nucleotide is composed of three parts: a five-carbon sugar known as ribose, a phosphate group, and one of four bases attached to each ribose, either adenine (A), cytosine (C), guanine (G), or uracil (U). The structure of RNA is basically a repeating chain of ribose and phosphate moieties, with one of the four bases attached to each ribose. The structure and function of the RNA vary depending on its sequence and length. *See* Nucleotide; Ribose.

In its basic structure, RNA is quite similar to DNA. It differs by a single change in the sugar group (ribose instead of deoxyribose) and by the substitution of uracil for the base thymine (T). Typically, RNA does not exist as long double-stranded chains as does DNA, but rather as short single chains with higher-order structure due to base pairing and tertiary interactions within the RNA molecule. Within the cell, RNA usually exists in association with specific proteins in a ribonucleoprotein complex.

The nucleotide sequence of RNA is encoded in genes in the DNA, and it is transcribed from the DNA by a complementary templating mechanism that is catalyzed by one of the RNA polymerase enzymes. In this templating scheme, the DNA base T specifies A in the RNA, A specifies U, C specifies G, and G specifies C.

Transfer RNA. These small RNAs (70–90 nucleotides) that act as adapters to translate the nucleotide sequence of mRNA into protein sequence. They do this by carrying the appropriate amino acid to the ribosome during the process of protein synthesis. Each cell contains at least one type of tRNA specific for each of the 20 amino acids, and usually several types. The base sequence in the mRNA directs the appropriate amino acid-carrying tRNAs to the ribosome to ensure that the correct protein sequence is made. *See* Protein.

Ribosomal RNA. Ribosomes are complex ribonucleoprotein particles that are the site of protein synthesis, that is, the process of linking amino acids to form proteins. The RNA components of the ribosome account for more than half of its weight.

Like tRNAs, rRNAs are stable molecules and exist in complex folded structures. Each of these rRNAs is essential in determining the exact structure of the ribosome. In addition, the rRNAs, rather than the ribosomal proteins, are likely the basic functional elements of the ribosome. *See* RIBOSOMES.

Messenger RNA. Whereas most types of RNA are the final products of their genes, mRNA is an intermediate in information transfer. It carries information from DNA to the ribosome in a genetic code that the protein-synthesizing machinery translates into protein. Specifically, mRNA sequence is recognized in a sequential fashion as a series of nucleotide triplets by tRNAs via base pairing to the three-nucleotide anticodons in the tRNAs. There are specific triplet codons that specify the beginning and end of the protein-coding sequence. Thus, the function of mRNA involves the reading of its primary nucleotide sequence, rather than the activity of its overall structure. Messenger RNAs are typically shorter-lived than the more stable structural RNAs, such as tRNA and rRNA. *See* GENETIC CODE.

Small nuclear RNA. Small RNAs, generally less than 300 nucleotides long and rich in uridine (U), are localized in the nucleoplasm (snRNAs) and nucleolus (snoRNAs) of eukaryotic cells. There they take part in RNA processing, such as intron removal during eukaryotic mRNA splicing and posttranscriptional modification that occurs during production of mature rRNA. *See* INTRON.

Catalytic RNA. RNA enzymes, or ribozymes, are able to catalyze specific cleavage or joining reactions either in themselves or in other molecules of nucleic acid. *See* CATALYSIS; RIBOZYME.

Viral RNA. While most organisms carry their genetic information in the form of DNA, certain viruses, such as polio and influenza viruses, have RNA as their genetic material. The viral RNAs occur in different forms in different viruses. For example, some are single-stranded and some are double-stranded; some occur as a single RNA chromosome while others are multiple. In any case, the RNA is replicated as the genetic material and either its sequence, or a complementary copy of itself, serves as mRNA to encode viral proteins. The RNA viruses known as retroviruses contain an enzyme that promotes synthesis of complementary DNA in the host cell, thus reversing the typical flow of information in biological systems. *See* ANIMAL VIRUS; RETROVIRUS; VIRUS.

Other types of RNA. There are RNAs that serve other important and diverse cellular functions. For example, a ribonucleoprotein enzyme is responsible for replication of chromosome ends. Also, there is an essential RNA component in a ribonucleoprotein complex that ensures that membrane and secreted proteins are synthesized in the appropriate cellular location.

RNA molecules can function both as carriers of genetic information and as enzymes. The discoveries of RNA catalysis and of the central role of rRNA in protein synthesis have led to an enhanced appreciation of RNA as the probable original informational macromolecule, preceding both the more specialized DNA and protein molecules in evolution. *See* MOLECULAR BIOLOGY; NUCLEIC ACID.   [A.L.Be.; M.W.G.]

Ribose A water-soluble pentose, also known as D-ribose (see first structural formula), which, together with 2-deoxy-D-ribose, makes up the carbohydrate constituents of nucleic acids, which are found in all living organisms. The universal occurrence of nucleic acids in all living cells makes this pentose highly interesting to biochemists and biologists. The type of nucleic acid that yields D-ribose is referred to as ribonucleic acid (RNA). D-Ribose is a constituent not only of the nucleic acids, but also of several vitamins and coenzymes. As in the nucleic acids, this sugar occurs in the furanose

D-Ribose   α-D-Ribofuranose

configuration (see second structural formula) in these natural products. *See* COENZYME; DEOXYRIBOSE; NUCLEIC ACID; VITAMIN.   [W.Z.H.]

Ribosomes   Small particles, present in large numbers in every living cell, whose function is to convert stored genetic information into protein molecules. In this synthesis process, a molecule of messenger ribonucleic acid (mRNA) is fed through the ribosome, and each successive trinucleotide codon on the messenger is recognized by complementary base-pairing to the anticodon of an appropriate transfer RNA (tRNA) molecule, which is in turn covalently bound to a specific amino acid. The successive amino acids become linked together on the ribosome, forming a polypeptide chain whose amino acid sequence has thus been determined by the nucleic acid sequence of the mRNA. The polypeptide is subsequently folded into an active protein molecule. Ribosomes are themselves complex arrays of protein and RNA molecules, and their fundamental importance in molecular biology has prompted a vast amount of research, with a view to finding out how these particles function at the molecular level. *See* GENETIC CODE; PROTEIN; RIBONUCLEIC ACID (RNA).

Ribosomes are composed of two subunits, one approximately twice the size of the other. In the bacterium *Escherichia coli*, whose ribosomes have been the most extensively studied, the smaller subunit (30S) contains 21 proteins and a single 16S RNA molecule. The larger (50S) subunit contains 32 proteins, and two RNA molecules (23S and 5S). The overall mass ratio of RNA to protein is about 2:1. Cations, in particular magnesium and polyamines, play an important role in maintaining the integrity of the ribosomal structures. The ribosomes are considerably larger in the cytoplasm of higher organisms (eukaryotes). Nevertheless, all ribosomal RNA molecules have a central core of conserved structure, which presumably reflects the universality of the ribosomal function. *See* CELL (BIOLOGY); ORGANIC EVOLUTION.

The process of protein biosynthesis is essentially very similar in both prokaryotes and eukaryotes; what follows is a brief summary of what happens in *E. coli*. The first step is that an initiator tRNA molecule attached to the amino acid *N*-formyl methionine recognizes its appropriate codon on a mRNA molecule, and binds with the mRNA to the 30S subunit. A 50S subunit then joins the complex, forming a complete 70S ribosome. A number of proteins (initiation factors, which are not ribosomal proteins) are also involved in the process. At this stage, the initiator aminoacyl tRNA occupies one binding site, the P-site (peptidyl site), on the ribosome, while a second tRNA binding site (the A-site, or aminoacyl site) is free to accept the next aminoacyl tRNA molecule. In the subsequent steps, the elongation process aminoacyl tRNA molecules are brought to the A-site as ternary complexes together with guanosine triphosphate (GTP) and a protein factor (elongation factor Tu). Once an aminoacyl tRNA is in the A-site, the initiator amino acid (or at later stages the growing polypeptide chain) is transferred from the P-site tRNA to the A-site aminoacyl tRNA. It is not clear whether this peptidyl transferase activity requires the active participation of a ribosomal component. After peptide transfer has taken place, the peptide is attached to the A-site tRNA, and an "empty" tRNA molecule is at the P-site. The peptidyl tRNA complex must now be translocated to the P-site, in order to free the A-site for the next incoming tRNA molecule. Here again protein factors and GTP are involved, and it is probable that the empty tRNA occupies a third ribosomal site (exit or E-site) before finally leaving the complex. Studies show that elongation factor G hydrolyzes GTP to bring about translocation of the tRNA molecules. The protein chain is completed by the appearance of a "stop" codon in the mRNA. This is recognized by yet another set of protein factors, which causes the completed polypeptide chain to be released from the ribosome. At any one time a number of ribosomes are engaged in the reading of a single mRNA molecule, which leads to the appearance of polyribosomes (polysomes). *See* MOLECULAR BIOLOGY.

[R.Bri.; H.G.W.; S.Jo.]

Ribozyme   A ribonucleic acid (RNA) molecule that, like a protein, can catalyze specific biochemical reactions. Examples include self-splicing rRNA and RNase P, both involved in catalyzing RNA processing reactions (that is, the biochemical reactions that convert a newly synthesized RNA molecule to its mature form). Different ribozyme structures catalyze quite distinct RNA processing reactions, just as protein enzyme families that are composed of different structures catalyze different types of biochemical reactions.

Ribozymes share many similarities with protein enzymes, as assessed by two parameters that are used to describe a biological catalyst. The Michaelis-Menten constant K_m relates to the affinity that the catalyst has for its substrate, and ribozymes possess K_m values which are comparable to K_m values of protein enzymes. The catalytic rate constant describes how efficiently a catalyst converts substrate into product. The values of this constant for ribozymes are markedly lower than those values observed for protein enzymes. Nevertheless, ribozymes accelerate the rate of chemical reaction with specific substrates by 10^{11} compared with the rate observed for the corresponding uncatalyzed, spontaneous reaction. Therefore, ribozymes and protein enzymes are capable of lowering to similar extents the activation energy for chemical reaction. *See* ENZYME; PROTEIN; RIBONUCLEIC ACID (RNA).

[D.W.Ce.]

Ribulose   A pentose sugar, also known as D-riboketose and D-erythropetulose; it has never been prepared in crystalline form, and exists only as a syrup. The structural formula of ribulose is shown below.

$$
\begin{array}{c}
CH_2OH \\
| \\
C{=}O \\
| \\
HCOH \\
| \\
HCOH \\
| \\
CH_2OH
\end{array}
$$

Ribulose-5-phosphate occurs in animal and plant tissues. It can be converted to ribulose-l, 5-diphosphate by a phosphokinase enzyme acting in the presence of adenosine triphosphate (ATP). The ribulose-5-phosphate is also a significant intermediate in the carbohydrate metabolism through the pentose phosphate pathway. *See* CARBOHYDRATE METABOLISM; MONOSACCHARIDE.

[W.Z.H.]

Rickettsioses   Often severe infectious diseases caused by several diverse and specialized bacteria, the rickettsiae and rickettsia-like organisms. The best-known rickettsial diseases infect humans and are usually transmitted by parasitic arthropod vectors.

Rickettsiae and rickettsia-like organisms are some of the smallest microorganisms visible under a light microscope. Although originally confused with viruses, in part because of their small size and requirements for intracellular replication, rickettsiae and rickettsia-like organisms are characterized by basic bacterial (gram-negative) morphologic features. Their key metabolic enzymes are variations of typical bacterial enzymes. The genetic material of rickettsiae and rickettsia-like organisms likewise seems to conform to basic bacterial patterns. The genome of all rickettsia-like organisms consists of double-stranded deoxyribonucleic acid (DNA).

Rickettsiae enter host cells by phagocytosis and reproduce by simple binary fission. The site of growth and reproduction varies among the various genera.

Clinically, the rickettsial diseases of humans are most commonly characterized by fever, headache, and some form of cutaneous eruption, often including diffuse rash, as in epidemic and murine typhus and Rocky Mountain spotted fever, or a primary ulcer or eschar at the site of vector attachment, as in Mediterranean spotted fever and scrub typhus. Signs of disease may vary significantly between individual cases of rickettsial disease. Q fever is clinically exceptional in several respects, including the frequent absence of skin lesions.

All of the human rickettsial diseases, if diagnosed early enough in the infection, can usually be effectively treated with the appropriate antibiotics. Tetracycline and chloramphenicol are among the most effective antibiotics used; they halt the progression of the disease activity, but do so without actually killing the rickettsial organisms. Presumably, the immune system is ultimately responsible for ridding the body of infectious organisms. Penicillin and related compounds are not considered effective. *See* ANTIBIOTIC.

Most rickettsial diseases are maintained in nature as diseases of nonhuman vertebrate animals and their parasites. Human infection may usually be regarded as peripheral to the normal natural infection cycles, and human-to-human transmission is not the rule. However, the organism responsible for epidemic typhus (*Rickettsia prowazekii*) and the agent responsible for trench fever (*Rochalimaea quintana*) have the potential to spread rapidly within louse-ridden human populations. *See* ZOONOSES.

All known spotted fever group organisms are transmitted by ticks. Despite a global distribution in the form of various diseases, nearly all spotted fever group organisms share close genetic, antigenic, and certain pathologic features. Examples of human diseases include Rocky Mountain spotted fever (in North and South America), fièvre boutonneuse or Mediterranean spotted fever (southern Europe), South African tick-bite fever (Africa), Indian tick typhus (Indian subcontinent), and Siberian tick typhus (northeastern Europe and northern Asia). If appropriate antibiotics are not administered, Rocky Mountain spotted fever, for example, is a life-threatening disease. *See* INFECTIOUS DISEASE.   [R.L.Re.]

Rift Valley fever   An arthropod-borne (primarily mosquito), acute, febrile, viral disease of humans and numerous species of animals. Rift Valley fever is caused by a ribonucleic acid (RNA) virus in the genus *Phlebovirus* of the family Bunyaviridae. In sheep and cattle, it is also known as infectious enzootic hepatitis. First described in the Rift Valley of Africa, the disease presently occurs in west, east, and south Africa and has extended as far north as Egypt. Historically, outbreaks of Rift Valley fever have occurred at 10–15-year intervals in normally dry areas of Africa subsequent to a period of heavy rainfall.

In humans, clinical signs of Rift Valley fever are influenzalike, and include fever, headache, muscular pain, weakness, nausea, epigastric pain, and photophobia. Most people recover within 4–7 days, but some individuals may have impaired vision or blindness in one or both eyes; a small percentage of infected individuals develop a hemorrhagic syndrome and die.

Rift Valley fever should be suspected when high abortion rates, high mortality, or extensive liver lesions occur in newborn animals. The diagnosis is confirmed by isolating the virus from tissues of the infected animal or human. Control of the disease is best accomplished by widespread vaccination of susceptible animals to prevent amplification of the virus and, thus, infection of vectors. Any individual that works with infected animals or live virus in a laboratory should be vaccinated. *See* ANIMAL VIRUS; VACCINATION.

[C.A.Me.]

Rodentia   The mammalian order consisting of the rodents, often known as the gnawing mammals. This is the most diverse group of mammals in the world, consisting of over 2000 species, more than 40% of the known species of mammals on Earth today. Rodents range in size from mice, weighing only a few grams, to the Central American capybara, which is up to 130 cm (4 ft) in length and weighs up to 79 kg (170 lb). Rodents have been found in virtually every habitat and on every continent except Antarctica. Rodents have adapted to nearly every mode of life, including semiaquatic swimming (beavers and muskrats), gliding ("flying" squirrels), burrowing (gophers and African mole rats), arboreal (dormice and tree squirrels), and hopping (kangaroo rats and jerboas). Nearly all rodents are herbivorous, with a few exceptions that are partially insectivorous to totally omnivorous, such as the domestic rat. The great adaptability and rapid evolution and diversity of rodents are mainly due to their short gestation periods (only 3 weeks in some mice) and rapid turnover of generations.

The most diagnostic feature of the Rodentia is the presence of two pair of ever-growing incisors (one pair above and one below) at the front of the jaws. These teeth have enamel only on the front surface, which allows them to wear into a chisellike shape, giving rodents the ability to gnaw. Associated with these unique teeth are a number of other anatomical features that enhance this ability. Behind the incisors is a gap in the jaws where no teeth grow, called a diastema. The diastema of the upper jaw is longer than that of the lower jaw, which allows rodents to engage their gnawing incisors while their chewing teeth (molars and premolars) are not being used. The reverse is also true; rodents can use their chewing teeth (also called cheek teeth) while their incisors are disengaged.

The entire skull structure of rodents is designed to accommodate this task of separating the use of the different types of teeth. Rodent skulls have long snouts; the articulation of the lower jaw with the skull is oriented front to back rather than sideways as in other mammals; the jaw muscles (masseter complex) are extended well forward into the snout; and the number of cheek teeth is less than in most other mammals—all features unique to rodents.

The classification of rodents has always been difficult because of the great diversity of both Recent and fossil species. Traditionally, there are two ways that rodents have been divided: into three major groups based on the structure of the attachment of the jaw muscle on the skull (Sciuromorpha, Hystricomorpha, Myomorpha); or into two groups based on the structure of the lower jaw (Sciurognathi, Hystricognathi). The difficulty in using these groups (usually considered suborders or infraorders) is that the distinctive adaptations of one group of rodents are also present in others, derived in completely separate ways.

[W.W.K.]

Root (botany)   The absorbing and anchoring organ of vascular plants. Roots are simple axial organs that produce lateral roots, and sometimes buds, but bear neither leaves nor flowers. Elongation occurs in the root tip. The older portion of the root, behind the root tip, may thicken through cambial activity. Some roots, grass for example, scarcely thicken, but tree roots can become 4 in. (10 cm) or more in diameter near the stem. Roots may be very long. The longest maple (*Acer*) roots are usually as long as the tree is tall, but the majority of roots are only a few inches long. The longest roots may live for many years, while small roots may live for only a few weeks or months.

Root tips and the root hairs on their surface take up water and minerals from the soil. They also synthesize amino acids and growth regulators (gibberellins and cytokinins). These materials move up through the woody, basal portion of the root to the stem. The thickened, basal portion of the root anchors the plant in the soil. Thickened roots, such as carrots, can store food that is later used in stem growth. *See* CYTOKININ; GIBBERELLIN.

Roots usually grow in soil where: it is not too dense to stop root tip elongation; there is enough water and oxygen for root growth; and temperatures are high enough (above 39°F or 4°C) to permit root growth, but not so high that the roots are killed (above 104°F or 40°C). In temperate zones most roots are in the uppermost 4 in. (10 cm) of the soil; root numbers decrease so rapidly with increasing depth that few roots are found more than 6 ft (2 m) below the surface. Roots grow deeper in areas where the soil is hot and dry; roots from desert shrubs have been found in mines more than 230 ft (70 m) below the surface. In swamps with high water tables the lack of oxygen restricts roots to the uppermost soil layers. Roots may also grow in the air. Poison ivy vines form many small aerial roots that anchor them to bark or other surfaces.

The primary root originates in the seed as part of the embryo, normally being the first organ to grow. It grows downward into the soil and produces lateral second-order roots that emerge at right angles behind the root tip. Sometimes it persists and thickens to form a taproot. The second-order laterals produce third-order laterals and so on until there are millions of roots in a mature tree root system. In contrast to the primary root, most lateral roots grow horizontally or even upward. In many plants a few horizontal lateral roots thicken more than the primary, so no taproot is present in the mature root system.

Adventitious roots originate from stems or leaves rather than the embryo or other roots. They may form at the base of cut stems, as seen in the horticultural practice of rooting cuttings.   [B.F.W.]

Rotifera   A phylum of pseudocoelomate, microscopic, mainly free-living aquatic animals, characterized by an anterior ciliary apparatus, the corona, whose cilia when in motion have the appearance of a pair of rapidly rotating wheels. This structure is implicit in the phyletic name (literally "wheel bearers") and the older popular name wheel animalcules.

The Rotifera show considerable diversity in form and structure, but all are bilaterally symmetrical, pseudocoelomate animals possessing complete digestive, excretory, nervous, and reproductive systems, but lacking separate respiratory and circulatory systems. They possess two features unique to their phylum: the corona, which is a retractile trochal disk, and the mastax, which is a gizzardlike structure derived from the modified pharynx.

Rotifers are dioecious and sexually dimorphic; females are commoner than males, some of which are degenerate organisms lacking a mouth and digestive organs. Males, when produced in the life cycle, are short-lived and survive for only hours or at the most a few days.

The three major subdivisions of the Rotifera, now given class status, are the Seisonacea, Bdelloidea, and Monogononta.   [J.B.J.]

Rubella A benign, infectious virus disease of humans characterized by cold-like symptoms and transient, generalized rash. This disease, also known as German measles, is primarily a disease of childhood. However, maternal infection during early pregnancy may result in infection of the fetus, giving rise to serious abnormalities and malformations. The congenital infection persists in the infant, who harbors and sheds virus for many months after birth.

In rubella infection acquired by ordinary person-to-person contact, the virus is believed to enter the body through respiratory pathways. Antibodies against the virus develop as the rash fades, increase rapidly over a 2–3-week period, and then fall during the following months to levels that are maintained for life. One attack confers life-long immunity, since only one antigenic type of the virus exists. Immune mothers transfer antibodies to their offspring, who are then protected for approximately 4–6 months after birth. *See* IMMUNITY.

Live attenuated rubella vaccines have been available since 1969. The vaccine induces high antibody titers and an enduring and solid immunity. It may also induce secretory immunoglobulin (IgA) antibody in the respiratory tract and thus interfere with establishment of infection by wild virus. This vaccine is available as a single antigen or combined with measles and mumps vaccines (MMR vaccine). The vaccine induces immunity in at least 95% of recipients, and that immunity endures for at least 10 years. *See* BIOLOGICALS; VACCINATION.   [J.L.Me.]

Rust (microbiology) Plant diseases caused by fungi of the order Uredinales and characterized by the powdery and usually reddish spores produced. There are more than 4000 species of rust fungi. All are obligate parasites (require a living host) in nature, and each species attacks only plants of particular genera or species. Morphologically identical species that attack different host genera are further classified as special forms (*formae speciales*); for example, *Puccinia graminis* f. sp. *tritici* attacks wheat and *P. graminis* f. sp. *hordei* attacks barley. Each species or special form can have many physiological races that differ in their ability to attack different cultivars (varieties) of a host species. Rusts are among the most destructive plant diseases. Economically important examples include wheat stem rust, white pine blister rust, and coffee rust. *See* UREDINALES.

Rust fungi have complex life cycles, producing up to five different fruiting structures with distinct spore types that appear in a definite sequence. Macrocyclic (long-cycled) rust fungi produce all five spore types, whereas microcyclic (short-cycled) rust fungi produce only teliospores and basidiospores. Some macrocyclic rust fungi complete their life cycle on a single host and are called autoecious, whereas others require two different or alternate hosts and are called heteroecious. *See* FUNGI; PLANT PATHOLOGY.
                                    [E.A.M.]

S

Salmonelloses Diseases caused by *Salmonella*. These include enteritis and septicemia with or without enteritis. *Salmonella typhi*, *S. paratyphi A*, *B*, and *C*, and occasionally *S. cholerae suis* cause particular types of septicemia called typhoid and paratyphoid fever, respectively; while all other types may cause enteritis or septicemia, or both together.

Typhoid fever has an incubation period of 5–14 days. It is typified by a slow onset with initial bronchitis, diarrhea or constipation, a characteristic fever pattern (increase for 1 week, plateau for 2 weeks, and decrease for 2–3 weeks), a slow pulse rate, development of rose spots, swelling of the spleen, and often an altered consciousness; complications include perforation of the bowel and osteomyelitis. Typhoid fever leaves the individual with a high degree of immunity. Vaccination with an oral vaccine gives an individual considerable protection for about 3 years. The only effective antibiotic is chloramphenicol. *See* ANTIBIOTIC; IMMUNITY; VACCINATION.

Paratyphoid fever has a shorter course and is generally less severe than typhoid fever. Vaccination is an ineffective protective measure.

Enteric fevers, that is, septicemias due to types of *Salmonella* other than those previously mentioned, are more frequent in the United States than typhoid and paratyphoid fever but much less frequent than *Salmonella* enteritis. In children and in previously healthy adults, enteric fevers are most often combined with enteritis and have a favorable outlook. The organisms involved are the same as those causing *Salmonella* enteritis. Chloramphenicol or ampicillin are used in treatment. However, resistant strains have been observed. *See* DRUG RESISTANCE.

Inflammation of the small bowel due to *Salmonella* is one of the most important bacterial zoonoses. The most frequent agents are *S. typhimurium*, *S. enteritidis*, *S. newport*, *S. heidelberg*, *S. infantis*, and *S. derby*. The incubation period varies from 6 h to several days. Diarrhea and fever are the main symptoms; the intestinal epithelium is invaded, and early bacteremia is probable. Predisposed are persons with certain preexisting diseases (the same as for enteric fevers), very old and very young individuals, and postoperative patients. Antimicrobial treatment serves only to prolong the carrier state and has no effect on the disease.　　　　　　　　　　　[A.W.C.V.G.]

Salt gland A specialized gland located around the eyes and nasal passages in marine turtles, snakes, and lizards, and in birds such as the petrels, gulls, and albatrosses, which spend much time at sea. In the marine turtle it is an accessory lacrimal gland which opens into the conjunctival sac. In seagoing birds and in marine lizards it opens into the nasal passageway. Salt glands copiously secrete a watery fluid containing a high percentage of salt, higher than the salt content of urine in these species. As a consequence, these animals are able to drink salt-laden sea water without experiencing the dehydration necessary to eliminate the excess salt via the kidney route. See GLAND. [O.E.N.]

Salt marsh   A maritime habitat characterized by grasses, sedges, and other plants that have adapted to continual, periodic flooding. Salt marshes are found primarily throughout the temperate and subarctic regions.

The tide is the dominating characteristic of a salt marsh. The salinity of the tide defines the plants and animals that can survive in the marsh area. The vertical range of the tide determines flooding depths and thus the height of the vegetation, and the tidal cycle controls how often and how long vegetation is submerged. Two areas are delineated by the tide: the low marsh and the high marsh. The low marsh generally floods and drains twice daily with the rise and fall of the tide; the high marsh, which is at a slightly higher elevation, floods less frequently. See MANGROVE.

Salt marshes usually are developed on a sinking coastline, originating as mud flats in the shallow water of sheltered bays, lagoons, and estuaries, or behind sandbars. They are formed where salinity is high, ranging from 20 to 30 parts per thousand of sodium chloride. Proceeding up the estuary, there is a transitional zone where salinity ranges from 20 to less than 5 ppt. In the upper estuary, where river input dominates, the water has only a trace of salt. This varying salinity produces changes in the marsh—in the kinds of species and also in their number. Typically, the fewest species are found in the salt marsh and the greatest number in the fresh-water tidal marsh.

The salt marsh is one of the most productive ecosystems in nature. In addition to the solar energy that drives the photosynthetic process of higher rooted plants and the algae growing on the surface muds, tidal energy repeatedly spreads nutrient-enriched waters over the marsh surface. Some of this enormous supply of live plant material may be consumed by marsh animals, but the most significant values are realized when the vegetation dies and is decomposed by microorganisms to form detritus. Dissolved organic materials are released, providing an essential energy source for bacteria that mediate wetland biogeochemical cycles (carbon, nitrogen, and sulfur cycles). See BIOLOGICAL PRODUCTIVITY.

The salt marsh serves as a sediment sink, a nursery habitat for fishes and crustaceans, a feeding and nesting site for waterfowl and shorebirds, a habitat for numerous unique plants and animals, a nutrient source, a reservoir for storm water, an erosion control mechanism, and a site for esthetic pleasures. Appreciation for the importance of salt marshes has led to federal and state legislation aimed at their protection. [F.C.D.]

Sarcomastigophora   A subphylum of Protozoa, including those forms that possess flagella or pseudopodia or both. Organisms have a single type of nucleus, except the developmental stages of some Foraminiferida. Sexuality, if present, is syngamy, the fusion of two gametes. Spores typically are not formed. Flagella may be permanent or transient or confined to a certain stage in the life history; this is true also of pseudopodia. Both flagella and pseudopodia may be present at the same time.

Three superclasses are included: (1) Mastigophora, commonly flagellates, contains 19 orders. (2) Opalinata includes 1 order; these organisms were once considered as ciliates, but further research has indicated flagellate kinships. (3) Sarcodina comprises organisms which normally possess pseudopodia and are flagellated only in the developmental stages; 13 orders possess irregularly distributed lobose or filose and branching pseudopodia, while 7 orders have radially distributed axopodia, often with axial filaments.

Most of the plant flagellates will live in either fresh water or in both fresh and salt water. The zooflagellates are small and are not sufficiently abundant to enter markedly into the food chain. But the parasites and symbionts are of considerable interest economically and theoretically, for example, the trypanosomes and the peculiar xylophagous (wood-eating) symbionts of termites. In the termites these parasites actually digest the wood eaten by the host. Conspicuous in the ecology of marine waters are the dinoflagellates, radiolarians, and acantharians, especially in tropical waters of otherwise low productivity. *See* PROTOZOA.

[J.B.L.]

Savanna   The term savanna was originally used to describe a tropical grassland with more or less scattered dense tree areas. This vegetation type is very abundant in tropical and subtropical areas, primarily because of climatic factors. The modern definition of savanna includes a variety of physiognomically or environmentally similar vegetation types in tropical and extratropical regions. The physiognomically savannalike extratropical vegetation types (forest tundra, forest steppe, and everglades) differ greatly in environment and species composition.

In the widest sense savanna includes a range of vegetation zones from tropical savannas with vegetation types such as the savanna woodlands to tropical grassland and thornbush. In the extratropical regions it includes the "temperate" and "cold savanna" vegetation types known under such names as taiga, forest tundra, or glades. *See* GRASSLAND ECOSYSTEM; TAIGA; TUNDRA.

[H.Li.]

Scarlet fever   An acute contagious disease that results from infection with *Streptococcus pyogenes* (group A streptococci). It most often accompanies pharyngeal (throat) infections with this organism but is occasionally associated with wound infection or septicemia. Scarlet fever is characterized by the appearance, about 2 days after development of pharyngitis, of a red rash that blanches under pressure and has a sandpaper texture. Usually the rash appears first on the trunk and neck and spreads to the extremities. The rash fades after a week, with desquamation, or peeling, generally occurring during convalescence. The disease is usually self-limiting, although severe forms are occasionally seen with high fever and systemic toxicity. Appropriate antibiotic therapy is recommended to prevent the onset in susceptible individuals of rheumatic fever and rheumatic heart disease. *See* MEDICAL BACTERIOLOGY; RHEUMATIC FEVER; STREPTOCOCCUS.

[E.D.Gr.]

Schizophrenia   A brain disorder that is characterized by bizarre mental experiences such as hallucinations and severe decrements in social, cognitive, and occupational functioning. Patients with schizophrenia demonstrate a series of biological differences when compared to other groups of psychiatric patients. However, no biological marker has yet been found to conclusively indicate the presence of schizophrenia. A diagnosis is made on the basis of a cluster of symptoms reported by the patient, and of signs identified by the clinician.

People with schizophrenia may report perceptual experiences in the absence of a perceptual stimulus. Most common are auditory hallucinations, often reported in the form of words spoken to the person with schizophrenia. The language is often derogatory, and it can be tremendously frightening. *See* HALLUCINATION.

People with schizophrenia often maintain beliefs that are not held by the overwhelming majority of the general population. To be considered delusions, the beliefs must be unshakable. In many cases, these beliefs may be bizarre and stem from odd experiences. In some instances, the delusions have an element of suspicion to them, such as the belief that others are planning to cause the person harm. The delusions may or may not be related to hallucinatory experiences.

Many schizophrenics suffer from social isolation, lack of motivation, lack of energy, slow or delayed speech, and diminished emotional expression, often referred to as blunted affect. They may manifest an odd outward appearance due to the severity of their disorganization. This presentation may include speech that does not follow logically or sensibly, at times to the point of being incoherent. Facial expression may be odd or inappropriate, such as laughing for no reason. In some cases, people with schizophrenia may move in a strange and awkward manner. The extreme aspect of this behavior, referred to as catatonia, has become very rare since pharmacological treatments have become available.

Perhaps the most devastating feature of schizophrenia is the cognitive impairment found in most people with the disorder. On average, such people perform in the lowest 2–10% of the general population on tests of attention, memory, abstraction, motor skills, and language abilities.

The onset of schizophrenia generally occurs in people in the late teens to early twenties. However, schizophrenia is possible throughout the life span. While the onset of symptoms is abrupt in some people, others experience a more insidious process, including extreme social withdrawal, reduced motivation, mood changes, and cognitive and functional decline. The course of schizophrenia is normally characterized by episodes of relative remission in which only subtle symptoms remain, and episodes of exacerbation of symptoms, which are often caused by failure to continue treatment.

It is likely that there are various forms of schizophrenia, perhaps with different causes. Although schizophrenia appears to be inherited in some cases, the influence of genes is far from complete. Many arguments have been put forth regarding environmental factors that could cause schizophrenia. Very few of these theories are consistently supported.

Magnetic resonance imaging (MRI) has revealed that people with schizophrenia often have changes in the structure of their brain such as enlargement of the cerebral ventricles (the fluid-filled spaces in the brain close to the midline). Various brain regions have been found to be smaller in patients with schizophrenia, including the frontal cortex, temporal lobes, and hippocampi. In addition, studies of patients with schizophrenia have found patterns of abnormal activation of the brain while performing tests of memory and problem solving. *See* BRAIN; MEDICAL IMAGING.

Either a pharmacological or behavioral approach may be used in treating schizophrenia. A variety of antipsychotic medications have been used, and research continues into how to minimize the side effects which are often associated with such drugs. There are several targets for behavioral treatments in schizophrenia. Structured training programs have attempted to teach patients how to function more effectively in social, occupational, and independent living domains. Family interventions have been designed to provide a supportive environment for patients, and have been demonstrated to reduce risk of relapse. Another behavioral treatment area is teaching patients how to cope with hallucinations and delusions. Most patients with schizophrenia do not spontaneously recognize their symptoms as unusual and their experiences as unreal. Cognitive-behavioral treatments have been employed to help patients realize the nature of their symptoms and to develop plans for coping with them. *See* PSYCHOPHARMACOLOGY; PSYCHOTHERAPY.   [R.S.E.K.; P.D.H.]

Sclerenchyma   Single cells or aggregates of cells whose principal function is thought to be mechanical support of plants or plant parts. Sclerenchyma cells have thick secondary walls and may or may not remain alive when mature. They vary greatly in form and are of widespread occurrence in vascular plants. Two general types, sclereids and fibers, are widely recognized, but since these intergrade, the distinction is sometimes arbitrary.   [N.H.B.]

Second messengers   Molecules used to transmit signals within cells. These molecules trigger a cascade of events by activating other cellular components. The ability of cells to respond to specific extracellular molecules, or agonists, is crucial to growth, development, and homeostasis of multicellular organisms. Signal transduction refers to the movement of a signal initiated outside the cell into the cell interior. Many agonists induce the stimulation of cell growth, differentiation, or expression of specific genes. Signal transduction pathways must, therefore, include mechanisms for the initiation of signals at the cell surface membrane (plasma membrane), as well as a mechanism by which these signals traverse the interior of the cell (cytoplasm), and induce the desired target response. The pathways involve cascades of sequential molecular activation steps that are organized into three major components: (1) a receptor that recognizes and binds agonists, (2) second messengers, or signal transducing molecules, that couple receptors to intracellular pathways, and (3) effectors or molecules responsible for the ultimate response. A central feature of all signaling cascades is that they discriminate among a variety of signals and provide a mechanism for signal amplification. *See* SIGNAL TRANSDUCTION.   [D.M.Ra.]

Secretion   The export of proteins by cells. With few exceptions, in eukaryotic cells proteins are exported via the secretory pathway, which includes the endoplasmic reticulum and the Golgi apparatus. Secreted proteins are important in many physiological processes, from the transport of lipids and nutrients in the blood, to the digestion of food in the intestine, to the regulation of metabolic processes by hormones. *See* CELL (BIOLOGY); CELL ORGANIZATION.

Proteins destined for export are synthesized on ribosomes attached to the outside of the rough endoplasmic reticulum, a portion of the endoplasmic reticulum that is specialized for the synthesis of secretory proteins and most of the cell's membrane proteins. After they are folded, the proteins enter small vesicles in which they are transported to the Golgi apparatus. When the proteins reach the last cisterna of the Golgi, a highly tubulated region known as the *trans*-Golgi network, they are sorted and packaged again into transport vesicles, some of which are in the form of elongated tubules. From here, there are two pathways that proteins can take to the cell surface, depending on the cell type. Proteins can be transported directly to the plasma membrane (constitutive secretion) or to secretory granules (regulated secretion). *See* ENDOPLASMIC RETICULUM; GOLGI APPARATUS.

In all cells, there exists a constitutive secretion pathway whereby vesicles and tubules emerging from the *trans*-Golgi network fuse rapidly with the plasma membrane. The emerging vesicles and tubules attach to microtubules, cytoskeletal elements emanating from the Golgi region, that accelerate their transport to the plasma membrane. *See* ABSORPTION (BIOLOGY); CELL MEMBRANES.

In cells that secrete large amounts of hormones or digestive enzymes, most secretory and membrane proteins emerging from the *trans*-Golgi network are not immediately secreted, but are stored in membrane-bounded secretory granules. Secretory granules release their contents into the extracellular space in a process known as exocytosis, when their membranes fuse with the plasma membrane. Exocytosis occurs only after the cell receives a signal, usually initiated by the binding of a hormone or neurotransmitter to a receptor on the cell surface. The receptor triggers a signal transduction cascade that results in increased concentrations of second messengers such as cyclic adenosine

3′, 5′-monophosphate and phosphatidylinositol triphosphate. In most secretory cells, the second messengers or the hormone receptors themselves trigger the opening of calcium channels through which calcium ions stream into the cytoplasm. Calcium initiates the docking of the secretory granules with the plasma membrane and the activation of the fusion apparatus. *See* ENZYME; HORMONE; SIGNAL TRANSDUCTION.

In exceptional cases, proteins can be exported directly from the cytoplasm without using the secretory pathway. One such protein is fibroblast growth factor, a hormone involved in the growth and development of tissues such as bone and endothelium. Several interleukins, proteins that regulate the immune response, are also released via an unconventional route that may involve transport across the plasma membrane through channel proteins. These channels have adenosine 5′-triphosphatase (ATPase) enzyme activity and use the energy derived from the hydrolysis of ATP to catalyze transport. *See* CELLULAR IMMUNOLOGY.   [M.Ri.]

Secretory structures (plant)   Cells or organizations of cells which produce a variety of secretions. The secreted substance may remain deposited within the secretory cell itself or may be excreted, that is, released from the cell. Substances may be excreted to the surface of the plant or into intercellular cavities or canals. Some of the many substances contained in the secretions are not further utilized by the plant (resins, rubber, tannins, and various crystals), while others take part in the functions of the plant (enzymes and hormones). Secretory structures range from single cells scattered among other kinds of cells to complex structures involving many cells; the latter are often called glands.

Epidermal hairs of many plants are secretory or glandular. Such hairs commonly have a head composed of one or more secretory cells borne on a stalk. The hair of a stinging needle is bulbous below and extends into a long, fine process above. If one touches the hair, its tip breaks off, the sharp edge penetrates the skin, and the poisonous secretion is released.

Glands secreting a sugary liquid—the nectar—in flowers pollinated by insects are called nectaries. Nectaries may occur on the floral stalk or on any floral organ: sepal, petal, stamen, or ovary.

The hydathode structures discharge water—a phenomenon called guttation—through openings in margins or tips of leaves. The water flows through the xylem to its endings in the leaf and then through the intercellular spaces of the hydathode tissue toward the openings in the epidermis. Strictly speaking, such hydathodes are not glands because they are passive with regard to the flow of water.

Some carnivorous plants have glands that produce secretions capable of digesting insects and small animals. These glands occur on leaf parts modified as insect-trapping structures. In the sundews (*Drosera*) the traps bear stalked glands, called tentacles. When an insect lights on the leaf, the tentacles bend down and cover the victim with a mucilaginous secretion, the enzymes of which digest the insect. *See* INSECTIVOROUS PLANTS; VENUS' FLYTRAP.

Resin ducts are canals lined with secretory cells that release resins into the canal. Resin ducts are common in gymnosperms and occur in various tissues of roots, stems, leaves, and reproductive structures.

Gum ducts are similar to resin ducts and may contain resins, oils, and gums. Usually, the term gum duct is used with reference to the dicotyledons, although gum ducts also may occur in the gymnosperms.

Oil ducts are intercellular canals whose secretory cells produce oils or similar substances. Such ducts may be seen, for example, in various parts of the plant of the carrot family (Umbelliferae).

Laticifers are cells or systems of cells containing latex, a milky or clear, colored or colorless liquid. Latex occurs under pressure and exudes from the plant when the latter is cut.

[K.E.]

Seed   A fertilized ovule containing an embryo which forms a new plant upon germination. Seed-bearing characterizes the higher plants—the gymnosperms (conifers and allies) and the angiosperms (flowering plants). Gymnosperm (naked) seeds arise on the surface of a structure, as on a seed scale of a pine cone. Angiosperm (covered) seeds develop within a fruit, as the peas in a pod. *See* FLOWER; FRUIT.

Structure.   One or two tissue envelopes, or integuments, form the seed coat which encloses the seed except for a tiny pore, the micropyle (see illustration). The micropyle is near the funiculus (seed stalk) in angiosperm seeds. The hilum is the scar left when the seed is detached from the funiculus. Some seeds have a raphe, a ridge near the hilum opposite the micropyle, and a bulbous strophiole. Others such as nutmeg possess arils, outgrowths of the funiculus, or a fleshy caruncle developed from the seed coat near the hilum, as in the castor bean. The embryo consists of an axis and attached cotyledons (seed leaves). The part of the axis above the cotyledons is the epicotyl (plumule); that below, the hypocotyl, the lower end of which bears a more or less developed primordium of the root (radicle). The epicotyl, essentially a terminal bud, possesses an apical meristem (growing point) and, sometimes, leaf primordia. The seedling stem develops from the epicotyl. An apical meristem of the radicle produces the primary root of the seedling, and transition between root and stem occurs in the hypocotyl. *See* APICAL MERISTEM; ROOT (BOTANY); STEM.

Two to many cotyledons occur in different gymnosperms. The angiosperms are divided into two major groups according to number of cotyledons: the monocotyledons and the dicotyledons. Mature gymnosperm seeds contain an endosperm (albumen or nutritive tissue) which surrounds the embryo. In some mature dicotyledon seeds the endosperm persists, the cotyledons are flat and leaflike, and the epicotyl is simply

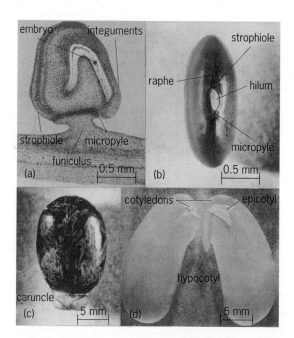

Seed structures. (*a*) Median longitudinal section of pea ovule shortly after fertilization, showing attachment to pod tissues. (*b*) Mature kidney bean. (*c*) Mature castor bean. (*d*) Opened embryo of mature kidney bean.

an apical meristem. In other seeds, such as the bean, the growing embryo absorbs the endosperm, and food reserve for germination is stored in fleshy cotyledons. The endosperm persists in common monocotyledons, for example, corn and wheat; and the cotyledon, known as the scutellum, functions as an absorbing organ during germination. Grain embryos also possess a coleoptile and a coleorhiza sheathing the epicotyl and the radicle, respectively. The apical meristems of lateral seed roots also may be differentiated in the embryonic axis near the scutellum of some grains.

Many so-called seeds consist of hardened parts of the fruit enclosing the true seed which has a thin, papery seed coat. Among these are the achenes, as in the sunflower, dandelion, and strawberry, and the pits of stone fruits such as the cherry, peach, and raspberry. Many common nuts also have this structure. Mechanisms for seed dispersal include parts of both fruit and seed. See POPULATION DISPERSAL.

Economic importance. Propagation of plants by seed and technological use of seed and seed products are among the most important activities of modern society. Specializations of seed structure and composition provide rich sources for industrial exploitation apart from direct use as food. Common products include starches and glutens from grains, hemicelluloses from guar and locust beans, and proteins and oils from soybeans and cotton seed. Drugs, enzymes, vitamins, spices, and condiments are obtained from embryos, endosperms, and entire seeds, often including the fruit coat. Most of the oils of palm, olive, and pine seeds are in the endosperm. Safflower seed oil is obtained mainly from the embryo, whereas both the seed coat and embryo of cotton seed are rich in oils. See FOOD; PLANT ANATOMY; REPRODUCTION (PLANT).   [R.M.R.]

Physiology. Physical and biochemical processes of seed growth and germination are controlled by genetic and environmental factors. Conditions of light, temperature, moisture, and oxygen affect the timing and ability of a seed to mature and germinate. Seed development (embryogenesis) is concerned with the synthesis and storage of carbohydrate, protein, and oil to supply nutrients to the germinating seedling prior to soil emergence. Seed development occurs in several stages: rapid cell division, seed fill, and desiccation. The timing of each stage is species-specific and environmentally influenced.

Dormancy. Seed dormancy is the inability of a living seed to germinate under favorable conditions of temperature, moisture, and oxygen. Dormancy does not occur in all seeds, but typically occurs in plant species from temperate and colder habitats. This process allows for a delay in seed germination until environmental conditions are adequate for seedling survival. At least three types of seed dormancy are recognized: primary, secondary (induced), and enforced. Primary dormancy occurs during seed maturation, and the seed does not germinate readily upon being shed. Secondary and enforced dormancy occur after the seed is shed and may be caused by adverse environmental factors such as high or low temperature, absence of oxygen or light, low soil moisture, and presence of chemical inhibitors. Seeds with secondary dormancy will not germinate spontaneously when environmental conditions improve, and need additional environmental stimuli. Seeds with enforced dormancy germinate readily upon removal of the environmental limitation. Regulation of dormancy may be partly controlled by hormones. See DORMANCY.

Dormancy is terminated in a large number of species when an imbibed seed is illuminated with white light. Biochemical control of this process is related to the functioning of a single pigment, phytochrome, frequently located in the seed coat or embryonic axis. Phytochrome imparts to the seed the ability to interpret light quality, such as that under an existing vegetative canopy, and to distinguish light from dark with respect to its position in the soil. Phytochrome also is affected by temperature and is involved in the seasonal control of the ending of dormancy. Hormones that promote germination

of dormant seeds include gibberellins, cytokinins, ethylene, and auxins.

Germination. Germination is the process whereby a viable seed takes up water and the radicle (primary root) or hypocotyl emerges from the seed under species-specific conditions of moisture, oxygen, and temperature. Dormant seeds must undergo additional environmental stimuli to germinate. The germinating seed undergoes cell expansion, as well as increases in respiration, protein synthesis, and other metabolic activities prior to emergence of the growing seedling.   [C.A.L.]

Sensation   A term commonly used to refer to the subjective experience resulting from stimulation of a sense organ, for instance, a sensation of warm, sour, or green. As a general scientific category, the study of sensation is the study of the operation of the senses. Sense receptors are the means by which information presented as one form of energy, for example, light, is converted to information in the form used by the nervous system, that is, impulses traveling along nerve fibers. *See* SENSE ORGAN.

Each sense has mechanisms and characteristics peculiar to itself, but all display the phenomena of absolute threshold, differential threshold, and adaptation. Not until sufficient stimulation impinges on a receptor can the presence of a stimulus be detected. The quantity of stimulation required is known as the absolute threshold. Not until a sufficient change occurs in some aspect of a stimulus can the change be detected. The magnitude of the change required is called the differential threshold. Under steady stimulation there is a decrease in sensitivity of the corresponding sense, as indicated by a shift in the absolute threshold and in the magnitude of sensation. After the stimulation ceases, sensitivity increases. An obvious example of visual adaptation occurs when one goes from bright to dim surroundings or vice versa.

With fairly good accuracy humans can localize visual objects, sounds, and cutaneous contacts and can discriminate the spatial orientation of the body and its members. With rather poor accuracy humans can localize many of the stimuli originating within the body.

With the exception of hearing, in which sense localization depends on differences in the acoustic stimuli reaching the two ears, there appears to be a common principle involved in giving spatially separated receptors their different local signs. Stimulation at different points on the receptive surface results in peaks of electrical activity at different loci in the brain. In no sense is there anything like a private wire from each sensory cell to a corresponding point in the brain. In fact, there are so many opportunities for a signal to go astray on its way from the receptor to the brain that it is surprising that spatial discrimination is as good as it is. Nevertheless, there is clear evidence that, by a combination of anatomical and functional arrangements, spatial differences at the receptor level are translated into topologically similar spatial differences in brain activity. *See* HEARING (HUMAN).

The nerve fibers between receptor and brain do not serve merely as transmitters of sensory information. Their interconnections enable them to influence one another's sensitivity and to perform logical operations like those carried out inside computers. As a result the information arriving in the sensory areas of the brain is not merely a more or less faithful replica of that presented to the receptors but in addition has had certain aspects of the information selected for special signaling. *See* CHEMICAL SENSES; SOMESTHESIS; TASTE; VISION.   [J.F.H.]

Sense organ   A structure which is a receptor for external or internal stimulation. A sense organ is often referred to as a receptor organ. External stimuli affect the sensory structures which make up the general cutaneous surface of the body, the exteroceptive area, and the tissues of the body wall or the proprioceptive area. These somatic area receptors are known under the general term of exteroceptors. Internal stimuli which originate in various visceral organs such as the intestinal tract or heart affect the visceral sense organs or interoceptors. A receptor structure is not necessarily an organ; in many unicellular animals it is a specialized structure within the organism. Receptors are named on the basis of the stimulus which affects them, permitting the organism to be sensitive to changes in its environment.

Photoreceptors are structures which are sensitive to light and in some instances are also capable of perceiving form, that is, of forming images. Light-sensitive structures include the stigma of phytomonads, photoreceptor cells of some annelids, pigment cup ocelli and retinal cells in certain asteroids, the eye-spot in many turbellarians, and the ocelli of arthropods. The compound eye of arthropods, mollusks, and chordates is capable of image formation and is also photosensitive. *See* PHOTORECEPTION.

Phonoreceptors are structures which are capable of detecting vibratory motion or sound waves in the environment. The most common phonoreceptor is the ear, which in the vertebrates has other functions in addition to sound perception. *See* EAR.

Statoreceptors are structures concerned primarily with equilibration, such as the statocysts found throughout the various phyla of invertebrates and the inner ear or membranous labyrinth filled with fluid.

The sense of smell is dependent upon the presence of olfactory neurons, called olfactoreceptors, in the olfactory epithelium of the nasal passages among the vertebrates. *See* OLFACTION.

The sense of taste is mediated by the taste buds, or gustatoreceptors. In most vertebrates these taste buds occur in the oral cavity, on the tongue, pharynx, and lining of the mouth; however, among certain species of fish, the body surface is supplied with taste buds as are the barbels of the catfish. *See* TASTE.

The surface skin of vertebrates contains numerous varied receptors associated with sensations of touch, pain, heat, and cold. *See* CHEMICAL SENSES; CUTANEOUS SENSATION; SENSATION.   [C.B.C.]

Serology   The division of biological science concerned with antigen-antibody reactions in serum. It properly encompasses any of these reactions, but is often used in a limited sense to denote laboratory diagnostic tests, especially for syphilis. The techniques of blood grouping have come from the study of antigen-antibody reactions in serum, as have techniques for identification of genetic polymorphism and quantitation of numerous serum proteins. With these advances came the means for developing transfusion therapy with cells and plasma. In addition, these techniques led to identification of antibodies involved in incompatibility reactions, such as in erythroblastosis fetalis, and the development of effective measures to prevent their occurrence. Further, extension of these techniques to identification of antigens on white cells led to effective methods of histocompatibility typing, facilitating organ transplantation. *See* TRANSPLANTATION BIOLOGY.   [D.R.]

Serotonin   A compound, also known as 5-hydroxytryptamine (5-HT), derived from tryptophan, an indole-containing amino acid. It is widely distributed in the animal and vegetable kingdoms. In mammals it is found in gastrointestinal enterochromaffin cells, in blood platelets, and in brain and nerve tissue. Serotonin is a local vasoconstrictor, plays a role in brain and nerve function and in regulation of gastric secretion and intestinal peristalsis, and has pharmacologic properties. It is inactivated by monoamine oxidases (MAO-A and -B), enzymes that also inactivate other neurotransmitters such as norepinephrine and dopamine.

Serotonin is concentrated in certain areas of the brain; the hypothalamus and midbrain contain large amounts, while the cortex and cerebellum contain low concentrations. Like most neurotransmitters, it is stored in granules inside nerve endings, and is thus not exposed to inactivation by monoamine oxidases until it is released into the synaptic space between nerves. When a serotonin-containing nerve fires, serotonin is released and can bind to any one of a series of at least 14 distinct downstream serotonin receptors (5-HT receptors). Release of serotonin or other stored neurotransmitters can also be induced by alkaloids such as reserpine, which have been used as tranquilizing agents in the treatment of nervous and mental disorders. Although pharmacologic doses of serotonin produce a type of sedation and other depressant conditions of the nervous system, several types of clinically useful antidepressants, such as monoamine oxidase (MAO) inhibitors, tricyclic antidepressants, and selective serotonin reuptake inhibitors (SSRIs), act by increasing the amount of active serotonin in nerve synapses in particular brain regions. Conversely, various conditions that lower serotonin levels are associated with depression, suggesting that normal to slightly elevated serotonin levels tend to elevate mood and prevent depression. *See* AFFECTIVE DISORDERS; BRAIN; NERVOUS SYSTEM (VERTEBRATE); NEUROSECRETION; PSYCHOPHARMACOLOGY.

[M.K.S.; B.A.St.]

Serum The liquid portion that remains when blood is allowed to clot spontaneously and is then centrifuged to remove the blood cells and clotting elements. It has approximately the same volume (55%) as plasma and differs from it only by the absence of fibrinogen. *See* FIBRINOGEN.

Blood serum contains 6–8% solids, including macromolecules such as albumin, antibodies and other globulins, and enzymes; peptide and lipid-based hormones; and cytokines; as well as certain nutritive organic materials in small amounts, such as amino acids, glucose, and fats. Somewhat less than 1% of the serum consists of inorganic substances. Small amounts of respiratory gases are dissolved in the serum, as is the gas nitric oxide, which serves as a chemical messenger and vasodilator. Small amounts of waste material are also present. These substances, along with other small molecules which are not bound to blood proteins, are filtered out as blood flows through the kidney. *See* BLOOD; KIDNEY.

Certain types of sera, both human and animals, are used in clinical medicine. Immune serum and hyperimmune serum either are developed by naturally occurring disease or are deliberately prepared by repeated injection of antigens to increase antibody titer for either diagnostic tests or the treatment of active disease. These sera are referred to as antisera, since they have a specific antagonistic action against specific antigens. *See* ANTIBODY; ANTIGEN; BIOLOGICALS; IMMUNITY.

By custom, the clear portion of any liquid material of animal origin separated from its solid or cellular elements is also referred to as sera. These fluids are more properly referred to as effusions. *See* SEROLOGY.

[R.Str.; B.A.St.]

Sex determination The genetic mechanisms by which sex is determined in all living organisms. The nature of the genetic basis of sex determination varies a great deal among the various forms of life.

There are two aspects of sexuality: the primary form involves the gametes, and the secondary aspect is gender. In its broadest usage the term "sex" refers to the processes that enable species to exchange materials between homologous chromosomes, that is, to effect recombination. Generally, recombination is essential to their mechanism for reproduction. For most organisms this involves, either exclusively or as one stage in the life cycle, the formation of special cells, known as gametes, by meiosis. *See* GAMETOGENESIS.

Most sexually reproducing species produce two different kinds of gametes. The relatively large and sessile form, an ovum or egg, usually accumulates nutriments in its cytoplasm for the early development of the offspring. The relatively mobile form, a sperm (or pollen grain in many plants), contributes little beyond a haploid chromosome set. Thus the primary form of sex differentiation determines which kind of gamete will be produced. The formation of gametes usually involves the concomitant differentiation of specialized organs, the gonads, to produce each kind of gamete. The ova-producing gonad is usually known as an archegonium or ovary (in flowering plants it is part of a larger organ, the pistil or carpel); the gonad producing the more mobile gametes is usually known as a testis in animals and an antheridium or stamen in plants. *See* OVARY; OVUM; SPERM CELL; TESTIS.

In most animals and many plants, individuals become specialized to produce only one kind of gamete. These individuals usually differ not only in which kind of gonad they possess but also in a number of other morphological and physiological differences, or secondary sex characteristics. The latter may define a phenotypic sex when present, even if the typical gonad for that sex is absent or nonfunctional. The form that usually produces ova is known as female; the one that usually produces sperm or pollen is known as male. Since some sexual processes do not involve gametes, the more universal application of the term "gender" refers to any donor of genetic material as male and the recipient as female.

In plants, sexual reproduction is not always accompanied by the kinds of differentiation described above. The majority of plant species are monoecious, with both kinds of gonads on the same plant. Plants that bear male and female gonads on separate plants are dioecious. They occur in about 60 of the 400 or so families of flowering plants, 20 of which are thought to contain exclusively dioecious species. *See* REPRODUCTION (PLANT).

Although the sexes are distinct in most animals, many species are hermaphroditic; that is, the same individual is capable of producing both eggs and sperm. This condition is particularly common among sessile or sluggish, slowly moving forms. Some hermaphroditic and monoecious species are homothallic; that is, the eggs and sperm of the same individual can combine successfully; but most are heterothallic, the gametes being capable only of cross-fertilization, often evolving special mechanisms to ensure its occurrence.

Sex differentiations are often accompanied by consistent chromosomal dimorphisms, leading to the presumption that the chromosomal differences are related to, and possibly responsible for, the sex differences. Indeed, the chromosomes that are not alike in the two sexes were given the name sex chromosomes. Some workers use the term "heterosomes" to distinguish them from the autosomes, which are the chromosomes that are morphologically identical in the two sexes.

In most species, one of the sex chromosomes, the X chromosome, normally occurs as a pair in one gender but only singly in the other. The gender with two X chromosomes is known as the homogametic sex, because each of its gametes normally receives an X chromosome after meiosis. The gender with only one X chromosome generally also has a morphologically different sex chromosome, the Y chromosome. The X and Y chromosomes usually pair to some extent at meiosis, with the result that the XY is the heterogametic sex, with half its gametes containing an X and half containing a Y. Geneticists noted that the fundamental dimorphism of X and Y chromosomes lies in their genic contents: X chromosomes of the species share homologous loci, just as do pairs of autosomes, whereas the Y chromosome usually has few, if any, loci that are also represented on the X. Thus X and Y chromosomes are sometimes very similar in shape or size but are almost always very different in genetic materials.

The major factor in sex differentiation in humans is a locus on the short arm of the Y chromosome designated *SRY* or *SrY* (for sex-determining region of the Y). This comparatively small gene contains no introns and encodes for a protein with only 204 amino acids. The protein appears to be a deoxyribonucleic acid (DNA)-binding type that causes somatic cells of the developing gonad to become Sertoli cells that secrete a hormone, Müllerian inhibiting substance (MIS), that eliminates the Müllerian duct system (the part that would produce major female reproductive organs). The gonad is now a testis, and certain cells in it become the Leydig cells that produce testosterone, which causes the primordial Wolffian duct system of the embryo to develop the major male reproductive organs. If no MIS is produced, further development of the Müllerian duct structures occurs, and in the absence of testosterone the Wolffian ducts disappear, producing the normal female structures. Embryos lacking *SRY* or having mutated forms of it normally become females even if they are XY. This system of sex determination is called Y-dominant. It appears to be characteristic of almost all mammals, even marsupials, plus a few other forms. While *SRY* is the primary gene, many other genes, both autosomal and X-chromosomal, are involved in the course of developing the two sexes in mammals. *See* Human genetics; Mutation.   [M.Le.]

Sex-influenced inheritance   Inherited characteristics that are conditioned by the sex of the individual. These traits are determined by genes that act differently in the two sexes. The usual result is that a given trait appears preponderantly in one sex. The reasons for such inheritance are neither the chromosomal location of the responsible genes, which may therefore be autosomal as well as X-linked, nor the normal sex-determining mechanism of the species. *See* Sex determination.

A special class of sex-influenced genes can be called sex-limited. These are manifested in only one sex because the other lacks the requisite organs. Some examples are milk production in cows and egg production in chickens.

Some traits are sex-influenced because of genes that interact with a substance that is not produced equally in males and females. An example is early pattern baldness. Since male-to-male transmission occurs, the responsible gene must be autosomal. There is a preponderance of this trait in males because the action of the gene depends on the level of male hormones (androgens) present. *See* Gene action.

Some sex differences in expression of inherited traits may result from genetic imprinting. Genetic imprinting refers to different expression of chromosomes, parts of chromosomes, or single genes, depending on which of the two sexes they are inherited from. To achieve imprinting, some genetic materials can be modified during gamete production or early embryonic development in one of the two sexes, so the traits determined by the imprinted genes are expressed differently than would be expected under typical mendelian inheritance. A growing body of evidence points to methylation of cytosine residues in the context of cytosine-guanine (CpG) dinucleotides as the mechanism of imprinting. Such methylation, especially if it occurs in the promoter regions of genes, can nullify the ability of the genes to be transcribed. Certain genes that can be imprinted will be methylated in the production of sperm, others in the production of ova, and they can be reactivated by demethylation when they pass through gametogenesis in the opposite sex. It is still not known why certain alleles are subject to imprinting while others are not, and why they are more likely to be imprinted in one sex than the other.

Imprinting can involve amplification of genes rather than inactivation; that is, as the gene passes through gametogenesis in one of the sexes, sections of it become duplicated and the gene thereby is enlarged. This is seen in neuroblastoma, where one commonly finds an increased number of DNA segments containing the *N-myc* protooncogene: such amplification is correlated with poor prognosis of the disease. In an overwhelming proportion of cases, it is the paternal *N-myc* gene that is amplified, suggesting that imprinting is responsible. A similar phenomenon occurs in Huntington's chorea, an autosomal dominant condition that usually does not become manifested until middle age or beyond. Earlier manifestation, often even in childhood, is associated with amplification of certain segments of DNA in the gene; but the amplifications, if they occur, are only in *HC* genes inherited from fathers. *See* DEOXYRIBONUCLEIC ACID (DNA); GENETICS; HUMAN GENETICS; OOGENESIS; SEX DETERMINATION; SEX-LINKED INHERITANCE; SPERMATOGENESIS.   [M.Le.]

Sex-linked inheritance   The inheritance of a trait (phenotype) that is determined by a gene located on one of the sex chromosomes. Genetic studies of many species have been facilitated by focusing on such traits because of their characteristic patterns of familial transmission and the ability to localize their genes to a specific chromosome. As the ability to map a gene to any of an organisms chromosomes has improved markedly, reliance on the specific pattern of inheritance has waned.

The expectations of sex-linked inheritance in any species depend on how the chromosomes determine sex. For example, in humans, males are heterogametic, having one X chromosome and one Y chromosome, whereas females are homogametic, having two X chromosomes. In human males, the entire X chromosome is active (not all genes are active in every cell), whereas one of a female's X chromosomes is largely inactive. Random inactivation of one X chromosome occurs during the early stages of female embryogenesis, and every cell that descends from a particular embryonic cell has the same X chromosome inactivated. The result is dosage compensation for X-linked genes between the sexes. A specific gene on the long arm of the X chromosome, called XIST at band q13, is a strong candidate for the gene that controls X inactivation. This pattern of sex determination occurs in most vertebrates, but in birds and many insects and fish the male is the homogametic sex. *See* SEX DETERMINATION.

In general terms, traits determined by genes on sex chromosomes are not different from traits determined by autosomal genes. Sex-linked traits are distinguishable by their mode of transmission through successive generations of a family. In humans it is preferable to speak in terms of X-linked or Y-linked inheritance.

Red-green color blindness was the first human trait proven to be due to a gene on a specific chromosome. The characteristics of this pattern of inheritance are readily evident. Males are more noticeably or severely affected than females; in the case of red-green color blindness, women who have one copy of the mutant gene (that is, are heterozygous or carriers) are not at all affected. Among offspring of carrier mothers, on average one-half of their sons are affected, whereas one-half of their daughters are carriers. Affected fathers cannot pass their mutant X chromosome to their sons, but do pass it to all of their daughters, who thereby are carriers. A number of other well-known human conditions behave in this manner, including the two forms of hemophilia, Duchenne muscular dystrophy, and glucose-6-phosphate dehydrogenase deficiency that predisposes to hemolytic anemia. *See* COLOR VISION.

Refined cytogenetic and molecular techniques have supplemented family studies as a method for characterizing sex-linked inheritance and for mapping genes to sex chromosomes in many species. Over 400 human traits and diseases seem to be encoded by genes on the X chromosome, and over 200 genes have been mapped. Among mammals, genes on the X chromosome are highly conserved. Thus, identifying a sex-linked trait in mice is strong evidence that a similar trait, and underlying gene, exists on the human X chromosome. *See* GENETICS; HUMAN GENETICS; SEX-INFLUENCED INHERITANCE.

[R.E.Py.]

Sexual dimorphism   Any difference, morphological or behavioral, between males and females of the same species. In many animals, the sex of an individual can be determined at a glance. For example, roosters have bright plumage, a comb, and an elaborate tail, all of which are lacking in hens. Sexual dimorphism arises as a result of the different reproductive functions of the two sexes and is a consequence of both natural selection and sexual selection. Primary differences such as the structure of the reproductive organs are driven by natural selection and are key to the individual's function as a mother or father. Other differences such as the peacock's (*Pavo cristatus*) enormous tail are driven by sexual selection and increase the individual's success in acquiring mates. *See* ORGANIC EVOLUTION.

A less obvious sexual dimorphism is the difference in size of male and female gametes. In nearly all cases, the sperm (or pollen) are substantially smaller and more numerous than the ova. Eggs are large because they contain nutrients essential for development of the embryo. However, the sole purpose of sperm is to fertilize the egg. Sperm do not contain any nutrients and can therefore be small. For the same investment of nutrients, a male can produce more sperm than a female can produce eggs. Human males, for example, produce about 300 million motile sperm per ejaculate, whereas females normally produce only one egg (30,000 times larger than a single sperm) per month. *See* GAMETOGENESIS; REPRODUCTION (ANIMAL); REPRODUCTIVE SYSTEM.

In nearly all animal groups (apart from mammals and birds), females are larger than males because larger females tend to produce more eggs and contribute more young to the next generation. In contrast, size does not appear to limit males' ability to produce sperm. However, among mammals and birds males are generally the larger sex. Differences in body size and shape can be caused by factors other than reproductive success. Sexual dimorphism can arise as a consequence of competition between the sexes over resources, or because the sexes use different resources. For example, in many species of snake, males and females use different habitats and eat different food, which has led to differences in their head shape and feeding structures.

Plants also differ in showiness. Many plants bear both male and female flowers (simultaneous hermaphrodites), but male flowers are sometimes larger and more conspicuous. For example, the female catkins of willow are dull gray compared with the bright yellow male catkins, because male flowers compete with each other to attract pollinators. In plant species with separate sexes (dioecious), males tend to produce more flowers than females. For example, males of the American holly (*Ilex opaca*) produce seven times as many flowers as females in order to increase their chances of pollen transfer to females. *See* FLOWER; POLLINATION.

Animals and plants show marked sexual dimorphism in other traits. Calling, singing, pheromones, and scent marking can all be explained by competition between males and by female mate choice. *See* ANIMAL COMMUNICATION.

Associated with morphological sexual dimorphism are several behavioral differences between males and females. Many of these are related to locating a mate, competition between males, and female choosiness. Animals also show sexual dimorphism relating to their roles as parents. Many parents continue to provide for their young after birth, with the female performing the bulk of the care in most species. Female mammals suckle their young, whereas males cannot because they lack mammary glands. However, some mammals (such as gibbons and prairie voles) and many birds share parental duties, with both males and females feeding and protecting the young.

[A.M.Du.; N.W.]

Sexually transmitted diseases   Infections that are acquired and transmitted by sexual contact. Although virtually any infection may be transmitted during intimate contact, the term sexually transmitted disease is restricted to conditions that are largely dependent on sexual contact for their transmission and propagation in a population. The term venereal disease is literally synonymous with sexually transmitted disease but traditionally is associated with only five long-recognized diseases (syphilis, gonorrhea, chancroid, lymphogranuloma venereum, and donovanosis). Sexually transmitted diseases occasionally are acquired nonsexually (for example, by newborn infants from their mothers, or by clinical or laboratory personnel handling pathogenic organisms or infected secretions), but in adults they are virtually never acquired by contact with contaminated intermediaries such as towels, toilet seats, or bathing facilities. However, some sexually transmitted infections (such as human immunodeficiency virus infection, viral hepatitis, and cytomegalovirus infection) are transmitted primarily by sexual contact in some settings and by nonsexual means in others. *See* GONORRHEA; SYPHILIS.

The sexually transmitted diseases may be classified in the traditional fashion, according to the causative pathogenic organisms, as follows:

Bacteria
  Chlamydia trachomatis
  Neisseria gonorrhoeae
  Treponema pallidum
  Mycoplasma genitalium
  Mycoplasma hominis
  Ureaplasma urealyticum
  Haemophilis ducreyi
  Calymmatobacterium granulomatis
  Salmonella species
  Shigella species
  Campylobacter species
Viruses
  Human immunodeficiency viruses
    (types 1 and 2)
Herpes simplex viruses
    (types 1 and 2)
  Hepatitis viruses B, C, D
  Cytomegalovirus
  Human papillomaviruses
  Molluscum contagiosum virus
  Kaposi sarcoma virus
Protozoa
  Trichomonas vaginalis
  Entamoeba histolytica
  Giardia lamblia
  Cryptosporidium and related species
Ectoparasites
  Phthirus pubis (pubic louse)
  Sarcoptes scabiei (scabies mite)

Sexually transmitted diseases may also be classified according to clinical syndromes and complications that are caused by one or more pathogens as follows:

1. Acquired immunodeficiency syndrome (AIDS) and related conditions
2. Pelvic inflammatory disease
3. Female infertility
4. Ectopic pregnancy
5. Fetal and neonatal infections
6. Complications of pregnancy
7. Neoplasia
8. Human papillomavirus and genital warts
9. Genital ulcer-inguinal lymphadenopathy syndromes
10. Lower genital tract infection in women
11. Viral hepatitis and cirrhosis
12. Urethritis in men
13. Late syphilis
14. Epididymitis
15. Gastrointestinal infections
16. Acute arthritis
17. Mononucleosis syndromes
18. Molluscum contagiosum
19. Ectoparasite infestation

See ACQUIRED IMMUNE DEFICIENCY SYNDROME (AIDS); DRUG RESISTANCE; HEPATITIS.

Most of these syndromes may be caused by more than one organism, often in conjunction with nonsexually transmitted pathogens. They are listed in the approximate order of their public health impact.   [H.H.Ha.]

Siderophores   Low-molecular-mass molecules that have a high specificity for chelating or binding iron. Siderophores are produced by many microorganisms, including bacteria, yeast, and fungi, to obtain iron from the environment. More than 500 different siderophores have been identified from microorganisms. Some bacteria produce more than one type of siderophore. *See* BACTERIA; FUNGI; YEAST.

Iron is required by aerobic bacteria and other living organisms for a variety of biochemical reactions in the cell. Although iron is the fourth most abundant element in the Earth's crust, it is not readily available to bacteria. Iron is found in nature mostly as insoluble precipitates that are part of hydroxide polymers. Bacteria living in the soil or water must have a mechanism to solubilize iron from these precipitates in order to assimilate iron from the environment. Iron is also not freely available in humans and other mammals. Most iron is found intracellularly in heme proteins and ferritin, an iron storage compound. Iron outside cells is tightly bound to proteins. Therefore, bacteria that grow in humans or other animals and cause infections must have a mechanism to remove iron from these proteins and use it for their own energy and growth needs. Siderophores have a very high affinity for iron and are able to solubilize and transport ferric iron (Fe^{3+}) in the environment and also to compete for iron with mammalian proteins such as transferrin and lactoferrin. The majority of bacteria and fungi use siderophores to solubilize and transport iron. Microorganisms can use either siderophores produced by themselves or siderophores produced by other microorganisms. *See* IRON METABOLISM.

The many different types of siderophores can generally be classified into two structural groups, hydroxamates and catecholate compounds. Despite their structural differences, all form an octahedral complex with six binding coordinates for Fe^{3+}.

Siderophores have potential applications in the treatment of some human diseases and infections. Some siderophores are used therapeutically to treat chronic or acute iron overload conditions in order to prevent iron toxicity in humans. Individuals who have defects in blood cell production or who receive multiple transfusions can sometimes have too much free iron in the body. However, in order to prevent infection during treatment for iron overload, it is important to use siderophores that cannot be used by bacterial pathogens.

A second clinical application of siderophores is in antibiotic delivery to bacteria. Some gram-negative bacteria are resistant to antibiotics because they are too big to diffuse through the outer-membrane porins. However, siderophore-antibiotic combination compounds have been synthesized that can be transported into the cell using the siderophore receptor. *See* ANTIBIOTIC; DRUG RESISTANCE.   [P.A.So.]

Signal detection theory   A theory in psychology which characterizes not only the acuity of an individual's discrimination but also the psychological factors that bias the individual's judgments. Failure to separate these two aspects of discrimination had tempered the success of theories based upon the classical concept of a sensory threshold. The theory provides a modern and more complete account of the process whereby an individual makes fine discriminations.

The theory of signal detection has two parts of quite different origins. The first comes from mathematical statistics and is a translation of the theory of statistical decisions. The major contribution of this part of the theory is that it permits a determination of the individual's discriminative capacity, or sensitivity, that is independent of the judgmental bias or decision criterion the individual may have had when the discrimination was made. The second part of the theory comes from the study of electronic communications. It provides a means of calculating for simple signals, such as tones and lights, the best discrimination that can be attained. The prediction is based upon physical measurements of the signals and their interfering noise.

This opportunity to compare the sensitivity of human observers with the sensitivity of an "ideal observer" for a variety of signals is of considerable usefulness, and of growing interest, in sensory psychology. Signal detection theory has been applied to several topics in experimental psychology in which separation of intrinsic discriminability from decision factors is desirable. Included are attention, imagery, learning, conceptual judgment, personality, reaction time, manual control, and speech.

The analytical apparatus of the theory has been of value in the evaluation of the performance of systems that make decisions based on uncertain information. Such systems may involve only people, or people and machines together, or only machines, Examples come from medical diagnosis, where clinicians may base diagnostic decisions on a physical examination, or on an x-ray image, or where machines make diagnoses, perhaps by counting blood cells of various types.   [J.A.Sw.]

Signal transduction   The transmission of molecular signals from a cell's exterior to its interior. Molecular signals are transmitted between cells by the secretion of hormones and other chemical factors, which are then picked up by different cells. Sensory signals are also received from the environment, in the form of light, taste, sound, smell, and touch. The ability of an organism to function normally is dependent on all the cells of its different organs communicating effectively with their surroundings. Once a cell picks up a hormonal or sensory signal, it must transmit this information from the surface to the interior parts of the cell—for example, to the nucleus. This occurs via signal transduction pathways that are very specific, both in their activation and in their downstream actions. Thus, the various organs in the body respond in an appropriate manner and only to relevant signals. *See* CELL (BIOLOGY).

All signals received by cells first interact with specialized proteins in the cells called receptors, which are very specific to the signals they receive. These signals can be in various forms. The most common are chemical signals, which include all the hormones and neurotransmitters secreted within the body as well as the sensory (external) signals of taste and smell. The internal hormonal signals include steroid and peptide hormones, neurotransmitters, and biogenic amines, all of which are released from specialized cells within the various organs. The external signals of smell, which enter the nasal compartment as gaseous chemicals, are dissolved in liquid and then picked up by specialized receptors. Other external stimuli are first received by specialized receptors (for example, light receptors in the eye and touch receptors in the skin), which then convert the environmental signals into chemical ones, which are then passed on to the brain in the form of electrical impulses.

Once a receptor has received a signal, it must transmit this information effectively into the cell. This is accomplished either by a series of biochemical changes within the cell or by modifying the membrane potential by the movement of ions into or out of the cell. Receptors that initiate biochemical changes can do so either directly via intrinsic enzymatic activities within the receptor or by activating intracellular messenger molecules. Receptors may be broadly classified in four groups that differ in their mode of action and in the molecules that activate them.

The largest family of receptors are the G-protein-coupled receptors (GPCRs), which depend on guanosine triphosphate (GTP) for their function. Many neurotransmitters, hormones, and small molecules bind to and activate specific G-protein-coupled receptors.

A second family of membrane-bound receptors are the receptor tyrosine kinases (RTKs). They function by phosphorylating themselves and recruiting downstream signaling components.

Ion channels are proteins open upon activation, thereby allowing the passage of ions across the membrane. Ion channels are responsive to either ligands or to voltage changes across the membrane, depending on the type of channel. The movement of ions changes the membrane potential, which in turn changes cellular function. *See* Biopotentials and ionic currents.

Steroid receptors are located within the cell. They bind cell-permeable molecules such as steroids, thyroid hormone, and vitamin D. Once these receptors are activated by ligand, they translocate to the nucleus, where they bind specific DNA sequences to modulate gene expression. *See* Steroid.

The intracellular component of signal propagation, also known as signal transduction, is receptor-specific. A given receptor will activate only very specific sets of downstream signaling components, thereby maintaining the specificity of the incoming signal inside the cell. In addition, signal transduction pathways amplify the incoming signal by a signaling cascade (molecule A activates several molecule B's, which in turn activate several molecule C's) resulting in an appropriate physiological response by the cell.

Several small molecules within the cell act as intracellular messengers. These include cAMP, cyclic guanosine monophosphate (cGMP), nitric oxide (NO), and Ca^{2+} ions. Increased levels of Ca^{2+} in the cell can trigger several changes, including activation of signaling pathways, changes in cell contraction and motility, or secretion of hormones or other factors, depending on the cell type. Increased levels of nitric oxide cause relaxation of smooth muscle cells and vasodilation by increasing cGMP levels within the cell. Increasing cAMP levels can modulate signaling pathways by activating the enzyme protein kinase A (PKA).

One of the most important functions of cell signaling is to control and maintain normal physiological balance within the body. Activation of different signaling pathways leads to diverse physiological responses, such as cell proliferation, death, differentiation, and metabolism. Signaling pathways in cells may also interact with each other and serve as signal integrators. For example, negative and positive feedback loops in pathways can modulate signals within a pathway; positive interactions between two signaling pathways can increase duration of signals; and negative interactions between pathways can block signals. *See* Cell nucleus; Cell organization; Endocrine system (vertebrate); Noradrenergic system.   [P.T.R.; R.I.]

Sipuncula   A phylum of sedentary marine vermiform coelomates that are unsegmented, but possibly distantly related to the annelids; they are commonly called peanut worms. Two classes are defined: Sipunculidea and Phascolosomatidea. In all there are 17 genera and approximately 150 species living in a wide variety of oceanic habitats within the sediment or inside any protective shelter such as a discarded mollusk shell, foraminiferan test, or crevice in rock or coral.

Adult sipunculans range in trunk length from 2 to over 500 mm (0.08 to over 20 in.). The shape of the body ranges from almost spherical to a slender cylinder. Sipunculans have a variety of epidermal structures (papillae, hooks, or shields). Many species lack color, but shades of yellow or brown may be present. Internal anatomy is relatively simple. The digestive tract has a straight esophagus and a double-coiled intestine extending toward the posterior end of the body and back terminating in a rectum, sometimes bearing small cecum. A ventral nerve cord with lateral nerves and circumenteric connectives to the pair of cerebral ganglia are present. Two or four pigmented eyespots may be present on the cerebral ganglia, and a chemoreceptor (nuchal organ) is usually present.

Knowledge of the reproductive biology of sipunculans is scanty, and good information on breeding cycles is unavailable for most genera. Most sipunculans are dioecious and lack any sexual dimorphism. These worms play a part in the recycling of detritus and probably consume smaller invertebrates in the process. They are in turn preyed on by fishes and probably other predators (including humans).   [E.B.Cu.]

Sirenia An order of herbivorous aquatic placental mammals, commonly known as sea cows, that includes the living manatees and dugongs and the recently exterminated Steller's sea cow. The order has an extensive fossil record dating from the early Eocene Epoch, some 50 million years ago.

The earliest known sirenians were quadrupedal and capable of locomotion on land. Fossils clearly document the evolutionary transition from these amphibious forms to the modern, fully aquatic species, which have lost the hindlimbs and transformed the forelimbs into paddlelike flippers. The living species have streamlined, fusiform bodies with short necks and horizontal tail fins like those of cetaceans, but no dorsal fins. The skin is thick and nearly hairless. The nostrils are separate, and the ears lack external pinnae.

Sirenians typically feed on aquatic angiosperms, especially seagrasses, but in ecologically marginal situations they also eat algae and even some animal material. They are normally found in tropical or subtropical marine waters, but some have become adapted to fresh water or colder latitudes. Body sizes have ranged from less than 3 m up to 9–10 m (30–33 ft). Sirenians mate and give birth in the water, bearing a single calf (occasionally twins) after about 13–14 months of gestation and then nursing it from one pair of axillary mammae. The closest relatives of sirenians among living mammals are the Proboscidea (elephants).   [D.P.D.]

Skin The entire outer surface of the body and the principal boundary between the external environment and the body's internal environment of cells and fluids. Skin serves as the primary barrier against the intrusion of foreign elements and organisms into the body, and also as a large and complex sense organ through which animals explore and learn about the external world. In addition, skin functions to maintain the homeostasis of the body's constituents, acting as a barrier to the loss of various ions and nutrients by diffusion. For terrestrial animals, it also serves as an effective barrier to water loss, without which most land animals would rapidly become desiccated and die.

The skin of humans and other mammals can be divided into two distinct regions, the epidermis and the dermis.

The epidermis is the outermost layer of the skin. It varies in thickness from 0.1 mm in most of the protected areas of the skin to approximately 1 mm in those regions exposed to considerable friction, such as the soles of the feet and palms of the hands. The epidermis consists of a great many horizontally oriented layers of cells. The outermost layer, the stratum corneum, consists of many layers of this packed cellular debris, forming an effective barrier to water loss from lower layers of the skin. The lowest levels of stratum germinativum constitute the portion of the skin that contains melanocytes, cells that produce the dark pigment melanin. Different levels of melanin secretion are responsible for the large range of pigmentation observed among humans.

The dermis plays a supportive and nutritive role for the epidermis. The epidermis has no blood supply of its own. However, nutrients and oxygen are apparently provided by diffusion from the blood supply of the underlying dermis. The average thickness of the dermis is 1–3 mm. It is in this layer that the sebaceous and sweat glands are located and in which the hair follicles originate. The products of all these sets of glands are derived from the rich blood supply of the dermis. Hair, sweat glands, and mammary glands (which are modified sweat glands) are skin inclusions unique to mammals. *See* HAIR; THERMOREGULATION.   [A.F.Be.]

Sleep and dreaming   Sleep is generally defined as an easily reversible (with strong or meaningful sensory stimuli), temporary, periodic state of suspended behavioral activity, unresponsiveness, and perceptual disengagement from the environment. Sleep should not be considered a state of general unconsciousness. The sleeper is normally unconscious (but not always) of the nature of events in the surrounding environment. However, the sleeper's attention may be fully engaged in experiencing a dream. And if reportability is accepted as a sufficient condition for conscious mental processes, any dream that can be recalled must be considered conscious. Dreaming, then, can be simply defined as the world-modeling constructive process through which people have experiences during sleep, and a dream is just whatever the dreamer experienced while sleeping.

Nature of sleep. In general, biological organisms do not remain long in states of either rest or activity. For example, if a cat's blood sugar level drops below a certain point, the cat is motivated by hunger to venture from its den in search of a meal. After satisfying the urge to eat, the cat is no longer motivated to expend energy tracking down prey; now its biochemical state motivates a return to its den, to digest in peace, conserve energy, and generally engage in restful, regenerative activities, including sleep. This example tracks a cat through one cycle of its basic rest-activity cycle (BRAC). Such cyclic processes are ubiquitous among living systems.

Sleep and wakefulness are complementary phases of the most salient aspects of the brain's endogenous circadian rhythm, or biological clock. Temporal isolation studies have determined the biological clock in humans to be slightly longer than 24 hours. Several features of sleep are regulated by the circadian system, including sleep onset and offset, depth of sleep, and rapid eye movement (REM) sleep intensity and propensity. In the presence of adequate temporal cues (for example, sunlight, noise, social interactions, and alarm clocks), the internal clock keeps good time, regulating a host of physiological and behavioral processes. *See* BIOLOGICAL CLOCKS; NORADRENERGIC SYSTEM.

Sleep is not a uniform state of passive withdrawal from the world; a version of the BRAC continues during sleep, showing a periodicity of approximately 90 minutes. There are two distinct kinds of sleep: a quiet phase (also known as quiet sleep or QS, slow-wave sleep) and an active phase (also known as active sleep or AS, REM sleep, paradoxical sleep), which are distinguished by many differences in biochemistry, physiology, psychology, and behavior. Recordings of electrical activity changes of the brain (electroencephalogram or EEG), eye movements (electrooculogram or EOG), and chin muscle tone (electromyogram or EMG) are used to define the various stages and substages of sleep.

Sleep cycle. If sleepy enough, most people can fall asleep under almost any condition. After lying in bed for a few minutes in a quiet, dark room, drowsiness usually

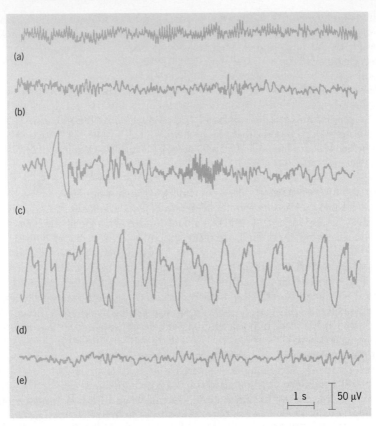

Human EEG associated with different stages of sleep and wakefulness.
(*a*) Relaxed wakefulness (eyes shut) shows rhythmic 8–12-Hz alpha waves.
(*b*) Stage 1 non-REM sleep shows mixed frequencies, especially 3–7-Hz theta
waves. (*c*) Stage 2 non-REM sleep shows 12–14-Hz sleep spindles and
K-complexes. (*d*) Delta sleep shows large-amplitude (>75 μV) 0.5–2-Hz delta
waves. (*e*) REM sleep shows low-amplitude, mixed frequencies with sawtooth
waves.

sets in. The subjective sensation of drowsiness can be objectively indexed by a corresponding change in brain waves (EEG activity): formerly continuous alpha rhythms
(see illustration) gradually break up into progressively shorter trains of regular alpha
waves and are replaced by low-voltage mixed-frequency EEG activity. When less than
half of an epoch [usually the staging epoch is the 20–30 seconds it takes to fill one
page of polygraph (sleep recording) paper] is occupied by continuous alpha rhythm,
sleep onset is considered to have occurred and stage 1 sleep is scored. At this stage,
the EOG usually reveals slowly drifting eye movements (SEMs) and muscle tone might
or might not decrease. Awakenings at this point frequently yield reports of hypnagogic
(leading into sleep) imagery, which can often be extremely vivid and bizarre.

Stage 1 is a very light stage of sleep described by most subjects as "drowsing" or
"drifting off to sleep." Normally, it lasts only a few minutes before further EEG changes
occur, defining another sleep stage. It is at this point that startlelike muscle jerks known
as hypnic myoclonias or hypnic jerks occasionally briefly interrupt sleep. As the subject
descends deeper into sleep, the EEG of stage 2 sleep is marked by the appearance of
relatively high-amplitude slow waves called K-complexes as well as 12–14-Hz rhythms

called sleep spindles. The EOG would generally indicate little eye movement activity, and the EMG would show somewhat decreased muscle tone. Reports of mental activity from this stage of sleep are likely to be less bizarre and more realistic than those from stage 1. However, light sleepers sometimes report lengthy and vivid dreams upon awakening from stage 2 sleep.

After several minutes in stage 2, high-amplitude slow waves (delta waves) gradually begin to appear in the EEG. When at least 20% of an epoch is occupied by these (1–2-Hz) delta waves, stage 3 is defined. Usually this slow-wave activity continues to increase until it completely dominates the appearance of the EEG. When the proportion of delta EEG activity exceeds 50% of an epoch, the criterion for the deepest stage of sleep, stage 4, is met. During stages 3 and 4, often collectively referred to as delta sleep, the EOG shows few genuine eye movements but is obscured by the high-amplitude delta waves. Muscle tone is normally low, although it can be remarkably high, as when sleepwalking or sleep-talking occurs. Recall of mental activity on arousal from delta sleep is generally very poor and fragmentary and is more thoughtlike than dreamlike. It should be noted that cognitive functioning immediately after abrupt wakening from sleep is likely to carry over some of the characteristics of the preceding sleep state. This phenomenon, known as sleep inertia, can be used as an experimental tool for studying cognition during different stages of sleep.

After about 90 minutes, the progression of sleep stages is reversed, back through stage 3 and stage 2 to stage 1 again. But now the EMG shows virtually no activity at all, indicating that muscle tone has reached its lowest possible level, and the EOG discloses the occurrence of rapid eye movements—at first only a few at a time, but later in dramatic profusion. This is REM (or active) sleep. Breathing rate and heart rate become more rapid and irregular, and both males and females show signs of sexual arousal. Brain metabolic rate increases to levels that typically exceed the waking state average. This state of intense brain activation is normally accompanied by experiences that seem vividly real while they last, but often vanish within seconds of waking. When people are abruptly awakened from REM sleep, 80–90% of the time they recall vivid and sometimes extremely detailed dreams.

While all this activity is happening in the brain, the body remains almost completely still (except for small twitches), because it is temporarily paralyzed during REM sleep to prevent dreams from being acted out. The brainstem system that causes the paralysis of REM sleep does not always inactivate immediately upon awakening. The resulting experience, known as sleep paralysis, can be terrifying, but it is quite harmless and normal if it occurs only occasionally. However, frequent sleep paralysis can be a symptom of a disorder of REM sleep called narcolepsy. *See* Sleep disorders.

After a REM period lasting perhaps 5 to 15 minutes, a young adult will typically go back through the preceding cycle stages, dreaming vividly three or four more times during the remainder of the night, with two major modifications. First, decreasing amounts of slow-wave EEG activity (stages 3 and 4 or delta sleep) occur in each successive cycle. Later in the night, after perhaps the second or third REM period, no delta sleep appears on the EEG at all, only non-REM, stage-2, and REM sleep. Second, as the night proceeds, successive REM periods tend to increase in length, up to a point. The fact that for humans most REM occurs in the last portion of the sleep cycle as dawn approaches suggests that REM serves a function related to preparation for waking activity.

Finally, after four or five periods of dreaming sleep, the sleeper wakes up (for perhaps the tenth time during the night) and gets up for the day. It may be difficult to believe that brief awakenings occur this frequently during an average night; however, they are prompty forgotten. This retrograde amnesia is a normal feature of sleep: information in short-term memory at sleep onset is usually not transferred into more permanent storage.

Evolution and function of sleep. Most organisms are adapted to either the dark or light phase of the day. Therefore, a biological process that limits activity to the phase of the cycle to which the organism is adapted will enhance survival. Most likely sleep developed out of the rest phase of the BRAC, allowing organisms to minimize interactions with the world during the less favorable phase, while engaging in a variety of internal maintenance operations. The fact that different species have many differences in sleep structure, process, and function fits with the idea that sleep serves the specific adaptive needs of each species. Quiet sleep appears to be an older form of sleep with simpler and more universal functions related to energy conservation, growth, and restoration. Active sleep is a mammalian invention with functions that appear to be related to specifically mammalian needs. The portion of total sleep composed of REM is at its highest level perinatally: newborn humans spend 8 hours per day in REM sleep, with even more time during the last 6 weeks before birth. The time of maximal REM corresponds to the time of maximal growth of the brain. A number of theorists suggest that this points to the main evolutionary function of REM: to provide a source of endogenous stimulation supporting the unfolding of genetic programming and self-organization of the brain. The fact that REM time does not decrease to zero after the full development of the nervous system suggests secondary adaptive advantages afforded by REM during adulthood, which may include facilitation of difficult learning and preparation of the brain for optimal functioning on arousal.

Although the modern understanding of sleep and dreaming has had the benefit of half a century of scientific research, there are still no simple and conclusive answers to the questions of why we sleep.

Dreams. From the biological perspective, the basic task of the brain is to predict and control the organism's actions and regulate those actions to achieve optimal outcomes (in terms of survival and reproduction). To accomplish this task, the brain in some sense internally "models" the world. The waking brain bases the features of its world model primarily on the current information received from the senses and secondarily on expectations derived from past experience. In contrast, the sleeping brain acquires little information from the senses. Therefore in sleep, the primary sources of information available to the brain are the current motivational state of the organism and past experience. According to this theory, dreams result from brains using internal information to create a simulation of the external world, in a manner directly parallel to the process of waking perception, minus most sensory input. *See* PERCEPTION.   [S.LaB.]

Smallpox   An acute infectious viral disease characterized by severe systemic involvement and a single crop of skin lesions that proceeds through macular, papular, vesicular, and pustular stages. Smallpox is caused by variola virus, a brick-shaped, deoxyribonucleic acid-containing member of the Poxviridae family. Strains of variola virus are indistinguishable antigenically, but have differed in the clinical severity of the disease caused. Following a 13-year worldwide campaign coordinated by the World Health Organization (WHO), smallpox was declared eradicated by the World Health Assembly in May 1980. Smallpox is the first human disease to be eradicated.

Humans were the only reservoir and vector of smallpox. The disease was spread by transfer of the virus in respiratory droplets during face-to-face contact. Before vaccination, persons of all ages were susceptible. It was a winter-spring disease; there was a peak incidence in the drier spring months in the Southern Hemisphere and in the winter months in temperate climates. The spread of smallpox was relatively slow. The incubation period was an average of 10–12 days, with a range of 7–17 days.

Fifteen to forty percent of susceptible persons in close contact with an infected individual developed the disease.

There were two main clinically distinct forms of smallpox, variola major and variola minor. Variola major, prominent in Asia and west Africa, was the more severe form, with widespread lesions and case fatality rates of 15–25% in unvaccinated persons, exceeding 40% in children under 1 year. From the early 1960s to 1977, variola minor was prevalent in South America and south and east Africa; manifestations were milder, with a case fatality rate of less than 1%.

There is no specific treatment for the diseases caused by poxviruses. Supportive care for smallpox often included the systemic use of penicillins to minimize secondary bacterial infection of the skin. When lesions occurred on the cornea, an antiviral agent (idoxuridine) was advised.

Edward Jenner, a British general medical practitioner who used cowpox to prevent smallpox in 1796, is credited with the discovery of smallpox vaccine (vaccinia virus). However, the global smallpox eradication program did not rely only on vaccination. Although the strategy for eradication first followed a mass vaccination approach, experience showed that intensive efforts to identify areas of epidemiologic importance, to detect outbreaks and cases, and to contain them would have the greatest effect on interrupting transmission. In 1978, WHO established an International Commission to confirm the absence of smallpox worldwide. The recommendations made by the commission included abandoning routine vaccination except for laboratory workers at special risk. *See* ANIMAL VIRUS; VACCINATION.

[J.Bre.]

Smut (microbiology) The dark powdery masses of "smut spores" (teliospores) that develop in living plant tissues infected by species of *Ustilago*, *Tilletia*, and similar plant parasitic fungi. Molecular and ultrastructural data show that smut fungi comprise two phylogenetically distinct lines within the Basidiomycota; recent classification places them in two different classes, Ustilaginomycetes and Urediniomycetes. Ustilaginomycetes contains most of the smut fungi, and several groups of morphologically distinct, nonsmut plant parasites, including *Exobasidium*, *Graphiola*, and *Microstroma*. Smut fungi belonging to the genus *Microbotryum*, best known as anther smuts of Caryophyllaceae, are now placed within the Urediniomycetes with rust fungi and allied taxa. Ustilaginomycetes and Urediniomycetes also contain a number of saprotrophic, yeastlike fungi that are related to the plant parasitic smuts. Yeastlike saprotrophs that produce teliospores include *Tilletiaria* in the Ustilaginomycetes, and *Leucosporidium*, *Rhodosporidium*, and *Sporobolomyces* in the Urediniomycetes. Yeastlike saprotrophs in the Ustilaginomycetes that do not form teliospores but reproduce in another manner similar to *Ustilago* and *Tilletia* include *Pseudozyma* and *Tilletiopsis*, respectively. *See* FUNGI.

Teliospores of plant parasitic smut fungi form in a fruiting structure called a sorus. Sori are commonly produced in the inflorescence, leaves, or stems of the host, although the root is the site of sorus formation in smuts belonging to the genus *Entorrhiza*. Teliospores develop within the sorus by conversion of dikaryotic mycelial cells into thick-walled resistant spores within which paired nuclei fuse. Meiosis also occurs in teliospores of some smut fungi, but meiotic division is more characteristic of the tubular basidium that develops at germination.

There are 1200 species and 50 different genera of known smut fungi that infect over 4000 species of angiosperms. Smut fungi occur on both monocotyledonous and dicotyledonous hosts but are most economically important as pathogens of barley, corn, oats, onions, rice, sorghum, sugarcane, and wheat. Control of smut diseases varies with species and includes fungicidal seed treatments and use of resistant crop varieties. *See* BASIDIOMYCOTA; PLANT PATHOLOGY.

[J.R.Ba.; L.M.Ca.]

Social hierarchy   A fundamental aspect of social organization that is established by fighting or display behavior and results in a ranking of the animals in a group. Social, or dominance, hierarchies are observed in many different animals, including insects, crustaceans, mammals, and birds. In many species, size, age, or sex determines dominance rank. Dominance hierarchies often determine first or best access to food, social interactions, or mating within animal groups.

When two animals fight, several different behavioral patterns can be observed. Aggressive acts and submissive acts are both parts of a fight. Aggression and submission, together, are known as agonistic behavior. An agonistic relationship in which one animal is dominant and the other is submissive is the simplest type of dominance hierarchy. In nature, most hierarchies involve more than two animals and are composed of paired dominant-subordinate relationships. The simplest dominance hierarchies are linear and are known as pecking orders. In such a hierarchy the top individual (alpha) dominates all others. The second-ranked individual (beta) is submissive to the dominant alpha but dominates the remaining animals. The third animal (gamma) is submissive to alpha and beta but dominates all others. This pattern is repeated down to the lowest animal in the hierarchy, which cannot dominate any other group member.

Other types of hierarchies result from variations in these patterns. If alpha dominates beta, beta dominates gamma, but gamma dominates alpha, a dominance loop is formed. In some species a single individual dominates all members of the social group, but no consistent relationships are formed among the other animals. In newly formed hierarchies, loops or other nonlinear relationships are common, but these are often resolved over time so that a stable linear hierarchy is eventually observed.

Males often fight over access to females and to mating with them. Male dominance hierarchies are seen in many hooved mammals (ungulates). Herds of females use dominance hierarchies to determine access to food. Agonistic interactions among females are often not as overtly aggressive as those among males, but the effects of the dominance hierarchy can easily be observed. In female dairy cattle, the order of entry into the milking barn is determined by dominance hierarchy, with the alpha female entering first. *See* REPRODUCTIVE BEHAVIOR.

Because dominant animals may have advantages in activities such as feeding and mating, they will have more offspring than subordinate animals. If this is the case, then natural selection will favor genes for enhanced fighting ability. Heightened aggressive behavior may be counterselected by the necessity for amicable social interactions in certain circumstances. Many higher primates live in large groups of mixed sex and exhibit complex social hierarchies. In these groups, intra- and intersexual dominance relationships determine many aspects of group life, including feeding, grooming, sleeping sites, and mating. Macaque, baboon, and chimpanzee societies are characterized by cooperative alliances among individuals that are more important than individual fighting ability in maintaining rank. *See* PRIMATES.

Social hierarchies provide a means by which animals can live in groups and exploit resources in an orderly manner. In particular, food can be distributed among group members with little ongoing conflict. Another motivation for group living is mutual defense. Even though subordinates receive less food or have fewer opportunities to mate, they may have greatly increased chances of escaping predation. *See* BEHAVIORAL ECOLOGY; POPULATION ECOLOGY; SOCIAL MAMMALS; TERRITORIALITY.   [M.D.Bre.]

Social insects   Insects that share resources and reproduce cooperatively. The shared resources are shelter, defense, and food (collection or production). After a period of population growth, the insects reproduce in several ways. As social insect groups grow, they evolve more differentiation between members but reintegrate into a more closely organized system known as eusocial. These are the most advanced societies with individual polymorphism, and they contain insects of various ages, sizes, and shapes. All the eusocial insects are included in the orders Isoptera (termites) and Hymenoptera (wasps, bees, and ants). *See* INSECTA; POLYMORPHISM (GENETICS).

The social insects have evolved in various patterns. In the Hymenoptera, the society is composed of only females; males are produced periodically for their sperm. They usually congregate and attract females, or they visit colonies with virgin females and copulate there. In the Hymenoptera, sex is determined largely by whether the individual has one or two sets of chromosomes. Thus the queen has the power to determine the sex of her offspring: if she lets any of her stored sperm reach the egg, a female is produced; if not, a male results. In the more primitive bees and wasps, social role (caste) is influenced by interaction with like but not necessarily related individuals. The female that can dominate the others assumes the role of queen, even if only temporarily. Domination is achieved by aggression, real or feigned, or merely by a ritual that is followed by some form of salutation by the subordinates. This inhibits the yolk-stimulating glands and prevents the subordinates from contributing to egg production; if it fails to work, the queen tries to destroy any eggs that are laid. Subordinate females take on more and more of the work of the group for as long as the queen is present and well. At first, all the eggs are fertilized and females develop, with the result that virgin females inhabit the nest for the first batches. They are often undernourished, and this, together with their infertility, reduces their urge to leave the nest and start another one. Such workers are said to be produced by maternal manipulation.

Reproductive ants, like termites, engage in a massive nuptial flight, after which the females, replete with sperm, go off to start a new nest. At some stage after the nuptials, the reproductives break off their wings, which have no further use. Workers, however, never have wings because they develop quickly and pass right through the wing-forming stages; their ovaries and genitalia are also reduced. Ant queens can prevent the formation of more queens; as with the honeybee, they do this behaviorally by using pheromones. They also force the workers to feed all larvae the same diet. To this trophogenic caste control is added a blastogenic control; eggs that are laid have a developmental bias toward one caste or another. This is not genetic; bias is affected by the age of the queen and the season: more worker-biased eggs are laid by young queens and by queens in spring. In some ants, workers mature in various sizes. Since they have disproportionately large heads, the biggest workers are used mainly for defense; they also help with jobs that call for strength, like cutting vegetation or cracking nuts.

Social insects make remarkable nests that protect the brood as well as regulate the microclimate. The simplest nests are cavities dug in soil or soft wood, with walls smoothed and plastered with feces that set hard. Chambers at different levels in the soil are frequently connected by vertical shafts so that the inhabitants can choose the chamber with the best microclimate. Termites and ants also make many different types of arboreal nests. These nests are usually made of fecal material, but one species of ant (*Oecophylla*) binds leaves together with silk produced in the salivary glands of their larvae that the workers hold in their jaws and spin across leaves. A whole group of ants (for example, *Pseudomyrmex*) inhabit the pith of plants.

Social bees use wax secreted by their cuticular glands and frequently blended with gums from tree exudates for their nest construction. Cells are made cooperatively by a curtain of young bees that scrape wax from their abdomen, chew it with saliva, and mold it into the correct shape; later it is planed and polished. With honeybees the hexagonal comb reaches perfection as a set of back-to-back cells, each sloping slightly upward to prevent honey from running out. The same cells are used repeatedly for brood and for storage; or they may be made a size larger for rearing males. Only the queen cell is pendant, with a circular cross section and an opening below.   [M.V.B.]

Social mammals   Mammals that exhibit social behavior. This may be defined as any behavior stimulated by or acting upon another animal of the same species. In this broad sense, almost any animal which is capable of behavior is to some degree social. Even those animals which are completely sedentary, such as adult sponges and sea squirts, have a tendency to live in colonies and are social to that extent. Social reactions are occasionally given by species other than the animals' own; an example would be the relations between domestic animals and humans.

The postnatal development of each species is closely related to the social organization typical of the adults. Every highly social animal has a short period early in life when it readily forms attachments to any animal with which it has prolonged contact. The process of socialization begins almost immediately after birth in ungulates like the sheep, and the primary relationship is formed with the mother. In dogs and wolves the process does not begin until about 3 weeks of age, at a time when the mother is beginning to leave the pups. Consequently the strongest relationships are formed with litter mates, thus forming the foundation of a pack. Many rodents stay in the nest long after birth; primary relationships are therefore formed with nest mates. Young primates are typically surrounded by a group of their own kind, but because they are carried for long periods the first strong relationship tends to be with the mother.

Mammals may develop all types of social behavior to a high degree, but not necessarily in every species. Mammals have great capacities for learning and adaptation, which means that social relationships are often highly developed on the basis of learning and habit formation as well as on the basis of heredity and biological differences. The resulting societies tend to be malleable and variable within the same species and to show considerable evidence of cultural inheritance from one generation to the next. Mammalian societies have been completely described in relatively few forms, and new discoveries will probably reveal the existence of a greater variety of social organization.

Basic human social organization and behavior obviously differs from that of all other primates, although it is related to them. At the same time, the range of variability of human societies as seen in the nuclear family does not approach that in mammals as a whole. Human societies are characterized by the presence of all fundamental types of social behavior and social relationships rather than by extreme specialization. *See* ETHOLOGY; HUMAN ECOLOGY; REPRODUCTIVE BEHAVIOR.   [J.P.S.]

Soil ecology   The study of the interactions among soil organisms, and between biotic and abiotic aspects of the soil environment. Soil is made up of a multitude of physical, chemical, and biological entities, with many interactions occurring among them. Soil is a variable mixture of broken and weathered minerals and decaying organic matter. Together with the proper amounts of air and water, it supplies, in part, sustenance for plants as well as mechanical support.

Abiotic and biotic factors lead to certain chemical changes in the top few decimeters (8–10 in.) of soil. The work of the soil ecologist is made easier by the fact that the surface 10–15 cm (4–6 in.) of the A horizon has the majority of plant roots, microorganisms, and fauna. A majority of the biological-chemical activities occur in this surface layer.

The biological aspects of soil range from major organic inputs, decomposition by primary decomposers (bacteria, fungi, and actinomycetes), and interactions between microorganisms and fauna (secondary decomposers) which feed on them. The detritus decomposition pathway occurs on or within the soil after plant materials (litter, roots, sloughed cells, and soluble compounds) become available through death or senescence. Plant products are used by microorganisms (primary decomposers). These are eaten by the fauna which thus affect flows of nutrients, particularly nitrogen, phosphorus, and sulfur. The immobilization of nutrients into plants or microorganisms and their subsequent mineralization are critical pathways. The labile inorganic pool is the principal one that permits subsequent microorganism and plant existence. Scarcity of some nutrient often limits production. Most importantly, it is the rates of flux into and out of these labile inorganic pools which enable ecosystems to successfully function. *See* ECOLOGY; ECOSYSTEM; GUILD; SOIL; SYSTEMS ECOLOGY.   [D.C.C.]

Somatic cell genetics   The study of mechanisms of inheritance in animals and plants by using cells in culture. In such cells, chromosomes and genes can be reshuffled by parasexual methods, rather than having to depend upon the chromosome segregation and genetic recombination that occur during the meiotic cell divisions preceding gamete formation and sexual reproduction. Genetic analysis is concerned with the role of genes and chromosomes in the development and function of individuals and the evolution of species. Genetic analysis of complex multicellular organisms classically required multiple-generation families, and fairly large numbers of progeny of defined matings had to be scored. As a result, analysis of animals and plants with long generation times, small families, or lack of controlled matings was difficult and slow. Somatic cell genetics circumvents many of these limitations. It has enhanced the scope and speed of genetic analysis in higher plants and animals, especially when combined with the powerful techniques of molecular biology and the ability to generate fertile plants and animals from single cultured cells. With these methods, every gene in any species of interest can be identified and mapped to its position on a particular chromosome, its functions determined, and its evolutionary relationships to genes in other species revealed. Cross-species comparisons have provided essential insights into such poorly understood areas as embryonic differentiation and the development of complex nervous systems. *See* EMBRYONIC DIFFERENTIATION; MOLECULAR BIOLOGY.

Foreign genes (transgenes) can be introduced into somatic cells, which grow and differentiate into complete organisms whose sexual reproduction permits both the analysis of the effects of the introduced gene and the development of stocks with desirable characteristics. Transgenic plants have tremendous potential in the development of plants resistant to insects; to viral, fungal, or bacterial disease; and to environmental stress. Transgenic animals are generated in ever-increasing numbers because of their usefulness in studying cell differentiation, morphogenesis, and function. *See* GENE ACTION; GENETIC ENGINEERING; GENETICS.   [O.J.M.]

Somatostatin   A naturally occurring regulatory peptide that carries out numerous functions in the human body, including the inhibition of growth hormone secretion from the anterior pituitary gland. Somatostatin consists of 14 amino acids; two cysteine residues are joined by a disulfide bond so that the peptide forms a ring structure. A larger variant of this peptide, called somatostatin-28, is produced in some cells and has an additional 14 amino acids attached at the amino-terminal end of normal somatostatin (somatostatin-14).

Somatostatin acts primarily as a negative regulator of a variety of different cell types, blocking processes such as cell secretion, cell growth, and smooth muscle contraction. It is secreted from the hypothalamus into the portal circulation and travels to the anterior pituitary gland, where it inhibits the production and release of both growth hormone and thyroid-stimulating hormone. Many tissues other than the hypothalamus contain somatostatin, suggesting that this peptide has numerous roles.

Each of the functions of somatostatin is initiated by the binding of the peptide to one or more of five different cell-surface receptor proteins, thereby activating one or more intracellular G-proteins and initiating biochemical signaling pathways within the cell. *See* SIGNAL TRANSDUCTION.

Analogs of somatostatin have been synthesized that are smaller, more potent, longer-lasting, and more specific in their biological effects than natural somatostatin. Some of these analogs have become useful as drugs. *See* ENDOCRINE SYSTEM (VERTEBRATE); HORMONE; NEUROSECRETION; PITUITARY GLAND.   [W.H.Si.]

Somesthesis   A general term for the somatic sensibilities aroused by stimulation of bodily tissues such as the skin, muscles, tendons, joints, and the viscera. Six primary qualities of somatic sensation are commonly recognized: touch-pressure (including temporal variations such as vibration), warmth, coolness, pain, itch, and the position and movement of the joints. These basic sensory qualities exist because each is served by a different set of sensory receptors (the sensory endings of certain peripheral nerve fibers) which differ not only in their sensitivities to different types of stimuli, but also in their connections to structures within the central nervous system.

The somatic sensory pathways are dual in nature. One major part, the lemniscal system, receives input from large-diameter myelinated peripheral nerve fibers (for example, those serving the sense of touch-pressure). The second major somatic pathway is called the anterolateral system. It receives input from small-diameter myelinated and unmyelinated peripheral nerve fibers carrying pain and temperature information. *See* CUTANEOUS SENSATION; PROPRIOCEPTION.   [R.LaM.]

Speciation   The process by which new species of organisms evolve from preexisting species. It is part of the whole process of organic evolution. The modern period of its study began with the publication of Charles Darwin's and Alfred Russell Wallace's *Theory of Evolution by Natural Selection* in 1858, and Darwin's *On the Origin of Species* in 1859.

Belief in the fixity of species was almost universal before the middle of the nineteenth century. Then it was gradually realized that all species continuously change, or evolve; however, the causative mechanism remained to be discovered. Darwin proposed a mechanism. He argued that (1) within any species population there is always some heritable variation; the individuals differ among themselves in structure, physiology, and behavior; and (2) natural selection acts upon this variation by eliminating the less fit. Thus if two members of an animal population differ from each other in their ability to find a mate, obtain food, escape from predators, resist the ravages of parasites and pathogens, or survive the rigors of the climate, the more successful will be more likely than the less successful to leave descendants. The more successful is said to have greater fitness, to be better adapted, or to be selectively favored. Likewise among plants: one plant individual is fitter than another if its heritable characteristics make it more successful than the other in obtaining light, water, and nutrients, in protecting itself from herbivores and disease organisms, or in surviving adverse climatic conditions. Over the course of time, as the fitter members of a population leave more descendants than the less fit, their characteristics become more common.

This is the process of natural selection, which tends to preserve the well adapted at the expense of the ill adapted in a variable population. The genetic variability that must exist if natural selection is to act is generated by genetic mutations in the broad sense, including chromosomal rearrangements together with point mutations. *See* GENETICS; MUTATION.

If two separate populations of a species live in separate regions, exposed to different environments, natural selection will cause each population to accumulate characters adapting it to its own environment. The two populations will thus diverge from each other and, given time, will become so different that they are no longer interfertile. At this point, speciation has occurred: two species have come into existence in the place of one. This mode of speciation, speciation by splitting, is probably the most common mode. Two other modes are hybrid speciation and phyletic speciation; many biologists do not regard the latter as true speciation.

Many students of evolution are of the opinion that most groups of organisms evolve in accordance with the punctuated equilibrium model rather than by phyletic gradualism. There are two chief arguments for this view. First, it is clear from the fossil record that many species persist without perceptible change over long stretches of time and then suddenly make large quantum jumps to radically new forms. Second, phyletic gradualism seems to be too slow a process to account for the tremendous proliferation of species needed to supply the vast array of living forms that have come into existence since life first appeared on Earth. *See* ANIMAL EVOLUTION; POPULATION GENETICS; SPECIES CONCEPT. [E.C.P.]

Species concept
The species is the fundamental unit of organization of the taxonomic system; of interactions between organisms as described by geneticists and ecologists; and of evolution as studied by phylogeneticists. As a category the term species resists definition; thus, a species concept is adopted as a framework within which biologists of various persuasions delineate the taxa with which they work at the species level. However, no universal concept has been accepted by all biologists for two fundamental reasons: (1) Different groups of organisms in nature are organized differently in terms of reproductive mechanisms and patterns; in degrees of differentiation among species in morphological, genetic, physiological, behavioral, biochemical, and other types of characters; and in the modes of speciation that have given rise to the members of the group. (2) The philosophy, training, working methods, and goals of different of biologists affect the manner in which each perceives the coherence or diversity of the biological world in general and that of the group of organisms in question in particular.

According to the taxonomic concept, a species consists of groups of individuals (populations) that are morphologically similar to one another, and differ morphologically from other such groups. There are several important ideas expressed in this concept. First, there is internal cohesiveness; that is, the members of the species share certain characteristics. Second, there is external distinction because other species have different characteristics, and thus species may be distinguished from one another. Third, the characteristics that a species possesses may be easily observed because they are phenotypic; that is, a species may be identified by its appearance.

Difficulty in applying the taxonomic concept arises with certain groups of organisms. Bacteria are often identified by physiological and biochemical tests requiring sophisticated laboratories and equipment; in addition, the mutation rate in bacteria is so high that the various traits used to identify them can change rapidly. In insects, the morphological differences between species may be very slight and easily overlooked. In certain groups of plants, hybridization and polyploidy have led to a continuous range of variation of characters, in which no discontinuities sufficient to distinguish species can be discerned. Critics claim that the purely phenetic approach of the taxonomic concept may not reflect real genetic or breeding relationships. However, this concept provides guidelines by which species may be recognized by ordinary (nonexperimental) means. The composition of a species so recognized can then be subjected to hypothesis testing within the framework of other concepts. *See* BACTERIAL TAXONOMY; TAXONOMIC CATEGORIES.

According to the biological concept, a species is composed of groups of individuals (populations) that normally interbreed with one another. The fundamental ideas expressed by this concept are that the internal cohesiveness of a species is maintained by the exchange of genes through sexual reproduction (gene flow) and that the distinctness of the species is maintained by reproductive isolation (barriers to gene flow) from other groups of populations. If two populations do not exchange genes, they belong to separate species regardless of their morphological similarity.

This concept works well in those groups of organisms that are exclusively outbreeding, such as birds and mammals. However, it is difficult to apply to plants, in which interbreeding between morphologically very distinct species and even genera is common. Also, those organisms that do not reproduce sexually present problems of classification. Even in sexually reproducing organisms, populations that are morphologically identical but reproductively separated by geographic distance (disjuncts) present problems of classification within the framework of the concept. The populations might interbreed if they were in contact, but this can be determined only under artificial conditions and not in nature. However, the development of the biological species concept has contributed greatly to making taxonomy an evolutionary science because of its emphasis on the identification of genetic, rather than the very possibly superficial phenetic, relationship among organisms.

According to the evolutionary concept, a species is a lineage of ancestor-descendant populations that maintains its identity from other such lineages and that has its own evolutionary tendencies and historical fate. The important ideas expressed in this concept are the following. (1) All organisms, regardless of their mode of reproduction, belong to some evolutionary species. (2) Species need be reproductively isolated from one another to the extent that they maintain their distinction from other species. (3) There may or may not be a morphological discontinuity between species but, if there is, it is reasonable to hypothesize that more than one species is present. If there is not, other data such as that on breeding relationships may be used to recognize species.

The evolutionary concept encompasses the taxonomic concept, the biological concept, and other more narrowly defined concepts—for example, the ecological species, the genetic species, and the paleospecies. It is operational in that it provides guidelines for the recognition of species and for testing of hypotheses concerning membership in each species; it also is compatible with the Linnaean taxonomic hierarchy. As it becomes more widely used by working systematists, problems and difficulties with the concept may appear that will require its refinement. However, the evolutionary concept may in the long run be more acceptable to a wider group of biologists than any other yet proposed. *See* TAXONOMY.   [M.A.La.]

Speech   A set of audible sounds produced by disturbing the air through the integrated movements of certain groups of anatomical structures. Humans attach symbolic values to these sounds for communication. There are many approaches to the study of speech.

Speech production.   The physiology of speech production may be described in terms of respiration, phonation, and articulation. These interacting processes are activated, coordinated, and monitored by acoustical and kinesthetic feedback through the nervous system.

Most of the speech sounds of the major languages of the world are formed during exhalation. Consequently, during speech the period of exhalation is generally much longer than that of inhalation. The aerodynamics of the breath stream influence the rate and mode of the vibration of the vocal folds. This involves interactions between the pressures initiated by thoracic movements and the position and tension of the vocal folds. *See* RESPIRATION.

The phonatory and articulatory mechanisms of speech may be regarded as an acoustical system whose properties are comparable to those of a tube of varying cross-sectional dimensions. At the lower end of the tube, or the vocal tract, is the larynx. It is situated directly above the trachea and is composed of a group of cartilages, tissues, and muscles. The upper end of the vocal tract may terminate at the lips, at the nose, or both. The length of the vocal tract averages 6.5 in. (16 cm) in men and may be increased by either pursing the lips or lowering the larynx.

The larynx is the primary mechanism for phonation, that is, the generation of the glottal tone. The vocal folds consist of connective tissue and muscular fibers which attach anteriorly to the thyroid cartilage and posteriorly to the vocal processes of the arytenoid cartilages. The vibrating edge of the vocal folds measures about 0.92–1.08 in. (23–27 mm) in men and considerably less in women. The aperture between the vocal folds is known as the glottis. The tension and position of the vocal folds are adjusted by the intrinsic laryngeal muscles, primarily through movement of the two arytenoid cartilages. *See* LARYNX.

When the vocal folds are brought together and there is a balanced air pressure to drive them, they vibrate laterally in opposite directions. During phonation, the vocal folds do not transmit the major portion of the energy to the air. They control the energy by regulating the frequency and amount of air passing through the glottis. Their rate and mode of opening and closing are dependent upon the position and tension of the folds and the pressure and velocity of airflow. The tones are produced by the recurrent puffs of air passing through the glottis and striking into the supralaryngeal cavities.

Speech sounds produced during phonation are called voiced. Almost all of the vowel sounds of the major languages and some of the consonants are voiced. In English, voiced consonants may be illustrated by the initial and final sounds in the following words: "bathe," "dog," "man," "jail." The speech sounds produced when the vocal folds are apart and are not vibrating are called unvoiced; examples are the consonants in the words "hat," "cap," "sash," "faith." During whispering all the sounds are un-voiced.

The rate of vibration of the vocal folds is the fundamental frequency of the voice (F0). It correlates well with the perception of pitch. The frequency increases when the vocal folds are made taut. Relative differences in the fundamental frequency of the voice are utilized in all languages to signal some aspects of linguistic information.

Many languages of the world are known as tone languages, because they use the fundamental frequency of the voice to distinguish between words. Chinese is a classic example of a tone language. There are four distinct tones in Chinese speech. Said with a falling fundamental frequency of the voice, *ma* means "to scold." Said with a rising fundamental frequency, it means "hemp." With a level fundamental frequency it means "mother," and with a dipping fundamental frequency it means "horse." In Chinese, changing a tone has the same kind of effect on the meaning of a word as changing a vowel or consonant in a language such as English.

The activity of the structures above and including the larynx in forming speech sound is known as articulation. It involves some muscles of the pharynx, palate, tongue, and face and of mastication.

The primary types of speech sounds of the major languages may be classified as vowels, nasals, plosives, and fricatives. They may be described in terms of degree and place of constriction along the vocal tract.

The only source of excitation for vowels is at the glottis. During vowel production the vocal tract is relatively open and the air flows over the center of the tongue, caus-ing a minimum of turbulence. The phonetic value of the vowel is determined by the resonances of the vocal tract, which are in turn determined by the shape and position of the tongue and lips.

The nasal cavities can be coupled onto the resonance system of the vocal tract by lowering the velum and permitting airflow through the nose. Vowels produced with the addition of nasal resonances are known as nasalized vowels. Nasalization may be used to distinguish meanings of words made up of otherwise identical sounds, such as *bas* and *banc* in French. If the oral passage is completely constricted and air flows only through the nose, the resulting sounds are nasal consonants. The three nasal consonants in "meaning" are formed with the constriction successively at the lips, the hard palate, and the soft palate.

Plosives are characterized by the complete interception of airflow at one or more places along the vocal tract. The places of constriction and the manner of the release are the primary determinants of the phonetic properties of the plosives. The words "par," "bar," "tar," and "car" begin with plosives. When the interception is brief and the constriction is not necessarily complete, the sound is classified as a flap. By tensing the articulatory mechanism in proper relation to the airflow, it is possible to set the mechanism into vibrations which quasiperiodically intercept the airflow. These sounds are called trills.

These are produced by a partial constriction along the vocal tract which results in turbulence. Their properties are determined by the place or places of constriction and the shape of the modifying cavities. The fricatives in English may be illustrated by the initial and final consonants in the words "vase," "this," "faith," "hash."

The ability to produce meaningful speech is dependent in part upon the association areas of the brain. It is through them that the stimuli which enter the brain are interrelated. These areas are connected to motor areas of the brain which send fibers to the motor nuclei of the cranial nerves and hence to the muscles. Three neural pathways are directly concerned with speech production, the pyramidal tract, the extrapyramidal, and the cerebellar motor paths. It is the combined control of these pathways upon nerves arising in the medulla and ending in the muscles of the tongue, lips, and larynx which permits the production of speech. See NERVOUS SYSTEM (VERTEBRATE).

Six of the 12 cranial nerves send motor fibers to the muscles that are involved in the production of speech. These nerves are the trigeminal, facial, glossopharyngeal, vagus, spinal accessory, and the hypoglossal. See PSYCHOACOUSTICS; PSYCHOLINGUISTICS.

[W.S.Y.W.]

Speech perception   A term broadly used to refer to how an individual understands what others are saying. More narrowly, speech perception is viewed as the way a listener can interpret the sound that a speaker produces as a sequence of discrete linguistic categories such as phonemes, syllables, or words. See PSYCHOLINGUISTICS.

Classical work in the 1950s and 1960s concentrated on uncovering the basic acoustic cues that listeners use to hear the different consonants and vowels of a language. It revealed a surprisingly complex relationship between sound and percept. The same physical sound (such as a noise burst at a particular frequency) can be heard as different speech categories depending on its context (as "k" before "ah," but as "p" before "ee" or "oo"), and the same category can be cued by different sounds in different contexts. Spoken language is thus quite unlike typed or written language, where there is a relatively invariant relationship between the physical stimulus and the perceived category.

The reasons for the complex relationship lie in the way that speech is produced: the sound produced by the mouth is influenced by a number of continuously moving and largely independent articulators. This complex relationship has caused great difficulties in programming computers to recognize speech, and it raises a paradox. Computers readily recognize the printed word but have great difficulty recognizing speech. Human listeners, on the other hand, find speech naturally easy to understand but have to be taught to read (often with difficulty). It is possible that humans are genetically predisposed to acquire the ability to understand speech, using special perceptual mechanisms usually located in the left cerebral hemisphere. See HEMISPHERIC LATERALITY.

Building on the classical research, the more recent work has drawn attention to the important contribution that vision makes to normal speech perception; has explored the changing ability of infants to perceive speech and contrasted it with that of animals; and has studied the way that speech sounds are coded by the auditory system and how speech perception breaks down in those with hearing impairment. There has also been substantial research on the perception of words in continuous speech.

Adult listeners are exquisitely sensitive to the differences between sounds that are distinctive in their language. The voicing distinction in English (between "b" and "p") is cued by the relative timing of two different events (stop release and voice onset). At a difference of around 30 milliseconds, listeners hear an abrupt change from one category to another, so that a shift of only 5 ms can change the percept. On the other hand, a similar change around a different absolute value, where both sounds are heard as the same category, would be imperceptible. The term categorical perception refers to this inability to discriminate two sounds that are heard as the same speech category.

Categorical perception can arise for two reasons: it can have a cause that is independent of the listener's language—for instance, the auditory system may be more sensitive to some changes than to others; or it can be acquired as part of the process of learning a particular language. The example described above appears to be language-independent, since similar results have been found in animals such as chinchillas whose auditory systems resemble those of humans. But other examples have a language-specific component. The ability to hear a difference between "r" and "l" is trivially easy for English listeners, but Japanese perform almost at chance unless they are given extensive training. How such language-specific skills are developed has become clearer following intensive research on speech perception in infants.

Newborn infants are able to distinguish many of the sounds that are contrasted by the world's languages. Their pattern of sucking on a blind nipple signals a perceived change in a repeated sound. They are also able to hear the similarities between sounds such as those that are the same vowel but have different pitches. The ability to respond to such a wide range of distinctions changes dramatically in the first year of life. By 12 months, infants no longer respond to some of the distinctions that are outside their native language, while infants from language communities that do make those same distinctions retain the ability. Future experience could reinstate the ability, so it is unlikely that low-level auditory changes have taken place; the distinctions, although still coded by the sensory system, do not readily control the infant's behavior.

Although conductive hearing losses can generally be treated adequately by appropriate amplification of sound, sensorineural hearing loss involves a failure of the frequency-analyzing mechanism in the inner ear that humans cannot yet compensate for. Not only do sounds need to be louder before they can be heard, but they are not so well separated by the ear into different frequencies. Also, the sensorineurally deaf patient tolerates only a limited range of intensities of sound; amplified sounds soon become unbearable (loudness recruitment).

These three consequences of sensorineural hearing loss lead to severe problems in perceiving a complex signal such as speech. Speech consists of many rapidly changing frequency components that normally can be perceptually resolved. The lack of frequency resolution in the sensorineural patient makes it harder for the listener to identify the peaks in the spectrum that distinguish the simplest speech sounds from each other; and the use of frequency-selective automatic gain controls to alleviate the recruitment problem reduces the distinctiveness of different sounds further. These patients may also be less sensitive than people with normal hearing to sounds that change over time, a disability that further impairs speech perception.

Some profoundly deaf patients can identify some isolated words by using multichannel cochlear implants. Sound is filtered into different frequency channels, or different parameters of the speech are automatically extracted, and electrical pulses are then conveyed to different locations in the cochlea by implanted electrodes. The electrical pulses stimulate the auditory nerve directly, bypassing the inactive hair cells of the damaged ear. Such devices cannot reconstruct the rich information that the normal cochlear feeds to the auditory nerve. *See* HEARING (HUMAN); PERCEPTION; PSYCHOACOUSTICS; SPEECH.

[C.J.Da.]

Sperm cell   The male gamete. The typical sperm of most animals has a head containing the nucleus and acrosome, a middle piece with the mitochondria, and a tail with the 9 + 2 microtubule pattern (see illustration). Sperm, as well as the acrosome shape, varies with the species. The nucleus consists of condensed chromatin (deoxyribonucleic acid, DNA) and histone proteins. The acrosome, which is derived from the Golgi complex, contains hydrolytic enzymes, that is, hyaluronidase capable of lysing the egg coats at fertilization. Actin molecules which aid in the interaction between sperm and egg are found in the area between the acrosome and nucleus.

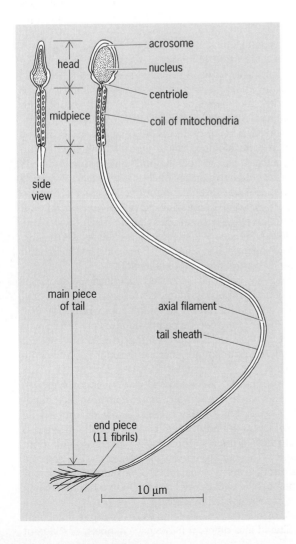

Diagram of a human spermatozoon, based on electron micrographs.

The mitochondria in the middle piece apparently provide the energy necessary for the motility created by the tail. The tail has a central core, or axial filament, made up of nine double tubules and two central tubules. *See* CILIA AND FLAGELLA.

Many groups, including nematodes, myriapods, and crustaceans, have atypical sperm which lack a flagellum and are presumably nonmotile. The sperm of *Ascaris* is round and moves by ameboid means. The crustacean sperm have a large acrosome of several components. In the anomurans a middle with mitochondria and arms filled with microtubules precedes the nucleus. In the true crabs the nucleus forms arms which possess microtubules and also surrounds the many component acrosomes. The nucleus of crustacean sperm does not condense with maturation as it does in typical sperm mentioned above. *See* SPERMATOGENESIS.   [G.W.H.]

Spermatogenesis

Spermatogenesis   The differentiation of spermatogonial cells (primordial germ cells in the testes) into spermatozoa (see illustration).

Spermatogonial divisions occur continuously throughout the life of mammals; these divisions both maintain the stem cell population (spermatogonial cells) and supply cells which develop into sperm. Clusters of spermatogonia maintain communication through

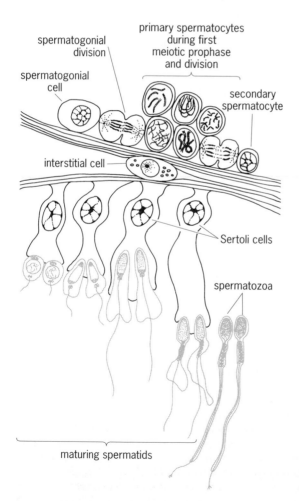

Cellular events in human spermatogenesis.

cytoplasmic bridges, and these groups become primary spermatocytes when they syn-
chronously enter the first meiotic prophase. The first meiotic prophase is characterized
by a series of remarkable changes in chromosome morphology, which are identical
to those seen in the corresponding stage of oogenesis. The secondary spermatocyte
produced by this division then undergoes a division in which the chromosomes are not
replicated; the resulting spermatids contain half the somatic number of chromosomes.
See MEIOSIS.

The spermatids become embedded in the cytoplasm of Sertoli cells, and there undergo the distinctive changes which result in formation of spermatozoa. These morphological transformations include the conversion of the Golgi apparatus into the acrosome
and progressive condensation of the chromatin in the nucleus. A centriole migrates to
a position distal to the nucleus and begins organizing the axial filament which will form
the motile tail of the sperm. Mitochondria may fuse to form a nebenkern as is the case
for many vertebrates, or there may be less extensive fusion as in mammals. In all cases
the resulting structures become located around the axial filament in the midpiece. The
cytoplasm of the spermatid is reflected distally away from the nucleus during spermatid
maturation; eventually, most of the cytoplasm is sloughed off and discarded.

The Sertoli cells are thought to provide nutrition for the developing sperm, because
their cytoplasm contains large stores of glycogen which diminish as spermatids mature.
There is no direct evidence for this nutritive function, but some forms of male sterility
are associated with the failure to produce normal Sertoli cells. Electron microscopy
has revealed distinct plasma membranes surrounding the two cell types at the points of
contact, and thus the Sertoli cell-spermatid relationship is not syncytial as once thought.

Spermatogenesis is cyclical to a varying extent depending on the species, and under
endocrine control. Spermatogenesis is maintained and regulated by male steroid hormones such as testosterone, which is produced by the interstitial or Leydig cells found
in the connective tissue of the testis. Interstitial cells, in turn, are stimulated by luteinizing hormone (LH) which is produced by the pituitary gland. The male testis-regulating
hormone was formerly known as interstital cell-stimulating hormone (ICSH), but it is
now known to be identical to LH. *See* GAMETOGENESIS; TESTIS.   [S.J.B.]

Sphingolipid   Any lipid containing the long-chain amino alcohol sphingosine
(structure **1**) or a variation of it, such as dihydrosphingosine, phytosphingosine (structure **2**), or dehydrophytosphingosine. Sphingosine itself is synthesized by condensing

$$CH_3(CH_2)_{12}CH=CH-CH-CH-CH_2OH$$
$$\begin{array}{cc} | & | \\ OH & NH_2 \end{array}$$

(1)

$$CH_3(CH_2)_{13}CH-CH-CH-CH_2OH$$
$$\begin{array}{ccc} | & | & | \\ OH & OH & NH_2 \end{array}$$

(2)

a long-chain fatty acid with the amino acid serine.

Sphingosine is converted into a variety of derivatives to form the family of sphingolipids. The simplest form is a ceramide which contains a sphingosine and a fatty
acid residue joined by an amide linkage. Ceramide is the basic building block of practically all of the naturally occurring sphingolipids. It can be further modified by the
addition of a phosphorylcholine at the primary alcohol group to form sphingomyelin, a
ubiquitous phospholipid in the plasma membranes of virtually all cells. Modification of

a ceramide by addition of one or more sugars at the primary alcohol group converts it to a glycosphingolipid, which occurs widely in both the plant and animal kingdoms. See GLYCOSIDE; LIPID.

Sphingolipids participate in diverse cellular functions. A number of inheritable diseases that can cause severe mental retardation and early death occur as the result of a deficiency in one or more of the degradative enzymes, resulting in the accumulation of a particular sphingolipid in tissues. These diseases are collectively called sphingolipidoses and include Niemann-Pick disease, Gaucher disease, Krabbe disease, metachromatic leukodystrophy, and several forms of gangliosidoses, such as Tay-Sachs disease. Functionally, glycosphingolipids are known to serve as important cell-surface molecules for mediating cell-to-cell recognition, interaction, and adhesion. They also serve as receptors for a variety of bacterial and viral toxins. Many glycosphingolipids can modulate immune responses as well as the function of hormones and growth factors by transmitting signals from the exterior to the interior of the cell. A number of glycolipids are also found to participate in a variety of immunological disorders by serving as autoantigens. Other sphingolipids and their metabolites may serve as second messengers in several signaling pathways that are important to cell survival or programmed cell death (apoptosis). See AUTOIMMUNITY. [R.K.Y.]

Spirometry   The measurement, by a form of gas meter, of volumes of gas that can be moved in or out of the lungs. The classical spirometer is a hollow cylinder (bell) closed at its top. With its open end immersed in a larger cylinder filled with water, it is suspended by a chain running over a pulley and attached to a counterweight. The magnitude of a gas volume entering or leaving is proportional to the vertical excursion of the bell. Volume changes can also be determined from measurements of flow, or rate of volume change, that can be sensed and recorded continuously by a transducer that generates an electrical signal. The flow signal can be continuously integrated to yield a volume trace.

The volume of gas moved in or out with each breath is the tidal volume; the maximal possible value is the vital capacity. Even after the most complete expiration, a volume of gas that cannot be measured by the above methods, that is, the residual volume, remains in the lungs. It is usually measured by a gas dilution method or by an instrument that measures blood flow in the lungs. Lung volumes can also be estimated by radiological or optical methods.

At the end of an expiration during normal resting breathing, the muscles of breathing are minimally active. Passive (elastic and gravitational) forces of the lungs balance those of the chest wall. In this state the volume of gas in the lungs is the functional residual capacity or relaxation volume. Displacement from this volume requires energy from natural (breathing muscles) or artificial (mechanical) sources. See RESPIRATION. [A.B.O.]

Spleen   An organ of the circulatory system present in most vertebrates, lying in the abdominal cavity usually in close proximity to the left border of the stomach.

In humans the spleen normally measures about 1 by 3 by 5 in. (2.5 × 7.5 × 12.5 cm) and weighs less than $1/2$ lb (230 g). It is a firm organ with an oval shape and is indented on its inner surface to form the hilum, or stalk of attachment to the peritoneum. This mesentery fold also carries the splenic artery and vein to the organ.

The spleen is an important part of the blood-forming, or hematopoietic, system; it is also one of the largest lymphoid organs in the body and as such is involved in the defenses against disease attributed to the reticuloendothelial system. Although the chief functions of the spleen appear to be the production of lymphocytes, the probable formation of antibodies, and the destruction of worn-out red blood cells, other less well-understood activities are known. For example, in some animals it may act as a reservoir for red blood cells, contracting from time to time to return these cells to the bloodstream as they are needed. In the fetus and sometimes in later life, the spleen may be a primary center for the formation of red blood cells. Another function of the spleen is its role in biligenesis. Because the spleen destroys erythrocytes, it is one of the sites where extrahepatic bilirubin is formed. *See* BILIRUBIN.   [W.J.B.]

Sporozoa   A subphylum of Protozoa, typically with spores. The spores are simple and have no polar filaments. There is a single type of nucleus. There are no cilia or flagella except for flagellated microgametes in some groups. In most Sporozoa there is an alternation of sexual and asexual stages in the life cycle. In the sexual stage, fertilization is by syngamy, that is, the union of male and female gametes. All Sporozoa are parasitic. The subphylum is divided into three classes—Telosporea, Toxoplasmea, and Haplosporea. *See* HAPLOSPOREA; PROTOZOA.   [N.D.L.]

Squamata   The dominant order of living reptiles composed of the lizards and snakes. The group first appeared in Jurassic times and today is found in all but the coldest regions. Various forms are adapted for arboreal, burrowing, or aquatic lives, but most squamates are fundamentally terrestrial. There are about 4700 Recent species: 2200 lizards and 2500 snakes.

The order is readily distinguished from all known reptiles by its highly modified skull; an enlarged and movable quadrate; and a temporal opening that is lost or reduced in many forms. No other reptiles show these modifications, which allow for great kinesis in the lower jaw since it articulates with the quadrate. In addition, the order is distinct from other living reptile groups because its members have no shells or secondary palates and the males possess paired penes.

Traditionally the Squamata have been divided into two major subgroups, the lizards, suborder Sauria, and the snakes, suborder Serpentes. The latter group is basically a series of limbless lizards, and it is certain that snakes are derived from some saurian ancestor. There are many different legless lizards, and it has been suggested that more than one line has evolved to produce those species currently grouped together as snakes.

Sauria. The majority of saurians are insectivorous, but a few feed on plants while others, notably the Varanidae and allies, feed on larger prey including birds and mammals. The largest living lizard is the Komodo dragon (*Varanus komodoensis*).

The majority of lizards are quadrupedal in locomotion and are usually ambulatory scamperers or scansorial. Some forms are bipedal, at least when in haste. The coloration of each species of lizard is characteristic. Most forms exhibit marked differences in coloration between the sexes, at least during the breeding season, and frequently the young are markedly different from the parents. Color changes occur in rapid fashion among some species, and all are capable of metachrosis or changing color to a certain extent. *See* SEXUAL DIMORPHISM.

There are but two species of venomous lizards, both members of the genus *Heloderma*, in the family Helodermatidae: the Gila monster (*H. suspectum*) and the beaded lizard (*H. horridum*).

Serpentes. Snakes are basically specialized, limbless lizards which probably evolved from burrowing forms but have now returned from subterranean habitats to occupy terrestrial, arboreal, and aquatic situations. The following characteristics are typical of all serpents. There is no temporal arch so that the lower jaw and quadrate are very loosely attached to the skull. This gives the jaw even greater motility than is the case in lizards. The body is elongate with 100–200 or more vertebrae, and the internal organs are elongate and reduced. A spectacle covers the eye.

The largest living snake is the Indian python (*Python reticulatus*), which reaches 30 ft (9 m) in length and a weight of 250 lb (113 kg). The largest venomous snake is the king cobra (*Ophiophagus hannah*), of southern Asia, which is known to attain a length of 18 ft (5.5 m).

The senses of snakes are fundamentally similar to those of all terrestrial vertebrates. Great dependence is placed upon olfaction and the Jacobson's organs (olfactory canals in the nasal mucosa). The tongue of all snakes is elongate and deeply bifurcated. When not in use it can be retracted into a sheath located just anterior to the glottis, but it is protrusible and is constantly being projected to pick up samples for the Jacobson's organs from the surrounding environment. Snakes are deaf to airborne sounds and receive auditory stimuli only through the substratum via the bones of the head. The eyes are greatly modified from those in lizards, and there is no color vision. Some groups are totally blind and have vestigial eyes covered by scales or skin.

Four basic patterns of locomotion are found in snakes, and several may be used by a particular individual at different times. The most familiar type is curvilinear. Snakes using rectilinear locomotion move forward in a straight line, without any lateral undulations, by producing wavelike movements in the belly plates. Laterolinear locomotion, or sidewinding, is used primarily on smooth or yielding surfaces and is very complex. Concertina locomotion movement resembles the expansion and contraction of that musical instrument.

The vast majority of living snakes are harmless to humans, although a number are capable of inflicting serious injury with their venomous bites. The venom apparatus has evolved principally as a method of obtaining food, but it is also advantageous as a defense against attackers. Fangs are teeth modified for the injection of venom into the victim, and the venom glands are modified salivary glands connected to the grooved fangs by a duct. Special muscles are present in all proglyphous snakes to force the venom into the wound. The venom itself is a complex substance containing a number of enzymes. Certain of these enzymes attack the blood, others in the nervous system, and some are spreaders.
[J.M.S.]

Stain (microbiology) Any colored, organic compound, usually called dye, used to stain tissues, cells, cell components, or cell contents. The dye may be natural or synthetic. The object stained is called the substrate. The small size and transparency of microorganisms make them difficult to see even with the aid of a high-power microscope. Staining facilitates the observation of a substrate by introducing differences in optical density or in light absorption between the substrate and its surround or between different parts of the same substrate. In electron microscopy, and sometimes in light microscopy (as in the silver impregnation technique of staining flagella or capsules), staining is accomplished by depositing on the substrate ultraphotoscopic particles of a metal such as chromium or gold (the so-called shadowing process); or staining is done by treating the substrate with solutions of metallic compounds such as uranyl acetate or phosphotungstic acid. Stains may be classified according to their molecular structure. They may also be classified according to their chemical behavior into acid, basic, neutral, and indifferent. This classification is of more practical value to the biologist. See MEDICAL BACTERIOLOGY.
[J.P.Tr.]

Staphylococcus A genus of bacteria containing at least 28 species that are collectively referred to as staphylococci. Their usual habitat is animal skin and mucosal surfaces. Although the genus is known for the ability of some species to cause infectious diseases, many species rarely cause infections. Pathogenic staphylococci are usually opportunists and cause illness only in compromised hosts. *Staphylococcus* *aureus*, the most pathogenic species, is usually identified by its ability to produce coagulase (proteins that affect fibrinogen of the blood-clotting cascade). Since most other species of staphylococci do not produce coagulase, it is useful to divide staphylococci into coagulase-positive and coagulase-negative species. Coagulase-negative staphylococci are not highly virulent but are an important cause of infections in certain high-risk groups. Although *Staphylococcus* infections were once readily treatable with antibiotics, some strains have acquired genes making them resistant to multiple antimicrobial agents. *See* BACTERIA; DRUG RESISTANCE; MEDICAL BACTERIOLOGY.

Staphylococcus cells are spherical with a diameter of 0.5–1.5 micrometers. Clumps of staphylococci resemble bunches of grapes when viewed with a microscope, owing to cell division in multiple planes. The staphylococci have a gram-positive cell composition, with a unique peptidoglycan structure that is highly cross-linked with bridges of amino acids. *See* STAIN (MICROBIOLOGY).

Most species are facultative anaerobes. Within a single species, there is a high degree of strain variation in nutritional requirements. Staphylococci are quite resistant to desiccation and high-osmotic conditions. These properties facilitate their survival in the environment, growth in food, and communicability.

In addition to genetic information on the chromosome, pathogenic staphylococci often contain accessory elements such as plasmids, bacteriophages, pathogenicity islands (DNA clusters containing genes associated with pathogenesis), and transposons. These elements harbor genes that encode toxins or resistance to antimicrobial agents and may be transferred to other strains. Genes involved in virulence, especially those coding for exotoxins and surface-binding proteins, are coordinately or simultaneously regulated by loci on the chromosome. *See* BACTERIAL GENETICS; BACTERIOPHAGE; PLASMID; TRANSPOSONS.

Most *Staphylococcus aureus* infections develop into a pyogenic (pus-forming) lesion caused by acute inflammation. Inflammation helps eliminate the bacteria but also damages tissue at the site of infection. Typical pyogenic lesions are abscesses with purulent centers containing leukocytes, fluid, and bacteria. Pyogenic infections can occur anywhere in the body. Blood infections (septicemia) can disseminate the organism throughout the body and abscesses can form internally.

Certain strains of *S. aureus* produce exotoxins that mediate two illnesses, toxic shock syndrome and staphylococcal scalded skin syndrome. In both diseases, exotoxins are produced during an infection, diffuse from the site of infection, and are carried by the blood (toxemia) to other sites of the body, causing symptoms to develop at sites distant from the infection. Toxic shock syndrome is an acute life-threatening illness mediated by staphylococcal superantigen exotoxins. Staphylococcal scalded skin syndrome, also known as Ritter's disease, refers to several staphylococcal toxigenic infections. It is characterized by dermatologic abnormalities caused by two related exotoxins, the type A and B exfoliative (epidermolytic) toxins. *See* CELLULAR IMMUNOLOGY; TOXIC SHOCK SYNDROME.

Staphylococcal food poisoning is not an infection, but an intoxication that results from ingestion of staphylococcal enterotoxins in food. The enterotoxins are produced when food contaminated with *S. aureus* is improperly stored under conditions that allow the bacteria to grow. Although contamination can originate from animals or the environment, food preparers with poor hygiene are the usual source. Effective methods for preventing staphylococcal food poisoning are aimed at eliminating contamination through common hygiene practices, such as wearing gloves, and proper food storage to minimize toxin production. *See* FOOD POISONING.

Coagulase-positive staphylococci are the most important *Staphylococcus* pathogens for animals. Certain diseases of pets and farm animals are very prominent. *Staphylococcus aureus* is the leading cause of infectious mastitis in dairy animals.   [G.Boh.]

Stem   The organ of vascular plants that usually develops branches and bears leaves and flowers. On woody stems a branch that is the current season's growth from a bud is called a twig. The stems of some species produce adventitious roots. *See* ROOT (BOTANY).

General characteristics. While most stems are erect, aerial structures, some remain underground, others creep over or lie prostrate on the surface of the ground, and still others are so short and inconspicuous that the plants are said to be stemless, or acaulescent. When stems lie flattened immediately above but not on the ground, with tips curved upward, they are said to be decumbent, as in juniper. If stems lie flat on the ground but do not root at the nodes (joints), the stem is called procumbent or prostrate, as in purslane. If a stem creeps along the ground, rooting at the nodes, it is said to be repent or creeping, as in ground ivy.

Most stems are cylindrical and tapering, appearing circular in cross section; others may be quadrangular or triangular.

Herbaceous stems (annuals and herbaceous perennials) die to the ground after blooming or at the end of the growing season. They usually contain little woody tissue. Woody stems (perennials) have considerable woody supporting tissue and live from year to year. A woody plant with no main stem or trunk, but usually with several stems developed from a common base at or near the ground, is known as a shrub.

[N.A.]

External features. A shoot or branch usually consists of a stem, or axis, and leafy appendages. Stems have several distinguishing features. They arise either from the epicotyl of the embryo in a seed or from buds. The stem bears both leaves and buds at nodes, which are separated by leafless regions or internodes, and sometimes roots and flowers (see illustration).

The nodes are the regions of the primary stem where leaves and buds arise. The number of leaves at a node is usually specific for each plant species. In deciduous plants which are leafless during winter, the place of former attachment of a leaf is marked by the leaf scar. The scar is formed in part by the abscission zone formed at the base of the leaf petiole. The stem regions between nodes are called internodes. Internode length varies greatly among species, in different parts of the same stem, and under different growing conditions.

Lenticels are small, slightly raised or ridged regions of the stem surface that are composed of loosely arranged masses of cells in the bark. Their intercellular spaces are

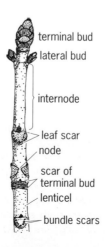

terminal bud
lateral bud
internode
leaf scar
node
scar of terminal bud
lenticel
bundle scars

Winter woody twig (horse chestnut) showing apical dominance. (*After E. W. Sinnott and K. S. Wilson, Botany: Principles and Problems, 5th ed., McGraw-Hill, 1955*)

continuous with those in the interior of the stem, therefore permitting gas exchange similar to the stomata that are present before bark initiation.

There are three major types of stem branching: dichoto-mous, monopodial, and sympodial. Dichotomy occurs by a division of the apical meristem to form two new axes. If the terminal bud of an axis continues to grow and lateral buds grow out as branches, the branching is called monopodial. If the apical bud terminates growth in a flower or dies back and one or more axillary buds grow out, the branching is called sympodial. Often only one bud develops so that what appears to be single axis is in fact composed of a series of lateral branches arranged in linear sequence.

The large and conspicuous stems of trees and shrubs assume a wide variety of distinctive forms. Columnar stems are basically unbranched and form a terminal leaf cluster, as in palms, or lack obvious leaves, as in cacti. Branching stems have been classified either as excurrent, when there is a central trunk and a conical leaf crown, as in firs and other conifers, or as decur-rent (or deliquescent), when the trunk quickly divides up into many separate axes so that the crown lacks a central trunk, as in elm. *See* TREE.   [J.B.F.]

Internal features. The stem is composed of the three fundamental tissue systems that are found also in all other plant organs: the dermal (skin) system, consisting of epidermis in young stems and peridem in older stems of many species; the vascular (conducting) system, consisting of xylem (water conduction) and phloem (food conduction); and the fundamental or ground tissue system, consisting of parenchyma and sclerenchyma tissues in which the vascular tissues are embedded. The arrangement of the vascular tissues varies in stems of different groups of plants, but frequently these tissues form a hollow cylinder enclosing a region of ground tissue called pith and separated from the dermal tissue by another region of ground tissue called cortex. *See* CORTEX (PLANT); EPIDERMIS (PLANT); PHLOEM; PITH; SCLERENCHYMA; XYLEM.

Part of the growth of the stem results from the activity of the apical meristem located at the tip of the shoot. The derivatives of this meristem are the primary tissues; epidermis, primary vascular tissues, and the ground tissues of the cortex and pith. In many species, especially those having woody stems, secondary tissues are added to the primary. These tissues are derived from the lateral meristems, oriented parallel with the sides of the stem: cork cambium (phellogen), which gives rise to the secondary protective tissue periderm, which consists of phellum (cork), phellogen (cork cambium), and phelloderm (secondary cortex) and which replaces the epidermis; and vascular cambium, which is inserted between the primary xylem and phloem and forms secondary xylem (wood) and phloem. *See* APICAL MERISTEM; LATERAL MERISTEM.

The vascular tissues and the closely associated ground tissues—pericycle (on the outer boundary of vascular region), interfascicular regions (medullary or pith rays), and frequently also the pith—may be treated as a unit called the stele. The variations in the arrangement of the vascular tissues serve as a basis for distinguishing the stelar types. The word stele means column and thus characterizes the system of vascular and associated ground tissues as a column. This column is enclosed within the cortex, which is not part of the stele.   [J.E.Gu.]

Stem cells   Cells that have the ability to self-replicate and give rise to specialized cells. Stem cells can be found at different stages of fetal development and are present in a wide range of adult tissues. Many of the terms used to distinguish stem cells are based on their origins and the cell types of their progeny.

There are three basic types of stem cells. Totipotent stem cells, meaning their potential is total, have the capacity to give rise to every cell type of the body and to form an entire organism. Pluripotent stem cells, such as embryonic stem cells, are capable of generating virtually all cell types of the body but are unable to form a functioning organism. Multipotent stem cells can give rise only to a limited number of cell types. For example, adult stem cells, also called organ- or tissue-specific stem cells, are multipotent stem cells found in specialized organs and tissues after birth. Their primary function is to replenish cells lost from normal turnover or disease in the specific organs and tissues in which they are found.

Totipotent stem cells occur at the earliest stage of embryonic development. The union of sperm and egg creates a single totipotent cell. This cell divides into identical cells in the first hours after fertilization. All these cells have the potential to develop into a fetus when they are placed into the uterus. The first differentiation of totipotent cells forms a hollow sphere of cells called the blastocyst, which has an outer layer of cells and an inner cell mass inside the sphere. The outer layer of cells will form the placenta and other supporting tissues during fetal development, whereas cells of the inner cell mass go on to form all three primary germ layers: ectoderm, mesoderm, and endoderm. The three germ layers are the embryonic source of all types of cells and tissues of the body. Embryonic stem cells are derived from the inner cell mass of the blastocyst. They retain the capacity to give rise to cells of all three germ layers. However, embryonic stem cells cannot form a complete organism because they are unable to generate the entire spectrum of cells and structures required for fetal development. Thus, embryonic stem cells are pluripotent, not totipotent, stem cells.

Embryonic germ (EG) cells differ from embryonic stem cells in the tissue sources from which they are derived, but appear to be similar to embryonic stem cells in their pluripotency. Human embryonic germ cell lines are established from the cultures of the primordial germ cells obtained from the gonadal ridge of late-stage embryos, a specific part that normally develops into the testes or the ovaries. Embryonic germ cells in culture, like cultured embryonic stem cells, form embryoid bodies, which are dense, multilayered cell aggregates consisting of partially differentiated cells. The embryoid body-derived cells have high growth potential. The cell lines generated from cultures of the embryoid body cells can give rise to cells of all three embryonic germ layers, indicating that embryonic germ cells may represent another source of pluripotent stem cells.

Much of the knowledge about embryonic development and stem cells has been accumulated from basic research on mouse embryonic stem cells. Since 1998, however, research teams have succeeded in growing human embryonic stem cells in culture. Human embryonic stem cell lines have been established from the inner cell mass of human blastocysts that were produced through in vitro fertilization procedures. The techniques for growing human embryonic stem cells are similar to those used for growth of mouse embryonic stem cells. However, human embryonic stem cells must be grown on a mouse embryonic fibroblast feeder layer or in media conditioned by mouse embryonic fibroblasts. Human embryonic stem cell lines can be maintained in culture to generate indefinite numbers of identical stem cells for research. As with mouse embryonic stem cells, culture conditions have been designed to direct differentiation into specific cell types (for example, neural and hematopoietic cells).

Adult stem cells occur in mature tissues. Like all stem cells, adult stem cells can self-replicate. Their ability to self-renew can last throughout the lifetime of individual organisms. But unlike embryonic stem cells, it is usually difficult to expand adult stem cells in culture. Adult stem cells reside in specific organs and tissues, but account for a very small number of the cells in tissues. They are responsible for maintaining a stable state of the specialized tissues. To replace lost cells, stem cells typically generate intermediate cells called precursor or progenitor cells, which are no longer capable of self-renewal. However, they continue undergoing cell divisions, coupled with maturation, to yield fully specialized cells. Such stem cells have been identified in many types of adult tissues, including bone marrow, blood, skin, gastrointestinal tract, dental pulp, retina of the eye, skeletal muscle, liver, pancreas, and brain. Adult stem cells are usually designated according to their source and their potential. Adult stem cells are multipotent because their potential is normally limited according to their source and their potential. Adult stem cells are multipotent because their potential is normally limited to one or more lineages of specialized cells. However, a special multipotent stem cell that can be found in bone marrow, called the mesenchymal stem cell, can produce all cell types of bone, cartilage, fat, blood, and connective tissues.

Blood stem cells, or hematopoietic stem cells, are the most studied type of adult stem cells. The concept of hematopoietic stem cells is not new, since it has been long realized that mature blood cells are constantly lost and destroyed. Billions of new blood cells are produced each day to make up the loss. This process of blood cell generation called hematopoiesis, occurs largely in the bone marrow. Another emerging source of blood stem cells is human umbilical cord blood. Similar to bone marrow, umbilical cord blood can be used as a source material of stem cells for transplant therapy. However, because of the limited number of stem cells in umbilical cord blood, most of the procedures are performed for young children of relatively low body weight.

Neural stem cells, the multipotent stem cells that generate nerve cells, are a new focus in stem cell research. Active cellular turnover does not occur in the adult nervous system as it does in renewing tissues such as blood or skin. Because of this observation, it had been a dogma that the adult brain and spinal cord were unable to regenerate new nerve cells. However, since the early 1990s, neural stem cells have been isolated from the adult brain as well as fetal brain tissues. Stem cells in the adult brain are found in the areas called the subventricular zone and the ventricle zone. Another location of brain stem cells occurs in the hippocampus, a special structure of the cerebral cortex related to memory function. Stem cells isolated from these areas are able to divide and to give rise to nerve cells (neurons) and neuron-supporting cell types in culture.

Stem cell plasticity refers to the phenomenon of adult stem cells from one tissue generating the specialized cells of another tissue. The long-standing concept of adult organ-specific stem cells is that they are restricted to producing the cell types of their specific tissues. However, a series of studies have challenged the concept of tissue restriction of adult stem cells. Although the stem cells appear able to cross their tissue-specific boundaries, crossing occurs generally at a low frequency and mostly only under conditions of host organ damage. The finding of stem cell plasticity carries significant implications for potential cell therapy. For example, if differentiation can be redirected, stem cells of abundant source and easy access, such as blood stem cells in bone marrow or umbilical cord blood, could be used to substitute stem cells in tissues that are difficult to isolate, such as heart and nervous system tissue. *See* CELL DIFFERENTIATION; EMBRYOLOGY; EMBRYONIC DIFFERENTIATION; GERM LAYERS; HEMATOPOIESIS; REGENERATION (BIOLOGY); TRANSPLANTATION BIOLOGY.   [C.Wa.]

Stereoscopy   The phenomenon of simultaneous vision with two eyes, producing a visual experience of the third dimension, that is, a vivid perception of the relative distances of objects in space. In this experience the observer seems to see the space between the objects located at different distances from the eyes.

Stereopsis, or stereoscopic vision, is believed to have an innate origin in the anatomic and physiologic structures of the retinas of the eyes and the visual cortex. It is present in normal binocular vision because the two eyes view objects in space from two points, so that the retinal image patterns of the same object points in space are slightly different in the two eyes. The stereoscope, with which different pictures can be presented to each eye, demonstrates the fundamental difference between stereoscopic perception

of depth and the conception of depth and distance from the monocular view. *See* Vision.
[K.N.O.]

Sterilization   An act of destroying all forms of life on and in an object. A substance is sterile, from a microbiological point of view, when it is free of all living microorganisms. Sterilization is used principally to prevent spoilage of food and other substances and to prevent the transmission of diseases by destroying microbes that may cause them in humans and animals. Microorganisms can be killed either by physical agents, such as heat and irradiation, or by chemical substances.

Heat sterilization is the most common method of sterilizing bacteriological media, foods, hospital supplies, and many other substances. Either moist heat (hot water or steam) or dry heat can be employed, depending upon the nature of the substance to be sterilized. Moist heat is also used in pasteurization, which is not considered a true sterilization technique because all microorganisms are not killed; only certain pathogenic organisms and other undesirable bacteria are destroyed. *See* Pasteurization.

Many kinds of radiations are lethal, not only to microorganisms but to other forms of life. These radiations include both high-energy particles as well as portions of the electromagnetic spectrum. *See* Radiation biology.

Filtration sterilization is the physical removal of microorganisms from liquids by filtering through materials having relatively small pores. Sterilization by filtration is employed with liquid that may be destroyed by heat, such as blood serum, enzyme solutions, antibiotics, and some bacteriological media and medium constituents. Examples of such filters are the Berkefeld filter (diatomaceous earth), Pasteur-Chamberland filter (porcelain), Seitz filter (asbestos pad), and the sintered glass filter.

Chemicals are used to sterilize solutions, air, or the surfaces of solids. Such chemicals are called bactericidal substances. In lower concentrations they become bacteriostatic rather than bactericidal; that is, they prevent the growth of bacteria but may not kill them. Other terms having similar meanings are employed. A disinfectant is a chemical that kills the vegetative cells of pathogenic microorganisms but not necessarily the endospores of spore-forming pathogens. An antiseptic is a chemical applied to living tissue that prevents or retards the growth of microorganisms, especially pathogenic bacteria, but which does not necessarily kill them.

The desirable features sought in a chemical sterilizer are toxi-city to microorganisms but nontoxicity to humans and animals, stability, solubility, inability to react with extraneous organic materials, penetrative capacity, detergent capacity, noncorrosiveness, and minimal undesirable staining effects. Rarely does one chemical combine all these desirable features. Among chemicals that have been found useful as sterilizing agents are the phenols, alcohols, chlorine compounds, iodine, heavy metals and metal complexes, dyes, and synthetic detergents, including the quaternary ammonium compounds.
[C.F.N.]

Steroid   Any of a group of organic compounds belonging to the general class of biochemicals called lipids, which are easily soluble in organic solvents and slightly soluble in water. Additional members of the lipid class include fatty acids, phospholipids, and triacylglycerides. The unique structural characteristic of steroids is a four-fused ring system. Members of the steroid family are ubiquitous, occurring, for example, in plants, yeast, protozoa, and higher forms of life. Steroids exhibit a variety of biological functions, from participation in cell membrane structure to regulation of physiological events. Naturally occurring steroids and their synthetic analogs are used extensively in medical practice.

Each steroid contains three fused cyclohexane (six-carbon) rings plus a fourth cyclopentane ring (see illustration). Naturally occurring steroids have an

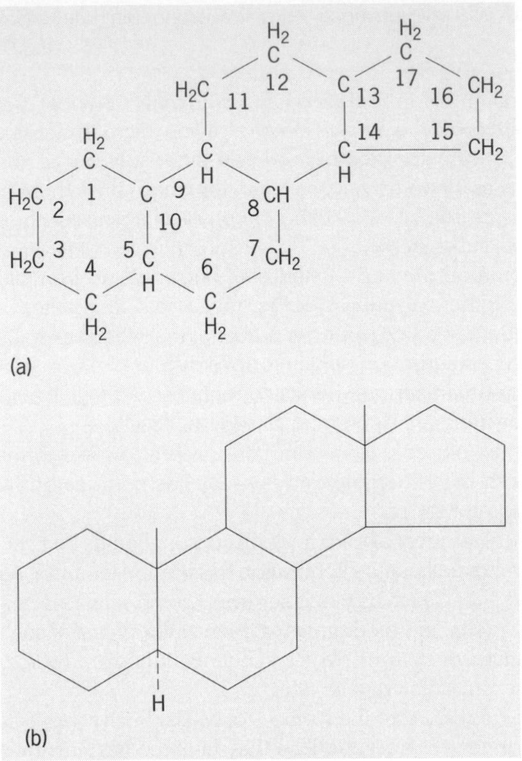

(a)

(b)

Steroid skeleton. (*a*) Structure and numbering. (*b*) Shorthand formulation; the lines attached to the rings represent methyl groups.

oxygen-containing group at carbon-3. Shorthand formulas for steroids indicate the presence of double bonds, as well as the structure and position of oxygen-containing or other organic groups.

The most abundant steroid in mammalian cells is cholesterol. The levels and locations of planar cholesterol molecules, embedded in the phospholipid bilayers that form cell and organelle membranes, are known to influence the structure and function of the membranes. A second major function of cholesterol is to serve as a precursor of steroids acting as physiological regulators (such as the steroid hormones). Enzyme systems present in a hormone-secreting gland convert cholesterol to the hormone specific for that gland. For example, the ovary produces estrogens (such as estradiol and progesterone); the testis produces androgens (such as testosterone); the adrenal cortex produces hormones that regulate metabolism (such as cortisol) and sodium ion transport (such as aldosterone). A third major function of cholesterol is to serve as a precursor of the bile acids. These detergentlike molecules are produced in the liver and stored in the gall bladder until needed to assist in the absorption of dietary fat and fat-soluble vitamins and in the digestion of dietary fat by intestinal enzymes. *See* CELL MEMBRANES; CHOLESTEROL; STEROL.

Some examples of diseases treated with naturally occurring or synthetic steroids are allergic reactions, arthritis, some malignancies, and diseases resulting from hormone deficiencies or abnormal production. In addition, synthetic steroids that mimic an action of progesterone are widely used oral contraceptive agents. Other synthetic steroids are designed to mimic the stimulation of protein synthesis and muscle-building action of naturally occurring androgens. *See* HORMONE; LIPID.   [M.E.D.]

Sterol   Any of a group of naturally occurring or synthetic organic compounds with a steroid ring structure, having a hydroxyl (—OH) group, usually attached to carbon-3. This hydroxyl group is often esterified with a fatty acid (for example, cholesterol ester). The hydrocarbon chain of the fatty-acid substituent varies in length, usually from 16 to 20 carbon atoms, and can be saturated or unsaturated. Sterols commonly contain one or more double bonds in the ring structure and also a variety of substituents attached to the rings. Sterols and their fatty-acid esters are essentially water insoluble. For transport in an aqueous milieu (for example, the bloodstream of mammals), sterols and other lipids are bound to specific proteins, forming lipoprotein particles. These particles are classified based on their composition and density. One lipoprotein class is abnormally high in the blood of humans prone to heart attacks.

Sterols are widely distributed in nature. Modifications of the steroid ring structure are made by specific enzyme systems, producing the sterol characteristic for each species, such as ergosterol in yeast. The major regulatory step in the sterol biosynthetic pathway occurs early in the process. Drugs that lower blood cholesterol levels in humans are designed to inhibit this regulatory enzyme. In addition to their conversion to sterols, several intermediates in the pathway are precursors of other important biological compounds, including chlorophyll in plants, vitamins A, D, E, and K, and regulators of membrane functions and metabolic pathways.

A universal role of sterols is to function as part of membrane structures. In addition, some insects require sterols in their diets. Cholesterol also serves as a precursor of steroid hormones (estrogens, androgens, glucocorticoids, and mineralocorticoids) and bile acids. *See* CHOLESTEROL; STEROID.   [M.E.D.]

Streptococcus   A large genus of spherical or ovoid bacteria that are characteristically arranged in pairs or in chains resembling strings of beads. Many of the streptococci that constitute part of the normal flora of the mouth, throat, intestine, and skin are harmless commensal forms; other streptococci are highly pathogenic. The cells are gram-positive and can grow either anaerobically or aerobically, although they cannot utilize oxygen for metabolic reactions. Glucose and other carbohydrates serve as sources of carbon and energy for growth. All members of the genus lack the enzyme catalase. Streptococci can be isolated from humans and other animals.

Streptococcus pyogenes is well known for its participation in many serious infections. It is a common cause of throat infection, which may be followed by more serious complications such as rheumatic fever, glomerulonephritis, and scarlet fever. Other beta-hemolytic streptococci participate in similar types of infection, but they are usually not associated with rheumatic fever and glomerulonephritis. Group B streptococci, which are usually beta-hemolytic, cause serious infections in newborns (such as meningitis) as well as in adults. Among the alpha-hemolytic and nonhemolytic streptococci, *S. pneumoniae* is an important cause of pneumonia and other respiratory infections. Vaccines that protect against infection by the most prevalent capsular serotypes are available. The viridans streptococci comprise a number of species commonly isolated from the mouth and throat. Although normally of low virulence, these streptococci are capable of causing serious infections (endocarditis, abcesses). *See* PNEUMONIA.   [K.Ru.]

Stress (psychology)   Generally, environmental events of a challenging sort as well as the body's response to such events. Of particular interest has been the relationship between stress and the body's adaptation to it on the one hand and the body's susceptibility to disease on the other. Both outcomes involve behavioral and brain changes as well as psychosomatic events, that is, changes in body function arising from the ability of the brain to control such function through neural output as well as hormones. One problem is that both environmental events and bodily responses have been referred to interchangeably as stress. It is preferable to refer to the former as the stressor and the latter as the stress response. The stress response consists of a cascade of neural and hormonal events that have short- and long-lasting consequences for brain and body alike. A more serious issue is how an event is determined to be a stressor. One view is to define a stressor as an environmental event causing a negative outcome, such as a disease. Another approach is to view stressors as virtually any challenge to homeostasis and to regard disease processes as a failure of the normal operation of adapative mechanisms, which are part of the stress response. With either view, it is necessary to include psychological stressors, such as fear, that contain implied threats to homeostasis and that evoke psychosomatic reactions. These are reactions that involve changes in neural and hormonal output caused by psychological stress. Psychosomatic reactions may lead to adaptive responses, or they may exacerbate disease processes. Whether the emphasis is on adaptation or disease, it is essential to understand the processes in the brain that are activated by stressors and that influence functions in the body. *See* HOMEOSTASIS; PSYCHOSOMATIC DISORDERS.

Among the many neurotransmitter systems activated by stress is noradrenaline, produced by neurons with cell bodies in the brainstem that have vast projections up to the forebrain and down the spinal cord. Stressful experiences activate the noradrenergic system and promote release of noradrenaline; severe stress leads to depletion of noradrenaline in brain areas such as the hypothalamus. This release and depletion of noradrenaline stores results in changes at two levels of neuronal function: phosphorylation is triggered by the second-messenger cyclic AMP and occurs in the presynaptic and postsynaptic sites where noradrenaline is released and where it also acts; synthesis of new protein is induced via actions on the genome. Both processes enhance the ability of the brain to form noradrenaline when the organism is once again confronted with a stressful situation. Other neurotransmitter systems may also show similar adaptive changes in response to stressors. *See* NORADRENERGIC SYSTEM.

Stress also activates the neurally mediated discharge of adrenaline from the adrenal medulla and of hypothalamic hormones that initiate the neuroendocrine cascade, culminating in glucocorticoid release from the adrenal cortex. Thus, the activity of neurons triggered by stressful experiences, physical trauma, fear, or anger leads to hormone secretion that has effects throughout the body. Virtually every organ of the body is affected by stress hormones. The hypothalamic hormone (corticotrophin-releasing hormone) that triggers the neuroendocrine cascade directly stimulates the pituitary to secrete ACTH. In response to certain stressors, the hypothalamus also secretes vasopressin and oxytocin, which act synergistically with corticotrophin-releasing hormone on the pituitary to potentiate the secretion of ACTH. Various stressors differ in their ability to promote output of vasopressin and oxytocin, but all stressors stimulate release of corticotrophin-releasing hormone. Other hormones involved in the stress response include prolactin and thyroid hormone; the metabolic hormones insulin, epinephrine, and glucagon; and the endogenous opiates endorphin and enkephalin. *See* ENDORPHINS.

Of all the hormones in the endocrine cascade initiated by stress, the glucocorticoids are the most important because of their widespread effects throughout the body and in the brain. The brain contains target cells for adrenal glucocorticoids secreted in stress, and receptors in these cells are proteins that interact with the genome to affect expression of genetic information. Thus, the impact of stress-induced activation of the endocrine cascade that culminates in glucocorticoid release is the feedback of glucocorticoids on target brain cells. The effect is to alter the structure and function of the brain cells over a period of time ranging from hours to days.

In the case of noradrenaline, glucocorticoids have several types of feedback effects that modify how the noradrenergic system responds to stress. Glucocorticoids inhibit noradrenaline release, and they reduce the second-messenger response of brain structures such as the cerebral cortex to noradrenaline. Glucocorticoid feedback also affects the serotonin system, facilitating serotonin formation during stress but at the same time altering the levels of several types of serotonin receptors in different brain regions, which has the net effect of shifting the balance within the serotonergic system. Taken together, evidence points to a role of glucocorticoid secretion in leading to restoration of homeostatic balance by counteracting the acute neural events such as increased activity of noradrenaline and serotonin, which are turned on by stressful experiences. Other neurotransmitter systems may also respond to glucocorticoid action. Moreover, the other hormones activated by stress have effects on the brain and body that must be considered. *See* SEROTONIN.

In general, stress hormones are protective and adaptive in the immediate aftermath of stress, and the organism is more vulnerable to many conditions without them. However, the same hormones can promote damage and accelerate pathophysiological changes, such as bone mineral loss, obesity, and cognitive impairment, when they are overproduced or not turned off. This wear-and-tear on the body has been called allostatic load. It is based upon the notion that allostasis is the active process of maintaining stability, or homeostasis, through change, and allostatic load is the almost inevitable cost to the body of doing so.

Stress hormone actions have important effects outside the brain on such systems as the immune response. Glucocorticoids and catecholamines from sympathetic nerves and the adrenal medulla participate in the mobilization and enhancement of immune function in the aftermath of acute stress. These effects improve the body's defense against pathogens but can exacerbate autoimmune reactions. When they are secreted chronically, the stress-related hormones are generally immunosuppressive; such effects can be beneficial in the case of an autoimmune disease but may compromise defense against a virus or bacterial infections. At the same time, glucocorticoids are important agents for containing the acute-phase response to an infection or autoimmune disturbance. In the absence of such containment, the organism may die because of the excessive inflammatory response. *See* IMMUNOLOGY.

Besides affecting the immune response, stressors are believed to exacerbate endogenous depressive illness in susceptible individuals. Major depressive illness frequently results in elevated levels of cortisol in the blood. It is not clear whether the elevated cortisol is a cause or strictly a result of the brain changes involved in depressive illness. *See* AFFECTIVE DISORDERS.   [B.McE.]

Sucrose   An oligosaccharide, α-D-glucopyranosyl β-D-fructofuranoside, also known as saccharose, cane sugar, or beet sugar. The structure is shown below. Su-

crose is very soluble in water and crystallizes from the medium in the anhydrous form. The sugar occurs universally throughout the plant kingdom in fruits, seeds, flowers, and roots of plants. Honey consists principally of sucrose and its hydrolysis products. Sugarcane and sugarbeets are the chief sources for the preparation of sucrose on a large scale. Another source of commercial interest is the sap of maple trees. *See* OLIGOSACCHARIDE.

[W.Z.H.]

Swamp, marsh, and bog   Wet flatlands, where mesophytic vegetation is a really more important than open water, which are commonly developed in filled lakes, glacial pits and potholes, or poorly drained coastal plains or floodplains. Swamp is a term usually applied to a wetland where trees and shrubs are an important part of the vegetative association, and bog implies lack of solid foundation. Some bogs consist of a thick zone of vegetation floating on water.

Unique plant associations characterize wetlands in various climates and exhibit marked zonation characteristics around the edge in response to different thicknesses of the saturated zone above the firm base of soil material. Coastal marshes covered with vegetation adapted to saline water are common on all continents. Presumably many of these had their origin in recent inundation due to post-Pleistocene rise in sea level. *See* MANGROVE.   [L.B.L.]

Swim bladder   A gas-filled sac found in the body cavities of most bony fishes (Osteichthyes). The swim bladder has various functions in different fishes, acting as a float which gives the fish buoyancy, as a lung, as a hearing aid, and as a soundproducing organ. In many fishes it serves two or three of these functions, and in the African and Asiatic knife fishes (Notopteridae) it may serve all four. The swim bladder contains the same gases that make up air, but often in different proportions.   [R.McN.A.]

Sympathetic nervous system   The portion of the autonomic nervous system concerned with nonvolitional preparation of the organism for emergency situations. *See* AUTONOMIC NERVOUS SYSTEM.

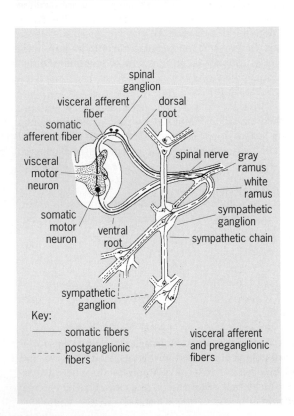

The visceral reflex arc and the sympathetic chain. (*After B. A. Houssay et al., Human Physiology, 2d ed., McGraw-Hill, 1955*)

The sympathetic nervous system is best understood in mammals. It consists of two neuron chains from the thoracic and lumbar regions of the spinal cord to viscera and blood vessels. The first or preganglionic neuron has its cell body in the spinal cord and sends its axon to synapse with a postganglionic sympathetic neuron, which lies either in a chain of sympathetic ganglia paralleling the spinal cord or in a sympathetic ganglion near the base of the large blood vessels vascularizing the alimentary viscera. The postganglionic axons are longer than the preganglionic axons and extend to glands or smooth muscles of viscera and blood vessels. Sensory visceral nerve fibers innervate blood vessels and viscera and carry sensory information to the spinal cord, thus providing a visceral reflex (see illustration). *See* NERVOUS SYSTEM (VERTEBRATE); PARASYMPATHETIC NERVOUS SYSTEM.
[D.B.W.]

Synaptic transmission   The physiological mechanisms by which one nerve cell (neuron) influences the activity of an anatomically adjacent neuron with which it is functionally coupled. Brain function depends on interactions of nerve cells with each other and with the gland cells and muscle cells they innervate. The interactions take place at specific sites of contact between cells known as synapses. The synapse is the smallest and most fundamental information-processing unit in the nervous system. By means of different patterns of synaptic connections between neurons, synaptic circuits are constructed during development to carry out the different functional operations of the nervous system.

The simplest type of synapse is the electrical synapse (see illustration), which consists of an area of unusually close contact between two cells packed with channels that span the two membranes and the cleft between them. Electrical synapses are also known as gap junctions. Electrical and metabolic communication between two cells is established by the components of the gap junctions. A variety of influences, including calcium ions, pH, membrane potential, neurotransmitters, and phosphorylating enzymes, may act on the channels to regulate their conductance in one direction (rectification) or both directions.

Electrical synapses are present throughout the animal kingdom. In vertebrates, they are numerous in the central nervous systems of fish as well as in certain nuclei of the mammalian brain, in regions where rapid transmission and synchronization of activity is important. Electrical synapses also interconnect glial cells in the brain. *See* BIOPOTENTIALS AND IONIC CURRENTS; CELL PERMEABILITY.

The most prevalent type of junction between nerve cells is the chemical synapse (see illustration). At chemical synapses neurotransmitters are released from the presynaptic cell, diffuse across the synaptic clefts, and bind to receptors on the postsynaptic cell. Chemical synapses are found only between nerve cells or between nerve cells and the gland cells and muscle cells that they innervate. The neuromuscular junction, that is, the junction between the axon terminals of a motoneuron and a muscle fiber, is a prototypical chemical synapse. Three basic elements constitute this synapse: a presynaptic process (in this case, the motoneuron axon terminal) containing synaptic vesicles; an end plate (a specialized site of contact between the cells); and a postsynaptic process (in this case, the muscle cell). The postsynaptic membrane contains receptors for the transmitter substance released from the presynaptic terminal.

The chemical substance that serves as the transmitter at the vertebrate neuromuscular junction is acetylcholine (ACh). Within the nerve terminal, acetylcholine is concentrated within small spherical vesicles. At rest, these vesicles undergo exocytosis at low rates, releasing their acetylcholine in quantal packets to diffuse across the cleft and bind to and activate the postsynaptic receptors. Each quantum gives rise to a small depolarization of the postsynaptic membrane. These miniature end-plate potentials are rapid, lasting only

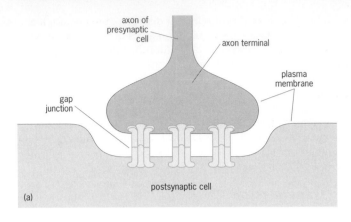

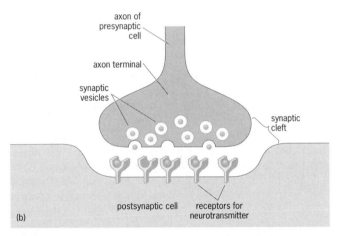

Types of synapses. (*a*) **An electrical synapse, showing the plasma membranes of the presynaptic and postsynaptic cells linked by gap junctions.** (*b*) **A chemical synapse, showing neurotransmitters released by the presynaptic cell diffusing across the synaptic cleft and binding to receptors on the postsynaptic membrane.**

some 10 milliseconds, and small in amplitude, only some 500 microvolts, below the threshold for effecting any response in the muscle. They represent the resting secretory activity of the nerve terminal.

When an organism wants to move its muscles, electrical impulses known as action potentials are generated in the motoneurons. These are conducted along the axon and invade the terminal, causing a large depolarization of the presynaptic membrane. This opens special voltage-gated channels for calcium ions, which enter the terminal and bind to special proteins, causing exocytosis of vesicles simultaneously. Calcium ions are the crucial link between the electrical signals in the presynaptic neuron and the chemical signals sent to the postsynaptic neuron. The combined action of this acetylcholine on postsynaptic receptors sets up a large postsynaptic depolarization, which exceeds the threshold for generating an impulse in the surrounding membrane, and causes the muscle to contract. The action of acetylcholine at its receptor is terminated by an enzyme, acetylcholinesterase, which is present in the synaptic cleft and hydrolyzes the acetylcholine to acetate and choline.

In order for neurotransmission to continue, synaptic vesicles have to be regenerated. Vesicles are rapidly and efficiently reformed in the nerve terminal by endocytosis. Specific neurotransmitter transporters within the membrane then fill the synaptic vesicle with appropriate neurotransmitter. The regenerated vesicle either returns to the plasma membrane where it rejoins the releasable pool of vesicles, or remains in the nerve terminal as part of a reserve pool. *See* ACETYLCHOLINE; MUSCLE.

In the central nervous system the presynaptic process containing synaptic vesicles is most often an axon terminal and the postsynaptic process a dendrite, making an axodendritic synapse, but other relationships are also seen. The effect of transmitter on a postsynaptic cell is either excitatory or inhibitory, meaning that it either depolarizes or hyperpolarizes the membrane. Whether a transmitter has an excitatory or inhibitory effect on a cell is determined by the type of ion able to pass through the cell's receptor channels.

There are two principal types of central synapses.

Type 1 central synapses commonly release an amino acid transmitter, such as glutamate, whose action produces an excitatory postsynaptic potential. At low levels of activity the glutamate binds to the glutamate receptor and activates a relatively small conductance increase for sodium and potassium ions. Glutamate is the transmitter at many excitatory synapses throughout the central nervous system. The type 2 central synapse is usually associated with inhibitory synaptic actions. The most common inhibitory transmitter is gamma-amino butyric acid (GABA). Most inhibitory interneurons in different regions of the brain make these kinds of synapses on relay neurons in those regions. The GABA receptor is a complex channel-forming protein with several types of binding sites and several conductance states.

Other classes of synaptic transmitter substances include the biogenic amines, such as the catecholamines, norepinephrine and dopamine, and the indoleamine 5-hydroxytryptamine (also known as serotonin). *See* DOPAMINE; NORADRENERGIC SYSTEM; SEROTONIN.

A final type of transmitter substance consists of a vast array of neuropeptides. They are a diverse group and include substances that stimulate the release of hormones; those that act at synapses in pain pathways in the brain (the endogenous morphinelike substances, enkephalins and endorphins); and many of still undetermined functions. Peptides may act also indirectly, modifying the state of a receptor in its response to other transmitter substances, and they may do this in an activity-dependent manner. In view of the complexity and slow time course of many of their effects, these peptides are often referred to as neuromodulators. *See* ENDORPHINS; HORMONE.

At central synapses, rapid responses to transmitters (typically within milliseconds) are most commonly the result of direct synaptic transmission, in which the receptor itself is the ion channel. Such receptors are referred to as ionotropic. There are, however, other receptor molecules for each of the neurotransmitters, and many of these are not themselves ion channels. They are known as metabotropic receptors, and they affect neurotransmission indirectly via a set of intermediary proteins called G-proteins. Activated G-proteins have a variety of effects on synaptic processes. Some are mediated by direct interactions with ion channels. However, many other effects are mediated by activation of cellular second messenger systems involving messengers such as calcium and cyclic adenosine monophosphate (cyclic AMP). The time courses for effects caused by activation of G-protein-coupled receptors is much longer than that of ionotropic channels (milliseconds), reflecting the lifetime of the activated G-protein subunits (seconds) and second messengers (seconds to minutes). Such longer lasting signals greatly increase the complexity of chemical neurotransmission and synaptic modulation. *See* SECOND MESSENGERS.

The synapse is a dynamic structure whose function is very dependent on its activity state. In this way the synapse is constantly adjusted for its information load. At glutamatergic synapses, high levels of input activity bring about a different transmission state. The buildup of postsynaptic depolarization relieves the normal block of a specialized glutamate receptor channel, permitting influx of calcium ions into the postsynaptic process. Since the conductance of the channel is dependent on the depolarization state of the membrane, it is said to have a voltage-gated property, in addition to being ligand-gated by its transmitter. The calcium ion acts as a second messenger to bring about a long-lasting increase in synaptic efficacy, a process known as long-term potentiation. The conjunction of increased pre- and postsynaptic activity to give an increase in synaptic efficacy is called Hebbian, and is believed to be the type of plasticity mechanism involved in learning and memory. *See* LEARNING MECHANISMS; MEMORY.

The synapse is one of the primary targets of drug actions. The first example to be identified was the arrow poison curare, which blocks neuromuscular transmission by binding to acetylcholine receptor sites. Many toxic agents have their actions on specific types of receptors; organic fluorophosphates, for example, are widely used pesticides that bind to and inactivate acetylcholinesterase. Most psychoactive drugs exert their effects at the synaptic level. *See* NERVOUS SYSTEM (VERTEBRATE); NEUROBIOLOGY.   [G.M.Sh.; P.I.H.]

Syphilis   A sexually transmitted infection of humans caused by *Treponema pallidum* ssp. *pallidum*, a corkscrew-shaped motile bacterium (spirochete). Due to its narrow width, *T. pallidum* cannot be seen by light microscopy but can be observed with staining procedures (silver stain or immunofluorescence) and with dark-field, phase-contrast, or electron microscopy. The organism is very sensitive to environmental conditions and to physical and chemical agents. The complete genome sequence of the *T. pallidum* Nichols strain has been determined. The nucleotide sequence of the small, circular treponemal chromosome indicates that *T. pallidum* lacks the genetic information for many of the metabolic activities found in other bacteria. Thus, this spirochete is dependent upon the host for most of its nutritional requirements. *See* BACTERIAL GENETICS; IMMUNOFLUORESCENCE.

Syphilis is usually transmitted through direct sexual contact with active lesions and can also be transmitted by contact with infected blood and tissues. If untreated, syphilis progresses through various stages (primary, secondary, latent, and tertiary). Infection begins as an ulcer (chancre) and may eventually involve the cardiovascular and central nervous systems, bones, and joints. Congenital syphilis results from maternal transmission of *T. pallidum* across the placenta to the fetus. *See* SEXUALLY TRANSMITTED DISEASES.

Treponema pallidum is an obligate parasite of humans and does not have a reservoir in animals or the environment. Syphilis has a worldwide distribution. Its incidence varies widely according to geographical location, socioeconomic status, and age group. Although syphilis is controlled in most developed countries, it remains a public health problem in many developing countries. Studies have shown that syphilis is a risk factor for infection with the human immunodeficiency virus (HIV) since syphilitic lesions may act as portals of entry for the virus. There is little natural immunity to syphilis infection or reinfection.

Parenteral penicillin G is the preferred antibiotic for treatment of all stages of syphilis. Alternative antibiotics for syphilis treatment include erythromycin and tetracycline. There is currently no vaccine to prevent syphilis. However, it is anticipated that information obtained from the *T. pallidum* genome sequence will lead to further improvements in diagnostic tests for syphilis and to the eventual development of a vaccine that would prevent infection. *See* ANTIBIOTIC.   [L.V.S.]

Systems ecology   The analysis of how ecosystem function is determined by the components of an ecosystem and how those components cycle, retain, or exchange energy and nutrients. Systems ecology typically involves the application of computer models that track the flow of energy and materials and predict the responses of systems to perturbations that range from fires to climate change to species extinctions. Systems ecology is closely related to mathematical ecology, with the major difference stemming from systems ecology's focus on energy and nutrient flow and its borrowing of ideas from engineering. Systems ecology is one of the few theoretical tools that can simultaneously examine a system from the level of individuals all the way up to the level of ecosystem dynamics. It is an especially valuable approach for investigating systems so large and complicated that experiments are impossible, and even observations of the entire system are impractical. In these overwhelming settings, the only approach is to break down the research into measurements of components and then assemble a system model that pieces together all components. An important contribution of ecosystem science is the recognition that there are critical ecosystem services such as cleansing of water, recycling of waste materials, production of food and fiber, and mitigation of pestilence and plagues. See ECOLOGICAL COMMUNITIES; ECOLOGICAL ENERGETICS; ECOLOGY; ECOSYSTEM; GLOBAL CLIMATE CHANGE; THEORETICAL ECOLOGY.   [P.M.Ka.]

T

Taiga A zone of forest vegetation encircling the Northern Hemisphere between the arctic-subarctic tundras in the north and the steppes, hardwood forests, and prairies in the south. The chief characteristic of the taiga is the prevalence of forests dominated by conifers. The dominant trees are particular species of spruce, pine, fir, and larch. Other conifers, such as hemlock, white cedar, and juniper, occur locally, and the broad-leaved deciduous trees, birch and poplar, are common associates in the southern taiga regions. Taiga is a Siberian word, equivalent to "boreal forest." *See* TUNDRA.

The northern and southern boundaries of the taiga are determined by climatic factors, of which temperature is most important. However, aridity controls the forest-steppe boundary in central Canada and western Siberia. In the taiga the average temperature in the warmest month, July, is greater than 50°F (10°C), distinguishing it from the forest-tundra and tundra to the north; however, less than four of the summer months have averages above 50°F (10°C), in contrast to the summers of the deciduous forest further south, which are longer and warmer. Taiga winters are long, snowy, and cold—the coldest month has an average temperature below 32°F (0°C). Permafrost occurs in the northern taiga. It is important to note that climate is as significant as vegetation in defining taiga. Thus, many of the world's conifer forests, such as those of the American Pacific Northwest, are excluded from the taiga by their high precipitation and mild winters.

[J.C.Ri.]

Taste Taste, or gustation, is one of the senses used to detect the chemical makeup of ingested food—that is, to establish its palatability and nutritional composition. Flavor is a complex amalgam of taste, olfaction (smell), and other sensations, including those generated by mechanoreceptor and thermoreceptor sensory cells in the oral cavity. Taste sensory cells respond principally to the water-soluble chemical stimuli present in food, whereas olfactory sensory cells respond to volatile (airborne) compounds. *See* CHEMICAL SENSES; SENSATION.

The sensory organs of gustation are termed taste buds. In humans and most other mammals, taste buds are located on the tongue in the fungiform, foliate, and circumvallate papillae and in adjacent structures of the throat. There are approximately 5000 taste buds in humans, although this number varies tremendously. Taste buds are goblet-shaped clusters of 50 to 100 long slender cells. Microvilli protrude from the apical (upper) end of sensory cells into shallow taste pores. Taste pores open onto the tongue surface and provide access to the sensory cells. Individual sensory nerve fibers branch profusely within taste buds and make contacts (synapses) with taste bud sensory cells. Taste buds also contain supporting and developing taste cells.

The basic taste qualities experienced by humans include sweet, salty, sour, and bitter. (In some species, pure water also strongly stimulates taste bud cells). A fifth taste, umami, is now recognized by many as distinct from the other qualities. Umami is a

Japanese term roughly translated as "good taste" and is approximated by the English term "savory." It refers to the taste of certain amino acids such as glutamate (as in monosodium glutamate) and certain monophosphate nucleotides. These compounds occur naturally in protein-rich foods, including meat, fish, cheese, and certain vegetables.

The middorsum (middle top portion) of the tongue surface is insensitive to all tastes. Only small differences, if any, exist for the taste qualities between different parts of the tongue. No simple direct relationship exists between chemical stimuli and a particular taste quality except, perhaps, for sourness (acidity). Sourness is due to H^+ ions. The taste qualities of inorganic salts are complex, and sweet and bitter tastes are elicited by a wide variety of diverse chemicals.   [C.P.; N.Cha.; S.Rop.]

Taxis A mechanism of orientation by means of which an animal moves in a direction related to a source of stimulation. There exists a widely accepted terminology in which the nature of the stimulus is indicated by a prefix such as phototaxis (light), chemotaxis (chemical compounds), geotaxis (gravity), thigmotaxis (contact), rheotaxis (water current), and anemotaxis (air current). The directions toward or away from the stimulus are expressed as positive or negative, respectively. Finally, the sensory and locomotory mechanisms by means of which the orientation is achieved are denoted by a second type of prefix forming a compound noun with taxis. Positive phototropotaxis thus describes a mechanism by means of which an animal carries out a directed movement toward a source of light along a path which permits the animal's paired eyes to receive equal intensities of light throughout the movement.   [O.E.L.]

Taxonomic categories Any one of a number of formal ranks used for organisms in a traditional Linnaean classification. Biological classifications are orderly arrangements of organisms in which the order specifies some relationship. Taxonomic classifications are usually hierarchical and comprise nested groups of organisms. The actual groups are termed taxa. In the hierarchy, a higher taxon may include one or more lower taxa, and as a result the relationships among taxa are expressed as a divergent hierarchy that is formally represented by tree diagrams. In Linnaean classifications, taxonomic categories are devices that provide structure to the hierarchy of taxa without the use of tree diagrams. By agreement, there is a hierarchy of categorical ranks for each major group of organisms, beginning with the categories of highest rank and ending with categories of lowest rank, and while it is not necessary to use all the available categories, they must be used in the correct order (see table).

Conceptually, the hierarchy of categories is different than the hierarchy of taxa. For example, the taxon Cnidaria, which is ranked as a phylum, includes the classes Anthozoa (anemones), Scyphozoa (jellyfishes), and Hydrozoa (hydras). Cnidaria is

Categories commonly used in botanical and zoological classifications, from highest to lowest rank

Botanical categories	Zoological categories
Divisio	Phylum
Classis	Class
Ordo	Order
Familia	Family
Genus	Genus
Species	Species

a particular and concrete group that is composed of parts. Anthozoa is part of, and included in, Cnidaria. However, categorical ranks are quite different. The category "class" is not part of, nor included in, the category "phylum." Rather, the category "class" is a shelf in the hierarchy, a roadmark of relative position. There are many animal taxa ranked as classes, but there is only one "class" in the Linnaean hierarchy. This is an important strength of the system because it provides a way to navigate through a classification while keeping track of relative hierarchical levels with only a few ranks for a great number of organisms.

When Linnaeus invented his categories, there were only class, order, family, genus, and species. These were sufficient to serve the needs of biological diversity in the late eighteenth century, but were quite insufficient to classify the increasing number of species discovered since 1758. As a result, additional categorical levels have been created. These categories may use prefixes, such as super- and sub-, as well as new basic levels such as tribe. An example of a modern expanded botanical hierarchy of ranks between family and species is:

Familia
Subfamilia
Tribus
Subtribus
Genus
Subgenus
Sectio
Subsectio
Series
Subseries
Species

Linnaean categories are the traditional devices used to navigate the hierarchy of taxa. But categories are only conventions, and alternative logical systems, such as those used by phylogenetic systematists (cladists), are frequently used. See ANIMAL SYSTEMATICS; CLASSIFICATION, BIOLOGICAL; PHYLOGENY; PLANT TAXONOMY; ZOOLOGICAL NOMENCLATURE.

[E.O.W.]

Taxonomy   The arrangement or classification of objects according to certain criteria. Systematics is a broader term applied to all comparative biology, including taxonomy. For classifying plants and animals, where the term taxonomy is most often applied, the criteria are characters of structure and function.

A given character usually has two or more states. These variations are used as the basis of biological classification, grouping together like species (in which the majority of the character states are alike) and separating unlike species (in which many of the character states are different). Since the acceptance by biologists of the concept of organic evolution, more and more effort has been made to produce systems of classification that conform to phylogenetic (that is, evolutionary) relationships. Taxonomy is thus concerned with classification, but ultimately classification itself depends upon phylogeny—the amount, direction, and sequence of genetic changes. Scientists try to classify lines, or clusters of lines, of descent. This has not always been the case, and in the past various other criteria have been used, such as whether organisms were edible (ancient times) and whether flowers had five stamens or four or some other number (Linnaean times). Modern taxonomists generally agree that the patterns or clusters of diversity they observe in nature, such as the groups of primates, the rodents, and the bats, are the objective results of purely biological processes acting at different times and places in the past. At the least, animal and plant taxonomy provides a method of communication, a system of naming; at the most, taxonomy provides a framework for the embodiment of all comparative biological knowledge. *See* ANIMAL SYSTEMATICS; CLASSIFICATION, BIOLOGICAL; NUMERICAL TAXONOMY; ORGANIC EVOLUTION; PHYLOGENY; PLANT TAXONOMY.   [W.H.Wa.]

Temperature adaptation   The ability of animals to survive and function at widely different temperatures as a result of specific physiological adaptations. Temperature is an all-pervasive attribute of the environment that limits the activity, distribution, and survival of animals.

Changes in temperature influence biological systems, both by determining the rate of chemical reactions and by specifying equilibria. Because temperature exerts a greater effect upon the percentage of molecules that possess sufficient energy to react (that is, to exceed the activation energy) than upon the average kinetic energy of the system, modest reductions in temperature (for example, from 77 to 59°F or from 25 to 15°C, corresponding to only a 3% reduction in average kinetic energy) produce a marked depression (two- to threefold) in reaction rate. In addition, temperature specifies the equilibria between the formation and disruption of the noncovalent (electrostatic, hydrophobic, and hydrogen-bonding) interactions that stabilize both the higher levels of protein structure and macromolecular aggregations such as biological membranes. Maintenance of an appropriate structural flexibility is a requirement for both enzyme catalysis and membrane function, yet cold temperatures constrain while warm temperatures relax the conformational flexibility of both proteins and membrane lipids, thereby perturbing biological function. *See* CELL MEMBRANES; ENZYME.

Animals are classified into two broad groups depending on the factors that determine body temperature. For ectotherms, body temperature is determined by sources of heat external to the body; levels of resting metabolism (and heat production) are low, and mechanisms for retaining heat are limited. Such animals are frequently termed poikilothermic or cold-blooded, because the body temperature often conforms to the temperature of the environment. In contrast, endotherms produce more metabolic heat and possess specialized mechanisms for heat retention. Therefore, body temperature is elevated above ambient temperature; some endotherms (termed homeotherms or warm-blooded animals) maintain a relatively constant body temperature. There is no natural taxonomic division between ecto- and endotherms. Most invertebrates, fish, amphibians, and reptiles are ectotherms, while true homeothermy is restricted to birds and mammals. However, flying insects commonly elevate the temperature of their thoracic musculature prior to and during flight (to 96°F or 36°C), and several species of tuna retain metabolic heat in their locomotory musculature via a vascular countercurrent heat exchanger. *See* HIBERNATION; THERMOREGULATION.   [J.R.Ha.]

Tendon   A cord connecting a muscle to another structure, often a bone. A tendon is a passive material, lengthening when the tension increases and shortening when it decreases. This characteristic contrasts with the active behavior of muscle. Away from its muscle, a tendon is a compact cord. At the muscle, it spreads into thin sheets called aponeuroses, which lie over and sometimes within the muscle belly. The large surface area of the aponeuroses allows the attachment of muscle fibers with a total cross-sectional area that is typically 50 times that of the tendon. *See* MUSCLE.

Tendons are living tissues that contain cells. In adult tendons, the cells occupy only a very small proportion of the volume and have a negligible effect on the mechanical properties. Like other connective tissues, tendon depends on the protein collagen for its strength and rigidity. The arrangement of the long, thin collagenous fibers is essentially longitudinal, but incorporates a characteristic waviness known as crimp. The fibers lie within a matrix of aqueous gel. Thus, tendon is a fiber-reinforced composite (like fiberglass), but its collagen is much less stiff than the glass and its matrix is very much less stiff than the resin. *See* COLLAGEN.

The function of tendons is to transmit force. They allow the force from the muscle to be applied in a restricted region. For example, the main muscles of the fingers are in the forearm, with tendons to the fingertips. If the hand had to accommodate these muscles, it would be too plump to be functional. Tendon extension can also be significant in the movement of a joint. For example, the tendon which flexes a human thumb joint is about 7 in. (170 mm) long. The maximum force from its muscle stretches this tendon about 0.1 in. (2.9 mm), which corresponds to rotation of the joint through an angle of about 21°. *See* JOINT (ANATOMY).

Some tendons save energy by acting as springs. In humans, the Achilles tendon reduces the energy needed for running by about 35%. This tendon is stretched during the first half of each step, storing energy which is then returned during takeoff. This elastic energy transfer involves little energy loss, whereas the equivalent work done by muscles would require metabolic energy in both stages. *See* CONNECTIVE TISSUE; MUSCULAR SYSTEM.   [R.F.K.]

Terrestrial ecosystem   A community of organisms and their environment that occurs on the land masses of continents and islands. Terrestrial ecosystems are distinguished from aquatic ecosystems by the lower availability of water and the consequent importance of water as a limiting factor. Terrestrial ecosystems are characterized by greater temperature fluctuations on both a diurnal and seasonal basis than occur in aquatic ecosystems in similar climates. The availability of light is greater in terrestrial ecosystems than in aquatic ecosystems because the atmosphere is more transparent than water. Gases are more available in terrestrial ecosystems than in aquatic ecosystems. Those gases include carbon dioxide that serves as a substrate for photosynthesis, oxygen that serves as a substrate in aerobic respiration, and nitrogen that serves as a substrate for nitrogen fixation. Terrestrial environments are segmented into a subterranean portion from which most water and ions are obtained, and an atmospheric portion from which gases are obtained and where the physical energy of light is transformed into the organic energy of carbon-carbon bonds through the process of photosynthesis.

Terrestrial ecosystems occupy 55,660,000 mi^2 (144,150,000 km^2), or 28.2%, of Earth's surface. Although they are comparatively recent in the history of life (the first terrestrial organisms appeared in the Silurian Period, about 425 million years ago) and occupy a much smaller portion of Earth's surface than marine ecosystems, terrestrial ecosystems have been a major site of adaptive radiation of both plants and animals. Major plant taxa in terrestrial ecosystems are members of the division Magnoliophyta (flowering plants), of which there are about 275,000 species, and the division Pinophyta (conifers), of which there are about 500 species. Members of the division Bryophyta (mosses and liverworts), of which there are about 24,000 species, are also important in some terrestrial ecosystems. Major animal taxa in terrestrial ecosystems include the classes Insecta (insects) with about 900,000 species, Aves (birds) with 8500 species, and Mammalia (mammals) with approximately 4100 species. *See* ANIMAL SYSTEMATICS; PLANT TAXONOMY; TAXONOMY.

Organisms in terrestrial ecosystems have adaptations that allow them to obtain water when the entire body is no longer bathed in that fluid, means of transporting the water from limited sites of acquisition to the rest of the body, and means of preventing the evaporation of water from body surfaces. They also have traits that provide body support in the atmosphere, a much less buoyant medium than water, and other traits that render them capable of withstanding the extremes of temperature, wind, and humidity that characterize terrestrial ecosystems. Finally, the organisms in terrestrial ecosystems have evolved many methods of transporting gametes in environments where fluid flow is much less effective as a transport medium.

The organisms in terrestrial ecosystems are integrated into a functional unit by specific, dynamic relationships due to the coupled processes of energy and chemical flow. Those relationships can be summarized by schematic diagrams of trophic webs, which place organisms according to their feeding relationships. The base of the food web is occupied by green plants, which are the only organisms capable of utilizing the energy of the Sun and inorganic nutrients obtained from the soil to produce organic molecules. Terrestrial food webs can be broken into two segments based on the status of the plant material that enters them. Grazing food webs are associated with the consumption of living plant material by herbivores. Detritus food webs are associated with the consumption of dead plant material by detritivores. The relative importance of those two types of food webs varies considerably in different types of terrestrial ecosystems. Grazing food webs are more important in grasslands, where over half of net primary productivity may be consumed by herbivores. Detritus food webs are more important in forests, where less than 5% of net primary productivity may be consumed by herbivores. *See* FOOD WEB; SOIL ECOLOGY.

There is one type of extensive terrestrial ecosystem due solely to human activities and eight types that are natural ecosystems. Those natural ecosystems reflect the variation of precipitation and temperature over Earth's surface. The smallest land areas are occupied by tundra and temperate grassland ecosystems, and the largest land area is occupied by tropical forest. The most productive ecosystems are temperate and tropical forests, and the least productive are deserts and tundras. Cultivated lands, which together with grasslands and savannas utilized for grazing are referred to as agroecosystems, are of intermediate extent and productivity. Because of both their areal extent and their high average productivity, tropical forests are the most productive of all terrestrial ecosystems, contributing 45% of total estimated net primary productivity on land. *See* DESERT; ECOLOGICAL COMMUNITIES; ECOSYSTEM; FOREST AND FORESTRY; GRASSLAND ECOSYSTEM; SAVANNA; TUNDRA.   [S.J.McN.]

Territoriality   Behavior patterns in which an animal actively defends a space or some other resource. One major advantage of territoriality is that it gives the territory holder exclusive access to the defended resource, which is generally associated with feeding, breeding, or shelter from predators or climatic forces. Feeding and breeding territories can be mobile, such as when an animal defends a newly obtained food source or a temporarily receptive mate. Stationary territories often serve multiple functions and include access to food, a place to rear young, and a refuge site from predators and the elements.

Territoriality can be understood in terms of the benefits and costs accrued to territory holders. Benefits include time saved by foraging in a known area, energy acquired through feeding on territorial resources, reduction in time spent on the lookout for predators, or increase in number of mates attracted and offspring raised. Costs usually involve time and energy expended in patrolling and defending the territorial site, and increased risk of being captured by a predator when engaged in territorial defense.

Because territories usually include resources that are in limited supply, active defense is often necessary. Such defense frequently involves a graded series of behaviors called displays that include threatening gestures such as vocalizations, spreading of wings or gill covers, lifting and presentation of claws, head bobbing, tail and body beating, and finally, direct attack. Direct confrontation can usually be avoided by advertising the location of a territory in a way that allows potential intruders to recognize the boundaries and avoid interactions with the defender. Such advertising may involve odors that are spread with metabolic by-products, such as urine or feces in dogs, cats, or beavers, or produced specifically as territory markers, as in ants. Longer-lasting territorial marks can involve visual signals such as scrapes and rubs, as in deer and bear. See CHEMICAL ECOLOGY; ETHOLOGY; POPULATION ECOLOGY; REPRODUCTIVE BEHAVIOR.   [G.S.H.]

Testis   The organ of sperm production. In addition, the testis (testicle) is an organ of endocrine secretion in which male hormones (androgens) are elaborated. In the higher vertebrates (reptiles, birds, and mammals), the testes are paired and either ovoid or elongated in shape. In mammals, the testes are usually ovoid or round. In many species (for example, humans) they are suspended in a pouch (scrotum) outside the main body cavity; in other species they are found in such a pouch only at the reproductive season; in still others the testicles are permanently located in the abdomen (for example, in whales and bats).

Within a firm and thick capsule of connective tissue, the tunica albuginea, the testis contains a varying number of thin but very long seminiferous tubules which are the sites of sperm formation. Essentially, these tubules are simple loops which open with both their limbs into a network of fine, slitlike canals, the rete testis. From this the sperm drains through a few, narrow ducts, the ductuli efferentes, into the epididymis, where sperm mature and are stored.

The seminiferous tubules comprise most of the testis, and in different species vary greatly in complexity. Each tubule is surrounded by a layer of thin cells which is contractile and enables the tubules to wriggle slowly. The spaces between tubules are filled with connective tissue, blood vessels, an extensive network of very thin-walled lymph vessels, and secretory cells, the interstitial cells or cells of Leydig, which secrete male hormone.

The sperm cells, spermatozoa, develop in the wall of the seminiferous tubules, either periodically, as in most vertebrates, or continually, as in humans. Most of the cells in the tubules are potential spermatozoa (spermatogenic or germ cells). Nursing cells (Sertoli cells) are interspersed at regular intervals between them. The Sertoli cells support and surround the developing spermatogenic cells and provide a specialized environment, which is absolutely necessary for normal sperm development. See SPERM CELL.

Spermatogenesis in the testis is the result of a balance between proliferation and differentiation, and cell degeneration or apoptosis. Apoptosis of the spermatogenic cells is largely hormonally controlled, and specifically directed apoptosis occurs in conditions of testicular damage due to environmental insults such as heat, radiation, or chemical toxicants. Recovery of spermatogenesis is possible provided the stem cells are not depleted by these processes. See SPERMATOGENESIS.   [M.P.H.; E.C.R.R.]

The functions of the testis are dependent on the secretion of gonadotropic hormones, the release of which from the pituitary gland is in turn regulated by the central nervous system. In mammals, male-hormone production resides in the Leydig cells, located in the intertubular tissue of the testes.

The principal androgenic hormone released by the testis into the bloodstream is testosterone. The testis is able to form cholesterol and to convert this via a number of pathways to testosterone. Testosterone may be further metabolized into estrogens in the testis. The production of estrogens in the male varies quite widely among species, from relatively low in humans to very high, for example in stallions and boars. Estrogens are important in the development and proper function of the ducts which drain the testis (the rete testis and ductuli efferentes), even in species with relatively low levels of estrogens. *See* ANDROGEN.

Testosterone synthesis is normally limited by the rate of pituitary gonadotrophin secretion: administration of the luteinizing hormone or of chorionic gonadotrophin results in increased testosterone synthesis and release within minutes. These hormones also stimulate growth and multiplication of Leydig cells. Hypophysectomy leads to cessation of androgen formation. *See* ADENOHYPOPHYSIS HORMONE; PITUITARY GLAND.

At the ambisexual stage of embryonic development, the testis promotes the growth of the paired Wolffian ducts and their differentiation into the epididymis, vasa deferentia, and seminal vesicles; the fetal testis also causes masculinization of the urogenital sinus, fusion of the labioscrotal folds in the midline, and development of the genital tubercle into a phallus. *See* EMBRYOLOGY.

Toward puberty, increased secretion of testosterone stimulates the growth of the penis, scrotum, and male accessory glands responsible for the formation of the seminal plasma, for example, the prostate and seminal vesicles. The hormone brings about the appearance of secondary sex characters, such as the male-type distribution of hair and body fat and lowered pitch of voice in man, the growth of the comb and wattles in birds, the clasping pads of amphibians, or the dorsal spine of certain fishes.

Unlike the ovary, the testis remains functional throughout life, with ongoing spermatogenic development. However, the efficiency of spermatogenesis falls away, and androgen levels begin to fall due to a declining Leydig cell activity. These events can lead to reduced fertility, and androgen insufficiency problems in later life in some men. *See* REPRODUCTIVE SYSTEM.   [M.P.H.; H.R.L.]

Thallobionta   One of the two commonly recognized subkingdoms of plants, encompassing the euglenoids and various classes of algae. In contrast to the more closely knit subkingdom Embryobionta, the Thallobionta (often also called Thallophyta) are diverse in pigmentation, food reserves, cell-wall structure, and flagellar structure. The Thallobionta are united more by the absence of certain specialized tissues or organs than by positive resemblances. They do not have the multicellular sex organs commonly found in most divisions of Embryobionta. Many of the Thallobionta are unicellular, and those which are multicellular seldom have much differentiation of tissues. None of them has tissues comparable to the xylem found in most divisions of the Embryobionta, and only some of the brown algae have tissues comparable to the phloem found in most divisions of the Embryobionta.

A large proportion of the Thallobionta are aquatic, and those which grow on dry land seldom reach appreciable size. The Thallobionta thus consist of all those plants which have not developed the special features that mark the progressive adaptation of the Embryobionta to life on dry land. *See* PLANT KINGDOM.   [A.Cr.]

Theoretical ecology   The use of models to explain patterns, suggest experiments, or make predictions in ecology. Because ecological systems are idiosyncratic, extremely complex, and variable, ecological theory faces special challenges. Unlike physics or genetics, which use fundamental laws of gravity or of inheritance, ecology has no widely accepted first-principle laws. Instead, different theories must be invoked for different questions, and the theoretical approaches are enormously varied. A central problem in ecological theory is determining what type of model to use and what to leave out of a model. The traditional approaches have relied on analytical models based on differential or difference equations; but recently the use of computer simulation has greatly increased. *See* ECOLOGICAL MODELING; ECOLOGY.

The nature of ecological theory varies depending on the level of ecological organization on which the theory focuses. The primary levels of ecological organization are (1) physiological and biomechanical, (2) evolutionary (especially applied to behavior), (3) population, and (4) community.

At the physiological and biomechanical level, the goals of ecological theory are to understand why particular structures are present and how they work. The approaches of fluid dynamics and even civil engineering have been applied to understanding the structures of organisms, ranging from structures that allow marine organisms to feed, to physical constraints on the stems of plants.

At the behavioral evolutionary level, the goals of ecological theory are to explain and predict the different choices that individual organisms make. Underlying much of this theory is an assumption of optimality: the theories assume that evolution produces an optimal behavior, and they attempt to determine the characteristics of the optimal behavior so it can be compared with observed behavior. One area with well-developed theory is foraging behavior (where and how animals choose to feed). Another example is the use of game theory to understand the evolution of behaviors that are apparently not optimal for an individual but may instead be better for a group. *See* BEHAVIORAL ECOLOGY.

The population level has the longest history of ecological theory and perhaps the broadest application. The simplest models of single-species populations ignore differences among individuals and assume that the birth rates and death rates are proportional to the number of individuals in the population. If this is the case, the rate of growth is exponential, a result that goes back at least as far as Malthus's work in the 1700s. As Malthus recognized, this result produces a dilemma: exponential growth cannot continue unabated. Thus, one of the central goals of population ecology theory is to determine the forces and ecological factors that prevent exponential growth and to understand the consequences for the dynamics of ecological populations. *See* POPULATION ECOLOGY.

Modifications and extensions of theoretical approaches like the logistic model (which uses differential equations to explain the stability of populations) have also been used to guide the management of renewable natural resources. Here, the most basic concept is that of the maximum sustainable yield, which is the greatest level of harvest at which a population can continue to persist. *See* ADAPTIVE MANAGEMENT.

The primary goal of ecological theory at the community level is to understand diversity at local and regional scales. Recent work has emphasized that a great deal of diversity in communities may depend on trade-offs. For example, a trade-off between competitive prowess and colonization ability is capable of explaining why so many plants persist in North American prairies. Another major concept in community theory is the role of disturbance. Understanding how disturbances (such as fires, hurricanes, or wind storms) impacts communities is crucial because humans typically alter disturbance. *See* BIODIVERSITY; ECOLOGICAL COMMUNITIES.   [A.Has.]

Theria   One of the four subclasses of the class Mammalia, including all living mammals except the monotremes. The Theria were by far the most successful of the several mammalian stocks that arose from the mammallike reptiles in the Triassic. The subclass is divided into three infraclasses: Pantotheria (no living survivors), Metatheria (marsupials), and Eutheria (placentals). Therian mammals are characterized by the distinctive structural history of the molar teeth. The fossil record shows that all the extremely varied therian molar types were derived from a common tribosphenic type in which three main cusps, arranged in a triangle on the upper molar, are opposed to a reversed triangle and basinlike heel on the lower molar. *See* MAMMALIA.   [D.D.D./F.S.S.]

Thermal ecology   The examination of the independent and interactive biotic and abiotic components of naturally heated environments. Geothermal habitats are present from sea level to the tops of volcanoes and occur as fumaroles, geysers, and hot springs. Hot springs typically possess source pools with overflow, or thermal, streams (rheotherms) or without such streams (limnotherms). Hot spring habitats have existed since life began on Earth, permitting the gradual introduction and evolution of species and communities adapted to each other and to high temperatures. Other geothermal habitats do not have distinct communities.

Hot-spring pools and streams, typified by temperatures higher than the mean annual temperature of the air at the same locality and by benthic mats of various colors, are found on all continents except Antarctica. They are located in regions of geologic activity where meteoric water circulates deep enough to become heated. The greatest densities occur in Yellowstone National Park (Northwest United States), Iceland, and New Zealand. Source waters range from 40°C (104°F) to boiling (around 100°C or 212°F depending on elevation), and may even be superheated at the point of emergence. Few hot springs have pH 5–6; most are either acidic (pH 2–4) or alkaline (pH 7–9).   [C.Wi.]

Thermoregulation   The processes by which many animals actively maintain the temperature of part or all of their body within a specified range in order to stabilize or optimize temperature-sensitive physiological processes. Body temperatures of normally active animals may range from 32 to 115°F (0 to 46°C) or more, but the tolerable range for any one species is much narrower.

Animals are commonly classified as warm-blooded or cold-blooded. When the temperature of the environment varies, the body temperature of a warm-blooded or homeothermic animal remains high and constant, while that of a cold-blooded or poikilothermic animal is low and variable. However, supposedly cold-blooded reptiles and insects, when active, may regulate body temperatures within 2–4°F (1–2°C) of a species-specific value. Supposedly warm-blooded mammals and birds may allow their temperature to drop to 37–68°F (5–20°C) during hibernation or torpor. Further, optimal temperature varies with organ, time of day, and circumstance. Thus, this classification is often misleading.

A better classification is based on the principal source of heat used for thermoregulation. Endotherms (birds, mammals) use heat generated from food energy. Ectotherms (invertebrates, fish, amphibians, reptiles) use heat from environmental sources. This classification also has limitations, however. For example, endotherms routinely use external heat sources to minimize the food cost of thermoregulation, and some ectotherms use food energy for thermoregulation. *See* PHYSIOLOGICAL ECOLOGY (ANIMAL).

Behavior is the most obviously active form of thermoregulation. Most animals are mobile, sensitive to their environment, and capable of complex behaviors. The simplest thermoregulatory behavior consists of moving to a favorable location. Operative temperature may also be altered by changing posture in one place. Lizards face the sun to minimize the area exposed to solar heating, or orient broadside to maximize it, and some ground squirrels use their tail as a sunshade. Some reptiles and amphibians also expand or contract pigmented cells in their skin to increase or decrease solar heating. *See* CHROMATOPHORE.

Evaporation is an effective means of cooling the body. Evaporation from the respiratory mucous membranes is the most common mechanism. Evaporation from the mucous membranes cools the nose during inhalation. During exhalation, water vapor condenses on the cool nasal membranes and is recovered. Evaporation can be greatly increased by exhaling from the mouth to prevent condensation. Additional increases in evaporation result from panting, that is, rapid breathing at the resonant frequency of the respiratory system. Evaporation from the eyes and the mucous membranes of the mouth and tongue is another source of cooling. Water is also evaporated from the skin of all animals, and can be varied for thermoregulation. Some desert frogs control evaporation by spreading an oily material on the skin. Reptiles, birds, and mammals have relatively impermeable skins, but evaporation can be increased by various means. The sweat glands in the skin of mammals are particularly effective and are one of the few purely thermoregulatory organs known. *See* SKIN.

Changes in circulation can be used to regulate heat flow. Countercurrent heat exchange is used to regulate heat flow to particular parts of the body while maintaining oxygen supply. Large vessels may be divided into intermingled masses of small vessels to maximize heat exchange, forming an organ called a rete. However, retes can be bypassed by alternative circulation paths to regulate heat flow. Many animals living in warm environments have a rete that regulates brain temperature by cooling the arterial blood supply to the brain with blood draining from the nasal membranes, eyes, ears, or horns. *See* CARDIOVASCULAR SYSTEM.

Heat exchange with the environment is limited by the fur of mammals, feathers of birds, and furlike scales or setae of insects. Erection or compression of this insulation varies heat flow. Insulation thickness varies over the body to exploit variations in local operative temperature. Thermal windows are thinly insulated areas that are either shaded (abdomen of mammals, axilla of birds and mammals) or of small size (ears, face, legs) so that solar heating is minimized.

The oxidation of foodstuffs within the metabolic pathways of the body releases as much heat as if it were burned. Basal metabolism is the energy use rate of a fasting animal at rest. Activity, digestion, and thermoregulation increase metabolism above the basal rate. Endothermy is the utilization of metabolic heat for thermoregulation. Birds and mammals are typical examples, but significant endothermy also occurs in large salt-water fish, large reptiles, and large flying insects. Endotherms regulate only the temperature of the body core, that is, the brain, heart, and lungs. The heat production of these metabolically active organs is often supplemented with heat produced in muscles. Heat produced as a by-product of activity may substitute partially for thermoregulatory heat production, and imposes no thermoregulatory energy cost. In contrast, shivering produces heat only for thermoregulation and results in an extra cost. Some animals have specialized heater organs for nonshivering thermogenesis, which is more efficient than shivering. Brown adipose tissue is a fatty tissue with a high density of mitochondria. It is found in the thorax of mammals, especially newborns and hibernators, and it warms the body core efficiently. *See* METABOLISM.

The variety of mechanisms used in thermoregulation indicates a corresponding complexity in neural control. Temperature sensors distributed over the skin respond nearly immediately to changes in the environment and provide the major input. Nearly all parts of the central nervous system also respond to local thermal stimulation. These peripheral and central thermal inputs are integrated at a series of centers beginning in the spinal cord. This series clearly extends to the cerebral cortex, as a learning period is required before behavioral thermoregulation reaches maximum precision. Various components respond to the rate of temperature change as well as the difference between preferred and actual temperature. The neuroendocrine system then regulates metabolic heat production, the sympathetic nervous system controls blood flow, and the cerebral cortex controls behavioral thermoregulation. *See* ENDOCRINE SYSTEM (VERTEBRATE); HOMEOSTASIS; NERVOUS SYSTEM (VERTEBRATE).   [G.Ba.]

Thiamine   A water-soluble vitamin found in many foods; pork, liver, and whole grains are particularly rich sources. It is also known as vitamin B_1 or aneurin. The structural formula of thiamine is shown below.

Thiamine deficiency is known as beriberi in humans and polyneuritis in birds. Muscle and nerve tissues are affected by the deficiency, and poor growth is observed. People with beriberi are irritable, depressed, and weak. They often die of cardiac failure. Wernicke's disease observed in alcoholics is associated with a thiamine deficiency. This disease is characterized by brain lesions, liver disease, and partial paralysis, particularly of the motor nerves of the eye. As is the case in all B vitamin diseases, thiamine deficiency is usually accompanied by deficiencies of other vitamins.   [S.N.G.]

Thirst and sodium appetite   The sensations caused by dehydration, the continuing loss of fluid through the skin and lungs and in the urine and feces while there is no water intake into the body. Thirst becomes more and more insistent as dehydration worsens. Water and electrolytes are needed to replace losses, and an adequate intake of sodium as well as water is important for maintaining blood volume. Normally, the amounts of water drunk and taken in food are more than enough to maintain hydration of the body, and the usual mixed diet provides all the electrolytes required.

Deficit-induced drinking occurs when a deficit of fluid in one or both of the major fluid compartments of the body serves as a signal to increase drinking. Cellular dehydration, detected by osmoreceptors, causes thirst and vasopressin release. Hypovolemia (low blood volume), detected by volume receptors in the heart and large veins and the arterial baroreceptors, causes immediate thirst, a delayed increase in sodium appetite, activation of the renin-angiotensin system, and increased mineralocorticoid and vasopressin secretion. Increases or decreases in amounts drunk in disease may result from normal or abnormal functioning of mechanisms of thirst or sodium appetite.

Cellular dehydration. Observations using a variety of osmotic challenges have established that hyperosmotic solutions of solutes that are excluded from cells cause more drinking than equiosmolar amounts of solutes that penetrate cells. Thus, the osmotic shift of water out of the cells caused by the excluded solutes provides the critical stimulus to drinking. Continuing water loss in the absence of intake is perhaps a more significant cause of cellular dehydration than administration of an osmotic load, but the same mechanisms apply.

Sharing in the overall cellular dehydration are osmoreceptors which initiate the responses of thirst and renal conservation of water. Osmoreceptors are mainly located in the hypothalamus. The nervous tissue in the hypothalamus surrounding the anterior third cerebral ventricle and, in particular, the vascular organ of the lamina terminalis also respond to osmotic stimuli. Osmoreceptors initiating thirst work in conjunction with osmoreceptors initiating antidiuretic hormone (ADH) release to restore the cellular water to its prehydration level. In addition to reducing urine loss, ADH may lower the threshold to the onset of drinking in response to cellular dehydration and other thirst stimuli. The cellular dehydration system is very sensitive, responding to changes in effective osmolality of 1–2%.

Hypovolemia. The cells of the body are bathed by sodium-rich extracellular fluid that corresponds to the aquatic environment of the unicellular organism. Loss of sodium from the extracellular fluid is inevitably accompanied by loss of water, resulting in hypovolemia with thirst followed by a delayed increase in sodium appetite. If not corrected, continuing severe sodium loss eventually leads to circulatory collapse.

Stretch receptors in the walls of blood vessels entering and leaving the heart and in the heart itself are thought to initiate hypovolemic drinking. Volume receptors in the venoatrial junctions and receptors that register atrial and ventricular pressure respond to the underfilling of the circulation with a reduction in inhibitory nerve impulses to the thirst centers, which results in increased drinking. Angiotensin II and other hormones (such as aldosterone and ADH) are also involved in this response. Arterial baroreceptors function in much the same way as the volume receptors on the low-pressure side of the circulation, exerting continuous inhibitory tone on thirst neurons. A fall in blood pressure causes increased drinking, whereas an acute rise in blood pressure inhibits drinking. The anterior third cerebral ventricle region, which is implicated in angiotensin-induced drinking, plays a crucial role in hypovolemic drinking, body fluid homeostasis, and blood pressure control.

Renin-angiotensin systems. It is believed that drinking caused by hypovolemic stimuli partly depends on the kidneys. The renal thirst factor is the proteolytic enzyme renin, which is secreted into the circulation by the kidney in response to hypovolemia. Renin cleaves an inactive decapeptide, angiotensin I, from angiotensinogen, an α_2-globulin that is synthesized in the liver and released into the circulation. Angiotensin I is converted to the physiologically active octapeptide angiotensin II during the passage of blood through the lungs. Angiotensin II is an exceptionally powerful stimulus of drinking behavior in many animals when administered systemically or into the brain. Increased activation of the renin-angiotensin system may sometimes account for pathologically increased thirst in humans. Angiotensin II also produces (1) a rise in arterial blood pressure, release of norepinephrine from sympathetic nerve endings, and secretion of adrenomedullary hormones; and (2) water and sodium retention by causing release of ADH from the posterior pituitary and stimulation of renal tubular transport of sodium through direct action on the kidney and indirectly through increased aldosterone secretion from the adrenal cortex. *See* ALDOSTERONE; KIDNEY.

Neuropharmacology. Many substances released by neurons, and in some cases by neuroglial cells, affect drinking behavior when injected into the brain and may interact with the brain and modify angiotensin-induced drinking. Substances may stimulate or inhibit drinking, or both, depending on the species and the conditions of the experiment. Acetylcholine is a particularly powerful stimulus to drinking in rats, and no inhibitory effects on drinking have been described. Histamine also seems to be mainly stimulatory. However, a lengthening list of neuroactive substances, including norepinephrine, serotonin, nitric oxide, opioids, bombesin-like peptides, tachykinins, and neuropeptide Y, may either stimulate or inhibit drinking with varying degrees of effectiveness, depending on the species or the site of injection in the brain. Natriuretic peptides, prostaglandins, and gamma-amino butyric acid seem to be exclusively inhibitory. *See* ACETYLCHOLINE; NEUROBIOLOGY; SYNAPTIC TRANSMISSION.

Many hormones also affect water or sodium intake. Relaxin stimulates water intake, and ADH (or vasopressin) lowers the threshold to thirst in some species. Vasopressin injected into the third cerebral ventricle may stimulate water intake, suggesting a possible role for vasopressinergic neurons. Increased sodium appetite in pregnancy and lactation depends partly on the conjoint action of progesterone, estrogen, adrenocorticotrophic hormone (ACTH), cortisol, corticosterone, prolactin, and oxytocin. Aldosterone and other mineralocorticoids, the stress hormones of the hypothalamo-pituitary-adrenocortical axis, corticotrophin, ACTH, and the glucocorticoids also stimulate sodium intake. *See* NEUROHYPOPHYSIS HORMONE.

The effect of many of these substances on drinking behavior shows both species and anatomical diversity. The multiplicity of effects of many of these substances makes it impossible to generalize on their role in natural thirst, but none of these substances seems to be as consistent and as universal a stimulus of increased thirst and sodium appetite as angiotensin.   [J.T.F.]

Throat   The region that includes the pharynx, the larynx, and related structures. Both the nasal passages and the oral cavity open into the pharynx, which also contains the openings of the Eustachian tubes from the ears. The lower portion of the pharynx leads into the esophagus and the trachea or windpipe. The rather funnel-shaped pharynx is suspended from the base of the skull and the jaws; it is surrounded by three constrictor muscles that function primarily in swallowing. *See* EAR; PHARYNX.

The larynx, or voice box, is marked externally by the shield-shaped thyroid cartilage which forms the Adam's apple. The larynx contains the vocal cords that act as sphincters for air regulation and permit phonation. The lower end of the larynx is continuous with the trachea, a tube composed of cartilaginous rings and supporting tissues. *See* LARYNX.

The term throat is also used in a general sense to denote the front (ventral side) of the neck.   [T.S.P.]

Thymosin   A polypeptide hormone synthesized and secreted by the endodermally derived reticular cells of the thymus gland. Thymosin exerts its actions in several loci: (1) in the thymus gland, either on precursor stem cells derived from fetal liver or from bone marrow, or on immature thymocytes, and (2) in peripheral sites, on either thymic-derived lymphoid cells or on precursor stem cells. The precursor stem cells, which are immunologically incompetent whether in the thymus or in peripheral sites, have been designated as predetermined T cells or T_0 cells, and mature through stages termed T_1 and T_2, each reflecting varying degrees of immunological competence. Thymosin promotes or accelerates the maturation of T_0 cells to T_1 cells as well as to the final stage of a T_2. In addition to this maturation influence, the hormone also increases the number of total lymphoid cells by accelerating the rate of proliferation of both immature and mature lymphocytes. *See* IMMUNITY.   [A.W.]

Thyrocalcitonin   A hormone, the only known secretory product of the parenchymal or C cells of the mammalian thyroid and of the ultimobranchial glands of lower forms.

In conjunction with the parathyroid hormone, thyrocalcitonin is of prime importance in regulating calcium and phosphate metabolism. Its major function is to protect the organism from the dangerous consequences of elevated blood calcium. Its sole known effect is that of inhibiting the resorption of bone. It thus produces a fall in the concentration of calcium and phosphate in the blood plasma because these two minerals are the major constituents of bone mineral and are released into the bloodstream in ionic form when bone is resorbed. *See* BONE; PARATHYROID GLAND; PARATHYROID HORMONE.

Thyrocalcitonin also causes an increased excretion of phosphate in the urine under certain circumstances, but a question remains as to whether this is a direct effect of the hormone upon the kidney or an indirect consequence of the fall in blood calcium which occurs when the hormone inhibits bone resorption. *See* THYROID GLAND.   [H.Ras.]

Thyroid gland   An endocrine gland found in all vertebrates that produces, stores, and secretes the thyroid hormones. In humans, the gland is located in front of, and on either side of, the trachea (see illustration). Thyrocalcitonin, one hormone

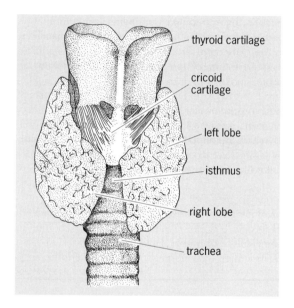

thyroid cartilage

cricoid cartilage

left lobe

isthmus

right lobe

trachea

Ventral view of human thyroid gland shown in relation to trachea and larynx. (*After C. K. Weichert, Elements of Chordate Anatomy, 3d ed., McGraw-Hill, 1967*)

of the thyroid gland, assists in regulating serum calcium by reducing its levels. The iodine-containing hormones thyroxine and triiodothyronine regulate metabolic rate in warm-blooded animals and are essential for normal growth and development. To produce these, the thyroid gland accumulates inorganic iodides from the bloodstream and unites them with the amino acid tyrosine. This activity is regulated by thyrotropic hormone from the anterior lobe of the pituitary gland. *See* THYROID HORMONE; THYROXINE.
                                                                                    [G.C.Ke.]

Thyroid hormone   Any of the chemical messengers produced by the thyroid gland, including thyrocalcitonin, a polypeptide, and thyroxine and triiodothyronine, which are iodinated thyronines. *See* HORMONE; THYROCALCITONIN; THYROID GLAND; THYROXINE.   [H.Ras.]

Thyroxine A hormone secreted by the thyroid gland. Thyroxine (structure **1**) is quite similar chemically and in biological activity to triiodothyronine (**2**). Both

$$(1)$$

$$(2)$$

are derivatives of the amino acid tyrosine and are unique in being the only iodine-containing compounds of importance in the economy of all higher forms of animal life. The thyroid gland avidly accumulates the small amount of iodine in the diet. This iodine is oxidized to iodide ion in the gland and then reacts with tryosine to form mono- and diiodotyrosine. These latter are then coupled to form either thyroxine or triiodothyronine. *See* THYROID GLAND.

The maintenance of a normal level of thyroxine is critically important for normal growth and development as well as for proper bodily function in the adult. Its absence leads to delayed or arrested development. It is one of the few hormones with general effects upon all tissues. Its lack leads to a decrease in the general metabolism of all cells, most characteristically measured as a decrease in nucleic acid and protein synthesis, and a slowing down of all major metabolic processes.   [H.Ras.]

Tissue An aggregation of cells more or less similar morphologically and functionally. The animal body is composed of four primary tissues, namely, epithelium, connective tissue (including bone, cartilage, and blood), muscle, and nervous tissue. The process of differentiation and maturation of tissues is called histogenesis. *See* HISTOLOGY.   [C.B.C.]

Tissue typing A procedure involving a test or a series of tests to determine the compatibility of tissues from a prospective donor and a recipient prior to transplantation. The immunological response of a recipient to a transplant from a donor is directed against many cell-surface histocompatibility antigens controlled by genes at many different loci. However, one of these loci, the major histocompatibility complex (MHC), controls antigens that evoke the strongest immunological response. The human MHC is known as the HLA system, which stands for the first (A) human leukocyte blood group system discovered. *See* CELLULAR IMMUNOLOGY; HISTOCOMPATIBILITY.

The success of transplantation is greatly dependent on the degree of histocompatibility (identity) between the donor and recipient, which is determined by the HLA complex. When the donor and recipient have a low degree of histocompatibility, the organ is said to be mismatched, and the recipient mounts an immune response against the donor antigen. By laboratory testing, the degree of antigenic similarity between the donor and the recipient and the degree of preexisting recipient sensitization to donor antigens (and therefore preformed antibodies) can be determined. This is known as cross-matching.

Phenotyping of HLA-A, -B, and -C (ABC typing) of an individual is determined by reacting that individual's lymphocytes with a large panel of antisera directed against specific HLA antigens. The procedure is known as complement-mediated cytotoxicity assay. The person's lymphocytes are incubated with the different antisera and complement is added. Killing of the cells being tested indicates that they express the HLA antigens recognized by the particular antiserum being used. Killing of potential donor lymphocytes in the complement-mediated cytotoxicity assay is a contraindication to transplantation of tissue from that donor. See COMPLEMENT; HYPERSENSITIVITY; IMMUNOASSAY.

In addition to its important role in organ transplantation, determination of the HLA phenotype is useful in paternity testing, forensic medicine, and the investigation of HLA-disease associations. See TRANSPLANTATION BIOLOGY.   [M.W.Fl.; T.Moh.]

Tonsil   Localized aggregation of diffuse and nodular lymphoid tissue found in the region where the nasal and oral cavities open into the pharynx. The tonsils are important sources of blood lymphocytes. They often become inflamed and enlarged, necessitating surgical removal.

The two palatine (faucial) tonsils are almond-shaped bodies measuring 1 by 0.5 in. (2.5 by 1.2 cm) and are embedded between folds of tissue connecting the pharynx and posterior part of the tongue with the soft palate. These are the structures commonly known as the tonsils. The lingual tonsil occupies the posterior part of the tongue surface. It is really a collection of 35–100 separate tonsillar units, each having a single crypt surrounded by lymphoid tissue. Each tonsil forms a smooth swelling about 0.08–0.16 in. (2–4 mm) in diameter. The pharyngeal tonsil (called adenoids when enlarged) occupies the roof of the nasal part of the pharynx. This tonsil may enlarge to block the nasal passage, forcing mouth breathing. See LYMPHATIC SYSTEM.   [T.Sn.]

Tooth   One of the structures found in the mouth of most vertebrates which, in their most primitive form, were conical and were usually used for seizing, cutting up, or chewing food, or for all three of these purposes. The basic tissues that make up the vertebrate tooth are enamel, dentin, cementum, and pulp (see illustration).

Enamel is the hardest tissue in the body because of the very high concentration, about 96%, of mineral salts. The remaining 4% is water and organic matter. The

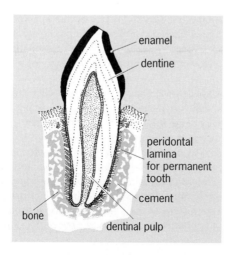

enamel

dentine

peridontal lamina for permanent tooth

cement

bone

dentinal pulp

Structure of a tooth.

enamel has no nerve supply, although it is nourished to a very slight degree from the dentin it surrounds. The fine, microscopic hexagonal rods (prisms) of apatite which make up the enamel are held together by a cementing substance.

Dentin, a very bonelike tissue, makes up the bulk of a tooth, consisting of 70% of such inorganic material as calcium and phosphorus, and 30% of water and organic matter, principally collagen. The rich nerve supply makes dentin a highly sensitive tissue; this sensitivity serves no obvious physiological function.

Cement is a calcified tissue, a type of modified bone less hard than dentin, which fastens the roots of teeth to the alveolus, the bony socket into which the tooth is implanted. A miscellaneous tissue, consisting of nerves, fibrous tissue, lymph, and blood vessels, known as the pulp, occupies the cavity of the tooth surrounded by dentin.

The dentition of therian mammals, at least primitively, consists of four different kinds of teeth. The incisors (I) are usually used for nipping and grasping; the canines (C) serve for stabbing or piercing; the premolars (Pm) grasp, slice, or function as additional molars; and the molars (M) do the chewing, cutting, and grinding of the food. Primitively the placentals have 40 teeth and the marsupials 50.

In therian mammals, probably because of the intricacies and vital importance of tooth occlusion, only part of the first (or "milk") dentition is replaced. This second, or permanent, dentition is made up of incisors, canines, and premolars; as a rule only one premolar is replaced in marsupials. Although the molars erupt late in development and are permanent, that is, not replaced, they are part of the first, or deciduous, dentition.

[F.S.S.]

Toxic shock syndrome   A serious, sometimes life-threatening disease usually caused by a toxin produced by some strains of the bacterium *Staphylococcus aureus*. The signs and symptoms are fever, abnormally low blood pressure, nausea and vomiting, diarrhea, muscle tenderness, and a reddish rash, followed by peeling of the skin.

Toxic shock syndrome was first reported in 1978 in seven pediatric patients. However, in 1980 hundreds of cases were reported among young women without apparent staphylococcal infections. Epidemiologists observed that the illness occurred predominantly in young women who were menstruating and were using tampons, especially those that contained so-called superabsorbent synthetic materials. A toxin [toxic shock syndrome toxin number 1 (TSST-1)] that occurs in some strains of staphylococci was later identified. These bacteria are known to proliferate in the presence of foreign particles in human infections, and it has been postulated that the tampons acted as foreign particles, allowing toxin-producing staphylococci to multiply in the vagina.

Several hundred cases of toxic shock syndrome not associated with menstruation have been reported. In these cases, which occurred in males as well as females, there was almost always an overt staphylococcal infection. Susceptibility may depend on lack of antibodies to the toxin that occur in most adults.

The toxin has been shown to occur in only about 1% of the staphylococcal strains studied. Moreover, there is some evidence that the syndrome may be caused also by other staphylococcal toxins, particularly enterotoxins. Cases of toxic shock syndrome that were caused by streptococci have been reported. A toxin distinct from TSST-1 appears involved. Persons with the symptoms of toxic shock syndrome should receive immediate medical care to reduce the chance of death. *See* STAPHYLOCOCCUS; TOXIN.

[J.O.Co.]

Toxin   Properly, a poisonous protein, especially of bacterial origin. However, non-proteinaceous poisons, such as fungal aflatoxins and plant alkaloids, are often called toxins. See AFLATOXIN; ALKALOID.

Bacterial exotoxins are proteins of disease-causing bacteria that are usually secreted and have deleterious effects. Several hundred are known. In some extreme cases a single toxin accounts for the principal symptoms of a disease, such as diphtheria, tetanus, and cholera. Bacteria that cause local infections with pus often produce many toxins that affect the tissues around the infection site or are distributed to remote organs by the blood. See CHOLERA; DIPHTHERIA; STAPHYLOCOCCUS.

Toxins may assist the parent bacteria to combat host defense systems, to increase the supply of certain nutrients such as iron, to invade cells or tissues, or to spread between hosts. Sometimes the damage suffered by the host organism has no obvious benefit to the bacteria. For example, botulinal neurotoxin in spoiled food may kill the person or animal that eats it long after the parent bacteria have died. In such situations it is assumed that the bacteria benefit from the toxin in some other habitat and that the damage to vertebrates is accidental. See FOOD POISONING.

Certain bacterial and plant toxins have the unusual ability to catalyze chemical reactions inside animal cells. Such toxins are always composed of two functionally distinct parts termed A and B, and they are often called A-B toxins. The B part binds to receptor molecules on the animal cell surface and positions the toxin upon the cell membrane. Subsequently, the enzymically active A portion of the toxin crosses the animal cell membrane and catalyzes some intracellular chemical reaction that disrupts the cell physiology or causes cell death. See IMMUNOLOGIC CYTOTOXICITY.

A large group of toxins breach the normal barrier to free movement of molecules across cell membranes. In sufficient concentration such cytolytic toxins cause cytolysis, a process by which soluble molecules leak out of cells, but in lower concentration they may cause less obvious damage to the cell's plasma membrane or to its internal membranes. See CELL MEMBRANES; CELL PERMEABILITY.

Tetanus and botulinal neurotoxins block the transmission of nerve impulses across synapses. Tetanus toxin blockage results in spastic paralysis, in which opposing muscles contract simultaneously. The botulinal neurotoxins principally paralyze neuromuscular junctions and cause flaccid paralysis.

Gram-negative bacteria, such as *Salmonella* and *Hemophilus*, have a toxic component in their cell walls known as endotoxin or lipopolysaccharide. Among other detrimental effects, endotoxins cause white blood cells to produce interleukin-1, a hormone responsible for fever, malaise, headache, muscle aches, and other nonspecific consequences of infection. The exotoxins of toxic shock syndrome and of scarlet fever induce interleukin-1 and also tumor necrosis factor, which has similar effects. See ENDOTOXIN; SCARLET FEVER; TOXIC SHOCK SYNDROME.

Toxoids are toxins that have been exposed to formaldehyde or other chemicals that destroy their toxicities without impairing immunogenicity. When injected into humans, toxoids elicit specific antibodies known as antitoxins that neutralize circulating toxins. Such immunization (vaccination) is very effective for systemic toxinoses, such as diphtheria and tetanus. See ANTIBODY; IMMUNITY; VACCINATION.   [D.M.Gi.]

Toxin-antitoxin reaction   A term used in serology to denote the combination of a toxic antigen with its corresponding antitoxin. If the antitoxin is derived from any species other than the horse, precipitation occurs over a wide range of reactant ratios, $20 \times$ or more, as in other antigen-antibody reactions. With horse antitoxin, flocculation occurs only if toxin and antitoxin are near equivalence, a twofold excess of either reactant giving soluble complexes. In most instances, the reaction results in partial or complete neutralization of the toxic activity of the antigen. *See* ANTIBODY; ANTIGEN; ANTITOXIN; NEUTRALIZATION REACTION (IMMUNOLOGY); SEROLOGY.   [H.P.T.]

Transamination   The transfer of an amino group from one molecule to another without the intermediate formation of ammonia. Enzymatic reactions of this type play a prominent role in the formation and ultimate breakdown of amino acids by living organisms. Enzymes that catalyze such reactions are widely distributed and are termed transaminases, or amino-transferases. Perhaps the most prominent transamination reactions in higher animals are those in which glutamate is formed from α-ketoglutarate and other amino acids. *See* PROTEIN METABOLISM.   [E.E.S.]

Transduction (bacteria)   A mechanism for the transfer of genetic material between cells. The material is transferred by virus particles called bacteriophages (in the case of bacteria), or phages. The transfer method differentiates transduction from transformation. In transformation the genetic material (deoxyribonucleic acid) is extracted from the cell by chemical means or released by lysis. *See* BACTERIAL GENETICS; BACTERIOPHAGE; DEOXYRIBONUCLEIC ACID (DNA); TRANSFORMATION (BACTERIA).

The transduction mechanism has two features to distinguish it from the more usual mechanism of gene recombination, the sexual process. The most striking feature is the transfer of genetic material from cell to cell by viruses. The second feature is the fact that only a small part of the total genetic material of any one bacterial cell is carried by any particular transducing particle. However, in general transduction, all of the genetic material is distributed among different particles.

Transduction is not accomplished by all bacteriophages. It is done by some that are classified as "temperate." When such temperate bacteriophages infect sensitive bacteria, some of the bacteria respond by producing more bacteriophage particles. These bacteria donate the transducing material. Other bacteria respond to the infection by becoming more or less permanent carriers of the bacteriophage, in a kind of symbiotic relationship; these are called lysogenic bacteria. Bacteria in this latter class survive the infection, and it is among these that transduced cells are found. The proportion of bacteria in any culture that responds to infection in either manner can be influenced by the particular environment at the time of infection. *See* LYSOGENY.

Certain phages carry out a more restricted kind of transduction. They carry only a specific section of bacterial genetic material; they transduce only a few genes. Retroviruses carry out specific or restricted transduction. It has long been known that these viruses can cause the formation of tumors (oncogenesis) in animals. It is now known that these viruses exchange a small portion of their genome for a mutant cellular gene that has a role in gene regulation or replication. These viruses carrying mutant genes infect cells, causing them to be transformed into tumor cells. *See* ANIMAL VIRUS; RETROVIRUS.   [N.D.Z.]

Transformation (bacteria)   The addition of deoxyribonucleic acid (DNA) to living cells, thereby changing their genetic composition and properties. The recipient bacteria are usually closely related to the donor strain. The process may occur in natural conditions, for example, in a host animal infected with two parasitic strains, and indeed it might play a part in the rapid evolution of pathogenic bacteria. There are several species of bacteria in which transformation has been achieved in the laboratory.

That bacterial transformation is true genetic transmission on a small scale, rather than controlled mutation, is demonstrated by the following characteristics: (1) A specific trait is introduced, coming always from donors bearing the trait. (2) The trait is transferred by determinant, genelike material far less complex than whole cells or nuclei, and this material, DNA, is known to be present in gene-carrying chromosomes. (3) The trait is inherited by the progeny of the changed bacteria. (4) The progeny produce, when they grow, increased amounts of DNA carrying the specific property. (5) The traits are transferred as units exactly in the patterns in which they appear or in which they are induced by mutation. (6) The DNA transmits the full potentialities of the donor strain, whether these are in an expressed or in a latent state. (7) The traits are often attributable to the presence of a specific gene-determined enzyme protein. (8) Certain groups of determinants may occur "linked" within DNA molecules, just as genes may be linked, and if so, heat denaturation, radiation, or enzyme action will inactivate or separate them just to the extent that they can damage or break apart the DNA molecules. (9) Linked determinants, while transforming a new cell, may become exchanged (recombined) between themselves and their unmarked or unselective alternate forms in such a way that they bring about genetic variation, and in a pattern indicating the existence of larger organized genetic units. *See* BACTERIAL GENETICS; GENE.

Through the application of a number of procedures prior to adding the DNA, transformation was extended first to many different bacterial species and then to eukaryotic cells. Today almost any cell type can be transformed. In some cases, tissues can be injected directly with naked DNA and transformed. However, unlike with bacteria, the naked DNA adds almost anywhere in the genome rather than recombining with its indigenous homolog. However, with special highly selective procedures, homologous recombination can be obtained. By treating embryonic stem cells and adding them to embryos that then go to term, specific and nonspecific transgenic animals can be obtained (for example, mice). *See* GENETIC ENGINEERING.

When the source of the DNA is some entity capable of independent replication, such as a virus or plasmid, the phenomenon is called transfection. If foreign DNA is then inserted into these entities, the result is recombinant DNA that can lead to transduction. *See* MOLECULAR BIOLOGY; TRANSDUCTION (BACTERIA). [R.D.H.; N.D.Z.]

Transplantation biology The science of transferring a graft from one part of the body to another or from one individual to another. The graft may consist of an organ, tissue, or cells. If donor and recipient are the same individual, the graft is autologous. If donor and recipient are genetically identical (monozygotic), it is syngeneic. If donor and recipient are any other same-species individuals, the graft is allogeneic. If the donor and recipient are of different species, it is called xenogeneic.

In theory, virtually any tissue or organ can be transplanted. The principal technical problems have been defined and, in general, overcome. Remaining major problems concern the safety of methods used to prevent graft rejection and the procurement of adequate numbers of donor organs.

Living volunteers can donate one of a pair of organs, such as a kidney, only one of which is necessary for normal life. Volunteer donors may also be employed for large unpaired organs such as small bowel, liver, or pancreas, segments of which can be removed without impairment of function. Living donors can also provide tissues capable of regeneration; these include blood, bone marrow, and the superficial layers of the skin. In the case of a vital, unpaired organ, such as the heart, the use of cadaver donors is obligatory. In practice, with the exception of blood and bone marrow, the great majority of transplanted organs are cadaveric in origin, a necessity that presents difficult logistic problems.

Autografts are used for an increasing number of purposes. Skin autografts are important in the treatment of full-thickness skin loss due to extensive burns or other injuries.

Provided that the grafts comprise only the superficial levels of the skin, the donor sites reepithelialize spontaneously within a week or two. The saphenous vein of the ankle is frequently transplanted to the heart to bypass coronary arteries obstructed by atherosclerosis. Autologous hematopoietic stem cell transplantation is sometimes used to restore blood cells to cancer patients who receive forms of chemotherapy that are lethal to their bone marrow.

The most serious problem restricting the use of allografts is immunological. Because cells in the donor graft express on their surface a number of genetically determined transplantation antigens that are not present in the recipient, allografts provoke a defensive reaction analogous to that evoked by pathogenic microorganisms. As a consequence, after a transient initial period of apparent well-being, graft function progressively deteriorates and the donor tissue is eventually destroyed. The host response, known as allograft rejection, involves a large number of immunological agents, including cytotoxic antibodies and effector lymphocytes of various types. There are a few special exemptions from rejection that apply to certain sites in the body or to certain types of graft. For example, the use of corneal allografts in restoring sight to individuals with corneal opacification succeeds because of the absence of blood vessels in the host tissue.

Successful transplantation of allografts such as kidneys and hearts currently requires suppressing the recipient's immune response to the graft without seriously impairing the immunological defense against infection. Treatment of individuals with so-called immunosuppressive drugs and other agents prevents allograft rejection for prolonged periods, if not indefinitely. Under cover of nonspecific immunosuppression, the recipient's immune system appears to undergo an adaptation to the presence of the graft, allowing the dosage of the drugs to be reduced. However, in almost all successfully transplanted individuals, drug therapy at some low dose is required indefinitely. *See* IMMUNOSUPPRESSION.

An individual's response against an allograft is directed against a large number of cell-surface transplantation antigens controlled by allelic genes at many different loci. However, in all species, one of these loci, the major histocompatibility complex (MHC), transcends all the other histocompatibility loci in terms of its genetic complexity and the strength of the antigenic response it controls. In humans, the MHC, known as the HLA (human leukocyte antigen) complex, is on the sixth chromosome; its principal loci are designated A, B, C, DR, and DQ. The allelic products of the HLA genes can be detected by serology, polymerase chain reaction technology, or microcytotoxicity assays. The ABO red cell antigens are also important because they are expressed on all tissues. *See* BLOOD GROUPS; HISTOCOMPATIBILITY.

In kidney transplants between closely related family members, the degree of HLA antigen matching can be determined very precisely, and there is a very good correlation between the number of shared HLA antigens and the survival of the graft. With grafts from unrelated donors, HLA matching is more difficult and can delay transplantation, but it may be beneficial. HLA matching is not as clearly beneficial in the case of most other solid organ grafts, and no attempt is made to HLA-match heart, lung, liver, and pancreas grafts. With few exceptions, however, most donors and recipients are matched for the expression of ABO blood group antigens.

Bone marrow transplantation presents a unique problem in its requirements for HLA matching and for immunosuppression in advance of grafting. In addition to the possibility of rejection of the graft by the recipient, by virtue of immunologically competent cells still present in the recipient, bone marrow grafts can react against the transplantation antigens of their hosts. These are known as graft-versus-host reactions, and they can be fatal. *See* IMMUNOLOGY.

The immunological events that lead to the rejection of xenografts are different from and less well understood than those responsible for allograft rejection. The small number of xenografts attempted to date have failed. In particular, xenografts are susceptible to hyperacute rejection by humans. This is due to the presence of certain glycoproteins in blood vessels of many species that are recognized by antibodies present in the blood of all humans.   [J.P.Mo.; R.E.Bi.; D.L.Gr.; A.A.R.]

Transposons   Types of transposable elements which comprise large discrete segments of deoxyribonucleic acid (DNA) capable of moving from one chromosome site to a new location. In bacteria, the transposable elements can be grouped into two classes, the insertion sequences and the transposons. The ability of transposable elements to insert into plasmid or bacterial virus (bacteriophage) which is transmissible from one organism to another allows for their rapid spread. *See* BACTERIOPHAGE; PLASMID.

The insertion sequences were first identified by their ability to induce unusual mutations in the structural gene for a protein involved in sugar metabolism. These insertion sequences are relatively small (about 500–1500 nucleotide pairs) and can only be followed by their ability to induce these mutations. Most bacterial chromosomes contain several copies of such insertion sequence elements.

The transposons are larger segments of DNA (2000–10,000 base pairs) that encode several proteins, usually one or two required for the movement of the element and often an additional protein that imparts a selective advantage to the host containing a copy of that element. The structure of many transposons suggests they may have evolved from the simpler insertion sequence elements.

All transposable elements, both the simple insertion sequence elements and the more complex transposons, have a similar structure and genetic organization. The ends of the element represent recognition sites and define the segment of DNA undergoing transposition. A short sequence present at one end of the element is repeated in an inverted fashion at the other end. These terminal inverted repeats are characteristic for each element.

Members of a widespread group of transposons, the Tn3 family, all have a similar structure and appear to move by a similar mechanism. Transposase, one protein encoded by the element, promotes the formation of intermediates called cointegrates, in which the element has been duplicated by replication. A second element-encoded protein, resolvase, completes the process by converting the cointegrates into the end products of transposition, a transposon inserted into a new site. A third protein encoded by the Tn3 element imparts resistance to the antibiotic ampicillin.

Transposons are known that encode resistances to almost all antibiotics as well as many toxic metals and chemicals. In addition, some transposons have acquired the ability to direct the synthesis of proteins that metabolize carbohydrates, petroleum, and pesticides. Other transposable elements produce enterotoxins that cause travelers to become ill from drinking water contaminated with bacteria carrying the element. The broad spectrum of activities encoded by the transposable elements demonstrates the strong selective advantage that has accompanied their evolution.

Transposable elements are not restricted to prokaryotes. Yeast as well as higher eukaryotes have DNA segments that move and cause mutations. The eukaryotic elements have much in common with their prokaryotic counterparts: the termini of the elements are composed of inverted repeats, and many of the larger elements are composed of two small insertion sequence-like regions flanking a unique central region. One class of eukaryotic virus, the ribonucleic acid (RNA) retrovirus, also has this structure and is thought to integrate into the host chromosome through a transpositionlike mechanism. *See* ANTIBIOTIC; GENE; GENE ACTION; RETROVIRUS; VIRUS.   [R.Re.]

Tree   A perennial woody plant at least 20 ft (6 m) in height at maturity, having an erect stem or trunk and a well-defined crown or leaf canopy. However, no sharp lines can be drawn between trees, shrubs, and lianas (woody vines). The essence of the tree form is relatively large size, long life, and a slow approach to reproductive maturity. The difficulty of transporting water, nutrients, and storage products over long distances and high into the air against the force of gravity is a common problem of large treelike plants and one that is not shared by shrubs or herbs.

Classification.   Almost all existing trees belong to the seed plants (Spermatophyta). An exception are the giant tree ferns which were more prominent in the forests of the Devonian Period and today exist only in the moist tropical regions. The Spermatophyta are divided into the Pinophyta (gymnosperms) and the flowering plants, Magnoliophyta (angiosperms). The gymnosperms bear their seed naked on modified leaves, called scales, which are usually clustered into structures called cones—for example, pine cones. By contrast the seed of angiosperms is enclosed in a ripened ovary, the fruit. See MAGNOLIOPHYTA; PINOPHYTA.

The orders Cycadales, Ginkgoales, and Pinales of the Pinophyta contain trees. *Ginkgo biloba*, the ancient maidenhair tree, is the single present-day member of the Ginkgoales. The Cycadales, characteristic of dry tropical areas, contain many species which are small trees. The Pinales, found throughout the world, supply much of the wood, paper, and building products of commerce. They populate at least one-third of all existing forest and include the pines (*Pinus*), hemlocks (*Tsuga*), cedars (*Cedrus*), spruces (*Picea*), firs (*Abies*), cypress (*Cupressus*), larches (*Larix*), Douglas-fir (*Pseudotsuga*), sequoia (*Sequoia*), and other important genera. The Pinales are known in the lumber trade as softwoods and are popularly thought of as evergreens, although some (for example, larch and bald cypress) shed their leaves in the winter.

In contrast to the major orders of gymnosperms which contain only trees, many angiosperm families are herbaceous and include trees only as an exception. Only a few are exclusively arborescent. The major classes of the angiosperms are the Liliopsida (monocotyledons) and the Magnoliopsida (dicotyledons). The angiosperm trees, commonly thought of as broad-leaved and known as hardwoods in the lumber market, are dicotyledons. Examples of important genera are the oaks (*Quercus*), elms (*Ulmus*), maples (*Acer*), and poplars (*Populus*).

The Liliopsida contain few tree species, and these are never used for wood products, except in the round as posts. Examples of monocotyledonous families are the palms (Palmae), yucca (Liliaceae), bamboos (Bambusoideae), and bananas (Musaceae).

Morphology.   The morphology of a tree is similar to that of other higher plants. Its major organs are the stem, or trunk and branches; the leaves; the roots; and the reproductive structures. Almost the entire bulk of a tree is nonliving. Of the trunk, branches, and roots, only the tips and a thin layer of cells just under the bark are alive. Growth occurs only in these meristematic tissues. Meristematic cells are undifferentiated and capable of repeated division. See FLOWER; LATERAL MERISTEM; LEAF; ROOT (BOTANY); STEM.

Growth.   Height is a result of growth only in apical meristems at the very tips of the twigs. A nail driven into a tree will always remain at the same height, and a branch which originates from a bud at a given height will never rise higher. The crown of a tree ascends as a tree ages only by the production of new branches at the top and by the death and abscission of lower, older branches as they become progressively more shaded. New growing points originate from the division of the apical meristem and appear as buds in the axils of leaves. *See* APICAL MERISTEM; BUD; PLANT GROWTH.

In the gymnosperms and the dicotyledonous angiosperms, growth in diameter occurs by division in only a single microscopic layer, three or four cells wide, which completely encircles and sheaths the tree. This lateral meristem is the cambium. It divides to produce xylem cells (wood) on the inside toward the core of the tree and phloem cells on the outside toward the bark. In trees of the temperate regions the growth of each year is seen in cross section as a ring. *See* PHLOEM; XYLEM.

Xylem elements become rigid through the thickening and modification of their cell wall material. The tubelike xylem cells transport water and nutrients from the root through the stem to the leaves. In time the xylem toward the center of the trunk becomes impregnated with various mineral and metabolic products, and it is no longer capable of conduction. This nonfunctional xylem is called heartwood and is recognizable in some stems by its dark color. The light-colored, functional outer layer of the xylem is the sapwood. *See* WOOD ANATOMY.

The phloem tissue transports dissolved carbohydrates and other metabolic products manufactured by the leaves throughout the stem and the roots. Most of the phloem cells are thin-walled and are eventually crushed between the bark and the cambium by the pressures generated in growth. The outer bark is dead and inelastic but the inner bark contains patches of cork cambium which produce new bark. As a tree increases in circumference, the old outer bark splits and fissures develop, resulting in the rough appearance characteristic of the trunks of most large trees.

In the monocotyledons the lateral cambium does not encircle a central core, and the vascular or conducting tissue is organized in bundles scattered throughout the stem. The trunk is not wood as generally conceived although it does in fact have secondary xylem. *See* FOREST AND FORESTRY; PLANT PHYSIOLOGY; PLANT TAXONOMY. [F.T.L.]

Tree physiology The study of how trees grow and develop in terms of genetics; biochemistry; cellular, tissue, and organ functions; and interaction with environmental factors. While many physiological processes are similar in trees and other plants, trees possess unique physiologies that help determine their outward appearance. These physiological processes include carbon relations (photosynthesis, carbohydrate allocation), cold and drought resistance, water relations, and mineral nutrition.

Three characteristics of trees that define their physiology are longevity, height, and simultaneous reproductive and vegetative growth. Trees have physiological processes that are more adaptable than those in the more specialized annual and biennial plants. Height allows trees to successfully compete for light, but at the same time this advantage creates transport and support problems. These problems were solved by the evolution of the woody stem which combines structure and function into a very strong transport system. Simultaneous vegetative and reproductive growth in adult trees causes significant competition for carbohydrates and nutrients, resulting in decreased vegetative growth. Trees accommodate both types of growth by having cyclical reproduction: one year many flowers and seeds are produced, followed by a year or more in which few or no flowers are produced.

Carbon relations. While biochemical processes of photosynthesis and carbon assimilation and allocation are the same in trees and other plants, the conditions under which these processes occur in trees are more variable and extreme. In evergreen species, photosynthesis can occur year round as long as the air temperature remains above freezing, while some deciduous species can photosynthesize in the bark of twigs and stem during the winter.

Carbon dioxide fixed into sugars moves through the tree in the phloem and xylem to tissues of high metabolism which vary with season and development. At the onset of growth in the spring, sugars are first mobilized from storage sites, primarily in the secondary xylem (wood) and phloem (inner bark) of the woody twigs, branches, stem, and roots. The sugars, stored as starch, are used to build new leaves and twigs, and if present, flowers. Once the new leaves expand, photosynthesis begins and sugars are produced, leading to additional leaf growth. Activation of the vascular cambium occurs at the same time, producing new secondary xylem and phloem. In late spring, the leaves begin photosynthesizing at their maximum rates, creating excess sugars which are translocated down the stem to support further branch, stem, and root growth. From midsummer through fall until leaf abscission (in deciduous trees) or until temperatures drop to freezing (in evergreen trees), sugars replenish the starch used in spring growth. Root growth may be stimulated at this time by sugar availability and warm soil temperatures. Throughout the winter, starch is used for maintenance respiration, but sparingly since low temperatures keep respiration rates low. *See* PHLOEM; PHOTOSYNTHESIS; XYLEM.

In adult trees, reproductive structures (flowers in angiosperms or strobili in gymnosperms) develop along with new leaves and represent large carbohydrate sinks. Sugars are preferentially utilized at the expense of leaf, stem, and root growth. This reduces the leaf area produced, affecting the amount of sugars produced during that year, thereby reducing vegetative growth even further. The reproductive structures are present throughout the growing season until seed dispersal and continually utilize sugars that would normally go to stem and root growth.

Cold resistance. The perennial nature of trees requires them to withstand low temperatures during the winter. Trees develop resistance to freezing through a process of physiological changes beginning in late summer. A tree goes through three sequential stages to become fully cold resistant. The process involves reduced cell hydration along with increased membrane permeability. The first stage is initiated by shortening days and results in shoot growth cessation, bud formation, and metabolic changes. Trees in this stage can survive temperatures down to 23°F (−5°C). The second stage requires freezing temperatures which alter cellular molecules. Starch breakdown is stimulated, causing sugar accumulation. Trees can survive temperatures as low as −13°F (−25°C) at this stage. The last stage occurs after exposure to very low temperatures (−22 to −58°F or −30 to −50°C), which increases soluble protein concentrations that bind cellular water, preventing ice crystallization. Trees can survive temperatures below −112°F (−80°C) in this stage. A few days of warmer temperatures, however, causes trees to revert to the second stage.

Water relations. Unlike annual plants that survive drought as seeds, trees have evolved traits that allow them to avoid desiccation. These traits include using water stored in the stem, stomatal closure, and shedding of leaves to reduce transpirational area. All the leaves can be shed and the tree survives on stored starch. Another trait of some species is to produce a long tap root that reaches the water table, sometimes tens of meters from the soil surface. On a daily basis, trees must supply water to the leaves for normal physiological function. If the water potential of the leaves drops too low, the stomata close, reducing photosynthesis. To maintain high water potential, trees use water stored in their stems during the morning which is recharged during the night. *See* PLANT-WATER RELATIONS.

Transport and support. Trees have evolved a means of combining long-distance transport between the roots and foliage with support through the production of secondary xylem (wood) by the vascular cambium. In older trees the stem represents 60–85% of the aboveground biomass. However, 90% of the wood consists of dead cells. These dead cells function in transport and support of the tree. As these cells develop and mature, they lay down thick secondary walls of cellulose and lignin that provide support, and then they die with the cell lumen becoming an empty tube. The interconnecting cells provide an efficient transport system, capable of moving 106 gal (400 liters) of water per day. The living cells in the wood (ray parenchyma) are the site of starch storage in woody stems and roots. *See* PLANT TRANSPORT OF SOLUTES.

Mineral nutrition. Nutrient deficiencies are similar in trees and other plants because of the functions of these nutrients in physiological processes. Tree nutrition is unique because trees require lower concentrations, and they are able to recycle nutrients within various tissues. Trees adapt to areas which are low in nutrients by lowering physiological functions and slowing growth rates. In addition, trees allocate more carbohydrates to root production, allowing them to exploit large volumes of soil in search of limiting nutrients. Proliferation of fine roots at the organic matter-mineral soil interface where many nutrients are released from decomposing organic matter allows trees to recapture nutrients lost by leaf fall. *See* PLANT MINERAL NUTRITION; PLANT PHYSIOLOGY; TREE.

[J.D.Jo.]

Triglyceride A simple lipid. Triglycerides are fatty acid triesters of the trihydroxy alcohol glycerol which are present in plant and animal tissues, particularly in the food storage depots, either as simple esters in which all the fatty acids are the same or as mixed esters in which the fatty acids are different. The triglycerides constitute the main component of natural fats and oils.

The generic formula of a triglyceride is shown below, where RCO_2H, $R'CO_2H$, and

$$CH_2 - OOC - R$$
$$|$$
$$CH - OOC - R'$$
$$|$$
$$CH_2 - OOC - R''$$

$R''CO_2H$ represent molecules of either the same or different fatty acids, such as butyric or caproic (short chain), palmitic or stearic (long chain), oleic, linoleic, or linolenic (unsaturated). Saponification with alkali releases glycerol and the alkali metal salts of the fatty acids (soaps). The triglycerides in the food storage depots represent a concentrated energy source, since oxidation provides more energy than an equivalent weight of protein or carbohydrate. *See* LIPID METABOLISM.

The physical and chemical properties of fats and oils depend on the nature of the fatty acids present. Saturated fatty acids give higher-melting fats and represent the main constituents of solid fats, for example, lard and butter. Unsaturation lowers the melting point of fatty acids and fats. Thus, in the oil of plants, unsaturated fatty acids are present in large amounts, for example, oleic acid in olive oil and linoleic and linolenic acids in linseed soil. *See* LIPID.

[R.H.G.; H.E.Ca.]

Trophic ecology The study of the structure of feeding relationships among organisms in an ecosystem. Researchers focus on the interplay between feeding relationships and ecosystem attributes such as nutrient cycling, physical disturbance, or the rate of tissue production by plants and the accrual of detritus (dead organic material). Feeding or trophic relationships can be represented as a food web or as a food chain. Food webs depict trophic links between all species sampled in a habitat, whereas food chains simplify this complexity into linear arrays of interactions among trophic levels. Thus, trophic levels (for example, plants, herbivores, detritivores, and carnivores) are amalgamations of species that have similar feeding habits. (However, not all species consume prey on a single trophic level. Omnivores are species that feed on more than one trophic level.) *See* ECOLOGY; ECOSYSTEM; FOOD WEB.

The three fundamental questions in the field of trophic ecology are: (1) What is the relationship between the length of food chains and plant biomass (the relative total amount of plants at the bottom of the food chain)? (2) How do resource supply to producers (plants) and resource demand by predators determine the relative abundance of organisms at each trophic level in a food chain? (3) How long are real food chains, and what factors limit food chain length?

A central theory in ecology is that "the world is green" because carnivores prevent herbivores from grazing green plant biomass to very low levels. Trophic structure (the number of trophic levels) determines trophic dynamics (as measured by the impact of herbivores on the abundance of plants). Indirect control of plant biomass by a top predator is called a trophic cascade. Cascades have been demonstrated to varying degrees in a wide variety of systems, including lakes, streams, subtidal kelp forests, coastal shrub habitats, and old fields. In all of these systems, the removal of a top predator has been shown to precipitate dramatic reductions in the abundance of species at lower trophic levels. Food chain theory predicts a green world when food chains have odd numbers of trophic levels, but a barren world (plants suppressed by herbivores) in systems with even numbers of trophic levels.

Although predators often have strong indirect effects on plant biomass as a result of trophic cascades, both predation (a top-down force) and resource supply to producers (a bottom-up force) play strong roles in the regulation of plant biomass. The supply of inorganic nutrients at the bottom of a food chain is an important determinant of the rate at which the plant trophic level produces tissue (primary production, or productivity). However, the degree to which nutrient supply enhances plant biomass accrual depends on two factors: (1) how many herbivores are present (which in turn depends on how many trophic levels there are in the system) and (2) the degree to which the herbivores can respond to increases in plant productivity and control plant biomass. The relative importance of top-down (demand) versus bottom-up (supply) forces is well illustrated by lake systems, in which the supply of phosphorus (bottom-up force) and the presence of piscivorous (fish-eating) fish (top-down force) have significant effects on the standing stock of phytoplankton, the plant trophic level in lake water columns. *See* BIOLOGICAL PRODUCTIVITY; BIOMASS; FRESH-WATER ECOSYSTEM; PHYTOPLANKTON.

Increases in productivity may act to lengthen food chains. However, food chain length may be limited by the efficiency at which members of each trophic level assimilate energy as it moves up the food chain; the resilience of the chain (measured as the inverse of the time required for all trophic levels to return to previous abundance levels after a disturbance); and the size of the ecosystem—small habitats are simply not large enough to support the home range or provide ample habitat for larger carnivorous species. *See* ECOLOGICAL ENERGETICS; SYSTEMS ECOLOGY; THEORETICAL ECOLOGY.   [J.L.S.; L.R.G.]

Tuberculosis   An infectious disease caused by the bacillus *Mycobacterium tuberculosis*. It is primarily an infection of the lungs, but any organ system is susceptible, so its manifestations may be varied. Effective therapy and methods of control and prevention of tuberculosis have been developed, but the disease remains a major cause of mortality and morbidity throughout the world. The treatment of tuberculosis has been complicated by the emergence of drug-resistant organisms, including multiple-drug-resistant tuberculosis, especially in those with HIV infection. *See* ACQUIRED IMMUNE DEFICIENCY SYNDROME (AIDS).

Mycobacterium tuberculosis is transmitted by airborne droplet nuclei produced when an individual with active disease coughs, speaks, or sneezes. When inhaled, the droplet nuclei reach the alveoli of the lung. In susceptible individuals the organisms may then multiply and spread through lymphatics to the lymph nodes, and through the bloodstream to other sites such as the lung apices, bone marrow, kidneys, and meninges.

The development of acquired immunity in 2 to 10 weeks results in a halt to bacterial multiplication. Lesions heal and the individual remains asymptomatic. Such an individual is said to have tuberculous infection without disease, and will show a positive tuberculin test. The risk of developing active disease with clinical symptoms and positive cultures for the tubercle bacillus diminishes with time and may never occur, but is a lifelong risk. Only 5% of individuals with tuberculous infection progress to active disease. Progression occurs mainly in the first 2 years after infection; household contacts and the newly infected are thus at risk.

Many of the symptoms of tuberculosis, whether pulmonary disease or extrapulmonary disease, are nonspecific. Fatigue or tiredness, weight loss, fever, and loss of appetite may be present for months. A fever of unknown origin may be the sole indication of tuberculosis, or an individual may have an acute influenzalike illness. Erythema nodosum, a skin lesion, is occasionally associated with the disease.

The lung is the most common location for a focus of infection to flare into active disease with the acceleration of the growth of organisms. There may be complaints of cough, which can produce sputum containing mucus, pus- and, rarely, blood. Listening to the lungs may disclose rales or crackles and signs of pleural effusion (the escape of fluid into the lungs) or consolidation if present. In many, especially those with small infiltration, the physical examination of the chest reveals no abnormalities.

Miliary tuberculosis is a variant that results from the blood-borne dissemination of a great number of organisms resulting in the simultaneous seeding of many organ systems. The meninges, liver, bone marrow, spleen, and genitourinary system are usually involved. The term miliary refers to the lung lesions being the size of millet seeds (about 0.08 in. or 2 mm). These lung lesions are present bilaterally. Symptoms are variable.

Extrapulmonary tuberculosis is much less common than pulmonary disease. However, in individuals with AIDS, extrapulmonary tuberculosis predominates, particularly with lymph node involvement. Fluid in the lungs and lung lesions are other common manifestations of tuberculosis in AIDS. The lung is the portal of entry, and an extrapulmonary focus, seeded at the time of infection, breaks down with disease occurring.

Development of renal tuberculosis can result in symptoms of burning on urination, and blood and white cells in the urine; or the individual may be asymptomatic. The symptoms of tuberculous meningitis are nonspecific, with acute or chronic fever, headache, irritability, and malaise.

A tuberculous pleural effusion can occur without obvious lung involvement. Fever and chest pain upon breathing are common symptoms.

Bone and joint involvement results in pain and fever at the joint site. The most common complaint is a chronic arthritis usually localized to one joint. Osteomyelitis is also usually present.

Pericardial inflammation with fluid accumulation or constriction of the heart chambers secondary to pericardial scarring are two other forms of extrapulmonary disease.

The principal methods of diagnosis for pulmonary tuberculosis are the tuberculin skin test (an intracutaneous injection of purified protein derivative tuberculin is performed, and the injection site examined for reactivity), sputum smear and culture, and the chest x-ray. Culture and biopsy are important in making the diagnosis in extrapulmonary disease.

A combination of two or more drugs is used in the initial therapy of tuberculous disease. Drug combinations are used to lessen the chance of drug-resistant organisms surviving. The preferred treatment regimen for both pulmonary and extrapulmonary tuberculosis is a 6-month regimen of the antibiotics isoniazid, rifampin, and pyrazinamide given for 2 months, followed by isoniazid and rifampin for 4 months. Because of the problem of drug-resistant cases, ethambutol can be included in the initial regimen until the results of drug susceptibility studies are known. Once treatment is started, improvement occurs in almost all individuals. Any treatment failure or individual relapse is usually due to drug-resistant organisms. *See* Drug resistance.

The community control of tuberculosis depends on the reporting of all new suspected cases so case contacts can be evaluated and treated appropriately as indicated. Individual compliance with medication is essential. Furthermore, measures to enhance compliance, such as directly observed therapy, may be necessary. *See* Mycobacterial diseases.   [G.Lo.]

Tumor viruses   Viruses associated with tumors can be classified in two broad categories depending on the nucleic acid in the viral genome and the type of strategy to induce malignant transformation.

RNA viruses. The ribonucleic acid (RNA) tumor viruses are retroviruses. When they infect cells, the viral RNA is copied into deoxyribonucleic acid (DNA) by reverse transcription and the DNA is inserted into the host genome, where it persists and can be inherited by subsequent generation of cells. Transformation of the infected cells can be traced to oncogenes that are carried by the viruses but are not necessary for viral replication. The viral oncogenes are closely similar to cellular genes, the proto-oncogenes, which code for components of the cellular machinery that regulates cell proliferation, differentiation, and death. Incorporation into a retrovirus may convert proto-oncogenes into oncogenes in two ways: the gene sequence may be altered or truncated so that it codes for proteins with abnormal activity; or the gene may be brought under the control of powerful viral regulators that cause its product to be made in excess or in inappropriate circumstances. Retroviruses may also exert similar oncogenic effects by insertional mutation when DNA copies of the viral RNA are integrated into the host-cell genome at a site close to or even within proto-oncogenes. *See* Retrovirus.

RNA tumor viruses cause leukemias, lymphomas, sarcomas, and carcinomas in fowl, rodents, primates, and other species. The human T-cell leukemia virus (HTLV) types I and II are endemic in Southeast Asian populations and cause adult T-cell leukemia and hairy-cell leukemia.

DNA viruses. DNA viruses replicate lytically and kill the infected cells. Transformation occurs in nonpermissive cells where the infection cannot proceed to viral replication. The transforming ability of DNA tumor viruses has been traced to several viral proteins that cooperate to stimulate cell proliferation, overriding some of the normal growth control mechanisms in the infected cell and its progeny. Unlike retroviral oncogenes, DNA virus oncogenes are essential components of the viral genome and have no counterpart in the normal host cells. Some of these viral proteins bind to the protein products of two key tumor suppressor genes of the host cells, the retinoblastoma gene and the p53 gene, deactivating them and thereby permitting the cell to replicate its DNA and divide. Other DNA virus oncogenes interfere with the expression of cellular genes either directly or via interaction with regulatory factors. There is often a delay of several years between initial viral infection in the natural host species and the development of cancer, indicating that, in addition to virus-induced transformation, other environmental factors and genetic accidents are involved. A specific or general impairment of the host immune responses often plays an important role.

DNA tumor viruses belong to the families of papilloma, polyoma, adeno, hepadna, and herpes viruses and produce tumors of different types in various species. DNA tumor viruses are thought to play a role in the pathogenesis of about 15–20% of human cancers. These include Burkitt's lymphoma, nasopharyngeal carcinoma, immunoblastic lymphomas in immunosuppressed individuals and a proportion of Hodgkin's lymphomas that are all associated with the Epstein-Barr virus of the herpes family; and liver carcinoma associated with chronic hepatitis B virus infection. *See* ANIMAL VIRUS; EPSTEIN-BARR VIRUS; MUTATION.

[M.G.Ma.]

Tundra   An area supporting some vegetation beyond the northern limit of trees, between the upper limit of trees and the lower limit of perennial snow on mountains, and on the fringes of the Antarctic continent and its neighboring islands. The term is of Lapp or Russian origin, signifying treeless plains of northern regions. Biologists, and particularly plant ecologists, sometimes use the term tundra in the sense of the vegetation of the tundra landscape. Tundra has distinctive characteristics as a kind of landscape and as a biotic community, but these are expressed with great differences according to the geographic region.

Characteristically tundra has gentle topographic relief, and the cover consists of perennial plants a few inches to a few feet or a little more in height. The general appearance during the growing season is that of a grassy sward in the wetter areas, a matted spongy turf on mesic sites, and a thin or sparsely tufted lawn or lichen heath on dry sites. In winter, snow mantles most of the surface. By far, most tundra occurs where the mean annual temperature is below the freezing point of water, and perennial frost (permafrost) accumulates in the ground below the depth of annual thaw and to depths at least as great as 1600 ft (500 m).

[W.S.B.]

Twins (human)   Two babies born to a mother at one birth. There are two types of twins, monozygotic and dizygotic. Members of a twin pair are called co-twins.

Controversy surrounding the definition of a twin arose with the advent of reproductive technologies enabling the simultaneous fertilization of eggs, with separate implantation. The unique "twinlike" relationships that would result between parents and cloned children (who would be genetically identical to their parents) also challenge current conceptions of twinship. Monozygotic twins are clones (genetically identical individuals derived from a single fertilized egg), but parents and cloned children would not be twins for several reasons, such as their differing prenatal and postnatal environments.

Monozygotic twins. The division of a single fertilized egg (or zygote) between 1 and 14 days postconception results in monozygotic twins. They share virtually all their genes and, with very rare exception due to unusual embryological events, are of the same sex. A common assumption is that because monozygotic co-twins have a shared heredity, their behavioral or physical differences are fully explained by environmental factors. However, monozygotic twins are never exactly alike in any measured trait, and may even differ for genetic reasons.

Sometimes chromosomes fail to separate after fertilization, causing some cells to contain the normal chromosome number (46) and others to contain an abnormal number. This process, mosaicism, results in monozygotic co-twins who differ in chromosomal constitution. There are several other intriguing variations of monozygotic twinning. Splitting of the zygote after day 7 or 8 may lead to mirror-image reversal in certain traits, such as handedness or direction of hair whorl. The timing of zygotic division has also been associated with placentation. Monozygotic twins resulting from earlier zygotic division have separate placentae and fetal membranes (chorion and amnion), while monozygotic twins resulting from later zygotic division share some or all of these structures. Should the zygote divide after 14 days, the twins may fail to separate completely.

This process, known as conjoined twinning, occurs in approximately 1 monozygotic twin birth out of 200. The many varieties of conjoined twins differ as to the nature and extent of their shared anatomy. Approximately 70% of such twins are female. There do not appear to be any predisposing factors to conjoined twinning. *See* MOSAICISM.

Dizygotic twins. Dizygotic twins result when two different eggs undergo fertilization by two different spermatozoa, not necessarily at the same time. Dizygotic twins share, on average, 50% of their genes, by descent, so that the genetic relationship between dizygotic co-twins is exactly the same as that of ordinary brothers or sisters. Dizygotic twins may be of the same or opposite sex, outcomes that occur with approximately equal frequency.

There are some unusual variations of dizygotic twinning. There is the possibility of polar body twinning, whereby divisions of the ovum prior to fertilization by separate spermatozoa could result in twins whose genetic relatedness falls between that of monozygotic and dizygotic twins. Blood chimerism, another variation, refers to the presence of more than one distinct red blood cell population, derived from two zygotes, and has been explained by connections between two placentae. In humans, chimerism can occur in dizygotic twins. Superfecundation is the conception of dizygotic twins following separate fertilizations, usually within several days, in which case each co-twin could have a different father. Superfetation, which refers to multiple conceptions occurring several weeks or even one month apart, may be evidenced by delivery of full-term infants separated by weeks or months and by the birth or abortion of twin infants displaying differential developmental status.

Epidemiology. According to conventional twinning rates, monozygotic twins represent approximately one-third of twins born in Caucasian populations and occur at a rate of 3–4 per 1000 births. The biological events responsible for monozygotic twinning are not well understood. It is generally agreed that monozygotic twinning occurs randomly and not as a genetically transmitted tendency. Some recent evidence from Sweden suggests an increased tendency for mothers who are monozygotic twins to bear same-sex twins themselves; further work will be needed to resolve this question.

Dizygotic twinning represents approximately two-thirds of twins born in Caucasian populations. The dizygotic twinning rate is lowest among Asian populations (2 per 1000 births), intermediate among Caucasian populations (8 per 1000 births), and highest among African populations (50 per 1000 births in parts of Nigeria). The natural twinning rate increases with maternal age, up to between 35 and 39 years, and then declines. Dizygotic twinning has also been linked to increased parity, or the number of children to which a woman has previously given birth. Mothers of dizygotic twins are also significantly taller and heavier, on average, than mothers of monozygotic twins and singletons. Dizygotic twinning appears to be genetically influenced, although the pattern of transmission within families is unknown.

Twinning rates have risen dramatically since about 1980 mainly due to advances in fertility treatments (for example, in vitro fertilization and ovulation induction), but also due to delays in the child-bearing years. The increase has mainly involved dizygotic twinning in which multiple ovulation and maternal age matter.   [N.L.S.]

U

Urea A colorless crystalline compound, formula CH_4N_2O, melting point $132.7°C$ ($270.9°F$). Urea is also known as carbamide and carbonyl diamide, and has numerous trade names as well. It is highly soluble in water and is odorless in its purest state, although most samples of even high purity have an ammonia odor. The diamide of carbonic acid, urea has the structure below.

$$H_2N - \overset{\overset{O}{\|}}{C} - NH_2$$

Urea occurs in nature as the major nitrogen-containing end product of protein metabolism by mammals, which excrete urea in the urine. The adult human body discharges almost 50 g (1.8 oz) of urea daily. Urea was first isolated in 1773 by G. F. Rouelle. By preparing urea from potassium cyanate (KCNO) and ammonium sulfate (NH_4SO_4) in 1828, F. Wöhler achieved a milestone, the first synthesis of an organic molecule from inorganic starting materials, and thus heralded the modern science of organic chemistry. *See* NITROGEN; PROTEIN METABOLISM.

Because of its high nitrogen content (46.65% by weight), urea is a popular fertilizer. About three-fourths of the urea produced commercially is used for this purpose. After application to soil, usually as a solution in water, urea gradually undergoes hydrolysis to ammonia (or ammonium ion) and carbonate (or carbon dioxide). Another major use of urea is as an ingredient for the production of urea-formaldehyde resins, extremely effective adhesives used for laminating plywood and in manufacturing particle board, and the basis for such plastics as malamine. *See* FERTILIZER; UREA-FORMALDEHYDE RESINS.

Other uses of urea include its utilization in medicine as a diuretic. In the past, it was used to reduce intracranial and intraocular pressure, and as a topical antiseptic. It is still used for these purposes, to some extent, in veterinary medicine and animal husbandry, where it also finds application as a protein feed supplement for cattle and sheep. Urea has been used to brown baked goods such as pretzels. It is a stabilizer for nitrocellulose explosives because of its ability to neutralize the nitric acid that is formed from, and accelerates, the decomposition of the nitrocellulose. Urea was once used for flameproofing fabrics. Mixed with barium hydroxide, urea is applied to limestone monuments to slow erosion by acid rain and acidic pollutants. [R.D.Wa.]

Uric acid The main excretory end product of protein metabolism in certain species of birds and reptiles. In mammals, uric acid is derived from purines; in higher primates, including humans, it is excreted as such and is not oxidized to allantoin, the main excretory purine metabolism product of most species. In humans, uric acid levels are increased following excessive intake of dietary purines, primary synthesis in certain diseases (gout, Lesch-Nyhan syndrome), endogenous nucleic acid metabolism (leukemia, an abnormal number of erythrocytes in blood, chemotherapy-induced tumor lysis), and restricted renal excretion (renal diseases, ketoacidosis, lacticidosis, diuretics). Uric acid levels are lowered by the use of drugs causing increased uric acid excretion, and by renal tubular defects. *See* Liver; Nucleic acid; Protein metabolism; Purine.   [M.K.S.]

Urinary system   The urinary system consists of the kidneys, urinary ducts, and bladder. Similarities are not particularly evident among the many and varied types of excretory organs found among vertebrates. The variations that are encountered are undoubtedly related to problems with which vertebrates have had to cope in adapting to different environmental conditions.

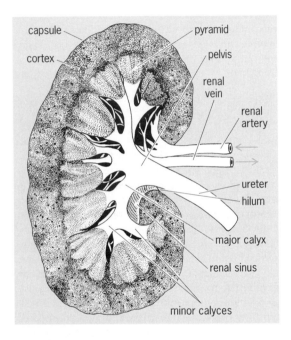

Fig. 1. Sagittal section of a human metanephric kidney (semidiagrammatic). (*After C. K. Weichert and W. Presch, Elements of Chordate Anatomy, 4th ed., McGraw-Hill, 1975*)

Kidneys. In reptiles, birds, and mammals three types of kidneys are usually recognized: the pronephros, mesonephros, and metanephros. These appear in succession during embryonic development, but only the metanephros persists in the adult.

The metanephric kidneys of reptiles lie in the posterior part of the abdominal cavity, usually in the pelvic region. They are small, compact, and often markedly lobulated. The posterior portion on each side is somewhat narrower. In some lizards the hind parts may even fuse. The degree of symmetry varies.

The kidneys of birds are situated in the pelvic region of the body cavity; their posterior ends are usually joined. They are lobulated structures with short ureters which open independently into the cloaca.

A rather typical mammalian metanephric kidney (Fig. 1) is a compact, bean-shaped organ attached to the dorsal body wall outside the peritoneum. The ureter leaves the medial side at a depression, the hilum. At this point a renal vein also leaves the kidney and a renal artery and nerves enter it. The kidneys of mammals are markedly lobulated in the embryo, and in many forms this condition is retained throughout life. *See* Kidney.

[C.K.W.]

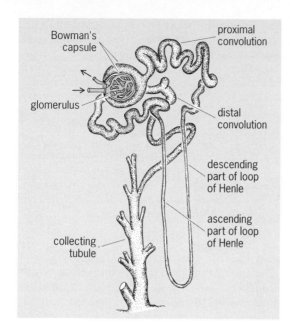

Fig. 2. A mammalian metanephric tubule, showing the renal corpuscle and secretory and collecting portions. (*After C. K. Weichert and W. Presch, Elements of Chordate Anatomy, 4th ed., McGraw-Hill, 1975*)

Urinary bladder. At or near the posterior ends of the nephric ducts there frequently is a reservoir for urine. This is the urinary bladder. Actually there are two basic varieties of bladders in vertebrates. One is found in fishes in which the reservoir is no more than an enlargement of the posterior end of each urinary duct. Frequently the urinary ducts are conjoined and a small bladder is formed by expansion of the common duct. The far more common type of bladder is that exhibited by tetrapods. This is a sac which originates embryonically as an outgrowth from the ventral side of the cloaca. Present in all embryonic life, it is exhibited differentially in adults. All amphibians retain the bladder, but it is lacking in snakes, crocodilians, and most lizards; birds, also, with the exception of the ostrich, lack a bladder. It is present in all mammals.

[T.W.T.]

Physiology. Urine is produced by individual renal nephron units which are fundamentally similar from fish to mammals (Fig. 2); however, the basic structural and functional pattern of these nephrons varies among representatives of the vertebrate classes in accordance with changing environmental demands. Kidneys serve the general function of maintaining the chemical and physical constancy of blood and other body fluids. The most striking modifications are associated particularly with the relative amounts of water made available to the animal. Alterations in degrees of glomerular development, in the structural complexity of renal tubules, and in the architectural disposition of the various nephrons in relation to one another within the kidneys may all represent adaptations made either to conserve or eliminate water.

Regulation of volume. Except for the primitive marine cyclostome *Myxine*, all modern vertebrates, whether marine, fresh-water, or terrestrial, have concentrations of salt in their blood only one-third or one-half that of seawater. The early development of the glomerulus can be viewed as a device responding to the need for regulating the volume of body fluids. Hence, in a hypotonic fresh-water environment the osmotic influx of water through gills and other permeable body surfaces would be kept in balance by a simple autoregulatory system whereby a rising volume of blood results in increased hydrostatic pressure which in turn elevates the rate of glomerular filtration. Similar devices are found in fresh-water invertebrates where water may be pumped out either as the result of work done by the heart, contractile vacuoles, or cilia found in such specialized "kidneys" as flame bulbs, solenocytes, or nephridia that extract excess water from the body cavity rather than from the circulatory system. Hence, these structures which maintain a constant water content for the invertebrate animal by balancing osmotic influx with hydrostatic output have the same basic parameters as those in vertebrates that regulate the formation of lymph across the endothelial walls of capillaries. *See* OSMOREGULATORY MECHANISMS.

Electrolyte balance. A system that regulates volume by producing an ultrafiltrate of blood plasma must conserve inorganic ions and other essential plasma constituents. The salt-conserving operation appears to be a primary function of the renal tubules which encapsulate the glomerulus. As the filtrate passes along their length toward the exterior, inorganic electrolytes are extracted from them through highly specific active cellular resorptive processes which restore plasma constituents to the circulatory system.

Movement of water. Concentration gradients of water are attained across cells of renal tubules by water following the active movement of salt or other solute. Where water is free to follow the active resorption of sodium and covering anions, as in the proximal tubule, an isosmotic condition prevails. Where water is not free to follow salt, as in the distal segment in the absence of antidiuretic hormone, a hypotonic tubular fluid results.

Nitrogenous end products. Of the major categories of organic foodstuffs, end products of carbohydrate and lipid metabolism are easily eliminated mainly in the form of carbon dioxide and water. Proteins, however, are more difficult to eliminate because the primary derivative of their metabolism, ammonia, is a relatively toxic compound. For animals living in an aquatic environment ammonia can be eliminated rapidly by simple diffusion through the gills. However, when ammonia is not free to diffuse into an effectively limitless aquatic environment, its toxicity presents a problem, particularly to embryos of terrestrial forms that develop wholly within tightly encapsulated eggshells or cases. For these forms the detoxication of ammonia is an indispensable requirement for survival. During evolution of the vertebrates two energy-dependent biosynthetic pathways arose which incorporated potentially toxic ammonia into urea and uric acid molecules, respectively. Both of these compounds are relatively harmless, even in high concentrations, but the former needs a relatively large amount of water to ensure its elimination, and uric acid requires a specific energy-demanding tubular secretory process to ensure its efficient excretion. *See* UREA; URIC ACID.

Urine concentration. The unique functional feature of the mammalian kidney is its ability to concentrate urine. Human urine can have four times the osmotic concentration of plasma, and some desert rats that survive on a diet of seeds without drinking any water have urine/plasma concentration ratios as high as 17. More aquatic forms such as the beaver have correspondingly poor concentrating ability.

The concentration operation depends on the existence of a decreasing gradient of solute concentration that extends from the tips of the papillae in the inner medulla of the kidney outward toward the cortex. The high concentration of medullary solute is achieved by a double hairpin countercurrent multiplier system which is powered by the active removal of salt from urine while it traverses the ascending limb of Henle's loop (Fig. 2). The salt is redelivered to the tip of the medulla after it has diffused back into the descending limb of Henle's loop. In this way a hypertonic condition is established in fluid surrounding the terminations of the collecting ducts. Urine is concentrated by an entirely passive process as water leaves the lumen of collecting ducts to come

into equilibrium with the hypertonic fluid surrounding its terminations. *See* URINE.
[R.P.F.]

Urine   An aqueous solution of organic and inorganic substances, mostly waste products of metabolism. The kidneys maintain the internal milieu of the body by excreting these waste products and adjusting the loss of water and electrolytes to keep the body fluids relatively constant in amount and composition. The urine normally is clear and has a specific gravity of 1.017–1.020, depending upon the amount of fluid ingested, perspiration, and diet. The increase in specific gravity above that of water is due to the presence of dissolved solids, about 60% of which are organic substances such as urea, uric acid, creatinine, and ammonia; and 40% of which are inorganic substances such as sodium, chloride, calcium, potassium, phosphates, and sulfates. Its reaction is usually acid (pH 6) but this too varies with the diet. It usually has a faint yellow color due to a urochrome pigment, but the color varies depending upon the degree of concentration, and the ingestion of certain foods (for example, rhubarb) or cathartics. It usually has a characteristic aromatic odor, the cause of which is not known. *See* KIDNEY; UREA; URIC ACID; URINARY SYSTEM.
[R.Str.]

Urodela   One of the orders of the class Amphibia, also known as the Caudata. The members of this order are the tailed amphibians, or salamanders, and are distinguished superficially from the frogs and toads (order Anura) by the possession of a tail, and from the caecilians (order Apoda) by the possession of limbs. Salamanders resemble lizards in that members of both groups normally have a relatively elongate body, four limbs, and a tail. The similarity is however, only superficial. The most obvious external difference, the moist glandular skin of the amphibian and dry scaly skin of the reptile, is underlain by the numerous characters that distinguish reptiles from amphibians. *See* ANURA.

The vast majority of salamanders are well under a foot (0.3 m) in length. The largest is the giant salamander of Japan and China, which may attain a length of 5 ft (1.5 m). A close relative, the hellbender, which lives in streams in the eastern United States, grows to over 2 ft (0.6 m) in length.

Four well-developed limbs are typically present in salamanders, but the legs of the mud eel (*Amphiuma*) of the southeastern United States are very tiny appendages and of no use in locomotion. The sirens (*Siren* and *Pseudobranchus*), also aquatic salamanders of the same region, have undergone even further degeneration of the limbs and retain only tiny forelimbs. Salamanders with normal limbs usually have four toes on the front feet and five on the rear, though a few have only four on all feet. A feature of the Urodela not shared with the Anura is the ability to regenerate limbs.

The moist and highly vascularized skin of a salamander serves as an organ of respiration, and in some forms shares with the buccal region virtually the whole burden. In one entire family of salamanders, the Plethodontidae, lungs are not present. Even in those forms with lungs and gills, dermal respiration plays a very important part. The tympanum is absent in salamanders and the middle ear is degenerate. Hence these animals are deaf to airborne sounds. Undoubtedly correlated with this is the reduction of voice; salamanders are mute or produce only slight squeaking or, rarely, barking sounds when annoyed. However, salamanders can detect sounds carried through ground or water.

Salamanders live in a variety of aquatic or moist habitats. Many forms are wholly aquatic, living in streams, rivers, lakes, and ponds. Others live on land most of the year but must return to water to breed. The most advanced species live out their lives in moist places on land or, in the case of some tropical species, in trees, and never go in the water.

Producing the young alive rather than by laying eggs is very rare among salamanders. The eggs of salamanders may be deposited in water or in moist places on land. Presumably, aquatic breeding is the more primitive. Fertilization is external in most of the Cryptobranchoidea, internal by means of spermatophores in the remaining suborders.

About 300 species of salamanders are known to be living today, and these are distributed among about 54 genera. The greatest concentration of families and genera of salamanders is found in the eastern United States, and these animals are one of the few major groups of vertebrate animals that is distinctly nontropical. No salamander occurs south of the Equator in the Old World, and only 18 species of the evolutionarily advanced family Plethodontidae are found as far south as South America in the New World. *See* AMPHIBIA.   [R.G.Z.]

Uterus   The hollow, muscular womb, being an enlarged portion of the oviduct in the adult female. An adult human uterus, before pregnancy, measures $3 \times 2 \times 1$ in. ($7.5 \times 5 \times 2.5$ cm) in size and has the shape of an inverted, flattened pear. The paired Fallopian tubes enter the uterus at its upper corners; the lower, narrowed portion, the cervix, projects into the vagina (see illustration). Normally the uterus is tilted slightly forward and lies behind the urinary bladder.

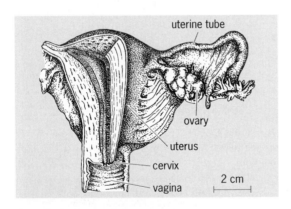

Human uterus and associated structures. (*After L. B. Arey, Developmental Anatomy, 7th ed., Saunders, 1965*)

The lining, or mucosa, responds to hormonal stimulation, growing in thickness with a tremendous increase in blood vessels during the first part of the menstrual cycle. If fertilization does not occur, the thickened vascular lining is sloughed off, producing the menstrual flow at the end of the cycle, and a new menstrual cycle begins with growth of the mucosa. When pregnancy occurs, the mucosa continues to thicken and forms an intimate connection with the implanted and enlarging placenta. *See* MENSTRUATION; REPRODUCTIVE SYSTEM.   [W.J.B.]

V

Vaccination Active immunization against a variety of microorganisms or their components, with the ultimate goal of protecting the host against subsequent challenge by the naturally occurring infectious agent. The terms vaccine and vaccination were originally used only in connection with Edward Jenner's method for preventing smallpox, introduced in 1796. In 1881 Louis Pasteur proposed that these terms should be used to describe any prophylactic immunization. Vaccination now refers to active immunization against a variety of bacteria, viruses, and parasites (for example, malaria and trypanosomes). *See* SMALLPOX.

Implicit within Jenner's method of vaccinating against smallpox was the recognition of immunologic cross-reactivity together with the notion that protection can be obtained through active immunization with a different, but related, live virus. It was not until the 1880s that the next immunizing agents, vaccines against rabies and anthrax, were introduced by Pasteur. Two facts of his experiments on rabies vaccines are particularly noteworthy.

First, Pasteur found that serial passage of the rabies agent in rabbits resulted in a weakening of its virulence in dogs. During multiple passages in an animal or in tissue culture cells, mutations accumulate as the virus adapts to its new environment. These mutations adversely affect virus reproduction in the natural host, resulting in lessened virulence. Only as the molecular basis for virulence has begun to be elucidated by modern biologists has it become possible to deliberately remove the genes promoting virulence so as to produce attenuated viruses.

Second, Pasteur demonstrated that rabies virus retained immunogenicity even after its infectivity was inactivated by formalin and other chemicals, thereby providing the paradigm for one class of noninfectious virus vaccine, the "killed"-virus vaccine.

Attenuated-live and inactivated vaccines are the two broad classifications for vaccines. Anti-idiotype antibody vaccines and deoxyribonucleic acid (DNA) vaccines represent innovations in inactivated vaccines. Recombinant-hybrid viruses are novel members of the live-virus vaccine class recently produced by genetic engineering.

Because attenuated-live-virus vaccines reproduce in the recipient, they provoke both a broader and more intense range of antibodies and T-lymphocyte-associated immune responses than noninfectious vaccines. Live-virus vaccines have been administered subdermally (vaccinia), subcutaneously (measles), intramuscularly (pseudorabies virus), intranasally (infectious bovine rhinotracheitis), orally (trivalent Sabin poliovirus), or by oropharyngeal aerosols (influenza). Combinations of vaccines have also been used. Live-virus vaccines administered through a natural route of infection often induce local immunity, which is a decided advantage. However, in the past, attenuated-live virus vaccines have been associated with several problems, such as reversion to virulence, natural spread to contacts, contaminating viruses, lability, and viral interference. *See* ANIMAL VIRUS; VIRULENCE; VIRUS CLASSIFICATION; VIRUS INTERFERENCE.

Noninfectious vaccines include inactivated killed vaccines, subunit vaccines, synthetic peptide and biosynthetic polypeptide vaccines, oral transgenic plant vaccines, anti-idiotype antibody vaccines, DNA vaccines, and polysaccharide-protein conjugate vaccines. With most noninfectious vaccines a suitable formulation is essential to provide the optimal antigen delivery for maximal stimulation of protective immune responses. Development of new adjuvant (a substance that enhances the potency of the antigen) and vector systems is pivotal to produce practical molecular vaccines. *See* ANTIBODY; ANTIGEN; IMMUNITY.   [S.Kit.]

Vacuole   An intracellular compartment, bounded by a single membrane bilayer, which functions as a primary site of protein and metabolite degradation and recycling in animals, but serves additional complex functions in fungi and plants (see illustration). Scientists who study vacuoles also define them as the terminal product of the secretory pathway. The secretory pathway functions to transport protein and metabolite-containing membrane vesicles from sites of synthesis or uptake to the vacuole. *See* CELL MEMBRANES; CELL METABOLISM; GOLGI APPARATUS; SECRETION.

In animals, a lytic vacuole known as the lysosome typically functions to process macromolecules. Such macromolecules can be targeted to the lysosome from sites of synthesis. For example, proteins that assemble incorrectly in the endoplasmic reticulum (ER) can be degraded in the lysosome and their constituent amino acids recycled. Proteins that can serve as nutrients are also targeted to the lysosome from the cell surface. An important process for the recycling of cytoplasm in eukaryotic cells is autophagy, in which molecules or organelles are encapsulated in membrane vesicles that fuse with the lysosome. *See* ENDOCYTOSIS; ENDOPLASMIC RETICULUM; LYSOSOME.

In the mammalian immune system, macrophages and neutrophils take up particles and pathogens in the process of phagocytosis, during which the pathogen is eventually digested in the lysosome. A number of diseases in humans can be caused when intracellular pathogens evade destruction in the lysosome. *See* PHAGOCYTOSIS.

In fungi, vacuoles can serve functions not found in animals. Besides a lytic function, they serve in the storage of ions as well as amino acids for protein synthesis. In yeast, vacuoles can also function in the destruction and recycling of cellular organelles, such

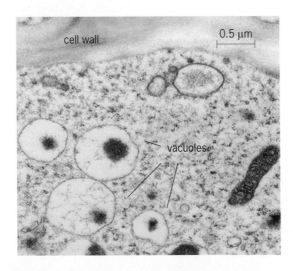

Electron micrograph of a barley root tip cell, showing multiple vacuoles within the cytoplasm.

as peroxisomes, which help protect the cell from toxic oxygen-containing molecules. The process of peroxisome digestion by vacuoles is known as pexophagy.

The most complex vacuoles are found in plants. Some contain hydrolytic enzymes and store ions similar to those found in lysosomes, whereas others serve a role in storing pigments which impart color to flowers to attract pollinators. Specialized ER-derived vacuoles in plant seeds, known as protein bodies, function in the storage of proteins called prolamines that are common in the endosperm of cereals. Upon germination, the proteins are degraded and used as a source of amino acids and nitrogen for the growing plant. Toxins, such as alkaloids, are stored in vacuoles in parts of the plant, such as the leaves, which are subject to frequent herbivory. Scientists have learned that plants produce and store in their vacuoles a vast array of unique chemicals which may, in addition to their natural functions, have medicinal value. *See* PLANT CELL.

Another unique function that vacuoles serve in plants is in cell growth. As a consequence of the accumulation of ions, metabolites, and water, plant vacuoles are under considerable internal osmotic pressure. The vacuolar membrane in plants, known as the tonoplast, as well as the cell itself would burst under this pressure if not for the rigid wall that surrounds the cells. The resulting turgor pressure provides mechanical stability to plant stems. Loss of osmotic pressure in the vacuole due to a lack of water results in plant wilting. The osmotic pressure of the vacuoles also provides the driving force that allows plants to grow by enlarging their cell volume. Enzymes reduce the rigidity of the cell wall, which permits cell expansion under the force of turgor. This is a fundamental process in plants and explains why vacuoles can occupy as much as 95% of the volume of some cells. *See* CELL WALLS (PLANT). [G.R.Hi.; N.Ra.]

Vernalization   The induction in plants of the competence or ripeness to flower by the influence of cold, that is, temperatures below the optimal temperature for growth. Vernalization thus concerns the first of the three phases of flower formation in plants. In the second stage, for which a certain photoperiod frequently is required, flowers are initiated. In the third stage flowers are unfolded. *See* FLOWER; PHOTOPERIODISM; PLANT GROWTH. [K.N.Z.]

Vertebrata   The major subphylum of the phylum Chordata, comprising the backboned animals, including humans. The subphylum is sometimes called the Craniata, because of the common possession of a cranium or braincase, but that term has dropped out of use in scientific nomenclature.

The characteristic features of the Vertebrata are a vertebral column, or backbone, and a cranium, which protects the central nervous system (brain and spinal cord) and major sense organs; the presence of bone, which is a tissue unique to vertebrates; and a neural crest of nerve cells that remain after the formation of the central nervous system. Other distinctive vertebrate features are a kidney, with the nephron as its functional unit; a heart; red and white blood cells; a liver and a pancreas; specialized sense organs, such as a complex eye, a lateral-line system, ears, and a sense of smell; several unique endocrine organs, such as the pituitary and thyroid; and a complex skin comprising an epidermis and dermis. *See* CHORDATA.

Vertebrates evolved from a lower chordate similar to the present-day Cephalochordata (amphioxus). They originated in fresh water and developed a kidney as their organ of water balance. They became free-swimming, with several evolutionary lines invading the oceans. The main line of evolution in the vertebrates, that which led to the tetrapods, remained in fresh waters.

The Vertebrata are divided into the following eight classes, which are arranged into several partly overlapping informal groups, and often two superclasses, Pisces and

Tetrapoda, are used to differentiate the aquatic and the terrestrial vertebrates. *See*
PISCES (ZOOLOGY).

Superclass Pisces	Superclass Tetrapoda
Class: Agnatha	Class: Amphibia
Placodermi	Reptilia
Chondrichthyes	Aves
Osteichthyes	Mammalia

The term Gnathostomata designates the seven classes of jawed vertebrates, in contrast to the jawless Agnatha. The Anamniota include the Pisces (fishes) and the Amphibia (amphibians). The Amniota consists of the Reptilia, Aves, and Mammalia. *See*
AMNIOTA; ANIMAL KINGDOM.   [W.J.B.]

Vertebrate brain (evolution)   A highly complex organ consisting of sensory and motor systems that constitutes part of the nervous system. Virtually all of
the brain systems that are found in mammals occur in birds, reptiles, and amphibians,
as well as in fishes and sharks. These systems have become more complex and sophisticated as the adaptive requirements of the animals changed. Occasionally, new
sensory systems arose, most likely as specializations of existing systems; however, some
of these disappeared as animals left the aquatic world. Some sensory systems arose
and declined several times in different lineages. In spite of the many changes in brain
structure, some of them quite dramatic, the evolution of the nervous system, from the
earliest vertebrates through to those of today, has been relatively conservative. *See*
NERVOUS SYSTEM (INVERTEBRATE); NERVOUS SYSTEM (VERTEBRATE).

Central nervous system.   The nervous system consists of two main divisions: the
central nervous system, which is made up of the brain and the spinal cord, and the
peripheral nervous system. The peripheral nervous system consists of the nerves that
bring information from the outside world via the sensory systems, and the nerves that
carry information from the body's interior to the spinal cord and brain. These nerves
also convey commands from the brain and spinal cord to the external muscles that
move the skeleton, as well as to various internal organs and glands. *See* CENTRAL
NERVOUS SYSTEM.

The brain consists of a variety of systems, some of which are sensory and deal
with the acquisition of information from the internal and external environments. Other
systems are motor and are involved with the movement of the skeletal muscles; the
muscles of the internal organs, such as the heart and the digestive and respiratory
systems; and the secretions of certain glands, such as the salivary and tear glands. The
bulk of the brain, however, is composed of systems that are integrative and organize,
coordinate, and direct the activities of the sensory and motor systems. These integrative
systems regulate such processes as sleep and wakefulness, attention, the coordination of
various muscle groups, emotion, social behavior, learning, memory, thinking, planning,
and other aspects of mental life. Social behavior itself is highly complex and includes
such interactions between individuals as courtship, mating, parental care, and the
organization and structure of groups of individuals. *See* BRAIN; MOTOR SYSTEMS.

Development.   The nervous system develops in the embryo as a hollow tube. The
remnants of this hollow tube in the adult are known as the brain ventricles and are
filled with the cerebrospinal fluid. Two types of overall brain organization are found
among vertebrates based on the relationship of the neurons to these ventricles. In
brains with laminar organization, the neurons have not migrated very far from the

layer immediately surrounding the hollow ventricular core of the brain. This type of organization is typical of amphibia and is also found in the brains of some sharks, fishes (especially those in which their skeletons are partly or mostly made of cartilage rather than bone), and lampreys. In contrast, in the brains of those vertebrates with the elaborated type of organization, the neurons have migrated from the zone around the ventricles to occupy nearly all of the interior of the brain. This type of organization is typical of reptiles, mammals, birds, fishes (with fully bony skeletons), as well as skates, rays, some sharks, and hagfishes.

In general, brain size or weight varies in proportion to the size of the body. In some species, however, brain size or weight is greater than would be expected for that body weight, for example, in humans, chimpanzees, and porpoises. Birds have brains that are comparable to those of mammals of equivalent body weight. In fact, crows have brain weights that would be expected of a small primate of equivalent body weight. In contrast to birds and mammals, amphibians, reptiles, and bony fishes have relatively small brains for their body weights, as do jawless fishes.

Subdivisions of brain. The brain is divided into a hindbrain, a midbrain, and a forebrain.

Hindbrain. The hindbrain is a region that contains nerve endings that receive information from the outside world and from the body interior; these are known as sensory cranial nerves. The neuron groups upon which they terminate are known as sensory cranial nuclei. Also found in the hindbrain are motor nerves that control internal and skeletal muscles and glands, which are called motor cranial nerves; the neuron groups from which they originate are known as motor cranial nerve nuclei.

Many animals possess senses that humans do not possess. One such is the lateral line sense, which derives from receptors located in the lateral line organ which can easily be seen on most bony fishes as a thin, horizontal line running the length of the body from behind the gill opening to the tail. Other lateral line organs can be found on the head and jaws. These organs contain mechanoreceptors that respond to low-frequency pressure waves that might be produced by other fishes nearby or the bow wave of a fast-swimming predator about to strike. Lateral line systems and a special region of the hindbrain dedicated to lateral line sense are found in fishes and sharks, jawless fishes, and bony fishes of various sorts.

Electroreception is another way of dealing with a murky environment. Scientists have described two types of electroreception: active and passive. The receptors are also located in the lateral line canals and sometimes on the skin. Animals with passive electroreception, such as sharks and rays, platypuses, and echidna, can detect the presence of the very weak electric fields that are generated around a living body, which they then follow to capture their prey. Animals with active electroreception generate stronger electric fields around themselves using specialized electric organs. By detecting changes in these electric fields, they can derive a picture of their environment. Electrosensory cranial nerves terminate in a region of the hindbrain known as the electrosensory area. A second group of active electrosensory fishes are capable of generating electric fields so powerful they can stun a prey or an enemy. Among these are the electric eel, the electric catfish, and an electric shark (the torpedo). These animals also use their low-level electric fields to detect objects and creatures in the environment.

Not only did the hindbrain change in response to sensory evolution, but it also underwent major motor transformations; for example, motor-neuron groups involved in swallowing, chewing, and salivating evolved as a consequence of the transition to land and the loss of the water column to carry food from the opening of the mouth into the throat.

The hindbrain also contains two important coordinating or integrating systems: the cerebellum and the reticular formation. The functions of the cerebellum are varied; they include the integration of a sense of balance with aspects of movement and motor learning and motor memory, as well as playing an important role in electrosensory reception.

The reticular formation coordinates the functions of various muscle groups. For example, the actions of the jaws and tongue must be coordinated so that an animal does not eat its own tongue while eating its meal. It also coordinates the motor-neuron groups that control the air column that enters and leaves the mouth and throat, which produces the various vocalizations of land animals, including speech. The reticular formation also is involved in sleep, wakefulness, and attention.

Midbrain. The midbrain contains the motor cranial nerves that move the eyes. It also contains neuron groups that are organized to form maps of visual space, auditory space, and the body. These maps are coordinated with each other such that a sudden, unexpected sound will cause the head and eyes to move to the precise region of space from which the sound originated. In those animals that make extensive use of sound localization, such as owls and bats, the map areas of the midbrain are very highly developed. In addition, certain snakes, such as rattlesnakes and boa constrictors, have infrared detectors on the snout or under the eyes that can sense the minute heat from a small animal's body at a distance of 1 m (3 ft) or more. The midbrains of these animals also have infrared maps that are in register with the auditory, visual, and body maps to permit the animal to correlate all the necessary information to make a successful strike on prey in virtually total darkness.

Forebrain. The forebrain is a very complex region that consists of the thalamus, the hypothalamus, the epithalamus, and the cerebrum or telencephalon. In addition, the forebrain contains the limbic system, which has components in all regions of the forebrain as well as continuing into the midbrain. The thalamus processes and regulates a large quantity of the information that enters and emanates from the forebrain. As the cerebrum increases in size and complexity in land animals, the thalamus increases accordingly. The hypothalamus regulates autonomic functions as well as behaviors such as feeding, drinking, courtship and reproduction, parental, territoriality, and emotional, which it controls in conjunction with the limbic system. The hypothalamus also regulates the endocrine system. The size and complexity of the hypothalamus, relative to the rest of the brain, is greatest in fishes and sharks; it declines considerably in proportion to the rest of the brain in land animals. The epithalamus contains the pineal gland, which is involved in various biological rhythms that depend on daylight, including seasonal changes. In some animals, such as certain reptiles, the pineal takes on the form of an eye, located on the top of the head and known as the parietal eye. This eye has a lens and a primitive retina that capture light and transmit information, such as the amount of daylight, to the hypothalamus. The epithalamus, like the hypothalamus, is relatively smaller in the brains of land animals.

The greatest evolutionary expansion of the forebrain is seen in the cerebrum. The cerebrum consists of an outer layer, the pallium, and a series of deep structures, known as the subpallium. The subpallium is composed of the corpus striatum, the amygdala, and the hippocampus. The outer layer of the cerebrum in mammals is known as the cerebral cortex. Considerable debate surrounds the evolutionary relationship between the cerebral cortex of mammals and the pallium and subpallium of nonmammals. Most specialists, however, seem to agree that the mammalian cortex arose from the pallium and certain regions of the subpallium. The cerebrum is relatively small in animals with laminar brains and larger in those with complex brains. Scientists have only begun to catalog the many complicated behavioral functions of the cerebrum. Among them appear to be memory, thinking and reasoning, and planning. With the advent of life on the land, the cerebrum underwent an extreme degree of elaboration in reptiles and birds and especially in mammals. *See* ENDOCRINE SYSTEM (VERTEBRATE).   [W.Ho.]

Vestibular system   The system that subserves the bodily functions of balance and equilibrium. It accomplishes this by assessing head and body movement and position in space, generating a neural code representing this information, and distributing this code to appropriate sites located throughout the central nervous system. Vestibular function is largely reflex and unconscious in nature.

The centrifugal flow of information begins at sensory hair cells located within the peripheral vestibular labyrinth. These hair cells synapse chemically with primary vestibular afferent nerve fibers, causing them to fire with a frequency code of action potentials that include the parameters of head motion and position. These vestibular afferents, in turn, enter the brain and terminate within the vestibular nuclei and cerebellum. Information carried by the firing patterns of these afferents is combined within these central structures with incoming sensory information from the visual, somatosensory, cognitive, and visceral systems to compute a central representation of head and body position in space. This representation is called the gravito-inortial vector and is an important quantity that the central nervous system employs to achieve balance and equilibrium. *See* BRAIN; NERVOUS SYSTEM (VERTEBRATE); POSTURAL EQUILIBRIUM; REFLEX.

The vestibular labyrinth is housed within the petrous portion of the temporal bone of the skull along with the cochlea, the organ of hearing (Fig. 1). The receptor element or primary motion sensor within the labyrinth is the hair cell (Fig. 2). Hair cells respond to bending of their apical sensory hairs by changing the electrical potential across their cell membranes. These changes are called receptor potentials, and the apical surface

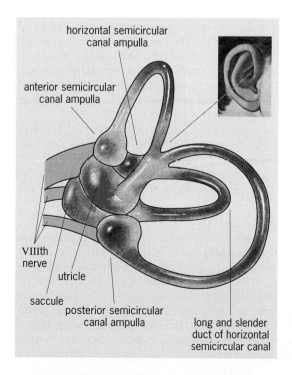

horizontal semicircular canal ampulla

anterior semicircular canal ampulla

VIIIth nerve

utricle

saccule

posterior semicircular canal ampulla

long and slender duct of horizontal semicircular canal

Fig. 1. The vestibular labyrinth is located within the inner ear. It communicates with the brain via the VIIIth nerve. Each of the three semicircular canals has an ampulla and a long and slender duct. The utricle primarily senses motion in an earth-parallel plane, while the saccule primarily senses motion and gravity in an earth-perpendicular plane.

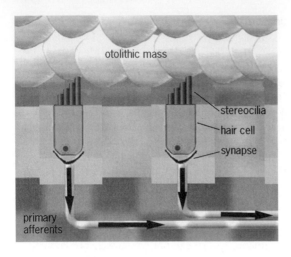

otolithic mass

stereocilia

hair cell

synapse

primary
afferents

Fig. 2. Otolithic macula at rest. The arrows within the primary afferents or VIIIth nerve fibers indicate spontaneous activity in these fibers in the absence of motion of the otolithic mass relative to the hair cell stereocilia. (The otolithic membrane is not illustrated for clarity.)

of the hair cell thus functions as a mechanical-to-electrical transducer. The frequency of the resulting action potentials in the VIIIth cranial (vestibulocochlear) nerve encodes the parameters of angular and linear motion. See BIOPOTENTIALS AND IONIC CURRENTS; EAR (VERTEBRATE); SYNAPTIC TRANSMISSION.

Hair cells are the common sensory element in both the angular and linear labyrinthine sensors as well as within the cochlea. The particular frequency of energy that hair cells sense within these diverse end organs arises because of the accessory structures surrounding the hair cells. Thus, angular motion is sensed by the semicircular canals, linear motion by the otolith organs, and sound energy by the cochlea.

The primary afferents innervated by hair cells are the peripheral processes of bipolar neurons having cell bodies located in Scarpa's ganglion within the internal auditory meatus. The central processes of these cells contact neurons in the brainstem of the central nervous system. The vestibular nuclei complex is defined as the brainstem region where primary afferents from the labyrinth terminate. It is composed of four main nuclei: the superior, medial, lateral, and descending nuclei. The axonal projections of vestibular nuclear neurons travel to all parts of the neuraxis, including the brainstem, cerebellum, spinal cord, and cerebrum. See MOTOR SYSTEMS.

In all vertebrates, there is an efferent system that originates from cell bodies within the central nervous system and terminates upon labyrinthine hair cells and primary afferents. The efferent vestibular system is presently a subject of intense study but undoubtedly is in place to enhance vestibular function. It is interesting that evolution felt it necessary to modify incoming vestibular information before it could enter the central nervous system.   [S.M.H.]

Vibrotaction   The response of tactile nerve endings to varying forces on the skin and to oscillatory motion of the skin. Grasping, holding, and tactile exploration of an object are part of everyday experience. The performance of all these activities is dependent on the dynamic response of specialized nerve endings located in the skin.

Knowledge of the neural and psychophysical processes involved in vibrotaction is necessary to develop effective tactile communication systems, such as vibrotactile pagers, and multipin vibrotactile stimulators used to produce images on an extended skin surface. Potential users range from business people to the visually and hearing impaired: potential applications range from activities involving visual and aural sensory saturation (such as pilots in high stress situations) to those requiring sensory stimulation (for example, virtual reality).

Small electrical impulses, or action potentials, generated by a single nerve ending can be recorded by inserting a microelectrode into the arm of an alert human subject and positioning the electrode tip in a nerve fiber. Studies of the action potentials produced when the skin is locally depressed at a fingertip have identified activity in four networks of distinctive nerve endings lying within 1–2 mm of the skin surface. These nerve endings, which transform skin motion into neural signals, consist of physically and functionally different mechanoreceptors.

Three types of mechanoreceptor in the fingertip have been implicated in vibrotaction. One of these is a population of slowly adapting mechanoreceptors (SA type I, or SAI); their action potentials persist for some time after a transient skin indentation. The two others are populations of rapidly adapting receptors (FAI and FAII types). Type I receptors respond only to skin indentation within a few millimeters of the nerve ending, whereas type II receptors also respond to stimuli at a greater distance from the nerve ending. A fourth mechanoreceptor type appears to respond primarily to skin stretch (denoted SAII). *See* CUTANEOUS SENSATION; MECHANORECEPTORS.   [A.J.Br.]

Viral inclusion bodies   Abnormal structures which appear within the cell nucleus, the cytoplasm, or both, during the course of virus multiplication. In general, the inclusion bodies are concerned with the developmental processes of the virus. In some virus infections, such as molluscum contagiosum, inclusion bodies may be simply masses of maturing virus particles. In other infections (herpes simplex), typical inclusion bodies do not appear until after the virus has multiplied. Such inclusions may be remnants of the process of virus multiplication.

The presence of inclusion bodies is often important in diagnosis. A cytoplasmic inclusion in nerve cells, the Negri body, is pathogenic for rabies. *See* RABIES; VIRUS.
[J.L.Me.]

Viroids   The smallest known agents of infectious disease. Conventional viruses are made up of nucleic acid encapsulated in protein (capsid), whereas viroids are uniquely characterized by the absence of a capsid. In spite of their small size, viroid ribonucleic acids (RNAs) can replicate and produce characteristic disease syndromes when introduced into cells. Viroids thus far identified are associated with plants.

Nine different viroids have been described from widely separated geographical locations and from an assortment of herbaceous and woody plants. Viroid infections in some plant species produce profound disease symptoms ranging from stunting and leaf epinasty to plant death, whereas infections in other species produce few detectable symptoms compared to uninoculated control plants. Viroids generally have a restricted host range, although several viroids can infect the same hosts and cause similar symptoms in these hosts. Good controls are not available for diseases caused by these small infectious agents other than indexing procedures to provide viroid-free propagules. *See* PLANT VIRUSES AND VIROIDS; VIRUS.   [R.K.Ho.]

Virulence   The ability of a microorganism to cause disease. Virulence and pathogenicity are often used interchangeably, but virulence may also be used to indicate the degree of pathogenicity. Scientific understanding of the underlying mechanisms of virulence has increased rapidly due to the application of the techniques of biochemistry, genetics, molecular biology, and immunology. Bacterial virulence is better understood than that of other infectious agents.

Virulence is often multifactorial, involving a complex interplay between the parasite and the host. Various host factors, including age, sex, nutritional status, genetic constitution, and the status of the immune system, affect the outcome of the parasite-host interaction. Hosts with depressed immune systems, such as transplant and cancer patients, are susceptible to microorganisms not normally pathogenic in healthy hosts. Such microorganisms are referred to as opportunistic pathogens. The attribute of virulence is present in only a small portion of the total population of microorganisms, most of which are harmless or even beneficial to humans and other animals. *See* OPPORTUNISTIC INFECTIONS.

The spread of an infectious disease usually involves the adherence of the invading pathogen to a body surface. Next, the pathogen multiplies in host tissues, resisting or evading various nonspecific host defense systems. Actual disease symptoms are from damage to host tissues caused either directly or indirectly by the microorganism's components or products.

Most genetic information in bacteria is carried in the chromosome. However, genetic information is also carried on plasmids, which are independently replicating structures much smaller than the chromosome. Plasmids may provide bacteria with additional virulence-related capabilities (such as pilus formation, iron transport systems, toxin production, and antibiotic resistance). In some bacteria, several virulence determinants are regulated by a single genetic locus. *See* BACTERIA; CELLULAR IMMUNOLOGY; PLASMID; VIRUS.   [B.Wi.]

Virus   Any of a heterogeneous class of agents that share three characteristics: (1) They consist of a nucleic acid genome surrounded by a protective protein shell, which may itself be enclosed within an envelope that includes a membrane; (2) they multiply only inside living cells, and are absolutely dependent on the host cells' synthetic and energy-yielding apparatus; (3) the initial step in multiplication is the physical separation of the viral genome from its protective shell, a process known as uncoating, which differentiates viruses from all other obligatorily intracellular parasites. In essence, viruses are nucleic acid molecules, that is, genomes that can enter cells, replicate in them, and encode proteins capable of forming protective shells around them. Terms such as "organism" and "living" are not applicable to viruses. It is preferable to refer to them as functionally active or inactive rather than living or dead.

The primary significance of viruses lies in two areas. First, viruses destroy or modify the cells in which they multiply; they are potential pathogens capable of causing disease. Many of the most important diseases that afflict humankind, including rabies, smallpox, poliomyelitis, hepatitis, influenza, the common cold, measles, mumps, chickenpox, herpes, rubella, hemorrhagic fevers, and the acquired immunodeficiency syndrome (AIDS) are caused by viruses. Viruses also cause diseases in livestock and plants that are of great economic importance. *See* ACQUIRED IMMUNE DEFICIENCY SYNDROME (AIDS); PLANT PATHOLOGY.

Second, viruses provide the simplest model systems for many basic problems in biology. Their genomes are often no more than one-millionth the size of, for example, the human genome; yet the principles that govern the behavior of viral genes are the same as those that control the behavior of human genes. Viruses thus afford unrivaled opportunities for studying mechanisms that control the replication and expression of genetic material. *See* HUMAN GENOME PROJECT.

Although viruses differ widely in shape and size (see illustration), they are constructed according to certain common principles. Basically, viruses consist of nucleic acid and protein. The nucleic acid is the genome which contains the information necessary for virus multiplication and survival, the protein is arranged around the genome in the

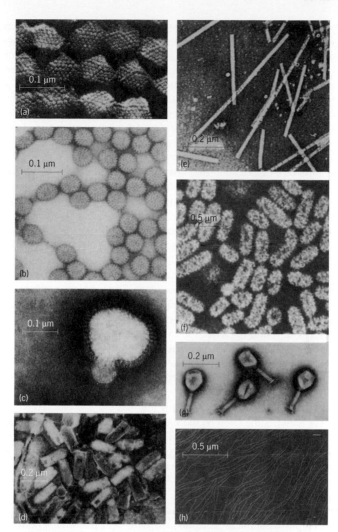

Electron micrographs of highly purified preparations of some viruses.
(*a*) Adenovirus. (*b*) Rotavirus. (*c*) Influenza virus (*courtesy of George Leser*). (*d*) Vesicular stomatitis virus. (*e*) Tobacco mosaic virus. (*f*) Alfalfa mosaic virus. (*g*) T4 bacteriophage. (*h*) M13 bacteriophage.

form of a layer or shell that is termed the capsid, and the structure consisting of shell plus nucleic acid is the nucleocapsid. Some viruses are naked nucleocapsids. In others, the nucleocapsid is surrounded by a lipid bilayer to the outside of which "spikes" composed of glycoproteins are attached; this is termed the envelope. The complete virus particle is known as the virion, a term that denotes both intactness of structure and the property of infectiousness.

Viral genomes are astonishingly diverse. Some are DNA, others RNA; some are double-stranded, others single-stranded; some are linear, others circular; some have plus polarity, other minus (or negative) polarity; some consist of one molecule, others of several (up to 12). They range from 3000 to 280,000 base pairs if double-stranded, and from 5000 to 27,000 nucleotides if single-stranded. *See* VIRUS CLASSIFICATION.

Viral genomes encode three types of genetic information. First, they encode the structural proteins of virus particles. Second, most viruses encode enzymes capable of transcribing their genomes into messenger RNA molecules that are then translated by host-cell ribosomes, as well as nucleic acid polymerases capable of replicating their genomes; many viruses also encode nonstructural proteins with catalytic and other functions necessary for virus particle maturation and morphogenesis. Third, many viruses encode proteins that interact with components of host-cell defense mechanisms against invading infectious agents. The more successful these proteins are in neutralizing these defenses, the more virulent viruses are.

The two most commonly observed virus-cell interactions are the lytic interaction, which results in virus multiplication and lysis of the host cell; and the transforming interaction, which results in the integration of the viral genome into the host genome and the permanent transformation or alteration of the host cell with respect to morphology, growth habit, and the manner in which it interacts with other cells. Transformed animal and plant cells are also capable of multiplying; they often grow into tumors, and the viruses that cause such transformation are known as tumor viruses. See RETROVIRUS; TUMOR VIRUSES.

There is little that can be done to interfere with the growth of viruses, since they multiply within cells, using the cells' synthetic capabilities. The process, interruption of which has met with the most success in preventing virus multiplication, is the replication of viral genomes, which is almost always carried out by virus-encoded enzymes that do not exist in uninfected cells and are therefore excellent targets for antiviral chemotherapy. Another viral function that has been targeted is the cleavage of polyproteins, precursors of structural proteins, to their functional components by virus-encoded proteases; this strategy is being used with some success in AIDS patients. See CYTOMEGALOVIRUS INFECTION; HERPES; INFLUENZA.

Antiviral agents on which much interest is focused are the interferons. Interferons are cytokines or lymphokines that regulate cellular genes concerned with cell division and the functioning of the immune system. Their formation is strongly induced by virus infection; they provide the first line of defense against viral infections until antibodies begin to form. Interferons interfere with the multiplication of viruses by preventing the translation of early viral messenger RNAs. As a result, viral capsid proteins cannot be formed and no viral progeny results.

By far the most effective means of preventing viral diseases is by means of vaccines. There are two types of antiviral vaccines, inactivated virus vaccines and attenuated active virus vaccines. Most of the antiviral vaccines currently in use are of the latter kind. The principle of antiviral vaccines is that inactivated virulent or active attenuated virus particles cause the formation of antibodies that neutralize a virulent virus when it invades the body. See ANIMAL VIRUS; PLANT VIRUSES AND VIROIDS; VACCINATION; VIRUS, DEFECTIVE.   [W.K.J.]

Virus, defective   A virus that by mutation has lost the ability to be replicated in the host cell without the aid of a helper virus. The virus particles (virions) contain all the viral structural components; they can attach, penetrate, and release their nucleic acid (RNA; DNA) within the host cell. However, since the mutation has destroyed an essential function, new virions will not be made unless the cell was simultaneously infected with the helper virus, which can provide the missing function. Only then will the cell produce a mixed population of new helper and defective viruses. Occasionally, when their nucleic acids become integrated in the DNA of the host cell, defective viruses persist in nature by propagation from mother cell to daughter cell. *See* ANIMAL VIRUS; MUTATION.

The most important group of defective viruses are deletion mutants. They are derived from their homologous nondefective (wild-type) virus through errors in the nucleic acid replication that result in the deletion of a fragment in the newly synthesized molecules. The defective nucleic acid must be capable of self-replication, at least in the presence of the wild-type virus, and must combine with other viral components to form a particle in order to exit the cell.

The defective RNA tumor viruses are deletion mutants. Mammalian and most avian sarcoma viruses require a nondefective leukemia virus as a helper virus. Usually the specificity for a certain type of host cell exhibited by the defective virion depends on the helper virus, indicating that one of the virion surface proteins has been furnished by the helper virus gene. These proteins are involved in interactions with cellular surface receptors, and thus determine whether a cell can serve as a host for viral infection.

[M.E.Re.]

Virus classification   There is no evidence that viruses possess a common ancestor or are in any way phylogenetically related. Nevertheless, classification along the lines of the Linnean system into families, genera, and species has been utilized. Based on the organisms they infect, the first broad division of viruses is into bacterial, plant, and animal viruses. Within these classes, other criteria for subdivision are used. Among these are general morphology; envelope or the lack of it; nature of the genome (DNA or RNA); structure of the genome (single- or double-stranded, linear or circular, fragmented or nonfragmented); mechanisms of gene expression and virus replication (positive- or negative-strand RNA); serological relationship; host and tissue susceptibility; pathology (symptoms, type of disease).

Animal viruses. The families of animal viruses are sometimes subdivided into subfamilies; the suffix -virinae may then be used. The subgroups of a family or subfamily are equivalent to the genera of the Linnean classification. *See* ANIMAL VIRUS.

The animal DNA viruses are divided into five families: Poxviridae, Herpesviridae, Adenoviridae, Papovaviridae, and Parvoviridae. RNA animal viruses may be either single-stranded or double-stranded. The single-stranded are further subdivided into positive-strand and negative-strand RNA viruses, depending on whether the RNA contains the messenger RNA (mRNA) nucleotide sequence or its complement, respectively. Further, the RNA genes may be located on one or several RNA molecules (nonfragmented or fragmented genomes, respectively). The positive-strand RNA animal viruses contain six families: Picornaviridae, Calciviridae, Coronaviridae, Togaviridae, Retroviridae, and Nodamuraviridae. The nucleocapsid of negative-strand RNA animal viruses contains an RNA-dependent RNA polymerase required for the transcription of the negative strand into the positive mRNAs. Virion RNA is neither capped nor polyadenylated. The group is divided into five families: Arenaviridae, Orthomyxoviridae, Paramyxoviridae, Rhabdoviridae, and Bunyaviridae. The double-stranded RNA animal viruses contain only one group, the Reoviridae.

Bacterial viruses. Bacterial viruses are also known as bacteriophages or phages. They may be tailed or nontailed. Nontailed phages are further subdivided into those with envelopes and those without. Tailed phages, which do not have envelopes, are divided into three families: Myoviridae, Styloviridae, and Pedoviridae. The group of nontailed DNA bacteriophages contains seven families, each with a distinctive morphology: Tectiviridae, Corticoviridae, Inoviridae, Microviridae, Leviviridae, Plasmaviridae, and Cystoviridae. Only the latter two families have envelopes. *See* BACTERIOPHAGE.

Plant viruses. Plant viruses are divided into groups, rather than families, except those which belong to families of rhabdo viridae and reoviridae. The group, and correspondingly subgroup and type, can be viewed as analogous to family, genus, and species, respectively. Most common among plant viruses are those with a single-stranded, capped but not polyadenylated, positive-strand RNA. *See* PLANT VIRUSES AND VIROIDS.   [M.E.Re.]

Virus interference   Inhibition of the replication of a virus by a previous infection with another virus. The two viruses may be unrelated, related, or identical. In some cases, virus interference may take place even if the first virus was inactivated. The term mutual exclusion has been applied to this phenomenon in bacterial viruses.

Several mechanisms of interference can be distinguished: (1) Inactivation of cell receptors by one virus may prevent subsequent adsorption and penetration by another virus. (2) The first virus may inhibit or modify cellular enzymes or proteins required for replication of the superinfecting virus. (3) The first virus may generate destructive enzymes or induce the cell to synthesize protective substances which prevent superinfection. (4) The first virus may generate defective interfering particles or mutants which may inhibit the replication of the infecting virus by competing with it for a protein (or enzyme) available in limited quantities; this type of viral interference has been called autointerference, and depends on a greater replicative efficiency of the defective interfering particles or mutants, compared to the infecting virus. *See* ANIMAL VIRUS; VIRULENCE; VIRUS; VIRUS, DEFECTIVE.   [M.E.Re.]

Vision   The sense of sight, which perceives the form, color, size, movement, and distance of objects. Of all the senses, vision provides the most detailed and extensive information about the environment. In the higher animals, especially the birds and primates, the eyes and the visual areas of the central nervous system have developed a size and complexity far beyond the other sensory systems.

Visual stimuli are typically rays of light entering the eyes and forming images on the retina at the back of the eyeball (Fig. 1). Human vision is most sensitive for light comprising the visible spectrum in the range 380–720 nanometers in wavelength. In general, light stimuli can be measured by physical means with respect to their energy, dominant wavelength, and spectral purity. These three physical aspects of the light are closely related to the perceived brightness, hue, and saturation, respectively.

Anatomical basis for vision. The anatomical structures involved in vision include the eyes, optic nerves and tracts, optic thalamus, primary visual cortex, and higher

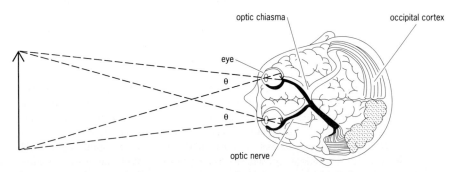

Fig. 1. Diagram showing the eyes and visual projection system. The visual angle θ is measured in degrees.

visual areas of the brain. The eyes are motor organs as well as sensory; that is, each eye can turn directly toward an object to inspect it. The two eyes are coordinated in their inspection of objects, and they are able to converge for near objects and diverge for far ones. Each eye can also regulate the shape of its crystalline lens to focus the rays from the object and to form a sharp image on the retina. Furthermore, the eyes can regulate the amount of light reaching the sensitive cells on the retina by contracting and expanding the pupil of the iris. These motor responses of the eyes are examples of involuntary action that is controlled by various reflex pathways within the brain. *See* EYE (VERTEBRATE).

The process of seeing begins when light passes through the eye and is absorbed by the photoreceptors of the retina. These cells are activated by the light in such a way that electrical potentials are generated. These potentials serve to generate nerve responses in various successive neural cells in the vicinity of excitation. Impulses emerge from the eye in the form of repetitive discharges in the fibers of the optic nerve, which do not mirror exactly the excitation of the photoreceptors by light. Complex interactions within the retina serve to enhance certain responses and to suppress others. Furthermore, each eye contains more than a hundred times as many photoreceptors as optic nerve fibers. Thus it would appear that much of the integrative action of the visual system has already occurred within the retina before the brain has had a chance to act.

The optic nerves from the two eyes traverse the optic chiasma. Figure 1 shows that the fibers from the inner (nasal) half of each retina cross over to the opposite side, while those from the outer (temporal) half do not cross over but remain on the same side. The effect of this arrangement is that the right visual field, which stimulates the left half of each retina, activates the left half of the thalamus and visual cortex. Conversely the left visual field affects the right half of the brain. This situation is therefore similar to that of other sensory and motor projection systems in which the left side of the body is represented by the right side of the brain and vice versa.

The visual cortex includes a projection area in the occipital lobe of each hemisphere. Here there appears to be a point-for-point correspondence between the retina of each eye and the cortex. Thus the cortex contains a "map" or projection area, each point of which represents a point in visual space as seen by each eye. Other important features of an object such as its color, motion, orientation, and shape are simultaneously perceived. The two retinal maps are merged to form the cortical projection area. This allows the separate images from the two eyes to interact with each other in stereoscopic vision, binocular color mixture, and other phenomena. In addition to the projection areas on the right and left halves of the cortex, there are visual association areas and other brain regions that are involved in vision. Complex visual acts, such as form recognition, movement perception, and reading, are believed to depend on widespread cortical activity beyond that of the projection areas. *See* BRAIN.

Scotopic and photopic vision. Night animals have eyes that are specialized for seeing with a minimum of light. This type of vision is called scotopic. Day animals have predominantly photopic vision. They require much more light for seeing, but their daytime vision is specialized for quick and accurate perception of fine details of color, form, and texture, and location of objects. Color vision, when it is present, is also a property of the photopic system. Human vision is duplex; humans are in the fortunate position of having both photopic and scotopic vision. Some of the chief characteristics of human scotopic and photopic vision are enumerated in the table.

Scotopic vision occurs when the rod receptors of the eye are stimulated by light. The outer limbs of the rods contain a photosensitive substance known as visual purple or rhodopsin. This substance is bleached away by the action of strong light so that the scotopic system is virtually blind in the daytime. In darkness, however, the rhodopsin

Characteristics of human vision		
Characteristic	Scotopic vision	Photopic vision
Photochemical substance	Rhodopsin	Cone pigments
Receptor cells	Rods	Cones
Speed of adaptation	Slow (30 min or more)	Rapid (8 min or less)
Color discrimination	No	Yes
Region of retina	Periphery	Center
Spatial summation	Much	Little
Visual acuity	Low	High
Number of receptors per eye	120,000,000	7,000,000
Cortical representation	Small	Large
Spectral sensitivity peak	505 nm	555 nm

is regenerated by restorative reactions based on the transport of vitamin A to the retina by the blood. One experiences a temporary blindness upon walking indoors on a bright day, especially into a dark room. As the eyes become accustomed to the dim light the scotopic system gradually begins to function. This process is known as dark adaptation. Complete dark adaptation is a slow process during which the rhodopsin is restored in the rods. A 10,000-fold increase in sensitivity of is often found to occur during a half-hour period of dark adaptation. By this time some of the rod receptors are so sensitive that only one photon is necessary to trigger each rod into action. Faulty dark adaptation or night blindness is found in persons who lack rod receptors or have a dietary deficiency in vitamin A. This scotopic vision is colorless or achromatic.

Normal photopic vision has the characteristics enumerated in the table. Emphasis is placed on the fovea centralis, a small region at the very center of the retina of each eye.

Foveal vision is achieved by looking directly at objects in the daytime. The image of an object falls within a region almost exclusively populated by cone receptors, closely packed together in the central fovea, each of which is provided with a series of specialized nerve cells that process the incoming pattern of stimulation and convey it to the cortical projection area. In this way the cortex is supplied with superbly detailed information about any pattern of light that falls within the fovea centralis.

Peripheral vision takes place outside the fovea centralis. Vision extends out to more than 90° from center, so that one can detect moving objects approaching from either side. This extreme peripheral vision is comparable to night vision in that it is devoid of sharpness and color.

There is a simple anatomical explanation for the clarity of foveal vision as compared with peripheral vision. The cones become less and less numerous in the retinal zones that are more and more remote from the fovea. In the extreme periphery there are scarcely any, and even the rods are more sparsely distributed. Furthermore, the plentiful neural connections from the foveal cones are replaced in the periphery by network connections in which hundreds of receptors may activate a single optic nerve fiber. This mass action is favorable for the detection of large or dim stimuli in the periphery or at night, but it is unfavorable for visual acuity (the ability to see fine details of an object) or color vision, both of which require the brain to differentiate between signals arriving from closely adjacent cone receptors.

Space and time perception. Vernier and stereoscopic discrimination are elementary forms of space perception. Here, the eye is required to judge the relative position of one object in relation to another (Fig. 2). The left eye, for example, sees the lower

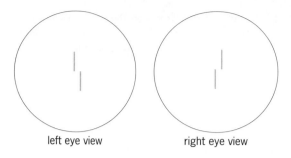

left eye view   right eye view   **Fig. 2. Vernier and stereoscopic discriminations of space.**

line as displaced slightly to the right of the upper. This is known as vernier discrimination. The eye is able to distinguish fantastically small displacements of this kind, a few seconds of arc under favorable conditions. If the right eye is presented with similar lines that are oppositely displaced, then the images for the two eyes appear fused into one and the subject sees the lower line as nearer than the upper. This is the principle of the stereoscope. Again it is true that displacements of a few seconds of arc are clearly seen, this time as changes in distance. The distance judgment is made not at the level of the retina but at the cortex where the spatial patterns from the separate eyes are fused together. The fineness of vernier and stereoscopic discrimination transcends that of the retinal mosaic and suggests that some averaging mechanism must be operating in space or time or both.

The spatial aspects of the visual field are also of interest. Good acuity is restricted to a narrowly defined region at the center of the visual field. Farther out, in the peripheral regions, area and intensity are reciprocally related for all small sizes of stimulus field. A stimulus patch of unit area, for example, looks the same as a patch of twice the same area and half the luminance. This high degree of areal summation is achieved by the convergence of hundreds of rod receptors upon each optic nerve fiber. It is the basis for the ability of the dark-adapted eye to detect large objects even on a dark night.

In daytime vision, spatial inhibition, rather than summation, is most noticeable. The phenomenon of simultaneous contrast is present at a border between fields of different color or luminance. This has the effect of heightening contours and making forms more noticeable against their background.

The temporal characteristics of vision are revealed by studying the responses of the eye to various temporal patterns of stimulation. When a light is first turned on, there is a vigorous burst of nerve impulses that travel from the eye to the brain. Continued illumination results in fewer and fewer impulses as the eye adapts itself to the given level of illumination. Turning the light off elicits another strong neural response. The strength of a visual stimulus depends upon its duration as well as its intensity. Below a certain critical duration, the product of duration and intensity is found to be constant for threshold stimulation. A flash of light lasting only a few milliseconds may stimulate the eye quite strongly, providing its luminance is sufficiently high. A light of twice of the original duration will be as detectable as the first if it is given half the original luminance.

Voluntary eye movements enable the eyes to roam over the surface of an object of inspection. In reading, for example, the eyes typically make four to seven fixational pauses along each line of print, with short jerky motions between pauses. An individual's vision typically takes place during the pauses, so that one's awareness of the whole object is the result of integrating these separate impressions over time.

A flickering light is one that is going on and off (or undergoing lesser changes in intensity) as a function of time. At a sufficiently high flash rate (called the critical frequency of fusion, cff) the eye fails to detect the flicker, and the light pulses seem to fuse to form a steady light that cannot be distinguished from a continuous light that has the same total energy per unit of time. As the flash rate is reduced below the cff, flicker becomes noticeable, and at very low rates the light may appear more conspicuous than flashes occurring at higher frequency. The cff is often used clinically to indicate a person's visual function as influenced by drugs, fatigue, or disease. *See* COLOR VISION; PERCEPTION.   [L.A.R.; C.E.Ste.]

Vitamin   An organic compound required in very small amounts for the normal functioning of the body and obtained mainly from foods. Vitamins are present in food in minute quantities compared to the other utilizable components of the diet, namely, proteins, fats, carbohydrates, and minerals.

Synthetic and natural vitamins usually have the same biological value. Different vitamins, which are often not related to each other chemically or functionally, are conventionally divided into a fat-soluble group (vitamins A, D, E, and K) and a water-soluble group [vitamin C (ascorbic acid) and the various B vitamins: thiamine, vitamin B, riboflavin, vitamin B_2, vitamin B_6, niacin, folic acid, vitamin B_{12}, biotin, and pantothenic acid]. The vitamins, particularly the water-soluble ones, occur almost universally throughout the animal and plant kingdoms individual articles on each vitamin.

The B vitamins function as coenzymes that catalyze many of the anabolic and catabolic reactions of living organisms necessary for the production of energy; the synthesis of tissue components, hormones, and chemical regulators; and the detoxification and degradation of waste products and toxins. On the other hand, vitamin C and the fat-soluble vitamins do not function as coenzymes. Vitamins C and E and β-carotene (a precursor of vitamin A) act as antioxidants, helping to prevent tissue injury from free-radical reactions. In addition, vitamin C functions as a cofactor in hydroxylation reactions. Vitamin D has hormonelike activity in calcium metabolism; vitamin A plays a critical role in night vision, growth, and maintaining normal differentiation of epithelial tissue; and vitamin K has a unique posttranscriptional role in the formation of active blood-clotting factors. *See* ANTIOXIDANT; CAROTENOID; COENZYME.
                    [L.J.M.]

Vocal cords   The pair of elastic, fibered bands inside the human larynx. The cords are covered with a mucous membrane and pass horizontally backward from the thyroid cartilage (Adam's apple) to insert on the smaller, paired arytenoid cartilages at the back of the larynx. The vocal cords act as sphincters for air regulation and may be vibrated to produce sounds. Separation, approximation, and alteration of tension are produced by action of laryngeal muscles acting on the pivoting arytenoids. Vibration of the cords produces fundamental sounds and overtones. These can be modified by the strength of the air current, the size and shape of the glottis (the opening between the cords), and tension in the cords. *See* LARYNX; SPEECH.   [W.J.B.]

Water-borne disease   Disease acquired by drinking water contaminated at its source or in the distribution system, or by direct contact with environmental and recreational waters. Water-borne disease results from infection with pathogenic microorganisms or chemical poisoning.

These pathogenic microorganisms include viruses, bacteria, protozoans, and helminths. A number of microbial pathogens transmitted by the fecal-oral route are commonly acquired from water in developing countries where sanitation is poor. Viral pathogens transmitted via fecally contaminated water include hepatitis viruses A and E. Important bacterial pathogens transmitted via fecally contaminated water in the developing world are *Vibrio cholerae*, enterotoxigenic *Escherichia coli*, *Shigella*, and *Salmonella enterica* serotype Typhi. Water-borne protozoan pathogens in the developing world include *Giardia lamblia* and *Entamoeba histolytica*. The major water-borne helminthic infection is schistosomiasis; however, transmission is not fecal-oral. Another water-borne helmenthic infection is dracunculiasis (guinea worm infection).

In developed countries, fecal contamination of drinking water supplies is less likely. However, there have been outbreaks of diseases such as shigellosis and giardiasis associated with lapses in proper water treatment, such as cross-contamination of wastewater systems and potable water supplies. Animals are therefore more likely to play a role in water-borne disease in developed countries. Bacterial pathogens acquired from animal feces such as nontyphoid *S. enterica*, *Campylobacter jejuni*, and *E. coli* serotype O157:H7 have caused outbreaks of water-borne disease in developed countries where water is not properly chlorinated. Hikers frequently acquire *G. lamblia* infections from drinking untreated lake and stream water. *Giardia lamblia* may have animal reservoirs and can persist in the environment. A recently recognized pathogen apparently resistant to standard chlorination and filtration practices is the protozoan *Cryptosporidium parvum*. This organism is found in the feces of farm animals and may enter water supplies through agricultural runoff.

Chemical poisoning of drinking water supplies causes disease in both developing and developed countries. Lead, copper, and cadmium have been frequently involved. *See* CHOLERA; ESCHERICHIA; MEDICAL PARASITOLOGY.   [S.L.M.]

Wetlands   Ecosystems that form transitional areas between terrestrial and aquatic components of a landscape. Typically they are shallow-water to intermittently flooded ecosystems, which results in their unique combination of hydrology, soils, and vegetation. Examples of wetlands include swamps, fresh- and salt-water marshes, bogs, fens, playas, vernal pools and ponds, floodplains, organic and mineral soil flats, and tundra. As transitional elements in the landscape, wetlands often develop at the interface between drier uplands such as forests and farmlands, and deep-water aquatic systems such as lakes, rivers, estuaries, and oceans. Thus, wetland ecosystems are characterized by the presence of water that flows over, ponds on the surface of, or saturates the soil for at least some portion of the year.

Vegetated wetlands are dominated by plant species, called hydrophytes, that are adapted to live in water or under saturated soil conditions. Adaptations that allow plants to survive in a water-logged environment include morphological features, such as pneumatophores (the "knees," or exposed roots, of the bald cypress), buttressed tree trunks, shallow root systems, floating leaves, hypertrophied lenticels, inflated plant parts, and adventitious roots. Physiological adaptations also allow plants to survive in a wetland environment. These include the ability of plants to transfer oxygen from the root system into the soil immediately surrounding the root (rhizosphere oxidation); the reduction or elimination of ethanol accumulation due to low concentrations of alcohol dehydrogenase; and the ability to concentrate malate (a nontoxic metabolite) instead of ethanol in the root system. See ROOT (BOTANY).

Wetlands differ with respect to their origin, position in the landscape, and hydrologic and biotic characteristics. For example, work has focused on the hydrology as well as the geomorphic position of wetlands in the landscape. This hydrogeomorphic approach recognizes and uses the fundamental physical properties that define wetland ecosystems to distinguish among classes of wetlands that occur in riverine, depressional, estuarine or lake fringe, mineral or organic soil flats, and slope environments.

The extent of wetlands in the world is estimated to be $2–3 \times 10^6$ mi^2 ($5–8 \times 10^6$ km^2), or about 4–6% of the Earth's land surface. Wetlands are found on every continent except Antarctica and in every clime from the tropics to the frozen tundra. Rice paddies, which comprise another 500,000–600,000 mi^2 ($1.3–1.5 \times 10^6$ km^2), can be considered as a type of domesticated wetland of great value to human societies worldwide. See MANGROVE; SALT MARSH; TUNDRA.

Wetlands are often an extremely productive part of the landscape. They support a rich variety of waterfowl and aquatic organisms, and represent one of the highest levels of species diversity and richness of any ecosystem. Wetlands are an extremely important habitat for rare and endangered species.

Wetlands often serve as natural filters for human and naturally generated nutrients, organic materials, and contaminants. The ability to retain, process, or transform these substances is called assimilative capacity, and is strongly related to wetland soil texture and vegetation. The assimilative capacity of wetlands has led to many projects that use wetland ecosystems for wastewater treatment and for improving water quality. Wetlands also have been shown to prevent downstream flooding and, in some cases, to prevent ground-water depletion as well as to protect shorelines from storm damage. The best wetland management practices enhance the natural processes of wetlands by maintaining conditions as close to the natural hydrology of the wetland as possible.

The world's wetlands are becoming a threatened landscape. Loss of wetlands worldwide currently is estimated at 50%. Wetland loss results primarily from habitat destruction, alteration of wetland hydrology, and landscape fragmentation. Global warming may soon be added to this list, although the exact loss of coastal wetlands due to sea-level rise is not well documented. Worldwide, destruction of wetland ecosystems primarily has been through the conversion of wetlands to agricultural land. The heavy losses of wetlands in the world, coupled with the recognized values of these systems, have led to a number of policy initiatives at both the national and international levels. See ECOSYSTEM; RESTORATION ECOLOGY.   [W.J.M.; P.L.Fi.; L.C.Le.; S.R.St.]

Whooping cough   An acute infection of the tracheobronchial tree caused by *Bordetella pertussis*, a bacteria species exclusive to infected humans. The disease (also known as pertussis) follows a prolonged course beginning with a runny nose, and finally develops into violent coughing, followed by a slow period of recovery. The coughing stage can last 2–4 weeks, with a whooping sound created by an exhausted individual rapidly breathing in through a narrowed glottis after a series of wrenching coughs. The classical disease occurs in children 1–5 years of age, but in immunized populations infants are at greatest risk and adults with attenuated (and unrecognized) disease constitute a major source of transmission to others. *Bordetella pertussis* is highly infectious, particularly following face-to-face contact with an individual who is coughing. The disease is caused by structural components and extracellular toxins elaborated by *B. pertussis*. Multiple virulence factors produced by the organism play important roles at various stages of pertussis.

A vaccine produced from whole *B. pertussis* cells and combined with diphtheria and tetanus toxoids has been used throughout the world for routine childhood immunization. Concern over vaccine morbidity has caused immunization rates to decline in some developed countries. These drops in immunization rates have often been followed by widespread outbreaks of disease, including deaths. Considerable effort has been directed toward the development of a vaccine which would minimize side effects but maintain efficacy. A new acellular vaccine is available and has fewer side effects than the whole-cell vaccine. *See* Diphtheria; Vaccination.

Although *B. pertussis* is susceptible to many antibiotics, their use has little effect once the disease reaches the coughing stage. Erythromycin is effective in preventing spread to close contacts and in the early stage.   [K.J.R.]

Wood anatomy   Wood is composed mostly of hollow, elongated, spindle-shaped cells that are arranged parallel to each other along the trunk of a tree. The characteristics of these fibrous cells and their arrangement affect strength properties, appearance, resistance to penetration by water and chemicals, resistance to decay, and many other properties.

Just under the bark of a tree is a thin layer of cells, not visible to the naked eye, called the cambium. Here cells divide and eventually differentiate to form bark tissue to the outside of the cambium and wood or xylem tissue to the inside. This newly formed wood (termed sapwood) contains many living cells and conducts sap upward in the tree. Eventually, the inner sapwood cells become inactive and are transformed into heartwood. This transformation is often accompanied by the formation of extractives that darken the wood, make it less porous, and sometimes provide more resistance to decay. The center of the trunk is the pith, the soft tissue about which the first wood growth takes place in the newly formed twigs. *See* Stem.

In temperate climates, trees often produce distinct growth layers. These increments are called growth rings or annual rings when associated with yearly growth; many tropical trees, however, lack growth rings. These rings vary in width according to environmental conditions.

Many mechanical properties of wood, such as bending strength, crushing strength, and hardness, depend upon the density of wood; the heavier woods are generally stronger. Wood density is determined largely by the relative thickness of the cell wall and the proportions of thick- and thin-walled cells present. *See* Wood properties.

In hardwoods (for example, oak or maple), these three major planes along which wood may be cut are known commonly as end-grain, quarter-sawed (edge-grain) and plain-sawed (flat-grain) surfaces (see illustration).

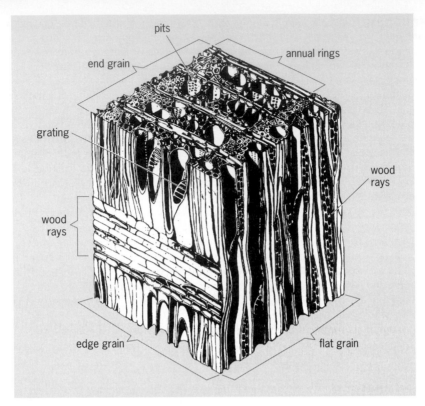

Structure of a typical hardwood. (*USDA*)

Hardwoods have specialized structures called vessels for conducting sap upward. Vessels are a series of relatively large cells with open ends, set one above the other and continuing as open passages for long distances. In most hardwoods, the ends of the individual cells are entirely open; in others, they are separated by a grating. On the end grain, vessels appear as holes and are termed pores. The size, shape, and arrangement of pores vary considerably between species, but are relatively constant within a species.

Most smaller cells on the end grain are wood fibers which are the strength-giving elements of hardwoods. They usually have small cavities and relatively thick walls. Thin places or pits in the walls of the wood fibers and vessels allow sap to pass from one cavity to another. Wood rays are strips of short horizontal cells that extend in a radial direction. Their function is food storage and lateral conduction. *See* PARENCHYMA; SECRETORY STRUCTURES (PLANT).

The rectangular units that make up the end grain of softwood are sections through long vertical cells called tracheids or fibers. Because softwoods do not contain vessel cells, the tracheids serve the dual function of transporting sap vertically and giving strength to the wood. The wood rays store and distribute sap horizontally.

The principal compound in mature wood cells is cellulose, a polysaccharide of repeating glucose molecules which may reach 4 μm in length. These cellulose molecules are arranged in an orderly manner into structures about 10–25 nm wide called microfibrils. The microfibrils wind together like strands in a cable to form macrofibrils that measure about 0.5 μm in width and may reach 4 μm in length. These cables are as strong as an equivalent thickness of steel.

This framework of cellulose macrofibrils is cross-linked with hemicelluloses, pectins, and lignin. Lignin, the second most abundant polymer found in plants, gives the cell wall rigidity and the substance that cements the cells together. *See* CELL WALLS (PLANT); PLANT ANATOMY; TREE.   [R.B.M.]

Xylem   The principal water-conducting tissue and the chief supporting system of higher plants. This tissue and the associated phloem constitute the vascular system of vascular plants. Xylem is composed of various kinds of cells, living or nonliving. The structure of these cells differs in their functions, but characteristically all have a rigid and enduring cell wall that is well preserved in fossils.

In terms of their functions, the kinds of cells in xylem are those related principally to conduction and support, tracheids; to conduction, vessel members; to support, fibers; and to food storage, parenchyma. Vessel members and tracheids are often called tracheary elements. The cells in each of the four categories vary widely in structure. *See* PARENCHYMA.

Xylem tissues arise in later stages of embryo development of a given plant and are added to by differentiation of cells derived from the apical meristems of roots and stems. Growth and differentiation of tissues derived from the apical meristem provide the primary body of the plant, and the xylem tissues formed in it are called primary. Secondary xylem, when present, is produced by the vascular cambium. *See* LATERAL MERISTEM.

In the trade, softwood is a name for xylem of gymnosperms (conifers) and hardwood for xylem of angiosperms. The terms do not refer to actual hardness of the wood. Woods of gymnosperms are generally composed only of tracheids, wood parenchyma, and small rays, but differ in detail. Resin ducts are present in many softwoods. Woods of angiosperms show extreme variation in both vertical and horizontal systems, but with few exceptions have vessels.   [V.I.C.; K.E.]

Xylose   A pentose sugar, referred to in the early literature as L-xylose. It is present in many woody materials. The polysaccharide xylan, which is closely associated with cellulose, consists practically entirely of D-xylose. Corncobs, cottonseed hulls, pecan shells, and straw contain considerable amounts of this sugar. This pentose sugar is also a component of the hemicelluloses and the rare disaccharide, primeverose. *See* CARBOHYDRATE.   [W.Z.H.]

Y

Yeast A collective name for those fungi which possess, under normal conditions of growth, a vegetative body (thallus) consisting, at least in part, of simple, single cells. The cells making up the thallus occur in pairs, in groups of three, or in straight or branched chains consisting of as many as 12 or more cells. Vegetative reproduction is characterized by budding or fission. Sexual reproduction also occurs in yeast, and is differentiated from that of other fungi by sexual states that are not enclosed in a fruiting body. Yeasts are a phylogenetically diverse group of organisms that occur in two divisions of fungi (Ascomycotina and Basidiomycotina) and 100 genera. The 700 or more species that have been described possibly represent only 1% of the species in nature, so the majority of the yeasts have yet to be discovered. Yeast plays a large part in industrial fermentation processes such as the production of industrial enzymes and chemicals, food products, industrial ethanol, and malt beverage and wine; in diseases of humans, animals and plants; in food spoilage; and as a model of molecular genetics. *See* GENETIC ENGINEERING; MEDICAL MYCOLOGY.

The shape and size of the individual cells of some species vary slightly, but in other species the cell morphology is extremely heterogeneous. The shape of yeast cells may be spherical, globose, ellipsoidal, elongate to cylindrical with rounded ends, more or less rectangular, pear-shaped, apiculate or lemon-shaped, ogival or pointed at one end, or tetrahedral. The diameter of a spherical cell may vary from 2 to 10 micrometers. The length of cylindrical cells is often 20–30 μm and, in some cases, even greater.

The asexual multiplication of yeast cells occurs by a budding process, by the formation of cross walls or fission, and sometimes by a combination of these two processes. Yeast buds are sometimes called blastospores or blastoconidia. When yeast reproduces by a fission mechanism, the resulting cells are termed arthrospores or arthroconidia.

Yeasts are categorized into two groups, based on their methods of sexual reproduction: the ascomycetous (Division Ascomycotina) and basidiomycetous (Division Basidiomycotina) yeasts.

The sexual spores of the ascomycetous yeasts are termed ascospores, which are formed in simple structures, often a vegetative cell. Such asci are called naked asci because of the absence of an ascocarp, which is a more complex fruiting body found in the higher Ascomycetes. If the vegetative cells are diploid, a cell may transform directly into an ascus after the 2n nucleus undergoes a reduction or meiotic division. *See* ASCOMYCOTA.

Certain yeasts have been shown to be heterothallic; that is, sporulation occurs when strains of opposite mating type (usually indicated by "a" and α) are mixed on sporulation media. However, some strains may be homothallic (self-fertile), and reduction division and karyogamy (fusion of two haploid nuclei) take place during formation of the sexual spore. Yeasts that produce sporogenous cells represent the teleomorphic form of the life cycle. In cases, in which sexual cycles are unknown, the yeast represents the asexual or anamorphic form. A species of yeast may be originally discovered in the anamorphic form and named accordingly; subsequently, the sexual state may be found and a name applied to represent the teleomorph. Consequently, the anamorphic and teleomorphic names will differ.

Basidiospores and teliospores are the sexual spores that are produced in the three classes of basidiomycetous yeasts: Urediniomycetes, Hymenomycetes, and Ustilaginomycetes. Sexual reproduction and life cycle in these yeasts is typical of other basidiomycetes in that it can include both unifactorial (bipolar) and bifactorial (tetrapolar) mating systems. *See* BASIDIOMYCOTA.

Some yeasts have the ability to carry out an alcoholic fermentation. Other yeasts lack this property. In addition to the fermentative type of metabolism, fermentative yeasts as a rule have a respiratory type of metabolism, whereas nonfermentative yeasts have only a respiratory, or oxidative, metabolism. Both reactions produce energy, with respiration producing by far the most, which is used in part for synthetic reactions, such as assimilation and growth. Part is lost as heat. In addition, small or sometimes large amounts of by-products are formed, including organic acids, esters, aldehydes, glycerol, and higher alcohols. When a fermenting yeast culture is aerated, fermentation is suppressed and respiration increases. This phenomenon is called the Pasteur effect. *See* FERMENTATION.

Yeasts are ubiquitous in nature. They exist on plants and animals; in waters, sediments, and soils; and in terrestrial, aquatic, and marine habitats. Yeasts require oxygen for growth and reproduction; therefore they do not inhabit anaerobic environments such as anoxic sediments. Many species have highly specific habitats, whereas others are found on a variety of substrates in nature.   [J.W.Fe.; H.J.P.]

Yeast infection   An infection mainly caused by fungi of the genus *Candida*. Although members of the genus *Candida* continue to be the most common agents of yeast infections, numerous nosocomial (related to medical treatment) factors have altered this etiologic pattern over the last 20 years. Reports in professional publications have described over 200 species in 25 yeast genera as being associated with human infections. *See* FUNGAL INFECTIONS; FUNGI; YEAST.

Etiologic agents. *Candida*, species particularly *C. albicans*, cause almost 70% of all yeast infections. However, recent changes in medical practices such as the use of broad-spectrum antibiotics, steroids, and immunosuppressive drugs, along with the recognition of new and highly debilitating diseases [for example, acquired immune deficiency syndrome (AIDS)], have increased the diversity of the agents of these infections. Species that were once rarely encountered in patient specimens (for example, *C. parapsilosis*, *C. krusei*, and *C. guilliermondii*) are being isolated with increased frequency. Equally important is the fact that yeasts that have never been described as the cause of human infections, (for example, *Blastoschizomyces capitatus*, *C. dubliniensis*, and *Trichosporon cutaneum*) are now being associated, albeit rarely, with human disease. *See* ACQUIRED IMMUNE DEFICIENCY SYNDROME (AIDS); OPPORTUNISTIC INFECTIONS.

Predisposing factors. Since yeasts are not as adept as other microbial pathogens at evading or overwhelming the body's immune defenses, they generally require some disruption in the natural protective mechanisms of humans to initiate an infection. Minor breaks in the skin (such as those caused by a cut or scrape) to more significant disruptions in the integrity of the skin (as created by the delivery of medications or nutrients through intravenous catheters) can provide the means by which the yeasts on human skin may enter the body and potentially initiate an infection. The use of broad-spectrum antibacterial agents eliminates a large portion of the normal bacterial flora, allowing the yeasts in the mouth and intestines to grow rapidly and seed the blood to create a temporary benign infection or a chronic, potentially life-threatening infection. Natural hormonal imbalances as created by pregnancy or diabetes mellitus, as well as those caused by the use of medications such as corticosteroids, depress the immune system and predispose the individual to possible yeast infections. The common use of immunosuppressive drugs, and the depressed immunity associated with newer human diseases such as AIDS cause a decrease in the immune system's ability to prevent and eliminate yeast infections. Finally, the longer human life expectancy created by modern medical practices has contributed to an ever-increasing population of senior citizens with naturally lowered resistance to all forms of microbial infections. *See* IMMUNOSUPPRESSION.

Clinical symptomology. Although yeast infections usually affect the skin and mucous membranes, the illness can take several different forms, each with different symptoms. For example, in newborns and infants, candidiasis can appear as reddening and blisterlike lesions of skin infections (diaper rash), or it can present as white-gray lesions on the mucosal tissue lining the oral cavity (thrush). The symptoms observed in the vast majority of yeast infections mimic those of other microbial pathogens and thus are generally of little value in establishing their etiology. The diagnosis of most yeast infections involves obtaining detailed medical histories from patients, conducting extensive physical examinations, analyzing clinical laboratory data, and utilizing the education, training, and experience of the attending physicians and infectious disease specialists. *See* CLINICAL MICROBIOLOGY.

Treatment. The introduction of the first clinically effective antifungal antibiotic (nystatin) closely followed the use of antibacterial drugs (penicillin). However, nystatin was found to be effective only when brought into direct contact with the infectious agent. The broad-spectrum and fungicidal (killing fungi) activity of amphotericin B, another member of the same chemical family, maintains its use as the drug of choice for several yeast infections and as the antifungal of last resort when all other antibiotics have failed. Two closely related families of drugs, the azoles and triazoles, were introduced in the early 1970s and quickly established themselves as the first-line antibiotics for yeast infections. However, the newer triazoles are fungistatic (limiting growth) rather than fungicidal. As a result, recurrences of infection happen frequently once therapy is discontinued. Although new antifungal antibiotics continue to be introduced, the perfect drug with broad-spectrum and fungicidal activity, easy delivery, and limited side effects has yet to be found. *See* ANTIBIOTIC; ANTIMICROBIAL AGENTS.   [I.F.S.]

Yellow fever   An acute, febrile, mosquito-borne viral disease characterized in severe cases by jaundice, albuminuria, and hemorrhage. Inapparent infections also occur.

The agent is a flavivirus, an arbovirus of group B. The virus multiplies in mosquitoes, which remain infectious for life. After the mosquito ingests a virus-containing blood meal, an interval of 12–18 days (called the extrinsic incubation period) is required for it to become infectious. *See* ANIMAL VIRUS; ARBOVIRAL ENCEPHALITIDES.

The virus enters the body through a mosquito bite and multiplies in lymph nodes, circulates in the blood, and localizes in the liver, spleen, kidney, bone marrow, and lymph glands. The severity of the disease and the major signs and symptoms which appear depend upon where the virus localizes and how much cell destruction occurs. The incubation period is 3–6 days. At the onset, the individual has fever, chills, headache, and backache, followed by nausea and vomiting. A short period of remission often follows.

On about the fourth day, the period of intoxication begins with a slow pulse relative to a high fever and moderate jaundice. In severe cases, there are high levels of protein in the urine, and manifestations of bleeding appear; the vomit may be black with altered blood; and there is an abnormally low number of lymphocytes in the blood. When the disease progresses to the severe stage (black vomit and jaundice), the mortality rate is high. However, the infection may be mild and go unrecognized. Diagnosis is made by isolation of the virus from the serum obtained from an individual as early as possible in the disease, or by the rise in serum antibody. *See* ANTIBODY; COMPLEMENT-FIXATION TEST; NEUTRALIZATION REACTION (IMMUNOLOGY).

There are two major epidemiological cycles of yellow fever: classical or urban epidemic yellow fever, and sylvan or jungle yellow fever. Urban yellow fever involves person-to-person transmission by *Aedes aegypti* mosquitoes in the Western Hemisphere and West Africa. This mosquito breeds in the accumulations of water that accompany human settlement. Jungle yellow fever is primarily a disease of monkeys. In South America and Africa, it is transmitted from monkey to monkey by arboreal mosquitoes (*Haemagogus* and *Aedes* species) that inhabit the moist forest canopy. The infection in animals ranges from severe to inapparent. Persons who come in contact with these mosquitoes in the forest can become infected. Jungle yellow fever may also occur when an infected monkey visits a human habitation and is bitten by *A. aegypti*, which then transmits the virus to a human.

Vigorous mosquito abatement programs have virtually eliminated urban yellow fever. However, with the speed of modern air travel, the threat of a yellow fever outbreak exists where *A. aegypti* is present. An excellent attenuated live-virus vaccine is available. *See* VACCINATION.   [J.L.Me.]

Yersinia   A genus of bacteria in the Enterobacteriaceae family. The bacteria appear as gram-negative rods and share many physiological properties with related *Escherichia coli*. Of the 11 species of *Yersinia*, *Y. pestis*, *Y. enterocolitica*, and *Y. pseudotuberculosis* are etiological agents of human disease. *Yersinia pestis* causes flea-borne bubonic plague (the black death), an extraordinarily acute process believed to have killed over 200 million people during human history. Enteropathogenic *Y. pseudotuberculosis* and *Y. enterocolitica* typically cause mild chronic enteric infections. The remaining species either promote primary infection of fish (*Y. ruckeri*) or exist as secondary invaders or inhabitants of natural environments (*Y. aldovae*, *Y. bercovieri*, *Y. frederiksenii*, *Y. intermedia*, *Y. kristensenii*, *Y. mollaretii*, and *Y. rohdei*). *See* MEDICAL BACTERIOLOGY; PLAGUE.   [R.R.B.]

Yolk sac   An extraembryonic membrane which extends through the umbilicus in vertebrates. In some elasmobranchs, birds, and reptiles, it is laden with yolk which serves as the nutritive source of embryonic development.

In mammals, as in birds, the yolk sac generally develops from extraembryonic splanchnopleure, and extends beneath the developing embryo. A blood vessel network develops in the mammalian yolk sac lining. Though these blood vessels are empty, they play an important role in absorbing nourishing food and oxygen from the mother. Thus, although the yolk sac in higher mammals may be considered an evolutionary vestige from its yolky-egged ancestors, it still serves important functions in the young embryo. As the embryo ages, the yolk sac shrinks in size, and the allantois takes over the role of nutrition. *See* ALLANTOIS.   [S.B.O.]

Z

Zoological nomenclature The system of naming animals that was adopted by zoologists and detailed in the International Code of Zoological Nomenclature, which applies to both living and extinct animals. The present system is founded on the 10th edition of C. Linnaeus's *Systema Naturae* (1758) and has evolved through international agreements culminating in the Code adopted in 1985. The primary objective of the Code is to promote the stability of the names of taxa (groups of organisms) by providing rules concerning name usage and the activity of naming new taxa. The rules are binding for taxa ranked at certain levels and nonbinding on taxa ranked at other levels. *See* ANIMAL SYSTEMATICS.

Zoological nomenclature is built around four basic features. (1) The correct names of certain taxa are either unique or unique combinations. (2) These names are formed and treated as Latin names and are universally applicable, regardless of the native language of the zoologist. (3) The Code for animals is separate and independent from similar codes for plants and bacteria. (4) No provisions of the Code are meant to restrict the intellectual freedom of individual scientists to pursue their own research.

There are four common reasons why nomenclature may change. (1) New species are found that were once considered parts of other species. (2) Taxonomic revisions may uncover older names or mistakes in identification of types. (3) Taxa may be combined, creating homonyms that require replacement. (4) Concepts of the relationships of animals change. Stability is subservient to progress in understanding animal diversity.

The articles in the Code are directed toward the names of taxa at three levels. The family group includes taxa ranked as at the family and tribe levels (including super- and subfamilies). The genus group includes taxa below subtribe and above species. The species group includes taxa ranked as species or subspecies. Taxa above the family group level are not specifically treated, and their formation and use are not strictly regulated. For each group, provisions are made that are either binding or recommended.

Binominal nomenclature. The basis for naming animals is binominal nomenclature, that is, a system of two-part names. The first name of each species is formed from the generic name, and the second is a trivial name, or species epithet. The two names agree in gender unless the specific epithet is a patronym (named for a person). The combination must be unique; no other animal can have the same binominal. The formal name of a species also includes the author, so the formal name for humans is *Homo sapiens* Linnaeus. The genus, as a higher taxon, may have one or many species, each with a different epithet. *Homo* includes *H. sapiens, H. erectus, H. habilis,* and so forth. One feature of the Linnaean binominal system is that species epithets can be used over and over again, so long as they are used in different genera. *Tyrannosaurus rex* is a large dinosaur, and *Percina rex* is a small fresh-water fish. The epithet *rex* is not the species name of *Percina rex* because all species names are binominal in form. It is recommended that names of genera and species be set in a different typeface from normal text; italics is conventional. Different names for the same species are termed synonyms, and the senior synonym is usually correct (principle of priority). Modern species descriptions are accompanied by a description that attempts to show how the species is different from others, and the designation of one or more type specimens.

Higher taxa. All higher taxonomic names have one part (uninominal) and are plural. Names of taxa of the family and genus groups must be unique. The names of genera are in Latin or latinized, are displayed in italics, and may be used alone. The names of the family group are formed by a root and an ending specific to a particular hierarchical level: family Hominidae (root + idae), subfamily Homininae (root + inae). The endings of superfamilies (root + oidea) and tribes (root + ini) are recommended but not mandated. The endings of taxa higher than the family group vary. For example, orders of fishes are formed by adding -iformes to the root (Salmoniformes), while in insects the ending is usually -ptera (Coleoptera). *See* CLASSIFICATION, BIOLOGICAL; TAXONOMIC CATEGORIES.   [E.O.W.]

Zoology   The science that deals with knowledge of animal life. With the great growth of information about animals, zoology has been much subdivided. Some major fields are anatomy, which deals with gross and microscopic structure; physiology, with living processes in animals; embryology, with development of new individuals; genetics, with heredity and variation; parasitology, with animals living in or on others; natural history, with life and behavior in nature; ecology, with the relation of animals to their environments; evolution, with the origin and differentiation of animal life; and taxonomy, with the classification of animals. *See* DEVELOPMENTAL BIOLOGY; GENETICS; PARASITOLOGY; PHYLOGENY; PLANT EVOLUTION; TAXONOMY.   [T.I.S.]

Zoonoses   Infections of humans caused by the transmission of disease agents that naturally live in animals. People become infected when they unwittingly intrude into the life cycle of the disease agent and become unnatural hosts. Zoonotic helminthic diseases, caused by parasitic worms, involve many species of helminths, including nematodes (roundworms), trematodes (flukes), cestodes (tapeworms), and acanthocephalans (thorny-headed worms). Helminthic zoonoses may be contracted from domestic animals such as pets, from edible animals such as seafood, or from wild animals. Fortunately, most kinds of zoonotic helminthic infections are caused by rare human parasites.

The best-recognized example of a food-borne zoonotic helminthic disease is trichinosis, caused by the trinchina worm, *Trichinella spiralis*, a tiny nematode. People commonly become infected by eating inadequately prepared pork, but a sizable proportion of victims now contract the worms by eating the meat of wild carnivores, such as bear. Trichinosis is usually a mild disease, manifested by symptoms and signs of intestinal and muscular inflammation, but in heavy infections damage done by the larvae to the heart and central nervous system can be life threatening. Because of public awareness about properly cooking pork and federal regulations about feeding pigs, trichinosis has become uncommon in the United States. People who eat inadequately prepared marine fish may become infected with larval nematodes. Of the many potential (and rare) helminthic zoonoses from wild animals in the United States, *Baylisascaris procyonis* is particularly dangerous. The nematode is highly prevalent in raccoons, the definitive host. *See* MEDICAL PARASITOLOGY; NEMATA.   [D.E.No.]

Zooplankton   Animals that inhabit the water column of oceans and lakes and lack the means to counteract transport currents. Zooplankton inhabit all layers of these water bodies to the greatest depths sampled, and constitute a major link between primary production and higher trophic levels in aquatic ecosystems. Many zooplankton are capable of strong swimming movements and may migrate vertically from tens to hundreds of meters; others have limited mobility and depend more on water turbulence to stay afloat. All zooplankton, however, lack the ability to maintain their position against the movement of large water masses.

Zooplankton can be divided into various operational categories. One means of classification is based on developmental stages and divides animals into meroplankton and holoplankton. Meroplanktonic forms spend only part of their life cycles as plankton and include larvae of benthic worms, mollusks, crustaceans, echinoderms, coral, and even insects, as well as the eggs and larvae of many fishes. Holoplankton spend essentially their whole existence in the water column. Examples are chaetognaths, pteropods, larvaceans, siphonophores, and many copepods. Nearly every major taxonomic group of animals has either meroplanktonic or holoplanktonic members.

Size is another basis of grouping all plankton. A commonly accepted size classification scheme includes the groupings: picoplankton (<2 micrometers), nanoplankton (2–20 μm), microplankton (20–200 μm), mesoplankton (0.2–20 mm), macroplankton (20–200 mm), and megaplankton (>200 mm).

The classic description of the trophic dynamics of plankton is a food chain consisting of algae grazed by crustacean zooplankton which are in turn ingested by fishes. This model may hold true to a degree in some environments such as upwelling areas, but it masks the complexity of most natural food webs. Zooplankton have an essential role in linking trophic levels, but several intermediate zooplankton consumers can exist between the primary producers (phytoplankton) and fish. Thus, food webs with multiple links to different organisms indicate the versatility of food choice and energy transfer and are a more realistic description of the planktonic trophic interactions.

Size is of major importance in planktonic food webs. Most zooplankton tend to feed on organisms that have a body size smaller than their own. However, factors other than size also modify feeding interactions. Some phytoplankton are noxious and are avoided by zooplankton, and others are ingested but not digested. Furthermore, zooplankton frequently assume different feeding habits as they grow from larval to adult form. They may ingest bacteria or phytoplankton at one stage of their life cycle and become raptorial feeders later. Other zooplankton are primarily herbivorous but also ingest heterotrophic protists and can opportunistically become carnivorous. Consequently, omnivory, which is considered rare in terrestrial systems, is a relatively common trophic strategy in the plankton. In all food webs, some individuals die without being consumed and are utilized by scavengers and ultimately by decomposers (bacteria and fungi). *See* ECOLOGY; ECOSYSTEM; MARINE ECOLOGY; PHYTOPLANKTON.   [R.W.Sa.]

Zygomycetes

Zygomycetes   A class of terrestrial fungi in the phylum Zygomycota, comprising organisms commonly known as the bread molds. Sexual reproduction is by the formation of zygospores. Asexual reproduction is by endospores (sporangiospores) produced in sporangia, or uni- or multispored sporangiola or merosporangia, conidia, yeast cells, chlamydospores, or arthrospores. These fungi occur as haustorial (having food-absorbing cells in the host) or nonhaustorial parasites of fungi, plants, or animals (including humans), or as saprobes, especially in soil or dung; but other substrates with soluble nutrients may also contain Zygomycetes. Some taxa are endo- or ectomycorrhizal on vascular plants.

The mature spore-bearing structures are dry and readily dispersed by air currents, or are wet and are distributed by direct contact with small animals or are ingested by animals and disseminated in their feces. Water droplets also may disperse the spores or the intact spore-bearing structures.

Classification is based on mode of nutrition, morphology of the zygospore (if formed), type of asexual reproduction, branching pattern of sporophores, and frequency of septa (if formed) and septal morphology. Zygomycetes are currently placed in seven orders: Dimargaritales, Endogonales, Entomophthorales, Glomales, Kickxellales, Mucorales, and Zoopagales. Zygomycetes are distributed worldwide, although many taxa are rarely encountered; they may be relatively common on a particular host or substrate. *See* EUMYCOTA; FUNGI.   [G.L.Be.]

1
Appendix

2
Contributors

3
Index

BIBLIOGRAPHIES

AGRICULTURE

Adams, C.R., K. Bamdford, and M.P. Early, *Principles of Horticulture*, 3d ed., 1998.
Barrick, R.K., and H. Harmon, *Animal Science*, 1984.
Blakely, J., and D.H. Bade, *The Science of Animal Husbandry*, 5th ed., 1989.
Brady, N.C. (ed.), *Advances in Agronomy*, vols. 28–45, 1976–1991.
Ensminger, M.E. (ed.), *Animal Science*, 9th ed., 1991.
Heath, E., et al., *Forages: The Science of Grassland Agriculture*, 4th ed., 1985.
Lockhart, J.A., and A.J. Wiseman, *Introduction to Crop Husbandry: Including Grassland*, 6th ed., 1988.
Martin, J.H., et al., *Principles of Field Crop Production*, 4th ed., 1986.
Miller, D.A., *Forage Crops*, 1984.
Rechcigl, M., Jr. (ed.), *Handbook of Agricultural Productivity*, vol. 1: *Plant Productivity*, vol. 2: *Animal Productivity*, 1982.
Sparks, D.L. (ed.), *Advances in Agronomy*, vols. 47–49, 1992–1993.

Journals:
Agronomy Journal, American Society of Agronomy, bimonthly.
Journal of Agricultural Science (England), bimonthly.
Journal of Animal Science, American Society of Animal Science, monthly.

ANATOMY

Chee, A.N., *Anatomy and Physiology: A Dynamic Approach*, 4th ed., 1991.
Fong, E., and A. Senisiscott, *Body Structures and Functions*, 10th ed., 2003.
Guyton, A., *Physiology of the Human Body*, 6th ed., 1984.
Marieb, E.N., *Human Anatomy and Physiology*, 6th ed., 2003.
Schlossberg, L., and G.D. Zuidema, *The John Hopkins Atlas of Human Functional Anatomy*, 4th ed., 1997.
Tortora, G., *Principles of Anatomy and Physiology*, Learning Guide, 10th ed., 2002.
Williams, P.L., et al., *Gray's Anatomy*, Deluxe Set, 38th rev. ed., 1995.

Journals:
Anatomical Record, Wiston Institute Press, monthly.
Journal of Anatomy (England), bimonthly.

ANTHROPOLOGY AND ARCHEOLOGY

Campbell, B.J. Loy, *Humankind Emerging,* 8th ed., 1999.
Ember, C.R., M. Ember, and P. Perengrine, *Anthropology*, 10th ed., 2001.
Fagan, B., *World Prehistory: A Brief Introduction*, 8th ed., 2002.
Fagan, B.M., *People of the Earth*, 11th ed., 2003.
Klein, R.G., and B. Edgar, *The Dawn of Human Culture*, 2002.
Renfrew, C., and P. Bahn, *Archaeology: Theories, Methods and Practice*, 3d ed., 2000.
Strier, K.B., *Primate Behavioral Ecology*, 1999.
Thomas, D.H., *Archaeology*, 3d ed., 1997.
Whitten, P., and D.E. Hunter, *Anthropology: Contemporary Perspectives*, 8th ed., 2000.

Journals:
Evolutionary Anthropology, Wiley-Liss, monthly.

BIOCHEMISTRY

Alberts, B., et al., *Molecular Biology of the Cell*, 4th ed., 2002.
Devlin, T.M. (ed.), *Textbook of Biochemistry*, 5th ed., 2001.
Elliott, W.H., and D.C. Elliott, *Biochemistry and Molecular Biology*, 2d ed., 2001.
Horton, H.R., et al., *Principles of Biochemistry*, 3d ed., 2002.
Murray, R.K., et al., *Harper's Illustrated Biochemistry*, 2003.
Nelson, D., and M. Cox, *Lehninger Principles of Biochemistry*, 4th ed., 2004.
Stipanuk, M.H., *Biochemical and Physiological Aspects of Human Nutrition*, 2000.
Stryer, L., *Biochemistry Extended*, 2002.
Van Holde, K.E., C. Johnson, and P. Ho, *Principles of Physical Biochemistry*, 1998.
Voet, D., and J. Voet, *Biochemistry*, 3d ed., 2004.

Journals:
Annual Review of Biochemistry, annually.
Archives of Biochemistry and Biophysics, biweekly.
Biochemical Journal, biweekly.
Biochemistry, Centcom Ltd., biweekly.
Biochimica et Biophysica Acta, 100+ issues per year.
European Journal of Biochemistry, semimonthly.
Journal of Biological Chemistry, American Society of Biological Chemists, semimonthly.
Trends in Biochemical Sciences, monthly.

BIOMEDICAL ENGINEERING

Bronzino, J.D. (ed.), *The Biomedical Engineering Handbook*, 2d ed., 2000.
Domach, M.F., *Introduction to Biomedical Engineering*, 2004.
Dyro, J.F. (ed.), *Clinical Engineering Handbook*, 2004.
Khandpur, R.S., *Biomedical Instrumentation*, 2005.
Kutz, M. (ed.), *Standard Handbook of Biomedical Engineering & Design*, 2003.

Journals:
Annals of Biomedical Engineering, monthly.
Annual Review of Biomedical Engineering, annually.
IEEE Transactions on Biomedical Engineering, monthly.

BIOPHYSICS

Austin, R.H., and S. Chan, *Biophysics for Physicists*, 2003.
Cerdonio, M., and R.W. Noble, *Introductory Biophysics*, 1988.
Kreighbaum, E., and K. Barthels, *Biomechanics: A Qualitative Approach for Studying Human Movements*, 4th ed., 1995.
Sybesma, C. (ed.), *Biophysics: An Introduction*, 1989.
Valenta, J. (ed.), *Biomechanics*, 1993.
Wainwright, S.A., et al., *Mechanical Design in Organisms*, 1982.

Journals:
Annual Review of Biophysics and Bioengineering, annually.
Biophysical Journal, monthly.

CELL AND MOLECULAR BIOLOGY

Alberts, B., et al., *Molecular Biology of the Cell*, 4th ed., 2002.
Drew, H.R., et al., *Understanding DNA: The Molecule and How It Works*, 3d ed., 2004.

Lodish, H., et al., *Molecular Cell Biology*, 5th ed., 2003.
Pollard, T., *Cell Biology*, 2d ed., 2002.
Watson, J.D., et al., *Molecular Biology of the Gene*, 5th ed., 2003.

Journals:
Cell, biweekly.
Current Opinion in Cell Biology, bimonthly.
EMBO Journal, European Molecular Biology Organization, bimonthly.
Journal of Cell Biology, monthly.
Journal of Molecular Biology, biweekly.
Molecular and Cellular Biology, American Society for Microbiology, monthly.
Molecular Biology, bimonthly.
Molecular Biology of the Cell, monthly.
Nature Cell Biology, monthly.
Trends in Cell Biology, monthly.

CONSERVATION

Dasmann, R.F., *Environmental Conservation*, 6th ed., 2004.
Frankham, R., J.D. Ballou, and D.A. Briscoe, *A Primer of Conservation Genetics*, 2004.
Hambler, C., *Conservation* (Studies in Biology), 2004.
Meffe, G.K., and C.R. Carroll, *Principles of Conservation Biology*, 3d ed., 2005.
Kircher, H.B., *Our Natural Resources and Their Conservation*, 7th rev. ed., 1992.
Owen, O., and D.D. Chiras, *Natural Resources Conservation: An Ecological Approach*,
    5th ed., 1990.
Primack, R.B., *Essentials of Conservation Biology*, 2004.

Journals:
American Institute for Conservation Journal, semiannually.
Audubon Magazine, Audubon Society, bimonthly.
Conservation, bimonthly.
New York State Conservationist, New York State Department of Environmental Conservation,
    bimonthly.

DEVELOPMENTAL BIOLOGY

Beysens, D., G. Forgacs, and F. Gaill, *Interplay of Genetic and Physical Processes in the
    Development of Biological Form*, 1995.
Browder, L.W., C.A. Erickson, and W.R. Jeffrey, *Developmental Biology*, 3d ed., 1991.
Carlson, B.M., *Human Embryology and Developmental Biology*, 2d ed., 1999.
Gilbert, S.F., *Developmental Biology*, 6th ed., 2000.
Hall, B.K., *Evolutionary Developmental Biology*, 1998.
Oppenheimer, S.B., *Introduction to Embryonic Development*, 3d rev. ed., 1988.
Russo, V.E., et al., *Development: The Molecular Genetic Approach*, 1993.
Vander Zanden, J.W., et al., *Human Development*, 7th updated edition, 2002.

Journals:
Current Opinion in Genetics and Development, bimonthly.
Developmental Biology, monthly.
Excerpta Medica, Section 21: Developmental Biology and Teratology, 10 issues per
    year.
Genes and Development, Cold Spring Harbor Laboratory Press, bimonthly.
Roux' Archives of Developmental Biology, semiannually.

ECOLOGY

Bolen, E.G., and W.L. Robinson, *Wildlife Ecology and Management*, 5th ed., 2002.
Conner, J.K., and D.L. Hartl, *A Primer of Ecological Genetics*, 2004.
Gotelli, N.J., *A Primer of Ecology*, 3d ed., 2001.
Molles, Jr., M.C., *Ecology: Concepts and Applications*, 2d ed., 2002.
Pianka, E.R., *Evolutionary Ecology*, 6th ed., 1999.
Ricklefs, R.E., and G. Miller, *Ecology*, 4th ed., 1999.
Roughgarden J., et al. (eds.), *Perspectives in Ecological Theory*, 1989.
Smith, R.L., and T. Smith, *Ecology and Field Biology*, 6th ed., 2001.
Walker, L.R., and R. del Moral, *Primary Succession and Ecosystem Rehabilitation* (Cambridge Studies in Ecology), 2003.
Westman, W.E., *Ecology Impact, Assessment and Environmental Planning*, 1985.

Journals:

Annual Review of Ecology and Systematics, annually.
Ecological Monographs, Ecological Society of America, quarterly.
Ecology, Ecological Society of America, 6 issues per year.
Journal of Environmental Sciences, Institute of Environmental Sciences, bimonthly.

EMBRYOLOGY

See Developmental biology.

EVOLUTION

Bell, G., *Selection: The Mechanisms of Evolution*, 1996.
Futuyma, D.J., *Evolutionary Biology*, 3d ed., 1998.
Hall, B.K., *Evolutionary Developmental Biology*, 2d ed., 1998.
Li, W.-H., *Molecular Evolution*, 1997.
Strickberger, M.W., *Evolution*, 3d ed., 2000.
Williams, G.C., *Adaptation and Natural Selection: A Critique of Some Current Evolutionary Thought*, 1996.

Journals:

Evolution, The Society for the Study of Evolution, bimonthly.
Journal of Molecular Evolution, Springer-Verlag, New York, bimonthly.

FORESTRY

Anderson, D., and I.I. Holland (eds.), *Forests and Forestry*, 4th ed., 1997.
Gholz, H.L. (ed.), *Agroforestry: Realities, Possibilities and Potentials*, 1987.
Landsberg, J.J., and S.T. Gower, *Applications of Physiological Ecology to Forest Management*, 1996.
Leuschner, W.A., *Introduction to Forest Resource Management*, 1992.
Matthews, J.D., *Silvicultural Systems*, 1991.
Sharpe, G.W., and C. Hendes, *Introduction to Forestry*, 6th ed., 1995.
Shugart, H.H., *A Theory of Forest Dynamics: The Ecological Implications of Forest Succession Models*, 2003.
Young, A., *Agroforestry for Soil Conservation* (Science and Practice of Agroforestry), 1989.

Journals:

Forest Products Journal, Forest Products Research Society, monthly.
Forest Science, Society of American Foresters, quarterly.
Journal of Forestry, Society of American Foresters, monthly.

GENETIC ENGINEERING

Bourgaize, D.B., T.P. Jewell, and R. Bruiser, *Introduction to Biotechnology*, 1999.
Nicholl, D.S.T., *An Introduction to Genetic Engineering*, 2002.
Primrose, S.B., R.W. Old, and R.M. Twyman, *Principles of Gene Manipulation*, 6th ed., 2002.
Setlow, J.K. (ed.), *Genetic Engineering: Principles and Methods*, 2002.
Singer, M., and P. Berg, *Exploring Genetic Mechanisms*, 1997.
Watson, J.D., *Recombinant DNA*, 2d ed., 1995.
Weaver, R.F., *Molecular Biology*, 3d ed., 2005.

Journals:

Biotechnology News, biweekly.
Biotechnology Progress, bimonthly.
Genetic Engineering News, biweekly.
Nature Biotechnology, monthly.

GENETICS

Dobzhansky, T., *Genetics and the Origin of Species*, 1982.
Hall, J.C., J.C. Dunlap, and T. Friedman, *Advances in Genetics*, vol. 49, 2003.
Hartwell, L., et al., *Genetics: From Genes to Genomes*, 2004.
King, R.C., and W.D. Stansfield, *Dictionary of Genetics*, 6th ed., 2002.
Klug, W.S., and M.R. Cummings, *Concepts of Genetics*, 6th ed., 2002.
Scriver, C.R., et al., *The Metabolic Basis of Inherited Disease*, 8th ed., 2001.
Starr, C., and Taggart, R., *Cell Biology and Genetics* (with CD-ROM and InfoTrac), 10th ed., 2003.
Vogel, F., and A.G. Motulsky, *Human Genetics: Problems and Approaches*, 1997.
Watson, J.D., and A. Berry, *DNA: The Secret of Life*, 2003.
Watson, J.D., et al., *Molecular Biology of the Gene*, 5th ed., 2003.

Journals:

American Journal of Human Genetics, bimonthly.
Annual Review of Genetics, annually.
Annual Review of Genomics and Human Genetics, annually.
Gene, semiweekly.
Genetics, Genetics Society of America, monthly.
Journal of Heredity, American Genetic Association, bimonthly.
Molecular and General Genomics, monthly.

IMMUNOLOGY

R. Coico et al., *Immunology: A Short Course*, 5th ed., 2003.
Goldsby, R.A., T.J. Kindt, and B.A. Osborne, *Kuby Immunology*, 4th ed., 2003.
Janeway, C.A., et al., *Immunobiology: The Immune System in Health and Disease*, 5th ed., 2001.
Parham, P., *The Immune System*, 2000.
Parslow, T.G., et al., *Medical Immunology*, 10th ed., 2001.
Sell, S., and E. Max, *Immunology, Immunopathology, and Immunity*, 6th ed., 2001.

Journals:

Advances in Immunology, annually.
Annual Review of Immunology, annually.
Immunobiology, 10 issues per year.
Immunology, Abstracts (England), monthly.
Immunology Letters, bimonthly.

Journal of Immunology, American Association of Immunologists, monthly.
Trends in Immunology, Elsevier, monthly.

INVERTEBRATE ZOOLOGY

See Zoology.

MEDICAL MICROBIOLOGY

Brooks, G.F., et al., *Jawetz, Melnick & Adelberg's Medical Microbiology*, 23d ed., 2004.
Levinson, W., *Medical Microbiology and Immunology*, 8th ed., 2004.
C.A. Mims, H.M. Dockrell, and R.V. Goering, *Medical Microbiology*, 3d ed., 2004.
Ryan, K.J., and C.G. Ray, *Sherris Medical Microbiology: An Introduction to Infectious Diseases*, 4th ed., 2003.

Journals:

Annual Review of Microbiology, annually.
Antimicrobial Agents and Chemotherapy, monthly.
Journal of Clinical Microbiology, monthly.
Journal of Medical Microbiology, monthly.

MEDICINE AND PATHOLOGY

Johnson, L.R., and J.H. Byrne (eds.), *Essential Medical Physiology*, 3d ed., 2003.
Kasper, D.L., et al. (eds.), *Harrison's Principles of Internal Medicine*, 15th ed., 2004.
Kumar, V., N. Fausto, and A. Abbas, *Robbins & Cotran Pathologic Basis for Disease*, 7th ed., 2004.
Rosai, J., *Rosai and Ackerman's Surgical Pathology*, 9th ed., 2004.
Tamparo, C., and M.A. Lewis, *Diseases of the Human Body*, 3d ed., 2000.
Williams, R.H., et al., *Williams Textbook of Endocrinology*, 10th ed., 2002.

Journals:

American Journal of Cardiology, monthly.
American Journal of Diseases of Children, American Medical Association, monthly.
American Journal of Medical Technology, American Society for Medical Technology, monthly.
American Journal of Medicine, monthly.
American Journal of Pathology, monthly.
American Journal of Surgery, monthly.
Annals of Internal Medicine, American College of Physicians, monthly.
Cancer, American Cancer Society, semimonthly.
Cardiovascular News, monthly.
Circulation, American Heart Association, monthly.
Contemporary Surgery, monthly.
Endocrinology, monthly.
Human Pathology, monthly.
JAMA: Journal of the American Medical Association, monthly.
Journal of Nuclear Medicine, monthly.
Modern Medicine, monthly.
New England Journal of Medicine, weekly.

MICROBIOLOGY

Balows, A. (ed.), *Manual of Clinical Microbiology*, 5th ed., 1991.
Balows, A., et al., *The Prokaryotes*, 2d ed., 1992.

Garrity, G., D.R. Boone, and R.W. Castenholz (eds.), *The Bergey's Manual of Systematic Bacteriology*, 2d ed., 2001.

Lengeler, J., H.G. Schlegel, and G. Drews, *Biology of the Prokaryotes*, 1999.

Maddigan, M.T., J. Martinko, and J. Parker, *Brock Biology of Microorganisms*, 10th ed., 2002.

Tortora, G.J., C.L. Case, and B.R. Funke, *Microbiology: An Introduction*, 2003.

Journals:

Advances in Applied Microbiology, annually.

Advances in Microbial Physiology, irregularly.

Annual Reviews of Microbiology, annually.

Applied and Environmental Microbiology, monthly.

International Journal of Systematic and Evolutionary Microbiology, bimonthly.

Journal of Bacteriology, biweekly.

Journal of General Microbiology (England), monthly.

Microbiological Reviews, American Society for Microbiology, quarterly.

Microbiology, monthly.

Microbiology and Molecular Biology Reviews, quarterly.

MICROSCOPY

Bradbury, S., *An Introduction to the Optical Microscope*, vol. 1., 1989.

Briggs, A., *An Introduction to Scanning Acoustic Microscopy* (Microscopy Handbooks no. 12), 1986.

Duke, P.J., and A.G. Michette (eds.), *Modern Microscopy: Techniques and Applications*, 1990.

Goldstein, J.I., et al., *Scanning Electron Microscopy and X-Ray Microanalysis*, 3d ed., 2003.

Johari, O., et al. (eds.), *Scanning Electron Microscopy*, 1983.

Mayer, O., and D.J. Mayer, *Clinical Wide-Field Specular Microscopy*, 1984.

Shotton, D.M. (ed.), *Electronic Light Microscopy: The Principles and Practice of Video-enhanced, Contrast Digital Intensified Fluorescence, and Confocal, and Scanning Light Microscopy*, 1993.

Slayter, E.M., and H.S. Slayter, *Light and Electron Microscopy*, 1992.

Wilson, T.C., and J.R. Sheppard, *Theory and Practice of Scanning Optical Microscopy*, 1984.

Wilson, T. (ed.), *Confocal Microscopy*, 1990.

Wischnitzer, S., *Introduction to Electron Microscopy*, 3d ed., 1981.

Journals:

Micron, quarterly.

Microscope, Cutter Laboratories, 10 issues per year.

The Microscope, McCrone Research Institute, quarterly.

MOLECULAR BIOLOGY

See Cell and molecular biology.

MYCOLOGY

Ainsworth, G.C., et al., *Ainsworth and Bisby's Dictionary of Fungi*, 9th ed., 2001.

Burnett, J.H., *Fungal Populations and Species* (Life Science), 2003.

Carlile, M.J., et al., *The Fungi*, 2d ed., 2001.

Khachatourians, G.G., et al., *Applied Mycology and Biotechnology: Fungal Genomics*, 2003.

Ulloa, M., and R.T. Hanlin, *Illustrated Dictionary of Mycology*, 2000.

Watanabe, T., *Pictorial Atlas of Soil and Seed Fungi: Morphologies of Cultured Fungi and Key to Species*, 2d ed., 2002.

Journals:
FEMS Yeast Research, Elsevier, quarterly.
Fungal Genetics and Biology, Elsevier, 9 issues per year.
Medical Mycology, Taylor & Francies, bimonthly.
Mycological Research, British Mycological Society, monthly.
Mycologist, British Mycological Society, monthly.

NEUROPSYCHOLOGY

Beaumont, J.G., P. Kenealy, and M.J. Rogers, *The Blackwell Dictionary of Neuropsychology*, 1996.
Gazzaniga, M.S., R.B. Ivry, and G.R. Manguan, *Cognitive Neuroscience: The Biology of the Mind*, 2d ed., 2002.
Heilman, K., and E. Valenstein, *Clinical Neuropsychology* (Medicine), 2003.
Kolb, B., and I.Q. Whishaw, *Fundamentals of Neuropsychology*, 2003.
M.D. Lezak, *Neuropsychological Assessment*, Oxford University Press, 2004.
Loring, D.W., and K.J. Meador, *Dictionary of Neuropsychology*, 1999.
Spreen, O., and E. Strauss, *Compendium of Neuropsychological Tests: Administration, Norms, and Commentary*, 2d ed., 1998.

NEUROSCIENCE

Bear, M., B. Conners, and M. Paradiso, *Neuroscience: Exploring the Brain*, 2d ed., 2002.
Butler, A.B., and W. Hodos, *Comparative Vertebrate Neuroanatomy: Evolution and Adaptation*, 1996.
Cooper, J.R., F.E. Bloom, and R.H. Roth, *Biochemical Basis of Neuropharmacology*, 8th ed., 2002.
Kandel, E.R., J.H. Schwartz, and T.M. Jessell (eds.), *Principles of Neuroscience*, 4th ed., 2000.
Levitan, I.B., and L. Kaczmarek, *The Neuron*, 3d ed., 2001.
Nestler, E.J., S.E. Hyman, and R.C. Malenka, *Molecular Basis of Neuropharmacology*, 2001.
Nicholls, J.G., et al., *From Neuron to Brain*, 4th ed., 2001.
Purves, D., et al. (eds.), *Neuroscience*, 3d ed., 2004.
Shepherd, G.M. (ed.), *Synaptic Organization of the Brain*, 5th ed., 2003.
Shepherd, G.M., *Neurobiology*, 3d ed., 1994.

Journals:
Annual Review of Neuroscience, Annual Reviews, yearly.
Journal of Neuroscience, Society for Neuroscience, weekly.
Nature Neuroscience, Nature Publishing, monthly.
Neuron, Cell Press, bimonthly.
Trends in Neurosciences, Elsevier, monthly.

PALEONTOLOGY

Benton, M.J., and J. Sibbock, *Vertebrate Paleontology*, 2000.
Briggs, D., D. Erwin, and F.J. Collier, *The Fossils of the Burgess Shale*, 1995.
Briggs, D.E.G., and P.R. Crowther, *Palaeobiology II*, 2002.
Carroll, R., *Vertebrate Paleontology and Evolution*, 1987.
Clack, J.A., *Gaining Ground: The Origin and Early Evolution of Tetrapods*, 2002.
Gould, S.J., *The Book of Life: An Illustrated History of the Evolution of Life on Earth*, 2d ed., 2001.

Jackson, J.B.C., S. Lidgard, and A.H. Cheetham, *Evolutionary Patterns: Growth, Form, and Tempo in the Fossil Record*, 2001.

Knoll, A.H., *Life on a Young Planet: The First Three Million Years of Evolution on Earth*, 2003.

Lowell, D., and T. Rowe, *The Mistaken Extinction: Dinosaur Evolution and the Origin of Birds*, 1997.

Minkoff, E.C., E.H. Colbert, and M. Morales, *Colbert's Evolution of the Vertebrates*, 2001.

Prothero, D.R., *Bringing Fossils to Life: An Introduction to Paleobiology*, 2003.

Rudwick, M.J., *The Meaning of Fossils: Episodes in the History of Paleontology*, 2d ed., 1985.

Simpson, G.G., *Life in the Past: An Introduction to Paleontology*, 2003.

Vermeij, G.J., *Evolution and Escalation: An Ecological History of Life*, 1987.

Willis, K., and J. McElwain, *The Evolution of Plants*, 2002.

Journals:

Journal of Paleontology, Society of Economic Paleontologists and Mineralogists, bimonthly.

Journal of Vertebrate Paleontology, Society of Vertebrate Paleontology, quarterly.

Palaeontology, Palaeontological Association, bimonthly.

Paleobiology, Paleontology Society, quarterly.

PHARMACOLOGY

Hardman, J.G., and L.E. Limbird (eds.), *Goodman and Gilman's The Pharmacological Basis of Therapeutics*, 10th ed., 2001.

Katzung, B.G. (ed.), *Basic and Clinical Pharmacology*, 8th ed., 2000.

Licino, J., and M.-L. Wong, *Pharmacogenomics: The Search for Individualized Therapies*, 2002.

Neal, M.J., *Medical Pharmacology at a Glance*, 4th ed., 2002.

Physicians' Desk Reference, 2004.

Journals:

Advances in Pharmacology and Chemotherapy, irregularly.

American Pharmacy, American Pharmaceutical Association, monthly.

Biochemical Pharmacology, monthly.

Excerpta Medica, Section 80: Pharmacology and Toxicology, 30 issues per year.

Hospital Pharmacy Today, monthly.

PHYSIOLOGY

Berne, R.M., et al. (eds.), *Physiology*, 5th ed., 2003.

Costanzo, L.S., *Physiology*, 1998.

Dantzler, W.H., *Comparative Physiology*, 1997.

Fong, E., *Body Structures and Functions*, 1998.

Ganong, W.A., *Review of Medical Physiology*, 21st ed., 2003.

Guyton, A.C., and J.E. Hall, *Textbook of Medical Physiology*, 10th ed., 2001.

Malvin, R.L., et al., *Concepts of Human Physiology*, 1997.

Porterfield, S.P., *Endocrine Physiology*, 2d ed., 2001.

Prosser, C.L., *Comparative Animal Physiology*, 4th ed., 1991.

Randall, D., et al., *Eckert Animal Physiology: Mechanisms and Adaptations*, 2001.

Rhoades, R.A., and R.G. Pflanzer, *Human Physiology*, 4th ed., 2002.

Sherwood, L., H. Klandorf, and P.H. Yancy, *Animal Physiology*, 2005.

Sperelakis, N., *Cell Physiology Source Book: A Molecular Approach*, 2001.

Journals:
American Journal of Physiology, American Physiological Society, monthly.
Annual Review of Physiology, annually.
Journal of Comparative Physiology, A: Sensory, Neural, and Behavioral Physiology, and B: Systematic and Environmental Physiology, irregularly.
Journal of General Physiology, monthly.
Journal of Physiology (England), monthly.
Physiological Reviews, American Physiological Society, quarterly.

PLANT ANATOMY

Bowes, B.G., *A Colour Atlas of Plant Structure*, 1996.
Dickison, W.C., *Integrative Plant Anatomy*, 2000.
Fahn, A., *Plant Anatomy*, 4th ed., 1990.
Mauseth, J.D., *Plant Anatomy*, 1988.
Nabors, M., *Introduction to Botany*, 2004.
Northington, D.K., et al., *The Botanical World*, 2d ed., 1995.
Pearson, L.C., *The Diversity of Evolution of Plants*, 1995.
Raven, P.H., R.F. Evert, and S.E. Eichhorn, *Biology of Plants*, 1999.
Rudall, P., *Anatomy of Flowering Plants: An Introduction to Structure and Development*, 1987.

PLANT PATHOLOGY

Agrios, G.N., *Plant Pathology*, 4th ed., 1997.
Dickinson, M., and J. Beynon (eds.), *Molecular Plant Pathology*, 2000.
Lucas, G.B., C.L. Campbell, and L.T. Lucas, *Introduction to Plant Diseases: Identification and Management*, 2d ed., 1992.
Lucas, J.A., *Plant Pathology and Plant Pathogens*, 1998.
Matthews, R.E., et al., *Plant Virology*, 4th ed., 2001.
Sinclair, W.A., H. Lyon, and W.T. Johnson, *Diseases of Trees and Shrubs*, 1987.
Strange, R.N., *Introduction of Plant Pathology*, 2003.
Talbot, N., *Plant-Pathogen Interactions*, 2004.
Vidhyasekaran, P., *Concise Encyclopedia of Plant Pathology*, 2004.
Zamir K.P. (ed.), *Fungal Disease Resistance in Plants: Biochemistry, Molecular Biology, and Genetic Engineering*, 2004.

Journals:
Annual Review of Phytopathology, annually.
Plant Disease, American Phytopathological Society, monthly.

PLANT PHYSIOLOGY

Baker, N.R., *Photosynthesis and the Environment* (Advances in Photosynthesis), 1996.
Bewley, J.D., and M. Black, *Seeds: Physiology Development and Germination* (The Language of Science), 2d ed., 1994.
Blankenship, R.E., *Molecular Mechanisms of Photosynthesis*, 2002.
Chrispeels, M.J., and D.E. Sadava, *Plants, Genes, and Crop Biotechnology*, 2d ed., 2003.
Davies, P.J., *Plant Hormones: Physiology, Biochemistry and Molecular Biology*, 1995.
Epstrin, E., and A.J. Bloom, *Mineral Nutrition of Plants: Principles and Perspectives*, 2d ed., 2004.
Kramer, P.J., and J.S. Boyer, *Water Relations of Plants and Soils*, 1995.

Leyser, O., and S. Day, *Mechanisms in Plant Development*, 2003.
Raven, P.H., et al., *Biology of Plants*, 6th ed., 1998.
Taiz, L., and E. Zeiger, *Plant Physiology*, 3d ed., 2002.

Journals:
Current Opinion in Plant Biology, Elsevier, bimonthly.
The Plant Cell, American Society of Plant Biologists, monthly.
Plant Cell and Environment, monthly.
Plant Journal, bimonthly.
Plant Physiology, American Society of Plant Biologists, monthly.
Planta, Springer-Verlag, monthly.
Trends in Plant Science, monthly.

PSYCHIATRY

American Psychiatric Association, *Diagnostic and Statistical Manual of Mental Disorders*, text revision, 4th ed., 1994.
Freud, S., et al., *Outline of Psychoanalysis*, rev. ed., 1989.
Garfield, S.L., *Psychotherapy: An Eclectic Integrative Approach* (Wiley Series on Personality Processes), 2d ed., 1995.
Tasman, A., J. Kay, and J.A. Lieberman, *Psychiatry*, 2d ed., vols. 1 and 2, 2003.
Waldinger, R.J., *Psychiatry for Medical Students*, 3d ed., 1997.

Journals:
American Journal of Psychiatry, American Psychiatric Association, monthly.
Psychiatric News, American Psychiatric Association, biweekly.

PSYCHOLOGY

Aronson, E., *The Social Animal*, 8th ed., 1999.
Carlson, N.R., *Physiology of Behavior*, 7th ed., 2000.
Gerow, J.R., *Essentials of Psychology*, 2d ed., 1996.
Gerow, J.R., and K. Bordens, *Psychology: An Introduction*, 7th ed., 2001.
Kalat, J.W., *Introduction to Psychology*, 6th ed., 2001.

Journals:
American Psychologist, American Psychological Association Inc., monthly.
Annual Review of Psychology, annually.
Contemporary Psychology, American Psychological Association, Inc., monthly.

SYSTEMATICS

Avise, J.C., *Phylogeography: The History and Formation of Species*, 2000.
Brooks, D.R., and D.A. McLennan, *The Nature of Diversity: An Evolutionary Voyage of Discovery*, 2002.
Ereshefsky, M., *The Poverty of the Linnaean Hierarchy: A Philosophical Study of Biological Taxonomy*, 2001.
Felsenstein, J., *Inferring Phylogenies*, 2004.
Ghiselin, M.T., *Metaphysics and the Origin of Species*, 1997.
Hillis, D.M., C. Moritz, and B.K. Mable (eds.), *Molecular Systematics*, 2d ed., 1996.
Schuh, R.T., *Biological Systematics: Principles and Applications*, 2000.
Wilson, R.A. (ed.), *Species: New Interdisciplinary Essays*, 1999.

Journals:
Cladistics, Willi Hennig Society, bimonthly.
Systematic Biology, Society of Systematic Zoology, bimonthly.

VERTEBRATE ZOOLOGY

See Zoology.

VETERINARY MEDICINE

Aiello, S.E. (ed.), *The Merck Veterinary Manual,* 8th ed., 1998.
Ettinger, S.J., and E.C. Feldman, *Textbook of Veterinary Internal Medicine,* 4th ed., 1995.
Fenner, W.R., *Quick Reference to Veterinary Medicine,* 3d ed., 2000.
Howard, J.L., and R.A. Smith, *Current Veterinary Therapy 4: Food Animal Practice,* 1999.
Timoney, J.F., *Hagan and Bruner's Microbiology and Infectious Diseases of Domestic Animals,* 8th ed., 1988.

VIROLOGY

Belshe, R.B., *Textbook of Human Virology,* 2d ed., 1990.
Diener, T.O. (ed.), *The Viroids* (The Viruses), 1987.
Dimmock, N.J., P.D. Griffiths, and C.R. Madeley (eds.), *Control of Virus Diseases,* 1990.
Fields, B.N., *Virology* 3d ed., 1995.
Flint, S.J., et al. (eds.), *Principles of Virology: Molecular Biology, Pathogenesis, and Control,* 2d ed., 2000.
ICTVdB: The Universal Virus Database of the International Committee on Taxonomy of Viruses, maintained by C. Büchen-Osmond [http://www.ncbi.nlm.nih.gov/ICTVdB/ICTVdBintro.htm].
Knipe, D.M. *Fundamental Virology,* 4th ed., 2001.
Matthews, R.E., et al., *Matthew's Plant Virology,* 4th ed., 2001.
Nathanson, N. (ed.), *Viral Pathogenesis,* 1997.
Voyles, B.A., *Biology of the Viruses,* 2d ed., 2002.
Wagner, E.K., and M.J. Hewlett, *Basic Virology,* 1999.

Journals:
Advances in Virus Research, irregularly.
Excerpta Medica, Section 47: Virology, 10 issues per year.
Journal of Virology, American Society for Microbiology, bimonthly.

ZOOLOGY

Alcock, J., *Animal Behavior: An Evolutionary Approach,* 7th ed., 2001.
Barnes, R.D., R.S. Fox, and E.E. Ruppert, *Invertebrate Zoology,* 7th ed., 2003.
Bond, C.E., *Biology of Fishes,* 2d ed., 1996.
Dorit, R., W.F. Walker, and R.D. Barnes, *Zoology,* 1991.
Feduccia, A., and E. McCrady, *Torrey's Morphogenesis of the Vertebrates,* 5th ed., 1991.
Grzimek, B. (ed.), *Grzimek's Encyclopedia of Mammals,* 2d ed., 1989.
Hickman, C.P., L.S. Roberts, and A. Larson, *Integrated Principles of Zoology,* 11th ed., 2000.
Hildebrand, M., and G. Goslow, *Analysis of Vertebrate Structure,* 5th ed., 2001.
Kardong, K.V., *Vertebrates,* 2d ed., 1998.
Linzey, D.W., *Vertebrate Biology,* 2001.
McFarland, D., *Animal Behavior, Psychobiology, Ethology, and Evolution,* 3d ed., 1998.
Meglitsch, P.A., and F.R. Schram, *Invertebrate Zoology,* 3d ed., 1991.
Miller, S.A., and J.P. Harley, *Zoology,* 6th ed., 2004.

Pearse, V., et al., *Living Invertebrates*, 1987.
Pough, F., et al., *Vertebrate Life*, 6th ed., 2001.

Journals:

Integrative and Comparative Biology, Society for Integrative and Comparative Biology,
   bimonthly.
Journal of Zoology, monthly.

Equivalents of commonly used units for the U.S. Customary System and the metric system

1 inch = 2.5 centimeters (25 millimeters)
1 foot = 0.3 meter (30 centimeters)
1 yard = 0.9 meter
1 mile = 1.6 kilometers

1 acre = 0.4 hectare
1 acre = 4047 square meters

1 gallon = 3.8 liters
1 fluid ounce = 29.6 milliliters
32 fluid ounces = 946.4 milliliters

1 quart = 0.95 liter
1 ounce = 28.35 grams
1 pound = 0.45 kilogram
1 ton = 907.18 kilograms

$°F = (1.8 \times °C) + 32$

1 centimeter = 0.4 inch
1 meter = 3.3 feet
1 meter = 1.1 yards
1 kilometer = 0.62 mile

1 hectare = 2.47 acres
1 square meter = 0.00025 acre

1 liter = 1.06 quarts = 0.26 gallon
1 milliliter = 0.034 fluid ounce

1 gram = 0.035 ounce
1 kilogram = 2.2 pounds
1 kilogram = 1.1×10^{-3} ton

$°C = (°F − 32) ÷ 1.8$

1 inch = 0.083 foot
1 foot = 0.33 yard (12 inches)
1 yard = 3 feet (36 inches)
1 mile = 5280 feet (1760 yards)

1 quart = 0.25 gallon (32 ounces; 2 pints)
1 pint = 0.125 gallon (16 ounces)
1 gallon = 4 quarts (8 pints)

1 ounce = 0.0625 pound
1 pound = 16 ounces
1 ton = 2000 pounds

Conversion factors for the U.S. Customary System, metric system, and International System

A. Units of length

Units	cm	m	in.	ft	yd	mi
1 cm	= 1	0.01*	0.3937008	0.03280840	0.01093613	6.213712×10^{-6}
1 m	= 100.	1	39.37008	3.280840	1.093613	6.213712×10^{-4}
1 in.	= 2.54*	0.0254	1	0.08333333...	0.02777777...	1.578283×10^{-5}
1 ft	= 30.48	0.3048	12.*	1	0.3333333...	$1.893939... \times 10^{-4}$
1 yd	= 91.44	0.9144	36.	3.*	1	$5.681818... \times 10^{-4}$
1 mi	$= 1.609344 \times 10^{5}$	1.609344×10^{3}	6.336×10^{4}	5280.*	1760.	1

B. Units of area

Units	cm²	m²	in.²	ft²	yd²	mi²
1 cm²	= 1	10^{-4}*	0.1550003	1.076391×10^{-3}	1.195990×10^{-4}	3.861022×10^{-11}
1 m²	$= 10^{4}$	1	1550.003	10.76391	1.195990	3.861022×10^{-7}
1 in.²	= 6.4516*	6.4516×10^{-4}	1	$6.944444... \times 10^{-3}$	7.716049×10^{-4}	2.490977×10^{-10}
1 ft²	= 929.0304	0.09290304	144.*	1	0.7777777...	3.587007×10^{-8}
1 yd²	= 8361.273	0.8361273	1296.	9.*	1	3.228306×10^{-7}
1 mi²	$= 2.589988 \times 10^{10}$	2.589988×10^{6}	4.014490×10^{9}	2.78784×10^{7}*	3.0976×10^{6}	1

C. Units of volume

Units		m³	cm³	liter	in.³	ft³	qt	gal
1 m³	=	1	10^6	10^3	6.102374×10^4	35.31467×10^{-3}	1.056688	264.1721
1 cm³	=	10^{-6}	1	10^{-3}	0.06102374	3.531467×10^{-5}	1.056688×10^{-3}	2.641721×10^{-4}
1 liter	=	10^{-3}	1000.*	1	61.02374	0.03531467	1.056688	0.264 1721
1 in.³	=	1.638706×10^{-5}	16.38706*	0.0163870 6	1	5.787037×10^{-4}	0.01731602	4.329004×10^{-3}
1 ft³	=	2.831685×10^{-2}	28316.85	28.31685	1728.*	1	2.992208	7.480520
1 qt	=	9.463529×10^{-4}	946.3529	0.9463529	57.75	0.0342014	1	0.25
1 gal (U.S.)	=	3.785412×10^{-3}	3785.412	3.785412	231.*	0.1336806	4.*	1

D. Units of mass

Units		g	kg	oz	lb	metric ton	ton
1 g	=	1	10^{-3}	0.03527396	2.204623×10^{-3}	10^{-6}	1.102311×10^{-6}
1 kg	=	1000.	1	35.27396	2.204623	10^{-3}	1.102311×10^{-3}
1 oz (avdp)	=	28.34952	0.02834952	1	0.0625	2.834952×10^{-5}	3.125×10^{-5}
1 lb (avdp)	=	453.5924	0.4535924	16.*	1	4.535924×10^{-4}	$5. \times 10^{-4}$
1 metric ton	=	10^6	1000.*	35273.96	2204.623	1	1.102311
1 ton	=	907184.7	907.1847	32000.	2000.*	0.9071847	1

Conversion factors for the U.S. Customary System, metric system, and International System (cont.)

E. Units of density

Units	$g \cdot cm^{-3}$	$g \cdot L^{-1}, kg \cdot m^{-3}$	$oz \cdot in.^{-3}$	$lb \cdot in.^{-3}$	$lb \cdot ft^{-3}$	$lb \cdot gal^{-1}$
$1\ g \cdot cm^{-3}$ = 1	1	1000.	0.5780365	0.03612728	62.42795	8.345403
$1\ g \cdot L^{-1}, kg \cdot m^{-3}$ = 10^{-3}	10^{-3}	1	5.780365×10^{-4}	3.612728×10^{-5}	0.06242795	8.345403×10^{-3}
$1\ oz \cdot in.^{-3}$ = 1.729994	1.729994	1729.994	1	0.0625	108.	14.4375
$1\ lb \cdot in.^{-3}$ = 27.67991	27.67991	27679.91	16.	1	1728.	231.
$1\ lb \cdot ft^{-3}$ = 0.01601847	0.01601847	16.01847	9.259259×10^{-3}	5.787037×10^{-4}	1	0.1336806
$1\ lb \cdot gal^{-1}$ = 0.1198264	0.1198264	119.8264	4.749536×10^{-3}	4.329004×10^{-3}	7.480519	1

F. Units of pressure

Units	$Pa, N \cdot m^{-2}$	$dyn \cdot cm^{-2}$	bar	atm	$kgf \cdot cm^{-2}$	mmHg (torr)	in. Hg	$lbf \cdot in.^{-2}$
$1\ Pa, 1\ N \cdot m^{-2}$ = 1	1	10	10^{-5}	9.869233×10^{-6}	1.019716×10^{-5}	7.500617×10^{-3}	2.952999×10^{-4}	1.450377×10^{-4}
$1\ dyn \cdot cm^{-2}$ = 0.1	0.1	1	10^{-6}	9.869233×10^{-7}	1.019716×10^{-6}	7.500617×10^{-4}	2.952999×10^{-5}	1.450377×10^{-5}
1 bar = 10^{5}*	10^{6}	10^{6}	1	0.9869233	1.019716	750.0617	29.52999	14.50377
1 atm = 101325*	1013250	1013250	1.01325	1	1.033227	760.	29.92126	14.69595
$1\ kgf \cdot cm^{-2}$ = 98066.5	980665	980665	0.980665	0.9678411	1	735.5592	28.95903	14.22334
1 mmHg (torr) = 133.3224	1333.224	1333.224	1.333224×10^{3}	1.315789×10^{-3}	1.3595510×10^{-3}	1	0.03937008	0.01933678
1 in. Hg = 3386.388	33863.88	33863.88	0.03386388	0.03342105	0.03453155	25.4	1	0.4911541
$1\ lbf \cdot in.^{-2}$ = 6894.757	68947.57	68947.57	0.06894757	0.06804596	0.07030696	51.71493	2.036021	1

G. Units of energy

Units	g mass (energy equiv)	J	eV	cal	cal$_{IT}$	Btu$_{IT}$	kWh	hp-h	ft-lbf	ft$^3 \cdot$ lbf $\cdot$ in.$^{-2}$	liter-atm
1 g mass (energy equiv)	= 1	8.987552×10^{13}	5.609589×10^{32}	2.148076×10^{13}	2.146640×10^{13}	8.518555×10^{10}	2.496542×10^{7}	3.347918×10^{7}	6.628878×10^{13}	4.603388×10^{11}	8.870024×10^{11}
1 J	$= 1.112650 \times 10^{-14}$	1	6.241509×10^{18}	0.2390057	0.2388459	9.478172×10^{-4}	$2.777777\ldots \times 10^{-7}$	3.725062×10^{-7}	0.7375622	5.121960×10^{-3}	9.869233×10^{-3}
1 eV	$= 1.782662 \times 10^{-33}$	1.602177×10^{-19}	1	3.829294×10^{-20}	3.826733×10^{-20}	1.518570×10^{-22}	4.450490×10^{-26}	5.968206×10^{-26}	1.181705×10^{-19}	8.206283×10^{-22}	1.581225×10^{-21}
1 cal	$= 4.655328 \times 10^{-14}$	4.184*	2.611448×10^{19}	1	0.9993312	3.965667×10^{-3}	$1.1622222\ldots \times 10^{-6}$	1.558562×10^{-6}	3.085960	2.143028×10^{-2}	0.04129287
1 cal$_{IT}$	$= 4.658443 \times 10^{-14}$	4.1868*	2.613195×10^{19}	1.000669	1	3.968321×10^{-3}	1.163×10^{-6}	1.559609×10^{-6}	3.088025	2.144462×10^{-2}	0.04132050
1 Btu$_{IT}$	$= 1.173908 \times 10^{-11}$	1055.056	6.585141×10^{21}	252.1644	251.9958	1	2.930711×10^{-4}	3.930148×10^{-4}	778.1693	5.403953	10.41259
1 kWh	$= 4.005540 \times 10^{-8}$	3600000.*	2.246943×10^{25}	860420.7	859845.2	3412.142	1	1.341022	2655224.	18349.06	35529.24
1 hp-h	$= 2.986931 \times 10^{-8}$	2364519.	1.675545×10^{25}	641615.6	641186.5	2544.33	0.7456998	1	1980000.*	13750.	26494.15
1 ft-lbf	$= 1.508551 \times 10^{-14}$	1.355818	8.462351×10^{18}	0.3240483	0.3238315	1.285067×10^{-3}	3.766161×10^{-7}	$5.050505\ldots \times 10^{-7}$	1	$6.944444\ldots \times 10^{-3}$	0.01338088
1 ft$^3 \cdot$ lbf $\cdot$ in.$^{-2}$	$= 2.172313 \times 10^{-12}$	195.2378	1.218578×10^{21}	46.66295.	46.63174	0.1850497	5.423272×10^{-5}	$7.272727\ldots \times 10^{-5}$	144.*	1	1.926847
1 liter-atm	$= 1.127393 \times 10^{-12}$	101.325	6.3242109×10^{20}	24.21726	24.20106	0.09603757	2.814583×10^{-5}	3.774419×10^{-5}	74.73349	0.5189825	1

*Numbers followed by an asterisk are definitions of the relation between the two units.

ABO blood group system

Blood group	RBC (red blood cell) antigens	Possible genotypes	Plasma antibody
A	A	AA or A/O	Anti-B
B	B	B/B or B/O	Anti-A
O	—	C/O	Anti-A and anti-B
AB	A and B	A/B	—

Amino acid abbreviations

Ala	Alanine	Leu	Leucine
Arg	Arginine	Lys	Lysine
Asn	Asparagine	Met	Methionine
Asp	Aspartic acid	Phe	Phenylalanine
Cys	Cysteine	Pro	Proline
Gln	Glutamine	Ser	Serine
Glu	Glutamic acid	Thr	Threonine
Gly	Glycine	Trp	Tryptophan
His	Histidine	Tyr	Tyrosine
Ile	Isoleucine	Val	Valine

Universal (standard) genetic code*

RNA BASES:

RNA BASES:	U	C	A	G
U	UUU ⎤ Phe UUC ⎦ UUA ⎤ Leu UUG ⎦	UCU ⎤ UCC ⎥ Ser UCA ⎥ UCG ⎦	UAU ⎤ Tyr UAC ⎦ UAA ⎤ Stop UAG ⎦	UGU ⎤ Cys UGC ⎦ UGA Stop UGG Trp
C	CUU ⎤ CUC ⎥ Leu CUA ⎥ CUG ⎦	CCU ⎤ CCC ⎥ Pro CCA ⎥ CCG ⎦	CAU ⎤ His CAC ⎦ CAA ⎤ Gln CAG ⎦	CGU ⎤ CGC ⎥ Arg CGA ⎥ CGG ⎦
A	AUU ⎤ AUC ⎥ Ile AUA ⎦ AUG Met	ACU ⎤ ACC ⎥ Thr ACA ⎥ ACG ⎦	AAU ⎤ Asn AAC ⎦ AAA ⎤ Lys AAG ⎦	AGU ⎤ Ser AGC ⎦ AGA ⎤ Arg AGG ⎦
G	GUU ⎤ GUC ⎥ Val GUA ⎥ GUG ⎦	GCU ⎤ GCC ⎥ Ala GCA ⎥ GCG ⎦	GAU ⎤ Asp GAC ⎦ GAA ⎤ Glu GAG ⎦	GGU ⎤ GGC ⎥ Gly GGA ⎥ GGG ⎦

*Each of the 64 codons found in mRNA specifies an amino acid (indicated by the common three-letter abbreviation) or the end of the protein chain (stop). U, uracil; C, cytosine; A, adenine; G, guanine.

Some functions of essential vitamins

Vitamins	Functions	Best sources	Deficiency	Daily recommended dietary allowance (RDA) for adults	
				Men	Women
FAT-SOLUBLE					
Vitamin A (retinoids, carotenes)	Maintenance of vision in dim light, growth, reproduction	Fish liver oils; liver; dairy products; yellow, orange, and green plants; carrots; sweet potatoes	Poor growth and night vision; blindness	900 µg or 3000 IU	700 µg or 2330 IU
Vitamin D (cholecalciferol)	Rickets-preventive factor, calcification of bones, calcium and phosphorus metabolism	Fish oils, fortified dairy products	Rickets, osteomalacia	5 µg or 200 IU* (ages 19–50) 10 µg or 400 IU* (ages 50–70) 15 µg or 600 IU* (ages 70+)	5 µg or 200 IU* (ages 19–50) 10 µg or 400 IU* (ages 50–70) 15 µg or 600 IU* (ages 70+)
Vitamin E (tocopherols)	Antioxidant, membrane integrity and metabolism, heme synthesis	Grains and vegetable oils	Neuropathy	15 mg or 22 IU	15 mg or 22 IU
Vitamin K	Blood-clotting factor	Green vegetables	Bleeding	120 µg	90 µg

	Function	Sources	Deficiency	RDA	RDA
WATER-SOLUBLE					
Ascorbic acid (vitamin C)	Antiscorbutic (scurvy-preventive) factor, collagen formation, neurotransmitter synthesis	Citrus fruits, fresh vegetables, potatoes	Scurvy	90 mg	75 mg
Thiamine (vitamin B-1)	Antiberiberi factor, energy utilization, particularly from carbohydrates	Pork, liver, whole grains	Beriberi	1.2 mg	1.1 mg
Riboflavin (vitamin B-2)	Energy utilization, protein metabolism	Milk, egg white, liver, leafy vegetables	Cheilosis, glossitis	1.3 mg	1.1 mg
Niacin (vitamin B-3)	Antipellagra factor, energy release from carbohydrate, fat, and protein	Yeast, wheat germ, meats	Pellagra	16 mg	14 mg
Vitamin B-6 (pyridoxine, pyridoxal, pyridoxamine)	Coenzyme for protein metabolism	Whole grains, yeast, egg yolk, liver	Skin disorders; convulsion in infants	1.3 mg (ages 19–50) 1.7 mg (ages 50+)	1.3 mg (ages 19–50) 1.5 mg (ages 50+)
Pantothenic acid	Metabolism of protein, carbohydrate, fat	Liver, kidney, green vegetables, egg yolk		5 mg*	5 mg*
Folate	Transfer of one-carbon units in metabolism	Liver, deep-green leafy vegetables	Macrocytic anemias	400 µg	400 µg
Vitamin B-12 (cobalarrin)	Blood formation, nervous tissue metabolism	Liver, kidney, yeast	Skin disorders	2.4 µg	2.4 µg
Biotin	Synthesis and oxidation of fatty acids and carbohydrates	Liver, meats	Pernicious anemia	30 µg*	30 µg*

*Adequate intake (AI); used when there is insufficient data to establish an RDA.

SOURCES Facts About Dietary Supplements, NIH Clinical Center, National Institutes of Health, http://www.cc.nih.gov/ccc/supplements/intro.html; Dietary Reference Intakes: Vitamins, Food and Nutrition Board, National Academy of Science, www4.nationalacademies.org/iom/iomhome.nsf/WFiles/webtablevitamins/$file/webtablevitamins.pdf.

Major groups of viruses*

Group	Host	Morphology	Examples of viruses
Class I viruses: double-stranded DNA genomes			
Myoviridae	Bacteria	Complex	T4
Siphoviridae	Bacteria	Complex	λ
Podoviridae	Bacteria	Complex	T7
Papovaviridae	Animal	Naked icosahedral	Polyomavirus, SV40
Adenoviridae	Animal	Naked icosahedral	Adenovirus
Herpesviridae	Animal	Enveloped icosahedral	Herpes simplex, varicella-zoster
Poxviridae	Animal	Complex	Smallpox, vaccinia
Hepadnaviridae	Animal	Enveloped icosahedral	Hepatitis B
Caulimoviruses	Plant	Naked icosahedral	Cauliflower mosaic
Class II viruses: single-stranded DNA genomes			
Microviridae	Bacteria	Naked icosahedral	ϕX174
Parvoviridae	Animal	Naked icosahedral	Parvovirus, adeno-associated virus
Geminiviruses	Plant	Fused-pair icosahedral	Maize streak
Class III viruses: double-stranded RNA genomes			
Reoviridae	Animal	Naked icosahedral	Reovirus, rotavirus
Class IV viruses: positive-strand RNA genomes			
Leviviridae	Bacteria	Naked icosahedral	MS2, Qβ
Picornaviridae	Animal	Naked icosahedral	Poliovirus, rhinovirus, hepatitis A, coxsackievirus
Togaviridae	Animal	Enveloped icosahedral	Sindbis
Coronaviridae	Animal	Enveloped helical	Murine hepatitis
Potyvirus	Plant	Naked helical	Potato Y
Tymovirus	Plant	Naked icosahedral	Turnip yellow mosaic
Tobamovirus	Plant	Naked helical	Tobacco mosaic
Comovirus	Plant	Naked icosahedral	Cowpea mosaic
Class V viruses: negative-strand RNA genomes			
Rhabdoviridae	Animal and plant	Enveloped helical	Rabies, vesicular stomatitis
Paramyxoviridae	Animal	Enveloped helical	Mumps, measles, parainfluenza
Filoviridae	Animal	Enveloped helical	Ebola
Orthomyxoviridae	Animal	Enveloped helical	Influenza A, B
Bunyaviridae	Animal	Enveloped helical	Phlebovirus
Arenaviridae	Animal	Enveloped helical	Lassa
Class VI viruses: retroviruses			
Retroviridae	Animal	Enveloped icosahedral	Human immunodeficiency virus (HIV)

*Reproduced with permission from B.A. Voyles, *The Biology of Viruses*, 2d ed., McGraw-Hill, 2002.

Cranial nerves of vertebrates

Number	Name	Fiber types	Peripheral origin or destination	Vertebrates possessing this nerve
—	Terminal	Somatic sensory	Anterior nasal epithelium	Almost all
I	Olfactory	Special sensory	Olfactory mucosa	All
—	Vomeronasal	Special sensory	Vomeronasal mucosa	Almost all
II	Optic	Special sensory	Retina of eye	All
III	Oculomotor	Somatic motor	Four extrinsic eye muscles	All
IV	Trochlear	Somatic motor	One extrinsic eye muscle	All
V	Trigeminal	Special visceral motor	Muscles of mandibular arch derivative	All
		Somatic sensory	Most of head	All
VI	Abducens	Somatic motor	One extrinsic eye muscle	All
—	Anterior lateral line	Special sensory	Lateral line organs of head	Fish and larval amphibians
VII	Facial	Special visceral motor	Muscles of hyoid arch derivative	All
		General visceral motor	Salivary glands	All
		Somatic sensory	Small part of head	All
		Visceral sensory	Anterior pharynx	All
		Special sensory	Taste, anterior tongue	All
VIII	Vestibulocochlear	Special sensory	Inner ear	All
—	Posterior lateral line	Special sensory	Lateral line organs of trunk	Fish and larval amphibians
IX	Glossopharyngeal	Special visceral motor	Muscles of third branchial arch	All
		General visceral motor	Salivary gland	All
		Somatic sensory	Skin near ear	All
		Visceral sensory	Part of pharynx	All
		Special sensory	Taste, posterior tongue	All
X	Vagus	Special visceral motor	Muscles of arches 4–6	All
		General visceral motor	Most viscera of entire trunk	All
		Visceral sensory	Larynx and part of pharynx	All
		Special sensory	Taste, pharynx	All
XI	Spinal accessory	Special visceral motor	Some muscles of arches 4–6	Reptiles, birds, mammals
XII	Hypoglossal	Somatic motor	Muscles of tongue and anterior throat	Reptiles, birds, mammals

Classification of living organisms

Domain Archaea[d]
  Phylum Crenarchaeota
    Class Thermoprotel
      Order Thermoproteales
      Order Desulfurococcales
      Order Sulfolobales
  Phylum Euryarchaeota
    Class Methanobacteria
      Order Methanobacteriales
  Class Methanoccoci
      Order Methanococcales
      Order Methanomicrobiales
      Order Methanosarcinales
    Class Halobacteria
      Order Halobacteriales
    Class Thermoplasmata
      Order Thermoplasmatales
    Class Thermococci
      Order Thermococcales
    Class Archaeoglobi
    Class Methanopyrl
      Order Methanopyrales

Domain Bacteria
  Phylum Aquificae
    Class Aquificae
      Order Aquificales
  Phylum Thermotogae
    Class Thermotogae
      Order Thermotogales
  Phylum Thermodesulfobacteria
    Class Thermodesulfobacteria
      Order Thermodesulfo-
        bacteriales
  Phylum Deinococcus-Thermus
    Class Deinococci
      Order Deinococcales
      Order Thermales
  Phylum Chryslogenetes
    Class Chrysiogenetes
      Order Chrysiogenales
  Phylum Chloroflexi
    Class Chloroflexi
      Order Chloroflexales
      Order Herpetosiphonales
  Phylum Thermomicrobia
    Class Thermomicrobia
      Order Thermomicrobiales
  Phylum Nitrospira
    Class Nitrospira
      Order Nitrospirales

Phylum Deferribacteres
  Class Deferribacteres
    Order Deferribacterales
Phylum Cyanobacteria
  Class Cyanobacteria
Phylum Chlorobi
  Class Chlorobia
    Order Chlorobiales
Phylum Proteobacteria
  Class Alphaproteobacteria
    Order Rhodospirillales
    Order Rickettsiales
    Order Rhodobacterales
    Order Sphingomonadales
    Order Caulobacterales
    Order Rhizobiales
  Class Betaproteobacteria
    Order Burkholderiales
    Order Hydrogenophilales
    Order Methylophilales
    Order Neisseriales
    Order Nitrosomonadales
    Order Rhodocyclales
  Class Cammaproteobacteria
    Order Chromatiales
    Order Acidithiobacillales
    Order Xanthomonadales
    Order Cardiobacteriales
    Order Thiotrichales
    Order Legionellals
    Order Methylococcales
    Order Oceanospirillales
    Order Pseudomonadales
    Order Alteromonadales
    Order Vibrionales
    Order Aeromonadales
    Order Enterobacteriales
    Order Pasteurellales
  Class Deltaproteobacteria
    Order Desulfurellales
    Order Desulfovibrionales
    Order Desulfobacterales
    Order Desulfuromona-
      dales
    Order Syntrophobac-
      terales
    Order Bdellovibrionales
    Order Myxococcales
  Class Epsilonproteobacteria
    Order Campylobacterales
Phylum Firmicutes

  Class Clostridia
    Order Clostridiales
    Order Thermoanaerobac-
      teriales
    Order Haloanaerobiales
  Class Mollicutes
    Order Mycoplasmatales
    Order Entomoplasmatales
    Order Acholeplasmatales
    Order Anaeroplasmatales
  Class Bacilli
    Order Bacillales
    Order Lactobacillales
Phylum Actinobacteria
  Class Actinobacteria
    Subclass Acidimicrobidae
      Order Acidimicrobiales
        Suborder Acidimicro-
        bineae
    Subclass Rubrobacteridae
      Order Rubrobacterles
        Suborder Rubrobacter-
        ineae
    Subclass Coriobacteridae
      Order Coriobacteriales
        Suborder Cariobacter-
        ineae
    Subclass Sphaerobacteridae
      Order Sphaeriobacteriales
        Suborder Sphaerobacter-
        ineae
    Subclass Actinobacteridae
      Order Actinomyietales
        Suborder Actiomycineae
        Suborder Micrococcineae
        Suborder Corynebacter-
        ineae
        Suborder Micromonospor-
        ineae
        Suborder Propionibacter-
        ineae
        Suborder Pseudonocard-
        ineae
        Suborder Streptomyc-
        ineae
        Suborder Streptosporang-
        ineae
        Suborder Frankineae
        Suborder Glycomycineae
      Order Bifidobacteriales
Phylum Planctomycetes

Classification of living organisms (*cont.*)

Class Planctomycetacia
  Order Planctomycetales
Phylum Chlamydiae
  Class Chlamydiae
    Order Chlamydiales
Phylum Spirochaetes
  Class Spirochaetes
    Order Spirochaetales
Phylum Fibrobacteres
  Class Fibrobacteres
    Order Fibrobacterales
Phylum Acidobacteria
  Class Acidobacteria
    Order Acidobacteriales
Phylum Bacteroidetes
  Class Bacteroidetes
    Order Bacteroidales
  Class Flavobacteria
    Order Flavobacteriales
  Class Sphingobacteria
    Order Sphingobacteriales
Phylum Fusobacteria
  Class Fusobacteria
    Order Fusobacteriales
Phylum Verrucomicrobia
  Class Verrucomicrobiae
    Order Verrucomicrobiales
Phylum Dictyoglomus
  Class Dictyoglomi
    Order Dictyoglomales

Domain Eukarya[b]

Kingdom Protista
  Phylum Metamonada
  Phylum Trichozoa
  Subphylum Parabasala
    Class Trichomonadea
    Class Hypermastigotea

Subkingdom Neozoa
  Phylum Choanozoa
  Phylum Amoebozoa
  Subphylum Lobosa
  Subphylum Conosa
    Class Archamoebae
    Class Mycetozoa
  Phylum Foraminifera
  Phylum Percolozoa
  Phylum Euglenozoa
    Class Euglenoidea

Class Saccostomae
Phylum Sporozoa
  Subphylum Gregarinae
  Subphylum Coccidiomorpha
  Subphylum Perkinsida
  Subphylum Manubrispora
Phylum Ciliophora
Phylum Radiozoa
Phylum Heliozoa
Phylum Rhodophyta
  Class Rhodophyceae
    Subclass Banglophycidae
      Order Bangiales
      Order Compsopogonales
      Order Porphyridiales
      Order Rhodochaetales
    Subclass Florideophycidae
      Order Acrochaetiales
      Order Ahnfeltiales
      Order Balbianiales
      Order Balliales
      Order Batrachospermales
      Order Bonnemaisoniales
      Order Ceramiales
      Order Colaconematales
      Order Corallinales
      Order Gelidiales
      Order Gigartinales
      Order Gracilarlales
      Order Halymeniales
      Order Hildenbrandiales
      Order Nemaliales
      Order Palmariales
      Order Plocamiales
      Order Rhodogorgonales
      Order Rhodymeniales
      Order Thoreales
Phylum Chrysophyta
  Class Bacillariophyceae
    Subclass Bacillariophycidae
      Order Achnanthales
      Order Bacillariales
      Order Cymbellales
      Order Dictyoneidales
      Order Lyrellales
      Order Mastogloiales
      Order Naviculales
      Order Rhopalodiales
      Order Surirellales
      Order Thallassiophysales
    Subclass Biddulphiophycidae

      Order Anaulales
      Order Biddulphiales
      Order Hemlaulales
      Order Triceratiales
    Subclass Chaetocerotophycidae
      Order Chaetocerotales
      Order Leptocylindrales
    Subclass Corethrophycidae
      Order Cymatosirales
    Subclass Coscinodiscophycidae
      Order Arachnoidiscales
      Order Asterolamprales
      Order Aulacoseirales
      Order Chrysaanthemodiscales
      Order Coscinodiscales
      Order Ethmodiscales
      Order Melosirales
      Order Orthoseirales
      Order Parallales
      Order Stictocyclales
      Order Stictodiscales
    Subclass Cymatosirophycidae
      Order Cymatosirales
    Subclass Eunotiophycidae
      Order Eunotiales
    Subclass Fragilariophycidae
      Order Ardissoneales
      Order Cyclophorales
      Order Climacospheniales
      Order Fragllariales
      Order Licmorphorales
      Order Protoraphidales
      Order Rhabdonematales
      Order Rhaphoneidales
      Order Striatellales
      Order Tabellariales
      Order Thalassionematales
      Order Toxariales
    Subclass Lithodesmiophycidae
      Order Lithodesmialescidae
    Subclass Rhizosoleniophycidae
      Order Rhizosoleniales
    Subclass Thalassiosirophycidae
      Order Thalassiosirales
  Class Bolidophyceae
    Order Bolidomonadales
  Class Chrysomerophyceae
    Order Chrysomeridales
      nom. nud.
  Class Chrysophyceae
    Order Chromulinales

Classification of living organisms (*cont.*)

Order Hibberdiales
Class Dictyochophyceae
Order Dictyochales
Order Pedinellales
Order Rhizochromulinales
Class Eustigmatophyceae
Order Eustigmatales
Class Pelagophyceae
Order Pelagomonadales
Order Sarcinochrysidales
Class Phaeophyceae
Order Ascoseirales
Order Chordariales
Order Cutleriales
Order Desmarestiales
Order Dictysiphonales
Order Dictyotales
Order Durvillaeales
Order Ectocarpales
Order Fucales
Order Laminariales
Order Scytosiphonales
Order Sphacelariales
Order Sporochnales
Order Tilopteridiales
Class Phaeothamniophyceae
Order Phaeothamniales
Order Pleurochloridellales
Class Pinguiophyceae
Order Pinguiochrysidales
Class Raphidophyceae
Order Rhaphidomonadales
Class Synurophyceae
Order Synurales
Class Xanthophyceae
(=Tribophyceae)
Order Botrydiales
Order Chloramoebales
Order Heterogloeales
Order Mischococcales
Order Rhizochloridales
Order Tribonematales
Order Vaucheriales
Phylum Cryptophyta
Class Cryptophyceae
Order Cryptomonadales
Order Cryptococcales
Phylum Glaucocystophyta
Class Glaucocystophycaae
Order Cyanophorales
Order Glaucocystales

Order Gloeochaetales
Phylum Prymnesiophyta
(=Haptophyta)
Class Pavlovophyceae
Order Pavlovales
Class Prymnesiophyceae
Order Coccolithales
Order Isochrysidales
Order Phaeocystales
Order Prymneslales
Phylum Dinophyta
Class Dinophyceae
Order Actiniscales
Order Blastodiniales
Order Chytriodiniales
Order Desmocapsales
Order Desmomonadales
Order Dinophysales
Order Gonyaulacales
Order Gymnodiniales
Order Kokwitziellaless
Order Nannoceratopslales
Order Noctilucales
Order Oxyrrhinales
Order Peridiniales
Order Phytodiniales
Order Prorocentrales
Order Ptychodiscales
Order Pyrocysales
Order Suessiales
Order Syndiniales
Order Thoracosphaerales
Phylum Chlorophyta
Class Charophyceae
Order Charales
Order Chlorokybaees
Order Coleochaetales
Order Klebsormidiales
Order Zygnematales
Class Chlorophyceae
Order Chaetophorales
Order Chlorococcales
Order Cladophorales
Order Odeogoniales
Order Sphaeropleales
Order Volvocales
Order Pleurastrales
Class Prasinophyceae
Order Chlorodendrales
Order Mamiellales
Order Pseudoscourfeldiales

Order Pyramimonidales
Class Trebouxiophyceae
Order Trebouxiales
Class Ulvophyceae
Order Bryopsidales
Order Caulerpales
Order Codiolales
Order Dasycladales
Order Halimedales
Order Prasioeales
Order Siphonocladales
Order Trentepohliales
Order Ulotrichales
Order Ulvales
Phylum Euglenophyta
Class Euglenophyceae
Order Euglenales
Order Euglenamorphales
Order Eutreptiales
Order Heteronematales
Order Rhabdomonadales
Order Sphenomonadales
Phylum Acrasiomycota
Class Acrasiomycetes
Order Acrasiales
Phylum Dictyosteliomycota
Class Dictyosteliomycetes
Order Dictyosteliales
Phylum Myxomycota
Class Myxomycetes
Order Liceales
Order Echinosteliales
Order Trichiales
Order Physarales
Order Stemonitales
Order Ceratiomyxales
Class Protosteliomycetes
Order Protosteliales
Phylum Plasmodiophoromycota
Class Plasmodiophoromy-
cetes
Order Plasmodiophorales
Phylum Oomycota
Class Oomycetes
Order Saprolegniales
Order Salilagenidiales
Order Leptomitales
Order Myzocytiopsidales
Order Rhipidiales
Order Pythiales
Order Peronosporales

Classification of living organisms (*cont.*)

Phylum Hyphochytriomycota
Class Hyphochytriomycetes
Order Hyphochytriales
Phylum Labyrinthulomycota
Class Labyrinthulomycetes
Order Labyrinthulales
Phylum Chytridiomycota
Class Chytridiomycetes
Order Blastocladiales
Order Chytridiales
Order Monoblepharidales
Order Neocallimastigales
Order Spizellomycetales
Phylum Zygomycota
Class Trichomycetes
Order Amoebidiales
Order Asellariales
Order Eccrinales
Order Harpellales
Class Zygomycetes
Order Mucorales
Order Dimargaritales
Order Kickxellales
Order Endogonales
Order Glomales
Order Entomophthorales
Order Zoopagales
Phylum Ascomycota
Class Archiascomycetes
Order Taphrinales
Order Schizosaccharomyce-
tales
Class Saccharomycetes
Order Saccharomycetales
Class Plectomycetes
Order Eurotiales
Order Ascosphaerales
Order Onygenales
Class Laboulbeniomycetes
Order Laboulbeniales
Order Spathulosporales
Class Pyrenomycetes
Order Hypocreales
Order Melanosporales
Order Microascales
Order Phylachorales
Order Ophiostomatales
Order Diaporthales
Order Calosphaceriales
Order Xylariales
Order Sordariales

Order Meliolales
Order Halosphaeriales
Class Discomycetes
Order Medeolarlales
Order Rhytismatales
Order Ostropales
Order Cyttariales.
Order Helotiales
Order Neolectales
Order Gyalectales
Order Lecanorales
Order Lichinales
Order Peltigerales
Order Pertusariales
Order Teloschistales
Order Caliciales
Order Pezizales
Class Loculoascomycetes
Order Coryneliales
Order Dothideales
Order Myriangiales
Order Arthoniales
Order Pyrenulales
Order Asterinales
Order Capnodiales
Order Chaetothyriales
Order Patellariales
Order Pleosporales
Order Melanommatales
Order Trichotheliales
Order Verrucariales
Phylum Basidiomycota
Class Basidiomycetes
Subclass Heterobasidiomy-
cetes
Order Agricostibales
Order Atractiellales
Order Auriculariales
Order Heterogastridiales
Order Tremellales
Subclass Homobasidiomycetes
Order Agaricales
Order Boletales
Order Bondarzewiales
Order Cantharellales
Order Ceratobasidiaes
Order Cortinariales
Order Dacrymycetales
Order Fistulinales
Order Ganodermatales
Order Gautieriales

Order Gomphales
Order Hericiales
Order Hymenoghaetales
Order Hymenogastrales
Order Lachnocladiales
Order Lycoperdales
Order Melanogastrales
Order Nidulariales
Order Phallales
Order Poriales
Order Russulales
Order Schizophyllales
Order Sclerodermatales
Order Stereales
Order Thelephorales
Order Tulasnellales
Order Tulostomatales
Class Ustomycetes
Order Cryptobasidiales
Order Cryptomycocola-
cales
Order Exobasidiales
Order Graphiolales
Order Platyglocales
Order Sporidiales
Order Ustilaginales
Class Tellomycetes
Order Septobasidiales
Order Uredinales
Phylum Deuteromycota
(Asexual Ascomycetes
and Basidiomycetes)
Class Hyphomycetes
Order Hyphomycetales
Order Stibeilales
Order Tuberculariales
Class Agonomycetes
Order Agonomycetales
Class Coelomycetes
Order Melanconiales
Order Sphaeropsidales
Order Pycnothyriales

Kingdom Plantae

Subkingdom Embryobionta
Division Hepaticophyta
Class Junermanniopsida
Order Calobryales
Order Jungermanniales
Order Metzgeriales

Classification of living organisms (*cont.*)

Class Marchantiopsida
   Order Sphaerocarpales
   Order Monocleales
   Order Marchantiales
Division Anthocerotophyta
   Class Anthocerotopsida
    Order Anthocerotales
Division Bryophyta
   Class Sphagnicopsida
    Order Sphagnicales
   Class Andreaeopsida
    Order Andreaeles
   Class Bryopsida
    Order Archidiales
    Order Bryales
    Order Buxbaumiales
    Order Dicranales
    Order Encalyptales
    Order Fissidentales
    Order Funariales
    Order Grimmiales
    Order Hookeriales
    Order Hypnobryales
    Order Isobryales
    Order Orthotrichales
    Order Pottiales
    Order Orthotrichales
    Order Seligerales
    Order Splachnales
Division Lycophyta
   Class Lycopsida
    Order Isoetales
    Order Lycopodiales
    Order Selaginellales
Division Polypodiophyta
   Class Polypodopsida
    Order Equisetales
    Order Marattiales
    Order Ophioglossales
    Order Polypodiales
    Order Psilotales
Division Pinophyta
   Class Ginkgopsida
    Order Ginkgoales
   Class Cycadopsida
    Order Cycadales
   Class Pinopsida
    Order Pinales
    Order Podocarpales
    Order Gnetales
Division Magnoliophyta

|unplaced orders|
   Order Ceratophyllales
   Order Chloranthales
Class Amborellopsida
   Order Amborellales
Class Austrobaileyales
   Order Austrobaileyales
Class Liliopsida
   Order Acorales
   Order Alismatales
   Order Arecales
   Order Asparagales
   Order Commelinales
   Order Dioscoreales
   Order Liliales
   Order Pandanales
   Order Poales
   Order Zingiberales
Class Magnoliopsida
   Order Magnoliales
   Order Laurales
   Order Piperales
   Order Canellales
Class Nymphaeopsida
   Order Nymphaeales
Class Rosopsida
   |unplaced orders|
   Order Berberidopsidales
   Order Buxales
   Order Gunnerales
   Order Proteales
   Order Saxifragales
   Order Santalales
   Order Trochodendrales
   Subclass Caryophyllidae
    Order Caryophyliales
    Order Dilleniales
   Subclass Ranunculidae
    Order Ranunculales
   Subclass Rosidae
    |unplaced orders|
    Order Crossosomatales
    Order Geraniales
    Order Myrtales
    Order Vitales
    Superorder Rosanae
    Order Celastrales
    Order Cucurbitales
    Order Fabales
    Order Fagales
    Order Malpighiales

    Order Oxalidales
    Order Rosales
    Order Zygophyllales
    Superorder Malvanae
    Order Brassicales
    Order Malvales
    Order Sapindales
   Subclass Asteridae
    |unplaced order|
    Order Boraginales
    Superorder Cornanae
    Order Cornales
    Superorder Ericanae
    Order Ericles
    Superorder Lamianae
    Order Garryales
    Order Gentianales
    Order Lamiales
    Order Solanales
    Superorder Asteranae
    Order Apiales
    Order Aquifoliales
    Order Asterales
    Order Dipsacales

Kingdom Animalia

Subkingdom Parazoa
   Phylum Porifera
    Subphylum Cellularia
     Class Demospongiae
     Class Calcarea
    Subphylum Symplasma
     Class Hexactinellida
   Phylum Placozoa

Subkingdom Eumetazoa
   Phylum Cnidaria
   (=Coelenterata)
    Class Scyphozoa
     Order Stauromedusae
     Order Coronatae
     Order Semaeostomeae
     Order Rhizostomeae
    Class Cubozoa
     Order Cubomedusae
    Class Hydrozoa
     Order Hydroida
     Order Milleporina
     Order Stylasterina
     Order Trachylina

Classification of living organisms (*cont.*)

Order Siphonophora
Order Chondrophora
Order Actinulida
Class Anthozoa
Subclass Alcyonaria
  (=Octocorallia)
Order Stolonifera
Order Gorgonacea
Order Alcyonacea
Order Pennatulacea
Subclass Zoantharia
  (=Hexacorallia)
Order Actinaria
Order Corallimorpharia
Order Scleractinia
Order Zoanthinaria
  (=Zoanthidea)
Order Ceriantharia
Order Ptychodactiaria
Order Antipatharia
Phylum Ctenophora
Class Tentaculata
Order Cydippida
Order Platyctenida
Order Lobata
Order Cestida
Order Ganeshida
Order Thalassocalycida
Class Nuda
Order Beroida
Phylum Platyhelminthes
Class Turbellaria
Order Acoela
Order Rhabdocoela
Order CatenulIda
Order Macrostomida
Order Nemertodermatida
Order Lecithoepitheliata
Order Polycladida
Order Prolecithophora
  (=Holocoela)
Order Proseriata
Order Tricladida
Order Neorhabdocoela
Class Cestoda
Subclass Cestodaria
Subclass Eucestoda
Order Caryophyllidea
Order Spathebothriidea
Order Trypanorhyncha
Order Pseudophyllidea

Order Tetraphyllidea
Order Cyclophyllidea
Class Monogenea
Class Trematoda
Subclass Digenea
Order Strigeidida
Order Azygiida
Order Echinostomida
Order Plagiorchiida
Order Opisthorchiida
Subclass Aspidogastrea
  (=Aspidobothrea)
Phylum Mesozoa
Class Orthonectida
Class Rhombozoa
Order Dicyemida
Order Heterocyemida
Phylum Myxozoa
  (=Myxospora)
Phylum Nemertea
  (=Rhynchocoela,
  Nemertinea)
Class Anopia
Order Palaeonemertea
  (=Palaeonemertini)
Order Heteronemertea
Class Enopia
Order Hoplonemertea
  (=Hoplonemertini)
Order Bdelionemertea
Phylum Gnathostomuilda
Order Filospermoidea
Order Bursovaginoidea
Phylum Gastrotricha
Order Chaetonotida
Order Macrodasyida
Phylum Cycliophora
Phylum Rotifera
Class Monogononta
Order Ploima
Order Flosculariaceae
Order Collothecaceae
Class Bdelloidea
Class Seisonidea
Phylum Acanthocephaia
Class Archiacanthocephaia
Class Eoacanthocephaia
Class Palaeacanthocephala
Phylum Nematoda (=Nemata)
Class Adenophorea
Subclass Enoplia

Order Enoplida
Order Dorylaimida
Order Trichocephalida
Order Mermithida
Subclass Chromadoria
Class Secernentea
Subclass Rhabditia
Order Rhabditida
Order Ascaridida
Order Strongylida
Subclass Spiruria
Order Spirurida
Order Camallanida
Subclass Diplogasteria
Phylum Nematomorpha
Class Nectonematoida
Class Gordioida
Phylum Priapulida
Phylum Kinorhyncha
  (=Echinoderida)
Class Cyclorhagida
Class Homalorhagida
Phylum Loricifera
Phylum Mollusca
Subphylum Aculifera
Class Polyplacophora
Class Aplacophora
Subclass Neomeniophora
  (=Solenogastres)
Subclass Chaetodermomor-
  pha
  (=Caudofoveata)
Subphylum Conchifera
Class Monoplacophora
Class Gastropoda
Subclass Prosobranchia
Order Archaeogastropoda
Order Mesogastropoda
  (=Taenioglossa)
Order Neogastropoda
Subclass Opisthobranchia
Order Cephalaspidea
Order Runcinoidea
Order Acochlidioidea
Order Sacoglossa
  (=Ascoglossa)
Order Anaspidea
  (=Aplysiacea)
Order Notaspidea
Order Thecosomata
Order Gymnosomata

Classification of living organisms (*cont.*)

Order Nudibranchia
Subclass Pulmonata
  Order Archaeopulmonata
  Order Basommatophora
  Order Stylommatophora
  Order Systellommato-
  phora
Class Bivalvia
  (=Pelecypoda)
Subclass Protobranchia
  (=Palaeotaxodonta,
  Cryptodonta)
Subclass Pteriomorphia
Subclass Paleoheterodonta
Subclass Heterodonta
Subclass Anomalodesmata
Class Scaphopoda
Class Cephalopoda
Subclass Nautiloidea
Subclass Coleoidea
  (=Dibranchiata)
  Order Sepioidea
  Order Teuthoidea
  (=Decapoda)
  Order Vampyromorpha
  Order Octopoda
Phylum Annelida
Class Polychaeta
  Order Phyllodocida
  Order Spintherida
  Order Eunicida
  Order Spionida
  Order Chaetopterida
  Order Magelonida
  Order Psammodrilida
  Order Cirratulida
  Order Flabelligerida
  Order Ophelilda
  Order Capitellida
  Order Owenilda
  Order Terebellida
  Order Sabellida
  Order Protodrilida
  Order Myzostomida
Class Clitellata
Subclass Oligochaeta
  Order Lumbriculida
  Order Haplotaxida
Subclass Hirudinea
  Order Rhynchobdeilae
  Order Arhynchobdellae

Order Branchiobdellida
Order Acanthobdellida
Class Pogonophora
  (=Siboglinidae)
Subclass Perviata
  (=Frenulata)
Subclass Obturata
  (=Vestimentifera)
Class Echiura
  Order Echiura
  Order Xenopneusta
  Order Heteromyota
Phylum Sipuncula
Phylum Arthropoda
Subphylum Chelicerata
  Class Merostomata
    Order Xiphosura
  Class Arachnida
    Order Scorpiones
    Order Uropygi
    Order Amblypygi
    Order Araneae
    Order Ricinulei
    Order Pseudoscorpiones
    Order Solifugae
    (=Solpugida)
    Order Opiliones
    Order Acari
  Class Pycnogonida
    (=Pantopoda)
Subphylum Mandibulata
  Class Myriapoda
    Order Chilopoda
    Order Dipiopoda
    Order Symphyia
    Order Pauropoda
  Class insecta (=Hexapoda)
  Subclass Apterygota
    Order Thysanura
    Order Collembola
  Subclass Pterygota
    Superorder Hemime-
    tabola
    Order Ephemeroptera
    Order Odonata
    Order Blattaria
    Order Mantodea
    Order isoptera
    Order Grylioblattaria
    Order Orthoptera
    Order Phasmida

    (=Phasmatoptera)
    Order Dermaptera
    Order Embiidina
    Order Plecoptera
    Order Psocoptera
    Order Anoplura
    Order Mallophaga
    Order Thysanoptera
    Order Hemiptera
    Order Homoptera
  Superorder Holometabola
    Order Neuroptera
    Order Coleoptera
    Order Strepsiptera
    Order Mecoptera
    Order Siphonaptera
    Order Diptera
    Order Trichoptera
    Order Lepidoptera
    Order Hymenoptera
  Class Crustacea
  Subclass Cephalocarida
  Subclass Malacostraca
    Superorder Syncarida
    Superorder Hoplocarida
    Order Stomatopoda
    Superorder Peracarida
    Order Thermosbaenacea
    Order Mysidacea
    Order Cumacea
    Order Tanaidacea
    Order Isopoda
    Order Amphipoda
    Superorder Eucarida
    Order Euphausiacea
    Order Decapoda
  Subclass Branchiopoda
    Order Notostraca
    Order Cladocera
    Order Conchostraca
    Order Anostraca
  Subclass Ostracoda
    Order Myodocopa
    Order Podocopa
  Subclass Mystacocarida
  Subclass Copepoda
    Order Calanoida
    Order Harpacticoida
    Order Cyclopoida
    Order Monstrilloida
    Order Siphonostomatoida

Classification of living organisms (*cont.*)

Order Poecilostomatoida
Subclass Branchiura
Subclass Pentastomida
Order Cephalobaenida
Order Porocephalida
Subclass Tantulocarida
Subclass Remipedia
Subclass Cirripedia
Order Acrothoracica
Order Ascothoracica
Order Thoracica
Order Rhizocephala
Phylum Tardigrada
Class Heterotardigrada
Class Mesotardigrada
Class Eutardigrada
Order Parachela
Order Apochela
Phylum Onychophora
Phylum Phoronida
Phylum Brachiopoda
Class inarticulata
Order Lingulida
Order Acrotretida
Class Articulata
Order Rhynchonellida
Order Terebratulida
Phylum Bryozoa
(=Ectoprocta, polyzoa)
Class Phylactolaemata
Class Stenolaemata
Class Gymnolaemata
Order Ctenostomata
Order Chellostomata
Phylum Entoprocta
(=Kamptozoa)
Phylum Chaetognatha
Class Sagittoidea
Order Phragmophora
Order Aphragmophora
Phylum Echinodermata
Subphylum Crinozoa
Class Crinoidea
Order Millericrinida
Order Cyrtocrinida
Order Bourgueticrinida
Order Isocrinida
Order Comatulida
Subphylum Asterozoa
Class Stelleroidea
Subclass Somasteroidea

Subclass Ophiuroidea
Order Phrynophiurida
Order Ophiurida
Subclass Asteroidea
Order Platyasterida
Order Paxillosida
Order Valvatida
Order Spinulosida
Order Forcipulata
Order Brisingida
Class Concentricycloidea
Subphylum Echinozoa
Class Echinoidea
Order Cidaroida
Order Echinothuroida
Order Diadematoida
Order Arbacioida
Order Temnopleuroida
Order Echinoida
Order Holectypoida
Order Clypeasteroida
Order Spatangoida
Class Holothuroidea
Order Dendrochirotida
Order Aspidochirotida
Order Elasipodida
Order Apodida
Order Molpadiida
Phylum Hemichordata
Class Enteropneusta
Class Pterobranchia
Phylum Chordata
Subphylum Urochordata
(=Tunicata)
Class Ascidiacea
Order Aspiousobranchia
Order Phlebobranchia
Order Stolidobranchia
Class Larvacea
(=Appendicularia)
Class Thaliacea
Order Pyrosomida
Order Doliolida
Order Salpida
Subphylum Cephalochordata
(=Acrania)
Phylum Chordata^c
Subphylum Vertebrata
Superclass Agnatha
Class Myxini
Order Myxiniformes

Class Cephalaspidomorphi
Order Petromyzontiformes
Superclass Gnathostomata
Class Chondrichthyes
Subclass Holocephali
Order Chimaeriformes
Subclass Elasmobranchii
Order Hexanchiformes
Order Squaliformes
Order Pristiophoriformes
Order Squatiniformes
Order Pristiformes
Order Rhinobatiformes
Order Torpediniformes
Order Myliobatiformes
Order Heterodontiformes
Order Orectolobiformes
Order Lamniformes
Order Carchiniformes
Class Sarcopterygii
Subclass Coelacanthimor-
morpha
Order Coelacanthiformes
Subclass Porolepimorpha
and Dipnol
Order Ceratodontiformes
Order Lepidosireniformes
Class Actinopterygii
Subclass Chondrostei
Order Polypteriformes
Order Acipenseriformes
Subclass Neopterygii
Order Semionotiformes
Order Amiiformes
Division Teiestei
Subdivision Osteoglosso-
morpha
Order Osteoglossiformes
Subdivision Elopomorpha
Order Elopiformes
Order Albuliformes
Order Anguilliformes
Order Saccopharyngi-
formes
Subdivision Clupeomorpha
Order Clupeiformes
Subdivision Euteleostei
Superorder Ostariophysi
Order Gonorthynchiformes
Order Cypriniformes
Order Characiformes

Classification of living organisms (*cont.*)

Order Siluriformes
Order Gymnotiformes
Superorder Protacanthop-
  terygii
Order Esociformes
Order Osmeriformes
Order Salmoniformes
Superorder Stenopterygii
Order Stomiformes
Order Ateleopodiformes
Superorder Cyclosqua-
  mata
Order Aulopiformes
Superoder Scopelo-
  morpha
Order Myctophiformes
Superorder Lampridio-
  morpha
Order Lampridiformes
Superorder Polymixio-
  morpha
Order Polymixiiformes
Superorder Paracanthop-
  terygii
Order Percopsiformes
Order Ophidiiformes
Order Gadiformes
Order Batrachoidiformes
Order Lophiiformes
Superorder Acanthop-
  terygil
Order Mugiliformes
Order Atherinomorpha
Order Beloniformes
Order Cyprinodontiformes
Order Stephanoberyci-
  formes
Order Beryciformes
Order Zeiformes

Order Gasterosteiformes
Order Synbranchiformes
Order Scorpeaniformes
Order Perciformes
Order Pleurnectiformes
Order Tetraodontiformes
Class Amphibia
Subclass Lissamphibia
Order Gymnophiona
Order Caudata (Urodela)
Order Anura–frogs and
  toads
Class Reptilia
Subclass Anapsida
  Order Testudines
Subclass Diapsida
  Order Sphenodonta
  Order Squamata
  Suborder Lacertilia
  Suborder Serpentes
  Order Crocodylia
Infraclass Eoaves
  Order Struthioniformes
  Order Tinamiformes
Infraclass Neoaves
  Order Craciformes
  Order Galliformes
  Order Anseriformes
  Order Turniciformes
  Order Piciformes
  Order Galbuliformes
  Order Bucerotiformes
  Order Upupiformes
  Order Trogoniformes
  Order Coraciiformes
  Order Coliiformes
  Order Cuculiformes
  Order Psittaciformes
  Order Apodiformes

Order Trochiliformes
Order Musophagiformes
Order Strigiformes
Order Columbiformes
Order Grulformes
Order Ciconliformes
Suborder Charadrii
Suborder Ciconii
Order Passeriformes
Class Mammalia (Synapsida)
Order Monotremata
Order Didelophimorphia
Order Paucituberculata
Order Microbiotheria
Order Dasyuromorphia
Order Peramelemorphia
Order Notoryctemorphia
Order Diprotodontia
Order Xenarthra
Order insectivora
Order Scandentia
Order Dermoptera
Order Chiroptera
Order Primates
Order Carnivora
Order Cetacea
Order Sirenia
Order Proboscidea
Order Perissodactyla
Order Hyracoidea
Order Tubulidentata
Order Artiodactyla
Order Pholidota
Order Rodentia
Suborder Sciurognathi
Suborder Hystricognathi
Order Lagomorpha
Order Macroscelidea

[a]Derived from G. M. Garrity et. al., *Taxonomic Outline of the Prokaryotes* Release 2, January 2002, Springer-Verlag. New York. http://dx.doi.org/10.1007/bergeysouthline. Readers interesed in determning taxonomic composition of lower taxa may obtain this document, free of charge.

[b]Condensed from Jan A. Pechnik, *Biology of the Inverlebrates*, 4th ed., McGraw-Hill, 2000.

[c]Condensed from Donald Linzey. *Vertebrate Biology*. Appendix 1: Classification of Living Vertebrates, McGraw-Hill, 2001.

Note: The contributions of the following to the updating of this classification scheme are gratefully acknowledged: Dr. Craig Balley: Dr. Mark Chase: Dr. George M. Garrity: Dr. S.C. long; Dr. Robert Knowlton; Dr. Donald Linzey.

BIOGRAPHICAL LISTING

Abel, John Jacob (1857–1938), American pharmacologist and physiologist. Isolated epinephrine, and insulin in crystal form.

Addison, Thomas (1793–1860), English physician. Identified pernicious anemia and Addison's disease of the adrenal cortex.

Adler, Alfred (1870–1937), Austrian psychiatrist and psychologist. Founded the school of individual psychology.

Adrian of Cambridge, Edgar Douglas Adrian, Baron (1889–1977), English physiologist. Investigated physiology of nervous system; showed that change in electric potential in electroencephalograph is due to electrical activity of cortex; Nobel Prize, 1932.

Afzelius, Adam (1750–1837), Swedish botanist. Founded the Linnaean Institute.

Agassiz, Jean Louis Rudolphe (1807–1873), Swiss-born American naturalist. Wrote books on ichthyology, especially relating to classification.

Agre, Peter (1949–), American medical doctor and scientist. Discovered water channels in cell membranes; Nobel Prize, 2003.

Allen, Edgar (1892–1943), American biologist. Discovered estrogen; investigated hormonal mechanisms controlling female reproductive cycle.

Allen, Willard Myron (1904–1993), American physician. With G. W. Corner, discovered progesterone, and proved it necessary for development of embryo in early pregnancy; with O. Wintersteiner, synthesized crystalline progesterone.

Altman, Sidney (1939–), American chemist. Discovered an unusual enzyme that contains ribonucleic acid (RNA) in addition to a protein, leading to the discovery that RNA molecules have catalytic properties similar to those of enzymes; Nobel Prize, 1989.

Anfinsen, Christian Boehmer (1916–1995). American biochemist. Discovered how three-dimensional structures of ribonuclease and other proteins are formed; Nobel Prize, 1972.

Arber, Werner (1929–), Swiss molecular biologist. Determined the molecular mechanism of host-controlled restriction modification of bacterial viruses and discovered the restriction enzymes; Nobel Prize, 1978.

Aristotle (384–322 B.C.), Greek philosopher. Exponent of the methodology and division of sciences; contributed to physics, astronomy, meteorology, psychology, and biology.

Audubon, John James (1785–1851), Haitian-born American ornithologist and artist. Made drawings and paintings of birds and animals.

Avicenna (979–1037), Arab physician. Wrote the medical text *Canon Medicinae*.

Axel, Richard (1946–), American molecular biologist. Recognized along with Linda Buck for pioneering research of the olfactory system, which led to the discovery of the genes and proteins involved in the transmission of olfactory information. Later independent work clarified the cellular and molecular mechanisms underlying the olfactory system. Nobel Prize, 2004.

Axelrod, Julius (1912–), American biochemist and pharmacologist. Showed that many drugs act by modifying storage of neurotransmitters at nerve terminals; made discoveries concerning metabolism, and mechanisms for formation and inactivation of norepinephrine; Nobel Prize, 1970.

Baer, Karl Ernst von (1792–1876), Estonian embryologist. Discovered the mammalian ovum and the notochord; developed the theory of embryonic germ layers.

Balfour, Francis Maitlant (1851–1882), English biologist. Founder of comparative embryology.

Baltimore, David (1938–), American virologist. Investigated interaction between ribonucleic acid tumor viruses and genetic material; independently of H. M. Temin, discovered reverse transcriptase; Nobel Prize, 1975.

Bang, Bernhard Laurits Frederik (1848–1932), Danish veterinarian. Discovered method of eradicating bovine tuberculosis; discovered *Brucella abortus*, the agent of contagious abortion (Bang's disease) and brucellosis.

Banting, Frederick Grant (1891–1941), Canadian physician. With J. J. R. Macleod and C. H. Best, discovered insulin and its role in diabetes; Nobel Prize. 1923.

Bárány, Robert (1876–1936), Austrian physician. Developed new methods of diagnosing ear diseases; Nobel Prize, 1914.

Barr, Murray Llewellyn (1908–1995), Canadian anatomist. Discovered the Barr body on the X chromosome of the human female.

Bartholin, Kaspar (1655–1738), Danish physician. Discovered Bartholin's glands of the vagina and a sublingual duct.

Bartholin, Thomas (1616–1680), Danish physician. Discovered lymphatic glands; described the lymphatic system.

Bassham, James Alan (1922–), American chemist. Helped to elucidate basic photosynthetic carbon cycle.

Bates, Henry Walter (1825–1892), English naturalist. Discovered Batesian mimicry among butterflies and moths.

Bayliss, William Maddock (1860–1924), English physiologist. Did research on electrophysiology of heart action; discovered the hormone secretin.

Beadle, George Wells (1903–1989), American geneticist. With E. L. Tatum, proved that genes affect heredity by controlling cell chemistry; Nobel Prize, 1958.

Beaumont, William (1785–1853), American physician. Did pioneering studies of digestion and gastric juices.

Beebe, Charles William (1877–1962), American naturalist. Pioneer in deep-sea exploration; made ornithological collections.

Behring, Emil Adolph von (1854–1917), German bacteriologist. Produced diphtheria and tetanus antitoxins; Nobel Prize, 1901.

Békésy, Georg von (1889–1972), Hungarian-born American physicist. Studied hearing processes, especially inner-ear mechanics; Nobel Prize, 1961.

Bell, Charles (1774–1842), Scottish anatomist. Discovered that sensory and motor nerves are anatomically and functionally distinct.

Benacerraf, Baruj (1920–), American immunologist. Discovered immune-response (Ir) genes that control specific immune responses to thymus-dependent antigens; Nobel Prize, 1980.

Berg, Paul (1926–), American biochemist. Investigated the biochemistry of deoxyribonucleic acid (DNA) and designed a technique for gene splicing; Nobel Prize, 1980.

Bergey, David Hendricks (1860–1937), American bacteriologist. Authority on classification of bacteria.

Bergström, Sune Carl (1916–2004), Swedish biochemist and medical scientist. Studied the metabolism of unsaturated fatty acids and determined the chemical structure of prostaglandins; Nobel Prize, 1982.

Bernard, Claude (1813–1878), French physiologist. Studied digestion; discovered that glycogen is produced by the liver.

Berthelot, Pierre Eugène Marcellin (1827–1907), French chemist. Founder of thermochemistry; first to synthesize organic compounds; demonstrated nitrogen fixation.

Best, Charles Herbert (1899–1978), Canadian physiologist and medical researcher. Associated with F. G. Banting and J. J. R. Macleod in the discovery of insulin.

Bichat, Marie François Xavier (1771–1802), French anatomist and physiologist. Founder of animal histology; originated the term "tissues," and distinguished 21 types in his particular scheme.

Binet, Alfred (1857–1911), French psychologist. Investigated development and measurement of intelligence.

Bishop, John Michael (1936–), American virologist and biochemist. With H. Varmus, researched the genetic basis of human cancers; their work led to the identification of over 50 cellular genes that can become oncogenes; Nobel Prize, 1989.

Black, James (1924–), British pharmacologist. Developed the first beta blocker drug, propranolol; also credited with the discovery of another important class of drugs, the H2 antagonists; Nobel Prize, 1988.

Blobel, Günter (1936–), German-born American cell and molecular biologist. Discovered that proteins carry signals that help direct their movement among the organelles of the cell; Nobel Prize, 1999.

Bloch, Konrad Emil (1912–2000), German-born American biochemist. Traced the transformations of fat and carbohydrate metabolites to cholesterol; Nobel Prize, 1964.

Blumberg, Baruch Samuel (1925–), American physician and biologist. Research leading to a test for hepatitis viruses in blood and to an experimental hepatitis vaccine; Nobel Prize, 1976.

Boerhaave, Hermann (1668–1738), Dutch physician. A great teacher at the University of Ley-den; wrote the physiology textbook *Institutiones Medicae*.

Bordet, Jules Jean Baptiste Vincent (1870–1961), Belgian physiologist. Made discoveries in immunology; with O. Gengou, developed the technique of the complement fixation reaction; Nobel Prize. 1919.

Bose, Jagadis Chandra (1858–1937), Indian plant physiologist and physicist. Founded the Bose Research Institute in Calcutta; investigated photosynthesis, "nervous mechanism" of plants, and other plant subjects.

Bovet, Daniel (1907–1992), Swiss-born Italian pharmacologist. Research on synthetic compounds that inhibit the action of the vascular system and skeletal muscles; Nobel Prize, 1957.

Boyer, Paul D. (1918–), American chemist. Made major contributions toward elucidating the enzymatic mechanism underlying the synthesis of adenosine triphosphate (ATP) by proposing the binding change mechanism; Nobel Prize, 1997.

Brenner, Sydney (1927–), South African-born British molecular biologist. Established the nematode *Caenorhabditis elegans* as an experimental model system for studying genetic regulation of cell division, cell specialization, and organ development in multicellular animals. Also credited with the identification of messenger ribonucleic acid (mRNA). Nobel Prize, 2002.

Breuer, Josef (1842–1925), Austrian neurologist. Evolved abreaction method for treatment of neuroses.

Bright, Richard (1789–1858), English physician. Made biochemical study of disease; researched Bright's disease of the kidneys.

Brown, Michael S. (1941–), American biochemist and geneticist. With Joseph L. Goldstein, discovered low-density lipoprotein receptors and their function in cholesterol metabolism; Nobel Prize, 1985.

Buchner, Eduard (1860–1917), German chemist. Studied alcoholic fermentation of sucrose; Nobel Prize, 1907.

Buck, Linda (1947–), American molecular biologist. Recognized along with Richard Axel for pioneering research of the olfactory system, which led to the discovery of the large gene family encoding the different odorant receptors located on the membrane of olfactory receptor cells. Later independent work clarified the olfactory system, from the molecular level to the organization of the cells. Nobel Prize, 2004.

Buffon, Georges Louis Leclerc, Comte de (1707–1788), French naturalist. Compiled *Histoire Narurelle*, a monumental work on natural history.

Burnet, Frank Macfarlane (1899–1985), Australian immunologist. With P. B. Medawar, studied the body's tolerance of antigenic substances; Nobel Prize, 1960.

Butenandt, Adolph Friedrich Johann (1903–1995), German chemist. Researched sex hormones; Nobel Prize (declined), 1939.

Calvin, Melvin (1911–1997), American chemist. With J. A. Bassham, traced the path of carbon in photosynthesis; Nobel Prize, 1961.

Cardano, Geronimo, or Jerome Cardan (1501–1576), Italian physician and mathematician. Wrote on algebra, medicine, and astronomy; invented the Cardan shaft.

Carlsson, Arvid (1923–), Swedish pharmacologist. Did research on dopamine, leading to the discovery of its role as a key neurotransmitter in the brain and in the control of movement; the development of L-dopa, a precursor of dopamine, into a drug to treat Parkinson's disease; the elucidation of the mode of action of antipsychotic drugs, which affect synaptic transmission by blocking dopamine receptors; and work (along with that of Paul Greengard and Eric Kandel) leading to the elucidation of the molecular mechanisms involved in slow synaptic transmission in the nervous system; Nobel Prize, 2000.

Carver, George Washington (1864–1943), American botanist. Did research on industrial uses of the peanut.

Cech, Thomas R. (1947–), American chemist. By studying the single-cell organisms *Tetrahymena* and *Thermophila*, discovered that molecules of ribonucleic acid (RNA) have catalytic properties similar to those of enzymes; Nobel Prize, 1989.

Chain, Ernst Boris (1906–1979), German-born British biochemist. With H. W. Florey, worked on the chemical structure of penicillin and its first clinical trials; Nobel Prize, 1945.

Charcot, Jean Martin (1825–1893), French neurologist. Director of the Salpetrière clinic, where he made systematic clinical studies of chronic nervous disorders, including cerebrospinal disease.

Ciechanover, Aaron (1947–), Israeli medical doctor and scientist. Discovered ubiquitin-mediated protein degradation; Nobel Prize, 2004.

Claude, Albert (1899–1983), American cytologist, born in Luxembourg. Pioneered in applying electron microscopy to cell studies and in using centrifuge to separate cell components; Nobel Prize. 1974.

Cohen, Stanley (1922–), American biochemist. With R. Levi-Montalcini, made landmark studies of nerve growth factor and its functions; Nobel Prize, 1986.

Cohn, Ferdinand Julius (1828–1898), German botanist. A founder of bacteriology; did research in plant pathology; first to classify bacteria according to genus and species.

Cole, Kenneth Stewart (1900–1984), American biophysicist. Research on structure and function of living cell membranes and nerve membranes in particular, concentrating on electrical approach; with brother, R. H. Cole, introduced Cole-Cole plot of dielectric behavior.

Conant, James Bryant (1893–1978), American chemist. Researched free radicals, hemoglobin, and chlorophyll; contributed to atomic energy development.

Corey, Elias James (1928–), American chemist. Developed theories and methods of organic chemical synthesis that have made possible the production of a wide variety of complex biologically active substances and useful chemicals; Nobel Prize, 1990.

Cori, Carl Ferdinand (1896–1984), and **Cori, Gerty Theresa Radnitz** (1896–1957). Czechoslovakian-born American biochemists. Discovered the enzymatic mechanism of glucose-glycogen interconversion and the effects of hormones on this mechanism; Nobel Prize, 1947.

Corner, George Washington (1889–1981), American medical biologist. Contributed to understanding of anatomical details of menstrual cycle and functions of estrogen and progesterone.

Cornforth, John Warcup (1917–), Australian-born British chemist. Investigated stereochemistry of enzyme-catalyzed reactions; Nobel Prize, 1975.

Cournand, André Frédéric (1895–1988), French-born American physician. Studied normal and abnormal human cardiovascular and pulmonary functions; Nobel Prize, 1956.

Crick, Francis Harry Compton (1916–2004), English molecular biologist. With J. D. Watson, proposed a double-helix structure for the deoxyribo-nucleic acid molecule; Nobel Prize, 1962.

Cushing, Harvey (1869–1930), American surgeon. Innovator in neurosurgical techniques; research on function and diseases of the pituitary gland.

Cuvier, Georges Léopold Chrétien Frédéric Dagobert, Baron (1769–1838), French naturalist. Made a detailed classification of the animal kingdom; wrote on comparative anatomy.

Dale, Henry Hallett (1875–1968), British pharmacologist and physiologist. Isolated acetylcholine and recognized its effect to be similar to that brought about by parasympathetic nerves; Nobel Prize, 1936.

Dam, Carl Peter Henrik (1895–1976), Danish biochemist and nutritionist. Discovered vitamin K and studied its role in human hemorrhagic disease; Nobel Prize, 1943.

Darwin, Charles Robert (1809–1882), English naturalist. Proposed far-reaching theory of evolution of species and theory of natural selection in his *Origin of Species*.

Dausset, Jean (1916–), French biologist and medical scientist. Studied antigen in human leukocytes and their role in transplant acceptance or rejections; Nobel Prize, 1980.

de Duve, Christian René (1917–), Belgian biochemist and cytologist. Refined centrifuge technique for studying cell components; discovered lysosomes; Nobel Prize, 1974.

Deisenhofer, Johann (1943–), German chemist. With R. Huber and M. Hartmut, elucidated the structure of a bacterial protein that performs photosynthesis; Nobel Prize, 1988.

Delbruck, Max (1906–1981), German-born American biologist. Pioneered in molecular biology; research on bacterial viruses; Nobel Prize, 1969.

De Vries, Hugo (1848–1935), Dutch botanist. Formulated the mutation theory of evolution.

Dick, George Frederick (1881–1967), American physician and bacteriologist. Isolated scarlet fever streptococci, developed scarlet fever streptococcus antitoxin, and developed Dick test.

Djerassi, Carl (1923–), Austrian-born, American chemist. Synthesized the first oral contraceptive.

Dobzhansky, Theodosius (1900–1975), Russian-born American biologist. Elucidated the mechanisms of heredity and variation through studies of *Drosophila*.

Doherty, Peter C. (1940–), Australian-born American immunologist. Collaborated with R. M. Zinkerngagel in the discovery of specificity of cell-mediated immune defense; Nobel Prize, 1996.

Dolsy, Edward Adelbert (1893–1986), American biochemist. Isolated pure crystalline compounds important to human health, such as sex hormones and vitamins; Nobel Prize, 1943.

Domagk, Gerhard (1895–1964), German biochemist. Discovered sulfamidocrysoidin, the first synthetic microbial of broad clinical usefulness. Nobel Prize (declined), 1939.

Donnan, Frederick George (1870–1956), Irish chemist born in Ceylon. Research in chemical kinetics; originated the Donnan theory of membrane equilibrium.

Duane, William (1872–1935), American physicist and radiologist. Developed treatment of cancer by radioisotopes and x-rays; with F. L. Hunt, discovered Duane-Hunt law of x-rays.

Du Bois-Reymond, Emil (1818–1896), German physiologist. Pioneer work in electrical properties of living tissues, especially nerves.

Ducrey, Augusto (1860–1940), Italian dermatologist. Discovered *Hemophilus ducreyi,* the agent of chancroid.

du Vigneaud, Vincent (1901–1978), American biochemist. Synthesized a polypeptide hormone, oxytocin: worked on other biologically important sulfur compounds; Nobel Prize, 1955.

Eccles, John Carew (1903–1997), Australian physiologist. Elucidated the action of nerve impulses across zones of close contact between nerve cells; Nobel Prize, 1963.

Edelman, Gerald Maurice (1929–), American biochemist. Worked to determine chemical structure of immunoglobulins; Nobel Prize, 1972.

Ehrlich, Paul (1854–1915), German bacteriologist. Research in chemotherapy, notably the discovery of Salvarsan for treatment of syphilis; pioneered in the study of hematology and immunity; Nobel Prize, 1908.

Eijkman, Christiaan (1858–1930), Dutch physician. Studied dietary deficiency disease, in particular beriberi; Nobel Prize, 1929.

Einthoven, Willem (1860–1927), Dutch physiologist born in Java. Used the string galvanometer to record electrical activity of the heart, thereby inventing the electrocardiograph; Nobel Prize, 1924.

Elion, Gertrude Belle (1918–1999), American biochemist. With G. H. Hitchings, pioneered research that led them to the development of drugs for the treatment of leukemia, malaria, gout, herpes, bacterial and fungal infections, and autoimmune diseases and organ-transplant rejection; Nobel Prize, 1988.

Enders, John Franklin (1897–1985), American microbiologist. With F. C. Robbins and T. H. Weller, discovered the capacity of poliomyelitis virus to grow in various tissue cultures; Nobel Prize, 1954.

Erasistratus (3d century B.C.), Greek physician and anatomist. Founder of physiology; distinguished between the cerebrum and cerebellum, and sensory and motor nerves.

Erlanger, Joseph (1874–1965), American physiologist. With H. S. Gasser, created new methods for amplifying and recording electrical impulses in nerves; research on the function of the synapse; Nobel Prize, 1944.

Ernst, Richard R. (1933–). Swiss chemist. Developed methods that transformed nuclear magnetic resonance (NMR) spectroscopy from a tool with a narrow application to a key analytical technique in chemistry as well as many other fields: Nobel Prize, 1991.

Euler-Chelpin, Hans Karl August Simon von (1873–1964), German-Swedish chemist. Research on enzyme action and fermentation of sugars; Nobel Prize, 1929.

Fabricius, Hieronymus, or Girolamo Fabrizio (ca. 1533–1619), Italian anatomist. Made painstaking descriptions of valves in veins; did comparative research in animal embryology.

Fallopio, Gabriele (1523–1562), Italian anatomist. Discovered Fallopian tubes; gave first clear description of organs of inner and middle ear.

Fechner, Gustav Theodor (1801–1887), German psychologist. Founded psychophysics; developed the Fechner law concerning intensity of sensation produced by a stimulus.

Fibiger, Johannes Andreas Grib (1867–1928), Danish pathologist. First to produce cancer experimentally; Nobel Prize, 1926.

Finsen, Niels Ryberg (1860–1904), Danish physician. Originated ultraviolet light therapy for certain diseases; Nobel Prize, 1903.

Fischer, Edmond H. (1920–), American biochemist. With E. G. Krebs, discovered phosphorylation processes that play a critical role in cell-protein regulation; they isolated the first protein kinase, a class of enzymes that transfer phosphate from adenosinetriphosphate to proteins; Nobel Prize, 1992.

Fischer, Emil Hermann (1852–1919), German chemist. Synthesized many natural substances, including purines, D-glucose and other sugars, and the first nucleotide; studied polypeptides and proteins; Nobel Prize, 1902.

Fischer, Hans (1881–1945), German organic chemist. Investigated and synthesized pyrrole pigments; studied structure of chlorophylls; Nobel Prize, 1930.

Fisher, Ronald Aylmer (1890–1962), English geneticist and statistician. Developed statistical techniques for analysis of variance, and for use and validation of small samples; developed theory of the evolution of dominance.

Fleming, Alexander (1881–1955), British bacteriologist. Discovered lysozyme and penicillin; Nobel Prize, 1945.

Florey, Howard Walter (1898–1968), British pathologist born in Australia. Contributed, with E. B. Chain, to development of penicillin as a chemotherapeutic agent; Nobel Prize, 1945.

Forssmann, Werner Theodor Otto (1904–1979), German physician. Developed the technique of cardiac catheterization; Nobel Prize, 1956.

Freud, Sigmund (1856–1939), Austrian psychoanalyst. Founder of psychoanalysis, with emphasis on dream interpretation and free association; developed a theory of personality involving id, ego, and superego, and stressing importance of the libido.

Frisch, Karl von (1886–1982), Austrian zoologist. Discovered means by which bees communicate information about the distance and direction of food; Nobel Prize, 1973.

Furchgott, Robert F. (1916–), American pharmacologist. Discovered endothelium-derived relaxing factor (EDRF), a signaling molecule in the cardiovascular system that makes vascular smooth muscle cells relax (Louis J. Ignarro, working independently and with Furchgott, later concluded that EDRF was nitric oxide); Nobel Prize, 1998.

Gajdusek, Daniel Carleton (1923–), American physician and virologist. Discovered causal virus and transmission mechanism of kuru; Nobel Prize, 1976.

Galen (2d century), Greek physician and medical writer. Wrote treatises long used as textbooks; experimented on animal nervous systems; made anatomical descriptions of structure and functions of body parts.

Gamow, George (1904–1968), Russian-born American physicist. Made theoretical contributions to nuclear physics, astronomy, and biology; with E. Teller, formulated the selection rule for beta emission: proposed theoretically the genetic code.

Gasser, Herbert Spencer (1888–1963), American physiologist. With J. Erlanger, provided a new method for recording electrical impulses of nerves; studied functions of nerve fibers; Nobel Prize, 1944.

Gesner, Konrad von (1516–1565), Swiss naturalist. Wrote *Historia Animalium*, beginning zoology as a science.

Gilbert, Walter (1932–), American biochemist. Developed methods for determining nucleotide sequence (independently of F. Sanger), advancing the technology of DNA recombination; Nobel Prize, 1980.

Gilman, Alfred G. (1941–), American pharmacologist. With M. Rodbell, discovered G-proteins and their role in cellular signal transduction; Nobel Prize, 1994.

Goldstein, Joseph L. (1940–), American biochemist and geneticist. With M. S. Brown, discovered low-density lipoprotein receptors and their function in cholesterol metabolism; Nobel Prize, 1985.

Golgi, Camillo (1843–1926), Italian physician. Pioneered in the study of histology of the nervous system; discovered the Golgi bodies; Nobel Prize, 1906.

Granit, Rangar Arthur (1900–1991), Finnish-born Swedish physiologist. Research on vision and on motor control by afferent neurons; Nobel Prize, 1967.

Greengard, Paul (1925–), American neurobiologist. Discovered the mechanism by which dopamine and other chemical neurotransmitters (such as norepinephrine and serotonin) affect the nervous system—work contributing to the elucidation of the molecular mechanisms involved in slow synaptic transmission in the nervous system; Nobel Prize, 2000.

Guillemin, Roger Charles Louis (1924–), French-born American physiologist. With A. V. Schally, isolated and analyzed peptide hormones secreted in hypothalamic region of brain which control anterior pituitary hormone secretion; Nobel Prize, 1977.

Gullstrand, Allvar (1862–1930), Swedish ophthalmologist. Discovered intracapsular accommodation of the eye lens; improved techniques for studying eye structure; Nobel Prize, 1911.

Haeckel, Ernst Heinrich (1834–1919), German biologist. Studied various invertebrates; classified animals as uni- and multicellular organisms; proposed the theory of recapitulation: ontogeny repeats phylogeny.

Hahnemann, Christian Friedrich Samuel (1775–1843), German physician. Founder of homeopathy.

Haldane, John Bourdon Sanderson (1892–1964), British geneticist and physiologist. Pioneered in mathematical treatment of population genetics; studied respiration in humans; wrote about enzymes.

Haldane, John Scott (1860–1936), British physiologist. Research on respiration, particularly the effects of high and low atmospheric pressures.

Hansen, Armauer (1841–1912), Norwegian bacteriologist. Discovered the bacillus of leprosy, or Hansen's disease.

Harden, Arthur (1865–1940), English chemist. Research on enzymes and alcoholic fermentation; Nobel Prize, 1929.

Hartline, Haldan Keffer (1903–1983), American biophysicist. Elucidated cellular electrical activity in the eye and optic nerve; Nobel Prize, 1967.

Hartwell, Leland H. (1939–), American geneticist. Discovered more than 100 genes that control the cell cycle and introduced the concept of cell cycle checkpoints, ordered groups of genes and protein which halt progress through the cell cycle if DNA is damaged, allowing time for DNA repair; Nobel Prize, 2001.

Harvey, William (1578–1657), English anatomist and physician. Described the true circulation of blood and the action of the heart.

Havers, Clopton (1665–1702), English osteologist. Provided the first full discussion of Haversian lamellae and Haversian canals.

Haworth, Walter Norman (1883–1950), English chemist. Synthesized ascorbic acid; studied carbohydrates, including the structure of sugars; Nobel Prize, 1937.

Helmholtz, Hermann Ludwig Ferdinand von (1821–1894), German physicist. anatomist, and physiologist. Physiological research on the nervous system and the human eye and ear, and theoretical work on conservation of force in physics; invented the ophthalmoscope.

Hench, Philip Showalter (1896–1965), American physiologist. Discovered that ACTH and cortisone could be used to treat rheumatoid arthritis; Nobel Prize, 1950.

Henle, Friedrich Gustav Jacob (1809–1885), German pathologist and anatomist. Wrote *Handbuch der Rationellen Pathologie*, integrating the study of physiology and pathology; discovered looped portion of the kidney tubules, and the epithelium.

Hershey, Alfred Day (1908–1997), American biologist. With M. Chase, experimented with bacteriophage, confirming earlier indications that the material basis of heredity is contained in nucleic acids; Nobel Prize, 1969.

Hershko, Avram (1937–), Israeli medical doctor and scientist. Discovered ubiquitin-mediated protein degradation; Nobel Prize, 2004.

Hess, Walter Rudolf (1881–1973), Swiss physiologist. Discovered the organizer function of the middle brain in coordinating activity of internal organs; developed technique of using electrodes to stimulate localized brain areas; Nobel Prize, 1949.

Hevesy, George von (1886–1966), Hungarian chemist. Experimented with radioisotope indication, leading to the technique of isotope tracing of biological and chemical processes; Nobel Prize, 1943.

Heymans, Corneille (1892–1968), French-Belgian physiologist. Investigated the carotid sinus in connection with the mechanism of breathing; Nobel Prize, 1938.

Hill, Archibald Vivian (1886–1977), English physiologist. Worked on heat loss and oxygen consumption in muscle contraction; Nobel Prize, 1922.

Hippocrates (460?–377 B.C.), Greek physician. Known as the father of medicine; writings attributed to him contain clinical observations of diseases, descriptions of surgical practice, and the Hippocratic doctrine of the four humors.

Hitchings, George Herbert (1905–1998), American biochemist. With G. B. Elion, pioneered research that led them to the development of drugs for the treatment of leukemia, malaria, gout, herpes, bacterial and fungal infections, and autoimmune diseases and organ-transplant rejection; Nobel Prize, 1988.

Hodgkin, Alan Lloyd (1914–1998), British biophysicist. With A. Huxley, devised a system of mathematical equations describing the nerve impulse; presented evidence for the sodium theory of nervous conduction; Nobel Prize, 1963.

Hodgkin, Dorothy Crowfoot (1910–1994), Egyptian-born British chemist. Determined the structure of the vitamin B_{12} molecule through x-ray crystallographic analysis; Nobel Prize, 1964.

Hodgkin, Thomas (1798–1866), English physician. First to describe Hodgkin's disease, a glandular disorder.

Hofmeister, Wilhelm Friedrich Benedict (1824–1877), German botanist. Did fundamental work on plant embryology; explained the alternating life cycles of mosses and ferns.

Holley, Robert William (1922–1993), American biochemist. With coworkers, made first determination of a nucleotide sequence of a nucleic acid; Nobel Prize, 1968.

Hopkins, Frederick Gowland (1861–1947), English biochemist. Discovered the amino acid tryptophan and the tripeptide glutathione; did experimental work leading to the discovery of vitamins; Nobel Prize, 1929.

Horvitz, H. Robert (1947–), American geneticist and neurobiologist. Identified and characterized the genes controlling programmed cell death in the nematode *Caenorhabditis elegans*. Showed that these genes interact with each other in cell death and correspond to existing genes in humans. Nobel Prize, 2002.

Houssay, Bernardo Alberto (1887–1971), Argentine physiologist. Research on the functions and effects of the hypophysis, including its relationship to carbohydrate metabolism; Nobel Prize, 1947.

Howell, William Henry (1860–1945), American physiologist. Discovered heparin; isolated thrombin and thromboplastin; discovered Howell-Jolly bodies; proved that blood platelets are formed in lungs.

Hubel, David Hunter (1926–), American neurobiologist. Contributed to the study of the processing of visual information in the brain; Nobel Prize, 1981.

Huber, Robert (1937–), German chemist. With J. Deisenhofer and M. Hartmut, elucidated the structure of a bacterial protein that performs photosynthesis; Nobel Prize, 1988.

Huggins, Charles Brenton (1901–1997), Canadian-born American surgeon and cancer researcher. Developed treatment of cancers using endocrinologic methods; Nobel Prize, 1966.

Hunt, R. Timothy (1943–), British biologist who discovered cyclins, proteins that regulate cyclin-dependent kinase activity, and found that their periodic degradation is an important general control mechanism of the cell cycle; Nobel Prize, 2001.

Huxley, Andrew Fielding (1917–), British physiologist. With A. L. Hodgkin, discovered the ionic mechanism involved in excitation in the cell membrane of peripheral nerves; Nobel Prize, 1963.

Ignarro, Louis J. (1941–), American pharmacologist. Working independently and with Robert Furchgott, he concluded that endothelium-derived relaxing factor was identical to nitric oxide; Nobel Prize, 1998.

Ingenhousz, Jan (1730–1799), Dutch physician and naturalist. Demonstrated the cycle of photosynthesis in plants.

Jacob, François (1920–), French biologist. Discovered episomes, a class of genetic elements; with J. Monod, proposed the concepts of messenger ribonucleic acid and of the operon; Nobel Prize, 1965.

James, William (1842–1910), American psychologist and writer. Coformulator of James-Lange theory that emotions are the perception of physiological changes.

Janet, Pierre Marie Félix (1859–1947), French psychologist. Studied hysteria, obsession, and neurosis; wrote a textbook on the theory of hysteria.

Jenner, Edward (1749–1823), English physician. Discovered vaccination.

Jerne, Niels Kaj (1911–1994), Swiss immunologist. Formulated three important theories involving the immune system: how the body produces specific antibodies, how the immune system develops and matures, and how the various interrelated aspects of the immune response are coordinated by the body; Nobel Prize, 1984.

Jung, Carl Gustav (1875–1961), Swiss psychologist and psychiatrist. Evolved a theory of complexes; founded the analytical school of psychoanalysis and psychotherapy.

Kandel, Eric R. (1929–), Austrian-born American neurobiologist. Discovered that protein phosphorylation plays an important role in the molecular mechanisms underlying learning and memory formation; his work contributed to the elucidation of the molecular mechanisms involved in slow synaptic transmission in the nervous system; Nobel Prize, 2000.

Karrer, Paul (1889–1971), Swiss chemist. Pioneering research on vitamins A and B$_2$ and on the flavins and carotenoids; Nobel Prize, 1937.

Katz, Bernard (1911–2003), German-born British physiologist. Made discoveries concerning mechanism for release of transmitter substances at nerve-muscle junction; Nobel Prize, 1970.

Kendall, Edward Calvin (1886–1972), American biochemist. Chemical investigation of the adrenal cortex, leading to the isolation of crystalline cortical hormones, especially cortisone; Nobel Prize, 1950.

Kendrew, John Cowdery (1917–1997), British molecular biologist. First to successfully determine the structure of a protein; Nobel Prize, 1962.

Khorana, Har Gobind (1922–), Indian-born American biochemist. Synthesized complicated nucleic acids: proved that genetic code consists of nonoverlapping triplets of bases without gaps between triplets; Nobel Prize, 1968.

Kitasato, Shibasaburo (1852–1931), Japanese bacteriologist. Independently of A. E. J. Yersin, discovered the bacillus of bubonic plague; isolated bacilli of symptomatic anthrax, dysentery, and tetanus.

Klebs, Edwin (1834–1913), German pathologist. Described diphtheria (Klebs-Löffler) bacillus; studied bacteriology of malaria, anthrax, and tuberculosis.

Klug, Aaron (1926–), South African-born British biochemist. Developed crystallographic electron microscopy and elucidated biologically important nucleic acid-protein complexes; Nobel Prize, 1982.

Koch, Robert (1843–1910), German physician and bacteriologist. Studied cholera, tuberculosis, and bubonic plague; showed a specific bacillus to be the cause of anthrax; discovered the tubercle bacillus; Nobel Prize, 1905.

Kocher, Emil Theodor (1841–1917), Swiss surgeon. Studied the functions and malfunctions of the thyroid gland; Nobel Prize, 1909.

Köhler, Georges J. F. (1946–1995), Swiss immunologist. With C. Milstein, discovered a laboratory technique for producing monoclonal antibodies, highly uniform immune bodies that are selective in responding to target substances; Nobel Prize, 1984.

Kornberg, Arthur (1918–), American biochemist. Discovered deoxyribonucleic acid polymerase, providing the first rational enzymatic mechanism for the replication of genetic material of the cell; Nobel Prize, 1959.

Kossel, Albrecht (1853–1927), German chemist. Investigated the chemistry of cells and of proteins; Nobel Prize, 1910.

Krafft-Ebing, Richard, Baron von (1840–1902), German neurologist. Authority on psychological disorders and their forensic implications; wrote *Psychopathia Sexualis*, a collection of case histories.

Krebs, Edwin Gerhard (1918–), American biochemist. With E. H. Fischer, discovered phosphorylation processes that play a critical role in cell-protein regulation; they isolated the first protein kinase, a class of enzymes that transfer phosphate from adenosine triphosphate to proteins; Nobel Prize, 1992.

Krebs, Hans Adolf (1900–1981), German-born British biochemist. Elucidated metabolic pathways, including the tricarboxytic acid cycle; Nobel Prize, 1953.

Krogh, Schack August Steenberg (1874–1949), Danish physiologist. Discovered the regulation of the vasomotor mechanism of capillaries; devised the nitrous oxide method for measuring human circulation; Nobel Prize, 1920.

Kuhn, Richard (1900–1967), German chemist. Research on the structures and synthesis of vitamins and carotenoids; Nobel Prize, 1938 (declined).

Lamarck, Jean Baptiste Pierre Antoine de Monet, Chevailer de (1744–1829), French naturalist. Proposed theory that changes in animal and plant structure are caused by changes in environment; classified animals into vertebrates and invertebrates.

Landsteiner, Karl (1868–1943), Austrian-born American pathologist. Discovered human blood groups and factors M and N; with A. S. Weiner, discovered the Rh factor; Nobel Prize, 1930.

Lange, Carl Georg (1834–1900), Danish physician and psychologist. With W. James, proposed the James-Lange theory of emotion.

Langerhans, Paul (1847–1888), German pathologist and anatomist. Studied human and animal microscopical anatomy, particularly structures of skin and pancreas; discovered islets of Langerhans.

Laveran, Charles Louis Alphonse (1845–1922), French physician. Discovered the malaria parasite; researched sleeping sickness; Nobel Prize, 1907.

Lederberg, Joshua (1925–), American geneticist. With E. L. Tatum, discovered genetic recombination in bacteria and organization of genetic material; Nobel Prize, 1958.

Leloir, Luis Federico (1906–1987), French-born Argentine biochemist. Discovered sugar nucleotides and their role in carbohydrate biosynthesis; Nobel Prize, 1970.

Levi-Montalcini, Rita (1909–), Italian biologist. With S. Cohen, made landmark studies of nerve growth factor and its functions; Nobel Prize, 1986.

Lewis, Edward B. (1918–2004), American geneticist. Shared in discoveries showing the genetic involvement of early embryonic development with C. Nusselin-Volhard and E. F. Wieschaus; Nobel Prize, 1995.

Leydig, Franz von (1821–1908), German histologist and anatomist. Founder of comparative histology; promoted use of microscope in anatomical study; described cells in testes believed to secrete male hormones.

Lipmann, Fritz Albert (1899–1986), German-born American biochemist. Formulated general rules for the biotechnology of energy transmission; discovered coenzyme A; Nobel Prize, 1953.

Lister, Joseph, 1st Baron (1827–1912), English surgeon. Introduced antiseptics to surgery; pioneered in bacteriology.

Loewi, Otto (1873–1961), German pharmacologist. Investigated nerve impulses; proved the role of ace-tylcholine in nerve impulse transmission; Nobel Prize, 1936.

Löffler, Friedrich August Johannes (1852–1915). German bacteriologist. Isolated the diphtheria (Klebs-Löffler) bacillus; developed protective serum against foot-and-mouth disease.

Lorenz, Konrad Zacharias (1903–1989), Austrian zoologist. Pioneered in study of animal behavior patterns; discovered imprinting in birds; Nobel Prize, 1973.

Luria, Salvador Edward (1912–1991), Italian-born American biologist. Devised fluctuation test to demonstrate and study spontaneous mutations in bacteria and viruses; Nobel Prize, 1969.

Lwoff, André Michael (1902–1994), French biologist. Explained the phenomenon of lysogeny in bacteria; Nobel Prize, 1965.

Lynen, Feodor (1911–1979), German biochemist. Research on the formation of the cholesterol molecule; discovered chemistry of biotin; Nobel Prize, 1964.

MacKinnon, Roderick (1956–), American medical doctor and scientist. Determined structure and mechanism of ion channels in cell membranes; Nobel Prize, 2003.

Macleod, John James Rickard (1876–1935), Scottish physiologist. Shared in discovery of insulin with F. G. Banting and C. H. Best; Nobel Prize, 1923.

Magnus, Heinrich Gustav (1802–1872), German physicist and chemist. Made first quantitative analysis of blood gases; showed that arterial blood has higher oxygen content than venous blood; discovered Magnus effect.

Malpighi, Marcello (1628–1694), Italian anatomist. Discovered the capillaries; made microscopic studies in embryology; discovered the Malpighian layer of the epidermis and the Malpighian corpuscles in the kidney.

Mariotte, Edmé (?-1684), French physicist and physiologist. Discovered blind spot; studied circulation of sap in plants, collisions of bodies, properties of air, refraction and color of light, hydrostatics, hydraulics, and meteorology.

McClintock, Barbara (1902–1992), American geneticist. Discovered mobile genetic elements known as jumping genes; Nobel Prize, 1983.

Meckel, Johann Friedrich (1781–1833), German anatomist and embryologist. Gave first comprehensive description of birth defects; described Meckel's cartilage; discovered Meckel's diverticulum.

Medawar, Peter Brian (1915–1987), Brazilian-born British biologist and medical scientist. Discovered acquired immunological tolerance; Nobel Prize, 1960.

Mendel, Gregor Johann (1822–1884), Austrian botanist. Formulated Mendel's laws of heredity, the foundation of genetics.

Merrifield, Robert Bruce (1921–), American biochemist. Developed methods of protein synthesis, including solid-phase peptide synthesis that produces proteins by assembling amino acids sequentially into peptide chains; Nobel Prize, 1984.

Metchnikoff, Élie (1845–1916), Russian-born French zoologist and bacteriologist. Work on cholera and immunology; Nobel Prize, 1908.

Meyerhof, Otto Fritz (1884–1951), German physiologist. Studied the glycogen-lactic acid cycle of muscles; Nobel Prize, 1923.

Michaelis, Leonor (1875–1949), German-born American biochemist. Developed theory of kinetics of enzyme-catalyzed reactions.

Michel, Hartmut (1948–), German chemist. With J. Deisenhofer and R. Huber, elucidated the structure of a bacterial protein that performs photosynthesis; Nobel Prize, 1988.

Milstein, César (1927–2002), British immunologist. With Georges J. F. Köhler, discovered a laboratory technique for producing monoclonal antibodies, highly uniform immune bodies that are selective in responding to target substances; Nobel Prize, 1984.

Minot, George Richards (1885–1950), American physician. With W. P. Murphy, first to recognize the value of liver therapy for pernicious anemia; studied arthritis, cancer, and vitamin B deficiency; Nobel Prize, 1934.

Mitchell, Peter (1920–1992), British chemist. Explained how plant and animal cells store and transfer energy by creating protonic gradients in the oxidative and photosynthetic phosphorylation processes; Nobel Prize, 1978.

Mohl, Hugo von (1805–1872), German botanist. Worked on the anatomy and physiology of higher plant forms; discovered protoplasm.

Moniz, Antonio Egas (1874–1955), Portuguese neurosurgeon. Developed cerebral angiography; introduced the prefrontal lobotomy; Nobel Prize, 1949.

Monod, Jacques (1910–1976), French biologist. With F. Jacob, proposed the concepts of messenger ribonucleic acid and of the operon; Nobel Prize, 1965.

Moore, Stanford (1913–1982), American biochemist. With W. H. Stein, developed technique for determining amino acid sequence in proteins, and applied it to ribonuclease; Nobel Prize, 1972.

Morgagni, Giovanni Battista (1682–1771), Italian anatomist. Founded pathological anatomy; first to describe liver cirrhosis.

Morgan, Thomas Hunt (1866–1945), American geneticist, embryologist, and zoologist. Proposed the chromosome theory of heredity; Nobel Prize, 1933.

Muller, Hermann Joseph (1890–1967), American geneticist. Studied genetic mutation rates under natural and artificial conditions; discovered the effect of x-rays on mutation rate; Nobel Prize, 1946.

Müller, Johannes Peter (1801–1858), German physiologist and anatomist. Proposed the principle of specific nerve energies, concerning stimuli to sense organs; discovered the Müllerian duct, an early embryonic structure.

Mullis, Kary B. (1944–), American chemist. Invented the polymerase chain reaction (PCR) method used for studying DNA molecules; Nobel Prize, 1993.

Murad, Ferid (1936–), American pharmacologist. Analyzed the action of nitroglycerin and related vasodilating compounds, leading to the discovery that they release nitric oxide, which relaxes smooth muscle cells; his work, along with the research of Robert F. Furchgott and Louis J. Ignarro, led to the discovery of nitric oxide as a signaling molecule in the cardiovascular system; Nobel Prize, 1998.

Murphy, William Parry (1892–1987), American physician. With G. R. Minot, first to suggest liver diet as a treatment for pernicious anemia; Nobel Prize, 1934.

Murray, Joseph (1919–), American physician. Performed the first successful transplant of a human organ, a kidney; with E. D. Thomas, helped define and then overcome the immunological mechanisms behind organ rejection; Nobel Prize, 1990.

Nathans, Daniel (1928–1999), American biologist. Pioneered in the use of restriction enzymes to study the structure and functions of deoxyribonucleic acid (DNA) molecules; Nobel Prize, 1978.

Neher, Erwin (1944–), German biophysicist. With B. Sakmann, using the "patch clamp" technique they developed, showed how individual ion channels control the passage of charged ions into and out of cells; Nobel Prize, 1991.

Nicolle, Charles Jules Henri (1866–1936), French physician. Discovered the louse to be the transmission vector of typhus; Nobel Prize, 1928.

Nirenberg, Marshall Warren (1927–), American biochemist. Pioneered in deciphering genetic code; Nobel Prize, 1968.

Noguchi, Hideyo (1876–1928), Japanese bacteriologist. First to produce pure cultures of syphilis spirochetes; discovered the parasite of yellow fever.

Northrop, John Howard (1891–1987), American biochemist. Isolated several enzymes and proved them to be proteins; isolated the first bacterial virus; established the chemical nature of enzymes and viruses; Nobel Prize, 1946.

Nurse, Paul M. (1949–), British biologist. Identified, cloned, and characterized a key regulator of the cell cycle, cyclin-dependent kinase; Nobel Prize, 2001.

Nüsslein-Volhard, Christiane (1942–), German developmental biologist. Using *Drosophila*, she and Eric Wieschaus identified and classified a small number of genes that are important in determining the body plan and the formation of body segments; their work, along with that of American development biologist Edward B. Lewis, led to the discovery of important genetic mechanisms which control early embryonic development; Nobel Prize, 1995.

Ochoa, Severo (1905–1993), Spanish-born American biochemist. Discovered a bacterial enzyme that synthesizes ribonucleic acid from nucleoside diphosphates; first to synthesize a ribonucleic acid; Nobel Prize, 1959.

Orr, John Boyd, Baron (1880–1971), Scottish physiologist and nutritionist. Work on animal nutrition; pioneer in science of human nutrition; Nobel Peace Prize, 1949.

Paget, James (1814–1899), English surgeon and pathologist. Studied pathology of tumors and bone and joint diseases; described osteitis deformans (Paget's disease).

Palade, George Emil (1912–), Rumanian born American cytologist. Applied electron microscope and centrifuge techniques to study of ultrastructure of cells; discovered ribosomes; Nobel Prize, 1974.

Papanicolaou, George Nicholas (1883–1962), Greek-born American cytologist and anatomist. Developed the Papanicolaou test for diagnosis of uterine cervical and endometrial cancer.

Paracelsus, Philippus Aureolus, real name Theophrastus Bombastus von Hohenheim (1493–1541), Swiss physician. Emphasized use of chemicals in medicine; advocated that diseases are specific and require specific remedies.

Paré, Ambroise (1509–1590), French surgeon. Advocated the treatment of wounds by tying arteries with ligatures rather than by cauterization; proposed improvements in operating methods.

Parkinson, James (1755–1824), English physician and paleontologist. Described parkinsonism.

Pasteur, Louis (1822–1895), French biologist. Founder of microbiology; discovered the role of bacteria in fermentation; discovered anaerobic bacteria; developed the pasteurization process; demonstrated the efficacy of vaccination, especially for rabies.

Pavlov, Ivan Petrovich (1849–1936), Russian pathologist. Discovered the nerve fibers affecting heart action and the secretory nerves of the pancreas; research on the physiology of digestive glands; studied conditioned reflexes; Nobel Prize, 1904.

Pearl, Raymond (1879–1940), American biologist and statistician. Applied statistics to the study of population changes; introduced logistic curve describing population growth.

Pearson, Karl (1857–1936), English applied mathematician, statistician, and biometrician. Pioneered in application of statistics to biology; introduced chi-square test.

Perutz, Max Ferdinand (1914–2002), Austrian-born British crystallographer and molecular biologist. Worked on the structure of hemoglobin; introduced the method of isomorphous replacement with heavy atoms into protein crystallography; Nobel Prize, 1962.

Pfeiffer, Richard Friedrich Johann (1858–1945), German bacteriologist. Discovered Pfeiffer's bacillus in influenza; described Pfeiffer's reaction for determination of cholera.

Piaget, Jean (1896–1980), Swiss psychologist. Elucidated development of cognitive functions in the child.

Poiseuille, Jean Léonard Marie (1797–1869), French physiologist and physicist. Studied physiology of arterial circulation; invented improved methods for measuring blood pressure; discovered Hagen-Poiseuille law independently of G. H. L. Hagen.

Porter, Rodney Robert (1917–1985), British biochemist. Research to determine chemical structure of immunoglobulins; Nobel Prize, 1972.

Prusiner, Stanley B. (1942–), American neurologist. Discovered prions, a new biological agent of infection; Nobel Prize, 1997.

Purkinje, Johannes Evangelista (1787–1869), Czech physiologist. Discovered the Purkinje effect in eye physiology and Purkinje cells in the cerebral cortex.

Ramón y Cajal, Santiago (1852–1934), Spanish histologist. Isolated the neuron and made discoveries concerning nerve cells in gray matter and the spinal cord; Nobel Prize, 1906.

Rathke, Martin Heinrich (1793–1860), German biologist. Discovered gill slits and gill arches in embryo birds and mammals, and Rathke's pocket in developing vertebrates.

Ray or Wray, John (1627?–1706), English naturalist. Identified the difference between mono- and dicotyledons; arranged plants according to their natural form, the foundation of the natural system of classification.

Réaumur, René Antoine Ferchault de (1683–1757), French entomologist. Worked in biology and metallurgy; invented the Réaumur thermometer scale.

Reichstein, Tadeus (1897–1996), Polish-born Swiss organic chemist. Isolated about 30 of the 40 substances produced by the adrenal cortex; synthesized and described the structure and properties of many of these substances; Nobel Prize, 1950.

Richet, Charles Robert (1850–1935), French physiologist. Studied serum therapy and discovered anaphylaxis; Nobel Prize, 1913.

Robbins, Frederick Chapman (1916–2003), American microbiologist. Discovered that poliomyelitis virus can be grown in various human tissue cultures; Nobel Prize, 1954.

Roberts, Richard J. (1943–), British geneticist. Independently of P. Sharp, discovered split genes; Nobel Prize, 1993.

Robinson, Robert (1886–1975), English chemist. Worked on plant pigments, alkaloids, and phenanthrene derivatives; Nobel Prize, 1947.

Rodbell, Martin (1925–1998), American pharmacologist. With A. Gilman, discovered G-proteins and the role of these proteins in cellular signal transduction; Nobel Prize, 1994.

Rose, Irwin (1926–), American biochemist. Discovered ubiquitin-mediated protein degradation; Nobel Prize, 2004.

Ross, Ronald (1857–1932), British physician. Proved that malaria is transmitted by the female *Anopheles* mosquito; Nobel Prize, 1902.

Rous, Francis Peyton (1879–1970), American physician and virologist. Produced cancer in chickens by inoculating them with filterable virus procured from tissue of chickens with tumors; Nobel Prize, 1966.

Roux, Pierre Paul Emile (1853–1933), French physician and bacteriologist. Helped develop modern serum therapeutics, especially concerning diphtheria.

Sabin, Albert Bruce (1906–1993), Polish-born American physician and virologist. Studied nature, mode of transmission, and epidemiology of human poliomyelitis; developed oral polio virus vaccine.

Sachs, Julius von (1832–1897), German botanist. Studied the connection between sunlight and chlorophyll; worked on heliotropism and geotropism.

Sakmann, Bert (1942–), German physiologist. With E. Neher, using the "patch clamp" technique they developed, showed how individual ion channels control the passage of charged ions into and out of cells: Nobel Prize, 1991.

Salk, Jonas Edward (1914–1995), American physician. Produced killed-virus vaccine effective in preventing poliomyelitis.

Samuelsson, Bengt Ingemar (1934–), Swedish biochemist and medical scientist. Studied prostaglandin metabolism and the formation of prostaglandin from arachidonic acid; Nobel Prize, 1982.

Sanctorius, real name Santorio Santorio (1561–1636), Italian physician. Invented the clinical thermometer; experimented with metabolism.

Sanger, Frederick (1918–), English chemist. Determined the exact order of amino acids in insulin; first to establish amino acid sequence for a protein; developed methods for determining nucleotide sequences (independently of W. Gilbert), advancing the technology of DNA recombination; Nobel Prizes. 1958 and 1980.

Schally, Andrew Victor (1926–), Polish-born American physiologist. With R. Guillemin, isolated and analyzed peptide hormones secreted in hypothalmic region of brain which control anterior pituitary hormone secretion; Nobel Prize, 1977.

Servetus, Michael (1511–1553), Spanish physician. Discovered the pulmonary circulation and the purification of the blood by the lungs.

Sharp, Phillip A. (1944–), American geneticist. Independently of R. Roberts, discovered split genes; Nobel Prize, 1993.

Sherrington, Charles Scott (1861–1952), English physiologist. Studied the neuron and its function and other aspects of the nervous system; Nobel Prize, 1932.

Skou, Jens C. (1918–), Dutch chemist. Discovered an ion-transporting enzyme—sodium, potassium-stimulated adenosine triphosphatase (Na^+, K^+-ATPase)—maintaining the balance of sodium and potassium ions in the living cell; Nobel Prize, 1997.

Smith, Hamilton Othanel (1931–), American geneticist. Isolated a restriction enzyme that cleaves deoxyribonucleic acid (DNA) molecules at a specific site; Nobel Prize, 1978.

Smith, Michael (1927–2000), Canadian chemist. Made fundamental contribution toward oligonucleotide-based, site-directed mutagenesis and its development for protein studies within DNA-based chemistry; Nobel Prize, 1993.

Snell, George Davis (1903–1996), American immunogeneticist. Demonstrated the x-ray induction of mutational changes in a mammal; contributed to the study of immunological systems and to the development of transplant immunology; Nobel Prize, 1980.

Sörensen, Sören Peter Lauritz (1868–1939), Danish biochemist. Did pioneer work on hydrogen ion concentration; invented the symbol pH.

Spemann, Hans (1869–1941), German zoologist. Studied embryonic development and discovered the organizer function of certain tissues; Nobel Prize, 1935.

Sperry, Roger Wolcott (1913–1994), American neuroscientist. Discovered the functional split between the left and right hemispheres of the brain; Nobel Prize, 1981.

Stanley, Wendell Meredith (1904–1971), American biochemist. Discovered that a virus is a nucleoprotein and can be crystallized; Nobel Prize, 1946.

Stein, William Howard (1911–1980), American biochemist. With S. Moore, developed technique for determining amino acid sequence in proteins, and applied it to ribonuclease; Nobel Prize, 1972.

Sulston, John E. (1942–), British geneticist. Using the nematode *Caenorhabditis elegans* as a model system, discovered that specific cells in the cell lineage always die through programmed cell death. Described the visible steps in the cellular death process and demonstrated the first mutations of genes participating in programmed cell death. Nobel Prize, 2002.

Sumner, James Batcheller (1887–1955), American biochemist. First to isolate an enzyme in pure, crystalline form and characterize it as a protein; Nobel Prize, 1946.

Sutherland, Earl Wilbur, Jr. (1915–1974), American physiologist. Uncovered intermediary role of cyclic adenylic acid in the mechanism of hormone control over human metabolic activities; Nobel Prize, 1971.

Svedberg, Theodor (1884–1971), Swedish chemist. An authority on colloid chemistry (dispersed phase); developed a centrifuge for colloidal particles and protein molecules; Nobel Prize, 1926.

Sydenham, Thomas (1624–1689), English physician. Gave classic descriptions of gout, venereal disease, fevers, hysteria, and Sydenham's chorea.

Szent-Györgyi, Albert von Nagyrapolt (1893–1986), Hungarian biochemist. Isolated vitamin C; research on combustion processes in plant and animal tissues, muscular contraction, and cell division; Nobel Prize, 1937.

Tanaka, Koichi (1959–), Japanese engineer. Developed soft desorption ionization method for mass spectrometric analyses of biological macromolecules; Nobel Prize, 2002.

Tatum, Edward Lawrie (1909–1975), American biochemist and geneticist. Researched the relation of genes to biochemical reactions in bacterial, yeast, and mold cells; with G. W. Beadle, discovered the phenomenon of genetic recombination in bacteria; Nobel Prize, 1958.

Temin, Howard Martin (1934–1994), American virologist. Proposed that genetic information is transferred from ribonucleic acid tumor viruses to deoxyribonucleic acid; independently of D. Baltimore, discovered reverse transcriptase; Nobel Prize, 1975.

Theiler, Max (1899–1972), South African physician and virologist. Developed a vaccine to prevent human yellow fever; Nobel Prize, 1951.

Theorell, Axel Hugo Teodor (1903–1982), Swedish biochemist. Made discoveries concerning the nature and mode of action of oxidative enzymes; Nobel Prize, 1955.

Thomas, Edward Donnall (1920–), American physician. Performed the first successful transfer of bone marrow from one individual to another; with J. Murray, helped define and then overcome the immunological mechanisms behind organ rejection; Nobel Prize, 1990.

Tinbergen, Nikolaas (1907–1988), Dutch-born British zoologist. Pioneered in study of social behavior of animals and their responses to complex stimuli; conducted experimental studies of the effects of selection pressures and evolutionary response to them; Nobel Prize, 1973.

Tiselius, Arne Wilhelm Kaurin (1902–1971), Swedish biochemist. Research on electrophoresis and absorption analysis; made discoveries concerning the complex nature of serum proteins; Nobel Prize, 1948.

Todd of Trumpington, Alexander Robertus Todd, Baron (1907–1997), British chemist. Worked on the structure and synthesis of nucleotides, and nucleotide coenzymes, and the related problem of phosphorylation; Nobel Prize, 1957.

Tonegawa, Susumu (1939–), Japanese immunologist. Discovered how a limited number of genes are capable of producing a vast number of diverse antibodies, each designed for a specific invading foreign substance; Nobel Prize, 1987.

Vane, John Robert (1927–), English pharmacologist. Discovered prostaglandin X (prostacyclin) and the role of aspirinlike drugs as blocking agents in the prostaglandin synthesis; Nobel Prize, 1982.

Varmus, Harold (1939–), American researcher in molecular virology and oncogenesis. With J. M. Bishop, researched the genetic basis of human cancers; their work led to the identification of over 50 cellular genes that can become oncogenes; Nobel Prize, 1989.

Vesalius, Andreas (1514–1564), Belgian anatomist in Italy. Known as the father of modern anatomy; corrected many of Galen's mistaken doctrines.

Virtanen, Artturi Ilmari (1895–1973), Finnish biochemist. Research on problems of human nutrition and agriculture; investigated acidity (pH) and biological nitrogen fixation; Nobel Prize, 1945.

Von Euler, Ulf Svante (1905–1983), Swedish physiologist. Identified norepinephrine as neurotransmitter of sympathetic nervous system; isolated and characterized norepinephrine storage granules in nerves; Nobel Prize, 1970.

Wagner von Jauregg (Wagner-Jauregg), Julius (1857–1940), Austrian psychiatrist. Developed use of malarial infection to treat general paresis; Nobel Prize, 1927.

Waksman, Selman Abraham (1888–1973), Russian-born American bacteriologist. Isolated the antibiotic streptomycin; Nobel Prize, 1952.

Wald, George (1906–1997), American biologist and biochemist. Discovered the role of vitamin A in vision; Nobel Prize, 1967.

Walker, John E. (1941–), British chemist. Made major contributions toward elucidating the enzymatic mechanism underlying the synthesis of adenosine triphosphate (ATP) by clarifying the structural conditions of the enzyme; Nobel Prize, 1997.

Wallace, Alfred Russel (1823–1913), English naturalist. Originated, independently of C. Darwin, theory of natural selection; postulated Wallace's line regarding geographical distribution of animals.

Warburg, Otto Heinrich (1883–1970), German physiologist. Worked on chemistry of respiration and on cancer; Nobel Prize, 1931.

Wassermann, August von (1866–1925), German physician. Discovered the Wassermann test for the detection of syphilis.

Watson, James Dewey (1928–), American biochemist. With F. H. C. Crick, determined the double-helix structure of deoxyribonucleic acid; Nobel Prize, 1962.

Watson, John Broadus (1878–1958), American psychologist. Founded the behaviorist school of psychology.

Weber, Ernst Heinrich (1795–1878), German anatomist and physiologist. Discovered Weberian apparatus; applied hydrodynamics to study of blood circulation; discovered inhibitory power of vagus nerve; proposed Weber's law of stimuli.

Weil, Adolf (1848–1916), German physician. Gave classic description of Weil's disease.

Weismann, August (1834–1914), German biologist. Contributed to the theory of heredity, which he attributed to variations in "germ-plasm."

Weller, Thomas Huckle (1915–), American virologist and parasitologist. Isolated the virus of chickenpox and herpes zoster and proved the common etiology of the two diseases; first to propagate German measles virus; Nobel Prize, 1954.

Whipple, George Hoyt (1878–1976), American pathologist. Studied anemia and liver treatment; Nobel Prize, 1934.

Wieland, Heinrich (1877–1957), German chemist. Studied bile acids, chlorophyll, and hemoglobin; Nobel Prize, 1927.

Wieschaus, Eric F. (1947–), American developmental biologist. Using *Drosophila*, he and the German developmental biologist Christiane Nüsslein-Volhard identified and classified a small number of genes that are important in determining the body plan and the formation of body segments; their work, along with that of American development biologist Edward B. Lewis, led to the discovery of important genetic mechanisms which control early embryonic development; Nobel Prize, 1995.

Wiesel, Torsten Nils (1924–), Swedish physiologist. Contributed to the study of the processing of visual information in the brain; Nobel Prize, 1981.

Wilkins, Maurice Hugh Frederick (1916–2004), English biophysicist born in New Zealand. Made x-ray diffraction studies that contributed to the structural determination of deoxyribonucleic acid; Nobel Prize, 1962.

Willstätter, Richard (1872–1942), German chemist. Worked on plant pigments; investigated alkaloids and their derivatives; Nobel Prize, 1915.

Windaus, Adolf (1876–1959), German chemist. Worked on sterols; discovered that ultraviolet light activates ergosterol and gives vitamin D_2; Nobel Prize, 1928.

Wright, Almroth Edward (1861–1947), British physician and pathologist. Studied parasitic disease; introduced inoculation against typhoid.

Wundt, Wilhelm Max (1832–1920), German physiologist and psychologist. Founded the first laboratory for experimental psychology.

Wüthrich, Kurt (1938–), Swiss chemist. Developed nuclear magnetic resonance spectroscopy for determining the three-dimensional structure of biological macromolecules in solution; Nobel Prize, 2002.

Yalow, Rosalyn Sussman (1921–), American medical physicist. Developed a radioimmunoassay technique to detect and measure minute levels of substances such as hormones in the body; Nobel Prize, 1977.

Yersin, Alexandre Émile Jean (1863–1943), Swiss bacteriologist. Discovered the bubonic plague bacillus in Hong Kong, working independently of S. Kitasato, and developed a serum for it.

Young, Thomas (1773–1829), English physicist and physician. Discovered the effect of the ciliary muscle on the shape of the eye lens (the mechanism of accommodation).

Zernike, Fritz (1888–1966), Dutch physicist. Developed the phase-contrast microscope, making possible the first microscopic examination of the internal structure of living cells; Nobel Prize, 1953.

Zinkernagel, Rolf M. (1944–), Swiss-born American immunologist and physician. Shared in the discovery of the specificity of cell-mediated immune defense with P. C. Doherty; Nobel Prize, 1996.

Zinsser, Hans (1878–1940), American bacteriologist. Developed methods of immunization against typhus.

Contributor Initials

Each article in the Encyclopedia is signed with the contributor's initials. This section gives all such initials. The contributor's name is provided. The contributor's affiliation can then be found by turning to the next section.

A

A.A.R.   Aldo A. Rossini
A.B.   Alexander Baumgarten
A.Bre.   Alan Breier
A.Bu.   Allison Butts
A.Bur.   Alan Burkhalter
A.B.O.   Arthur B. Otis
A.Ci.   Alex Ciegler
A.Cr.   Arthur Cronquist
A.C.Ca.   A. Charles Catania
A.C.L.   Alcinda C. Lewis
A.E.Bro.   Arthur E. Broadus
A.E.Fr.   A. E. Freeman
A.E.Wo.   Albert E. Wood
A.Fe.   Alan Feduccia
A.F.Be.   Albert F. Bennett
A.G.Hu.   Arthur G. Humes
A.Has.   Alan Hastings
A.Ho.   Arthur Horwich
A.H.B.   Alan H. Brush
A.H.St.   Alfred H. Sturtevant
A.J.Br.   Anthony J. Brammer
A.J.C.   Aaron J. Ciechanover: Protein
A.J.C.   Alan J. Charig: Reptilia etc.
A.J.F.G.   A. J. F. Griffiths
A.J.R.   A. J. Rowell
A.Ko.   Allan Konopka
A.L.   Anton Lang
A.Lar.   Allan Larson
A.L.Be.   Ann L. Beyer
A.L.Bi.   A. L. Bisno
A.L.deW.   A. L. de Week
A.L.Ko.   Arthur L. Koch
A.M.Ma.   Abe M. Macher
A.M.Pa.   Ana M. Parma
A.M.W.   Andrew M. Weitzenhoffer
A.M.We.   Adrian M. Wenner
A.McC.   Allysa McCabe
A.Me.   Anthony Mescher
A.N.P.   Arthur N. Popper
A.R.A.   Arthur R. Ayers
A.R.B.   Anna Ruth Brummett
A.R.I.   Anthony R. Ives
A.R.J.   Arthur R. Jensen
A.R.M.   Armand R. Maggenti
A.R.Mo.   Aage R. Møller
A.San.   Anthony Sanchez
A.Se.   Amita Sehgal
A.S.L.H.   A. S. L. Hu
A.T.   Albert Tyler
A.Tu.   Angelo Turturro
A.W.   Abraham White
A.We.   Alison Weiss
A.W.C.   Arthur W. Cooper
A.W.C.V.G.   Alexander W. C. von Graevenitz
A.W.F.   Arthur W. Francis
A.W.G.   Arthur W. Galston: Reproduction (plant)
A.W.G.   Arthur W. Guy: Electrotherapy
A.W.W.   Andrew W. Wayne

B

B.A.M.   Brian A. Maurer
B.A.St.   Bruce A. Stanley
B.Bro.   Barbara Brodsky
B.C.S.   B. C. Sutton
B.D.D.   Bernard D. Davis
B.E.S.G.   Brian E. S. Gunning
B.F.   Bernard Frank
B.F.W.   B. F. Wilson
B.Hog.   Brigid Hogan
B.H.Ki.   Bryan H. King
B.H.McC.   Bayard H. McConnaughey
B.I.   Brent Iverson
B.J.D.M.   Bastiaan J. D. Mccusc
B.J.K.   Brian J. Kilbey
B.J.Mu.   Brent J. Muus

B.Kal.   Bengt Kallen
B.McE.   Bruce McEwen
B.Ro.   Barry Rosen
B.S.   Bobb Schaeffer
B.S.Gl.   Benjamin S. Glick
B.S.M.   Bernard S. Meyer
B.S.N.   Bodil Schmidt-Nielsen
B.T.B.   Bernard T. Bormann
B.T.S.   Bradley T. Scheer
B.Wi.   Brian Wilkinson
B.Y.Ta.   Bernard Y. Tao

C

C.A.F.   Charles A. Francis
C.A.H.   Carol A. Hoffman
C.A.L.   Cadence A. Lowell
C.A.Me.   Charles A. Mebus
C.A.Sp.   Carol A. Spiegel
C.B.C.   Charles B. Curtin
C.B.G.   C. B. Gillies
C.B.V.N.   Cornelis B. Van Niel
C.B.W.   Curtis B. Wilson
C.C.L.   Ching Chun Li
C.C.La.   Conrad C. Labandeira
C.De.   Carter Denniston
C.E.Ba.   Clinton E. Ballou
C.E.LaM.   C. E. LaMotte
C.E.St.   C. Edward Stevens
C.E.Ste.   Charles E. Sternheim
C.F.E.R.   Clyde F. E. Roper
C.F.N.   Charles F. Niven, Jr.
C.G.G.   Chauncey G. Goodchild
C.G.J.   Clive G. Jones
C.H.   Cadet Hand
C.Ha.   Carlyn Halde
C.H.L.   Choh Hao Li
C.J.Da.   C. J. Darwin
C.J.Ka.   Clarence J. Kado
C.K.W.   Charles K. Weichert
C.L.F.W.   C. L. F. Woodcock
C.L.Ma.   Clement L. Markert
C.L.Mas.   Colin L. Masters
C.L.R.   Charles L. Rulfs
C.M.G.   Carlos M. Grilo
C.M.S.   Cheng-Mei Shaw
C.No.   Charles Noback
C.O.   Cristian Orrego
C.P.   Carl Pfaffmann
C.Pa.   Camille Parmesan
C.P.L.   Charles P. Lyman
C.R.Ca.   C. Ronald Carroll
C.S.Co.   Christine S. Cozzens
C.S.M.   Craighton S. Mauk
C.V.   Charles Vitek
C.Wa.   Chen Wang
C.Wi.   Conrad Wickstrom
C.W.B.   Carl W. Boothroyd

D

D.A.C.   David A. Clark
D.A.D.   Donald A. Dewsbury
D.A.Mi.   Dorothy A. Miller
D.Bl.   Donald Blough
D.B.M.   David B. Meyer
D.B.So.   David B. South
D.B.W.   Douglas B. Webster
D.C.   David Cohen
D.C.C.   David C. Coleman
D.C.J.   Donald C. Jackson
D.C.M.   David C. Morrison
D.D.C.   Denise Dellarosa Cummins
D.D.D.   D. Dwight Davis
D.D.Fo.   Dennis D. Focht
D.E.G.   David E. Giannasi
D.E.J.   Dorothy E. Jegla

D.E.No.   Donald E. Norris
D.F.Ow.   Denis F. Owen
D.G.M.   Douglas G. Mook
D.He.   Donald Heyneman
D.Ho.   Derek Horton
D.H.O.   Douglas H. Ohlendorf
D.J.C.   Donald J. Cohen
D.J.D.   David J. Dabbs
D.J.Ev.   Doyle J. Evans, Jr.
D.J.Fu.   Douglas J. Futuyma
D.J.K.   D. J. Kushner
D.J.L.   Douglas J. Loftus
D.J.St.   Dan J. Stein
D.J.S.B.   Donald J. S. Barr
D.L.Gr.   Dale L. Greiner
D.L.Pa.   Darwin L. Palmer
D.L.S.   David L. Spector: Cell nucleus
D.L.S.   David L. Stocum: Animal morphogenesis
D.M.C.   D. Martinez-Carrera
D.M.Ca.   Don M. Carlson
D.M.DeL.   Dwight M. DeLong
D.M.Fi.   David M. Findlay
D.M.G.   David M. Greenberg
D.M.Pr.   David M. Prescott
D.N.La.   Daniel N. Lapedes
D.O'H.   David O'Hagan
D.P.D.   Daryl P. Domning
D.R.   Donald Raum
D.Ru.   Dorothea Rudnick
D.R.J.   David R. Jones
D.R.Pr.   Donald R. Prothero
D.Sim.   Daniel Simberloff
D.Sk.   David Skelly
D.S.C   Dennis S. Charney
D.S.P.   David S. Palermo
D.T.L.   David T. Lykken
D.V.Mo.   Donald V. Moore
D.W.   Daniel Wellner
D.W.Ce.   Daniel W. Celander
D.W.Me.   David W. Meinke
D.X.F.   Daniel X. Freedman

E

E.A.Ad.   Edward A. Adelberg
E.A.B.   Edward A. Boyden
E.A.F.   E. A. Freundt
E.A.M.   Eugene A. Milus
E.B.Cu.   Edward B. Cutler
E.B.F.   E. B. Ford
E.B.L.   Edward B. Lewis
E.C.A.   Ellsworth C. Alvord, Jr.
E.C.P.   E. C. Pielou
E.C.R.R.   Edward C. Roosen-Runge
E.D.Gr.   Ernest D. Gray
E.E.F.   Eberhard E. Fotz
E.E.S.   Esmond E. Snell
E.Fr.   Ernesto Freire
E.F.Lo.   Elizabeth F. Loftus
E.Gry.   Ellen Gryj
E.G.C.   Elizabeth G. Cutter
E.G.St.   Edward G. Stuart
E.G.W.   Ernest G. Wever
E.Ha.   Everett Hausen
E.Ho.   Eric Holtzman
E.H.C.   Edward H. Cole
E.H.H.   Elbert H. Hadley
E.Jo.   Edward Johnson
E.Jor.   E. Jordan
E.L.   E. Lazarides
E.L.P.   E. Lowe Pierce
E.L.V.C.   Ernest L. Van Campenhout
E.L.Y.   Ellis L. Yochelson
E.Ma.   E. Margoliash
E.M.B.   Elliott M. Blass
E.O.B.   Elgene O. Box
E.O.W.   Edward O. Wiley
E.P.G.   E. Patrick Groody
E.P.Go.   Eric P. Goosby

E.R.L.   E. R. Leadbetter
E.W.Ge.   Erwin W. Gelfand
E.W.V.   Edward W. Voss, Jr.

F

F.A.L.C.   F. A. L. Clowes
F.A.M.   Frederick A. Murphy
F.B.S.   Frank B. Salisbury
F.Co.   F. Collins: Human Genome Project
F.Co.   Friedrich Constabel: Breeding (plant)
F.C.D.   Franklin C. Daiber
F.C.P.Y.   Frank C. P. Yin
F.F.R.   Frank F. Richards
F.K.McK.   Frank K. McKinney
F.L.Sc.   Frederick L. Schuster
F.M.D.   Frank Matthews Dugan
F.P.H.   Frederick P. Heinzel
F.R.Vo.   Fred R. Volkmar
F.S.R.   Fred S. Rosen
F.S.S.   Frederick S. Szalay
F.T.A.   Fredrich T. Addicott
F.T.L.   F. Thomas Ledig
F.V.   Friedrich Vogel: Human genetics
F.V.B.   Ferdinando V. Boero
F.Wi.   Fred Wilt

G

G.   Govindjee
G.Al.   Gene Alexander
G.A.A.   Gregory A. Ahern
G.A.B.   Gerald A. Berkowitz
G.Ba.   George Bakken
G.Boh.   Greg Bohach
G.B.B.   Günther B. Blobel
G.B.M.   Gairdner B. Moment
G.C.B.   George C. Brainard
G.C.Ke.   George C. Kent, Jr.
G.E.Pe.   Gertrude E. Perlmann
G.E.W.P.   Gerhard W. E. Plaut
G.Hr.   Geza Hrazdina
G.H.F.   George H. Fried
G.H.O.   Gordon H. Orians
G.J.   Giles Johnson
G.J.C.   Gerald J. Canter
G.J.W.   George J. Wilder
G.L.   Gary Levy
G.LeB.   Gretchen LeBuhn
G.Lo.   George Lordi
G.L.Be.   Gerald L. Benny
G.L.Gi.   Gerald L. Gilardi
G.L.St.   G. Ledyard Stebbins
G.M.   George Mandler
G.Mo.   Giuliana Moreno
G.M.L.   George M. Lordi
G.M.M.   George M. Malacinski
G.M.S.   George M. Savage
G.M.Sh.   Gordon M. Shepherd
G.P.   George Papageorgiou
G.Pas.   Gavril Pasternak
G.Po.   Guido Pontecovo
G.P.Kr.   Graham P. Krasen
G.R.Ca.   G. R. Carter
G.R.Hi.   Glenn R. Hicks
G.Slu.   Greenfield Sluder
G.S.H.   Gene S. Helfman
G.S.K.   George S. Kobayashi
G.S.S.   Gary S. Stein
G.S.W.   George S. Wilson
G.W.H.   Gertrude W. Hinsch
G.W.Ha.   Gerald W. Hart
G.W.Hay.   G. W. Hay
G.W.Sa.   Gary W. Saunders
G.Z.   Geoffrey Zubay

H

H.A.   Herbert Athenstaedt
H.A.B.   Horace A. Barker
H.Cl.   Hartwig Cleve
H.Cr.   Howard Crum
H.Di.   Hugh Dingle
H.D.P.   Harry D. Patton
H.E.Ca.   Herbert E. Carter
H.E.We.   H. E. Wendler
H.G.   Harold Goodglass
H.G.W.   H. G. Wittmann

H.H.F.   H. Hugh Fudenberg
H.H.Ha.   H. Hunter Handsfield
H.J.L.   Harry J. Lipner
H.J.P.   Herman J. Phaff
H.Le.   Henry Leland
H.Lei.   Hoyle Leigh
H.Li.   Helmut Lieth
H.L.H.   Howard L. Hamilton
H.L.O.   H. L. Ostergaard
H.L.Sc.   Hilary Lappin-Scott
H.M.T.   Howard M. Temin
H.O.H.   Harlyn O. Halverson
H.P.S.   Hanns-Peter Schultze
H.P.T.   Henry P. Treffers
H.P.W.   Hilda P. Willett
H.Ras.   Howard Rasmussen
H.R.L.   Hans R. Lindner
H.Sa.   Helmut Sauer
H.S.Be.   H. Stanley Bennett
H.T.L.   Helen Tappan Loeblich
H.Wh.   Harry Wheeler
H.Wi.   Hugh Wilcox
H.W.Bl.   H. Weston Blaser
H.W.J.   Holger W. Jannasch
H.W.K.   Harold W. Keller
H.W.Mo.   Harland W. Mossman

I

I.B.W.   Irwin B. Wilson
I.Fr.   Irwin Fridovich
I.F.S.   Ira F. Salkin
I.G.   Isidore Gersh
I.Gi.   Ian Gibbons
I.J.Go.   Ira J. Goldberg
I.L.B.   I. Lehr Brisbin, Jr.
I.M.P.   Ingrid M. Parker
I.P.T.   Irwin P. Ting
I.R.   Irvin Rock
I.R.M.   Ian R. Mackay
I.Z.   Israel Zelitch

J

J.A.Do.   James A. Doyle
J.A.Pe.   Jan A. Pechenik
J.A.Ri.   James A. Rillema
J.A.Sw.   John A. Swets
J.Bi.   Joseph Biederman
J.Bre.   Joel Breman
J.B.D.   John B. Dunning, Jr.
J.B.Da.   James B. Dale
J.B.F.   Jack B. Fisher
J.B.G.   Jeffrey B. Graham
J.B.J.   J. B. Jennings
J.B.Jo.   Jeremy B. Jones
J.B.L.   James B. Lackey
J.B.M.   J. B. Messerger
J.Co.   Jerome Cohen
J.Cr.   Joel Cracraft
J.C.Ri.   J. C. Ritchie
J.C.Ro.   Jerome C. Rozen, Jr.
J.C.Sc.   Jack C. Schultz
J.D.C.   J. Donald Capra
J.D.Jo.   Jon D. Johnson
J.D.Ro.   J. David Robertson
J.E.Ba.   John E. Banks
J.E.Bla.   James E. Blankenship
J.E.F.   James E. Ferrell
J.E.Gu.   James E. Gunckel
J.E.Wi.   Judith E. Winston
J.F.Cr.   James F. Crow
J.F.F.   James T. Fitzsimons
J.F.H.   John F. Hahn
J.F.L.   J. F. Loneragan
J.F.Web.   Jacqueline F. Webb
J.G.   John Garcia
J.Ge.   John Gergely
J.Gi.   J. Gijskuenen: Chemostat
J.Gi.   Jacques Gilloteaux: Gallbladder
J.Ho.   James Hodgdon
J.H.Cr.   John H. Crowe
J.H.T.   J. Herbert Taylor
J.J.   Jules Janick
J.J.Ka.   James J. Kasmierczak
J.J.Ma.   John J. Marchalonis
J.J.Se.   J. John Sepkoski, Jr.
J.K.   Jan Klein
J.K.M.   June Kan-Mitchell

J.K.Ri.   J. Keith Rigby
J.K.St.   Jeffrey K. Stone
J.L.Br.   Judith L. Bronstein
J.L.La.   J. L. Larimer
J.L.Me.   Joseph L. Melnick
J.L.Mey.   Judy L. Meyer
J.L.S.   John L. Sabo
J.L.St.   Janet L. Stein
J.L.T.   J. L. Turk
J.Mas.   Jeam Massion
J.Mein.   J. Meinwald
J.M.Ba.   Janice M. Bahr
J.M.F.   Jean-Marie Franc
J.M.M.   James M. Manning
J.M.Q.   John M. Quarles
J.M.S.   Jay M. Savage
J.M.Tr.   James M. Trappe
J.N.Bu.   Judith N. Burstyn
J.N.F.   Jordan N. Fink
J.O.C.   John O. Corliss
J.O.Co.   Jay O. Cohen
J.P.M.   Joseph P. Mascarenhas
J.P.Mo.   John P. Mordes
J.P.S.   John P. Scott
J.P.Tr.   J. P. Truant
J.P.W.   Jon P. Woods
J.R.B.   James R. Bamburg
J.R.Ba.   J. R. Bandoni
J.R.G.T.   John R. G. Turner
J.R.Ha.   Jeffrey R. Hazel
J.R.M.   Joan R. Marsden
J.R.P.   Julian R. Pleasants
J.R.Po.   Jeffrey R. Powell
J.R.Ra.   John R. Raper
J.R.S.F.   J. R. S. Fincham
J.S.   Julius Schachter
J.Sc.   Jonathan Schooler
J.S.G.   Joseph S. Gots
J.S.R.   John S. Ryland
J.S.Ro.   James S. Robertson
J.Tr.   John Trowsdale
J.T.F.   James T. Fitzsimons
J.T.G.   Joseph T. Gregory
J.Va.   Jacob Vaya
J.W.Be.   J. W. Bennett
J.W.Br.   Jason W. Brown
J.W.C.   J. W. Costerton
J.W.Ez.   John W. Ezzell
J.W.Fe.   Jack W. Fell
J.W.Fo.   Jackson W. Foster
J.W.H.   J. Woodland Hastings
J.W.St.G.   Joseph W. St. Geme
J.W.T.   John W. Taylor
J.W.V.   James W. Valentine

K

K.At.   Kenji Atoda
K.E.   Katherine Esau
K.E.M.   Kenneth E. Moyer
K.F.K.   Karl F. Koopman
K.G.F.   Karen Grady Ford
K.Hu.   Keith Hutchison
K.H.M.   Kenneth H. Mann
K.J.   Kjell Johansen
K.J.McN.   Kenneth J. McNamara
K.J.R.   Kenneth J. Ryan
K.J.W.   Kimerly J. Wilcox
K.L.C.   Karen L. Chobor
K.L.D.   Kenneth L. Duke
K.M.   Karl Maramorosch
K.M.C.   Kenneth Mark Colby
K.M.N.   Kenneth M. Noll
K.N.O.   Kenneth N. Ogle
K.N.P.   Kathleen N. Potter
K.N.Z.   Klaus Napp-Zinn
K.P.A.   Kenneth P. Able
K.Ru.   Kathryn Ruoff
K.Sh.   Ken Shortman
K.S.Th.   Keith S. Thomson
K.S.W.   Katherine S. Waldmann
K.T.   Keith Thomson
K.U.S.   Karl U. Smith
K.V.S.   Karlene V. Schwartz

L

L.A.C.   Louis A. Chiodo
L.A.Gr.   Les A. Grivell

L.A.R.　Lorrin A. Riggs
L.B.　Lane Barksdale
L.B.L.　Luna B. Leopold
L.B.R.　Lee B. Reichman
L.Co.　Lee Conch
L.C.L.　Leonard C. Lutter
L.C.Le.　Lyndon C. Lee
L.E.M.　Lawrence E. Marks
L.E.Mo.　Leonard E. Mortenson
L.E.W.　L. E. Wittmers
L.F.S.　Lee F. Schuchardt
L.G.　Leonard Goland
L.Gre.　Larry Green
L.H.　Leonard Hayflick
L.H.W.　Laura Hood Watchman
L.J.A.　Leslie J. Audus
L.J.Kl.　Lewis J. Kleinsmith
L.J.M.　Lawrence J. Machlin
L.Lo.　L. Lorand
L.M.C.　Lucy M. Cranwell
L.M.Ca.　Lori M. Carris
L.P.　Lester Packer
L.P.C.　Leo P. Clements
L.R.G.　Leah R. Gerber
L.V.S.　Lola V. Stamm

M

M.A.Je.　Michael A. Jenike
M.A.L.　Max A. Lauffer
M.A.La.　Meredith A. Lane
M.A.Ma.　Michelle A. Marvier
M.A.R.　Martin A. Rizack
M.A.Ric.　Michael A. Rice
M.A.W.　Michael A. Walsh
M.Bl.　Meredith Blackwell
M.Bo.　Mark Bothwell
M.B.McC.　Mary B. McCann
M.B.St.　Murray B. Stein
M.Ch.　Martha Christensen
M.C.C.　M. C. Chang
M.C.McK.　Malcolm C. McKenna
M.C.W.　Mark C. Willingham
M.C.Wo.　Marc S. Wold
M.D.　Michael Doudoroff
M.Do.　Mike Doyle
M.D.Br.　Michael D. Brown
M.D.Bre.　Michael D. Bree
M.D.C.　M. Donald Cave
M.D.U.　Michael D. Uhler
M.Ed.　Marshall Edelson
M.E.D.　Mary E. Dempsey
M.E.Re.　M. E. Reichmann
M.E.Ri.　Mary E. Rice
M.E.T.　Helmet E. Thiess
M.F.　Milton Fingerman
M.F.F.　Michael F. Fay
M.F.R.　Mark F. Reynolds
M.G.　Martin Gibbs
M.Go.　Marjorie Goldfarb
M.G.Ma.　Maria G. Masucci
Mo.H.　Monto Ho
M.Ha.　Michael Hanna
M.H.C.　Marvin H. Carruthers
M.J.　Mark Johnson
M.J.Ca.　Michael J. Cavey
M.J.Cou.　Mary J. Coulombe
M.J.Kr.　Mary Jeanne Kreek
M.J.K.H.　Michael J. K. Harper
M.J.Po.　Margaret J. Polley
M.Kl.　Maren Klich
M.K.S.　Morton K. Schwartz
M.L.　Martin Lotz
M.La.　Meredith Lane
M.Le.　M. Levitan
M.My.　Michelle Mynlieff
M.M.B.　M. M. Brooke
M.M.Ba.　M. M. Barry
M.P.H.　Mark P. Hedger
M.P.S.　Martin P. Schreibman
M.Ri.　Michael Rindler
M.Ru.　Manfred Ruddat
M.R.C.　Michael R. Cummings
M.R.J.S.　M. R. J. Salton
M.Sy.　Megan Sykes
M.S.G.　Michael S. Gazzaniga
M.S.Mi.　Malcolm S. Mitchell
M.V.B.　M. V. Brian
M.W.A.　M. W. Adams
M.W.C.　Mark W. Chase
M.W.Fl.　M. Wayne Flye

M.W.G.　Michael W. Gray
M.W.T.　Margaret R. Thompson
M.Y.D.　M. Yusoff Dawood
M.Y.W.　Michelle Y. Walker
M.Z.　Milton Zaitlin

N

N.A.　Nelle Ammons
N.Ar.　Naveen Arya
N.B.C.　Nancy B. Clark
N.B.S.　N. B. Simmons
N.Cha.　Nirupa Chaudhari
N.D.L.　Norman D. Levine
N.D.Z.　Norton D. Zinder
N.G.　Nigel Girgraph
N.G.D.　Nancy G. Dengler
N.Ho.　Nigel Holder
N.H.B.　Norman H. Boke
N.H.G.　Nafsika H. Georgorapadakou
N.J.Go.　Nicholas J. Gottelli
N.K.M.　N. Karle Mottet
N.L.S.　Nancy L. Segal
N.Ra.　Natasha Raikhel
N.Sh.　Nathan Sharon
N.T.S.　Nelson T. Spratt, Jr.
N.W.　Nina Wedell

O

O.D.R.　Oscar D. Ratnoff
O.E.L.　Otto E. Lowenstein
O.E.N.　Olin E. Nelsen
O.H.　Olga Hartman
O.J.M.　Orlando J. Miller
O.L.F.　Oscar L. Frick
O.R.A.　O. Roger Anderson

P

P.A.E.　Peter A. Edwards
P.A.Ma.　Preston A. Marx
P.A.McL.　Patsy A. McLaughlin
P.A.So.　Pamela A. Sokol
P.B.C.　Philip B. Cowles
P.Ch.　Patrick Choy
P.C.M.　Paul C. Marino
P.C.Si.　P. C. Silva
P.D.C.　Paul D. Carey
P.D.H.　Philip D. Harvey
P.Fr.　Peter Frumhoff
P.F.M.　Paul F Maderson
P.G.Ri.　Paul G. Risser
P.H.Ho.　Peter H. Homann
P.I.H.　Phyllis I. Hanson
P.J.D.　Peter J. Davies
P.J.McN.　Peter J. McNamara
P.K.　Peter Karlson
P.Ka.　Peter Kareiva
P.K.M.　Pamela K. Mulligan
P.L.C.　Peter L. Carlton
P.L.Fi.　Peggy L. Fiedler
P.M.Ac.　Phillip M. Achey
P.M.B.　Percy M. Butler
P.M.Ka.　P. M. Kareiva
P.M.M.R.　Peter M. M. Rae
P.Ran.　Peter Randerson
P.Ri.　Paul Risser
P.Ro.　Patricia Rosa
P.R.M.　Peter R. Marker
P.S.　Peter Satir
P.Sae.　Peter Saenger
P.Sc.　Paul Schimmel
P.Si.　Philip Siekevitz
P.S.H.　Paul S. Hoffman
P.S.S.　Pill-Soon Song
P.T.M.　Paul T. Magee
P.T.R.　Prahlad T. Ram
P.V.　Peter Villiger
P.W.B.　Philip W. Brandt
P.W.P.　Peter W. Price

R

R.Ad.　Robert Ader
R.Au.　Robert Austrian

R.A.Fin.　Richard A. Finkelstein
R.A.Go.　Richard A. Goodman
R.A.Ra.　Richard A. Rachubinski
R.Bri.　R. Brimacombe
R.B.C.　Richard B. Couch
R.B.He.　Ronald B. Herberman
R.B.M.　Regis B. Miller
R.Ch.　Robert Chen
R.C.MacD.　Robert C. McDonald
R.C.Mo.　Raymond C. Moore
R.D.B.　Robert D. Barnes
R.D.Ber.　R. D. Berger
R.D.H.　Rollin D. Hotchkiss
R.D.M.　Reginald D. Manwell
R.D.Ma.　R. D. Martin
R.D.V.　Richard D. Vierstra
R.D.Wa.　Robert D. Walkup
R.E.Bi.　Rupert E. Billingham
R.E.H.　Robert E. Hungate
R.E.Ho.　Ralph E. Hoffman
R.E.K.　R. E. Kallio
R.E.Py.　Reed E. Pyeritz
R.E.St.　Robert E. Stall
R.F.Bo.　R. F. Bozarth
R.F.K.　Robert F. Ker
R.G.　Raymond Giese
R.Go.　Ronald Gold
R.Gov.　R. Govindjee
R.G.E.M.　R. G. E. Murray
R.G.M.　R. G. Martin
R.G.No.　R. Glenn Northcutt
R.G.W.A.　Richard G. W. Anderson
R.G.Z.　Richard G. Zweifel
R.Hog.　Robert Hogan
R.Hol.　Robert Holt
R.H.E.　Richard H. Eyde
R.H.F.H.　R. H. F. Hunter
R.H.G.　Roy H. Gigg
R.H.P.　R. H. Pearce
R.H.R.　Robert H. Rownd
R.H.T.　Richard H. Tedford
R.I.D.　Ralph I. Dorfman
Ri.H.　Richard Hong
R.I.MacD.　Ruby I. MacDonald
R.J.F.　Robert J. Foster
R.J.K.　R. J. Keddy
R.J.R.　Rupert J. Riedel
R.Kor.　Roger Korus
R.K.Ho.　R. K. Horst
R.K.Y.　Robert K. Yu
R.Lev.　Rachmiel Levine
R.L.Ca.　Ronald L. Calabrese
R.L.He.　Robert L. Heinrikson
R.L.Hu.　Robert L. Hulbary
R.L.M.　R. L. Mower
R.L.Moe.　Richard L. Moe
R.L.Re.　Russell L. Regnery
R.L.W.　Ray L. Watterson
R.McN.A.　R. McNeill Alexander
R.Mur.　Robert Murphy
R.M.A.　Ronald M. Atlas
R.M.Al.　R. McNeill Alexander
R.M.B.　Reeve M. Bailey
R.M.Fe.　Rodney M. Feldman
R.M.K.　Richard M. Klein
R.M.R.　Roger M. Reeve
R.O'Ra.　Ronan O'Rahilly
R.Pe.　Roger Penrose
R.P.H.　Richard P. Hall
R.P.Hi.　Robert P. Higgins
R.P.Le.　Rafael Pont-Lezica
R.P.W.　Robert P. Wagner
R.Re.　Randall Reed
R.Ri.　Ralph Riley
R.Ro.　Richard Roberts: Restriction enzyme
R.Ro.　Robert Rosen: Mathematical biology
R.Ros.　Robert Roskoski, Jr.
R.R.B.　Robert R. Brubaker
R.R.C.　Rita R. Colwell
R.R.F.　Richard R. Fay
R.R.J.　Robert R. Jacobson
R.S.　Rudolf Schmid
R.Sk.　Richard Skalak
R.Str.　Reuben Straus
R.S.E.K.　Richard S. E. Keefe
R.S.H.　R. Scott Hawley
R.S.Le.　Richard S. Lewis
R.S.McE.　Robert S. McEwen

R.S.W. Ralph S. Wolfe
R.S.Y. Rosalyn S. Yalow
R.T.D. Raymond T. Damian
R.T.Ha. Richard T. Hanlin
R.T.J. Richard T. Jones
R.U. R. Ullrich
R.V. Richard Vallee
R.We. Richard Wetzel
R.W.But. Robert W. Butler
R.W.H. Robert W. Holmes
R.W.Po. Robert S. Pozos
R.W.Sa. Robert W. Sanders
R.W.T. Raymond W. Tennant

S

S.A.L. Simon A. Levin
S.A.Mo. Stephen A. Morse
S.A.R. Scott A. Redhead
S.B.O. Steven B. Oppenheimer
S.B.P. Steward B. Peck
S.B.Se. Shlomo Bar-Sela
S.C. Sydney Chapman
S.Chi. Shu Chien
S.Co. Sheryl Coombs
S.C.H. Standish C. Hartman
S.C.J. Shung-Chang Jong
S.C.Jo. S. C. Jong
S.Gr. S. Granick
S.G.B. S. Gaylen Bradley
S.H. Sven Horstadius
S.Jo. S. Joseph
S.J.B. Spencer J. Berry
S.J.Co. Steven J. Collins
S.J.Ga. Stephen J. Galli
S.J.McN. Samuel J. McNaughton
S.Kit. Saul Kit
S.LaB. Stephen LaBerge
S.L.G. Sol L. Garfield
S.L.M. Steve L. Moseley
S.M.F. Sydney M. Finegold
S.N.G. Stanley N. Gershoff
S.Pi. Stuart Pimm
S.P.H. Samuel P. Hammar
S.P.P. Sybil P. Parker
S.Rop. Stephen Roper
S.R.G. Steven R. Goodman
S.R.St. Scott R. Stewart
S.So. Stevern Southwick
S.S.D. S. Sovonick-Dunford
S.U.W. S. U. Walkley
S.V. Steve Vogel
S.W.P. Stephen W. Porges
S.W.Pe. S. William Pelletier

T

T.A.Wa. Thomas A. Waldmann
T.A.Z. Thomas A. Zanoni
T.B.T. Thomas B. Turner
T.C.R. Theodore C. Ruch
T.C.Wh. T. C. Whitmore
T.D.S. Thomas D. Sharkey
T.E.D. T. E. Dawson
T.E.M. Thomas E. Miler
T.E.S. Thomas E. Schroeder
T.Ha. Terry Harrison
T.I.S. Tracy I. Storer
T.J.B. Thomas J. Bouchard
T.J.G. Timothy J. Gaudin
T.L.Ha. Thomas L. Hale
T.L.O.W. Terry L. Orr-Weaver
T.L.W. Timothy L. White
T.Moh. T. Mohanakumar
T.M.Ba. T. M. Barkley
T.M.Ch. T. Ming Chu
T.M.F. Thomas M. Frost
T.M.K. Todd M. Kana
T.N.T. Thomas N. Taylor
T.Po. Thomas Pollard
T.P.S. Theodore P. Schilb
T.R.Sm. T. R. Smithson
T.Sc. Tim Schowalter
T.Sn. Theodore Snook
T.S.P. Thomas S. Parsons
T.W.C. Thomas W. Cronin
T.W.D. T. Wijesekera Dolphin
T.Y.L. Tae Young Lee

U, V

U.L. Ulrich Luttge
V.Ah. Vernon Ahmadjian
V.A.F. Victoria A. Fromkin
V.C.C. Valeria Cizerski Culotta
V.G.A. Vincent G. Allfrey
V.I.C. Vernon I. Cheadle
V.J.W. Verner J. Wulff
V.K.S. V. K. Sawhney
V.L.E. Virginia L. Ernster
V.W. Virginia Walbot

W

W.An. Warren Andrew
W.A.B. William A. Brodsky
W.A.Be. William A. Beresford
W.A.Li. Werner A. Lindenmaier

W.A.V. Wesley A. Volk
W.B. William Bradford
W.Be. William Bemis
W.Bu. Willy Burgdorfer
W.B.C. William B. Campbell
W.Ca. William Cain
W.D.H. Willard D. Hartman
W.D.Hu. William D. Hummon
W.D.R.H. W. D. Russell-Hunter
W.E.B. William E. Bell
W.E.D. William E. Dossel
W.E.S. W. E. Sterrer
W.F.Mo. William F. Morris
W.F.W. Warren F. Walker, Jr.
W.G.A. Warren G. Abrahamson
W.G.W. W. Gordon Whaley
W.Ho. William Hodos
W.H.K. William H. Konigsberg
W.H.Si. William H. Simmons
W.H.Wa. Warren H. Wagner, Jr.
W.J.A. William J. Adelman, Jr.
W.J.B. Walter J. Bock
W.J.Hag. William J. Hagan, Jr.
W.J.J. W. John Judd
W.J.M. William J. Mitsch
W.Ku. Wietse Kuis
W.K.J. W. K. Joklik
W.L.Ny. William L. Nyhan
W.L.S. Waldo L. Schmitt
W.Ma. Walter Mannheim
W.McG. William McGinnis
W.Mil. William Milsom
W.Po. William Porter
W.P.B. William P. Banks
W.Re. Walter Reid
W.R.Br. Winslow R. Briggs
W.R.L. Werner R. Loewenstein
W.R.P. William R. Philipson
W.R.R. William R. Riedel
W.Sh. William Shive
W.S.Y.W. William S.-Y. Wang
W.S.B. William S. Benninghof
W.S.Br. Willard S. Bromley
W.T.K. William T. Keeton
W.W.B. William W. Ballard
W.W.Bro. William W. Bromer
W.W.K. William W. Korth
W.W.Sp. Wesley W. Spink
W.Z.H. William Z. Hassid

X, Y

X.J.M. X. J. Musacchia
Y.C.F. Y. C. Fung
Y.W. Y. Waisel

Contributor Affiliations

This list comprises all contributors to the Encyclopedia. A brief affiliation is provided for each author. This list may be used in conjunction with the previous section to fully identify the contributor of each article.

A

Able, Dr. Kenneth P. Department of Biological Sciences, State University of New York, Albany.

Abrahamson, Prof. Warren G., II. Department of Biology, Bucknell University, Lewisburg, Pennsylvania.

Achey, Prof. Phillip M. Institute of Food and Agricultural Sciences, University of Florida.

Adams, Prof. M. W. Department of Crop and Soil Sciences, Michigan State University.

Addicott, Prof. Fredrick T. Department of Botany, University of California, Davis.

Adelberg, Dr. Edward A. Department of Microbiology, Yale University.

Adelman, Dr. William J., Jr. National Institutes of Health, Bethesda, Maryland.

Ader, Prof. Robert. Department of Psychiatry, University of Rochester, New York.

Ahearn, Prof. Gregory A. Department of Zoology, University of Hawaii, Manoa.

Ahmadjian, Dr. Vernon. Department of Biology, Clark University, Worcester, Massachusetts.

Alexander, Dr. Gene. Laboratory of Neurosciences, National Institutes of Aging and Health, Bethesda, Maryland.

Alexander, Prof. R. McNeill. Department of Biology, University of Leeds, England.

Allfrey, Dr. Vincent G. Department of Cell Biology, Rockefeller University.

Alvord, Dr. Ellsworth C., Jr. Department of Neuropathology, University of Washington.

Ammons, Dr. Nelle. Retired; Department of Biology, West Virginia University.

Anderson, Dr. O. Roger. Lamont-Doherty Geological Observatory, Palisades, New York.

Anderson, Prof. Richard G. W. Department of Cell Biology and Neuroscience, University of Texas Southwestern Medical Center, Dallas.

Andrew, Dr. Warren. Chairman, Department of Anatomy, School of Medicine, Indiana University.

Athenstaedt, Dr. Herbert. Director, Institut für Molekular-Physikalische Physiologie, Hanover, Germany.

Atlas, Dr. Ronald M. Department of Biology, University of Louisville, Kentucky.

Atoda, Dr. Kenji. Professor of Zoology, Tohoku University, Sendai, Japan.

Audus, Dr. Leslie J. Professor of Botany (retired), Bedford College, University of London, England.

Austrian, Dr. Robert. Department of Research Medicine, School of Medicine, University of Pennsylvania.

Ayers, Arthur R. Assistant Professor, Cellular and Development Biology, Harvard University.

B

Bahr, Dr. Janice M. Professor of Animal Science and Physiology, Department of Animal Sciences, College of Agriculture, University of Illinois, Urbana-Champaign.

Bailey, Dr. Reeve M. Deceased; formerly, Curator of Fishes, Museum of Zoology, University of Michigan.

Bakken, Prof. George S. Center Director, Center for Biodiversity Studies, Indiana State University, Terre Haute.

Ballard, Prof. William W. Department of Biological Sciences, Dartmouth College.

Ballou, Prof. Clinton E. Department of Molecular and Cell Biology, University of California, Berkeley.

Bamburg, Prof. James R. Department of Biochemistry, Colorado State University.

Banks, Prof. William P. Chairperson, Department of Psychology, Pomona College, Claremont, California.

Barker, Dr. Horace A. Department of Biochemistry, University of California, Berkeley.

Barkley, Prof. T. M. Division of Biology, Kansas State University.

Barksdale, Dr. Lane. Department of Microbiology, School of Medicine, New York University Medical Center.

Barr, Dr. Donald J. S. Principal Research Scientist, Centre for Land and Biological Resources Research, Ottawa, Ontario, Canada.

Barry, Dr. Michelle M. Department of Medical Microbiology and Immunology, University of Alberta, Edmonton, Canada.

Bar-Sela, Dr. Shlomo. Department of Medicine, Allergy-Immunology Section, Medical College of Wisconsin.

Baumgarten, Dr. Alexander. Department of Laboratory Medicine, School of Medicine, Yale University.

Bell, Dr. William E. Department of Pediatrics, University of Iowa.

Bennett, Prof. Albert F. Department of Ecology and Evolutionary Biology, University of California, Irvine.

Bennett, Dr. H. Stanley. Department of Molecular, Cellular and Developmental Biology, University of Colorado.

Bennett, Prof. Joan W. Department of Cell and Molecular Biology, Tulane University, New Orleans, Louisiana.

Benninghoff, Dr. William S. Department of Botany, University of Michigan.

Benny, Dr. Gerald L. Department of Plant Pathology, University of Florida, Gainesville.

Beresford, Dr. William A. Department of Anatomy, West Virginia University.

Berger, Dr. Richard D. Department of Plant Pathology, University of Florida.

Berkowitz, Dr. Gerald A. Institute for Photobiology of Cells and Organelles, Brandeis University.

Berry, Dr. Spencer J. Department of Biology, Wesleyan University.

Beyer, Dr. Ann L. Department of Microbiology, University of Virginia.

Biederman, Dr. Joseph. Pediatric Psychopharmacological Unit, Massachusetts General Hospital, Boston.

Billingham, Dr. Rupert E. Department of Biology, University of Texas Health and Science Center, Dallas.

Bisno, Dr. A. L. Veterans Administration Medical Center, Miami, Florida.

Blackwell, Dr. Meredith. Department of Plant Biology, Louisiana State University, Baton Rouge.

Blankenship, Dr. James E. Department of Physiology and Biophysics, Marine Biomedical Institute, University of Texas, Galveston.

Blaser, Prof. H. Weston. Department of Botany, University of Washington.

Blass, Dr. Elliott M. Department of Psychology, Johns Hopkins University.

Blobel, Dr. Günter B. Department of Cell Biology, Rockefeller University, New York; Nobelist.

Blough, Prof. Donald S. Department of Psychology, Brown University.

Bock, Dr. Walter J. Professor of Evolutionary Biology, Department of Biological Sciences, Columbia University.

Boero, Dr. Ferdinando. Professor of Zoology, Università di Lecce, Dipartimento di Biologia, Stazione di Biologia Marina, Lecce, Italy.

Bohach, Dr. Greg. Department of Microbiology, Molecular Biology, and Biochemistry, University of Idaho, Moscow.

Boke, Dr. Norman H. George Lynn Cross Research Professor of Botany, University of Oklahoma.

Boothroyd, Dr. Carl W. Department of Plant Pathology, Cornell University.

Bormann, Dr. Bernard T. Department of Forest Sciences, Oregon State University, Corvallis.

Bothwell, Dr. Mark. Biochemical Sciences Laboratory, Princeton University.

Bouchard, Prof. Thomas J. Chairman, Department of Psychology, University of Minnesota.

Box, Dr. Elgene O. Department of Geography, University of Georgia.

Boyden, Prof. Edward A. Department of Biological Structure, School of Medicine, University of Washington.

Bozarth, Dr. Robert F. Department of Life Science, Indiana State University, Terre Haute.

Bradley, Prof. S. Gaylen. Department of Microbiology and Immunology. Virginia Commonwealth University, Richmond.

Brainard, Dr. George C. Department of Neurology, Thomas Jefferson University, Jefferson Medical College, Philadelphia, Pennsylvania.

Brammer, Dr. Anthony J. Institute for Microstructural Science, National Research Council of Canada, Ottawa, Ontario.

Brandt, Dr. Philip W. Department of Anatomy, College of Physicians and Surgeons, Columbia University.

Breed, Dr. Michael D. Environmental Population and Organismic Biology, University of Colorado.

Breier, Dr. Alan. Department of Psychiatry, Yale University School of Medicine, and Connecticut Mental Health Center, New Haven.

Breman, Dr. Joel D. Division of Parasitic Diseases, Centers for Disease Control, Department of Health and Human Services, Atlanta, Georgia.

Brian, Dr. M. V. Institute of Terrestrial Ecology, Furzebrook Research Station, Wareham, England.

Briggs, Dr. Winslow R. Department of Plant Biology, Carnegie Institution of Washington, Stanford, California.

Brimacombe, Dr. R. Max-Planck Institut für Molekulare Genetik, Berlin, Germany.

Brisbin, Dr. I. Lehr. Savannah River Ecology Laboratory, University of Georgia, Aiken, South Carolina.

Broadus, Dr. Arthur E. Associate Professor of Medicine, Department of Medicine, Yale University.

Brodsky, Dr. Barbara. Department of Biochemistry, UMDNJ–Robert Wood Johnson Medical School, Piscataway, New Jersey.

Brodsky, Dr. William A. Mount Sinai School of Medicine of the City University of New York; Institute for Medical Research and Studies, New York.

Bromley, Willard S. Consulting Forester and Association Consultant, New Rochelle, New York.

Bronstein, Dr. Judith. Department of Ecology and Evolutionary Biology, University of Arizona, Tucson.

Brooke, Dr. M. M. Deceased; formerly, Deputy Chief, Licensure and Development Branch, Center for Disease Control, U.S. Public Health Service, Atlanta, Georgia.

Brown, Dr. Jason W. Institute for Research in Behavioral Neuroscience, Department of Neurology, New York University Medical Center.

Brown, Michael D. Department of Biochemistry and Molecular Biology, Colorado State University.

Brubaker, Prof. Robert R. Department of Microbiology, Michigan State University, East Lansing.

Brummett, Prof. Anna Ruth. Associate Professor of Biology and Associate Dean, Oberlin College.

Brush, Dr. Alan H. Department of Biology, University of Connecticut.

Burgdorfer, Dr. Willy. Scientist Emeritus, Laboratory of Pathology, Rocky Mountain Laboratories, National Institutes of Health, Department of Health and Human Services, Hamilton, Montana.

Burkhalter, Dr. Alan. Department of Pharmacology, School of Medicine, University of California, San Francisco.

Burstyn, Dr. Judith N. Department of Chemistry, University of Wisconsin, Madison.

Butler, Dr. Percy M. Egham, Surrey, United Kingdom.

Butler, Dr. Robert W. Department of Psychology, Child Development and Rehabilitation Center, Oregon Health Sciences University, Portland.

Butts, Prof. Allison. Professor Emeritus of Metallurgy and Materials Science, Lehigh University.

C

Cain, Dr. William S. John B. Pierce Foundation Laboratories, New Haven, Connecticut.

Calabrese, Dr. Ronald L. Department of Biology, Emory University.

Campbell, Dr. William B. Professor and Chairman, Department of Pharmacology and Toxicology, Medical College of Wisconsin, Milwaukee.

Canter, Prof. Gerald J. Department of Communicative Disorders, Northwestern University.

Capra, Dr. J. Donald. Department of Microbiology, Southwestern Medical School, University of Texas, Dallas.

Carlson, Dr. Don M. Division of Biological Sciences, University of California, Davis.

Carlton, Dr. Peter L. Department of Psychiatry, University of Medicine and Dentistry of New Jersey, Rutgers Medical School.

Carroll, Dr. C. Ronald. Institute of Ecology, University of Georgia, Athens.

Carruthers, Dr. Marvin H. Department of Chemistry, University of Colorado.

Carter, Dr. G. R. Professor Emeritus, Department of Patho-biology, Virginia-Maryland Regional College of Veterinary Medicine, Virginia Polytechnic Institute and State University, Blackburg.

Carter, Prof. Herbert E. Vice Chancellor for Academic Affairs, University of Illinois.

Catania, Prof. A. Charles. Department of Psychology, University of Maryland.

Cave, Dr. M. Donald. Department of Anatomy, University of Arkansas for Medical Sciences.

Cavey, Michael J. Department of Biology, University of Calgary, Alberta, Canada.

Celander, Dr. Daniel W. Department of Microbiology, University of Illinois, Urbana.

Chang, Dr. M. C. Worcester Foundation for Experimental Biology, Shrewsbury, Massachusetts.

Chapman, Dr. Sydney. Deceased; formerly, High Altitude Observatory, University of Colorado.

Charney, Dr. Dennis S. Department of Psychiatry, Yale University School of Medicine, and Connecticut Mental Health Center, New Haven.

Chaundhari, Dr. Nirupa. University of Miami School of Medicine, Department of Physiology and Biophysics, Rosentiel Medicial Sciences Building, Miami, Florida.

Cheadle, Prof. Vernon I. Chancellor, University of California, Santa Barbara.

Chen, Dr. Robert T. Medical Epidemiologist, Infant Immunization Section, Centers for Disease Control, Surveillance Investigations and Research Branch, Atlanta, Georgia.

Chien, Dr. Shu. Institute for Biomedical Engineering, University of California, La Jolla, California.

Chiodo, Prof. Louis A. Chairperson, Department of Pharmacology, Texas Tech University Health Sciences Center, Lubbock.

Chobor, Karen L. Institute for Research in Behavioral Neuroscience, Department of Neurology, New York University Medical Center.

Choy, Dr. Patrick C. Department of Biochemistry, University of Manitoba Faculty of Medicine, Winnipeg, Canada.

Christensen, Dr. Martha. Professor Emeritus, Department of Botany, University of Wyoming, Laramie.

Chu, Dr. T. Ming. Roswell Park Memorial Institute, Buffalo, New York.

Ciechanover, Dr. Aaron J. Department of Biochemistry, The Bruce Rappaport Faculty of Medicine, Technion-Israel Institute of Technology.

Ciegler, Dr. Alex. Southern Regional Research Center, USDA Science and Education Administration, New Orleans.

Clark, Dr. David A. Department of Medicine, McMaster University, Ontario, Canada.

Clark, Dr. Nancy Barnes. Department of Physiology and Neurobiology, University of Connecticut.

Clements, Dr. Leo P. Emeritus Professor of Anatomy, School of Medicine, Creighton University.

Cleve, Dr. Hartwig. Institute for Anthropology and Human Genetics, University of Munich, Germany.

Clowes, Dr. F. A. L. Botany Department, University of Oxford, England.

Cohen, Dr. David. National Magnetic Laboratory, Massachusetts Institute of Technology.

Cohen, Dr. Donald J. Assistant Professor, Child Study Center, Yale University.

Cohen, Dr. Jay O. Deceased; formerly, Microbiologist, Department of Health and Human Services, Public Health Service, Centers for Disease Control, Atlanta, Georgia.

Cohen, Dr. Jerome. Department of Psychiatry, Medical School, Northwestern University.

Colby, Dr. Kenneth Mark. Department of Psychiatry and Behavioral Sciences, School of Medicine, University of California, Los Angeles.

Cole, Dr. Edward H. Department of Immunopathology, Scripps Clinic and Research Foundation, La Jolla, California.

Coleman, Dr. David C. Department of Entomology, University of Georgia.

Collins, Dr. Francis. Department of Health and Human Services, National Human Genome Research Institute, Bethesda, Maryland.

Collins, Dr. Steven J. Department of Clinical Neurosciences, St. Vincent's Hospital, Melbourne, and Department of Pathology, University of Melbourne, Australia.

Colwell, Dr. Rita R. Department of Microbiology, Division of Agricultural and Life Sciences, University of Maryland.

Constabel, Dr. Fred. Plant Biotechnology Institute, National Research Council, Saskatoon, Saskatchewan, Canada.

Coombs, Dr. Sheryl. Professor of Hearing Sciences, Parmly Hearing Institute, Loyola University, Chicago, Illinois.

Cooper, Dr. Arthur W. Department of Botany, North Carolina State University.

Corliss, Dr. John O. Department of Zoology, University of Maryland.

Costerton, Dr. J. William F. Department of Biology, University of Calgary, Alberta, Canada.

Couch, Dr. Richard B. Professor of Naval Architecture and Marine Engineering, Ship Hydrodynamics Laboratory, University of Michigan.

Coulombe, Dr. Mary J. Director, Timber Access and Supply, American Forest and Paper Association, Washington, D.C.

Cowles, Prof. Philip B. Professor Emeritus of Microbiology, School of Medicine, Yale University.

Cozzens, Christine S. Biology Laboratory, Harvard University.

Cracraft, Dr. Joel. Department of Ornithology, American Museum of Natural History, New York.

Cranwell, Dr. Lucy M. Department of Geosciences, University of Arizona.

Cronin, Dr. Thomas. Department of Biological Sciences, University of Maryland, Baltimore County.
Cronquist, Dr. Arthur. Director of Botany, New York Botanical Gardens, Bronx, New York.
Crow, Dr. James F. Department of Genetics, University of Wisconsin.
Crowe, Dr. John H. Department of Zoology, University of California, Davis.
Crum, Dr. Howard. Herbarium, University of Michigan.
Culotta, Prof. Valeria Cizewski. Associate Professor, Johns Hopkins University School of Public Health, Department of Environmental Health Sciences, Baltimore, Maryland.
Cummings, Dr. Michael R. Department of Biological Sciences, University of Illinois.
Curtin, Dr. Charles B. Department of Biology, Creighton University.
Cutler, Dr. Edward B. Department of Biology, Utica College of Syracuse University.
Cutter, Dr. Elizabeth G. Department of Cryptogamic Botany, University of Manchester, England.

D

Dabbs, Dr. David J. Pathologist, Department of Pathology, University of Washington.
Daiber, Dr. Franklin C. College of Marine Studies, University of Delaware.
Dale, Dr. James B. Veteran Affairs Medical Center, Memphis, Tennessee.
Damian, Dr. Raymond T. Department of Zoology, Franklin College of Arts and Sciences, University of Georgia.
Darwin, Dr. C. J. Experimental Psychology, University of Sussex, England.
Davies, Dr. Peter J. Department of Botany, Cornell University.
Davis, Dr. Bernard D. Deceased; formerly, Bacterial Physiology Unit, Harvard Medical School.
Davis, D. Dwight. Deceased; formerly, Curator of Vertebrate Anatomy, Chicago Museum of Natural History.
Dawood, Dr. M. Yusoff. Department of Obstetrics and Gynecology, University of Illinois College of Medicine, Chicago.
Dawson, Dr. Todd E. Ecology and Systematics, Cornell University, Carson Hall, Ithaca, New York.
DeLong, Dr. Dwight M. College of Biological Sciences, Ohio State University.
Dempsey, Prof. Mary E. Department of Biochemistry, University of Minnesota Medical School, Minneapolis.
Dengler, Dr. Nancy G. Department of Botany, University of Toronto, Ontario, Canada.
Denniston, Dr. Carter L. Department of Medical Genetics, University of Wisconsin, Madison.
de Week, Dr. A. L. Institut für Klinische Immunologic Inselspital, Universitat Bern, Switzerland.
Dewsbury, Dr. Donald A. Department of Psychology, University of Florida, Gainesville.
Dingle, Prof. Hugh. Department of Entomology, College of Agricultural and Environmental Sciences, University of California, Davis.
Domning, Dr. Daryl P. Department of Anatomy, Howard University, Washington, DC.
Dorfman, Dr. Ralph I. Senior Vice President and Director, Syntex Research Center, Palo Alto, California.
Dossel, Dr. William E. Professor and Chairman, Department of Anatomy, School of Medicine, Creighton University.
Doudoroff, Dr. Michael. Deceased; formerly, Department of Bacteriology, University of California, Berkeley.
Doyle, Prof. James A. Department of Biological Sciences, University of California, Davis.
Doyle, Prof. Michael P. Director, Center for Food Safety and Quality Enhancement, University of Georgia, Griffin.
Dugan, Dr. Frank M. American Type Culture Collection, Manassas, Virginia.
Duke, Kenneth L. Department of Anatomy, Duke University Medical Center.
Dunning, Dr. John B., Jr. Department of Forestry and Natural Resources, Purdue University.

E

Edelson, Dr. Marshall. Department of Psychiatry, Yale University.
Edwards, Dr. Peter A. Department of Biological Chemistry, University of California School of Medicine, Los Angeles.
Ernster, Dr. Virginia L. Department of Epidemiology and International Health, School of Medicine, University of California, San Francisco.
Esau, Prof. Katherine. Department of Botany, University of California, Santa Barbara.

Evans, Dr. Doyle J. Chief, Bacterial Enteropathogens Laboratory, Veterans Affairs Medical Center, Houston, Texas.
Eyde, Dr. Richard H. Department of Botany, Smithsonian Institution.
Ezzell, Dr. John W. Chief, Special Pathogens Branch, U.S. Army Medical Research Institute, Fort Detrick, Maryland.

F

Fay, Dr. Richard R. Parmly Hearing Institute and Department of Psychology, Loyola University of Chicago, Illinois.
Feduccia, Dr. Alan. Department of Biology, University of North Carolina, Chapel Hill.
Feldmann, Dr. Rodney M. Department of Geology, Kent State University, Kent, Ohio.
Fell, Dr. Jack W. University of Miami, Rosenstiel School of Marine and Atmospheric Science, Marine Biology and Fisheries, Key Biscayne, Florida.
Ferrell, Dr. James E., Jr. Department of Molecular Pharmacology, Stanford University, School of Medicine.
Fetz, Dr. Eberhard E. Department of Physiology and Biophysics, University of Washington School of Medicine.
Fiedler, Dr. Peggy L. Piedmont, California.
Fincham, Prof. J. R. S. Department of Genetics, University of Leeds, England.
Findlay, Dr. David M. Department of Orthopedics and Trauma, University of Adelaide, Royal Adelaide Hospital, Adelaide, Australia.
Finegold, Dr. Sydney M. Chief, Infectious Disease Section, Veterans Administration Wadsworth Hospital Center, Los Angeles, California.
Fingerman, Dr. Milton. Department of Biology, Tulane University.
Fink, Prof. Jordan N. Chief, Allergy- Immunology Section, Department of Medicine, Medical College of Wisconsin.
Finkelstein, Dr. Richard. Department of Microbiology, University of Missouri School of Medicine, Columbia.
Fisher, Dr. Jack B. Fairchild Tropical Garden and Research Center, Miami, Florida.
Fitzsimons, James T. Physiological Laboratory, University of Cambridge, United Kingdom.
Flye, Prof. M. Wayne. Surgery, Microbiology and Immunology, Washington University School of Medicine, St. Louis, Missouri.
Focht, Prof. Dennis D. Department of Soil and Environmental Sciences, University of California, Riverside.
Ford, Prof. E. B. Deceased; formerly, Genetics Laboratory, Department of Zoology, Oxford University, England.
Ford, Dr. Karen Grady. Department of Biology, College of Charleston, South Carolina.
Foster, Prof. Jackson W. Deceased; formerly, Professor of Microbiology, University of Texas.
Foster, Dr. Robert J. Department of Physics, San Jose State University.
Franc, Dr. Jean-Marie. Laboratoire d'Histologie et Biologie Tissulaire, Universite Claude Bernard, Villeurbanne, France.
Francis, Dr. Arthur W. Union Carbide Corporation, Tarrytown, New York.
Frank, Prof. Bernard. Deceased; formerly, Professor of Watershed Management, Colorado State University.
Freeman, Dr. A. E. Department of Animal Science, Iowa State University.
Freedman, Dr. Daniel X. Department of Psychiatry and Behavioral Sciences, University of California School of Medicine.
Freire, Prof. Ernesto. Director, Biocalorimetry Center, Johns Hopkins University, Baltimore, Maryland.
Freundt, Dr. E. A. Institute for Medical Microbiology, Aarhus University, Denmark.
Frick, Dr. Oscar L. Department of Pediatrics, University of California Medical Center.
Fridovich, Dr. Irwin. Department of Biochemistry, Duke University Medical Center.
Fried, Dr. George H. Brooklyn College, City University of New York.
Fromkin, Dr. Victoria A. Dean, Vice Chancellor, Graduate Programs, Department of Linguistics, University of California, Los Angeles.
Frost, Dr. Thomas M. Center for Limnology, University of Wisconsin.
Frumhoff, Dr. Peter. Department of Entomology, University of California, Davis.
Fudenberg, Dr. H. Hugh. Section of Hematology and Immunology, San Francisco Medical Center, University of California.
Fung, Prof. Y. C. Department of Applied Mechanics, University of California, San Diego.
Futuyma, Dr. Douglas J. Section of Ecology and Systematics, Cornell University.

G

Galli, Prof. Stephen J. Department of Pathology, Beth Israel Hospital, Boston, Massachusetts.

Galston, Dr. Arthur W. Department of Biology, Yale University.

Garcia, Dr. John. Department of Psychology, University of California, Los Angeles.

Garfield, Dr. Sol L. Department of Psychology, Washington University.

Gaudin, Dr. Tim. Department of Biological and Environmental Science, University of Tennessee, Chattanooga.

Gazzaniga, Dr. Michael S. Professor of Psychology and Social Sciences in Medicine, State University of New York, Stony Brook.

Gelfand, Prof. Erwin W. Chief, Division of Immunology and Rheumatology, Hospital for Sick Children, Toronto, Ontario, Canada.

Georgorapadakou, Dr. Nafsika H. Department of Infectious Diseases, DuPont Research Laboratories, Wilimington, Delaware.

Gerber, Leah R. National Center for Ecological Analysis and Synthesis, Santa Barbara, California.

Gergely, Dr. John. Department of Muscle Research, Boston Biomedical Research Institute, Boston, Massachusetts.

Gersh, Prof. Isidore. Research Professor, Department of Animal Biology, School of Veterinary Medicine, University of Pennsylvania.

Gershoff, Prof. Stanley N. Department of Nutrition, Harvard School of Public Health, Boston, Massachusetts.

Giannasi, Dr. David E. Department of Botany, University of Georgia.

Gibbons, Dr. Ian. Kewala Laboratory, University of Hawaii.

Gibbs, Dr. Martin. Institute for Photobiology of Cells and Organelles, Brandeis University.

Giese, Raymond. Department of Mechanical Engineering, University of Minnesota.

Gigg, Roy H. Chemistry Division, National Institute for Medical Research, London, England.

Gilardi, Dr. Gerald L. Microbiology Laboratory, North General Hospital, New York.

Gilloteaux, Dr. Jacques. Professor of Cell Biology and Anatomy, Lake Erie College of Osteopathic Medicine, Erie, Pennsylvania.

Glick, Dr. Benjamin. University of Chicago, Cummings Life Science Center, Chicago, Illinois.

Goland, Dr. Leonard. Executive Vice President, Dynasciences Corporation, Los Angeles, California.

Gold, Dr. Ronald. Hospital for Sick Children, Toronto, Ontario, Canada.

Goldberg, Dr. Ira J. Department of Medicine, Columbia College of Physicians and Surgeons, Division of Metabolism and Nutrition, New York.

Goldfarb, Dr. Marjorie S. School of Oceanography, University of Washington, Seattle.

Goodchild, Dr. Chauncey G. Candler Professor of Biology, Emory University.

Goodglass, Dr. Harold. Director, Psychology Research, Veterans Administration Hospital, Boston, Massachusetts.

Goodman, Dr. Richard A. Division of Public Health, Emory University.

Goodman, Dr. Steven R. Chair, Department of Cell Biology and Neuroscience, University of South Alabama College of Medicine, Mobile, Alabama.

Goosby, Dr. Eric P. AIDS Education and Training Centers Program, U.S. Public Health Service, Rockville, Maryland.

Gotelli, Dr. Nick. Department of Biology, University of Vermont, Burlington.

Gots, Dr. Joseph S. Department of Microbiology, School of Medicine, University of Pennsylvania.

Govindjee, Dr. Department of Botany and Department of Physiology and Biophysics, University of Illinois, Urbana.

Govindjee, Dr. Rajni. Retired; formerly, Department of Botany, University of Illinois, Urbana.

Graham, Dr. Jeffrey B. Scripps Institution of Oceanography, La Jolla, California.

Granick, Dr. S. Department of Biochemistry, Rockefeller University.

Gray, Dr. Ernest. Variety Club Children's Hospital, Department of Pediatrics, University of Minnesota.

Greenberg, Prof. David M. Department of Biochemistry, School of Medicine, University of California, San Francisco.

Gregory, Dr. Joseph T. Professor of Paleontology and Curator of Lower Vertebrates, Museum of Paleontology, University of California, Berkeley.

Greiner, Dr. Dale L. Professor of Medicine, University of Massachusetts Medical School, Worcester.

Griffiths, Dr. A. J. F. Department of Botany, University of British Columbia, Vancouver, Canada.

Grilo, Dr. Carlos M. Director of Psychology, Yale Psychiatric Institute, New Haven, Connecticut.

Grivell, Dr. Les A. Afdeling Moleculaire Biologie, Laboratorium voor Biochemie, Universiteit van Amsterdam, Netherlands.

Groody, Dr. E. Patrick. Integrated Genetics, Framingham, Massachusetts.

Gunckel, Prof. James E. Department of Botany, Rutgers University.

Gunning, Dr. Brian E. S. Department of Botany, Queen's University, Belfast, Ireland.

Guy, Dr. Arthur W. Bioelectromagnetism Research Laboratory, School for Medicine and College of Engineering, University of Washington, Seattle.

H

Hadley, Dr. Elbert H. Assistant Dean (retired), College of Liberal Arts and Sciences, and Professor of Chemistry, Southern Illinois University.

Hagan, Dr. William J., Jr. Department of Chemistry, College of St. Rose, Albany, New York.

Hahn, Dr. John F. Department of Psychology, University of Virginia.

Halde, Dr. Carlyn. Department of Microbiology and Immunology, School of Medicine, University of California, San Francisco.

Hall, Dr. Richard P. Deceased; formerly, Professor of Zoology, University of California, Los Angeles.

Halvorson, Dr. Harlyn O. Department of Biochemistry, University of Minnesota.

Hamilton, Dr. Howard L. (Retired) Department of Biology, University of Virginia.

Hammar, Dr. Samuel P. The Diagnostic Specialties Laboratory, Washington.

Hand, Dr. Cadet. Bodega Marine Laboratory, University of California, Bodega Bay.

Handsfield, Dr. H. Hunter. Director, Sexually Transmitted Disease Control Program, Seattle-King Country Public Health Department, Harborview Medical Center, Seattle, Washington.

Hanlin, Dr. Richard T. Department of Plant Pathology, University of Georgia, Athens.

Hanna, Dr. Michael. Assistant Professor of Biology, Rensselaer Polytechnic Institute.

Hanson, Dr. Phyllis. Department of Cell Biology and Physiology, Washington University School of Medicine, St. Louis, Missouri.

Harper, Dr. Michael J. K. Department of Obstetrics and Gynecology, University of Texas Health Science Center, San Antonio.

Harrison, Prof. Terry. Department of Anthropology, New York University, New York.

Hart, Prof. Gerald W. Chair, Department of Biochemistry and Molecular Genetics, University of Alabama, Birmingham.

Hartman, Dr. Olga. Deceased; formerly, Allan Hancock Foundation, University of Southern California.

Hartman, Dr. Standish C. Department of Chemistry, Boston University.

Hartman, Dr. Willard D. Associate Professor of Biology and Curator in Invertebrate Zoology, Peabody Museum of Natural History, Yale University.

Harvey, Dr. Philip D. Professor of Psychiatry, Mount Sinai School of Medicine, New York.

Hassid, Prof. William Z. Deceased; formerly, Department of Biochemistry, University of California, Berkeley.

Hastings, Dr. Alan. Division of Environmental Studies, University of California at Davis.

Hastings, Prof. J. Woodland. Biological Laboratories, Department of Cellular and Development Biology, Harvard University.

Hawley, Dr. R. Scott. Department of Genetics, Section of Molecular and Cellular Biology, University of California at Davis.

Hay, Prof. George W. Department of Chemistry, Queen's University, Ontario, Canada.

Hayflick, Prof. Leonard. Center for Gerontological Studies, University of Florida.

Hazel, Prof. Jeffrey R. Department of Zoology, Arizona State University.

Hedger, Dr. Mark. Institute of Reproduction and Development, Monash University, Clayton, Australia.

Heinrikson, Dr. Robert L. Department of Biochemistry, University of Chicago.

Heinzel, Dr. Frederick P. Department of Medicine, Division of Infectious Diseases, University of California, School of Medicine, San Francisco.

Helfman, Dr. Gene S. Department of Zoology, University of Georgia.

Herberman, Dr. Ronald B. Chief, Biological Development Branch, National Cancer Institute, Frederick Cancer Research Facility, Frederick, Maryland.

Heyneman, Dr. Donald. Chair, Health and Medical Sciences Program, University of California, Berkeley.

Hicks, Dr. Glenn R. Associate Director, Plant Biotechnology, Exelixis Pharmaceuticals, South San Francisco, California.

Higgins, Dr. Robert P. Curator, Department of Invertebrate Zoology, National Museum of Natural History, Smithsonian Institution.

Hinsch, Dr. Gertrude W. Department of Biology, University of South Florida.

Hodgdon, Dr. James. Naval Health Research Center, San Diego, California.

Hodos, Dr. William. Department of Psychology, University of Maryland, College Park.

Hoffman, Dr. Paul. Department of Microbiology and Immunology, Faculty of Medicine, Dalhousie University, Halifax, Nova Scotia, Canada.

Hoffman, Dr. Ralph E. Yale Psychiatric Institute, School of Medicine, Yale University.

Hogan, Dr. Brigid. Mill Hill Laboratories, Imperial Cancer Research Fund, London.

Hogan, Dr. Robert. Department of Psychology, Johns Hopkins University.

Holder, Dr. Nigel. Anatomy and Human Biology Group, Biomedical Sciences Division, Kings College, University of London.

Holmes, Dr. Robert W. Department of Biological Sciences, University of California, Santa Barbara.

Holtzman, Dr. Eric. Deceased; formerly, Department of Biological Sciences, Columbia University.

Homann, Prof. Peter H. Institute of Molecular Biophysics, Florida State University.

Horst, Dr. R. K. Department of Plant Pathology, Cornell University.

Horstadins, Prof. Sven. Professor Emeritus of Zoology, University of Uppsala, Sweden.

Horton, Prof. Derek. Department of Chemistry, American University, Washington, D.C.

Horwich, Dr. Arthur. Yale University School of Medicine, Howard Hughes Medical Institute, New Haven, Connecticut.

Hotchkiss, Prof. Rollin D. Department of Cellular Physiology, Rockefeller University.

Hu, Dr. A. S. L. Department of Biochemistry, University of Kentucky.

Hulbary, Dr. Robert L. Department of Botany, University of Iowa.

Humes, Dr. Arthur G. Department of Biology, Boston University.

Hummon, Dr. William D. Department of Zoological and Biomedical Sciences, Ohio University.

Hungate, Prof. Robert E. Department of Bacteriology, University of California, Davis.

Hunter, Dr. R. H. F. School of Agriculture, University of Edinburgh, Scotland.

Hutchison, Dr. Keith. Department of Biology, Brandeis University.

I

Iverson, Dr. Brent L. Department of Chemistry and Biochemistry, University of Texas, Austin.

Ives, Dr. Anthony R. Department of Zoology, University of Wisconsin, Madison.

J

Jackson, Donald C. Division of Biology and Medicine, Brown University.

Jacobson, Dr. Robert. Chief of the Clinical Branch, Department of Health and Human Services, Gillis W. Long Hansen's Disease Center, Carville, Louisiana.

Janick, Prof. Jules. Department of Horticulture, Purdue University.

Jannasch, Dr. Holger W. Senior Scientist, Woods Hole Oceanographic Institution, Woods Hole, Massachusetts.

Jegla, Dr. Dorothy E. Department of Biology, Kenyon College, Gambier, Ohio.

Jenike, Dr. Michael A. Research Psychiatrist, Massachusetts General Hospital, Harvard Medical School.

Jennings, Dr. J. B. Department of Pure and Applied Zoology, University of Leeds, England.

Jensen, Prof. Arthur R. School of Education, University of California, Berkeley.

Johansen, Dr. Kjell. Department of Zoophysiology, University of Aarhus, Denmark.

Johnson, Dr. Edward. Department of Cell Biology, Rockefeller University.

Johnson, Dr. Giles. School of Biological Sciences, University of Manchester, United Kingdom.

Johnson, Dr. Jon D. Department of Forestry, University of Florida, Gainesville.

Joklik, Dr. W. K. Department of Microbiology and Immunology, Duke University Medical Center.

Jones, Dr. Clive G. Institute of Ecosystem Studies, New York Botanical Garden, Millbrook, New York.

Jones, Dr. David R. Department of Zoology, University of British Columbia, Canada.

Jones, Dr. Jeremy B. Department of Biological Sciences, University of Nevada, Las Vegas.

Jones, Dr. Richard T. Department of Biochemistry, University of Oregon Medical School.

Jordan, Dr. Elke. Department of Health and Human Services, National Human Genome Research Institute, Bethesda, Maryland.

Joseph, Dr. Simpson. Department of Chemistry and Biochemistry, University of California, La Jolla.

Judd, Dr. W. John. Department of Pathology, University of Michigan, Ann Arbor.

K

Kallen, Dr. Bengt. Department of Embryology, University of Lund, Sweden.

Kallio, Dr. R. E. School of Life Sciences, University of Illinois, Urbana.

Kana, Dr. Todd M. Horn Point Laboratory, Cambridge, Maryland.

Kan-Mitchell, Dr. June. School of Medicine, University of Southern California.

Kareiva, Prof. Peter. Department of Zoology, University of Washington, Seattle.

Karlson, Dr. Peter. Insitut für Physiologische Chemie, Philipps-Universitat, Marburg, Germany.

Keddy, Prof. Rex J. Schonland Research Center for Nuclear Sciences, University of Witwatersrand, Johannesburg, South Africa.

Keefe, Dr. Richard S. E. Department of Psychiatry, Duke University Medical Center, Durham, North Carolina.

Keeton, Dr. William T. Deceased; formerly, Professor and Chairman, Section of Neurobiology and Behavior, Langmuir Laboratory, Division of Biological Science, Cornell University.

Keller, Harold W. Associate Professor, Department of Microbiology and Immunology, Wright State University.

Kent, Dr. George C., Jr. Professor Emeritus, Louisiana State University; Authors' Services, Inc., Baton Rouge, Louisiana.

Ker, Dr. Robert F. Department of Pure and Applied Biology, University of Leeds, United Kingdom.

Kilbey, Dr. Brian J. Department of Genetics, Institute of Animal Genetics, University of Edinburgh, Scotland.

King, Dr. Bryan H. Professor of Psychiatry and Pediatrics, Department of Psychiatry, Dartmouth Hitchcock Medical Center, Lebanon, New Hampshire.

Kit, Dr. Saul. Novagene Inc., Houston, Texas.

Klein, Dr. Jan. Max Planck Insitut für Biologie, Abteilung Immungenetik, Tubingen, Germany.

Klein, Prof. Richard M. Department of Botany, University of Vermont.

Kleinsmith, Prof. Lewis J. Division of Biological Sciences, University of Michigan.

Klich, Dr. Maren. Microbiologist, Food and Feed Safety Research, U.S. Department of Agriculture–Agricultural Research Service, New Orleans, Louisiana.

Kobayashi, Dr. George. Washington University School of Medicine, Saint Louis, Missouri.

Koch, Prof. Arthur L. Department of Biology, Indiana University.

Konigsberg, Dr. William H. Department of Molecular Biophysics, Yale University.

Konopka, Dr. Allan E. Department of Biological Sciences, Purdue University.

Koopman, Dr. Karl F. Department of Mammalogy, American Museum of Natural History, New York.

Korth, Dr. William W. Rochester Institute of Vertebrate Paleontology, Penfield, New York.

Korus, Dr. Roger A. Chairperson, Department of Chemical Engineering, College of Engineering, Buchanan Engineering Laboratory, University of Idaho.

Krasan, Dr. Graham P. Lecturer in Pediatrics and Communicable Diseases, University of Michigan Medical School, Ann Arbor.

Kreek, Dr. Mary Jeanne. Rockefeller University.

Kuis, Wietse. Department of Molecular and Experimental Medicine, Research Institute of Scripps Clinic, La Jolla, California.

Kushner, Dr. D. J. Department of Microbiology, University of Toronto, Ontario, Canada.

L

Labandeira, Dr. Conrad C. Department of Paleobiology, National Museum of Natural History, Smithsonian Institution, Washington, DC.

LaBerge, Dr. Stephen. Department of Psychology, Stanford University, Stanford, California.

LaMotte, Dr. Clifford E. Botany Department, Iowa State University.

Lane, Dr. Meredith A. Director, University of Kansas Herbarium, Lawrence.

Lang, Dr. Anton. Department of Botany, MUS-DOE Plant Research Laboratory, Michigan State University.

Lapedes, Daniel N. Deceased; formerly, Editor in Chief, "McGraw-Hill Encyclopedia of Science and Technology," McGraw-Hill, Inc., New York.

Lappin-Scott, Hilary. Department of Biology, University of Calgary, Alberta, Canada.

Larimer, Dr. J. L. Department of Zoology, University of Texas, Austin.

Lazarides, Dr. E. Department of Biology, California Institute of Technology.

Leadbetter, Prof. E. R. Department of Biology, Amherst College.

LeBuhn, Dr. Gretchen. Department of Biological Sciences, Florida State University, Tallahassee.

Ledig, Dr. F. Thomas. School of Forestry, Yale University.

Lee, Lyndon C. L. C. Lee & Associates, Inc., Seattle, Washington.

Lee, Dr. Tae Young. Department of Chemistry, Seoul National University, Seoul, Korea.

Leigh, Dr. Hoyle. Department of Psychiatry, University of California, San Francisco, and Director, Fresno Division, Fresno, California.

Leland, Dr. Henry. Department of Psychology, Ohio State University.

Leopold, Dr. Luna B. Department of Geology and Geophysics, University of California, Berkeley.

Levine, Dr. Norman D. College of Veterinary Medicine, University of Illinois, Urbana.

Levine, Dr. Rachmiel. City of Hope National Medical Center, Duarte, California.

Levitan, Dr. Max. Department of Cell Biology, Mount Sinai School of Medicine, New York.

Lewis, Dr. Alcinda C. Institute of Ecosystem Studies, New York Botanical Garden, Millbrook.

Lewis, Prof. Edward B. Department of Biology, California Institute of Technology; Nobelist.

Lewis, Dr. Richard S. Department of Psychology, Pomona College, Claremont, California.

Li, Dr. Ching Chun. Graduate School of Public Health, University of Pittsburgh.

Li, Prof. Choh Hao. Deceased; formerly, Hormone Research Laboratory, University of California Medical Center, San Francisco.

Lieth, Dr. Helmut. Department of Biochemistry, University of North Carolina.

Lindenmaier, Dr. Werner A. Hoffmann- LaRoche, Inc., Nutley, New Jersey.

Lindner, Dr. Hans R. Department of Biodynamics, Weizmann Institute of Science, Rehovoth, Israel.

Lipner, Prof. Harry J. Department of Biological Science, Florida State University.

Loeblich, Dr. Alfred R., Jr. Department of Earth and Space Sciences, University of California, Los Angeles.

Loewenstein, Dr. Werner R. College of Physicians and Surgeons, Columbia University.

Loftus, Dr. Douglas J. Laboratory of Cell Biology, National Cancer Institute, Bethesda, Maryland.

Loftus, Prof. Elizabeth F. Professor of Psychology, Department of Psychology, University of Washington, Seattle.

Loneragan, Prof. J. F. School of Environmental and Life Science, Murdoch University, Perth, Australia.

Lorand, Dr. L. Department of Biochemistry and Molecular Biology, Northwestern University.

Lordi, George M. Department of Medicine, College of Medicine and Dentistry, Newark, New Jersey.

Lotz, Dr. Martin. Department of Molecular and Experimental Medicine, Research Institute of Scripps Clinic, La Jolla, California.

Lowell, Cadence A. Department of Biology, Central State University, Wiberforce, Ohio.

Lowenstein, Prof. Otto E. Department of Zoology, University of Birmingham, England.

Lutter, Dr. Leonard. Molecular Biology Research Program, Henry Ford Hospital, Detroit, Michigan.

Luttge, Prof. Ulrich. Institut für Botanik, Technische Hochschule Darmstadt, Darmstadt, Germany.

Lykken, Dr. David T. Department of Psychiatry, University of Minnesota, Minneapolis.

Lyman, Prof. Charles P. Department of Medical Sciences, Harvard University.

M

MacDonald Ruby I. Department of Biochemistry, Molecular, and Cell Biology, Northwestern University.

Macher, Dr. Abe M. Medical Consultant, AIDS Education and Training Centers Programs, U.S. Public Health Service, Rockville, Maryland.

Machlin, Dr. Laurence J. Department of Vitamins and Clinical Nutrition, Hoffmann-LaRoche, Inc., Nutley, New Jersey.

Mackay, Dr. Ian R. Center for Molecular Biology and Medicine, Monash University, Clayton, Australia.

Maderson, Dr. Paul F. Department of Biology, Brooklyn College.

Magee, Paul T. Department of Microbiology, School of Medicine, Yale University.

Maggenti, Dr. Armand R. Division of Nematology, University of California, Davis.

Malacinski, Dr. George M. Department of Biology, Indiana University.

Mandler, Dr. George. Department of Psychology, University of California, San Diego.

Mann, Dr. Kenneth H. Fisheries Research Board of Canada, Dartmouth, Nova Scotia.

Mannheim, Prof. Walter. Med. Zentrum filr Hygiene, Universitat Marburg, Germany.

Manning, Dr. James M. Department of Biochemistry, Rockefeller University.

Manwell, Dr. Reginald D. Department of Zoology, College of Liberal Arts, Syracuse University.

Maramorosch, Dr. Karl. Department of Entomology, Rutgers University, New Brunswick, New Jersey.

Marchalonis, Dr. John J. Chairperson, Department of Biochemistry, Medical University of South Carolina.

Margollash, Dr. E. Department of Biochemistry, Northwestern University.

Marino, Dr. Paul. Department of Biology, College of Charleston, South Carolina.

Markert, Prof. Clement L. Department of Biology, Yale University.

Martin, Prof. R. D. Anthropologisches Institut, Universitat Zurich-Irchel, Zurich, Switzerland.

Martin, R. G. National Institutes of Health, Bethesda, Maryland.

Martínez-Carrera, Dr. D. College of Postgraduates in Agricultural Sciences, Mushroom Biotechnology, Puebla, Mexico.

Marvier, Dr. Michelle A. Department of Biology, Santa Clara University, Santa Clara, California.

Marx, Dr. Preston A. California Primate Research Center, University of California, Davis.

Mascarenhas, Prof. Joseph P. Department of Biological Sciences, State University of New York, Albany.

Massion, Dr. Jean. Laboratoire de Neurobiologie et Mouvements, Centre de Recherche en Neurosciences Cognitives, Marseille, France.

Masters, Dr. Colin L. Head of the National Creutzfeldt-Jakob Disease Registry, Department of Pathology, University of Melbourne, Australia.

Masucci, Dr. Maria G. Microbiology and Tumor Biology Center, Karolinska Institute, Stockholm, Sweden.

Mauk, Dr. Craighton S. Research Associate, Department of Horticultural Science, Mountain Horticultural Crops Research and Extension Center, School of Agriculture and Life Sciences, North Carolina State University, Fletcher.

Maurer, Dr. Brian A. Department of Fisheries and Wildlife, Michigan State University, East Lansing.

McCabe, Dr. Allyssa. Eliot-Pearson Department of Child Study, Tufts University.

McCann, Dr. Mary B. Nutrition Program, Center for Disease Control, Health Services and Mental Health Administration, U.S. Department of Health, Education and Welfare, Rockville, Maryland.

McConnaughey, Dr. Bayard H. Department of Biology, University of Oregon.

McEwan, Prof. Robert S. Deceased; formerly, Professor Emeritus, Oberlin College.

McEwen, Dr. Bruce. Harold and Margaret Milliken Hatch Laboratory of Neuroendocrinology, Rockefeller University, New York.

McGinnis, Prof. William. Department of Molecular Biophysics and Biochemistry, Yale University.

McKenna, Dr. Malcolm C. Frick Curator, American Museum of Natural History, New York.

McKinney, Prof. Frank K. Department of Geology, Appalachian State University, Boone, North Carolina.

McLaughlin, Dr. Patsy. Shannon Point Marine Center, Western Washington University, Anacortes.

McNamara, Dr. Ken J. Senior Curator, Invertebrate Paleontology, Western Australian Museum, Perth, Western Australia.

McNamara, Dr. Peter. Department of Medical Microbiology, University of Wisconsin, Madison.

McNaughton, Prof. Samuel J. Department of Biology, Syracuse University.

Mebus, Dr. Charles A. Laboratory Chief, Foreign Animal Disease Diagnostic Laboratory, U.S. Department of Agriculture, Greenport, New York.

Meinke, Dr. David. Department of Botany and Microbiology, Oklahoma State University.

Meinwald, Dr. J. Department of Chemistry, Cornell University.

Melnick, Dr. Joseph L. Department of Virology and Epidemiology, Baylor College of Medicine.

Mescher, Prof. Anthony L. Anatomy Section, School of Medicine, Medical Sciences Program, Indiana University.

Messenger, Dr. John B. Department of Zoology, University of Sheffield, United Kingdom.

Meyer, Dr. Bernard S. Department of Botany, Ohio State University.

Meyer, Dr. David B. Department of Anatomy, Wayne State University School of Medicine.

Meyer, Dr. Judy L. Institute of Ecology, University of Georgia.

Miller, Dr. Dorothy A. Wayne State University School of Medicine, Center for Molecular Medicine and Genetics, Detroit, Michigan.

Miller, Prof. Orlando J. Wayne State University School of Medicine, Center for Molecular Medicine and Genetics, Detroit, Michigan.

Miller, Dr. Regis B. Project Leader, Center for Wood Anatomy Research, Forest Products Laboratory, U.S. Department of Agriculture, Forest Service, Madison, Wisconsin.

Milsom, Dr. William K. Department of Zoology, University of British Columbia, Vancouver, Canada.

Milus, Dr. E. A. Department of Plant Pathology, University of Arkansas, Fayetteville.

Mitchell, Dr. Malcolm S. Comprehensive Cancer Center, Kenneth Norris, Jr. Cancer Research Institute, University of Southern California, Los Angeles.

Mitsch, Prof. William J. Graduate Program Environmental Science, School of Natural Resources, Ohio State University, Columbus.

Moe, Dr. Richard L. Department of Botany, University of California, Berkeley.

Mohanakumar, Dr. T. Department of Surgery, Washington University School of Medicine, St. Louis, Missouri.

Møller , Prof. Aage R. Department of Neurological Surgery, University of Pittsburgh.

Moment, Dr. Gairdner B. Department of Biological Sciences, Goucher College, Towson, Maryland.

Mook, Dr. Douglas G. Department of Psychology, University of Virginia.

Moore, Dr. Raymond C. Deceased; formerly, Department of Geology, University of Kansas.

Mordes, Dr. J. P. Department of Medicine, University of Massachusetts Medical School, Worcester.

Moreno, Dr. Giuliana. Institute of Cellular Pathology, Paris, France.

Morris, Dr. William F. Department of Zoology, Duke University, Durham, North Carolina.

Morrison, Dr. David C. Associate Director, Basic Research Programs, Department of Microbiology, University of Kansas Medical Center, Kansas City.

Morse, Dr. Stephen A. Director, Division of Sexually Transmitted Diseases Laboratory Research, Centers for Disease Control and Protection, Atlanta, Georgia.

Mortenson, Leonard E. Department of Biological Sciences, Purdue University.

Moseley, Dr. Steve L. Department of Microbiology, University of Washington School of Medicine, Seattle.

Mossman, Prof. Harland W. Emeritus Professor, Department of Anatomy, University of Wisconsin.

Mottet, Dr. N. Karle. Professor of Pathology and Director of Hospital Pathology, University Hospital, University of Washington.

Moyer, Dr. Kenneth E. Department of Psychology, Carnegie-Mellon University.

Mulligan, Dr. Pamela K. Formerly, Department of Biochemistry, University of North Carolina.

Murphy, Dr. Frederick A. Centers for Disease Control, Department of Health and Human Services, Tucker, Georgia.

Murphy, Dr. Robert L. Division of Infectious Diseases, Northwestern University Medical School, Chicago, Illinois.

Murray, Prof. R. G. E. Department of Microbiology and Immunology, Health Sciences Centre, University of Western Ontario, London, Canada.

Musacchia, Dr. X. J. Department of Physiology and Space Science Research Center, University of Missouri.

Muus, Dr. Bent J. Research Biologist, Danish Institute for Fishery and Marine Research, Charlottenund, Denmark.

Mynlieff, Dr. Michelle. Department of Biology, Marquette University, Milwaukee, Wisconsin.

N

Napp-Zinn, Prof. Klaus. Botanical Institute, Cologne, Germany.

Nelsen, Dr. Olin E. Department of Biology, University of Pennsylvania.

Noback, Dr. Charles R. Department of Anatomy, Columbia University.

Noll, Dr. Kenneth. Department of Microbiology, University of Illinois, Urbana-Champaign.

Northcutt, Dr. R. Glenn. Department of Anatomy, Case Western Reserve University.

Nyhan, Prof. William L. Department of Pediatrics, University of California, La Jolla.

O

Ogle, Dr. Kenneth N. Section of Biophysics, Mayo Clinic, Rochester, Minnesota.

O'Hagan, Dr. David. Department of Chemistry, University of Durham, United Kingdom.

Ohlendorf, Dr. Douglas H. Genex Corporation, Gaithersburg, Maryland.

Oppenheimer, Dr. Steven B. Department of Biology, California State University, Northridge.

O'Rahilly, Dr. Ronan. Carnegie Embryological Laboratories, University of California, Davis.

Orians, Dr. Gordon. Department of Zoology, University of Washington, Seattle.

Orrego, Dr. Cristian. Department of Biology, Brandeis University.

Orr-Weaver, Dr. Terry. Whitehead Institute for Biomedical Research, Cambridge, Massachusetts.

Ostergaard, Dr. H. L. Department of Biology, University of California, Los Angeles.

Otis, Dr. Arthur B. Department of Physiology, College of Medicine, University of Florida.

Owen, Dr. Denis F. Department of Biology, Oxford Polytechnic.

P

Packer, Dr. Lester. University of California, Department of Molecular and Cell Biology, Berkeley, California.

Palermo, Dr. David S. Department of Psychology, Pennsylvania State University.

Palmer, Prof. Darwin L. Chief, Veterans Administration Hospital, Medical Center, Department of Medicine, Infectious Disease Division, University of New Mexico School of Medicine.

Papageorgiou, George. Research Associate, Department of Botany, University of Illinois, Urbana.

Parker, Sybil P. Formerly, Editor in Chief, "McGraw-Hill Encyclopedia of Science and Technology," McGraw-Hill Book Co., New York.

Parma, Dr. Ana. International Pacific Halibut Commission, Seattle, Washington.

Parmesan, Dr. Camille. National Center for Ecological Analysis and Synthesis, Santa Barbara, California.

Parsons, Dr. Thomas S. Department of Zoology, University of Toronto, Ontario, Canada.

Pasternak, Dr. Gavril W. Attending Neurologist, Department of Neurology, Memorial Hospital, Sloan-Kettering Institute Cancer Center, New York.

Patton, Dr. Harry D. Chairman, Department of Physiology-Biophysics, School of Medicine, University of Washington.

Pearce, Prof. R. H. Department of Pathology, Faculty of Medicine, University of British Columbia, Canada.

Pechenik, Dr. Jan. Department of Biology, Tufts University, Medford, Massachusetts.

Peck, Dr. Stewart B. Department of Biology, Carleton University, Ottawa, Ontario, Canada.

Pelletier, Dr. S. William. Director, Institute for Natural Product Research, University of Georgia, Athens.

Penrose, Prof. Roger. Mathematical Institute, University of Oxford, England.

Perlmann, Dr. Gertrude E. Deceased; formerly, Rockefeller University.

Pfaffmann, Dr. Carl. Department of Psychology, Rockefeller University.

Phaff, Dr. Herman J. Department of Food Science and Technology, College of Agriculture and Environmental Science, University of California, Davis.

Philipson, Dr. William R. Department of Botany, University of Canterbury, Christchurch, New Zealand.

Pielou, Dr. E. C. Department of Biology, University of Lethbridge, Alberta, Canada.

Pierce, Prof. E. Lowe. Department of Zoology, University of Florida.

Pimm, Dr. Stuart. Department of Zoology, University of Tennessee, Knoxville.

Pleasants, Dr. Julian R. International Committee on Laboratory Animals, Lobund Laboratory, University of Notre Dame.

Pollard, Dr. Thomas. Department of Cell Biology and Anatomy, Johns Hopkins University School of Medicine, Baltimore, Maryland.

Pont-Lezica, Dr. Rafael. Department of Biology, Washington University, St. Louis, Missouri.

Pontecorvo, Dr. Guido. Imperial Cancer Research Fund Laboratories, London, England.

Popper, Dr. Arthur N. Director, Neuroscience and Cognitive Science Program, Department of Biology, University of Maryland, College Park.

Porges, Dr. Steven. Department of Human Development, University of Maryland, College Park.

Potter, Dr. Kathleen N. Department of Microbiology, University of Texas Southwestern Medical Center, Dallas.

Powell, Jeffrey R. Department of Biology, Yale University.

Pozos, Dr. Robert S. Sustained Performance Program Manager, Department of the Navy, Naval Health Research Center, Department of Defense, San Diego, California.

Prescott, David M. Department of Molecular, Cellular and Developmental Biology, Boulder, Colorado.

Price, Dr. Peter W. Department of Entomology, Northern Arizona University.

Prothero, Dr. Donald R. Chair, Department of Geology, Occidental College, Los Angeles, California.

Pyeritz, Prof. Reed E. Director, Center for Medical Genetics, Allegheny Health, Education and Research Foundation, Pittsburgh, Pennsylvania.

Q, R

Quarles, Dr. John M. Department of Medical Microbiology & Immunology, Texas A & M University, College Station.

Rachubinski, Dr. Richard A. Department of Cell Biology and Anatomy, University of Alberta, Edmonton, Alberta, Canada.

Rae, Dr. Peter M. M. Molecular Diagnostics, Inc., West Haven, Connecticut.

Raikhel, Dr. Natasha V. Department of Energy, Michigan State University, East Lansing.

Ram, Dr. Prahlad T. Department of Pharmacology, Mount Sinai School of Medicine, New York.

Randerson, Dr. Peter. Department of Applied Biology, University of Wales Institute of Science and Technology, Cardiff.

Raper, Dr. John R. Professor of Botany, Harvard University.

Rasmussen, Dr. Howard. Department of Biochemistry, School of Medicine, University of Pennsylvania.

Ratnoff, Dr. Oscar D. Department of Medicine, Case Western Reserve University.

Raum, Dr. Donald. Center for Blood Research, Boston, Massachusetts.

Redhead, Dr. Scott A. Mycologist, Biosystematics Research Centre, Agriculture Canada, Research Branch, Central Experimental Farm, Ottawa, Ontario, Canada.

Reed, Dr. Randall. Department of Molecular Biology and Genetics, School of Medicine, Johns Hopkins University.

Reeve, Dr. Roger M. Western Regional Research Laboratory, U.S. Department of Agriculture, Albany, California.

Regnery, Dr. Russell. Supervisory Research Microbiologist, Viral and Rickettsial Zoonoses Branch, Department of Health and Human Services, Centers for Disease Control and Prevention, Atlanta, Georgia.

Reichman, Lee B. Department of Medicine, College of Medicine and Dentistry, Newark, New Jersey.

Reichmann, Dr. M. E. Department of Microbiology, University of Illinois.

Reid, Dr. Walter V. World Resources Institute, Washington, D.C.

Reynolds, Mark F. Graduate Research Assistant, Department of Chemistry, University of Wisconsin, Madison.

Rice, Dr. Mary E. Associate Curator, Division of Worms, Smithsonian Institution.

Rice, Dr. Michael. Department of Fish, Animal and Veterinary Science, University of Rhode Island, Kingston, Rhode Island.

Richards, Dr. Frank F. Department of Medicine, Yale University.

Riedel, Dr. Rupert J. Department of Zoology, University of North Carolina.

Rigby, Dr. J. Keith. Department of Geology, Brigham Young University.

Riggs, Dr. Lorrin A. Department of Psychology, Brown University.

Riley, Dr. Ralph. Plant Breeding Institute, Cambridge, England.

Rillema, Prof. James A. Professor of Physiology, Department of Physiology, School of Medicine, Wayne State University.

Rindler, Dr. Michael. Associate Professor of Cell Biology, New York University School of Medicine, New York.

Risser, Dr. Paul G. Vice President for Research, University of New Mexico.

Ritchie, Dr. J. C. Department of Biology, Trent University, Peterborough, Ontario, Canada.

Rizack, Dr. Martin A. Department of Medicine, Rockefeller University.

Roberts, Dr. Richard J. Cold Spring Harbor Laboratories, Cold Spring Harbor, New York.

Robertson, Dr. J. David. Department of Anatomy, Duke University Medical Center.

Robertson, Dr. James S. Medical Department, Medical Physics Division, Brookhaven National Laboratory, Upton, New York.

Rock, Dr. Irwin. Department of Psychology, University of California, Berkeley.

Roosen-Runge, Prof. Edward C. Department of Biological Structure, School of Medicine, University of Washington.

Roper, Dr. Stephen D. University of Miami School of Medicine, Department of Physiology and Biophysics, Miami, Florida.

Rosa, Dr. Patricia. National Institutes of Health and Allergies, Rocky Mountain Laboratories, Hamilton, Montana.

Rosen, Prof. Barry. Department of Biological Chemistry, University of Maryland.

Rosen, Dr. Fred S. President, Center for Blood Research, Department of Pediatrics, Harvard Medical School, Children's Hospital Medical Center, Boston, Massachusetts.

Rosen, Dr. Robert. Department of Physiology and Biophysics, Faculty of Medicine, Dalhousie University, Halifax, Nova Scotia, Canada.

Roskoski, Dr. Robert, Jr. Department of Biochemistry and Molecular Biology, Louisiana State University, New Orleans.

Rossini, Dr. Aldo A. Professor of Medicine, and Director, Division of Diabetes, University of Massachusetts Medical School, Worcester.

Rowell, Prof. A. J. Department of Geology, University of Kansas.

Rownd, Dr. Robert H. Department of Molecular Biology, Northwestern Medical School.

Ruch, Prof. Theodore C. Director, Regional Primate Research Center; Professor, Department of Physiology and Biophysics, School of Medicine, University of Washington.

Ruddat, Dr. Manfred. Department of Molecular Genetics and Cell Biology, University of Chicago, Barnes Laboratory.

Rudnick, Dr. Dorothea. Department of Biology, Albertus Magnus College, Yale University.

Rulfs, Dr. Charles L. Department of Chemistry, University of Michigan.

Ruouff, Dr. Kathryn L. Francis Blake Bacteriology Laboratories, Department of Microbiology and Molecular Genetics, Massachusetts General Hospital, Harvard Medical School, Boston, Massachusetts.

Russell-Hunter, Prof. W. D. Professor of Zoology, Department of Biology, Syracuse University.

Ryan, Dr. Kenneth J. Department of Pathology, University of Arizona Medical Center, Tucson.

Ryland, Prof. John S. Head of Biology, School of Natural Resources, University of the South Pacific, Laucala Bay, Suva, Fiji.

S

Sabo, Dr. John L. National Center for Ecological Analysis and Synthesis, Santa Barbara, California.

Saenger, Dr. Wolfram. Max Planck-Institut für Experimentelle Medizen, Gottingen, Germany.

Salisbury, Dr. Frank B. Plant Science Department, Utah State University.

Salkin, Dr. Ira F. Wadsworth Center, New York Department of Health, Albany, New York.

Sanchez, Dr. Anthony. Research Officer, Department of Health and Human Services, Centers for Disease Control and Prevention, Atlanta, Georgia.

Sanders, Dr. Robert W. Department of Zoology, University of Georgia.

Satir, Dr. Peter. Chairman, Department of Anatomy and Structural Biology, Albert Einstein College of Medicine.

Sauer, Prof. Helmut. Department of Biology, Texas A&M University.

Saunders, Dr. Gary W. Department of Biology, University of New Brunswick, Fredericton, New Brunswick, Canada.

Savage, Dr. George M. Director, Product Research and Development, Upjohn International Inc., Kalamazoo, Michigan.

Savage, Dr. Jay M. Department of Biological Sciences, University of Southern California.

Sawhney, Dr. V. K. Department of Biology, University of Saskatchewan, Saskatoon, Canada.

Schachter, Dr. Julius. Department of Laboratory Medicine, University of California, San Francisco.

Schaeffer, Dr. Bobb. Chairman and Curator, American Museum of Natural History, New York.

Scheer, Dr. Bradley T. Professor Emeritus, Department of Biology, University of Oregon.

Schimmel, Dr. Curt. Silicon Graphics, Inc., Mountain View, California.

Schmid, Dr. Rudolf. Department of Botany, University of California, Berkeley.

Schmidt-Nielsen, Dr. Bodil. Department of Zoology, Duke University.

Schmitt, Dr. Waldo L. Deceased; formerly, Zoologist Emeritus, Department of Zoology, Smithsonian Institution.

Schooler, Dr. Jonathan. Learning, Research, and Development Center, University of Pittsburgh.

Schowalter, Prof. Timothy D. Department of Entomology, Oregon State University, Corvallis.

Schreibman, Dr. Martin P. Department of Biology, Brooklyn College, City University of New York.

Schroeder, Dr. Thomas E. Friday Harbor Laboratories, University of Washington.

Schuchardt, Dr. Lee F. Merck, Sharp, and Dohme, West Point, Pennsylvania.

Schultz, Dr. Jack. Gypsy Moth Research Center, Department of Entomology, College of Agriculture, Pesticide Research Laboratory and Graduate Study Center, Pennsylvania State University.

Schultze, Dr. Hanns-Peter. Curator of Vertebrate Paleontology, Museum of Natural History, University of Kansas.

Schuster, Prof. Frederick L. Department of Biology, Brooklyn College.

Schwartz, Dr. Karlene V. Department of Biology, University of Massachusetts, Boston.

Schwartz, Dr. Morton K. Department of Biochemistry, Memorial Hospital, New York.

Scott, Dr. John P. Director, Center for Research on Social Behavior, Bowling Green State University.

Segal, Dr. Nancy L. Department of Psychology, California State University, Fullerton.

Sehgal, Dr. Amita. Howard Hughes Medical Institute, Department of Neuroscience, University of Pennsylvania School of Medicine, Philadelphia.

Sepkoski, Dr. J. John, Jr. Department of Geophysical Sciences, Henry Hinds Laboratory, University of Chicago.

Sharkey, Dr. Thomas D. Department of Botany, University of Wisconsin.

Sharon, Prof. Nathan. Department of Membrane Research and Biophysics, Weizmann Institute of Science, Rehovot, Israel.

Shaw, Dr. Cheng-Mei. Laboratory of Neuropathy, Department of Pathology, University of Washington School of Medicine.

Shepherd, Dr. Gordon M. Yale University Medical School.

Shive, Prof. William. Department of Chemistry and Clayton Foundation Biochemical Institute, University of Texas, Austin.

Shortman, Dr. Ken. Head, Lymphocyte Differentiation Unit, The Walter and Eliza Hall Institute of Medical Research, Melbourne, Australia.

Siekevitz, Dr. Philip. Department of Cell Biology, Rockefeller University, New York.

Silva, Dr. Paul C. Department of Botany, University of California, Berkeley.

Simberloff, Prof. Daniel. Department of Biological Science, Florida State University.

Simmons, Dr. Nancy. Department of Mammology, American Museum of Natural History, New York.

Simmons, Dr. William H. Department of Biochemistry and Biophysics, Loyola University Medical Center, Maywood, Illinois.

Skalak, Dr. Richard. Deceased; formerly, Founding Director, Institute for Mechanics and Materials, University of California, San Diego.

Skelly, Dr. David. School of Forestry and Environmental Studies, Yale University, New Haven, Connecticut.

Sluder, Dr. Greenfield. Senior Scientist, Worcester Foundation for Experimental Biology, Shrewsbury, Massachusetts.

Smith, Prof. Karl U. Director, Behavioral Cybernetics Laboratory, and Professor of Psychology, University of Wisconsin.

Smithson, Dr. T. R. Head of School, Science Maths and Information Technology, Cambridge Regional College, Kings Hedges Campus, Cambridge, United Kingdom.

Snell, Dr. Esmond E. Department of Biochemistry, University of California, Berkeley.

Snook, Dr. Theodore. Department of Anatomy, School of Medicine, University of North Dakota.

Sokol, Dr. Pamela A. Department of Microbiology and Infectious Diseases, University of Calgary Health Sciences Center, Calgary, Alberta, Canada.

Southwick, Dr. Steven. Department of Psychiatry and Connecticut Mental Health Center, School of Medicine, Yale University.

Sovonick-Dunford, Dr. S. Department of Biological Sciences, University of Cincinnati.

Spector, Dr. David L. Senior Staff Scientist, Cold Spring Harbor Laboratory, Cold Spring Harbor, New York.

Spiegel, Dr. Carol A. Director, Clinical Microbiology, Department of Pathology and Laboratory Medicine, University of Wisconsin Hospital and Clinics, Madison.

Spink, Dr. Wesley W. Regents, Professor of Medicine, School of Medicine, University of Minnesota.

Spratt, Dr. Nelson T., Jr. Department of Zoology, University of Minnesota.

St. Geme, Dr. Joseph W. Associate Professor of Pediatrics and Molecular Microbiology, Department of Pediatrics, Washington University School of Medicine, St. Louis, Missouri.

Stall, Prof. Robert E. Plant Pathology Department, Institute of Food and Agricultural Sciences, University of Florida.

Stamm, Dr. Lola. Department of Epidemiology, School of Public Health, University of North Carolina, Chapel Hill.

Stanley, Dr. Bruce A. Department of Cellular and Molecular Physiology, College of Medicine, Pennsylvania State University, Hershey.

Stebbins, Prof. G. Ledyard. Department of Genetics, College of Agriculture, University of California, Davis.

Stein, Dr. Gary S. Department of Biochemistry and Molecular Biology, J. Hillis Miller Health Center, College of Medicine, University of Florida.

Stein, Dr. Janet L. Department of Biochemistry and Molecular Biology, J. Hillis Miller Health Center, College of Medicine, University of Florida.

Stein, Dr. Murray B. Anxiety & Traumatic Stress Disorders Research Program, University of California, La Jolla.

Sternheim, Dr. Charles E. Director of Undergraduate Studies, Department of Psychology, University of Maryland, College Park.

Sterrer, Dr. W. E. Bermuda Biological Station, St. George's West.

Stevens, Dr. C. E. College of Veterinary Medicine, North Carolina State University, Raleigh.

Stewart, Scott R. L. C. Lee & Associates, Inc., Seattle, Washington.

Stocum, Dr. David L. Department of Genetics and Development, University of Illinois.

Stone, Dr. Jeffrey K. Department of Botany and Plant Pathology, Oregon State University, Corvallis.

Storer, Dr. Tracy I. Deceased; formerly, Department of Zoology, University of California, Davis.

Straus, Dr. Reuben. Providence Medical Center, Portland, Oregon.

Stuart, Dr. Edward G. Deceased; formerly, West Virginia School of Medicine.

Sturtevant, Prof. Alfred H. Thomas Hunt Morgan Professor of Biology, Emeritus, California Institute of Technology.

Sutton, Dr. B. C. Head of Taxonomic and Identification Services, Mycological Institute, Ferry Lane, Surrey, United Kingdom.

Swets, Dr. John A. Bolt Beranek and Newman, Inc., Cambridge, Massachusetts.

Szalay, Dr. Frederick S. Department of Vertebrate Paleontology, American Museum of Natural History, New York.

T

Tao, Dr. B. Y. School of Agricultural and Biological Engineering, Purdue University, West Lafayette, Indiana.

Taylor, Prof. J. Herbert. Institute of Molecular Biophysics, Florida State University.

Taylor, Prof. John W. Department of Plant Biology, University of California, Berkeley.

Taylor, Prof. Thomas N. Department of Biology, University of Kansas, Lawrence.

Tedford, Dr. Richard H. Department of Vertebrate Paleontology, American Museum of Natural History, New York.

Temin, Dr. Howard M. McArdle Laboratory for Cancer Research, University of Wisconsin Medical Center.

Thiess, Helmut E. Washington, D.C.

Thompson, Dr. Margaret R. Departments of Medical Genetics and Pediatrics, University of Tronoto and the Hospital for Sick Children, Toronto, Ontario, Canada.

Thomson, Dr. Keith S. President, Academy of Natural Sciences, Philadelphia, Pennsylvania.

Ting, Dr. Irwin P. Department of Botany and Plant Sciences, University of California, Riverside.

Trappe, Dr. James M. Department of Forest Science, Oregon State University, Corvallis.

Treffers, Dr. Henry P. Professor of Pathology, School of Medicine, Yale University.

Trowsdale, Dr. John. Professor of Immunology, Department of Pathology, Cambridge University.

Truant, J. P. Advance Medical & Research Center, Inc., Pontiac, Michigan.

Turk, Prof. J. L. Department of Pathology, Royal College of Surgeons of England.

Turner, Prof. J. R. G. Department of Genetics, University of Leeds, United Kingdom.

Turner, Dr. Thomas B. Professor of Microbiology and Dean Emeritus, School of Medicine, Johns Hopkins University.

Turturro, Dr. Angelo. National Center for Toxicological Research, Department of Health and Human Services, Jefferson, Arkansas.

Tyler, Prof. Albert. Deceased; formerly, Division of Biology, California Institute of Technology.

U

Uhler, Dr. Michael D. Department of Biological Chemistry, University of Michigan, Ann Arbor.

Ullrich, Dr. Robert C. Department of Botany, University of Vermont, Burlington.

V

Valentine, Dr. J. W. Department of Geology, University of California, Santa Barbara.

Vallee, Dr. Richard. Principal Scientist, Worcester Foundation for Experimental Biology, Shrewsbury, Massachusetts.

Van Campenhout, Prof. Ernest L. Deceased; formerly Professor of Anatomy, Histology, and Embryology, School of Medicine, University of Louvain, Belgium.

Van Niel, Dr. Cornelius B. Deceased; formerly, Hopkins Marine Station, Pacific Grove, California.

Vaya, Dr. Jacob. Migal-Galilee Technological Center, Rosh-Pina, Israel.

Vierstra, Dr. Richard. Horticulture Department, University of Wisconsin.

Villiger, Peter. Research Associate, Department of Molecular and Experimental Medicine, Research Institute of Scripps Clinic, La Jolla, California.

Vitek, Dr. Charles. Medical Epidemiologist, HIV Vaccine Section, Division of HIV/AIDS Prevention, Centers for Disease Control and Prevention, Atlanta, Georgia.

Vogel, Dr. Friedrich. Institute for Anthropology and Human Genetics, Im Neuenheimer Feld, Germany.

Vogel, Prof. Steven. Department of Zoology, Duke University, Durham, North Carolina.

Volk, Dr. Wesley A. Department of Microbiology, School of Medicine, University of Virginia.

Volkmar, Dr. Fred R. Child Study Center, Yale University.

Von Graevenitz, Alexander W. C. Department of Medical Microbiology, University of Zurich, Switzerland.

Voss, Prof. Edward W., Jr. Department of Microbiology, University of Illinois, Urbana.

W

Wagner, Dr. Robert P. Department of Zoology, University of Texas, Austin.

Wagner, Dr. Warren H., Jr. Department of Botany, University of Michigan.

Waisel, Prof. Y. Department of Botany, Tel Aviv University, Israel.

Walbot, Dr. Virginia. Department of Biological Sciences, Stanford University.

Waldmann, Katherine S. National Institutes of Health, Department of Health and Human Services, Bethesda, Maryland.

Waldmann, Dr. Thomas A. Chief, Metabolism Branch, National Institutes of Health, Department of Health and Human Services, Bethesda, Maryland.

Walker, Michelle Y. Davis, California.

Walker, Dr. Warren F., Jr. Department of Biology, Oberlin College.

Walkley, Dr. S. U. Department of Neuroscience, Rose F. Kennedy Center for Research in Mental Retardation and Human Development, Albert Einstein College of Medicine, Bronx, New York.

Walkup, Dr. Robert D. Department of Chemistry and Biochemistry, Texas Tech University.

Walsh, Dr. Michael A. Department of Biology, Utah State University.

Wang, Prof. William S. Y. Project On Linguistic Analysis, University of California, Berkeley.

Watterson, Dr. Ray L. Department of Zoology, University of Illinois, Urbana.

Wayne, Dr. Andrew W. Department of Haematology, Kings College Hospital, London, England.

Webb, Dr. Jacqueline. Villa Nova, Pennsylvania.

Webster, Dr. Douglas B. Department of Otorhinolaryngology and Biocommunication, Louisiana State University Medical Center.

Wedell, Dr. Nina. School of Biology, University of Leeds, United Kingdom.

Weichert, Dr. Charles K. Professor of Zoology and Dean, College of Arts and Sciences, University of Cincinnati.

Weiss, Dr. Allison. Department of Molecular Genetics, Biochemistry, and Microbiology, University of Cincinnati, Ohio.

Weitzenhoffer, Dr. Andre M. Veterans Administration Hospital, Oklahoma City, Oklahoma.

Wellner, Dr. Daniel. Department of Biochemistry, Cornell University Medical College.

Wendler, Dr. Helen E. Department of Biology, Massachusetts Institute of Technology.

Wenner, Prof. Adrian M. Department of Biological Sciences, University of California, Santa Barbara.

Wetzel, Dr. Richard. College of William and Mary, Virginia Institute of Marine Science, School of Marine Science, Gloucester Point, Virginia.

Whaley, Dr. W. Gordon. Cell Research Institute, University of Texas, Austin.

Wheeler, Dr. Harry E. Department of Plant Pathology, University of Kentucky.

White, Dr. Abraham. Consulting Professor of Biochemistry, Stanford University; School of Medicine; Distinguished Scientist, Institute of Biological Sciences, Syntex Research.

White, Dr. Tim. School of Forest Resources, University of Florida, Gainesville.

Whitmore, Dr. T. C. Department of Geography, University of Cambridge, United Kingdom.

Wickstrom, Dr. Conrad. Department of Biological Sciences, Kent State University.

Wilcox, Dr. Hugh. State University College of Forestry, Syracuse University.

Wilcox, Dr. Kimerly J. Dight Laboratories, University of Minnesota.

Wilder, Dr. George J. Department of Biological Sciences, University of Illinois, Chicago.

Wiley, Prof. Edward O., III. Curator, Natural History Museum, University of Kansas, Lawrence.

Wilkinson, Dr. Brian J. Department of Biological Sciences, Illinois State University.

Willett, Prof. Hilda P. Director of Graduate Studies, Department of Microbiology, Duke University Medical Center, Durham, North Carolina.

Willingham, Dr. Mark C. National Institutes of Health, National Cancer Institute, Bethesda, Maryland.

Wilson, Dr. B. F. Department of Forestry and Wildlife Management, University of Massachusetts.

Wilson, Dr. Curtis B. Department of Immunopathology, Scripps Clinic and Research Foundation, La Jolla, California.

Wilson, Prof. George S. Department of Chemistry, University of Kansas, Lawrence.

Wilson, Dr. Irwin B. Department of Chemistry and Biochemistry, University of Colorado.

Wilt, Dr. Fred. Department of Zoology, University of California, Berkeley.

Winston, Dr. Judith E. Assistant Curator, Department of Invertebrates, American Museum of Natural History, New York.

Wittmann, H. G. Max-Planck Institut für Molekulare Genetik, Berlin, Germany.

Wittmers, Dr. L. E. School of Medicine, University of Minnesota.

Wold, Dr. Marc. Department of Biochemistry, University of Iowa College of Medicine, Iowa City.

Wolfe, Dr. Ralph S. Marine Biological Laboratory, Woods Hole, Massachusetts.

Wood, Dr. Albert E. (Retired) Department of Biology, Amherst College.

Woodcock, C. L. F. Professor of Zoology, University of Massachussetts.

Woods, Dr. Jon P. Assistant Professor, Department of Medical Microbiology and Immunology, University of Wisconsin Medical School, Madison.

Wulff, Dr. Verner J. Associate Director of Research, Masonic Medical Research Laboratory, Utica, New York.

Y

Yalow, Dr. Rosalyn S. Senior Medical Investigator, Veterans Administration Hospital, New York.

Yin, Prof. Frank C.-P. Department of Medicine, Johns Hopkins Schools of Medicine, Baltimore, Maryland.

Yochelson, Dr. Ellis L. Geological Survey, U.S. Department of the Interior, Washington, D.C.

Yu, Dr. Robert K. Department of Biochemistry and Molecular Biophysics, Virginia Commonwealth University School of Medicine, Richmond.

Z

Zaitlin, Dr. Milton. Associate Director, Biotechnology Program, Plant Pathology, Cornell University.

Zanoni, Thomas A. Taxonomist, Jardin Botanico Nacional, Santo Domingo, Dominican Republic; and Honorary Research Associate, New York Botanical Garden.

Zinder, Dr. Norton D. Department of Microbial Genetics, Rockefeller University.

Zubay, Dr. Geoffrey. Sherman Fairchild Center for the Life Sciences, Department of Biological Sciences, Columbia University.

Zweifel, Dr. Richard G. Curator, Department of Herpetology, American Museum of Natural History, New York.

Index

The asterisk indicates page numbers of an article title.

C